SCHOOL-BASED FAMILY COUNSELING: TRANSFORMING FAMILY-SCHOOL RELATIONSHIPS

Brian Gerrard
University of San Francisco

Marcel Soriano
California State University, Los Angeles

Editors

Institute for School-Based Family Counseling

ISBN-13: 978-1490934822
ISBN-10: 1490934820

Cover design by Jocelyn Aceves

SCHOOL-BASED FAMILY COUNSELING: TRANSFORMING FAMILY-SCHOOL RELATIONSHIPS

Table of Contents

PART I   SCHOOL-BASED FAMILY COUNSELING: FOUNDATIONS

1   **School-Based Family Counseling: an overview**
Marcel Soriano and Brian Gerrard   2

2   **School-Based Family Counseling: a re-emerging paradigm**
Brian Gerrard   16

3   **Ethical, Training, and Supervision Issues in School-Based Family Counseling**
Marcel Soriano   37

PART II   SCHOOL-BASED FAMILY COUNSELING: PREPARING FOR CHANGE

4   **How to Develop an Integrative School-Based Family Counseling Case Conceptualization**
Brian Gerrard   51

5   **How to Assess Change in School-Based Family Counseling**
Brian Gerrard   116

6   **How to Form a Partnership with Schools**
Judy Giampaoli   137

7   **How to Form a Partnership with the Family**
Kristin Velazquez Kenefick and Sarah Hudson   144

PART III   SCHOOL-BASED FAMILY COUNSELING CHANGE STRATEGIES: FAMILY-INTERVENTION FOCUS

8   **How to do Parent/Guardian Consultation: an Integrative Behavior-Process Consultation Approach**
Margaret Garcia and Michele D. Wallace   154

9   How to do Conjoint Family Counseling
Michael Carter   172

10   How to Help a Child Through Couple Relationship Strengthening
Hans Everts   211

PART IV   SCHOOL-BASED FAMILY COUNSELING CHANGE STRATEGIES: SCHOOL-INTERVENTION FOCUS

11   How to do Teacher Consultation: an Integrative Behavior-Process Consultation Approach
Margaret Garcia and Michelle D. Wallace   235

12   How to Provide Group Counseling in the School
George Hong   248

13   How to do a Crisis Intervention in a School
Theresa Kruczek and Lauren Young   262

PART V   SCHOOL-BASED FAMILY COUNSELING CHANGE STRATEGIES: FAMILY-PREVENTION FOCUS

14   How to Provide a Parent Education Workshop
Nancy Rosenbledt   277

15   How to Lead a Parent/Guardian Support Group
Allan Morotti   301

PART VI   SCHOOL-BASED FAMILY COUNSELING CHANGE STRATEGIES: SCHOOL-PREVENTION FOCUS

16   How to Help Teachers Develop Productive Working Relationships with Families: the CORE Model of Family-School Collaboration
Kathleen M. Minke   312

17   How to Develop a School-wide Classroom Management Program
Lindsey K. Ma   329

18   How to Plan and Carry Out a Guidance Group
Allan Morotti and Judith Morotti   344

19 **How to Facilitate a Classroom Meeting**
   Gema Macias   *363*

PART VII SCHOOL-BASED FAMILY COUNSELING: SPECIFIC APPLICATIONS

A. *FAMILY AND COMMUNITY FACTORS AFFECTING STUDENTS*

20 **The Role of Parental Tolerance in Student Mental Health**
   Virginia Corina Samaniego   *374*

21 **Looking for "Home" in a Trans-national World: Migration and School- Based Family Counseling**
   Maria Marchetti-Mercer   *382*

22 **Teachers' Stories of Children Coping with Family Change: a Hong Kong Hybrid Case**
   Pattie Yuk Yee Luk-Fong   *395*

23 **Excluded Student-Excluded Parent: The Experience and Reflections of Parents Whose Teenagers are Excluded from School**
   Andrew Smith   *407*

24 **Assessing Individual or Family Dynamics through the Collage Life-Story ElicitationTechnique (CLET)**
   Gertina J. van Schalkwyk   *419*

B. *SCHOOL-BASED FAMILY COUNSELING: FAMILY-INTERVENTION APPLICATIONS*

25 **Family Involvement in School-Based Treatment of Childhood Trauma**
   Theresa Kruczek   *441*

26 **Therapeutic Storytelling Intervention Group Therapy**
   Ron Phillips   *455*

27 **Creativity and Healing: Expressive Arts and Families**
   Nancy Iverson and Andrea Bass   *473*

28 Resilience-Oriented Family Systems Approach: A Model for School-Based Family Counseling with Parents and Siblings of Children with a Life-threatening Illness
Martha Markward   *491*

C. *SCHOOL-BASED FAMILY COUNSELING: SCHOOL-INTERVENTION APPLICATIONS*

29 The Calgary Transitions Mental Health Classrooms: A 16 Year Old Collaborative Program
Terisita José   *502*

30 Therapeutic Interventions Following an Incident of Violence in a School: A South African Case Study
Maria Marchetti-Mercer   *518*

31 Se Se Puede: A Service Learning School Support Project
Nancy Iverson and Andrea Bass   *529*

32 Crisis Intervention on Campus: A School-Based Family Counseling Approach
Chris Trailer   *544*

33 Group Intervention to Address the Emotional Aspects of Children with Learning Disorders and Their Parents
Zipora Shechtman   *552*

D. *SCHOOL-BASED FAMILY COUNSELING: FAMILY-PREVENTION APPLICATIONS*

34 Promoting School Success Through Mentor Families
Dale Fryxell   *571*

35 Developing Migrant Family Resilience
Hans Everts   *579*

E. *SCHOOL-BASED FAMILY COUNSELING: SCHOOL-PREVENTION APPLICATIONS*

36 *Kiwi Ace*: A School-Based Preventive Depression Program
Barbara Woods   *605*

37 Coping with School Bullying: Students and Experts' Views on Effective Strategies
Phillip T. Slee   *615*

38 The Hong Kong "Uncle Long Legs" Letter Box Project
Frederick Yeung Ka Ching, Queenie Lai Kwan Chan and Daby Kwan Wah Tam   *624*

F.   CASE STUDIES IN SCHOOL-BASED FAMILY COUNSELING

39 The Girl Who Believed She Would Never Be Good Enough
Heidi Petrow   *638*

40 School-Based Family Counseling: An Integration of Psychodynamic, Cognitive-Behavioral and Family Systems Approaches
Salome Dineros   *648*

41 Organizational Development in Schools: Impact on School-Based Family Counseling
Steven D. Pomerantz   *656*

42 A Day in the Life of a School-Based Family Counselor
Sean Faulkner   *668*

G.   EXAMPLES OF SCHOOL-BASED FAMILY COUNSELING PROGRAMS

43 The Copper River Project: Laying the Foundation for School-Based Family Counseling with Alaska's Indigenous Populations
Allan Morotti   *680*

44 The California State University, Los Angeles Masters of Science Degree in School-Based Family Counseling
Michael Carter and Emily J. Hernandez   *693*

45 *Mission Possible*: a 30 year University-Schools Partnership in School-Based Family Counseling
Brian Gerrard   *709*

46 Joining School-Based Counseling Teams: School Certification for Connecticut Marriage and Family Therapists
Kathleen C. Laundy, Ralph S. Cohen and Kit Bishop   *726*

47 Connecticut MFT Models for School-Based Family Counseling: Medical
    Family Therapy and the Longitudinal Overview of Growth in Systems
    (LOGs)
    Kathleen C. Laundy   740

48 *Mission Possible*: A Private Practice Model for Implementing School-Based
    Family Counseling
    Christine Tippett   752

49 The M.Ed. Specialization in School-Based Family Counseling at the Hong
    Kong Institute of Education
    Pattie Luk-Fong   765

50 The Origins of School-Based Family Counseling in Southern California:
    Practical Partnership, Leadership and School Reform
    Marcel Soriano   780

PART IX   FUTURE DEVELOPMENTS IN SCHOOL-BASED FAMILY COUNSELING

51 School Counseling and Family Services in Southeast Asia: Towards the
    Development of School-Based Family Counseling
    Gertina van Schalkwyk   792

List of Contributors

Andrea Bass
Family Therapist
San Francisco, California, USA

Kit Bishop
Daisy Ingraham School
Westbrook, Connecticut, USA

Michael Carter
California State University, Los Angeles
Los Angeles, California, USA

Queenie Lai Kwan Chan
Evangelical Lutheran Church Social Service
Hong Kong

Frederick Yeung Ka Ching
The University of Hong Kong
Hong Kong

Ralph S. Cohen
Central Connecticut State University
New Britain, Connecticut, USA

Salome Dineros
lately University of San Francisco
San Francisco, California, USA

Hans Everts
lately Faculty of Education, University of Auckland
Auckland, New Zealand

Sean Faulkner
University of San Francisco
San Francisco, California, USA

Dale Fryxell
Chaminade University
Honolulu, Hawaii, USA

Margaret Garcia
California State University, Los Angeles
Los Angeles, California, USA

Brian Gerrard
University of San Francisco
San Francisco, California, USA

Judy Giampaoli
University of San Francisco
San Francisco, California, USA

Emily J. Hernandez
California State University, Los Angeles
Los Angeles, California, USA

George Hong
California State University, Los Angeles
Los Angeles, California, USA

Sarah Hudson
Adler School of Professional Psychology
Chicago, Illinois, USA

Nancy Iverson
California-Pacific Medical Center, San Francisco and
Living with Loss, Support for Families of Children with Disabilities
San Francisco, California, USA

Terisita J. José
University of Calgary
Calgary, Alberta, Canada

Kristin Velazquez Kenefick
Adler School of Professional Psychology
Chicago, Illinois, USA

Theresa Kruczek
Ball State University
Muncie, Indiana, USA

Kathleen C. Laundy
Central Connecticut State University
New Britain, Connecticut, USA

Pattie Yuk Yee Luk-Fong
lately Hong Kong Institute of Education
Tai Po, New Territories, Hong Kong

Lindsey K. Ma
San Gabriel High School
San Gabriel, California, USA

Gema Macias
Richard Garvey Intermediate School
Rosemead, California, USA

Maria Marchetti-Mercer,
University of Witswatersrand
Johannesburg, South Africa

Martha Markward
University of Missouri
Columbia, Missouri, USA

Kathleen M. Minke
University of Delaware
Newark, Delaware, USA

Allan Morotti
University of Alaska Fairbanks
Fairbanks, Alaska

Judith Morotti
Family Counselor
Fairbanks, Alaska, USA

Heidi Petrow
Family Counselor
Sacramento, California, USA

Ron Phillips
Counties Manukau District Health Board
New Zealand

Steven D. Pomerantz
University of San Francisco
Sacramento, California, USA

Nancy Rosenbledt
University of San Francisco
San Francisco, California, USA

Virginia Corina Samaniego
Pontificia Universidad Católica Argentina
Buenos Aires, Argentina

Gertina J. van Schalkwyk
University of Macao
Macao, (SAR), China

Zipora Shechtman
University of Haifa
Haifa, Israel

Phillip T. Slee
Flinders University
Adelaide, South Australia, Australia

Andrew Smith,
Bethlehem Tertiary Institute
Tauranga, New Zealand

Marcel Soriano
California, State University, Los Angeles
Los Angeles, California, USA

Daby Kwan Wah Tam
Evangelical Lutheran Church Social Service
Hong Kong

Christine Tippett
University of San Francisco
Sacramento, California, USA

Chris Trailer
University of San Francisco
San Francisco, California, USA

Michele D. Wallace
California State University, Los Angeles
Los Angeles, California, USA

Barbara Woods
St. Mary's College
Wellington, New Zealand

Lauren Young
Ball State University
Muncie, Indiana, USA

PART I

SCHOOL-BASED FAMILY COUNSELING: FOUNDATIONS

Chapter 1
School-Based Family Counseling: An Overview

Marcel Soriano   Brian Gerrard

"Psychology and education are two phases of the same reality and the same problem."
- Alfred Adler

OVERVIEW: *This chapter defines School-Based Family Counseling (SBFC) and describes its unique strengths and possible applications. The chapter lays out the foundation for the ensuing chapters, each showing the myriad ways in which the model serves children, families, schools and the greater community.*

SBFC: A DEFINITION

SBFC is an approach to helping children succeed at school and overcome personal, interpersonal, and family problems. SBFC integrates counseling approaches used in schools and with families within a broad based systems meta-model. It is used to conceptualize the child's problems in the context of all her/his interpersonal networks: family, peer group, classroom, school (teacher, principal, other students), and community. When a child is referred to the SBFC professional, the child's problem may involve one or all of these interpersonal networks. However, irrespective of the level of interpersonal network affected, the SBFC professional will relate positively with the child's family in order to reinforce positive change with the child. Moreover, the SBFC professional will also help bring about changes

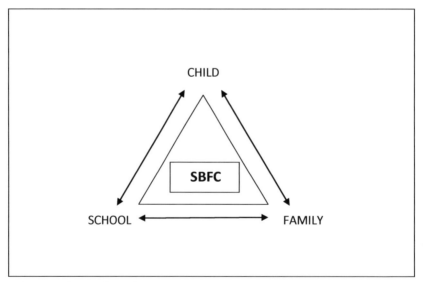

Figure 1.1 The Central Role of Family and School

*Note: Part of this chapter is adapted with permission from the International Journal for School-Based Family Counseling, (2008)1, 1.

necessary with the school system in order to help realign the school with the needs of the child, just as he/she would help by responding to the needs of the child when the family system is in disarray. A SBFC approach may be used by any mental health professional (e.g. counselor, family therapist, psychologist, school psychologist, social worker, school social worker, psychiatrist, nurse, or physician) or educator (e.g. principal or teacher). While not all of these professionals will be trained to the same level of skill in each SBFC modality, each is in a position to help a child by working with the child's two most important systems: home and school. For example, a teacher could help a shy child to integrate more effectively with her class by seating the child near a friendly peer. In addition, the teacher could meet with the parents and encourage them to help the child with homework. These two interventions in the child's school and home environments could just as easily have been made by a school or an agency mental health professional using a SBFC orientation.

Any mental health professional or educator who uses SBFC skills to help a child

---

Figure 1.2 Definition: SBFC Professional

Counselors
Family Counselors
Marital and Family Therapists
Mental Health Counselors
Principals
Psychiatrists
Psychologists
Social Workers
School Counselors
School Nurses
School Psychologists
School Social Workers
Teachers

Figure 1.3 Professionals who do SBFC

The term "school-based" is not meant to refer to the site at which the counseling occurs. Rather, it is meant to refer to the focus or primacy given to promoting school success. There are six basic types of School-Based Family Counseling, depending on whether the family counseling occurs at the school or at a community agency (see Table 1.1). School-sited SBFC is conducted on site at the school and the school-based family counselor is identified as a member of the school staff. This is in contrast to the traditional school counseling model in which the counselor is not trained to provide therapeutic interventions for the family. Agency-sited SBFC is conducted at an agency site by the school-based family counselor, who receives client referrals from parents and schools. However, the agency-sited SBFC professional is intimately "linked" with the school, often spelled out in agreements or memoranda of understanding documents. The point here is that the agency-sited school-based family counselor is regarded as a member of the school's support team, and he/she will visit the schools in order to foster a personal connection with school staff and with parents. This is in contrast to most traditional family therapy and community counseling models, in which the counselor is not trained to work in school systems.

The specific skills typically required of the school-based family counselor are shown in Table 1.2. As can be seen from this table, the skill set required of the school-based family counselor covers specific school counseling skills (such as, career counseling and guidance groups), as well as specific family counseling skills (such as, couples counseling and family counseling). Of the 23 skill/competency areas listed, 10 are held in common by both school counselors and family counselors.

THE NEED FOR SBFC

The need for SBFC arises from the challenges of traditional school counseling and family counseling (agency based) models in dealing with children who are failing at school because of family problems. A survey of the student clients of SBFCs in San Francisco (Gerrard, 1990) showed that over 85% of the children referred by teachers, parents, or self-referred had significant problems at home. The family problems included: marital discord, parents divorcing, custody problems, substance abuse, older siblings involved in gangs, sexual and physical abuse, parental neglect, single parents overwhelmed by economic and emotional problems, spouse abuse, and chaotic families with little parental control. Carlson and Sincavage (1987) conducted a survey of 110 members of the National Association of School Psychologists and reported that family variables were seen as highly relevant to children's school problems. Crespi and Hughes (2004) describe some of the crises affecting adolescents in schools: alcohol and drug addiction, teenage pregnancy, divorce, abuse, and family discord. The authors present an argument for school-based mental health services for adolescents as a way to offset restrictions imposed by managed care. Stinchfield (2004) describes research that indicates that traditional office-based therapy is not always effective with at-risk families and advocates family-based therapy that includes involvement of school personnel.

There is considerable research demonstrating that dysfunctional families (characterized by conflict, anxiety, low cohesion, and emotional problems of parents) are associated with a variety of problems affecting children. These problems include: behavior problems (Henderson, Sayger & Horne, 2003; Morris, Silk, Steinberg, Sessa, Avenevoli & Essex, 2002); deliberate self harm (Evans, Hawton & Rodham, 2005); delinquency (Coll, Thobro, & Haas, 2004; Cashwell &Vacc, 1996); depression (Schneiders, Nicolson, Berkhof, Feron, van Os & de Vries, 2006; Sigfusdottir, Farkas & Silver, 2004; Sourander, Multimaki, Nikolakaros, Haavisto, Ristkari, Helenius, Parkkola, Piha, Tamminan, Moilanen, Kumpulainen & Almqvist, 2005); risky peer behavior (Goldstein, Davis-Kean & Eccles, 2005; Jeltova, Fish & Revenson, 2005); social isolation (Elliott, Cunningham, Linder, Colangelo & Gross, 2005); substance abuse (Henry, Robinson & Wilson, 2004); and suicide attempt (Yip, Liu, Lam, Stewart, Chen & Fan, 2004; Wild, Flisher & Lombard, 2004; Hacker, Suglia, Fried, Rappaport & Cabral, 2006).

These negative effects of the family on children extend to the school. According to Crespi, Gustafson and Borges (2006) school psychologists are increasingly being confronted with students affected by family problems: "With one in six children raised in alcoholic families, with divorce impacting approximately 60% of families, and with such issues as...parental neglect, as well as sexual and physical abuse affecting large numbers of children and youths, many practitioners are interested in interventions which can directly affect children in school settings." (p.67). Researchers have documented the negative effects on children's academic performance caused by lack of family support (Lagana, 2004; Chiam, 2003; Ponsford & Lapadat, 2001); marital disruption and divorce (Sun & Li, 2002); mother absence

Table 1.1 Six Types of SBFC Service Delivery Programs

Program Type	Site of Counseling	Main Accountability of SBFC Personnel	Personnel Providing SBFC	Administrative Control of Program
1. School-sited: In-service Training	School	School	School Counselor School Psychologist School Social Worker Teacher	School
2. School-sited: Family Therapy Staff	School	School	Family Therapists	School
3. School-sited: University-School Collaborative	School	School	Family Therapy Graduate Students	School/ University
4. School-sited: Agency-School Collaborative	School	School	Family Therapists	School/Agency
5. Community-sited: Agency	Community: Agency	Agency	Family Therapists	Agency
6. Community-sited: Private Practice	Community: Private Office	Family Therapist in Private Practice	Family Therapist	Family Therapist

Program Type	Clinical Control of Program	Advantages	Disadvantages	Examples*
1. School-sited: In-service Training	School	Low cost, Utilizes existing personnel	Extensive in-service training required	Nicoll (1992) Merril, Clark, Varvil, Sickle & McCall (1991) Bemak & Cornely (2002)
2. School-sited: Family Therapy Staff	School	Utilizes experienced family therapists	Requires hiring of new personnel	Kramer (1977), Kronick (2005)
3. School-sited: University-School Collaborative	University	Cost effective for schools and parents	Inexperience of graduate students	Albaum (1990), Hillis, Gerrard, Soriano, Girault, Carter & Hong (1991), Carter (2003)
4. School-sited: Agency-School Collaborative	Agency	Cost effective for Schools	Parents pay fee	Barksdale (1979) , Blatt & Starr (1977), Klein (2004)
5. Community-sited: Agency	Agency	Utilizes community resources	Parents pay fee, Reluctance of families to participate	McGuire & Lyons (1985), Long & Burnett (2005)
6. Community-sited: Private Practice	Family therapist	Utilizes community resources	Parents pay fee, Reluctance of families to participate	Freund & Cardwell (1977), Wetchlet (1986)

Note: The term "School-Based" in "SBFC" refers to the critical importance of the role of the school rather than the school site, specifically.

* References for Examples are found in Chapter 2.

Table 1.2 Examples of Different Skills/Competencies Performed by the School-Based Family Counselor Shown as Traditional Skills Taught to Family Counselors and to School Counselors in North America

Counseling Approach	Traditional Skill/Competency Taught
School Counseling and Family Counseling (skills common to both)	Child counseling
	Group counseling
	Child advocacy
	Child assessment
	Parent consultation
	Awareness of ethical issues
	Referral to community resources
	Program evaluation
	Multicultural counseling
	Community intervention*
School Counseling	Teacher consultation
	Teacher education (e.g. classroom discipline)
	Career counseling
	Guidance groups
	Classroom meetings
	School law
	Academic planning
Family Counseling	Family counseling
	Couples counseling
	Family assessment
	Family law
	Parent education
	Parent support groups

*emerging skill area

(Heard, 2007); and parental loss (Abdelnoor & Hollins, 2004). Other researchers have noted the positive correlation between children's aggression at school and variables such as: family aggression (Fitzpatrick, Dulin & Piko, 2007; Miller, Miller, Trampush, McKay, Newcorn & Halperin, 2006) and negative home experiences (Fryxell & Smith, 2000).

There are also a number of studies focusing on how healthy family functioning helps children succeed at school. Zimmer-Gembeck and Locke (2007) found support for a Family Primacy Model exemplified by adolescents with more positive family relationships using more effective coping strategies at home and at school. Lambert and Cashwell (2004) state that preadolescents who perceived effective communication with their parents had low school-based aggression. Steward, Jo, Murray, Fitzgerald, Neil, Fear & Hill (1998) found that students who used family members for solving problems had higher GPA's than students who did not rely on their families. Amatea, Smith-Adcock, and Villares (2006) describe a family resilience framework that school counselors can use to help families promote students' learning.

Resmini (2004) points out that in some cases for a particular child the school itself may function like a dysfunctional family exposing the child to abuse and neglect by peers and teachers. Resmini states: "Some schools can bear a strong resemblance to the proverbial dysfunctional home, particularly for the student who has learning differences or different interests. Teachers often are taxed by the large number of students in their class, and therefore they are apt to ignore the needs of the student with differences." (p.222). Resmini recommends a family systems approach be used to assist these children both at home and at school.

When children's problems are seen through the lens of the education researcher (Adelman & Taylor, 2011), the focus becomes one of looking for the "barriers to student achievement". These indeed are often the same barriers described above with respect to the family. However, beyond the family system, research accumulated over the past twenty years by the National Clearing House which is based at UCLA's School Mental Health Project (see http://smhp.psych.ucla.edu/temphome.htm) suggests that the problems are not always due to dysfunctional families, but may lie in the way school systems are structured as well as the way support services, including counseling, targets problems after they impact the child's learning, then apply "counseling" interventions that amount to band aids to a serious wound. This is not to say that counseling is not seen as important, but rather that traditional school interventions are piecemeal approaches that lack an understanding of the three contextual systems that are critical to optimal child development, the family, the school and the community. Thus when Johnny experiences a hostile, adversarial divorce between his/her parents, the negative effects of this hostility, turmoil and instability weigh heavily on his/her ability to function well in school. SBFC professionals, on the other hand, are skilled at working with all three systems, often generating school and community support since they "see" the wisdom of involving key stake-holders in the helping process.

School counselors, who typically have no training (or only one survey course) in family counseling, are not equipped to intervene effectively with the families of these students. Family counseling is one of the more difficult forms of counseling and learning to do it well requires extensive training and supervision. When school personnel determine that there is a family problem affecting a student, they often refer the family to a community mental health agency for family counseling. Most school principals are familiar with the phenomenon of families that are referred for family counseling, but they fail to go. Many of these "resistant" families are involved in a power struggle with school personnel. The families resent being sent for therapy because of the implicit message that the family (i.e. the parent) is sick or irresponsible. While seeing a therapist may be a sign of social status or trendiness with some people, with many, especially with minority families, therapy holds a stigma. "Seeing a therapist" is viewed within these families' communities as a sign one is "crazy." Family therapists who are themselves very familiar with the concept of triangulation (in which two family members form a coalition against a third family member, who is often the family scapegoat or "identified patient") are often perceived by parents as involved in a triangulation in which the school and the family therapist are in a coalition and "ganging up" on the parents. SBFC minimizes this triangulation because the school-based family counselor is not seen as a "third party" but rather is viewed as part of the school system. The SBFC professional is an advocate for the child, the family, and the school. The counseling focus is on working with parents and families to help their children succeed in school.

STRENGTHS OF SBFC

School-Based Family Counseling has six strengths:
        Systems Focus

Strength-based
Partnership with Parents
Multi-culturally sensitive
Child Advocacy role
Promotion of school transformation

SYSTEMS FOCUS

SBFC emphasizes that students are part of multiple systems: family, school, peer group, and the larger community. Family and school, however, play a critical role especially at the primary and middle school levels. These represent critical periods where change can be more easily implemented to help children. They are also the levels where appropriate interventions can have optimal positive results. What is unique about the SBFC systems orientation is its emphasis on family systems theory which is change focused and connected to practical family counseling techniques for implementing change. Likewise, family systems theory recognizes the interdependence of various systems in our society--be they the school, the family, or the community context—as well as the vulnerability of the child depending on these systems for his/her development. Because of the flexibility of family systems theory, it can also be used to conceptualize relationship dynamics in the "school family." Evidence of the growing, albeit not always enthusiastic recognition of "systems" thinking in our society is the preface to the document, "Creating Caring Relationships to Foster Academic Excellence: Recommendations for Reducing Violence in California Schools (Dear, Soriano et al, 1995). This document was the summation of three years' worth of research on school violence and the degree to which the educational community is prepared to respond to acts of violence in schools. The Preface states in part, "The problems in the schools are but a reflection of the problems in society; the solution to those problems lies in understanding the systemic nature and interdependence of schools, families and communities." (Dear, Soriano et al., 1995).

STRENGTH-BASED

Unlike the traditional paradigm for professional education whereby training and practice of professionals is done "irrespective" of other professionals, SBFC relies on the familiarity, respect and understanding of various professionals who have an interest in the child and his/her family. SBFC requires significant distancing away from the "silo" training model that results in separate interventions that may directly or indirectly undermine efforts of other professionals. Like the proverbial "blind leading the blind" counselors who "counsel" the child, but fail to work with the parents or with the teacher(s) (who may be unaware of the child's home ordeals) may actually do more harm than good, as the intervention with the child may fail to address the root of the problem. Also, unlike therapy models based on the DSM, SBFC is not pathology-based, but rather strength-based. SBFC is a strength-based approach in that the focus of counseling is on promoting wellness and student success. When parents, guardians, and other family members are approached by the SBFC professional it is in order to help a child succeed in school. This is in sharp contrast to the school contacting the family and recommending they "go for counseling" in order to deal with "family problems" that are having a negative effect on the student. This normalizes and de-pathologizes the counseling situation for the child and family.

PARTNERSHIP WITH PARENTS

Increasingly, government   professional licensing bodies have published research showing the importance of effective partnerships with parents. For example, in the document entitled, "Preparing

Educators for Partnerships with Families", the California Commission on Teacher Credentialing states: "A growing number of citizens and educators believe that any workable solution to the problems facing education must include a re-conceptualization of the ways schools work with families and communities. Family involvement in the education of children is known to be critical for effective schooling. Collaboration between schools and homes has repeatedly been found to improve students' achievement, attitudes toward learning, and self esteem. School-home partnerships benefit not only students, but families, schools and teachers." (Ammon, 1998, p. 3). SBFC professionals "walk the talk" by essentially adopting the paradigm that says, the client is the child and family; and the intervention must be inclusive of involvement with the family, the school and the community. Parents and guardians are approached as true partners and persons of authority and wisdom who are in a unique position to provide guidance to the student and the school. This view has much in common with the CBT view of the importance of the "therapeutic alliance." However, this goes a step further in framing this counselor-parent/guardian alliance as fully collaborative in helping a third party: the child. That is, the parents are approached as "co-helpers."

MULTI-CULTURALLY SENSITIVE

Considerable research has shown that western individualistic models of helping are culturally inappropriate with many collectivist cultures, including Asian, Latino, African and Middle Eastern, among others (Sue & Sue, 2008; Hong, Garcia & Soriano, in press). For example, a majority of Mexican immigrants do not share the Western assumptive set that when one has a family problem, one goes to a therapist. Instead, the assumptive set of most traditional Mexicans is to seek guidance from a family elder, from a priest or even a "curandero" (an indigenous healer). Thus counselors offering "therapy" or "counseling" meet with great resistance, even when the problems are significantly stressful. However, an SBFC professional understands that while a Mexican client may resist "counseling" he/she would eagerly seek "educational help" for his/her child or adolescent. Thus the reframing of "counseling" into a psycho-educational model of service reaches both parents and their children.

Going to a school or agency to consult with the counselor on how to help one's child succeed in school is something that many parents are willing to accept (especially if the counselor emphasizes that she/he needs the parents' help). This normalizes the counseling and reframes it in a way that de-stigmatizes coming for counseling. As the school-based family counselor works with the parents and family to help the child, trust is built which permits the counselor to eventually work on other family's issues affecting the child. School-based family counseling is a multi-culturally sensitive approach because it engages parents and families as partners with the school-based family counselor in working to promote the success of the child at school (Soriano, 2004).

CHILD ADVOCACY ROLE

The ethical standards for professional conduct in the helping professions require the clinician to take a stance as an advocate for the client. This is particularly so in the case of the most vulnerable member in a family, a school or in the community: this is the child. Moreover, as society becomes increasingly complex and taxing on families, schools and communities, abuse and neglect of children continues to be an underreported but growing problem. Often this is not necessarily with malicious intent, but due to overwhelmed parents and educators. In SBFC the client is the child, the family, and the school. The SBFC professional acts as an advocate for all three. However, emphasis is given to being an advocate to the child because children are more vulnerable than families or schools. This requires a balancing act by the SBFC professional who must act in the child's best interests while also acting in the best interests of the family and the school. In essence, the SBFC professional is multilingual and multi-visional; he/she learns the language of schools, the language of counseling and the language of families, while understanding the world view of each of them.

PROMOTION OF SCHOOL TRANSFORMATION

As stated earlier when quoting the California Commission on Teacher Credentialing (CCTC), "the problems in the schools are but a reflection of the problems in society" (Dear, 1995). The challenges facing students in public schools are intimately related to the problems facing educators. Any way one looks at the needs of children and adolescents, the structure of the school is not congruous with the life cycle reality of a developing child, a growing adolescent or a diverse, evolving family. This was captured in national milestone publications like "Lost in the Shuffle," "Caught in the Middle" or "Second to None." These are all professional documents and books stating that we essentially forgot to think of the child when configuring the structure of schools. Consequently, a major focus of SBFC philosophy is to put the child and his/her family back in the equation. In an ASCD Journal article, Rick Allen (2010) states: "Whether they call it "middle school" or "junior high school," educator advocates who seek to shine the light on best practices for young adolescent students believe grades 5-9 are pivotal in students' academic careers and should be a key element of school reform. In the last 10 years, with the intense focus on developing solid reading and math skills in early elementary students, lowering the high school dropout rate, and preparing students for college and careers, the needs of middle school students have been overlooked, say middle school experts" (Allen, 2010). Moreover, the SBFC professional knows that the same holds true for the structure of elementary and high schools. SBFC professional counselors are leaders whose vision, illustrated in Figure 1.1, includes the promotion of collaboration and true school reform that places the child and family first.

In SBFC the school, as well as the family, has an obligation to change in order to promote student success and resilience. Schools that have authoritarian or chaotic leadership in the classroom or in the school overall can have a destructive effect on children, as well as a demoralizing effect on teachers and others in the school. The SBFC professional will not only assess the child's behavior and the family's structure and dynamics, but will also assess the organizational structure and dynamics of the child's classroom and school. It is admittedly more difficult to promote school transformation, particularly if the SBFC professional is an intern or recently graduated. Nevertheless, the SBFC professional is in a unique position to initiate small but important changes with principals and teachers by virtue of the counselor's SBFC systems skills.

SBFC: AS A PHILOSOPHICAL WAY OF LIFE

For those of us who work with children, whether at a school, an agency or in private practice, it is difficult to conceive of working with them without in some way first determining those adults who impact them in one way or the other. In some cases the impact is positive, as in my own case (MS) when as a young adolescent my teachers Mr. Menzies or Mr. Freeman took interest in me and took time to meet my family, thereby establishing a personal relationship that steered me in the right path, and turned me on to learning. In one case Mr. Freeman, my history teacher, counseled my mother about ways to navigate the school system, as she was a Mexican immigrant with little schooling in Mexico, let alone in the complexity of the US system of education. Thus when I work with children, I instantly seek to see them in the context of the school and the family, before any attempt to intervene with my counseling. In summary, the SBFC approach to counseling is a social justice approach aimed at empowering children, families and schools, and the communities in which they exist.

HOW TO USE THIS BOOK

This book is organized around the SBFC model (see Figure 1.4). The SBFC model illustrates the primary focus of SBFC: on the family and on the school; on prevention and on intervention. The SBFC model shows the four quadrants: School-Intervention, School-Prevention, Family-Intervention, and Family-Prevention. These four quadrants delineate the four areas in which SBFC professionals typically work. School counselors typically work on the school side. Family counselors typically practice on the Family side. SBFC professionals use an integrated approach working across all four quadrants. The SBFC model is an intervention model that directs attention to specific types of helping interventions.

Family-Intervention: This refers to interventions that focus on promoting family change when family problems are having a negative effect on a student. It also refers to interventions that promote family support to help a student, even when the family is not a source of stress for the student. Examples include: Parent/Guardian Consultation (Parents/Guardians), Couple Counseling (Parents), Conjoint Family Counseling (Family), and Family Counseling with Individuals (Student or family member). Part III presents chapters for working remedially with families.

School-Intervention: This refers to interventions that are required in a school after a problem has clearly developed. Examples of problems include: a bullying incident affecting the entire school or classroom; death of a teacher or student; an incident of violence occurring at school; a group of students all dealing with a similar problem (e.g. parents divorcing). Examples of interventions include: Workshop on Cyberbullying (Students and Teachers), Crisis Intervention (School); Support Groups (Student). Part IV presents chapters for working remedially with students.

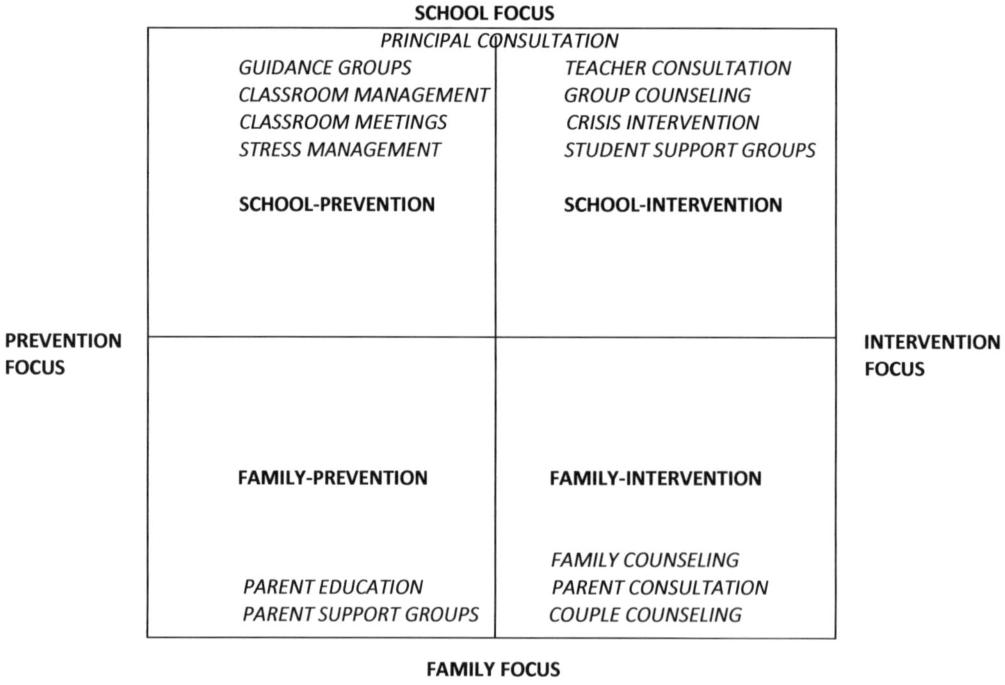

SCHOOL FOCUS

PRINCIPAL CONSULTATION	
GUIDANCE GROUPS	*TEACHER CONSULTATION*
CLASSROOM MANAGEMENT	*GROUP COUNSELING*
CLASSROOM MEETINGS	*CRISIS INTERVENTION*
STRESS MANAGEMENT	*STUDENT SUPPORT GROUPS*
SCHOOL-PREVENTION	**SCHOOL-INTERVENTION**

PREVENTION FOCUS — **INTERVENTION FOCUS**

FAMILY-PREVENTION	**FAMILY-INTERVENTION**
	FAMILY COUNSELING
	PARENT CONSULTATION
PARENT EDUCATION	*COUPLE COUNSELING*
PARENT SUPPORT GROUPS	

FAMILY FOCUS

Figure 1.4 The SBFC Model

Family-Prevention: This refers to interventions that help parents, guardians, and families to develop skills that prevent future problems. Examples include: Family Communication Skills Workshop (Family), Parenting Skills Workshop (Parents and Guardians). Part V presents chapters for working preventively with parents, guardians, and families.

School-Prevention: this refers to interventions that focus on teaching students and/or teachers skills that could prevent future problems. Examples include: Social Skills Training; Stress Management (Students) and Classroom Discipline; Stress Management (Teachers). Part VI presents chapters for working preventively with schools.

Part VII Special Applications in SBFC contains detailed examples of cases and unique programs designed as interventions across the four quadrants of the SBFC Model. As a SBFC professional you will typically work in at least two SBFC quadrants at a time when there is a serious problem affecting a student. Depending on the nature of the problem experienced by a student or students you may end up working in all four quadrants. What we find helpful about this model is the simple way it keeps us focused on working systemically with home and school. This is the heart of the SBFC approach: the integrative use of interventions linking family and school.

REFERENCES

Abdelnoor, A. & Hollins, S. (2004). The effect of childhood bereavement on secondary school performance. *Educational Psychology in Practice, 20 (1),* 43-54.

Adelman, H.S. & Taylor, L. (1998). Reframing mental health in schools and expanding school reform. Educational Psychologist, 33(4), 135-152.

Allen,R. (2010;) Retrieved from ASCD Journal Update, http://www.ascd.org/publications/ newsletters/education-update/jul10/vol52/num07/Caught-in-the-Middle.aspx

Amatea, E., Daniels, H., Bringman, N., & Vandiver, F. (2004). Strengthening counselor-teacher-family connections: the family-school collaborative consultation project. *Professional School Counseling, 8 (1),* 47-52.

Ammon, S. M. (1998). Preparing Educators for Partnerships with Families: Report of the Advisory Task Force on Educator Preparation for Parent Involvement. Sacramento, CA: California Commission on Teacher Credentialing.

Carlson, C. & Sincavage, J. (1987). Family-oriented School Psychology practice: Results of a national survey of NASP members. *School Psychology Review, 16 (4),* 519-526.

Cashwell, C. & Vacc, N. (1996). Family functioning and risk behaviors: influences on adolescent delinquency. *School Counselor, 44 (2),* 105-114.

Coll, K., Thobro, P., & Haas, R. (2004). Relational and purpose development in youth offenders. *Journal of Humanistic Counseling Education and Development, 43 (1),* 41-46.

Crespi, T., Gustafson, A., & Borges, S. (2006). Group counseling in the schools: Considerations for child and family issues. *Journal of Applied School Psychology, 22 (1),* 67-85.

Crespi, T. & Hughes, T. (2004). School-based mental health services for adolescents: School psychology in contemporary society. *Journal of Applied School Psychology, 20 (1),* 67-78.

Dear, J.D. (1995). Creating Caring Relationships to Foster Academic Excellence: Recommendations for Reducing Violence in California Schools. Sacramento, CA: CCTC.

Elliott, G., Cunningham, S., Linder, M., Colangelo, M., & Gross, M. (2005). Child physical abuse and self-perceived social isolation among adolescents. *Journal of Interpersonal Violence,*

20 (12), 1663-1684

Evans, E., Hawton, K. & Rodham, K. (2005). In what ways are adolescents who engage in self-harm or experience thoughts of self-harm different in terms of help-seeking, communication and coping strategies? *Journal of Adolescence, 28 (4),* 573-587.

Fitzpatrick, K., Dulin, A., & Piko, B. (2007). Not just pushing and shoving: school bullying among African American adolescents. *Journal of School Health, 77 (1),* 16- 22.

Fryxell, D. & Smith, D. (2000). Personal, social, and family characteristics of angry students. *Professional School Counseling, 4 (2),* 86-94.

Gerrard, B. (1990). *The mission possible family counseling program.* Unpublished report: School of Education, University of San Francisco, San Francisco.

Gerrard, B. (2008). School-Based Family Counseling: Overview, trends, and recommendations for future research. *International Journal for School-Based Family Counseling,1,* 6-24.

Goldstein, S., Davis-Kean, P. & Eccles, J. (2005). Parents, peers and problem behavior: a longitudinal investigation of the impact of relationship perceptions and characteristics on the development of adolescent problem behavior. *Developmental Psychology, 41 (2),* 401-413.

Hacker, K., Suglia, S., Fried, L., Rappaport, N. & Cabral, H. (2006). Developmental differences in risk factors for suicide attempts between ninth and eleventh graders. *Suicide and Life-threatening Behavior, 36 (2),* 154-166.

Heard, H. (2007). Fathers, mothers, and family structure: family trajectories, parent gender, and adolescent schooling. *Journal of Marriage and Family, 69 (2),* 435-450.

Henderson, A., Sager, T. & Horne, A. (2003). Mothers and sons: a look at the relationship between child behavior problems, marital satisfaction, maternal depression, and family cohesion. *Family Journal: Counseling and Therapy for Couples and Families, 11 (1),* 33-41.

Henry, C., Robinson, L., & Wilson, S. (2004). Adolescent perceptions of their family system, parents' behavior, self-esteem, and family life. *Journal of Child and Adolescent Substance Abuse, 13 (2),* 29-59.

Jeltova, I., Fish, M. & Revenson, T. (2005). Risky sexual behaviors in immigrant adolescent girls from the former soviet union: Role of natal and host culture. *Journal of School Psychology, 43 (1),* 3-22.

Lagana, M. (2004). Protective factors for inner-city adolescents at risk of school dropout: family factors and social support. *Children & Schools, 26 (4),* 211-220.

Lambert, S. & Cashwell, C. (2004). Preteens talking to parents: perceived communication and school-based aggression. *Family Journal: Counseling for Couples and Families, 12* (2), 122-128.

Miller, C., Miller, S., Trampush, J., McKay, K., Newcorn, J., & Halperin, J. (2006). Family and cognitive factors: modeling risk for aggression in children and ADHD. *Journal of the American Academy of Child and Adolescent Psychiatry, 45 (3),* 355-363.

Morris, A., Silk, J., Steinberg, L., Sessa, F., Avenevoli, S., & Essex, M. (2002). Temperamental vulnerability and negative parenting as interacting predictors of child adjustment. *Journal of Marriage and Family, 64 (2),* 461-471.

Ponsford, K. & Lapadat, J. (2001). Academically capable students who are failing in high school: Perceptions about achievement. *Canadian Journal of Counselling, 35 (2),* 137-156.

Schneiders, J., Nicolson, N., Berkhof, J., Feron, F., van Os, J., & de Vries, M. (2006). Mood reactivity to daily negative events in early adolescence: relationship to risk for psychopathology. *Developmental Psychology, 42 (3),* 543-554.

Sigfusdottir, I., Farkas, G., & Silver, E. (2004). The role of depressed mood and anger in the relationship between family conflict and delinquent behavior. *Journal of Youth and Adolescence, 33 (6),* 509-515.

Soriano, M., Soriano, F.I. & Jimenez, E. (1994). School Violence Among Culturally Diverse Populations: Sociocultural and Institutional Considerations. School Psychology Review, 23(2), (216-235).

Sourander, A., Multimaki, P., Nikolakaros, G., Haavisto, A., Ristkari, T., Helenius, H., Parkkola, K., Piha, P., Tamminen, T., Moilanen, I., Kumpulainen, K. & Almqvist, F. (2005). Childhood predictors of psychiatric disorders among boys: a prospective community-based follow-up study from age 8 to early adulthood. *Journal of the American Academy of Child and Adolescent Psychiatry, 44 (8),* 756-767

Steward, R., Jo, H., Murray, D., Fitzgerald, W., Neil, D., Fear, F., and Hill, M. (1998). Psychological adjustment and coping styles of urban African American high school students. *Journal of Multicultural Counseling and Development, 26 (2),* 70-82

Stinchfield, T. (2004). Clinical competencies specific to family-based therapy. C*ounselor Education and Supervision, 43 (4),* 286-292.

Sue, D.W. & Sue, D. (2008*). Counseling the culturally diverse: Theory and practice* (5th Edition). NJ: John Wiley & Sons.

Sun, Y. & Li, Y. (2002). Children's well-being during parents' marital disruption process: a pooled time-series analysis. *Journal of Marriage and Family, 64 (2),* 472- 488.

Wild, L., Flisher, A. & Lombard, C. (2004). Suicidal ideation and attempts in adolescents: associations with depression and six domains of self-esteem. *Journal of Adolescence, 27 (6),* 611-624.

Yip, P., Liu, K., Lam, T., Stewart, S., Chen, E. & Fan, S. (2004). Suicidality among high school students in Hong Kong, SAR. *Suicide and Life-threatening Behavior, 34 (3),* 284-297.

Zimmer-Gembeck, M. & Locke, E. (2007). The socialization of adolescent coping behaviours: relationships with families and teachers. *Journal of Adolescence, 30 (1),* 1-16.

Chapter 2
SBFC: A Re-emerging Paradigm

Brian Gerrard

OVERVIEW: This chapter broadly surveys the School-Based Family Counseling (SBFC) literature from its beginnings in Adler's guidance clinics in the 1920's to the present day. Although the current literature is mainly descriptive and Amerocentric in nature, it reveals a growing support for SBFC across mental health disciplines. Challenges include a need for more evidence-based research, cross-cultural research, and evaluation of different SBFC models and training approaches. Several recommendations for strengthening the SBFC field are made.

ALFRED ADLER: PIONEER IN SBFC

The earliest example of SBFC conducted on a large scale is that of the psychiatrist Alfred Adler in the 1920's (see Figure 2.1).

Figure 2.1 Alfred Adler: Pioneer in SBFC

* Note: This chapter is based on a reprint with permission from the International Journal for School-Based Family Counseling, (2008)1, 1.

Adler describes how he began his work with schools:

> In 1898 I wrote my first article developing my idea of the relation between
> medicine in the larger sense and the school. Later, in connection with an
> extension class, I conducted a clinic. But it was only a small beginning and a
> very unsatisfactory one in the face of the great need for child guidance. Thus
> was born the plan to teach the teachers, for through the school I could reach
> hundreds of children at once.
>
> (Adler, 1927, p.490)

By 1934 Adler in collaboration with the Vienna school system had developed over 30 child guidance clinics (Ansbacher & Ansbacher, 1956). He frequently referred to them as "advisory" clinics. Most were based in schools; some were based in the community. However, irrespective of the site of the guidance clinic, Adler used an integrated counseling approach that emphasized helping children by working collaboratively with parents, teachers, and psychologists. Adler frequently conducted family counseling interviews in auditoriums before an audience of teachers, mental health workers, and parents. Adler describes his school-based counseling approach as follows:

> The purpose of these clinics is to put the knowledge of modern psychology at the
> service of the educational system. A competent psychologist who understands
> not only psychology, but the life of the teachers and parents as well, joins with
> the teachers and holds a consultation clinic on a certain day. On that day the
> teachers will have a meeting, and each one will bring up his particular cases
> of problem children. They will be cases of lazy children, children who corrupt the
> class, children who steal, etc. The teacher describes his particular cases,
> and then the psychologist will contribute his own experiences. Then the discussion
> starts. What are the causes? When did the situation develop? What should be done?
> The family life of the child and his whole psychological development is analyzed.
> With their combined knowledge, the group comes to a decision as to what should be
> done with a particular child.
>
> At the next session the child and the mother are both present. The mother
> will be called in first...Then the mother tells her side of the story, and a
> discussion starts between the mother and the psychologist.....When, finally,
> the method of influencing the child is agreed upon, the child enters the room.
> He sees the teacher and the psychologist, and the psychologist talks to him
> but not about his mistakes. The psychologist speaks as in a lecture, analyzing
> objectively - but in a manner that the child can grasp - the problems and the
> reasons and the ideas that are responsible for the failure to develop properly....
>
> This summary account will give an indication of the possibilities
> that can be realized from the fusion of psychology and education. Psychology
> and education are two phases of the same reality and the same problem.
>
> (Adler, 1930, pp.187-189)

This approach was consistent with Adler's philosophy that a child should not be treated in isolation and that those involved with children would learn in an audience-demonstration format. We see here the elements both of a systems theory and an emphasis on prevention (through education). It could be argued that the first family counseling was conducted by Adler and that it was SBFC. In 1934 all of Adler's child guidance clinics were closed with the coming to power of the Nazis. Following World War II, by 1954, five child guidance clinics were again operating in Vienna (Ansbacher & Ansbacher, 1956). Other Adlerians, especially Dreikers, have emphasized both school and home intervention (Dreikers, 1958, 1965, 1968; Piercy, 1972). Mozak (1971) has described the application of Adlerian principles to an entire school system in the United States. Clearly, SBFC has important roots in Adlerian psychology.

MODERN LITERATURE ADVOCATING A FAMILY SYSTEMS EMPHASIS FOR PROMOTING SCHOOL SUCCESS

THE SCHOOL COUNSELING AND SCHOOL PSYCHOLOGY LITERATURE

The value of a family systems approach when working with a child on a school problem has been attested to by a large number of school counselors and school psychologists (Amatea & Finnette, 1981, 1984; Basal, 1989; Braden & Sherrard, 1987; Bundy & Gumaer, 1984; Capuzzi, 1981; Capuzzi & North, 1984; Carson, 1987; Cooper & Upton, 1990; Downing, 1983; Fine & Gardner, 1991; Fine & Holt, 1983; Ford, 1986; Golden, 1983; Ilowit, 1995; Johnston & Zemitzsch, 1988; Klein, 1981; Kraus, 1998; Lockhart & Keys, 1998; Matthews & Menna, 2003; McComb, 1981; McDaniel, 1981; Mullis & Edwards, 2001; Paget, 1987; Palmo, Lowry, Weldon & Scioscia, 1988; Peeks, 1989, 1993; Ryan, Barham & Fine, 1985; Sawatzky & Pare, 1996; Shepard-Tew & Creamer, 1998;Smith, 1977; Tucker & Bernstein, 1979; Wendt & Zake, 1984; Wilcoxon, 1986; Wilcoxon & Comas, 1987; and Young, 1979).

An important, early article on SBFC by Friesen (1976) is visionary in its call for school counselors to embrace family counseling. Friesen (1977) recommends that SBFCs use four basic approaches to working with families: family life education, family enrichment, family consultation, and marital and family counseling. Goodman and Kjonaas (1984) conducted a SBFC pilot project and concluded that school counselors can, with proper training, do family counseling. Ford (1986) argues that because of growing problems experienced by families and declining parent involvement in schools, learning about family counseling is a necessary next step in the professional development of school counselors, teachers, and principals. Johnston and Zemitzsch (1988) describe the dangers of school intervention programs that focus exclusively on the individual student and ignore the student's other subsystems (family, peer, and community). They advocate a family systems approach that addresses all these subsystems (including the school subsystem) and suggest that school psychologists should begin using family counseling instead of referring students to outside agencies.

Fine and Gardner (1991) contend that having a developmental and family systems orientation is more important for the elementary school counselor than a specific set of techniques. Hinkle, author of the book *Family Counseling in the Schools*, makes a case that school counselors are in a unique position to appreciate, and to utilize, a family systems approach (Hinkle, 1992, 1993). According to Hinkle, many school counselors find family counseling more effective than lengthy individual counseling in the school setting. Even when a referral to a community agency is warranted, the school counselor is more likely to make a successful referral if she/he first conducts a family interview. Nicoll (1992) describes a brief family counseling/family consultation model for school counselors that can be used within the parent-teacher conference setting.

Woody and Woody (1994) in an important article titled "The Fourth Revolution: Family Counseling in the Schools" advocate family counseling as a core counseling approach for use in schools.

Williams (1994) emphasized the need for coordination between the family system, the school system, and community-based mental health systems. Edwards and Foster (1995) recommend uniting the family and school system as a way to empower school counselors. Widerman (1995) emphasized the importance of positive family influence in successful school education and recommended family systems-oriented school counseling as the way to promote this. Lewis (1996) recommends that family counseling be the focus of interventions performed by school counselors. Weiss (1996) describes the work of the Centre for Family-School Collaboration at the Ackerman Institute for Family Therapy. The goal of the Centre, founded in 1981, is to "change the structure of family-school relationships from those characterized by alienated and adversarial interactions to ones which were collaborative and mutually supportive. Our conception was that the school could function as a genuine partner to the family of each school child." (p. 211). Evans and Carter (1997) gave a detailed definition of the role of school-based family counselor along with a case study illustrating comprehensive SBFC intervention strategies with children, teachers, and parents. Colbert (1996), Keys and Bemack (1997), Aviles (1999), Ho (2001), Bryan & Holcomb-McCoy (2004) recommend that school counselors play a leadership role in a school-family-community linked services model for developing comprehensive prevention and intervention programs. Bemak and Cornely (2002) describe the School and Family Intervention (SAFI) Model as an effective approach for school counselors to work with marginalized students and their families.

THE FAMILY COUNSELING LITERATURE

The ratio of articles in the family counseling literature advocating a school emphasis compared to the number of articles in the school counseling/school psychology literature advocating a family emphasis, is about 1:4. This suggests that school counselors and school psychologists are more involved with families than family therapists are involved with schools. Nevertheless, there is a growing awareness among family therapists that family systems theory, which is the dominant paradigm in family therapy, implies not only working with the other members of a child's family, but also working with all the subsystems of which a child is part, including the school subsystem (Cowie, Quinn, Gunning & Gunning, 1998; Palmatier, 1998; Rotter & Boveja, 1999).

Gerald Patterson, at the Oregon Social Learning Center, did pioneering work in the application of behavior therapy to aggressive children with integrated interventions made by parents, siblings, peers, and teachers. The book *Living with children: New methods for parents and teachers* is a classic in the SBFC literature (Patterson & Gullion, 1968). Phillips (1975) was one of the earliest family therapists to recommend that marriage and family counseling be provided through public schools as a way of reaching out to the community. McDaniel (1981) emphasizes the importance of collaboration between family therapists and school counselors. Guerin and Katz (1984) describe five types of problems common to the family with a child experiencing school problems (the child-centered family): emotional vulnerability in the family, conflict with a parent, conflict with a teacher or principal, an enmeshed relationship with a teacher that promotes peer resentment, and parent-teacher conflict. In addition, there are five types of triangles that can be involved in a child's school-related problems: parent-parent-child, parent-sibling-child, sibling-sibling-child, parent-child-teacher, and grandparent-parent-child.

Vazquez-Nuttal, Avila-Vivas and Morales-Barreto (1984) describe the advantages of using a family therapy approach with Latino school children because of the strong emphasis on the family in Latino families. Wetchler (1986) describes a macrosystemic model of family therapy treatment of school problems in which the school and family are viewed as the locus of the problem and treatment consists of the therapist working with the child in each subsystem separately first, and then rejoining the two subsystems in a more functional relationship. Taylor (1986) describes how children can get triangled into a "go-between" role between parents and teachers when ambivalence exists between the home and school systems. Lusterman (1988) describes a case study in which the circumplex model is used to map the dynamics occurring in a child's family and school. McGuire, Manghi and Tolan (1989) recommend that the family therapist conceptualize school behavior problems as part of a home-school system problem. Ron, Rosenberg, Melnick and Pesses (1990) point out that often family therapy alone is insufficient because the child is caught between the dysfunctional interaction between home and school. Inter-systems intervention is required in such cases. Long and Burnett (2005) discuss the importance of couples counseling as an approach for dealing with school-related violence.

Several family therapists have described the use of family therapy to help improve children's academic/school problems (Andrey, Burille, Martinez & Rey, 1978; Freund & Cardwell, 1977; Igarashi, 1992; McGuire & Lyons, 1985; Reimondi, Lockwood & Brannigan, 1981; Wetchler, 1986). Friesen & Der (1978) used a randomized control group design to compare the effectiveness of parent consultation combined with teacher consultation and child counseling with a) teacher consultation and child counseling, b) child counseling, and c) a no treatment group.

A variety of outcome measures were used with 70 grade 4-6 students: the Walker Problem Behavior Identification Checklist, the Werry-Quay classroom observation measure, and measures of reading ability and child self-concept. The three counseling interventions were carried out over four months by graduate counseling students. Counseling compared to no counseling showed significant gains only in reading ability. The teacher consultation and child counseling approach showed more significant gains for reading than did the parent consultation (combined with teacher consultation and child counseling) approach. The researchers concluded that the counselors administering the parent consultation were dealing in many instances with severe family problems that in the future would justify a reduced client load to permit adequate counseling focus on the three modalities used (with parent, teacher, and child). The lack of impact of all three interventions on classroom behavior and self-concept measures suggests possible limitations due to using inexperienced counselor and time-limited counseling.

Santa-Barbara (1979) conducted an outcome study on the effects of brief family therapy on 279 families. Eighty therapists participated in the study and there was a six month follow-up. There were no significant improvements in children's academic performance, compared to control subjects, but there was a significant improvement in classroom behavior. Blechman, Taylor and Schrader (1981) utilized a randomized control group design to investigate the effectiveness of family problem-solving (contingency contracting between parents and children, guided by a problem-solving game) and found it superior to a home note comparison group and the control group in helping academically weak children improve mathematics skills. McGuire and Lyons (1985) describe a community agency-based program to which 17 families were referred by schools because of an underachieving child. After treatment 83% of the children in these families had improved in grades and in classroom behavior.

A causal comparative study by Almonte (2005) assessing the effectiveness of a multicultural counseling program found significant improvements in counselor ratings for classroom behavior, grades, at-home behavior, and DSM GAF scores for students receiving 2 or more family/parent counseling sessions as compared with control group students who received only individual counseling. While this study suggests that increased family contact by the school counselor was beneficial, it must be noted that there was no random assignment of subjects to treatment conditions. The family therapy literature also contains several descriptions of SBFC programs that are university-school partnerships in which graduate family counseling students carry out internships in schools (Albaum, 1990; Carter, 1997; Friesen, 1974; Gerrard, 1993; Hillis, Gerrard, Soriano, Girault, Carter & Hong, 1991; Smith, 1989).

THE SOCIAL WORK AND SPECIAL EDUCATION LITERATURE

In the social work literature, Long (1988) describes the importance of understanding the families of latch key children in order for school personnel to help those families. Wattenberg and Kagle (1986) describe their study of 83 families referred out by school social workers for family therapy. Dicocco, Chalfin and Olson (1987) describe a family therapy program that is a partnership between a community family counseling agency and a public school system. Although in none of these studies is family systems theory emphasized as an integral part of the school social worker's role, there is an awareness of the importance of family variables affecting schoolchildren.

The authors of four articles advocate family counseling as being an important part of the School Social Worker's role (Fine & Jennings, 1985; McCard, 1987; Millard, 1990 (a); Millard, 1990 (b)). Blatt and Staff (1977) describe a collaborative relationship between a child guidance center and an elementary school which resulted in the development of an outreach family therapy mini-clinic in the school. McDonald-Joy (1977) advocates a Montessori schooling approach for the children of alcoholics as a way of raising the children's self-esteem and thereby enhancing treatment of the parent(s) and overall family functioning. This study is interesting because it makes a case for an educational intervention with the child as having an important systems effect on the rest of the family.

In the Special Education literature there are a limited number of references to family counseling as being a valuable part of the Special Education specialist's role. Farago (1988) advocates the use of siblings in therapy as a way to help school children. Dawson and McHugh (1986) describe the use of a family systems approach in a school to reduce attendance problems among children with emotional and behavioral problems. Dawson and McHugh (1987) describe case studies of students whose problems are exacerbated by teacher-parent communication difficulties and give examples of how teachers can make home visits as part of a family systems approach to changing students' behavior. Sixteen students participating in the *Youth in Psychoeducational Services* (YIPS) program received family counseling, in addition to academic and behavioral treatment: 58% showed improvement on a behavior rating checklist, 93% improved in reading achievement, 86% improved in spelling, and 71% improved in reading (District of Columbia Public Schools, 1981).

While the school counseling, school psychology, family therapy, social work, and special education literature contains parallel themes emphasizing the value of intervening in both family and school in order to help children with difficulties at school, this literature is mostly descriptive in nature.

LITERATURE ON COMPREHENSIVE SBFC PROGRAMS

The first comprehensive SBFC program was that developed by Adler and is described in detail above. More recent SBFC programs are described below. Friesen (1974) developed one of the first outreach SBFC programs in a school district through a university-school partnership (between the University of British Columbia and Richmond School District). A community counseling center based in a school was staffed by masters and doctoral students in counseling who used a family systems orientation with school clients. Kramer (1977) describes a family counseling program for alienated secondary school students. The program, at Berkeley High School in California, was supervised by the principal and counselor and was staffed by licensed family therapists. Barksdale (1979) describes a collaborative program between a school district and a community mental health agency. Over two years an outreach SBFC program was developed at one elementary school, then extended in the second year to four additional schools.

Merrill, Clark, Varvil, Sickle, and McCall (1991) describe what may be a model approach for implementing a program in SBFC that is based on retraining of existing school mental health professionals. Over a nine-year period school psychologists and school social workers in the Topeka Public Schools have participated in the SBFC program. Co-therapy teams use a problem solving family systems approach with an average of two families a year. Team members are closely supervised by an experienced family therapy supervisor. The SBFC team members also participate in a bi-monthly seminar that focuses on learning family therapy skills. Data for a five-year period showed that 137 families had been served.

Opuni (1995) describes the Houston Independent School District's *Beating the Odds (BTO)* program, initiated in 1988. BTO provides in-school counseling, community outreach, family case management, and specialized teacher training to assist at-risk secondary students. Opuni credits the BTO program with helping to curb the district's high dropout rate and for improving mathematics achievement with the students involved in the program. Gerrard (1996) outlines the formation of the University of San Francisco's *Mission Possible* program, a university-schools partnership in SBFC that was begun in San Francisco school in 1984 and has now operated for 25 years. Mission Possible places master's level trainees in Marital and Family Therapy in public and private schools where the trainees function as school-counselors, but using a family systems orientation. Since 1984 more than 10,000 at-risk elementary and middle school children and their families, and over 100 San Francisco-Bay area schools have been served. Robbins and Carter (1998) describe a school counseling program called *Family Builders* which was initiated by the Archdiocese of Louisville, Kentucky. The purpose of this program is to help teachers and parents correct undesirable behavior in students through a home/school/community partnership emphasizing recognition of parents as children's primary educators. Repka (1999) reviews the services offered by the Seton Center in New Jersey, which augments support provided by the teacher and principal with parenting classes, parent support groups, and an emphasis on early intervention and prevention.

Carter (2003) describes the Mission Possible program at California State University, Los Angeles. This program places trainees in CSULA's master's degree SBFC program in public schools in the greater Los Angeles schools. This program has provided service to over 30 Los Angeles schools since 1988. Carns and Carns (2003) describe the evolution of a SBFC center in central Texas. Klein (2004) reports on *Community Agency School Services (CASS)*, a program administered by the school district in Frederick County, Maryland. The CASS program consists of 10 licensed master's level social workers each of whom is assigned to a high school feeder area. The program provides case management and referrals for family counseling, housing, and health care for families with problems that may negatively impact their children's learning. Klein indicates that in 2003 more than 700 families were assisted. Amatea, Daniels, Bringman and Vandiver (2004) describe the *Family-School Collaborative Consultation Project*, a three year project of school-wide change initiated by a team of administrators, school counselors, and counselor educators. The primary goal of the project is to create strong working relationships between school counselors, teachers, and students' families. Chafouleas and Whitcomb (2004) present evaluation data from the *Placement Prevention Program* which integrates school, family, and community resources with an emphasis on working closely with families. The authors report that through the use of crisis intervention, counseling, intensive supervision, preventive programming, and mentoring the program has achieved its goal of reducing the number of out-of-home placements and the goal of increasing student success at home and at school has been partially met. Lochman and Wells (2004) report that a randomized control group evaluation of the *Coping Power Program* demonstrated lower rates of covert delinquent behavior and improved classroom behavior in at-risk adolescent boys who received the full program with parent and child intervention components.

SBFC services have also been implemented through school-based health centers called comprehensive school health programs (CSHPs). CSHPs typically provide services and programs covering a wide variety of areas affecting children: health and mental health screening, health services, health education, family planning, family education, schoolwide health promotion, food service, nutrition counseling, school environment, counseling, drug prevention counseling, parent education, physical education, and family, school, and community partnerships (Dryfoos, 1994; Kronick, 2005; Kuersten, 1998; Tyson, 1999; Weist, Rubin, Moore, Adelsheim & Wrobel, 2007). The locating of a comprehensive health center in a school reduces fragmentation of services (Dolan, 1996). Examples of specific programs are: the *School Based Youth Services* program of New Jersey (Dolan, 1996); the *Homan Square Project* in Chicago (Hollinger-Smith, 1998); the *Full Service Schools Program* in Knoxville, Tennessee (Kronick, 2005); and a CSHP program in Providence, Rhode Island school district and Animas, New Mexico (Marx

& Northrop (2000). Ho (2001) and Bryan (2005) have emphasized that school counselors have an important role to play in the provision of CSHPs and school-family-community partnerships through roles such as team facilitator, collaborator, and child advocate. It is important to note that while all CSHPs employ some form of counseling, the degree to which a family systems approach is used varies considerably. Some programs emphasize a traditional mental health approach emphasizing DSM diagnosis and child counseling; others utilize some form of parent education; and some use a strong family systems approach and emphasize family counseling.

Carter and Perluss (2003) have described one of the first master's graduate degree programs in SBFC at California State University, Los Angeles. Graduates of this program which emphasizes integration of school counseling and family counseling approaches within a family systems framework, are eligible for the Pupil Personnel Services credential (which permits them to work in public schools as school counselors), as well as the Marital and Family Therapy license. Carter and Evans (2003) have outlined a detailed step-by-step approach for implementing a comprehensive SBFC program. Terry (2002) describes a one-semester unit course entitled "Family Counseling in the Schools." Some of the books most widely used in university and in-service SBFC training are: *Preparation, Collaboration and Emphasis on the Family in School Counseling for the New Millennium* (Duhon & Manson, 2000); *The Handbook of Family-School Intervention: A Systems Perspective* (Fine & Carlson, 1991); *Family Counseling in School Settings* (Giblin & Walsh, 1998); *Family Counseling in the Schools* (Hinckle & Wells, 1995); and *Integrating School and Family Counseling: Practical Solutions* (Miller, 2002.

FAMILY COUNSELING APPROACHES USED IN SBFC

Some of the family counseling theoretical approaches used in SBFC are: Adlerian family therapy (Arciniega & Newton, 1981; Baideme, Kern & Taffel-Cohen, 1979; Kern & Carlson, 1981; Nicoll, 1984); Eclectic Systems Therapy (Sawatzky, Eckert & Ryan, 1993); Behavioral Family Therapy (Blechman, Taylor, & Schrader,1981; Horne & Walker, 1984; Snyder, Cramer, Afrank & Patterson, 2005); Family of Origin Therapy, Humanistic Family Therapy, and Behavioral Family Therapy (Ford, 1986); Multiple Group Family Therapy (Dombalis & Erchal, 1987); Parent Training (Beutler, 1979; Carr & Carr, 1974; Stapp & Whittlesey, 1972); Psychodynamic and Gestalt Family Therapy (Smith, 1978); Psychodynamic Cognitive-Behavioral Systems therapy (Dineros, 2003); Strategic Family Therapy (Amatea, 1989; Conoley, 1987; Lewis, 1986; McDaniel, 1981; Nelson, 2006; O'Connor & LaSala, 1988; Stone & Peeks, 1986; Webb-Watson, 1988); Structural Family Therapy (Carlson & Sincavage, 1987; Fish & Jain, 1988; Goodman & Kjonaas, 1984); Structural/Strategic Family Therapy (Dicocco, Chalfin & Olson, 1987; Wetchler, 1986); and Solution-Focused Brief Therapy (Williams, 2000). This represents a broad range of traditional family therapy approaches being applied in the school setting.

Specific techniques used in SBFC include: couples counseling (Everts, 2003); collaborative drawing (Van Velsor & Cox, 2000); conjoint family counseling (Albaum, 1990; Arciniega & Newton, 1981; Casey & Buchan, 1991; Carlson & Sincavage, 1987; Conoley, 1987; Dawson & McHugh, 1986; Dombalis & Erchul, 1987; Dowling & Taylor, 1989; Ewashen, 1988; Fine & Gardner, 1991; Ford, 1986; Golden, 1986, 1988; Goodman & Kjonaas, 1984; Peeks, 1989; Stone & Peeks, 1986; Smith, 1989; Stark, Brookman & Frazier, 1990; William & Hugman, 1982); crisis intervention (Trailer, 2004); divorce group counseling with children (Bundy & Gumaer, 1984; Graver, 1987; Prokop, 1990); family autobiography (Holcomb-McCoy, 2004); family change group counseling (Costa & Stiltner, 1994); family drawing (Colba & Brazelton, 1994); the family-school problem-solving meeting (Weiss,1992); letter writing (Yeung, 2005); evidence-based parent training (Valdez, Carlson & Zanger, 2005; mentor families (Fryxell, 2003); parent communication training (Williamson, 1997); parent conferences (Bowman & Goldberg, 1983; Conrad, 1989; Dawson & McHugh, 1987); rituals (Parker, 1999); therapeutic storytelling (Fortune, 2005); and working with grandfamilies (Edwards, 1998).

The literature contains articles describing the value of a family approach in dealing with a wide variety of specific student situations: abuse (Moletsane, 2005); academic difficulties (Stone & Peeks, 1986; Taylor, 1982); alienated students (Kramer, 1977); bereavement (Ayyash-Abdo, 2001; Iverson, 2003); depression (Stark, Brookman & Frazier, 1990; Woods, 2005); developmentally immature students (Campion, 1984); disruptive students (Ewashen, 1988; Williams, 1988); drinking violation (Ford, 1986); dysfunctional families (Bilynsky & Vernaglia, 1999); elective mutism (Lazarus, Gavilo & Moore, 1983); fighting (Canfield, Ballard, Osmon & McCune, 2004); gifted students (Colangelo, 1988; Lester & Anderson, 1981; Zuccone & Amerikaner,1986); HIV/AIDS (Eloff, 2003); homework (Margolis, McCabe & Alber, 2004); improvement of mathematics skills (Blechman, Taylor & Schrader, 1981); learning disabled students (Perose & Perosa, 1981); married students (O'Brian, 1976); parental abuse and neglect (Griggs & Gale, 1977); prejudice towards students with cancer (Tan, 2004); racism (Fusick & Bordeau, 2004); school phobia (Cerio, 1997); school violence (Marchetti-Mercer, 2003); single parent families (Weiers, 1986); social anxiety (Fisher, Masia-Warner & Klein, 2004); special education students (Ferreira, 2003); stepfamilies (Kosinksi, 1983; Medler, 1985; Poppen & White, 1984); substance abuse (Lambie & Rokutani, 2002); suicide (Maples, Packman, Abney, Daugherty, Casey & Pirtle, 2005); and trauma (Kruczek, 2005). The literature describes six main benefits of SBFC for schools: improved academic functioning of the students receiving SBFC, lessening of students' emotional and behavioral problems, decreased classroom disruption of other students, improved functioning of the students at home, improved relationships between schools and families with children having school problems, and cost effectiveness (Albaum, 1990; Stone & Peeks, 1986).

Dowling and Taylor (1989) point out that parents experience SBFC as more accessible and less threatening than going to a traditional clinic. Bobele and Conran (1988) and Colapinto (1988) describe some of the difficulties that arise when school personnel refer students' families to outside agencies for family counseling. There is a danger of the therapist becoming triangulated into a conflict between the school and the family and focusing on the family prematurely rather than viewing the problem as one within the larger school-family system. Carter (1992) has suggested that parents experience less threat with SBFC because the focus of the counseling is academic - "helping the child succeed at school" - rather than dealing exclusively with "family problems." This definition of the family counseling as school-focused reframes family counseling for the parents and family in a way that makes it more socially acceptable.

Quirk, Fine and Roberts (1991) point out that the potential resistance of teachers to parents being more involved in academic decisions is lessened by the family counselor being a part of the school team. Soriano (2003) has described the value of SBFC as transforming and reframing psychological services as educational services and thereby making counseling more accessible to minority families. The SBFC model is a multi-culturally sensitive one that overcomes many of the stigmatizing limitations of traditional DSM-based mental health models that fail to meet the needs of immigrant communities (Soriano, 2005). Examples of this are the multi-culturally relevant programs developed by Everts (2003) and Igoa (2006). Everts (2003) has described a SBFC intervention program with Asian migrant families and their children in which traditional Western counseling programs and techniques were adapted to make them more culturally relevant to the migrant parents and children. Igoa (2006) has developed a teacher approach to SBFC with immigrant children that employs basic counseling strategies and artwork to empower children and their parents.

CHALLENGES IN IMPLEMENTING SBFC

The literature also identifies several problems in the implementation of SBFC. Some of the difficulties in implementing a family systems therapy approach in schools are: a lack of parental cooperation and disparities between home and school behavior (Feldman, Peer, & Altman, 1984). Wendt and Zake (1984) discuss the advantages of training school psychologists in family dynamics and family therapy, but point out that the family systems approach is complex and requires extensive coursework. This has important implications for in-service training and university curricula. Golden (1983) suggests that family therapy is too complex for school counselors, although school counselors can make brief interventions with functional families.

Although the literature reviewed above contradicts Golden's position (there are many studies of school counselors using family therapy techniques effectively), Golden's article indicates the importance of adequate training in family therapy for school counselors. Alessi (1989) states that practicing family therapy in schools involves more complex ethical issues than those usually encountered in private, outpatient practice. Hansen, Green and Kutner (1989), and Mynuson and Noreen (1998) indicate that when school counselors and school psychologists increase their involvement with families, ethical issues related to training and competence and to welfare of consumers are raised. Fine and Holt (1981) identify five obstacles to the school psychologist using family counseling: the school psychologist's competence to do family counseling, resistance to using family counseling, the absence of research in SBFC, difficulties in identifying the client system, and the complexity of system dynamics. Quirk, Fine, and Roberts (1991) describe a number of difficulties associated with family-school systems interventions: school personnel resisting a wider systems focus that includes the family and community; the need for school counselors to do evening work (to accommodate parents); and ethical dilemmas arising from viewing the teacher as a client as opposed to a partner in consultation. Samis (1993) surveyed 249 elementary school counselors and found that they had a preference to do individual counseling with children and teacher consultation rather than to do parent consultation. This suggests that many elementary school counselors might be reluctant to do family counseling because of insufficient training in parent consultation.

Woody (1989) describes the need for curriculum revision in universities to help school psychologists learn SBFC and anticipates that professional defensiveness might be the result. This would seem to be a normal process in the re-visioning of any professional role. Stone and Peeks (1986) describe how some counselors not trained in family systems thinking may have difficulty shifting away from an "individual" psychological way of conceptualizing. Many mental health professionals trained in the diagnostic model of the American Psychiatric Association, called the Diagnostic and Statistical Manual (or DSM), conceptualize mental health problems as mental disorders in individuals. Family therapists generally view the client who presents for therapy as "the identified patient" who is often the symptom bearer for a dysfunctional family system. The DSM emphasis on individual pathology may make it difficult for some mental health professionals to adopt a systems viewpoint which is central to the practice of SBFC.

RECOMMENDATIONS FOR FUTURE RESEARCH

There are several observations that can be made about the abovementioned literature. First, the literature reveals a growing interest in SBFC that cuts across disciplines: school counseling, school psychology, family therapy, school social work, and special education. School practitioners in each of these fields have written about the importance of a family systems theoretical viewpoint in working with children with school difficulties. This represents an important paradigm shift in the conceptualization of counseling school children. In particular, the school counseling literature has given increasing emphasis to the role of the family as it affects children's school behavior and academic performance. Following Adler's impressive 10 year implementation in the 1920's of a SBFC program through 30 guidance clinics linked with Vienna schools, there followed a relative 30 year hiatus after World War II. The literature suggests a strong resurgence of interest in SBFC beginning in the 1970's and continuing into the present. The Adlerian emphasis on a broad school district involvement involving multiple schools has been continued by programs such as the Center for Family-School Collaboration at the Ackerman Institute for Family Therapy and the Mission Possible programs at the University of San Francisco and California State University, Los Angeles.

Second, the literature suggests that there are at least six main types of SBFC service delivery program currently being used: 1) School-sited: In-service Training, 2) School-sited: Family Therapy Staff, 3) School-sited: University-School Collaborative, 4) School-sited: Agency-School Collaborative, 5) Community-sited: Agency, and 6) Community-sited: Private Practice. Table 1.1 lists the six SBFC service delivery program types and compares each one on site of counseling, accountability of SBFC personnel, personnel providing the SBFC, administrative and clinical control of the program, advantages and disadvantages, and examples of representative

programs. The literature suggests that SBFC occurs in a variety of ways, but what all have in common is the emphasis on linking family intervention with school intervention. The relative effectiveness of these different SBFC delivery approaches is unknown. Since the literature reviewed above is primarily US-based, the reader should not assume that there are only 6 types of SBFC delivery approaches.

Third, the literature suggests that the skills needed of persons practicing SBFC are those typically practiced by school counselors, school social workers, and by family counselors. Table 1.2 lists some of the typical skills common to school counseling and family counseling as traditionally practiced in North America. As can be seen from this table, the skill set required of the SBFC professional potentially covers specific school counseling skills (such as career counseling and guidance groups) as well as specific family counseling skills (such as couples counseling and family counseling). Of the 23 skill/competency areas listed 10 are held in common by both school counselors and family counselors. It should be noted that this list is not meant to be exhaustive or to exclude counseling functions performed by other mental health professionals or by important non-mental health professionals, such as educators or peer helpers, e.g. the mentor families described by Fryxell (2003).

Fourth, the SBFC literature reviewed above is primarily descriptive. There is a relative absence of outcome studies, particularly studies comparing SBFC in its various forms with traditional approaches to school counseling. While the logic of combining school and family counseling interventions is compelling, the evidence-based support is sparse.

Fifth, the SBFC literature as it currently exists is primarily US-based and reflects what is primarily an Amerocentric perspective on counseling. There are other important cultural perspectives on ways to help children through home-school intervention and these perspectives need to be investigated and given "voice." For example, there are some schools in South Africa where the students are mostly orphans and live in a home connected to the school (Adams, 2003). In this context, the school functions as a sort of family and the counseling is provided by the teachers who are also parent figures. This echos Adler's belief that teachers are ideally suited to help children overcome psychological problems.

Sixth, the literature also reveals important ethical issues around the level of training needed to do SBFC. Family counseling is a type of group counseling and can be a challenge for counselors who are introverts or who have been trained in only individual counseling. There is a need for SBFC academic programs that are integrated, that is, programs that are not just a splicing together of Family Therapy and School Counseling/School Psychology/School Social Work/Special Education programs, but have a genuinely eco-systemic view of the family-school system (as well as the child's peer and community subsystems).

I would like to offer the following suggestions for a preliminary SBFC research agenda to address some of the challenges described above. First, there is a need for greater documentation of the effectiveness of SBFC using rigorous research designs. Outcome research is needed using traditional between-groups and within-groups experimental designs (as well as mixed designs) evaluating the effectiveness of SBFC in its various forms in comparison with traditional forms of school counseling. To paraphrase the specificity hypothesis:

What forms of SBFC work best with what type of students, parents, and families for what problems, as delivered by which helpers under what conditions...

Attention should be given to:

a) The focus of the counseling: i) parent consultation, ii) conjoint parent and child counseling, iii) conjoint parent, child and family (e.g. sibling, grandparent, etc.) counseling, iv) teacher consultation, v) peer counseling, vi) child counseling with a relationship/family focus. It should be noted that not all family systems interventions are conjoint: some approaches can be used with individuals, as in Bowen therapy and some of the strategic therapies. The intervention is made with an individual, but the counselor is guided by a family systems theory and utilizes relationship change techniques with the client (e.g. behavior rehearsal to help a child communicate more effectively with a parent). This is in contrast to intra-psychic approaches that do not give a primary focus to relationship change.

b) Who the helper is: i) mental health professional, ii) teacher, iii) principal, iv) peer, iv) other adult (e.g. mentor family).

c) The theoretical orientation used: e.g. Cognitive-Behavioral, Narrative, Structural, Brief, Strategic, Solution-Focused, etc.

d) The SBFC service delivery model used (see Table 1.1).

e) The grade level of the students: i) elementary school, ii) middle school, iii) secondary school. In the North American context most mental health professionals seem to believe that the family has less influence on older adolescents and that it is therefore more efficacious to intervene at the elementary level for preventative reasons and because the family can exert a more corrective influence. This assumption cannot be made of other cultural contexts.

Researchers should consider using the Friesen & Der (1978) study as a possible model for SBFC investigation. The main strengths of their research were: a) use of a randomized control group pretest posttest design, b) comparison of multiple counseling treatments, c) use of objective assessments of academic performance and classroom behavior, and d) stratified random sampling of schools to control for socio-economic variables. Their report is useful in that it includes detailed training materials as well as sample letters and strategies used to develop a collaborative relationship with parents.

Second, qualitative and quantitative research should be conducted on the various forms of SBFC practiced internationally. As proposed by Everts (2006a) a survey should be conducted of members of the *Oxford Symposium in SBFC* to determine current best practices of SBFC around the world. At the 2006 Oxford Symposium in SBFC members were polled on their research interests as a first step in the formation of international research teams. The formation of these international research teams should continue as recommended by Everts (2006b). This international research could lead to a valuable broadening of the definition of SBFC and the sharing of new SBFC interventions. The *International Journal of SBFC* could play a valuable role in stimulating international research on SBFC.

Third, research is needed on the most effective ways to train practitioners in SBFC. Some noteworthy examples in the literature include the in-service model described by Merrill et al (1991), the California State University, Los Angeles SBFC masters program (Carter, 2003), and the Personalismo training program (Almonte, 2005).

Fourth, research should be conducted on different SBFC assessment models. There may be an advantage to using assessment models that can be applied in both home and school settings, e.g. the circumplex model (Lusterman, 1988). The advantage may have to do with keeping the counselor focused on the child's relationships with significant others at school and at home and assist in identifying similar relationship patterns occurring in both settings. Resmini (2004) has noted that for some children the situation at school replicates the dysfunctional family environment. Research is needed to determine whether this type of cross-setting assessment facilitates treatment gains.

Fifth, research should be conducted on the various administrative and organizational obstacles to implementing SBFC programs. Examples of these obstacles include: opposition by colleagues who may have a different theoretical orientation; opposition by educational administrators; and dealing with institutional blockages that may interfere with counseling interventions linking children, schools, universities, and families. Most counselors only have to deal with problems within one organization, i.e. their school or agency. SBFC program developers invariably work with multiple groups and organizations that require flexible problem-solving across organizational boundaries. Frequently these different organizational units can behave like dysfunctional families and impede successful SBFC program implementation (Yeung, 2007). Descriptive research, both qualitative and quantitative, would be valuable in delineating the variety of administrative and organizational challenges experienced by SBFC practitioners and possibly suggest strategies for dealing effectively with these challenges.

SUMMARY

These research suggestions are not meant to be exhaustive and are intended to stimulate discussion. This review of the literature suggests that the paradigm of SBFC so strongly launched by Adler in the 1920's, has re-emerged in the 1970's to cross disciplines and establish itself as a meaningful approach to school counseling now utilized by a wide variety of mental health professional and educators. As with all new paradigms the challenge is to now put it to further evidence-based testing.

REFERENCES

Adams, Q. (2003). Lecture on South African orphan schools given at the First *Oxford Symposium in SBFC* held at Keble College, Oxford, August 10 - 15, 2003.

Adler, A. (1927). A doctor remakes education. *Survey, 58,* 490-495.

Adler, A. (1930). *The education of children*. Chicago: Gateway.

Albaum, J. (1990). *A cost free counseling model for high risk elementary students.* Paper presented at the Annual Convention of the American Psychological Association, 98th, Boston, M.A. August 10-14, 1990.

Alessi, G. (1989). Ethical issues facing school psychologists in family therapy: A commentary. *Professional School Psychology, 4 (4),* 265-271.

Allen, S. & Tracy, E. (2004). Revitalizing the role of home visiting by school social workers. *Children and Schools, 26 (4),* 197- 208.

Almonte, L. (2005). The impact of the personalismo experiential training program on counselor trainee effectiveness. *Dissertation Abstracts International*.

Amatea, E., Smith-Adcock, S. & Villares, E. (2006). From family deficit to family strength: viewing families' contributions to children's learning from a family resilience perspective. *Professional School Counseling, 9 (3),* 177-189.

Ansbacher, H. & Ansbacher, R. (1956). *The individual psychology of Alfred Adler*. New York: Harper Perennial.

Arciniega, M. & Newlon, B. (1981). A theoretical rationale for crosscultural family counseling. *School Counselor, 29 (2),* 89-96.

Aviles, R., Guerrero, M., Howarth, H., & Thomas, G. (1999). Perceptions of Chicano/Latino students who have dropped out of school. *Journal of Counseling and Development, 77 (4),* 465- 473.

Ayyash-Abdo, H. (2001). Childhood bereavement: what school psychologists need to know. *School*

Psychology International, 22 (4), 417-433.

Bemak, F. & Cornely, L. (2002). The SAFI model as a critical link between marginalized families and schools: a literature review and strategies for school counselors. *Journal of Counseling & Development, 80 (3),* 322-331.

Bilynsky, N. & Vernaglia, E. (1999). Identifying and working with dysfunctional families. *Professional School Counseling, 2 (4),* 304 -313.

Bryan, J. (2005). Fostering educational resilience and achievement in urban schools through school-family-community partnerships. *Professional School Counseling, 8 (3),* 219-225.

Bryan, J. & Holcomb-McCoy, C. (2004). School counselors' perceptions of their involvement in school-family-community partnerships. *Professional School Counseling, 7 (3),* 162-175.

Canfield, B., Ballard, M., Osmon, B., & McCune, C. (2004). School and family counselors work together to reduce fighting at school. *Professional School Counseling, 8 (1),* 40-50.

Capuzzi, D. & Noeth, R. (1984). Counselor skills: Expectancies for the future, part one. *School Counselor, 31 (3),* 205-294.

Carlson, C. (1987). Resolving school problems with Structural Family Therapy. *School Psychology Review, 16 (4),* 457-468.

Carns, A. & Carns, M. (1997). A systems approach to school counseling. *School Counselor, 44 (3),* 218-223.

Carns, M. & Carns, A. (2003). The evolution of a SBFC center in central Texas. *Proceedings of the 2003 Oxford Symposium in SBFC.* San Bruno: Institute for School-Based Family Counseling.

Carter ,M. (1990). Personal Communication.

Carter, M. & Evans, W. (2003). A procedural model for assessment and treatment in SBFC. *Proceedings of the 2003 Oxford Symposium in SBFC.* San Bruno: Institute for School-Based Family Counseling.

Carter, M. & Perluss, E.(2003). Developments in training school-based family counselors: the School-Based Family Counseling (SBFC) graduate program at California State University, LosAngeles. *Proceedings of the 2003 Oxford Symposium in SBFC.* San Bruno: Institute for School-Based Family Counseling.

Casey, J. & Buchan, G. (1991). Family approaches to school psychology: Brief strategic family intervention. *School Psychology International, 12 (4),* 349-353.

Cerio, J. (1997). School phobia: a family systems approach. *Elementary School Guidance & Counseling, 31 (3),* 180-191.

Chafouleas, S. & Whitcomb, M. (2004). Integrating home, school, and community resources: Evaluation of a district-wide prevention program. *Reclaiming Children and Youth: the Journal of Strength-based Interventions, 12 (4),* 203-215.

Cobla, D. & Brazelton, E. (1994). The application of family drawing tests with children in remarriage families: understanding familial roles. *Elementary School Guidance and Counseling, 29 (2),* 129-136.

Colangelo, N. (1988). Families of gifted children: The next ten years. *Roeper Review, 11 (1),* 16-18.

Colapinto, J. (1988). Avoiding a common pitfall in compulsory school referrals. *Journal of Marital and Family Therapy, 14 (1),* 89-96.

Colbert, R. (1996). The counselor's role in advancing school and family partnerships. *School Counselor, 44 (2),* 100-104.

Colpin, H., Vandemeulebroecke, L., & Ghesquiere, P. (2004). Supporting the educational career of children from divorced families: Parents' experiences and the role of the school. *British Journal of Sociology of Education, 25 (3),* 275-289.

Conoley, J. (1987). Strategic family intervention: Three cases of school-aged children. *School Psychology Review, 16 (4),* 469-486.

Conrad, M. (1989). Informing parents that their children may be handicapped. *School Counselor, 36 (5),* 380-383.

Costa, L. & Stiltner, B. (1994). Why do the good things always end and the bad things go on forever: a family change counseling group. *School Counselor, 41 (4),* 300- 304.

Cowie, K., Quinn, K., & Gunning, M. (1998). School/home issues related to grief and loss within the families of disabled students: a systems approach. *Family Journal: Counseling and Therapy for Couples and Families, 6 (2),* 141-146.

Davis, K. (2001). Structural-strategic family counseling: a case study in elementary school counseling. *Professional School Counseling, 4 (3),* 180-186.

Dawson, N. & McHugh, B. (1986). Application of a family systems approach in an education unit. *Maladjustment and Therapeutic Education, 4 (2),* 48-54.

Dawson, N. & McHugh, B. (1987). Learning to talk to parents. *British Journal of Special Education, 14 (3),* 119-121.

Dicocco, B., Chalfin, S. & Olson, J. (1987). Systemic family therapy goes to school. *Social Work in Education, 9 (4),* 209-221.

Dineros, S. (2003). A psychodynamic cognitive-behavioral systems approach to school-based family counseling. *Proceedings of the 2003 Oxford Symposium in School- Based Family Counseling.* San Bruno: Institute for School-Based Family Counseling.

Dolan, L. (1996). New Jersey's school based youth services program. *New Schools, New Communities, 12 (3),* 48-52.

Dombalis, A. & Erchul, W. (1987). Multiple family group therapy: A review of its applicability to the practice of School Psychology. *School Psychology Review, 16 (4),* 487-497.

Dowling, E. & Taylor, D. (1989). The clinic goes to school: Lessons learned. *Maladjustment and Therapeutic Education, 7 (1),* 24-29.

Downing, J. (1983). A positive way to help families. *Elementary School Guidance and Counseling, 17 (3),* 208-213.

Dreikurs, R. (1958). *Children: The challenge.* New York: Norton.

Dreikurs, R. & Cassel, P. (1965). *Discipline without tears.* New York: Harper & Row.

Dreikurs, R. (1968). *Maintaining sanity in the classroom.* New York: Harper & Row.

Dryfoos, J. (1994). *Full-service schools: a revolution in health and social services for children, youth, and families.* San Francisco: Jossey-Bass.

Dunst, C. & Trivette, C. (1987). Enabling and empowering families: Conceptual and intervention issues. *School Psychology Review, 16* (4), 443-456.

Edwards, D. & Foster, M. (1995). Uniting the family and school systems: a process of empowering the school counselor. *School Counselor, 42 (4),* 277-282.

Edwards, O. (1998). Helping grandkin--grandchildren raised by grandparents: expanding psychology in the schools. *Psychology in the Schools, 35 (2),* 173-181.

Ehrlich, M. (1983). Psychofamilial correlates of school disorders. *Journal of School Psychology, 21 (3),* 191-199.

Eloff, I. (2003). Mapping assets in SBFC. *Proceedings of the 2003 Oxford Symposium in SBFC.* San Bruno: Institute for School-Based Family Counseling.

Evans, W. & Carter, M. (1997). Urban SBFC: role definition, practice applications, and training implications. *Journal of Counseling and Development, 75 (5),* 366-374.

Everts, H. (2003) Integrating pastoral care in schools with the enhancement of family resilience: a New Zealand project for migrant families. *Proceedings of the 2003 Oxford Symposium in SBFC.* San Bruno: Institute for School-Based Family Counseling.

Everts, H. (2006a) Personal communication.

Everts, H. (2006) The contribution of the Oxford symposia to school-based family counseling: development of a vision and its implications for research. A paper delivered at the Fourth *Oxford*

Symposium in SBFC held at Brasenose College, Oxford, August 6 – 11, 2006.

Ewashen, G. (1988). School suspension alternatives. *Education Canada, 28 (1),* 49.

Exum, H. (1983). Key issues in family counseling with gifted and talented black students. *Roeper Review, 5 (3),* 28-31.

Ferreira, R. (2003). SBFC in a South African school for special education. *Proceedings of the 2003 Oxford Symposium in School-based Family Counseling.* San Bruno: Institute for School-Based Family Counseling.

Farago, S. (1988). Expanding the horizon: Sibling contributions to the ecological model. *Perception, 23,* 3.

Fine, M. & Gardner, A. (1991). Counseling and education services for families: An empowerment perspective. *Elementary School Guidance and Counseling, 26 (1),* 33- 44.

Fine, M. & Holt, P. (1981). The family-school relationship: A systems perspective. Paper presented at the *Annual Convention of the American Psychological Association,* 89th, Los Angeles, CA, August, 24-26.

Fine, M. & Holt, P. (1983a). Intervening with school problems: A family systems perspective. *Psychology in the Schools, 20 (1),* 59-66.

Fine, M. & Holt, P. (1983b). Corporal punishment in the family: A systems perspective. *Psychology in the Schools, 20 (1),* 85-92.

Fine, M. & Jennings, J. (1985). What parent education can learn from family therapy. *Social Work in Education, 8 (1),* 14-30.

Fish, M. & Jain, S. (1988). Using systems theory in school assessment and intervention: A structural model for school psychologists. *Professional School Psychology, 3 (4),* 291-300.

Fisher, P., Masia-Warner, C., & Klein, R. (2004). Skills for social and academic success: a school-based intervention for social anxiety disorder in adolescents. *Clinical Child and Family Psychology Review, 7 (4),* 241-249.

Ford, R. (1989). *Family Counseling strategies in the schools.* ERDS, Washington.

Fortune, S. (2005). Therapeutic storytelling intervention (TSI) in school-based family counseling. *Proceedings of the 2005 Oxford Symposium in School-based Family Counseling.* San Bruno: Institute for School-Based Family Counseling.

Friesen, J. (1976) Family counselling – a new frontier for school counselors. *Canadian Counsellor, 10 (4),* 180-184.

Friesen, J. (1977) The school and family facilitation. *School guidance worker, 33 (2),* 31-34.

Fryxell, D. (2003) Three models for providing mental health services to students and their families: Training mentor families; drug prevention for teenage girls; primary school adjustment project. *Proceedings of the 2003 Oxford Symposium in School-based Family Counseling.* San Bruno: Institute for School-Based Family Counseling.

Gerrard, B. (1993). *The school success program.* Unpublished report: Center for Child and Family Development, School of Education, University of San Francisco, San Francisco.

Gerrard, B. & Perry, K. (1995). *Report to the GAP Foundation on the School Success Program.* Unpublished report: University of San Francisco, San Francisco.

Gilbert, J. (1996). School social workers as family therapists: a dialectical-systemic-constructivist model. *Social Work in Education, 18 (4),* 222-236.

Golden, L. (1990). *Brief family consultation in schools.* Highlights: an ERIC/CAPS Digest. ERIC Clearinghouse on Counseling and Personnel Services, Ann Arbor, Michigan.

Golden, L. (1988). Quick assessment of family functioning. *School Counselor, 35 (3),* 179-184.

Golden, L. (1986). Identifying families who benefit from brief interventions. Paper presented at the *Annual Convention of the American Association for Counseling and Development,* Los Angeles, CA, April 20-23.

Golden, L. (1983). Brief family interventions in a school setting. *Elementary School Guidance and Counseling, 17 (4),* 288-293.

Goodman, R. and Kjonaas, D. (1984). Elementary school family counseling: A pilot project. *Journal Counseling and Development, 63 (4),* 255-257.

Graver, C. (1987) Group counseling program helps students deal with divorce. *NASSP Bulletin, 71 (499),* 32-34.

Handy, L. (2004). Children with social-emotional issues and the family systems approach. *Reclaiming Children and Youth: The Journal of Strength-based Interventions, 12 (4),* 222-228.

Hansen, J., Green, S. & Kutner, K. (1989). Ethical issues facing school psychologists working with families. *Professional School Psychology, 4 (4),* 245-255.

Hanselman, P. (1989). Countering rejection anxiety. *School Counselor, 36 (5),* 376-379.

Hillis, R., Gerrard, B., Soriano, M., Girault, E., Carter, M. & Hong, P. (1991). Mission Possible: a School Based Family Counseling Program. Paper presented at the A*merican Psychological Association Annual Conference,* Los Angeles.

Ho, B. (2001). Family-centered, integrated services: opportunities for school counselors. *Professional School Counseling, 4 (5),* 357-361.

Holcomb-McCoy, C. (2004). Using the family autobiography in school counselor preparation: an introduction to a systemic perspective. *Family Journal: Counseling and Therapy for Couples and Families, 12 (1),* 21-25.

Holcomb-McCoy, C. & Mitchell, N. (2005). A descriptive study of urban school counseling programs. *Professional School Counseling, 8 (3),* 203-215.

Hollinger-Smith, L. (1998). Partners in collaboration: the Homan Square project. *Journal of Professional Nursing, 14 (6),* 344-349.

Howit, G. (1995). School-based outreach network counseling. *School Counselor, 43 (2),* 93-96.

Igoa, C. (2006). The inner world of the immigrant child: a case study. A paper delivered at the Fourth *Oxford Symposium in SBFC* held at Brasenose College, Oxford, August 6 – 11, 2006.

Iverson, N. (2003). Living with loss, learning to heal: Children, families, communities and schools. *Proceedings of the 2003 Oxford Symposium in School-based Family Counseling.* San Bruno: Institute for School-Based Family Counseling.

Johnston, J. & Fields, P. (1981). School consultation with the "classroom family". *School Counselor, 29 (2),* 140-146.

Johnston, J. & Zemitzsch, A. (1988). Family power: An intervention beyond the classroom. *Behavioral Disorders, 14 (1),* 69-79.

Keys, S. & Bemak, F. (1997). School-family-community linked services: a school counseling role for changing times. *School Counselor, 44 (4),* 255-263.

Klein, E. (2004). Forging partnerships to meet family needs. *School Administrator, 61 (7),* 40-45.

Khamis, V. (2005). Post-traumatic stress disorder among school age Palestinian children. *Child Abuse and Neglect, 29 (1),* 81-95.

Kosinski, F. (1983). Improving relationships in stepfamilies. *Elementary School Guidance and Counseling, 17 (3),* 200-207.

Kraus, I. (1998). A fresh look at school counseling: a family systems approach. *Professional School Counseling, 1 (4),* 12-17.

Kronick, R. (2005). *Full service community schools: prevention of delinquency in students with mental illness and/or poverty.* New York: Charles C. Thomas.

Kruczek, T. (2005). Family involvement in school-based treatment of childhood trauma. *Proceedings of the 2005 Oxford Symposium in SBFC.* San Bruno: Institute for School-Based Family Counseling

Kuersten, J. (1998). Comprehensive school health programs: an idea whose time has come. *Our Children, 23 (6),* 6-10.

Kwame, A. (1995). Beating the odds: a support program for at-risk students. *ERS Spectrum*, *13 (2)*, 37-43.

Lambie, G. & Rokutani, L. (2002). A systems approach to substance abuse identification and intervention for school counselors. *Professional School Counseling*, *5 (5)*, 353- 359.

Lester, C. & Anderson, R. (1981). Counseling with families of gifted children: The school counselor's roles. *School Counselor*, *29 (2)*, 147-151.

Lewis, W. (1996). A proposal for initiating family counseling interventions by school counselors. *School Counselor*, *44 (2)*, 93-99.

Lochman, J. & Wells, K. (2004). The coping power program for preadolescent aggressive boys and their parents: outcome effects at the 1-year follow-up. *Journal of Consulting and Clinical Psychology*, *72 (4)*, 571-578.

Lockhart, E. & Keys, S. (1998). The mental health counseling role of school counselors. *Professional School Counseling, 1 (4)*, 3-6.

Long, L. (1988). Providing assistance to latchkey families. *Pointer*, *33 (1)*, 37-40.

Long, L. & Burnett, J. (2005). Teaching couples counseling: an integrative model. F*amily Journal: Counseling and Therapy for Couples and Families*, *13 (3)*, 321-327.

Lusterman, D. (1988). School-family intervention and the circumplex model. *Journal of Psychotherapy and the Family*, *4 (12)*, 267-283.

Mainor, P. (2001). Family matters. *Tribal College Journal*, *12 (4)*, 10-13.

Maples, M., Packman, J., Abney, P., Daugherty, R., Casey, J., & Pirtle, L. (2005). Suicide by teenagers in middle school: a postvention team approach. *Journal of Counseling & Development, 83 (4)*, 397-405.

Marchetti-Mercer, M. (2003). Therapeutic interventions in the aftermath of school violence: Guidelines for mental health professionals. Proceedings: Oxford Symposium in School-Based Family Counseling. San Francisco, CA: Institute for School-Based Family Counseling.

Margolis, H., McCabe, P., & Alber, S. (2004). Resolving struggling readers' homework difficulties: How elementary school counselors can help. *Educational Psychologist*, *15 (1)*, 79-110.

Margolin, S. (2001). Interventions for nonaggressive peer-rejected children and adolescents: a review of the literature. *Children and Schools*, *23 (2)*, 73-83.

Markward, M. & Bride, B. (2001). Oppositional defiant disorder and the need for family-centered practice in schools. *Children and Schools*, *23 (2)*, 73-83.

Marx, E. & Northrop, D. (2000). Partnerships to keep schools healthy. *Educational Leadership*, *57(6)*, 22-24.

Matthews, D. & Menna, R. (2003). Solving problems together: Parent/school/community collaboration at a time of educational and social change. *Education Canada*, *42 (1)*, 20-23.

McCard, K. (1987). School Social Work interventions with families problems and prospects. In McCullagh, J. & McCullagh, A. (Eds.) *School social work interventions with behaviorally disordered children: Practical applications of theory*. Iowa State Dept. of Education, Des Moines.

McGuire, D. & Lyons, J. (1985). A transcontextual model for intervention with problems of school underachievement. *American Journal of Family Therapy*, *13 (3)*, 37-45.

McGuire, D., Manghi, E. & Tolin, P. (1989). The family school system: The critical focus for structural/strategic therapy with school behavior problems. *Journal of Psychotherapy and the Family*, *6 (34)*, 108-127.

Miller, L. (Ed.) (2002). *Integrating school and family counseling: practical solutions*. Alexandria, VA.: American Counseling Association.

Medler, B. (1985). Identification and treatment of stepfamily issues for counselors and teachers. Paper presented at the *Annual Convention of the American Association for Counseling and Development*, New York, NY, April 25.

Melcer, D. (1981). Family therapy and the school system. Paper presented at the *Annual Meeting of the National Council on Family Relations*, Milwaukee, WI, October, 1317.

Millard, T. (1990a). School-based social work and family therapy. *Adolescence, 25 (98),* 401-408.

Millard, T. (1990b). School-based Social Work and Family Therapy. *Family Therapy, 17(1),* 83-90.

Moletsane, M. (2005). Resilience in abused South African youth: a case study. *Proceedings of the 2005 Oxford Symposium in SBFC.* San Bruno: Institute for School-Based Family Counseling.

Mozak, H. (1971). Strategies for behavior change in schools: consultation strategies. *Counseling Psychologist, 3,* 58-62.

Mullis, F. & Edwards, D. (2001). Consulting with parents: applying family systems concepts and techniques. *Professional School Counseling, 5 (2),* 116-123.

Nelson, J. (2006). For parents only: a strategic family therapy approach in school counseling. *Family Journal: Counseling and Therapy for Couples and Families, 14* (2), 180-183.

O'Connor, J. & LaSala, M. (1988). An invariant intervention of last resort: treatment of chronic school failure in adolescents. *Journal of Strategic and Systemic Therapies, 7 (3),* 53-66.

Ozer, E. (2005). The impact of violence on urban adolescents: longitudinal effects of perceived school connection and family support. *Journal of Adolescent Research, 20 (2),* 167-192.

Paget, K. (1987). Systemic family assessment: Concepts and strategies for school psychologists. *School Psychology Review, 16 (4),* 429-442.

Palmatier, L. (Ed.) (1998). *Crisis counseling for a quality school community: applying William Glasser's choice therapy.* New York: Routledge.

Parese, S. (2002). "It ain't like she's my mother:" Tyanna's red flag intervention. *Reclaiming Children and Youth, 10 (4),* 246-250.

Parker, R. (1999). The art of blessing: Teaching parents to create rituals. *Professional School Counseling, 2 (3),* 218-225.

Patterson, C. (1986). Some strategies for readers. *Journal of Counseling and Development, 65 (4),* 204.

Patterson, G. & Guillon, E. (1968). *Living with children: new methods for parents and teachers.* Champaign, Il.: Research Press.

Peeks, B. (1989). Farm families in crisis: The school counselor's role. *School Counselor, 36 (5),* 384-388.

Perosa, L. & Perosa, S. (1981). The school counselor's use of structural family therapy with learning disabled students. *School Counselor, 29 (2),* 152-155.

Prokop, M. (1990). Children of divorce: Relearning happiness. *Momentum, 21 (2),* 72-73.

Rayment, J. (2006). Child and youth care as psychotherapy. *Reclaiming Children and Youth: the Journal of Strength-based Interventions, 15 (2),* 85-88.

Repka, J. (1999). Seton Center: a family systems approach. *Momentum, 30 (1),* 14-16.

Robbins, T. & Carter, M. (1998). Family builders: counseling families in Catholic schools. *Momentum, 29 (3),* 31-33.

Ron, K., Rosenberg, R., Melnick, T. & Pesses, D. (1990). Family therapy alone is not enough: Or, the dirty story of Dorian. *Contemporary Family Therapy, 12 (1),* 35-48.

Rotter, J. & Boveja, M. (1999). Family therapists and school counselors: a collaborative endeavor. *Family Journal: Counseling and Therapy for Couples and Families, 7 (3),* 276-279.

Ryan, B., Barham, R. & Fine, M. (1985). The functional role of school problems in a child's family. *Interchange, 16 (4),* 113.

Sheridan, S. & Kratochwill, T. (2007). *Conjoint behavioral consultation: Promoting family-school connections and interventions* New York: Springer.

Siu, A. & Shek, D. (2005). Relations between social problem solving and indicators of interpersonal and family well-being among Chinese adolescents in Hong Kong. *Social Indicators Research, 71 (1-3),* 517-539

Smith, A. (1977). Encountering the family system in school related behavior problems. A paper presented at the *National Association of School Psychologists Convention*, Cincinnati, Ohio, March.

Smith, D. (1989). A joint venture in counselor education: The Clovis family counseling center. *Counselor Education and Supervision, 28 (3),* 253-258.

Snyder, J., Cramer, A., Afrank, J. & Patterson, G. (2005) The contributions of ineffective discipline and parental hostile attributions of child misbehavior to the development of conduct problems at home and school. *Developmental psychology, 41 (1),* 30-41.

Soriano, M. (2004). SBFC: a caring, culturally congruent bridge to diverse communities. *Proceedings of the 2004 Oxford Symposium in SBFC*. San Bruno: Institute for School-Based Family Counseling.

Stark, K., Brookman, C. & Frazier, R. (1990). A comprehensive school-based treatment program for depressed children. *School Psychology Quarterly, 5 (2),* 111-140.

Stone, G. & Peeks, B. (1986a). The use of strategic family therapy in the school setting: A case study. *Journal of Counseling and Development, 65 (4),* 200-203.

Stone, G. & Peeks, B. (1986b). Some strategies for readers: Response to Patterson. *Journal of Counseling and Development, 65 (4),* 204.

Tan, V. (2004). Evaluation of a school-based cancer education programme and its impact on peer acceptance for children with cancer. *Proceedings of the 2004 Oxford Symposium in SBFC*. San Bruno: Institute for School-Based Family Counseling.

Taylor, D. (1986). The child as go between: Consulting with parents and teachers. *Journal of Family Therapy, 8 (1),* 79-89.

Taylor, G. (2000). *Parental involvement: a practical guide for collaboration and teamwork for students with disabilities*. New York: C.C. Thomas

Terry, L. (2002). Family counseling in the schools: a graduate course. *Family Journal: Counseling and Therapy for Couples and Families, 10 (4),* 419-428.

Thomas, C. & Corcoran, J. (2003). Family approaches to attention deficit hyperactivity disorder: a review to guide school social work practice. *Children and Schools, 25 (1),* 19-34.

Trailer, C. (2004). Crisis intervention in SBFC. *Proceedings of the 2004 Oxford Symposium in SBFC*. San Bruno: Institute for School-Based Family Counseling.

Tyson, H. (1999). A load off teachers' backs: coordinated school health programs. *Phi Delta Kappan, 80 (5),* 1-8.

Valdez, C., Carlson, R., & Zanger, D. (2005). Evidence-based parent training and family interventions for school behavior change. *School Psychology Quarterly, 20 (4),* 403- 433.

Van Velsor, P. & Cox, D. (2000). Use of collaborative drawing technique in school counseling practicum: an illustration of family systems. *Counselor Education and Supervision, 40 (2),* 141-152.

Wattenberg, S. & Kagle, J. (1986). School social work referrals for family therapy. *Social Work in Education, 8 (4),* 231-242.

Webb-Watson, L. (1988). Larger system interviewing: Expanding resources for change. *Family Therapy Collections, 24,* 119-130.

Weist, M., Rubin, M., Moore, E., Adelsheim, S., & Wrobel, G. (2007). Mental health screening in schools. *Journal of School Health, 77 (2),* 53-58.

Wendt, R. & Zake, J. (1984). Family systems therapy and school psychology: Implications for training and practice. *Psychology in the Schools, 21 (2),* 204-210.

Wetchler, J. (1986). Family therapy of school-focused problems: A macrosystemic perspective. *Contemporary Family Therapy, 8 (3),* 224-240.

Widerman, J. & Widerman, E. (1995). Family systems-oriented school counseling. *School Counselor, 43 (1),* 66-73.

Wilcoxon, A. (1986). Family counseling practices: Suggested reading guide for School Counselors. *School Counselor, 33 (4),* 272-278.

Wilcoxon, A. & Comas, R. (1987). Contemporary trends in family counseling: What do they mean for the school counselor? *School Counselor,* 34 *(3),* 219-225.

Williams, G. (1988). School counselors using group counseling with family-school problems. *School Counselor, 35 (3),* 169-178.

Williams, G. (2000). The application of solution-focused brief therapy in a public school setting. *Family Journal: Counseling and Therapy for Couples and Families, 8 (1),* 76-78.

Williamson, L. (1997). Parents as teachers of children program (PATCH). *Professional School Counseling, 1 (2),* 7-12.

Woods, B. (2005). A school-based preventive depression programme trial. *Proceedings of the 2005 Oxford Symposium in SBFC.* San Bruno: Institute for School-Based Family Counseling.

Woody, R. (1989). Working with families: A school psychology training perspective. *Professional School Psychology, 4 (4),* 257-260.

Yeung, K. (2005). Innovative collaboration with schools: "Uncle-long-legs" letter box and "Y2K ICQ counseling project." *Proceedings of the 2005 Oxford Symposium in SBFC.* San Bruno: Institute for School-Based Family Counseling.

Yeung, K. (2007) Comment made during the presentation Quality parenting project: implications for SBFC from the study of core values on parenting. Paper presented at the Fifth *Oxford Symposium in School-Based Family Counseling* held at Robert Black College, University of Hong Kong, June 24 – 29, 2007.

Zuccone, C. & Amerikaner, M. (1986). Counseling gifted underachievers: A family systems approach. *Journal of Counseling and Development, 64 (9),* 590-592.

Chapter 3

Ethical and Legal Guidelines for Implementing a School-Based Family Counseling Services Program

Marcel Soriano

OVERVIEW: This chapter provides a legal and ethical framework for guiding professionals who work in schools in a helping capacity. It lays out the potential legal and ethical challenges that must be addressed when practicing outside the boundaries of traditional counselor training. It also provides rationale advancing School Based Family Counseling as an effective approach to serving children and families within the context of schools.

BACKGROUND: LAW, ETHICS, AND SBFC

It is often said that law and ethics are some times at opposite polarities when it comes to giving guidance to counselors on decisions to undertake when helping clients. The paradigm for legal discourse is seen as black or white, true or false, legal or illegal. Ethical discourse, on the other hand, takes on a more nuanced, relativistic stance between black and white, adding gradients of gray to be considered. Ethical decision making is more like the rainbow, with hues of diverse colors and intensities that defy simple yes or no responses. In fact, law and ethics are often contradictory. Imagine, for example, a counselor working with an undocumented Mexican client who smokes marijuana. From the legal perspective the counselor accepts the client and his/her behavior, but he/she might mention the fact that it is illegal, or that the drug may have long-term adverse consequences, leading to possible dependency implications.

From an ethical perspective, however, a counselor must also inform the client of the risk of deportation, even if he/she is prescribed marijuana, since federal law still lists it as an illegal drug. The counselor must also make him/her aware that in some communities law enforcement detains undocumented arrestees and turns them over to the Immigration and Customs Enforcement (ICE) Department. Thus, failing to inform his/her client increases the risk of an accusation of unethical conduct against the provider. This illustrates some of the complexity that lies between law and ethics. Some actions are legal, but may be unethical, while others are ethical but may be illegal.

This discussion is relevant as we will see when we continue our discussion of legal and ethical conduct by school-based family counselors (SBFCs) who essentially straddle boundaries not traditionally faced by school counselors, school social workers, school psychologists, marriage and family therapists or psychologists working in schools. SBFC professionals from a variety of licensure backgrounds see the wisdom of working systemically with the child and the family, with teachers and other professionals who have an interest in the child, but who work with the child in ways that can potentially raise ethical and legal challenges. The intent of this chapter is to help SBFC professionals reduce, if not entirely avoid, the risk of an allegation of unethical or unprofessional conduct.

THE SCHOOL AND ITS EVOLVING CULTURAL CONTEXT

Traditional public schools represent an organizational culture originally designed to provide a context for academic teaching and learning. However, the progressive education movement in the early nineteenth and into the 20th Centuries, pioneered by child advocates such as John Dewey (Ratner, 1939), redefined the school's mission as one inclusive of preparation of civic minded citizens who are fully prepared for living in a civil society. A further expansion of the role of the public school, has taken place over the past three or four decades in order to accommodate a changing philosophy that is more developmentally sensitive and inclusive of special needs children and their parents. This has been accomplished due to the growing body of literature that suggests that a good academic learning outcome is dependent on a strong partnership with parents (Dear, 1995; Gestwicki, 2010). Thus the school and its academic domain has evolved over the years to include the development of career and personal/social domains, now codified in the current standards for counselor preparation (ASCA, 2012).

However, a strong partnership with parents is contingent on parents who are informed and are actively engaged with the school. This strong partnership is also essential with community professionals who must feel "at home" in the schools. Nonetheless, while the picture is slowly but surely changing, schools remain by and large devoted to academic teaching and learning, often hesitant to allow, much less invite "outsiders" into their domains (Soriano, Soriano & Jimenez, 1994; Hong, Garcia & Soriano, in press). However, there are sufficient structural changes in the role and function of schools, as well as sufficient external pressure stemming from the complexity of problems in society, to make the schools a viable option to provide some degree of solution to these problems. It is here that School-Based Family Counseling can make a significant contribution toward addressing the needs of children and families in a diverse and changing society.

THE STRANGERS IN SCHOOLS

The range of professionals who interact with educators in today's American schools is wide and diverse. Beside teachers and administrators, schools now house school counselors, school psychologists, school social workers, speech pathologists, occupational therapists, marriage, family and child therapists, nurses, psychologists, police officers, probation officers, drug abuse counselors, and many others, not including volunteer parents. Each of these professionals, however, is trained based on what I refer to as the "silo" model that does not allow one to take a systems perspective in order to account for the complexity of problems requiring this comprehensive vision. As a model, School Based Family Counseling holds the vision of professionals who connect the "strangers" in the school and together wrap their professionally diverse arms around the child and family's needs. The challenge then is to find ways to convert a silo model into a systems model without ethical challenges. Herein lays the need to explore potential ethical challenges and address each one.

For purposes of discussion in this chapter, each professional working in the schools is assumed to be familiar with his/her profession's code of ethics. Moreover, whether we are talking about a school counselor's Code of Ethics developed by the American School Counseling Association (ASCA), or the School Social Worker's Code of Ethics developed by the National Association of Social Workers, or any of the other professionals listed above, each professional should already be well versed with his or her ethical code of conduct. Therefore, the intent of this chapter is not to replicate the ethical code for school social workers, school counselors, marriage and family therapists, school psychologists or clinical psychologists who might work in the schools.

These ethical codes (See Appendix A) already provide each licensed professional with their respective standards for ethical conduct. The intent here is to provide a framework that may help guide the practicing professionals to evolve their work as School Based Family Counselors but do so while remaining ethically within the scope of their training, thus minimizing potential ethical challenges. Additionally, it is our hope that professionals learn to work ethically and effectively with other professionals serving children and their families in the schools.

In today's public school, each professional works within the scope of his or her training supported and anchored by his or her license (or credential). These professionals are the product of professional "silos," institutions of higher learning that specialize in developing professionals who are skilled in their specific narrow domains, but do so without the benefit of endorsing a systems perspective to accommodate the complexities of the real world. Consequently, these professionals are left to their own initiative to learn, understand and collaborate with other professionals whose training is equally specialized for a specific domain, such as testing in the case of the school psychologist. In fact, it is this author's observation that in most instances, faculty who train and supervise school counselors, school psychologists, marriage and family therapists, etc. in the same department or administrative unit do not know one another's literature or curriculum and instructional approaches to serve children and families. Rarely do they team teach or collaborate across curricular areas, even if the content is complementary. Ironically, this lack of modeled collaboration is exactly what we expect of the service professional once in the schools! Needless to say, our students continue to model what they were taught, professional isolation and a reluctant and awkward collaboration. SBFC shifts this paradigm completely upside down. However, there are ethical risks that must be addressed.

When working as a SBFC professional, professionals are essentially "going against the current" by going beyond what their training institution said they would be doing. The school counselor, for example, is not trained to "counsel" with parents, but merely to consult with parents and provide them with guidance and information about their child. So why have a chapter on ethical guidelines for SBFC? SBFC responds to a new "systems-oriented" paradigm in child and family services. This paradigm recognizes the interdependence of children and parents within the school and community. Stated poetically in the words of John Donne, "no man is an island", we are all part of the continent and as such we are interconnected to one another. Thus the old silo-trained model of professional work in schools is necessarily being replaced by the new paradigm of school-based services, including family counseling. However, legal and ethical challenges are likely to be raised and must be understood in order to avoid increases in risk of ethical violations or violations of statutes governing professional practice. For example, a school counselor may be accused of an ethical violation, not to mention a legal one, by providing "therapy" to a parent when the counselor had no training to do so. Here the counselor needs to know the difference between "psychotherapy" and "counseling and guidance" in the preparation of his/her defense, or simply to educate the public about the differences. Actively listening to parents, or being empathic may be therapeutic and helpful to parents, and yet it is not unethical. Thus when the school counselor works with families within the American School Counseling Association's Standards (ASCA) relating to the personal and social domains, he/she is not outside the scope of practice as a school counselor. On the other hand, if the couple experiences violence, or one of the members suffers from major depressive disorder, the school counselor would be ill advised to provide such services. Here the school counselor would serve as a conduit for a referral to a psychotherapist.

RELATIONSHIP TO THE SBFC MODEL: ETHICS, LAW AND THE CHANGING SCHOOL CONTEXT

The previous discussion on the nature of legal versus ethical professional conduct is important when working as a SBFC professional, regardless of license and/or credential. This is due to the fact that all licenses or credentials for professional practice apply a general principle that essentially states that the bearer of the license limits the scope of his/her work based on (a) successful academic training, (b) supervised practical experience face to face with clients in a classroom or clinical setting, and (c) independent practice experience under the supervision of a licensed, experienced professional (APA, 2010; ACA, 2011; NASW, 2010). Consequently, it is illegal for a school counselor to perform psychotherapy, unless he/she is also a licensed MFT, a licensed LCSW or licensed psychologist. On the other hand, it is equally <u>unethical</u> for a school counselor to walk away and not respond to the needs of a child or a parent with serious emotional problems. For the school counselor or school psychologist to respond to the emotional needs of a child or his/her parents <u>is</u> ethical. This means involving his/her family, not as a psychotherapist, but as a professional concerned with the welfare of the child and his/her family. Counselors are trained to consult and guide parents to other professionals when they identify a need for adjunct services beyond those provided by the school counselor. The issue of whether or not there is a bridge of ethical standards or a violation of law depends on how the counselor responds to the perceived need. The action can result in a malpractice claim, or an allegation of client abandonment, but it can equally result in praise for the counselor's preventive and timely responsiveness to the need. The intent of this chapter, therefore, is to embrace a paradigm shift away from the silo model of counseling and move towards a model that recognizes the efficacy of working systemically with the whole family and the community, but to do so ethically and within the legal bounds of the law. The rest of this chapter highlights the important principles and conditions guiding professionals working as SBFC professionals.

SBFC AS A NEW PARADIGM IN HELPING: GUIDANCE FOR AVOIDING ETHICAL CHALLENGES

The philosophy and moral principles undergirding the SBFC model transcend the individual helping professional who may be trained as a counselor, psychologist or social worker. This philosophy and the moral principles are grounded in what Corey, Corey & Callahan (2012) call the "six basic moral principles to guide decision making" (p. 17). These include autonomy, nonmaleficence, beneficence, justice, fidelity and veracity. These moral principles are the foundation upon which ACA, APA and NASW, the three major helping professional associations (in the USA), base their professional codes of ethics. (For a more comprehensive discussion of these principles and case examples from each of the three professions, the reader is referred to Corey et. al, 2007). For our purposes, however, the three most important moral principles guiding SBFC are nonmaleficence, beneficence and justice.

NONMALEFICENCE

This moral principle signals to the counselor (the word "counselor" will be used in this chapter in a generic manner to include counselors, social workers and psychologists) that above anything else we do no harm. Potential harm may include delivering services for which the individual has not had any training and supervised practical experience. A school counselor who is not trained to do marital therapy runs the risk of harming vulnerable partners. Here, personal knowledge of, and a good working relationship with professionals who are capable of providing couple's therapy is an a-priori requirement. The ethical course of action would have this school counselor assist the couple to access and arrange for therapy right in the school. Increasingly such school counselors are obtaining training and supervision in these services and are dual-licensed. These are the ideal SBFC professionals, but the SBFC model does not require dual licensure. Rather, the model requires depth in understanding the professional community of helpers and what each of them brings to the table. Nonmaleficence requires us to not remain ignorant and arrogant by thinking we can do it all, even with good intention, or by our ignorance of the professionals who possess the skills needed. Nonmaleficence would also warn us not to be blind to the obvious need due to our lack of training, vision or insight that come from training and experience. Walking away from a perceived client need potentially harms the client and the helping professions in general.

An alternative to be considered is the "skill retrofitting" of existing personnel working in schools by offering training in couple or family therapy. However, this would require changes in licensure laws, similar to what is currently being done with the re-certification of Licensed Professional Counselors across the country. In another effort to see these skills among existing school personnel, Woody (1989) suggests curriculum revision for school psychologists and other Pupil Personnel professionals to help them learn SBFC skills. However, this again would require legislative action.

BENEFICIENCE

Most of us who become helpers or healers subscribe to this moral principle by becoming motivated to "help others" and seek their welfare. A strong ethical covenant under beneficence is the requirement to think beyond the client's psychological needs and consider his or her ecological and physical needs. We know the intimate connection between psyche and soma, between the body and the spirit, between the cognitive and affective domains. The philosophy and ethics in SBFC requires a more systems orientation to the person, inclusive of the emotional as well as physical needs, the relational as well as the social/community needs. Beneficence as a moral principle in SBFC suggests that the counselor harness resources through personal contacts for referrals to the community. More importantly, it requires that the counselor see beyond the trained "counselor's" eyes and acquire "social worker's" eyes, employment and housing services professional eyes, etc. The SBFC professional is essentially a "multivisional" professional who is capable of collaborating with others who are equally committed to the welfare of children and families. In many ways counselors are behind the times in terms of fully appreciating the interconnectedness of psychological, social and economic and physical wellbeing. At the national level, the social work profession has long recognized this interconnectedness and has worked systemically to address family's needs. However, psychologists, counselors and marriage family therapists are now getting on the bandwagon by recognizing the importance of addressing the whole person, than a single characteristic of human beings. In fact, the recognition of the centrality of the school in meeting the needs of families preventively, has now moved center stage in many states, especially in California, New York, Wisconsin and Florida (Hong, Garcia & Soriano, in press).

Recently the California State Department of Education under the leadership of its Superintendent Tom Torlakson convened a Student Mental Health Policy Workgroup (SMHPW) with funding from the California Mental Health Services Authority (CalMHSA). The CalMHSA is an organization of county governments working to improve mental health outcomes for individuals, families and communities. The initiative sought consultation with Dr. Brian Gerrard from the University of San Francisco and Drs. Marcel Soriano (this author) and Michael Carter, from California State University, Los Angeles. The significance of this initiative is that it follows and underscores the values undergirding the moral principle of "beneficence." It also gives great hope to those of us who seek to realize the new paradigm in school-based services. Furthermore, it follows similar trends in school based services models advanced by the previous superintendent of public instruction, Jack O'Connell.

JUSTICE

The principle of justice requires that we be committed to equity, fairness and a level playing field for all. SBFC professionals must be aware of social and institutional biases that differentially affect some segments of society more so than others. This ethical principle requires a willingness to move away from the fence and take on advocacy positions on behalf of those on the margin in society. The principle of justice requires that we acknowledge that despite the advances achieved in civil rights during the 1960s and '70s, ethnic minorities, women, persons with disabilities, and many other segments in society still face an uphill battle when it comes to equitable distribution of resources. SBFC requires a recognition that the promise of the fruits in society still remain out of reach for many children and their families. For example, many children and families who need mental health services, but cannot afford them, can access such services through a SBFC professional based in the school. In some cases these services can be provided at home, thereby avoiding the barrier of lack of transportation.

In 2010, under the leadership of Jack O'Connell, the previous California Superintendent of Public Instruction, the California Standards for the School Counseling Profession, Student Assistance Programs made considerable progress in highlighting the urgent need to close the achievement gap affecting significant numbers of ethnic minority students. These standards addressed issues of justice and equity by promoting three models of services quite similar in substance to SBFC (California Department of education, 2010). Their concern is a just and equitable system of education that levels the playing field for all learners and includes the following models for counseling in schools. The *Counselor Model* utilizes a community-based contracted person or in-house school personnel as the source for student assistance program services (SAPs). The second model is the *Community Agency Model*. This utilizes a contracted external agency provider that brings skilled clinicians into the schools to work with students and their families. The third one is the *Core Team Model* where a central group of six to eight multidisciplinary on-campus personnel who have been trained by experienced consultants to provide integrated services to students, but do so with the whole family. The point here is that there is now clear evidence of concern at the top of state and national leadership for a new paradigm in counseling children and their families. This was recently echoed by President Obama when speaking of his Health Care Reform and when referring to the recent incidents of school violence requiring counseling interventions, rather than armed guards at schools (New Republic, December 21, 2012). These California examples of changes in vision for school based family counseling are evident in other states (Welfel, 2013). School mental health has become a major priority across the country with the most recent school shootings in various states, including Colorado, New Jersey, Connecticut, Pennsylvania, among others. In fact, many states are now developing comprehensive counseling and guidance models as a way to promote full service schools inclusive of family services (Hong, Garcia & Soriano, in press). The intent of this discussion on moral principles is to help us appreciate the importance of a moral foundation to help guide our ethical decision making in SBFC. This is the moral foundation that guides SBFC's leadership at the Institute for Child and Family Development at the University of San Francisco, as well as the Oxford symposium in School-Based Family Counseling held each year to highlight the application of this model in schools and in other countries around the world.

SCOPE OF PRACTICE

Earlier we identified the three stages in professional development as that which includes coursework, supervised practicum experience and supervised independent practice prior to licensure. Scope of practice is that statement codified in law that defines what services each professional is trained to perform. Typically the statement is standard-based, with stated competencies that are behaviorally anchored. This helps to define the scope of practice, that range of skills and therapeutic interventions capably performed by the trained professional. Also previously, we stated that a school counselor is not trained to perform psychotherapy, but can provide counseling services that are indeed therapeutic in nature, but are not psychotherapy. Psychotherapy implies the presence of pathology or deeply rooted problems requiring diagnostic skills, as well as clinical skills. Counseling, on the other hand, implies assistance, guidance and support by a counselor who is familiar with academic, vocational/career and personal-social concerns typical of children and adolescents. Both therapist and counselor must establish a warm, caring and responsive relationship with the client. Thus in this realm they are both the same. However, where the problem may lie is when the SBFC professional may lack the training as a therapist and yet attempt to perform therapy when his/her training is in school counseling and he/she attempts to do family therapy. The ethical course of action for the SBFC professional lacking the training and licensing in psychotherapy is to provide only those services for which he/she is trained and refer to those who are trained as therapists to do therapy. Again, more and more colleges and universities are combining both to address their needs and better serve children and families.

As a general guide to graduate students, this author offers the following recommendation. When working with children and adolescents, the younger your client, the more urgent the need to involve parents as the major focus of your interventions. Children are amazingly resilient when provided with nurturance, security, and a caring and loving relationship. The acting out child signals in most cases the absence of one of these ingredients. Thus no amount of skilled interventions will replace those elements. This is where ethical SBFC professionals may have an edge on traditional counselors in that they recognize their "client" as the entire family, not the acting out child alone. It would seem unethical, therefore, to target the child for clinical interventions without considering the entire family system and its nesting within the school and community systems. In other words, the "client" is defined as the child and his/her associated systems. Ethical interventions, therefore, must be systemic, not one-dimensional and narrow.

PROFESSIONAL COMPETENCE

Legal competence implies meeting licensure requirements within the boundaries of a profession. Ethical competence, on the other hand, suggests a wider and deeper sense of professional training, experience and understanding of the diverse client community and of the professionals who take on a helping role with these diverse clients. Ethical competence implies an understanding of professional boundaries and the scope of professional practice established in our society. In the context of schools and the SBFC model, ethical competence requires the SBFC professional to understand the diverse professionals who work with children and families in the community. This includes school psychologists, school social workers, child welfare and attendance professionals, school nurses, pediatricians, clinical social workers, protective services social workers, psychiatrists, marriage, family therapists, licensed clinical social workers, psychologists, priests and ministers, probation officers, deans of students and other administrators who are in a capacity to help children and their families. As one can see, the list is only partial and indeed others in the school and the community can be enlisted to be "helpful" with the child and family. However, the point to be made here is that professional and ethical competence requires SBFC professionals to possess unique professional qualities, inclusive of knowledge and skills in order to be successful SBFC professionals. Furthermore, professional competence requires a respectful attitude toward other professionals and an understanding of school culture.

ETHICS AND AN EXPANDING PROFESSIONAL SBFC ROLE

Earlier I spoke of a "new paradigm" in SBFC and the training and re-training of professional counselors who work in schools as the product of what I refer to as the "silo training model" of professional preparation. The problem with the old model for training of "helpers" is that it is inconsistent with the realities in the schools and communities where they are found. The result is that we continue to produce one-dimensional professionals for a multidimensional world! Faculty in most training institutions don't model cross-disciplinary collaboration and consultation in their teaching, so how could we expect newcomers to the counseling profession to be effective and competent collaborators. Moreover, we don't teach the scope of practice for each helping professional, but expect ethical and professionally competent helpers to effectively and ethically work together as they help children and families. Thus, the new paradigm must ultimately require universities and colleges to change their own paradigm for training professionals in order to meet professional and ethical standards. The new paradigm requires that we apply the same standard for determining when a professional acted in a professional manner. This is typically determined when one compares a given action by a professional in comparison to the judgment and professional actions that would be taken by an equally trained, competent professional. The only difference being that the new paradigm for professional conduct will include the "<u>real world</u>" conditions faced by children and families in today's society! Furthermore, in order to effectively meet these ethical standards, current professionals must be "retooled" with this knowledge and skill in order to effectively work with families in our complex society.

There is another reason to change the current counselor-training paradigm, if not for the wisdom of holistic, systems-based, integrated services model. President Obama's new Health Care Overhaul (Welfel, 2013) being implemented across the country will require thousands more health care providers, including more psychologists, marriage family therapists and professional counselors. However, we simply don't have enough professionals to meet that national (Mishak, 2013). California, New York and other states with large urban populations are aggressively preparing for the large wave of newly insured children, adolescents and adults who up to now have lacked health care insurance. The challenge is that we are seeing more people with a health insurance card and no professionals available to meet that need. Thus many states' legislatures are proposing "expanding professional boundaries" in the scope of practice by health care professionals. And although the focus of these efforts is primarily medical health care, the same reality is true for mental health, as there are not enough mental health professionals available to meet a growing need. For example, as of this writing, this author has seen an exponential increase in Medical beneficiaries seeking mental health services under the "Healthy Families" program funded by Medicare! And although there are both legal, ethical and professional challenges that must be addressed, this alone may result in strong support for expanding the boundaries of school counselors, school social workers and other mental health professionals to become effective SBFC professionals.

CHALLENGES OF IMPLEMENTING A SBFC MODEL

In a very relevant discussion about the challenges of implementing an SBFC model, Gerrard (this volume, Chapter 2) presents a review of the literature exploring the feasibility of school counselors or school psychologists, for example, doing family therapy and the difficulties of ethically and professionally being able to do so (Wendt and Zake, 1984; Golden, 1983). Citing others (Alessi, 1989), Gerrard (this volume, Chapter 2) optimistically suggests that schools in various communities already embrace SBFC in practice due to the urgent necessity to address the myriad complex family problems affecting children and adolescents in schools. Moreover, in light of the previous discussion about the Health Care Overhaul, the future of SBFC appears bright with promise of ushering the new paradigm for professional standards in training future professional counselors to work in schools and communities. However, while this may be the case in the foreseeable future, to remain ethically and professionally within bounds, I urge caution and a mid-point stage that first embraces the knowledge of the rich variety of professionals who now work in the schools by training all current helpers to understand the scope of their practice and exercise restraint in practicing beyond the scope of the individual's training and supervised practice experience.

To address this ethical challenge, the author proposes a progressive series of steps toward embracing the implementation of a School Based Family Counseling Model. Table 3.1 presents a view of current scope of practice conditions and the projected and desired conditions for a successful ushering of the SBFC Paradigm. Under the current "silo" training paradigm, professionals are trained but remain ignorant of others outside their professional boundaries, while having to work with families whose needs require their full understanding of complex issues requiring skills and competencies in school, community and family domains. Clinicians often voice disparaging remarks of school counselors as not being able to address obvious clinical and family needs (even when they are skilled, though not trained). School personnel, on the other hand, often criticize clinicians for "pathologizing" children and their families, failing to see that they are often victims of societal ills of poverty, discrimination and lack of access to resources. The point here is that each is suspicious and critical of the other. Table 3.1 also

Table 3.1 Expanding the Scope of Practice in Professional Counseling

Stage of SBFC Training	School Counselor/Psychologist	MFT, LCSW or Psychologist
Current Paradigm	Training for narrow specialty Difficulty in seeing child in context of family and school Treats academic or learning issues only Does not understand scope of practice of other health care providers Has trouble consulting and/or collaborating with other professionals Limits parent work to consultation and/or informing on child's progress	Training for wider, family and system-focused, excluding school culture Difficulty understanding school culture Treats psychological or family issues, but excludes school issues. Assumes scope of practice precludes emotional, or psychological skills. Has trouble collaborating with school personnel. Limits parent work to clinical issues, not school bound issues.
Future SBFC Paradigm	All pupil services professionals, including counselors and school psychologists will be trained by multi-disciplinary faculty for a wider family-based focus and social systems perspective. Professionals see child in context of family, school and community. Treats academic, learning issues in context of family, while consulting and referring to other professionals when reaching intense, remedial focus. Fully understands scope of practice and relevance for prevention or remedial focused interventions. Is a skilled collaborator and works "seamlessly" well with other professionals. Is skilled and comfortable working with parents, informing them of academic, social and emotional needs and wisdom of "therapy" when at the level of remedial focus.	All clinicians are trained to understand the strategic value of involvement in schools and understand school culture. Professional clinicians see child in context of school and its influence on wellness and prevention. Treats clinical and family issues holistically and in consultation with school personnel and other health care professionals, including school nurses, teachers and others who know the child. Fully understands the expanded scope of practice of school personnel and embraces them with an attitude of acceptance as peers and helps guide prevention efforts in schools. Is a skilled collaborator and feels "at-home" in schools. Is skilled and comfortable working with teachers, school administrators, counselors and other school personnel; He/she advises on prevention focus initiatives.

suggests what the new SBFC paradigm might look like. This would be a world in which professional respect and relevant appreciation for each other would promote prevention and early intervention. Clinicians whose focus is primarily remedial would be able to focus in this level of intervention, but not at the exclusion of preventive collaboration with school personnel in seeing that the referrals to remedial focused interventions remain in the prevention focused level, thus maximizing student wellness and academic achievement. The point here is that there is plenty of room for both, the prevention focus and the remedial focus professionals. However, the difference is in the results. The SBFC paradigm suggests greater prevention success and less suffering; it suggests greater student achievement and a more vibrant family in our society.

ISSUES OF PRIVACY, CONFIDENTIALITY AND OTHER LEGAL MATTERS

While the new paradigm promises to usher a new era of collaboration and professional conduct appropriate to serving clients more effectively, there are additional ethical and legal issues that must be addressed in the foreseeable future, including compliance with law and ethical professional standards. A professional axiom in the mental health and pupil services professions is the importance of privacy. Privacy is the cornerstone of the professional counselor's ability to serve clients, regardless of profession. The school counselor enjoys the same promise of privacy to the client and his/her parents as other licensed clinicians in their practice. In fact, pupil service professionals in some states, such as California, enjoy greater latitude in the application of client privilege than non-school, licensed professionals. For example, the California Education Code (CEC, 2012) affords the school counselor and school psychologist the ability to work with students twelve years or older without parental consent, except when the professional counselor deems the student to not be sufficiently competent to make decisions (Hong, Garcia & Soriano, in press).

Nonetheless, in most cases where the parent is included in the counseling relationship, the issue is how to protect privacy, yet share information with appropriate professionals when it is in the best interest of the child or family. There are instances, for example, where sharing information with others may be contraindicated. Here the principles of consultation and professional collaboration must defer to the interests of the client. The competent client, as in the case of a minor whose parent is involved in treatment, must be allowed to chose whether or not it is appropriate to consult, collaborate or otherwise share information with other collaborative professionals. This is no different under the SBFC or future paradigm than the current paradigm. The difference, if there is one, is in the desire and intent of the professional counselor to acknowledge and account for the strengths of other professionals whose skills are capable of contributing to client success.

In the SBFC model, ethical and legal mandates must be addressed in the same way that they are addressed today. Child abuse reporting must continue to be enforced; the Health Insurance Portability and Accountability Act (HIPAA) must be enforced equally under both models (Reinhardt, 2013). However, the new SBFC paradigm will most likely result in greater "portability" and "accountability" as the new world of professional relationships will require respect and a greater knowledge of each professional and his/her scope of training and professional practice. Our vision in SBFC is to understand the crucial role schools play in the lives of children and their families. The pupil services professional is placed in a critical position to make a difference in our preventive focus model, while ideally suited to provide some level of remedial focus services in a preventive fashion while referring clients who are clearly in the remedial focus domain and require more intensive treatment. Thus this promises to provide greater access and accountability for services rendered and greater achievement and success for children and adolescents in our schools (Reinhardt, 2013).

With regard to privacy, confidentiality and privilege, the same principles that apply in the current model of training and professional conduct would be applicable in the SBFC model. Even when professional judgment suggests the importance of consulting with others, including parents and other professionals, informed consent must apply in order to protect the client and his/her relationship with the professional counselor. Moreover, since privilege, that legal right accorded to adult clients and competent minors in some states (see California Title 5 Code of Regulations and Welfare and Institutions Code) is controlled by the competent client, only an informed, signed release allows the professional to share information with others. This includes in some cases minors over the age of twelve who may choose to keep information private from their parents or legal guardians (Welfel, 2013; Taylor & Adelman, 1989; Taylor & Adelman, 1998). However, in most cases skilled clinicians seek to skillfully and sensitively involve the parent or do so in states where this is legally required.

SUMMARY AND RECOMMENDATIONS FOR ETHICAL IMPLEMENTATION OF AN SBFC PROGRAM

A quick review of Table 3.1 provides us with a clearer understanding of the current challenges and opportunities that lie ahead. As a delightful stanza in the musical "The Music Man" states, "Oh we have trouble, right here in River City, with a Capital T and that stands for…," we do indeed have trouble in the manner in which children, adolescents and their families are being served by the current work force of professionals who work in schools and communities. For the school counselor or school psychologist, the scope of practice as currently trained is too limited to address the myriad needs clients have in today's schools and communities. For the clinician working outside or even within the school, their challenge is to more fully appreciate the important role played by schools and the professionals who work in them. With few exceptions usually related to the individual's background and interests, most clinicians are not familiar with school culture, its language and issues affecting students and the professionals who work in the school. Thus a more intensive training focus would go far toward enabling them to better consult, collaborate and serve clients in the schools.

Given the changing nature of health care and the limited resources available to meet a growing population of children and families in need of mental health services, a final recommendation is for more intensive and extensive research, both quantitative and qualitative, that addresses the ethical and legal challenges identified in this chapter, while assuring a more uniform and effective way to serve children and families in our society. Some of these challenges will require legislative changes in law, while others are being "re-interpreted" or expanded by judicial case interpretation of existing law. It is hoped that as more professional educators come on board with the new paradigm, the community of future professional counselors will more adequately address the evolving trends and needs of clients.

REFERENCES

Alessi, G. (1989). Ethical issues facing school psychologists in family therapy: A commentary. *Professional School Psychology*, *4 (4)*, 265-271.

ASCA National Model (2012). American School Counseling Association (ASCA): A Framework for School Counseling Programs (3rd Edition). Alexandra, VA: Author.

ASCA School Counselor (2012*). Ins & Outs of Ethics & Law*. American School Counselor Association, Author.

Corey, G., Corey, M. S. & Callahan, P. (8th Edition, 2012*). Issues and Ethics in the Helping Professions*. Belmont, CA: Thomson Brooks/Cole.

Ford, G.G. (2006*). Ethical Reasoning for Mental Health Professionals*. Thousand Oaks, CA: Sage Publications, Inc.

Gestwicki, C. (2010*). Home, School & Community Relations* (7th Edition). Belmont, CA: Wadsworth Cengage Learning.

Golden, L. (1983). Brief family interventions in a school setting. *Elementary School Guidance and Counseling*, *17 (4)*, 288-293.

Hong, G., Garcia, M. & Soriano, M. (in press), Responding to the challenge: Preparing Mental Health Professionals for the Changing U.S. Demographics. Chapter in Paniagua et al., (in press).

Mishak, M.J. (2013). State Lacks Doctors to Fill Needs. Los Angeles Times, February 10, 2013, California Section, p. A35.

Ratner, J. (1939). *Intelligence in the Modern World: John Dewey's Philosophy.* New York: Random House, Inc.

Reinhardt, R. (2013). Evaluating cloud-based practice management systems. *Counseling Today*, 55 (8). American Counseling Association.

Stone, C, Hermann, M & Williams, R. (2012). Asked & Answered: School Counseling Legal and Ethical Issues. *ASCA School Counselor*, 49 (5), p. 6.

Taylor, L. & Adelman, H.S. (1989) Reframing the confidentiality dilemma to work in children's best interests. *Professional Psychology: Research and Practice*, 20, 79-83.

Taylor, L. & Adelman, H.S. (1998). Confidentiality: Competing principles, inevitable dilemmas. *Journal of Educational and Psychological Consultation*, 9, 267-275.

Welfel, E.R. (2013). *Ethics in Counseling & Psychotherapy: Standards, Research and Emerging Issues.* Belmont, CA: Brooks/Cole.

Wendt, R. & Zake, J. (1984). Family systems therapy and school psychology: Implications for training and practice. *Psychology in the Schools, 21 (2),* 204-210.

RESOURCES

Websites for Professional Codes of Ethics for Major Helping Professions

The following links provide the latest ethics standards or statements for professional conduct.

American Association for Marriage and Family Therapy (July 1, 2012)
> http://www.aamft.org/imis15/content/legal_ethics/code_of_ethics.aspx

American Counseling Association (2005)
> http://www.ncblpc.org/Laws_and_Codes/ACA_Code_of_Ethics.pdf

American Psychological Association (2002)
> http://www.apa.org/ethics/code/index.aspx

American School Counseling Association (2010)
> http://www.schoolcounselor.org/files/EthicalStandards2010.pdf

Commission on Rehabilitation Counselor Certification Code of Ethics (2010).
> http://www.crccertification.com/filebin/pdf/CRCCodeOfEthics.pdf

National Association of School Psychologists (NASP).
> http://www.nasponline.org/standards/2010standards.aspx

National Association for Social Workers (2008)
> http://www.socialworkers.org/pubs/code/code.asp

National Association for School Social Work (2012)
> http://sswaa.org/associations/13190/files/naswschoolsocialworkstandards.pdf

PART II

SCHOOL-BASED FAMILY COUNSELING:
PREPARING FOR CHANGE

Chapter 4
How to Develop An Integrative School-Based Case Conceptualization

Brian Gerrard

OVERVIEW: *This chapter describes an integrative Multicultural, Developmental, CBT, Family Systems, Strength-Based approach to SBFC case conceptualization using the SBFC Model as a meta-framework.*

DEFINITION

Case conceptualization refers to the theoretical lens through which the SBFC professional thinks about her client's problems and strengths. The case conceptualization has three main goals: first, to help the SBFC professional to understand the client's situation (Diagnosis); second, to facilitate setting a meaningful and attainable goal for counseling (Goal-setting); and third, to help the SBFC professional to select treatment strategies (Intervention Plan).

ILLUSTRATIVE CASE STUDY

To illustrate how the different case conceptualization models can be applied, we will use a hypothetical case involving Luis, a Latino student age 11.

Luis was referred to counseling by his teacher, Miss Jones, because he has been inattentive in class and often tearful when spoken to. The SBFC professional Barbara interviewed Luis and discovered he was being bullied by an older boy, Mark. Miss Jones' view of this is that "boys will be boys" and that she has a difficult time monitoring what happens in a large class of 30 students. The principal reports that there have been instances of bullying, especially cyberbullying, in other grade levels in the school. Janice learned in a phone call with Luis' mother, Mrs. Janet Rodriguez, that Luis has been sad since his mother and father separated. Mrs. Rodriguez reports that she has been separated from her husband for 6 months and that things are very tense between them. Luis is angry with his father who now rarely calls Luis.

USING THE SBFC MODEL AS AN INTEGRATING FRAMEWORK

The SBFC Model (shown in Figure 4.1) is a framework for conceptualizing SBFC interventions. It consists of four quadrants based on whether the intervention is school-focused or family-focused; remedial or preventive. The SBFC quadrants may be summarized as follows:
Family-Intervention: This refers to interventions that focus on promoting family change when family problems are having a negative effect on a student. It also refers to interventions that promote family support to help a student, even when the family is not a source of stress for the student.
School-Intervention: This refers to interventions that are required in a school after a problem has clearly developed.

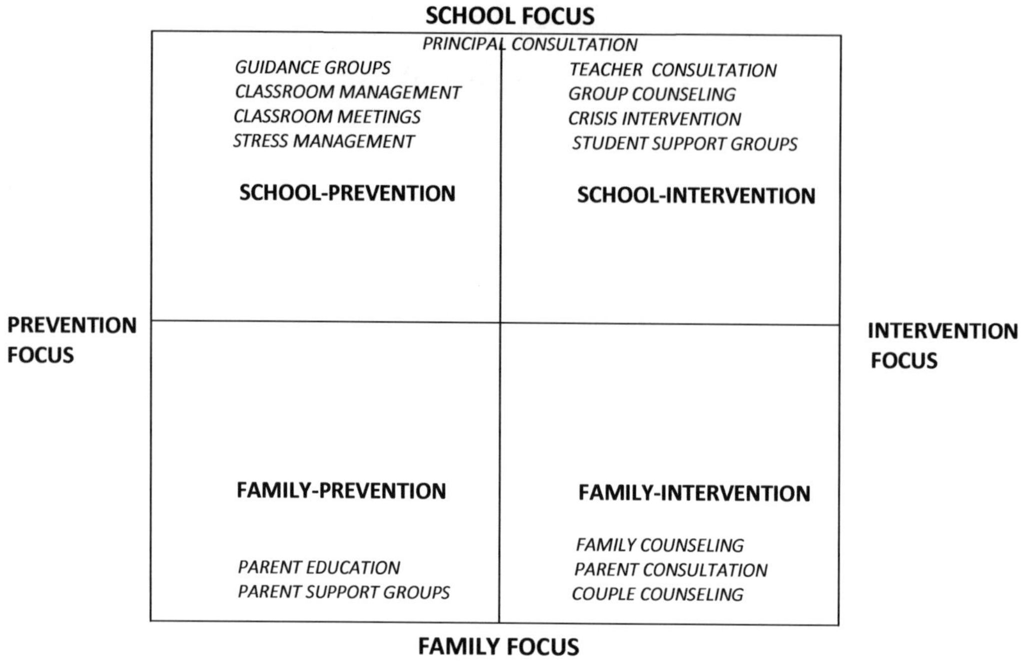

SCHOOL FOCUS

PRINCIPAL CONSULTATION

GUIDANCE GROUPS
CLASSROOM MANAGEMENT
CLASSROOM MEETINGS
STRESS MANAGEMENT

SCHOOL-PREVENTION

TEACHER CONSULTATION
GROUP COUNSELING
CRISIS INTERVENTION
STUDENT SUPPORT GROUPS

SCHOOL-INTERVENTION

PREVENTION FOCUS

INTERVENTION FOCUS

FAMILY-PREVENTION

PARENT EDUCATION
PARENT SUPPORT GROUPS

FAMILY-INTERVENTION

FAMILY COUNSELING
PARENT CONSULTATION
COUPLE COUNSELING

FAMILY FOCUS

Figure 4.1 The SBFC Model

Family-Prevention: This refers to interventions that help parents, guardians, and families to develop skills that prevent future problems. *School-Prevention*: this refers to interventions that focus on teaching students and/or teachers skills that could prevent future problems.

Example: The Case of Luis
A counselor applying the SBFC Model to Luis' situation would likely consider the following interventions:

Family-Intervention:
> *Parent Consultation* to assist Mrs. Rodriguez in helping Luis deal with the feeling of loss around his father and being bullied at school.
> *Parent Consultation* to facilitate Mr. Rodriguez resuming parenting with Luis.
> *Parent Consultation* to assist Mr. and Mrs. Rodriguez in cooperating with each other in parenting Luis.
> *Parent Consultation* with Mark's parents to deal with Mark's bullying behaviors.
> *Family Counseling with Individuals* to teach Luis and Mark CBT coping skills for   managing stress related to family and peers.

School-Intervention:

Student Support Group for Luis and other children dealing with parental separation and divorce.
Teacher Consultation to help Miss Jones develop classroom discipline skills to   minimize bullying in her classroom.
Classroom Meeting with Luis's class and Mark's class to develop anti-bullying norms   in the classroom and develop peer support for Luis.

School-Prevention:

Bullying Prevention Workshop (*Guidance Group*) for the school to develop greater cohesion among students.
Bullying Prevention Workshop for teachers and school staff to build skills in identification and intervention.

Family-Prevention:

Bullying Prevention Workshop for parents and guardians to provide information on identification and prevention of bullying.

In Figure 4.2 you will find a decision tree that may be useful in determining which SBFC Model quadrants to work in. There may be interventions you can think of for your clients that are not listed in the decision trees. The purpose of the decision trees is to encourage you to think flexibly about working systemically across the four SBFC quadrants.

FIVE APPROACHES TO CASE CONCEPTUALIZATION

The five theoretical approaches we recommend you use in conceptualizing your SBFC cases are: Multicultural, Developmental, Cognitive-Behavioral, Family Systems, and Strength-Based. We would like to state at the outset that there are more than five approaches to case conceptualization that could be used in SBFC. We decided to focus on these because they are popular in the school and family counseling literature, they have evidence-based support, and we have used them successfully in supervising SBFC students over a 30 year period.

We recommend that all five approaches be used in an integrative fashion. Within each general theoretical approach we discuss more than one model illustrating the approach. For example, we review three different Strength-Based Approaches: Maslow's Hierarchy of Needs, Seligman's Positive Psychology, and Epston and White's Narrative Therapy. The reason for this broad perspective is to highlight that there are "many ways to Rome" and to promote flexibility of approach.

HOW TO USE A MULTICULTURAL COUNSELING MODEL IN CASE CONCEPTUALIZATION

A multicultural counseling approach has often been described as the "fourth force" in counseling, a designation that highlights its importance. A multicultural counseling approach is a social justice approach. It emphasizes that many clients suffer from discrimination based on factors such as ethnicity, gender, sexual orientation, age, religion, disability, and social class. Further, it emphasizes that counselors should do something about it. Madanes (2010) has argued that most instances of "mental illness" have to do with interpersonal situations involving social injustice. For this reason she believes that the most important competency a counselor can have is to be a social activist.

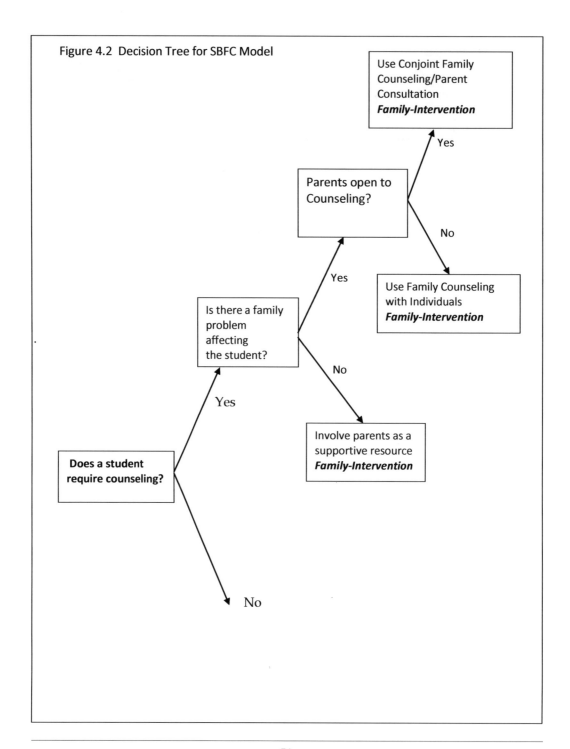

Figure 4.2 Decision Tree for SBFC Model

Use Conjoint Family Counseling/Parent Consultation
Family-Intervention

Parents open to Counseling?

Yes

No

Use Family Counseling with Individuals
Family-Intervention

Is there a family problem affecting the student?

Yes

No

Involve parents as a supportive resource
Family-Intervention

Yes

Does a student require counseling?

No

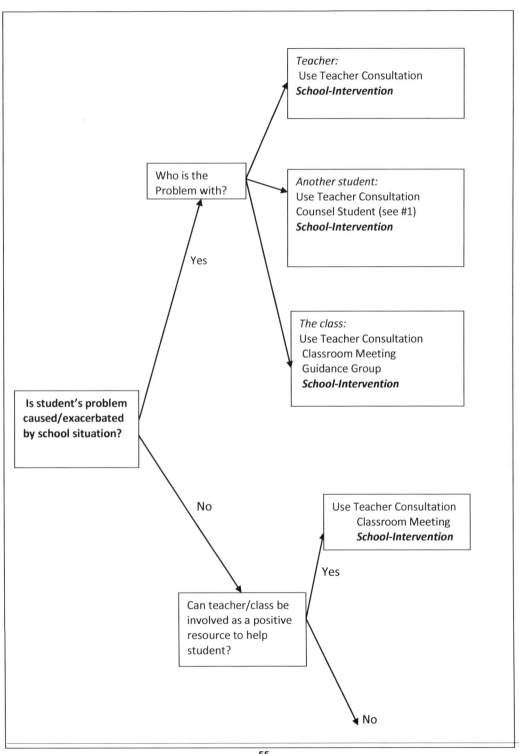

Teacher:
 Use Teacher Consultation
School-Intervention

Who is the
Problem with?

Another student:
Use Teacher Consultation
Counsel Student (see #1)
School-Intervention

The class:
Use Teacher Consultation
 Classroom Meeting
 Guidance Group
School-Intervention

Yes

**Is student's problem
caused/exacerbated
by school situation?**

No

Use Teacher Consultation
 Classroom Meeting
School-Intervention

Yes

Can teacher/class be
involved as a positive
resource to help
student?

No

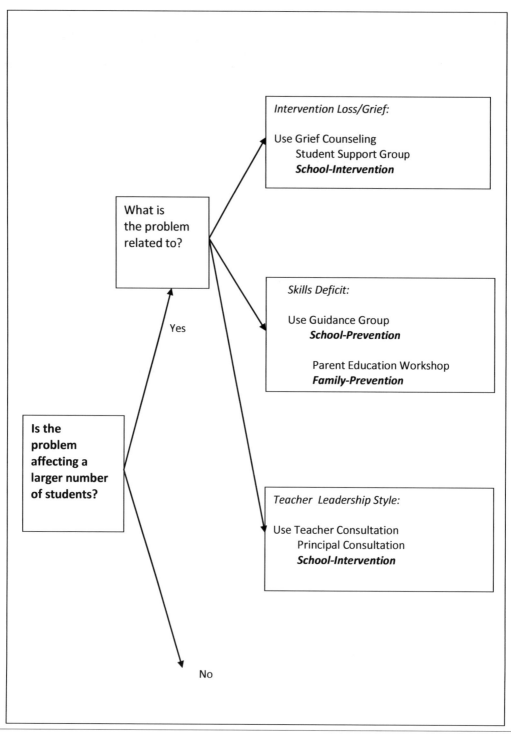

Intervention Loss/Grief:

Use Grief Counseling
    Student Support Group
    School-Intervention

What is
the problem
related to?

Skills Deficit:

Use Guidance Group
    School-Prevention

    Parent Education Workshop
    Family-Prevention

Yes

Is the
problem
affecting a
larger number
of students?

Teacher Leadership Style:

Use Teacher Consultation
    Principal Consultation
    School-Intervention

No

Schools are not immune from the problems of discrimination and prejudice that occur in the larger community. Anyone who has spent time in a school knows that schools contain student sub-groupings and cliques based on ethnicity and values. Children who are bullied are typically those who are perceived as "different" in some way. In some schools many older white teachers are from a middle class background while their minority students may be from a lower social class. These differences in age, ethnicity, and social class can lead to problems in the classroom between teachers and students. The 1950's stereotype that boys are good at math and science and girls are good at the arts and home economics was certainly a factor in the research demonstrating that male mathematics teachers for many years would call on boys for answers and ignore the girls (despite the fact that girls have an aptitude for mathematics equal to that of boys). Teachers who hold a bias towards some students being "smart" can have a profound effect on the students viewed as "smart" and those viewed as "not smart."

In a famous study by Rosenthal and Jacobson (1968), described in their book Pygmalion in the Classroom, teachers were told that one group of students had a very high IQ and that another group of students had a very low IQ. In fact both groups of students had equivalent IQ levels. At the end of the school year both the grades and the IQ levels of each group of students had changed significantly: the "smart" students showed improvement; the "not smart" students did not. The researcher's conclusion was that teacher expectation and attention to students accounted for these differences. If a teacher has a prejudicial attitude toward a student or group of students it can have a profound impact on student learning. The same would be true for a counselor affected by prejudice or bias.

The concept of multicultural competency, as described by Sue et al (1982), involves three components:

1) Beliefs and attitudes:

Do you genuinely value diversity?

Do you have empathy for persons very different from yourself and holding values different from your own?

Did you grow up in a family that had prejudicial or stereotyped attitudes about persons from different cultural backgrounds?

Do you hold any of these prejudicial or stereotyped attitudes?

2) Knowledge:

Are you aware of research documenting the fact that persons who are viewed as "different" often are discriminated against?

Have you ever witnessed an act of discrimination?

Have you read any literature describing the history and struggles of different groups viewed as "different" by the dominant culture?

Do you know what "white male privilege is?"

Do you know why many minority persons do not utilize mental health counseling?

Are you aware that when most persons seek help for emotional problems the first person they go to is not a counselor? Do you know why that is?

3) Skills:

Do you know how to make friends with a client who is ambivalent about receiving counseling from you?

Are you experienced in a variety of counseling approaches both directive and non-directive?

Can you tailor your counseling interventions to meet the needs of your clients?

Do you tend to use a "one size fits all" approach to counseling?

If the help your client wants is from a non-therapist (for example, a priest, rabbi, iman, or native healer) would you be able to support that?

What is your assessment of your competence in each of the above multicultural competence areas?

We recommend that when you are working with a client who is culturally different that you consider doing the following:

1) Approach your client with an attitude of respect and from a "one-down" rather than a "top-down" expert position.

2) Be aware of any prejudicial attitudes you may have towards persons like your client.

3) Approach your client with what in zen is called "beginner mind." That is, make no assumptions about your client's values, goals, ability, or challenges. Instead, take the position that you want to learn who your client is from your client. Be open about aspects of your client's experience about which you are ignorant and invite your client to teach you.

4) Set aside stereotypes about your client's particular ethnic group, gender, etc and explore the within-group differences demonstrated by your client.

5) Use the Person-Centered counseling skills of empathy, warmth, respect, and genuineness.

6) Discuss with your client whether he/she has any concerns about working with you if you are culturally very different from your client.

7) At the end of you counseling session, ask your client if there were any things he/she would have liked to talk about that didn't get discussed.

8) If your client is reluctant to talk, acts suspicious of you, or expresses reservations about counseling, respond with empathy and do not take it personally.

9) Find out your client's idea of the counseling relationship and process. It may be very different from what you expect. Consider being flexible in how you implement any techniques.

Diagnosis: As you can see from the above recommendations, we emphasize developing a relationship of trust with your client and not plunging too swiftly into change techniques. If you are successful in establishing a relationship of trust with your client, you will be in a stronger position to find out who he/she really is and what his/her unique challenges are. You will also be more likely to learn what your client's values are and how these might affect you working together.

The Example of Luis
Barbara, Luis' SBFC professional, is Caucasian. When she met with Luis' mother, Mrs. Rodriguez, she addressed her reluctance for counseling in the following fashion.

Mrs. Rodriguez: "I don't see why Luis needs counseling. That boy Mark who is bullying him needs counseling. And so does that teacher who does nothing when my son is bullied."
Barbara: "I can understand your feeling that way. Luis has been treated unfairly and the teacher has a responsibility to stop it."
Mrs. Rodriguez: "So why did you ask to see me? It is very hard for me to come here during the day."

Barbara: *"I appreciate very much that you came Mrs. Rodriguez because you are the expert on your son. I wanted to meet with you so I could have the benefit of your wisdom about Luis. I will be more effective in helping Luis if I really understand him and what he is going through. As his mother you are the best person to know Luis."*

Mrs. Rodriguez: *"The teachers don't care about Luis. All they do is complain about him?"*

Barbara: *"You feel that the teachers are prejudiced towards him?"*

Mrs. Rodriguez: *"Yes."*

Barbara: *"If that is happening I will do everything I can to put a stop to it. It is the teacher's role to help Luis."*

Mrs. Rodriguez: *"You are not like other people at the school."*

Barbara: *"I am here to help your son succeed at school and with your help I know we can help Luis."*

As can be seen in this example, Barbara showed empathy for Mrs. Rodriguez and validated her perception that some teachers at the school were not treating Luis fairly. As a next step, the SBFC professional would investigate Mrs. Rodriguez' concern and perhaps observe Luis in some of his classes in order to observe teacher interaction with Luis and other minority children.

Case Planning and Intervention: For the above example, the SBFC professional should be aware of the importance of *personalismo* (the quality of developing a personal, friendly relationship) among Latino families and assess whether this value was present in Luis' family. She should also investigate whether Mark's bullying behavior towards Luis, and the teacher's ignoring the bullying, was based on prejudice (Mark and the teacher are both Caucasian). In addition to taking steps to stop the bullying, the SBFC professional should assess the need for a classroom meeting to discuss diversity issues related to bullying. She should also meet with the principal to discuss holding preventive workshops on bullying for students, teachers, and parents. These anti-bullying workshops would also address diversity issues since the victim is often someone who is culturally different.

HOW TO USE A DEVELOPMENTAL MODEL IN CASE CONCEPTUALIZATION

We recommend you use three developmental models:

> 1) The Individual Life Cycle Model
>
> 2) The Family Life Cycle Model
>
> 3) The Client Readiness for Change Model

1. THE INDIVIDUAL LIFE CYCLE MODEL

Diagnosis: Life cycle models have as their central thesis that most persons pass through different stages that require the individual to negotiate a developmental task. If the task is successfully mastered, the individual continues until confronted with the next developmental task. If the developmental task is not successfully mastered, then the individual will experience a problem which may continue into later developmental periods. Table 4.1 lists the developmental stages described by Erikson (1963) and which span birth to old age. Table 4.2 describes some typical developmental tasks faced by children and which SBFC professionals are likely to encounter (Masten & Coatsworth, 1998).

The Example of Luis

In Erikson's Life Cycle model Luis would be considered in the Ego Identity vs. Role Confusion stage. The bullying behavior by Mark and the distancing behavior of Luis' father would add to Luis' challenges in negotiating this stage and developing an integrated sense of his own personal identity. The absence of his father as a role model to guide him and questions about his own "manliness" in dealing with the bully will contribute to Luis' role confusion.

Table 4.1 Erikson's Developmental Stages

Developmental Stage	Typical Age	Developmental Task
1. Trust vs. Mistrust	Birth-1 year	Develop trust for the mother
2. Autonomy vs. Shame and Doubt	1 - 3 years	Develop a sense of self-control and autonomy
3. Initiative vs. Guilt	4 - 5 years	Develop a positive identification with parents as role models
4. Industry vs. Inferiority	6 - 11 years	Develop feelings of competence and mastery
4. Ego Identity vs. Role Confusion	Early adolescence	Develop an integrated sense of personal identity
6. Intimacy vs. Isolation	Late adolescence-early adulthood	Develop intimate relationship(s)
7. Generativity vs. Self-absorption	Adulthood	Develop ability to guide the next generation
8. Ego Integrity vs. Despair	Late adulthood	Develop appreciation of one's strengths and acceptance of one's challenges

Goal-setting and Intervention Plan: Because Life Cycle models are essentially descriptive, interventions used with these models typically come from other theoretical approaches. The goal is to help the individual master the developmental task he/she is struggling with. An example of different interventions that could be used with an adolescent having difficulty with "Successful transition to secondary schooling" are: CBT coping skills for managing stress, developing friendship skills for overcoming loneliness, teacher consultation to promote teacher reinforcement of positive classroom behaviors, parent counseling to deal with family stress associated with job difficulties for parents.

Table 4.2 Typical Developmental Tasks Faced By Children

Age Period	Task
Infancy to preschool	Attachment to caregiver(s) Language Differentiation of self from environment Self-control and compliance
Middle childhood	School adjustment (attendance, appropriate conduct) Academic achievement (e.g. learning to read, do arithmetic) Getting along with peers (acceptance, making friends) Rule-governed conduct (following rules of society for moral behavior and prosocial conduct)
Adolescence	Successful transition to secondary schooling Academic achievement (learning skills needed for higher education or work) Involvement in extracurricular activities (e.g. athletics, clubs) Forming close friendships within and across gender Forming a cohesive sense of self: identity

Reprinted with permission from Masten, A.S. & Coatsworth, J.D. (1998). The development of competence in favorable and unfavorable environments: Lessons from research on successful children. *American Psychologist, 53*, p.207.

2. THE FAMILY LIFE CYCLE MODEL

Diagnosis: Just as individuals go through life stages and are presented with specific developmental tasks, so do families. Table 4.3 shows a traditional stage sequence for families as described by Carter & McGoldrick (1999). Carter and McGoldrick also developed useful tables illustrating developmental stages for divorcing and remarried families (see Tables 4.4 and 4.5).

Goal-setting and Intervention Plan: The above-mentioned Carter and McGoldrick tables list the specific developmental issues that must be mastered for the family to successfully move forward. A weakness of developmental theory is that it is descriptive in nature and does not specify the interventions most likely to promote stage mastery. Nevertheless, the Carter and McGoldrick tables identify clear family goals that a SBFC professional could use to help a student affected by a "stuck" family. Most of the developmental goals listed in these tables represent goals familiar to all family counselors, irrespective of theoretical orientation. In terms of family counseling interventions specifically designed for developmental stages, Jay Haley's book Uncommon Therapy describes how strategic therapist Milton Erickson designed interventions to move a couple or family through different developmental "stuck-points" from birth to old age (Haley, 1993).

Table 4.3 Stages of the Family Life Cycle

Family Life Cycle Stage	Emotional Process of Transition: Key Principles	Second-Order Changes in Family Status Required to Proceed Developmentally
Leaving home: single young adults	Accepting emotional and financial responsibility for self	a) Differentiation of self in relation to family of origin b) Development of intimate peer relationship c) Establishment of self in respect to work and financial independence
The joining of families through marriage: the new couple	Commitment to new system	a) Formation of marital system b) Realignment of relationships with extended families and friends to include spouse
Families with young children	Accepting new members into the system	a) Adjusting marital system to make space for children b) Joining in child rearing, financial and household tasks c) Realignment of relationships with extended family to include parenting and grandparenting roles
Families with Adolescents	Increasing flexibility of family boundaries to permit children's independence and grandparents' frailties	a) Shifting of child-parent relationships to permit adolescent to move into and out of system b) Refocus on midlife marital and career issues c) Beginning of shift to caring for older generation
Launching children and moving on	Accepting a multitude of exits from and entries into the family system	a) Renegotiation of marital system as a dyad b) Development of adult-to-adult relationships between grown children and their parents c) Realignment of relationships to include in-laws and grandchildren d) Dealing with disabilities and death of parents (grandparents)
Families in later life	Accepting the shifting generational roles	a) Maintaining own and/or couple functioning and interests in face of

physiological decline
b) Support for more central role of
   middle generation
c) Making room in the system for the
   wisdom and experience of the
   elderly; supporting the older
   generation without
   overfunctioning for them
d) Dealing with loss of spouse,
   siblings, and other peers and
   preparation for death

Source: Reprinted with permission Carter, B. & McGoldrick, M. (Eds).(1999). The expanded family life cycle: Individual, family, and social perspectives (3rd ed.). Boston: Allyn & Bacon, p.2

Table 4.4 An Additional Stage of the Family Life Cycle for Divorcing Families

Phase		Emotional Process of Transition: Prerequisite Attitude	Developmental Issues
Divorce	The decision to divorce	Acceptance of inability to resolve marital tensions sufficiently to continue relationship	Acceptance of one's own part in the failure of the marriage
	Planning the breakup of the system	Supporting viable arrangements for all parts of the system	a) Working cooperatively on problems of custody, visitation, and finances b) Dealing with extended family about the divorce
	Separation	a) Willingness to continue cooperative co-parental relationship and joint financial support of children	a) Mourning loss of intact family b) Restructuring marital and parent-child relationships and finances; adaptation to living apart
		b) Work of resolution of attachment to spouse	c) Realignment of relationships with extended family; staying connected with spouse's extended family
	The divorce	More work on emotional divorce; overcoming hurt, anger, guilt, etc.	a) Mourning loss of intact family; giving up fantasies of reunion b) Retrieval of hopes, dreams, expectations from the marriage c) Staying connected with extended families

Post-divorce family	Single parent (custodial household or primary residence)	Willingness to maintain financial responsibilities, continue parental contact with ex-spouse, and support contact of children with ex-spouse and his or her family	a) Making flexible visitation arrangements with ex-spouse and family b) Rebuilding own financial resources c) Rebuilding own social network
	Single parent (noncustodial)	Willingness to maintain financial responsibilities and parental contact with ex-spouse and to support custodial parent's relationship with children	a) Finding ways to continue effective parenting b) Maintaining financial responsibilities to ex-spouse and children c) Rebuilding own social network

Source: Reprinted with permission Carter & McGoldrick, 1999, p. 375

Table 4.5 Remarried Family Formulation: A Developmental Outline

Step	Prerequisite Attitude	Developmental Issues
1. Entering the new relationship	Recovery from loss of first marriage (adequate emotional divorce)	Recommit to marriage and to forming a family with readiness to deal with complexity and ambiguity
2. Conceptualizing and planning new marriage and family	Accepting one's own fears and those of new spouse and children about remarriage and forming a stepfamily Accepting need for time and patience for adjustment to complexity and ambiguity of: 1. Multiple new roles 2. Boundaries: space, time, membership and authority 3. Affective issues: guilt, loyalty conflicts, desire for mutuality, unresolvable past hurts	a) Work on openness in the new relationships to avoid pseudomutuality b) Plan for maintenance of cooperative financial and co-parental relationships with ex-spouses c) Plan to help children deal with fears, loyalty conflicts, and membership in two systems d) Realign relationships with extended family to include new spouse and children e) Plan maintenance of connections for children with extended family of ex-spouse
3. Remarriage and reconstruction of family	Final resolution of attachment to previous spouse and ideal of "intact" family; acceptance of a different model of family with permeable boundaries	a) Restructure family boundaries to allow for inclusion of new spouse-stepparent b) Realign relationships and financial arrangements throughout

subsystems to permit
interweaving of several systems

c) Make room for relationships with
all children with biological
(noncustodial) parents,
grandparents, and other extended
family

d) Share memories and histories to
enhance stepfamily integration

Source: Reprinted with permission Carter & McGoldrick, 1999, p. 377

The Example of Luis
The Family Life Cycle issues facing Luis' family are shown in Table 4.6

Table 4.6 Family Life Cycle Issues for Rodriguez Family

Family Life Cycle Phase	Developmental Task*
Families with Adolescents	Need to refocus on midlife and marital issues
Separation	Willingness to continue co-operative parenting
	Need for joint financial support of children
	Restructuring marital and parental relationships
	Mourning loss of intact family

* examples from Carter & McGoldrick, 1999

3. THE CLIENT READINESS FOR CHANGE MODEL

Diagnosis: This model was developed by Prochasa, DiClemente, & Norcross (1992) in order to describe the stages many clients go through when deciding to engage in counseling and make changes to improve their lives. These stages are described in Table 4.7. What is particularly useful is their idea that many clients are at a Precompletion stage in which they do not see a need for counseling. The implication is that counselors should not assume that in an initial session with a client that they have a "customer." The term customer is used in Strategic Therapy to describe a person who wants counseling and is open to making changes to improve themselves and their relationships with others. In supervision we have frequently observed the phenomenon of a beginning intern report that they have had multiple sessions with a client but the client appears to have no goals. The counselor is frustrated and feels that she is just "spinning her wheels." This typically is the situation of an interview with someone who is at a Precontemplation Stage of readiness for counseling. We sometimes tell the intern that the problem is that they "don't have a client yet" or that the interviewee "hasn't bought into being a client yet."

Table 4.7 Client Readiness to Change Stages

Readiness for Change Stage	Description
Precontemplation	Individual does not see the need for counseling.
Contemplation	Client is open to considering the need for counseling.
Preparation	Client is open to planning for change.
Action	Client implements change.
Maintenance	Client takes steps to maintain change and prevent relapse

There are many reasons for a potential client to be in the Precontemplative Stage:

The "client" may not be psychological-minded and have the view that the problem does not require counseling.

The "client" may believe that their problem is more spiritual in nature and better dealt with by their priest, rabbi, or iman.

The "client" may be interested in counseling but have reservations about whether you are the right counselor for them.

The "client" may have a negative stereotype of counseling based on the portrayal of counselors on TV (all mostly "crazy" or troubled), or, based on the portrayal of counseling in film and television that requires uncovering of vulnerable feelings of inadequacy (i.e. deficit-focused counseling).

The "client" may lack insight into how they are contributing to their own difficulties.

Table 4.8 shows an ideal situation for beginning counseling with all the parties showing a readiness for and openness to counseling. Unfortunately, this type of situation is rare. Tables 4.9 and 4.10 show situations in which only the teacher or only the student is ready for counseling.

Goal-setting and Intervention Plan: In this model the initial goal is to facilitate the "client" to move out of a Precomtemplative stage or a Contemplative stage to a Preparation stage. In dealing with a person in the Precontemplative stage, we recommend that you approach this person with an open attitude and not assume that a client's deficit, such as fear or lack of insight, is the reason for reluctance to enter into counseling. Counseling is only one way of dealing with problems in life. We all need to be aware that

Table 4.8 An Ideal SBFC Readiness for Change Situation on Beginning Counseling

Readiness for Change Level	Teacher	Student	Parent/Guardian	Parent/Guardian
Precontemplation				
Contemplation	x	x	x	x
Preparation				
Action				
Maintenance				

Table 4.9 SBFC Example of Teacher as the Customer

Readiness for Change Level	Teacher	Parent/Guardian	Parent/Guardian	Student
Precontemplation		X	X	X
Contemplation				
Preparation	X			
Action				
Maintenance				

Table 4.10 SBFC Example of Student as the Customer

Readiness for Change Level	Student	Parent/Guardian	Parent/Guardian	Teacher
Precontemplation		X	X	X
Contemplation				
Preparation	X			
Action				
Maintenance				

there are many paths to healing. Most persons having relationship problems seek help from a priest, rabbi, or iman, rather than a counselor. Not all persons who seek counseling are improved by it. The counseling literature suggests that in about 7% of cases, clients get worse after seeking counseling. We adhere to the view that as counselors we have to earn the right to work in depth with a client's most vulnerable feelings and concerns. The way we do this is by taking the time to establish a relationship of trust with the "client" through our use of empathy, warmth, and respect. Research on premature termination of counseling indicates that approximately 50% of clients engage in premature termination. That is, the "client" comes for 1-6 sessions, then drops out (Barrett, Chua, Crits-Christolph, Gibbons & Thompson, 2008). This suggests a failure, fairly widespread, to help the "client" move out of a Precontemplation stage. Research by Shimokawa, Lambert & Smart (2010) suggests that when the counselor who makes an extra effort to ensure that the counseling is focusing on the client's concerns by using a feedback form at the end of each session, premature termination rates drop significantly.

The Example of Luis:

Table 4.11 SBFC Readiness for Change Situation for Luis

Readiness for Change Level	Luis	Mother	Father	Teacher	Mark	Mark's Family
Precontemplation			x		x	x
Contemplation		x		x		
Preparation	x					
Action						
Maintenance						

HOW TO USE A CBT MODEL FOR CASE CONCEPTUALIZATION

Because of the popularity and usefulness of CBT models we will be reviewing four:
1) The ABC Behavioral Model
2) Lazarus' Multimodal Assessment Model
3) Christensen's Social Interactional Model
4) Ellis' ABC Model

1. THE ABC BEHAVIORAL MODEL

Diagnosis: The ABC Behavioral assessment model examines Antecedents, Behavior, and Consequences for the client (Spiegler & Guevremont, 2003). Antecedents are prior conditions or events that trigger the occurrence or non-occurrence of a client's behavior. Behavior refers to the client's response to antecedent stimuli. Behavior may be overt (saying and doing something) or covert (thinking, feeling, or a physiological response). Consequences refer to the presence or absence of events that reinforce a behavior and cause the behavior to maintain, increase, or decrease. Table 4.12 gives some examples of common antecedents, behaviors, and consequences affecting children.

Table 4.12 Examples of Antecedents, Behavior, and Consequences for Children

Antecedent	Behavior	Consequence
No one in class initially speaks to a new student Lucy	Lucy thinks:"No one likes me" and doesn't speak to anyone because she anticipates being rejected	Lucy feels relieved that she wasn't overtly rejected. Her feelings of relief reinforce further avoidance of classmates.
Ben's father watches TV turned up loud	Ben can't concentrate on homework so watches TV with his father	Ben and father enjoy watching TV together. Ben is reinforced for not doing homework.
Margaret's mother is lonely since her divorce	Margaret feels ill each day and wants to stay at home rather than go to school	Margaret's mother feels less lonely and Margaret is reinforced for staying at home
Billy frequently gets out of his seat in class	Miss Smith his grade 4 teacher yells at Billy to sit down	Billy sits down when yelled at but 30 minutes later is out of his seat again. Billy's sitting down is a reinforcer for Miss Smith's yelling
Billy feels bored by Miss Smith's teaching	Billy gets out of his seat to look around the room	Miss Smith yells at him to sit down but 30 minutes later he is out of his seat again. Miss Smith's yelling is a reinforcer for Billy's out of seat behavior

Lena's mother tells her to do her homework	Lena asks her father for permission to go outside and play	Her father gives Lena permission to go outside and play. Lena is reinforced for not doing homework.
Sarah's parents are arguing	Sarah plays her radio too loud	Sarah's parents stop arguing and yell at Sarah. Sarah (who is very frightened when her parents fight) is reinforced for her "interrupting" behavior.

The Example of Luis:
An ABC Behavioral Analysis for Luis might look like this (see Table 4.13).

Table 4.13 An ABC Behavioral Analysis for Luis

Antecedent	Behavior	Consequence
1. Mark is angry at his parents	Mark bullies Luis and takes Luis' lunch	Luis gives up his lunch and Miss Jones turns a "blind eye" to the incident. Mark is reinforced for bullying Luis.
2. Luis is bullied at school	Luis tries to talk to his mother about being bullied (but eventually gives up "bothering" her)	Luis' mother says: "Not now I'm exhausted."
3. Luis wants to contact his father to tell him about soccer	Luis leaves his father a message on the phone (but eventually stops calling)	Luis' father never returns Luis' calls

Goal-setting and Intervention Plan: Some different intervention strategies that could be used to address the three situations described in Table 4.13 are shown in Table 4.14

Table 4.14 Goals and Sample Interventions for Table 4.13

Antecedent	Behavior	Consequence
1. *Goal:* Decrease Mark's anger at parents	*Goal:* Provide Mark with alternative way to cope with anger	*Goal:* Provide aversive consequence for bullying
Strategy: Family counseling	*Strategy:* Anger management	*Strategy:* Teacher to provide Mark with detention
2. *Goal:* Eliminate bullying	*Goal:* Improve Luis' communication skills with his mother	*Goal:* Improve mother's communication skills
Strategy: Teach Luis assertion	*Strategy:* Coach Luis on timing; behavior rehearsal of request skills	*Strategy:* Parenting skills training for Luis' parents
3.	*Goal:* Improve Luis' communication skills with father	*Goal:* Improve father's relationship with Luis
	Strategy: Have Luis write his father instead of phoning	Strategy: Counselor to develop working alliance with father; parenting skills training

2. LAZARUS' MULTIMODAL ASSESSMENT MODEL

Diagnosis: The Multimodal Assessment model was developed by Lazarus (2006) because he felt that traditional behavior therapy focused too narrowly on behavior to the exclusion of other important parts of the personality. According to Lazarus, a comprehensive treatment plan would assess how the client was functioning in seven key areas:

Behavior –your actions: what you do and say
Affect – your emotions
Sensation – your body sensations and tensions
Imagery – your fantasies and imagined scenarios
Cognition – your thoughts and attributions
Interpersonal – your interaction with others and how they relate to you
Drug/Physiological- how your body is affected

Lazarus called this the BASIC ID using D for drugs to indicate the Physiological dimension.

You can obtain your client's BASIC ID diagnosis by asking questions that tap each of the seven dimensions:

Behavior: "What do you typically say or do with_____(problematic situation or person)?"

Affect: "What sort of emotions or feeling do you typically have with_____?"

Sensation: "What sensations or tensions do you experience when_____?"

Imagery: "What images or fantasies do you have when dealing with_____?"

Cognition: "What does it mean to you when_____?"
"What kinds of thoughts do you have about_____?"

Interpersonal: "What does (name person) typically do when_____?"
"How does (name person) treat you when_____?"

Drug/Physiological: "When you are dealing with_____, how is your body affected?"
(e.g. "Feel ill, sleep affected, need medication, etc").

The BASIC ID assessment may be of a client's a) life situation in general, b) relationship with a specific person or group, or c) specific incident involving another person or group. As illustrated below for Behavior, the wording for specific levels of ID BASIC assessment will differ:

BASIC ID Assessment of a Client's Life Situation
"What do you generally do during a typical day?"
"What are some things you do that you would like to do more of?"
"What sort of behaviors would you like to do less of?"

BASIC ID of Relationship with a Specific Person or Group
"What do you say and do when you are with_____?"

BASIC ID of Specific Incident Involving Another Person or Group
"When_____occurred, what did you say or do?"

When doing a BASIC ID assessment, it is useful to use the multimodal assessment questions to map out all three levels: life situation, specific relationship, and specific incident. Box 4.1 shows how to ask multimodal assessment questions for a specific incident.

Goal-setting and Intervention Plan
After investigating your client's situation using multimodal assessment, the next step is to prepare a table briefly listing any problems in the seven BASIC ID categories, then identify possible treatment options that address the identified problems.

Box 4.1 <u>Multimodal Assessment for a Specific Incident</u>

Step 1: Identify a *specific incident* (identify time, place, person). Stick with this single incident.

  "I'd like to ask you some questions to get a clear idea of how you experienced this incident. Would that be alright?"

Step 2: Ask BASIC ID questions. OK to alternate with active listening. Start with any modality and move from one to another. Try to ask *at least two questions* for each modality. Use the spaces provided to check off the modalities you investigated.

_____ **B**ehavior: "What did you say?"
                        "What did you do?"

_____ **A**ffect: "How did you feel?"
                        "What emotions did you have? At the time? Later?"

_____ **S**ensation: "Did you experience any tensions in your body?"
                        "Was your breathing affected?"

_____ **I**magery: "Did you have any images or fantasies about him/her/yourself?"

_____ **C**ognition: "What did this incident mean to you? About him/her? Your relationship? Yourself?"

_____ **I**nterpersonal: "What did she/he say? Do?"

_____ **D**rug/Physiological: " How was your body affected at the time? Later?"
                        (e.g. "Did you feel ill, have to sleep?")
                        "Did you try to lower stress by soothing your body in some way eating, drinking, taking medication, etc.?"

A multimodal assessment table for Luis showing problem areas and proposed interventions is shown as Table 4.15.

Table 4.15 Multimodal Assessment (BASIC ID) for Luis

Modality	Problem	Proposed Intervention
Behavior	Non-assertive when bullied	Problem solving Assertion training Behavior Rehearsal
Affect	Sadness (re father) Anxiety and depression (re being bullied)	Art therapy Cognitive restructuring
Sensation	Muscle tension at school	Systematic muscle relaxation Diaphragmatic Breathing
Imagery	Images of being attacked Nightmares	Cognitive Restructuring (using positive imagery)
Cognition	"I am weak and helpless" "My father doesn't love me" "No one wants to be my friend"	Cognitive restructuring
Interpersonal	Lacks friends Parents too busy to attend to Luis' needs	Seat Luis near a sympathetic student Teach parents listening skills Arrange weekly phone call with father
Drug/ Physiological	Difficulty sleeping, nightmares	Systematic Muscle Relaxation before bedtime

In dealing with a case like Luis', a SBFC professional would also generate a multimodal assessment for the bully, and also one for Luis' mother if she were willing to enter counseling to help her son. Additional multimodal assessments might also be done for other persons such as Mark's parents and the teacher, Miss Jones.

3. CHRISTENSEN'S SOCIAL INTERACTIONAL MODEL

Diagnosis: The social interactional model developed by Christensen (Christensen & Pass, 1983) assesses for sources of client interpersonal stress called Troublesome Social Stimuli. According to Christensen most relationship stress is caused by specific behavioral triggers or Troublesome Social Stimuli (TSS). The TSS Model is shown in Figure 4.3. The seven most common TSS are shown in Table 4.16.

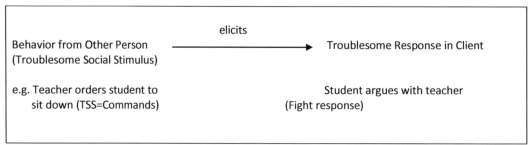

Figure 4.3 The TSS Model

Table 4.16 Seven Common Troublesome Social Stimuli (TSS)

TSS	Description from Client's Point of View
Commands	Other person gives order or strong request to client
Anger	Other person speaks to client in angry tone, yells, or gives angry look
Criticism	Other person criticizes client, points out clients mistake.
Depression/Sadness	Other person is sad or depressed in presence of client
Unresponsiveness	Other person makes no response to comment or presence of client
Impulsivity	Other person acts odd or irrational in client's presence
Affection	Other person expresses warmth, caring for client

It is important to note that the TSS is a behavior engaged in by your client's Other Person (who may be a family member, teacher, student, or any other person with whom your client is having difficulty). The seven common TSS may not all be troublesome for them. The purpose of conducting a TSS assessment is to determine which of these common interpersonal stressors are, in fact, a challenge for your client. If a TSS is troublesome your client will likely show one or more of the following responses shown in Table 4.17. Also shown in Table 4.18 are responses that indicate that the "TSS" is not, in fact, troublesome for your client.

The fundamental difference between the Tolerate responses and the responses indicating that the TSS is troublesome is that the Tolerate responses are characterized by your client being relatively calm and free to choose his/her response. The troublesome responses are compulsive and reflex-like for your client, who may be aware that she is not responding in a way she likes. Diagnosis involves systematically asking your client about her responses to specific TSS with the Other Person. The TSS Relationship Assessment Form shown as Box 4.2 may be used to collect this information.

Table 4.17 Common Responses to a TSS Indicating the TSS is Troublesome

Response	Description
Tense	Client's muscles tense up Client may be silent A "freeze" response
Leave	Client removes himself/herself from the presence of the other person A "flight" response
Change	Client tries to get other person to stop engaging in the TSS through deflecting responses such as pleading, apologizing, denying, joking.
Change-Fight	A change response where the client criticizes or becomes aggressive towards the other person A "fight" response

Table 4.18 Common Responses to a TSS Indicating that the TSS is not Troublesome

Response	Description
Tolerate	Client is able to tolerate the TSS Client does not show a Tense, Leave, or Change response
Tolerate sub-category:	
Assertive	Client chooses to make an assertive response
Ignore	Client chooses to ignore the TSS
Positive	Client chooses to respond with warmth or empathy

There are two main ways to use the form:
1) ask your client for an example for each of the seven TSS, or
2) ask your client to select the 3 TSS that she is most concerned about and collect data on these.
When collecting this behavioral assessment information, follow these steps:

Step 1. Teach your client about TSS and common responses to them.

Step 2. Invite your client to do a TSS assessment of their relationship with the Other Person.

Box 4.2 Relationship Assessment Form for Troublesome Social Stimuli

Client:_____   Relationship with:_____

Troublesome Social Stimuli For each of the following TSS identify a recent, typical incident in which the other person demonstrated the TSS	Stimulus How did the other person display the TSS? What did they say? do? What was their voice tone? facial expression?	Response What did you say/do in response? What was your voice tone? Did you feel tension? Breathing affected?	Classification of Your Response **Troublesome:** *Tense (T) Fight (F) Leave(L) Change(C)* **Tolerating:** *Assertive (A) Calm (C) Ignore (I) Positive (P)*
Commands			Troublesome: __Tense __ Fight __ Leave __ Change Tolerating: __ Assertive __ Calm __ Ignore __ Positive
Criticism			Troublesome: __Tense __ Fight __ Leave __ Change Tolerating: __ Assertive __ Calm __ Ignore __ Positive
Anger			Troublesome: __Tense __ Fight __ Leave __ Change Tolerating: __ Assertive __ Calm __ Ignore __ Positive

Depression/Sadness			Troublesome: __Tense __ Fight __ Leave __ Change Tolerating: __ Assertive __ Calm __ Ignore __ Positive
Unresponsiveness			Troublesome: __Tense __ Fight __ Leave __ Change Tolerating: __ Assertive __ Calm __ Ignore __ Positive
Impulsivity			Troublesome: __Tense __ Fight __ Leave __ Change Tolerating: __ Assertive __ Calm __ Ignore __ Positive
Affection			Troublesome: __Tense __ Fight __ Leave __ Change Tolerating: __ Assertive __ Calm __ Ignore __ Positive

Step 3. Select the first TSS and ask for a recent, specific, typical example of the TSS. If your client gives a general example, ask if they can identify a specific incident in which the Other Person emitted the TSS behavior. Remember that the TSS behavior is always that of the Other Person, not your client. Use the behavioral assessment questions listed on the form to guide your inquiry. Make brief notes on the form to record your client's responses.

Step 4. Ask your client how she responded to the TSS using the behavioral assessment questions provided on the form. Be aware that their response may be classified in more than one category, eg. "I tensed up, then left the room." Check to see if your client had any urges as these can indicate a response tendency. You can also assess the strength of your client's Tense responses on a 1 to 10 scale (10 = very high tension).

Step 5. Collect information on the next TSS and continue with steps 3 and 4 until the assessment is complete.

Step 6. Ask your client to look at the TSS assessment form with you and tell you if they see any pattern. Common patterns are a similar stress response across TSS, e.g. your client responds with a Tense response to each TSS or a unique response to one TSS, eg. a tense response to Commands and Anger, but a Fight response to Criticism.

The Example of Luis:
A TSS Relationship Analysis for Luis revealed the following TSS and response patterns for key persons in his life (Table 4.19).

Table 4.19 Summary of Luis' TSS and Responses

Other Person	TSS from this Person	Luis's Typical Response
Mark	Commands (to give up lunch)	Tense (10/10), urge to run away
Father	Unresponsive (to Luis' request to spend Time with Luis)	Tense (6/10)
Mother	Criticism (about concerns made by Luis' teacher)	Tense (8/10)

Goal-setting and Intervention Plan: In Christensen's social interactional approach to counseling (called Interpersonal Coping Skills) the counseling goal for Luis would be to determine if he would like to learn to tolerate the TSS from Mark, Father, and Mother in order to be able to choose a different set of responses. For example, to be able to say no to Mark in a way that is assertive but does not provoke aggression from Mark; to be able to communicate more effectively with his father in order to develop a closer relationship with him; and to be able to not feel tense when his mother criticizes him. The CBT counseling techniques most typically used to promote these changes are: Desensitization to the TSS, Cognitive Restructuring to replace catastrophic thoughts triggered by the TSS, and Assertiveness Training and Behavior Rehearsal to build more effective communication skills (see Chapter 11).

4. ELLIS' A-B-C MODEL

Diagnosis: The cognitive assessment model developed by Ellis (Ellis & Maclaren, 2005)   and used in his Rational Emotive Behavior Therapy (REBT) approach emphasizes the identification of your client's irrational beliefs. In Ellis' ABC model, A represents the Activating Event that triggers client stress. C stands for the Consequences which are typically stress, upset emotions, and non-assertive or aggressive behaviors. B stands for the Beliefs that the client has about the Activating Event. According to Ellis A does not cause C. Negative emotional Consequences are instead caused by irrational or catastrophic thoughts at B. Some common irrational beliefs are:

> I must be loved and approved of and if I am not it is terrible.
> If I make a mistake it is terrible and I am a bad person.
> If someone else makes a mistake it is terrible and they are a bad person.
> The possibility that something bad might happen to me means I must be constantly worried.
> I must have someone stronger to be dependent on in order to survive.
> I will never find love

According to Ellis our self worth becomes tied up with the approval of others or our performance. Similarly, our assessment of the worth of others may become tied to their performance. What makes the beliefs listed above irrational or dysfunctional is that they magnify things out of proportion to the triggering situation.

To conduct an ABC cognitive assessment follow these steps:

Step 1. Explain Ellis' ABC model to your client and invite your client to collaborate with you in applying it to her situation.

Step 2. Using paper, computer screen or white board, map out your client's situation for the A (Activating Event) and the C (Consequences).

Step 3. Ask your client what they were thinking at B that made them so stressed. Show your client the list of common irrational beliefs listed above and see if any fit. If your client is having difficulty identifying an irrational belief and you have a good idea about one that might fit, test it out:
"Could it be you believe_____?"
"Many people in your situation would have the thought_____.
Is it possible you had that thought too?"

You can also help your client identify their irrational beliefs by using a technique called The Vertical Arrow Technique (or the Downward Arrow Technique), developed by Burns (1999). To use this technique ask your client: "What does it mean to you that (refer to the Activating Event)?" For example, "What does it mean to you that your mother criticized you?" When your client makes her response to this, continue to explore the meaning to your client.

Example:
Counselor: "What does it mean to you that your father didn't respond to your letter?"
Luis: "It means he was too busy with work."
Counselor: "And if your father is too busy with work to reply to your letter what does that mean?"
Luis: "It means I'm not important to him." (Note: this belief could be true. However, it is more likely that it is not true and that the father is avoiding the mother, or is having emotional or work problems, or is not aware of the emotional impact on his son.") At this point the counselor has uncovered a core irrational belief which is probably: "If my father doesn't love me, it's terrible and my fault."

The Example of Luis
An REBT ABC analysis for Luis is shown as Table 4.20.

Table 4.20 Summary of Irrational Beliefs Experienced by Luis

Activating Event	Irrational Belief	Consequences
1. Bully takes his lunch	"I made a mistake (failed to stand up for myself), and am weak and stupid"	Depressed, anxious
2. Father doesn't respond to letters	"My father doesn't love me and so I am a bad son"	Sad, doesn't phone father
3. Mother seems preoccupied	"My mother does not approve of me and I can't stand it"	Anxious, doesn't tell mother about bully

Goal-setting and Treatment Plan: The REBT counseling goal for Luis would be to help him to a) identify when he is having an irrational belief, and b) to teach him effective ways to dispute or challenge his irrational beliefs in order to replace them with more rational beliefs (see Cognitive Restructuring in Chapter 11).

HOW TO USE A FAMILY SYSTEMS MODEL FOR CASE CONCEPTUALIZATION

Family Systems models diagnose relationships rather than individuals. This section will describe two approaches to a Family Systems case conceptualization: Bowen Theory and the Circumplex Model.

1. BOWEN THEORY

Diagnosis: The family systems theory of Murray Bowen (Bowen, 1978) is considered by family counselors to be one of the most important theoretical contributions in the field of family counseling. A minimal Bowen Theory case conceptualization would address the following elements:

> a) Genogram

> b) Triangles and scapegoating

> c) Family projection process

> d) Differentiation of self

a) Genogram
The Genogram is a sort of family tree diagram that displays the family members across generations (see Figure 4.4). Conventional symbols are used to indicate gender and type of relationship. Brief information concerning names, ages, health status, etc can be added. The purpose of the genogram is to aid you in identifying the web of family relationships affecting your client. Bowen also used the genogram to identify learned patterns of interaction that were passed from one generation to another (called the "multigenerational transmission of neurosis").

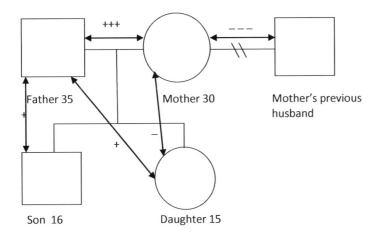

Father 35   Mother 30   Mother's previous husband

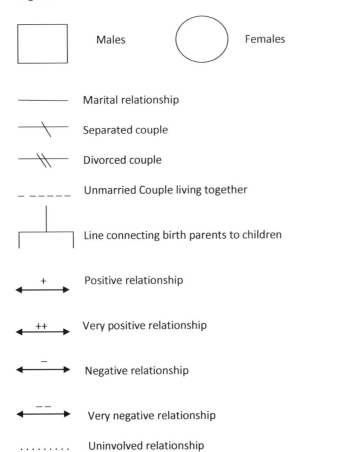

Son 16   Daughter 15

Legend:

☐   Males   ◯   Females

———   Marital relationship

—／—   Separated couple

—／／—   Divorced couple

– – – – – –   Unmarried Couple living together

    Line connecting birth parents to children

←—+—→   Positive relationship

←—++—→   Very positive relationship

←—−—→   Negative relationship

←—−−—→   Very negative relationship

· · · · · · · ·   Uninvolved relationship

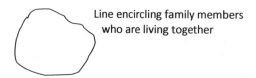

Line encircling family members
who are living together

Figure 4.4 Example of a Genogram

b) Triangles and Scapegoating

Bowen felt that when there was marked tension between two family members a common way to reduce this tension was by forming triangles. A triangle is most typically a coalition of two against one. Figure 4.5 shows a scapegoating triangle where the parents have a tense relationship with each other and displace their tension onto the child. This is sometimes referred to as a detouring triangle because the hostility between the couple is being projected onto the child as a way to reduce anxiety.

Figure 4.5 A Scapegoating Triangle

Figure 4.6 shows a triangle where the mother has a tense relationship with the father and she forms a coalition with the child against the father.The value of triangle analysis is that it will help you to understand more thoroughly the web of family relationships influencing a client. What may at first appear to be just a problem between a child and a mother may actually have its origin in a problem between the parents.

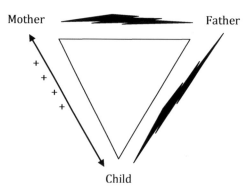

Figure 4.6 Coalition of Parent and Child Against Parent

c) Family Projection Process

This is the process where families project onto a particular family member a particular characteristic or identity. For example, in a family with severe marital discord, the parents may project onto a child their own hostile feelings and perceive the child as a "bad boy or girl". Repeated messages given to the child about his/her "badness" ("You are so inconsiderate", "you are a selfish girl", "why can't you behave", "you are trouble", "you're going to end up in trouble with the law") reinforce a negative self-image in the child and can become a self-fulfilling prophesy if the child takes on the persona being projected onto him/her.

d) Differentiation of Self

The goal of counseling in Bowen Theory and Therapy is to help clients to differentiate or emotionally separate themselves from their family. Bowen used the term "undifferentiated family ego mass" to describe enmeshed families in which members were not able to develop opinions that differed from those of the family. A Bowenian goal of counseling is to help clients to take "I think this" and "I feel this" positions that might be different from other family members while maintaining a constructive relationship with those family members. A Differentiation of Self Scale is sometimes used to indicate the degree to which a client has differentiated from his/her family (see Table 4.21).

Table 4.21 The Differentiation of Self Scale

Differentiation Level	Description	Example
76-100	Interdependent	Able to take "I" positions separate from family of origin while maintaining constructive contact with family members
51-75	Independent	Able to take "I" positions separate from family of origin but may experience difficulty maintaining these positions when in the presence of family members
26-50	Counter-dependent	Able to take "I" positions separate from family of origin, but does so in a rebellious way
1-25	Dependent	Unable to take "I" positions separate from family members

The Example of Luis

A Bowenian analysis of Luis's situation might look like the following. A genogram for Luis and his family is shown as Figure 4.7. As can be seen in the diagrammed relationships, Luis has a slightly positive relationship with his mother, Janet, and a neutral relationship with his father, Ramon. Ramon has a poor relationship with both his parents and also with his wife. Jane, however, has a good relationship with both of her parents. Janet's parents also have a positive relationship with Luis. If you were dealing with this family system, some things to think about would be:

> How to help Ramon and Janet improve their parenting relationship
> Increasing the connection between Luis and his father
> Helping Ramon develop a more positive relationship with his parents
> Enlisting the aid of Janet's parents as support for Luis and Jane

There appear to be two problematic triangles operating in this family system. One involves a coalition between Ramon and his mother against Janet. The second appears to be a coalition of Mary and Ramon against Jose.

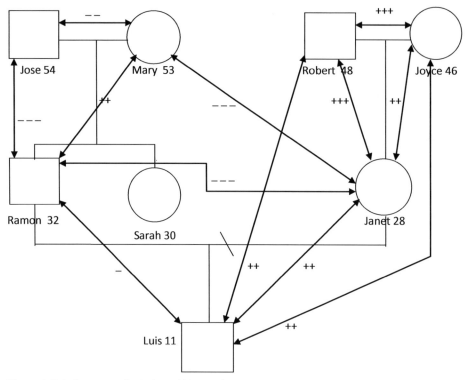

Figure 4.7 A Genogram for Luis and his Family

A third involves a coalition of Janet and Luis against Robert. The latter triangle is common when parents are at odds with each other and a child is used as an ally by one parent. It would be important to determine whether Janet is "parentifying" Luis to some extent by projecting onto him positive attributes of her own parents as she looks for allies against Ramon. Similarly, it is possible that Ramon, detecting his son's anger towards him, may be projecting onto Luis some of the negative attributes of Ramon's father. That is to say, through the projections of his parents, Luis is being given messages that he has a particular role to play in his parent's marital discord: rescuer to his mother and persecutor to his father.

Differentiation of Self Scale ratings for the family members would likely be as follows:

Luis	25
Janet	65
Ramon	45
Jose	45
Mary	55
Robert	75
Joyce	75

Goal-setting and Intervention Plan: A counselor using the Bowenian model would likely take the following steps in initiating treatment: a) Detriangulation of Luis from the conflict between Ramon and Janet; b) Strengthening of the relationship between Luis and Ramon; c) Enlistment of the support of Robert and Joyce; d) Helping Ramon deal with Janet without bringing in his mother. The general therapeutic approach would be to help each family member to differentiate themselves within their specific relationships.

2. THE CIRCUMPLEX MODEL

Diagnosis: David Olson's Circumplex Model is a widely used approach for family assessment and case planning (Olson, Russell & Sprenkle, 1989). The Circumplex Model with its 16 sub-categories is shown in Figure 4.8. The Circumplex Model is a relationship assessment approach: it does not diagnose individuals. Families are assessed on two key variables: Cohesion and Flexibility. Cohesion refers to the degree of closeness between family members and ranges between Enmeshed (overly close) and Disengaged (lacking in closeness). In-between these two extremes are more functional levels of cohesion: Connected (a constructive close relationship) and Separated (a constructive, caring but more independent relationship). Flexibility refers to the way power, authority, and structure are handled in the relationship and ranges between Chaotic (overly flexible and lacking in structure) and Rigid (lacking in flexibility and having a too much structure). In-between these two extremes are more functional levels of Flexibility: Flexible (an egalitarian, collaborative relationship) and Structured (a relationship characterized by clear but considerate leadership). In summary, each dimension- Cohesion and Flexibility- has 4 levels. The outer two are more extreme and the inner two are more characteristic of healthy relationships. The instruments Olsen uses to assess Cohesion and Flexibility (as well as Communication)- FACES II- have excellent reliability and validity.

The Circumplex Model was designed to primarily assess family systems . However it can be used to diagnose any relationship. You can use it to diagnose an entire family, or a single relationship. Our experience is that it is generally more useful to use the Circumplex Model to diagnose different dyads (two person groupings).

Examples include:
Student-Mother
Student-Father
Mother-Father
Student-Teacher
Parent-Teacher
Teacher-Class
Student-Class
Principal-Parent
Student-SBFC professional

As Lusterman (1989) has shown, the Circumplex Model can also be used to diagnose relationships within the school and between the school and the family. This makes the Circumplex Model extremely useful for trans-system assessment (i.e. an approach that can be used flexibly for diagnosis in different systems). Table 4.22 gives brief examples of the different Circumplex Model categories for family and school situations.

COHESION

| | DISENGAGED | SEPARATED | CONNECTED | ENMESHED |
| low | | | | high |

	DISENGAGED	SEPARATED	CONNECTED	ENMESHED
CHAOTIC (high)	<u>Chaotically Disengaged</u>	*Chaotically Separated*	*Chaotically Connected*	<u>Chaotically Enmeshed</u>
FLEXIBLE	*Flexibly Disengaged*	**Flexibly Separated**	**Flexibly Connected**	*Flexibly Enmeshed*
STRUCTURED	*Structurally Disengaged*	**Structurally Separated**	**Structurally Connected**	*Structurally Enmeshed*
RIGID (low)	<u>Rigidly Disengaged</u>	*Rigidly Separated*	*Rigidly Connected*	<u>Rigidly Enmeshed</u>

FLEXIBILITY (high ↑ / low ↓)

Note:

<u>Underlined</u>: Extreme family/relationship types

Italics: Families/relationships with issues

Bold: More functional families/relationships

Figure 4.8 The Circumplex Model

Table 4.22 Brief Examples of Circumplex Model Categories

Circumplex Category	Brief Example for Family and School

Cohesion:

> Enmeshed
>
> *Family:*
> Parent may be overprotective of child
> Partner A is very dependent on Partner B
> Family member interrupts and speaks for another family member
> Family time is required
>
> *School:*
> Teacher may be overprotective of student ("teacher's pet")
>
> Connected
>
> *Family:*
> Family members have a warm, respectful relationship
> Family member A listens to and appreciates feelings of Family member B
> Family time is valued
>
> *School:*
> Teacher and student have a warm, respectful relationship
> Teacher and parent have a warm, respectful relationship
>
> Separated
>
> *Family:*
> Family members are caring but engage in a lot of independent activity
> Family time is valued but occurs less often
>
> *School*
> Teacher is respectful of student and parent
>
> Disengaged
>
> *Family:*
> Family members lack emotional closeness with each other
> Family time is avoided
> Relationships characterized by coldness or hostility
>
> *School:*
> Teacher is coldly matter of fact or demonstrates lack of caring towards student and/or parent

Circumplex Category	Brief Example for Family and School

Flexibility:

Chaotic

Family:
Parents/guardians are not in charge: no clear family hierarchy
Conversations are a "free for all"
Family rules are unclear ; Family rules not enforced

School:
Teacher lacks classroom discipline skills
Teacher has difficulty getting students to remain in seats or focus
Teacher unable to implement lesson plan

Flexible

Family:
Parents/guardians use egalitarian leadership style
Children included in decision making often by consensus

School:
Teacher is willing to modify lesson plan to accommodate student interests

Structured

Family:
Parents/guardians make the rules, but consider children's views

School:
Teacher is clearly in charge, but occasionally modifies lesson plan to accommodate student interests

Rigid

Family:
Parents/guardians make the rules in an arbitrary fashion
A family rule is almost never changed despite the circumstances

School:
Teacher is inflexible about the rules or lesson plan
Student failure to conform is swiftly punished

Because the Circumplex Model can be used to diagnose any relationship, it can also be used to diagram a wide variety of relationship within and across family and school:

teacher-parent
teacher-principal
teacher-student
principal-parent
principal-student
student-student
counselor-teacher
counselor-parent
counselor-student
student-class
school-family

This is extremely useful when thinking systemically about a client's relationships and ecosystemic context.

The Example of Luis

A Circumplex Model diagnosis for the significant relationships involving Luis is shown as Figure 4.9. As can be seen there are three extreme relationships, all Disengaged: Luis and Mark (Rigidly-Disengaged), Luis's Mother and Father (Rigidly-Disengaged), and Mark and his family (Chaotically-Disengaged). In addition, Luis has a Disengaged relationship with his father (Structurally-Disengaged). Both the teacher and his mother have a more positive Structurally-Separated relationship with Luis. None of the diagrammed relationships are in the Connected area.

Goal-setting and Intervention Plan: Figure 4.10 shows how the Circumplex Model can be used to develop treatment goals for Luis. The arrows show the direction a SBFC would likely try to shift relationships affecting Luis.

First, the counselor should block further bullying of Luis at school by:

a) asking the teacher to monitor Mark's classroom behavior and establish a swift consequence for further bullying behaviors; b) meeting with Mark and his parents to help the parents establish a more stable family climate and maintain increased disciplinary control of Mark; c) helping Mark to develop coping skills with his family in order to manage his stress and not displace his feelings onto Luis or another child.

Second, the counselor should:a) teach Luis coping and assertion skills to help Luis deal with bullying; b) encourage the teacher and Luis' mother to develop a more Connected relationship with Luis in order to provide him with greater support.

Third, the counselor should: a) work to develop greater closeness between Luis and his father (i.e. move their relationship from Disengaged to Separated); b) help Luis' parents to develop a positive relationship based on collaborative parenting (i.e. move their relationship from Rigidly-Disengaged to Structurally-Separated). Olsen recommends that when working to improve a relationship, you initially work on one Circumplex dimension (Cohesion or Flexibility) at a time. He also recommends making small steps, i.e. trying to initially shift the relationship into the adjacent cell (e.g. moving from Rigid to Structured, rather than trying to too suddenly move the relationship to Flexible). Box 4.3 is of a worksheet you can use for your case planning.

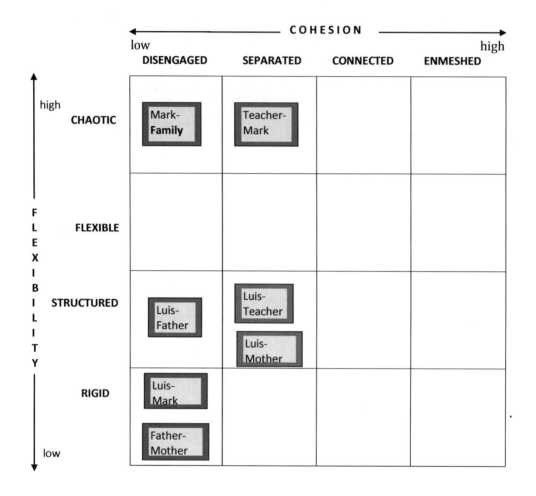

Figure 4.9 Circumplex Model Diagnosis for Luis

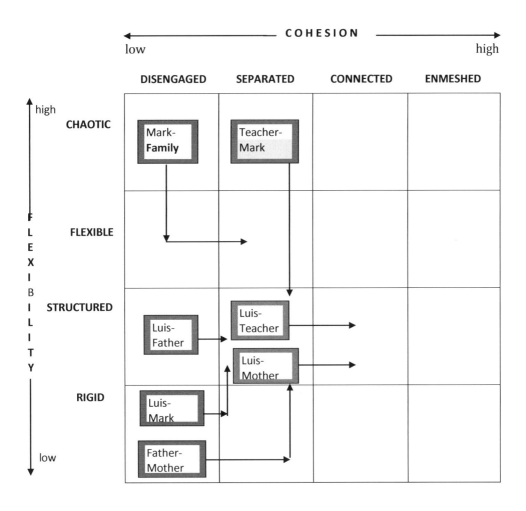

Figure 4.10 Circumplex Model Goals for Luis

Box 4.3   Circumplex Model Worksheet   Client:_____

COHESION
low   high

	DISENGAGED	SEPARATED	CONNECTED	ENMESHED
CHAOTIC				
FLEXIBLE				
STRUCTURED				
RIGID				

FLEXIBITY

high

HOW TO USE A STRENGTH-BASED MODEL FOR CASE CONCEPTUALIZATION

In this section we will describe four strength-based models for case conceptualization: 1) Maslow's Hierarchy of Needs; 2) Seligman's Positive Psychology approach; 3) Narrative Therapy approach, and 4) Type Development.

1) Maslow's Hierarchy of Needs
Diagnosis: This model will be familiar to most readers as it is covered in every introductory psychology text. According to Maslow there are five levels of need that all human beings have: Physiological, Safety, Belonging, Esteem, and Self-actualization (see Figure 4.11)(Maslow, 1968) .

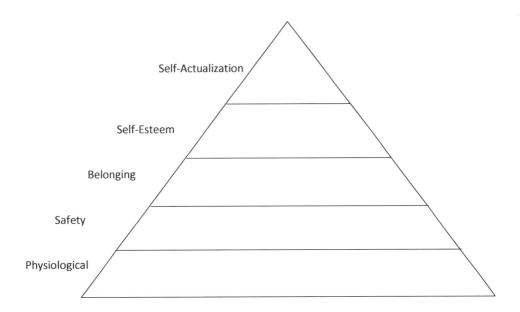

Figure 4.11   Maslow's Hierarchy of Needs

Table 4.23 gives a brief definition of each need level and the consequences if that need is not met. It was Maslow's belief that if a lower level need was not met the individual would have difficulty meeting the need at the levels above. For example, if a child fears for her safety at school because of a bully, she is unlikely to be able to concentrate on achieving through study or enjoy time with friends. Subsequent research has suggested that culture plays a large role in the effect of a need not being met on the other needs and that a linear relationship between the needs cannot be assumed. Nevertheless the importance of satisfying basic human needs seems compelling and directs us to an examination of the extent to which a client's basic human needs are being met.

Table 4.23 Examples of Maslow's Need Levels

Need Level	Description	Consequence if not met
Physiological	The body needs: need for food, water, air, temperature regulation, being free of disease	Illness, death
Safety	The need to be free from danger	Anxiety, fear
Belonging	The need to love and be loved	Loneliness
Esteem	The need to be valued by self and others for one's competence and achievements	Anxiety, low self-esteem
Self-actualization	The need to develop one's full potential; to be creative and experience fun	Boredom

To use a Maslow approach with clients you investigate the extent to which your client's needs are being met in each need level. Areas in which needs are being strongly met can be used to help deal with a crisis or problem (for example, by using existing friendships to buffer against financial stress). Areas in which needs are not being met can become a focus of counseling to strengthen your client generally (for example, a client who has low self esteem because of poor grades could develop competence in something other than grades, such as sports, such that his/her self-esteem increases and this facilitates a sense of self-efficacy in being able to increase grades).

A couple that is fighting all the time (Belonging Needs not being met) may have Esteem Needs not being met at work which help to "fuel" marital dissatisfaction. In this example a counselor would want to help the couple to develop better communication skills. However, if the couple's Esteem Needs remain unmet, then each partner's overall life satisfaction will be less- a situation that is unlikely to promote a happier marriage. By helping a couple meet their Esteem Needs (perhaps by providing some career counseling), will facilitate a stronger relationship between them. The basic principle is: help your client to be happier by strengthening their ability to meet all their basic needs in addition to the need level that contains the presenting problem (e.g. marital discord).

The Example of Luis
A Maslow needs analysis for Luis' situation (for Luis, Mark, and Luis' parents) is shown as Figure 4.12. This type of analysis identifies need levels that are not being met: e.g. for Luis the Safety, Belonging, Esteem and Self-Actualization needs.

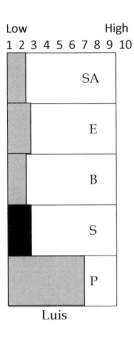

Low | High
1 2 3 4 5 6 7 8 9 10

Luis

Only Luis' Physiological needs are being met. Because of his Safety needs not being met (due to bullying), his Esteem needs are lower because on inability to concentrate in school. In addition, his Belonging needs are not being met because his father is under-involved with Luis and his mother is preoccupied with supporting herself and Luis financially. The dark shading indicates the need area initially affected by the presenting problem.

Figure 4.12 Maslow Needs Analysis for Luis

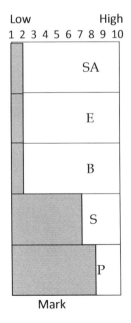

Low | High
1 2 3 4 5 6 7 8 9 10

Mark

Mark, like Luis, has unmet needs in the area of Belonging, Esteem and Self-Actualization. Mark's unmet Belonging and Esteem needs are primarily related to his chaotic family environment, poor parenting, and marital discord.

Figure 4.13 Maslow Needs Analysis for Mark

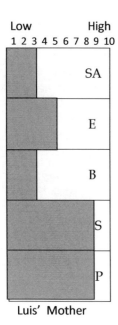

Luis' Mother

Low   High
1 2 3 4 5 6 7 8 9 10

SA
E
B
S
P

Luis' mother, Janet, has her Safety and Physiological needs met. However, her Belonging needs are not being met, partly due to her conflict with her separated husband and partly due to the fact she has a weak support network and few friends.

Figure 4.14 Maslow Needs Analysis for Luis' Mother

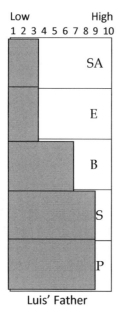

Luis' Father

Low   High
1 2 3 4 5 6 7 8 9 10

SA
E
B
S
P

Luis' father has adequately met Safety, Physiological, and Belonging needs. Unlike his wife he has several male friends who provide support. However his Esteem needs and his Self-Actualization needs are not being met. At work he has been repeatedly criticized by his supervisor and is on probation.

Figure 4.15 Maslow Needs Analysis for Luis' Father

Goal-setting and Intervention Plan: Once the counselor has identified a need that is not being met, the next step is to identify different ways the need could be met and then develop a plan, with the client's support, to meet the need. This strategy is followed even if the unmet need area seems unrelated to the presenting problem. The goal is to improve the overall functioning of the client. Table 4.24 shows a preliminary plan for fulfilling the need areas for Luis and his mother. A comprehensive treatment plan would extend to the father and include Mark and his family.

Table 4.24 Plan for Promoting Fulfillment of Needs for Luis and his Mother

Family Member	Unmet Need	Proposed Strategy to Meet Need
Luis	Safety	End bullying through: -Counseling for Mark and his family -Getting Mark's teacher to monitor Mark -Teaching Luis coping and assertion skills -Enlisting class support for Luis
	Belonging	Help Luis become closer to father Remove Luis from his parent's conflict by counseling parents Have teacher seat Luis next to a sympathetic student Assist Luis in developing friendship skills Mother to allow Luis to have a friend visit
	Esteem	Encourage Luis to participate in school soccer team Have teacher encourage Luis in his schoolwork
	Self-Actualization	Encourage Luis' mother to spend one evening a week in a fun activity with Luis Discuss with Luis' mother the possibility of enrolling his in a soccer camp for the summer
Luis' Mother (Janet)	Belonging	Teach Janet coping skills for lowering her stress when dealing with her husband Explore with Janet ways of expanding her social network
	Esteem	Assist Janet with career planning so she can find a better, more interesting job which will pay more
	Self-Actualization	Encourage Janet to take up tennis again - a sport that she gave up when she married but which gave her great pleasure

2. POSITIVE PSYCHOLOGY

Diagnosis: Positive Psychology, as described by Dr. Martin Seligman, addresses the "missing half" of counseling: promoting personal strengths (Seligman & Csikszentmihalyi, 2000). According to Seligman almost all counseling and psychotherapy is obsessively focused on identifying psychological problems and eliminating them. What is missing is a focus on strengthening clients generally and promoting their positive attributes. The reason for doing this is that it promotes client happiness, improves health, and is a major buffer for stress. Seligman's position is that this is not an either/or situation. As counselors we should both eliminate client problems and deficits and help clients be happier and more fulfilled. This position is consistent with helping clients to be more self-actualized and to meet more of their needs through the development of their strengths. A list of 24 strengths that are assessed in Seligman's Brief Strengths Test (available at http://www.authentichappiness) are:

Love of learning
Fairness
Forgiveness and mercy
Humor
Creativity
Open-mindedness
Perspective
Integrity
Love
Kindness
Social intelligence
Citizenship
Leadership
Humility/Modesty
Prudence
Self-regulation
Gratitude
Hope
Curiosity
Persistence
Appreciation of beauty and excellence
Spirituality
Bravery
Vitality

A Positive Psychology assessment may be conducted by asking your client questions like:
What are you most proud of?
What about you do you consider your greatest strengths?
What positive quality do you admire that you want to develop further in yourself?
What would be a small step you could take to put more of_____ (e.g. joy, creativity, fun, etc) into your life?

The Example of Luis
When Luis was asked these questions, he responded in this fashion:

Counselor: "What are you most proud of?"
Luis: "My soccer playing. I scored a goal last week!"
Counselor: "What do you consider your greatest strengths?"
Luis: "When my team is behind in scoring I never give up. I always try to help someone when they are in trouble."
Counselor: "What positive quality do you admire that you want to develop further in yourself?"
Luis: "Well, sometimes I feel like giving up. I'd like to get better at not feeling that way."
Counselor: "What would be a small step you could take to put more off "not giving up" into your life?"
Luis: "Well, the next time my team is behind and I miss a goal, I could try to think more about getting the next goal."

Goal-setting and Intervention Plan: As can be seen in the above example, the client clearly sets the goal and identifies the next step in strengthening a positive area of his life. The counselor would follow through at the next session to see how the strength-building assignment went. A more directed assignment that Seligman sometimes gives clients who wish to strengthen gratitude in their life is called "The Gratitude Visit." The client is asked to identify a person who had a profound influence on his/her life and to whom the client has never told. The assignment is to first write out a description of what the person did that was so helpful and then a description of the impact that help had on the client's life. Next, the client schedules an appointment to meet with the person and at the meeting reads the letter to him/her. Seligman reports that this assignment is deeply moving for both the client and the other person.

3. NARRATIVE THERAPY

Diagnosis: In Narrative Therapy, one of the strength-based therapies, diagnosis involves identifying "unique outcomes" which are positive incidents that contradict a client's negative story about their life and identity (White & Epston, 1990). Generally, in any client's life, there are a mix of both positive and negative events (Figure 4.16). Clients, however, tend to emphasize the negative events and overlook the positive events. The story about their lives becomes a "problem-saturated account" (Figure 4.17). The Narrative Therapist searches for a "unique outcome" which is a positive incident reflecting a client strength (Figure 4.18). For example, with a client who feels helpless and dependent, the counselor may look for an incident where the client behaved independently. With a client who feels incompetent, the counselor will look for an incident where the client behaved with competence.

The Example of Luis
The following dialogue shows how a counselor using a Narrative Therapy approach would identify and then focus on a unique outcome for Luis.

Counselor: "If you were to give a name to what is happening to you at school with Mark, what name would you give it?"
Luis: "Bullied!"
Counselor: "How has bullied been affecting you?"
Luis: "I find it hard to concentrate in class and I've been getting bad grades. My mom is upset with me."
Counselor: " Have there been any days when Bullied didn't get the better of you?"

Luis: *"Well, once I complained to the principal and she spoke to the teacher and Mark left me alone for about 2 weeks."*
Counselor: *"Wow! That was amazing what you did. What name would you give to describe what you did in talking to the principal?"*
Luis: *"Braveheart."*
Counselor: *" It sounds like Braveheart represents courage or braveness. Most students would be reluctant to speak to the principal. How did you learn this quality of Braveheart?"*

Goal-setting and Intervention Plan: Rather than focus on the client's deficits (the "problem-saturated account"), the counselor instead focuses on a client's strength and makes that the focus of the counseling. The counselor shows strong interest in the client's incident demonstrating a strength and explores with the client what it means about the client's identity, as well as ways to strengthen that quality.

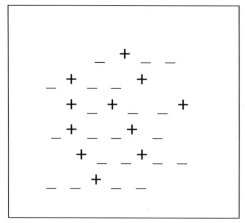

Figure 4.16 Positive and Negative Incidents in a Client's Life

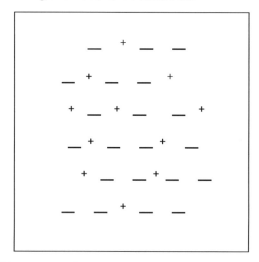

Figure 4.17 The Problem-Saturated Account: Failure Identity

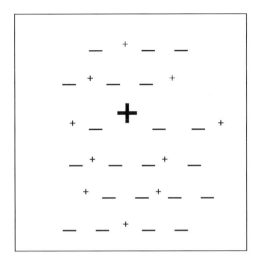

Figure 4.18 Focusing on Unique Outcomes: Building Success Identity

HOW TO USE THE DSM IN CASE CONCEPTUALIZATION

Because of its widespread use in mental health, you may wish to use the American Psychiatric Association's DSM approach to diagnosis. The DSM V typically uses a multi-axial diagnosis as shown in Table 4.24.

Table 4.25 DSM Multi-axial Diagnosis

Axis	Description
I	Mental Disorders
II	Personality Disorders and Mental Retardation
III	General Medical Conditions
IV	Psychosocial and environmental problems
V	Global Assessment of Functioning Scale (1-100)

SIX REASONS TO USE THE DSM

1. This is the most widely used mental health diagnostic system and is used internationally. It especially enjoys wide use amongst psychiatrists and psychologists. Many agencies require the use of the DSM by clinicians and failure to use or understand DSM terminology may be viewed as a lack of professional competence.

2. The multi-axial system is useful in providing a broad-spectrum picture of a client, especially through the use of Axes III and IV.

3. Many HMO's will not reimburse a client unless there is a DSM diagnosis.

4. Most of the efficacy and effectiveness studies conducted on counseling techniques use the DSM as a diagnostic system. That is, often when an effective counseling approach has been demonstrated, it is for application to a particular DSM axis I or II category.

4. The Global Assessment of Functioning (GAF) Scale has demonstrated reliability.

6. The V-codes (see Table 4.26) allow for diagnosis of relationship problems.

Table 4.26 DSM-IV TR codes for Relational Assessment

V code	Description
V61.1	Partner Relational Problem
V61.20	Parent-Child Relational Problem
V61.21	Child Neglect
	Physical/Sexual Abuse of a Child
V61.8	Sibling Relational Problem
V62.2	Occupational Problem
V62.3	Academic Problem
V62.4	Acculturation Problem
V62.82	Bereavement
V62.89	Phase of Life Problem
	Religious or Spiritual Problem
V71.01	Adult Antisocial Behavior
V71.02	Child or Adolescent Antisocial Behavior
V71.09	No diagnosis or Condition (on Axis I or Axis II)

SIX REASONS TO NOT USE THE DSM

1. Almost all of the DSM Axis I and II categories lack adequate reliability for clinical use. Spitzer, the architect of the DSM, set a kappa correlation coefficient of .70 as the minimum level required for clinical use of a category.

A high Kappa (generally 0.70 and above) indicates good agreement as to whether or not the patient has a disorder within that diagnostic class.

(Spitzer et al, 1979: 816-817)

Appendix F of the DSM III contained data from the first major reliability study conducted on the DSM. Almost all of the Axis I disorders for children and for adults were below the .70 kappa standard set by Spitzer. Eighty-six percent of the diagnostic categories failed to reach the .70 standard on both of the reliability trials conducted. In the DSM III R , Appendix F was removed and no subsequent reliability data has been published in the DSM.

Based on Appendix F data the mean reliability scores for some of the more common diagnoses that might be used with children are shown as Table 4.28.

Table 4.28 Kappa Scores for Common Axis I Diagnoses for Children

DSM Category	Mean Kappa Score
CONDUCT DISORDER	.61
ADHD	.54
ADJUSTMENT DISORDER	.51
AFFECTIVE DISORDER	.41
ANXIETY DISORDER	.35

These are, as a group, low scores. It should be kept in mind that the DSM reliability trials are conducted by psychiatrists trained in the use of the DSM. The low scores indicate a failure of the raters to agree on a diagnosis. In contrast, the kappa reliability scores for Mental Retardation (1.00) and Substance Abuse (.77) are high. However, these conditions are relatively easy to observe.

Reliability studies conducted 30 years later show no improvement in scores. Table 4.29 summarizes DSM reliability data collected over a 30 year period (Frances, 2012). Allen Frances, M.D., Professor Emeritus, Duke University and task force leader for the DSM-IV makes the following criticisms of the DSM-V and previous versions of the DSM (Frances, 2012):

> The results of the DSM-5 field trials are a disgrace to the field. For context, in previous   DSMs a diagnosis had to have a kappa reliability of about 0.6 or above to be considered acceptable.   A reliability of 0.2 to 0.4 has always been considered completely   unacceptable, not much above chance agreement. No predetermined publication date justifies business as usual in the face of these terrible field trial results, which are even   more striking given that they were obtained in academic settings with trained and skilled interviewers, highly selected patients, and no time pressure (the results in real-world settings would be much lower). Reliability this low for so many diagnoses gravely undermines the credibility of DSM-5 as a basis for administrative coding, treatment selection, and clinical research.

2. When a diagnostic system has poor reliability, it cannot be valid.

3. The DSM contains many labels widely considered stigmatizing: e.g. Borderline, Narcissistic, Bi-Polar, and these stamp a "mental illness" label on a client. This has been referred to as the pathologizing of everyday behavior. One of the reasons many clients do not seek counseling is because they do not want to appear "loco" i.e. crazy. The DSM lacks a focus on resilience or client strengths.

4. The DSM has a history of pathologizing homosexuals, women, and minorities. In 1968 the DSM II diagnosed Homosexuality as one of 10 sexual deviations. In 1987 this diagnosis was removed due to political action by gay activists. In 1986 women therapists and feminists managed to have a proposed diagnosis for the DSM III-R (301.89 Masochistic Personality Disorder) dropped, out of concern that women would have been assigned this diagnosis disproportionately because of gender bias in the diagnostic criteria. Loring and Powell (1988), in a study of 488 psychiatrists, found a disproportionate assignment of paranoid schizophrenic disorder given to black males and a disproportionate assignment of paranoid personality disorder given to black males and females. The researchers concluded: "Clinicians appear to ascribe violence, suspiciousness, and dangerousness to black clients even though the case studies are the same as the case studies for the white clients."

4. The DSM is an intra-psychic diagnostic model and lacks a systems perspective. This deficiency is expressed by the following quote from Dr. William Glasser: "For every crazy person out there, there is someone who made them crazy and that is the person who is really crazy."

6. A growing number of critics have pointed to the fact that the DSM advisory board has ties with pharmaceutical companies. This raises questions about the objectivity of the DSM diagnostic criteria which are used by psychiatrists to prescribe medication as the primary intervention for mental disorder. U.S. News & World Report in 2007 reported that ,of 27 APA Task Force Members, only 8 had no ties with pharmaceutical companies. This means 70% of the APA Task Force had ties. This is a matter for concern because:

> ...studies have repeatedly shown a connection between authors who receive
> income from drug companies and published papers favoring the firm's
> products. The papers also tend to underreport negative side effects.
> -U.S. News & World Report, 2007, Dec. 31, 25-26

As can be seen, the advantages of the DSM are balanced by its disadvantages. If you decide to use the DSM in a SBFC context, we recommend the following:

1. Do not assign an Axis I diagnosis until you have seen a child at least 5 times – particularly if you suspect one of the unreliable diagnostic categories listed in Table 4.29.

2. If you believe that a particular Axis I category may be stigmatizing for a child, or lead to pathologizing of the child's behavior by the school or family, or promote a "failure identity" in the child, then assign a more benign diagnosis. Examples of less stigmatizing diagnoses include: 309 Adjustment Disorder or one of the 25 v-codes (such as v61.20 Parent-Child Relational problem). This is considered a "social justice" perspective in utilizing the DSM.

3. Do not assign one of the stigmatizing Axis II personality disorders to any child. Use V71.09 No diagnosis or 799.9 Diagnosis deferred.

4. Use the more constructive Axis III: General Medical Conditions; Axis IV: Psychosocial and Environmental Conditions; and Axis V: Global Assessment of Functioning Scale.

Table 4.29 Kappa Reliability Statistics for the DSM

	DSM-5	DSM-IV	ICD-10	DSM-III
Generalized anxiety disorder (GAD)	0.20	0.65	0.30	0.72
Post-traumatic stress disorder (PTSD)	0.67	0.59	0.76	0.55
Schizophrenia	0.46	0.76	0.79	0.81
Bipolar disorder type I	0.54		0.69	
Major depressive disorder (MDD)	0.32	0.59	0.53	0.80
Major neurocognitive disorder	0.78		0.60	0.91
Mild neurocognitive disorder	0.50			
Alcohol use disorder	0.40		0.71	0.80
Hoarding	0.59			
Binge-eating disorder (BED)	0.56			
Bipolar disorder type II	0.40			
Mixed anxiety-depressive disorder	0.06			
Attenuated psychosis syndrome	0.46			
Obsessive-compulsive personality disorder (OCD)	0.31			
Antisocial personality disorder	0.22			
Autism spectrum disoder	0.69	0.85	0.77	0.01
Attention-deficit hyperactivity disorder (ADHD)	0.61	0.59	0.85	0.50
Disruptive mood dysregulation disorder (DMDD)	0.50			
Oppositional defiant disorder (ODD)	0.41	0.55		0.66
Conduct disorder	0.48	0.57	0.78	0.61

Source: Frances (2012) Reprinted with permission.

The Example of Luis
An example of a social justice DSM diagnosis for Luis is shown as Table 4.30.

Table 4.30 Social Justice DSM Diagnosis for Luis

Axis	Diagnosis
I	309 Adjustment Disorder V Other Relationship Problem
II	V 71.09 No diagnosis
III	None
IV	Bullied at school Mother and father separated with tense relationship Mother overworked with job stress
V	GAF= 60

SUMMARY

Whether you use the case conceptualization models described here, or even other models, we encourage you to consider how the model can be applied within the context of the SBFC model quadrants. A detailed worksheet is provided in Box 4.4 to aid you in developing your case conceptualization.

REFERENCES

American Psychiatric Association. (2000). *Diagnostic and statistical manual of mental disorders* (4th ed., text revision). Washington,DC: Author.

Barrett M. S., Chua W. J., Crits-Christoph P., Gibbons M. B., Thompson D. Early withdrawal from mental health treatment: Implications for psychotherapy practice. *Psychotherapy: Theory, Research, Practice, Training*. 2008;45:247–267.

Bowen, M. (1978). *Family therapy in clinical practice*. New York: Aronson.

Breggin, P. (1991) *Toxic psychiatry: why therapy, empathy and love must replace the drugs, electroshock and biochemical theories of the "new psychiatry."* New York: St. Martin's Press.

Burns, D. (1999). *The feeling good handbook*. New York: Plume.

Caplan, P. (1994.) *They say you're crazy: how the world's most powerful psychiatrists decide who's normal.* New York: Perseus Books.

Carter, B. & McGoldrick, M. (Eds.). (1999). *The expanded family life cycle: Individual, family, and social perspectives* (3rd ed.). Boston: Allyn & Bacon.

Christensen, C. & Pass, L. (1983). *Social interactional approach to counseling/psychotherapy.* Toronto: Ontario Institute for Studies in Education.

Dineen, Tana (1996). *Manufacturing victims: what the psychology industry is doing to people.* Toronto: Robert Davies.

Ellis, A. & Maclaren, C. (2005). *Rational emotive behavior therapy: a therapist's guide.* Atascadero, CA: Impact Publishers.

Erikson, E. (1963). *Childhood and society.* New York: Norton.

Frances, A. (2012). Newsflash From APA Meeting: DSM-5 Has Flunked Its Reliability Tests. *The Huffington Post*, 05/08.

Frances, A. (2012). DSM 5 in distress: The DSM's impact on mental health practice and research. (Reprinted from Psychology Today, 2012, May 5).

Glasser, W. (2004).*Warning: psychiatry can be hazardous to your mental health.* New York: HarperCollins.

Haley, J. (1993). Uncommon therapy: the psychiatric techniques of Milton H. Erickson, M.D. New York: W. W. Norton.

Kirk, S. & Kutchins, H. (1992). *The selling of DSM: The rhetoric of science in psychiatry.* New York: Hawthorne.

Kirk, S. & Kutchins, H. (1994). "The myth of the reliability of DSM" *Journal of Mind and Behavior*, 15:71- 86.

Lusterman, D. (1989). School-family intervention and the circumplex model. in Olson, D. H. Russell, C.S. & Sprenkle, D.H. (Eds.). (1989*). Circumplex model: Systemic assessment and treatment of families.* Binghampton, N.Y.: Haworth Press.

Lazarus, A. (2006). *Brief but comprehensive psychotherapy: The multimodal way.* New York: Guilford Press.

Loring, M. & B. Powell (1988) Gender, race and DSM III: A study of the objectivity of psychiatric diagnostic behavior. *Journal of Health and Social Behavior, 29*, March.

Kutchins, H. and Kirk, S. (1997.) *Making us crazy DSM: The psychiatric bible and the creation of mental disorders.* New York: The Free Press.

Moynihan, R. & Cassels, A. (2005) *Selling sickness: how the world's biggest pharmaceutical companies are turning us all into patients.* New York: Nation Books.

Madanes, C. (2006). *The therapist as humanist, social activist, and systemic thinker...and other selected papers. Phoenix, AZ: Zeig, Tucker & Thiesen, Inc.*

Maslow, A. (1968*). Toward a psychology of being* (2nd.ed.). New York: Van Nostrand.

Masten, A.S. & Coatsworth, J.D. (1998). The development of competence in favorable and unfavorable environments: Lessons from research on successful children. *American Psychologist, 53*, 205-220.

Olson, D. H. Russell, C.S. & Sprenkle, D.H. (Eds.). (1989). Circumplex model: Systemic assessment and treatment of families. Binghampton, N.Y.: Haworth Press.

Prochasa, J. , DiClemente, C. & Norcross, J. (1992). In search of how people change: applications to addictive behaviors. *American Psychologist, 47*, 1102-1114.

Rosenthal, R. & Jacobson, L. (1968). *Pygmalion in the classroom: teacher expectation and pupils' intellectual developmen*t. New York: Holt, Rinehart & Winston.

Schwab-Stone, M. (2000). NIMH Diagnostic Interview Schedule for Children Version IV (NIMH DISC-IV): Description, Differences from Previous Versions, and Reliability of Some Common Diagnoses. *Journal of the American Academy of Child and Adolescent Psychiatry*, 1,1.

Seligman, M. E. & Csikszentmihalyi, M. (2000). Positive psychology: An introduction. *American Psychologist, 55*, 5-14.

Shimokawa, K. , Lambert, M., & Smart, D. (2010). Enhancing treatment outcome of patients at risk of treatment failure: meta-analytic and mega-analytic review of a psychotherapy quality assurance system. *J Consult Clin Psychol.* 2010 Jun;78(3):298-311.

Spitzer, R., Forman, J. & Nee, J. (1979). DSM-III field trials: I. Initial interrater diagnostic reliability. *American Journal of Psychiatry, 136*, 815-817.

Spiegler, M.D. & Guevremont, D.C. (2003). *Contemporary behavior therapy.* (4th ed.). Belmont: CA: Wadsworth.

Sue, D. W., Bernier, J.E., Durran, A. Feinberg, L., Pedersen,P., Smith, E.J. & Vasquez-Nuttall, E. (1982). Position paper: Cross-cultural counseling competencies. *The Counseling Psychologist, 10*, 45-52.

White, M. & Epston, D. (1990). *Narrative means to therapeutic ends*. New York: Norton.

Box 4.4   SBFC Case Conceptualization Worksheet

Client:_____   Date:_____

Assessment	Proposed Interventions
The SBFC Model School-Prevention_____ School-Intervention_____ Family-Prevention_____ Family-Intervention_____	 _____ _____ _____ _____
Multicultural Counseling Model _____ _____ _____ _____	 _____ _____ _____ _____
Developmental Models Individual Life Cycle Stage/Task: _____	 _____

Family Life Cycle Stage/Task:

_____   _____

Readiness for Counseling Level:

_____   _____

CBT Models

Behavioral ABC Model:
Antecedent_____   _____

_____   _____

Behavior_____   _____

_____   _____

Consequences_____   _____

_____   _____

Multimodal Model:
Behavior_____   _____

_____   _____

Affect_____   _____

_____   _____

Sensation_____   _____

_____   _____

Imagery_____   _____

_____   _____

Cognition_____   _____

_____   _____

Interpersonal_____   _____

_____   _____

Drug/Physiological_____   _____

_____   _____

Social Interactional Model
Troublesome Social Stimuli:
1)_____   _____

2)_____   _____

3)_____   _____

Dominant Response Pattern:

1)_____   _____

2)_____   _____

3)_____   _____

REBT Model (Ellis's A-B-C Model)
Irrational/Dysfunctional Beliefs Present:
1)_____   _____

2)_____   _____

3)_____   _____

Family Systems Models

Bowen Model
1) Genogram

2) Triangles:

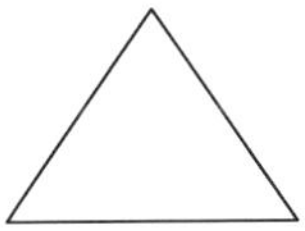

3) Family Projection Process:

_____

_____

4) Differentiation of Self Scale:

Person   Rating

_____   _____

_____   _____

_____   _____

_____   _____

Circumplex Model Dyad Diagnosis

Family dyads:

1)_____

2)_____

3)_____

4)_____

5)_____

School dyads:
1)_____   _____

2)_____   _____

3)_____   _____

Strength-Based Models
Maslow Hierarchy of Needs Model:

Person   Need Areas
                          to Strengthen

1)_____   _____   _____

2)_____   _____   _____

3)_____   _____   _____

Positive Psychology Model:

Basic Strengths:
1)_____   _____

2)_____   _____

3)_____   _____

Narrative Therapy Model:

Unique Outcomes:

_____   _____

_____   _____

_____   _____

DSM Model

Axis I:_____   _____

_____   _____

Axis II:_____   _____

_____   _____

Axis III:_____   _____

_____   _____

Axis IV:_____   _____

_____   _____

_____   _____

Axis V: _____   _____

Additional Diagnoses: Additional Interventions:

Chapter 5
How to Assess Change in School-Based Family Counseling

Brian Gerrard

OVERVIEW: This chapter describes challenges and solutions in assessing change in SBFC. Strategies for evaluating change at child, school, and family levels are reviewed.

BACKGROUND

Assessing change in SBFC is important for two reasons. The first is as *ongoing feedback* to the SBFC professional on whether particular counseling strategies are having the desired effect. Based on this type of feedback the counselor may decide to continue, modify, or replace a counseling strategy.

Example: Sarah, a SBFC professional at Washington Middle School has been counseling Stacey, age 14, on how to improve her grades in Mathematics and English. After two months of coaching Stacey in how to use better study habits, Sarah notes that Stacey's grades in bi-weekly Math and English assignments have not improved. Further investigation by Sarah reveals that Stacey has nowhere quiet at home to do her homework using her new study habits. Sarah, with Stacey's approval, meets with Stacey's mother Janet and secures her help in arranging a quiet study space in the kitchen for Stacey.

In this example the counselor realizes from Stacey's grades that the intervention is not working and leads to a different intervention with Stacey's mother that is designed to facilitate Stacey's studying.

The second is as *outcome data* to show that counseling goals have been met.

Example: As Sarah (in the above example) continues counseling Stacey, she discovers that Stacey's family is experiencing severe stress due to financial problems. Stacey's mother Janet meets with Sarah three times during which Sarah helps Janet improve her resume and think through job alternatives. Shortly later Janet obtains a position as a bank clerk and this helps stabilize the family income and lower everyone's stress. At the end of the school year Stacey's grades in Math and English have improved from C's to B+ and A respectively. During her first session with Sarah, Janet rated the stress in her family as being a 9 out of 10 (on a 1-10 scale with 10 = extremely high).Janet now rates the family stress as 2 out of 10. Using the DSM-IV GAF scale, Sarah rates Stacey's functioning as having gone from 65 to 80.

Having objective, tangible ways to assess client change are of critical importance in this age of accountability and evidence-based support. In mental health professional training programs there is typically always a required course in psychological assessment. The literature on child, school, and family assessment is large and complex. Graduate students taking these courses are exposed to the three types of reliability, the 6 types of validity, the need for assessment, and the many standardized and non-standardized methods for assessing change. However, despite this widespread training, our experience - which includes over 30 years of teaching doctoral and masters students in research methods, psychological assessment, and counseling program evaluation - is that many counselors do not use these rigorous methods to assess client change. Why is this and what can be done about it?

ASSESSMENT CHALLENGES IN SBFC

There are several challenges experienced by mental health professionals working with schools with respect to measuring change:

1. High student-counselor ratios: The student-counselor ratio recommended by the (e.g.) American School Counseling Association (ASCA) is 250:1 however the national average is 471:1. This places a great strain on the counselor who given the choice between spending time counseling a student and time evaluating change, may view the time spent counseling as more important.

2. Counselor personality type: Extensive research on the relationship between career choice and personality using the Myers-Briggs Type Inventory suggests that depending on personality type some counselors will be less interested in assessment. The psychological type dimensions most likely associated with an interest in assessment are Sensing (S) - preference for focusing on details -, Thinking (T) - preference for approaching problems logically -, and Judging (J) - preference for being organized. The psychological type dimensions most likely associated with a lack of interest in assessment are Intuition (N) - preference for being visionary and seeing beyond surface details -, Feeling (F) - preference for being harmonious -, and Perceiving (P) - preference for being flexible in decision making. Developing and carrying out a counseling evaluation, often involving using statistics, requires the counselor to use the Sensing, Thinking, Judging parts of her personality. Counselors scoring high on Intuition, Feeling, Perceiving may find it challenging to develop and carry out client evaluations if these counselors have not done "type development" (i.e. developed their non-preferred personality dimensions).

3. Narrow professional training paradigms: Many traditional academic training programs train mental health professionals on assessment in only a limited area of the SBFC Model. For example, school counselors are typically trained to assess school-related behaviors, but not family behaviors; family counselors are trained in family assessment approaches, but typically not trained in classroom or school-related assessment. This "narrowness" in professional training can lead a counselor to concentrate on assessing either school-related change or family-related change (but not both).

4. Social desirability and SBFC assessment: Social desirability refers to the tendency for people to want to "look good", rather than deviant on psychological tests. No parent wants to be viewed by their child's school as a "bad parent." When a SBFC professional tries to get a parent evaluation of change with the parent's child (focusing on school or home), it is normal for parents to be concerned about how the evaluation data will be used and how it will make the parent appear to the principal and school staff. There is a power differential in the relationship between the school and the family. Although minority families are more likely to feel this power differential, it can affect any parent. Carter (2010) has described a situation in which minority parents were asked to evaluate the functioning of their child before and after counseling using an inventory. The post-counseling scores were consistently worse because the parents wanted to present a very positive picture of their child and family when they completed the pre-counseling inventory. As a relationship of trust developed with the SBFC professionals over the course of counseling, the parents felt more secure in revealing problems without worrying about "losing face." In this context it should be noted that minority parents are more likely than Caucasian parents to view mental health counseling as a sign that one is "crazy."

5. Organizational policies regarding assessment: If a school or counseling center does not have a policy that counseling outcome assessment is essential, SBFC professionals may perceive this as a license to be lax in conducting assessments of counseling effectiveness. An example of this is a study by Riger and

Staggs (2011) which found that fewer than 10% of state funders of counseling agencies dealing with domestic violence require outcome assessment.

6. Fiscal and Time Costs Associated with Standardized Assessment: The gold standard in assessment is represented by standardized tests that have been rigorously assessed for reliability and validity, and that have norms for different populations and age groups. These tests generally need to be purchased which may posed a challenge for financially strapped school administrators. In addition, to effectively use most standardized tests, the counselor must be familiar with the manual that describes how to use the test and interpret the scores. This places an additional time demand on a counselor who may be in a school with a high student to counselor ratio. Finally, while there are some standardized tests that can be completed in a short amount of time (10-15 minutes) by a teacher or parent, many are longer and can be experienced by the teacher or parent as burdensome. Finally, standardized tests leave no doubt in a parent's mind that their child is being "formally tested" and "psychologically evaluated." This can make parents nervous if a strong relationship of trust is not present between parent and counselor and lead to assessment validity being compromised.

ADVANTAGES OF SBFC ASSESSMENT

The abovementioned challenges to conducting SBFC assessment are offset by the advantages:

1. Corrective Feedback for the SBFC professional: As described at the beginning of this chapter, without some form of assessment on how a client is functioning the counselor has no idea of whether a particular counseling approach is working. With assessment feedback the counselor is in a position to continue an effective approach or replace an ineffective one.

2. Outcome Evaluation for Counselor, Client, School and Family: Outcome evaluation permits the counselor, client, school and family to know when the original counseling goal has been reached. Grades improve, disruptive classroom behaviors cease, attendance increases, family stress decreases, etc. Endless counseling is never viewed as therapeutic. Through outcome evaluation it is possible to determine improvement and its extent.

3. Funding Implications of Counseling Assessment: In a climate of recession and decreased funding for schools and mental health, clear outcome data demonstrating the effectiveness of a counseling program may help to keep that program off the "chopping block." During 2011-12 funding cutbacks in California schools resulted in student-counselor ratios of 800:1 and in many schools principals saved money for other "essential" programs by cutting school counselor/mental health counselor positions. During that period in San Francisco, the Mission Possible SBFC program (described in Chapter 45) was in 26 schools where principals of 20 schools indicated that had they not had access to Mission Possible SBFC professionals they would not have been able to afford any mental health professionals in their schools.

HOW TO CONDUCT A SBFC ASSESSMENT

Generally speaking, a SBFC assessment should include a pre-test and a post-test in order to show change before and after SBFC. In addition to assessing change in the student (e.g. grades, attendance, self-esteem, etc.), when there is a clear family problem there should be an assessment of change in the family (e.g. lower family stress, fewer arguments, improved parenting, etc.). Table 5.1 lists four types of SBFC assessment that can be applied to assess child behaviors at home and at school. A limited number of examples are shown to facilitate comparison.

1. INTERVIEW

Examples of interview questions for students, teachers, and parents/guardians are shown in Box 5.1 and Box 5.2. For this type of change assessment to be valid it is essential the SNFC counselor have a relationship of trust developed with the interviewee. Social desirability is the main threat to this type of assessment. Social desirability refers to the tendency of persons being interviewed to say things that they believe the interviewer wants to hear, that is, to make a "socially desirable" response. This can lead a student or parent to say that things are fine, when in fact they may not be. The more skilled the SBFC professional is at developing rapport with students, teachers, and parents, the more likely that the interview will yield valuable information. This means that the SBFC professional must be equally open to hearing "bad news", i.e. that the interviewee feels there has been no change in a child's behavior.

2. TAILORED INVENTORY

Examples of tailored inventories are shown in Box 5.3 and Box 5.4. This simplest form of tailored inventory is based on the likert scale (developed by Rensis Likert). The person completing the inventory is asked to indicate the degree of agreement or disagreement with specific statements by checking one of 6 columns containing the headings:

Strongly Agree	SA
Moderately Agree	MA
Slightly Agree	SLA
Slightly Disagree	SD
Moderately Disagree	MD
Strongly Disagree	SD

Table 5.1 Four Types of Assessment

1. Qualitative

A) Interview

Description	The counselor conducts an in-depth interview to assess the child's functioning.
Person Completing Assessment	Child, Parent, Teacher
Example	Child Interview: "How are things at school?" "How are things at home?" Parent Interview: " How is your child doing at school?" 　　　　　　　　　　" How is your child doing at home?" Teacher Interview: "How is _____ doing in your class?"
Advantages	Inexpensive. The interview format tends to promote trust which can increase the validity of this assessment approach. Easy to administer.

| Disadvantages | May lack reliability. |
| | Risk of interviewer bias affecting the interview. |

B) Drawing/Art
Description	The counselor invites the child to draw, color, or paint.
Person Completing Assessment	Child
Example	Counselor: "Draw a picture of anything you like."
	"Can you draw me a picture of how you are feeling right now?"
	Analysis is made of the style and content of the drawing, e.g. presence of negative images (such as guns, knives) and presence of positive images (such as sports, family outing).
Advantages	Inexpensive.
	Easy to administer.
	Readily accepted by children- an assessment approach frequently experienced as soothing by children.
Disadvantages	May lack reliability and validity.
	Pictures can be ambiguous, open to multiple interpretations.

---

2. Quantitative: Non-standardized

Tailored Inventory

Description	Counselor-constructed inventory assessing a specific behavior.
Person Completing Assessment	Counselor, Child, Parent, Teacher
Example	The inventory consists of sentence stems describing specific behaviors which are then rated on a 6 point likert scale: SA=Strongly Agree, MA= Moderately Agree; SLA= Slightly Agree, SLD= Slightly Disagree, MD= Moderately Disagree, SD= Strongly Disagree)

Counselor and Teacher Form
Student studies quietly in class   SA   MA   SLA   SLD   MD   SD

Child Form
I study quietly in class   SA   MA   SLA   SLD   MD   SD
Parent Form
My child studies quietly at home   SA   MA   SLA   SLD   MD   SD

| Advantages | Easy to administer. |

Inexpensive.
Measures behavior of interest.
Is typically brief because of focus on behaviors of interest for change.

Disadvantages May lack reliability, validity.
Requires counselor time to construct inventory.

---

3. Quantitative: Behavior

A) Direct Observation

Description
which

An adult observes the child and keeps a tally of the frequency with different behaviors occur.

Person Completing
Assessment

Counselor, Teacher, Parent

Example

Adult counts the number of times a child engages in a specific behavior (e.g. whining).

	Mon	Tue	Wed	Thu	Fri
Number of times Sally whined	8	6	7	5	8

Advantages

Direct assessment of a behavior of interest.
Good reliability and validity.
Inexpensive.

Disadvantages

Requires adult to spend time monitoring child's behavior.

b) School Record Data
Description

School records containing information on school-related behaviors: grades, attendance, detentions, and disciplinary actions.

Person Completing
Assessment

Counselor (typically)

Example

School data for Sally	Before Counseling	After Counseling
a) Grades:		
Mathematics	C-	B+
English	C	B
b) Days absent		
(Out of 60 school days)	20	5

Advantages	Data readily available in school records; already collected.
	Good reliability, validity.
	Outcome data very relevant to school success.

| Disadvantages | Parent permission required to use school data. |
| | Counselor time required to extract data from school files. |

---

4. Quantitative: Standardized

Standardized Tests

| Description | These are measures that have been subjected to extensive research on their reliability and validity. |

| Person Completing Assessment | Counselor, Child, Teacher, Parent |

| Example | The Child Behavior Checklist is a self-report inventory measuring child behaviors for the following sub-categories: Social Withdrawal, Somatic Complaints, Anxiety/Depression, Social Problems, Thought Problems, Attention Problems, Delinquent Behavior, and Aggressive Behavior. It comes in Youth, Parent, and Teacher forms. |

Advantages	Very good reliability.
	Very good validity generally.
	Some measures (e.g. CBCL) have a short administration time (10-15 minutes).
	Represent the "gold standard" in assessment; essential for research funding.

Disadvantages	Can be expensive: many standardized tests must be purchased.
	The evaluator will generally need to read and understand the manual accompanying the test.
	If the parent or child feels they are being formally psychologically tested and there is a lack of trust in the relationship, validity may be compromised.
	Some standardized tests are lengthy (which improves subscale reliability) and teachers and parents may feel they take too long to complete.

Box 5.2 Qualitative Questions to Evaluate Degree of Change from Counseling

General Principles: This is phase 2 of a qualitative assessment. At this point the counselor should have established a relationship of trust with the person being interviewed. This being the case the counselor can ask fairly directly about change in reference to specific counseling goals.

A) Questions for the Student

1. When we originally began meeting, your goal was to_____. Do you feel you have met that goal?

2. When we started meeting, you were having difficulty with _____. How are things now?

3. You were having some challenges with your _____ subject. How are you doing now in that subject?

4. We have been meeting now for _____ weeks. What do you feel you have accomplished?

B) Questions for the Teacher

1. How is the student doing now in your class?

2. What improvements have you noticed? Can you give me a specific example?

3. What behaviors, if any, do you feel still need improvement? Can you give me a specific example?

4. Have you had any recent contact with the student's parents/guardian? How helpful have they been in encouraging the student to improve?

C) Questions for the Parent/Guardian

1. When I first spoke to you, you expressed some concerns about how your child was doing at school with respect to _____. How do you feel about how your child is doing now?

2. How do you feel about how the school has been doing to help your child succeed?

3. What changes have you noticed with respect to how your child is doing at_____?

4. Is there anything about how your child is doing at school that you would like to see improved?

Box 5.3 How to Construct a Tailored Inventory

Step 1: Identify a behavior you want to assess.
        Examples might include:
        a) classroom behavior:
                -paying attention
                -working quietly
                -staying in seat
                -working cooperatively with other
                -complying with teacher's requests
        b) at-home behavior:
                - doing homework
                - complying with parent's request
                - playing cooperatively with siblings
                - doing chores

Step 2: Prepare likert scale items that assess the behaviors you want to assess.

Example for Teacher Inventory:

Student works quietly in class	SA	MA	SLA	SLD	MD	SD
Student works cooperatively with other students	SA	MA	SLA	SLD	MD	SD

Step 3: Format the items you want onto a sheet that can be given to teachers, Parents, or Students. Examples of a generic Tailored Inventory are shown in Box 4.4

Sometimes the respondent is asked to circle the abbreviation that indicates the extent of their agreement. If numbers are assigned to each level: Strongly Agree=7, Strongly Disagree=1, etc. then before/after scores can be easily obtained to summarize extent of change (see Box. 5.5).

In the examples given the items are all worded so that agreement indicates the presence of a positive behavior.

      The tailored inventory can be easily constructed to assess any behavior the SBFC professional, or referring parent/guardian, teacher, or student, is concerned about. The main strengths of the tailored inventory are that it assesses the exact behaviors that are of concern, it can be easily constructed and scored, and it is free. Because the number of items are generally limited, it can also be completed quickly by teachers and parents/guardians. It can also be administered to parents/guardians over the telephone (or via email). Again, the validity of the tailored inventory - like the interview- depends on there being a relationship of trust present between the SBFC professional and the person completing the tailored inventory.

Box 5.4 Example of a Tailored Inventory

The following brief tailored inventories were constructed for a 10 year old student whose parents and teacher were concerned about the student being non-compliant at home and school, being inattentive in the classroom, and not completing assigned work.

A) Student Version

Name of Student:_____ Date:_____

Instructions: Please read each statement below and indicate the degree to which you agree with the statement by placing a check mark (V) in the appropriate column to the right.

	Strongly Agree	Moderately Agree	Slightly Agree	Slightly Disagree	Moderately Disagree	Strongly Disagree
1. I concentrate on my work in class						
2. I stay in my seat in class						
3. I do what my teacher asks						
4. I work well with other students						
5. I always do my homework						
6. I do what my parents tell me						
7. I get along with my brothers & sisters						
8. I enjoy school						

B) Teacher Version

Name of Teacher:_____

Name of Student:_____ Date:_____

Instructions: Please read each statement below and indicate the degree to which you agree with the statement by placing a check mark (V) in the appropriate column to the right.

The student:	Strongly Agree	Moderately Agree	Slightly Agree	Slightly Disagree	Moderately Disagree	Strongly Disagree
1. Concentrates on assignments in class						
2. Stays in her/his seat in class						
3. Complies with my requests						
4. Works well with other students						
5. Completes assigned homework						
6. Seems to enjoy my class						

B) Parent/Guardian Version

Name of Parent/Guardian:_____

Name of Student:_____   Date:_____

Instructions: Please read each statement below and indicate the degree to which you agree with the statement by placing a check mark (V) in the appropriate column to the right.

My child:	Strongly Agree	Moderately Agree	Slightly Agree	Slightly Disagree	Moderately Disagree	Strongly Disagree
1. Is doing well at school						
2. Completes homework						
3. Does what I ask her/him to do						
4. Gets along with his/her siblings						
5. Gets along with her/his teachers						
6. Seems to enjoy school						

3A DIRECT OBSERVATION OF BEHAVIOR

The direct observation of a child's behavior by a parent, teacher, or SBFC professional has the advantage of measuring in the child's everyday environment the negative behaviors that brought the child to counseling and the desired positive behaviors. Behavioral observation also avoids stigmatizing labels (e.g. from the DSM). The main disadvantage associated with behavioral observation is that the adult observing the behavior must do it in "real time". For a teacher this means that each time the child demonstrates a particular behavior, the teacher must make a notation the behavior occurred. Similarly, a parent would need to keep track of the child's at home behavior as it occurs. For behaviors such as compliance with an adult's request, it is fairly obvious when the behavior of compliance or refusal occurs as this behavior is directed toward the adult. However, other behaviors, such as working cooperatively with other students or playing cooperatively with siblings, require greater vigilance on the part of a busy teacher or parent. However, SBFC professionals can make it easier for teachers and parents to make a behavioral observation record by limiting the observation period to a class period, an hour, or a day. Sample behavioral observation sheets that can be used to record children's behaviors are shown in Box 5.6. Box 5.7 shows how a simple data analysis can be conducted using before/after Behavior Observation forms.

3B RECORDED INFORMATION

This category includes traditional recorded information on student behavior that is kept in school files and can be accessed with parent/guardian approval: grades, attendance, detentions, expulsions, visits to principal's office. This behavioral data is particularly useful because it measures some of the traditional behaviors associated with school success (especially grades and attendance). Because this information is collected routinely by schools, it is available as a convenient before/after measure of change. However, the SBFC professional must take the time to obtain parent consent and to comb through the school files for the information.

Box 5.5 Tailored Inventory: Before/After Example

An example of a tailored inventory completed before counseling and then after counseling is shown below.

A) Before Counseling (Teacher Version)

The student:	6 Strongly Agree	5 Moderately Agree	4 Slightly Agree	3 Slightly Disagree	2 Moderately Disagree	1 Strongly Disagree
1. Concentrates on assignments in class					X	
2. Stays in her/his seat in class					X	
3. Complies with my requests						X
4. Works well with other students				X		
5. Completes assigned homework					X	
6. Seems to enjoy my class					X	

B) After Counseling (Teacher Version)

The student:	6 Strongly Agree	5 Moderately Agree	4 Slightly Agree	3 Slightly Disagree	2 Moderately Disagree	1 Strongly Disagree
1. Concentrates on assignments in class			X			
2. Stays in her/his seat in class	X					
3. Complies with my requests		X				
4. Works well with other students		X				
5. Completes assigned homework		X				
6. Seems to enjoy my class		X				

Scoring would be done by assigning scores (1 to 7) to each before/after statement

	Before	After
1. Concentrates on assignments in class	2	4
2. Stays in her/his seat in class	2	6
3. Complies with my requests	1	5
4. Works well with other students	3	5
5. Completes assigned homework	2	5
6. Seems to enjoy my class	2	5
Mean score	2.0	5.0

Box 5.6 Forms for Recording Direct Observation of Behavior

Behavior Observation Form

Name of Student Observed:_____

Name of Observer:_____

Length of Observation Period: _____ class period (Date:_____ Time:_____)

                           _____ 1 hour (Date:_____ Time:_____)

                           _____ 1 day (Date:_____)

Behavior to be Observed:

Negative behavior (want less of): _____

Positive behavior: (want more of):_____

Instructions: Each time the positive or negative behavior occurs, make a tally mark in the appropriate column.

Negative Behavior:	Positive Behavior:

128

Behavioral Observation Form (for Weekly Observation)

Name of Student Observed:_____

Name of Observer:_____

Observation Period: Week of:_____

Behavior to be Observed:
Negative behavior (want less of): _____

Positive behavior: (want more of):_____

Instructions: Each time the positive or negative behavior occurs, make a tally mark in the appropriate column.

Day	Negative Behavior:	Positive Behavior:
Monday		
Tuesday		
Wednesday		
Thursday		
Friday		
Saturday		
Sunday		

Box 5.7 Data Analysis for Behavioral Observation Forms

Example: The example below shows a teacher's Behavioral Observation Forms at beginning of counseling and at end of counseling for a 10 year old student. The behaviors observed were: Negative : Out of seat Positive: Working quietly for 15 minutes
Observation period: 3 class periods each day

Summary Sheet for Beginning of Counseling

Day	Negative Behavior: Out of seat	Positive Behavior: Working quietly
Monday	~~IIII~~ ~~IIII~~ 10	 0
Tuesday	~~IIII~~ 5	II 2
Wednesday	~~IIII~~ IIII 9	 0
Thursday	III 3	III 3
Friday	~~IIII~~ ~~IIII~~ IIII 14	 0
Saturday		
Sunday		
Total:	41	5

Summary Sheet for End of Counseling

Day	Negative Behavior: Out of Seat	Positive Behavior: Working quietly
Monday	II 2	IIII III 8
Tuesday	 0	IIII IIII 10
Wednesday	I 1	IIII 4
Thursday	 0	IIII IIII IIII 14
Friday	II 2	IIII I 6
Saturday		
Sunday		
Total:	5	42

4. STANDARDIZED TESTS

Standardized tests are instruments that have been extensively assessed for reliability and validity, and which often come with norms so that scores can be compared with a reference group (e.g. of similar children). The use of standardized instruments are important when doing research and may be required by some foundations funding a SBFC project.

A challenge in using standardized instruments is that many must be purchased and require extensive training to use. This puts these instruments beyond the reach of the SBFC professional with a huge caseload or a limited budget. It can also be difficult to locate the specific instruments for a particular situation. However, <u>Measures for Clinical Practice and Research: A Sourcebook</u> by Fischer and Corcoran (2007) is a user-friendly two volume book containing copies of standardized inventories and questionnaires that SBFC professionals will find valuable in helping them to evaluate whether to use a specific ineventory. Examples of the variety of instruments available in this book (over 120 child and family instruments) are shown in Box 5.8. Additional standardized instruments listed by the California Evidence-Based Clearinghouse (CEBC) are shown in Box 5.9.

SUMMARY

This chapter is not meant to be an exhaustive review of assessment methodology related to children and families. It is intended as a brief overview of the different types of change assessment that SBFC professionals can use.

Our recommendations for SBFC assessment of change in clients are as follows:

1. Use at least one of the assessment approaches with SBFC clients.

2. Consider assessing the student's behavior from multiple sources: e.g. parent, teacher, student, SBFC professional.

3. Be aware that the longer the instrument, the more it looks like a "psychological test", and the lower the level of trust between the SBFC professional and the person completing the instrument, the more likely that that instrument will be rejected or the results rendered meaningless.

4. The SBFC professional should be open to assessment that shows change has not occurred or is occurring too slowly and regard this information as of immense value in case planning.

Box 5.8 Examples of Brief Standardized Tests

From Fischer, J. and Corcoran, K. (2007). *Measures for clinical practice and research: a sourcebook*. 4th Ed. Vol. 1 & 2. Oxford: Oxford University Press.

This book contains a description of 63 Family and 58 Child instruments. A copy of each instrument
  is included along with a brief description and information on scoring, reliability, validity, norms,
  a primary referenceand how to order copies.

Examples of Instruments for Children

Adolescent Concerns Evaluation
Adolescent Coping Orientation for Problem Experiences
Assertiveness Scale for Adolescents
Behavioral Self-Concept Scale
Behavioral Rating Index for Children
Child report of Posttraumatic Symptoms and
  Parent Report of Posttraumatic Symptoms
Child's Attitude Toward Father and Mother Scales
Children and Adolescent Social and Adaptive Functioning Scale
Children's Loneliness Questionnaire
Depression Self-Rating Scale
Elementary School Success Profile
Homework Problem Checklist
Hopelessness Scale for Children
How I Feel
Impulsivity Scale
Index of Peer Relations
Inventory of Parent and Peer Attachment
Mood Thermometers
Multi-Attitude Suicide Tendency Scale
Multi-group Ethnic Identity Measure
Peer and Self-Rating Scale
Persistence Scale for Children
Positive and Negative Suicide Ideation Inventory
Self-Concept Scale for Children

Examples of Instruments for Families

Adolescent-Family Inventory of Life Events and Changes
Adult-Adolescent Parenting Inventory
Family Adaptability and Cohesion Evaluation Scale
Family Assessment Device
Family Beliefs Inventory
Family Celebrations Index
Family Coping Index
Family Coping Inventory
Family Empowerment Scale
Family Hardiness Index
Family Inventory of Life Events and Changes
Family Inventory of Resources for Management
Family Member Well-Being
Family Organized Cohesiveness Scale
Family Pressures Scale-Ethnic
Family Problem-Solving Communication
Family Times and Routines Index
Family Traditions Scale
Healthy Families Parenting Inventory
Index of Brother and Sister Relations
Index of Family Relations
Index of Parental Attitudes
Kansas Family Life Satisfaction Scale
Kansas Parental Satisfaction Scale
Parent Affect Test
Parent's Report
Parent-Child Relationship Survey
Parental Attachment Scale
Parental Authority Questionnaire
Parental Nurturance Scale
Parental Tolerance Scale
Parenting Scale
Self-Report Family Instrument

Box 5.9 The California Evidence-Based Clearinghouse (CEBC)
Alphabetical Listing of Screening and Assessment Tools for Child Welfare

Ages and Stages Questionnaire (ASQ)

Behavior Assessment System for Children (BASC™)

Behavioral and Emotional Rating Scale (2nd Edition): Youth Rating Scale (BERS-2)

Child Abuse Potential Inventory (CAP)

Child and Adolescent Needs and Strengths-Mental Health (CANS-MH)

Child Behavior Checklist for Ages 1.5-5 (CBCL/1.5-5)

Child Behavior Checklist for Ages 6-18 (CBCL/6-18)

Child Exposure to Domestic Violence Scale (CEDV)

Child PTSD Symptom Scale (CPSS)

Children's Depression Inventory (CDI)

Eyberg Child Behavior Inventory (ECBI)

Family Assessment Form (FAF)

Family Assessment Measure III (FAM-III)

Keys to Interactive Parenting Scale (KIPS)

Mood and Feelings Questionnaire (MFQ)

North Carolina Family Assessment Scale (NCFAS)

Ohio Youth Problems, Functioning, and Satisfaction Scales (Ohio Scales)

Parenting Stress Index and Parenting Stress Index-Short Form (PSI/PSI-SF)

Pediatric Symptom Checklist-17 (PSC-17)

Protective Factors Survey (PFS)

Screen for Childhood Anxiety Related Emotional Disorders (SCARED)

Strengths and Difficulties Questionnaire (SDQ)

REFERENCES

American School Counselor Association (n.d.). Student to school counselor ratios. Retrieved October 21, 2012 from http://www.schoolcounselor.org/content.

Carter, M. , Evans, W., Zapata, J. & Taifa, A. (2011). School-based family counseling evaluation: warm feelings, perilous paradigms & perilous hopes. *International Journal for School-Based Family Counseling*, 3, 1-12.

Riger, S. & Staggs, S. (2011). A nationwide survey of state-mandated evaluation practices for domestic violence agencies. Journal of Interpersonal Violence, 26, 1, 50-70.

RESOURCES

At this url there are hyperlinks with reviews on each CEBC instrument and contact information: http://www.cebc4cw.org/assessment-tools/

Chapter 6
How to Form a Partnership with Schools

Judy Giampaoli

OVERVIEW: *School-Based Family Counseling (SBFC) serves as a bridge to culturally diverse families in accessing mental health services for students and promoting student learning and achievement (Soriano, 2004). It is incumbent upon the SBFC professional professional to become an integral part of the school community. This chapter will focus on the practical steps to take in forming a partnership with the school community and meeting the counseling needs of the students at a school site.*

BACKGROUND

During the first week at his school placement, Paul, a School-Based Family Counseling intern, was told part of his job would be to supervise the hallways during passing period. Not wanting to appear uncooperative, Paul complied with the request, even though this task was inappropriate to his role in the school.

School-Based Family Counselors are sometimes viewed as the counselor in the traditional role of a school counselor. School staff are often so pleased to have a counselor at their school, they may make requests that would reflect the role of a school guidance counselor or other support staff. School-Based Family Counselors, most often licensed MFTs, Social Workers, or interns, provide a unique service to the school community, that of "providing a vehicle for helping teachers and parents enable children to be more successful in the classroom,"(Evans & Carter,1997) academically, socially and emotionally. The following outline will assist trainees, interns and new School-Based Family Counselors with guidelines to forming a positive and productive partnership with their school.

THE SCHOOL

The most successful School-Based Family Counselors have developed excellent rapport and clear communication with the key stakeholders in the school community. While everyone has experienced school firsthand as a child, SBFCs will now be re-entering a school setting where they will be a member of the school staff. They will be challenged to become familiar with the school vision, procedures and norms while developing a professional identity and establishing professional standards.

Carolyn, an MFT intern in an elementary school, built a strong family counseling program at a school that had never had SBFC counseling available to students and families. Her alliance with the principal was invaluable in developing a counseling referral process, and a support system for making parent contact. Making herself available to consult with teachers expanded the impact of her work with students. "By developing a partnership with the Principal and teachers at my school, I was able to establish a strong counseling component that supported students in need." Upon completing her traineeship, Carolyn was offered employment at the school and continues to do school-based family counseling at this high need school. Also she is now able to coach new interns in building the necessary skills to becoming effective school-based family counselors.

Communication is the key to a successful partnership with schools, beginning with the introductory meeting with the school administrator and continuing with regularly scheduled meetings throughout the school year.   Establishing a school-based family counseling program is a learning process for the administrators, staff, students and families.   Each school community is unique with expectations and procedures that are in place to meet the needs of the students, families and staff at that specific school. The initial task of the SBFC professional is to begin to understand the culture of the school, as well as define and negotiate the roles and responsibilities of the SBFC professional for the school.

The size of the student body plays a big part in how a school is organized. The SBFC professional can expect to have more direct contact with the Principal of a smaller school because there is generally less support staff available. Keep in mind however, that because less staff are available to assist in the day-to-day administration of the school and activities, the principal of a smaller school assumes many roles each day. In fact, Principals of smaller schools often serve as counselor or social worker to students and parents and look forward to assistance in dealing with the numerous social and emotional issues that surface in the course of a day at school. In a larger school, SBFCs may have limited access to the Principal, working instead with an Assistant Principal or assigned to a Counseling staff member. Larger schools may have a counseling department and have an established system for referring students needing therapeutic support.

THE PRINCIPAL

1. THE PRINCIPAL'S ROLE

The principal, as leader of the school, is responsible for everything that occurs at a school. Everything that occurs on campus is of concern to the principal from the obvious, such as the effectiveness of the instructional program, to any crisis that may occur at a moment's notice and require immediate attention. While flexibility, ability to maintain priorities and effective multi-tasking are some of the characteristics of an effective principal, he/she is also a problem solver, and a caring individual who puts children first. In fact, the presence of the SBFC professional at the school may be a result of the principal seeing a need for support services at the school and looking for the best ways to address those needs. An appreciation of the principal's role in the school will assist in the development of a workable communication plan between the SBFC professional and the site principal.

2. MEETING THE PRINCIPAL

 An SBFC intern at an elementary school site reported that the new principal did not have an available confidential space for her and did not believe it was important to have an office. He stated, "Why can't the counselor meet with a student on the playground or in the cafeteria?" What would you say to this principal regarding the need for office space?

The first meeting with the principal is an important one. The Principal is an ally and may serve as a conduit between the SBFC professional and staff, students and families in developing the counseling program at the school. Principals are generally very pleased to have counseling services available to their students and families. The responsible principal needs to be knowledgeable about the skills and abilities of the SBFC professional as well as potential counseling activities the SBFC professional may perform at the site . This may include individual or family therapy, group counseling, consultation with staff and presentations to various stakeholders.

The SBFC professional should come prepared with a resume and a list of questions or requests to discuss at this initial meeting. Keep in mind the principal will lead this meeting and is interested in getting an impression of the SBFC professional and evaluating their skills and talents. The principal will be considering professional demeanor and how well the SBFC professional conduct herself/himself. The

SBFC professional's task during this meeting is to introduce oneself to the Principal, and to discuss the role of a School-Based Family Counselor. The SBFC professional should consider sharing the strengths she/he brings to this work, previous work with children and families or other work experiences that will assist the SBFC professional in being a member of the school team. At this first meeting, the SBFC professional's enthusiasm about the assignment, how she/he anticipates helping children, families and staff and the willingness to learn will provide the principal with needed information to assess how the SBFC professional can be best utilized in the school.

Established procedures are a part of every school. At this first meeting, the SBFC professional will learn some of the basic practices that are a part of the daily program at the school as well as the principal's expectations. Sometimes a school will have an orientation packet for new staff or volunteers. These packets can be most helpful and can include: a school schedule, faculty roster, activities calendar, student and faculty handbook. It is important that the SBFC professional become familiar with general school procedures and routines. Over time, the SBFC professional will learn the finer points of the daily program.

In addition, during this first meeting, the SBFC professional may have basic requests, including determining an office space, securing a mailbox and perhaps taking a tour of the school. Upon completion of the first meeting with the principal, the SBFC professional will begin to develop the elements of the School-Based Family Counseling program for this school site and become familiar with the school community.

3. ESTABLISHING A CONSISTENT MEETING TIME

Whether the SBFC professionals consulting/contact person and referral source is the Principal, Assistant Principal, or Counselor, it is important to establish a regularly scheduled meeting time. The principal/contact person is the staff member who will assist the SBFC professional in organizing the referral process making regular, weekly means of communicating essential to counseling duties and responsibilities. In some schools, this person has the responsibility of making counseling referrals directly to SBFC, in others, a student support team is established to make referrals for a variety of services. However referrals are made at individual schools, this contact person will often have a good knowledge of the children and families in the school and will serve as an effective resource for the SBFC professional. This established consultation time, even if a brief 15-30 minutes, will go far in helping the SBFC professional establish direction, priorities and strategies for success at the school. Through these meetings SBFC will learn best ways to approach other members of the school community including parents, teachers and students as well as receiving counseling referrals for students and families in need of support.

If the contact person is not able to arrange weekly meetings, an alternative means should be established to maintain regular, weekly communication. It is important to avoid working in isolation with little or no communication with the contact person.

4. THE PRINCIPAL'S SECRETARY

The Principal's secretary is another ally to the SBFC professional and the importance of getting to know them cannot be underestimated. They will be able to provide the SBFC professional with needed materials, keys, access to a phone in a confidential location or ideas about the best time to meet with the Principal. School secretaries have forms, schedules and are a wealth of information about the day's events at the school, upcoming field trips, assemblies, or early dismissal days that will disrupt the counseling schedule. Getting to know the secretary and building rapport will help the SBFC professional avoid disturbing the principal for small matters.

INTRODUCING YOURSELF TO THE SCHOOL COMMUNITY

Patricia, an Intern at a K-8 school, always made the effort to be present for the Morning Assembly when students, parents and teachers gathered to hear from the Principal about the upcoming activities and announcements, inspiring thoughts and daily lessons. After a couple of months of attendance, Patricia had gotten to know some parents, and as information spread about counseling services, parents began to speak with her, make referrals for their children, and arrange meetings. Persistence and your presence pays off.

As early as possible in the SBFC professional's tenure at the school, formal and informal introductions should be made to staff, students and families. Be visible and approachable. Being present prior to the start of school, or at the end of each day will give the school community access to the SBFC professional. Many students are not shy about asking who the new staff person is and what she/he does when the SBFC professional appears on the playground during recess or lunch. Being visible and available to parents as they deliver their children to school or pick them up in the afternoon is also an informal way to meet parents.

1. INTRODUCTION TO TEACHERS AND STAFF

In a more formal manner, it is useful to develop a letter of introduction to be presented to staff at the beginning of the school year. As a new member of the school community the faculty need to learn about the SBFC professional, as well as services to be provided and consultation opportunities available to them in order to begin to establish a relationship with the SBFC professional. At one of the first faculty meetings, the SBFC professional can be introduced and be given some time to provide staff with the letter of introduction along with referral forms, and some of the specifics of the counseling program. In addition, it is important for staff to know how the SBFC professional can be contacted, their days on campus, and office location.

2. INTRODUCTION TO STUDENTS

Formal introductions to students can take place in a brief classroom introduction/presentation with the permission of the teacher. Elementary, middle or high school presentations may look quite different, however being visible, giving students an explanation about the role of the SBFC professional at the school and letting students know how they can arrange an appointment to meet with the counselor may be the encouragement a student needs to make a self-referral.

3. INTRODUCTION TO PARENTS AND CAREGIVERS

Parent newsletters are filled with important information regarding school life. Check with the Principal or parent organization President to see if a letter of introduction can be published in the weekly bulletin or parent newsletter along with a description of the School-Based Counseling Program. Also, parent organizations often invite guest speakers to their meetings. Making yourself available for a more formal introduction at a parent meeting enables the SBFC professional to inform parents of services as well as have an opportunity to talk with parents and caregivers in a more personal way.

MANAGING THE SBFC PROGRAM

Now that the SBFC professional has been presented to key members of the school community, the counselor is ready to implement the school-based family counseling program.

1. REFERRALS

The SBFC professional has now established office hours and has developed a process for accepting referrals with support from the Principal. Sometimes referrals are made to a Student Support Services Committee to be discussed at regularly scheduled meetings that are charged with coordinating support for students with physical and/or mental health needs. The SBFC professional would do well to become a member of this or other mental health- related committees at the school. Some schools submit all referrals to the Principal, some schools make referrals directly to the counselor.

Once the SBFC professional has received a referral from the Principal, teachers, parents or committee, the first step is to gather information. Identify the reason for the referral by speaking to the referring party to discuss their concerns. If a student is self-referred, the SBFC professional may meet once to assess for safety, before requiring parent permission to establish a counseling relationship with the student.

2. STUDENTS

When students are referred to the SBFC professional, and not self-referred, they may be confused as to why they have been called from class or feel embarrassed about going to a counselor. Or, some students may feel a great sense of relief and appreciate the opportunity to solve their problem or address a serious or painful issue with a counselor. Whichever the case, SBFC professionals must be sensitive to the needs of the student when making arrangements for counseling sessions.

An important step in this process is identifying a time for the student to be seen. Parents may be interested in providing counseling for their child, however, may express concern about loss of class time. A review of the student's schedule and consultation with key personnel to establish optimum session times is important in avoiding conflicts during academic hours and reassuring parents. Also, make certain that the means for releasing the student from class is comfortable for the student and negotiated with the teacher ahead of time.

3. CONFIDENTIALITY

It is important that the SBFC professional take necessary steps to maintain confidentiality in the process of counseling students in a school setting. Staff are often very interested in the well-being of their students and take a personal interest in students' success. The SBFC professional may be asked specifics of counseling sessions, which may not be divulged. Be prepared with a statement that will serve as a gentle reminder about the rules of confidentiality to someone who asks for specifics.

Also, students may share information with the SBFC professional that requires further action. It is possible the SBFC professional may need to assess and perhaps report to the authorities. The SBFC professional will communicate with their supervisor about the need to make the report and consult with Child Protective Services, if there is uncertainty about whether to report or not. While not required, it is helpful to inform the Principal of the action taken, especially if the SBFC professional is at the school on a part time basis. The Principal will then be alerted to steps to be taken for the safety of the child. In addition, there may be a social worker or other personnel who may interview the student during the school day and perhaps on a day when the SBFC professional is not present.

3. PARENT PERMISSION

Douglas, a SBFC trainee at a middle school, was given a referral early in September. Before seeing the student, he contacted the parent to introduce himself and begin the process for gaining permission to see the 7th grader. The parent naturally wanted to know the source of the referral, what the problem was and why she hadn't been notified about concerns before now, before the problem had escalated to the need for a therapist. While the trainee did his best to answer the parent's concerns she had felt blind-sided and unprepared for this call, and was unwilling to consider having her child enter into counseling.

When the referral has been submitted by a teacher, administrator or other staff member, it is recommended the SBFC professional elicit their assistance in making contact with the parent. Often they have had previous parent contact as a result of scheduled conferences or school events. It is useful for the staff member or Principal to make the initial contact with the parents to inform them of the referral for counseling. Their discussion of the issues and concerns and referral for counseling services is often effective in establishing the need for counseling and gaining agreement from the parents.

Once that initial contact has been made, the parent will expect a call from the SBFC professional counselor. During the initial contact the SBFC professional can invite the parent to come to the school to meet or discuss the referral by phone. The SBFC professional can follow-up by sending home a packet of information including a permission form which will need to be signed prior to scheduling the student's counseling sessions.

Knowledge of the home language prior to making contact is necessary. Translations of parent permission forms may be necessary, as well as utilizing a translator in making contact with the parents. When the home language of the client differs from the SBFC professional, counseling services can become challenging. However, schools can sometimes provide translation services for families. It is important for the SBFC professional to learn of any arrangements that may be utilized, with parent permission.

Sensitivity to and understanding of differences of race, culture, language as well as the SBFC professionals own assumptions and biases will strengthen the effectiveness of a school-based family counselor. "Lack of such understanding may hinder effective intervention" (Bolton-Brownlee, 1987).

4. PARENT INVOLVEMENT

Parents are often less intimidated when receiving counseling services in the familiar setting of school (American Academy of Pediatrics, 2004). The school environment may not hold the stigma of a mental health setting for them, and they may feel more cultural compatibility at the school. Since an intervention may be ineffective if it is directed at one part of a family system, arranging for parent participation in counseling sessions must take into consideration the parents' schedule. Maintaining flexible hours to accommodate parents is something to be negotiated with the school principal.

CHALLENGES AND SOLUTIONS

THE NEED FOR EDUCATING THE SCHOOL COMMUNITY TO SBFC

Some of the common problems School-Based Family Counselors may face in building their practice at a school include parent participation, student participation, collaboration with staff and maintaining confidentiality. These common problems point out the need for laying the groundwork at the school by being available to talk with parents, teachers and students on an informal basis as well as being available to make educational presentations early in the year and perhaps on an ongoing basis. Making presentations to parent groups and classroom presentations to students will allow for discussions regarding reasons for seeking counseling, demystifying the counseling process, and in general, will raise awareness of the program at the school.

Some staff may not share a commitment to the school-based family counseling program and may not permit their students to be seen during their teaching hours. Making presentations to faculty or consulting with teachers individually may offer the SBFC professional the opportunity for the teachers to get to become familiar with the SBFC professional and begin building a positive working relationship. Finding opportunities to discuss issues such as the importance of working collaboratively to support a child's success in school, arranging counseling session times, developing an understanding of their concerns in depth, as well as providing them with an understanding of the need for confidentiality will demonstrate the SBFC professionals interest in supporting their students. And finally, the simple act of reminding the school community how the SBFC professional can be reached and their availability can increase access to counseling services for all.

MAINTAINING YOUR FOCUS

As in any working environment, there are differing opinions, conflicts and controversies that can arise among faculty members. In schools, these differences can be about educational philosophies, about how to teach, how to address student/family needs or any number of school issues. The SBFC professional may be asked to align with one group or another, offer opinions on controversies that present themselves during the course of the school year. Seeking consultation with the principal/contact person and maintaining open communication will allow the SBFC professional to gain perspective and decide how they will choose to proceed.

As the SBFC professional becomes a part of this dynamic environment called school, it is important that she/he continue to develop as a professional, to seek ways to be a part of the school, continue to learn effective modalities for working with students and families, and build trusting relationships with the principal and faculty. These efforts will assist the SBFC professional in developing a deeper understanding of their role as a School Based Family Counselor and how they can best serve clients and the school.

There is a saying among educators, "Victory is in the classroom," meaning triumph for students comes when they are able to focus on classroom activities, perform academically and successfully work together with their classmates and teachers. Through the SBFC professionals therapeutic work with students, the family system and the school, victory in the classroom can be possible for children who have been marginalized by circumstance or experience.

REFERENCES

American Academy of Pediatrics,Committee on School Health, (Lead Authors: Taras, H., Young, T.), (2004), School-based mental health services. *Pediatrics*, 113, (6), 1839-1845.

Bolton-Brownlee, Ann (1987), Issues in Multicultural Counseling. ERIC/CAPS Digest, ED279995.

Evans, W., & Carter, M., (1997), Urban school-based family counseling: role definition, practice applications and training implications. *Journal of Counseling and Development*, 75,May/June.

Soriano, M (2004) School-based family counseling: A caring, culturally congruent bridge to diverse communities. A paper presented at the second annual Oxford Symposium in School-Based Family Counseling, Keble College, Oxford University, England.

Chapter 7
How to Form a Partnership with the Family

Kristin Velazquez Kenefick and Sarah Hudson

OVERVIEW: *In traditional school-based counseling models in the USA, the counselor is seen as an agent of the school, and parents are seldom involved in the counseling process. They may be kept abreast of the child's misbehavior, but are rarely sought as collaborators in the child's education. As a result, family issues that may be affecting the child's functioning in school are not addressed, and the child's academic and emotional functioning shows little improvement as a result. This chapter examines the challenges of implementing a school-based Adlerian mental health program on the West Side of Chicago, in the heart of the inner city. Adler believed that children are best understood in the context of their families and communities. He and his colleagues went into inner-city schools and initiated guidance clinics adjoining them with the aim of reducing delinquency. He was the first of the major theoreticians to consult directly with teachers and parents within the school structure. In this school-based Adlerian mental health program, teacher and parent consultation, counseling, and psychological testing are offered in an integrated way. Working closely with parents and teachers is the cornerstone of this program. The chapter explores various social and institutional impediments that discourage the engagement of parents, especially with regard to cross-cultural issues, socioeconomic issues, and child abuse. The chapter examines various challenges in working with teachers, such as the influences of school culture, hierarchy, and pedagogy, and reports on effective strategies being implemented to overcome these barriers.*

BACKGROUND

Children and adolescents in the United States are experiencing significant mental health problems with higher frequency. Current reviews approximate that as many as one in five children has a diagnosable disorder, and that one in ten has a disorder that significantly affects his or her functioning in school, at home, and in the community (Tolan & Dodge, 2005). Low-income children of color are at higher risk for behavioral problems and psychological disorders due to their impoverished and stressful environments, lower socioeconomic status, and poor access to mental health services (President's Commission on Mental Health, 1978). African American youth (10-19 years old) make up 14.7 percent of the total youth population in the USA (U.S. Bureau of Census, 2001). "As a result of generations of discrimination and deprivation, African American adolescents have developed high rates of psychological and behavioral disorders, as well as certain problematic psychosocial behaviors," (Gibbs, 2003). African American families typically do not search for treatment for their children and adolescents who may be experiencing psychological problems, and more typically are referred
for treatment by schools, the child welfare system, and/or juvenile court (Boyd-Franklin, 1989).

As increasing numbers of children are developing significant mental health problems with higher frequency, there is poorer access to mental health services for lower socioeconomic status (SES) clients. Some clients of diverse ethnic backgrounds may also be reluctant to seek out services voluntarily. Therefore, schools must develop innovative mental health programs to address these complex needs.

Alfred Adler's approach toward treatment of children's mental health marked a radical departure from that of others of his time. Based on his theory of Individual Psychology, Adler focused on holism (the person is an indivisible unit), teleology (the purpose of one's behavior), phenomenology (the unique perspective of each person), soft determinism, and social- field theory (a person cannot be understood outside of his or her context) (Mosak & Maniacci, 1999). He applied these principles to children and developed over 30 child guidance clinics, most of which were located within the schools of Vienna (Ansbacher, 1956).

The process Adler used when working with children in a school setting not only involved family, but teachers and school staff as well. Once a student had been referred the clinician would hold a meeting with teachers to better understand the student, their concerns, and collaborate with them to find solutions. "The teacher describes his particular cases, the psychologist shares his own related experiences then the discussion starts. What are the causes? When did the situation develop? What should be done? The family life of the child and his whole psychological development are analyzed. With their combined knowledge, the group comes to a decision as to what should be done with a particular child," (Adler, 2006, p. 181).

Next, the psychologist would invite the family to a meeting, which the teacher may or may not attend. The psychologist would first speak with the parents to hear their perspective of the problem and then propose some solutions to help address the purpose of the child's misbehavior. Then the child would be invited in to the room for a conversation. While discussing the problem the psychologist would incorporate ideas about how the child may have felt discouraged and then propose solutions. (Adler, 2006). In this way the teachers, psychologist, family and child all share the same understanding regarding the solution to the problem.

This chapter presents a school-based Adlerian mental health program, in which teacher and parent consultation, counseling, and psychological testing are offered in an integrated fashion. Working closely with parents and teachers is the cornerstone of this program. The paper explores various social and institutional impediments that discourage the engagement of parents, especially with regard to cross-cultural issues, socioeconomic issues, and child abuse. The paper examines various challenges in working with teachers, such as the influences of school culture, hierarchy, and pedagogy, and reports on effective strategies being implemented to overcome these barriers. To illustrate these points, the paper will contrast a case example from a traditional school based counseling model with an Adlerian SBFC approach.

PSYCHOLOGICAL TESTING

Psychological assessment was one of the main areas of service offered to the students of this school.

Leo is a 12 year-old African American male in the sixth grade at an inner-city Catholic middle school. He is struggling academically, and many of his grades are in the failing range. He is new to the school this year. Leo also displays some behavioral problems in the class, such as not listening to the teacher, getting out of his seat frequently, talking to his classmates, and appearing distracted. Leo's teacher recommended psychological testing at the end of the first quarter to determine if he has a learning disorder or some other clinical issue that may be getting in the way of his learning.

In traditional school counseling models, the psychologist would call an Individualized Educational Plan (IEP) meeting with members of the school. The school counselor, teacher, principal, or other administrator would meet prior to testing to discuss the child's difficulties and narrow the assessment question. The parent would be invited to attend this meeting, but if the parent did not attend, the meeting would proceed without the parent. In most cases, the child would not be invited to this meeting. Following this meeting, testing would proceed. When testing was completed, the same group would convene. Again, the parent would be invited to this meeting, which would proceed with or without his or her participation.

TRADITIONAL SCHOOL-BASED COUNSELING (TSBC) VIGNETTE

The school social worker attempted to call Leo's mother and left several messages. Leo's mother did not return the calls. The IEP meeting was scheduled, but Leo's mother did not attend. The school personnel agreed on a testing battery, and testing was completed without the parent's input. When the testing was completed, the team decided not to even attempt to call Leo's mother again, since she never returned the original phone calls. Leo was diagnosed with ADHD, and a recommendation was made for him to be medicated by a psychiatrist. A letter was sent home to Leo's mother instructing her to take Leo to a psychiatrist for an evaluation and possible medication management.

This scenario likely would never transpire in an Adlerian-based approach, in which inclusion of parents is central. The first step in the process is for the clinician to set up an intake appointment with the parent/legal guardian. Working with inner-city children and families can be challenging. Due to multiple stressors, sometimes parents/guardians do not return phone calls. Sometimes families do not have working phones, or answering devices, so getting in touch with parents can be difficult, requiring persistence and creative ways of contact. Sending notes home with the student, mailing letters, and calling emergency contact numbers are all alternative ways to get in touch with a parent/guardian who does not have access to a phone. We believe that a comprehensive assessment cannot be completed without the input of the parent/guardian, and that schools are obligated to take these steps to engage parents in their children's psychological assessment.

ADLERIAN SCHOOL-BASED FAMILY COUNSELING (ASBFC) VIGNETTE

The clinician called Leo's mother and left two messages. When the messages were not returned, the clinician asked the teacher how Leo gets home from school. The teacher indicated that in the past, his mother would pick him up, but recently his aunt Betty was meeting him after school to take him home. The clinician decided that day to accompany Leo outside to speak briefly with Leo's aunt. Without divulging the reason for wanting to speak with his mother, the clinician introduced himself to the aunt as a member of the school, and asked how Leo's mother was doing. The aunt became tearful and disclosed that Leo's mother was struggling with cancer and had recently undergone major surgery. She was recovering slowly, and the extended family had all come together to help out with caring for Leo and his mother. They were not currently staying in their home, so the calls were not returned. The aunt agreed to deliver the message to Leo's mother with a number to reach the clinician by phone. Within one week of receiving the message, Leo's mother returned the call. It was agreed that due to Leo's mother's medical condition, an intake could be completed by phone. This was accomplished the following week. During the IEP meeting, Leo's mother participated via speaker-phone.

During the intake interview with the parent/guardian, it is critical to get the parent's input on the child's difficulties and explore any interventions the parent recommends. In many cases, children's problems in school are related to issues in the home life of the child. Through consideration of the child's context we then have a more accurate understanding of the purpose of the child's behavior. According to Rudolf Dreikurs, "even the worst kind of behavior has a purpose," (Dreikurs, 1971, p. 83). One of the outcomes of the intake may be to recommend services for other members of the family, which may or may not be available at the school. In our program, if the entire family is experiencing a difficult time, we offer services to the child and his/her family on-site at the school.

Leo's mother explained that she had been diagnosed with breast cancer the previous August, right before school started. Leo's grandmother died of breast cancer two years ago, and he was very close to her. So Leo started the school year with a great deal of anxiety about his mother's health. Leo's father has never been involved in his life, and Leo does not have any siblings, so his mother is his primary caregiver and support.

Once the intake is completed with the parent/guardian, critical information obtained from the parent can be explored with the child during his/her intake. Knowing the family history is critical, as children and adolescents are often reluctant to disclose personal information about their families. However, if the clinician has this information in mind, he or she may use this information to elicit the child's feeling about the family situation.

Leo initially appeared defensive with the clinician during his intake interview. When the clinician asked about his family and relationship with his mother, Leo responded that everything was "fine" and there were no difficulties. After several attempts to elicit affect in an open-ended way, the clinician disclosed to Leo that he knew Leo's mother had been ill and was wondering how Leo was feeling about his mother's illness. Leo broke down and started crying, saying he was terrified that his mother would die, as his grandmother had died a couple of years ago. Given the emotionality of Leo's response, the remainder of the time was spent offering support and discussing coping skills and possible outside supports for Leo in lieu of testing. The testing was postponed until the following session, at which time Leo was connected to the clinician and cooperated wonderfully with the testing battery.

Following psychological testing, a feedback session is conducted. In this session, it is critical to integrate the information obtained from the parent/guardian, child, teacher, psychological tests, and outside collateral reports. In many cases, sensitive personal information is revealed that may not be appropriate to be shared with school personnel. Other times, information obtained about the family that affects the child (such as Leo's mother's illness) is necessary to share with school personnel. In either case, the parent/guardian should be informed first in a private feedback session with the examiner. Together, the parent/guardian can decide what the he or she is comfortable sharing with school staff. Additionally, hearing the feedback in private allows the parent/guardian to ask questions he or she may not feel comfortable asking in front of a group of school personnel. The examiner may also make recommendations about other family members that he/she would not make in front of school personnel.

When testing was completed, the clinician called Leo's aunt to inform his mother that the testing was completed. By this time his mother was recovering well, and indicated that she would very much like to meet in person for the feedback session. She also asked if her sister (Leo's aunt Betty) could attend the meeting, since she was helping to care for Leo. The clinician met with Leo, his mother, and his aunt the following week. He shared with them that although Leo was displaying many symptoms indicative of ADHD in the classroom, since these symptoms only began after Leo's mother's diagnosis of cancer the previous August, Leo did not in fact have ADHD. Rather, Leo was suffering from an adjustment disorder with anxiety. Leo's IQ was in the average range, but his achievement scores were significantly below his current grade. This was likely due to the fact that he had been attending public schools prior to his enrollment at this Catholic school. Tutoring was recommended to bring him up to grade level by the end of the academic year.

Following the family feedback session, the family and clinician met with school personnel. The clinician made a more formal presentation of the testing material to the school staff. The teacher was relieved to hear that Leo did not have ADHD. Leo's mother shared her medical history with the school and received a great deal of support.

COUNSELING

In traditional school counseling programs, children are referred for services because they are exhibiting problems in the classroom. Parents are contacted to give consent, and are often interviewed briefly over the phone. These intake interviews tend to be focused on the child and his/her functioning, rather than on the family as a whole. For example, rarely is the parent asked if the parent is experiencing any problems. Furthermore, the phone may serve as a barrier for the parent to distance himself/herself from the social worker. Often, clients interviewed in person display behavioral cues to the interviewer that a particular issue should be explored further. When interviewed over the phone, these cues are often not evident.

Following consent for services, children are typically seen either individually or in a group setting with peers. Rarely, if ever, are parents engaged in the counseling process. The focus of the counseling is helping the child to function better in the classroom setting.

TRADITIONAL SCHOOL-BASED COUNSELING (TSBC) VIGNETTE

In the traditional school-based counseling model, Leo was diagnosed with ADHD and a letter was sent home to his mother recommending a psychiatric evaluation. Leo's aunt followed up with the recommendation and called the local community mental health center for an appointment. There was a six month wait for an appointment, and she placed Leo's name on the list. Meanwhile, in school, things did not change. Leo continued to struggle academically and began to exhibit more and more behavioral problems. After getting into a fight with a peer, he was sent to the school social worker. The school social worker met with Leo and began to teach him coping skills for his feelings. But in the back of her mind, she really did not believe this would be helpful, as Leo had been diagnosed with ADHD and needed medication. Although the social worker did ask Leo if there was anything happening at home that was bothering him, Leo did not want to talk about his mother's illness. Every time he talked about it, he began to cry, and didn't want the social worker to see this side of him. So week after week they talked about coping skills for anger related to peer issues, when really the heart of the issue was Leo's grief about his mother's illness and fear for her life. Leo was also sent to a group with peers who also shared the diagnosis of ADHD to discuss ways to manage their behavior in the classroom.

In Adlerian counseling, parents are seen as partners in working with their children. Counseling, even in the school setting, would not be attempted without the parents' participation. Minimally, the parent(s) would meet in person with the clinician for a comprehensive intake about the child and family. The clinician would inquire about the social context in which the client grew up, the family constellation (ordinal and psychological birth order), and the exogenous factor (current trigger) that precipitated the symptoms.

ADLERIAN SCHOOL-BASED FAMILY COUNSELING (ASBFC) VIGNETTE

During the intake with Leo's mother, it was revealed that Leo's parents were not married when he was conceived. They had been dating on and off for several years, and when Leo's mother became pregnant, Leo's father indicated that he did not want to have responsibility for a child. He encouraged Leo's mother to terminate the pregnancy, but Leo's mother had always dreamt of having a child, and felt that she could rear him with the support of her extended family. Leo's mother was in her late 30's at the time of his conception, and she did not know if she would ever find a mate with whom to have another child, so she continued the pregnancy and never saw Leo's father again.

The first several months of Leo's life were very stressful, as his mother was balancing working and caring for a newborn infant alone. As Leo's mother and grandmother were very close, his grandmother suggested that she and Leo move in with her so that Leo's mother could work fewer hours to spend more time with her baby. Leo and his mother lived with his maternal grandmother for five years, which allowed his mother to work flexible hours, finish a college degree, and receive the support of her extended family. When Leo started school, he and his mother rented an apartment one block away from his grandmother. His mother obtained full-time employment and Leo went to his grandmother's home after school every day until his mother picked him up. Leo developed a very close relationship with his grandmother. Given this relationship, it is understandable that his grandmother's death from breast cancer and mother's subsequent diagnosis of breast cancer would create great anxiety and distress for Leo.

In addition to meeting with the parent for an intake, Adlerian counselors work closely with parents on an ongoing basis. Sometimes the focus of the counseling is helping parents to develop more appropriate parenting strategies.   Other times, family members are included in the counseling process. Adler himself acknowledged the importance of understanding the context of the child. "The honest psychologist cannot shut his eyes to social conditions which prevent the child from becoming a part of the community", (Ansbacher, 1964). What is important is not to treat the child in isolation, but to understand the family context and include parent(s) and extended family members when possible.

Following testing, the clinician offered several treatment options that included working with Leo in the school setting, referring Leo and his family for outpatient counseling, and/or meeting with Leo and his family within the school setting. Since Leo's mother would be returning to work in a few weeks and working the second shift at a hospital as a nurse, it would be unlikely that they could attend family counseling in an outpatient clinic. But since she dropped Leo off to school in the morning, it was agreed that Leo and his mother could be seen together during the first period every other week. During alternating weeks, Leo would meet individually for counseling. Leo's aunt would join them every so often, as she was integrally involved in the family life and caregiving.

The teacher agreed to the plan to release Leo from first period every other week so he and his mother could participate in family counseling together. Leo was seen during lunchtime on the off weeks. Within two months, Leo's behavior began to change. As he received support from his teacher and school counselor and learned how to cope with his feelings, he began to attend to his work. Slowly his grades began to improve. By the next quarter, most of his grades had improved, although he continued to struggle with subjects in which he historically had not done well.

CHILD PROTECTION ISSUES

One day, Leo came to school with a black eye. His classroom teacher immediately noticed his eye and asked him what happened. Leo disclosed that his mother's new boyfriend hit him. Leo's mother had been dating a man seriously, and mid-way through the academic year, he moved in with Leo and his mother. Leo loved his mother's boyfriend, and fantasized about his mother marrying him. It was the first time Leo had a stable male adult in his life, and he was very excited about the developing relationship.

One day after school, instead of going to his grandmother's house, he went straight home. He knew his mother's boyfriend had a day off work, and Leo hoped to play basketball with him. He was surprised to find that his mother's boyfriend at the kitchen table, surrounded by beer cans. He thought the man was acting strange, and smelled like beer. When Leo asked him to play basketball, he became angry and started yelling at Leo. Leo was so shocked and dismayed, he began yelling back, and the man hit Leo in the face. Leo's eye swelled up and was bruised. He ran out of the house to his grandmother's home. Since his mother was working a double shift at the hospital, Leo spent the night with his grandmother and had not even seen his mother when he went to school the next day.

When working with children and adolescents, inevitably the issue of child protection will emerge with students in the school setting. In the USA, there are laws regarding making reports of child abuse and neglect. School administrators and school employees, educational advocates, and truant officers are required by law to report suspicions of child abuse or neglect. Schools often have very strict mandated reporting procedures that all personnel must follow.

In many traditional school-based counseling programs, when abuse or neglect is suspected, a call to the state child abuse hotline is made. In Illinois, the child welfare agency responsible for investigating allegations of child abuse is the Department of Children and Family Services (DCFS). When a child presents in school with a physical injury, and reports that this injury was inflicted by a parent or caregiver, a call to the DCFS hotline is made. It is possible for the reporter to remain anonymous, and many times the school will choose not to disclose its identity. It is not required that the parent be contacted first. A DCFS investigator will make a visit to the home and school within 24 hours to assess the child's safety and determine if the child should be removed from the home. The child may be temporarily removed from the home until a formal court petition can be made to request that the child enter into DCFS custody and be placed in foster care.

TRADITIONAL SCHOOL-BASED COUNSELING (TSBC) VIGNETTE

After meeting with Leo, the school social worker made an anonymous call to DCFS. The report was accepted, and an investigator came to Leo's school to talk to him. She saw his eye and noted his report about his mother's boyfriend hitting him. Next, the caseworker went to the home. It was late in the day, and Leo's mother was sleeping, as she had worked a double shift the night before. She answered the door half asleep. The caseworker came into the home and questioned Leo's mother about the alleged physical abuse. Leo's mother said she did not know about any altercation, and refused to believe that her boyfriend would harm her son. Given that she did not believe her son had been hurt, the investigator made a decision to remove Leo from his mother's home and place him in temporary foster care. Leo's mother became enraged upon hearing this, and began yelling and arguing with the investigator. The investigator felt threatened, and left the home quickly to get back to the school and take Leo to a temporary foster home. The investigator also considered Leo's mother to be "angry and dangerous," and made a recommendation that she not be awarded visitation with her son until she completed anger management classes.

As Adlerian counselors, we see the parent as our partners in the counseling process. Therefore, the idea of making an anonymous call to a child protection agency is inconceivable. As the parent is viewed as a partner to the counselor, the first thing the counselor will want to do is to talk to the parent about the allegation and engage the parent in the report making. As the counselor already has a relationship with the parent, he or she will call the parent and request an immediate meeting. If the meeting cannot take place in person, the counselor will talk with the parent over the phone. The counselor will inform the parent of the child's report, and discuss with the parent the need to make a report to the D.C.F.S. hotline. The parent's feelings and reactions will be discussed and processed. The parent will be invited by the counselor to make the call. The very act of inviting the parent to make the call is empowering in the midst of a very disempowering situation. The counselor will remain with the parent while the call is made, and will walk the parent through the investigation process, offering support and information throughout. In Illinois, for example, the counselor will suggest to DCFS that the counselor will be available to talk to the investigator about the child and family and offer background information on the case.

ADLERIAN SCHOOL-BASED FAMILY COUNSELING (ASBFC) VIGNETTE

The clinician was notified by Leo's teacher that he had a black eye. The clinician met with Leo and he disclosed that his mother's boyfriend hit him the night before. Immediately, the clinician called Leo's mother at home. She answered the phone in a sleepy state. The clinician told her there was an emergency and that the clinician needed to meet with her immediately at the school. Although Leo's mother was exhausted, she dressed and went to the school. She had a good relationship with the clinician, and knew that he would not insist that she come to the school unless it was necessary. Upon seeing her son's black eye, she became concerned and asked him what happened. He told her about the incident the day before. The clinician explained the need to make a report to the child abuse hotline, and invited her to make the report herself. At first, Leo's mother was very angry with the clinician, and wanted to leave and take Leo home. The clinician remained calm and continued to engage her in conversation, empathizing with her feelings and stressing the importance of her cooperation in the process. The clinician explained that if she did not cooperate and agree to protect her son, he could be placed in foster care.

After about one hour, Leo's mother finally agreed to make the call herself. The report was accepted and the clinician gave his contact information to the investigator. The next day, before going out to the home, the investigator contacted the clinician and was given background information on the case and family. The investigator visited with Leo in school, and then went to the home. Since Leo's mother knew that an investigator would be coming, she took a day off of work and had time to prepare herself for the home visit. Although she was very angry about this investigation, she now understood the importance of cooperating with the authorities and the risk of Leo being removed from her home. Therefore, she told her boyfriend to move out immediately even though she felt ambivalent about the decision. When the investigator came to the home, she was pleased that Leo's mother had acted to protect her son, and had made the report herself. Therefore, Leo remained in the home and the case was opened for intact family services. Under this program, a caseworker comes to the home weekly to offer supportive services to the family and help the family to stabilize.

SUMMARY

Traditional school counselors may believe that their work is easier if they do not engage the parent in the counseling process. However, as the vignettes demonstrated, by not engaging the parents in the process, traditional school counselors may be missing the heart of the problem for the child, and therefore not helping the child heal.

Adlerian SBFC professionals, by contrast, view the parent(s) and family as their equal partner(s). As such, the parent and family are engaged from the beginning of counseling and throughout testing and/or counseling. As a result, the context of the child's problems is understood, and interventions may be appropriately implemented. If progress is stalled, the parent is consulted so that the intervention may be revised. Although this approach may be considered by some to be more time-consuming for the clinician, it is more likely that progress will result.

REFERENCES

Adler, A. (2006). *Education for prevention.* Stein, H.T. (Ed.). Bellingham: Classical Adlerian Translation Project.

Ansbacher, H.L., & Ansbacher, R.R. (Eds.) (1964). *The individual psychology of Alfred Adler.* New York: Harper Torchbooks.

Boyd-Franklin, N. *Black Families in Therapy: A Multisystems Approach.* New York: Guilford Press, 1989.

Dreikurs, R. (1971). *Social equality: The challenge of today.* Chicago: Adler School of Professional Psychology.

Gibbs, J. T. (2003). African American Children and Adolescents. In Gibbs and Haung (Eds.), *Children of Color: Psychological interventions with culturally diverse youth* (pp. 95-144) . San Franciso, CA: John Wiley & Sons, Inc.

Mosak, H.H. & Maniacci, M. (1999). *A primer of Adlerian psychology: The analytic, behavioral, cognitive psychology of Alfred Adler.* New York: Routledge.

President's Commission on Mental Health. *Mental Health in America: 1978,* Vol.1 Washington, D. C.

Tolan, P. H., & Dodge, K. A. (2005). Children's mental health as a primary care and concern: A system for comprehensive support and service. *American Psychologist, 60,* 601-614.

U. S. Bureau of the Census. *Statistical Abstract of the United States: 2001.* (21st ed.) Washington, D.C.: U.S. Department of Commerce, 2001.

PART III

SCHOOL-BASED FAMILY COUNSELING CHANGE STRATEGIES: FAMILY-INTERVENTION FOCUS

SCHOOL FOCUS

School-Prevention	School-Intervention
Family-Prevention	**Family-Intervention**

PREVENTION FOCUS

INTERVENTION FOCUS

FAMILY FOCUS

Chapter 8
How to do Parent/Guardian Consultation:
An Integrative Behavior-Process Consultation
Approach

Margaret Garcia and Michele D. Wallace

OVERVIEW: This chapter provides basic concepts, skills, and mindsets for school-based family counselors to consider when taking a behavioral approach to parent/guardian consultation. The importance of adhering to a consultation model will be emphasized and illustrated with the case of Jacob. Additionally, we will recommend the application of Process Consultation (PC) along with Behavioral Consultation (BC) as an integration of consultation models that fully involve and expose the parents/guardians to problem-solving. Steps in the consultation process, strategies and resources are addressed.

BACKGROUND

The two authors of this chapter come from different backgrounds in consultation. One of us has strong foundations in Mental Health Consultation based on the work of Gerald Caplan (Caplan & Caplan, 1998) with origins in psychoanalytic theory. The other has provided extensive parent consultation from a behavior analytic approach based on the principles and procedures developed by B.F. Skinner and other influential behavior analysts. These are two very different, almost contrary models of consultation. An advanced understanding of the models allows the consultant to begin using one and then transitioning to the other if that turns out to be best depending on how the case progresses but that will not be addressed in this chapter. Both models are taught at California State University, Los Angeles but only the school psychology and school counseling graduate students are exposed to both, along with other models such as Adlerian. Graduate students are encouraged to select only one model and adhere to it closely in order to guide their approach to the case. Which model is best? It depends. First and foremost, it's important to know a model and its underlying theory. It provides structure to the problem identification and analysis and provides the basis for interventions developed to reduce the problem and increase success. This chapter will focus on a behavioral approach to consultation with the recommendation that it be imbedded in process consultation based on the work of Edgar Schein (1999).

Often, the novice school-based counselor will want to rely on his or her counseling or interviewing skills when serving as a consultant to parents. While there are critical communication skills that intersect counseling, interviewing, and consultation, one must recognize the differences and learn to employ the applicable skill set and tap into the appropriate knowledge base when serving as a consultant.

CONSULTATION VERSUS COUNSELING

Unlike the traditional school counselor, the SBFC professional works directly with families not just to improve school functioning of their child but to improve family functioning to meet the needs of the child and family and in turn improve school success for the child. When the SBFC professional provides counseling or therapy for a family, serving as the helper and the family members as the clients, that is direct intervention. But there are times when direct intervention is not ideal and when families should be encouraged and supported in providing their own interventions with the guidance of a professional consultant. Consultants provide indirect interventions by working with the consultee (the parent or guardian) who directly works with the identified client (the child).

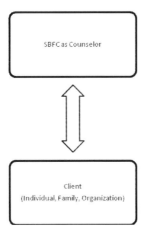

Figure 8.1 Counselor Client Dyadic Relationship

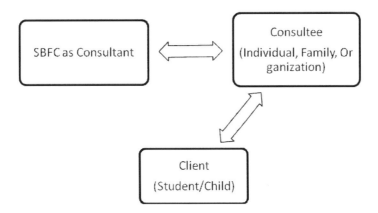

Figure 8.2 Consultant - Consultee - Client Triad

In Behavioral Consultation the consultant may directly observe the client in order to gather information in the form of direct assessments. But in that case, one should be trained in Applied Behavior Analysis and be familiar with various methods of data collection and recording of direct observations in order to determine the function of a target behavior. This chapter will focus on some basics in taking a behavior analytic approach when consulting with parents.

THE CASE OF JACOB

Jacob is a fifth grade student who had been retained in the third grade due to significant delays in his academic achievement. At every grade level since kindergarten, Jacob's teachers have expressed concerns about his ability to attend and his apparent inability to stay seated, and to avoid talking out of turn. But he has never been assessed for special education as the parents have refused to sign assessment plans claiming that Jacob is fine at home. His current teacher, Mrs. Davis, reports Jacob's reading skills to be at the mid-fourth grade level and his math skills to be slightly below the fourth grade level. Mrs. Davis believes he would catch up to his grade peers if he completed more classwork and particularly if he completed homework of which he currently submits none. It's now the spring semester and Jacob hasn't turned in completed homework assignments since February and very few before then.

Jacob's father, Frank works full-time as a mechanic at a major car dealership. Jacob's mother, Linda works full-time as a receptionist at a dentist office about 10 miles from home and is taking classes two nights a week to become a dental hygienist. Jacob's parents have been married for 15 years and have three children including Angela (14 years old), Jacob (12 years old), and Matthew (8 years old). Angela is an above average student attending the eighth grade at the local middle school and Matthew is performing at grade level attending third grade where Jacob also attends. Frank reports that he is of Mexican descent on his paternal side and Greek/Italian on his maternal side. Linda reports that she is second generation born in the United States with grandparents immigrated from Mexico. The family lives in a middle class neighborhood in a Los Angeles suburb where the population is 39% Latino/Hispanic, 27% Armenian, 16% Asian, 2% African American, 10% two or more ethnicities, <1% Native American, and 5% other.

Linda gets home from work by 5pm on nights she doesn't take classes and about 9:30pm on the two nights she does take classes. Frank is usually home by 7pm but also works half days Saturday and has Mondays off. Except for Mondays the parents aren't home when Angela, Jacob, and Matthew return home from school. Grandma picks up Matthew and Jacob from school and Angela prefers to walk home with friends. Grandma takes care of the kids (e.g., feeds them snacks, works on homework with them, starts dinner) until their parents get home.

Sandra, the SBFC professional at Jacob's school contacted Linda via her mobile phone number to set up an appointment to discuss Jacob's lack of homework completion and his classroom disruptions. Linda could not be available except early in the morning as she had to be at work by 8am and she preferred not to meet early on the mornings after she got home late. She suggested that Frank meet with Sandra on one of his Mondays off. Frank was reluctant but knew that his availability on Mondays made it difficult for him to make excuses.

RELATIONSHIP TO THE SBFC MODEL

School-Prevention: Chapter 12 will address teacher consultation which is more directly tied to prevention of school related challenges. However, parent consultation can certainly result in preventing school problems whether they are academic, social, or emotional. This can happen in at least two ways. First, if the parent implements effective strategies to remediate a behavior problem at home, the child likely learned skills that could generalize to the school environment which would be preventive if the child were not already experiencing school problems. If Linda and Frank come up with a plan to improve Jacob's homework completion, Jacob may also show improvement in completing classwork but this would be remedial rather than preventive. Second, if the parent has other children, experiencing success with an intervention may result in the parent generalizing that success with the other children which again may have benefits at the school level. Although Angela and Michael are not currently experiencing academic problems, Frank and Linda may be better able to help them maintain that success after realizing the support that Jacob needed from home.

School-Intervention: The SBFC professional contacted Jacob's parents due to problems in his classroom performance as well as his failure to complete homework assignments. If Sandra can effectively work with Frank and Linda to improve Jacob's homework and general skills in attending to and persevering with on-task behavior, they can share their strategies with Jacob's teacher.

Family-Prevention: Because the consultee who works directly with the client has the opportunity to gain knowledge, skills, and problem-solving ability, the consultee becomes better able to apply those skills to future situations of a similar nature and will be more likely to prevent problems from occurring. Rather than rely on the SBFC professional to directly intervene with Jacob, the parents themselves provide the intervention. This does not mean that Linda and Frank would not need additional consultation in the future for Jacob or any of their children. But they now have a better awareness of Jacob's behavior and their own actions or non-actions that contributed to it. Moreover, they could possibly recognize how changing their own actions or non-actions could prevent or remediate future problems.

Family-Intervention: Mrs. Davis has resources at the school site that she can turn to for help with students in her classroom. But when it comes to parents, they are often contacted about their child's problem behavior but not provided with the knowledge and skills to address the problem directly. They are simply expected to use their typical disciplinary methods with special attention to the presenting problem. Linda and Frank had been informed for years that Jacob demonstrates difficulty with attending in class and he creates class disruptions by leaving his seat instead of doing his work. But because they claimed not to see the problem at home, they didn't participate in any problem-solving and refused to have Jacob considered for special education services. Remediation of problems within the family in this case will begin with first recognizing that there is a problem at home and that Jacob's struggles are not limited to the classroom. But rather than simply inform the parents or invite them for a conference to discuss Jacob's performance, Mrs. Davis asked the SBFC professional to contact the family. Sandra opted to approach the parents as a consultant rather than as a counselor.

EVIDENCE-BASED SUPPORT

Behavioral consultation as spelled out by Kratochwill and Bergan (1990) has led to many examples of parents increasing desired behavior and/or decreasing problem behavior. For example, behavior consultation has led to parents implementing effect treatment programs designed to treat pediatric feeding issues (Mueller, et al., 2003); reduce sleep problems (Ashbaugh & Pect, 1998); modify child noncompliance (Rotto & Kratochwill, 1994); reduce the amount of television watched by children (Wolfe, Mendes, & Factor, 1984); promote play-based verbal initiations (Reagon & Higbee, 2009); and improve reading (Gortmaker, et al., 2007), to name a few. Some have utilized behavioral consultation to set up behaviorally based treatment programs for children with autism in their home, specifically to teach parents how to implement discrete-trail teaching as well as train others to use such procedures (Lafasakis & Sturmey, 2007). In fact, the behavioral journals are filed with a variety of examples illustrating the use behavioral consultation, be it with parents, teachers, or other caregivers, to improve the behavior and lives of clients as well as the family or educational unit. What seems to be missing from this evidence, is the lasting effects of such an approach on the consultee (in this case the parent). Most outcomes reported are based upon parental adherence to specific treatment protocols as child outcomes. It seems as the field has been mostly concerned with outcomes and not necessarily the process. By incorporating Process Consultation within a behavioral framework, process as well as outcome can be evaluated. Let me share an interesting story of behavioral consultation paired with process consultation story. One of the authors (Michele) was providing consultation to a family that was struggling with their child's feeding disorder. The child was a typically developing 6 year old that only ate French fries, yogurt, and fish crackers. During the behavioral consultation process, Process Consultation was also utilized. In the end, not only could the parents implement the effective treatment procedure for the feeding disorder, but the mom was able to utilize the problem solving logic that had been modeled to identify why her other daughter consistently bugged her whenever she was on the phone, develop an appropriate intervention, and effectively modify her daughter's bugging behavior all without the help of the behavioral consultant. This story is a clear demonstration of not only focusing on the outcomes (i.e., getting the child to eat and mom to implement the program with high fidelity), but the process as well (i.e., getting the parent to see that what she does or doesn't do affects her child's behavior and understanding and modifying environmental events can effectively change behavior).

PROCEDURE

Behavioral consultation is primarily an indirect intervention with an emphasis on problem-solving and consists of four basic stages: problem identification, problem analysis, treatment implementation, and treatment evaluation (Kratochwill & Bergan, 1990; Sheridan & Elliott, 1991). These stages designate the steps that are required to go from specifying the problem to determining a solution with evidence of its effectiveness. The four stages of Behavioral Consultation as applied to the case of Jacob are illustrated within the phases of Process Consultation.

STAGE 1: PROBLEM IDENTIFICATION

The first step is to define the problem in behavioral terms which is not as simple as it may seem. Operational definitions allow the consultant and consultee to form a common understanding of the observable behavior and should be clear, objective, and include instances of what counts and what doesn't count. For example, an operational definition of "refusing to do homework" might be: Jacob says "no, I don't want to and you can't make me" when his grandmother tells him it is time to do his homework. In addition, Jacob walks away from the table and his grandmother. It does not include Jacob sitting down at the table and saying he doesn't know how to do the work. The next step is to tentatively identify the behavior in terms of antecedent, situation, and consequent conditions. This is an ecological approach that is highly contextualized so an understanding of what happens in the moment cannot be considered without recognizing what preceded and followed the event. Antecedent events whether distant or proximal will affect behavior but discriminative stimuli or signals that indicate if reinforcement is available are events closer to the target behavior and are more under the control of the parent or consultee. Also to be considered are the establishing operations that affect the potency of a reinforcer. For instance, in the case of Jacob it will be noted that he has easy access to video games at home so this reduces its effectiveness as a reinforcer just as food treats would not be effective if a child is satiated even if he loves the treats being offered. Next, the intensity, sequencing, and frequency of the target behavior should be tentatively determined in order to establish a procedure for collection of baseline data.

STAGE 2: PROBLEM ANALYSIS

Once the consultant and consultee have identified the problem, they will evaluate and obtain an agreement on the sufficiency and adequacy of baseline data. If appropriate, they will conduct a functional behavioral assessment prior to discussing and agreeing upon a goal for behavior change. The functional behavioral assessment could include an indirect assessment, a descriptive assessment, and/or a functional analysis (Note: it is best practice to use all three methods when determining the why of a behavior problem).The behavior change goal could involve increasing a behavior such as doing homework and staying in seat or reducing a behavior such as talking out of turn or walking about the classroom, talking to peers, or making noises during independent work time. Basically, there are four primary functions of behavior to consider: Attention (from peers or adults), Escape (from person, task, environment), Tangible (desire for a specific item or activity), or Automatic (the behavior produces its own reinforcement, for example it feels good or alleviates pain). The next step is to design an intervention plan specifying the conditions to be changed and the implementation of the treatment plan. The consultant and consultee will discuss how data will continue to be collected and recorded.

STAGE 3: TREATMENT IMPLEMENTATION

At this stage it should be determined whether the consultee has the skills needed to effectively implement the treatment plan. It is critical for the behavioral consultant to recognize forms of resistance or any issues that may affect treatment integrity. Parents may believe that slight variations or ad-libbing an intervention are harmless or should serve the same purpose, but any deviation from the agreed upon plan make it difficult to monitor the effectiveness of the original treatment plan and may even reinforce the behavior we are trying to reduce. Moreover, some interventions fall apart, or don't work, if they are not implemented with full integrity.This is similar to physicians who struggle with patient honesty in reporting the taking of medications as prescribed. If the patient reports that the medication isn't working, a different dosage or a different medication may be prescribed. But if the patient did not take the medication as prescribed to avoid side effects for example, the doctor may be changing the treatment plan that actually had the most promise if delivered with integrity. So it is important for the consultant to monitor the data collection procedures and determine whether the plan is proceeding as designed. Based upon the data analysis, the consultant can determine whether any revisions in the treatment plan arenecessary.

Sometimes expert consultants who know the literature that supports the intervention as applied to the given case will fail to recognize the family stressors or cultural values that could make implementation of the plan as designed doomed to fail. Open discussions and changes to the treatment plan along with altered expectations for results could be more likely to yield positive outcomes than an insistence on sticking with the original plan. Thus, it is important to note these family stressors or cultural values before embarking on a specific plan. For example, if the parents will not tolerate any talking back to an elder, then ignoring the behavior may not be an option. Once the parents experience success with a plan that meets their needs,they may expand their skills and improve treatment integrity.

STAGE 4: TREATMENT EVALUATION

It is at this stage where we determine if the goals of consultation have been met. We evaluate the effectiveness of the treatment plan and discuss strategies and tactics regarding the continuation, planning for generalization and maintenance, modification, or termination of the intervention. At this point consultation can be terminated or follow-up sessions should be scheduled. The consultant should be cautious about fostering dependency by the consultee but should also provide follow-up support if the need is anticipated. Even scheduling a brief check-in a few weeks after the last session could help the consultee maintain the successful intervention. Moreover, a good consultant will make sure the consultee is obtaining the needed support from their environment so that they are not dependent on the consultant for all aspects of support (e.g., making sure other family members acknowledge their efforts and provide support).

PROCESS CONSULTATION

Based on ten principles, process consultation as described by Schein (1999) offers a good structure for any model of consultation including behavioral. This can be particularly helpful when a school-based counselor enters into a consultation relationship with a parent regarding behavioral concerns and while having a stronger knowledge of systems theory than of behavior and social learning theory. It helps the consultant focus on problem-solving and to make decisions on the best model of consultation that will serve the consultee's needs.

TEN PRINCIPLES OF PROCESS CONSULTATION

1. Always try to be helpful. This may seem obvious but should not be taken for granted by those of us in the helping professions. Many things can get in the way of how we choose to define our helping role. For instance, one might think it helpful to advise parents to implement research-based strategies in working with their child. This could be the case, but if the parents don't fully understand how the problem was defined they may not implement the intervention with integrity and it may not yield good results. But if rather than tell the parents what is expected to work the consultant involves the parents in the process of identifying and analyzing the problem, the parents will become better equipped to fully address the problem and its solutions. But this takes more time and patience on everyone's part. Frank and Linda for example, may feel pressed for time and would prefer that Sandra, the SBFC professional simply provide strategies for them to consider and not take the time to engage in long discussions of Jacob and their actions relating to his behavior. However, ensuring that Frank and Linda understand how they are contributing to Jacob's behavior will help them change their behavior to change Jacob's behavior in the current situation and in the future.

2. Always stay in touch with the current reality. The consultant must avoid offering advice based on an ideal or even based on someone else's experiences, good or bad. Frank and Linda work full-time and are not home most afternoons when their children are expected to do their homework. When they do get home, it's dinner time or bed time and that leaves little time for quality interactions. So suggesting a plan where Frank or Linda sit with Jacob one-on-one for two hours doing his homework and providing a lot of individualized attention, although it may be evidence based, would not work within the current reality.

3. Access your ignorance. This is one of our favorite points made by Schein. It refers to our tendency to rely on assumptions without even realizing it. Consultants, especially those new to the field will often ask themselves "What do I know about this case?" We spend a lot of energy trying to relate what the consultee is saying to what we know about the client or the client's culture, or the kind of presenting problem and the research surrounding it. We need to spend more energy accessing our ignorance. What do you NOT know about the case? In many respects, behavioral consultants take this very seriously placing great attention on operationalizing the target behaviors and its occurrence, and the details of what happens before and after. Little is left to assumption when done right. Some things are left without further investigation by behavioral consultants but that tends to be deliberate. Behavioral consultants for example will choose to remain ignorant about what a child may have been thinking or feeling because there is no direct way to measure it and the focus is on observable behavior. It's not that thoughts and feelings are irrelevant, it's just that behavior serves a purpose for the child that should not be inferred based on internal events that cannot be directly observed. We (or the consultee) can change the "purpose" but we cannot change the child's feelings (nor should we).

4. *Everything you do is an intervention*. Through process consultation the SBFC professional will serve as a model for how to think about the case. Every question the consultant asks the consultee is part of the consultative intervention. When Sandra asks Frank and Linda questions about how they react to Jacob's behavior at home, she isn't just gathering information in preparation of offering advice for an intervention. Sandra is intervening with Jacob's parents by directing their attention to aspects of the case that are important in understanding it from a behavioral perspective. For example, she is trying to get the parents to understand that Jacob does certain things to either get attention, avoid homework, or because it feels good and to focus less on the fact that he is the family comedian. Beyond her questions, Sandra's expressed anxiety levels may also be part of the intervention. She may choose to present a sense of urgency or a sense of calm depending on the situation. If Frank and Linda do not perceive a problem at home with Jacob's behavior, Sandra may need to help build a little anxiety to motivate problem identification and problem solving. This isn't to say that Sandra would promote panic or worry, but would instead model a recognition of the problem as immediate in nature and deserving of attention. Sandra may ask "Does Jacob realize that his missing homework is affecting his overall performance and may also affect his transition to middle school in the fall?" This inquiry serves to direct the parents' attention to Jacob's perspective and how his current behavior is placing him at risk.

5. *It is the consultee who owns the problem and the solution*. Leave your ego at the door when serving as a consultant. Recognize that the consultee is the expert on his or her own situation and may or may not find your input valuable. Parents should be free to accept or reject your input. It doesn't mean that they don't care when they opt not to follow through on suggested strategies or that they did not benefit from the process. Avoid taking the stance of "Why did I spend this time working with these parents when they don't even accept my input?" Regardless of whether they accept your input, you have opened up the way they view the problem, which is a success.

6. *Go with the flow*. While it is good to be prepared with questions and ideas, the parents may go in a direction that is different than what you planned. A behavioral consultant should not interrupt the parent who persists in describing his or her feelings rather than their actions, at least not at first. It is important to reflect back to the parent what you have heard and to demonstrate empathy. Furthermore, the family's culture helps them to maintain a sense of stability and preserves a lifestyle they value. The consultant has to learn to work within a culture that is different than her own and can do so by going with the flow. You can always prompt the parents back to the agenda after listening and reflecting their feelings. Moreover, it may be that once their feelings are validated, they will be more inclined to discuss the matter from an objective stand point.

7. *Timing is crucial*. Don't blurt out a question the moment it enters your mind. Take note and ask the question when the time is right. Remember the fourth principle, everything is an intervention. Your questions are most effective when asked at the right time. Be deliberate and patient so that the consultee can gain the most from your inquiry. Process consultation involves phases of inquiry that we will present in the next section. The phases are sequential and should be timed to serve their purpose before moving to the next phase.

8. Be constructively opportunistic with confrontive interventions. One of the most difficult skills to learn as a consultant is recognizing when one is being confrontive. This will be illustrated in the next section but one example of a confrontive intervention is "Have you tried praising him when he begins doing his homework?" This is confrontive because it implies that the parents should have considered this action. This inquiry is fine but not before exploring what the parents have already tried.

9. Everything is data. Errors will always be observed and are the prime source for learning. If you ask a question that appears to have elicited a negative reaction from the consultee, don't dwell in fear that you have ruined the consultative relationship or lost the trust of the consultee. Whether you were mistaken in your line of inquiry or did what the most experienced of consultants would have done, if the intervention resulted in a negative reaction from a parent, take note and learn from it. Use the recovery skills you might use in counseling to regain positive momentum in the process of consultation. Allow the consultee to assert his or her reactions to your inquiry without getting defensive. This will promote open communication and give you the opportunity to gather more data about the consultee's perspectives on the matters being addressed.

10. When in doubt, share the problem. A good consultant should recognize the value of consultation and seek it out as a consultee when appropriate. While respecting federal and state laws and confidentiality, a SBFC professional can share a case with a colleague who can offer a different problem solving perspective.

PHASES OF INQUIRY IN PROCESS CONSULTATION

All consultation sessions should begin with some basic structuring that establishes timing of the session, confidentiality and exceptions to it, and then should transition to formal consultation. The three basic phases of inquiry in process consultation are Pure Inquiry, Exploratory Diagnostic Inquiry, and Confrontive Inquiry. Whether the consultation was initiated by the SBFC professional or the parent, consultation should begin in Pure Inquiry. However, if the consultation was initiated by the parent, the SBFC professional should begin with silence, allowing the parent to present the problem. The SBFC professional should only ask questions that will prompt the parent to tell their story, sharing the problem from his or her perspective without censorship from the consultant. Given that Sandra initiated the consultation session, she does not begin with silence but attempts to allow Jacob's father to present the problem as he sees it.

Pure Inquiry: Behavioral Consultation does not yet begin because this is when the consultant enters the relationship without an agenda or preconceived notion for how to approach the case. Clearly Sandra has ideas and is aware of problem behaviors that need to be addressed, but to be effective at involving the parents Sandra needs to gain a better understanding of how they view the situation.

Sandra: "Thank you for meeting with me Mr. Rodriguez. I know this is your day off so I really appreciate you taking the time to join me in a discussion about Jacob's behavior. I asked you to meet with me because Mrs. Davis has indicated that Jacob hasn't turned in any completed homework for several weeks and often doesn't complete his classwork. I can talk to Mrs. Davis about Jacob's behavior in the classroom at another time. I'd like to use this time to focus on your experience with Jacob at home and to see if I can be of help to you and Mrs. Rodriguez. Is that okay with you?"

Frank: "I usually leave these things up to Linda, my wife because I don't get home until late. But she started taking classes to get her certification as a dental hygienist so now some nights she gets home later than I do. My mother-in-law helps us watch the kids when we aren't home but I guess she hasn't really been making sure they're getting their homework done. She does so much for us that I don't feel right asking her to do more. But I will talk to Jacob about it and we will make sure he gets it done."

At this point Sandra has questions and even ideas to suggest but she holds back to keep this phase in Pure Inquiry, getting an idea of the problem from Frank's perspective. For instance, Sandra notices that Frank is viewing the problem as something recent, possibly triggered by Linda's new class schedule. But Sandra knows that throughout his school record teachers have documented Jacob's difficulty completing tasks. She also can't help but wonder how Jacob's parents plan to "make sure" he gets his homework completed but asking about it now would be premature and challenging to the consultee.

Sandra: "How is Jacob's behavior at home?"

Frank: "He's a good kid. He's a typical twelve year-old, you know. He'd rather play his video games or watch TV than do homework." (Sandra makes it a point not to hypothesize the function of Jacob's behavior but mentally notes Frank's recognition of Jacob's preferred activities.) "Esther, my mother-in-law usually blames Jacob when the kids fight. Sometimes Angela and Matthew complain that Jacob won't leave them alone but Matthew also likes playing with his big brother."

Sandra: "How much time does Esther spend with the kids?" Sandra wants to know more about Jacob's behavior but she prefers to know it based on the consultee's direct observations rather than hearing about it twice removed.

Frank: "She picks them up from school every day except Mondays when I'm home. It's a big help and she stays with them until Linda gets home from work around five or when I get home around seven. But Linda works late on Mondays and Wednesdays – I mean she gets home late because she goes to class after work. But the rest of the week I'm the one who gets home later and I'm too tired to help the kids with homework."

Although Sandra doesn't think Frank will not be involved with any interventions the rest of the week, she decides to focus on Mondays so that she can learn more about Frank's interactions with the kids.

Sandra: "I know it has already been a week, but can you tell me what you can remember about Jacob's behavior last Monday?"

Frank: "What do you mean? I don't really remember anything special about it."

Sandra: "Did Jacob do his homework that day?"

Frank: "Well, I think Angela did hers but I don't think Jacob and Matthew had homework last Monday. I know I asked them about it. Jacob said he didn't have any and Matthew said he already did his at school." Sandra knows that Mrs. Davis assigns homework every night plus assigns classwork to be completed at home if it wasn't completed at school that day. But she does not confront Frank with this knowledge. Instead she is trying to gather more information from Frank's perspective. Sandra also avoids asking confrontive questions such as "Do you check their homework to make sure its done?"

Sandra: "When is the last time you had a chance to observe Jacob doing homework?" (This question borders on confrontive but Sandra takes a chance because she needs to understand Frank's recognition of the problem).

Frank: "I don't think he gets homework on Mondays when I'm home but he usually waits until the last minute to do the homework he gets on Friday that he's supposed to turn in on Monday morning. Our weekends are pretty busy. I work half days on Saturday so Sundays are the only day we all have together as a family when none of us are working or in school. We sleep in and go to church then we usually visit with my parents or Linda's parents for the rest of the day. By the time we get home on Sundays, we usually don't have the energy to make the kids do their homework. They are tired too so I really wish the teachers didn't assign homework on the weekends. It really shouldn't eat into our family time so much. I know it's important but enough is enough. I mean we all come home after a nice day but get frustrated when we have to deal with getting the kids to do homework. Really it's just Jacob's homework but we try to get Angela to help him and she complains because she feels like it's punishment for her because *she already did her homework. I guess I don't blame her but it shouldn't feel like punishment to help your brother."*

      Sandra continues to gather information through Pure Inquiry and summarizes her session with Mr. Rodriquez.

Sandra: "Mr. Rodriguez, I'd like to summarize our meeting and discuss plans for meeting again. You and Mrs. Rodriguez both work full-time and count on your mother-in-law to help watch the kids for a few hours after school during the week. You only have two days off per week, Sundays and Mondays, but they are usually devoted to shared family activities or taking care of household chores. Angela and Matthew tend to get their homework done with little need for prompting from you or Mrs. Rodriguez or your mother-in-law. But you do make it a point to ask them about it and acknowledge them for getting it done. But Jacob often claims he doesn't have homework or when he does admit to having it, he struggles to get it done and says it's too hard. You often rely on Angela to help him but she complains that he doesn't want her help, he wants her to give him the answers or he keeps doing other things and that makes Angela mad because she wants to get it over with. Is that right?"

Frank: "Yeah, I guess we need to figure out a way to help Jacob but Mrs. Davis should also stop giving him so much work to do. It's too much pressure on him and he never seems to get it done."

Sandra: "Can we meet again next week to collaborate on coming up with a plan to help Jacob with his homework at home?"

Frank: "If you have any ideas for me now I will be sure to try them instead of waiting for next week."

Sandra: "I don't have any suggestions yet but I would like to discuss the problem in more detail next week so that we can truly understand the problem and come up with a plan that will be best for Jacob and your family. I'd also like you to use this afternoon to gather more information that might be helpful to our discussion next week. Note Jacob's behavior with regard to homework and how he responds to your prompts to do it. Is that okay?" Frank reluctantly agrees and they schedule a meeting for next week.

      Exploratory Diagnostic Phase of Inquiry: During this phase, the consultant provides more structure to the line of questioning and provides a model for thinking about the case. It involves three areas of inquiry that include asking about the consultee's feelings or reactions in response to a specific event, exploring the consultee's hypotheses or beliefs about reasons for the client's behavior or their own responses, and thirdly, exploring actions taken or contemplated. In this case, the structure for the exploratory diagnostic inquiry will be provided by the behavioral consultation model which will carry over into the next phase of Confrontive Inquiry. Table 8.1 provides a comparison of the Exploratory and Confrontive levels of inquiry relative to the stages of Behavioral Consultation.

Table 8.1 Process and Behavioral Consultation as Applied to Jacob

Process Consultation Phases of Inquiry	Stages of Behavioral Consultation	Case of Jacob
Pure Inquiry Ask questions that allow the Consultee to provide his or her own perspective. This should be uncensored and the Consultant should avoid redirecting the discussion unless the Consultee wanders far from the presenting problem.	The first stage of BC does not formally begin in Pure Inquiry as this is the point where the Consultee presents the story from his or her own perspective with minimal directing from the Consultant. However the beginnings of identifying the problem will emerge.	Sandra allows Frank to discuss his views of Jacob's behavior. Aside from providing rationale for holding the consultation meeting (lack of homework completion), Sandra does not identify the problem. Frank only begins to acknowledge the problem through Sandra's open and closed questions.

Exploratory Diagnostic Inquiry In this phase the Consultant approaches the presenting problem with a specific model in mind. The questions asked serve to gather more information and to direct the Consultee's attention to specific aspects of the case.	*Stage 1 Identifying the Problem* The Consultant will ask questions that allow the Consultee to more operationally define the problem and/or target behavior.	Jacob's homework completion is defined as sitting at a table at home with materials ready, working on the assignment until complete. The behavior that we want to increase is working on the assignment. Although Jacob has turned in no homework for several weeks, that is an emphasis on outcomes rather than behaviors. In actuality, Jacob does spend measurable time on homework but rarely completes it. The behaviors we want to decrease are arguing/playing with siblings, watching TV, and playing video games during homework time.
a) Exploring Reactions Ask questions that bring out the details of a specific case. Be sure to have the Consultee talk about a specific incident of the problem behavior. While acceptable during Pure Inquiry, in this phase, do not allow the Consultee to explain the problem in generalities such as "He always..." or "He never..." Use this step of the Exploratory Phase to ask the Consultee how he or she responds to client's behavior.	*Stage 1* continues with the Consultant asking questions that address the antecedents and consequences of the target behaviors. More specifically, the Consultant asks about the Consultee's actions around the target behavior.	Questions Sandra asks at this Phase/Stage: "What was happening right before you told Jacob to do his homework?" "How did you tell him to do his homework?" "What did Jacob do when you told him to do his homework?" "How did you respond when Jacob said he didn't have homework?" "How did you respond when Jacob said he left his homework materials at school?"
b) Exploring Hypotheses At this step, ask questions such as "Why do you think he responded that way?" or "What purpose do	*Stage 2 Problem Analysis* Hypothesize the function of the client's behavior (Attention, Escape, Tangible, Automatic)	Sandra has Frank fill out an indirect assessment that focuses on the purpose behind Jacob's behavior, that models for Frank that in order to

you think that behavior is serving for him?" "What does he get out of that behavior?" "Why did you respond the way you did?"		understand why Jacob does what he does he needs to understand why.
c) *Exploring Actions Taken or Contemplated* Be certain to ask the Consultee what he or she has already tried to address the problem. This helps the Consultee to understand the perception of resources including their own knowledge and skills. The Consultant provides enough opportunity for the Consultee to discuss what has already been tried along with how well it worked or didn't work and the reasons behind the outcomes.	*Stage 2 Problem Analysis* It may be determined that the Consultee knows what might work and has seen improvement with certain strategies but such strategies may not be feasible to continue. It could be that punishment is effective but the Consultant will work toward positive interventions. Further, punishment serves to reduce behavior and parents often use it when their actual intent is to increase a behavior.	After completing the survey, Frank realizes that Jacob not only gets to do other things, but more importantly he gets out of doing his homework by either arguing, playing video games, and yes, by being sent to his room. Although Frank and Linda do not hit their kids, in many households if a child doesn't do homework the child may be spanked. To increase behavior such as doing homework, the parent should be reinforcing on-task behavior rather than punishing the absence of it.
Confrontive It's at this phase of Inquiry that the Process Consultant asks about specific strategies to consider and will offer their expert perspective on the problem and why it is occurring. In the Confrontive phase, the Consultee can be direct about addressing the evidence that supports an intervention and the knowledge and skills that need to be developed to implement the plan effectively.	*Stage 3* *Treatment Implementation* It's at this stage that the Consultant offers a great deal of direct feedback about the details of an effective treatment plan. If the Consultee lacks appropriate skills, the Consultant may take the opportunity to teach the skill.	Sandra will ask questions such as: "Does Jacob respond the same way to his grandmother and mother as he does to you?" "How does Angela interact with Jacob when she helps him with his homework?" "How can the assignment be made less aversive for Jacob?" "Does Angela (or Esther, Linda, Frank) know how to help him with the skills he needs to do the assignment?" Sandra will need to help Frank involve other family members such a Linda, Esther, and Angela so that the treatment plan is not dependent only on Frank's presence.

	Stage 4 Treatment Evaluation Here is where the Consultant and Consultee will determine whether a plan has been successful; Consultation may continue to help the family generalize to another behavior or to another setting. Consultation may be terminated or it may lead to involving other parties such as the teacher.	

Result of Sandra's work with the Rodriguez family: Sandra has a basic understanding of the family setting during opportunities for the children to complete their homework assignments. She begins with a focus on Monday afternoons because that is when Frank can provide the clearest picture. Sunday evenings and other nights of the week are to be considered as well but Sandra knows that variations in the week from day to day make it difficult to establish a general plan. She begins with a focus on Mondays.

Frank brings Jacob and Michael home from school and lets them get snacks and play for about half an hour. Angela walks home from school and usually gets a snack and then sits at the dining room table to do her homework while watching TV. Sandra learns that the antecedent is that Frank prompts Jacob and Michael to do their homework when he sees Angela has started to do hers.

Jacob's behavior in response to the prompt is typically to claim that he doesn't have any homework. But after talking with Sandra the previous week, Frank told Jacob that he must have homework and that if he didn't start doing it he would have to go to his room without TV or games until dinner. Frank tells Jacob he doesn't believe him and that he must do his homework or go to his room. Jacob adjusts his claim and states that he left his homework at school. Frank sends Jacob to his room (Consequence). After completing the survey, Frank realizes that Jacob not only gets to do other things, but more importantly he gets out of doing his homework by either arguing, playing video games, and by being sent to his room. Prior to gaining this information possible hypotheses could be considered for the function of Jacob's behaviors listed above. Could it be to get Angela's or Matthew's attention? Is he trying to get his parents' attention? Could it be to gain access to preferred activities such as watching TV or playing video games? Could it be that he has difficulty sitting still and getting up to move around reduces discomfort? What Sandra and Frank determined is that Jacob's behavior and the consequences served to help him escape the task. Having access to preferred activities also served to maintain the avoidant behaviors.

Sandra also allowed Frank to further explore his ideas that Jacob's teacher gave him too much homework. The work was difficult for Jacob to do independently but it was also a lot to get done because it typically included unfinished classwork. Sandra agreed to work with Frank and Linda to meet with Mrs. Davis about only giving Jacob the same amount of homework that she gives to her other students, maybe even less at first, and that Sandra will work with the teacher about a plan to increase his work completion in class (this will be addressed in Chapter 12), allowing the parents to focus on a more reasonable work load, increasing the likelihood of success. To address the difficulty of the tasks assigned Sandra would again work with Mrs. Davis. At home, ideas to support Angela or one another in teaching Jacob the skills he needs to complete a task would depend on input from Mrs. Davis.

In sum, the function of Jacob's behavior is Escape. To increase on-task behavior Sandra and Frank decided to take two strategies: reduce the aversion of the tasks and give Jacob opportunities to take breaks he earns or to complete his work sooner. If he stays on task for 10 minutes, he may earn a stretch break for two minutes. This serves to give him a break from the work (escape) and to provide him with a feeling of movement he enjoys (automatic). This consultation has not focused on diagnosing a possible attention deficit hyperactivity disorder because the label may not serve to help determine the function. But enough evidence has been available that suggests Jacob does have difficulty sitting still in his seat. The caution in giving short breaks is that sometimes children have difficulty transitioning between activities. Part of evaluating the treatment plan will be in determining how frequently the breaks should be and how long they should last. If Jacob returns to the homework task on his own or within a few seconds (be specific) of being prompted, his behavior should be reinforced. While gaining attention may not be the primary function, verbal praise may suffice to reinforce Jacob's compliance with returning to the task. Another possible reinforcer may be a visual reminder that his on-task behavior is being recognized and counting toward his next break. For instance, starting a timer as soon as he returns to the task may help him to realize how soon he can earn his next break. Another caution to consider with giving breaks is that they may turn what could be a half hour assignment into a 45 minute or one hour assignment. Total time on task is not the only thing to consider as the amount of time that elapses from the start to the end of an assignment could result in the total activity feeling more aversive. During treatment evaluation these details can be observed by the parents and discussed with the consultant on follow up sessions.

MULTICULTURAL COUNSELING CONSIDERATIONS

SBFC professionals may recognize that Behavioral Consultation and the treatment plans that result when done well have significant support in the literature but may at times seem quite prescriptive. During treatment implementation and treatment evaluation the SBFC professional should consider cultural issues that could affect treatment integrity. For example, if a child sasses back to the grandparent who refuses to buy him candy when they are shopping at a supermarket, the mother may not ignore his behavior as this may appear to condone such displays of disrespect to elders. So rather than ignore his backtalk or outburst, mother may yell at him or may even slap him. Another possibility is that she gives in right away to avoid the argument in the first place. Consultants shouldn't disregard the importance of displaying respect for elders and accept that tolerating certain behaviors are unacceptable (cussing, threatening). Another consideration is that the details elicited by the Behavioral Consultation involve a scrutiny of behavior that may feel too invasive within certain cultural groups.

Rogers (2000) identifies six cross-cultural consultation competencies, many of which go beyond consultation and apply to all roles of the SBFC professional:

Understanding one's own and others' culture
Developing cross-cultural communication and interpersonal skills
Examining cultural embeddedness of consultation
Using qualitative methodologies
Acquiring culture-specific knowledge
Knowledge and skill in use of interpreters

Sheridan (2000) notes that although Behavioral Consultation (BC) and Conjoint Behavioral Consultation (CBC) have significant support in the literature for their effectiveness in addressing challenging behaviors, little research has been done on their applications in multicultural settings. Sheridan points out that the structural elements of BC and CBC are often the focus of research but that consultation itself is relational in nature and this is an area that needs further study among Behavioral Consultants. We have partially addressed this through the use of Process Consultation along with BC, but the effectiveness of this proposed framework is yet to be investigated. Nonetheless, even within the structural features of BC, consultants can address cultural values and issues to through improved relational skills and better awareness of how problems are identified, analyzed, and treated from different cultural viewpoints (Holcomb-McCoy, 2009). Sheridan, Eagle, & Doll (2006) found that over an eight year study of graduate students in school psychology training programs, CBC was perceived to be effective whether in settings with or without diversity. They looked at behavioral change, goal attainment, acceptability, and reported satisfaction with the elements of CBC.

Generally speaking, BC is typically based on single-case research design; thus it offers excellent opportunity for addressing the specific cultural aspects of the problem in the setting in which it occurs. The difficulty arises when consultants either fail to recognize cultural variables or when the behavior occurs across settings such as at home and in the classroom.

CHALLENGES AND SOLUTIONS

From our experience working with graduate students in SBFC at California State University, Los Angeles, we find that one challenge in preparing them to conduct BC is that it tends to be inconsistent with their general skill repertoire when conducting family counseling. Our SBFC graduate students will often hold less value for an approach that limits focus to measureable tightly operationalized behaviors than they do for methods that invite consideration of thoughts and feelings of the client. There is a tendency to believe that behavior analysts are too sterile in their approach to the presenting problem because there is a greater emphasis on structure than on relationships during the problem-solving process. Some behavioral consultants may come across as too dogmatic or pay minimal attention to building relationships in the consultation process and the criticism is often deserved. Many have complained about the high level of jargon that behaviorists use in working with non-behavioral clients, consultees, and colleagues. However, BC has strength in its evidence of effective outcomes and goal attainment leaving no doubt that the approach is quite effective at reducing unwanted behaviors and increasing desired behaviors. We find that one way to improve BC is to align it with Process Consultation (PC) and have provided this as a way to address the shortcomings of a BC approach, especially as applied by SBFC professionals.

As indicated in the previous section, BC can be applied in multicultural settings but very little research has been done in this area. We hope to address this as we study the effectiveness of our PC/BC framework. Integrating these two models holds promise for modeling problem-solving for the consultee in a manner that will promote better skill development and improved functioning in face of current and future problems.

SUMMARY

School-Based Family Counselors are in a good position to engage parents in consultation that allows them to implement their own treatment plans. With practice and experience, SBFCs can learn to differentiate their direct intervention skills such as family counseling from their indirect intervention skills such as in consultation. We know we may have complicated this chapter by not only introducing the SBFC professional to Behavioral Consultation but also Process Consultation. We encourage the use of Process Consultation with any model of consultation including Mental Health Consultation and Adlerian Consultation. It allows the consultant to more fully involve the consultee in problem solving through active inquiry. Consultees first present the problem from their own perspectives, and that helps to improve cultural awareness in the consultant. It also makes it more palatable for the consultee to discuss solutions as they are not simply being "prescribed" by the expert. The case of Jacob will be presented again in Chapter 12 How to do Teacher Consultation: A Behavioral Approach. Jacob's case will be discussed from the teacher's perspective using the same format of PC/BC integration of consultation models.

REFERENCES

Ashbaugh, R., & Pecks, S. M. (1998). Treatment of sleep problems in a toddler: A replication of the faded bedtime with response cost protocol. *Journal of Applied Behavior Analysis*, 31, 127-129.

Caplan, G. &Caplan R.B. (1998).*Mental health consultation and collaboration*. San Francisco, CA: Jossey Bass.

Gortmaker, V. J., Daly III, E. J., McCurdy, M., Persampieri, M. J., & Hergenrader, M. (2007). Improving reading outcomes for children with learning disabilities: Using brief experimental analysis to develop parent-tutoring interventions. *Journal of Applied Behavior Analysis*, 42, 659-664.

Guli, L.A. (2005). Evidence-based parent consultation with school-related outcomes. *School Psychology Quarterly*, 20(4), 455-472.

Holcomb-McCoy, C. (2009). Cultural considerations in parent consultation. *Professional Counseling Digest* (ACAPCD-25). Alexandria, VA: American Counseling Association.

Ingraham, C. L. (2000). Consultation through a multicultural lens: Multicultural and cross-cultural consultation in schools. *School Psychology Review*, 29(3), 320–343.

Kampwirth, T.J. & Powers, K.M. (2012).*Collaborative consultation in the schools: Effective practices for students with learning and behavior problems* (4th ed.). Boston, MA: Pearson.

Kratochwill, T. R., & Bergan, J. R. (1990).*Behavioral consultation in applied settings: An individual guide*. New York, NY: Plenum.

Lafasakis, M., & Sturmey, P. (2007). Training parent implementation of discrete-trial teaching: effects on generalization of parent teaching and child correct responding. *Journal of Applied Behavior Analysis*, 40, 685-689.

Mayer, G.R., Sulzer-Azaroff, B., & Wallace, M.D. (2012).*Behavior analysis for lasting change* (2^{nd}ed.). Cornwall-on-Hudson, NY: Sloane.

Mueller, M. M., Piazza, C. C., Moore, J. W., Kelley, M. E., Bethke, S. A., Pruett, A. E., Oberdorff, A. J., &

Layer, S. A. (2003).Training parents to implement pediatric feeding protocols. *Journal of Applied Behavior Analysis*, 36, 545-562.

Reagon, K. A., & Higbee, T. S. (2009). Parent-implemented script fading to promote play-based verbal initiations in children with autism. *Journal of Applied Behavior Analysis*, 42, 659-664.

Rogers, M. (2000).Examining the cultural context of consultation. *School Psychology Review*, 29(3), 414-418.

Rotto, P. C., & Kratochwill, T. R. (1994). Behavioral consultation with parents: Using competency-based training to modify child noncompliance. *School Psychology Review*, 23(4), 669-693.

Schein, E. (1999). *Process consultation revisited: Building the helping relationship*. Reading, MA: Addison-Wesley.

Sheridan, S.M. (2000). Considerations of multiculturalism and diversity in behavioral consultation with parents and teachers. *School Psychology Review*, 29(3), 344-353.

Sheridan, S.M., Eagle, J.W., & Doll, B. (2006).An examination of the efficacy of conjoint behavioral consultation with diverse clients. *School Psychology Quarterly*, 21(4), 396-417.

Sheridan, S.M. & Elliott, S.N. (1991). Behavioral consultation as a process for linking the assessment and treatment of social skills. *Journal of Educational and Psychological Consultation*, 2(2), 151-173.

Tarver Behring, S., & Ingraham, C. L. (1998). Culture as a central component to consultation: A call to the field. *Journal of Educational and Psychological Consultation*, 9, 57–72.

Wolfe, D. A., Mendes, M. G., & Factor, D. (1984). A parent administered program to reduce children's television viewing. *Journal of Applied Behavior Analysis*, 17, 267-272.

RESOURCES

Center for Effective Collaboration and Practice (http://cecp.air.org/fba/default.asp)
This website offers descriptions of functional behavioral assessments and offers tools and examples that support understanding of its applications.

Intervention Central (http://www.interventioncentral.org/behavioral-intervention-modification)
This site offers many resources for behavior interventions and ready-to-use forms that can be helpful in developing plans.

The Iris Center (http://iris.peabody.vanderbilt.edu/resources.html)
This site offers excellent resources and tutorial in many areas pertaining to students with disabilities including culturally relevant classroom management strategies.

NICHCY National Dissemination Center for Children with Disabilities
(http://nichcy.org/schoolage/behavior/athome)
This site is specifically intended as a resource for parents and provides many articles and resources regarding behavior for children with disabilities that can be applied to all children.

OSEP Technical Assistance Center on Positive Behavior Interventions and Supports
(http://www.pbis.org/)
This site has excellent resources for positive behavioral, school-wide interventions.

PENT Positive Environments, Network of Trainers (http://www.pent.ca.gov/)
This site is offered by the California Department of Education and is filled with useful materials including PowerPoint presentations of various topics relating to behavior.

Chapter 9
How to do Conjoint Family Counseling

Michael Carter

OVERVIEW: *This chapter is about how to implement conjoint family counseling in clinical settings, including the schools. It encompasses: 1) counselor preparation prior to engaging in conjoint family counseling, 2) the basic processes of conjoint family counseling including family evaluation, family feedback with narrative of cultural and historical factors, most important issues and crisis management, treatment plan formulation, implementation of conjoint family counseling, and termination, 3) school-based conjoint family counseling, 4) multicultural factors and 5) evidence-based support.*

BACKGROUND

The following chapter is based on my experiences training beginning graduate students in the art of family therapy at California State University, Los Angeles, a highly diverse university in an urban, economically challenged neighborhood. This graduate training program, a Masters of Science degree in School-Based Family Counseling (SBFC), is described in more detail elsewhere in this book in Chapter 45. The specific training in Family Therapy and SBFC that is the focus of this chapter takes place over the course of an entire academic year and involves 11 weeks of lecture followed by 22 weeks of clinical practice with direct, live supervision and an additional 11 weeks of lecture. This comprises a total of 164 hours of direct lecture, clinical experience and supervision. This chapter is an attempt to encapsulate this extensive level of training into a brief description. It is hoped that this discussion can give the reader an understanding of the basic concepts of family therapy and indications for further training. Understanding and being able to implement family counseling can often help counselors feel less intimidated by new experiences involving interpersonal conflict and can empower them to help others to resolve conflicts in a variety of settings, including the school. At the end of the chapter is a section on specific applications to SBFC.

FAMILY EVALUATION

When I first began to conduct and teach conjoint family counseling, I used Karpel & Strauss' multidimensional model of family evaluation, based on the work of Ivan Boszormenyi-Nagy, to try to make sense of what I was seeing in family therapy (Karpel& Strauss, 1983). Their book, Family Evaluation, although written in 1983, is highly recommended for anyone interested in conjoint family therapy and will be referred to throughout this chapter. Their description of family evaluation and the assessment of the Factual, Individual, Systemic, and Ethical dimensions enabled me organize my interviews and observations of families more cohesively. This led to obtaining information that created a more comprehensive view of family functioning and the determination of the most important issues for the whole family. These issues then became the focus of developing more effective treatment plans with prioritization of specific goals and delineation of the concrete and specific steps necessary to accomplish these.

Skill in family therapy requires knowledge of individual cognitive and emotional development and understanding of what these look like in natural settings from infant to grandparent. It also requires familiarity with the stages of the family life cycle, and normal and abnormal responses to stage transitions for a family from the birth of a child to the aging and death of parents. Family therapy involves the willingness to bring out conflict and the skills to resolve it in ways that help each member develop greater awareness and compassion for each other. These skills enable a counselor to feel prepared to handle a lot of what happens in assisting parents to help their children develop, especially in the emotional and behavioral areas.

This chapter is primarily focused on the process of conducting weekly conjoint family counseling over the course of a five-month period. Conjoint family counseling in schools, however, is a much more condensed process because you need to help the family change quickly to reduce anxiety so that children can become available for learning. This is especially important at the elementary and middle school level where the family has the most influence over a child's daily life. The end of every school year provides a clear and concrete evaluation of your work because of the academic, emotional, and behavioral benchmarks for student development. And kids don't learn if they don't find a way to manage their emotions effectively and to follow directions. Schools are responsible for dealing directly with behavior at school and the emotions underlying them, but families must be the main protagonists in teaching appropriate behavioral and emotional self-control. Families have to be the main teachers of these critical skills, but schools can help empower parents to be more effective by providing school-specific parent training and targeted intervention for school-related problems.

The role of the school should be to alert the family about problems in child development, provide brief intervention targeted towards school behavior, and to refer families to agencies that actively promote the connection between family mental health and child success in school. This can be very difficult because many parents and school personnel still have problems understanding the importance of this connection. This makes the skills of conjoint family therapy even more critical to implementing effective school interventions, because the counselor must be able to quickly facilitate change in adults' perceptions as well as children's. Still, it is important to remember that SBFC has more time-sensitive requirements for change and specific outcomes and a more condensed process to accomplish these. A final consideration is that all effective conjoint family counseling must incorporate a deep understanding of cultural background and individual history, both in families and in schools.

COUNSELOR PREPARATION FOR CONJOINT FAMILY COUNSELING

Before attempting to conduct conjoint family counseling, a counselor must be specifically prepared for the challenges of working with families. This preparation is critical to the overall success of implementing conjoint family counseling. The first level of preparation for the counselor is to understand the importance of unconditional positive regard for each family member. While this is a core requirement for any effective counseling, it is often more challenging when conducting family therapy because of the family archetypes that often cause counter-transference. This counter-transference may involve issues related to the counselor's experience with their own mother and father, and may subconsciously inhibit the counselor's ability to be empathic with a father or mother who is exhibiting difficulty, particularly during conflict.

In individual and group counseling, there is typically less need for confrontation, and counter-transference issues can be dealt with after the session without compromising rapport or the therapeutic process. In family counseling, however, a counselor is sometimes required to interrupt and confront a father or mother when they are engaged in behavior that may cause emotional damage to a child or each other. This type of confrontation is very difficult for counselors who are not aware of their own issues regarding their family, mother or father. This often results in the counselor either overreacting or under-reacting to the situation, which can have disastrous effects on the welfare of a family member or the effectiveness of the intervention.

This unconditional positive regard for each family member is also important because of the fact that many parents and other family members feel very defensive when in the presence of their family. This defensiveness may make it very difficult to interact with these family members because their transference may cause hypersensitivity to negative reactions from the counselor. If the counselor reacts defensively to the client, this puts great pressure on rapport and may result in the client discontinuing counseling.

Family counseling is also very different from individual or group counseling because it typically involves dealing with a high degree of interpersonal conflict and requires a more active and directive approach. At its core, effective family counseling often requires counselors to help a family to address the unresolved conflicts that create so much anxiety for family members, especially children. In fact, when helping families to address domestic violence, an important goal is for the family to interrupt or "shut down" their arguments at home and to resume them under the more controlled setting of the counseling office. Salvador Minuchin, one of the pioneers of family therapy, termed this process "enactment", whereby the counselor attempts to bring family arguments into the counseling session. This allows the counselor to observe typical family interactions, which Minuchin believes reveals the hierarchical structure of the family (Minuchin& Fishman, 1981). In order to benefit from these observations, however, a counselor must remain calm and clearheaded when dealing with these "family disturbance" situations that most police officers dread more than any other call.

How does a counselor remain calm and clearheaded when attempting to manage the most intense interpersonal conflicts of others? The first step is to be very self-aware of the thoughts and feelings that one has about one's own family of origin, especially when growing up. When implementing family counseling, these unconscious thoughts and feelings about our own past often reduce the counselor's ability to remain objective and empathic when interacting with families.

One exercise that can assist a counselor to become more aware of their own family issues involves conducting a family evaluation of one's own family of origin (mother, father, siblings and any extended members of the family who live in the home)(see Box 9.1).

Box 9.1 The Family Evaluation Paper

The family evaluation paper is a comprehensive, <u>objective</u> study of your own family of origin (i.e., the family consisting of you, your siblings, your parents, and grandparents.) Focus on a time in your family's history when a problem clearly existed and that you clearly remember. Imagine that the family sought counseling to address this problem and that <u>you</u> are the family counselor that they have chosen. Your task is to write a comprehensive and objective evaluation of the family <u>from the perspective of the family counselor</u>. You must include the following:

a. Construct a genogram of your family at the time of the crisis including your grandparents, your parents' generation and your own generation; include the year that this is happening and the Identified Patient (See page 79 & 80 in Karpel& Strauss).

b. Describe the presenting problem <u>and</u> identify the stage(s) in the developmental life cycle (Karpel& Strauss-Ch. 2) that your family was in when the problem occurred. If more than one stage, which is most important and why.

c. Analyze and describe the family's current structure and dynamics (i.e. <u>Factual</u>, <u>Individual</u>, <u>Systemic</u>, and <u>Ethical</u> dimensions) with respect to the presenting problem, cultural and historical factors, and any other issues that you may have identified.

d. Describe the <u>most important issues</u> for the family <u>as you see them</u>, including how the presenting problem fits in (e.g., separation anxiety resulting from Father-Child symbiosis).

Once an understanding of the basic concepts of family evaluation has been gained, students are asked to conduct a written evaluation of their own family of origin. They are asked to recall a time when they were growing up when their family experienced a crisis and to imagine that their family actually sought out family counseling. They are asked to use a family crisis that occurred when the student was at least 10 years old so that they are able to recall the basic facts of the situation. The students are then required to write a family evaluation through the eyes of the fictional family therapist that their family would work with. This evaluation must be objectively written and the student is discussed in the third person as just another member of the family.

Students report that, while this paper requires no library work, citations or footnotes, it is often the most difficult paper that they have ever written. This is because it requires the student to truly explore each family member's unique position and point of view as well as the interactive dynamics of their family of origin. When conducted in a genuine fashion with a truthful attempt to remain objective, this exercise can enable the student to gain a deeper understanding of the past and current issues regarding their family of origin. This awareness can then serve as a critical reference point when working with families and counter-transference.

BASIC PROCESSES OF CONJOINT FAMILY COUNSELING

THE FIRST TELEPHONE CONTACT

Conjoint family therapy begins with the first telephone contact with the client. As with most counseling strategies, the establishment of rapport is the first most critical process. This begins by clearly communicating to the client the need for the whole family to be involved in order to assist the family member who may be the primary reason for why the family is seeking help. It is important to remember that many parents do not truly understand what counseling is about and may feel very defensive about a request for their child or themselves to be involved in therapy. They may have learned from their own culture or family that counseling is only for "crazy people" or that personal information should never be shared outside of the family. In these cases, it is critical to explain to the parents that this type of counseling is part of the educational process that helps children learn. For example,

> *"One of the most important parts of the learning process is the ability to pay close attention to verbal or written instructions. Whenever we are feeling strong emotions such as anxiety or frustration, it is difficult to maintain our attention on academic information. This often results in classroom behavior problems such as inattention to the teacher, not following directions, "daydreaming", or fidgeting. Counseling with the child and the family can help to address these emotions so that they do not interfere with the child's availability for learning and developing social relationships."*

In many cases involving referral for school-related problems, parents may feel that only the child needs to be involved in counseling. Helping parents to understand why their involvement is required is an important first step in establishing rapport. Some parents may ask:" if my child is having the problem why do I need to be involved." Great care should be taken in answering this question because parents may become defensive if it is implied that they need to be involved in counseling because they are the source of the problem. This is a natural phenomenon that has been labeled the" source-solution attribution" (Compas, Adelman, Freundl, Nelson, & Taylor, 1982). In a few words, a "source- solution attribution" occurs when parents assume that if the *solution* to a problem is their involvement, then the *source* of the problem must be themselves. It is important to interrupt this attribution by explaining to the parents that:

"While there may be many things that cause children difficulty, parents have a unique relationship with a child that puts them in the best position to be a part of helping to solve the child's problems."

Most parents readily accept these explanations, which may increase their willingness to be directly involved in conjoint family counseling. If not, it is important for the counselor to continue to push for full involvement by the family. As Carl Whitaker would say, this "battle for structure" must be won by the therapist(Whitaker & Keith, 1981). This is a critical aspect of effective conjoint family counseling. Once a commitment has been gained for the entire family to attend counseling, especially those that live in the home, the first session is then scheduled.

THE FIRST SESSION

The first session with the family is the most important because it sets the stage for all the sessions that follow. The most important thing to accomplish in this session is to make a strong connection with the family so that they will return for subsequent sessions. This rapport is more important than anything that is discussed and should always be the utmost priority. Some of the following suggestions will help to establish this connection, but mindfulness about what is happening during the session and sensitivity to how each person feels (especially those that have power in the family) will be most important.

1. Counselor Behaviors to Always be Mindful of:

a) Remember that you are ALWAYS modeling effective communication for the family
        --in how you LISTEN
--in how you ADDRESS each person NONVERBALLY
--in HOW you SPEAK to each person

b) Remember that you will also:
        --serve as an advocate, especially for children
        --be able to provide information and explore personal and community resources
        --assist the family in looking at what might come up in the   future.

2. Establishing Rapport:

a) Introductions:

i) *"Hello, my name is* _____ *. "*
Ask each person in the family: what their name is, where they work or go to school, and what they like to do for fun._Remember, you're establishing connections with each person--be warm and speak with each member in a manner appropriate to their developmental level. Also find out the names of any immediate family members not present.

ii) Thank them for coming:

> *"We know it's not easy to get here. Your being here today tells us that you must care*
> *a lot about yourself and your family."*

b) Discuss your view of what family counseling is about:

"As we begin, we wanted to tell you a little bit about what we hope this experience will be like. First, we know that every family has strengths and challenges. We want to learn more about the strengths in your family and how you can use these to work on the challenges that are facing your family right now and in the future. So, we see this as a learning process that improves communication between family members so that you all know where you stand with each other and how best to help each other. We also want to focus on how your family can help each person to be as successful as possible in school, work, and with friends."

Ask the family what they think of this:

"How does this sound to you?"

3. Expectations and Ground Rules:

a) Commitment to each other--

"We're all going to work together as a group to make this happen and we want to make the most of the time that we have available. We'll be here each week and we hope that you'll be able to be here each week as well. It's important to meet as <u>consistently</u> as possible so that you'll get the most out of this experience. We know that emergencies come up, but be sure to <u>call</u> as soon as possible if you can't be here so that we'll know that you're okay. Before you leave today, we'll give you our card with the phone number and appointment time."

b) Overview of counseling process:

"The first thing we need to do is to learn more about the strengths of the family and about the problems that you are going through right now. In order to do this, we'll talk with the whole family for little while, then we'll talk with the parents and the kids separately. We may also want to contact the school to develop a partnership with them to help your children be more successful. Then, as we learn more about what's going on, we'll work together to come up with some strategies to help make things better. Some ideas will help and some may not, but we'll keep working together to find out what works the best."

c) Communication and Confidentiality

<u>The importance of the family's openness about what's going on in their lives and what they think and feel about this:</u>

"One of the most important things that we'll work on is communication. A lot of problems are caused by misunderstandings between people about what's going on. In order to improve your ability to communicate with each other, we hope that you can all be as open as possible with us about:
What's going on in your lives and how you feel about things, and

What you think of what we say. We will have ideas and suggestions about what's going on and what might make things better, but we need to be sure that these fit with your ideas of what is best for your family. If you ever disagree, please let us know as soon as possible so that we can resolve any misunderstandings or differences."

Freedom for everyone to be open during sessions without fear of punishment:

"Another thing that will help make this experience more valuable is if everyone can speak freely without worrying about getting in trouble for what they say during the sessions here. We'd like to ask the parents' permission that no one will get in trouble for what is said here. There are a lot of thoughts and feelings that we all have and we can't help straighten things out unless everyone feels free to talk about things without worrying about getting in trouble. Is this okay with both parents?"

(REMEMBER to remind everyone of this promise at the end of this session and any future session involving conflict.)

Safety and protection of everyone:

"We're also responsible for dealing with issues of safety. What we talk about in here is confidential and won't be shared with anyone else unless there is a need to protect you or others. If we feel that someone might hurt themselves or someone else, we need to do whatever is necessary to make sure that that doesn't happen. If something like this comes up, we'll talk about it and work out a way to make sure that everyone is safe. Any questions?"

4. Exploration of the Presenting Problem:

a) The Presenting Problem:

"The first thing we'll talk about is what brings you here today. We want to find out what each of you thinks the family is here for?"

Explain that it is normal for each family member to have different views of what the family needs to work on. In general, start by asking the youngest member of the family what they think their family is here for and move up, finishing with the father or mother. This allows the children to have some input before the parents give more detailed descriptions. As the family talks, be sure to explore EACH person's perspective and SUMMARIZE what they say and how they feel. (As soon as you start to feel "overloaded" by the amount of information, it's time to summarize—e.g., *"Let me make sure that I understand what you're saying. You feel that ...."*). Then, check with that person to make sure that your perceptions are accurate. As you listen, think about how the problem may be related to normal stresses that occur during each of the Family Life Cycles that the family may be in at this time.

b) Reframing

A major component of the counselors' work during this family discussion is the reframing of what family members say about a problem into more positive words. It's often helpful to summarize what the family says in a way that frames the problem in terms of:

GOALS -what they want to have happen and

OBSTACLES - what <u>gets in the way</u> of reaching this goal.

For example, when someone says, *"Jimmy's teacher's a jerk, she doesn't care about anyone but herself!"*, a possible reframe might be: *"So you want Jimmy to do better in school, but you feel that the teacher doesn't care about him."*
Or, *"my husband wants me to be all lovey-dovey, but when it's time for the kids to do homework, he just sits around on his butt."* A possible reframe might be: *"So you think that your husband wants to be closer to you, but it's hard for you because you get angry when he won't help you with the kids."*

c) Interrupting:

You may have to interrupt some family members if they jump in to answer for others. If this is necessary, explain that you don't want to seem rude in interrupting, but that you need to hear EACH member's viewpoint so that you can help the <u>whole</u> family. It's also important for the family to help each family member to learn to express their own views.)

      If family members interrupt and disagree with each other, reiterate that it's natural for every person to have their own viewpoint and that each person will get a chance to give their view.

      If the parents start to discuss marital issues or other issues that violate healthy subsystem boundaries, then immediately interrupt them with a brief explanation of the types of issues that are best discussed together as a family (e.g., expectations of parents and children, family rules & consequences, etc.) and the types of issues that are best talked about in private (issues that the parents have with each other, or issues that the parents have with a child that might embarrass the child if discussed with siblings, etc.). Then ask the parents to save that discussion for   later when you will talk with them separately from the kids.

5. Choosing an Assessment Plan Depending Upon the Type of Presenting Problem:

There are typically three main types of presenting problems and a specific assessment plan is used to address each type.

   a) If the <u>Presenting Problem</u> concerns a problem that a child is experiencing at school, then begin the assessment with the SBFC Interview Procedure (Carter & Evans, 2008). This procedure involves interviewing the parents, children, and teacher with a focus on learning more about strengths, challenges, and what has been tried to address these challenges. Following this process, you will also complete the Family Evaluation Interview Procedure.

   b) If the <u>Presenting Problem</u> concerns a child or the family, but does <u>not</u> occur at school, then begin the assessment with the Family Evaluation Interview Procedure. This procedure involves interviewing the parents and children to learn more about individual strengths, challenges, and what each person thinks about what is going on in the family.

   c) If the <u>Presenting Problem</u> primarily concerns the relationship between the couple, then begin the assessment by interviewing the couple together and separately.

During the initial stages of counseling, it is often important to separate the parents and children at some point in order to better assess their individual viewpoints. This may be necessary during the first session, if parents start to discuss marital issues or individual issues come up that might cause anxiety to the children, or it may be done in subsequent sessions. When separating family members, remind them that this is a normal part of the evaluation process that will help you to more fully understand the family. Let them know that this information will not be shared with the family without the individual's permission unless someone's safety is at risk. Assure them that if something comes up during these discussions that needs to be addressed with the family, you'll find a way to include it in your work with the family without losing the trust of family members.

When working separately with the parents or couple, use the ADULT INTERVIEW FORM (See Box 9.2), and include the following:

-their viewpoint of the history of the problem and the family
-anything that they think that you need to know in order to help the family
-their viewpoint of how well the parents operate together as a team
-the general level of marital satisfaction

When working separately with the children, use the CHILD INTERVIEW FORM (See Box 9.3)

6. Summarizing the First Session:

It is unlikely that you will be able to complete the Assessment in the first session, but it is very important to save time to SUMMARIZE what has happened in the first session. After each person has given their view, tell the family that the plan is to address each of the problems that they have talked about, but that we'll have to work on one at a time in order to make progress so that everyone will feel better.

As you summarize what the family has done to deal with the problem remember to:

a) Acknowledge and praise the family for their effort in trying to make things better, even if it didn't seem to solve the problem. Remind them that if they continue to try, things will get better.

b) Assure the family that, while it will take time for things to get better, today is a great start because everyone knows more about the situation and we can now start to help the family to work together to improve the situation a little each day.

c) "Shut-down, Write-down"

Explain to the family the importance of trying to save their arguments for when they meet with the family counselor. Watching them argue will enable the counselor to learn about how they communicate their disagreements and resolve their differences. This will then help the counselor to work with the family to develop better ways of communicating and solving problems.

"So, if you start to get into any arguments while discussing anything that happened today and anyone starts to feel bad, then stop the discussion and help each person to write down what the argument was about. At the next family session, these arguments will be explored to see if they can be used to help the family learn how to communicate better and to resolve conflicts with fewer hurt feelings.

Box 9.2 **ADULT INTERVIEW FORM**

Their names (what they liked to be called):

Name   Age

_____   _____

_____   _____

How is their health?_____

Date of Last Physical Exam: _____Name of Doctor:_____

Any friends, any best friends?: _____

Current Employment <u>outside</u> the home?: _____

Previous employment: _____

Highest Level of Education: _____

Where did they go to school?_____

Best thing about work whether in or out of the home:_____

Worst thing about work : _____

Things they're good at (anything): _____

_____

Things they're <u>not</u> so good at: _____

Three wishes: 1)_____/_____

2) _____/_____

3) _____/_____

What would they change if they could change one thing in the <u>whole world</u>?:

_____

What would they change if they could change one thing in their family?:

_____ __

Box 9.2 con't

Explore their own relationships with family (What is the best/worst thing about) :

Father-Best,_____ Worst:_____

Mother-Best,_____ Worst:_____

Spouse-Best,_____Worst:_____

Oldest child-Best,_____ Worst:_____

 Father-Best,_____ Worst:_____

Next oldest child-Best_____ Worst:_____

Next oldest child-Best,_____Worst:_____

Next oldest child-Best,_____Worst:_____

How do you and your spouse get along? _____

What happens when your children don't do what You say? _____

What happens when your children don't do what the other parent says?_____

What happens when your child hits someone or destroy something?_____

What makes you feel happy? _____

What makes you feel bad? _____

What makes you sad? _____

What makes you mad? _____

What is the most fun thing about your family? _____

Is there anything else you think I need to know about your family? _____

Any questions for me? _____

 Is there anything you've said that you don't want me to share with your spouse or children? If so, circle those answers and indicate whether it's with the spouse or children or both.

Box 9.3 **CHILD INTERVIEW FORM**

Their name (what they liked to be called) _____

Age (do they know their birthday?) _____

Name of their school: _____

What Grade: _____

Name of Teacher(s): _____

_____

Best thing about school: _____

Worst thing about school: _____

Who are their friends?_____

Are any of them a best friend?_____

What things are they good at? (anything?): _____

_____

What things they're not so good at:? _____

_____

Three wishes: 1)_____/_____

2) _____/_____

3) _____/_____

What would they change if they could change one thing in the whole world?:

_____

What would they change if they could change one thing in their family?:

_____

Box 9.3 con't

Explore their own relationships within the family "What's the best thing about _____?:

Father-Best, _____

     Worst, _____

Mother- Best, _____

     Worst, _____

Sibling (Brother or sister)Best _____

     Worst _____

Other Sibling:Best_____

     Worst _____

How do mom and dad get along? _____

What happens when you don't do what MOM says? _____

What happens when you don't do what DAD says? _____

What happens when you hit someone or destroy something?_____

What makes you feel happy? _____

What makes you feel bad? _____

What makes you sad? _____

What makes you mad? _____

What is the most fun thing about your family? _____

Is there anything else you think I need to know about your family? _____

_____

Any questions for me? _____

 Is there anything you've said that you <u>don't </u>want me to share with your parents?
If so, circle those answers and indicate whether it's with the parents or children or both.

GET the <u>CONSENT FOR COUNSELING</u> FORM SIGNED AND, IF NECESSARY, GET <u>CONSENT TO RELEASE INFORMATION</u> FORM SIGNED.

Remind the family of next week's session date and time and then say good-bye.

COMPLETING THE FAMILY EVALUATION

The initial session begins the process of family evaluation. After seeing the family for the first time, the counselor needs to determine the Presenting Problem and which stages of the Family Life Cycle the family is currently involved with.

1) The Presenting Problem and Stages of the Family Life Cycle:

Another aspect of the family evaluation is the determination of the Presenting Problem. The Presenting Problem is the prevailing view of family members as to what is the main reason why the family is seeking therapy. This viewpoint typically encompasses the parents' perception of who is primarily responsible for the family's difficulties, but may also be influenced by children and extended family members. As the counselor listens to the family, it is useful to think about how the problem may be related to normal stresses that occur during each of the Family Life Cycles that the family may be in at this time.

As you summarize what the family has done to deal with the presenting problem, remember to:

A) <u>Acknowledge</u> and <u>praise</u> the family <u>for their effort</u> in trying to make things better, even if it didn't seem to solve the problem. Remind them that if they <u>continue to try</u>, things will get better.

B) Assure the family that, while it will take time for things to get better, today is a great start because everyone knows more about the situation and we can now start to help the family to work together to improve the situation a little each day.

In addition to the Presenting Problem, the counselor must determine which phase or phases of the family life cycle (described in Karpel and Strauss) the family is currently involved with. Briefly, these family life cycle stages include: Marriage, Birth of A Child, Individuation of a Child, Individuation of Adolescents, Departure of Children, and Aging and Death of Parents. These family life cycle stages are important because they reflect significant stages of individual development and their impact on family structure and functioning. It is often common for families to experience difficulties during transitions between one stage to another.

2. The Four Dimensional Analysis:

As described in Karpel and Strauss's <u>Family Evaluation</u>, the family evaluation involves four specific dimensions of focus: Factual, Individual, Systemic, and Ethical. Information about these four dimensions of the family is gathered through individual and group interviews with members of the family and through direct observations of the family interacting with each other. Completing the family evaluation regarding these four dimensions is an ongoing process that requires frequent revisions as more information is revealed by the family through the course of therapy. In Box 9.4 is a brief summarization of Karpel and Strauss's four dimensions and some examples of additional questions to obtain information concerning these from the family.

The Factual Dimension:

The Factual Dimension includes all of the facts regarding the family, both current and past. The process of obtaining information for the Factual dimension typically begins with an interview with the parents where a genogram is constructed and information regarding family history and current facts is obtained(please see McGoldrick&Gerson, 1988).The focus of the Factual dimension is to ascertain the specific facts of the family versus individual viewpoints. This distinction is critical in order to obtain an objective viewpoint of the family's current and past situation. Areas of focus include: information about each family member (name, age, date of birth, developmental milestones and current health, educational and employment history, current job or educational placement and level of functioning); information regarding dates of marriages, separation, divorce, illness and death of family members; and other pertinent facts.

The Individual Dimension:

Information about the Individual Dimension is typically gathered through individual interviews with each family member. These interviews are intended to obtain information about the respondent's viewpoints of their own life and other family members. In addition to the "circle of life" described above, it is often helpful to use a structured interview format for these interviews (See Child and Adult interview forms Appendix A & B).

At the beginning of each individual interview, it is important for the counselor to help the respondent understand the nature of the interview and their role in it. When interviewing children, the following may help in this regard:

> "I'm going to ask you some questions about you and your family. There are no wrong or right answers to these questions, but what's important is that you try to be honest about what you think and feel. What we talk about will be confidential, except if something comes up that might involve someone getting hurt. If that happens, we will talk about it so that no one will get hurt. I want to remember what you say, so I will be writing down your answers. Do you have any questions?"

As the interview questions are being asked, there are often opportunities to go beyond the respondent's immediate answer to survey deeper aspects of the issues relating to the question. The respondent may be open to this exploration, but the counselor must be mindful about the level of rapport and not push the respondent so early in the evaluation process.
After the respondent answers al lof the questions, the counselor then says:

> "Now that you are finished, is there anything that you have talked about that you do not want me to share with your parents? If so, I will circle those answers and I will not share them with your parents or others. Okay?"

When interviewing the parents, it is often good to include an individual interview with each of them at some point in the evaluation. Before these individual interviews with the parents occur, it is best to discuss how this information will be used. For example,

"We're now going to have a chance to interview each of you separately. This is important in order to obtain each of your individual viewpoints about things that you may not feel comfortable discussing in front of each other. I will not share this information with the other parent unless I feel that it is important and only after I have obtained your permission to share it. The only exception to this, again, is if something is said that requires action to protect someone's welfare. Do you have any questions?"

In addition to the content obtained from the "Circle of Life" Adult and Child interview forms, the counselor should explore the respondent's view of the Presenting Problem.

The Systemic Dimension:

The Systemic Dimension involves how the family interacts with each other. This dimension is primarily based on the Structural Family Therapy of Salvador Minuchin. Minuchin proposed that family structure is reflected in the Spousal, Parental, and Sibling Subsystems and in the interactions both within and across these subsystems. Information about the functioning and boundaries around each of these subsystems is obtained through individual interviews and through observations of family interactions.

Exploring the Spousal Subsystem:

The Spousal subsystem typically involves one or both of the parents or their significant others. The functions of this subsystem include the process of how each partner gets their needs met through interactions with the other. In learning about this subsystem, whether partners are married or not, it is often helpful to explore what are termed," the Four Tasks of Marriage." These include: Division of Labor, Finances, Issues Regarding Children, and Boundaries Around Friends and Family. Division of Labor involves how each partner feels about how equally the work of the family is divided. The following questions may be useful:

Division of Labor:
"If you take all of the work that you and your partner do both inside and outside of the home, how fairly do you feel that is divided?"

Finances:
"How equally are you and your partner involved in the family's finances? Do you each know how and in what way all of the family's money is earned and spent? How involved are both of you in decisions about these issues? Do you feel that you have an equal say in the family's finances?"

Boundaries Around Family and Friends:
"How well do you and your partner agree on the nature of the boundaries around your immediate family (i.e., the parents and children)? This includes physical boundaries such as who has the keys to the family's home or whether guests are expected to call before visiting; as well as interpersonal boundaries such as who is privy to personal information about what is going on inside the family."

Issues Regarding Children:

> *"How equally are you and the other parent involved in issues regarding your children? Do you make decisions on your own or after mutual agreement? How equally are the parental roles of nurturing and disciplining shared between parents?"*

In addition to the above issues, the spousal subsystem functions also include romance, sexual intimacy, and companionship.

In the past, the functions of the Spousal subsystem have been part of marital relationships. Increasingly, however, these functions are more often being satisfied outside of traditional marriages and exploration of this subsystem must incorporate these differences. When a family involves parents who are unmarried, separated or divorced, these functions may be satisfied by another adult without necessarily compromising family functioning. When this does not occur, however, there is an increased possibility that children will be allowed into the Spousal subsystem, often with disastrous consequences to the child's emotional and social development and the functioning of the whole family. In cases such as these, it is critically important for the counselor to help the single parent to identify more constructive ways of meeting spousal subsystem needs in order to safeguard their children.

Exploring the Parental Subsystem:

The Parental subsystem traditionally has been made up of both biological parents of the children. Today, however, the parental subsystem may contain many different constellations of persons. While it is often still important to include the biological parents of each child in the evaluation, it is often just as important to interview those persons primarily responsible for parenting functions. These may include extended family members such as grandparents, aunts, uncles, or cousins; close friends of one or both of the parents; and foster care or adoptive parents. Accordingly, it is important to ascertain from the parents who is typically involved in the parenting of their children, which may even include older children, and obtain the parents' written consent to contact and interview these persons if necessary.

When exploring the functioning of the parental subsystem, it is often helpful to begin by inquiring about the following aspects of each child's history:

-The circumstances surrounding the child's birth, especially any traumatic event that occurred in the family.
-How well the child reached developmental milestones such as walking, talking, toileting, and the development of social relationships.
-What techniques did the parents use in teaching the child to follow the Three Rules of Kindergarten: 1) Keep your hands and feet to your self, 2) Follow adult directions, and 3) Respect others and their property.

Developmentally, this teaching process should begin when the child is about 2 years old, but some parents begin much earlier. It is important to note that many parents may not be consciously aware of their role in teaching their children how to behave. Most rely upon their own cultural and familial experiences to make decisions regarding how best to deal with their children. Consequently, the discussion of the Three Rules of Kindergarten may cover unfamiliar ground for some parents. Many parents may feel uncomfortable discussing their own discipline techniques that include yelling or spanking. In these cases, it is often helpful to use the following words:

"Research shows that most parents use conscious and unconscious information and personal experience in deciding how to discipline their children. Research also indicates that children learn best when discipline methods are consistent across all environments, especially in school. That's why it's important for us to explore the specific techniques that you have used in the past so that any necessary modifications can be made in the present in order to maximize your child's academic and personal development."

Another aspect to explore in the parental subsystem with preadolescent or adolescent children concerns the "3 high-risk behaviors of adolescence" and the main protective factors to prevent these. Briefly, the 3 high-risk behaviors of adolescence concern; 1) issues regarding substance and alcohol abuse, 2) issues regarding romantic relationships, sexual behavior, and pregnancy, 3) issues related to the negative influence of peers, including involvement in gangs(Fraser, 2004).Parents often become anxious as their children approach adolescence and most parents will share their concern about these high-risk behaviors, which often have great ramifications for the future happiness of their children. Many parents, however, are not aware of the protective factors that can help to prevent significant problems regarding these high-risk behaviors

The three main protective factors to prevent negative experiences with these issues are: 1) a strong relationship with a parent or significant adult where the adolescent is able to talk about mistakes and sensitive topics, 2) when the adolescent is particularly adept in a meaningful skill such as a sport, artistic skill, or academics, and 3) when the adolescent has very close friends who are a positive influence(Fraser, 2004).For many children, the latter two protective factors are very difficult to achieve, especially during adolescence. Therefore, the main protective factor to focus upon for most parents is the nature of their relationship with their adolescent. This protective factor is maximized when children and their parents have a good relationship with clear and effective communication and a willingness to discuss mistakes constructively. An important factor in family evaluation is the exploration of these parent-child relationships.

Exploring the Sibling Subsystem:

The Sibling subsystem is usually made up of the children in the family. In today's families, this often includes stepbrothers and stepsisters, cousins, and other children from the extended families. The sibling subsystem is where children learn the skills necessary to interact effectively with their peers. In families where there is an only child, this learning may be difficult unless the parents arrange consistent interactions with children of the same age. This can be accomplished through ongoing relationships with extended family members or through organizations such as the Girl Scouts, AYSO, and the Boys and Girls Club.

Assessment of this subsystem can be accomplished through interviews with parents and children as well as through direct observation of the children in situations where the parents are not present. At times, the counselor may want to meet separately with the siblings as a group to interview them about how they feel about each other and what they like to do together. Another interesting technique is to have all of the children play a game together in front of the counselor. This often provides a more genuine assessment of the sibling subsystem then relying upon interviews.

Additional Aspects of the Systemic Dimension:

In addition to the assessment of subsystem functioning, other areas of the Systemic Dimension need to be explored. These include the existence of any alliances or coalitions within the family; issues related to power, communication, and roles; and the nature of the boundaries around each subsystem and those around the family itself. These are typically assessed through direct observation.

The Ethical Dimension:

The Ethical Dimension includes many areas that may be less apparent than other aspects of family functioning. These include issues related to loss, trust and trustworthiness, loyalty, entitlement and obligation, acknowledgment and claim, realistic accountability, legacy, and the revolving slate of family history. These aspects of families often take more time to ascertain than the other dimensions of Karpel and Strauss, but they often are critical to the long-term healing of a family. These parts of the Ethical dimension are often heavily affected by a family's cultural and historical background. It is important to include a family's unique history in the discussion of cultural background because these experiences can have a profound influence on how the family deals with ethnic and linguistic diversity. The information of the Ethical dimension is typically obtained through family members' narrations of family history and direct discussion of each of these elements with families.

One process used to access information about the family in interviews is to explore the various areas of life experienced both as a family and as an individual. This "circle of life" encompasses current and past functioning in health, work/school, finances, living arrangements, friends, immediate and extended family, personal goals, recreation, and romance. This exploration must honor the subsystem boundaries discussed below so that information sensitive to children will not be shared with them (e.g. financial stressors).

Additional Considerations in the Family Evaluation:

In completing a comprehensive family evaluation, there are additional considerations that need to be included, particularly when dealing with families with experiences of substance abuse, domestic violence, and significant trauma. Discussions of these types of issues are often very difficult for family members due to embarrassment and shame. It is usually best to ask parents direct questions about these issues in individual interviews towards the end of the family evaluation when they may feel more comfortable with the counselor. Specific examples of these types of questions may include:

"Have there been any problems in the family regarding alcohol or drug abuse now or in the past?"

If the parent answers in the affirmative, then specific questions regarding the type of substance, frequency of use, and desired benefit of the use should be asked.

"Have there been any instances during family conflict where family members have gotten physical or yelled at each other."

If the parent answers in the affirmative, then specific questions regarding the dates, the degree of intensity, and the short-term and long-term consequences of these situations should be asked.

"Has anyone in the family experienced significant physical or emotional trauma in the past?"

If the parent answers in the affirmative, then specific information regarding the dates, the nature, degree of intensity, and the short-term and long-term consequences of these traumatic situations should be obtained.

3. Family Feedback regarding the Counselor's Evaluation

After completing the family evaluation, the counselor then meets with the parents first without the children to give feedback regarding the family situation. Before doing so, however, the counselor should organize the information in terms of the strengths and challenges for each individual and the family as a whole. This analysis leads to information about the "Most Important Issues", which will eventually lead to a comprehensive treatment plan for the family. It's usually good to begin this process by asking the parents if they noticed any reaction or changes in their children after they were interviewed. It is also important to begin feedback to the parents by acknowledging the fact that the evaluation has been completed over a relatively short period of time, which may or may not have resulted in misperceptions on the part of the counselor. Following may be a helpful example of how to address this:

"It is important to remember that I have had a relatively short time to experience your family through interviews and direct observation. As I give you feedback, it's important for you to "try on" the information that I present in terms of what seems to fit with your perceptions of the truth and what doesn't. If you have any disagreements with what I say, it's very important for you to stop and tell me about these so that we can understand the truth."

The process of providing feedback to the family continues with a description of individual and family strengths and challenges. One family strength that can always be included is the family's willingness to seek outside assistance in order to be the best family that they can be. In addition, some family strengths may be framed as being related to the positive aspects of parenting. For example,

"Your children appeared to be very open and honest in my interviews with them. To me, this reflects a parental strength in that you have nurtured your children in such a way that they can trust someone whom you trust."

The discussion of individual strengths and challenges often requires skillful reframing on the part of the family counselor. For example, in a case involving an adolescent who is arguing with her parents, the counselor might say:

"One of strengths that I see in your daughter is her ability to clearly communicate the truth as she sees it, even if that makes others uncomfortable. It's important for you to directly acknowledge this strength to her so that you can also help her to learn how to manage it so that it doesn't hurt her relationships with others. How does this fit with what you think?"

After discussing family and individual strengths, the counselor then begins to talk of the challenges for the family. It's usually best to start with family challenges that are related to the stages of the family life cycle, which are also discussed in Karpel and Strauss's book. For example,

"One of the challenges that your family is facing at this time is related to the fact that your oldest child is in the beginning stages of adolescence. As you may know, there are many physical, psychological, and emotional changes that happen to your child and the whole family during this time of explosive development. This often results in more conflict within the family as everyone learns to manage all of the significant changes that are occurring. This stage is critically important to the development of the child's long-term independence and often involves increased anxiety in both the child and parent as the role of the parent moves from "manager" of the adolescent to "consultant" to the adolescent. This anxiety is often related to how everyone feels about the competence of the adolescent in operating more independently of the family in many aspects of life. The most important of these include self-care, self-control and discipline, academics and work, and social relationships with peers and family as well as others. During this stage, most families need to make changes in the way they operate in order to gradually promote more independence and this can be very difficult. That's why this is a great time for your family to be involved in counseling because we can help you to make these changes in the most effective way. How does this sound to you?"

You'll notice that these examples always end with a solicitation from the client regarding what they think about what the counselor has said. This "checking in" with the parents is a critical aspect of feedback. It enables the counselor to check the client's understanding of the feedback and it also expresses to the client the importance of their active reflection of what they think about what the counselor has said. This also establishes the collaborative nature of effective conjoint family counseling that is so crucial to long-term change and success.

4. Narrative About the family's cultural and historical factors and the Presenting Problem

In addition to family strengths and challenges, the counselor provides a narrative regarding the family's cultural and historical factors. This often includes an exploration of the family's specific cultural beliefs and family history and how these may affect individual family members' development and the presenting problem. Continuing with the previous example of the adolescent daughter, the counselor might say:

"It seems that you are having difficulty understanding how your daughter came to be so aggressive in her interactions with you. Mrs. Salazar, you have spoken of your childhood in Mexico where you felt your choices were limited because of the fact that you were a woman and that you came to this country to find a husband who respected women as equals. Since then, you and your husband have encouraged your three daughters to "speak their mind no matter what." Mr. Salazar has also said that he has raised his daughters to "be strong and don't let anyone mess with you." You both also indicate that you were never allowed to disagree openly with your own parents. Due to these factors, it would make sense that, while you want your daughter to express herself, you may also have an expectation that she will do so in a respectful fashion and not argue with you. However, many children in early adolescence, like your daughter, have not yet learned how to modulate the intensity of their voices when speaking about their feelings."

5. The Most important Issues and Current Crises:

Following this narrative discussion, the parents are then presented with the counselor's view of the family's most important issues and current crises, the latter being the initial focus of treatment. The counselor considers all of the information obtained from the family and then prioritizes "The Most Important Issues", including any crises that the family is currently involved with. The Most Important Issues usually are related to the Presenting Problem, although the counselor's view of the Presenting Problem is typically different from the family's because the counselor is objectively considering many more aspects of the family from the dimensional analysis.

      Throughout the evaluation process, the counselor is looking for any crises that need immediate attention before continuing with further treatment. These are typically any situation where someone may get hurt, either physically or emotionally, or basic needs (from the Factual Dimension) such health, food, rent, or other time-sensitive issues and these require the counselor to engage in Crisis Counseling, which typically involves:

1) Identifying the possible harm that may occur and helping the family to understand that immediate action must be taken to <u>prevent harm to anyone</u>.

2) Developing a specific behavioral plan to assist the family in helping each other to cope constructively with the crisis.

3) Assisting the family to recognize what the crisis reveals about their family dynamics and what they can do to prevent further occurrence of the crisis.

      After speaking with the parents, the counselor then gives feedback to the whole family with an emphasis on strengths and family life cycle stressors that normally challenge all families, while safeguarding any information that would increase anxiety.

TREATMENT PLAN

After providing feedback to the family regarding the most important issues and current crises, the counselor then develops and implements a treatment plan specific to these issues. As discussed previously, the counselor first identifies and prioritizes crisis issues according to immediate needs and short and long-term factors (e.g., harm to self or others, domestic violence, child abuse, substance abuse, health, work or school issues, etc.). Crisis counseling typically involves directive problem solving that maximizes the input and participation from all family members. Part of this process is to identify crisis factors that reflect long-standing issues within the family, which must be addressed in order to prevent further occurrence of these crises.

1. The Importance of Clear and Permeable Subsystem Boundaries

While crisis situations are dealt with and reduce in intensity, the counselor also pays attention to improving family structure, communication, and functioning. One of the first steps in restructuring the family typically involves creating more clear and permeable boundaries around each of the family's subsystems in order to improve their functioning. If these boundaries are rigid or diffuse, too little or too much information may be shared in the family. Rigid boundaries often lead to disengagement and alienation whereas diffuse boundaries often lead to family chaos and incompetence.

Rigid boundaries often prevent children from getting to know their parents and may cause children to feel as if their parents are not interested in them. For example, in more traditional families, mothers may be primarily responsible for interacting with and raising children, while fathers may be primarily responsible for providing for the physical resources that the family needs. This sometimes leads to a family dynamic where the father and children primarily communicate through the mother and they may have difficulty in directly interacting with each other. This often creates significant problems as children grow into adolescence and identity formation issues become prevalent. During this time, adolescents usually need access to information from their same-sex parent as well as the other. For example, adolescent daughters usually need to talk to their mothers about the physical and emotional aspects of becoming a woman during this identity formation stage of development. At the same time, daughters usually learn how to deal with men through the modeling and relationship they have with their father, especially during adolescence. When adolescents do not have access to these relationships, sometimes because of rigid boundaries, they often turn to other less credible sources of information and modeling such as other adolescents or media figures.

When a family has loose or diffuse boundaries around its subsystems, children often get access to information about issues that make them anxious but that they have no control over. These types of issues include finances, parental health, child-rearing decisions, and conflict between parents. If boundaries around the spousal subsystem are not firm, children may be triangulated into marital conflict, which often makes the child highly anxious and interferes with their academic and social functioning and development. If children are allowed into the parental subsystem, they may take on parental functions, which may give them too much power in the family and negatively affect the functioning of the sibling subsystem because of this inequity. While it is important for parents to be aware of what is happening with their children, when parents intrude into the sibling subsystem, the opportunity to develop close connections between siblings is often lost. Therefore, boundary-making is often a critical first step of the treatment plan.

It is important to note that many cultures and families may not value these boundaries and may even feel that they are counterproductive to family functioning and survival of the culture. Many of these viewpoints are related to their family or culture's past experiences across the generations, especially when more than two generations lived in one home. When three generations live together, it is likely that the oldest generation will cross subsystem boundaries because of anxiety about the welfare of the younger generation. Grandparents are used to telling their children what to do, so they may interfere with their children's parenting by telling them what to do with the grandchildren, or by "jumping" generations and directly telling the grandchildren what to do. When grandparents tell their own children what to do with the grandchildren, it often interferes with the parent's development of their own competence in parenting. When grandparents directly tell the grandchildren what to do, especially when this is inconsistent with what the parents are saying, the grandchildren may follow the grandparents' directions, but with reduced belief in their own parent's credibility. In past generations when grandparents typically lived with their children until death, this violation of boundaries may have still been sufficient in raising children as long as the grandparent was in the home. When the grandparent dies, or, in modern times when fewer grandparents live with their children, the resulting "vacuum of authority" may result in family chaos due to the lack of competence of the parents. Box 9.5 outlines a procedure for helping parents/guardians to develop a positive approach to discipline with children.

In order to address these issues, it is critically important that the counselor respectfully explore the parents' specific viewpoints regarding subsystem boundaries, particularly what they fear might happen if these are put in place. When the family feels that the counselor understands and respects their cultural and familial values, it is easier for the counselor to gently co-create effective subsystem boundaries that still respect cultural mores. The counselor may ask the parents to bring the grandparent

Box 9.5 <u>POSITIVE BEHAVIOR MANAGEMENT and the OBJECTIVE DISCIPLINE PROCEDURE</u>

Hi Everyone,

Just a reminder that it is critical to be optimistic and positive in your interactions with your kids.

First and foremost, try your best to "catch" your child "being good": whenever he's showing self-control and praise it specifically, no matter how small it may seem. Let her know how mature self-control is and how good it makes you feel about her now and for her future. This will be the most important and consistent ingredient for success.

Whenever she starts to act up, try to first help her to identify what he's feeling, especially what he might be worried about. Acknowledging that she's worried about something and trying to identify what it is will help her feel heard and hopefully calm her enough so that she can communicate to you what she thinks should happen so that she can feel less anxious.

Then, you can try to come up with 2 structured choices that might help, even if one of them is to write down what he wants so that he can talk to both parents or others at a later time about it or wait until I come over for our next appointment.

Also, be very judicious about the behaviors that you focus upon with your child. As we talked about, ignore most of the annoying behaviors (like singing and whistling) and focus on the physical behaviors like going into other's rooms and following directions.

 Only use the Break when she won't follow directions that are necessary for the rest of the family and be sure to give her a prompt ("If you _____, then _____ will happen") to help her know the consequences of her choices and actions. Remind all of your children that we have to all focus on the most important things first.

Remember, we have to focus on the most important behaviors first and "prime the pump" with success in order to create the positive momentum necessary to improve the other behaviors.

Lastly, keep focused on the big picture of your child's improvement, no matter how small.

If a crisis occurs and things seem to be spiraling downward, then suspend the consequences until you can talk to me and we'll figure it out and resume again.

Keep remembering that you have a good, talented and complex family that is improving (although certainly not as fast as we might like it to). Take care,

Michael Carter

OBJECTIVE DISCIPLINE PROCEDURE FOR NONCOMPLIANCE (with grounding)

WHEN: When your child has not obeyed a reasonable request that you have made and it is necessary that she comply.

* Remember, only give a demand when you are prepared to follow it through to the end, whatever the consequences might be!

HOW:

DEMAND---Clearly and simply tell the child what you want him to do.

Example: " _____ (child's name), you need to pick up your clothes and put them in the basket right now."

Silently, count to three (1-2-3)

----If the child obeys the demand, then PRAISE immediately!

*Remember when PRAISING, tell the child what a great job she did, or what a "big kid" she is because of her ability to follow directions. Be sure to SHOW her that you're pleased; words mean nothing without your expressions.

----If the child does not obey the demand, then: PROMPT!

PROMPT: Repeat the initial DEMAND and state the consequences if the child does not obey.

Example: "IF you don't pick up your clothes and put them in the basket right now, then you're going to have a "BREAK."

(NOTE:- Be sure to start the Prompt with the word "IF" and put emphasis on both the specific DEMAND and the consequence for not following directions.)

Silently count to three (1-2-3)

----If the child obeys the prompt, then PRAISE immediately!

----If the child does not obey the prompt, then:

FOLLOW THROUGH WITH NEGATIVE CONSEQUENCES!

FOLLOWING THROUGH WITH NEGATIVE CONSEQUENCES: In as unemotional a manner as possible, follow through with the consequences (e.g., send the child to a BREAK) while making clear to the child why she is getting consequences. Begin by telling the child why she is getting the BREAK and use the word "BECAUSE" first.

Example: "BECAUSE you did not follow directions, you have to go take a BREAK."

Once the child is sitting in the BREAK area, set the timer for five minutes and completely ignore the child for the entire BREAK period, as long as the child does not get up or move the chair or talk loudly or become a danger to self.

IF THE CHILD DOES NOT GO TAKE A BREAK, say: "IF you do not go take a BREAK right now, then you'll have two BREAKS."

If the child does not go to the BREAK, say:

"BECAUSE you have not taken a BREAK, you have two BREAKS. IF you do not go to BREAK right now, then you will be grounded off of everything until you serve the 2 BREAKS plus 30 minutes. You will be grounded starting right now, but your 30 minutes to get off of grounding will not start until after you have served the two BREAKS."

If the child does not go take a BREAK, then begin their grounding immediately, with a reminder of the above. (Note: Remember, the child does not have to sit in the chair during grounding, but has no privileges - electronics, favorite foods, etc.)

When the child goes to take the BREAK, set the timer for one BREAK. When that is finished, say to the child: "That's your first BREAK. But because you did not go take a BREAK, here is your second BREAK."

IF THE CHILD VIOLATES THE BOUNDARIES OF the BREAK (i.e., butt on the chair, the chair doesn't move and no loud talking), then tell the child that the BREAK will start over and RESET the timer.

If the child refuses to return to the BREAK, then say: "IF you do not go and take the BREAK right now, then you will be grounded off of everything until you serve the 2 BREAKs plus 30 minutes. You will be grounded starting right now, but your 30 minutes will not start until after you have served the two BREAKs."

NOTE: Remember that you must not interact with the child while she is in BREAK. You only speak to the child to give directions.

WHEN THE BREAK PERIOD IS OVER, ask the child ONCE: "Why did you have to take a BREAK?"

If they do not answer correctly, then tell the child ONCE why she got a BREAK. (Do not require the child to give the right answer-this will only lead to a power struggle).

Then direct the child:
A)If the situation permits, return the child to the original situation and require him to obey the original DEMAND.
-If the child obeys the demand, then PRAISE immediately!
-If the child does not obey the demand, then PROMPT and FOLLOW THROUGH WITH THE CONSEQUENCES , if necessary, WITHOUT DELAY!
NOTE: Of course, you don't require the child to repeat a negative behavior such as hitting again.

B)If the situation does not permit you to return to the original situation, then repeat to the child the consequences for not following directions.

"Remember, if you don't follow directions (or whatever the demand was), then you are going to have to go to BREAK. If you do not go to BREAK, then you will have two BREAKs."

Then, if the child has earned grounding, set the timer for 30 minutes to finish the grounding. If the child earns another BREAK during this time, then the timer is stopped until they have finished the BREAK and then it is restarted.

*After this whole procedure is finished, write down what happened and the results, and then try to create situations in which the child can earn positive attention for appropriate behavior, especially those that include a lot of interaction with you - IF you're emotionally ready for giving positives.

*Also be sure to create time when you can talk to the child about her choosing to refuse to follow directions (or whatever behavior resulted in the BREAK) and discuss what other choices were available that would not have resulted in negative consequences (e.g., complying with your demand and then talking about it, etc.).

*REMEMBER, CONSISTENCY is the most important factor of this procedure. CONSISTENCY in ALL 3 steps of the OBJECTIVE DISCIPLINE PROCEDURE, and just as importantly, CONSISTENCY in GIVING POSITIVECONSEQUENCES FOR APPROPRIATE BEHAVIOR!

LEVELS OF LEVERAGE (to be used whenever the child refuses to go to or remain in a BREAK).

*Remember to use the Prompt-Consequence statements with IF and BECAUSE at the beginning of each one.

Level 1. CONSEQUENCE: Another BREAK

Level 2. CONSEQUENCE: Immediate grounding off of all privileges (i.e., electronics, games, favorite foods, activities outside the home unless required, etc.) until the child serves the 2 BREAKs PLUS 30 minutes, with the 30 minutes beginning after the two BREAKs are completed.

Level 3. CONSEQUENCE: _____

or grandparents into the next counseling session so that the counselor can interact directly with these important players in the nuclear family system. If the grandparent attends, the counselor should arrange to have an individual interview with the grandparent as soon as possible. In this interview, the counselor has an opportunity to show respect for the grandparent's experience with child rearing while also reinforcing boundaries around subsystems. For example, the counselor may want to acknowledge the hierarchical position and experience of the grandparent in dealing with children and then place the grandparent in the role of "family consultant" who offers advice while still respecting the parenting role of their own children. In other words, the counselor gently refocuses the grandparent on their role in teaching their own children to be more competent in parenting the grandchildren rather than doing it themselves. Facilitating this "teaching" often allows the counselor to revisit past unresolved issues between the grandparent and parent that may have led to the parent's current level of incompetence and increased tension in the home. This also reinforces the importance of hierarchical structure and maintaining boundaries around subsystems while also co-opting the grandparents into an almost "co-therapist" role.

a) Boundary-Making with Families

There are many ways the counselor can help a family create more effective boundaries. From the first session, the counselor often needs to create physical boundaries around subsystems in order to discuss information that should not be shared outside of the subsystem. These physical boundaries (often in a separate room) ensure that these discussions will not be heard or shared with other family members and can also lead to the formation of psychological boundaries that can be enforced when physical boundaries are not possible. For example, when a counselor meets with the parents alone in a separate room, the counselor is modeling the need for boundaries around the spousal and parental subsystems. Then, the counselor can help the parents to understand what information can be shared with the children and what information will need to be discussed only when the parents are alone with each other. While parents usually agree to these boundaries, they often do not understand why boundaries around the sibling subsystem are necessary, so it's important for the counselor to carefully explain the information previously discussed regarding the negative consequences of violating any subsystem boundaries. Parents need to understand that their children will eventually need to learn to deal with and resolve their issues with each other and other peers without parental assistance. This is why the boundaries around the sibling subsystem should only be crossed when the physical and emotional welfare of the children is at stake.

b) Improving the Functioning of Subsystems

While establishing clear and permeable boundaries around the primary subsystems in the family, the counselor also focuses upon strengthening the functioning of each subsystem. This is accomplished by meeting with the members of a subsystem to specifically address each of the areas previously discussed in the family evaluation portion of this chapter. In general, these meetings focus on the following aspects of each subsystem: 1) the relationship history between the members of the subsystem including unresolved issues from the past, 2) current factors that affect the functioning of the subsystem such as communication, time spent with each other, positives and negative feelings, and 3) determining desired areas for improvement for the functioning of that subsystem. Following is a discussion of issues within each subsystem that are typically considered by the family counselor.

In a Spousal subsystem with two participants, the family counselor typically addresses functional issues such as the " 4 tasks of marriage", and individual preferences regarding more emotional issues such as expectations for romance, affection and sexual relationship (Burr, 1970). If the client is a single parent, then it is important to address how the spousal needs of the parent can be met without involving the children. For example,

"I know that you are a single parent whose divorce has just been finalized. I know that you have been primarily focused upon your children's needs, but it's also important to find a way to meet your own needs as an adult. These might include companionship, physical needs and emotional support to name a few. This is an important task to accomplish so that your children can be free to develop normally without worrying about taking care of you. You've talked of the friends that you had before you were married and how you haven't spent much time with them since then. Perhaps now is a good time to contact them so that you can reconnect and renew your relationships with them."

The Parental subsystem is often a major focus of treatment in conjoint family therapy. This is because the majority of family functions related to children are executed by members of this subsystem. This subsystem has traditionally consisted of the two biological parents of the child or children. Today, however, when the majority of American children will at some time live in a single-parent household, the members of the parental subsystem have become quite diverse. These participants may include parents' significant others, extended family members such as grandparents or aunts and uncles, or close friends and neighbors. What is most important for children is that whoever is part of the parental subsystem will be primarily focused on meeting the developmental needs of the children.

As was discussed in the section on family evaluation, an extensive history should be obtained from the parents regarding the developmental progress of each child and which parenting techniques were used with each child along the way. When children are younger, between the ages of two and six years, the main focus is on how well the child has learned the "3 rules of kindergarten" (i.e. Keep your hands and feet to yourself; Follow directions; and Be respectful of others and their property). During these discussions, it's important to ask parents to reflect on their own childhood memories and how these might affect the parenting of their own children. Of particular interest is what techniques their parents used to teach the "3 rules of kindergarten" and how this affected their feelings about their parents as they grew older. This is often the beginning of helping parents to see the connection between early childhood experiences of parental discipline and the quality of the parent-child relationship during adolescence. This is a good time to reiterate that this relationship constitutes the primary protective factor against the three high-risk behaviors of adolescence. This discussion typically leads to explanation and training of positive discipline techniques including the use of "time-outs".

For older children, the focus is typically centered on the" 3 outcomes of young adulthood." These three outcomes are achieved when the adult child (usually in their early 20's) is able to 1) be self-maintaining, 2) have one good friend, and 3) stay out of jail. These three outcomes may seem minimal, but if a child is able to accomplish these, they'll have a good chance of being happy and successful. Realizing each of these outcomes requires the child to develop a variety of skills related to these areas during adolescence. Being self-maintaining requires a person to be able to take care of all of their physical, financial, and psychological needs. These include taking care of one's health; cooking and cleaning; developing work skills to earn enough money to survive; living within one's means with a minimum of debt; and numerous other skills required to live independently. Having one good friend requires the ability to identify and control one's own emotions; express thoughts and feelings adequately and to listen carefully to others; to be flexible enough to accommodate the needs of others while also advocating for one's own needs; as well as a number of other relationship skills. Staying out of jail requires the ability to understand and follow rules; respect authority; and to understand the social consequences of human behavior. These "3 outcomes of young adulthood" often become the basis for the development of family rules within the household as children grow older. It's also necessary to acknowledge the increase ability of the adolescent to participate and give input into family discussions regarding decisions that affect them and to also take more responsibility for their part in implementing these.

Addressing the needs of the Sibling subsystem is always an area of focus in conjoint family therapy, even when there is only one child. As was discussed previously, the sibling subsystem is where children learn the skills necessary to interact effectively with their peers. In families where there is an only child, parents need to arrange consistent interactions with children of the same age. This can be accomplished through ongoing relationships with extended family members such as cousins, step-siblings or neighborhood children, or through organizations such as the Girl Scouts, AYSO, and the Boys and Girls Club, to name a few.

Strengthening the sibling subsystem often requires parents to act more like consultants than managers. In other words, rather than directly interacting with siblings or friends, the parent tries to unobtrusively observe these interactions and then provide feedback and coaching regarding pro-social behaviors. These include cooperation, sharing, showing empathy, saying "please" and "thank you", and other social manners that children primarily learn from parents. In situations involving a high degree of conflict between siblings, however, it's often necessary for parents to directly intervene, especially when physical or emotional harm may be occurring. Whenever this occurs, it's important for parents to actively discuss with the children why they're intervening and to teach conflict resolution skills that preserve the development of positive relationships between the siblings now and in the future. It's also critically important for parents to be conscious of any perceptions of parental favoritism and to address this directly. Few things destroy sibling relationships as much as parental favoritism.

2. Improving Family Communication Through Family Meetings and Dyad Work

Throughout the process of strengthening the functioning of the subsystems, the counselor tries to maximize any opportunities to improve family communication. This involves facilitating effective communication with the whole group in family meetings, and through the use of dyad work in meetings with two members.

When working with the whole family, it's important for the counselor to focus on helping each person to express themselves and feel heard. A major obstacle to effective family communication is the tendency for members to interrupt each other. When this occurs, the counselor can say:

"In most families, it's natural to have interruptions while talking with each other because we often think we know what the person will say and we want to respond as quickly as possible so that we can be heard. It's important to remember, though, that everyone wants to be heard and that each member of the family is growing and changing so these assumptions about what they're going to say may be incorrect. In order to help reduce interruptions, I'm going to ask your permission to allow me to be the only one who can interrupt. I don't mean any disrespect when I interrupt, but it's necessary so that I can help everyone to be heard. Is that okay?"

The above statement will often result in cooperation from family members, and soon only a few reminders from the counselor are necessary to reduce interruptions. If interruptions continue to hinder family communication, however, then it's often beneficial to use a pen or pencil as a symbolic microphone where only the person holding the "microphone" can speak and everyone else listens. One problem with this technique might occur if a family member won't give up the "microphone" and uses it to dominate the conversation, but the counselor can gently remind them that everyone want to be heard.

In addition to improving communication through family meetings, it's often necessary for the counselor to help two members of the family to communicate more effectively through the use of "dyad work." Briefly, "dyad work" involves having two members of the family communicate directly with each other with facilitation from the counselor. This facilitation typically involves the process described in the following example with two parents :

> "John and Mary, I know that the two of you have a disagreement about the curfew for your 15-year-old daughter. I would like you both to discuss this in a way so that each of you will feel heard by the other. So John, I would like you to face Mary and explain to her the most important reason for your view of the curfew time. Mary, I would like you to carefully listen to John and, after he is finished, I will ask you to reflect back to him the main points of what he said and then how he feels about this. Then, I will ask Mary to give her response to John, with John then reflecting back to Mary the main points of what she said and how she feels about it. Then, when we are sure that you both understand each other, we can work on acknowledging common viewpoints and resolving any differences."

Effective facilitation of communication is a critical part of improving the functioning of each subsystem and of the family in general. Family members may at first feel awkward in interacting in this dyadic manner because they may feel that it is artificial or takes too much time. It is important to explain, however, that many family conflicts are caused by ineffective communication and the resulting bad feelings when people do not feel that their comments or feelings are being considered. This dyadic work is one of the most fundamental and critical aspects of conjoint family counseling because it improves the understanding and resolution of issues that are so critical to healthy relationships between family members.

3. Building Family Resilience

In addition to dealing with crises, strengthening subsystem functioning and improving communication, any effective treatment plan should also include the building of family resilience. Family resilience is often related to the existence of positive experiences within the family that motivate family members to spend time with each other and stay together. Another aspect of resilience is the ability of the family to anticipate future stressors and to prevent family crises by preparing for these. The family counselor can assist the family in building resilience through the following processes.

Family Fun: One quality of healthy families is the willingness to spend time together. Most people like to spend time with those they can have fun with. Therefore, families need to create opportunities to have fun, especially in ways that maximize interactions with each other. In modern times, media and technology provide many different ways to have fun alone, which may have led to a decline in the ability to interact socially and have fun with others. In order to address this situation, it's important to help families to learn to have fun interacting with each other without the use of technology or media.
 Children's self-esteem often improves when they learn that their parents can have fun with them and game-playing also can help kids feel more confident in their relationships with peers, even without batteries. Family fun can happen in many unique ways and places, and it's important for parents to learn which activities are fun for each child as well as themselves and to understand that these change as the child develops.

Families are busier than ever and many do not create enough time to have fun together. When families attend counseling, they are forced to set aside at least a couple of hours per week to spend together, although most members do not consider this to be fun. Counselors can help families have fun together by keeping this as an area of focus throughout the process of conjoint family therapy. You may have noticed from the "Opening Session" section of this chapter that the counselor includes questions about fun during the very first introductions to family members. This not only provides the counselor with important information, but also sets the precedent that family counseling is about fun as well as problem-solving. During the family evaluation process, particularly when interviewing children and adolescents, the counselor can help to establish rapport through the use of humor and fun activities such as drawing and playing cards. It's often useful for the family counselor to observe the family playing a game together because most games involve communication, competition, and decision-making, which are all important aspects of family functioning. One of the most important aspects of family game-playing is determining which games maximize the participation of all members, particularly the younger ones who may be limited by their early stage of development. It seems helpful to begin with simple child card games such as" go fish" and "UNO" before moving on to more advanced activities.

TERMINATION OF CONJOINT FAMILY COUNSELING

As the family learns to deal with crises, improve family structure and functioning, and to address and resolve specific family problems, the process of termination begins. This is a gradual process that requires a great deal of observation and monitoring on the part of the family counselor to ensure that the family has progressed enough to be able to terminate conjoint family counseling. This process begins by introducing the concept of "family meetings", where the family takes more responsibility for facilitating what happens in the family counseling sessions. Conjoint family counseling often incorporates these meetings into the termination process so that the counselor can measure how well the family can work together without assistance.

1. Family Meetings

In a few words, family meetings are an opportunity for families to get together to discuss both the positive and negative things that are happening. Family members rotate taking the role of the facilitator who runs the meeting and monitors the communication rules. The family counselor helps the facilitator direct the initial family meetings to ensure maximum participation and success. The meeting usually begins with each family member having the opportunity to comment on something positive that's happening in their life and one thing that they would like to see improvement in. Then, the discussion turns to how the whole family can help make this happen.

2. Crisis Prevention through Family Life Cycle Preparation and Problem-Solving

Resilience can be enhanced when a family is able to anticipate problems that may come up in the future and learn to deal with them through a proactive family problem-solving process. As previously discussed, transitions into new stages of the family life cycle often create a great deal of stress and conflict in families. Specific explanations of family life cycle stages, especially those that are in the near future, can help a family to understand what adaptations they will need to make to be successful as their family develops. Discussion of the challenges of these transitions can provide an opportunity to explore the family's problem-solving process, of which they may not be aware. It's often useful to use the most recent family life cycle stage to explore how the family dealt with previous problems.

Exploring the Family Problem-Solving Process: For each problem that is discussed, restate the problem and then ask:

"What was done to try to solve the problem?"

"Was there any part of the solution that seemed to work?"

How did they know that it worked? Did the rest of the family think that it worked?

"Was there any part of the solution that did not seem to work?

"What made you feel like it didn't work? Why did you think it didn't work?"

"What other solutions were generated by the family regarding the problem?"

"What additional information did the family need in order to solve the problem?"

"Can any of the information above be used to address future problems?"

Family resilience can be enhanced by integrating the above concepts into the conjoint family counseling processes of family evaluation, treatment and termination. These can help the family to recognize and use their own resources to maintain healthy structure and communication and to solve family problems now and in the future.

Another important process is helping the family to identify if and when they might need to return for continued family counseling. The counselor can help the family to understand and identify individual and family symptoms that may indicate the existence of problems. Individual symptoms may include reduced functioning in any of the areas of the "Circle of Life" as well as maladaptive responses to specific situations. Family symptoms may include a reduction in the frequency of family fun and time spent together or an increase in family conflict or negative mood. When these occur, the family should reactivate the processes of family meetings and problem-solving. If the family does not improve significantly following these occurrences, then the family should contact the counselor sooner than later in order to prevent crises. Another important part of this process is to help the family gather the necessary referral information just in case these are necessary at a later date.

RELATIONSHIP TO THE SBFC MODEL

The skills of conjoint family therapy are a critical component of School-Based Family Counseling (SBFC). SBFC can be implemented by counseling professionals in the school who are trained in its core processes and who are able to work with students and their families with problems that are more complex and require more direct and close intervention (Carter & Evans, 2008). SBFC is a more specific conceptualization of how conjoint family counseling processes can be applied directly to dealing with a student's problems in the school environment that are related to the ability to follow directions, exercise self-control and show respect of others. School personnel may be in the best position to implement SBFC and improve student functioning because of the emphasis on school behavior and achievement versus mental health. Most parents are more willing to attend counseling sessions or "classes" at a school versus a community mental health clinic because they are often more interested in their child's education than obtaining therapy.

Conjoint family therapy applied in SBFC can also be useful for schools because of its collaborative and open processes. For example, SBFC can assist schools in child abuse reporting issues in a way that leads the family to get closer to the school in this process versus the frequent alienation caused by reporting parents for child abuse. This can be done in a way that ensures safety, compliance with reporting obligations, and respect of culture while also improving the student's academic functioning & social behavior. In addition, SBFC is also able to affect more family members than just the target child, like older brothers and sisters who may be dropping out and increasing the chaos in the child's academic development as well as potential crime in the community. Following is an actual case of the application of conjoint family counseling processes applied in SBFC in both a school and Clinic setting.

THE CASE OF MARLON

Marlon is a 5th grader in a public elementary school in Huntington Park, California, a very impoverished area of Central Los Angeles with a high immigrant population. Marlon displayed a profile of Attention Deficit Hyperactive Disorder (ADHD) in the classroom (e.g., difficulty following directions, concentrating, finishing tasks, and staying in his seat), and was also beginning to bully other students without apparent reason. Marlon has 2 younger brothers, one in 3rd grade and one in kindergarten. The brother in Kindergarten had missed over 30 days of school in the first semester. The father is of Mexican descent and the mother's cultural background is Western European: Irish and French.

Marlon's teacher followed the school's discipline system and one day, after Marlon caused another disruption in the classroom, she told him that she would have to call his parents. Upon hearing this, Marlon started crying and said that he was afraid of being "whipped by his father" when he got home. The teacher felt conflicted because of her duty as a teacher and mandated reporter, but also feared the possible consequences to Marlon if she acted on these obligations.

Situations such as these often result in reports not being made by anyone, and the child continues to languish in a high-risk situation that results in decreased student performance at best, and child injury and increased school liability at the worst. An additional problem is to what degree does the teacher's anxiety affect her ability to teach other students in class. If the report is made, how often does the parent blame the school, then disconnect, and move to another school, while making sure that the child will not say anything to a teacher again. How does this affect student attendance, achievement and dropout rates?

So, what are the options to address this type of situation through SBFC? In this case, there was a 2nd year SBFC fieldwork student interning in the school 10 hours/week under the supervision of a Licensed Marriage and Family Therapist familiar with SBFC. The teacher met with the Intern and disclosed what happened. The Intern then interviewed Marlon and then called the mother. She did not answer, so she called the father, explaining that there was an important incident that occurred at school involving his son and that he needed to come in immediately. When the father came in, the Intern explained that the session was confidential and also explained the limits of confidentiality and the duty to report. She then talked to the father about Marlon's behavioral difficulties in the classroom and how this was affecting him academically. She explained about what kids go through developmentally in the 5th grade and explored how he behaved at home and how he did his homework. She also explored the father's hopes for Marlon and the current state of their relationship.

The father was pretty open about Marlon's behavior at home and his fights with his brothers. The father also explained that he and Marlon's mother had separated again 3 months ago and that he was living out of his car except on the weekends when he saw his boys at the mother's apartment. The Intern acknowledged how difficult that must have been for the father and praised him for his continued involvement in his son's lives despite the difficulties. She then explored how father and mother dealt with Marlon's behavior at home. The father said that they yelled a lot and took things away, but that he couldn't spank his kids anymore because of a parenting class that he had to take last year. He said that the mother was too easy on the kids and let them do whatever they wanted to do. The intern acknowledged the father's frustration and talked of the three high -risk behaviors of adolescents and the main protective factor of a strong and open relationship with a parent and how this protective factor was affected by the yelling and negative nature of the discipline strategies that were being used at home.

The Intern then helped the father to understand what Marlon needed at this stage of development and then explained positive parenting and the use of a modified "break" or time-out system and how this could be used to improve Marlon's relationship with the father and mother. The father was pretty skeptical about this. The intern explained that this would be critical to Marlon's academic and employment future and that this would also help to calm down the other sons and perhaps help the mother to discipline more effectively.

The intern then informed the father what Marlon had said and that she had no choice but to call Child Protective Services to find out if a report needed to be made. She also explained that she would like to tell them that the father had come into the school willingly and that he understood the need for positive parenting and was committed to attending the Parent Training classes provided at the school site and further counseling sessions if necessary.

The father was quite upset, but the intern walked him through the probable process with CPS including the need to be open and honest with them if a report needed to be made and they came out to the house. She reiterated that she felt that the father wanted the best for all of his children and that this change in dealing with Marlon was necessary anyway. If he agreed to commit to the process, she could explain that to CPS. The report was made to CPS, which was the third report in the last year, and CPS went out and interviewed Marlon and his family and recommended that his father and mother follow-through with the parenting classes and work with the SBFC Intern.

Marlon's father and mother attended a session the following week with the Intern and were quite upset. They were able to talk about their feelings about the CPS visit, but also about their separation and its affects on their sons. The intern steered them back to the need for positive discipline to teach all of the children the "3 Rules of Kindergarten" and also began to address the absences of the Kindergartener. Marlon's mother began to understand the need for her youngest son to be in school rather than keeping her company at home. Mother was referred for daytime English classes at the local adult school and the father for anger-management classes. They were also referred to a Clinic that the Intern had a relationship with and who understood the need to emphasize the effect of parental conflict on their children's education. The Clinic had a 3-month waiting list, so the Intern saw the parents for two sessions to help them focus on working on their Co-Parenting relationship and positive discipline while waiting for a spot in the Clinic.

By the second week of the parents' involvement in SBFC, the teacher reported that Marlon's behavior had improved significantly and the referral to the school psychologist to assess Marlon regarding ADHD was put on hold. The parents attended the parenting classes, and the Kindergartener's attendance problems stopped for almost 2 months. Then, Marlon had a downturn in behavior and the SBFC brought the parents in again. They reported that they had come together in their work as parents in SBFC and that this had resulted in the father moving back in to the apartment, but that the parents' fights began again. The Intern again explained how this was affecting the children and how it would probably affect them in the future. She helped the parents to work together to devise a living plan that would minimize their contact with each other for the next month while waiting for services from the Clinic. The children's attendance and behavior improved over the next two weeks, but deteriorated thereafter.

Two weeks later, the whole family was seen at the Clinic, which has an SBFC focus and utilizes conjoint family counseling processes. During the first three weeks of their attendance, the family underwent the family evaluation process. The parents were interviewed together and separately, and the children were interviewed individually. During these interviews, it became apparent that the parents were still continuing the same dynamics from before the intervention of the SBFC intern. The father was living in the mother's apartment five out of seven days during the week, and was still considered the disciplinarian, while the mother maintained her nurturing role. During the conjoint interviews with both parents present, the parents presented a picture of harmony and togetherness.

In individual interviews, however, the mother expressed her frustration over the current living situation and her ambivalence about continuing the marriage. She said that the father had continued to make romantic overtures and reacted with anger when she did not respond positively. She said that, while they did not argue in front of the children, she felt that the children sensed the tension between them and that they were often interrupted by the children's fighting. As part of the evaluation process, the counselors obtained informed consent from the parents and contacted the school and conducted a brief interview with each of the children's teachers. These interviews revealed that Marlon's behavior in the school and the playground had deteriorated and that his youngest brother's absences had increased.

After completing the family evaluation, the counselors at the clinic focused on the immediate crises caused by the parents living together again. The parents were told during the feedback process that they needed to put their romantic and spousal relationship on hold while we focused on improving their co-parenting relationships. The counselors informed the parents that,

> "Right now, it's very difficult to predict what will happen in your romantic relationship. We do know, however, that even if you never spoke to each other again, your relationship as parents would still exist within the hearts of your children forever. Every child wants to love their mother and father, and hopes that their parents will at least be friends, if not married. Because of this, we need to begin by working on building a strong and effective co-parenting relationship that is based on mutual respect, direct communication, and trust in each other as parents. These three factors are also critical to the development of any healthy spousal relationship, but an enduring marriage ultimately depends upon the feelings of each spouse. We need to first focus on the development of this co-parenting relationship before considering your romantic relationship. In addition, most children continue to hope for a reunion of their parents and are typically devastated if attempts at reconciliation are not successful. Therefore, we recommend that you physically separate and limit any romantic interactions until we have stabilized your co-parenting relationship."

This strategy essentially created a boundary around the spousal subsystem and allowed the parents to focus solely on improving the functioning of the parental subsystem. This focus on establishing respect, communication, and trust, is a strategy that is often used in working with parents who are separating or threatening to divorce. This allows the counselor to continue to improve the functioning of the family in critical areas while temporarily forestalling the potentially destructive process of ending the marriage. Improving the effectiveness of the parental subsystem while parents are separated requires that both parents learn to take on the roles of nurturing and discipline like a single parent. This is important to any family because the sharing of these roles helps to reinforce that nurturing is not gender specific, and that discipline is not personal or arbitrary. This also leads to an improvement in the relationships each parent has with their children, which can soften feelings of rejection if other relationships deteriorate. In many cases, this strategy also allows the couple to explore their feelings about the marriage as they create a more constructive relationship with each other that can become a protective factor against the chaos of ending a romantic relationship if that occurs. This is ultimately what occurred in Marlon's family.

The counselors met with the parents for several sessions to implement positive discipline with the use of the" break" procedure. Very briefly, positive discipline involves assisting parents to understand and acknowledge the feelings and motivations underlying their children's inappropriate behavior. The parents are then taught to acknowledge the child's feelings while providing two age-appropriate behavioral choices. The" break" procedure involves an age-appropriate modification of timeout where the child must sit for a few minutes without parental attention. This procedure is typically used when children do not follow directions. This" break" also allows the parent to stop and reflect on the situation and how best to handle it and hopefully leads to a calm discussion with the child about the reasons why it is necessary to follow parents' directions. Following the break, the child is placed back in the original situation if possible, and then required to follow the original directions. As soon as the counselors feel that the parents are proficient in positive discipline and the" break" procedures, these procedures are explained in a family session and role-played so that the children know what to expect.

In Marlon's family, this aspect of conjoint family counseling was implemented over a period of several weeks and led to positive feedback from the parents, the children, and the school. The counselors then met with Marlon's mother and father individually and conjointly over several weeks to explore their feelings about the romantic relationship while reinforcing the positive benefits of their individual co-parenting. Eventually, both parents came to an understanding that there was not mutual interest in continuing the marriage and the parents decided to get a divorce. They continued counseling together with a focus on positive parenting with respect, communication and trust to maintain their children's attendance and homework completion while also getting assistance in mediation. During the termination process, the parents established separate residences and continued to co-parent with limited interactions between them. This allowed each parent to heal from the loss of the marital relationship and also reinforced their ability to be individually competent in parenting their children. Six months after termination of counseling in the clinic, all three children continued to maintain their attendance without behavioral referrals and improvement in homework completion.

This example of SBFC involved about 6 hours of the intern's time with the parents and about 9 hours of the Parent Empowerment Classes, but these were attended by almost 40 parents. The family attended 15 conjoint family counseling sessions at the Clinic. At follow-up six months later, the parents reported that despite the divorce, they felt that their children were doing better than ever and that this was the longest period of stability that their family had ever experienced. This successful outcome also included direct savings for the school including a marked increase in their Average Daily Attendance, a reduction in the school psychologist's caseload by at least one student (and probably the Kindergartener as well), and most importantly, a reduction in classroom and playground disruptions for the students in Marlon and his younger brothers' classes.

The above example reflects our finding that after a few SBFC sessions with the family, particularly conjoint family counseling with the parents, many of these high-maintenance students often start to improve in school, first behaviorally, and then academically. Sometimes, the student hasn't even been to the clinic or seen by the SBFC professional before improvement occurs, as long as their parents are meeting consistently with the counselor. This reflects the Prevention and Intervention aspects of SBFC and how they are combined with outside referrals for conjoint family counseling to address behavioral and attendance issues. This also reflects the power of the family, especially when parents are empowered.

MULTICULTURAL COUNSELING CONSIDERATIONS

One of the most important aspects of effective conjoint family counseling is the specific consideration of the cultural and historical backgrounds of the family. These factors must be included in the evaluation of the family in order to improve understanding and reduce resistance. An example of this is seen in section D of this chapter regarding the narrative process in providing feedback to the family. Notice how the counselor integrated into the narrative specific aspects of the cultural background of the mother and father and their unique history with their own family of origin.

It is critical to focus on family history as well as cultural background in order to avoid making faulty generalizations that can adversely affect the success of conjoint family therapy. Counselors often make assumptions regarding cultural background, particularly regarding variations within the same ethnic group. For example, some counselors assume that Latino clients are Mexican or Spanish or that Latino cultures are essentially the same. This often leads to misunderstandings that insult the client and cause irreparable damage to rapport and the effectiveness of conjoint family counseling. Of course, there are significant differences between all Latino cultures just as there are between every state in America. There are also significant differences within each family's experience of the same culture, just as there are variations between any two families living on the same street. Exploring these differences in the Factual dimension is a critical aspect of effective family evaluation, for it influences all subsequent processes of conjoint family counseling.

EVIDENCE-BASED SUPPORT

Over the past 10 years, there has been an increase in evidence-based support for the effectiveness of conjoint family counseling in helping children. Examples of this are shown in Box 9.6.

Box 9.6 Support for the Use of Conjoint Family Therapy

Asen, E. (2002). Outcome research in family therapy.*Advances in Psychiatric Treatment, 8*, 230-238.

Carr, A. (2009). The effectiveness of family therapy and systemic interventions for child-focused problems. *Journal of Family Therapy, 31*, 3-45.

Cookerly, J. R. (1973). The outcome of the six major forms of marriage counseling compared: a pilot study. *Journal of Marriage and Family, 35*, 4,608-611

Cottrell, D. & Boston, P. (2002). Practitioner review: The effectiveness of systemic family therapy for children and adolescents. *Journal of Child Psychology and Psychiatry, 43*, 5, 573-586.

DeWitt, K.N. (1978). The effectiveness of family therapy: a review of outcome research. *Archives of General Psychiatry, 35*, 5, 549-561.

Diamond, G. & Josephson, A. (2005). Family-Based Treatment Research: A 10-Year Update. *Journal of the American Academy of Child and Adolescent Psychiatry, 44*, 9, 872-887.

Rowe, C. L. (2010). Multidimensional Family Therapy: Addressing Co-occurring Substance Abuse and Other Problems Among Adolescents with Comprehensive Family-based Treatment. *Child and Adolescent Psychiatric Clinics of North America, 19*, 3, 563-576.

Stratton, P. (2005). Report on the Evidence Base of Systemic Family Therapy. Association for Family Therapy, Pages 1-12.

Williams, R. & Chang, S. (2000). A comprehensive and comparative review of adolescent substance abuse treatment outcome. *Clinical Psychology: Science and Practice, 7*, 138-166.

REFERENCES

Burr, W. R. (1970). Satisfaction the Various Aspects of Marriage Over the Life Cycle: A Random Middle Class Sample. Journal of Marriage and Family , 32, 1, 29-37.

Carter, M. J. & Evans, W.P. (2008). Implementing School-Based Family Counseling: Strategies, activities, and process considerations. International Journal for School-Based Family Counseling, 1(1), 1-21.

Compas, B. E., Adelman, H. S., Freundl, P. C., Nelson, P., & Taylor, L. (1982). Parental and child causal attributions during clinical interviews.Journal of Abnormal Child Psychology, 10(1), 77-83.

Fraser, M. W. (2004).Risk and resilience in childhood: An ecological perspective. Washington, DC: NASW Press

Karpel, M. A., & Straus, E. (1983). Family evaluation. Boston, MA: Allyn and Bacon.

McGoldrick, M., &Gerson, R. (1988).Genograms and the family life cycle. In Carter, E. A., & McGoldrick, M., Changing family life cycle (164-189). Boston, MA: Allyn and Bacon.

Minuchin, S. & Fishman, H. C. (1981). Family therapy techniques.Cambridge, MA: Harvard University Press.

Whitaker, C. A., & Keith, D. V. (1981). Symbolic-experiential family therapy. In A. S. Gurman& D. P. Kniskern (Eds.), Handbook of family therapy. New York: Brunner/Mazel.

CHAPTER 10
HOW TO HELP A CHILD THROUGH COUPLE RELATIONSHIP STRENGTHENING

Hans Everts

OVERVIEW: *This chapter describes how strengthening a couple's relationship makes an important contribution to its ability to provide effective parenting for troubled children in the context of School-Based Family Counseling (SBFC). The evidence-based concept of couple resilience (CR) is a core element in a variety of psycho-educational programs developed in New Zealand, and designed to prevent the development of serious problems in families facing major challenges such as migration or having refugee status. This chapter is a companion to chapter 34 on Developing Migrant Family Resilience.*

BACKGROUND

THE NEED FOR A FAMILY SYSTEMS PERSPECTIVE

The basic postulate of SBFC is that, when a child experiences difficulties at school, it is crucially important to look at its family – in order to help understand what makes the child behave the way it does, understand how the family m operates as a system that may contribute to that behavior, and to work with the family in helping the child cope with challenges in the school environment. Thus the helping professional needs to have a sound understanding of families as social systems, a social system designed to meet the needs of its individual members, to meet the requirements of the community (such as a proper education), and to maintain itself as an effective unit in the face of constant developmental change (Everts, 2003). As a social system, the family is made up of subsystems or subgroups. In most societies it is the parental subsystem that has an executive role: it has the greatest power and the greatest responsibility for setting the family's course in coping with life challenges. Such challenges include normative developmental changes (children growing up), paranormative events (economic hardship, accident, migration, disaster), and coping with the problems that affect its individual members (like a child's problems at school). The parenting couple, if there is one, seeks to understand what is happening, makes decisions, initiates action, and organizes other family members to participate in various aspects of that process. Not surprisingly, SBFC professionals will often set out to work with the parenting couple as principal allies in helping the troubled child (Gerrard, 2008). Employing a family systems framework thus provides an essential rationale for intervention strategies.

COUPLE RESILIENCE (CR) AS A CONCEPTUAL FRAMEWORK

The above perspective provides a compelling reason for the SBFC professional to understand how the parenting couple functions. In the same way that the family is a social system, the parenting couple constitutes a social system that exists to meet the personal needs of each partner, to take responsibility for meeting society's requirements, and to maintain itself as a functioning unit (Everts, 2003). For example, its ability to deal with a child's problems at school is very much a reflection of its integrity as a team. Conceptually, therefore, the SBFC professional must adopt a theoretical framework or rationale that explains how couples function – for better or worse. Practically, the SBFC professional must translate sucha rationale into purposeful and effective action strategies that enable counselor and couple to collaborate in dealing with family-based challenges – such as the ability of a child to cope with problems at school. The focus of this chapter is exactly on that issue – the delineation of a novel conceptual framework developed by the author to explain couple functioning, and the development of a set of associated, teachable intervention strategies that have been applied to working preventively with families at risk – issues that have not received any attention in the literature of SBFC to date. While conceptually interconnected with the SBFC paradigm, work with couples on their relationship is some distance removed from working with a child in its school environment. This poses a further challenge to the helping professional involved, as discussed in the next section.

The conceptual framework developed by the author to address the above matters is that of couple resilience (CR). CR refers to the relationship qualities and skills that a couple draws on to cope with family issues. The appropriate use of these resources may also help a couple to maintain its integrity as a functional team, or even strengthen the couple's relationship, as indicated by Froma Walsh in her research on family resilience (Walsh, 1996, 2006). Through a series of research investigations, described below, we postulated that a couple's close and strong relationship draws on four core elements: the wellness or integrity of the individual partners, the couple's emotional bonds, its relationship skills, and its support systems. These core elements can be subdivided into seventeen components (see below). The CR framework forms the conceptual basis for a range of intervention programs, developed in New Zealand, that aim to enhance couple strength, develop parenting skills, prevent family violence, and prepare couples for marriage as described in the Procedures section. An attractive feature of the CR framework is its positive nature. While recognizing the need to appreciate fully the negative aspects of human nature, it defines these more in terms of underdeveloped or absent strengths. Intervention focuses on developing these strengths. Our use of CR as a guiding framework is particularly relevant for SBFC where the counselor is seeking to prevent the escalation of problems, or where one is working with clients whose cultural values are in harmony with a strength-based approach. The CR project addresses both these issues.

MIGRATION AND CULTURAL ADAPTATION

In New Zealand, as in many other countries, migration is a fact of life that puts major pressures on families, schools, and thus SBFC (Everts, 2007; Everts, 2008; Everts & Wu, 2004; Soriano,2004; Vong, 2002). Apart from the challenges of physical adaptation, migrant families face theneed for cultural adaptation that affects family values, customs and patterns of relationship. Together, these place many migrant families into a crisis situation, offering hope and threatening disaster at the same time. This is truly a test of a couple's resilience (Kim, 2001). The influx of migrants from East Asia into New Zealand during the last 25 years created a perfect opportunity for us to develop and integrate the Migrant Family Resilience project (see chapter 34), the CR project of this chapter, and SBFC (Everts, 2004a; Everts, 2004b; Wong & Everts, 2002). This work was extended to include the refugee community, as one whose needs are even greater and more complex. While aspects of our work are, of course, unique to New Zealand, the underlying themes are universal and it is our hope that our experiences have relevance for SBFC in other countries.

PREVENTION
As with the MFR project described in chapter 34, the CR project addresses itself primarily to the issue of prevention – where problems are apparent in children, schools, families, and parenting couples, but where a briefer process of preventive intervention may stop the development of more serious problems demanding more intensive treatment. Such preventive intervention may often involve the use of a more

structured psycho-educational program, as noted in chapter 34. Intervention that is seen as educational and strength-based is frequently more familiar and acceptable to migrant families. The CR work described in this chapter has the advantage of being culturally relevant for certain client communities, and of attempting to address families at risk and teetering at the top of the cliff. It also falls clearly into the family/preventive quadrant of the SBFC paradigm (Gerrard, 2008).

EVOLUTION OF THE CR PROJECT

The author has been involved in exploring the concept of CR since the 1990's, as an outgrowth of his work in family systems and family therapy (Everts, 1999). This intersected with the development of the multicultural MFR project team, with representation from Taiwanese (Joy Tai), Afghan (Arif Saeid), Korean (Gus Lim) and Dutch (the author) perspectives providing a springboard for the conceptual and clinical initiatives outlined in this chapter. Once the concept of CR was clarified, it was first applied in the form of a couple enrichment program for Taiwanese clients (Shih & Tai, 2002). Shih's experience clarified that many Asian couples dislike discussing their relationship in front of or with strangers. The one exception has proved to be our recently-developed Building Strong Couples program, a 6-session pre-marriage training program trialed in New Zealand and China (Everts & Yang, 2012). While some distance removed from SBFC, this work addresses issues that precede those that face the SBFC professional, and thus are relevant to this chapter. The effect of Shih's project was to embed the CR theme into the parenting programs (Everts & Tai, 2003) described in chapter 34, with emphasis on the migrant couple's need to establish a good quality intimate relationship in its new environment, which can then translate into effective teamwork in the task of helping their children adapt to life in a new community and school system. That Parenting program was subsequently simplified somewhat as we extended its application to a range of refugee communities. There,two issues were found to be particularly urgent and therefore addressed in our project. Firstly, the critical period of first arrival was addressed through our Successful Families program. Secondly, the frequently-present issue of family violence was addressed in both the Successful Families and Protecting Family Happiness programs. All these programs are discussed in the Procedure section below.

RELATIONSHIP TO THE SBFC MODEL

While the conceptual model of SBFC contains four quadrants, attention in pertinent literature has focused on some more than others (Gerrard, 2008). Arguably, preventive work with families has received least attention of all quadrants to date. This chapter's primary focus is on that very quadrant. Conceptually, SBFC spans both the school and home systems, and places considerable importance on having a sound understanding of both. Historically, of course, the primary focus has been on the school as a system, as reflected in the very title of SBFC. Brian Gerrard, in his overview of the field (Gerrard, 2008) refers to family therapy, family counseling and working with parents. He notes that the latter end of that continuum is ill-defined in the literature cited, and that there is no outline of anything approaching a conceptual model of the parental subsystem that provides a template for working with them. This is the precise area addressed in the current chapter, with its analysis of the couple subsystem and of couple resilience – all within the context of a wider family systems perspective (Everts, 2003).

Similarly, in terms of his analysis of therapeutic intervention with families, Gerrard (2008) lists the possible use of family therapy, family counseling, parent education and parent support groups. In actual practice, the typical SBFC professional lacks both the time and the skill to undertake any such family orientated intervention with any degree of sophistication – which is hardly surprising, given the complexity of the task involved. Most likely, such counselors are primarily school-based, and have a limited involvement with families. Some others are primarily community-based, with some limited involvement in the school system. This chapter addresses itself to the latter group. This group represents the family side of the SBFC quadrant, within which there are two foci – a therapeutic one and a preventive one. Virtually all sources cited in Gerrard's article (Gerrard, 2008) focus on the family-therapeutic quadrant. The present chapter addresses the rather "empty" family-preventive area, with emphasis on working with the parenting couple, whose integrity as a team needs to be maximized before they can be expected to do an effective job of their parenting task. In that sense, we address the far corner of the SBFC paradigm. Gerrard includes the strategies of couple counseling, parent education and parent support groups under his rubric of family counseling (Gerrard, 2008, table 2) – ones barely attended to by the authors cited in his review of the literature, but ones central to this chapter. It should be noted, however, that separate quadrants do not imply different ways of working. Gerrard includes both educational and therapeutic interventions under family preventive work, and even the delivery of more structured psycho-educational programs requires the combined skills of educator and therapist. In addition, professionals working in the family preventive field will most probably need to work with others in an interdisciplinary manner to reach into the school system. SBFC does not only span the different systems of family and school, it also spans different professions working towards a shared inclusive goal. These issues were presented and discussed at an international symposium on SBFC counseling at the Institute of Education in Hong Kong in June 2011 (Everts, 2011a). This family-based preventive work highlighted in this chapter must therefore be integrated with that of others in this book who represent the other three quadrants.

EVIDENCE-BASED SUPPORT

COUPLE RESILIENCE (CR) AS A CONCEPTUAL FRAMEWORK

The concept of CR was originally developed using a field-based, qualitative model (Everts, 1999). Subjects were asked the following open-ended question (with minor variations in wording): "*Think of a couple you know well who have coped successfully with serious problems and who have held together, if not strengthened, their relationship in the process. What is it in their relationship that has helped them to cope?" Write down your answer in your own words.* This question was given over time to 602 subjects in 6 countries. Using a modified grounded theory approach, it was possible to identify 17 categories of response, which were grouped into 4 themes of personal resourcefulness, emotional bonds, action skills, and community support (Box 1 below). A detailed scoring guide was developed, and its validity and inter-examiner reliability checked on several of the samples. The non-comparable nature of samples does not permit a detailed cross-analysis of specific response patterns for the samples. However, The total pattern of responses highlights several themes, evident in Appendix A.

In terms of the four broad themes, a couple's emotional bonds constitute the most prominent resource that contributes towards its resilience, accounting for 43% of the total responses recorded (second to last column). This is followed, fairly equally, by its action skills (26%) and the personal resources of individual partners (22%). Lastly, but still worthy of note, is the couple's community support (9%). Thus CR, while broadly based, comprises a clear hierarchy of prominence in its contributing themes. At the level of more specific qualities and skills, the responses obtained provide an alternative perspective on the pattern of variables that contribute to a couple's resilience. If one divides the ranked frequency of total responses across samples into three levels, the following emerges (see last column). The top level of categories (ranks 1-6) includes love, commitment and tolerance (all aspects of emotional bonds), communication as an action skill, the presence of a support network in the wider community, and the personal quality of optimism. The second level of prominence (ranks 7-12) includes

Box 10.1   The Concept of Couple Resilience – A Brief Outline

Couple resilience has to do with resources, in the form of qualities and skills, which help a couple cope with challenge and stress. Listed below are seventeen such resources, in four groups, drawn from international research findings. Their level of importance is rated from (1) to (3) in accordance with their frequency of mention in that research.

Group One – Personal resources
Optimism – having hope and faith in the future, even in the middle of problems; having a sense of humour. (1)*
Awareness – having an awareness or understanding of self and others. (2)
Religious or spiritual faith – having a religious or spiritual faith. (2)
Personal strength – being tough, courageous or determined in the face of stress. (2)

Group two – Emotional bonds
Love, affection – having love, trust, caring or respect for each other. (1)
Commitment – being committed or faithful to each other; being determined to see things through together, for better or worse. (1)
Tolerance – being tolerant, patient, forgiving and flexible towards each other; being able to give and take. (1)
Similar values – having similar values, goals and beliefs to each other. (2)

Group three – Action skills
Communication skills – being able to listen, discuss, make decisions or solve problems together; able to express oneself; able to find solutions which leave both parties happy; able to not lose one's temper or panic. (1)
Past history – having a long or good past history with each other; having coped with or learned from past problems. (2)
Collaboration – being able to work together as a team to solve problems or cope with stress. (2)
Intimacy time – having time together in recreation, fun or rest that makes that relationship a better one. (3)
Self-Sacrifice – making personal sacrifices for the sake of the other. (3)
Physical resources – having money or possessions to help cope with difficulties. (3)

Group four – Community support
Support network – having other family members, friends, professionals, or even pets, available to support and help the couple. (1)
Self-protection –being able to protect oneself as a couple against the bad influence of others in the wider community. (3)
Role models – having role models (good or bad) that are available to the couple. (3)

*(1) core resources; (2) important resources; (3) resources that are of some help

similarity of values, awareness, religious or spiritual faith, personal strength, the couple's past history, and the ability to collaborate. The thirdlevel of categories (ranks 13-17) includes intimacy time, self-sacrifice, physical resources, self-protection and the presence of role models.

Both perspectives, which have a measure of consistency across different nationality samples, indicate that couples draw on a range of qualities and skills in coping with challenge, and in maintaining (or even enhancing) the quality of their relationship. Indicative as these research findings are, they cannot be taken as prescriptive for individual couples. Any one couple will develop its own set of resources that determine its success in coping with life challenges. However, our findings indicate that some such resources are more likely to be of help than others, and that a couple is well advised to develop as many qualities and skills as possible. These research findings have been used by the CR project team to develop the following range of couple strengthening programs and activities for use within a variety of ethnic communities in New Zealand and elsewhere.

Table 10.1 Couple strengthening programs and activities in the MFR Project

1. The core Parenting program (6 or 8 sessions) for migrant and refugee families – one session on "Strong Couples, Responsible Parents".
2. The Successful Families program (2 sessions) to facilitate the effective settlement of newly-arrived refugees – CR is its conceptual basis and primary content.
3. The Protecting Family Happiness program (4 sessions) – as follow-up to the Parenting program for migrant and refugee parents facing family strife - CR is a basis for effective parenting.
4. The Training the Trainers program – a 7 hour program for community resource personel supporting migrant or refugee couples and families.
5. The Making Strong Couples program (6 sessions) – focuses on couple strengthening and pre-marriage training for migrant and cross-cultural couples.

COUPLE STRENGTHENING IN MIGRANT FAMILY RESILIENCE (MFR) PROGRAMS

Within the wider context of our Migrant Family Resilience project (see chapter 34), we have incorporated the CR theme into the context of the Parenting program for migrant and refugee families. This is in line with the project's emphasis on relating couple functioning to parenting effectiveness, and thus to SBFC. Specifically, we have a session on Strong Couples, Responsible Parents early on in the standard Parenting program (see Box 2 below), and one on Home-School Relationships as the second-to-last session. The research results on that first session (see table 2 below) have been drawn from the operation of 31 Parenting programs over the last 9 years, 14 based on the original version of the program between 2003 and 2007 (Kim & Everts, 2007), and 17 on its revised version, used between 2007 and 2011. The initial 14 programs were used with ethnic Chinese and Korean parents, mostly the former. The latter 17 programs were used with 7 groups of ethnic Chinese parents (eg. Tai, 2010); 2 of Koreans; 7 groups of refugees from a variety of countries (eg. Saeid, 2010); and 2 groups of ethnic Chinese grandparents (Tai & Lai, 2011). Most groups rated the usefulness of the Strong Couples, Responsible Parents session on a 7-point rating scale. The results indicate that parents (and grandparents) in a large number of groups from a range of migrant and refugee communities rate the sessions on couple functioning and home-school relationships as highly or fairly useful within the context of a preventive Parenting program.

Table 10.2 Evaluation of Strong Couples, Responsible Parents session

Program	Rating							
	High 7	6	5	4	3	2	1	0
Initial program (14 groups, 163 respondents; 160 rated this item)	63	69	23	4	1			
Revised program (13 groups, 133 respondents; 126 rated this item)	61	38	23	3	1			
In a total of 6 groups, the Home-School Relationships topic was evaluated, with 57 out of 60 respondents rating the session, as follows:	23	20	7	7				
In 4 groups of refugee parents, ratings were simplified on account of literacy issues; 59 respondents were involved, 58 rated this item	*Liked a lot* 52			*liked a little* 6		*did not like* 0		

Even allowing for a culture-based tendency for respondents to be polite and say the "right thing", it indicates the perceived value of these themes. Both of them are closely related to a wide span of SBFC-related issues, ranging from couple functioning through parenting to home-school relationships. These themes, embedded within this program, are very relevant to a couple's task of effective parenting in a society that is new and challenging for their families and, without doubt, to the school system that receives their children. Detailed evaluation results on both forms of the Parenting program are available from the author.

THE SUCCESSFUL FAMILIES PROGRAM, AS USED WITH NEWLY-ARRIVED REFUGEES
The Successful Families program (MFR, 2009a) is 2-session program developed specifically to address the needs of newly-arrived refugees (see Procedure for details), and delivered by the author to some 24 groups over a period of two years. Ten groups were evaluated, comprising a total of 150 respondents who listed a total of 345 items when asked what they had liked or learned in the program. Responses were obtained from a variety of groups, predominantly from Burma, Bhutan and Colombia, but also

Session V: Strong Couples make Good Parents

AIM OF SESSION

To help participants see how having a strong couple relationship helps partners be more effective in their parenting.

SESSION STRUCTURE
1. Welcome, introduction to session, and teaching input on couples (20 min)
2. Discussion (15 min)
3. Questions (15 mins)
4. Teaching input on parenting team (10 mins)
5. Discussion (15 mins)
6. Questions (15 mins)
7. Couple resilience research (15 mins)
8. Conclusion and homework (15 mins)

Welcome, introduction, and teaching input on couples (large group, 20 min)
Hans welcomes participants. Review programme. Do a round on significant learning to date. Introduce topic. Teaching input on couples, translated, using handout 1.

Discussion (in small groups, 15 mins)
Discussion and application of points on what makes couples strong.

Questions (large group, 15 mins)
Discussion of further questions in the large group.

Teaching input on couples as parenting teams (large group, 10 mins)
Hans goes through relevant points in handout 1.

Discussion (in small groups, 15 mins)
Discussion and application of points made.

Questions (large group, 15 mins)
Discussion of further questions in the large group.

Couple resilience research (large group, 15 mins)
Hans introduces his research on couple resilience (handout 2).

Conclusion and homework (large group, 15 mins)
Hans asks participants what they found especially useful in this session. Affirmation of points made. Invitation to discuss material with spouse, if available.

© Migrant Family Resilience Project (2009)

from Iraq, Sudan, Burundi, Somalia, Ethiopia and Eritrea. A number of categories were derived and scored from the open-ended questionnaires (table 3):

Table 10.3   What participants learned or liked in the Successful Families program

Characteristic	N	Rank
Attitudes		
Love, respect, trust	66	1
Happiness, meeting emotional needs (4 A's)	25	7
Interaction		
Discussion, communication, talking, problem solving	51	2
Listening, patience, understanding, thinking	40	3
Family relationships		
Parents as team, leaders, model, work together, win-win	39	4
Need for fair rules and duties, being responsible	36	5
Exercising discipline with love	30	6
Maintaining self-control, managing anger	22	8
Rewarding good behavior	18	9
Being fair, parent-child collaboration, everyone wins	18	9

The specificity of these results must be treated with caution since language and literacy problems, copied or shared answers, and misunderstandings were noted. In broad terms, however, these results indicate that in this context there was consistent acknowledgement of core universal values, interaction strategies, and patterns of family relationship that were held in common by respondents regardless of nationality, religion, gender or age. These results also affirm the relevance of the essential elements of the CR model, as noted in the handout material for session 1 (see Box 3 below). This provides a basic starting point (not followed through in this project) for further longer-term preventive intervention with severely challenged families in a multicultural setting, addressing couple relationships, parenting, and ultimately the adaptation of children in school – thus articulating the very essence of SBFC.

PROTECTING FAMILY HAPPINESS PROGRAM-FOR PREVENTING FAMILY VIOLENCE

The four-session Protecting Family Happiness program (MFR, 2009b) is designed as a follow-up to the generic Parenting program for parents who struggle with problems of family quarrels, anger and violence. These themes are similar to what is addressed in the Successful Families program, but pursued in rather more detail. To date, two programs have been delivered to Afghan and Burmese refugee parents in a school catering for the settlement of both adult and child refugees from different countries. Evaluative data was collected from 19 participants who completed the evaluation questionnaire (see table 4).

Box 10.3   Session 1 Handout from the Successful Families Program

"Successful Families" Program (2011) - Session I Handout

Nine Suggestions for Making a Family Successful

1. **Make couples successful - happy and strong**
    A couple is successful when each partner is happy, when both love and respect each other, when they talk and work together as a team, and when they get support from others. A successful couple (if there is a couple) lies at the heart of a successful family.

2. **Parents work as a team to get things done.**
    The parent team is strong when they agree on how to run the family, and set a good example.

3. **Parents teach children how to be responsible by showing them.**
    Parents teach children to be responsible by inviting them to join in family decision making as soon as they are old enough.

4. **Doing the right thing is rewarded.**
    Reward and praise are more powerful than punishment - so reward and praise each other whenever people do the right thing.

5. **Doing the wrong thing is punished.**
    If someone breaks a rule, the agreed punishment is given. Losing out on reward or praise is often the best punishment.

6. **Be disciplined where it is important.**
    It is important for the whole family to agree on basic rules, rewards and punishments that are necessary in making it run well. Discipline means sticking to making them work.

7. **Punish in a fair way.**
    Ignore smaller issues; make some allowance for the situation. Give warning, then don't argue, don't give in, but punish as agreed.

8. **Punish with love and respect.**
    Show love and respect for the other person, even while you punish someone's behaviour. Don't lose your temper. Don't overdo the punishment.

9. **Talk about things that have gone wrong.**
    When people are calm, talk about what has happened, and what was learned. If something needs to be changed in how the family works, do it.

Bearing in mind the difficulties experienced by participants completing questionnaires (see Successful Families above), these results suggest that the themes addressed and the techniques used were generally appreciated, but that a number of participants were uncomfortable about some topics and some techniques. Thus, the program as constituted is worthwhile, but warrants further refinement. It also requires systematic follow-through in the community by trained resource personal, which was not done in our project.

Table10. 4   What participants like in the Protecting Families Happiness program

Question	Liked a Lot	Liked a Little	Did Not Like
How much did you like the different topics?			
Happy/unhappy families	17	1	0
Arguments and quarrels	13	4	2
Anger, violence and abuse	11	5	2
How the law can help	16	1	0
How much did you like the techniques we used?			
Teaching/demonstrations	18	1	0
Group discussion	13	6	0
Handout notes	14	4	0
Home activities	15	4	0

TRAINING THE TRAINERS

On two occasions, a group of community resource personnel were taken through a 7-hour Train the Trainers program, with focus on the generic Parenting program, in order to enable them to better support and follow up on clients who had gone through that program. Eleven counselors working for Asian Family Services and nine resource personnel from different refugee communities completed the evaluation questionnaire (see table 5 below). These results strongly indicate the importance of taking community resource personnel through the generic Parenting program and discussing their role in following through on that program with clients who have completed it, as well as others in the wider community. This does not, of course, enable them to run the Parenting program, and also requires that they receive ongoing supervision in this work.

PROCEDURE

COUPLE RESILIENCE

The CR framework is a novel one that has empirical support, conceptual integrity and practical applicability, as shown above. Its 4 broad themes and 17 categories have been used consistently in the structure of all programs described in the present chapter. In clinical practice, it allows the SBFC-orientated professional to affirm qualities and skills that couples have, to teach skills (like communication) that are missing, and to suggest action that helps couples to fulfil effectively its

systemic responsibilities (like parenting and collaborating with schools). As demonstrated by underpinning research, the CR framework has cross-cultural validity, even though the pattern of resources that enables a couple to be successful varies across couples and cultures.

Table 10.5 What participants like in the Train the Trainers program

Question	Liked a Lot	Liked a Little	Did Not Like
How much did you like the program we did today?	20	0	0
How much did you like the different topics?			
Listening skills	17	2*	0
Power of praise	18	1*	0
Dealing with arguments	17	2	0
Strong couples, good parents	18	1*	0
Effective discipline	18	1	0
Dangers of anger	17	1	0
How much did you like the techniques we used?			
Teaching/demonstrations	18	1	0
Group discussion	18	1	0
Handout notes	19	0	0
How will you use this program's information in your work?			
Will use with clients: 17			
Will use to guide staff in team: 1			
Will use in personal life: 5			
Will learn more: 2			

* Respondent indicated that she already knew the material

"Think of a couple you know well who have coped successfully with serious problems and who have held together, if not strengthened, their relationship in the process. What is it in their relationship that has helped them to cope? Write down your answer in your own words." We have put this question to students, helping professionals and clients in a wide range of contexts and countries. Writing down one's own answers; then having the CR framework (Box 1) explained; scoring these answers; and discussing the implications with one's partner, group, trainer, or counselor provides a powerful consolidation of personal and professional understanding of the CR framework. We recommend this process to anyone wishing to become familiar with CR. In addition, if someone is going to use this question in professional practice, it is necessary to master the use of the scoring guidelines (Everts, 2011b). Then, a SBFC professional is ready to learn to use one of this chapter's CR programs with the educational and therapeutic competence that is required for family prevention work in a range of cultural contexts, as envisaged by Brian Gerrard. This will enable the SBFC professional to enhance a couple's effectiveness in parenting troubled children, and in collaborating with school personnel in aiding the child's functioning there. Finally, it should be noted that the author has adapted the basic CR questionnaire to ask migrant and dual career couples about the resources they have drawn on to cope successfully with those respective challenges (Everts, 2000a; Everts, 2000b). No equivalent survey has been carried out with couples struggling with their children's problems at school. It would be very valuable to conduct such a SBFC-orientated survey, which may well elucidate more clearly the relationship between couple functioning, effective parenting, and home-school relationships.

COUPLE STRENGTHENING IN MIGRANT FAMILY RESILIENCE (MFR) PARENTING PROGRAMS

As noted above, the "Strong Couples Make Good Parents" session (see Box 2) is embedded in the generic Parenting program (MFR, 2007). Its rationale is based not on the notion that couples want to look at their relationship for its own sake (which, in our situation, they avoid doing in public), but that being effective as parents requires them to work together as a functional and resilient team. As a couple working with a SBFC preventive counselor, they face a parenting crisis that contains both opportunity and danger – both ying and yang as in the Chinese definition of crisis. With appropriate help, their child and their relationship may benefit; without it, both may suffer further. The way in which this session is handled as part of the MFR Parenting program is described in detail in the Procedure section of chapter 34, and the interrelationship between couple resilience and effective parenting is referred to repeatedly in other sessions of that program. Where further help with family discord is needed, a parent or parenting couple in our New Zealand project may be referred to the Protecting Family Happiness program, described below.

THE SUCCESSFUL PROGRAM, AS USED WITH NEWLY-ARRIVED REFUGEES

This two-session program covers similar content themes as the generic Parenting program, but in highly condensed form. It also includes a significant segment on problems of anger and family violence, which feature in many refugee families – illustrative of the corrosive effects that trauma and long-term displacement have on family systems and family members. Running this program posed a number of significant challenges to the author as its developer and deliverer over two years. Each group comprised members of freshly-arrived families from different refugee communities, included teenage children (and sometimes younger, even babies), unattached young adults, single parents, parent couples, and grandparents. Multiple, simultaneous translations addressed often-bewildered participants in the context of an overwhelmingly busy 6-week induction program in Auckland's refugee reception center.

Over the 24 programs run, the author developed a number of strategies that proved fitting, helped achieve the results cited above, and even helped some participants remember the program's content some two years later when the author met them again in a community education setting. Strong, direct, personal but culturally appropriate rapport establishment was necessary from the outset. Being older, male, a migrant himself, long married, a grandparent, and a professional teacher inspired respect. Constant affirmation created confidence and enthusiasm. Humor bonded the group and lightened the session's mood. Inviting questions and comments helped bring out content that could be woven back into the process. Finding and articulating underlying universal values provided necessary validation (or reframing) of non-negotiable attitudes, at the same time as establishing a willingness in participants to consider new learnings that would enhance successful family adaptation in a new society (see Box 3 above). The author's use of personal illustrative examples, both positive and negative, lent credibility to teaching points. Running this program validated core values about personal and family integrity held by the author. It also tested every one of his professional skills as counselor and educator. Within the very limited scope of its brief, the relative success of this preventive crisis-intervention program for family systems may connect with the work of other SBFC professionals in a conceptual or practical way that warrants further exploration.

PROTECTING FAMILY HAPPINESS PROGRAM-FOR PREVENTING FAMILY VIOLENCE

The generic Parenting program (MFR, 2007) is pre-structured to cover a series of sequential topics. That may be sufficient to meet the needs of some parents who are in an at-risk situation, and thus prevent the escalation of their children's problems at home or school. However, it is unlikely to meet the needs of parents whose problems are more severe. They need something more personalized and flexible. The Protecting Family Happiness program was developed for such parents and couples. Going through the generic Parenting program would have (hopefully) given them a background framework of understanding, a degree of trust in process and leadership, and motivation to be openly and honestly engaged. The Protecting Family Happiness program can be used as follow-up from either the generic Parenting or the Successful Families program – though the latter has not yet occurred in our project.

While broadly educational in orientation (which is more culturally acceptable to our migrant and refugee communities), the actual session process is relatively flexible and allows for more personalized interaction than its precursor. The evaluation feedback from the two groups run to date indicates that, while generally successful, the selection and preparation of participants is important if they are to be fully engaged in and benefit from the process. Even then, a family's typical drift back to homeostasis, and the complex nature of systemic change means that one of two follow-up activities are normally required. For one, the consolidation of change processes started in a preventive program typically requires ongoing monitoring and support in the community – by professional or semi-professional resource personnel (see below). Alternatively, more time and intensive individualized intervention may be necessary – by which time we are talking about family counseling rather than family prevention in Gerrard's typology. In summary, the Protecting Family Happiness program constitutes an appropriate follow-through for some couples or parents who have completed a generic Parenting program, but is likely to require either consolidation in the community, or more intensive therapeutic intervention – neither of which has been systematically explored in the present project. Comparison with the work done by others in this field from a SBFC perspective would be very interesting.

COUPLE RELATIONSHIP STRENGTHENING PROGRAMS

While not directly related to the task of parenting, our project has recently developed the "Making Strong Couples" program, a six-session couple strengthening program based on the CR model (MFR, 2012). Its session topics include personal wellbeing or integrity, the couple's emotional relationship, effective communication, and teamwork and effective action.

A program like this can be run for couples who wish to enhance a satisfactory relationship, or ones who want to improve an at-risk one. While such programs are popular in the wider community, we have found little appetite for them among migrant and refugee families (as noted above). There is, however, a level of interest in this program among younger migrants who are preparing for marriage. To date, the Making Strong Couples has been run for one such group in the Chinese community in Auckland, New Zealand, and two for groups in Shanghai. While feedback from these trial groups indicates that they found it relevant, supportive and challenging, the program remains one in the developmental phase (Everts & Yang, 2012).

The importance of this program for SBFC lies partly in its CR rationale, which has proved to be as relevant for pre-marriage couples as it is for couples struggling with their children's problems at school. It is also important from a family systems perspective, where preventive intervention with teenagers, unattached young adults, pre-marriage couples, and couples in the process of cultural transition helps address couple relationship and parenting issues before they reach crisis proportions. We hope that our experience on this issue can be related to that of others in SBFC. An abbreviated outline of the program is contained in Appendix B below.

TRAINING THE TRAINERS

The MFR project has operated over the past 10 years, with the aim of systematically developing preventive, family strengthening resources (described above) within the migrant and refugee community in Auckland, New Zealand. Where possible, we have sought to empower others to use these resources rather than build our own service delivery organization. To that end, we have built our own leadership team in order to train group leaders, community resource personnel, and organizational leaders. To date, only part of this goal has been met.

The *MFR leadership team* comprises a small group of multi-cultural helping professionals, with qualifications in psychology, counseling, social work, medicine and religious ministry. It includes both migrants and refugees, both clinicians and academics – Joy Tai originally from Taiwan, Arif Saeid from Afghanistan, Gus Lim from Korea, and the author from the Netherlands. We are all in leadership positions in our own communities, and all were trustees in the Diversity Trust until its wind-up in 2011. As a team, we took responsibility for the development of the rationale-based programs described in this chapter and chapter 34, their adaptation to and translation into the language of the recipients, the training of group leaders and community resource personnel, the actual running of programs, the conduct of evaluation and follow-up, and liaison with recipient organizations. The nature and quality of the team has been essential to the success of the MFR project to date.

As described in chapter 35, *group leaders* are qualified helping professionals who are inducted into leadership via an apprentice training process and, once certified, are required to continue receiving supervision and sharing evaluative data with the MFR project team. The training of *community resource personnel* is essential for the generalization of learning from the time-limited MRF programs in the community. Such people may have a professional or semi-professional background, be in a paid or voluntary role, typically are members of the particular community that they serve, but have not usually trained to run MFR programs themselves. In order to help support, follow up on and consolidate client learnings, they must know what the programs contain, personally accept the basic premises involved, and have the ability (under supervision) to generalize the outcomes of the MFR programs. Two formal training programs of this kind have been noted above, and more informal training has taken place for others. Two half-day workshops on this issue were also conducted at the Institute of Education in Hong Kong in June 2011 (Everts, 2011b) and at the University of Padjadjaran in Bandung, Indonesia in October 2011 (Everts, 2011d). Ongoing supervision of this work by members of the MFR leadership team has not been easy to sustain over time, and constitutes an ongoing challenge – especially with the winding-up of the Diversity Trust and the author's retirement from the University of Auckland.

Where the MFR project has worked with existing *community organizations*, we have deliberately engaged their executive teams in order to ensure that our programs are appropriate to their needs, and that they in turn will support and foster the continued use of the resources that we provide free of charge. This has worked well with a range of such community organizations, including Refugees as Survivors, the Refugee Education for Adults and Families center, Korean Saturday Schools, the Taiwanese Hwa Hsia Society, and the Auckland Family Counselling Service. Part of our reason for working with these organizations is that the work of several spans both family and educational activities, as reflective of SBFC thinking.

MULTICULTURAL COUNSELING CONSIDERATIONS

As noted throughout this chapter and in chapter 34, the entire project discussed here is multi-cultural in nature. No additional points are therefore made on this issue here.

CHALLENGES AND SOLUTIONS

Many of the general challenges facing this project have been noted in the equivalent section in chapter 34, and the reader is referred there for suggested solutions. Some challenges pertain more directly to the theme of this chapter, as follows:

1. *The long stretch from couple functioning to a child's school adjustment* – this requires helping professionals to have a conceptual framework and collegial network that stretches across that gap, whether they work at the family end or the school end of the continuum alluded to in the SBFC literature (Gerrard, 2008).

2. *Working across very different or incompatible belief systems* – one can compromise in a conflict of needs, but not in a conflict of values, so we have to work from within the value system of our clients to find core beliefs that are sufficiently universal to apply in both cultures (see Box 3). This is augmented by the argument that couples, if they wish to be successful as couples and parents in New Zealand, have to adapt. This is a challenge for us as representatives of the recipient community as well as for the new immigrants. While we have been able to make a successful start in this process within the context of our programs, such adaptation takes years, and requires further

preventive intervention as well as the support of within-community resource personnel – an example of the collegial network in action, referred to above.

3. *The possible presence of trauma* – as noted in chapter 34, the presence of post-traumatic stress in the history of couples, especially refugees, remains an issue that program leaders must be constantly aware of and able to have addressed. Individual trauma intervention may well be required before couples can be expected to develop a resilient relationship that allows them to collaborate in effective parenting in a new country. This is one of the reasons why a couple focus is relevant to SBFC work.

4. *The many configurations of couple/parenting relationships* –in our programs we have worked with informal as well as married couples, single parents with or without support from other family members, separated couples, one spouse whose partner is unable or unwilling to attend (eg. Kim, 2010), and grandparents with major parenting responsibilities. We have found that the principles of CR hold true in any intimate relationship between two, or even more, partners. Even when such a relationship is in the process of formation (eg, the pre-marriage program) or has broken down, reflection on what it consists of and how it can be created or recreated is seen as valuable in a situation where people are reflecting on the challenges of parenthood in a new context.

5. *The limited scope of the present project* – this chapter deals only with the unique nature of our research and our research-based clinical activities. In addition, as noted above, our research data collected is limited in validity and reliability, and our clinical experience is limited in extent. Thus the reader needs to be cautious in evaluating what has taken place in New Zealand, but hopefully be able to relate this to what is being done elsewhere, and work with us to enhance SBFC internationally.

SUMMARY

This chapter explores how preventive couple strengthening provides a necessary foundation for effective parenting for children under stress, and for ultimately aiding the collaboration between home and school – though that issue is not addressed here. The work described here is part of the overall Migrant Family Resilience project designed to help migrant and refugee families adapt to life in a new country and culture. This wider project is discussed in chapter 34.

The choice of a preventive approach to couple strengthening is made in part because, where possible, prevention is better than cure, and in part because the communities involved have a cultural preference for education rather than therapy. The concept of Couple Resilience provides the conceptual core of the project, with its emphasis on identifying the qualities and skills that enable a couple to have a close relationship, as well as one that deals effectively with life challenges. This concept has been tested and validated in a range of countries and cultures, culminating in the so-called CR framework. This CR framework connects very well with SBFC, insofar as its emphasis on effective parenting leads into the enhancement of home-school collaboration. To effect this connection, however, couple strengthening activities must be augmented by others that focus in the child's successful integration into the school system.

The couple strengthening project has focused its applied work on the adaptation of migrant and refugee families into the New Zealand community for a variety of reasons – the need for family integrity in a new environment, parents struggling to maintain responsibility, children entering a strange school environment, community leaders seeking help, and helping professionals being trained in New Zealand. The MFR project was well positioned to take on the challenge. The project's programs that address the parenting couple's needs include the session in the generic Parenting program, the Successful Families program, the Protecting Family Happiness one, the Making Strong Couples one, and a range of workshops designed to develop the skills of community resource personnel. The entire couple strengthening project is multi-cultural in its applications and supporting evidence and, while still in the process of developing its scope fully, is demonstrably relevant to the family prevention aspect of the SBFC paradigm. We hope that this chapter will encourage readers to relate aspects of the project to their own work so that our collective experience may enhance the international applications of SBFC.

REFERENCES

Everts, J.F. (1999). Couple resilience: A definition and analysis of the concept. *New Zealand Journal of Counselling, 20,* 47-65.

Everts, J.F. (2000b). *Resilience in working couples.* Auckland: University of Auckland, Faculty of Education: Research Report.

Everts, J.F. (2003). An integrated Model of Functioning for use in counselling and Reaction Pattern Research. Auckland: University of Auckland: Occasional Paper.

Everts, H. (2004a). *Vision and challenge in School-Based Family Counselling.* Paper presented at the Second Annual Oxford Symposium in SBFC. Oxford: Brasenose College.

Everts, H. (2004b). *Migant Family Resilience.* Paper presented at the Inaugural International Asian Health Conference. New Zealand: Auckland, November.

Everts, J.F. (2007). *Applying Principles of School-Based Family Counselling to Preventive Intervention with Migrant and Refugee Families.* Paper presented at the Fifth Oxford Symposium in School-Based Family Counselling. Hong Kong: University of Hong Kong, June.

Everts, J.F. (2008). Integrating supportive care in schools with the enhancement of family resilience – A New Zealand project for immigrant families. *International Journal for School-Based Family Counseling, 1,* 57-64.

Everts, J.F. (2011a). *Building resilience in migrant families – An illustration of School-Based Family Counseling in action.* Paper presented at the Symposium on School-Based Family Counseling. Hong Kong: Hong Kong Institute of Education, June 25th.

Everts, J.F. (2011b). *Resilient couples, strong families.* Workshop presented at the Symposium on School-Based Family Counseling. Hong Kong: Hong Kong Institute of Education, June 25th.

Everts, J.F. (2011d). *Building resilience in disaster-hit families.* Workshop presented at the 2011 Padjadjaran Conference on Psychology for a Better Future. Bandung, Indonesia, October 26th.

Everts, J.F. & Tai, J. (2003). A Parenting Programme for migrant families. Auckland: University of Auckland, Faculty of Education: Draft Program.

Everts, H. & Wu, P. (2004). *Identity and resilience in families facing cultural transition through migration - with illustrative reference to Chinese families in New Zealand and Taiwan.* Paper presented at the Third Biennial International Conference on Intercultural Research, National Taiwan Normal University, Taipei, May.

Gerrard, B. (2008). School-Based Family Counseling: Overview, trends, and recommendations for future research. *International Journal for School-Based Family Counseling, 1,* 6-24.

Kim, H. (2001). *Parenting skills and couple relationships of Korean parents who have migrated with adolescent children to New Zealand.* Auckland: University of Auckland: unpublished MEd dissertation.

Kim, H. & Everts, J.F. (2007). *An evaluation of the Parenting Programme.* Auckland: University of Auckland, Faculty of Education: Research Report. Lim, G. (2010).

Saeid, A. (2010). *An evaluation of the Parenting Programme for Afghan men.* Auckland: University of Auckland, Faculty of Education: Research Report.

Shih, S. & Tai, J. (2002). *Migrant Family Resilience: A study of the process af adaptation for 25 Taiwanese migrant families in New Zealand.* Auckland: University of Auckland: Unpublished Manuscript.

Soriano, M. (2004). *School-Based Family Counseling: A caring, culturally congruent bridge to diverse communities.* Paper presented at the Second Annual Oxford Symposium in SBFC. Oxford: Brasenose College.

Tai, J. (2004). *Effective parenting for Chinese families.* Auckland: University of Auckland: unpublished MEd. Dissertation.Tai, J. (2010). *An evaluation of the Parenting for Single Parents Programme.* Auckland: University of Auckland, Faculty of Education: Research Report.

Tai, J. & Lai, J. (2011). *An evaluation of the Parenting for Grandparents Programme.* Auckland: University of Auckland, Faculty of Education: Research Report.Vong, C. (2002). The impact of migration on the Chinese family. *New Zealand Journal of Counselling, 23,* 21-24.

Walsh, F. (1996). The concept of family resilience: Crisis and challenge. *Family Process, 35,* 261-281.

Walsh, F. (2006). *Strengthening family resilience (2nd ed).* New York: Guilford.

Wong, J. & Everts, H. (2002). How Chinese families develop resilience. *New Zealand Journal of Counselling, 23,* 25-32.

Wu, S. J. (2001). Parenting in Chinese American families. In N. B. Webb, *Culturally diverse parent-child and family relationships.* NY: Columbia University Press.

RESOURCES

Everts, J.F. (2011c). *Couple Resilience – Scoring Guidelines.* Auckland: University of Auckland, Faculty of Education: Resource Manual.

Parenting Programme for Korean Fathers. Auckland, New Zealand: University of Auckland, Faculty of Education: Draft Program.

Migrant Family Resilience Project (2007). *Parenting Programme.* Auckland: University of Auckland, Faculty of Education: Program Manual.

Migrant Family Resilience Project (2009a). *Successful Families Programme.* Auckland: University of Auckland, Faculty of Education: Program Manual.

Migrant Family Resilience Project (2009b). *Protecting Family Happiness Programme.* Auckland: University of Auckland, Faculty of Education: Program Manual.

Migrant Family Resilience Project (2010). *Parenting for Grandparents Programme.* Auckland: University of Auckland, Faculty of Education: Program Manual.

Migrant Family Resilience Project (2012). *Making Strong Couples Programme.* Auckland: University of Auckland, Faculty of Education: Program Manual.

APPENDIX A

COUPLE RESILIENCE – Summary of scores for all samples

Sample origin *	NZ	USA	NL	Mal	HK	Indo	Total	% of	Rank
No. of participants	162	80	154	165	22	19	602	Total R	

Number of Responses

Group 1 – Personal resourcefulness - a person's own qualities and skills

	NZ	USA	NL	Mal	HK	Indo	Total	% of	Rank
Optimism	41	23	51	14	5	8	142		6
Awareness	10	10	48	34	5	4	111		8
Religious faith	37	0	4	41	14	11	107		9
Personal strength	39	13	26	11	3	5	97		10
Total N for group 1	**127**	**46**	**129**	**100**	**27**	**28**	**457**	**22%**	
% of total sample N	*18%*	*14%*	*25%*	*28%*	*22 %*	*33%*			

Group two – Emotional bonds - feelings and attitudes towards one's partner

	NZ	USA	NL	Mal	HK	Indo	Total		Rank
Love, affection	99	72	94	46	19	6	336		1
Commitment	76	56	47	46	7	13	245		3
Tolerance	57	18	59	48	11	4	197		4
Similar values	52	50	6	10	10	3	131		7
Total N for group 2	**284**	**196**	**206**	**150**	**47**	**26**	**909**	**43%**	
% of total sample N	*41%*	*58%*	*40%*	*42%*	*39%*	*31%*			

Group three – Action skills – the couple's relationship skills

	NZ	USA	NL	Mal	HK	Indo	Total		Rank
Communicn skills	100	33	125	29	10	7	304		2
Past history	45	11	7	8	3	2	76		11
Collaboration	38	10	9	7	6	4	74		12
Intimacy time	24	2	14	2	4	2	48		13
Self-Sacrifice	0	3	5	19	4	3	34		14
Physical resources	4	1	0	5	4	0	14		15
Total N for group 3	**211**	**60**	**160**	**70**	**31**	**18**	**550**	**26%**	
% of total sample N	*30%*	*18%*	*31%*	*20%*	*26%*	*21%*			

Group four – Community support - the couple's wider community relationships

	NZ	USA	NL	Mal	HK	Indo	Total		Rank
Support network	63	23	19	21	16	12	154		5
Self-protection	0	9	3	10	0	0	22		16
Role models	13	1	1	4	0	1	20		17
Total N for group 4	**76**	**33**	**23**	**35**	**16**	**13**	**196**	**9%**	
% of total sample N	*11%*	*10%*	*4%*	*10%*	*13%*	*15%*			

| **Total sample N of Rs** | **698** | **335** | **518** | **355** | **121** | **85** | **2112** | | |

* NZ – New Zealand; NL – Netherlands; Mal – Malaysia; HK – Hong Kong; Indo – Indonesia

Appendix B: Making Strong Couple Program – Abbreviated Outline

Making Strong Couples Programme (2012) – Leader Guidelines

Session I: Introduction and Setting the Context

AIM OF SESSION To welcome participants, share expectations, overview the programme, introduce the concept of couple resilience, and look at what others want for their marriage.

SESSION STRUCTURE (for a 2 hour session)

1. Welcome and personal introductions; get expectations (put on board).

2. Brief overview of programme, relate to participant expectations; ground rules.

3. Explain importance of others' expectations in setting relationship context; share some such messages; reflect on their importance in couples.

4. In large group, share some of partner expectations and what learned in session.

5. Homework – talk more about that between sessions, report back at next session.

Session II: Personal Wellness or Integrity

AIM OF SESSION   Introduce the concept of personal wellness or integrity, have them understand and share aspects of each partner's qualities and skills of personal wellness.

SESSION STRUCTURE (for a 2 hour session)

1. Do a round, share reflections, affirm and sum up comments.

2. Complete CR questionnaire anonymously. Collect questionnaires afterwards (research).

3. Circulate and discuss handout on Personal Wellness (the first section in the CR model).

4. Complete Personal Wellness Questionnaire on partner, with example.

5. Share in pairs, listen, thank in turn.

6. Note and share own qualities, as above.

7. Make and discuss the final three points about making two people happy.

8. Conclude with a round of learnings, give homework – share and affirm more.

Session III: The Couple's Emotional Relationship

AIM OF SESSION To introduce the concept of the couple's emotional relationship or intimacy; have them understand and share examples of this in their relationship.

SESSION STRUCTURE (for a 2 hour session)

1. Introduction - do a round on homework, affirm, discuss the 3 couple relationship tasks.

2. The 4 A's – seek ideas, introduce and discuss 4 A's, share and illustrate in pairs.

3. In large group share learnings.

4. CR – circulate and discuss section 2 points from CR model, discuss in pairs, ask re role models and illustrate. Share in large group.

5. The five love languages – share, discuss, apply, rate importance, share in pairs.

6. Do round – learnings, homework – application of above.

Session IV: Effective Communication

AIM OF SESSION   To introduce the process and skills of communication; demonstrate, discuss, and practice them.

SESSION STRUCTURE (for a 2 hour session)

1. Introduction – do a round on homework, discuss, affirm each couple.

2. Introduce topic. Do another round and ask each couple one thing that they are happy with in their communication, and one thing that they are not happy with. Write on the board.
3. Note communication as 4 interlinked skills – listening, self-sharing, finding solutions, and acting (the last comes up in the next session). Relate to previous topics.

4. Listening – demonstrate poor listening, discuss, relate to handout points.

5. Demonstrate good listening, discuss, practice both in pairs.

6. Introduce you-message; discuss; demonstrate I-message; discuss; practice in pairs.

7. Demonstrate and discuss win-lose argument and win-win discussion; practice in pairs.

8. Self-control – go through points in handout; discuss.

9. Homework - couples select an issue, somewhat tricky, practice at home, report back.

Session V: Teamwork and Effective Action

AIM OF SESSION   Detail the relationship between collaborative teamwork, effective couple action and resilience.

SESSION STRUCTURE (for a 2 hour session)

1. Do a round to ask how their homework went. Discuss briefly, affirm each couple.

2. Introduce topic of teamwork in effective action, is built on all the preceding qualities and skills in the program; need for effective communication and successful collaboration.

3. Remind that good communication involves active listening and mutual sharing of thoughts; selection of best solutions; expression of mutual love and respect, commitment, and tolerance; and having the personal needs of each partner met (win-win).

4. Discuss and illustrate alternative forms of leadership in effective couple collaboration.

5. Go through other relationship skills on resource sheet; illustrate and discuss.

6. Discuss and illustrate support networks, role models and self-protection

7. Homework - couples select an issue, somewhat tricky, to practice on at home, report back.

Session VI: Conclusion

AIM OF SESSION
To sum up, evaluate what participants have learned, hand out certificates, and celebrate.

SESSION STRUCTURE (for a 2 hour session)

1. Do a round to ask how their homework went. Discuss briefly, affirm each couple.

2. Circulate Couple Resilience handout, go through it as a reminder of topics covered.

3. Note – good partnership starts with critical awareness of self, then of partner. Remember that the excitement of difference in the beginning of a relationship is not as important as the comfort of similarity in the long run. A good relationship takes time to mature; growth comes in fits and starts; we learn as much from our failures as we do from our successes. There is no recipe for a perfect relationship. Different sets of skills and qualities can build a happy and strong relationship. The more Couple Resilience resources, the better.

4. Evaluate programme; share learnings; hand out certificates; affirm contributions; celebrate.

PART IV

SCHOOL-BASED FAMILY COUNSELING CHANGE STRATEGIES: SCHOOL-INTERVENTION FOCUS

SCHOOL FOCUS

School-Prevention	## School-Intervention
Family-Prevention	Family-Intervention

PREVENTION FOCUS

INTERVENTION FOCUS

FAMILY FOCUS

Chapter 11
How to do Teacher Consultation: An Integrative Behavior-Process Consultation Approach

Margaret Garcia and Michele D. Wallace

OVERVIEW: *This chapter provides basic concepts, skills, and mindsets for school-based family counselors to consider when taking a behavioral approach to teacher consultation. The case of Jacob from Chapter 8 will be considered from the teacher's perspective. Also as in Chapter 8, we will recommend the application of process consultation along with behavioral consultation as an integration of consultation models that fully involve and expose the consultee to problem-solving.*

BACKGROUND

With backgrounds in Mental Health Consultation (Caplan & Caplan, 1998), Applied Behavior Analysis, and Adlerian Consultation, we have worked to provide our graduate students in the various Master's degree in Counseling Options good grounding in consultative services to parents/guardians and teachers. At California State University, Los Angeles, graduate students in School Psychology and School Counseling are required to take a course in School-Based Consultation in which they engage in a consultation relationship with one teacher for a minimum of three sessions. They learn to apply Process Consultation (Schein 1999) alongside one other model of consultation such as behavioral or mental health consultation. Consultants learn to consider what may be causing the teacher's current work difficulty such as lack of knowledge, lack of skill, lack of objectivity, or lack of confidence. When approaching a teacher to participate in consultation as part of their training requirements, our graduate students will usually be met with willingness and curiosity about whether the sessions will yield helpful results. This chapter will address some of the common issues that arise in providing teacher consultation including confidentiality, resistance, and barriers to treatment implementation. For example, when teachers are asked to think about a problem they are experiencing with one student, they often try to present a behavior problem demonstrated by several students and will settle for focusing on just one student by choosing the worst of the bunch. For example, they cite several students who engage in talking out of turn when they should be working quietly, or students who don't persevere on tasks. At other times, teachers report feeling rather satisfied with how well their classroom management works with the exception of just one student who makes things difficult for everyone else, such as the "class clown."

Most teacher training programs do not involve student teachers in consultation with support personnel such as school psychologists or school counselors. They learn to make referrals to special education staff for students with learning problems or refer students to the principal or "office" if they pose significant disruptions in the classroom. Alderman & Gimpel (1996) found that teachers are most likely to seek consultation from the school psychologist or school counselor for aggressive behaviors but tend to address disruptive behavior on their own. They also found that teachers first prefer to address problem behaviors on their own followed by consulting with other teachers, then the principal, followed by taking classes on behavior interventions. This may be due to perceptions of greater access to fellow teachers and the principal than to the school counselor.

There is a growing appreciation for the role of school psychologists and school counselors as teacher consultants. Many schools and school districts have implemented Response to Intervention (RTI) models of identifying and addressing students at risk. These are tiered approaches that provide basic preventive interventions at the primary level for all students including screening for academic and mental health risk factors. At the next tier, research-based interventions are provided for students who have been identified to be at risk due to low performance on progress-monitoring measures (secondary prevention). Finally, the third tier addresses students at highest risk in need of individualized interventions (tertiary prevention). There is less emphasis on identifying students for special education in a "wait-to-fail" approach and more emphasis on providing classroom consultation at the preventive level (Suga i& Horner, 2009).

THE CASE OF JACOB

As presented in Chapter 8, Jacob is a fifth grade student who had been retained in the third grade due to significant delays in his academic achievement. At every grade level since kindergarten, Jacob's teachers have expressed concerns about his ability to attend and his apparent inability to stay seated, and to avoid talking out of turn. But he has never been assessed for special education as the parents have refused to sign assessment plans claiming that Jacob is fine at home. His current teacher, Mrs. Davis, reports Jacob's reading skills to be at the mid-fourth grade level and his math skills to be slightly below the fourth grade level. Mrs. Davis believes he would catch up to his grade peers if he completed more classwork and particularly if he completed homework of which he currently submits none. It's now the spring semester and Jacob hasn't turned in completed homework assignments since February and very few before then.

Mrs. Davis has been teaching fifth grade at the same school for 9 years. Prior to that she taught third grade at a different school which was during first two years of her teaching career. She enjoys teaching the fifth grade and takes pride in preparing students for middle school. However, the drawback is the frustration she feels when a minority of her students struggle academically and she is forced to see them socially promoted to the sixth grade. This is Mrs. Davis's current concern with Jacob who has already been held back one grade but is still at least a year below grade level.

Jacob's parents have been married for 15 years and have three children including Angela (14 years old), Jacob (12 years old), and Matthew (8 years old). Angela is an above average student attending the eighth grade at the local middle school and Matthew is performing at grade level attending third grade where Jacob also attends. Frank reports that he is of Mexican descent on his paternal side and Greek/Italian on his maternal side. Linda reports that she is second generation born in the United States with grandparents immigrated from Mexico. The family lives in a middle class neighborhood in a Los Angeles suburb where the population is 39% Latino/Hispanic, 27% Armenian, 16% Asian, 2% African American, 10% two or more ethnicities, <1% Native American, and 5% other.

Sandra, the SBFC counselor at Jacob's school contacted agreed to meet with Mrs. Davis to discuss Jacob. As a result of their first meeting, Sandra agreed to reach out to Jacob's parents to address the lack of homework submitted as Mrs. Davis feels her attempts to involve them have been futile. She sends notes home and leaves messages on their cell numbers but typically receives no response. When she has spoken to either parent, they would promise to work on it but Mrs. Davis would still not receive homework from Jacob. When Mrs. Davis asks Jacob about it, he usually just shrugs his shoulders and avoids responding.

After meeting with Jacob's father, Sandra learns that Jacob is being sent home with homework plus unfinished school work that should have been done in class. She agreed to meet with Mrs. Davis about improving Jacob's classwork completion.

RELATIONSHIP TO THE SBFC MODEL

School-Prevention: School-based consultation is aimed at preventing school failure. Behavioral consultation is aimed at problem-solving to develop treatment plans that reduce problem behavior by helping the teacher to gain the knowledge and skills to intervene. As a result, teachers have new skills sets that can apply to other students with similar problems. Teachers become better equipped to define a problem behavior and hypothesize the function or purpose it serves for the student. The teacher also becomes more skilled at making observations and possibly how to use paraprofessionals (classroom aides) to implement a behavior support or intervention plan.

School-Intervention: The SBFC professional who uses behavioral consultation along with process consultation will recognize how well it prepares the teacher to directly address the problem behavior and often results in improved behaviors. Greater time on task, for example, may yield improved academic performance and growth toward meeting curricular standards. Consultation also serves to support remediation for aggressive behaviors, disruptive behaviors, and poor social skills.

Family-Prevention: Conjoint Behavioral Consultation (CBC) is basically behavioral consultation conducted with both the teacher and the family to address school-related problems. In the case of Jacob, CBC is not employed in the sense that Mrs. Davis does not meet with the Rodriguez family simultaneously with Sandra. Sandra instead meets with teacher and father on separate occasions. However, Sandra is able to serve as a collaborator for helping the caregivers in each setting to meet Jacob's needs in ways that complement the treatment plans for home and school.

Family-Intervention: Sandra's consultation with Mrs. Davis should either result in helping Mrs. Davis improve her communication skills with Jacob's parents or to implement a plan in her classroom that is independent of what occurs at home. For instance, Mrs. Davis can offer to help Jacob do his homework in her classroom after school or she can implement a reward system to reinforce Jacob's submission of completed homework assignments. But this would do little to address the needs of the family to help Jacob complete his work. When Jacob moves on to the sixth grade, not all of his teachers will make an effort to reinforce homework submission. By working with Sandra to involve the family, the opportunity to remediate problems in the home that address learning supports and other behavioral plans.

EVIDENCE-BASED SUPPORT

As indicated in Chapter 8, procedures following a behavioral approach in parent consultation have resulted in outcomes demonstrating the reduction of problem behaviors and the increase in desired behaviors. The Journal of Applied Behavior Analysis provides extensive examples of single case studies in which behavioral technologies have been implemented to improve behavior in home and agency settings. It does not offer as much in terms of school-based applications. The Journal of Behavior Assessment and Intervention in Children (Anderson et al. (2010) for example) disseminates more research outcomes applied to school settings. The School Psychology Review and The School Psychology Quarterly also publish in the areas of behavioral interventions in school settings, but are not limited to behavioral consultation.

A growing body of support is gathering for Conjoint Behavioral Consultation which involves the teachers and parents working in collaborative consultation with a school psychologist or school counselor (Sheridan, Eagle & Doll, 2006; Kratochwill, Bergan, Sheridan, & Elliott, 1996).

PROCEDURE

Behavioral consultation is primarily an indirect intervention with an emphasis on problem-solving and consists of four basic stages: problem identification, problem analysis, treatment implementation, and treatment evaluation (Kratochwill & Bergan, 1990; Sheridan & Elliott, 1991). These stages designate the steps that are required to go from specifying the problem to determining a solution with evidence of its effectiveness. The four stages of Behavioral Consultation are re-examined for the case of Jacob within the phases of Process Consultation with the teacher.

PROCESS CONSULTATION

Based on ten principles, process consultation as described by Schein (1999) offers a good structure for any model of consultation including behavioral. The ten principles will be briefly re-iterated here as applied to Jacob in the classroom. See Chapter 8 for how it applies to Jacob at home.

TEN PRINCIPLES OF PROCESS CONSULTATION

1. *Always try to be helpful.* At times, teachers will ask quite directly for ideas about what to do. We caution consultants to avoid providing quick answers. It may seem helpful to provide quick answers to an eager teacher, especially when you are providing evidence-based strategies. But unless the teacher has a very good handle on defining and analyzing the problem, a more helpful approach is to engage in active inquiry and problem-solving.

2. *Always stay in touch with the current reality.* When a teacher asks you "Have you ever taught before?" that is a good indication that you are demonstrating a lack of empathy for the teacher's current reality. Sometimes consultants offer suggestions that require the teacher to engage in an inordinate amount of data collection and responding when she has over twenty other students in her classroom demanding her attention. What works in an ideal setting will not always be feasible for the large class setting.

3. *Access your ignorance.* Don't be eager to demonstrate how much you know about behavioral terminology, attention-deficits, hyperactivity, relational aggression, etc. Instead, be willing to spend time clarifying statements and making sure your understanding of the teacher's view of the problem is clear. Don't make assumptions about the principal just because you already know the principal, for instance. Many times teachers will expect that you already know aspects of the case because you work with the same people and have worked with many students in their classrooms. Don't let this stop you from learning more about the case from the teacher's point of view. There are many times we have an impression of certain students in our graduate programs and are surprised to find out how rude they may be when interacting with staff or adjunct faculty. People present themselves differently in different settings and under varying circumstances.

4. *Everything you do is an intervention.* Through process consultation the SBFC professional will serve as a model for how to think about the case. This is going to extend beyond your immediate role in a consultation session to how you present yourself overall as a SBFC professional. Then of course, your inquiry and ability to demonstrate an understanding about the presenting problem first from the teacher's perspective and then from an objective framework that redirects the teacher's attention is very powerful as an intervention tool. Sandra will acknowledge to Mrs. Davis the importance of getting the parents more involved in Jacob's academic success, but she will also help Mrs. Davis recognize ways to support their success as well as her own success with Jacob in the classroom.

5. *It is the consultee who owns the problem and the solution.* Leave your ego at the door when serving as a consultant. The teacher is the expert on his or her classroom. Mrs. Davis knows her students, their

strengths and weaknesses, her support staff, her own abilities and competencies, etc. She may not reveal all the relevant details to the consultant, especially one whose time is difficult to access. Consider the media regarding student achievement. Whose reputations are really on the line? When measuring student success, it's the teachers who are held most directly accountable. Don't forget this and appreciate your role in supporting their success without trying to gain commendations when things go well. If teachers associate success in their classrooms with consultation sessions with you, your value will be recognized.

6. Go with the flow. As a SBFC professional your time will be tightly scheduled and your days will go by quickly before you've managed to complete everything on your to-do list. You may often feel overwhelmed with putting out fires, dealing with crises, meeting with teachers and administrators, holding regular counseling groups, and seeing students for individual counseling as well as families in their homes. But with all that, you may have more flexibility than the classroom teacher. Mrs. Davis cannot just schedule meetings throughout the day, she can't even leave her classroom to go to the bathroom when needed without getting someone to cover for her. She has many students who demand her attention before, during, and after class. When you schedule meetings with the teacher, go with the flow.

7. Timing is crucial. Don't blurt out a question the moment it enters your mind. Take note and ask the question when the time is right. Remember the fourth principle: everything is an intervention. Your questions are most effective when asked at the right time. Be deliberate and patient so that the teacher can gain the most from your inquiry. Process consultation involves phases of inquiry that we will present in the next section. The phases are sequential and should be timed to serve their purpose before moving to the next phase.

8. Be constructively opportunistic with confrontive interventions. One of the most difficult skills to learn as a consultant is recognizing when one is being confrontive. Consultants need to realize that questions such as "Did you talk to his parents?" or "Did you try ignoring him when he talks out of turn?" are Confrontive and should be avoided until one has fully gone through Exploratory Diagnostic Inquiry.

9. Everything is data. Errors will always be observed and are the prime source for learning. You won't always say and do the exact right thing during consultation and in response to what a teacher has told you. There doesn't exist an exact protocol to spell out the most correct line of questioning and responding to the consultee. Use your client observation skills to gauge reactions and learn from mistakes.

10. When in doubt, share the problem. A good consultant should recognize the value of consultation and seek it out as a consultee when appropriate. While respecting FERPA and HIPAA laws and confidentiality, a SBFC professional can share a case with a colleague who can offer a different problem solving perspective.

PHASES OF INQUIRY IN PROCESS CONSULTATION

All consultation sessions should begin with some basic structuring that establishes timing of the session, confidentiality and exceptions to it, and then should transition to formal consultation. The three basic phases of inquiry in process consultation are Pure Inquiry, Exploratory Diagnostic Inquiry, and Confrontive Inquiry. Whether the consultation was initiated by the SBFC professional or the parent, consultation should begin in Pure Inquiry. However, if the consultation was initiated by the parent, the

SBFC professional should begin with silence, allowing the parent to present the problem. The SBFC professional should only ask questions that will prompt the parent to tell their story, sharing the problem from his or her perspective without censorship from the consultant. Mrs. Davis initiated the consultation session so she should begin with silence after introducing the session.

Table 11.1 Process and Behavioral Consultation as Applied to Jacob

Process Consultation Phases of Inquiry	Stages of Behavioral Consultation	Case of Jacob
Pure Inquiry Ask questions that allow the Consultee to provide his or her own perspective. This should be uncensored and the Consultant should avoid redirecting the discussion unless the Consultee wanders far from the presenting problem.	The first stage of BC does not formally begin in Pure Inquiry as this is the point where the Consultee presents the story from his or her own perspective with minimal directing from the Consultant. However the beginnings of identifying the problem will emerge.	Sandra allows Mrs. Davis to discuss her views of Jacob's behavior. Mrs. Davis takes the opportunity to vent about the lack of parental involvement. She places a lot of emphasis on homework but also addresses Jacob's behavior surrounding his classwork.
Exploratory Diagnostic Inquiry In this phase the Consultant approaches the presenting problem with a specific model in mind. The questions asked serve to gather more information and to direct the Consultee's attention to specific aspects of the case.	*Stage 1 Identifying the Problem* The Consultant will ask questions that allow the Consultee to more operationally define the problem and/or target behavior.	Jacob's work completion is defined as sitting at his desk with materials ready, working on the assignment until complete. The problem behaviors are defined as getting out of his seat without permission, attempting to engage other students in off-task conversations. The behaviors that Mrs. Davis wants Jacob to increase are staying in his seat and working on the assignment. Jacob spends measurable time on classwork and often asks for help but not until Mrs. Davis prompts him to get to work.
a) Exploring Reactions Ask questions that bring out the details of a specific case. Be sure to have the Consultee talk about a specific incident of the problem behavior. While acceptable during Pure Inquiry, in this phase,	*Stage 1* continues with the Consultant asking questions that address the antecedents and consequences of the target behaviors. More specifically, the Consultant asks about the Consultee's actions around the target behavior.	Questions Sandra asks at this Phase/Stage: "What does Jacob do when you prompt the class to begin working independently?" "How do you react when Jacob

do not allow the Consultee to explain the problem in generalities such as "He always..." or "He never..." Use this step of the Exploratory Phase to ask the Consultee how he or she responds to client's behavior.		begins doing his work?" "How do you react when Jacob gets out of his seat?" "How did you respond when Jacob asked for help?" "How did the other students respond when Jacob got out of his seat?"
b)Exploring Hypotheses At this step, ask questions such as "Why do you think he responded that way?" or "What purpose do you think that behavior is serving for him?" "What does he get out of that behavior?" "Why did you respond the way you did?"	*Stage 2 Problem Analysis* Hypothesize the function of the client's behavior (Attention, Escape, Tangible, Automatic)	Sandra has Mrs. Davis fill out an indirect assessment that focuses on the purpose behind Jacob's behavior, that models for Mrs. Davis that in order to understand why Jacob does what he does she needs to understand why. When asked "Why do you think Jacob leaves his seat when you prompt him to do his work?"
c) Exploring Actions Taken or Contemplated Be certain to ask the Consultee what he or she has already tried to address the problem. This helps the Consultee to understand the perception of resources including their own knowledge and skills. The Consultant provides enough opportunity for the Consultee to discuss what has already been tried along with how well it worked or didn't work and the reasons behind the outcomes.	*Stage 2 Problem Analysis* It may be determined that the Consultee knows what might work and has seen improvement with certain strategies but such strategies may not be feasible to continue. It could be that punishment is effective but the Consultant will work toward positive interventions. Further, punishment serves to reduce behavior and parents often use it when their actual intent is to increase a behavior.	After completing the survey, Mrs. Davis considers that Jacob would prefer to leave his seat and do just about anything else than to stay in his seat to do his work. She notes that when he does stay in his seat, he fiddles with his papers and pencil or anything he can get his hands on. He doesn't initiate requests for help but does accept help when Mrs. Davis offers. On many occasions Jacob will leave his seat and talk to other students causing them distraction. On these occasions after multiple prompts seem futile, Mrs. Davis sends Jacob out of the classroom to either the front office or to a neighboring classroom.

Confrontive	Stage 3 Treatment Implementation	Sandra will ask questions such as:
It's at this phase of Inquiry that the Process Consultant asks about specific strategies to consider and will offer their expert perspective on the problem and why it is occurring. In the Confrontive phase, the Consultee can be direct about addressing the evidence that supports an intervention and the knowledge and skills that need to be developed to implement the plan effectively.	It's at this stage that the Consultant offers a great deal of direct feedback about the details of an effective treatment plan. If the Consultee lacks the appropriate skills, the Consultant may take the opportunity to teach the skill.	"Is Jacob able to do his work independently or does he need help?" "Is he getting a lot of attention from you aside from help?" "How can the assignment be made less aversive for Jacob?" "Does Jacob have more success at certain parts of the day?" "If so, is this due to the time of day or the type of assignment?" "Does sending unfinished work home with Jacob result in completion?" "How does this affect his homework?"
	Stage 4 Treatment Evaluation Here is where the Consultant and Consultee will determine whether a plan has been successful; Consultation may continue to help the family generalize to another behavior or to another setting. Consultation may be terminated or it may lead to involving other parties such as the teacher.	

Result of Sandra's work with Mrs. Davis and the Rodriguez family: Basically, Sandra has engaged in Active Inquiry with one of Jacob's parents and with his teacher. Through interviews and surveys, Sandra and Mrs. Davis have determined that Jacob tries to escape from work on a regular basis because the work is too difficult. He moves around at his desk a lot when he does stay in his seat so leaving his seat seems to serve his desire to escape the task and gain comfort from movement.

During Exploratory and Confrontive Consultation, Sandra recognized that Mrs. Davis hypothesized Jacob's behavior to be escape maintained, especially when she sends him out of the classroom. She knows that he may need extra help but she also knows that even with easier items, Jacob does not persevere on tasks for more than 5 minutes at a time unless she works with him directly, item by item. She generally finds Jacob to be a nice boy whose noncompliance is rarely accompanied by disrespectful comments, something Mrs. Davis has plenty of experience with over the years.

In sum, the function of Jacob's behavior is Escape. To increase on-task behavior Mrs. Davis is going to reduce the number of items Jacob needs to complete. But this was not an easy concession for her to make:

Sandra: "What would happen if you reduced the number of items so that Jacob did not feel so overwhelmed by the overall task?"

Mrs. Davis: "I wouldn't want the other kids to see that he is getting away with less work. What would they think if they knew that getting out of your seat was rewarded with less work?"

Sandra: "How much work do the other students currently think he is getting done?" They may not protest as much as you might imagine. They are likely aware of his distractedness and need for extra support. "

Overall, Mrs. Davis agrees to reducing the amount of work for the classroom and homework assignments. She also agrees to not send unfinished classwork home. Further, Mrs. Davis and Sandra develop a plan to increase Jacob's initiating requests for help appropriately. Mrs. Davis will ignore Jacob when he leaves his desk and offer reinforcers to students who remain seated and on task when Jacob wanders the aisles. When Jacob is in his seat working, Mrs. Davis offers praise and checks in to provide feedback and or help on the items he has completed to that point.

With all her experience, Mrs. Davis's work with Jacob is not unique. She has worked with many students who don't complete their work or create disruptions. But she was particularly frustrated with a lack of response from the parents. Sandra decided to work with Mrs. Davis in addressing how she attempts to communicate with the parents, who like Jacob seem to engage in escape or avoidance of either the work that will be involved in helping Jacob, or the blame they may feel from Mrs. Davis. The teacher is encouraged to avoid adding to the work load by keeping unfinished work in the classroom and by creating a reward system for Jacob for his submission of homework. Once he does submit the completed or even partially completed assignment, Mrs. Davis will contact the parents to report his progress and to thank them for their support.

MULTICULTURAL COUNSELING CONSIDERATIONS

SBFC professionals may recognize that Behavioral Consultation and the treatment plans that result when done well have significant support in the literature but may at times seem quite prescriptive. During treatment implementation and treatment evaluation the SBFC professional should consider cultural issues that could affect treatment integrity. It is critical to help teachers to take into account the student's culture and family when determining best practices. While cultural issues were not directly addressed in the case of Jacob, he does live in an environment where there are typically different views on the family's attitudes toward education. The Armenian families approach education differently than the Latino families but some will stereotype one as placing a greater value on education than the other. Many other factors contribute to a family's approach to education and value judgments should be avoided.

As listed in Chapter 8, Rogers (2000) identifies six cross-cultural consultation competencies, many of which go beyond consultation and apply to all roles of the SBFC:

1. Understanding one's own and others' culture
2. Developing cross-cultural communication and interpersonal skills
3. Examining cultural embeddedness of consultation
4. Using qualitative methodologies
5. Acquiring culture-specific knowledge
6. Knowledge and skill in use of interpreters

We recommend the work of Ingraham (2000) for learning more about multicultural consultee centered case consultation. She takes a mental health consultation approach rather than behavioral, but the concepts are critical for all those engaged in school-based consultation. Unlike working with families, with teachers the consultation triad could be one in which the consultee, the consultant, and the client, are all from different cultural backgrounds. We should also consider how problem-solving is affected when the teacher and SBFC share a culture that is different from the student's or if the student and SBFC share a culture different than the teacher's, etc. Taking a culture sensitive approach opens up the problem solving to more data to consider and this is conducive to Behavioral Consultation.

Sheridan (2000) notes that although Behavioral Consultation (BC) and Conjoint Behavioral Consultation (CBC) have significant support in the literature for their effectiveness in addressing challenging behaviors, little research has been done on their applications in multicultural settings. Sheridan points out that the structural elements of BC and CBC are often the focus of research but that consultation itself is relational in nature and this is an area that needs further study among Behavioral Consultants. We have partially addressed this through the use of Process Consultation along with BC, but the effectiveness of this proposed framework is yet to be investigated. Nonetheless, even within the structural features of BC, consultants can address cultural values and issues through improved relational skills and better awareness of how problems are identified, analyzed, and treated from different cultural viewpoints (Holcomb-McCoy, 2009). Sheridan, Eagle, & Doll (2006) found that over an eight year study of graduate students in school psychology training programs, CBC was perceived to be effective whether in settings with or without diversity. They looked at behavioral change, goal attainment, acceptability, and reported satisfaction with the elements of CBC.

Generally speaking, BC is typically based on single-case research design thus it offers excellent opportunity for addressing the specific cultural aspects of the problem in the setting in which it occurs. The difficulty arises when consultants either fail to recognize cultural variables or when the behavior occurs across settings such as at home and in the classroom.

CHALLENGES AND SOLUTIONS

One of the major barriers that our consultants experience in working with teachers is that the teachers are often tied to a specific classroom management approach that is not conducive to implementing treatment plans for individual students. On the one hand they seem to realize that their classroom management system is not working for certain students and ask for help in addressing the unique problems presented by those exceptions. On the other hand, teachers worry that making changes for one student will result in weakening a classroom management system that is otherwise effective for more of the students. For example, many teachers use a color card system in which all students start out at green but are told to flip their cards to yellow, red, or purple as they break classroom rules. Reinforcers are not necessarily available to students at the red and purple levels when it could be these students who are most in need of immediate reinforcement for good behavior. Many teachers report that they don't follow through on making problem students flip their cards because they would always be at the lowest levels. The inconsistency in their use adds to its ineffectiveness.

Resistance is also an issue that needs to be addressed by Behavioral Consultants. Although resistance impedes problem-solving, it is normal coping behavior intended more toward self-preservation than to stand in the way of improvement. Types of resistance include (Kampwirth & Powers, 2012):

1. The Direct Block – "No, I don't have time to meet with you."
2. "Yes, but…"–This form of resistance recognizes interventions might work for others but give reasons why it wouldn't work in their case.
3. "I did it but it didn't work" – The teacher may have tried something with good fidelity to the treatment plan or may report that they already tried something even though what they attempted is quite different from what you are suggesting.

4. The Reverse – The teacher agrees to follow through but has excuses for not actually implementing the plan.
5. Projected Threat – The plan may create more work or cause tension between the teacher and parents.
6. Guilt Trip – The teacher points out her multiple responsibilities overwhelming duties when faced with the extra work of implementing a treatment plan.
7. Tradition- What teachers are already doing works well enough and they don't want to change it for just one to a few students. This is often the case with the color card system that teachers use for classroom management.

Factors that increase resistance include the following and should be part of the problem solving process:

1. Ambiguity
2. Overwork
3. Complexity of the Intervention
4. Tradition or Habit
5. Sunk Costs (Resistance due to sunk cost is when a suggested intervention predicts better results than current practice but the consultee keeps the current practice because of the time and energy already invested into it.)
6. Upsetting the Power or Status Balance
7. Insensitivity to Cultural Differences, Sexual Orientation, and Gender

Another important caution pertains to those school counselors, SBFC professionals, or school psychologists who have entered the mental health field after having some teaching experience, especially when they are new to the field. These consultants need to be reminded that they are not serving as mentor teachers and should not be tapping into their pedagogical knowledge base and skill sets for problem-solving. If that is what the consultee needs then they should be encouraged to gain access to such mentoring. SBFC professionals are there to help problem-solve from a different knowledge base and skill set. More than content, it is process skills and problem-solving skills that are most critical to the consultation relationship.

As indicated in the previous section, BC can be applied in multicultural settings but very little research has been done in this area. We hope to address this as we study the effectiveness of our PC/BC framework. Integrating these two models holds promise for modeling problem-solving for the consultee in a manner that will promote better skill development and improved functioning in face of current and future problems.

SUMMARY

The case of Jacob has been presented from the teacher's perspective and should be examined in conjunction with how it is presented from the parent perspective in Chapter 8, which offers more detail. Ideally, the SBFC professional should work toward Conjoint Behavioral Consultation but the scheduling of those meetings will not always be feasible. Be prepared to meet only with teachers or families while encouraging open communication between them. Do not create a dependence on you as the mediator but take the opportunity to help each to develop problem-solving skills that include improved information sharing. We highly recommend the use of Process Consultation to make BC more appealing and more attentive to the importance of the relationship and not just the content of the message.

REFERENCES

Alderman, G.L. &Gimpel, G.A. (1996). The interaction between type of behavior problem and type of consultant: Teachers' preferences for professional assistance. *Journal of Educational & Psychological Consultation*, 7(4), 305-313.

Andersen, M.N., Hofstadter, K.L., Kupzyk, S., Daly III, E., Bleck, A.A., Collaro, A.L., &Jones, K.E. (2010).A guiding framework for integrating the consultation process andbehavior analytic practice in schools: The treatment validation consultation model. *Journal of Behavior Assessment and Intervention in Children*, 1(1), 53-84.

Butler, T. S., Weaver, A.D., Doggett, R. A., & Watson, T. S. (2002). Countering teacher resistance in behavioral consultation: recommendations for the school-based consultant. *The Behavior Analyst Today*,3(3). Retrieved from http://www.biomedsearch.com/article/Countering-teacher-resistance-in-behavioral/170020731.html.

Caplan, G. &Caplan R.B. (1998).*Mental health consultation and collaboration*. San Francisco, CA: Jossey Bass.

Guli, L.A. (2005). Evidence-based parent consultation with school-related outcomes. *School Psychology Quarterly*, 20(4), 455-472.

Holcomb-McCoy, C. (2009). Cultural considerations in parent consultation. *Professional Counseling Digest*(ACAPCD-25). Alexandria, VA: American Counseling Association.

Ingraham, C. L. (2000). Consultation through a multicultural lens: Multicultural and cross-cultural consultation in schools. *School Psychology Review, 29(3),* 320–343.

Kampwirth, T.J. & Powers, K.M. (2012).*Collaborative consultation in the schools: Effective practices for students with learning and behavior problems* (4th ed.). Boston, MA: Pearson.

Kratochwill, T. R., & Bergan, J. R. (1990).*Behavioral consultation in applied settings: An individual guide*. New York, NY: Plenum.

Kratochwill, T. R., & Bergan, J. R., Sheridan, S.M., & Elliott, S.N. (1998). Assumptions of behavioral consultation: after all is said and done more has been done than said. *School Psychology Quarterly*, 13(1), 63-80.

Mayer, G.R., Sulzer-Azaroff, B., & Wallace, M.D. (2012).*Behavior analysis for lasting change* (2nded.). Cornwall-on-Hudson, NY: Sloane.

McKenna, S.A., Rosenfield, S., & Gravois, T.A. (2009).Measuring the behavioral indicators of instructional consultation: a preliminary validity study. *School Psychology Review*, 38(4), 496-509.

Mueller, M.M., Sterling, H.E., & Moore, J.W. (2005).Towards developing a classroom-based functional analysis condition to assess escape-to-attention as a variable maintaining problem behavior. *School Psychology Review*, 34(3), 425-431.

Rogers, M. (2000).Examining the cultural context of consultation. *School Psychology Review*, 29(3), 414-418.

Schein, E. (1999). *Process consultation revisited: Building the helping relationship*. Reading, MA: Addison-Wesley.

Sheridan, S.M. (2000). Considerations of multiculturalism and diversity in behavioral consultation with parents and teachers. *School Psychology Review*, 29(3), 344-353.

Sheridan, S.M., Eagle, J.W., & Doll, B. (2006).An examination of the efficacy of conjoint Behavioral consultation with diverse clients. *School Psychology Quarterly*, 21(4), 396-417.

Sheridan, S.M. & Elliott, S.N. (1991). Behavioral consultation as a process for linking the assessment and treatment of social skills. *Journal of Educational and Psychological Consultation*, 2(2), 151-173.

Skinner, M.E. & Hales, M.R. (1992). Classroom teachers'" explanations" of student behavior: One possible barrier to the acceptance and use of applied behavior analysis procedures in the schools. *Journal of Educational & Psychological Consultation*, 3(3), 219-233.

Sugai, G. & Horner, R. (2009).Responsiveness-to-intervention and school-wide positive behavior supports: integration of multi-tiered system approaches. *Exceptionality*, 17:223–237.

DOI: 10.1080/09362830903235375

Tarver Behring, S., & Ingraham, C. L. (1998). Culture as a central component to consultation: A call to the field. *Journal of Educational and Psychological Consultation*, 9, 57–72.

RESOURCES

Center for Effective Collaboration and Practice (http://cecp.air.org/fba/default.asp)
This website offers descriptions of functional behavioral assessments and offers tools and examples that support understanding of its applications.

Intervention Central (http://www.interventioncentral.org/behavioral-intervention-modification)
This site offers many resources for behavior interventions and ready-to-use forms that can be helpful in developing plans.

The Iris Center (http://iris.peabody.vanderbilt.edu/resources.html)
This site offers excellent resources and tutorial in many areas pertaining to students with disabilities including culturally relevant classroom management strategies.

NICHCY National Dissemination Center for Children with Disabilities
(http://nichcy.org/schoolage/behavior/athome)
This site is specifically intended as a resource for parents and provides many articles and resources regarding behavior for children with disabilities that can be applied to all children.

OSEP Technical Assistance Center on Positive Behavior Interventions and Supports
(http://www.pbis.org/)
This site has excellent resources for positive behavioral, school-wide interventions.

PENT Positive Environments, Network of Trainers (http://www.pent.ca.gov/)
This site is offered by the California Department of Education and is filled with useful materials including PowerPoint presentations of various topics relating to behavior.

Chapter 12
How to Provide Group Counseling in the School

George K. Hong

OVERVIEW: *Group counseling is an important part of school counseling. Proficiency in group counseling is expected of school counselors. As specified by CACREP (Council for Accreditation of Counseling and Related Educational Programs), a national body for accreditation of counselor training programs, professionals in school counseling must have the knowledge and skills to provide group counseling (CACREP, 2009). This chapter addresses the strategies for implementing group counseling in the school setting. The advantages of group counseling will be examined along with the challenges in providing group counseling in the school setting. Possible topics for groups relevant for school-based family counseling will also be reviewed. Just like individual counseling, group counseling can be based on different theoretical approaches, such as psychodynamic, humanistic/existential, or cognitive behavioral, etc. This chapter is focused on the generic aspects group counseling that is applicable regardless of the counselor's theoretical orientation.*

RELATIONSHIP TO THE SBFC MODEL

Group counseling may be remedial or preventive and used with students as well as with parents and family members. Group counseling is a flexible approach used in all four areas of the SBFC Model: School-Intervention, School-Prevention, Family-Intervention and Family-Prevention.

RATIONALE FOR GROUP COUNSELING

When a counselor plans to provide group counseling in a school, the first question to ask is "Why groups?" Why not individual counseling? There are two main reasons for choosing group counseling.

PRACTICAL ADVANTAGE

Groups are an effective way to provide services in schools. The school is a venue where a limited number of counselors are expected to provide service to a large number of students. If a counselor uses the individual approach to counseling, he or she can at most serve 30 – 40 students a week, or even a semester if these students need to be seen for a number of sessions over a period of time. This is clearly insufficient to meet the needs of the student population. However, if group counseling is provided, the counselor can reach out to ten times the number of students or even more. This practical consideration alone should be sufficient to convince anyone of the value and need to provide group counseling in the schools.

THERAPEUTIC ADVANTAGE

In addition to this practical consideration, there are therapeutic advantages of group counseling. The literature has identified a number of therapeutic effects or factors that are particularly salient in group counseling. These therapeutic factors are ones that promote or lead to change and growth in clients.

The following are major ones frequently mentioned (Corey, Corey, & Corey, 2010; Forsyth, 2006; Yalom, 2005).

Universality. This refers to the recognition that one's problem or difficulty is shared by others. When a person realizes that s/he is not the only one suffering or facing a problem, the feeling of isolation and loneliness is often lessened. This therapeutic factor is most evident in support groups or self help groups where members share similar problem(s) and find solace in the company of one another.

Hope. When group members realize that others in the group can or have made progress, this gives them hope that they can improve also. Group leaders trying to maximize this therapeutic factor often use testimonials of members or invited outside speakers to encourage and inspire members towards change.

Vicarious Learning. Groups provide the opportunity for members to observe and watch how others address various problems and learn from their observations through vicarious or social learning. For example a member may observe how the group leader or another group member expresses himself or herself in an assertive and non-offensive manner and subtly learn to do so. Or they may learn appropriate ways of social interaction by watching how others interact.

Interpersonal Learning. A person may learn directly from other group members. In the interactions and exchanges in the group, a person gets feedback about one's personality, social skills, emotional state, or the way one is handling a life problem. The feedback may be direct and verbal, such as other members explicitly telling the person what they think. It may also be less direct, in the nonverbal reaction or body language of the other members indicating agreement, disagreement, approval, or disapproval. When necessary, the group leader can clarify and make these reactions understandable to the person and help him or her learn from the feedback.

Guidance. The group leader, as well as members, may give direct suggestions on what to do to address a problem, or they may offer advice and information on how to approach a certain problem. In groups where the members are more mature or high functioning, a lot of mutual advice and information sharing may occur. In groups where the members are less mature or lower functioning, the group leader may have to be the major source of information and advice.

Cohesion and Support. Groups that are cohesive are a valuable source of emotional support for the members. A cohesive group is one in which members accept one another, identify with one another, and sense a common purpose. This bond or cohesiveness develops over time as the members interact and get familiar with each other. It may be stronger in some groups and less so in others.

Self-disclosure. This involves sharing of one's important personal information with others in the group. The information shared may be critical incidents in one's life, one's problems or thoughts, one's emotion concerning certain events, or even one's emotion during the group meeting. Disclosing information about distressing situations or troublesome thoughts often helps to lower a person's tension and distress.

Catharsis. This refers to the venting of strong emotions that have been held up inside a person. Under proper guidance from the counselor, a group can provide a safe venue for one to ventilate their pent up emotions, be it anger, sorrow, anxiety, or joy. While catharsis may escalate a person's feeling of distress at the moment, proper working through of these emotions with the support from other members can make this a very therapeutic experience.

Altruism. The group provides opportunities for members to offer advice and support to one another. In helping others, a member can feel empowered. Instead of being helpless and dependent, the person becomes a helper and one's self efficacy is enhanced. The benefits of altruism or mutual assistance are often emphasized in self-help groups where members help one another or are even assigned as mentors for others.

Insight. Through the interactions in a group, members gain information about themselves. They may get direct or indirect feedback from other members and the leader. They may realize their similarities or differences with others in the group. This may lead them to gain insight or recognize personal qualities or dispositions previously unknown to them. Certain type of groups emphasize insight development. Experiential exercises, especially Gestalt type exercises, are often used along with discussion to enhance insight.

The therapeutic factors discussed here are not discrete, mutually exclusive factors. Some of them may overlap. Also, some may be more salient in one group or emphasized by certain theoretical orientations, while others may be more salient in others. The list here covers the major factors that contribute to the effectiveness of groups as a mode of counseling. Counselors should keep these factors in mind when planning a group or explaining the rationale for groups to school administrators, teachers, and parents. It is important to let other stakeholders know that in addition to being efficient or practical, group counseling has specific therapeutic advantages that individual counseling may not provide.

TYPES OF GROUPS FOR THE SCHOOL SETTING

There are many types of groups that can be offered for the school-aged population. They have been identified under different labels, such as task groups, psychoeducational groups, counseling groups, psychotherapy groups, self-help groups, and brief groups (Corey, Corey, & Corey, 2010; Erford, 2010), remedial, support, and preventive groups (Greenberg, 2003), or simply as psychotherapy groups as compared to developmental groups (Carroll, Bates, & Johnson, 2004). This chapter will use the focus or goals of a group as the major criterion for classification. It categorizes groups loosely into remedial groups, prevention groups, and developmental or training groups.

Remedial groups include both counseling groups and psychotherapy groups. Their goals are to address or resolve particular emotional or behavioral problems, or specific life problems of the participants. Examples include groups for anger management, impulse control, bullying, truancy, or poor self-esteem, etc. This also includes support groups for individuals experiencing stressful life situations, such as grief or bereavement, and support for children of divorced or separated parents etc.

Prevention groups are targeted at students who are not experiencing problems, but are at risk of developing them due to peer influence, family or community conditions, or other psychosocial and environmental factors which make them vulnerable. Prevention groups are intended to build up their resilience and develop the skills and knowledge to avoid getting into trouble. Examples include groups for drug and alcohol prevention and gang prevention, etc.

Developmental and training groups are offered to help students develop specific skills or insights. Participants in these groups are functioning adequately, and are not necessarily experiencing any psycho-emotional, behavioral, or academic problems. The groups are focused on development of more advanced insights, social skills, or specific interpersonal skills. Examples of such groups include leadership training, team building, conflict resolution, assertiveness training, or sensitivity training, etc.

All three types of groups may take the format of a psycho-education group which is often used in the school setting (Deluccia-Waack, 2006). Psycho-educational groups are typically structured and focused on particular themes with the purpose of imparting information and helping members acquire new skills and understanding through the group discussion and information given by the leader (Corey, Corey, & Corey, 2010). While this format is particularly suitable for prevention and training or developmental groups, it may also be applied to remedial groups whose members need more direct guidance.

SCHOOL RESOURCES AND PRACTICAL CONSIDERATIONS

While remedial, prevention, and training or developmental groups can be offered in the school setting, in practice more attention is given to the remedial and prevention groups. The number of students who need help, or who are at risk is usually quite high, especially in urban schools. Oftentimes the schools' resources, including the counselors' time and attention need to be directed at them rather than at "good students." This is an unfortunate situation. One needs to remember that groups can be effective in addressing problems, in preventing problems, as well as in helping students develop their interpersonal skills and potential.

GROUP COUNSELING AND GROUP THERAPY

Counselors in schools also need to take the school's educational mandate into consideration when offering group counseling. In general, the school administration recognizes the need for counseling, but often draws the line at psychotherapy. Loosely defined, counseling is aimed at individuals facing life problems and who are still functioning close to the average range, while psychotherapy is aimed at individuals who are experiencing severe distress or psychiatric problems and functioning way below the average range, i.e. those with significant impairment in their daily social-occupational functioning. The difference is often a matter of degree and there are gray areas concerning what exactly constitutes average functioning. Typically, the school administration would see psychotherapy, including group therapy, as the responsibility of mental health clinics or community clinics rather than the schools' responsibility. Also, most school counselors are trained to provide counseling rather than therapy. In this regard, counselors should be prudent in choosing the type of groups they plan to offer in a school. For example, anorexia and body image is an issue that has been gaining attention in mental health services for young people. However, anorexia is a psychiatric disorder that should be treated by trained mental health providers, preferably in clinics with medical support to monitor the clients' physical health. It will not be appropriate for a counselor to plan for such a group in a school. However, a counselor can consider offering a group for teenagers with body image problems, or experiencing poor self-esteem because of body image. It can be a remedial group for teenagers with these problems but have not developed anorexia yet. It can also be a preventive group to promote positive body image and self-esteem, including information on proper nutrition and healthy life style. In this regard, counselors can address the needs of the students without over-stepping professional boundaries or institutional mandates.

TOPICS FOR GROUPS IN THE SCHOOL SETTING

There are many topics appropriate for group counseling in the school setting. They may be targeted at students, parents, and school personnel. More suggestions can be found in the sample resources at the end of this chapter.

GROUPS FOR STUDENTS

When groups are designed for students, their focus may be remedial or preventive. It all depends on whether the target students have already developed the problems or are simply at-risk of developing them. The following are some of the common topics (Greenberg, 2003; Deluccia-Waack, 2006):
> *Development of study skills or study habits to improve academic achievement.*
> *Motivational group for low achievers, or for development of positive attitude towards school, dropout prevention.*

Anger or aggression control.
Bullying (groups for victims and groups for perpetrators).
Impulse control.
Assertiveness training.
Social skills training.
Self-esteem development.
Overcoming shyness.
Stress management.
Test anxiety management.
Career or college planning.
Groups for students with disabilities or chronic illness experiencing adjustment difficulties.
Groups for pregnant teens or teen parents.
Groups for gay/lesbian/transgender students in stress.
Groups for children dealing with parental divorce or separation.
Groups for grief or bereavement for death of loved ones.
Improving school adjustment for newcomers (can be at elementary, middle or high school).
Acculturation group for students who are new immigrants.
Students with family problems, such as sibling issues, blended families, or single parents, latch-key kids, etc.
Drug prevention group.
Gang prevention.
Coping with peer pressure and maintaining a healthy lifestyle (including drug, gang, and pregnancy prevention, etc.)
Crisis intervention groups in the aftermath of a community tragedy or disaster.

The list can go on, but the above suffices to give counselors a good idea of the range of issues that can be addressed in group counseling in the school setting.

GROUPS FOR PARENTS

In the context of school-based family counseling, counselors should broaden their vision to include parents as possible client population. Again, more traditional-minded school administrators would want to limit services to students only and refer parents to community agencies. However, since the parents' problems may be affecting the students' academic performance or school behavior, services for parents to address these problems are justifiable. From an administrative point of view, it is helpful to relate the goals of these groups for parents to the children. For example, topics of these groups may be specified as:

How to parent children or teens (can be designed for elementary, middle, or high school).
How to improve communication with children to promote their healthy development.
How to help children accept authority at home and in school.
Proper discipline and support for children to enhance healthy development and school performance.
Helping immigrant parents acculturate, understand and collaborate with the school to foster their children's development.

School-based family counseling emphasizes the link between the home and the school. The home environment will affect the children's development or psycho-emotional state, and consequently affect their behaviors and performance in school. Counselors need to be alert to the issues and distress parents may be facing and address them. No doubt there may be resistance from some school administrators. In such situations, counselors will need to be creative and flexible in justifying the need for providing groups to parents. Groups for parents may also be difficult as some parents who need them may not have the time to attend ongoing group sessions. Sometimes when groups for parents are not viable, the counselor may consider offering a psychoeducational workshop for parents which meets only once or twice instead of a series of weekly group sessions. Another alternative is a day-long group for parents over a single Saturday which is often easier for them than recurring weekly sessions.

GROUPS FOR SCHOOL PERSONNEL

Finally, counselors should not forget that teachers and administrators may also need group services. These may be support groups to address work-related stress or to address specific issues like reaction to a traumatic incident in the school, etc. It may also be focused on team-building to help the school personnel collaborate better in serving the students, or to help teachers develop greater cultural awareness to address the need of immigrants or ethnic minority students in their classes. While these groups are worthwhile, counselors must be aware of the possible complications of dual relationships in proving counseling to ones' colleagues. If possible, it may be prudent for counselors to exchange schools in leading these groups, i.e. lead the group in another school rather than one's own school. A school district may also need to call in counselors from the outside to provide such services.

MULTICULTURAL COUNSELING CONSIDERATIONS

GROUPS ADDRESSING ISSUES OF IMMIGRANTS

It is important to note that public schools in many urban areas of the U.S. are having an increasing number of immigrant students from diverse cultures. Many of these immigrant students are English-learners and have a difficult time adjusting to the U.S. school system. Parents, especially those from lower socioeconomic backgrounds, may also be facing language barriers and adjustment issues. They may be too preoccupied with work and other life issues to pay full attention to their children's psychosocial development. Even those who are proficient in English or financially well-off may not be familiar with the school system and youth culture in the U.S. When the children develop school problems, peer problems, or face academic issues, many immigrant parents are often at a loss of what to do. For example, what are they to do when the children tell them "In America, everyone does this... or that..." or accuse them of being "old-fashioned?" Acculturation groups are helpful to guide and inform these parents on proper behavior and expectation for their children. Similarly, acculturation groups can help the children to adapt and learn proper values and norms of U.S. society and discern between good and bad peer influence. Since all immigrant children have to enroll in schools, the school is the ideal setting to reach out to these children and parents. In this regard, school-based family counselors need to be alert to their needs and offer groups as needed.

PROCEDURE: STRATEGIES FOR FORMING AND LEADING A GROUP

Unlike individual counseling in which a counselor waits for the client to provide information on the presenting problem before formulating a treatment plan, group counseling, especially when provided in the school setting, typically requires the counselor to plan ahead of time (Corey, Corey, & Corey, 2010; Deluccia-Waack, 2006; Erford, 2010; Greenberg, 2003). At times this plan has to be written formally as a group proposal for approval by the school administration or an external funding source. Other times, it may simply be needed as a plan to guide the counselors themselves. The specific steps and practical strategies for forming and leading a group will be presented here. This discussion is focused on homogenous groups which are often offered in school settings. In these groups, members share common attributes, such as goals or age group. The various steps and issues to consider include: 1)

Needs Assessment, 2) Scheduling and Logistics, 3) Recruitment, 4) Screening, 5) Parental Consent, 6) Evaluation, 7) Critical Tasks and Considerations at the Early Stage, and 8) Critical Tasks and Considerations at Later Stages.

1. NEEDS ASSESMENT

The first questions to consider are: What are the goals of the group, or what problem(s) is the group aimed at addressing? Why does one need a group instead of just providing individual counseling? These are issues to address through a needs assessment (Deluccia-Waack, 2006; Erford, 2010; Greenberg, 2003).

A needs assessment involves an examination of the common problem(s) experienced by the student population in a particular school. Is it truancy? Underachievement? Aggressive behavior? Bullying? Poor self-esteem? Adjustment problems relating to immigration or simply as newcomers to the particular school or community? How prevalent is the problem, i.e. how many students may benefit from such a group? While formal surveys of parents and students or teachers can provide such information, these surveys typically involve too much time and resources and may not be more informative than less extensive approaches. Also formal surveys often set up unrealistic expectations that certain groups will be provided, even though the suggested groups are not appropriate for the school setting. An alternative to formal surveys is for a counselor to talk to teachers about what they perceive as the need. This can be done either formally at staff meetings or informally in individual or small group discussions, even over lunch. A counselor can also look at school data and student demographics to discern problem areas, such as attendance records, referrals/penalties for behavioral problems in class, dropout rates, drug or gang problems in the school or community, unsafe sex and pregnant teens, etc.

Once a problem area is identified, the counselor will have to estimate how many students will be willing to attend the group and whether they will get parents' permission to attend. For example, while one may want to offer a group for "children of substance abusers," it may not be feasible to do so in the school setting. Such children's groups are often provided in community clinics where the parents are receiving drug/alcohol counseling through self-referral or as mandated by the legal system. In a school setting, one simply cannot send letters to parents asking whether they are drug users and whether they give permission for their children to be in a group, even though the needs assessment show a high prevalence of drug use in the community. Here practicality is the key.

2. SCHEDULING AND LOGISTICS

Once the need has been ascertained, the next step is to consider some practical factors such as time, place, frequency and duration of the group (Corey, Corey, & Corey, 2010; Deluccia-Waack, 2006; Greenberg, 2003). The institutional constraints of the school can present certain hurdles. For example, finding a time slot in the regular school hours where students from different classes can attend is often a daunting task. Doing it after school may be possible, but transportation home when the students miss their assigned school bus, or other safety issues have to be considered. Sometimes the group may need to be provided at lunch break, even though this limits the length of the group. Some students are reluctant to lose their free time during lunch.

One also needs to consider the issue of space, i.e. is there a room available for the group sessions, especially one that provides privacy to the group? At times, one may be tempted to simply use the playground and have the members sit on the ground in a circle like a campfire. This may be fine for some developmental or training groups where privacy is of less concern. However, for remedial groups where privacy, confidentiality and stigma are important considerations, this may not a good idea as other students may see the circle and ask about the purpose or nature of the group.

Finally there is the issue of frequency and duration, i.e. how long would each group session be? And how often would each section be? How many sessions would be held? These again are often determined by the school environment. For example, the session may have to be limited to the length of one period or the duration of the lunch break, even though a longer session may be more desirable. One may have to limit the number of sessions to the number of the weeks in one term or semester, instead of having more sessions. In terms of frequency, the general practice is to offer weekly sessions. However, counselors can be creative and consider 2 sessions per week for students who need more intensive help, or long daily sessions over a 2 or 3 day weekend for prevention and developmental or training groups.

In sum there are no definite answers to the practical questions concerning time, place, frequency and duration. The counselor has to take the unique situation of each school into consideration. The discussion here is simply intended to alert the counselor that one needs to plan ahead of time rather than run into obstacles later on.

3. RECRUITMENT

Having formulated a plan for the group, the next step is recruiting members. In general, it is advisable to use a low key or inconspicuous approach to recruitment. Students are often concerned about letting others know they are receiving counseling, i.e. in a remedial group, and sometimes even in prevention group. Announcing over the school intercom or posting announcements on notice boards about formation of a "self-esteem group," "impulse control group," or "truancy group," are not likely to attract self referrals from students. This may also attract undue attention to eventual members or stigmatize them. While giving positive titles to groups is a common practice, using these titles in public announcements may lead to misunderstanding about the real purpose of the group and having the wrong students sign up.

In general, speaking to teachers and staff, and getting referrals from them is a good approach (Deluccia-Waack, 2006). One is simply recruiting 8 – 12 students for each group, and it is not worth shaking up the entire school to find these students. If it is really so difficult to locate these students, the counselor will have to re-consider whether the needs assessment has been properly done, i.e. is there really a need or demand for such a group? From a different perspective, an open announcement to all students or letters to all parents may result in too many volunteers or referrals. It will be too time-consuming for the counselor to screen potential members or make referrals for those who need other services instead of the group. Hence it is more practical to simply talk to the teachers and staff of the school and obtain referrals from them.

4. SCREENING OF MEMBERS

When a potential member is referred for the group, the counselor needs to screen the person to determine whether the group is suitable for him or her (Corey, Corey, & Corey, 2010; Deluccia-Waack, 2006; Gladding, 2012; Greenberg, 2003). The major issues to consider are: Is the person likely to participate in the discussion or activities of the group? Is the person too shy, too withdrawn, or too aggressive or disruptive? Is there a match between the person's needs and the goals of the group? The ultimate question is whether the person may benefit from the group. If not, the counselor has to refer the student to more appropriate services. The counselor has a responsibility towards each student who comes for help, whether self-referred or teacher/staff-referred. One should not be over-focused on identifying members for the group and neglect or ignore those who need other services. When a student is offered other services instead of the group, it is prudent for the counselor to explain to the referral source the rationale of doing so. Otherwise teachers and staff may be offended that the students they referred are "rejected" by the counselor.

5. PARENTAL CONSENT

Obtaining signed consent from parents is an important step in preparing for a group (Deluccia-Waack, 2006; Erford, 2010; Greenberg, 2003). Some administrators and counselors have the opinion that certain groups such as developmental or training groups do not require parental consent. However, it is always advisable to obtain parental consent, regardless of whether it is legally required or not (Corey, Corey, & Corey, 2010). While some parents are not easy to contact and some students may not be conscientious in passing paperwork to their parents, the additional work in getting the consent can prevent unnecessary complaints or even litigation later on. After all, what can be wrong to inform parents and let them have a say in the services offered to their children? If a parent objects to the services, it is better to know it before the group starts than receive a complaint from him or her after the child has already been in the group for a few sessions.

6. EVALUATION

In the context of today's emphasis on "evidence based practice" and for accountability, it is important for the counselor to document the success of the group in achieving it's goals (Corey, Corey, & Corey, 2010; Deluccia-Waack, 2006; Erford, 2010; Greenberg, 2003). One common way to evaluate success is to do pretest and posttest using standard personality, psychoemotional, or behavioral assessment questionnaires or instruments at the beginning and end of the group. However, one must be sure to include these in the parental consent form to avoid the misperception and legal concerns that a child is given "psychological testing" without parental permission. Evaluation may also be based on data from other sources, such as attendance records, academic grades, teachers/parent feedback, or even direct feedback from the group members on whether they find the group helpful. Planning for evaluation also helps the counselor to assess whether the goals set for the groups are realistic. For example in a 12-week anger management group, one can expect a child to show fewer incidents of anger-related incidents. However, it would be unrealistic to expect the child to be totally incident or anger free. Counselors must be careful to promise what they can deliver rather than setting the goals too high.

7. EARLY STAGES AND TASKS

When a group meets for the first time, the usual practice is to give a brief orientation to the members about the nature of the group, what to expect and how to behave in the group sessions. This includes a reiteration of the goals and objectives, clarifying them as needed.

Confidentiality. Confidentiality is a delicate issue in groups and needs to be clarified in the beginning. While a counselor has the obligation to observe confidentiality of client information unless there are legal exceptions, there is no legal penalty or anything to mandate group members to observe confidentiality except their own personal commitment (Corey, Corey, & Corey, 2010). Hence counselors need to discuss the limits of confidentiality in group sessions, emphasizing that it cannot be guaranteed. One should also remind group members not to post their group discussions on social media such as the internet or other devices, which are popular these days.

However, it is unrealistic to expect everyone, especially teenagers, to abide by these rules, since such activities are so ingrained in teen culture today. Moreover, since students in K-12 are typically minors, their parents usually have the right to inquire about their counseling progress and even content.

So it is important for counselors to explain the limits of confidentially in regard to the group members' parents. In the context of today's heightened sensitivity regarding inappropriate relationships with students and lewd conduct engaged by teachers and staff in the school, it may sound suspicious or even sinister to some parents if their children tell people that things in the group are "secret," or "what happens in the group stays in the group," and they "cannot tell others about what happens there." There are different ways to address this issue. One approach is to present the concept of confidentiality in vocabulary appropriate to the age level of the group members and to the school setting. Refrain from using words like "secret," and emphasize terms like "respecting others' privacy," "no gossiping" or "not talking about others behind their back." Moreover, members can talk about the activities and discussions of the group, or talk about what they personally did if they choose to, especially when parents ask. But they should avoid identifying who said what or did what. This may help to make the group less secretive or suspicious. It will also be less of a psychological burden or dilemma for students who are often told by parents and school personnel not to keep any secrets about what they encounter in the school.

Another approach is to be even more upfront and let group members know they can tell their parents anything when asked, rather than holding back. Also inform group members that the counselor may talk to parents, teachers and essential school personnel (e.g. administrators, or school nurse, etc.) whenever he or she decides it is important to do so. In other words, there is no confidentiality between the counselor and parents, teachers and other essential school personnel. This practice is acceptable as long as the counselor makes it clear to all group members and to parents giving consent for their group participation. When following this approach, it is essential that these limitations of confidentiality be specified in the parental consent form and reiterated in the ground rules as a reminder. This approach is a departure from the traditional practice of confidentiality in counseling and psychotherapy. However, counselors must be sensitive and responsive to the prevailing concerns about school personnel taking advantage of students or engaging in lewd conduct with them and asking them to keep these illicit and unethical activities secret. These concerns from the public are unfortunate realities that one must face in many school districts today.

Ground Rules. When formulating the ground rules, the counselor should follow the acronym KISS: Keep It Short and Simple. There is no need for an exhaustive list of rules that cover every contingency. Rather the rules should just cover the main issues in a way that is easy for members to remember. For example: 1) Be punctual; 2) Be respectful and polite towards each other; 3) Let others finish what they are saying; 4) Respect privacy (confidentiality); 5) All school regulations still apply. Try to phrase the rules in a positive way rather than a negative way ("Do not...") which may create a punitive tone for the group. Note the last rule (#5) is particularly important as some schools have regulations such as zero tolerance for possession of weapons or drugs. Specifying this rule prevents the awkward dilemma when a student discloses in the group that she or he is in possession or a weapon or drug.

Some counselors like to let members discuss and come up with the ground rules. However, students often do not have a good idea of the nature of group counseling and spend too much time on this task. In the context of time-limited groups, the time used for formulating the ground rules may be more productively used to address the goals and objectives of the group.

Group Discussions. In the early stages or the first few group sessions, the counselor needs to ease the members into the group discussion. Special attention should be paid to culture and gender issues (Corey, Corey, & Corey, 2010; Erford, 2010; Gladding, 2012; Greenberg, 2003). One should be sensitive to the issues concerning disclosing personal information to strangers or to the opposite gender in the group setting, and give members sufficient time to ease into the group. The counselor should also be alert to the participation level of any member, whether over-participation or under-participation, and guide him or her, including having brief individual meetings as needed.

When a group has warmed up over a few sessions and starts to focus more time on addressing the goals and objectives of the group, the counselor needs to be alert to certain issues that may develop.

Group Collusion. When group members becomes cohesive and develop an understanding of one another, they may consciously or unconsciously reinforce prevailing attitudes, opinions, behaviors or norms (Forsyth, 2006; Gladding, 2012). At times, this situation is also called group think. For example, group members may agree with a suggestion simply for the sake of agreement, or not to "rock the boat." This tendency may stifle productive discussions in the group. In the worst case scenario, it may result in an erroneous or even destructive decision. For example, the group may support the idea that a member who is threatened by a gang should stand up against the gang. This would result in the member getting physically hurt. A good way for the leader to prevent group collusion is to play the role of devil's advocate actively in group discussions (Forsyth, 2006; Gladding, 2012). In other words,the counselor should present arguments for an alternative viewpoint or course of action and encourage group members to question the prevailing opinion before agreeing.

Over-Earnestness. At times, young people may become overly eager when they are in a supportive and cohesive group. Some of them may unwittingly engage in risky behaviors to impress the counselor or group members or just out of earnestness in performing a group assignment. This situation is similar to an eager student taking extreme action to perform a homework assignment to impress the teacher or class. For example, a group member may talk to unsavory strangers in inappropriate situations to "build up one's assertiveness." Other times, a member may be taking inappropriate risk and disclose personal information that would be extremely stigmatizing if spread outside of the group (Gladding, 2012). The counselor needs to protect members from such behaviors when he or she senses over-earnestness or naivete. For example, the counselor can caution members about unsafe situations when giving group homework assignments, or remind members about confidentiality issues when one member has disclosed too much before the counselor could prevent it. It is also important to guide members on how to practice or generalize their new insights or skills in the outside world. Sometimes a very cohesive and supportive group may lead to drastic changes in some young people and they become out of sync with their peers or family in the world beyond the group.

Ending. When the group is approaching the last few sessions, the counselor should tune things down and prepare members for termination. Inoculation or preparing the members about difficulties or relapses after termination is a critical task here (Corey, Corey, & Corey, 2010; Gladding, 2012). For example, the counselor can discuss obstacles and difficulties after the group so that members will not be surprised or discouraged when they occur. One can also inform members of resources and what to do should they experience difficulties in the future. Another consideration at this stage is consolidating the gains in the group by summarizing and reviewing with members what the group has accomplished and how they will use what they have learned in their daily lives (Deluccia-Waack, 2006). This review process is very helpful for reinforcing growth and maintaining progress after the group is terminated.

Follow-Up. After a group is terminated, post-group or follow-up sessions at less frequent intervals can be held to monitor progress or to booster growth (Corey, Corey, & Corey, 2010; Gladding, 2012; Greenberg, 2003). While these sessions are good ideas, they are not always feasible or practical. For example, students' school schedules change from term to term, and they may also be in other activities once they have finished their group. Finding a time when all groups members can come again may be difficult. Some students, especially those in remedial groups related to conduct problems, may be reluctant to come and be reminded of their disciplinary record. If only part of the group return for the post-group sessions, those who come may feel let down, while those who cannot come or choose not to come may feel awkward or guilty. This may spoil the good feelings developed in the original group. The heavy workload of counselors in many schools may also make these post-group sessions difficult, since the counselors may have to move on to new groups. As an alternative, follow-up can be done through other venues, such as keeping track of the students' performance through periodic discussion with teachers and parents, or checking on the students' attendance and other relevant academic data. As long as the students are in the school, the counselor can follow-up with them informally or individually without actual post-group sessions.

ADDITIONAL CONSIDERATIONS IN GROUP COUNSELING IN SCHOOLS

There are a number of additional factors to consider when planning for group counseling in the school setting.

GROUP ACTIVITIES

Group activities or group exercises are often used to stimulate a discussion in groups (Carroll, Bates, & Johnson, 2004; Erford, 2010; Gladding, 2012). They can be ice-breakers to warm group members up and help them get acquainted in the initial sessions. Activities and exercises can be more emotionally intense in the later sessions to lead the members into examining and discussing specific issues or experience certain feelings. While group activities and exercises are often used, especially in groups with children and adolescents, they are not always required in a group. When members are mature and verbal, sometimes they can proceed with a topic without the help of exercises. There are many publications on group activities and exercises for different purposes. A few examples are included in the recommended resources at the end of this chapter.

AGE LEVEL AND MATURITY OF THE GROUP MEMBERS

Counselors should be aware that even though schools are classified as elementary school, middle school, and high school, each of these 3 levels contains a wide range of students in terms of age and maturity level (Gladding, 2012; Greenberg, 2003). First and second graders are different from fourth and fifth graders, even though both groups are in elementary school. Ninth graders just entering high school often have different concerns than 12 graders looking to graduate. Students of the same age may also have different degrees of maturity. These issues must be taken into consideration in planning the group. For example, the duration of a group session needs to take into account the attention span of the members' age group. In general, younger ones have a shorter attention span. The materials planned for discussions in the sessions should be appropriate to the maturity level of the members, i.e. their cognitive developmental level or comprehension need to be considered along with the nature of problems the group is targeted to address.

In general, groups for younger or less mature children need more structure and more direct guidance from the counselor than groups for high school students. Groups for the lower grades should also be more activity oriented as compared to high school groups which can be more verbal oriented, as younger members have less verbal skills than older ones. A smaller group size, say 5 or 6 members, may be needed for young children due to their attention span, while groups for high school students may be as large as 10 to 14 members.

VOLUNTARY VS. INVOLUNTARY GROUPS

In school settings, groups are typically voluntary in the sense that students have the choice to come or not. However, in remedial groups, sometimes children do not have too much freedom to choose. They are often there because their parents or teachers ask them to go. Some may even be required to be in counseling as a condition for continuing in the school. Counselors should be sensitive to the feelings of these reluctant members and engage them to participate actively, rather than naively thinking they really volunteer to come and will be eager to participate.

DUAL ROLE OF GROUP LEADERS

SBFC professionals need to be sensitive to the possible dual roles they have with students in a school (Gladding, 2012). On one hand, they are counselors to the students, but on the other hand they are also staff members of the school with certain administrative responsibilities. This by itself is not an ethical issue. However, sometimes counselors may get into a dilemma when a student discloses behaviors that are not tolerable by the school, e.g. possession of drugs or weapons. Thus it is wise to explain these issues at the very beginning of a group. Other times, a counselor may also have some teaching assignments or serve as a vice principal or dean in charge of attendance and discipline. These roles may be in conflict with a counselor role in the context of counseling. There is no simple solution to these problems, except staying on the alert for potential conflicts and avoiding them to the extent possible.

MEMBER OF THE SCHOOL TEAM

SBFC professionals should always remember that they are a member of the school team. They need to actively consult and liaise with their colleagues, i.e. teachers and other staff (Deluccia-Waack, 2006; Greenberg, 2003). Colleagues can provide valuable help in various stages of a group, such as information about the needs of the student population, referral and recruitment of group members, feedback on students for group evaluation, etc. One may also need teachers' cooperation in identifying a time slot suitable for the group. Above all, counselors need to be responsive to institutional culture, mandates, and constraints in planning their work, especially groups which involve students in different classes. Things will move more smoothly if the counselor has the support of the school personnel.

REFERENCES

CACREP (2009). Council for Accreditation of Counseling and Related Educational Programs 2009 Standards. Retrieved from http://www.cacrep.org/doc/2009%20Standards%20with%20cover.pdf

Carroll, M., Bates, M., and Johnson, C. (2004). *Group leadership: Strategies for group counseling leaders* (4th Ed.). Denver, CO: Love Publishing Co.

Corey, M. S., Corey G., and Corey, C. (2010). *Groups: Process and practice* (8th Ed.). Pacific Grove, CA: Brooks/Cole.

Delucia-Waack, J. L. (2006). *Leading psychoeducational groups for children and   adolescents.* Thousand Oaks, CA: Sage.

Erford, B. T. (2010). *Group work in the schools.* Boston: Pearson.

Forsyth, D. R. (2006). *Group dynamics* (4th Ed.). Pacific Grove, CA: Brooks/Cole.

Gladding, S. T. (2012). *Groups: A counseling specialty* (6th Ed.). Boston: Pearson.

Greenberg, K. R. (2003). *Group counseling in K-12 schools: A handbook for school counselors.* Boston: Allyn & Bacon.

Yalom, I. (2005). *Theory and practice of group psychotherapy* (5th Ed.). New York: Basic Books.

RESOURCES

The following are samples of resources for planning and leading groups:

ACTIVITIES & EXERCISES

Bevilacqua, L. J. (2002). *Group therapy homework planner.* New York: John Wiley & Sons.
> Contains a variety of exercises for different group topics. Handouts can be easily photocopied from the book.

Carrell, S. (2010). *Group exercises for adolescents: A manual for therapists* (3nd Ed.). Thousand Oaks, CA: Sage.
> Presents a variety of exercises for adolescent groups. Systemically lists objectives, materials, method, instructions, and concluding discussion or comments for each exercise.

Dossick, J., & Shea, E. (1995). *Creative therapy III: 52 more exercises for groups.* Sarasota, FL: Professional Resource Press.
> This is the third in a series of manuals, each containing 52 incomplete drawings that can be photocopied and given to group members to complete. Purpose, instructions, and topics for discussions are included for each drawing.

Haslett, D. C. (2005). *Group work activities in generalist practice.* Belmont, CA: Thomson Brooks/Cole.
> Contains a variety of exercises for different group settings.

GROUP PLANNING

Macgowan, M. J. (2008). *A guide to evidence-based group work.* New York, NY: Oxford University Press.
> Provides information on setting up evidence-based group work.

Paleg, K. & Jongsma, A. E. Jr. (2005). *The group therapy treatment planner, 2nd Ed.* New York: John Wiley & Sons.
> Detailed treatment plans with goals, objectives, and interventions for a variety of problems for group therapy.

The Journal for Specialists in Group Work. Thousand Oaks, CA: Sage.
> A source for current information on topics and issues in group counseling. 2007 Vol. 32 Issue 1 and Issue 2 are special issues on group work in the schools.

Chapter 13
How to do a Crisis Intervention in a School

Theresa Kruczek and Lauren Young

OVERVIEW: *This chapter demonstrates how Bronfenbrenner's bioecological model can be used to effectively plan and carry out a crisis intervention in a school.*

BACKGROUND

Crisis events and the effects of those events are like a pebble thrown into a pond. While the crisis itself is at the epicenter, the effects of those events ripple and spread widely. At the most basic level, crisis events affect individuals and the effects of the event do not occur in isolation. Post-traumatic reactions to trauma are influenced by a myriad of factors. It is for this reason that unidimensional, individual-focused approaches to crisis intervention are not likely to be successful. Consequently, Hobfoll, Watson, Bell, Bryant, Brymer, Friedman et al. (2007) identified five evidence based intervention principles to help guide crisis intervention and prevention efforts regardless of setting. The five principles include promoting a sense of safety, calming, a sense of self- and community efficacy, connectedness, and hope. Further, when providing school-based crisis intervention it is not possible, nor desirable, to intervene only at the level of individual students, teachers, or administration. A comprehensive systems approach which allows for both conceptualization and intervention at the individual, family, whole school, broader community, and administrative levels seems preferable.

Toward this end we provide an ecosystemic model that we feel aligns well with the school-based family counseling conceptual framework and which can capture the complexity of the trauma and recovery processes. Bronfenbrenner (1979) proposed one of the most well known ecosystemic models that he and a colleague later expanded to a bioecological model (Bronfenbrenner and Ceci, 1994). This later, expanded model can serve as a conceptual framework for understanding the effects of school-related traumatic events as well as intervening in the immediate aftermath of these events and designing prevention programs.

This bioecological perspective fits well with the core values of school counselors and provides a framework that utilizes our unique skills and perspectives. Specifically, a primary goal of school counselors is to promote healthy personal and social development across the lifespan. We also strive to facilitate academic and career adjustment, promote social advocacy, and emphasize multicultural aspects of experiences. These areas of focus contrast sharply with the bulk of the literature on crisis intervention to date which has tended to emphasize the individual effects of crises in the form of post-traumatic stress reactions and other negative mental health sequelae (e.g., Srinivasa, 2007). The majority of the literature on trauma and crisis situations has ignored other effects such as academic disruptions, multicultural, and social justice factors.

The news is regularly filled with examples of crisis situations that sometimes affect students directly, because they occurred within the school, and other times indirectly, as they involved students and their families in the broader community. The very nature of what event is identified as a relevant a crisis situation can vary depending on the school and the nature of the traumatic event. While most schools would define mass trauma or disasters experienced within the school or broader community as trauma the loss of a single student (as in the forthcoming case example) might be seen as a crisis event in some school's but not others. Therefore, schools need to be equipped with a flexible, comprehensive plan with intervention strategies relevant at a wide variety of systemic levels. Traumatic events commonly tax the individual and collective resources of students, teachers, families, and the community as a whole. Further, degradation of resources can have long-term implications for student development. In this chapter we will explore the effects these events have on individual survivors' psychological resources and well-being as well as key relationships within the family, school, peer, and community networks. We will provide a comprehensive model for crisis intervention based on our bioecological conceptual framework and integrated with Hobofoll et al.'s (2007) principles.

BIOECOLOGICAL MODEL FOR CRISIS INTERVENTION

Bronfenbrenner's ecosystemic model (1979) was initially proposed as an explanatory process for child development in which any given child's developmental trajectories are influenced by a number of nested subsystems. These systems affect the child's response to environmental events and ultimately the developmental outcomes for each child. In the later, expanded *bio*ecological model (Bronfenbrenner and Ceci, 1994) life transitions and life course were included as chronosystems and there was inclusion of biomedical factors such as temperament and emotional reactivity. Crisis situations are merely one type of life event that can be understood using the bioecological model and in this chapter we have applied this approach to school-based crisis intervention. Hoffman and Kruczek (2011) originally proposed this as a conceptual model for understanding the impact of mass disasters and trauma. See Figure 13.1 for a visual representation of the hierarchical, nested systems with the chronosystem influencing the levels across time and development. Each level will be described briefly below.

BIOPHYSICAL

Crisis situations result in automatic behavioral and biophysical reactions that are grounded in Selye's (1952) "fight or flight" response. Environmental stressors trigger reflexive neurochemical reactions that lead to arousal and hypervigilance (Cohen, Perel, DeBellis, Friedman & Putnam, 2002) and seem to be minimally influenced by higher cortical functioning (van der Kolk, 2003). LeDoux (1996) described these automatic reactions as a "fear conditioning" response that seems to precipitate classically conditioned reactions to environmental triggers associated with the event (Foa, Zinbarg, &Rothbaum, 1992). Cohen et al. (2002) suggest these reactions form the basis of the re-experiencing symptoms (such as nightmares and intrusive memories) associated with Post Traumatic Stress Disorder (PTSD). While we all demonstrate these automatic responses to stress, certain individual's appear to be more susceptible to long-term adverse reactions to crisis situations. There seems to be a genetic predisposition to stronger stress reactions and development of PTSD symptoms after exposure to a crisis (Chantarujikapong, et al., 2001; True & Lyons, 1999). For example, children are five times more likely to develop PTSD when they have a parent with PTSD (Sack, Clarke and Seeley, 1995).

While these biophysical responses to a crisis are important for understanding trauma reactions, school based family counselors must also address the life span developmental influences on reactions to and outcomes of crisis situations as well as the broader social contexts within which the individual student experiences these reactions. The other levels of the bioecological model provide the framework for these important areas.

MICROSYSTEMS

The next level of nested systems includes the microsystems. These systems are those that have the most immediate and direct influence on individual development and response to crisis events. These microsystems include families, peer networks, classmates, neighbors, and religious communities.

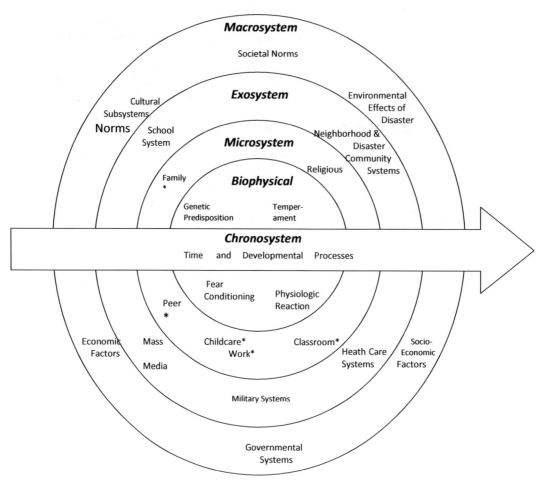

Figure 13.1: Bioecological Model
of Mass Trauma (Hoffman &
Kruczek, 2011)

* *Mesosystems* are the connections between systems for example the relationship between family and school

Student's parents additionally operate in the work setting and with their co-workers at a microsystemic level. One of the most consistent factors affecting trauma response for children and teens is the family's reaction to the trauma (Pfefferbaum, 1997; Pynoos, 1994; Siegel, 1998; Srinivasa, 2007). Additionally, children, teens and adults have all demonstrated within peer group symptom contagion in trauma responses (Brent, Perper, Moritz, & Allman, 1993; Tyano, Iancu, & Solomon, 1996).

EXOSYSTEMS

The exosystemic level includes wider social systems within which the student does not directly participate but which have indirect environmental influences on the child/teen and microsystems. Exosystems include the more immediate systems such as neighborhood and community systems, health care systems, school systems, and the mass media. The military system is an increasingly salient microsystem for a subset of students and their families. Recent disasters have highlighted the inadequacy of responses to mass trauma. However, schools in particular appear to have heeded the "wake up" call to improve their role in disaster response (Cook-Cottone, 2004).While there is an emerging literature on crisis preparedness in schools, the recommendations are based primarily on anecdotal responses to previous crisis situations (Cohen, 2004).

MACROSYSTEMS

The broadest level of the ecosystemic model includes macrosystems. The macrosystems are comprised of those larger cultural contexts such as cultural subsystem norms, broader societal norms, economic factors, sociopolitical factors, governmental systems, and in the case of natural and technological disasters, the environmental effects of the event. Race, ethnicity, and social class are correlated with response to trauma(McCann & Pearlman, 1990). Specifically, broader societal as well as cultural subsystem norms can foster or hinder adaptive coping (deSilva, 1999, p. 271).

MESOSYSTEMS

In Bronfenbrenner's (1986) original theory mesosystems referred to the bidirectional influence between the microsystems. He described them as the connections between the different contexts within the microsystemic level. For example, the mesosystemic influence on development included interactions between the family and school environments, family and peer relationships, and neighbors and families. In the 1994 revision of the model mesosytems were expanded and included the bidirectional influence of the nested systems on one another as well as the interactions within a particular level (Bronfenbrenner&Ceci, 1994). School-based crisis events affect individual students, teachers, and administrators within the broader context of the classroom, peer networks, and administrative hierarchies of the school system. These school system specific factors are grounded within the larger socioeconomic and cultural subsystems of the broader community and even society. Awareness and understanding of the bidirectional mesosystemic relationships of crisis situations can help us address the complexities needed in crisis response.

CHRONOSYSTEM AND DEVELOPMENTAL PROCESSES

Chronosystems include the life span developmental processes that are due to changes in the environment as a result of life transitions and life course events. These processes were added in the 1994 expanded model (Bronfenbrenner & Ceci, 1994). The expanded model also described proximal processes which refer to the primary mechanisms through which children learn to interact with the environment. Proximal processes are those reciprocal interactions the child has with people, objects, and symbols in order to grow and develop. These processes are expressed through the parent child relationships, peer relationships, play and leisure activities, learning paradigms, etc. Children and teens adaptation to crisis events are expressed through these proximal processes.

Crisis events directly and indirectly affect student's developmental trajectories. The student's progression through normative life transitions can be altered due to their experience of trauma. Further, the effect of these crisis events on family processes, school functions, and the broader community can indirectly affect the student. Chronosystem changes occur within multiple ecological contexts and these contexts include all the original levels of Bronfenbrenner's (1986) nested systems: microsystems, exosystems, macrosystems, and mesosystems. Therefore reaction of an student to a crisis situation can only be fully understood by evaluating the impact on developmental processes *and* the ecosystems within which the student functions.

Finally, the ultimate development of a student is bi-directionally influenced by internal developmental processes and external life experiences. When students encounter traumatic life events at critical life stages their internal developmental processes may be compromised as a result of negative physical, emotional, and cognitive reactions to the crisis event. For example, trauma experienced before the age of eleven results in a three times greater risk of later PTSD (Davidson & Smith, 1990) and separation from one's parents before the age of ten increases vulnerability to subsequent PTSD with later stressors (Davidson, 1991).

CASE DESCRIPTION

This section will apply the bioecological model to a specific crisis situation to illustrate the broad factors involved as well as highlight interventions at multiple levels and across various systems. This case example is loosely based on an actual crisis situation in which the first author of this chapter served as a school-based family counseling consultant. The crisis was precipitated by a natural disaster. A tornado struck in a small, rural, Midwestern community in the early hours of the morning on the first day of Spring Break. There is one Kindergarten-12th grade school that serves the community. The school has two wings, one houses primary school aged students and the other secondary school aged.

A family with four students suffered a direct hit of the tornado on their home. The parents in this family were divorced and the children's primary residence was with their mother. They had routine visitation with their father, who was an active alcoholic. When the tornado hit, the 14-year-old son was killed instantly and his 10-year-old brother was seriously injured. There were also two girls, ages 16 and 7. The girls and mother were less injured due to the placement of bedrooms in the home. The children all slept upstairs and the boys' room was on the corner of the house receiving the direct impact of the tornado. The bed of the boy who was killed was in front of a window. The girls' room was across the hall upstairs and the mother's room was downstairs on the opposite side of the house from impact. On the night of the tornado the youngest daughter was sleeping with her mother because she'd been afraid during the thunderstorms the evening preceding the tornado.

As this was a rural community (the house was in the country where the nearest neighbor was approximately 1/4 mile away) their house was the only one directly hit, although several nearby homes sustained significant damage. Further, even though the disaster struck while the students were on break, word of the tragedy spread quickly through the community and by mid-day most students and families were aware of the event. There were clear generational differences in mechanisms of communication. Parents tended to call or text one another. Students also used texts to inform their friends, but also used social media (primarily Facebook) to spread the word and discuss reactions.

The school counselor was out of state on vacation when she received word about the tragedy. As she was a former student of the first author, and the first author was supervising the current school counseling interns placed at the school, the counselor contacted the first author to serve as a consultant to address the immediate crisis. In consultation with the school administration, we recognized there was a need for students (and their families) to be able to gather to support one another based on a combination of direct communication, appraisal of social media postings, and the observation that students were spontaneously coming to school to gather on the playground. We therefore decided to collect as many teachers as possible and open the school to provide supportive sessions for students and families. The day following the disaster, we held a brief hour and a half meeting for teachers to: a) process their own reactions to the tragedy and b) become acquainted with the Hobfoll et al. (2007) principles (promoting a sense of safety, calming, self- and community efficacy, connectedness, and hope) to guide their own coping as well as that of their students. Students and families initially gathered in the gymnasium for one hour to connect informally and share as families and then those who wanted to meet in smaller age level groups broke up and met with teachers from that age level for an additional one to two hours (depending on age). The counseling interns and consultant met with parents.

The first week back after break the consultant met with the school counselor and school administrators to identify the bioecological issues and to devise a multisystemic intervention plan. Not only were immediate, initial needs discussed and identified, but a plan for longer term follow up and review also was put in place to track issues and needs as they arose. The specific issues with associated interventions follows.

First, there were chronosystem issues that factored into student and teacher responses related to the cohort of the deceased student. Specifically, his class had a gender imbalance with more males than females and this imbalance had been present since kindergarten. The lost student had been one of the few positive male leaders in their cohort. There were concerns about his loss generally and his loss as a positive leader among the group. Also, because students were affected across developmental levels there was recognition of a need for developmentally differentiated intervention with students and differentiated psycho-educational materials were needed for parents. Finally, the fact that the school was a K-12 setting highlighted the need for long term follow up in the aftermath of the trauma with not only the children in the family, but also with the larger student body who were affected via this loss and the broader impact of the disaster in the community.

The biophysical issues seemed most salient in the family with the immediate loss. However, as several other families had also experienced the environmental impact of the disaster, many of those students had biophysical reactions to the stressor that were present, but less obvious. Teachers and caregivers were apprised of warning signs for these reactions and encouraged to make counseling referrals accordingly. Those students who appeared to be experiencing an increase of fear reactions, hypervigilance, nightmares, avoidance/numbing, and other psychological sequelae of PTSD were either seen for individual counseling by the counseling interns or were referred to providers in the community at the preference of their families.

There were a host of microsystemic issues for the family, the classmates of the deceased and injured students, the student's in general, the teachers, and the religious groups of the families. There were immediate and long-term issues for the surviving family that were exacerbated by existing family dynamics. Initially, the school counselor made herself available as a support to the mother in regard to these issues, but later she determined that in order to best serve the needs of all family members, the mother could benefit from individual counseling with a private practitioner. One of the issues the family was dealing with was conflict between the parents over funeral arrangements owing to religious differences between the mother and father. This conflict spread beyond the immediate family to several other families with close affiliations to either parent through their respective religious communities. The parent's difficulties with conflict resolution were further exacerbated by father's active alcoholism, father's blaming mother for the loss, and mother's survivor guilt. The counselor remained available to the mother to help her facilitate grief-related coping and survivor guilt with her children and to promote their academic success. Two of the children had extended hospitalizations, and the brother returned to school in a wheelchair, all of which required academic accommodations.

Additional microsystemic issues were identified in regard to the classmates of the family members as well as the school in general. More specifically, many of the classmates of the deceased student were struggling with significant grief reactions. They were 8th graders and this early loss of a peer challenged many of their age typical "illusions of invulnerability". There was a noticed increase in behavioral issues in this class that teachers attributed to a combination of negative coping and the loss of positive leadership with the student's death. Initially, the counselor worked to provide psychoeducational lessons on the grieving process and work with students to develop positive coping strategies; however, these interventions were not generally well received. Subsequently, we worked with teachers to provide experiential activities appropriate to the subject content area to facilitate more adaptive coping. For example, in Language Arts we used directed readings and reaction papers. In Science we did a lesson on the environmental, economic, and societal impact of natural disasters. Art and music teachers provided more open-ended assignments that incorporated opportunities for personal expression and exploration of the Hobfoll et al. (2007) factors. Teachers, coaches, and counselors also worked with several of the other young men in the class to fill the positive leadership void left by this student's death.

Finally, the disaster affected the counselors, teachers, and administrators on several levels. The loss of life and injury of their students as well as the subsequent effect of the tragedy on their classroom environment specifically affected them. Several had family or friends whose homes sustained damage during the storm. There were a few who were affiliated with the conflicted religious communities. This combination of issues led us to recognize there was a need for staff support as well. The first author served as a facilitator for a series of support groups for the staff again grounded in the Hobfoll et al. principles (2007).

At the exosystemic level there was pressure stemming from the educational reform movement that resulted in some staff feeling conflicted about "devoting so much time" to the tragedy and school community's coping. While the school administration was quite supportive with the initial school-based interventions, they struggled at times with the follow up programming. When the counseling staff was able to help them see we could work with teachers to provide integrated curriculum that met not only the academic needs of the students, but also the personal and social needs of the students they were more receptive to longer term prevention and intervention efforts. Further, this disaster affected a significant number of families and even businesses in the community, albeit less drastically than the family who suffered the losses. As such, the disaster created a certain amount of broader "resource drain" for the school. While there was no intervention to address this issue, recognition of this broader impact at times helped assuage staff's frustrations.

Since the disaster occurred in a rural community there were limited trauma and rehabilitation treatment options at the local hospital. Therefore, two of the children (oldest sister and surviving son) in the surviving family were treated initially at a major medical center about an hour and a half drive away while the mother and youngest daughter were treated at the local hospital. Further, the surviving son had to spend about one month at a rehabilitation facility an hour away. This treatment in varied facilities created issues as the family originally was divided. The school nurse and counselor worked jointly with the hospitals to facilitate the injured student's transitions back to school.

A final exosystemic factor was the media. Initially, there were very dramatic photographs of the family's house in the local newspaper with a fairly sensationalistic headline about the family "sleeping through the disaster". Subsequently, there were a multitude of posts on the newspaper's webpage that were alternately supportive of the family and mother and condemning of her for not protecting her children. These contrasting views were similarly felt within the broader community although the majority sentiment was supportive. Additionally, the secondary student's use of social media around the disaster was significant. At first, it was the primary source of communicating the tragedy and then later became a mechanism for many students to process their grief reactions. One of the deceased student's best friends created a memorial site that many of the students continue to re-visit and post on. There is increased activity around the anniversary of the disaster, the deceased student's birthday, holidays, and major sporting events (he was on several sports teams). Throughout this site has been monitored by the counseling staff throughout the process, with the knowledge of the students, as a way of identifying students potentially in need of additional support.

The outermost level of systems is the macrosystems and many of the macrosystemic influences have been alluded to in earlier sections. There was little opportunity for school-based intervention at this level, however, awareness of the impact of these factors was often important in the crisis intervention process. First, there was the larger socioeconomic impact of the disaster on the community. There were also the cultural subsystem norms that resulted in conflict within the family and broader community. As counselors we worked to help those we had direct contact with be aware of and more accepting of each other's differences. There were also economic factors at play. The community was relatively economically depressed before the disaster and the disaster added an additional resource strain to a community already struggling. There were long-term economic issues for the surviving family of the deceased student (from medical bills and loss of their home), but also several of the other families who sustained damage to their homes.

RELATIONSHIP TO THE SBFC MODEL

As you can see the bioecological model and the specific case example contain the core elements of the SBFC Model. There are remedial and preventive efforts that occurred with not only the families affected by the disaster but also the broader school community. The bioecological model, in conjunction with the guiding principles recommended by Hobfoll and his colleagues (2007) provided a conceptual framework for crisis intervention that is congruent with SBFC.

EVIDENCE-BASED SUPPORT

Limited empirical research on school-based crisis intervention strategies exists; rather, there is much more research on individual approaches to treating trauma. The majority of the research that has been completed with respect to school-based crisis intervention approaches is on the Crisis Incident Stress Management (CISM) model for crisis intervention. This model originally was developed for emergency service personnel (Mitchell, 1983). The primary goal of this model is to reduce the traumatic effects of a stressful event by providing a safe place, education, and support to those affected. Similar to the CISM is a multiphasic critical incident stress debriefing (CISD), which consists of seven established phases (i.e., introduction phase, fact phase, thought phase, reaction phase, symptoms phase, teaching phase, and reentry phase) designed to be delivered as a single-session semi-structured intervention (Morrison, Russo, &Ilg, 2006).

A number of researchers have examined both the success and ineffectiveness of this approach with different groups. Morrison et al. (2006) reviewed a number of articles confirming empirical support for the model. Specifically, they found support for the use of the CISM with civilian and high-risk occupations groups, victims of armed robberies, child and adolescent victims of shipping disasters, emergency service personnel, and psychiatric workers after a traumatic work experience. Thus, it appears that there is some support for the CISM/CISD model with various populations. However, none of the aforementioned research evaluated the use of the CISM in school-based settings.

Morrison (2007) then conducted an evaluation of CISM that specifically examined the social validity of this model for school-based crisis intervention. Morrison utilized a qualitative, semi-structured interview procedure to query a group of school psychologists and social workers in an urban, Midwestern school district about their perception of the applicability of CISM for school-based crisis intervention. Morrison (2007) was primarily interested in capturing major themes, both positive and negative, related to the goals, procedures, and outcomes of the CISM model. Her findings suggested that 86% of respondents supported the CISM's allowed for emotional processing, support and normalization of participants post traumatic reactions. Further, CISM procedures were deemed appropriate for use in schools to provide a structured framework and common language for officials during crisis incidents. Although approval for the model was high, successful crisis intervention was believed to be in large part due to the knowledge and skills of the actual provider and not the model. However, those interviewed also felt CISM did not adequately address the developmental needs of school-age children, especially those from culturally diverse backgrounds. While some school professionals believed this was a major concern with the model, they also felt this deficit could be mitigated by knowledge and competencies held by individual providers. In sum, the model *could be* appropriate to addressing school-based crisis intervention needs, however, if provided by untrained professionals it could act in detrimental ways.

However, contrary to these perspectives, a number of researchers have reported empirical evidence refuting CISM's general effectiveness. Wei, Szumilas, and Kutcher (2010) conducted a meta-analytic review of the literature intended to provide a summary of evidence for the effectiveness of CISM/CISD as a commonly used crisis intervention in schools. Unfortunately, Wei and colleagues found research regarding the effectiveness of CISM/CISD in school settings was limited. That is, even though literature exists suggesting CISM/CISD models were effective in reducing symptoms of psychological distress in adults, there was little evidence supporting the efforts to translate these models into school-based crisis interventions with children. This finding, compounded by the lack of controlled studies supporting the use of these models in schools settings, is further evidence of the unfounded use of these models as interventions in schools (Wei et al., 2010).

Due to the differences in both research findings and opinion regarding the appropriateness of this highly publicized model for crisis intervention, it seems difficult to recommend this as the premiere model to use for school crises as has been done in the past. More recently, Hobfoll et al. (2007) identified five evidence based intervention principles to help guide crisis intervention and prevention efforts regardless of setting. The five principles include promoting a sense of safety, calming, a sense of self- and community efficacy, connectedness, and hope.

To be more explicit, these five established principles are believed by Hobfoll et al. (2007) to transcend specific approaches and instead provide responders with a more broad based guide for intervention practices following disaster or mass violence. Each principle is intended to assist in the process of establishing an intervention, and can be applied at both the individual and broader community level. These authors concede that specific interventions, with empirical support, already exist to help prevent or ameliorate PTSD reactions. They suggest that what is now needed are more integrative, "broad-scale", multisystemic interventions. Hobfoll and colleagues suggest their five principles are a start in that direction. We agree with Hobfoll and his colleagues (2007) that it is difficult to establish a simple, unidimensional model for crisis intervention in schools and instead call for a flexible approach due to the heterogeneity of traumatic events. We contend that integration of the principles suggested by Hobfoll et al., within a bioecological framework can allow for a comprehensive, flexible, and adaptable model for crisis intervention that is consistent with the principles of school-based family counseling. Further, we will provide more information regarding empirically supported components of effective crisis management (see the Procedure section below).

MULTICULTURAL COUNSELING CONSIDERATIONS

This section will address a broad approach to multicultural considerations when implementing crisis intervention strategies. A culturally aware approach that attends to the diverse needs of children, families, and communities is essential for the success of any type of crisis intervention. Ethnic diversity, however, is not the only multicultural consideration crisis teams need to attend to (Heath & Sheen, 2005). As the constellation of student populations in the United States becomes more diverse, consideration of the unique needs of specific cultural subgroups will become even more essential.

At this point, research focusing on providing culturally sensitive counseling in conjunction with crisis intervention with ethnically diverse populations is lacking (Canada, Heath, Money, Annandale, Fischer, & Young, 2006). Recognizing this concern, Canada et al. surveyed school counselors about the unique needs of students from culturally diverse backgrounds during crisis intervention. Their survey results illuminated a number of salient issues. Namely, these professionals cited a need to understand students' cultural backgrounds when implementing any effective crisis intervention. Similarly, community/home-related issues (i.e., barriers to families and/or communities accessing or rejecting services), communication/language issues (i.e., whether families/communities speak English or not, difficulty reaching families without phones, and difficulties disseminating information about the crisis and how to access services), and coping issues (i.e., how to respect others' beliefs about grief, death, loss, and coping in terms of individual cultural and religious beliefs) were all identified as leading concerns of school counselors when culturally sensitive crisis intervention. These concerns are related to a wide-range of cultural attitudes, beliefs, and experiences specific to both the individuals involved and the larger community population.

Canada et al. (2006) provided a number of implications and recommendations in light of these reported concerns. Specifically, these authors recommend crisis interventions be site specific and sensitive to the cultural context of the crisis or tragedy. This approach ensures a more personal, immediate, and culturally sensitive approach to the issues at hand. Further, the authors suggest performing a school-specific needs assessment to meet the individual needs of a community rather than prescribing to general culturally-specific approach. Finally, it was suggested for professionals to consult with religious and community leaders about customary interventions and to establish rapport for future community-based support. In total, these three considerations, although not exclusive, act to produce a more culturally aware and site-specific crisis intervention strategy.

Similarly, Jimerson, Brock, and Pletcher (2005) point to the considerations UNICEF has established for providing culturally grounded support services. These recommendations are as follows: (a) shift from a trauma approach to a community-based approach; (b) identify local professionals from various disciplines; (c) be aware of community heterogeneity; (d) promote and restore natural support networks and coping strategies that existed prior to the crisis; (e) utilize both traditional health methods and training on psychosocial needs, healing, and conflict resolution; (f) identify, incorporate, and promote local agencies and services; (g) understand community standards for socialization and healthy functioning; and (h) successful community integration sustains programs (Jimerson et al., 2005).

With these guidelines in mind, culturally competent school-based crisis interventions require an understanding of not just the children and families involved in the crisis but also the community as a whole. This broader multicultural focus will act to positively impact the quality of services provided to both schools and communities (Health & Sheen, 2005). Being culturally aware requires that professionals attend to the site- and community-specific factors, including culturally relevant coping, community/home influences, and communication factors related to a given crisis incident. Following UNICEF's suggestions might provide a strong foundation to cover various cultural considerations and further prepare for the most effective multicultural approach.

CHALLENGES AND SOLUTIONS

Similar to the previous sections, this portion will focus on general challenges that are encountered when implementing any school-based crisis intervention as well as potential solutions to such concerns.

Heath and Sheen (2005) recount a number of common problems with school crisis plans that occur on various systemic levels. First, they discuss how schools need to be proactive in their efforts to create or adapt a crisis plan that fits their individual needs. Individuals from all levels of personnel need to be included in this modification process to ensure the most effective plan possible. Secondly, plans need to be in a format that is easily understood and accessed by all those involved. That is, teachers, staff, administrators, and other support service personnel should have basic training on the crisis intervention to ensure it is ready to be implemented. Finally, crisis plans need to be periodically updated, which may require a grass-roots effort to keep plans current. This concern, however, is easily solved if someone is periodically assigned to keep controllable aspects of the intervention (e.g., the phone tree) current (Heath & Sheen, 2005).

Given the complexity of crisis intervention teams due to the lack consensus about the best approach to school-based crisis intervention, Adamson and Peacock (2007) sought to investigate specific details of crisis teams and how schools respond to crises. As part of this study they discovered a number of difficulties experienced by the school psychologists and thus provided solutions to these concerns. In continuation of prior suggestions from the crisis intervention literature the authors suggested performing periodic evaluations of crisis teams (Brock, Sandoval, & Lewis, 2001). They also suggest the use of crisis drills to provide opportunities to practice learned skills in the same manner as drills for fire and other natural disasters. Further, the authors suggest including parents and community members in the crisis preparation and response. This option provides awareness to the community and prepares them to assist in the crisis intervention if necessary. Finally, Adamson and Peacock (2007) suggested a number of workshops, in-service trainings, and other practice opportunities at the district level. Since school workers often follow the lead of districts' administrators, this suggestion will address that need and ensure a complete approach to school-based crisis intervention.

Similar to Adamson and Peacock, Crepeau-Hobson and Summers (2011) explored a number of themes discovered following a school-based shooting. To begin, familiarity with the school system was reported as one way to be more effective as a school-based crisis responder. Without this knowledge it would be difficult to adequately meet the needs of any school community. Further, responders suggested being able to address the needs of all those involved, including children and their parents. Another important aspect for the responder to be mindful of is the needs for flexibility. Due to the necessity for various outside responders, school-based crisis teams should maintain flexibility in response to both the school and the larger community's needs (Crepeau-Hobson & Summers, 2011).

On a more individual level, Crepeau-Hobson and Summers (2011) indicated the importance for school-based crisis responders to recognize the impact responding can have on them as responders. That is, data from their study revealed that many participants experienced reactions of secondary traumatic stress; therefore, even if the secondary trauma is transient in nature it is important to be mindful of this chance. Finally, the need for self-care and social support is highly important. Providing responders the opportunity to debrief with mental health professionals will assist with this (Crepeau-Hobson & Summers, 2011). In general, it appears that effective leadership is key to successful crisis intervention (Crepeau-Hobson, Sievering, Armstrong, & Stonis, 2012). Leaders should have awareness of crisis response resources available in the community so as to provide the most up-to-date and successful crisis intervention possible. Such an approach would help to disseminate knowledge throughout the crisis team and ultimately promote a flexible and cooperative approach to crisis management.

There is no step-by-step procedure for implementing a bioecological approach to crisis intervention. However, immediate interventions are likely to begin at the biophysical and microsystemic levels. Identification of relevant chronosystem, exosystem, and macrosystemic factors that would facilitate or hinder implementation of these interventions will help strengthen the likelihood of success and minimize challenges. Given the potential for long-term, adverse effects in the aftermath of trauma, it will be useful to identify short-term, immediate interventions and long term, follow up needs. Hobfoll et al.'s (2007) principles are particularly germane when developing the immediate interventions. There are also a variety of resources listed at the end of this chapter that can be useful in developing a comprehensive plan.

SUMMARY

It is clear that in these days and times, schools need to have a plan for dealing with crisis situations. Many crisis intervention plans focus on issues of securing the immediate safety of students. Further focus is on providing some type of CISM/CISD after the crisis ends even support for this approach is mixed. We feel that from a SBFC perspective we can contribute a general conceptual framework for addressing crisis situations that goes beyond CISM/CISD. Toward that end we have provided a comprehensive systems approach that allows for both conceptualization and intervention at the individual, family, whole school, broader community, and administrative levels.

REFERENCES

Adamson, A. D., & Peacock, G. G. (2007). Crisis response in the public schools: A survey of school psychologists' experiences and perceptions. *Psychology in the Schools, 44*, 749-764.

Brock, S. E., Sandoval, J., & Lewis, S. (2001). Preparing for crisis in the schools: A manual for building school crisis response teams (2nd ed.). New York: Wiley.

Bronfenbrenner, U. (1979). *The ecology of human development*. Cambridge, MA: Harvard University Press.

Bronfenbrenner, U., &Ceci, S. J. (1994). Nature-nurture reconceptualized in developmental perspective: A biological model. *Psychological Review, 101,* 568-586.

Canada, M., Heath, M. A., Money, K., Annandale, N., Fischer, L., & Young, E. L. (2006). Crisis intervention for students of diverse backgrounds: School counselors' concerns. *Brief Treatment and Crisis Intervention, 7*, 12-24.

Chantarujikapong, S. I., Scherrer, J. F., Xian, H., Eisen, S. A., Lyons, M. J., Goldberg, J., et al.(2001).A twin study of generalized anxiety disorder symptoms, panic disorder symptoms and post-traumatic stress disorder in men. *Psychiatric Residency, 103*, 133-145.

Cohen, S. (2004). Social relationships and health.*American Psychologist, 59*, 676-684.

Cohen, J. A., Perel, J. M., DeBellis, M. D., Friedman, M. J.,& Putnam, F. W. (2002). Treating traumatized children: Clinical implications of the psychobiology of posttraumatic stress disorder. *Trauma, Violence, & Abuse, 3*, 91-108.

Cook-Cottone, C.(2004). Childhood posttraumatic stress disorder: Diagnosis, treatment, and school reintegration. *School Psychology Review, 33*, 127-139.

Crepeau-Hobson, F., Sievering, K. S., Armstrong, C., &Stonis, J. (2012). A coordinated mental health crisis response: Lessons learned from three Colorado school shootings. *Journal of School Violence, 11*, 207-225.

Crepeau-Hobson, F., & Summers, L. L. (2011). The crisis response to a school-based hostage event: A case study. *Journal of School Violence, 10*, 281-298.

Davidson, J.R., Hughes, D., Blazer, D.G., & George, L. K. (1991). Post-traumatic stress disorder in the community: An epidemiological study. *Psychological Medicine, 21(3),* 713-721. doi:10.1017/S0033291700022352

Davidson, S., & Smith, R. (1990).Traumatic experiences in psychiatric outpatients. *Journal of Traumatic Stress Studies, 3,* 459-475.

deSilva, P.(1999). Cultural aspects of posttraumatic stress disorder. In W. Yule (Ed.), *Post traumatic stress disorders: Concepts and therapy* (pp. 116-137). New York: John Wiley & Sons.

Foa, E. B., Zinbarg, R., &Rothbaum, B. O. (1992). Uncontrollability and unpredictability in post-traumatic stress disorder: An animal model. *Psychological Bulletin, 112,* 218-238.

Heath, M. A., & Sheen, D. (2005). School-based crisis intervention: Preparing all personnel to assist. New York: Guilford Press.

Hobfoll, S. E., Watson, P., Bell, C. C., Bryant, R. A., Brymer, M. J., Friedman, M. J. et al. (2007). Five essential elements of immediate and mid-term crisis situations intervention: Empirical evidence. *Psychiatry, 70,* 283-315.

Hoffman, M.A., & Kruczek, T. (2011). A bioecological model of mass trauma: Individual, community and societal effects. *The Counseling Psychologist, 39,* 1087-1127. doi:10.1177/0011000010397932

Jimerson, S. R., Brock, S. E., &Pletcher, S. W. (2005). An integrated model of school crisis preparedness and intervention: A shared foundation to facilitate international crisis intervention. *School Psychology International, 26,* 275-296.

LeDoux, J. E. (1996). *The emotional brain: The mysterious underpinning of emotional life.* New York: Simon & Schuster.

McCann, L., & Pearlman, L. A. (1990). Vicarious traumatization: A framework for understanding the psychological effects of working with victims. *Journal of Traumatic Stress, 3,* 131-149.

Mitchell, J. T. (1983). When disaster strikes: The critical incident stress debriefing process. *Journal of Emergency Medical Services, 8,* 36-39.

Morrision, J. Q. (2007). Social validity of the critical incident stress management model for school-based crisis intervention. *Psychology in the Schools, 44,* 765-777.doi:10.1002/pits

Morrison, J. Q., Russo, C. J., &Ilg, T. J. (2006). School-based crisis intervention: Its effectiveness and role in broader crisis intervention plans. *International Journal of Educational Reform, 15,* 331-343.

Pfefferbaum, B. (1997). Posttraumatic stress disorder in children: A review of the past 10 years. *Journal of the American Academy of Child & Adolescent Psychiatry, 36,* 1503-1511.

Pynoos, R. S. (1994).Traumatic stress and developmental psychopathology in children and adolescents. In P. S. Pynoos (Ed.), *Posttraumatic stress disorder; A clinical review* (pp. 64- 98). Lutherville, MD: The Sidran Press.

Sack, W. H., Clarke, G. H., & Seeley, J.(1995).Posttraumatic stress disorder across two generations of Cambodian refugees. *Journal of the American Academy of Child & Adolescent Psychiatry, 34,* 1160-1166.

Selye, H. (1952). *The Story of the Adaptational Syndrome.* Montreal, Canada: Acta Inc.

Siegel, L. J. (1998). Children medically at risk. In R.J. Morris and T.R. Kratochivill (Eds.), *The practice of child therapy (2nd edition, pp. 325-366).* Boston: Allyn & Bacon.

Srinivasa, M. R. (2007). Mass violence and mental health: Recent epidemiological findings. *International Review of Psychiatry, 19,* 183-192. doi:10.1080/09540260701365460

True, W.R., & Lyons, M.J. (1999). Genetic risk factors for PTSD: A twin study. In R. Yehuda (Ed.), *Risk factors for posttraumatic stress disorder (pp. 68-71).* Washington DC: American Psychiatric Press.

Tyano, S, Iancu, I., Solomon, Z. (1996). Seven-year follow-up of child survivors of a bus-train collision. *Journal of the American Academy of Child and Adolescent Psychiatry, 35,* 365-373. doi:10.1097/00004583-199603000-00019 van der Kolk, B. A.(2003). The neurobiology of childhood trauma and abuse. *Child and Adolescent Clinics of North America 12*, 293– 317.

Wei, Y., Szumilas, M., &Kutcher, S. (2010). Effectiveness on mental health of psychological debriefing for crisis intervention in schools. *Educational Psychology Review, 22*, 339-347.

RESOURCES

Center for School Mental Health Assistance. (2002). Crisis intervention: A guide for school-based clinicians. Baltimore, MD: University of Maryland.

This online article is published by the University of Maryland's Center for school Mental Health Assistance and can be found at:
http://csmh.umaryland.edu/Resources/ResourcePackets/files/crisisintervention.pdf.
This article includes additional embedded resources for parents, teachers, educators, and clinicians.

http://smhp.psych.ucla.edu/qf/crisis_qt/
This online resource includes quick training aids for school-based crisis interventions. Sections   include fact sheets, general principles, handouts to organize a crisis team, handouts for crisis   responders, and additional resources.

http://smhp.psych.ucla.edu/qf/crisis_tt/crisisindex.htm
This online resource from *Center for Mental Health in Schools* at UCLA provides a training   tutorial for crisis assistance and prevention.

http://www.edpubs.gov
The U.S. Department of Education provides free publications, including those related to crisis preparedness and intervention, which can be found through this link.

PART V

SCHOOL-BASED FAMILY COUNSELING CHANGE STRATEGIES: FAMILY-PREVENTION FOCUS

SCHOOL FOCUS

School-Prevention	School-Intervention
Family-Prevention	Family-Intervention

PREVENTION FOCUS

INTERVENTION FOCUS

FAMILY FOCUS

Chapter 14
How to Provide a Parent Education Workshop

Nancy Rosenbledt

OVERVIEW: *This chapter describes the process in developing and implementing parent education for school-based family counselors to provide family-preventive services through psycho-educational trainings and workshops. Examples from parent education workshops within the school-based family counseling model framework are included in PowerPoint slide format from actual presentations based on best practices from a positive parenting perspective.*

BACKGROUND

Parents play a critical role in the development of their children, and therefore, can provide key components to effective intervention and prevention programs in the schools. Consequently, SBFC professionals working collaboratively with parents in targeting emotional, behavioral, and academic concerns is a vital partnership to ensuring their children's home/school success. SBFC professionals are in an optimal position to form an alliance with families and help them access and develop interventions that will remediate problems. Furthermore, it is in the best interest of the child to collaborate with the whole family, which includes extended family members and key adults in the child's life (Thompson, 2002). Nevertheless, common barriers that prevent parent involvement and therapeutic alliance must be identified and eradicated (Gimpel-Peacock & Collet, 2010).

Although parent training can be a very effective intervention, it not uncommon for SBFC professionals to encounter certain obstacles in implementing parent involvement intervention. One of the first obstacles involves parent expectations: if a child is having problems at school, then many parents believe it is not their problem, but the responsibility of the school to "fix it;" or parents who are receiving constant contact from the school about negative behaviors their child is exhibiting may feel overwhelmed and blamed, and therefore, inadequate as parents. Other reasons for the lack of parent involvement include: time conflicts between work and school schedules, cultural and language barriers, feeling uncomfortable or unwelcome in their child's school, lack of community support and transportation, and lack of understanding and support in the workplace (Thompson, 2002).

Emphasizing that SBFC professionals need parents' help in creating change by becoming collaborative partners can be an effective way of overcoming these obstacles. Let parents know that we may be the experts on behavioral change, but they have the expertise on their children and home situations. In additions, SBFC professionals need to focus on how much more important parents can be in having a greater impact in children's lives than the clinicians. Troubleshooting to overcome obstacles by teaching parents problem-solving skills may then be generalized to specific areas of concern and intervening effectively with children. Problem solving steps from Webster-Stratton's program (1998) can be taught as follows:

Identifying the problem
Identifying alternative solutions to the problem
Evaluating the outcomes of the different solutions
Choosing a solution to implement
Evaluating the success of the chosen solution

Motivational Interviewing based on the stages of change model can also be useful in helping parents engage in the parent training process (Prochaska and Diclemente, 2005):

Precontemplation: Parent is not yet ready to consider change or may be unaware that a problem exists. Provide evaluative feedback, validate parent's lack of readiness to change, but emphasize the decision to change is their decision to make. SBFC may need to proceed with the child and school staff alone.

Contemplation: Awareness that change is imminent. The SBFC professional validates parent's ambivalence, has discussion about realistic pros and cons and outcome expectations.

Preparation or action: Parents have realized that there is a problem and have either made changes recently or plan to do so soon. Interventions may focus on removing barriers and encouraging parents to think about small changes to which they can commit.

Maintenance or relapse: Parents have implemented a few changes and need assistance to continue with these behaviors. Other parents are eagerly participating and actively seeking help but need assistance in identifying concrete next steps and encouragement to maintain the changes they have already made. Others need help in anticipating possibility of relapse, triggers, and coping (what went wrong?)

RELATIONSHIP TO THE SBFC MODEL

Although schools cannot usurp the parenting process, they can provide parent effectiveness training and schools must partner with parents for the benefit of children (Gehrke, 1998). There are some basic principles SBFC professionals can institute to create effective school/home partnerships, however. SBFC professionals can acknowledge parents' right to teach their children values and beliefs that may be different from the mainstream. Parents need to be informed of the services SBFC professionals can and cannot offer. Parents need to be included to the maximum degree possible in the intervention process when children are having trouble. Parents should be regularly consulted and their responses seriously considered and implemented in the collaborative process. Finally, as mentioned previously, many homes have other adults besides parents who are involved in parenting children.

Offering some type of programming for parents to learn effective parenting skills is paramount to the SBFC Model in helping parents and families to develop skills that prevent future problems. Parent training is a preventive-family focus where SBFC professionals work with parents to reduce problematic behaviors that youth are exhibiting and to increase positive, pro-social behaviors both in home and school. Parents are instructed in a workshop format in the use and application of behavioral principles and methods (positive parenting principles) that have been found to be effective in reducing problematic child behaviors, such as positive reinforcement of appropriate behaviors and mild discipline (response cost) for inappropriate behaviors. Parent empowerment is emphasized as parents are viewed as key players in this process. In other words, change in child behavior comes through changes parents make in their responses to the child's behaviors.

Parents are first taught to attend to and praise and encourage positive behaviors that the child exhibits. Secondly, parents are taught to effectively use discipline skills, such as time-out and removal of privileges (Eisenstadt, Eyberg, McNeil, Newcomb, & Funderbun, 1993; Hanf, 1969). Furthermore, a social learning approach and active methods of training are implemented through the following steps:

Didactic instruction/description of the use of the skill.
Modeling of the skill.
Parental practice of the skill, with feedback provided by the SBFC professional.
Parental practice of the skill at home.

EVIDENCE-BASED SUPPORT

In a meta-analysis of studies examining the effects of behavioral parent training, Maughan, Christiansen, Jenson, Olympia, and Clark (2005) concluded that behavioral training was effective in reducing behavior problems in children. In an earlier meta-analysis, Serketich and Dumas (1996) also found support for the effectiveness of parent training in reducing problematic child behaviors, although unlike the former authors, Serketich and Dumas found that parent training was more effective with older children.

Parent Management Training-Oregon Model (PMTO) was designed to use family interventions to treat and prevent antisocial behavior problems in children and adolescents (Patterson et al., 1975; 1985; 1992). Both the shape and the contexts in which the model has been applied evolved since the early work of Patterson and his associates in the 1960s and 1970s. A summary of salient PMTO characteristics involve parenting comprised of coercive and positive parenting practices. Coercion occurs when one person uses aversive behavior to control the behavior of another. Examples of coercion are temper tantrums and threats by children and harsh punishment, both physical and psychological, as parental forms. This "dance" includes negative reciprocity and reinforcement.

Positive parenting practices involve a step-by-step procedure, with parents mastering one skill before adding new strategies to the parenting toolbox. The intervention is comprised of five dimensions demonstrated to serve as mediators of effects on child outcomes:

Scaffolding & positive reinforcement – breaking complex behaviors into achievable steps and encouraging approximation toward the goal and positive reinforcement to teach prosocial behaviors.

Limit setting – another teaching tool to discourage deviant behaviors with contingent small negative sanctions.

Monitoring – involves parental tracking of children's whereabouts, activities, peers, and behaviors while at home and away with appropriate adult supervision.

Problem solving – involves setting goals, developing strategies to achieve goals, committing to decision, action, and making relevant adjustments.

Positive involvement – includes the many ways that parents show their children love and interest.

Several studies using the PMTO model have shown that intervention benefits to parenting and reductions in deviant peer association have led to immediate and long-term reductions in negative youth outcomes. Furthermore, reciprocity in outcome effects help parents improve depression, financial stress, and police arrests (DeGarmo, Patterson, & Forgatch, 2004; Forgatch & DeGarmo, 2007).

Webster-Stratton's multicomponent program, Incredible Years, includes group parent training, individual child-focused, and teacher consultation components. In the parent training component, parents are taught to increase positive attention to their children through child-directed play, praise statements, and incentive programs. Parents also learn discipline techniques such as, ignoring, time-out, and logical and natural consequences. Finally, parent-specific skills are addressed including personal self-control, communication and problem-solving skills, strengthening social support, and self-care (Webster-Stratton & Reid, 2003). Analyses of treatment moderators (parents, teachers, and children) showed that intervention combinations that included parent training were generally more effective than those that did not; however, the addition of teacher training seemed to be significant for impulsive children (Beauchine, Webster-Stratton, & Reid, 2005). Results of Webster-Stratton's program indicate that reducing behavior problems in children and increasing use of effective discipline skills in parents were effective both immediately after and post treatment for up to a year (Webster-Stratton, 1998; Webster-Stratton et al., 2004). The best treatment responses were observed among children of parents who scored relatively low on verbal criticism and harsh parenting (Webster-Stratton, 2006).

Parent-Child Interaction Therapy (PCIT), a program based on parent training is aimed at parents of young children. In this program, parents are taught to use child-directed interaction, in which parents use play skills to implement positive attending and communication skills, including praise, reflection, imitation, description, and enthusiasm. Parents are then instructed on implementation of parent-directed interaction skills, including clear, effective command and time-out procedure (Brinkmeyer & Eyberg, 2003). In studies of the effectiveness of PCIT, parents reported a decrease in child behavior problems and parenting stress, more internal locus of control, and an increase in positive interactions with their children, i.e., praises, reflections, behavior descriptions, and decreases in negative parenting behavior during child-led play, i.e., questions, commands, criticisms (Bagner & Eyberg, 2007; Schuhmann, Foote, Eybert, Boggs, & Algina, 1998). Outcomes have been noted by researchers to have positive long-term effects even with an abbreviated form of PCIT (Hood & Eyberg, 2003; Nixon, Sweeney, Erickson, & Touyz, 2003).

The Triple P-Positive Parenting Program is a comprehensive parenting program that prevents behavior problems (Saunders, 1999) as follows: Treatment is geared toward information regarding parenting, shared through media outlets, tips sheets, etc. Parents participate in "anticipatory developmental guidance" with children who are considered to be at risk for behavior problems. Parents, whose children have mild behavior problems, are provided with information and specific intervention strategies to address the concerned problem. Parents who are considered to have children with specific behavior problems, but do not meet diagnostic criteria for a behavior disorder, learn specific parenting skills such as attending to positive behaviors and use of time-out to decrease inappropriate behaviors. Parents, who are experiencing additional difficulties such as, marital problems, depression, etc., are offered support.

An evaluation of PCIT revealed results that efficacy and effectiveness of the program, particularly with parents whose children manifested with mild behavior problems, demonstrated positive effects immediately post intervention and at 6-month follow up. Furthermore, the intervention produced reliable and significant reductions in oppositional, aggressive, and antisocial behavior and increases in prosocial behavior among children. The effects of treatment extend beyond multiple outcomes of the child where parent dysfunction and stress declined and family relations improved (Kazdin, Esveldt-Dawson, French, & Unis, 1987; Kazdin, Bass, Siegel, & Thomas, 1989; Kazdin, Siegel, & Bass, 1992).

Greene and Ablon's (2006) Collaborative Problem-Solving (CPS) intervention process has empirical support, yet contrasts with the above behavioral interventions in that CPS focuses on helping parents and children solve problems rather than applying behavioral contingencies to manage a child's behavior. Although results from a study by Greene et al.(2004) support CPS' effectiveness in decreasing oppositional behavior in children, more data are needed in order to address the validity for implementation by SBFC professionals.

Multisystemic therapy (MST) developed by Henggeler & Lee in 2003, is another evidence-based intervention geared toward children who engage in severe misconduct such as in juvenile offenders and those with serious mental health issues. MST is a family system's approach to treatment, involving the home, school, and community. Any combination of services, including family, peer, school, and individual interventions, medications, and family social support, may be delivered as needed. Studies have demonstrated many favorable effects for MST with juvenile offenders and their families (Borduin et al., 1995; Borduin, Henggeler, Blaske, & Stein, 1990; Brunk, Henggeler & Whelan, 1987; Hennggeler et al., 1986). Although the results of using MST are promising as demonstrated in decreases in substance use, rearrest, externalizing problems, and improvement in family functioning, however, because MST is so time-intensive, it is not feasible for SBFC professionals to implement other than to serve on the team and provide school-based interventions. Additional Evidence-Based Parenting Programs are briefly reviewed in Box 14.1.

Box 14.1 Additional Evidence-Based Parenting Programs

MEGASKILLS (Rich, 1992) focused on 10 values/traits presented to help parents with children ages 5-12 develop skills associated with school success:

Confidence	*Perseverance*
Motivation	*Caring*
Effort	*Teamwork*
Responsibility	*Common sense*
Initiative	*Problem solving*

ROOTS AND WINGS: RAISING RESILIENT CHILDREN (Wilmes, 2000) is designed to help parents learn how to provide positive influences for their children in the following areas:

Risk and protective factors
Standards about tobacco, alcohol, and drug use
Teachable moments (improving communication skills)
Setting boundaries, building bridges
Feelings
Rituals and traditions

BUILDING SUCCESSFUL PARTNERSHIPS: A GUIDE FOR DEVELOPING PARENT AND FAMILY INVOLVEMENT PROGRAMS (National PTA, 2000; www.PTA.org.) is research based in showing the importance of high levels of parent involvement to outcomes such as academic performance and prosocial behavior. The standards for parent improving parent/school collaboration aimed at helping students succeed are:

Communicating
Parenting
Student learning
Volunteering
School decision making
Collaborating with the community

SYSTEMIC TRAINING FOR EFFECTIVE PARENTING (STEP) (Dinkmeyer & McKay, 1997 is a video-based parenting program for parents of elementary school children and an audio-based parenting program for parents of teens. STEP program consists of nine sessions:

Understanding children's behavior and misbehavior
Understanding how children use emotions to involve parents
Encouragement
Communication: Listening
Communication: Exploring alternatives and expressing your ideas and feelings to children
Developing responsibility
Decision making for parents
The family meeting
Developing confidence and using your potential

THE NEXT STEP (SYSTEMIC TRAINING FOR EFFECTIVE PARENTING THROUGH PROBLEM SOLVING) (Dinkmeyer & McKay, 1997) is designed for parents who have participated in the previous mentioned program and want to gain additional practice in basic principles through a problem solving group:

Taking a fresh look at your parenting
Building self-esteem
How lifestyle beliefs affect parenting
Stress: Coping with changes and challenges
Making decisions as a family
Gentle strength and firm love

ACTIVE PARENTING NOW (Popkin, 2002) has two versions; a video-based parenting program for parents of children ages 5-12 and one for parents of teens:

The active parent
Winning cooperation
Responsibility and discipline
Understanding and redirecting behavior
Building courage, character, and self-esteem
The active family now

FAMILY TALK (Popkin, 1998) is designed to help families improve their communication skills using any of the following topics:

Family decisions   *Grandmother*
Television   *Mother's time*
Okay to feel sad   *Feeling alone*
Money   *Mom and Dad's time together*
Stress   *Minorities*
What's a step mom?   *Equality*
Honesty   *Choices*
Teasing

BOWDOIN PARENT EDUCATION PROGRAM (Bowdoin, 1993, 1996) is a research-based curriculum designed for "high-risk, low literacy" families who need simple and basic parenting skills. The video-based program is presented at parent meetings to help parents of children from ages 5-12 improve their self-concept and develop skills for school success:

How to develop values for responsible living
Help your child say "NO" to alcohol, tobacco, and drugs
Harmony at home
Healthy minds, healthy feelings
Expanding your child's reading ability
Expanding your child's math ability
The single parent

MULTICULTURAL COUNSELING CONSIDERATIONS

One of the most critical challenges facing school-based professionals is gaining competency in addressing the needs of an increasingly diverse student population (Coleman, 1995; House & Martin, 1998; Lee, 1995; Lewis & Hayes, 1991). In fact, it is projected that by 2020, most school-aged children attending public schools will come from diverse cultural and ethnic backgrounds (Campbell, 1994). Multicultural counseling competence refers to the SBFC professionals attitudes, beliefs, knowledge, and skills in working with people from different cultural groups including racial, ethnic, gender, social class, and sexual orientation (Arrendono et al., 1996. Accordingly, due to the increasing ethnic, social, and racial diversity of the U.S. school system, SBFC professionals need to possess appropriate levels of knowledge and skills to work with diverse students and their families (Durodoye, 1998; Hobson & Kanitz, 1996; Johnson, 1995).

These issues must be integrated within a context of family involvement where the SBFC professionals is accountable for understanding and generating awareness of specific cultural factors relevant to particular cultural groups. This includes knowledge to assess specific factors such as acculturation, language proficiency, and sociocultural history that are critical concerns for children's development in the schools (Paniagua, 1994; Vasquez-Nuthall, DeLeon, & Valle, 1990). Strategies that support multicultural competence within the context of family involvement consist of three components; parent education and support, school-family curriculum activities, and school staff-parent partnership efforts (Banks, 1993).

Parent Education and Support includes offering a lending library, parenting programs, and newsletters. Direct work, especially with immigrant parents, where the SBFC professional acts in the role of school-home-community liaison in support of navigating unfamiliar school systems (Atkinson & Juntunen, 1994). Casa and Furlong (1994) emphasize the advocacy role SBFC professionals play to increase parent participation and facilitate increased empowerment of parents and community.

School-Family Curriculum Activities includes discussion groups on racial or cultural issues, events where the entire school community celebrate their cultural diversity, parent participation in specific classroom curriculum activities (Ramsey & Derman-Sparks, 1992), and field trips and classroom presentations with discussion to explore concerns and ideas (Neugebauer, 1992). Furthermore, displays, performances, and literature throughout schools need to include representatives of people from diverse racial, ethnic, and cultural backgrounds engaged in meaningful activities.

Parent-Teacher Partnerships includes study teams, school advisory groups, and multicultural planning sessions for input on school policies and procedures (Ramsey & Derman-Sparks, 1992). As human development specialists, SBFC professionals make contributions that are proactive, collaborative, and integrative by providing services to students and their families. They need to become equipped with strategies that are responsive and proactive approaches to meet the needs of an increasingly diverse students population, which could mean providing human relations training, recognition and acknowledgment of divergent cultures, orientation and transition services, peer helper programs, conflict resolution and peer mediation programs, small group counseling, bilbliotherapy, and classroom guidance and teacher advisory programs.

Finally, systematic work on ethnicity and culture as moderators of treatment is needed. Professionals cannot assume that treatment developed primarily with a couple of cultural or ethnic groups will be applicable to other groups without modification. Many parent-child interactions and child-rearing practices are deeply woven into religious teachings and cultural beliefs and customs, for example, type of punishment, how and what demands are made on children, etc. It is reasonable, therefore, to expect ethnicity and culture to moderate intervention effects (Weisz & Kazdin, 2010).

CHALLENGES AND SOLUTIONS

As mentioned in the previous section, a fundamental challenge for SBFC professionals is involving and engaging challenging parents as key players and partners in their children's education. Therefore, SBFC professionals may need to be oriented to a positive psychology perspective and belief system (Wilde, 2005):

Belief #1: Parents love their kids in the best way they know how. Most people raise their children how their parents raised them, and most challenging parents did not have good role models as children.

Belief #2: Parents inability to believe negative behaviors attributed to their children is biologically/evolutionary rooted. That's how parents protect their progeny and keep their line of DNA moving forward in the next generation.

Belief #3: Carefully consider the requests made of parents as they have the skills, understanding, self-discipline, and organization to be successful in the implementation of plans.

Belief #4: With the exception of parents who have mental health issues, most of their behaviors would be predictable if professionals had access to the complex patterns that have been ingrained in their life histories. By keeping this in mind while unraveling these complex patterns will most likely engender successful engagement of challenging parents.

Belief #5: Imagining sitting in the parent's chair as if a SBFC professional were talking about your child, will dramatically increase your empathic understanding of parents.

Although behavioral parent training has shown empirical support in effectiveness, it does not work for all families and can end up alienating parents who interpret this approach as authoritarian, imposition of the parent's will, and conducted through a rigid process. Researchers have evaluated other interventions that involve working with parents as partners on the school team. In particular, Greene and Ablon (2006) provide a collaborative problem-solving (CPS) model which initially focuses on the antecedents of the child's problem behaviors. By learning what predicts the targeted behavior, parents, children, and school staff can engage in a CPS process to resolve the problem.

The first step in the CPS process is to identify skill deficits that are leading to misbehaviors as well as triggers associated with these behaviors. To identify pathways and triggers, the SBFC professional conducts a situational analysis in which the parent is asked to describe instances of child misbehavior. The SBFC professional's goal is to develop specific hypotheses about the child's behaviors based on the information the parent is describing. The SBFC professional determines if the behavior is a result of cognitive deficits or executive, language-processing, emotion regulation, cognitive flexibility, and/or social skills.

Once pathways and triggers have been determined, parents learn to predict misconduct episodes and use CPS skills of empathy, defining the problem, and invitation to proactively decrease them (Greene & Ablon, 2006). Parents use empathy to help acknowledge the child's concern and help define the problem from the child's perspective. As part of empathizing, parents attempt to clarify why the child is having problems simply by asking, "What's up?" Once the child's concerns are clear, parents continue to provide empathetic statements in validation of the child.

In the next step of defining the problem, parents raise their concerns. At this step, the SBFC professional may need to assist parents in defining their concerns so that there is something on which the parent and child will work collaboratively. The SBFC professional further clarifies by asking, "What specific concerns do you have about your child's behavior?"

Once concerns have been identified, the family is invited to brainstorm ideas for how to solve the problems in a way that is agreeable to both the child and parent. The word, "Let's" is emphasized in the invitation, by saying, for example, "Let's think of some ideas for how we can solve the problem." Although multiple solutions are generated, Greene and Ablon recommend that the final solution must be feasible, doable, and mutually satisfactory (2006). The use of CPS in the schools is the same intervention used by the SBFC professionals for parents as well as school personnel. Engaging the parents and school staff together in CPS appears to be a viable solution in obtaining a complete, integrated picture of the child's problem behavior and promotes effective home/school partnerships.

Finally, in keeping with best practices supported by efficacious effects of evidence-based programs, PowerPoint slides are included in this chapter as examples of simple strategies that can be implemented by parents to improve students' performance (See Appendix A).

PROCEDURE

In this section, parent training will be outlined that may be implemented in either a group workshop or individual format. Common elements of effective principles when designing and presenting parent training will be highlighted here. The presentation will focus on demonstrating the effectiveness of an aspect of SBFC professionals modeling services through a parent training workshop.

THEORY AND RESEARCH: SETTING THE FOUNDATION

Read the research on prevention programs. Identify existing prevention programs and resources for parent effectiveness training. Conduct a literature review and find significant professional/evidence-based research articles/resources that address prevention or intervention programs in SBFC regarding the topic.

Although parent training can be a very effective intervention, it is not uncommon to encounter certain obstacles in implementing this intervention. One of the first obstacles frequently observed involves parent expectations or an unawareness of what to expect when they seek assistance for their children. Frequently, parents view the problem as the child's and do not understand the need for their involvement. Therefore, it is important to get parent buy-in as the most effective method in modifying child's behaviors. The best recommendation for SBFCs is to adopt a collaborative approach by emphasizing a need to solicit parents' help in creating behavior change, i.e.; "co-counselors" in the process. In other words, SBFC professionals have the expertise in behavioral interventions and parents have the expertise on their children and their home situation with a focus on parents having a greater impact in their children's lives than clinicians.

Another obstacle encountered with parent training involves parents who view the training program as possibly negative and believe that the use of regular discipline may negatively impact their relationship with their child. The SBFC professional emphasizes the importance and appreciation children actually have for consistency and structure. The positive part of the parent training program is designed so that parents lay a positive foundation of interacting with their child before beginning the discipline component.

It is important for the SBFC counselor to understand and appreciate real obstacles a parent may face before implementing the training program. As skills are being introduced, it is important to anticipate prepare, and problem solve with parents as much as possible. For example, when discussing "special time," parents should think about when they can commit to this quality time, what they will do with their other children, and what problems they may encounter. There are typically multiple solutions to any given situation, so it is important that SBFC couselors be flexible in finding solutions that best fit for the family while still ensuring effective behavioral methods.

ASSESS NEED

Assess the needs in view of the factors creating risk, problematic behaviors, and/or skill deficits. "Prevention programming should always be designed to address needs and concerns identified by recipients of future services" (Capuzzi & Gross, 2008, p. 34). What does the research say what parents need as positive parenting principles? What are the salient needs of the school site population? How do SBFC professionals know?

Providing culturally appropriate services by assessing the resiliency, strengths, and protective factors of families is critical. Useful formal tools such as, standardized tests, well-researched measurement instruments, transcripts, attendance records, discipline/behavior files and informal assessments such as, observations/interviews with student, family, staff, and community members are all important data-gathering tools. (Center for Excellence in School Counseling and Leadership [CESCaL]). Interviews are frequently conducted as the first step in the assessment process. As discussed by Merrell (2008), interviews should generally cover the following areas:

Intrapersonal functioning: including information on feelings, eating/sleeping habits, understanding of reason for referral/interview.

Family relationships: including information regarding relationships with siblings and extended family, perceived family conflict/support, family routines.

Peer relationships: including report of friendships, activities enjoyed with friends, problems experienced in social situations.

School adjustment: including information on academic achievement, favored/less favored teachers and academic subjects, involvement in extracurricular activities.

Community involvement: including information in community-based activities (sports, clubs, religious organizations) and relationships with others in these contexts.

Observations are commonly used in school settings to obtain a direct picture of the behaviors in question. The SBFC professional can conduct observations in the classroom setting. Gathering observational data from both home and school can provide useful information and a picture of the problem across settings, but it is important to keep in mind that parents and teachers cannot always devote their full attention to the observational process and may need to be trained by the SBFC professional on remaining objective through functional behavioral analysis techniques. Comprehensive assessments can include self-report measures and rating scales in which the SBFC professional has achieved competency. By obtaining a data of the problem behaviors and the function that these behaviors serve, the SBFC professional will be in a better position to develop the most effective parent training intervention that is most likely to lead in a reduction of problematic behaviors children are exhibiting. Target the population, factors, and/or at-risk behaviors by using the results of the needs assessment. Research conducted of best and successful practices relative to similar populations, risk factors, or problems should be utilized.

PLANNING AND IMPLEMENTATION

Meet with appropriate staff and personnel to obtain input in planning for program support. The best prevention efforts have been based on collaborative, interdisciplinary teaming of members of the population to be served. A description of the program should be presented to the administration and staff for further review, revision, and refinement. Plan for staff development to provide for opportunities for questions and concerns to be addressed. Stakeholder collaboration is essential for strengths-based, culturally sensitive action plans to be effective in promoting student developmental outcomes. Identify appropriate school and community resources-adjunct services and referral options. Illustrate your partnerships with students' families and community. Provide evidence of your development as a learner and leader/collaborator with other professionals. Finally, plan variations for diversity in prevention programming that shows sensitivity and respect. Use knowledge of counseling diverse populations to apply counseling skills, techniques, and interventions within the context of the parent training program.

EVALUATE PROGRAM

Plan evaluation procedures prior to program implementation. Examine how your prevention planning and intervention services measure accountability and efficacy of the parent training program. Make appropriate recommendations for improvement of the family-preventive program based on the data (Center for School Counseling Outcome Research at University of Massachusetts at Amherst).

WORKSHOP MODEL

SBFC professionals may want to use a packaged program or create their own workshop for parents based on the needs assessment. The following training program format offers a diverse approach, yet provides for personalizing the material presented and for transfer of learning (Brigman, Mullis, Webb, & White, 2005):

Warm-up: Begin the training session with an activity or brief sharing of something positive tied to the theme of the session. Involve parents by having them think, write, and share in dyads their ideas, which is a safe way to get them into the topic. Ask for two or three volunteers to share their ideas with the larger group. This provides an opportunity for the SBFC professional to tie experiences back into the theme of the session, creating a rationale for parent involvement.

Ask before telling: Before offering information at any stage of the training, ask for parents' ideas first. The more SBFC professionals use parents' input, the more it becomes their program.

Introduction of information and skills: It is best to use the "Model, Rehearse, and Practice" method when providing information or introducing new ideas or skills. This approach keeps parents involved and leads to application of workshop skills and information.

Personalize and practice: After information is presented, allow time for personalizing and practice by asking parents to think, write, share, and practice in small groups. This kind of learning is essential for understanding to occur. Small groups then report their experience to the large group.

Process and summarize: Help parents summarize the workshop by providing time at the end to reflect on process questions:

> How involved was I in the activities and discussions?
> How did I feel during the activities and discussions?
> What did I learn or relearn?
> How can I use what I learned?

It is important to ask each parent to share with a partner or small group what s/he learned (goal). Allow volunteers to share ideas for application with the large group. This provides the SBFC professional an opportunity for encouragement, coaching, and reinforcement of key concepts.

Evaluate: Have simple written evaluations at the end of the workshop/training session (See Appendix B and C). Use the results to improve your next parent training and/or for positive public relations.

SUMMARY

In summary, parent training interventions for eliminating or reducing problematic behaviors in children have garnered significant empirical support in the research literature. Effective parent training components share a variety of common elements, including: a social learning orientation/format, including modeling skills in session, role plays or practice with feedback, and practice skills outside of sessions; a focus on changing existing environmental contingencies, frequently through a focus on creating changes in parents' behaviors; a dual focus on increasing adaptive behaviors and decreasing maladaptive/inappropriate behaviors; and the intervention techniques can be implemented by SBFC professionals in collaboration with school personnel and parents.

REFERENCES

Arredondo, P., Toporek, R., Brown, S.P., Jones, J., Locke, D.C., Sanchez, J. & Stadler, H. (1996). Operationalization of the multicultural counseling competencies. *Journal of Multicultural Counseling and Development, 70*, pp. 477-486.

Atkinson, D.R. & Juntunen, C.L. (1994). School counselors and school psychologists as school-home-community liaisons in ethically diverse schools. In Pederson, P. & Carey, J.C. (Eds.), *Multicultural counseling in the schools: A practical handbook* (pp. 103-119). Boston, MA: Allyn & Bacon.

Bagner, D.M. & Eyberg, S.M. (2007). Parent-child interaction therapy for disruptive behavior in children with mental retardation: A randomized controlled trial. *Journal of Clinical Child and Adolescent Psychology, 36,* pp. 418-429.

Banks, J. (1993). Multicultural education for young children: Racial and ethnic attitudes and their modifications. In Spodek, B. (Ed.), *Handbook of Research on the Education of Young Children* (pp. 246-258). New York: Macmillan.

Beauchaine, T.P., Webster-Stratton, C., & Reid, M.J. (2005). Mediators, moderators, and predictor of one-year outcomes among children treated for early-onset conduct problems: A latent growth curve analysis. *Journal of Consulting and Clinical Psychology, 73 (3),* pp. 371-388.

Borduin, C.M., Hengggeler, S.W., Blaske, D.M., & Stein, R. (1990). Multisystemic treatment of adolescent sexual offenders. *International Journal of Offender Therapy and Comparative Criminology, 35,* pp. 105-114.

Borduin, C.M., Mann, B.J., Cone, L.T., Hengggeler, S.W., Fucci, B.R., Blaske, D.M., et al., (1995). Multisystemic treatment of serious juvenile offenders: Long-term prevention of criminality and violence. *Journal of Consulting and Clinical Psychology, 63*, pp. 569-578.

Bowdoin, R. (1993; 1996). *Bowdoin method of parent education I. & II.* Brentwood, TN: Webster's International.

Brigman, G., Mullis, F., Webb, L., & White, J. (2005). *School counselor consultation: Skills for working effectively with parents, teachers, and other school personnel.* Hoboken, NJ: John Wiley and Sons.

Brinkmeyer, M. & Eyberg, S.M. (2003). Parent-child interaction therapy for oppositional children. In Kazdin, A.E. & Weisz, J.R. (Eds.). Evidence-based psychotherapies for children and adolescents (pp. 204-23). New York: Guilford Press.

Brunk, M. Henggeler, S.W., & Whelan, J.P. (1987). A comparison of multisystemic therapy and parent training in the brief treatment of child abuse and neglect. *Journal of Consulting and Clinical Psychology, 55,* pp. 311-318.

Campbell, P.R. (1994). *Population projections for states,, by age, race, sex: 1993-2000: Current population reports.* Washington, D.C.: U.S. Bureau of the Census.

Capuzzi, D. & Gross, D. (Eds.). (2008). *Youth at risk: A prevention resource for counselors, teachers, and parents (5th ed.),* p. 34. Alexandria, VA: American Counseling Association.

Casas, M. & Furlong, M.J. (1994). School counselors as advocates for increased Hispanic parent participation in schools. In Pederson, P. & Carey, J.C. (Eds.), *Multicultural counseling in the schools: A practical handbook* (pp. 121-155). Boston, MA: Allyn & Bacon.

Center for Excellence in School Counseling and Leadership [CESCaL] Web site. Pre- post tests, data reports, need assessments, and other vital resources developed for school-based family counselors).

Center for School Counseling Outcome Research at University of Massachusetts at Amherst [www.umass.edu/schoolcounseling] for research supporting school-based family counseling interventions.

Coleman, H.L.K. (1995). Cultural factors and the counseling process: Implications for school counselors. *The School Counselor, 42*, pp. 5-13.

DeGarmo, D.S. Patterson, G.R., & Forgatch, M.S. (2004). How do outcomes in a specified parent training intervention maintain or wane over time? *Prevention Science, 5*, pp. 75- 89.

Dinkmeyer, D.C. & McKay, G.D. (1997). *STEP (Systematic Training for Effective Parenting).* Circle Pines, MN: American Guidance Service.

Dinkmeyer, D.C. & McKay, G.D. (1997). *STEP/TEEN (Systematic Training for Effective Parenting of Teens).* Circle Pines, MN: American Guidance Service.

Durodoye, B.A. (1998). Fostering multicultural awareness among teachers: A tripartite model. *Professional School Counseling, 1 (5),* pp. 9-13.

Eisenstadt. T.H., Eyberg, S., McNeil, C.B., Newcomb, K., & Funderbunk, B. (1993). Parent-child interaction therapy with behavior problem children: Relative effectiveness of two stages and overall treatment outcome. *Journal of Clinical Child Psychology, 22*, pp. 42-51.

Forgatch, M.S. & DeGarmo, D.S. (2007). Accelerating recovery from poverty: Prevention effects for recently separated mothers. *Journal of Early and Intensive Behavioral Intervention, 4,* pp. 681-702.

Gimpel-Peacock, G. & Collet, B.R. (2010). *Collaborative home/school interventions: Evidence- based solutions for emotional, behavioral, and academic problems.* New York: Guilford Press.

Greene, R.W. & Ablon, J.S. (2006). *Treating explosive kids.* New York: Guilford Press.

Hanf, C. (1969). *A two stage program for modifying maternal controlling during mother-child (M-C) instruction.* Paper presented at the meeting of the Western Psychological Association, Vancouver, British Columbia, Canada.

Henggler, S.W. & Lee, T. (2003). Mulitsystemic treatment of serious conduct problems. In Kazdin, A.E. & Weisz, J.R. (Eds.), *Evidence-based psychotherapies for children and adolescent* (pp. 301-322). New York: Guilford Press.

Henggler, S.W., Rodick, J.D., Borduin, C.M., Hanson, C.L., Watson, S.M., & Urey, J.R. (1986). Multisystemic treatment of juvenile offenders: Effects on adolescent behavior and family interactions. *Developmental Psychology, 22*, pp. 132-141.

Hobson, S.M. & Kanitz, H.M. (1996). Multicultural counseling: An ethical issue for school counselors. *The School Counselor, 4 (3),* pp. 45-55.

Hood, K. & Eyberg, S.M. (2003). Outcomes of parent-child interaction therapy: Mothers' reports on maintenance three to six years after treatment. *Journal of Clinical Child and Adolescent Psychology, 32,* pp. 419-429.

House, R. & Martin, P.J. (1998). Advocating for better futures for all students: A new vision for school counselors. *Education, 119*, pp. 192-284.

Johnson, L.S. (1995). Enhancing multicultural relations: Intervention strategies for the school counselor. *The School Counselor, 43 (2)*, pp. 103-113.

Kazdin, A.E., Bass, D., Siegel, T., & Thomas, C. (1989). Cognitive-behavioral treatment and relationship therapy in the treatment of children referred for antisocial behavior. *Journal of Consulting and Clinical Psychology, 57,* pp. 522-535.

Kazdin, A.E., Esveldt-Dawson, K., French, N.H., & Unis, A.S. (1987). The effects of parent-management training and problem-solving skills training combined in the treatment of antisocial child behavior. *Journal of American Academy of Child and Adolescent Psychiatry, 26,* pp. 416-424.

Kazdin, A.E., Esveldt-Dawson, K., French, N.H., & Unis, A.S. (1987). Problem-solving skills training and relationship therapy in the treatment of antisocial child behavior. *Journal of American Academy of Child and Adolescent Psychiatry, 55,* pp. 1051-1062.

Kazdin, A.E., Siegel, T., & Bass, D. (1992). Cognitive-behavioral problem-solving skills training and parent management training in the treatment of antisocial behavior in children. *Journal of Consulting and Clinical Psychology, 60,* pp. 733-747.

Lee, C.C. (1995). *Counseling for diversity: A guide for school counselors and related professionals.* Alexandria, VA: American Counseling Association.

Lewis, A.C. & Hayes, S. (1991). Multiculturism and the school counseling curriculum. *Journal of Counseling and Development, 70*, pp. 119-125.

Maughan, D.R., Christiansen, E., Jenson, W.R., Olympia, D., & Clark, E. (2005). Behavioral parent training as a treatment for externalizing behaviors and disruptive behavior disorders: A meta-analysis. *School Psychology Review, 34.* pp. 267-286.

National PTA (2000). *Building successful partnerships: A guide for developing parent and family involvement programs.* Bloomington, IN: National Education Service.

Neugebauer, B. (Ed.). (1992). *Alike and different: Exploring our humanity with young children.* Washington, D.C.: National Association for the Education of Young Children.

Nixon, R.D., Sweeney, L. Erickson, D.B., & Touyz, S.W. (2003). Parent-child interaction therapy: A comparison of standard and abbreviated treatments for oppositional defiant pre- schoolers. *Journal of Counseling and Clinical Psychology, 71*, pp. 251-260.

Paniagua, F.A. (1994). *Assessing and treating culturally diverse clients: A practical guide.* Thousand Oaks, CA: Sage.

Patterson, G.R. Forgatch, M.S. (1985). Therapist behavior as a determinant for client noncompliance: A paradox for the behavior modifier. *Journal of Consulting and Clinical Psychology, 53*, pp. 846-851.

Patterson, G.R., Reid, J.B., & Dishion, T.J. (1992). *A social transactional approach: Vol. 4. Antisocial boys.* Eugene, OR: Castalia.

Patterson, G.R., Reid, J.B., Jones, R.R. & Conger, R. (1975). *A social learning approach to family intervention: Families and aggressive children.* Eugene, OR: Castalia.

Popkin, M.H. (1998). *Family talk.* Marietta, GA: Active Parenting.

Popkin, M.H. (2002). *Active parenting now.* Marietta, GA: Active Parenting.

Prochaska, J.O. & DiClemente, C.C. (2005). The transtheroretical approach. In Norcross, J.C. & Goldfried, M.R. (Eds.). *Handbook of psychotherapy integration (2nd Ed.).* pp. 147-171. New York: Oxford University Press.

Ramsey, P. & Derman-Sparks, L. (1992). Multicultural education reaffirmed. *Young Children, 47 (2),* pp. 10-11.

Rich, D. (1992). *MegaSkills.* Boston: Houghton Mifflin.

Serketich, W.J. & Dumas, J.E. (1996). The effectiveness of behavioral parent training to modify antisocial behavior in children: A meta-analysis. *Behavior Therapy, 27.* pp. 171-186.

Schuhmann, E.M., Foote, R., Eyberg, S.M., Boggs, S., & Algina, J. (1998). Parent-child interaction therapy: Interim report of a randomized trial with short-term maintenance. *Journal of Clinical Psychology, 27*, pp. 34-45.

Thompson, R.A. (2002). *School counseling: Best practices for working in the schools. (2nd ed.).* New York: Routledge Taylor & Francis Group.

Vasquez-Nuthall, E., DeLeon, B., & Valle, M. (1990). Best practices in considering cultural factors. In Thomas, A. & Grimes, J. (Eds.), *Best practices in School Psychology II* (pp. 219-235). Washington, D.C.: National Association of School Psychologists.

Webster-Stratton, C. (1998). Parenting conduct problems in Head Start children: Strengthening parenting competencies. *Journal of Consulting and Clinical Psychology, 66,* pp. 715-730.

Webster-Stratton, C. (2006). *The Incredible Years: A trouble-shooting guide for parents of children aged 3-8.* Seattle, WA: Incredible Years Press.

Webster-Stratton, C & Reid, M.J. (20003). The Incredible Years parent, teachers, and children training series: A multi-faceted treatment approach for young children with conduct problems. In Kazdin, A.E. & Weisz, J.R. (Eds.), *Evidence-based psychotherapies for children and adolescents* (pp. 224-240). New York: Guilford Press.

Webster-Stratton, C., Reid, M.J., & Hammond, M. (2004). Treating children with early-onset conduct problems: Intervention outcomes for parent, child, and teacher training. *Journal of Clinical Child and Adolescent Psychology, 33 (1),* pp. 105-124.

Weisz, J.R. & Kazdin, A.E. (Eds.). (2010). *Evidence-based psychotherapies for children and Adolescents (2nd ed.).* New York: Guilford Press.

Wilde, J. (2005). *80 creative strategies for working with challenging parents: A resource for elementary, middle & high school professional educators.* Chapin, SC: Youthlight, Inc.

Wilmes, D.J. (2000). Roots & wings: Raising resilient children. Center City, MN: Hazelden.

Appendix A: Sample Slides for a Parent Education Workshop

Slide 1

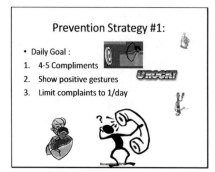

Parents need to create positive and upbeat home environments that are inviting and nurturing and kids know that you are available for emotional connection and support when needed by them. Research show that a 5:1 ratio of compliments to complaints keeps parent-child relationships intact.

Slide 2

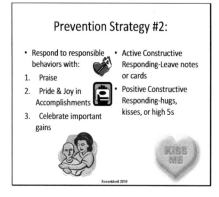

Set in motion purposeful positive relationships patterns that can strengthen and sustain connections.

Slide 3

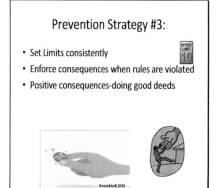

Experiment with positive consequences (time-limited) altruistic acts which tend to raise SE rather than always imposing taking away privileges or grounding.

Slide 4

Prevention Strategy #4:

- Model responsible use of substances
- Show ways to manage stress and emotional distress: exercising, meditating, yoga, engaging in meaningful activities and hobbies.

What do you do to manage your stress?

Slide 5

Prevention Strategy #5:

- Learn your kids' triggers for misbehavior
- Help them to learn distress management tools and strategies
- Practice using them at home with them

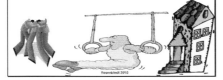

Monitor kids practicing using their coping strategies and tools at home. e.g. If your daughter is experiencing emotional stress, you can ask her: "Which tool do you think can be most helpful to you right now?"

Slide 6

Prevention Strategy #6:

- Know *where, when, what, & with whom* emotionally distressing episodes are most likely to occur.
- Intervene early with support, soothing, distraction, and whatever other strategy is effective.

Slide 7

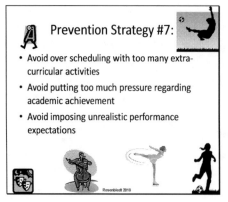

Prevention Strategy #7:

- Avoid over scheduling with too many extra-curricular activities
- Avoid putting too much pressure regarding academic achievement
- Avoid imposing unrealistic performance expectations

Rosenbledt 2010

Slide 8

Prevention Strategy #8:

- Reward with special privileges for staying on track, making better choices, and responsible behavior
- Spend time together as a family and engage in fun and meaningful activities

Rosenbledt 2010

Research indicates that the 2nd one is an important characteristic of strong families. The more parents and kids accrue positive experiences together, the more the relationship bonds will strengthen, which provides emotional insulation to better cope with their emotional distress and life stressors.

Slide 9

Prevention Strategy #9:

- Solicit feedback from your kids on how well you are doing in the parenting department.
- Welcome advice or suggestions they may have for improving the

  relationship.

Rosenbledt 2010

This shows kids how much you love and care about them and your willingness to go through great lengths to make the relationship better.

Slide 10

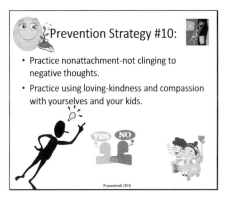

This will prevent parental burnout and you will be better able to be more present with your kids. This will help strengthen your relationships.

Slide 11

Here are the steps....

Slide 12

WHAT TO DO?????

- Decide what behaviors to ignore.
- When the behavior occurs, tell your child in a m[a] voice, "I'm not going to talk to you when you..." and label what the child is doing.
- Ignoring means that you remove all attention from your child.
- Be prepared for the behavior to get worse before it gets better & do not give in.
- To help ignore, engage in another task.
- Once your child stops, be sure to reinforce/praise for appropriate behavior.
- Rosenbledt 2010

Aggressive behaviors should not be ignored, but you will need to apply consequences. Ignoring is best used for minor misbehaviors especially involving crying, yelling, whining, pestering, etc. Tell the child only once. Avoid lecturing b/c this typically reinforces the child's negative behavior. You should not communicate or talk with your child in any way. This means avoiding eye contact as well as not talking to your child at all. This sounds simple, but is very hard to do. If you need to (and your child will be safe), you can leave the immediate area.If your child stops crying and begins doing a puzzle, you can say, "Great job putting that puzzle together. That looks like a lot of fun." Be sure to be genuine in your praise.

Slide 13

JOB CARD GROUNDING

- Alternative to time-out for older children:
1. Create 5-10 household jobs that your child can safely do.
2. Write a detailed description of each job on a separate card.
3. When breaks a rule, give 1-3 jobs to complete.

4. Grounded until jobs are completed.
5. Grounding ends when jobs are completed as determined by you.
6. Grounding period lasts as long as it takes to correctly complete jobs.

Rosenbleeft 2010

Approximately 15-30 minutes. Jobs should not be have to be completed immediately. Steps should be specific enough that your child knows what to do without asking you for additional guidance.

Draws card randomly from a container.

If jobs are not completed correctly, you should review the steps with your child and have them redo the job. This should not be viewed as negotiation. Important to stick to grounding until job cards have been completed.

If does job card immediately, grounding time will be very short or if s/he stalls, then grounding time may be quite long. Do not nag or remind your child about the jobs.

Slide 14

USING PRIVILEGES

- Positive Behaviors
- Daily Chores
- House Rules
- Rewards
- Automatic Privileges

Rosenbleeft 2010

Providing Privileges for Positive Behaviors: Generate a list of positive behaviors or extra chores your child can do to earn reinforcers/rewards. These should be rewards your child does not normally have access to or additional time in an activity your child has access to. Make sure to praise child w/reinforcer. Automatic Privileges: Expected daily chores are tied to privileges children automatically have access to. Give 1 warning and time frame by which the chore should be started. If fails to begin by specified time, take away 1 or more privilege. Generally best not to take away privileges for more than day. This way your child starts over w/a "clean slate" each morning, and you don't have to worry about running out of privileges to take away. House Rules: Whenever your child breaks one of the house rules, s/he should immediately lose 1 or more of the automatic privileges.

Slide 15

IMPLEMENTING PROBLEM-
SOLVING STEPS:

- Think ahead.
- Take a breath & make a plan.
- Think about solutions.
- Evaluate your solutions.
- Pick the best option & give it a try.
- How did it work?
- Decide what went wrong and what else you could try.

Rosenblodt 2010

Sometimes you can guess when a problem might be coming and prevent it. You don't have to come up with a solution right away. Give yourself a chance to relax and think. We usually make better decisions when we're not mad, scared, or embarrassed. You have to get to the real problem before you can solve it. Think about all the possibilities, even ones that don't seem practical. Go through each solution you came up with and think about what would happen (good & bad) if you used that solution. There will likely be one or two that seem best. Pick the very best and give it a try. If you're satisfied, congratulate yourself. Maybe another option would work better and could be used.

Slide 16

SANITY SAVER-5 RULES FOR HW COMPLIANCE

1. HW done in 1 place.
2. Workspace equipped w/appropriate materials.
3. Limiting access to study area during HW
4. Keeping noise to a minimum.
5. Starting HW at same time everyday.

Rosenblodt 2010

Sanity savers home program is a HW compliance and behavioral program for reinforcement implemented in the home setting. Students and parents together determine most appropriate HW time and place.

Parents check planner/assignment sheet for assignments and confirm that students has begun working on each. Praise if child is already working.

After 10 minutes of work time, check for on-task behavior. Assist w/HW tasks if needed and appropriate. HW probably should not be done in the bedroom. Background music may be soothing and a focusing tool for some children. Prompt student to organize HW materials to bring to school the next day.

Slide 17

WHAT TO SAY AND DO

- Check w/teacher about what will be expected & ask to be informed of assignments.
- HW time is for learning, even if no HW is due.
- Avoid power struggles.
- Give limited choices.

- Encourage daily!
- Show interest in child's work & help work through a problem.
- Participate in classroom & school functions.
- Consequences for not doing HW should be b/w your child and teacher and handled at school.

Rosenblect 2010

e.g.: Every Fri. is spelling test & every month a book is to be read, you can reinforce it at home.

"Kelly, as soon as you finish 30 minutes of reading you may watch a ½ hour of TV. If you argue there will be no TV this eve."

"Megan, I know you are upset about having to do HW. Let's see what you need to do before TV time."

"Maria, your HW is to read for 30 minutes tonight. Do you want to read to me or read by yourself."

"Jose, this has been a week of great effort on your part! You have done a lot of work! Let's spend time together building with the Lego set that you got for your birthday over the weekend."

Do not do the work for child.

"Marnie, I love you and I will be happy to help you. I know you will feel good when you accomplish this. I don't want to do the work for you and rob you of the opportunity to learn how to do it yourself."

Research shows children do better in school when parents take an interest and participate.

Slide 18

STEADY WARMTH

- Availability
- Comfort & Reassurance
- Set Warm Emotional Tone

Rosenblect 2010

Availability - Parents who are there when child wants to talk. Comfort & Reassurance – Keep up family traditions and identities. Parents who set the emotional tone make a conscious decision on how they treat and react to children. Parents can decide how to act to have the kind of home they desire when they set a warm emotional tone that feels safe, steady, and welcoming.

APPENDIX B

Workshop Evaluation

Today's workshop was:
Check one: ___ Very helpful ___ Helpful ___ Not at all helpful

---

Some of my ideas that were validated were:

_____

_____

_____

Some new ideas that I can use are:

_____

_____

_____

I liked:

_____

_____

_____

To make this workshop even better, I would:

_____

_____

_____

Additional comments:

_____

_____

_____

_____

THANK YOU!

Feedback to Workshop Facilitators

Title of workshop: _____

Name of workshop facilitator: _____

Please provide the following information with regard to your experience.

Warm-up: How did the "warm-up" help you get into the topic and ready to get involved?
Example/Comments:

Ask before Telling: What of your own ideas were you asked to share before information was presented?
Example/Comments:

Personalize and Practice: As information was shared, what were you asked to think about, write, or share of your own experiences as related to the topic at hand? How were you given an opportunity to practice what you were learning?
Example/Comments:

Process and Summarize: At the end of the session, what were you asked to reflect on regarding your involvement in the workshop and how will you use what you have learned or relearned?
Example/Comments:

Evaluate: Please give feedback about the effectiveness of the workshop in reaching targeted outcomes.
Example/Comments:

The most effective workshop strategy I experienced today was:

Something I might suggest for next time:

THANK YOU!

Chapter 15
How to Lead a Parent/Guardian Support Group

Allan A. Morotti

OVERVIEW: *A key element of School-Based Family Counseling programs is the Parent/Guardian Support Group. Support groups can be conceptualized as either a prevention activity (i.e., psycho-educational) or an intervention strategy (i.e., counseling). Regardless of their intended purpose, support groups follow a similar developmental pattern inherent in the group process itself. This chapter discusses the basic steps of how to formulate and carry out support groups, which have a prevention focus.*

BACKGROUND

The origins of support groups "in the United States can be traced back to the late nineteenth and early twentieth centuries, when millions of immigrants moved to American shores" (Encyclopedia of Mental Disorders, [EMD], n.d.). The purpose of these groups was to assist new immigrants in the acculturation process (EMD, n.d.). Groups of a similar purpose can still be found today across university campuses worldwide to assist foreign students in adjusting to their new home, as well as countries like New Zealand which have experienced increased immigration from southeast Asian countries (Everts, 2008). The parent/guardian support group (PGSG) commonly found associated with K-12 schools initially grew out of the work of Alfred Adler and his associate Rudolph Dreikurs (EMD, n.d.). In addition, some graduate programs in counseling such as the University of Oregon routinely offer no cost community based PGSGs based on Adlerian-Dreikursian principles of psychology.

Since the PGSG is preventive in scope, its focus is primarily educational in nature. Parenting programs like Systematic Training for Effective Parenting (Dinkmeyer, McKay,& Dinkmeyer, Jr., 1997), Positive Discipline (Nelson, 1987), or Developing Capable Young People (Glenn & Nelson, 1989) are some examples of pre-packaged curriculums. Typical components of these types of parenting programs include: a short description of their theoretical base, identified problematic behaviors most parents/guardians encounter in the child rearing process, a focus on communication skills that emphasize active listening skills and I statements, homework assignments, and a parent/guardian manual for participants to utilize. Group leaders conducting this type of a program may choose to include an experiential component or begin each session by asking participants to share successes or challenges when putting these strategies into practice in the home or community environment.

The other prominent PGSG format is more open-ended. This model uses an identified topic (e.g., blended families) as a means for bringing parents and guardians together who are dealing with a similar issue. Suggestions and topics for forming this type of group can originate from either school personnel or parents and guardians. While this group format does fold in the presenting concerns of the participants, the group leader(s) still define the parameters of the group so as to ensure the addressing of topics that are deemed necessary for the successful implementation of identified strategies.

What these PGSGs have in common is that they are educationally based. Corey (2012) writes:

> Psychoeducational groups serve a number of purposes: imparting information, sharing common experiences, teaching people how to solve problems, offering support, and helping people learn how to create their own support systems outside of the group setting. These groups can be thought of as educational and therapeutic groups in that they are structured along the lines of certain content themes. (p. 8)

Mental health and professional school counselors, as well as social workers and medical professionals, have been using psychoeducational groups as a prevention strategy since the 1930s (EMD, n.d.). Walsh (2010) and Erk (2008) both recommend the use of these groups for school-related and family issues. It is not uncommon for parents and guardians whose children are experiencing academic difficulty at school to feel alone, isolated, and experience more parental/guardian stress regardless of what may be identified as the underlying source of the child's problem(s) (e.g., developmental disability) (DeBonis, 2005; Levac, McCay, Merka, & Reddon-D'Arcy, 2008; Stahmer & Gist, 2001). PGSGs create a shared experience and common bond among the participants for mutual support (Haggman-Laitila & Pietila, 2009). In addition, the participants' ability to interact with an identified specialist (i.e., group leader) on their shared concern adds to the group's overall cohesiveness and satisfaction (Haggman-Laitila & Pietila 2009).

RELATIONSHIP TO THE SBFC MODEL

School-based family counseling (SBFC) "is an approach to helping children succeed at school and overcome personal and interpersonal problems" (Gerrard, 2008, p. 6). The overarching paradigm that SBFC is built on consists of school, family and systems models of counseling (Gerrard, 2008). The origins of SBFC can be traced back to Adler's work with the Vienna school system and the formation of child guidance clinics for parents and educators (Ansbacher & Ansbacher, 1956). Unlike the national model for school counseling developed by the American School Counselor Association (2005), SBFC encourages outreach to parents and guardians beyond the typical school day and environment. The significance of this difference cannot be over emphasized. SBFC not only addresses the student's academic performance, but also examines the quality of the interrelationships existing between the student, his/her family, and the systems of which they are a part.

Carl Rogers (1980), who is recognized as the founder of person-centered therapy, credits Adler (1931) as being one of the first theorists to embrace a holistic perspective of the individual and recognize his or her inherent value as a human being. Like Adler, Rogers believed an individual's actions are reflective of the variables present in that person's life. Only by understanding the individual as a whole can the therapist begin to assist the individual in moving towards wholeness and a more fulfilling life built on social interest and mutual respect (Adler, 1931).

PGSGs are one avenue for providing parents and guardians with information to better understand their child. In addition, Erk (2008) writes, "a counselor must understand what is developmentally expected at various times in a child's life" (p. 3). SBFC professionals are the ideal mental health provider for PGSGs because of their training and expertise in school and family counseling theories, coupled with a solid understanding of developmental psychology.

The sharing of information on a particular topic (e.g., depression in children) is a standard practice in the delivery of counseling services. This therapeutic component may take many forms, including PGSGs or parent education. Even though both terms share the term parent, they are distinctly different in practice. First of all parenting is commonly understood to mean the adult, parent(s) or guardian(s), who assume the primary responsibility of providing a safe, caring, and nurturing environment for the healthy development of the child into adulthood. "Parents acquire the knowledge and skills to perform this important role through their ethnic and cultural heritage, their kinship network, their friendships, their community, and the resources that are available to them" (Zepeda, Varela, & Morales, 2004, p. 7). These are all areas in which the SBFC professional possesses specialized training and knowledge.

As noted previously, parent education focuses on the development of positive parenting practices and is more of a learning activity (Zepeda et al., 2004). Parent support, on the other hand, "is the provision of services to assist parents or primary caregivers to develop and utilize available psychological and material resources to promote family self-sufficiency" (Zepeda et al., 2004, p. 10). To do this, SBFC professionals focus on the multiple systems that constitute the family's social network and represent its basis of parenting knowledge and practices. Furthermore, parent education "can be viewed as a subset of parent support in that it is often embedded and central to comprehensive, family-focused parent support programs". (Zepeda et al., 2004, p. 10). A primary role of the SBFC professionals is that of educator; therefore, regardless of the PGSG's intended purpose the SBFC professional is capable of integrating school, family or community services for providing the group participants with multiple strategies to meet their identified goals.

PGSGs may have either a family-preventive focus or more of a remedial emphasis. Certainly, PGSGs that utilize psycho-educational approaches will be conceptualized as preventive. By sharing parenting information and strategies, the SBFC professional provides parents and guardians with a greater array of child-rearing tools to improve both the child's academic efforts, as well as behavioral manifestations. PGSGs become remedial when participants move the focus of the group more towards a therapeutic experience. This may occur when parents and guardians have children who are experiencing chronic health issues. There is always a fine line between education and therapy when facilitating these types of groups. The facilitator whenever engaging in preventive activities is often called upon by the group participants to offer insight on a child's motivation. These parent/guardian queries and the facilitator's therapeutic-like responses blur the line between prevention and intervention (remedial) family services.

EVIDENCE-BASED SUPPORT

SBFC professionals who desire to offer PGSGs have a variety of pre-planned programs to choose from, or as noted previously can undertake developing their own model. Regardless of which approach is taken, successful PGSGs are tailored to the unique needs of that specific parent/guardian population. Partners in parenting (PIP) (Colorado State University: Colorado Family Education Resources & Training, [CSUCFERT, n.d.) is a program that blends these two approaches. One-hour sessions are held concurrently with family and youth meeting with their respective facilitators, followed by a one-hour joint session as a family. PIP states as a result of their program parents report better relationships with their children, fewer conduct problems in school, lower rates of drug use (CSUCFERT, n.d.). In a study by Wilson, Hahn, Gonzalez, Henry, and Cerbena (2011) utilizing a pre/post test design they found that parents who participated in a PIP program demonstrated improved parent-child relationships, parenting skills and attitudes.

Portwood, Lambert, Abrams, and Nelson (2011) studied the Adults and Children Together (ACT) Against Violence Parents Raising Safe Kids program. Using an experimental design with a random group assignment, participants in the ACT group were found to demonstrate improved caretaking behaviors (e.g., increased nurturing of the child, less physical punishment, reduction in harsh language) when compared to the group receiving traditional community-based support services. ACT is a parenting program developed by the American Psychological Association in conjunction with the National Association for the Education of Young Children. Knox, Burkhart, and Hunter (2011) also examined the effectiveness of the ACT program and reported similar results as the Portwood et al. (2011) study.

As noted previously, parents/guardians caring for a child on the Autism Spectrum Disorder (ASD) continuum might best be served by an ongoing PGSG. In a study conducted by Steiner (2011) utilizing a strengths-based approach (SBA) versus a deficit model to parent education with this population she found that the SBA resulted in improved parental affect, an increase in positive comments about the child, and more physical displays of affection towards the child. The study consisted of parents attending sessions with the therapist who would make either strengths-based comments about the child or highlight his or her deficits on an alternating basis.

Another parent education/support program that has demonstrated positive results with ASD children is the *Stepping Stones Triple P Positive Parenting Program (SSTP)*. Whittingham, Sofronoff, Sheffield and Sanders (2009) using a randomized control group model with 59 families found that parents in the PPP group demonstrated improvements in parenting approaches resulting in improved child behaviors. SSTP is a program especially designed for families who have a child with a disability. It teaches parents and guardians on how to manage the child's behaviors, develop appropriate discipline measures, understand the manifestation of developmental issues children with disabilities display, and how to enhance the parent/guardian relationship with the child (STPP, n.d.).
Numerous other studies (i.e., Roberts, Mazzucchelli, Studman, & Sanders, 2006; Sanders, 1999; Sanders, Markie-Dadds, Tully, & Bor, 2000) have found positive results when utilizing the SSTP with parents/guardians whose children have an identified disability.

The developers (i.e., Dinkmeyer, McKay & Dinkmayer, Jr., 1997; Glenn & Nelson, 1989; Nelson, 1997) of the pre-planned curriculums mentioned previously all report positive outcomes for participants who attend one of these parent/guardian psychoeducational groups. Outcomes include: improved parenting skills, increase in knowledge about child development, and lessening of parental/guardian stress regarding the child. It should be noted, however, that the data supporting these curriculums rely on self-report measures that can be subject to participants providing socially appropriate responses compromising the validity of the feedback.

PROCEDURE

The SBFC professional who desires to develop and facilitate a PGSG must begin by identifying what topic(s) the parents and guardians of his or her school population want to address. This can be accomplished through various means ranging from conducting a formal needs assessment of parents and guardians concerns to the SBFC professional's own knowledge of the types of issues present in this population. Once the SBFC professional has identified a focus for the group, he or she must then decide how to best construct it so as to provide the necessary knowledge and skill-building experiences for making it beneficial to the participants.

Logistically, the SBFC professional must determine: whether the group will be based on a particular psychological theory, co-facilitated or not, its size, how participants will be selected, time and place of meetings, frequency and length of meetings (usually once a week for two hours), whether it will be an ongoing group or have a set number of meetings, whether it will be an open or closed group, the degree of autonomy to be given to group members in determining how the group will function (e.g., selection of activities, sharing of experiences), consent and confidentiality issues.

Individuals participating in a school-community sponsored PGSG bring to the group their own histories of interactions with these systems. Most identified best practices interventions are built on cognitive-behavioral theories (e.g., Applied Behavioral Analysis, Rational Emotive Behavior Therapy, Reality Therapy). Nevertheless, one benefit of PGSGs is lessening the stress and feelings of isolation its members may be experiencing. As such, group facilitator(s) are encouraged to integrate other psychological theories into group interactions that rely on the expression of feelings (e.g., Humanistic-Existential, Multicultural, Feminist).

Corey and Corey (2006) have long recommended the co-leader model for group psychotherapy. Their reasons for this recommendation are many, but primarily center around the fact that it is easier for two facilitators to track group process rather than one. However, in the school environment it is unlikely that there will be two SBFC counselors assigned to the same school. Because of this, it is recommended that the size of the group be limited to eight-to-twelve participants. In addition, a group of this size fosters the development of "comradeship and intimacy but [is] large enough to stimulate the sharing of diverse backgrounds and ideas" (Santelli, 2002, cited in Parent to Parent USA, 2010).

Participant selection can be by invitation only or solicited through newsletters or other forms of advertisement. If the latter methods are selected, the SBFC professional will need to talk individually with the prospective participants to determine their suitability for the PGSG; keeping in mind that the overarching purpose of the group is psycho-educational in scope and not therapeutic. As a general rule, psycho-educational PGSGs usually have a pre-determined number of meetings and utilize a closed group format, meaning no new members will be allowed to join after the initial group meeting. Topics, such as children diagnosed with Autism Spectrum Disorder, may be best addressed through an ongoing and open group model. What this means is that the PGSG can continue meeting indefinitely and as participants exit the group new members will be allowed to join.

Similar to any type of group counseling experience, participants in PGSGs must complete informed consent forms and also agree to abide by the ethical obligations to maintain confidentiality. However, even when working with adults the informed consent form should be written in a clear, concise manner at a reading level comparable to a typical daily newspaper. It is recommended that the group's facilitator(s) ask questions of the participants to ensure their understanding of the consent form and their rights to withdraw from the group at any time without penalty, if they so choose.

Although, adults clearly understand the meaning of confidentiality it is a subject that merits thorough discussion. Some theorists recommend revisiting this topic at the start of every group session (Corey & Corey, 2006). Regardless of whether the facilitator adheres to this recommendation or not, establishing a safe and trusting environment is essential for PGSGs to function effectively. Participants must know that what they are willing to share will stay in the group. Schools are their own micro-societies, and to respect the privacy and rights of others in the group the participants must agree not to discuss what occurs in the group with anyone, including fellow participants, outside of the group. The only exceptions to this rule occur when there is a disclosure indicating harm to self or others, including all forms of abuse with protected populations (e.g., children or the elderly).

MULTICULTURAL COUNSELING CONSIDERATIONS

The American society and its public school system are experiencing a dramatic demographic change in their ethnic composition not seen since the turn of the 20th Century when immigrants from southern and eastern European countries immigrated in mass to the United States. Currently, 35% of the American population identifies as non-white (msnbc, 2010), and by 2042 the majority of Americans will be people of color (Quinones-Rosado, 2010). It is further estimated that by 2040 the majority of children attending K-12 schools will be non-Caucasian (National Education Association, [NEA], 2003). The fastest growing ethnic minority population within this group is children born with multiracial heritages (msnbc, 2010). Additionally, the teaching corps in the U.S. public school system is projected to remain primarily Caucasian through 2040 (NEA, 2003).

These statistics alone merit the SBFC professional's full attention. However, added to these phenomena is the knowledge among mental health professionals that ethnic minority children often face additional life challenges while growing into adulthood (Sue & Sue, 2008). Factors such as poverty or limited employment opportunities can negatively impact a student's performance, as well as socio-historical factors like prejudice and racism (Sue & Sue, 2008).

> Multicultural counseling [including group counseling] challenges the notion that
> problems are found exclusively within the person. Going beyond this stance of
> "blaming the victim," the multicultural approach emphasizes the social and cultural
> context of human behavior and deals with the self-in-relation. It is essential that

group workers recognize that many problems reside outside the person.

(Corey, 2012, p.11)

Since one of the primary purposes of PGSGs is to lessen feelings of isolation and stress among parents and guardians it is reasonable to assume that SBFC professionals will want to develop PGSGs specifically for this population to address their concerns. It is imperative that the SBFC professionals have a solid working knowledge of the sociocultural, historical, and political factors that have helped mold the worldviews of the parents and guardians of the children they interact with on a daily basis. Often times, the children of these individuals are considered to be at-risk for academic failure and eventual school dropout. Cárdenas (as cited in Montemayor, 2004, p. 1) explains:

> In successful programs for the education of at-risk school populations, there is a valuing of the students in ways in which they are not valued in regular and traditional school programs. In successful school programs, the student is valued, his language is valued, his heritage is valued, his family is valued, and, most important, the student is valued as a person.

SBFC professionals are well trained in both school and family counseling modalities. Their understanding of systems theories provides them with a knowledge base that embraces the totality of an individual's development and how it is affected by internal and external factors. Harpin (2010) notes that the majority of research supports a positive correlation between parent/guardian involvement and their student's academic achievement. Parents and guardians must feel welcomed at their child's school, one way for accomplishing this is by providing PGSGs focusing on the unique academic challenges children of color face.

In discussing multicultural counseling considerations SBFC professionals need to understand that the American public school system may be perceived by non-White parents and guardians as "agents of the dominant society" (Barnhardt, 1981, p. 2). The creation of PGSGs for this population can help to build trust between these individuals, the school, and the broader community. In addition, SBFC professionals can assume an advocacy role by working with and learning from the members of the PGSG innovative ways to build greater multicultural awareness and respect in the school environment. A strong positive relationship with parents and guardians can often offset the insecurities youths may feel about themselves. Parents need to nurture and understand the unique developmental processes of their children. The parent and child relationship has lasting effects over a lifetime. Through parents, children gain their sense of identity of who they are and where they came from.

Effective multicultural PGSGs start with the facilitator/therapist knowing more about his or her own cultural background and how that colors his or her worldview of others. While we are all more alike than different (Sullivan, 1953), the culturally effective practitioner must understand that individual differences are present in every interaction between two individuals. Differences such as age, gender, sexual orientation, SES, religious beliefs, language, race and ethnicity, and abilities or disabilities help define who we are in the eyes of others (Corey, 2012; Lee & Ramsey, 2006). In essence, our sense of self (i.e., self-concept) is a collection of our various cultural identities (Pedersen, 1997). The importance of understanding and appreciating these differences is vital to the development of effective multicultural PGSGs. Facilitator(s) and group members alike must learn the cultural language of the others for trust to develop among group members. Only then, can honest communication occur within the multicultural group setting.

CHALLENGES AND SOLUTIONS

One challenge inherent in all PGSGs is getting parents and guardians to join the group and commit to coming to each group session. One way this can accomplished is through advertising the proposed PGSG with the caveat that it will be scheduled to best fit the time schedules of a majority of the participants.

Inherent in this approach is the PGSG facilitator's willingness to be flexible with his or her time commitments.

Parents and guardians often have more than one child which raises childcare issues if they agree to participate in a group. A simple solution to this challenge is providing childcare services while the group is in session. There are numerous civic and school organizations (e.g., Girls Scouts, Boy Scouts, Student Council) that are willing to provide this type of childcare services. Often times, if the SBFC professional makes known to the school's Parent-Teacher Association (PTA) the need for childcare services, the PTA will not only contact one of the civic organizations, but also offer to pay a stipend for the services provided.

Another common challenge is scheduling PGSGs for working parents and guardians around their meal times. Once home after a day at work adults usually prefer not to go back out in the evening to attend meetings or other social events. However, one solution is to have food available for the participants to eat before the PGSG begins. The PGSG facilitator, the teaching staff, the PTA, or the participants themselves can volunteer to provide healthy snacks on a rotating schedule. Again, this is one of those informal strategies that help bond the group members together. The communal meal has long been used as a vehicle to bring people together for building supportive relationships. Current research (i.e., Fivush, Bohanek, & Zaman, 2011; Sen, 2010; Sterponi, 2009) highlights the many benefits of family meals in children's development, including the delay of sexual behaviors and use of drugs during the teen years.

Successful group experiences depend on multiple factors (e.g., suitability of group members); however, a critical element that is necessary for any successful group experience is the credibility of the group facilitator. The group facilitator can establish his or her credibility through the display of academic credentials, the sharing of professional experiences during pre-group meetings, or self-disclosure during group sessions. Nevertheless, self-disclosure during group must be used judiciously and be clearly beneficial to the group members themselves (Yalom, 2005). Perhaps, though, the presence of the SBFC professional may be the most influential with parents and guardians. Presence means being available to the parents and guardians when needed, visibility in the school and the community, participation in school and community activities; in other words, credibility is built through those innumerable daily interactions between the SBFC professional and those he or she serves.

Group participants' rights and confidentiality are always challenges every group facilitator faces. A clearly written informed consent document is always the first step in protecting group participants' rights. Basic components of any informed consent document include statements: about the purpose of the group; the group facilitator(s) education and training; any psychological risks the participants might be exposed to; under what circumstances confidentiality must be broken; and expectations about participants responsibilities to the other group members.

The maintaining of confidentiality is the core tenet around which group counseling activities are built. Participants must know that what they share with others in the group setting will be held in confidence. Confidentiality facilitates the building of trust. In this type of a safe environment participants can choose how vulnerable they wish to make themselves to the other group members. It is easy to understand how important this concept is in the school setting when parents and guardians may come into contact with one another through many different events. It is also essential that group participants understand that confidentiality must be broken when there is a disclosure of immanent harm to self or others, especially in relation to children and other protected populations.

One last item noteworthy of mention is socialization among group members outside of the group process time. This may or may not impede the work of the group. If members socialize and begin to form relationships that result in cliquish behaviors, then this will threaten the success of the group for all of its members. Yalom (2005) writes that any out-of-group socialization is detrimental to the group.

However, given a school's expectations regarding parent/guardian involvement in their child's education it is unlikely that there will never be a time when participants in a PGSG do not come into contact socially at a school event. Furthermore, while socialization may be detrimental to the group process, one of the primary goals of a PGSG is to develop supportive relationships among its members, leading to a social network of friends who come together as a community where there is no stigma attached to their child's behavior or health condition (New Hampshire Family Voices, n.d.) Therefore, while this topic should be addressed by the SBFC professional when discussing the participants' rights and responsibilities, it should be noted that participants are expected to adhere to this expectation within reason. For a more detailed discussion of this topic and the others noted above, the reader is referred to Corey's (2012) text on group counseling titled *Theory and Practice of Group Counseling (8th ed.)*.

SUMMARY

PGSGs are an ideal way for SBFC professionals to provide education and/or therapeutic services to a student's parents or guardians. Parents and guardians who join a support group can be facing issues ranging from common parenting concerns (e.g., discipline) to chronic health problems (e.g., autism). PGSGs create shared experiences for their participants which helps to lessen the members' feelings of isolation and frustration. They offer to their members the opportunity to learn new strategies for addressing their child's behaviors or health problems. PGSGs provide their participants with the opportunity to learn parenting strategies to be better able to assist their child to realize their full developmental potential. They also give families a forum for learning from other families who are facing similar challenges with their child how to better meet their own family's needs. SBFC professionals can assist the support group members with information about community organizations and resources that can be of assistance to them. In short, support groups bring together parents and guardians who share common experiences regarding their children so that they can create a community of support for one another.

REFERENCES

Adler, A. (1931). *What life should mean to you*. New York: Putman.

American School Counselor Association. (2005). *The ASCA national model: A framework for school counseling programs*. Alexandria, VA: Author.

Ansbacher, H.L. & Ansbacher, R.R. (1956).*The individual psychology of Alfred Adler*. New York: Harper Perennial.

Barnhardt, R. (1981). Culture, community and the curriculum. Retrieved February 9, 2005, from http:///www.ankn.uaf.edu/ccc2 , Alaska Native Knowledge Network, University of Alaska Fairbanks.

Colorado State University: Colorado Family Education Resources & Training. (n.d.). *Strengthening families*. Retrieved on April16, 2012 from:
http://www.coopext.colostate.edu/cfert/strengthening_families.shtml

Corey, G. (2012). *Theory and Practice of Group Counseling* (8th ed.). Belmont, CA: Thomson Brooks/Cole.

Corey, M.S., & Corey, G. (2006). *Groups: Process and practice* (7th ed.). Belmont, CA: Thomson Brooks/Cole.

DeBonis, J. (2005). *New Mexico developmental disabilities planning council: Parent support technical manual*. Retrieved on March 16, 2012 from:
http://www.nmddpc.com/uploads/parent-support-guide_0.pdf

Dinkmeyer, D., McKay, G., & Dinkmeyer, Jr., D. (1997). *The parents' handbook: Systematic training for effective parenting*. Circle Pines, MN: American Guidance Service.

Encyclopedia of Mental Disorders. (n.d.). Group therapy. Retrieved April 7, 2012 at: http://www.minddisorders.com/Flu-Inv/Group-therapy.html#b

Erk, R. (Ed.). (2008). *Counseling treatment for children and adolescents with DSM-IV Disorders* (2nd ed.). Upper Saddle River, NJ: Pearson.

Everts, H. (2008). Integrating supportive care in the schools with the enhancement of family resilience—a New Zealand project for immigrant families. *International Journal for School- Based Family Counseling*, 1(1), 57-64.

Fivush, R., Bohanek, J., & Zaman, W. (2011). Personal and intergenerational narratives in relation to adolescents' well-being. *New Directions for Child and Adolescent Development*, (131), 45-57.

Glenn, H. Stephen and Jane Nelsen (1989). *Raising self-reliant children in a self-indulgent world*. Rocklin, CA: Prima Publishing.

Haggman-Laitila, A., & Pietila, A. (2009). Preventive psychosocietal support groups: parents criteria for good quality. *Scandinavian Journal of Caring Sciences*, 23, 211-221.

Harpin, L. (2010). *Promising partnerships: Ways to involve parents in their children's education*. Lanham, MD: Rowman & Littlefield.

Knox, M., Burkhart, K. & Hunter, K. (2011). ACT against violence parents raising safe kids program: Effects on maltreatment-related parenting behaviors and beliefs. *Journal of Family Issues*, 32(1), 55-74.

Lee, C., & Ramsey, C. (2006). Multicultural counseling: A new paradigm for a new Century. In C.C. Lee (Ed*.), Multicultural Issues in Counseling: New Approaches to Diversity* (3rd ed., pp. 3-11). Alexandria, VA: American Counseling Association.

Levac, A., McCay, E., Merka, P., & Reddon-D'Arcy, M. (2008). Exploring parent participation in a parent training program for children's aggression: Understanding and illuminating mechanisms of change. *Journal of Child and Adolescent Psychiatric Nursing*, 21(2), 78-88.

Montemayor, A. (2004). *Excellent bilingual early childhood programs: A parents guide*. Retrieved April 15, 2012 from: http://www.eric.ed.gov/PDFS/ED484908.pdf

Nelson, J. (2011). *Positive discipline*. New York: Ballantine Books.

msnbc.com (2010). Census: Multiracial U.S. becomes more diverse. Retrieved June 10, 2010, from http://www.msnbc.com/id/37620349/ns/us_news-life/

Parent to Parent USA. (2010). Parent to parent guidance for recruiting and training Support parents. Retrieved April 10, 2012 from: www.P2USA.org

Pedersen, P. (1997). *Culture-Centered Counseling Interventions: Striving for Accuracy*.Thousand Oaks: CA: Sage.

Portwood, S., Lambert, R., Abrams, L., Nelson, E. (2011). An evaluation of the adults and children together (ACT) against violence parents raising safe kids program. *Journal of Primary Prevention*, 32(3-4), 147-160.

Quinines-Rosado, R. (2010). Where are Latinos in a future multiracial society? Yes magazine. Retrieved July 27, 2010, from http://www.yesmagazine.org/people/where-are-latinos-in-a-future-multiracial- **society**

Roberts, C., Mazzucchelli, T., Studman, L., & Sanders, M. (2006). Behavioral family intervention for children with developmental disabilities and behavioral problems. *Journal of Clinical Child and Adolescent Psychology*, 35(2), 180-193.

Rogers, C. (1980). *A way of being*. Boston: Houghton Mifflin.

Sanders, M. (1999). Triple p-positive parenting program: Towards an empirically validated multilevel parenting and family support strategy for the prevention of behavior and emotional problems in children. *Clinical Child and Family Psychology Review, 2*, 71-90.

Sanders, M., Markie-Dadds, C. Tully, L., & Bor, W. (2000). The triple p-positive parenting program: A comparison of enhanced, standard, and self-directed behavioral family intervention for parents of children with early onset conduct problems. *Journal of Consulting and Clinical Psychology, 68,* 624-640.

Sen, B. (2010). The relationship between frequency of family dinner and adolescent problem behaviors after adjusting for other family characteristics. *Journal of Adolescence*, 33(1), 187-196.

Stepping Stones Triple P. (n.d.). Retrieved April 16, 2012 from:
http://www10.triplep.net/?pid=2032

Stiener, A. (2011). A strengths-based approach to parent education for children with autism. *Journal of Positive Behavior Interventions*, 13(3), 178-190.

Sue, D.W. & Sue, D. (2008).*Counseling the culturally diverse: Theory and practice* (5th ed.). Hoboken, NJ: Wiley & Sons.

Stahmer, A., & Gist, K. (2001). The effects of an accelerated parent education program on technique mastery and child outcome. *Journal of Positive Behavior Interventions*, 3(2), 75- 82.

Sterponi, L. (2009). Accountability in family discourse: Socialization into norms and standards and negotiation of responsibility in Italian dinner conversations. *Childhood: A Global Journal of Child Research*, 16 (4), 441-459.

Sullivan, H.S. (1953). *The interpersonal theory of psychiatry.* New York, NY: Norton.

Walsh, J. (2010). *Psychoeducation in mental health*. Chicago, IL: Lyceum Books, Inc.

Whittingham, K., Sofronoff, K., Sheffiled, J., and Sanders, M. (2009). Stepping stones triple p: An rct of a parenting program with parent of a child diagnosed with an autism spectrum disorder. *Journal of Abnormal Child Psychology*, 37(4), 469-480.

Wilson, K., Hahn, L., Gonzalez, P., Henry, K., & Carbena, C. (2011). An evaluation of partners in parenting: A parent education curriculum implemented by county extension agents in Colorado. *Journal of Extension*, 49(4), Article 4RIB3.

Yalom, I. (2005). *The theory and practice of group psychotherapy* (5th ed.). New York: Basic Books.

Zepeda, M., Varela, F., & Morales, A. (2004). Promoting positive parenting practices through parent education. National Center for Infant and Early Childhood Health Policy, 13,pp. 1-40. Retrieved April 14, 2012 at: http://www.healthychild.ucla.edu/Publications/Documents/ParentEd.pdf

RESOURCES

Harpin, L. (2010). *Promising partnerships: Ways to involve parents in their children's education*. Lanham, MD: Rowman & Littlefield.

Knox, M., Burkhart, K. & Hunter, K. (2011). ACT against violence parents raising safe kids program: Effects on maltreatment-related parenting behaviors and beliefs. *Journal of Family Issues*, 32(1), 55-74.

Levac, A., McCay, E., Merka, P., & Reddon-D'Arcy, M. (2008). Exploring parent participation in a parent training program for children's aggression: Understanding and illuminating mechanisms of change. *Journal of Child and Adolescent Psychiatric Nursing*, 21(2), 78-88.

Nelson, J. (2011*). Positive discipline*. New York: Ballantine Books.

Stiener, A. (2011). A strengths-based approach to parent education for children with autism. *Journal of Positive Behavior Interventions*, 13(3), 178-190.

PART VI

SCHOOL-BASED FAMILY COUNSELING CHANGE STRATEGIES: SCHOOL-PREVENTION FOCUS

SCHOOL FOCUS

School-Prevention	School-Intervention
Family-Prevention	Family-Intervention

PREVENTION FOCUS

INTERVENTION FOCUS

FAMILY FOCUS

Chapter 16
How to Help Teachers Develop Productive Working Relationships with Families:
the CORE Model of Family-School Collaboration

Kathleen M. Minke

OVERVIEW: Positive relationships are the key to engaging families effectively in their children's education. This chapter provides an example of a professional development program for pre-service and in-service teachers that aims to build productive working relationships between families and schools in order to support students' academic success.

BACKGROUND

In 1991 I was a new assistant professor in the School Psychology Program at the University of Delaware. My dissertation research involved work with several infant/toddler programs that were trying to move from traditional, expert-driven models to more family-centered models of practice. It was clear that the greater trust that developed between parents and professionals, the more empowered parents were to actively engage in their children's educational programs and the more comfortable professionals were in encouraging that engagement (see Minke & Scott, 1993; 1995). When I arrived at the University of Delaware, I met Harleen S. (Honey) Vickers who had just been hired to coordinate the School Counseling Program in our department. She was an experienced school nurse who had a second career as a family therapist in an alternative school for adolescents with serious behavior problems. Her research involved examining patterns of family functioning with respect to student risk factors for dropping out of school (Vickers, 1994). We quickly learned that we had many shared interests, particularly in how parent-teacher relationships develop and how they influence child success.

Teachers in the United States typically receive limited training in skills that support the development of collaborative relationships (Epstein & Sanders, 2006). They are provided few tools with which to engage families or to manage difficult interactions with parents. Instead, they are most often trained in behavior management models that focus on short-term compliance through reward and punishment, approaches seen as counter-productive to the goal of relationship- building (Nicoll, 2002). School-based mental health service providers, including school psychologists, social workers, school counselors, and school-based family counselors, are a largely untapped resource for providing inservice training to teachers seeking to improve relationships with students and families. When these professionals' own training is grounded in family systems, ecological, and developmental theory, as well as an understanding of the organization and operation of schools, they are well-positioned to share this knowledge with teachers and other educators. We began to consider how to include this kind of knowledge in our graduate programs.

*This chapter is adapted with permission from Minke (2010).

Honey had been working for some years on developing a model that would capture an ecosystemic approach to family-school collaboration and provide guidance to teachers in developing and maintaining productive working relationships with parents. Over the next dozen years we worked together on the CORE Model of Family-School Collaboration, which posits positive relationships as the core element of collaboration and holds that the goal of every parent-teacher interaction is to have both parties feel more Connected, Optimistic, Respected and Empowered at the end of the interaction than they did at the beginning.We have used the model in a graduate course in family-school collaboration for school counselors, school psychologists, and special educators, and as part of student teaching preparation for elementary teacher education majors. In recent years (and following Honey's retirement), the CORE Model has been used to infuse family-school collaboration principles into Delaware's Positive Behavior Supports initiative.

PROGRAM DESCRIPTION: THE CORE MODEL OF COLLABORATION

Regardless of the setting in which training is delivered, several key components are always included. Participants are challenged to: 1) *think differently* about families and problems by taking a systems view; 2) *talk differently* with families and other professionals by using effective communication strategies; and 3) *behave differently* by developing relationship-building opportunities in their schools, including following specific formats for typical meetings that promote positive relationships (e.g., routine conferences, problem-solving meetings).

The training draws from systems theory (Bronfenbrenner, 1979), active listening and communication techniques (e.g., Cormier & Hackney, 2011), solution-oriented counseling (e.g., Murphy & Duncan, 2007), family-centered intervention (e.g., Dunst & Trivette, 1987), family empowerment (Cochran & Dean, 1991), and family-school consultation and collaboration models (Carlson, Hickman, & Horton, 1992; Weiss& Edwards, 1992). As noted above, the ideas and skills are summarized under the acronym "CORE." That is, following each encounter, the goal is to have families and professionals feel more Connected, Optimistic, Respected, and Empowered than they did prior to the encounter. Each element of the model is described below, primarily with reference to its application to in-service training for teachers.

THINKING DIFFERENTLY

Although effective family-school collaboration is supported by the use of specific communication and organizational strategies, technique alone is insufficient. Professionals' values and beliefs about families, problems, and helping relationships also must be addressed (Walker & Singer, 1993). We approach this in three ways.

First, we introduce traditional parent involvement efforts and highlight the ways in which these differ from collaborative approaches (see Table 16.1). There is ample evidence that not all parent involvement activities are equally desirable (e.g., Lareau, 1989; Lawson, 2003). When approached from a traditional perspective, attempts to involve families may be limited to programs designed to increase parents' presence at school, serving in ways deemed important by the school, with little attention to other ways parents support their children's education. When families do not respond as expected, teachers may feel unappreciated, parents may feel defensive, and promising programs may be quickly abandoned. The collaborative approach, in contrast, stresses development of shared goals built from the combined expertise of professionals, parents, and students. Plans are necessarily individualized to the particular values, goals, and needs of each student, family, and school community. Because the voices of multiple stakeholders are part of the decision-making process, greater success is anticipated.

Table 16.1 *Traditional vs. Collaborative Views of Parental Involvement in Schooling*

Traditional	Collaborative
Unidirectional We design activities to help the school achieve its goals, without consultation with parents regarding their goals and needs. We ask parents to volunteer to help teachers at school and to work with their children at home. We tell parents how to assist the school in "fixing" the child. Primary message: "We want you to…."	Transactional We work with families to develop plans that advance the shared goal of school success. We attend to the perceptions, beliefs, and preferences of parents, teachers, and students. We use these perceptions to plan interventions. Primary message: "How can we…"
Expert driven We summon parents to school to hear information; not to contribute information. We are the teachers & tellers; parents are the learners. Primary message: "I will tell you how…."	Multiple expertise We involve all stakeholders, including the child. We accept that each individual may have different, and equally valid, perceptions of the same situation. Primary message: "Help me understand…."
Universal We make recommendations to improve family participation in school and these are applied without understanding differing perceptions of individual families. Primary message: "One size fits all."	Individualized We respect and acknowledge differences and these differences are considered when interventions are planned. It is assumed that all families care about their child's education; it is understood that there may be barriers that prevent us from seeing that caring. Primary message: "Each child, family, teacher, and classroom is unique."

Second, we introduce basic systems principles. A large literature exists describing the systems-ecological (or ecosystemic) perspective and its application to family-school relationships (e.g., Christenson & Sheridan, 2001; Pianta, 1999). We selected two key concepts, wholeness and patterns of interaction, as the means to introduce educators to this perspective, especially the idea that children's behavior is inextricably linked to the contexts in which they are asked to function. Wholeness, the principle that every individual's behavior both influences and is influenced by the behavior of every other member of the system, encourages teachers to look beyond a single individual's behavior (usually the child's) in understanding challenging situations, and to look at how the entire system (e.g., classroom, school) contributes to the maintenance of difficulties. Using examples (see Figure 16.1), we demonstrate the idea that behavior patterns occur in repetitive, circular sequences, with each individual punctuating the interaction differently depending on their individual views of causation. When a problem is examined in this way, it allows educators to consider multiple perspectives, to give less attention to causation (i.e., who is to "blame"), and to increase attention to ways in which the pattern can be interrupted.

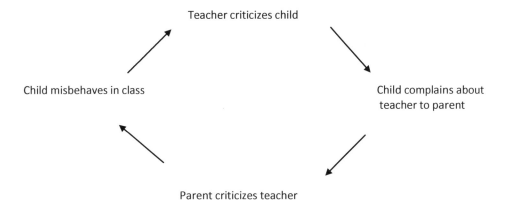

Teacher criticizes child

Child misbehaves in class

Child complains about
teacher to parent

Parent criticizes teacher

Figure 16.1   Circular pattern of interaction

The third component in "thinking differently" involves discussion of particular beliefs consistent with a collaborative approach (Table 16.2). The first element, Connection, relates to the importance of developing trusting relationships between educators and families. Trust is built when individuals feel valued, listened to and understood. Here we emphasize the need to not simply allow different views to be expressed, but also to elicit and embrace these differences. By using clear and open communication, such differences can be used constructively to arrive at more workable solutions and to develop greater trust and connection. The second element, Optimism, embraces the possibility of change and assumes that all persons are doing the best that they can with the resources and skills they have available to them at the time. We emphasize that each individual's behavior makes sense, at least to that person. Thus, the task is to understand the other's viewpoint, rather than judge it as right or wrong. Recalling the circular view of problems, we stress that problems do not reside within individuals but rather are system problems, and that blaming someone for a problem is both irrelevant and futile. The third element, Respect, acknowledges that each person is trustworthy and caring, with the right to different values. One important component of respect is that all participants are both experts and learners. Families have important information to contribute (and receive); teachers have important information to learn (and to share). Further, students themselves are considered key participants in their own education; in the CORE model, children's active participation in decisions that affect them is essential. However, parents' preferences regarding children's participation are always respected. The final element, Empowerment, facilitates feelings of competence of all participants by acknowledging each person's particular strengths and skills. Embedded in this element is the belief that power, responsibility and decision-making should be shared, and that unidirectional advice giving (i.e., school-to-home) is avoided.

The CORE elements and associated beliefs are actively taught, and participants are invited to discuss and debate the ideas. These discussions tend to be spirited and it is critical that facilitators model the skill of honoring participants' points of view while still challenging them to "try on" an alternative framework. Often it is through teachers' own examples that participants begin to change their thinking.

Table 16.2   CORE Elements and Beliefs

Element	Associated Beliefs
Connection	Trust develops when parties feel valued, listened to and understood
Optimism	All persons do the best they can
	No one person is to blame
	Problems are system problems; successes are system successes
Respect	Each person is both an expert and a learner
	Children are active participants
Empowerment	Power, responsibility and decision-making are aspects of a shared partnership
	Advice is avoided

TALKING DIFFERENTLY

Teaching basic communication strategies is a central focus of family-school collaboration training. These skills allow educators to enact beliefs central to the CORE Model, and are applicable in every interaction school personnel have with families (and with other professionals). Therefore, a substantial portion of the training is devoted to teaching and practicing skills very familiar to experienced school psychologists and counselors(see Table 16.3). Each skill is introduced individually, with detailed descriptions and examples. At the end of each discussion, participants practice through written activities (e.g., writing alternate responses to brief scenarios) and role-plays with partners.

Typically, some skills foster more discussion than others. For example, the concept of asking others' opinions first before offering your own often generates debate. Teachers frequently report that their role as education experts requires them to contribute their opinions. Soliciting others' opinions first challenges them to recognize that others, particularly parents, also have expertise that, when tapped, may independently generate a solution that the teacher was already thinking of suggesting. When this occurs, greater "buy in" can be expected in that participants are more likely to be invested in and execute interventions that come from their own ideas. Teachers are reminded that they can bring their own ideas into the discussion later, but by waiting and hearing what others have to say first, they are in a better position to tailor any suggestions to the specifics of the problem.

Table 16.3 Basic Communication Skills

Skill	Description	Examples
Attending to nonverbal communication	Increase your awareness of body language, tone, etc. Notice nonverbal communication of all the participants, including your own	"I noticed you were wringing your hands. I'm wondering if you are uncomfortable with what I just said." "I'm worried that I might be talking too fast and I feel like I may have interrupted you. What more did you want to say?"
Listening to understand and reflect	Be quiet and listen Avoid giving your personal experience or opinion Offer an empathic response	"You seem really worried about Johnny. Tell me more about what you are seeing with his reading."
Modeling the collaborative role	Resist the role of expert; ask for others' input before giving your ideas Avoid labeling, jargon, laundry lists, etc. Use effective questioning to elicit ideas from others	"Were there any other ideas that you had for helping Jane with her schoolwork?" "Sometimes I find it hard to get him interested in class projects. What have you found at home that really sparks his interest?"
Searching for strengths and positive qualities	When listening, identify strengths of the speaker When talking, emphasize the positive, highlight the parent's contributions	"He knows 24 of the 26 letters of the alphabet by heart. You have spent a lot of time help him learn them." "I can see that you have worked very hard to help Johnny be so respectful."
Reframing	Reconstruct a negative statement to have a positive meaning	"Johnny is very energetic" instead of "Johnny is very hyperactive." "Jane really likes to be in charge" rather than "Jane is very controlling."
Delivering negative information	Limit the amount of negative information delivered at any one time Be calm and communicate openness to other views Be brief, ask for a reaction after a few sentences	"Jane seems to have a hard time getting started with her work, especially if it is math. Have you noticed that yourself?" "Johnny has some trouble getting along with his classmates in the lunchroom and he sometimes gets into fights with other boys. What are your thoughts about that?"

Receiving negative information	Actively listen and try to understand the main concern and speaker's goal Reflect both content and emotion Do not defend yourself	"I can see that you are really upset about Johnny's math grades, and you think that he has been unfairly treated." "It sounds like you are angry about what happened on the playground. Tell me more about what happened."
Blocking blame	Use strategies to stop participants from blaming Validate others viewpoints Refocus the discussion Summarize	"I can see where constant questioning would distract you from your other responsibilities." "Here's what I think everyone has agreed on so far. Where can we go from here?"

From Minke & Anderson (2008); reprinted with permission.

Time is also spent working on delivering and receiving negative information, as teachers seem to have a particularly keen interest in this skill set. Participants practice delivering and receiving negative information in both written and oral forms. For example, participants practice responding orally to a parent who is very worried about the child's academic progress, and they practice responding in writing to a note from an angry parent. Once all of the skills have been practiced individually, participants are then given a set of scenarios in which they practice responding using all of the skills in combination, with coaching provided by the facilitators. In many cases, participants provide scenarios from their own experience for role-plays.

BEHAVING DIFFERENTLY: DEVELOPING "FAMILY FRIENDLY" PRACTICES

In this section of the training we illustrate ways in which the skills can be applied to various interactions among families and professionals in order to improve relationships. Three primary areas are explored.

First, we invite participants to consider what the physical plant of their school building communicates to families. For example, educators consider whether and how parents are welcomed to the school. Is there a welcome message printed in all languages represented in the school community? Are visitors greeted promptly and courteously? Is there physical space within the building for parents to meet with teachers, administrators, and other parents?

Second, we review two kinds of written communications: 1) communications (formal and informal) that are made to all families, and 2) personal written communications between individual teachers and families. Typical school forms (e.g., permission to evaluate, school discipline policy, requests for volunteers) are reviewed for readability and participants rewrite these to reflect collaborative principles. Drawing from actual examples of teacher-to-parent and school psychologist-to-parent written communications, participants consider the miscommunications and relationship damage that can occur when hastily written, poorly conceived notes and emails are sent. Again, activities are conducted in which these personal notes are revised to be more consistent with a collaborative approach.

Third, depending on the participants, we present one or two specific formats for conducting meetings with families. When school-based mental health service providers are the primary audience, a collaborative, solution-oriented problem-solving model is presented. This process is adapted primarily from Carlson, et al. (1992) and Weiss and Edwards (1992), and involves the mental health service provider as consultant. It focuses on developing a solvable complaint and shared goal for improvement, creating experiments for change, and monitoring outcomes. In all trainings, we also present a specific format for conducting routine family-school conferences (i.e., those conferences regularly scheduled for all students throughout the school year). Although only teachers are called on to conduct these kinds of meetings as a regular part of their professional roles, school-based mental health service providers are well qualified to conduct in-service training for teachers in these skills.

Traditional parent-teacher conferences tend to be ritualized experiences in which both parties demonstrate their concern for the child but little information is actually exchanged (Swap, 1993). Family-school conferences differ from traditional parent-teacher conferences in the following ways: 1) teachers, parents and students prepare in advance; 2) students are active participants; 3) teachers concentrate at least as much on receiving as giving information; 4) teachers focus on family and child strengths; and 5) the conference is a conversation; teachers are not "presenters" of information (see Minke & Anderson, 2003a for more detail). Training emphasizes that routine conferences should be used primarily as vehicles for relationship development and information exchange. Only minor behavioral or academic issues can be addressed in the usual 15-20 minute timeframe allotted for these meetings. When it becomes apparent that more intensive problem solving is needed, separate collaborative problem-solving meetings should be used. Table 16.4 overviews the steps of a Family-School Conference.

Table 16.4 Steps in Conducting Routine Family-School Conferences

Preparations:	
Parents	Provide parents information about purpose, length of meeting; set mutually agreeable time; ask parents for permission to include student; encourage them to invite other concerned adults to the meeting; provide parents a structure for thinking about what is going well and not well for the student and questions to be addressed in the conference
Students	Instruct students on their role in conferences; practice introductions of adults; elicit/record students' views of personal strengths and areas for improvement
Teachers	List several key points you want to make; gather work samples, test scores and other data; think of anecdotes to share that underscore your understanding of the students' unique qualities
Environment	Make space as comfortable as possible; place adult-sized chairs in a circle; avoid using the desk as a barrier

Start the meeting:

Ask student to introduce everyone to each other

Thank participants for coming and acknowledge their importance

Outline the process/agenda

Structure the discussion about strengths:

Remind student of preparations and ask for one strength

Elicit views of others on that strength

Offer your own view of that strength

Elicit next strength from student and repeat preceding steps

When student is finished, ask parents for additional strengths and repeat process

Repeat as needed for others in attendance

Offer any additional strengths you perceive and repeat process

Summarize

Structure the discussion about areas for improvement:

Ask student for one area for improvement

Elicit views of others on that area

Offer your own view of that area

Elicit next areas for improvement from student and repeat preceding steps

When student is finished, ask parents for additional areas of improvement and repeat process

Offer any additional area for improvement you perceive and repeat process

Summarize

Plan for future success:

Ask group to prioritize areas for improvement and select one

Brainstorm strategies to address this area; use student's ideas as much as possible

Develop consensus on the plan; be sure each person has a role

Summarize and plan follow-up:

Check that all participants have said all they want to say

Determine mutually agreeable follow up plans

Seek feedback on participants' experiences in the conference

As part of the invitation to family-school conferences, parents are encouraged to bring with them any extended family or community members with a particular interest in the student's academic success. They are also asked to complete a brief preparation form that asks them to record: 1) the student's primary strengths; 2) areas in which they would like the student to improve; and 3) questions that they wish to ask during the conference. Teachers engage in similar preparation and gather work samples, test scores, and other data that they want to include. Finally, students are also prepared for the conferences. Teachers explicitly instruct students in how to introduce their meeting participants to each other. This process sets up an expectation that students have an active role in the meeting. Students reflect on their own strengths and areas for improvement; teachers may include these as part of a writing assignment prior to the conference. It is important to note that participation is voluntary; parents choose whether or not their child will be present at the meeting.

During the meetings, teachers use the communication strategies taught to elicit information about the students' strengths and needs. They guide the conversation such that the student introduces most new information. Specifically, the student is asked first to discuss one area of strength. Teachers typically prompt and encourage the student to elaborate on this strength. Then other adults are asked to comment on this same strength, with the teacher offering his/her comments last. This "round robin" process continues through the child's self- identified strengths; students typically identify two or three strengths. Other adults (including the teacher) are given the opportunity to introduce additional strengths. Thus, the first part of the meeting is spent exploring what is going well for the student in some detail.

The process then is repeated for areas of needed improvement. That is, the student presents an idea that is thoroughly explored by others before additional ideas are presented. By the time it is the teacher's "turn" to present areas of needed improvement, most important topics have already been introduced by another participant, often the student. In this way, teachers frequently are relieved of the burden of "bearing the bad news," instead, students' self-identified concerns become the focus.

Finally, participants jointly develop a plan to support students' continued success. Teachers refrain from offering advice and suggestions, relying instead on the expertise of the student and family to generate ideas for improvement. These plans tend to be relatively simple. Follow-up often occurs by way of written communications among parents, student, and teacher.

CONCLUDING ACTIVITIES

Our workshop trainings, unlike our graduate course trainings, involve participant teams from particular schools. We typically start these trainings by asking the teams to write on chart paper all of the activities they currently have in place to involve parents in their children's education. These are usually impressive lists that form good building blocks for the workshop's content. At the end of the workshop, the teams are invited to return to the charts and consider how they can make adjustments to activities *already in place* that will make them more collaborative and more likely to build relationships with the families of their students. This reflection leads directly to an action plan activity that helps participants commit to at least a few small changes in their current practices.

By developing educators' skills in systemic thinking, effective communication, and productive family-school interventions, the CORE Model promotes positive relationships. These relationships may serve a preventive function in that minor problems are addressed quickly. If more significant behavior problems develop, an existing working relationship should make problem solving proceed more smoothly. The meeting structure presented above is easily adapted to more in-depth problem solving meetings and Individualized Education Plan meetings.

RELATIONSHIP TO THE SBFC MODEL

The CORE Model of Family-School Collaboration is considered a *School-Prevention* approach. Although family-school collaboration is clearly a transactional process, we developed the model from the perspective that it is the responsibility of schools to reach out effectively to the families of the students they serve. Many of the teachers we have worked with have asked for parallel training for parents, particularly in communication skills. However, we believe that when educators become more skilled in communication and proactive collaboration strategies, many of the difficulties they typically encounter with families are avoided. There is growing evidence that this premise is correct. For example, specific invitations for involvement from teachers (and from students) have been shown to be an important element in parents' decisions to become involved with their children's education (Anderson & Minke, 2007; Hoover-Dempsey, et al., 2005). Similarly, trusting relationships between parents and teachers are enhanced by effective communication and are related to important student outcomes (Adams & Christenson, 2000).

Still, it is likely that development of similar trainings for parents from a *Family-Prevention* perspective might also yield positive results. We have addressed this in a very limited way through several joint training sessions in which both parents of students with disabilities and the professionals working with them participated. These sessions, which were positively received by both parents and professionals, focused specifically on family-school meetings and covered many of the same concepts presented above (more information on these trainings is available from the author).

To utilize the CORE Model effectively, trainers must be well versed in eco-systemic thinking, counseling/communication skills, and consultation skills. However, these skills, which are shared by many helping professionals in the community, are not sufficient. It is critical that trainers also understand how schools function, the challenges faced by teachers in fulfilling multiple demands, and the practical constraints imposed on their efforts by high stakes testing and other mandates. Thus, school-based family counselors and other school-based mental health professionals, including school psychologists and counselors, are excellent candidates for supporting educators' efforts in reaching out to families in a prevention framework.

EVIDENCE-BASED SUPPORT

Most of the data we have collected is informal. Following in-service training sessions, participants complete an evaluation form that assesses the quality of the presenters, content, and materials. These data indicate that the training is well received. For example, participants during the 2002-03 academic year rated the quality of the workshop overall at 3.45 on a 4-point scale and the learning value of the workshop 3.41 on a 4-point scale. Similarly, 93% of the participants in a one-day workshop in 2006 rated the workshop as "effective" or "very effective" in enhancing their understanding of family-school collaboration. Participants in a 2011 brief workshop focused on collaborative meetings rated their learning at 4.53 on a 5-point scale. Unfortunately, these kinds of evaluations cannot reveal changes, if any, in participants' interactions with families subsequent to the workshops.

We conducted a somewhat more detailed evaluation of following a ten-session summer course (Minke & Anderson, 2003b). We assessed teachers' general teaching efficacy, efficacy for working with parents, and parent involvement practices. The study included teachers taking the family-school collaboration course (n = 27) and a comparison group of teachers taking other summer courses (n = 80) in a pretest/posttest design. Formal analyses showed little change between the two data collection points, in part because the teachers rated themselves very high prior to taking the course. For example, the pretest rating of efficacy for involving parents (in the experimental group) was a mean of 32.8 (sd = 6.0) on a scale with possible scores between 5 and 45; the posttest rating showed no significant change.

It is possible that the course had limited effects on teachers' views and behaviors. However, participants' answers to open-ended evaluation questions suggested that the course had positive outcomes. When asked what was the most important thing learned, 87% (n= 22) responded with at least one positive statement, many of which reflected agreement with one or more of the CORE beliefs. For example, one participant stated: "[I learned] that no one in particular is to blame for a student's problems in school. Time should be better spent on problem solving with parents and support staff (and students) rather than placing blame. Despite what we may believe as teachers, parents want the best for their child." Others noted the importance of the communication strategies and the routine conference procedures. One teacher wrote: "The steps to follow for a conference were beneficial. I felt less stress at my conferences this year and parents felt more involved."

When asked what, if anything, they disagreed with during the class, the majority (74%) indicated that they had no disagreements with the material. Those who did had concerns about feasibility (n =3), especially having enough time to involve families effectively, and others (n=4) indicated that they did not fully accept the CORE beliefs, noting that "some parents just can't be reached." Importantly, 80% (n = 24) of participating teachers stated that they made changes in family involvement practices following the course. Teachers mentioned maintaining a non-blaming, collaborative approach; increasing contacts with families, especially with positive comments; and including students in conferences. One teacher's comment summarized what we hope teachers gain from the course: "My students were active participants in parent conferences. I solicited information from parents prior to the meeting. All parents attended. About 95% of the students attended the conference with their parents. I plan on doing this again with every family in the spring."

We also completed an evaluation of the family-school conference process, which involved videotape analyses of traditional and family-school conferences, as well as interviews with parents and teachers following both conference types (Minke & Anderson, 2003a). Data indicated that both teachers and parents preferred the family-school conference style, with nearly all parents indicating that they would recommend the conference style to other families (96%; n=81). The family-school conferences were positive, conversational experiences in which students were central participants. Analyses of the meeting videos clearly demonstrated the active student role. Students engaged in dyadic exchanges with parents and/or teachers throughout the conferences, as evidenced by the percentage of 10-second intervals in which students spoke with another participant (mean = 25.4%; range = 7% – 52%). Their participation was supported by a relatively high level of direct elicitation from teachers; 81% of teacher questions were directed at students (range: 9-57 questions per conference). Significantly, 65.5% (n = 55) of parents noted the child's active participation as the thing they liked most about the conference. Parents and teachers reported that they learned more about the child and about each other during these conferences when compared to traditional conferences.

Clearly, additional evaluation data are needed beyond participant satisfaction, self-report of behavior change, and the single empirical study reported above. Still, it appears that the training in its various forms is appreciated by educators and influences their attitudes and behaviors in ways conducive to improved family-school relationships. Future research should investigate more specifically which elements of the training produce behavior change. In addition, research is needed to understand whether and how the training influences parent-child interactions. Finally, studies should address the ability of school- based mental health service providers to adapt the training for use in other settings.

MULTICULTURAL COUNSELING CONSIDERATIONS

Multicultural issues are addressed in several ways throughout the training. The eco-systemic framework invites participants to consider how multiple contextual variables, including culture, influence individuals' interactions and interpretations of one another's behavior. We emphasize the need for educators to seek to understand, rather than judge, parental behavior. When efforts to engage families are unsuccessful, educators are encouraged to systematically examine programs and activities for ways that they may not be meeting family needs rather than blame families for non-participation. Although these approaches are important in all parent-teacher interactions, they are particularly relevant when parents and teachers have differing cultural backgrounds as such differences can easily lead to miscommunication and misunderstanding.

Increasing awareness of these contextual variables must be matched with the capacity to respond to them. As part of the communication skills section of the training, educators are taught to attend and respond to both verbal and nonverbal communication on the part of families. Although we caution against simplistic notions of attributing particular nonverbal behaviors to particular cultural groups, we urge educators to use immediacy skills when they become aware of nonverbal cues that they are unsure how to interpret. The goal is to reduce miscommunication through respectful questioning and modification of interactions based on family preferences. Finally, when considering the extent to which the school is "family friendly," educators are asked to consider how diverse families are welcomed into the school. For example, participants are asked to problem solve about how linguistically diverse families experience the school environment and how they can be gain access to information that typically is provided in English.

CHALLENGES AND SOLUTIONS

The obstacles and solutions varied somewhat depending on the audience we were trying to reach. When we started this work, we were fortunate to have the support of the school psychology and school counseling programs, as well as the elementary teacher education program, within the School of Education at the University of Delaware in delivering this content. In addition, summer courses were easily created and delivered to in-service teachers. More recently, challenges have emerged as a result of changes in continuing education requirements and incentives for teachers in Delaware. University coursework has become more expensive and many teachers are opting for other avenues of continuing professional development. However, we continue to include this content in our school psychology graduate program (our school counseling program ended in 2004).

We have been successful in embedding this content into Delaware's statewide Positive Behavior Supports (DE-PBS) Initiative. Family-school collaboration is considered part of the school-wide or universal level of training for DE-PBS teams. We have one or two day training options for new school-based teams and we make efforts to embed content consistent with family-school collaboration in our other training modules. In my role as consultant to the project, I have been in a position to remind our state team members of the importance of family-school collaboration and to influence the inclusion of collaborative content throughout our project.

Time in school settings is exceedingly precious and there are multiple competing pressures on teachers to allocate their time effectively. We have faced challenges in finding time for continuing professional development training and time for interactions with families. As noted above, because collaboration is embedded in our overall DE-PBS process, we have at least some time built in for this content. However, follow up technical assistance is typically needed, especially if teams want to attempt family-school conferences or problem-solving meetings. We have not adequately addressed this problem. However, a training grant that would allow teachers to be compensated outside the school day for participating in follow-up technical assistance is a potential avenue for change.

It is significant that our approach makes efforts to avoid asking teachers to do something *more* than they are already doing; anyone who has spent time in schools knows that teachers' plates are overflowing with responsibilities. Rather, we ask teachers to look at things they already do and consider how they might do those things somewhat *differently* to make them more collaborative and more likely to promote positive family-school relationships. We reframe "parent involvement" activities as "relationship building opportunities" and provide guidance in how to make activities more successful. We offer opportunities for teachers to share their successes and learn from each other.

This practice seems particularly successful in building support for collaboration. For example, we encourage schools to include family members on their school-wide/universal planning and implementation teams. We offer lots of reasons why this is important. However, examples from the field are much more influential than our suggestions. One story that is shared concerns tardiness at an elementary school. Students in this school routinely arrived anytime between 8:15 and 8:45; late students disrupted literacy instruction and generally made it difficult to start the day on a positive note. As the team discussed possible solutions to this problem, a parent on the team asked, "Do parents know what time school starts?" Initially, teachers were surprised by this question, believing that, of course, parents know this information; it is sent home in any number of ways at the start of the year. However, having learned the value of data and the value of parent points of view, they decided to do a quick survey of parents to find out what time they thought school started. Parents responded with various times between 8:15 and 8:45! The team embarked on a new effort to communicate the start time of school and their problem with tardiness resolved. The teacher telling the story made clear that the team would not have come to this successful resolution without parent participation on the team.

With respect to time for interaction with families, we have noted anecdotally that some teachers choose to change their interaction patterns even without changes in school policies. Some teachers, for example, have chosen to continue family-school conferences with all students despite a school calendar that allows time for conferences only for students who are having academic or behavior difficulties. However, a more systematic approach to influencing school calendars and allocating time for conferences would be beneficial. We also are considering ways to work with other existing meeting structures (e.g., IEP meetings) to embed collaborative content without increasing teachers' responsibilities.

PROCEDURE

Steps for professionals interested in conducting similar training sessions mirror the three areas of the CORE Model: thinking, talking, and behaving differently. First, it is essential that facilitators have a deep understanding of a non-blaming, eco-systemic, collaborative approach to prevention and intervention. Participants often find this way of thinking challenging and can easily slip into parent blaming and hopelessness when they consider the obstacles that make connecting with families difficult. Facilitators must be able to respond quickly and persuasively to their questions and concerns in ways consistent with the CORE beliefs. School-based mental health professionals who developed an eco-systemic theoretical perspective as part of their graduate preparation will find this easier in all likelihood than those coming from other theoretical backgrounds. Similarly, it is important that facilitators understand the culture of schools and the significant pressures faced by educators. High stakes testing, accountability schemes, and resource limitations can lead to a degree of defensiveness in educators who feel under attack by forces they cannot control. They are unlikely to respond positively to facilitators who do not appear to "get it" with respect to the realities of schooling. Reviewing the recommended resources below, particularly Christenson and Sheridan (2001) and Minke (2006), will provide some of the necessary background knowledge in both of these areas.

Second, facilitators should have expertise in effective communication strategies and should feel comfortable leading experiential learning activities in groups. Again, school-based mental health service providers generally possess these skills, sometimes through training in individual, group, and family counseling and sometimes through consultation training. The importance of these skills can be seen in a quick example from one of our earliest training sessions. We asked teachers to role-play a problem solving interaction from their own experience. One teacher enthusiastically volunteered to play a parent with whom she had a problematic relationship. She was quite certain that this parent was one who would not respond to the kinds of skills we had been practicing. A second participant, somewhat more reluctantly, volunteered to play the teacher. I knew that the outcome of this entire training session rested on whether this particular exercise "worked." If it didn't, the whole group was going to conclude that certain parents just can't be dealt with and should be avoided. With some trepidation, I sat behind the "teacher" prompting her in providing empathic responses, clarifications, paraphrases, etc. I blocked her from trying to defend herself or explain her point of view until the "parent" had a chance to feel heard and understood. After a few minutes, we stopped and processed the exercise. The "parent" participant reported that she really was experiencing anger as she played the role and that she was astonished to feel that anger dissipate as the "teacher" used good active listening techniques. The "teacher" reported feeling empowered by using the techniques effectively and noted the importance of coaching in the exercise. I breathed a heavy sigh of relief and silently thanked my own mentors for helping me develop facilitation skills.

Finally, facilitators should tailor the training to the specific needs of the groups with which they work. The first two sections of the training need to be included for all groups but the actual activities targeted for change should be based on the views of the participants. Most often, we provide training that details ways to make a school more "family-friendly" but only overviews the conference and problem solving processes. Follow up training is needed for those groups that wish to become proficient in family-school conferences or problem solving. As noted earlier, finding time for follow up technical assistance has been an ongoing challenge in our schools.

Training materials from our workshops are available at the Delaware Positive Behavior Supports website (URL is below). These can be adapted to meet local needs.

SUMMARY

Productive family-school relationships support students' academic success and serve as a protective factor when problems arise in the school setting. However, teachers tend to receive limited preparation in ways to develop and maintain these kinds of relationships. The CORE Model of Family-School Collaboration is used to assist educators in this process. Training includes three major components: 1) thinking differently, in which teachers are encouraged to think eco-systemically and to consider broad contextual factors in understanding students, families, and the family-school connection; 2) communicating differently, in which specific active listening and empathic responding skills are taught, so that misunderstandings are less likely; and 3) behaving differently by modifying existing "parent involvement" activities to be more collaborative and family friendly. Content can be delivered through formal coursework or in-service workshops and includes discussion, role-plays, and action planning. Evaluation data are largely anecdotal but two more formal studies indicate that the training is effective in modifying teachers' interactions with families in ways that support positive relationships. There are ongoing challenges in finding time for productive family-school interactions in the school day as well as for training and follow-up technical assistance. We are encouraged, however, about embedding this content within a popular approach to school discipline, Positive Behavior Supports. Training materials are available online. Interested readers are welcome to adapt these materials to their own setting needs.

REFERENCES

Adams, K.S., & Christenson, S.L. (2000). Trust and the family-school relationship: Examination of parent-teacher differences in elementary and secondary grades. *Journal of School Psychology, 38*, 477–497.

Anderson, K.J., &Minke, K.M. (2007). Parent involvement in education: Toward an understanding of parents' decision-making. *Journal of Educational Research*.100, 311-322.

Bronfenbrenner, U. (1979). *The ecology of human development*. Cambridge, MA: Harvard University Press.

Carlson, C., Hickman, J., & Horton, C. (1992). From blame to solutions: Solution-oriented family-school consultation. In S. L. Christenson & J. C. Conoley (Eds.), *Home-school collaboration: Enhancing children's academic and social competence* (pp. 193-214). Silver Spring, MD: National Association of School Psychologists.

Cochran, M., & Dean, C. (1991). Home-school relations and the empowerment process. *Elementary School Journal, 91,* 261-269.

Cormier, S., & Hackney, H.L. (2011).*Counseling strategies and interventions*. Boston: Pearson Higher Ed.

Dunst, C. J., &Trivette, C. M. (1987). Enabling and empowering families: Conceptual and intervention issues. *School Psychology Review*, 16, 443-456.

Epstein, J. L., & Sanders, M. G. (2006). Prospects for change: Preparing educators for school, family, and community partnerships. *Peabody Journal of Education,* 81, 81-120.

Hoover-Dempsey, K. V., Walker, J. M. T., Sandler, H., M., Whetsel, D., Green, C. L., Wilkins, A. S., et al. (2005). Why do parents become involved? Research findings and implications. *Elementary School Journal*, 106, 105–130.

Lareau, A. (1989). *Home advantage: Social class and parental intervention in elementary education*. Philadelphia: Falmer Press.

Lawson, M. A. (2003). School-family relations in context: Parent and teacher perceptions of parent involvement. *Urban Education*, 38, 77-133.

Minke, K.M. (2010). Helping teachers develop productive working relationships with families: The CORE model of family-school collaboration. *International Journal for School-Based Family Counseling*, 2, 1-13 (may be retrieved online at http://www.schoolbasedfamilycounseling.com/journal.html).

Minke, K.M., & Anderson, K.J. (2008). Best practices in facilitating family-school meetings. In A. Thomas & J. Grimes (Eds.). *Best practices in school psychology –V* (pp. 969-982). Bethesda, MD: National Association of School Psychologists.

Minke, K. M. & Anderson, K. J. (2003a). Restructuring routine parent-teacher conferences: The family-school conference model. *Elementary School Journal*, 104, 49-69.

Minke, K.M. & Anderson, K.J. (2003b). Family-school collaboration: A CORE component of positive behavior supports. Presented at the First International Conference on Positive Behavior Support. March 28, 2003, Orlando, FL.

Minke, K.M. & Scott, M.M. (1993). The development of individualized family service plans: Roles for parents and staff. *Journal of Special Education, 27*, 82-106.

Minke, K.M. & Scott, M.M. (1995). Parent-professional relationships in early intervention: A qualitative investigation. *Topics in Early Childhood Special Education,15*, 335-352.

Murphy, J.J., & Duncan, B.L. (2007). *Brief intervention for school problems: outcome-informed strategies.* New York: Guilford.

Nicoll, W. G. (2002). Working with families: A rationale for school counseling programs. In L. D. Miller (Ed.), *Integrating School and Family Counseling: Practical Solutions* (pp. 31-49). Alexandria, VA: American Counseling Association.

Swap, S. M. (1993). *Developing home-school partnerships: From concepts to practice*. New York: Teachers College Press.

Vickers, H.S. (1994). Young children at risk: Differences in family functioning. *Journal of Educational Research, 87*(5), 262-270.

Vickers, H. S., Minke, K. M., & Anderson, K. A. (2002). Best practices in facilitating collaborative family-school routine conferences. In A. Thomas & J. Grimes (Eds.).*Best practices in school psychology –IV* (pp. 431-449). Bethesda, MD: National Association of School Psychologists.

Walker, B., & Singer, G. H. S. (1993). Improving collaborative communication between professionals and parents. In G. H. S. Singer & L.E. Powers (Eds.). *Families, disability, and empowerment: Active coping skills and strategies for family interventions* (pp. 285-315). Baltimore: Paul Brookes.

Weiss, H. M., & Edwards, M. E. (1992). The family-school collaboration project: Systemic interventions for school improvement. In S. L. Christenson & J. C. Conoley (Eds.), *Home-school collaboration:*

Enhancing children's academic and social competence (pp. 215-244). Silver Spring, MD: National Association of School Psychologists.

RESOURCES

Christenson, S.L., & Sheridan, S.M. (2001). *Schools and Families: Creating Essential Connections for Learning.* New York: Guilford.

This volume provides background knowledge on family-school collaboration and an excellent overview of how to develop improved family–school relationships at the school-wide level. Facilitators developing trainings for educators will also find it a good resource for presenting the rationale for improving family–school relationships.

Delaware Positive Behavior Supports: www.delawarepbs.org

Training materials referenced in this chapter can be obtained here.

Family Involvement Network of Educators: www.hfrp.org

Provides links to a variety of resources promoting family–school collaboration. Network membership is free and provides an e-newsletter, discussion board, and other resources.

Fujishin, R. (2000). *Creating communication: Exploring and expanding your fundamental communication skills*. San Francisco: Acada.

This brief volume provides an excellent review of verbal and nonverbal communication strategies and their application to leadership, small group, and interpersonal situations.

Minke, K. M. (2006). Parent-teacher relationships. In G. G. Bear & K. M. Minke (Eds.).*Children's needs II: Development, prevention, and intervention* (pp. 73-85). Bethesda, MD: National Association of School Psychologists.

This brief chapter outlines the importance of building positive relationships between parents and teachers and overviews some specific methods for accomplishing this goal.

Chapter 17
How to Develop a School-wide Classroom Management Program

Lindsey K. Ma

OVERVIEW: *In this chapter we are going to look at effective classroom management in a school's effort to build and incorporate the protocol of school based family counseling. We will look at a model that assesses the academic needs of kids, has systems that addresses the mental health needs that they bring into a school and a transition program that provides mentoring to the student transitioning from one level of schooling to the next, middle school to high school.*

BACKGROUND

Childhood memories are made in America's classrooms everyday. The classroom has become a sacred place where many of life's routines are established so that the love of learning and the taste of academic and social success can be discovered by America's youth and children. However, learning and completing school successfully does not happen in a vacuum or without disruption. Educators and today's teachers must have a skill set that not only facilitates fascinating engaging instruction, but that teachers must also befriend, support, counsel, and listen to the child in the classroom and in the school setting. Today, educators must strategically handle increasing disruptions and student behavior that results in disengagement in the learning environment, all of which is causing a nationwide media frenzy. Effective classroom management has become a hot topic because management of the classroom and student behavior increases academic achievement which impacts test results, and the student's social emotional affect.

Effective classroom management is transparent, one knows that a class of students is managed well when: students are listening and having an instructional exchange with one another, teachers are teaching and everyone in the learning environment is engaged in instruction. It is when students are not listening and lessons are not engaging that we see the manifestation of poor classroom management. So, with increasing office referrals for fighting, violence, incorrigible behavior, vandalism, truancy, drug use and a lack of discipline, how do schools and classroom teachers facilitate effective classroom management? Many of today's teachers have a skill set that includes practiced listening skills, sensitivity to student social-emotional needs and academic concerns and reflective questioning techniques that cause students to think, evaluate, and act. But still, communities, families and schools have growing concerns about the learning environment that their children are a part of daily. With diminishing resources, what can be done?

As America's classrooms address cultural and geographical diversity and address a number of different needs, school based programs need to move from a reactionary paradigm to a proactive paradigm in the arena of classroom management. Currently, consequences are administered for behavior that is rule violating in nature and positive behaviors may be recognized. As the negative behavior increases, the code of conduct increases its intensity by (Sugai and Horner, 2008; Gunter, Denny, Jack & Shores, 1993):

Monitoring and surveillance to catch the behavior,

Rules and sanctions for problem behavior are restated and reemphasized,

The continuum of punishment consequences for repeated rule-violations are extended,

Efforts are direct toward increasing the consistency with which school staff react to displays of antisocial behavior,

"Bottom-line' consequences are accentuated to inhibit future displays of problem behavior.

According to Mayer (1995), this paradigm is a result of low expectations and a history of severe antisocial behavior, which increases the intensity, and frequency of antisocial behavior. As negative behaviors increase, school districts, personnel and policy makers have been quick to establish and implement policies that address specific behaviors like zero-tolerance policies; the hiring of security personnel, addition of surveillance hardware and programs; adoption of school uniform policies, using in and out detention, suspension, and expulsion; and the building of alternative programs. School-wide programs that increase student engagement and impact the classroom management routine and philosophy emphasize prevention-based strategies. These programs break-up anti-social networks; increase opportunities to attain academic success; maintain positive classroom and learning climates; and prioritize prevention as a strategy that maintains a safe and orderly learning environment in the classroom, the school and the community. (Sugai and Horner; 2008; US Department of Health and Human Services, 2001).

Classroom practices and rules must achieve a positive learning environment while managing and preventing disruptive behaviors. According to Mayer (1995) and Mayer (1983), adopting constructive disciplinary parameters and procedures (the implementation of school-wide expectations and behaviors) generally lead to the reduction of negative behaviors associated with assault, vandalism and other anti-social behavior in the school and its classrooms. According to Nelson (1996), school wide programs with coordinated efforts in the classroom have demonstrated improvements in school discipline and academic engagement in the classroom. A positive approach with prevention should be emphasized.

The inclusion of children with problem behaviors exposes children to an active discipline system that addresses their social–emotional needs while providing them with exposure to positive opportunities and role models. When establishing systems that foster a positive climate, research indicates that: Punishment, exclusion, and embarrassment are ineffective when used without a proactive support system (Mayer, 1995); Positive/constructive behavioral principles are needed to organize successful support for individual students with problem behavior (Kerr & Nelson, 1983; Worley, Bailey, &Sugai, 1988); Effective instruction is linked to the reduction of problem behaviors (Lee, Sugai, & Horner, 1999), and; School-wide systems of behavior support are needed to reduce the disruptive and antisocial behavior and increase appropriate behavior (Horner & Sugai, 2000; Chapman & Hofweber, 2000).

As schools work to improve academic engagement in the classroom, research indicates that classroom management is a result of a number of factors that are synchronized and recognized and is a part of a school-wide discipline behavior management system. In the last ten years, education has more commonly referred to this system as Positive Behavior Support(PBS).PBS is a broad range of strategies that result in effective social and learning outcomes while minimizing and preventing negative behaviors. PBS is the combination of the following four elements (Sugai & Horner, 2002):Outcomes (academic achievement, social competence, employment options) that are uniquely defined and "valued" by the school's stakeholders (e.g. students, families, teachers, employers); An understanding of human behavior (how children behave and what they react to); Empirically validated practices for achieving identified outcomes; and, Implementation of practices in the context of the systems change needed for durable and generalized effects.

PROGRAM DESCRIPTION

The resolution to problem and chronic behaviors are more than mere classroom management strategies. Research indicates that school based programs and systems that react to student behaviors do not impact increased behavior management. In fact, reactionary measures like punishment increase the frequency of problem behaviors. School based program must integrate effective practices with four critical elements:

Relevant curriculum,

Meaningful educational assessments and evaluation,

Use of dwindling resources, and

Creation of a positive and caring school climate.

First, school-wide PBS is guided by an acknowledgement and evaluation of outcomes (where do you want the students to be academically, socially, and in their trajectory to school/work?). Schools should be able to clearly articulate measurable student and staff outcomes. Secondly, school-wide PBS is based in part by the implementation of curricula that is meaningful to the student and maximizes achievement. The curricula are also sustained and delivered by research-based practices. Schools should reflect upon their current practices and resist discarding proven practices just because there is a new initiative, curriculum or strategy that is being presented. According to Carnine (1997), consideration of new or different practices should be guided by questions of trustworthiness, effectiveness, efficiency, and relevance. He suggests asking the following reflective questions:

Are educationally and/or socially relevant outcomes specified?

Will the efficiency of outcome achievement be improved?

Is research accessible and supportive?

Are adoption costs justifiable?

Are sound conceptual and theoretical foundations indicated?

Are successful local applications available?

Does evidence exist to support a change in current practice?

Have previous practices been implemented with high fidelity?

Are supports in place to occasion and sustain implementation?

As a PBS model is implemented school-wide, the school must examine the systems or programs that are needed to ensure consideration of valued outcomes, research validated practices, and data driven decision-making. There should be a direct correlation between the school-wide system of behavior support and the classroom management system used in each of the classrooms of the school.

Using the metaphor of a pyramid, schools have listed their interventions in the pyramid where the services listed in the base of the pyramid are referred to as Tier 1: Benchmark Services. In this layer of the pyramid, all students have access to all of the services that collectively work to keep the student engaged in the classroom and at school. As the student demonstrates a need for more support, the student is referred to Tier 2 of the pyramid, where strategic services and programs are listed to further support the student to academic success. Finally, as a student demonstrates a need for more support, the school may recommend the services or programs listed in the top tier, Tier 3, intensive services and programs. When interventions are listed in this format and staff members are trained to facilitate and access the tiered services, to provide an intervention, the students have the opportunity to find success in the classroom and avoid the embarrassment that comes with negative consequences and punishment. Students who need more support, as demonstrated by a manifestation of negative anti-social behaviors, progress from the benchmark level to the next level of strategic services, usually referred to as Tier 2. As the services and programs from Tier 2 are exhausted, and the student still demonstrates anti-social and negative behaviors, intervention services are further identified and linked to the student, with intensive services, Tier 3, being linked to students for the most at-risk behaviors. This tiered intervention services are commonly referred to the Pyramid of Behavioral Intervention.

PYRAMID OF BEHAVIORAL INTERVENTION

Student behavior and especially misbehavior is always a daunting task and must be addressed in a proactive manner that includes the perspective of the whole school, classroom, non-classroom environment, and the individual student. In the Alhambra Unified School District in the San Gabriel Valley of Southern California, a strategic effort was made about four years ago to identify the progression of programs and services needed to support the student in the learning process at school. Each school in the school district identified three levels of intervention. The following steps were observed in the establishment of the pyramids of intervention (Sugai & Horner, 2008):

Step 1: Establish Leadership Team: form purpose statements, target groups, measurable outcome/progress indicators, membership and relationships with school improvement goals and objectives.

Step 2: Secure School-Wide Agreements and Supports: The Leadership Team must secure agreement from the staff for professional development needs in the area of PBS – Positive Behavior Support, a long term commitment to the effort, and the importance of taking a preventive and instructional approach to managing student behaviors.

Step 3: Develop Data-Based Action Plan: Collect a variety of student data including attendance and tardy patterns; office discipline referrals; detention, suspension and expulsion rates; and behavioral incidence data. The action plan should indicate: measurable outcomes, timeline, leadership and committee members; activities that lead to measurable outcomes, staff development and training, and resource and support needs.

Step 4: Arrange for High Fidelity of Implementation: The Leadership Team should secure a minimum of 80% agreement from the staff to support the program to prevent misbehaviors. Staff needs regular ongoing professional development so that the program is implemented with fidelity.

Step 5: Conduct Formative Data-Based Monitoring: Staff, students and parents need to see that the program is working and student data regarding elements like attendance, lower rate of office referrals, and higher levels of positive reinforcement is a result of the implementation of the school wide program.

As a result, leadership teams from the schools reviewed student data, secured buy-in, and established pyramids of intervention unique to each school. Programs and services for students were listed in each tier so that interventions were progressive and systematically implemented: Tier 1: The Benchmark of services; Tier 2: The Strategic level of intervention services and Tier 3: the Intensive level of services. Teachers, Counselors and Administrators refer to the pyramids regularly as students demonstrate their need for more support and the appropriate level of intervention is assigned. Please refer to Exhibit A, B, and C: sample pyramids of behavior from the elementary, secondary and alternative school settings to address and support student behavior. The alternative setting produced a referral form based on their Pyramid of Behavioral Intervention where the teacher checked off all of the interventions used at the benchmark level, Tier 1, before referring the student to strategic level, Tier 2, interventions.

CLASSROOM PLACEMENT AND ORGANIZATION

Typically, new teachers receive a challenging teaching assignment where classes are loaded with students who are most at-risk in their academic and behavioral progress. Students may or may not like school and have demonstrated minimal academic progress and demonstrated inappropriate behaviors while in class. Furthermore, these classes are loaded so that students with model behavior and/or satisfactory academic progress are placed in other class sections or their presence in these classes is nonexistent. We, as educators, call that your "baptism by fire" year. All the students who are not performing at grade level and demonstrate learning and social challenges are typically scheduled for the same sections of class but assigned to a typically more tenured educator. It is at most "challenging" to say the least for any teacher, who is assigned the former, let alone a first year teacher. Although this practice may be typical and a bit traditional, this archaic approach can breed issues at all levels of a school from the student, to the parent, to the teacher to the administrator. Many school districts and schools are developing systems to retire this practice.

The traditional approach of teacher assignments and scheduling students changed in the Alhambra Unified School District. In addition to the Pyramid of Behavioral Intervention, student schedules and the building of the master schedule at the secondary level was reorganized so that students who were at risk were not all placed in one class with one teacher. Rather, a cap on the number of students needing behavioral and academic interventions was placed on each of the core classes (Math, English/Language Arts, History/Social Studies and Science) so that one teacher would have no more than seven to eight students needing intervention in the classroom. Every teacher in the school would have at-risk students in their classes.

Placement of students was not haphazard. Guidance counselors, department chairs and administration used data collected from multiple assessment measures like the California Standards Test (CST), California English Language Development Test (CELDT), district benchmark assessment results, data and input from guidance counselor intake meetings, teacher recommendations, administration recommendations, and parent input were used to strategically build the master schedule and determine number of classes for each core curriculum and determine teacher assignments before placing students and building their class schedules. In the process, academic and behavioral expectations were raised and the student who was identified at-risk had access to academic interventions, model behavior and peer monitoring and mentoring. Communication regarding this change in building the master schedule to all departments at the secondary level was well received as a result of communication of the strategy in the Curriculum Council at the local secondary site. Each core department had to agree and establish consensus within its department as traditional teaching assignments would change as a result of this type of instructional intervention. More teachers were needed to support the change. And, administration anticipated that not all teachers would grasp the need for the change. However, the change in the scheduling method used to place students in classes impacted the at-risk student's success and behavior as all students were exposed to a higher set of academic expectations because the at-risk student was not tracked to one part of the schedule or one teacher of any core department. The advantage to this new scheduling set-up was a greater number of teachers in the school were addressing the needs and engaging the highly at-risk student in the core curriculum.

PYRAMID OF INSTRUCTIONAL DEVELOPMENT

At the same time, categorical or supplemental funds supported professional development of entire core departments, engaging teachers in effective practices like "checking for understanding", and "differentiating instruction". Funds were also used to integrate the resources of half-time Instructional Specialists in the curricular departments that demonstrated the most need to support the teachers with standards based lesson planning and department planning to include common assessments and differentiated instruction. The Instructional Specialists were given a partial teaching assignment at the secondary level, where they facilitated instruction, taught class, for two periods a day in their core area. The other part of the day was devoted to working with their department's teachers.

Intervention Advisors worked with students and parents targeting students who demonstrated both "Basic" and "Below Basic" bands of proficiency. The Intervention Advisor monitored student attendance and achievement. He/she called parents to:

Review warning notice grades.

Link academic support services.

Link peer support services.

Invite parents to Parent Teacher meetings and conferences.

Link mental health services to include counseling.

Review CST test results and California High School Exit Exam (CAHSEE) test results.

Provide academic counseling.

As a result, attendance for the 9th and 10th grade improved by 3.6%. The baseline attendance rate was 93.6% and increased to 97.2% as a result of the practices and programs developed by the Intervention Advisor. Students reported that they had an adult that cared about them and that they could access with their concerns. The Intervention Advisor had obtained her MA in Pupil Personnel Services – PPS.

MIDDLE SCHOOL TO HIGH SCHOOL TRANSITION PROGRAM

Effective transition programs are defined as ones that improve student attendance, achievement, and decrease retention. Schoolwide programs, like ones that address the transition from middle school to high school, impact classroom management.   To address the needs of the various constituencies, research suggests that effective transition programs have five or more diversified activities. The first most common activities include bringing the incoming students to visit the new school, hosting meetings with administration of both exiting and receiving schools to discuss programs, articulation, and having counselors from both the high school and middle school levels meet.

The second activity that schools must implement should target students, parents, and teachers. Parents and students usually have concerns regarding the academic environment and the school community and procedures.   All these should be addressed to ease the fears about transition. According to Cauley and Jovanovich (2006), schools typically do not address the social concerns of students. In addition, research recommends that the transition program should encompass the spring and summer seasons before entry into the new school.

Third, effective transition programs involve continuous planning among teams of teachers and school leaders.   Communication between teachers and school leaders should focus on the rising expectations for students, the necessary amount of preparation, and the high expectations and additional help that low-performing students may require to meet the standards.

Fourth, effective transition programs address specific groups of students who are likely to have the greatest difficulty with systemic transitions; girls, boys, students with behavior problems, low achievers, and minority or low socioeconomic students. Students with prior problem behaviors have difficulty successfully negotiating transitions because they do not have the social skills to adjust successfully to the new environment and continue getting into trouble.

According to Cauley and Jovanovich (2006), transition programs need to address the needs of students who are inadequately prepared for school and demonstrate difficulty making the transition from middle school to high school.   There are four areas of preparedness: academic success, independent and industrious work habits, conformity to adult standards and coping mechanisms for such activities as keeping track of assignments and resolving conflicts. Transition programs match the incoming student with an important adult who is committed to the student's academic and social success.

Helping middle school students make a successful transition to high school requires challenging middle school programs and activities that specifically address the transition from middle school to high school (Mizelle, 2005). Mizelle (2005) recommends that transition programs inform incoming the incoming freshman of high school programs and procedures. Activities should include the following (Mizelle, 2005):

Spring orientation, where high school counselors, students and administrators meet with the upcoming 9th graders to answer questions from students and parents.

Student shadowing, where 8th grade students spend time following a 9th grade student.

Student visitations, which allow the 8th grade students to spend time touring the high school campus and ask questions.

Beginning-of-school orientation, where new 9th grade students pick up their new fall schedule of classes and walk through their day.

Study skills or time management classes that are offered during the summer before 9th grade.

PARENT INVOLVEMENT

The parent involvement component is essential in establishing and designing an effective transition program. Parents who are involved in the high school tend to stay involved with their child's high school experience and have been involved in their child's schooling history. Parent involvement leads to higher grades, improved test scores, better attendance, positive attitude and behavior, and higher graduation rates (Mizelle, 2005). Also, students achieve more and are better adjusted individuals when parents are involved.

Parent involvement is the result of an intentional combined effort on the part of the middle school and high school. According to Epstein (1995 and 1996), school administrators need to inform parents about all transition activities and outreach/encourage parent participation to establish an effective transition program. Middle and high school administrators need to implement programs that keep parents involved in their child's education and school activities during the middle school years so that parents are comfortable with their involvement throughout the secondary years. Parents need to believe that their involvement makes a difference.

The child/student is not the only one that transitions into school. In fact, in K-12, the whole family transitions with a child from pre-school to Kindergarten, and from elementary school to middle school, and again from middle school to high school. At each transitional period, the outgoing and incoming school needs to establish programs that provide the family, parent and student critical information and opportunities for involvement. Students need to interact with people in their new school and surroundings before the start of school. According to Cognato (1999) and Mac Iver (1990), students who interacted with their new peers and adults in their new schools demonstrated fewer failing grades and missed fewer days of school than students who did not participate in transition programs.

By the time students transition to secondary education/high school, parents are no longer familiar with the programs and opportunities that are before them and thus, need information. Information and opportunities for involvement include: parent information meetings; discussions about ninth grade student schedules and high school graduation requirements; and a visit to the high school campus. Transition programs need to be meaningful and authentic so that the incoming student connects with other students, teachers and administration (Mizelle& Irvin, 2000).

CASE STUDY: A FRESHMAN TRANSITION PROGRAM

To that end, San Gabriel High School in the Alhambra Unified School District in Southern California established a yearlong ninth grade transition program called Motivating Matadors (MoMa) that grew out of their traditional annual freshman orientation day. The impact of the original orientation day was minimal, though fun, as data indicated that the ninth grade students demonstrated attendance issues, academic failure and unsatisfactory citizenship soared.

MoMa, the program, was a result of a need to support the incoming high school student and parent. Although the school had a fun two hour high school orientation event at the beginning of the freshman year, students, teachers, and parents wanted a program that would result in increased attendance; improved academic grades with no grade less than a "C"; knowledge of how to use the high school campus and all of its resources, develop positive and respectful communication skills, develop an appreciation of services and programs at school, encourage ninth grade students to join school activities and organizations, maintain satisfactory or high levels of citizenship and develop leaders. Administration, Teachers, and students soon developed a new Freshman Transition Program that addressed these goals through a series of year-long intentional mentoring relationships that took place regularly throughout the freshman year of high school.

The two-hour freshman orientation was replaced with a series of bi-monthly MoMa meetings that spanned the entire school year. All freshmen were required to attend these meetings. Freshmen were placed into small groups of about 20 students. The meetings were facilitated by upper-classmen and a volunteer teacher advisor. The meetings were conducted during lunch in the teacher's classroom. Arrangements were made with Food Services and Campus Security so that all freshmen were given a fast-pass during MoMa meeting dates to expedite lunch retrieval from the cafeteria so that a 35 minute meeting could be sustained. A myriad of topics were presented and discussed during the lunch-time club-like meetings. Topics included:

My First Month of School
Where do I get help?
How do I talk to my Teacher?
What is Homecoming?
Setting Goals – Passing my classes the first time.
What are final exams?

MoMa is a unique transition program in that is addresses the needs of the incoming freshman student, forges a mentoring relationship between the freshman and an upperclassmen or a teacher advisor, and facilitates and leadership component to develop leaders among the freshman class and for future MoMa.

Although parents of eighth grade students are contacted and invited to information nights and guidance counselors present high school information to students in the month of January with a series of follow-up meetings and conferences through May, the kick-off of the freshman year takes place on a Saturday in August where the entire incoming freshman class gathers in the high school football stadium for the Freshman Summit. On this hot summer day, the students from all feeder schools meet collectively for the first time. A number of team building exercises are facilitated in the morning hours of the summit to forge new friendships among students and better acquaint the students with their upperclassmen group facilitators called Student Motivators, as well as the adults, teacher advisors called Teacher Motivators. Students are placed in their small groups for the first time and face fun situations where they must work together to resolve situations. The Principal hosts a Bar-B-Que for lunch as the Associated Student Body (ASB) facilitates a club/activity/athletics recruitment fair while the upperclassmen (students in 10th/11th/12th grade) involved in visual and performing arts engage in a "flash mob" during the lunch hour, all in an effort to welcome the incoming student into the San Gabriel High School Community.

After lunch, goal-setting sessions are facilitated and a keynote speaker formally addresses the class about the highlights and challenges of high school, a whole new way of life. The speaker gives a personal account of classes to take, friends to make and places to go to access all kinds of help. Finally, in the last post lunch session, the incoming freshman is confronted with the pace of the next four years, and though fun, has much to accomplish: academically/scholastically, social emotionally, and physically. The speaker discusses goals and how to accomplish those goals in the next four years. After a time of personal reflection and goal setting, the Freshman Summit concludes and the freshman year has officially begun.

The parent portion of the Freshman Summit is called Pancakes with the Principal. The two-hour Saturday session for parents in the school's multi-purpose room where the Principal and the Assistant Principal of Instruction answered questions from the parents. The students are all in the stadium during this time. The demeanor of the meeting is casual. The Principal discusses student success at San Gabriel High School and his expectations. However, the purpose of the session is to address questions from the parents. Freshman Back To School Night, another opportunity to engage parents, is scheduled on the second day of the new school year and specifically focuses on course syllabi, introduction of the teachers and staff for the ninth grade students, student interventions and support services, and school resources.

Parent involvement is a huge factor that ensures and supports success at school. Opportunities for involvement are better received by the parent through personalized invitations from school representatives. Certainly, there is still a place for fliers and automated phone calls from the Administrator, but a personal invitation by the visible Principal in the parking lot, the Assistant Principal in the Guidance Office and the Teacher who is calling home makes a bigger impact in how that parent can be involved and supportive of their child's education.

RELATIONSHIP TO THE SBFC MODEL

The school is a natural setting for the delivery of intervention services for children. Because students spend a majority of their time in schools, interventions that assist the child in coping with the elements in the learning environment and targets the reduction of problem behaviors with a focus in improving social skills, with the teacher and schools staff members working towards the same goal is valuable and organic. It is imperative that schools facilitate programs that support the School Prevention quadrant in the SBFC Model. Activities, plans, policies and events need to address guidance of children and parents, school wide classroom management that prevents students from violating behavior codes of conduct.

The end result is academic achievement and a child that has been supported. Interventions that support the child and take place within the classroom can reduce referrals for more intensive interventions. According to Hoagwood and Erwin (1997), the effectiveness of combined school-based intervention that targets the reduction of problem behaviors through the use of cognitive-behavioral techniques, improvement in social skills, and teacher management of behaviors through consultation prove effective in engaging students and reducing at-risk behaviors. And, as the child experiences success in the classroom, assessments and referrals for services at the Intensive Tiers of the Pyramid of Intervention can be avoided.

EVIDENCE-BASED SUPPORT

According to Rones and Hoagwood (2000), programs that seek clarity in school rules impact classroom management and a reduction of aggressive and inappropriate behavior. Clear school wide behavioral and academic expectations will increase the effectiveness of classroom management. Many school districts have worked with their schools' leadership teams to establish a pyramid of intervention to reflect interventions that are delivered through a tiered concept. Interventions are listed in a pyramid with the base tier listing all benchmark services and programs that all students may access. As different students need more support, the student may access more services through the strategic level of intervention. If a student is still does not demonstrate success and behavior indicates a need for more support interventions identified at the Intensive level should be accessed.

In the classroom setting, teachers must organize their classrooms in ways that support the presentation and use of academic instruction and curriculum. For example, teachers must directly teach students expectations and routines for typical classroom activities. Teachers need to be prepared, facilitates protocol for: students to ask questions, getting the attention of the teacher, and problem solving.

DIRECT INSTRUCTION

Direct instruction that addresses the routines of the classroom need to take place at critical times during the school year, like the first weeks of school and the return from school holidays and breaks. Routines and expectations should be reviewed and communicated regularly and students who acclimate and engage need recognition from the teacher and other adults in the school(Paine, et.al, 1983; Wong & Wong, 1991). Teachers must engage and maximize fundamental behavior management practices. Students need to see that their teachers are monitoring their behaviors and in turn that adults are holding students accountable for their behavior. According to Latham (1992), teachers should give six to eight positive social engagements for every negative interaction to produce a positive social classroom climate and to support success in instructional engagement.

Although direct instruction may be a time in the lesson that the teacher imparts knowledge to the student, the student may not receive the knowledge. Differentiating the delivery of the lesson may cause more students to engage in the learning process and ultimately receive the knowledge. Cooperative groups and flexible grouping (Heacox, 2010) are instructional management strategies that create specific activities for students to be involved and engaged in what they are learning. The structured time that students have with one another when in a group around a topic gives students purpose to what they are learning and makes the process more meaningful. By increasing engagement in the classroom, misbehaviors are diminished.

CLASSROOM ENVIRONMENT

Organize the learning environment in a manner that supports the importance of learning and teaching. For example, student work samples should be posted; lesson objectives and the standards that the objective addresses should be communicated to the child in a verbal and visual format, positive rules and reinforcers should be posted in the classroom; and classroom supplies, materials and floor plans are factors in creating an engaging learning environment that maximizes student engagement and minimizes negative social behaviors.

SCHOOL ENVIRONMENT

The school environment is typically characterized as space that is outside the classroom and within the campus of the school. Unlike the classroom, the space is staffed with minimal school supervision, however, the setting is populated by a large number of students with high student-to-student interaction, and there is limited adult to student interaction. According to research (Colvin, Sugai, Good and Lee (1997) and Colvin and Lazar (1997), school wide expectations need to be addressed and taught so that students understand behavioral parameters and established routines in the school environment. Supervision in the non-classroom setting is overt, efficient and visible. Students must also have regular opportunities to practice behaviors that are expected of them. Staff members must play a part in active and overt supervision when students are not in the classroom setting. Active supervision is characterized by scanning the location, visibility (where the supervisor is routinely moving through a number of different locations) and prosocial (where the supervisor is making positive social contact with the student).

Classroom management techniques have also been used to reduce children's aggression. Rones and Hoagwood (2000) noted that the Good Behavior Game, a classroom based behavior management strategy for first-grade students, promoted positive behaviors by rewarding teams of students for their lack of negative, disruptive behaviors during specific periods of time. The characteristics of this game allowed the teacher/classroom facilitator to modify the duration of the game, the rewards for positive behaviors, and the reward delay. As the school year progressed with the implementation of this system the teacher had more classroom control and aggressive behavior declined.

According to Cunningham et.al (1998), Student Mediated Conflict Resolution Programs train and support students in peer mediation and conflict resolution. In this system a team of eight student mediators monitor the playground during an elementary school's recess and lunch periods and attempt to intervene in potential conflict situations by using the mediation and conflict resolution process. Peers approach their peers who appear to be at the start of a conflict and conducted mediation process in accordance to the mediation training that each mediator is invited to attend and complete. This type of program usually results in a reduction in aggressive playground behavior at the elementary school and increases communication among students.

The most memorable learning experience in school is the teacher who was able to engage all of the students. Effective classroom management is more than the implementation of effective classroom strategies in the classroom. Engaging students in classroom instruction is the end product of a focused Positive Behavior System in a school that strategically determines a pyramid of intervention where students who demonstrate a need for support are systematically linked to services or programs. At the same time, teachers, administrators and parents are also supported so that they are familiar with the procedures and systems that assist students.

Do the kids know what they are learning? Are teachers telling students what they are learning today? Are simple rhythms and memory devices used to engage kids in capturing information like dates? Although there is a place for lecture and rows of seats, student engage with the topic when they are moving around, talking about the concept and making mental and visual notes about what they are learning. It is not surprising the least number of office behavioral referrals come from classrooms that encourage thought, the spoken word and the exploration of ideas to capture the concept as well as application. Students rarely get into trouble when they are learning; they do misbehave however, when they are not engaged and not following the lesson. When the lesson is meaningful, the students will fall into line to learn it.

Figure 17.1 Sample of Pyramid of Intervention for Secondary Education

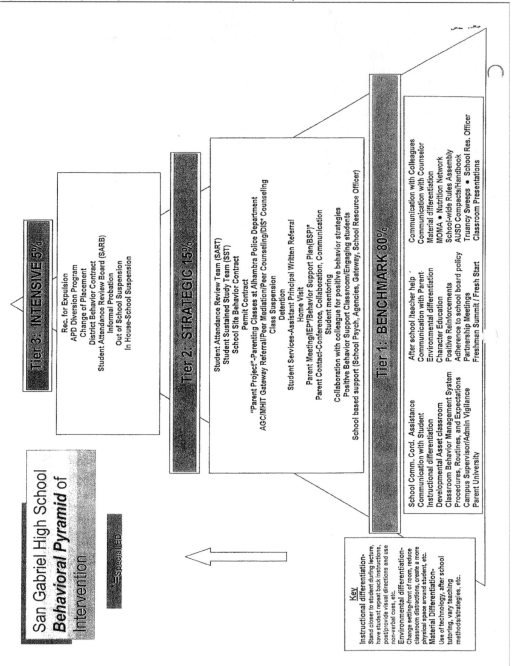

Figure 17.2 Sample of Pyramid of Intervention for Elementary

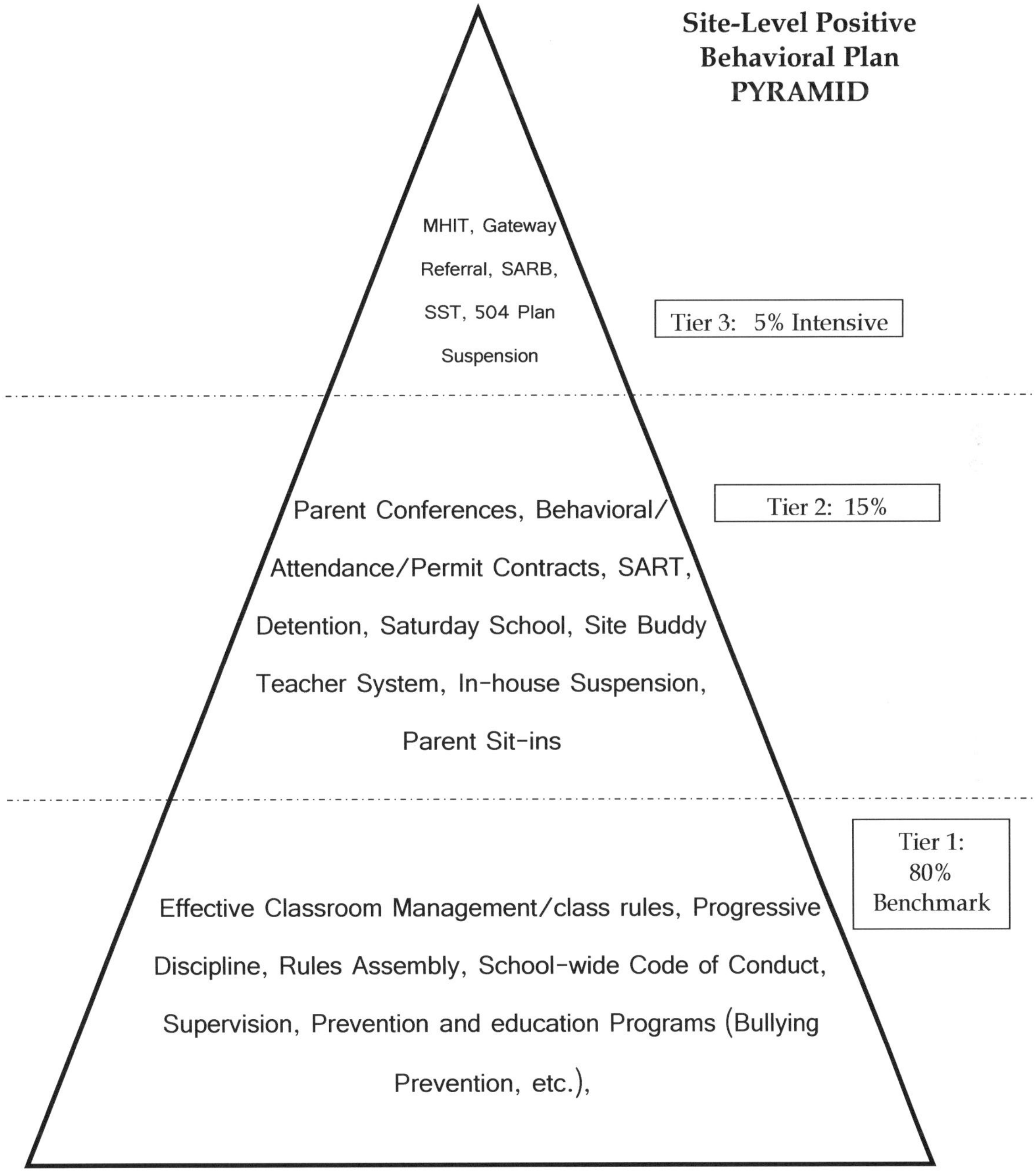

**Site-Level Positive
Behavioral Plan
PYRAMID**

MHIT, Gateway
Referral, SARB,
SST, 504 Plan
Suspension

Tier 3: 5% Intensive

Parent Conferences, Behavioral/
Attendance/Permit Contracts, SART,
Detention, Saturday School, Site Buddy
Teacher System, In-house Suspension,
Parent Sit-ins

Tier 2: 15%

Effective Classroom Management/class rules, Progressive
Discipline, Rules Assembly, School-wide Code of Conduct,
Supervision, Prevention and education Programs (Bullying
Prevention, etc.),

Tier 1:
80%
Benchmark

Figure 17.3   Sample of Pyramid of Behavioral Intervention for Alternative Settings

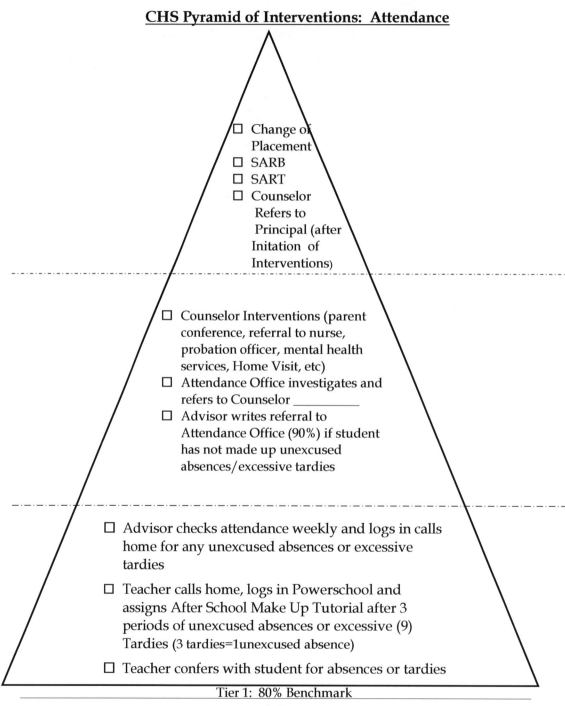

CHS Pyramid of Interventions: Attendance

☐ Change of Placement
☐ SARB
☐ SART
☐ Counselor Refers to Principal (after Initation of Interventions)

☐ Counselor Interventions (parent conference, referral to nurse, probation officer, mental health services, Home Visit, etc)
☐ Attendance Office investigates and refers to Counselor _____
☐ Advisor writes referral to Attendance Office (90%) if student has not made up unexcused absences/excessive tardies

☐ Advisor checks attendance weekly and logs in calls home for any unexcused absences or excessive tardies

☐ Teacher calls home, logs in Powerschool and assigns After School Make Up Tutorial after 3 periods of unexcused absences or excessive (9) Tardies (3 tardies=1unexcused absence)

☐ Teacher confers with student for absences or tardies

Tier 1: 80% Benchmark

REFERENCES

Cauley K.M., Jovanovich, D., (2006) Developing an effective transition program for students entering middle school or high school, The Clearing House, Vol. 80, No. 1, pp. 15 – 25.

Chapman, D., &Hofweber, C. (2000). Effective behavior support in British Columbia, *Journal of Positive Behavior Interventions*, 2, p. 235-237.

Cognato, C. A. (1999).*The effects of transition activities on adolescent self-perception and academic achievement during the progression from eighth to ninth grade.* Paper presented at the annual meeting of the National Middle School Association, Orlando.

Colvin, G., & Lazar, M. (1997). *The effective elementary classroom; Managing for success.*Longmont, CO: Sopris West.

Colvin, G., Sugai, G., Good, R., & Lee, Y. (1997). Effect of active supervision and precorrection on transition behaviors of elementary students. *School Psychology Quarterly,* 12, 344-363.

Epstein, J. L., (1995). School/family/community partnerships: Caring for the children we share. *Phi Delta Kappan* 76, pp. 701-712.

Epstein, J. L., (1996). Perspectives and previews on research and policy for school, family, and community partnerships. In A. Booth & J.F. Dunn (Eds.), *Family-school links: How do they affect educational outcomes?* (pp. 209-246). Mahwah, NJ: Lawrence Erlbaum.

Horner, R. H., &Sugai, G. (2000). School-wide behavior support: An emerging initiative (special issue). *Journal of Positive Behavioral Interventions,* 2, 231-232.

Gunter, P.L., Denny, R. K., Jack, S.L., Shores, R.E., &Neson, C.M. (1993). Aversive stimuli inacademic interactions between student with serious emotional disturbance and their teachers. *Behavioral Disorders,* vol. 19, p. 265-274.

Heacox, D., (2010).*Differentiating Instruction in the Regular* Classroom, Minneapolis, MN: Free Spirit Publishing.

Kerr, M. M., & Nelson, C.M. (1983). *Strategies for managing behavior problems in the classroom,* Columbus, OH: Merrill.

Latham, G. I. (1992). Interacting with at-risk children: The positive position. *Principal,* vol. 72(1), p. 26-30.

Mac Iver, D. J. (1990). Meeting the needs of young adolescents: Advisory groups, interdisciplinary teaching teams, and school transition programs. *Phi Delta* Kappan, 71(6), pp. 458 – 464.

Mayer, G. (1995). Preventing antisocial behavior in the schools. *Journal of Applied Behavior Analysis,* vol. 28, p. 467-478.

Mizelle, N.B. (2005). Moving out of middle school, *Educational Leadership.Vol. 62, 7, 56-60.*

Mizelle, N. B. and Irvin, J. L. (2000). Transition from middle school into high school. *Middle School Journal*, Vol. 31, No. 5, pp. 1-8.

Paine, S.C., Radicchi, J., Rosellini, L.C., Deutchman, L., and Darch, C.B. (1983). *Structuring your classroom for academic success.* Champaign, IL: Research Press.

Sugai, G., Horner, R., (2008). The evolution of discipline practices; School-wide positive behavior supports, *Child and Family Behavior Therapy*, vol. 24:1-2, 23-50.

US Department of Health and human services (2001). *Youth violence: A report of the Surgeon General.* Washington, DC: Office of the Surgeon General.

Wong, H. K., and Wong, R. T., (1991). *The first days of school: How to be an effective teacher.* Sunnyvale, CA: Harry K. Wong.

Worley, M. R., Bailey, D. P., Jr, and Sugai, G. (1988). *Effective teaching: Principles and procedures of applied behavior analysis with exceptional students.* Boston, MA: Allyn & Bacon.

Chapter 18
How to Plan and Carry Out a Guidance Group

Allan A. Morotti and Judith A. Morotti

***OVERVIEW:** This chapter describes what is considered by many as a lively addition to every developmentally-appropriate school-based family counseling program--the small group counseling experience. The authors discuss the origins of family counseling in the schools, the organizational steps to follow for developing small group counseling sessions, and highlight many of the reasons why School-Based Family Counselors are the ideal mental health professionals for providing these services.*

BACKGROUND

A central component in all school-based counseling programs is the guidance group (Gysbers & Henderson, 2006). Topics for these groups are as varied as the children and adolescents who constitute their membership. Set in the school environment they are ideal vehicles for the delivery of school-based family counseling (SBFC) services. They are time efficient, as well as affording the professional school counselor (PSC) the opportunity to interact with more students than possible through individual counseling sessions. Research studies (e.g., Bostick & Anderson, 2009; Gladding, 2008; Whiston & Quinby, 2009) have shown that group counseling is as effective as one-on-one counseling sessions for certain types of presenting concerns (e.g., academic performance, peer relations, social skills). Furthermore, Whiston and Quinby (2009) in their analysis of school counseling outcome research found that small group counseling interventions were more effective in facilitating behavioral changes in the individual rather than general classroom guidance activities.

While Irvin Yalom's (2005) *The Theory and Practice of Group Psychotherapy* is considered by many as the quintessential text on group counseling, the concepts that underlie this form of therapy were being espoused by Alfred Adler as early as the 1920s (Ansbacher & Ansbacher, 1956). Although, Adler did not practice group psychotherapy as it is known today, he did initiate a form of it in his child guidance clinics (Ansbacher & Ansbacher, 1956). Adler founded his first child guidance clinic in 1921 in Vienna, Austria. By 1922, he had begun the practice of holding live demonstrations in the clinic of parent and child counseling sessions. This method consisted of treating the children in front of and in cooperation with a group of adults. The common factor in this form of therapy and group therapy is that an individual's problems are discussed in front of a group and thus become objectified. (Ansbacher & Ansbacher, 1956, p. 348)

His goal in doing this was to make available to the general public the psychological principles of his day. Through this practice, Adler sought to use the language of the common man to demystify the practice of psychology and "to put the knowledge of modern psychology at the service of the educational system" (Adler, 1930, p. 187). In association with the Vienna school system Adler helped to found over 30 such clinics before his death in 1937 (Ansbacher & Ansbacher, 1956). After immigrating to the United States in 1937 Adler's associate, Rudolf Dreikurs, founded the first American child guidance clinic in Chicago. There, he began using the open forum model developed by Adler to provide parent education and training to the community (Adler School of Professional Psychology, n.d.). Variations of these clinics are still in existence today.

Educators and health professionals agree "mental well-being is a vital component of healthy child development" (Suldo, Friedrich, & Michalowski, 2010, p. 354). However, approximately one in five children or adolescents, ages nine to seventeen, is currently dealing with a diagnosable mental disorder (Suldo et al., 2010), and approximately only about 20% of those identified children receive any type of mental health services in a given year (National Alliance on Mental Illness, n.d.). The UCLA Center for Mental Health in Schools (n.d.) has published numerous briefs identifying mental health problems as a key impediment to students' academic performance. Steen, Bauman, and Smith (2007) write:

> A student who is distracted by grief (Abdelnoor& Hollins, 2004), or victimized by school bullies (Schwartz, Hopmeyer-Gorman, Nakamoto, & Toblin, 2005), or affected by his or her own or family members' substance abuse (Diego, Field, & Sanders, 2003), or upset by parental divorce (Kelly, 2000), is unlikely to demonstrate optimal academic performance. Small groups are particularly useful and effective in addressing such concerns (e.g., Samide & Stockton, 2002; Shechtman, 2002), which helps affected students to apply themselves to academic endeavors. (p.78)

Given the increased calls for greater accountability in public education today, especially of K-12 educators based on standardized student performance measures (i.e., standardized testing), it is imperative that as many barriers to student learning be remedied as possible. One of the primary functions of the PSC is to provide prevention, intervention, and remediation services to students for optimizing their academic performance. Developmentally-appropriate counseling and guidance programs are the vehicles through which these services can be delivered. In referencing Lockhart and Keys(1998), Bostick and Anderson (2009) write "Counseling and guidance programs are critical in addressing mental health problems that interfere with a student's ability to learn, to succeed, and to participate in the learning process" (p.428).

A central component of these programs are responsive services which are understood to mean individual and/or small group counseling services (Gysbers & Hendersen, 2006). According to Corey and Corey (2006), schools provide children and adolescents with more small group counseling opportunities than any other entity. Therefore, given the demand for greater teacher accountability coupled with instructional time limitations that restricts access to students, the delivery of small group counseling services are an ideal medium for providing students with academic, career, and personal/social counseling help. To underscore the importance of making counseling services available to students and families through the school environment, one need to look no further than the following statistics compiled by the Children's Defense Fund (2012):

Every second a public school student is suspended.*
Every 8 seconds a high school student drops out.*
Every 18 seconds a baby is born to an unmarried mother.
Every 20 seconds a public school student is corporally punished.*
Every 21 seconds a child is arrested.
Every 34 seconds a baby is born into poverty.
Every 42 seconds a child is confirmed as abused or neglected.
Every 42 seconds a baby is born without health insurance.
Every minute a baby is born to a teen mother.
Every 2 minutes a baby is born at low birth-weight.
Every 4 minutes a child is arrested for a drug offense.
Every 8 minutes a child is arrested for a violent offense.
Every 18 minutes a baby dies before his or her first birthday.
Every 45 minutes a child or teen dies from an accident.

Every 3 hours a child or teen is killed by a firearm.

Every 5 hours a child or teen commits suicide.

Every 5 hours a child is killed by abuse or neglect.

Every 16 hours a woman dies from complications of childbirth or pregnancy.

* Based on calculations per school day (180 days of seven hours each).

(Children's Defense Fund, 2012)

These statistics point out many of the barriers that impact students in their daily lives. Children who experience these events directly or indirectly are at greater risk of academic failure (Thomas, Rudolph, & Hendersen, 2011). Cognizant of these facts SBFC professionals work to assist students overcome whatever obstacles they may be confronted with by the two systems that most impact their lives—family and school (Carter & Evans, 2008).

RELATIONSHIP TO THE SBFC MODEL

Small group guidance/counseling groups fit well with the broader theoretical concepts underpinning the practice of SBFC. The primary purpose of guidance groups is to bring small groups of children together to participate in activities deemed preventive in nature. These groups are usually held outside of the regular classroom for a set period of time weekly. However, SBFC professionals working in the classroom setting might choose to randomly assign students to small groups to complete a multi-week project, such as: writing a script on saying "no" to drugs, acting it out, and video recording it so it can be shared with their classmates. On the other hand, small group counseling activities are remedial in nature. Again, these groups are always held outside of the student's regular classroom. Students are selected for these types of groups, because they have been identified as needing additional assistance in a particular area (e.g., academic, behavior, social).

The historical and theoretical roots of School-Based Family Counseling (SBFC) are firmly underpinned by the Adlerian School of Psychology. Adler's emphasis on prevention through parent education and his open forum model which employed an integrated, collaborative model of working with parents, educators, and mental health professionals was the forerunner of today's SBFC model (Gerrard, 2008). In addition to the teachings of Adler, SBFC also draws prominently on Bronfenbrenner's Ecological Systems Theory (1989) along with other system and family theorists (e.g., Carter & Evans, 2008; Stone & Peeks, 1986; Wetchler, 1986). The central tenant of these theories is that the individual does not exist in isolation, but is a member of a larger unit or system (e.g., family, school, religious organization, or country). The quality of interactions between these larger units or systems affects the individual in all aspects of his or her development, which in turn influences the individual's perceptions of that system, the individuals who comprise it, and his or her actions in relation to it. In other words, there are multiple bi-directional relationships existing simultaneously between the individual and the systems and also, between the systems themselves, such as: family and school or family and church. Therefore, in order to effect change in an individual the counselor must be able to understand how these systems interrelate and how one or more of them may be partly the basis for what is occurring.

> SBFC is an approach to helping children succeed at school and overcome personal and interpersonal problems. SBFC integrates school counseling and family counseling models within a broad based systems meta-model that is used to conceptualize the child's problems in the context of all of his or her interpersonal relationships: family, peer group, classroom, school (teacher, principal, other students), and community. (Gerrard, 2008, p. 6)

It is clear from Gerrard's (2008) article that the practice of SBFC utilizes a multidimensional approach to working with children and adolescents. This occurs through directed interventions, parent or teacher education, and/or family counseling. It endeavors to build trust between all the parties and employs a strength-based approach to counseling rather than a deficit model. "The SBFC professional is an advocate for the child, the family, and the school. The focus of the counseling is on working with parents and families to help their children succeed at school" (Gerrard, 2008, p.7). This, again, is an extension of Adler's theory because the SBFC professional reframes the child's behaviors as attempts to gain mastery over his or her environment. Through this process the SBFC professional encourages the partnership between parents, family and school as co-facilitators in the child's academic success. By focusing on the child's or adolescent's academic performance, the SBFC professional reduces the resistance parents may harbor towards examining broader family problems (Carter & Evans, 2008; Gerrard, 2008).

Small group counseling sessions in the school environment mirror many of the same interpersonal dynamics present in the student's family, peer group, or classroom. Perusse, Goodnough, and Lee (2009) note that:

> The multiple contextual factors that impact the lives of students shape the ways in which students process the content and dynamic interactions in groups. For example, factors such as socioeconomic status, race/ethnicity, gender, religious/spiritual beliefs and practices, sexual orientation, institutional barriers to learning, and family composition all become screens through which students filter the content of the group and the process dynamics that exist within the group. (p. 228)

For change to occur, both the individual and the system must make some accommodation to the other. SBFC professionals are trained in both school and family counseling modalities, providing them with the requisite professional skills required to navigate between these two systems. In addition, once the presenting concern is addressed and a plan of action is initiated to remedy the academic situation, the SBFC professional is free to direct his or her attention towards prevention activities designed for assisting the family unit to function more cohesively. Through this process the SBFC professional is able to draw attention to other factors present in the family that may be impacting the student's academic performance. By keeping the focus on how the family and school can work together as a unit to assist the student in his or her academic endeavors, resistance to the counseling process is lessened.

THE SBFC PROFESSIONAL AS EDUCATOR

One of the primary theoretical tenets that separate the practice of professional counseling and counseling psychology from other mental health disciplines is that counseling contains an educational component. No where is this more apparent than in the school setting where the counselor may be engaged in activities ranging from talking about what constitutes a healthy relationship to a classroom full of 8th graders to facilitating an after school parent education group on improving parent-teen communication. Once again, the origins of this tenet can be traced back to the child guidance centers founded first by Adler and, then, Dreikurs.

Education is prevention and nowhere is this more apparent than in the practice of SBFC. Ideally situated as the liaison between school and family, the SBFC professional is able to assume the role of educator through a variety of means. Some of these include: parent educator on topics specific to an identified family (e.g., separation anxiety), or as facilitator of a parent education group on a topic common to all families (e.g., discipline), discussing typical developmental milestones as a means to normalize behaviors is another. When working with families it is imperative to remember the following: (1) the parent is the child's first educator; (2) the parent determines what is best for his or child; (3) the child is an extension of the parent; (4) the parents' school experiences as students influences their perceptions of their child's school; and (5) the child seeks parental approval even when his or her actions may result in disapproval.

Working in the school environment makes the SBFC professional first an educator, and secondly a family counselor. Sharing knowledge and information pertinent on developmental issues common to all children and adolescents is an excellent way for building rapport with parents. This type of education is non-judgmental, and creates the opportunity for in depth discussion on a wider range of topics. An example of this can be seen when young adolescents move from concrete operational thinking patterns to more formal thought processes and become better able to identify inconsistencies in another's words or actions. This often manifests itself in the argumentative teenager, and the typical parent response of "what's happened to my beautiful child?" Helping the parent understand that the family is the child's first laboratory for practicing and trying out new behaviors does not necessarily lessen the pain of hurtful words, but it does bring a better understanding of adolescent development. Just as infants are driven to master standing and walking on their own, adolescents must do the same with their intellectual capacities. What SBFC professionals are always trying to do is help parents remember that:

> Children who achieve in school and develop important reading, critical thinking, problem solving, and communication skills are better able to cope with stressful and perhaps dangerous situations. Also, academic achievement enhances the development of a positive self-esteem and self-efficacy, both of which are necessary for children to experience emotional well-being and to achieve success. (Clarke, 2002, p. 5)

Returning to our argumentative teenager, the SBFC professional might suggest any number of ways to respond which hold the promise for better communication between parent and teen, than yelling at or threatening the teen with punishment. One strategy often employed and taken from Glasser's work (1998) is to listen and then respond by asking something like, "What would you like to have happen as a result of this discussion?"

The key to effective communication and relationship building is mutual respect. By modeling the behaviors we seek to develop in others, we are demonstrating through our actions respect for the other and laying foundation for building trust in the relationship. Other key areas where the SBFC professional may assume the role of educator are when providing consultation services to teachers, principals, other school personnel, and/or parents. In fact, Myrick (2002) identifies consultation as one of the three primary functions of the PSC, the other two being counseling and coordination services. Consultation means that significant adults in the student's life come together to discuss how they can better assist the student in becoming more successful in all aspects of the school experience, but especially academically. When functioning as a consultant, the SBFC professional is able to draw on school and community resources, as well as the family. The more resources available for the SBFC professional to utilize, the greater the possibility the proposed plan of action will have for being successful. Seldom are a student's difficulties at school the result of a single variable (e.g., poor test taking skills) alone. Therefore, it is imperative in the consultation process that the SBFC professional has a working knowledge of all available resources and how they can be integrated to benefit the student.

One other area that deserves mention in the educator realm is teacher in-service trainings. This is a natural extension of the SBFC professional's role as educator for it gives this individual the opportunity to offer focused trainings on topics of interest specific to the school and/or the district-at-large. Examples of such workshop topics include: classroom strategies for working with autism spectrum disordered students, using challenge activities to build social skills, cyber-bulling: what every teacher, parent and student needs to know about it, strategies for creating successful classroom meetings, building service learning activities into your health curriculum, wellness activities for educators. These topics draw from and integrate knowledge from many different disciplines (i.e., education, psychology, technology, health). In addition, they interface all the domains the SBFC professional works within—family, school, and community.

EVIDENCE-BASED SUPPORT

As noted previously, educators and educational systems are coming under ever-greater public scrutiny. With states facing decreasing financial resources and dwindling legislative support for blindly funding K-12 budget requests, these calls to accountability must be addressed. PSCs and their programs are often perceived as being an ancillary service in K-12 school systems and not central to a school's educational mission. This perception of PSCs and counseling services in general makes them expendable during difficult financial times. Therefore, it is imperative for PSCs to utilize a *best practices approach* in developing and implementing their school counseling programs. One method for accomplishing this is by drawing on evidence-based supported interventions (Carey & Dimmitt, 2006) and programs (Bostick & Anderson, 2009). To determine which interventions and programs to utilize as resources the SBFC must begin by conducting a needs assessment (Gysbers & Henderson, 2006) of the school. Ideally, this would be undertaken before the beginning of the school year and ask for input from students, parents, all school personnel, and community members-at-large. Having once collected and analyzed the data the SBFC can then proceed to identify potential resources specific to the school population (Johnson & Johnson, 2003) for the next academic year. The cornerstone for developing effective SBFC programs is the ongoing collection of data (Steen & Kaffenberger, 2007; Studer, Oberman, & Womack, 2006) for evaluating the counseling services provided. The collection and interpretation of valid reliable data makes continuous program improvement possible (Rowell, 2006).

One such evidence-based small group counseling program that has proven successful is the Social Skills Group Intervention, or S.S. GRIN (DeRosier, 2007). S.S. GRIN uses a cognitive-behavioral approach to address typical personal/social problems (e.g., teasing, peer pressure) common among students. Interventions are scripted with accompanying activities (e.g., role plays, modeling) (DeRossier, 2007). "Sessions focus on the development of verbal and nonverbal communication, initiation, cooperation, compromise, and negotiation skills. In addition, emotional regulation, impulse control, and perspective taking are emphasized" (Bostick & Anderson, 2009, p. 429). In a three-year study conducted by Bostick and Anderson (2009) implementing S.S. GRIN with 49 third grade students in a North Carolina elementary school, using a pre/post-test measurement regimen, they found statistical significance ($< .001$) for a reduction in both loneliness and social anxiety with an increase in the students' reading scores at the .001 level. While the researches urge caution in interpreting these findings because of a lack of a control group, they nevertheless recommend school counselors consider using the program.

A second evidence-based program that has received high marks is titled Student Success Skills (SSS). It is one of the few counseling curriculums to have been systematically evaluated and while used predominately with elementary school-aged children, it has also been shown to produce positive results with middle school students (Whiston & Quinby, 2009). Various studies (i.e., Brigman & Campbell, 2003; Campbell & Brigman, 2005; Webb, Brigman, & Campbell, 2005) have reported that students participating in SSS had higher achievement gains than the control group students. In a 2007 study Miranda, Brigman, and Pelusa found similar increases for Black, Hispanic, and Caucasian students. The program is delivered through large group guidance lessons with small group counseling activities being employed with students who need additional support. Similar to the S.S. GRIN curriculum, SSS utilizes cognitive-behavioral approaches to assist students manage personal/social issues. Students set goals, target areas for improvement, and practice strategies for achieving their goals (Webb et al., 2005).

PROCEDURE

Going about setting up, developing, and implementing a small group counseling experience in K-12 schools is a multi-step process. As mentioned previously, the SBFC professional must first determine through the needs assessment what are the predominant themes present in the school environment that are cause for concern. Secondly, the counselor must then select what evidence-based strategies would be best suited for intervening in these areas. In addition, the SBFC professional must answer the following questions before proceeding further: how large will the group be; when and how often will the group meet; how many total group meetings will there be and how long will each session last; will it be an open or closed group; will it be a homogenous or heterogeneous group; will participants be screened for suitability of membership; how will issues of consent and confidentiality be handled in the group (Crespi, 2009).

Time and access to students are critical variables in determining the answers to many of these questions. The increased demand for improving students overall academic performance as demonstrated through standard-based assessments leaves little time for supplementary activities that while beneficial to the student may not be deemed essential to academic performance by others. When determining the size of the group the SBFC professional has to consider the age of students and the purpose of the group. For example, younger children have a shorter attention span than older students, meaning when working with K-3 students the group size ought not to be larger than three or four students, with grades 4-6 no more than five, and with middle and high school students no more than 6-8 students. For small group counseling to be beneficial participants must feel safe and have the opportunity to share their perspectives. Additionally, if the purpose of the group is to help students learn how to be more on task and they have been diagnosed as having attention deficit hyperactivity disorder (ADHD), the SBFC professional might want to consider limiting the group size to three or four even if the students are in the 7th or 8th grade.

Teachers, as well as parents, are reluctant to have students released during core academic subject times (i.e., reading, language arts, mathematics). Therefore, when constructing small group meeting times, the SBFC professional must first get input from teachers for when they would consider releasing students for this activity before speaking with the student's parents. Elementary school teachers may have more flexibility during their academic day because they have their students for the entire day, while middle and high school teachers are limited to their subject time. It seems reasonable given the typical school day limitations that small group counseling sessions be held weekly for a period of 30-to-45 minutes.

Since small group counseling activities in schools usually are topic specific (e.g., social skills, anger management, grief) and comprised of students identified as needing additional assistance with developing a more effective set of coping skills in that area, it is best to follow a closed group format. Furthermore, the topic itself often determines whether the small group is homogenous or heterogeneous. If the topic is divorce the group most likely will be a blend of boys and girls across grade levels. On the other hand, if the topic is healthy body images the group will be made up entirely of one gender or the other. What must always be first and foremost in the SBFC professional's thinking is how can I create the safest environment for the students to encourage their fullest participation in the group?

These considerations lead to the question of screening or how to determine which students would be the most appropriate for the group. Common sense tells us not to put students together who are too far apart in age or developmental capabilities. It also tells us not to put students together who are extremely vulnerable to or disruptive. In these situations, one-on-one counseling is the more appropriate medium for assisting the student. If the students identified as possible group participants are known to the SBFC professional, the screening process might consist simply of asking the students if they would like to be part of the group. However, in the case of someone who is new to the school or not known to the SBFC professional, then it is in the best interests of all the parties (counselor and student) to meet and talk about the group to determine the student's appropriateness for it. The participant make-up of the group is the initial intervention for realizing the goals of the group.

There is ongoing debate about what constitutes consent and at what age it can be given. In most school settings at least up through the elementary grades, it is required to have parental consent for a child to receive counseling services. At the middle school and high school levels it is highly recommended if the counseling is of an ongoing nature. Since SBFC works with both schools and families, it is logical to assume that parental permission will be requested and forthcoming. However, the older the student the more power he or she has in determining his or her own consent. Consent implies that participation is voluntary and can be withdrawn at any time without any negative consequences. Because of this, it is important that the school and family partnership be firmly in place before initiating possible intervention strategies for assisting the student in overcoming any academic difficulties. One last item of note regarding consent--It is recommended to have two written consent forms. One form is for the parents and the other is for student. The student form should be written in age-appropriate language that the child can understand.

Of all the various components that comprise the small group counseling experience, confidentiality is often the most problematic. In short, confidentiality is meant to understand that what is said or transpires in the group stays in the group. This is critical for creating and maintaining a sense of safety and trust in the group process. The only exceptions to this cardinal rule of group process are when an individual discloses possible harm to self or others, or in cases of abuse and neglect. Young children do not possess the cognitive maturity to fully understand this concept and may disclose what is shared in the group with parents or friends. It is usually not until the later elementary years (grades 4-6) when the child's thinking matures into what Piaget (1952, cited in Ginsburg & Opper, 1969) described as concrete operational thought that the concept of confidentiality can be understood. However, one of the characteristics commonly ascribed to later childhood and adolescence is that of impulsivity. Youth in this age range (10-18) may inadvertently or purposefully reveal what someone has shared in the small group not realizing the possible long-term consequences of their actions. Additionally, the younger the child the more likely he or she is to reveal what transpires in a group when asked by a parent or another trusted adult, because they are authority figures and the child wishes to please them.

In sum, while small group counseling sessions provide the SBFC professional with many opportunities for initiating prevention and intervention activities they are not without potential drawbacks. For example, one author conducted small group exercises in an elementary school for children whose parents were incarcerated. Another group focused on children who had witnessed lethal violence in the home. These examples point out the, often times, sensitive nature of small group counseling and the ethical challenges the SBFC professional faces in maintaining confidentiality and protecting others' privacy.

MULTICULTURAL COUNSELING CONSIDERATIONS

While the ethnic mixture of America's public schools is growing more diverse daily and Caucasian students are beginning to become a minority group in many school districts throughout the United States, the teaching corps staffing those schools still remains predominately Caucasian (National Education Association, 2003). In referencing Holcomb-McCoy (2003), Steen, Bauman, and Smith (2007) write: "Considering the rapidly increasing linguistic and ethnic diversity of the student population in schools, school counselors are challenged to provide effective, relevant, and sensitive services to culturally diverse students, and small groups are effective in this regard" (p.72). All children experience similar developmental changes (e.g., puberty), however, children from differing cultural or ethnic backgrounds may be exposed to other external variables that impact their development. D.W. Sue and D. Sue (2008) have theorized that additional life stressors (e.g., poverty, prejudice, limited educational/employment opportunities) often associated with being a minority can impact the minority student's development.

With this in mind, it is necessary for SBFC professionals to have a working knowledge of the socio-cultural, historical, and political contexts shaping the learning environments of the students receiving counseling services through their schools. They must be knowledgeable of the social oppression a particular group may have or is currently experiencing at the hands of the dominant society. In referring back to what differentiates SBFC professionals from other PSCs, it is precisely this knowledge and ability to work effectively with the multiple systems affecting the student's learning. If a student experiences racial prejudice in the school or community environment because he or she is of a multiracial background, then the SBFC must initiate an intervention plan to assist the student in overcoming this additional barrier for developing a positive view of self. Small group counseling sessions are an ideal venue for accomplishing this goal. By participating in a *Making Friends Group,* students have the opportunity to learn about each other and grow to appreciate each other.

In essence, schools are microcosms of the larger society (Jones, 2004) and while it is not possible to be knowledgeable of every student's cultural needs, the SBFC professional can incorporate selected aspects of the cultural groups present in the school into his or her counseling program. Providing small group counseling services in a culturally responsive context helps students to learn to appreciate their differences as strengths and not as limitations (Barnhardt, 1997). Perusse et al. (2009) in reviewing the literature pertaining to the concept that small groups are well-suited for addressing the "culture and climate of the school" (p.226) write:

> There is a third category of groups that schools offer as well. These are groups that address the culture and climate of the school. Some of these groups include issues related to diversity awareness, bias and prejudice reduction, conflict resolution, and respect of self and others (Bradley, 2001; Nikels, Mims, & Mims, 2007). These groups may also address the cultural and institutional barriers to learning of certain groups of students (e.g., students of color; gay, lesbian, bisexual, and transgendered youth; lower socioeconomic status students. (p. 226)

The acquisition of knowledge and its application are complex processes. Students do not enter the formal schooling system as blank slates, but bring with them a cultural system of knowing rich in history and tradition. To help all students learn to the best of their abilities, schools themselves must learn how to incorporate and celebrate the diversity of their student bodies into their curriculum. SBFC professionals have a central role in helping to create a welcoming and tolerant school climate for all.

CHALLENGES AND SOLUTIONS

Many of the challenges in developing and delivering small group counseling services have been noted previously. These include: student and parent consent, confidentiality, scheduling difficulties, program accountability, teachers accountability for only students' academic success, maintaining student and parent privacy. Three others that directly impact the SBFC professional and his or her delivery of counseling services are: space restraints at the school site, lack of school personnel support, and legal concerns (Steen et al., 2007; Suldo et al., 2010).

To overcome these obstacles SBFC professionals must first understand the context in which they work (Perusse et al., 2009). The role and function of schools is to prepare and equip students with the needed skills to become contributing members to the society of which they are a part. Teachers and administrators are the individuals held responsible for this transformation through the formal schooling process. Academics will always come first in this environment. Therefore, SBFC professionals must be proactive in demonstrating to teachers, administrators, and parents the benefits they can provide to all students through their counseling program. This can be accomplished through the sharing of data highlighting the academic benefits of utilizing evidence-based counseling activities. Children who have spent the night hiding in a closet because of parental discord cannot be expected to come to school the next morning ready to learn. There must be built-in steps for understanding the child's situation.

While in today's educational climate academic achievement is being measured primarily through the use of standardized test measures, the actual learning process is more complex than the mere memorization of facts. True learning occurs when the student is able to organize and apply what they have learned in new and innovative ways. Parents, teachers, administrators and community members-at-large all want children to be academically successful. By educating these different constituencies as to how SBFC can help in this process especially through the offering of small groups, SBFC becomes a necessary addition to the academic mission of the school.

Respecting another's right to privacy and ensuring confidentiality are necessary prerequisites for the delivery of counseling services. In school settings these two prerequisites can be difficult to maintain because of space constraints. In addition, even when space is available its location may not be ideal for maintaining a person or family's anonymity. When one hears the term SBFC it is easy to understand that the individual would assume that counseling services take place on the school grounds. However, as Gerrard (2008) writes "the term 'school-based' is not meant to refer to the site at which the counseling occurs [but]…the focus given to promoting school success" (p. 6). Nevertheless, if the SBFC professional works at the school he or she might want to consider working a flex schedule around the core of the instructional day to have greater access to students, be better able to accommodate working parents, and be able to utilize a more desirable meeting space for parents and students due to a lessening of instructional time demands. The other available option would be using office space at a mental health agency, or contracting with a school district for use of space off campus. In sum, by assuming the role of educator with district staff, parents, and community members the SBFC professional can essentially avert many of the logistical challenges that might impede the full implementation of SBFC services, including small group counseling sessions.

SUMMARY

Small group counseling services are an important component of developmentally-appropriate school-based counseling programs. Small group counseling groups are time efficient, provide access to more students, and are reflective of the larger social world the child or adolescent lives in. This modality offers the PSC an array of topics and intervention strategies to select from in addressing whatever life challenges the student may be facing. Research studies (Adelman & Taylor, 2002; Parker, Rubin, Erath, Wojslawowicz, & Buskirk, 2006; Rubin, Bukowski, & Parker, 2006) have identified that the mental health problems of children and adolescents have a negative impact on their academic performance. Because of their expertise in both school and family counseling, SBFC professionals are ideally positioned to deliver the necessary mental health services to assist the student in bettering their academic performance. By focusing on the student's academic issues the SBFC professional can encourage both the student's family and the school to join together to remedy the student's academic difficulties.

REFERENCES

Adelman, H., & Taylor, L. (2002). Buidling comprehensive, multifaceted, and integrated   approaches   to address barriers to student learning. *Childhood Education*, 78, 261-268.

Adler, A. (1930). *The education of children*. Chicago: Gateway.

Adler School of Professional Psychology. (n.d.). Adler school timeline: History. Retrieved on March 16, 2011 from http://www.adler.edu

Ansbacher, H.L. &Ansbacher, R.R. (1956).*The individual psychology of Alfred Adler*. New York: Harper Perennial.

Barnhardt, R. (1997).Teaching/Learning across cultures: Strategies for success. Fairbanks, AK: Center for Cross-Cultural Studies, University of Alaska Fairbanks.

Bostick, D., & Anderson, R. (2009). Evaluating a small-group counseling program—A model for program planning and improvement in the elementary setting. *Professional School Counseling*, 12(6), 428-433.

Brigman, G., & Campbell, C. (2003). Helping students improve academic achievement and school success behavior. *Professional School Counseling*, 7, 91-98.

Bronfenbrenner, U. (1989). Ecological systems theory. In R. Vasta (Ed.), *Annals of child Development*, (Vol. 6, pp. 187-251). Greenwich, CT: JAI Press.

Campbell, C., &Brigman, G. (2005). Closing the achievement gap: A structural approach to group counseling. *The Journal for Specialists in Group Work*, 30, 67-82.

Carey, J. C., & Dimmitt, C. (2006). Resources for school counselors and counselor educators: The Center for School Counseling Outcome Research. *Professional School Counseling*, 9, 416– 420.

Carter, M., & Evans, W. (2008) Implementing school-based counseling strategies, activities, and process considerations. *International Journal for School-Based Family Counseling*, 1(1), 25- 39.

Children's Defense Fund. (2011).Moments in America for children .Retrieved on March 16, 2012 from http://www.childrensdefense.org/child-research-data-publications/moments-in- america-for-children.html

Clarke, A.S. (2002). Emotional distress among American Indian and Alaska Native students: Research findings. ERIC Digest. Charleston, WV: ERIC Clearinghouse on Rural Education and Small Schools. (ERIC Document No. ED459988)

Corey, M.S., & Corey, G. (2006). *Groups: Process and practice* (7th ed.). Belmont, CA: Thomson Brooks/Cole.

Crespi, T. D. (2009). Group counseling in the schools: Legal, ethical, and treatment issues in school practice. *Psychology In The Schools*, 46(3), 273-280.

DeRosier, M. (2007).Social skills group intervention (S.S.Grin): Group interventions and exercises   for enhancing children's communication, cooperation, and confidence (4th ed.).Cary, NC: 3-C Institute for Social Development.

Gerrard, B. (2008). School-based family counseling: Overview, trends, and recommendations for future research. *International Journal for School-Based Family Counseling*, 1(1), 6-24.

Gladding, S. (2008). *Group work: A counseling specialty* (5th ed.). Columbus, OH: Merrill Prentice Hall.

Glasser, W. (1998).*Choice theory: A new psychology of personal freedom*. New York: HarperCollins.

Ginsburg, H., &Opper, S. (1969). *Piaget's theory of intellectual development: An introduction*. Englewood Cliffs, NJ: Prentice-Hall.

Gysbers, N., & Henderson, P. (2006*). Developing and managing your school guidance program*   (3rd ed.). Alexandria, VA: American Counseling Association.

Johnson, S., & Johnson, C. (2003). Results-based guidance: A systems approach to student support programs. *Professional School Counseling*, 6, 180-184.

Jones, H. (2004). A research-based approach on teaching to diversity. *Journal of Instructional Psychology*, 31(1), 12-19.

Miranda, A., Webb, L., Brigman, G., & Peluso, P. (2007). Student Success Skills: A promising program to close the academic achievement gap for African American and Latino students. *Professional School Counseling*, 10, 490-497.

Myrick, R.D. (2002). Developmental guidance and counseling: A developmental approach (4th ed.). Minneapolis, MN: Educational Media Corporation.

National Alliance on Mental Illness. (n.d.). Child & adolescent action center: Facts on children's mental health in America. Retrieved March 16, 2011 from http://www.nami.org

National Education Association. (2003). Status of American public school teacher statistics. Retreived November 27. 2003: http://www.nea.org/edstats/images/statushighlights.pdf , Washington DC Distribution Center.

Parker, J., Rubin, K., Erath, S., Wojslawowicz, J., &Buskirk, A. (2006). Peer relationships, child development, and adjustment. In D. Cicchetti& D. Cohen (Eds.), Developmental psychopathology, Vol. 1: Theory and methods (2nd ed., pp. 96-161). New York: Wiley.

Perusse, R., Goodnough, G. E., & Lee, V. V. (2009). Group counseling in the schools. *Psychology In The Schools*, 46(3), 225-231.

Rowell, L. (2006). Action research and school counseling: Closing the gap between research and practice. *Professional School Counseling*, 9, 376-384.

Rubin, K., Bukowski, W., & Parker, J. (2006). Peer interactions, relationships, and groups. In N. Eisenberg (Ed.), Handbook of child psychology: Social, emotional, and personality development (6th ed., pp 571-645). New York: Wiley

Steen, S., Bauman, S., & Smith, J. (2007).Professional school counselors and the practice of group work. *Professional School Counseling*, 11(2), 72-80.

Steen, S., &Kaffenberger, C. J. (2007). Integrating academic interventions into small group counseling in elementary school. *Professional School Counseling*, 10(5), 516-519.

Stone, G., & Peeks, B. (1986). The use of strategic family therapy in the school setting: A case study. *Journal of Counseling and Development*, 65(4), 200-203.

Studer, J., Oberman, A., & Womack, R. (2006). Producing evidence to show counseling Effectiveness in the schools .*Professional School Counseling*, 9, 385-391.

Sue, D.W. & Sue, D. (2008).Counseling the culturally diverse: Theory and practice (5th ed.). Hoboken, NJ: Wiley & Sons.

Suldo, S. M., Friedrich, A., & Michalowski, J. (2010). Personal and systems-level factors that limit and facilitate school psychologists' involvement in school-based mental health services. *Psychology In The Schools*, 47(4), 354-373.

Thompson, C., Rudolph, L., &Hendersen, D. (2011). Counseling children (8th ed.). Belmont, CA: Wadsworth.

UCLA Center for Mental Health in Schools. (n.d.). School mental health project. Retrieved on March 16, 2011 from http://smhp.psych.ucla.edu

Villares, E., Lemberger, M., Brigman, G., Webb, L. (2011). Student success skills: An Evidence-based school counseling program grounded in humanistic theory. *Journal of Humanistic Psychology*, 50, 42-55.

Webb, L., Brigman, G., & Campbell, C. (2005). Linking school counselors and student success: A replication of the Student Success Skills approach targeting the academic and social competencies of students. *Professional School Counseling*, 2, 60-67.

Wetchler, J. (1986). Family therapy of school-focused problems: A macrosystematic perspective. *Contemporary Family Therapy*, 8, (3), 224-240.

Whiston, S. C., &Quinby, R. F. (2009). Review of school counseling outcome research. *Psychology In The Schools*, 46(3), 267-272.

Yalom, I. (2005).*The theory and practice of group psychotherapy*. New York: HarperCollins.

RESOURCES

Bostick, D., & Anderson, R. (2009). Evaluating a small-group counseling program—A model for program planning and improvement in the elementary setting. *Professional School Counseling*, 12(6), 428-433.

Crespi, T. D. (2009). Group counseling in the schools: Legal, ethical, and treatment issues in school practice. *Psychology In The Schools*, 46(3), 273-280.

DeRosier, M. (2007). Social skills group intervention (S.S.Grin): Group interventions and exercises for enhancing children's communication, cooperation, and confidence (4th ed.). Cary,NC: 3-C Institute for Social Development.

Perusse, R., Goodnough, G. E., & Lee, V. V. (2009). Group counseling in the schools. *Psychology In The Schools*, 46(3), 225-231.

Thompson, C., Rudolph, L., &Hendersen, D. (2011). Counseling children (8th ed.). Belmont, CA: Wadsworth.

Villares, E., Lemberger, M., Brigman, G., Webb, L. (2011). Student success skills: An Evidence-based school counseling program grounded in humanistic theory. *Journal of Humanistic Psychology*, 50, 42-55.

Webb, L., Brigman, G., & Campbell, C. (2005). Linking school counselors and student success: A replication of the Student Success Skills approach targeting the academic and social competencies of students. *Professional School Counseling*, 2, 60-67.

Social Skills Group Intervention

Program Topics
- Peer Acceptance
- Self-esteem
- Self-efficacy
- Social anxiety
- Depressive symptoms

The S.S. GRIN program consists of a ten hour long weekly sessions. Methods include modeling, reinforcement, and cognitive reframing of prosocial behavior, teaching through lecture, role-playing, brainstorming, playing games, and more.

Recommended Resources

To download or order the Social Skills Group Intervention program, please visit http://www.selmediainc.com/ssgrin/overview.

Student Success Skills

Program Topics
- Goal setting and reporting, progress monitoring, and success sharing
- Creating a caring, supportive, and encouraging community in the classroom
- Cognitive and memory skills
- Performing under pressure and managing test anxiety
- Building healthy optimism

Recommended Resources

To learn more about Student Success Skills, view a list of additional resources, or order a SSS manual, please visit http://www.studentsuccessskills.com.

For further information regarding the Student Success Skills program, please read the following:

Villares, E., Lemberger, M., Brigman, G., & Webb, L. (2011).Student success skills: An evidence-based school counseling program grounded in humanistic theory. *Journal of Humanistic Counseling, 50*, 42-55.

Webb, L. D., &Brigman, A. (2006). Student success skills: Tools and strategies for improved academic and social outcomes. *Professional School Counseling, 10*(2), 112-120.

Appendix 1 Supplemental Materials

Introduction to the Counselor-What does a counselor do?

Counseling helps students develop self-understanding, self-acceptance, and self-direction. The counselor works with individuals, small groups, and classes. Students may be counseled on academic, emotional, physical, personal and social concerns, or on career development. The counselor can help students develop positive self-concept; better communication skills; conflict resolution and decision making skills; positive peer relations, family relationships, and other adult relationships; career awareness, exploration, and decision making; course selection and career planning; and personal concerns, such as substance abuse, depression, school phobias, loss of a significant person, and adjusting to parental divorce.

Students can be referred to the counselor by a teacher or parents, or they may seek assistance on their own. Counseling can be individual, in groups, or in the form of guided classroom activities. Groups include students who share common concerns. Since students receive feedback from the counselor and their peers in a secure, caring environment the potential for personal growth and social development is greatly enhanced. Classroom activities are basically informational in nature and focus on preventing future concerns that may arise in the normal process of growth and development.

- -

I would like to visit each classroom to introduce myself to the students and let them know what a counselor may do in the elementary school. Please let me know a time that would be convenient to come visit your classroom for 15-20 minutes.

Teacher: _____   **Classroom Grade:** _____

Day of the Week: _____

Best Time: _____   **Alternate Time:** _____

Additionally, I would like to begin facilitating classroom guidance lessons focusing on the areas identified in the needs assessment survey. It is generally best if I am able to come in 4-6 week blocks so that I am able to make connections with the students, they can come to know what to expect from me, and there is some consistency and follow-through on topics. Please let me know if you would like me to complete lessons in your classroom. The following areas were identified as having highest needs: Students need to learn to

1. communicate more effectively with peers
2. be more accepting and kinder to peers

* plan and use time well (highest need area in 4th-6th grades)

3. develop good decision-making skills
4. develop a sense of responsibility
5. deal with peer pressure
6. work within the social group

* study skills (high need area in 4th 6th grades)

Topics of Interest: 1)_____ **2)** _____ **3)** _____

Time frame to Begin: _____

Number of visits:_____ **Length of Lesson:** _____

Day of the Week: _____ **How often (weekly/bi-weekly):** _____

Best Time: _____ **Alternate Time:** _____

Please return to my mailbox when completed. Thanks!

Counseling Referral Process

1. Complete the Counselor Referral Form (see below)

2. Meet with the counselor to discuss concerns

3. Teacher calls child's parent to discuss option of having child meet with the counselor.

   If ok, then let the parent know the counselor will call them to discuss the counseling process

   further.

   If not ok, then discuss with the counselor the possibility of setting up classroom visit times.

4. Counselor will set an appointment time with the teacher to meet with the student.

5. Counselor meets with the student

Counselor Referral Form

Date: _____

Teacher: _____ Classroom & Grade: _____

Comment or Concern: _____

_____

_____

Best day and time to touch base: _____

_____

358

I came to see you

Name: _____

Day/Date: _____

Teacher/Grade: _____

Notes: _____

_____

_____

_____

Parent/Guardian Consent Form: Consent for Group Counseling

Your permission is requested for your child, _____, to participate in group counseling activities. The group will involve _____ sessions and will run from _____ to _____. Each session will be about _____ minutes long and will take place during the school day (generally during recess or lunch), or possibly after school.

The group is entitled _____ and will include discussion of ideas, feelings, behaviors, attitudes, and opinions. The children will do some activities related to the topic, such as drawing, role-playing, relaxation exercises, and practicing new behaviors both in group and between sessions with family members and friends. For example, your child could be practicing telling you how she or he feels about a related issue.

Some of the session topics are:
_____
The children will have the opportunity to learn new skills and behaviors that may help their personal development and adjustment. The group will be led by the school counselor, _____.

Because counseling is based on a trusting relationship between counselor and the student, the group leader(s) will keep the information shared by group members confidential, except in certain situations in which there is an ethical responsibility to limit confidentiality. In the following circumstances you will be notified:
1.   If the child reveals information about harm to himself/herself of another person
2.   If the child reveals information about child abuse
3.   If the counselor's records are subpoenaed by the courts

By signing this form I give my informed consent for my child to participate in group counseling. I understand that:
- The group will provide an opportunity for members to learn and practice interpersonal skills, discuss feelings, share ideas, practice new behaviors and make new friends.

- Anything group members share in group will be kept confidential by the group leader(s) except in situations already noted.
- General information regarding the progress of your child in group may be discussed periodically, if requested by you.

Parent/Guardian: _____   Date: _____

Parent/Guardian: _____   Date: _____

Student: _____   Date: _____

Return to: _____   By: _____

Parent/Guardian Consent Form: Consent for Individual Counseling

Your permission is requested for your child, _____, to participate in individual counseling activities. Each session will be about _____ minutes long and will take place during the school day (generally during snack, recess or lunch), or possibly after school. Sessions will begin on _____ and continue until the child, the counselor, and the parent agree that the sessions are no longer necessary.

The main counseling session topic will be _____, but the sessions may explore other topics as well. The sessions will include discussion of ideas, feelings, behaviors, attitudes, and opinions. Your child may do some activities related to the topic, such as drawing, role-playing, relaxation exercises, and practicing new behaviors both in session and between sessions with family members and friends. For example, your child could be practicing telling you how she or he feels about a related issue.

Your child will have the opportunity to learn new skills and behaviors that may help their personal development and adjustment. The sessions will be led by the school counselor,

_____.

Because counseling is based on a trusting relationship between counselor and the student, the counselor will keep the information shared by your child confidential, except in certain situations in which there is an ethical responsibility to limit confidentiality. In the following circumstances you will be notified:
1. If the child reveals information about harm to himself/herself of another person
2. If the child reveals information about child abuse
3. If the counselor's records are subpoenaed by the courts

By signing this form I give my informed consent for my child to participate in individual counseling. I understand that:
- The counseling sessions will provide an opportunity for my child to learn and practice interpersonal skills, discuss feelings, share ideas, and practice new behaviors.
- Anything my child shares in sessions will be kept confidential by the counselor except in situations already noted.

- General information regarding the progress of your child in the counseling sessions may be discussed periodically, if requested by you.

Parent/Guardian: _____   Date: _____

Parent/Guardian: _____   Date: _____

Student: _____   Date: _____

Return to: _____   By: _____

CONSENT FORM FOR RELEASE OF INFORMATION

Student's Name: _____ Date of Authorization: _____
Social Security Number: _____ Birth Date: _____

I, _____, do hereby give my consent for the release of confidential information upon request regarding my son/daughter, _____,
      Student's Name

From/To: School: _____
               Attn: _____
               Address: _____
               Phone: _____ Fax: _____

I permit this confidential information to be sent to/from:

Agency: _____
Attn: _____
Address: _____
Phone: _____ Fax: _____

Method of Release: Phone / Fax / Mail

I give my permission to release the following specific confidential information:

_____
_____

361

I understand that any and all information in my records is protected under Federal laws and regulations governing Confidentiality of Records, 42 CFR Part 2, and cannot be disclosed without my written consent unless otherwise provided for in the regulations (in a covered life threatening emergence, child abuse or neglect, threatened or actual crime at this Program or against staff or appropriate by a judge). With this understanding, I am authorizing release of the above specified information for the purpose(s) note below. The recipient of this information may not disclose any of it without my further written consent as provided for by Federal Regulation 42 CFR Part 2.

Purpose and need for such disclosure: I understand that the information to be released includes information regarding the following:

_____Drug/alcohol abuse, assessment, treatment, rehabilitation, and compliance
_____Psychiatric assessment, treatment, and compliance
_____Counseling consultation

This consent is given voluntarily in writing by me for the above stated purpose and will remain in effect until the revocation date noted below, except for the action which has already been taken. I understand that this consent may be revoked by me at any time in a written statement.

Specification of the date which consent automatically expires: date:_____

_____   _____
Student Signature   Date

_____   _____
Parent/Guardian Signature   Date

_____   _____
Signature of Witness   Date

Chapter 19
How to Facilitate a Classroom Meeting

Gema Macias

OVERVIEW: *This chapter describes an integrative Systems, Developmental and Reality Therapy approach to classroom meetings within the SBFC Model framework.*

BACKGROUND

The first decade of the 21st Century ushered in a global economic downturn not seen since the Great Depression. The downturn, marked by high unemployment rates, both in the US and abroad, the failure of investment houses, tightened lending policies, reduced consumer spending and the collapse of a once booming housing market caused housing values to plummet at unprecedented rates. Thousands of homeowners found themselves with upended mortgages and, ultimately, in foreclosure. The subsequent glut of homes on the market resulted in existing homeowners losing equity, a major financial asset, in their homes. State and municipal governments across the United States were affected in turn by the reduced revenues in state and local taxes, particularly losses in real estate taxes and receipts from sales taxes. Reductions in local services such as police and fire protection, library services, and recreations services to children and teens ensued.

The causes of the economic downturn are complex but its impact on the American public school system is unmistakable. Reductions in funding at both the federal and state levels resulted in the curtailment or elimination of programs and services aimed at bolstering student achievement, reduction in teaching staff, the reduction or elimination of support services such as school counseling programs and the elimination of administration and central office personnel who once provided services and supports to students, families, site administrators and teachers. The average daily attendance, known as ADA, was directly impacted. The migration of families in search of adequate housing and employment left school districts with reduced ADA, the primary source of income for the local public school district.

White (2009) reports that California, a state hard hit by the downturn, suffered a loss of approximately 17,000 teaching and administrative positions since 2006. Remaining administrative staff found themselves covering multiple departments, the duties of which were sometimes outside their area of education, training and experience. Class sizes increased, site and central office support decreased, and students requiring additional support have few options for assistance. Past economic downturns have had similar effects though not to the degree seen in the 21st century. The federal education statutes No Child Left Behind (NCLB) and Individuals with Disability Education Act(IDEA) have accountability measures that remained unchanged. Calls for school reform based on persistent gaps in achievement between particular racial and ethnic minorities and the "white majority" , dismal high school drop-out rates and fears that the American school system is ill equipped to prepare its students for global competition in the sciences and technology continue to plague the public education system. Schools, with severely impacted budgets, are left to contend with unmitigated accountability measures, public outcry at the slow pace of school reform and the dilemma of meeting the needs of students arriving at their doorsteps with little preparation for school success.

The human toll of the downturn is evident in local neighborhoods and municipalities. Shuttered storefronts, homes standing darkened and vacant, long wait lists for services, large numbers of applicants for few employment positions and families sharing housing to reduce costs resulted in a climate of protest in which the unemployed, the underemployed and the ill-housed march, camp out in public places and otherwise take their frustration out on public officials or those in the financial services sector. Violence manifesting in riots in which thousands of dollars in damage to public and personal property add to the budget woes of beleaguered cities and schools. Demonstrations by teacher unions and community members at board of education meetings sometimes erupt into angry outbursts.

CHALLENGES AND SOLUTIONS

Bandura (1969) has shown that children emulate what they see. First it was television: programming containing images of violence; then came interactive computer games giving the player the ability to engage in virtual violence; the present has the internet with its instant access to images worldwide. Recently, it is handheld interactive instant messaging devices that allow unobtrusive access to social websites that give the illusion of friendship, provide instant communication not only to family and friends but to people unknown to the user and allow anyone to post a comment, as well as the opportunity to respond to the comments of others.

The impact on impressionable youth is undeniable. Young people, elementary school to through high school, see the sometimes bewildering manner in which adults make their opinions and expectations known. They bring to the classroom the images to which they are exposed and the messages, verbal and nonverbal, that surround them. With reduced resources to address their needs, teachers must continue the task of imparting instruction to meet state and federal mandates to a group of learners diverse in their racial and ethnic backgrounds, family ideologies, socio economic status and religious beliefs. Public schools are expected to be the neutral ground but also must address the violence that has spilled onto the campuses of public schools. The National Center for Educational statistics for 2010 found that students ages 12-18 were victims of about 828,000 nonfatal victimizations at school, including theft, simple assault (fights) and serious violent victimizations (rape, sexual assault, aggravated assault). That same year a greater number of students ages 12-18 report having experienced a greater number of victimizations at school than away from school. Schools have typically responded with greater security measures such as metal detectors, security cameras and drug-sniffing dogs. According to Glasser (2000) schools' attempt to control behavior through improved discipline with little to no corresponding attempt to create a more satisfying school. Schools, according to Glasser, need to do something to restructure classes so that they are more satisfying.

Until the early 1970's classroom management practices largely relied on stimulus response theories; that is, the idea that student behavior could be controlled. Current practices rely on the intentional development of a learning environment that directly involves students in the learning process, i.e., one that links that the cognitive demands of learning content with the social demands of exhibiting learning of the content. Examples include cooperative learning groupings, pair/share, graphic organizers that help students organize information, note-taking systems designed to stimulate questioning and interactive examinations using interactive media. Arriving at a time when students from diverse backgrounds can actively engage with one another and the teacher in a civil and respectful manner takes careful planning and the corresponding implementation of classroom structures designed to promote skills development, effective communication and problem-solving.

One such structure is the classroom meeting. Defined here as a time dedicated to discussion of issues important and relevant to the group (Emmet and Monsour, 1996), the classroom meeting was, in its present form, designed by William Glasser in his 1969 book, *Schools Without Failure*. Glasser believed that, in order to help students take responsibility for their learning, particularly their choices, schools must avoid stimulus response programs that control student behavior and develop schools that are conducive to helping develop intrinsic student motivation and hence, improve student achievement. Dreikurs (1972) specifically mentions the classroom meeting as a vehicle for modeling the democratic process of group problem-solving through developing empathy and group membership.

RELATIONSHIP TO THE SBFC MODEL

While the classroom meeting has been used as a classroom management technique, it is an ideal School-Prevention strategy for the school-based family counselor. In a climate of reduced resources and increased accountability, the school counselor must find methods to address student needs that are most effective, that reach the most students, and that have a positive and lasting impact on the school community and, ultimately, on the community at large. In 1993, Walsh and McCarroll recommended the school counselor move to a group focus, providing services such as teaching skills to groups, serving in the role of consultant to teachers and parents and serving as a link to community services agencies.

The skills taught in effective classroom meetings are the very skills used and taught by the school-based family counselor: group facilitation, active listening, open-ended questioning, problem-solving skills and conflict resolution skills. For this reason Emmet and Monsour (1996) note that the professional school counselor is a unique position to act as a consultant to school staff on the implementation of the classroom meeting. Edwards and Mullis (2003) suggest the school counselor can act as a consultant using counseling skills to encourage teachers during the implementation of the class meeting. These researchers further state the counselor can serve as a model to the teacher and initiate the implementation by co-leading classroom meetings. Classroom meetings meet a need that has been a source of frustration for school counselors: teaching social skills in isolation to troubled youth with disappointing results. The results are typically a student who may articulate the components of a skill and the process but is unable to apply the skill to the typical social setting.

Class meetings can be used to address a variety of problems. Helping students to develop effective conflict resolution skills, effective communication skills, discussion of interpersonal problems such as bullying and harassment, helping the teacher develop as sense of "community – here defined as a sense of belonging – in the classroom and even promote particular skills such as particular types of thinking (Curran, 2003). Most importantly, these skills can help students learn to hold civil, respectful discussions, the cornerstone of the democratic process. Halaby (2000), an advocate for the classroom meeting, found that students benefit from classroom meetings because they can see cause and effect of their actions since conflicts are named and repercussions of their actions are made public.

MULTICULTURAL COUNSELING CONSIDERATIONS

Since their introduction classroom meetings have been advocated as a vehicle to teach conflict resolution skills, effective communication skills, critical thinking skills and decision-making skills (Edwards, Mullis 2003). Effective classroom meetings can serve as a model of equality and inclusiveness and relationship –building because they provide the learning experiences missing in skills-based programs (Frey and Doyle, 2001). Classroom meetings can tap into intrinsic motivation by tapping into a student's interests and goals (Glasser 1988) rather than rely on the external controls of Stimulus Response found in typical classroom management programs.

Classroom meetings carry the potential of preventing classroom problems from arising. They can help student make better choices and can have a positive impact upon the participant's sense of belonging, power, freedom and enjoyment, constructs that are the foundation of Glasser's choice theory (1988). Students become skilled at identifying problems, seeking possible solutions, entering

discussions and holding each other accountable for implementing solutions (Knapp 2010). Classroom meetings held on a regular basis help build a community of learners within the classroom (Kriete, 2003). Students are known by name, thereby reducing the sense of isolation and alienation. They define behaviors for the victims
and perpetrators and the group in general. The participants develop a common understanding of the language used in the classroom. During group meetings the group members identify causes of problems and can see the results of their actions by hearing the reports from the group members at subsequent meetings.

Hess (2011) states that the school is the ideal location for students to learn how to hold respectful, civil discussions about controversial issues because students are more likely to encounter diversity in school than out:

> Students who engage in discussions learn how to make and defend an argument and analyze others' positions in constructive ways. They develop a better understanding of important content knowledge, especially content that is so difficult it can't be learned by merely listening to a lecture. Such discussion requires and produces intellectual rigor. At the same time, students who take part in high quality discussions of controversial issues become more interested in and tolerant of views different from their own (p. 70).

Nelson (1996) states that classroom meetings model the democratic processes of cooperation, mutual respect and social interest.

EVIDENCE-BASED SUPPORT

Research on the effectiveness of classroom meetings is scant. Marandola and Imber (1979) implemented the classroom meeting using the Glasser model in a classroom with preadolescent boys identified as learning disabled and who exhibited disturbances in behavior. Results suggest positive change, but the authors of the study give caution to generalizing the results because the size of the study was small and also note certain conditions that may have influenced results such as the study participants had established a relationship with the teacher prior to the study. In an action research study Emmett and Monsour (1996) applied Glasser's techniques to classroom meetings with children in grades two through five. They found the techniques useful in teaching students the attitudes and skills needed for successful conflict resolution in the classroom. Sisco (1992) reported elementary students who participated in classroom meetings exhibited fewer referrals for disciplinary issues to the main office. In a later study, Feldhusen and Feldhusen (2004) studied the effects of the classroom meeting on students identified as gifted. The results suggest classroom management can be enhanced via weekly class meetings in which gifted and talented students have the opportunity to offer ideas, solutions and creative insights. Angell (2004) studied the minutes from classroom meetings held over two years in a private school and concluded that classroom meetings appeared to allow students the opportunity for collective problem solving in turn contributing to a peaceful classroom environment.

Because there does not exist a standardized format for the classroom meeting it is difficult to measure its effectiveness. Edwards and Mullis (2003), conducting their own study on the research on the effectiveness of classroom meetings, cite possible reasons for the lack of reliable data. Teachers who employ the classroom meeting tend to follow a variety of agendas, use classroom meetings for a variety of reasons and vary in the frequency of use. Frey and Doyle (2001) describe a model of the classroom meeting with the goal of developing elementary school children's communication and problem-solving skills. Leachman and Victor (2003) used the classroom meeting to tap into students' goals and interests, leading to student-led classroom meetings. In an online article, Knapp (2010) describes a process for developing classroom meetings school-wide for the prevention of bullying on the school campus.

PROCEDURE

A basic classroom meeting has four components:
1. A regular meeting time
2. A regular meeting location
3. An agenda
4. A circle for seating arrangement

The ideal time to meet is immediately before a release time such as recess or lunch, dismissal to another class or the end of the school day. This prevents the meeting from spilling into time scheduled for a lesson or an activity.

The location for the meeting should remain the same. This builds familiarity and predictability for the group. An agenda should be posted. The agenda should be short and fit into the time frame set aside for the meeting. The agenda should be developed by group members; i.e., items included in the agenda may be items requested by students. Sometimes group members may not want to discuss an issue in public – it may be too personal to a group member. That item may be discussed and resolved in private with the teacher of the counselor.

A critical element is the use of the circle in a classroom meeting. It may be tempting to hold the meeting with students seated in their usual seating arrangement and the facilitator in a central location. This arrangement is convenient and avoids the brief disorganization of moving furniture to accommodate a circle. But the typical seating arrangement defeats the purpose of the classroom meeting: to include all group members. In a circle every group member is visible and is included in the group process. It may be cumbersome to move furniture but, with continued practice, students will quickly learn to move furniture with little disturbance and time.

A basic meeting format has three components:
1. An opening
2. A time for discussion
3. A closing

The opening may be a greeting, reviewing group norms or reviewing the agenda for the meeting. The discussion centers around the agenda item(s) posted. The closing may be a review of the lesson, agreements made and announcements relevant to the group. The facilitator should develop and pre-teach norms prior to the initial meeting. Include students in their development and ensure that students know and understand the norms. Norms should number five or fewer. More than five norms become difficult to implement. Norms should be stated in positive terms, i.e., stated in terms of what group members should do rather than what they should not do: One person speaks at a time replaces No side conversations.

Box 19.1 Sample Classroom Meeting Norms
1.Respect others (the idea that no person is belittled)
2.Maintain confidentiality (all information discussed in the meeting remains in the meeting)
3.Freedom to pass (no one is pressured to speak)
4.One person speaks at a time

It is important to teach and rehearse group discussion skills such as taking turns speaking, how to address group participants, active listening, and how to respond when a group member disagrees.

These skills are basic to effective communication and help students develop a repertoire of responses useful in a variety of situations.

The initial meeting may be short: 15 or 20 minutes. This meeting allows students to experience the meeting without the pressure of having to participate. The first meeting will be the group participant's first experience with the norms and newly acquired skills. The facilitator will serve as a model of the norms and skills.

The counselor must include the teacher at each level of implementation. This includes determining the reason for the classroom meetings. The skills of unconditional acceptance, attention to nonverbal communication, active listening, open-ended questioning and group facilitation are the skills of the school-based family counselor and not necessarily part of a teacher's repertoire of responses. The school-based family counselor may collaborate with teachers to plan meetings or co lead them and serve as the model for the skills of facilitation.

It is critical to identify the purpose of the classroom meeting. A full curriculum, continuous assessment and regular meetings to address student achievement are all on the teacher's agenda, not group facilitation. The best time to implement the classroom meeting is at the start of school year. The classroom meeting can be used to build cohesion among students for successful classroom instruction. The school-based family counselor can serve as consultant to teachers to identify issues that need attention in order to prevent issues from developing, to intervene early in the year to prevent escalation and to identify students who may need intensive intervention outside the classroom.

Box 19.2 Common classroom meeting purposes
Develop classroom routines
Teach pro-social skills
Teasing/bullying prevention or intervention
Teach conflict resolution skills with subsequent application in a safe environment.
Solve classroom disagreements
Discuss issues relevant to students
Develop leadership skills

The counselor should begin with teachers who are willing to implement the classroom meeting. The meetings may be short term with a particular goal such as teaching conflict resolution skills or communication skills or long term with the goal of having students eventually take responsibility for and lead the meetings. Some teachers may want to hold regular meetings. In this case the counselor may initially lead meetings serving as a model with the teacher as co-leader. The counselor eventually cedes the role of lead facilitator to the teacher and may remain a short time as co-facilitator or leave altogether. The counselor's role changes at this point to that of a consultant. The counselor may meet with participating teachers to debrief, identify problem areas in facilitating meetings and propose solutions to address difficulties.

When working with teachers it is important for the counselor to help the teacher understand the purpose of the classroom meeting. The school-based family counselor's role would be to assist the teacher in understanding that his/her role changes from that of managing a class and serving as disciplinarian in order to avoid using the meeting time as a forum for discipline. Along the same line, as consultant, the counselor helps teachers become aware of their responses to student responses and suggestions during classroom meetings. It would be easy to respond, "No, we can't do that" to suggestions the teacher believes would be difficult to implement rather than facilitating discussion and problem-solving.

Middle school and high school contexts pose unique challenges for implementation. Multiple teachers, rigid bell schedules, inflexible groupings and even staff perception can be obstacles to the implementation of the classroom meeting. In the departmentalized setting staff may believe the classroom meeting to be appropriate for the elementary-aged child and ineffective for older youth. It is precisely at the middle school and high school levels that the classroom meeting can be most beneficial. The preteen/ teen years are a time of developing independence and students at these ages increasingly look to their peers for inclusion, guidance and acceptance. During the teen years students begin to form intimate relationships and need to have the skills necessary to develop empathy, the cornerstone of caring about others. The skills developed in the classroom meeting can help students develop and practice these skills in the context of the supportive environment of the classroom meeting. It is also in the classroom meeting that youth can rehearse the skills of constructive dialogue and deal with differing points of view. Older students serve as mentors and models to younger students and can model the skills acquired in the classroom meeting for their younger counterparts. Suggestions for implementation in the departmentalized setting include implementing the classroom meeting during a homeroom period, implementing during a History or Social Science class on a monthly basis or as part of a leadership class.

CASE STUDY

Albert is a 13-year, 8th-month old male in the 8th grade. He is the only child born to a Native American mother and a Hispanic father. His parents were never married to one another and do not live together. Both are college graduates. Albert's mother works in a charter school as an aide and his father works as a behavior intervention therapist for a private company. Albert lives with his mother and sees his father four or more times a week. Parenting has been inconsistent. While the parents agree they must teach Albert to "make choices", they overrule Albert's "choices" and punish through restriction, isolation, withdrawing of privileges and activities and occasional corporal punishment such as a slap on the cheek.

At school Albert is identified as a student with a learning disability and receives special education services in a special day class setting. He engages in attention-seeking behaviors such as tapping students on the shoulder and running away, drawing pictures on the work of his peers, repeatedly asking to use the restroom or get a drink of water when he sees his peers ask the same and taking items lying on the desk of another student without permission. On one occasion, Albert snatched the cap off the head of another student and ran away from the student. The owner reacted by pursuing Albert, and, upon reaching him, reclaimed the cap, grasped one side of Albert's head and pushed it against a wall, causing a scrape on the side that hit the wall. A week later, Albert was found in possession of a cell phone reported missing. He denied having taken the cell phone and claimed a classmate gave it to him, telling him to hold it in his backpack for him. The classmate denied the claim. A week subsequent to that Albert was seen by his physical education teacher in the teacher's office taking candy out of the teacher's cabinet and putting it in his backpack.

When confronted with these concerns Albert's parents reacted by denying the validity of the concerns, claiming unfair treatment of their son at hands of the site administrator. They stated their son is being bullied although Albert denies being bullied or harassed by others. An agreement and subsequent plan developed with the father, the site administrator and Albert to help Albert avoid contact with the student whose cap Albert grabbed was unilaterally cancelled by the mother who claimed her son had a "right" to be in the company of whomever he chose.

Albert stays in the school's afterschool program. One afternoon, when retrieved from the program by his parents and still on school grounds, Albert's father pushed Albert on the shoulder against a wall and the mother slapped Albert on the cheek. The incident was witnessed by three of Albert's classmates who reported the altercation to school personnel the following day.

Interventions to consider in the case of Albert's situation:

Family-Intervention:

Making a suspected child abuse report

Parent consultation to assist parents in addressing their feelings surrounding Albert's school behavior

Parent consultation to develop consistent parenting skills

Family counseling to address the stress of raising a child with a disability

School-Intervention

Student support for children whose parents are separated

Classroom meeting with Albert's class to develop skills to learn conflict resolution skill and communication skills

School-Prevention

Classroom meetings to develop cohesion and inclusiveness in the classroom

Family-Prevention

Parenting skills workshop for parents to provide information on parenting when the parents are separated

Following is a sample dialogue from one of a series of classroom meetings in an 8th grade special education special day class with the goal of helping Albert and his classmates develop communication and conflict resolution skills:

Facilitator: (reviewing notes from the previous meeting) "Last week the group agreed to practice asking before joining an individual or group in an activity. How did it go?"

(Silence).

Jason: "Albert won't leave me alone; I stay away from him but he follows me and never asks. I am trying to stay out of trouble."

Albert (shaking his head): "No, no, that's not true; I don't follow him."

Marco (to Albert): "I saw you."

Facilitator: "Jason, what do you want to say to Albert?"

Jason: "I want Albert to leave me alone."

Facilitator: "Tell Albert what you would like him to do if he wants to join you."

(Silence).

Marco: "Albert has to ask if he could be with us at lunch but he never asks."

Albert (shaking his head): "I ask."

Jason: "No you don't, you just come up to us and last time you started calling Andrew names and Andrew didn't do nothing to you. You never ask. You have to ask."

Albert: "I didn't call Andrew names."

Facilitator (to the group): "Let's help each other out. When anyone wants to join a group, what does the new person need to do?"

Chorus: "Ask to see if its ok to join the group."

Facilitator: "Albert, what do you need to do if you want to join any group?"

Albert: "Ask."

Facilitator: "Jason, tell Albert what you need from him if he wants to join your group."

Jason (looking at Albert): "You have to ask first and you can't call people names."
Albert (looking down): "I'll ask."
Seth: "I ask."
Tiffany: "Me too."
Facilitator(to the group): "How can you help each other out?"
Tiffany: "We could remind each other to ask like we practiced."

In this sample dialogue, the facilitator kept the conversation focused on the agreed-upon skill and facilitated dialogue that addressed the skill. Note that the facilitator avoided turning the subject to the accusation of Albert's name-calling. The facilitator further avoided having a third party make the request for Jason, developing the communication skill of making a direct request to fill a need. The facilitator also used the group dynamic to reinforce the skill thereby supporting all students in learning to apply the skill. The facilitator may privately discuss the name-calling accusation with Jason and Albert to determine whether intervention is required.

REFERENCES

Angell, A.V. (2005). Making peace in elementary classrooms: A case for class meetings. *Theory and Research in Social Education*, Vol. 32 Issue 1, p.98-104.

Bandura, A. (1969). *Principles of behavior modification*. New York: Holt, Rinehart and Winston.

Curran, K. (2003). Thinking hats in the classroom. *Primary and Middle Years Educator*, Vol 1, Issue 3, p.11-13.

Dreikurs, R. & Cassel, P. (1972). *Discipline without tears*. New York: Hawthorne Books.

Edwards, D. & Mullis, F. (2003). Classroom meetings: Encouraging a climate of cooperation. *Professional School Counseling*, Vol. 7 Issue 1, p.20-28.

Emmet, J.D. & Monsour, F. (1996). Open classroom meetings: Promoting peaceful schools. *Elementary School Guidance and Counseling*, Vol. 31 Issue 1, p.3-10.

Feldhusen, J. & Feldhusen, H. (2004). The room meeting for gifted and talented students in an inclusion classroom. *Gifted Child Today*, Vol. 27 Issue 2, p.54-57.

Frey, A. & Doyle, H.D. (2001). Classroom meetings: A program model. *Children and Schools*, Vol. 23, Issue 4, p.212.

Glasser,W. (1969). *Schools without failure*. New York: Harper and Row.

Glasser,W. (1988). *Choice theory in the classroom*. New York: Harper Perennial.

Glasser,W. (2000). School violence from the perspective of William Glasser. *Professional School Counseling*, Vol. 4 Issue 2, p.77-80.

Halaby, M.H. (2000*). Belonging*. Massachussets: Brookline Books, Inc.

Hess, D. (2011). Discussions that drive democracy. *Educational Leadership*, Vol. 69 Issue 1, p.69- 73.

Knapp, J.R. (2010). Bully prevention through classroom meetings. Retrieved from http://www.articlesbase.com/childhood-educationarticles.

Kriete, R. (2003). Start the day with community. *Educational Leadership*, Vol.61 Issue 1, p.68-70.

Leachman, G. & Victor, D. (2003). Student-led classroom meetings. *Educational Leadership*, Vol. 60 Issue 6, p.64-68.

Marandola, P. & Imber, S. (1979). Glasser's classroom meeting: A humanistic approach to behavior change with preadolescent inner-city learning disabled children. *Journal of Learning Disabilities*, Vol.12 Issue 6, p.30-35.

National Center for Education Statistics (2011). Indicators of school crime and safety (Data file). Retrieved from http://www.nces.ed.gov/programs/crimeindicators.

Nelson, J. (1996). *Positive discipline*: Revised Edition. New York: Ballentine Books.

Sisco, S.C. (1992).Using goal setting to enhance self-esteem and create an internal locus of control in the at-risk elementary student. (ERIC ED 355017), Master's dissertation, Nova University.

Walsh, I.D. & McCarroll, L. (1993).The future role of the school counselor. *The School Counselor*, Vol. 41, p.48-53.

White, J. (2009). Budget cuts will hurt students. Association of California School Administrators. Retrieved from http://www.acsa.org.

PART VII

SCHOOL-BASED FAMILY COUNSELING: SPECIFIC APPLICATIONS

A. FAMILY AND COMMUNITY FACTORS AFFECTING STUDENTS

Chapter 20
The Role of Parental Tolerance in Student Mental Health

Virginia Corina Samaniego

OVERVIEW: *The study of parent-child interaction from a social cognitive view and the analysis of the impact of parent-child interaction on the health of children is important because of its potential for intervention and prevention. This research contributes to an understanding of issues that lead to health or disease in childhood and provides evidence which aids the planning of interventions.*

BACKGROUND

There are many different approaches to mental health problems during childhood. An important approach to the study of problems in children is provided by the Psychopathology of Development. As described by Rutter & Garmezy (1983), inherent limitations in the current database make premature any effort to construct a comprehensive global theory of psychopathology of development. A single theory is unlikely to be appropriate to explain all forms of childhood psychopathology or account for all family and child influences. Still, Psychopathology of Development theory is a useful framework for conceptualizing and understanding the psychopathology of a child.

Seen as a macro paradigm that subsumes a wide range of theories, it has been defined as "the study of the origins and course of Individual patterns of behavioral maladaptation" (Sroufe & Rutter, 1984, p.36). That is, it provides a framework from which to understand both the normal development as well as its deviations of maladaptive behavior.Lewis (2000) considers that a third aspect should be added, the maladaptive processes. It also states that underlying the study of developmental psychopathology is the principle of prediction, since the possibility of predicting maladaptive behavior not only has been seen as possible but as an important aspect in the field of developmental psychopathology. Thus, Lewis proposed a more comprehensive definition: "Developmental psychopathology is the study and prediction of maladaptive behaviors and processes across time" (Lewis, 2000, pg. 3). It does not focus on the study of childhood disorders, but it promotes the understanding and treatment of childhood disorders through the study of a wide variation of processes and outcomes. This perspective emphasizes the place of cultural and social family factors in predicting and understanding development changes. The focus on developmental psychopathology is on the normal patterns of development, continuities and discontinuities in behavior, and transformational interactions at different periods of development that produce adaptive or maladaptive outcomes. That's why a central theme of this approach is that in order to understand maladaptive behavior it is necessary to view it in relation to what is considered normative for a given period of development (Edelbrock, 1984).

The other perspective that contributes to the study of childhood disorders and their origin, development, prevention and treatment is Epidemiology. Because many diagnostic categories of childhood disorders are very much alike and are not firmly based on population data, epidemiological studies are needed to determine how the hypothetical disorders are distributed. In the same manner, many referrals of children to mental health services are caused by problems that most children manifest at some point in their development. This is why it is essential that research contributes to differentiate the psychopathological aspects from normal development of children. Developmental Epidemiology can contribute to the field of study of developmental psychopathology (Costello & Angold, 2000) as an approach that can unravel and predict aspects of the course of pathologies in infancy. Among the factors and processes to study in this framework, it is important to identify those that expose children to the risk of suffering lasting behavior problems versus those that are limited in time and are due to aspects of development. Thus we speak of proximate factors affecting the quality of parent-child interaction, and such contextual factors that are in the wider environment (Olson, Ceballo & Park, 2002).

Socialization strategies of parents have long been associated with the early development of child psychopathology, but it is also commonly recognized that children play an equally active role in influencing their social contexts (Pardini, 2008). For many preschoolers, aggression, defiant behavior and other externalizing problems represent struggles with self-regulation in normal development, problems that diminish after early infancy (Campbell, Shaw & Gillion, 2000). However, in some cases these problems continue through infancy and adolescence (Moffit & Caspi, 2001) and have consequences for the psychosocial functioning of an adult (Fergusson, Horwood & Ridder, 2004). Internalizing problems (anxiety and depressed mood) in their own way are less commonly identified in young children but increase throughout childhood and be predictive of continuous adaptation problems in later infancy (Gazelle & Ladd, 2003). The origin of many mental disorders in adults can be found in behavioral characteristics present in the first years of life (Rutter, Kim-Cohen & Maugham, 2006).

In many research and clinical studies, there are references, mainly to mothers, reflecting on their role as primary caregivers and containing the assumption that they are more accurate in observing children's problems (Kerr, Lunkenheimer & Olson, 2007). As proposed in the literature, there are differences between the perceptions of fathers and mothers (Samaniego, 2008) . However, the study of parents in their relationship with children has been neglected despite researchers pointing this out many years ago and noting that this study may actually contribute to a better understanding of the problem. The discrepancies between parent perceptions may indicate a real variation in children's behavior in different relational circumstances (Kerr, Lunkenheimer & Olson, 2007).

On the other hand there is agreement that families affect the development of children. The theoretical basis of this assumption, however, has evolved over time with a growing recognition that children live in complex and multi-determined environments (Bronfenbrenner, 1987). Prior to 1960 when major psychiatrists began to include families in the psychotherapy, there was little consideration given to the functioning of the family when a child was seen as a patient. When it began to be included, many times the family was considered only with respect to the mother-child relationship, and problems in children were viewed as the result of deficiencies in the mother. In many cases these conclusions were based on speculations rather than in direct observation of parent-child interactions (Fiese, Wilder & Bickman, 2000). Later, various researchers proposed interactive models of family dynamics where both the effect of parents on each other, and on the child, and the effect of a child on the parents, have been studied (Belsky, 1984).Due to methodological limitations, the researchers generally studied the individuals or dyads within families. However, many family theorists will argue that a family as a system has an identity and characteristic styles that are different than the sum of its parts. From that point, proposals have emerged to investigate the whole family as a system (Olson, Sprenkle & Russell, 1979). However, as described by Fiese et al. (2000), although there have been repeated calls to expand the scope of studies of development beyond dyads, family context remains an understudied area in the framework of developmental psychopathology. This area deserves more thorough investigation whenever studies have found the family to be associated with behavioral and emotional problems in boys and girls (Kroneman, Loeber, Hipwell & Koot, 2009).

As Petit and Arsiwalla state (2008) many efforts were made in the 1990s to develop conceptual models and to prove in a systematic way the bidirectionality in interactions and relationships between parents and children through a range of contexts and generate empirical evidence that supports these models. Theoretical models of social development changed into transactional and contextual ones, not focusing on who is affecting who, but rather focusing on the continuous dynamic (and bidirectional) interactions of the child with the family and social context. Sameroff's foundational contribution was pivotal in drawing attention towards more complex forms of transactions. Among the most cited models of transactional effects in the development of behavior problems in children we find the coercion model of Patterson and his colleagues (Patterson et al., 1992).

Several studies of cognitive processes suggest that parents that suffer certain problems conceptualize the behavior of their children in a way that undermines an effective parent-child interaction. It has been seen that parents with specific problems (for example: abusive parents, depressive parents, and parents of hyperactive children) have more negative expectations of their children and make more negative attributions for their behavior than parents of a normal population (Miller, 1995; Dix & Lochman, 1990). It has been found that abusive mothers judged negative behaviors of their own children as more internal and stable than negative behaviors of other children. This was exactly the opposite pattern for mothers in the control group (Miller, 1995). In addition, in comparison to the mothers control group, abusive mothers viewed positive behaviors of their children as more external and unstable (Larrance & Twentyman, 1983).

Most of the studies on bi-directionality are based on descriptive interpretations of parenting (Strassberg, 1997; Combs-Ronto et.al, 2009; Pardini, 2008; Pettit & Arsiwalla, 2008). However, other explanations have invoked models based on inferential interpretations as attributions that parents make about their children's behavior. Attributions constitute only one of a great variety of parental cognitions that have been studied, but the emphasis given to them is mainly because they provide a theoretical foundation and not only an empirical one as it happens with studies based on judgments. Early perceptions that parents make during the development of their children's skills influence the casual attributions they make about the child's performance later in the child's development (Miller, 1995). Dix and Cols (1986) noted that the assessments made by parents about their children's behaviors are linked to the degree of development of their children. As the child grows, parents think that behaviors are more caused by the child's personality and are more intentional and under the control of the child. Furthermore, the emotional reactions of parents towards bad behaviors are commonly related to their assessment of the cause of that behavior and become more negative as children get older.In contrast, positive emotion is not related to the attributions made to the child's positive behavior. The parents' attributions for their children's behavior is an important determinant in their emotional responses, which then mediate their behavioral reactions towards the child. If parents' attributions towards negative behaviors of their children are relatively internal, stable, and controllable, it is more likely that these attributions will lead to negative parental affective responses and to negative parental behaviors (Dix & Grusec, 1985). This emphasis on emotion as a mediator between attribution and response, derived from the cognitive-emotional model of Weiner (1980), has been supported by several studies (Bugental, Blue & Cruzcosa, 1989; Weiner, 1980). Dix & Lochman (1990) studied the reactions of parents to children's negative behaviors and found support for the hypothesis that attributions mediate the mothers' reactions through their effects upon the mothers' emotions.

There is an extensive literature that links child behavioral problems to severe discipline and negative attributions of mothers towards the behavior of a child (Dix & Lochman, 1990; Dix et al., 1989; Smith & O'leary, 1995; Strassberg, 1995, 1997; Wilson, Gardner, Burton& Leung, 2007)). This gives support to the existence of a processing trap in which the mother's negative attributions lead to the use of harsh discipline, which triggers the aversive behavior of a child, which consequently validates the attributions made by the mother (Snarr, Strassberg & Smith Slep, 2003). A central theoretical cognitive premise states that affective and behavioral reactions in close relationships are determined not only by the behavior of others but also, in a matter that is equally important, of how the behavior is cognitively processed (Baron & Byrne, 1998). These conceptualizations support the construct of parental tolerance understood as a structure of attributions, parenting styles and emotions that arise in the interaction with the child. It is considered that the attributes are only part of that interaction and that the mechanism turns out to be more complex.

There have been empirical studies that support the existence of the construct parental tolerance and which used a scale to investigate its presence and particular characteristics (Samaniego, 2004, 2010). The developed scale included certain dimensions such as dispositional attribution, intent, attribution of responsibility, affection- anger, affection- anxiety, expectation of resistance, strength in parenting style, verbosity, laxness and over-reactivity. This gave rise to three factors called: a) reactive affective behavior: which concentrates anger emotions , anxiety and behavior corresponding to a reactive parenting style b) attributive limit setting: involves setting limits when intentionality is identified in a child and, c) attributive: when there is a presence of intentionality , responsibility and dispositional attributions (Samaniego, 2010). Subsequent studies established that parental tolerance appears to be different according to the social position of families. We found that mothers with less education have lower levels of parental tolerance, taking the level of education of the mother as an indicator of the socioeconomic status of the family. The tolerance of these parents / mothers is also lower for boys than for girls. Finally and most importantly, parental tolerance was the most predictive variable of a higher degree of behavioral and emotional problems in children. The association found of parental tolerance with the degree of behavioral problems was even higher when considering the so-called externalizing problems (Samaniego, 2004). Since it was found that parental tolerance was the best predictor of the appearance of behavioral and emotional problems in children, it was necessary to inquire whether this tolerance was modified over time and what consequences this had on the mental health of children. In the study made, no changes were observed regarding the monitoring of parental tolerance. It was established that the construct turns out to be stable over time and that can be considered much a trait than a state (Samaniego, 2012).

In order to evaluate the relationship between the degree of behavioral problems and parental tolerance, multiple regression analyses were carried out, and it was found that the variable that best predicts the degree of problems in children is the previous level of severity of problems as well as parental tolerance as in other studies. (Berden, Althaus &Verhulst, 1990; Samaniego, 2005). The new contribution lies in that the nearest level of problems turns to be the best predictor of problems and that this influence decreases over time.

In the case of tolerance it is interesting to point out that what influences the occurrence of problems is the degree of synchronic tolerance with the symptoms. This suggests that what influences the appearance of child pathology is the interplay between the symptoms in the child and the reaction-tolerance in the parents dealing with these symptoms, possibly providing feedback to the circuit (Samaniego, 2012). This reinforces the idea of entrapment process (Snarr, 2003) and the possible occurrence of reciprocal causal influences and of self maintenance suggested by Bugental (1987).

The contributions of this study of parent-child interaction from a social cognitive point of view and the analysis of its consequences on the health of children are important for prevention and intervention. This provides evidence that assists the planning of interventions that temper the effects of negative influences on child mental health by intervening in parental psychological variables that mediates the appearance of child pathology.

RELATIONSHIP TO THE SBFC MODEL

Parental tolerance is an aspect present in parent-child interaction which may lead, together with other factors, to the presence of more symptomatology in children affecting their mental health. This is why it is necessary to work with the family and with parents on what to expect from their children regarding developmentally normal behavior. This is especially important for younger parents or parents with fewer children. These parents do not have previous experience and that may lead them to ignore the evolutionary aspects of development and thus being able to discriminate what is right, and what isn't, for the child's age. As a result, and particularly when exacerbated by stress, the parent may develop low parental tolerance for the child's behavior that can become a stable trait. School-based family counselors can play a critical role in helping to educate parents through parent education workshops held at school where the frame of reference is an educational one. This is an important SBFC family-prevention function that can promote parental tolerance by educating parents on what is developmentally normal behavior for children and by helping parents to understand how low parental tolerance can promote negative child behavior.

MULTICULTURAL COUNSELING CONSIDERATIONS

As multicultural considerations, it has been widely established that culture plays an important role in the socialization of children. In that sense, authors have developed parental ethnotheories which relate to knowledge and beliefs about the domain of parenting (Harkness and Super, 1995). Keller and colleagues (2007, cited on Berry, Poortinga, Breugelmans, Chasiotis & Sam, 2011), bringing evidence about the impact of these theories on eco-cultural contexts, found differences among mothers coming from different societies. They stated that mothers belonging to societies where there is a greater emphasis in the independent interpretation of the self focused on the autonomy and independence of the child while mothers in societies where the weight is more on a dependent self- construal pay more attention in relational aspects. Based on these and other examples Berry and colleagues (2011) concluded that different developmental features are included in the conceptualization of parental ethno-theories. The ones that we'd like to stand out are that, in the first place, parents do not only watch their own children but the ones in their same social environment, and then that "parents likely reflect the standards and expectations of the cultural environment they live in, not only in their treatment of children, but also in their perceptions"(p.51).

Articulating these ideas to the parental tolerance concept, we can assume that it will vary in each society considering that the content that will trigger the tolerance, namely expectations regarding the behavior of the children, will be different in each society so the parental response will be different as well. These aspects of socialization and the consequences in the children mental health remains essential taking into account that mainly mothers, female relatives or daughters are still the primary caregivers of children, and paternal care is comparatively uncommon as data coming from 189 cultures reveal (Berry, Poortinga, Breugelmans, Chasiotis & Sam, 2011).

SUMMARY

The challenge to include parental tolerance as one of the aspects to consider in relation to the development of psychopathology in children is to introduce the interactionist perspective between child and parents, not focusing on one or the other but emphasizing the development of the child in interaction. The SBFC approach has its theoretical basis in models that address the family situation so that the inclusion of parental tolerance as an SBFC goal is highly relevant.

REFERENCES

Baron, R. & Byrne, D. (1998). Psicología Social [*Social psychology*], (Eighth Edition), Madrid: Prentice Hall.

Belsky, J. (1984). The determinants of parenting: A process model, *Child Development*, 55, 83-96.

Berden G.F., Althaus M & Verhulst F. (1990) Major life events and change sin the behavioral functioning of children. *Journal of Child Psychology and Psychiatry,* 31, 6: 949-959.

Berry, J., Poortinga, Y., Breugelmans, S., Chasiotis, A. & Sam, D. (2011) *Cross-Cultural Psychology. Research and Applications,* Third edition. New York: Cambridge University Press.

Bronfenbrenner, U. (1987). *The ecology of human development*, Buenos Aires: Paidos.

Bugental, D.B.; Blue, J & Cruzcosa, M. (1989) Perceived control over caregiving outcomes: Implications for child abuse. *Developmental Psychology*, 25, 532-539

Combs-Ronto, L.A., Olson, S., Lunkenheimer, E. & Sameroff, A. (2009). Interactions between maternal parenting and children´s early disruptive behavior: bidirectional associations across the transition from preschool to school entry. *Journal of Abnormal Child Psychology,* 37, 1151-1163

Campbell, S.B., Shaw, D.S. & Gillion, M. (2000) Early externalizing behavior problems: Toddlers and preschoolers at risk for later maladjustment. *Development and Psychopathology*, 12, 467-488

Costello E. & Angold, A. (2000). Developmental epidemiology. A framework for developmental psychopathology. In A. Sameroff, M. Lewis & S. Miller (Eds.). *Handbook of developmental psychopathology* (Second Edition, pp. 57-73). New York: Springer.

Dix .T & Grusec, J (1985). Parent attribution processes in the socialization of children. In Siegel, I (ed.) *Parental beliefs systems*, (p. 201-233), Hillsdale NJ: Erlbaum.

Dix, T.; Ruble, D.N.; Grusec, J.E. & Nixon, S. (1986) Social cognition in parents. Inferential and affective reactions to children of three age levels. *Child Development*, 57, 879-894.

Dix, T.; Ruble, D.N. & Zambarano, R.J. (1989) Mother´s implicit theories of discipline: child effects, parent effects and the attribution process. *Child Development*, 60, 1373-1391.

Dix, T. & Lochman, J. E. (1990). Social cognition and negative reactions to children: A comparison of mothers of aggressive and nonaggressive boys. *Journal of Social & Clinical Psychology*, 9, 4, 418-438.

Edelbrock, C. (1984). Developmental considerations in Ollendick,*T. (ed.) Child Behavioral Assessment: principles and procedures*. New York: Pergamon Press.

Fergusson, D.M., Horwood, L.J. & Ridder E.M. (2004) Show me the child at seven: The consequences of conduct problems in childhood for psychosocial functioning in adulthood. *Journal of Child Psychology and Psychiatry,* 45, 1-13

Fiese, B., Wilder, J. & Bickman, N. (2000). Family context in developmental psychopathology, In Sameroff, M. Lewis & S. Miller (eds.), (pg. 115-134), *Handbook of developmental psychopathology*. New York: Springer.

Gazelle, H. & Ladd, G.W. (2003). Anxious solitude and peer exclusion: a diathesis-stress model on internalizing trajectories in childhood. *Child Development*, 74, 257-278.

Harkness, S. and Super, C.H. (eds.) (1995). *Parents' cultural belief systems: Their origins, expressions, and consequences.* New York: Guilford Press

Kerr, D., Lukenheimer, E. & Olson, S. (2007.) Assessment of child problem behaviors by multiple informants: a longitudinal study from preschool to school entry. *Journal of Child Psychology and Psychiatry*, 48, 967-975.

Kroneman, L., Loeber, R., Hipwell, A & Koot, H. (2009) Girls' disruptive behavior and its relationship to family functioning: a review. *Journal of Child and Family Studies*, 18, 259-273.

Lewis, M. (2000). Toward a development of psychopathology. Models, definitions and prediction. In A. Sameroff, M. Lewis & S. Miller (eds.). *Handbook of developmental psychopathology*, (2nd edition, pg. 3-22). New York: Springer.

Mash, E. & Dozois, D.(1996). Child psychopathology: A developmental systems perspective. In Mash, E. & Barkley, R. (eds.), *Child psychopathology*. New York: The Guildford Press.

Miller, S. A. (1995). Parents' attributions for their children's behavior. *Child Development*, 66, 1557-1584.

Moffit, T.E. & Caspi, A. (2001) Childhood predictors differentiate life course persistent and adolescence limited antisocial pathways among males and females. *Development and Psychopathology*, 13, 355-375.

Olson, D.H., Sprenkle, D.H. & Russell, (1979) Circumplex Model of marital and family systems I. Cohesion and adaptability dimensions, family types and clinical applications. *Family Process*, 18, 3-28

Olson, S.L., Ceballo, R. & Park, C. (2002) Early problem behavior among children from low income, mother- headed families: a multiple risk perspective. *Journal of Clinical Child and Adolescent Psychology*, 31, 419-430.

Pardini D. (2008) Novel insights into longstanding theories of bidirectional parent-child influences: Introduction to the special section. *Journal of Abnormal Child Psychology, 36*, 627-631.

Patterson, G.R. (2002). The early development of coercive family process. In J.B. Reid, G.R. Patterson & J.J. Snyder (eds.). *Antisocial behavior in children and adolescents: a developmental analysis and the Oregon model for intervention*. (pg. 25-44) Washington: APA.

Pettit, G. S. & Arsiwalla, D.D. (2008). Commentary on special Section on "Bidirectional parent-child relationships": the continuing evolution of dynamic, transactional models of parenting and youth behavior problems. *Journal of Abnormal Child Psychology, 36*, 711-718.

Rutter M & Garmezy N (1983) Developmental psychopathology In P. Mussen & Hetherington *Handbook of child psychology, Vol. 4: Socialization, personality and social development* (4th edition), (pp 775-911). New York: Wiley.

Rutter, M., Kim-Cohen, J. & Maugham, B. (2006). Continuities and discontinuities in psychopathology between childhood and adult life. *Journal of Child Psychology and Psychiatry, 47*, 276-295.

Samaniego, V.C. (2004). Parental tolerance towards child behavior: mediating factor? Unpublished Doctoral Dissertation, Universidad de Buenos Aires. Buenos Aires, Argentina.

Samaniego, V.C. (2005) Problemas comportamentales y sucesos de vida en niños de 6 a 11 años de edad. [Behavioral problems and life events in 6 to 11 years old children]. *Revista Psykhe*, 14, 2, 97-108.

Samaniego, V.C. (2008). El Child Behavior Checklist: Su Estandarización En Población Urbana Argentina. [The Child Behavior Checklist: its standardization in Argentine urban population] *Revista de Psicología .Pontificia Universidad Católica Argentina. 4 ,113-130*

Samaniego, V.C. (2010). Escala de Tolerancia parental hacia los comportamientos infantiles, elaboración y validación. [Parental tolerance scale towards infant behavior, building and validation]. *Revista Latinoamericana de Psicología*, 42 (2), 203-214.

Samaniego, V. C. (2012, july) *Parental Tolerance And Behavior And Emotional Problems In Children, A Cohort Study.* Paper presented at the 30th International Congress Of Psychology. Psychology Serving Humanity. Cape Town, South Africa.

Smith, A. M., & O'Leary, S. G. (1995). Attributions and arousal as predictors of maternal discipline. *Cognitive Therapy and Research*, 19, 459-471.

Snarr, J.D., Strassberg, Z. & Smith Slep, A. (2003) Making faces: testing the relation between child behavior problems and mother's interpretations of child emotion expressions. *Journal of Abnormal Child Psychology,* 31, 371-380.

Strassberg, Z. (1995). Social information processing in compliance situations by the mothers of behavior-problem boys. *Child Development*, 66, 376-389.

Strassberg, Z (1997). Levels of analysis in cognitive bases of maternal disciplinary dysfunction. *Journal of Abnormal Child Psychology,* 25, 3, 209.

Weiner, B. (1980) A cognition (attribution)-emotion-action model of motivated behavior: An analysis of judgments of help giving. *Journal of Personality and Social Psychology*, 39, 186-200.

Wilson, C., Gardner, F., Burton, J. & Leung, S. (2007) Maternal attributions and observed maternal behavior: are they linked? *Behavioral & Cognitive Psychotherapy*, 35, 165-178

CHAPTER 21

Looking for "Home" in a Trans-national World: Migration and School-Based Family Counseling

Maria Marchetti-Mercer

OVERVIEW: The search for "home" and a place where we can "belong" are experiences commonly shared by most people and may play a significant role in their lives and relationships. In this chapter, I will argue that it may be useful for School-Based Family Counselors to recognize and acknowledge this human need to belong and feel at "home";as this may impact on different families' experiences in their social context. I will begin by exploring how these concepts are linked to identity and culture and discuss how the family plays a role in their formation. I will focus on the phenomenon of migration as an expression of these concerns and explore how the different migration trends observed in our globalized world have had an enormous socio-psychological impact on societies all over the world. These phenomena are likely to find expression in the context of schools with children from very different family and cultural backgrounds and where mental health professionals are called upon to address issues of diversity in a respectful and therapeutically effective manner. In conclusion I will put forth some suggestions on how a School-Based Family Counseling model may benefit from incorporating some of these ideas.

BACKGROUND

Where do we find "home"?

The search for what "home" is and where it is to be found has led to a large body of work from a number of disciplines such as sociology, anthropology, psychology, geography, history, architecture and philosophy. (Marchetti-Mercer, Hurlin&Prinsloo, 2008).

The English word "Home", and what it represents, does not easily translate into other languages. Giamatti (1989) argues that,

> … No translation catches the associations, the mixture of memory and longing,…the aroma of inclusiveness, of freedom from wariness, that cling to the word home…. Home is a concept, not a place, it is a state of mind where self-definition starts; it is origins-the mix of time and place and smell and weather wherein one first realizes one is an original, perhaps like others, especially those one loves, but discrete, distinct, not to be copied. Home …remains in the mind as a place where reunion, if it were ever to occur, would happen…. It is about restoration of the right relations among things-and going home is where the restoration occurs, because that is where it matters most (p. 254).

The concept of "nostàlgia'" is often used to try to capture this wistfulness and yearning, which finds its roots in the Greek "nostos", which means return or the return home, and "algos", which means pain or sorrow. It was originally used to describe a source of organic diseases and was coined in 1688 by Johannes Hefer. It now points to a yearning for something, which is absent or even lost, and which holds emotional significance for an individual (Rubenstein, 2001).

Turner (1957, 1976 in Magat, 1999) sees home as a folk concept, which is prevalent in human discourse, and which can be a structure, a feeling, a metaphor or a symbol. He argues that home can be anything from a trailer, to one's land of origin or even the universe. It may vary from person to person and it may change over the course of one's life. Most saliently it may in fact refer to where one wants to die and be buried and not just where one wants to live. It may function as a centre, which integrates past, present and future and may ultimately contain some reconciliation between those concerns that are immediate and those that are ultimate (Magat, 1999). Rubenstein (2001) sees home more as an emotional space rather than just a physical structure or a geographical location, and links it to some of our earliest psychological experiences which may have a ripple effect throughout the rest of our lives. This view therefore holds a strong idealized dimension evoking strong feelings of nostalgia for that which could have been or could still be. Because of this strong emotive component it may remain a powerful driving force in people's lives (Machetti-Mercer,2006)

We also observe this search for "home" in many great literary works including children's literature. The search for the Paradise, which was lost after the fall of man was depicted by Milton in his epic poem. This theme has subsequently permeated many realms of our thinking and mythology. Although Homer's Odyssey is probably one of the most famous literary expressions of the struggle to return home, Dante also explored the theme in the "Divine Comedy" in the Purgatorio Canto VII. The brothers Grimm had Hansel and Gretel go to great lengths in order to return home (Marchetti-Mercer, 2006).

Looking for "home" can also be seen as a search for meaning in order to achieve spiritual and psychological liberation. McGoldrick (in McGoldrick, 1998) writes," Home is a space where we could all belong, with each other-strengthened by what we take from those who have come before us, creating a safe haven for those who are with us in our time, and insuring that we leave a safe space for our children and all those who will come after us" (p.216). Maya Angelou who came to live in Africa as part of her own search for "home" writes of, "the ache for home (which) lives in all of us, the safe place where we can go as we are and not be questioned." (Angelou, 1986, p. 54). However, issues of class, gender and race may prevent the majority of people from ever experiencing "home" as a safe place.

Can this search for "home" ever come to a resolution? Although Thomas Wolfe has argued that, "you can never go home again"(in Rubenstein, 2001, p.2) family therapists who have focused on the importance of our family-of-origin such as Framo (1976) have argued quite strongly that you can and should go home again. DiNicola (1997) is of the opinion that we in fact never leave our home, but as a snail is bound to its shell, so we too carry our home with us wherever we go. This latter idea is reminiscent of the words of Paolo Friere (1994) who argues that," No one leaves his or her world without having been transfixed by its roots, or with a vacuum for a soul. We carry with us the memory of many fabrics, a self soaked in our history, our culture; a memory, sometimes scattered, sometimes sharp and clear, of the streets of our childhood"(p.32).

In conclusion it is evident that the definition of "home" is an intricate one, almost impossible to encapsulate in a word or verb and at times even difficult to define. On the one hand it carries the memories of our childhood, our connection to our family- of- origin and our cultural and ethnic roots or even a geographical place, while on the other hand the "longing for home" is also an idealised and abstract concept which contains a number of fantasies around resolution, the end of conflict and the yearning for a place of safety where we can truly belong. In the final analysis I believe that this concept will hold very different meanings for everyone as well as different cultures (Marchetti-Mercer, 2006).

THE SEARCH FOR IDENTITY

McGoldrick (1993) argues that our sense of personal and even cultural identity are closely linked to the concept of "home", while Magat (1999) also maintains that "home" can provide us with a center, which is the indispensable origin of our identity. The debate around the nature and scope of the concept of identity clearly reflects the tensions between modernist and postmodernist approaches and has been widely documented (Sampson, 1993). A modernist approach emphasizes a well-defined sense of self and identity, as set out for example in the work of Geertz (1979), while postmodern approaches see self and identity as being determined by social structures and processes. They also tend to explore the role that history and ideologies play as exemplified in the work of Foucault (1988; 1988). The self is then to be seen as a fluid concept, which is strongly influenced by social contexts and experiences.

A more postmodern stance invites us to view personal identity as being influenced by different levels of experience, as well as influencing our relationships with a number of contexts. Who we are, and how we define ourselves are both irrevocably linked to where we come from, where we find ourselves and where we may be going. Making sense of these different levels of experience is essential in order to allow us to develop a sense of our identity and find out where we truly belong. However this process should not merely aim to achieve a fixed and one-dimensional sense of identity, as this journey is strongly linked to our social and historical experiences. It should rather try to make sense of, and find meaning in, the many ambiguities and contradictions that often inform whom we are (Marchetti-Mercer, 2006). Native Americans believe that an individual can only find completion only in relation to other people and by respecting one's past as well as place (Rubenstein, 2001). This is an important acknowledgement of the significance of our roots, both physical and historical, as well as the role that other people play in shaping who we are (Marchetti-Mercer, 2006). One's family of origin is one of the most significant social experiences in this respect, and I will discuss this next.

THE ROLE OF THE FAMILY

The family in which we are born and which provides us with our first home, often referred to as the family-of-origin, provides us our first sense of who we are. This primary experience can also be closely linked to geographical entities such as the place where we were born and where we spent our childhood. This is unlikely to be a similar experience for all people. Some may have never known their parents, some might have left their place of birth before they could even remember it; for some images of family and home might be extremely nurturing and reassuring, while for others they may elicit images of neglect and abuse.

However, it cannot be denied that our families-of-origin remain a strong point of reference from whence we learn what it means to belong (and sometimes also to be different) and which impacts on the development of our own personal identity. It is after all where we first get a name and furthermore a surname or family name, which links us to people and generations that came long before us. It is also in the context of our families that we acquire much of what is known as culture, which is also an important contributor to personal identity (Marchetti-Mercer, 2006).

CULTURE AND FAMILIES

The debate around an appropriate definition of what culture is also very complex highlighting the tensions between modern and postmodern approaches. On the one hand it a definition of culture may appear very simple, as it so intrinsic to our daily experience and the world in which we live. On the other hand any choice of definition will reflect our epistemology and will be influenced by power and social discourses. However as Laird (1998) reminds us," we cannot escape culture; we can only try to meet it on its own terms"(p.30).

Postmodern thinkers reject the traditional idea of culture as a static and fixed concept without taking into consideration the strong social and historical elements that in fact influence and transform it. They criticize traditional views, which may disguise certain ideologies used to protect some groups' own rights and privileges at the expense of other "cultures". A fixed view of culture may also lead us to assume that people from a specific ethnic background are all similar in their values, norms and behaviors, and resulting in stereotyping. Alternatively a strong emphasis on universality also holds some dangers. Andolfi (personal communication, 6 July 2005) speaks of a "globalization of mind" as a way of denying differences, which has become almost an extreme form of political correctness in our time where everyone should be exactly the same. The phenomenon of globalization has increasingly taken away the peculiarities and richness of cultural heritage unique to different countries. The dilemma lies in the fact that in our world not all cultures are considered equal and the dominant (usually Western) culture can easily become something that can be exploited in order to emphasize difference rather than encouraging diversity (Laird, 1998). Seeking out universalities and commonalities may be a useful exercise in that it may the beginning of dialogue between different people and introduces a critical element to any belief that one has an absolute take on the 'one truth" but should not become a means to ignore differences between people. Falicov's (1995) approach may be useful where she stresses that it is important to understand how common human experiences are approached by diverse groups of people, rather than to think in terms of ethnic groups or entities.

Psychology and family therapy in particular have long been struggling with the issue of culture as it relates specifically to the therapeutic context and there is a large body of work in family therapy literature that reflects this debate (for example, Friedman, 1980; Montalvo & Gutierrez, 1983; McGoldrick, 1993) Typical questions are as follows, Do we need "special knowledge" of other cultures in order to work as therapists in multicultural contexts? Can a therapist or counselor from a certain cultural background ever prove to be effective with a family from a different background? Can we use our own ethical norms to judge behaviors that reflect values different from our own?

I would like to propose that we all have a sense of what the accepted cultural norms, in the context in which we grew up and in which we live, are. These may not be always useful later in life and we may not always agree with them, but they undeniably influence our behaviors in a specific social context. Therefore our family-of-origin plays a central role in our understanding of culture. Pare' (1995) views families" as storying cultures" (p.12). He bases this concept on the use of the word culture by Howard (1991) who defines it as," a community of individuals who see the world in a particular manner-who share particular interpretations as central to the meaning of their lives and action" (p.190) and consequently views the "family-as-culture."

Similarly DiNicola (1997) believes that the life of a family represents a private world, which has its own expressive language, its own symbols and rules. He also draws parallels between the structures and functions of the two systems of culture and family with regard to the role they play in the shaping, as well as the claims they lay with regard to the identity of an individual. As we develop a cultural identity so there is also a cultural costume that accompanies it. This cultural costume is made up of the sayings and the mythology from the larger community in which the family lives and which also defines that family's experience (DiNicola, 1997). Consequently once we move outside of our family-of-origin, we are effectively moving into a foreign "culture" (Marchetti-Mercer,2006).A further useful contribution by DiNicola (1997) when dealing with cultural diversity, is the idea of "curiosity," as opposed to mere tolerance as he believes that the latter will only keep us closed up in our own worlds (Andolfi, 1997, p.ix).

In summary I believe we should recognise the role that families play in the development of our cultural identity and engage in a process driven by curiosity aware of the fact that every other person, every other family, every other community contains an element of unfamiliarity which may be worth knowing and understanding (Marchetti-Mercer, 2006).The phenomenon of migration is a very interesting embodiment of these issues and I will explore it next.

THE PHENONEMON OF MIGRATION AND THE SEARCH FOR "HOME"

No one will experience a sense of not belonging as much as the immigrant or exile that has had to leave the country of his/her birth to settle in a new country and find a new "home". Emigration from one's country is life changing and existing literature indicates that emigrants face a number of intra- and interpersonal challenges before and after emigration (for example Ainslie, 1998; Berry 2001; Falicov, 2007; Glick, 2010; Sluzki, 1979).

The different types of migration as well as the various reasons behind the decision to emigrate are anything but homogenous and have changed dramatically in the past century. In the late 19th and early 20th centuries a lot of emigration took place from Europe to America, Canada, Australia, New Zealand and also South Africa often as a means to escape political or economic hardships. Today we see many different trends, which reflect the socio-political dimensions of our times. Falicov (2007) observes that post 1965 the main source of migration to the U.S has consisted primarily of Latinos, Afro-Caribbeans and Asians. These should be seen as "new immigrants or transnationals" (Falicov, 2007, p.158). From the 1980's we have also witnessed the phenomenon of refugees and asylum seekers as the main type of migration. It is perhaps an irony that Europe which must have exported the largest percentage of emigrants in the 19th and 20th century is fast becoming the main destination of many migrants in the form of both refugee and exile. In South Africa we have observed a constant flux of migration both pre-and post-apartheid often linked to specific political events.

In the past emigration meant a total cut off of emotional and family ties due to the difficulty in communication. Today with the technologies available it is much easier and accessible for people to keep in touch with their countries of origin and the people they have left behind (Falicov, 2007). Consequently the phenomenon of globalization has greatly influenced the movement of people across countries and continents and much is being written about the transnational experiences of people with connections and loyalties across countries(for example Glick Schiller, Basch& Blanc-Szanton, 1992; Westwood &Phizacklea, 2000, Falicov, 2005; 2007). Glick Schiller et al (1992) argue that the new type of migrating population which has come about possesses networks, activities and ways of life reflective of both their host and original countries. As a result of this, two societies are being brought into one a single social field with their lives cutting across national boundaries. "Professional transients" who move mostly because of work opportunities bring about economic change and new cultural values in the countries in which they work; as well as in their own countries of origin when they eventually return (Castles & Davidson, 2000).

This perspective leads to a situation where belonging to only one nation is no longer a universal phenomenon nor perhaps even a desirable position. Christiansen and Hedetoft (2004) believe that the reality of "multiple belonging" may in fact be found in the social, cultural and political lives of many people. Castles and Davidson (2000) also point out that we are seeing an erosion of the context for a citizenship which is based on belonging to a single nation and that we must redefine citizenship based on the concept of globalization (Marchetti-Mercer, 2006). The transnationalism made possible in a globalized world with advanced technologies and ways of connecting across nations may hold the possibility of "living with two hearts rather than with one divided heart"(Falicov,2005,p.399). However, as an inescapably ambiguous position, this is likely to create a sense of discomfort as one continues to look for "home." In the past undergoing a process of assimilation and acculturation were often regarded as the optimal outcome for immigrants, although the difference between the two may be seen as subtle (Gordon, 1964).LaFramboise, Coleman & Gerton (1993)define these two as follows:

ASSIMILATION

This view postulates that a person entering a new culture needs to be absorbed into the dominant culture. Until this has taken place and he or she perceives an acceptance into the new culture, he or she will suffer from a sense of alienation and isolation (Marchetti-Mercer&Roos, 2006). However this model, which appears to be the one that is more often than not advocated for successful integration into a new society, has not escaped criticism as it," assumes that migrants and minorities are refugees of some sort, for political or economic reasons, who gratefully give up their attachments to other places and other ways of being "in the words of DiNicola (p.11, 1997). Falicov (1998) also argues the fact that the necessity often placed on assimilation is more reflective of a certain ideology rather than an empirical inevitability and may reflect the receiving society's inability to tolerate difference.

ACCULTURATION

This view holds that through this process a person must become a competent participant in majority culture, but will always be identified as a member of the minority culture. This often is an involuntary process as a person has no choice but to follow this route, more often than not to survive economically (LaFramboise et al, 1993). Bhugra (2004) points out that acculturation can be seen in terms of behavior such as language, religion, entertainment, food and shopping habits. It may also include other areas such as cognitive style, behavioral patterns and attitudes.

Whilst acculturation was seen as a positive outcome for immigrants in a pluralistic society (Falicov,2005) some research looking at the relationship between mental health and immigration indicates that attachment to one's old culture may in fact be beneficial. For example Vega (1998)argues that maintaining one's traditional culture may serve as a "buffer" to the negative mental health impact due to immigration (Marchetti-Mercer & Roos, 2006). The experience of transnationalism may be linked to an Alternation model which describes the process whereby it is possible for a person to know and understand two different cultures (LaFramboise et al, 1993). This implies that old cultural meanings are retained while simultaneously new cultural modes are acquired (Falicov, 1998) and can possibly be perceived as enriching.

EVIDENCE-BASED SUPPORT

Family therapists have attempted to address the issues of "home" and "belonging" and emigration in a number of ways as well as providing ways in which to deal with therapeutic issues related to the relationship between an adult individual and his or her family-of-origin. Although family therapy should in no way be seen as a homogeneous discipline as reflected by the major theoretical differences between its exponents, yet all these approaches in a way are based on the underlying assumption that individual problems are to be understood in a contextual framework which allows for a much richer explanation of human behavior. The more recent postmodern approaches focus on the narrative nature of problems and tend to see family problems as "stories gone awry" (Howard, 1991,p.326) and therefore in need of re-writing or mending.

HOME AND FAMILY THERAPY

Jay Haley (1980) who was one of the most important pioneers in the field of strategic therapy wrote a whole book on the phenomenon of leaving home describing the family dynamics at play during the sensitive transition of the adolescent leaving home. Murray Bowen (1978) provides some far reaching insights on the relationship between the individual and his/her family and has described the process that each person must go through when leaving the parental home in depth. He looks at achieving a balance between the experiences of belonging as opposed to separation and describes the goal of adult development to be individuation from one's family-of- origin, and becoming a differentiated individual.

Framo (1976) in his significant contributions to the field of intergenerational therapy argues very poignantly that one, "can and should go home again"(p.193) and believes that many marital and family difficulties are the manifestation of relationship problems of the spouses' families- of- origin. If members of a marital couple are able to go back to deal directly with past and present issues in their own families-of-origin there is a possibility for change to take place in their present times. Going back home can therefore be seen as a resolution of family-of-origin issues that have not been addressed.

These perspectives highlight the fact that ignoring one's own history is not possible as it is part of who we are and attempting to bury it may in fact make it more powerful (McGoldrick, 1999). However all the theories emphasize a process of moving away, or differentiating from, one's home. One could ask whether this emphasis on differentiation, while trying to stay connected, is not more of a Western concern and reflective of a very individualistic culture and not truly of relevance to other cultures. In general non-Western cultures and societies tend to value a more communal sense of identity, which reflect a tendency towards, "We are therefore, I am" (McGoldrick, 1993, p.335). The same spirit is reflected in the concept of ubuntu, which is a term used in several African languages and which in essence refers to the fact that one's humanity is affirmed by recognizing the humanity of others and establishing respectful human relations with them. One is therefore a person through other persons (Ramose, 1999). This once again highlights the fact that the need for "belonging" may differ for different people and communities (Marchetti-Mercer, 2006).

MIGRATION AND FAMILY THERAPY

Carlos Sluzkihas made a number of important contributions to our understanding of the impact of emigration on family life and wrote a seminal paper "Migration and family life" published in 1979 where he describes in great detail the processes and phases that a family goes through prior, during and post migration. More recently Celia Falicov has explored the transnational experience of emigrants (see Falicov, 2005; 2007). She argues very saliently that "Transnational lifestyles present theoretical and therapeutic challenges that demand new analytic frames for understanding family relationship and devising interventions. Work with immigrants requires a better integration of cultural and socio-political approaches with foundational aspects of the family therapy field "(Falicov, 2007, p.158).

Consequently she has proposed a specific model to address this, called the Multidimensional Ecosystemic Comparative Approach (MECA). This model highlights aspects of migration/acculturation, ecological context, family life cycle and family organization. Falicov (2007) is of the belief that when working with migrants there are three so-called contexts of living that must be taken into consideration, namely a) the relational, b) the community and c) the cultural-sociopolitical.

a) The relational context: According to Falicov (2007) the process of migration is likely to impact the relational context of the individual and family in a number of ways. Firstly a new definition of family life iss required. Secondly the family is likely to experience some form of relational stress which may already have started prior to emigration; and lastly some type of so-called acculturative stress is likely to be experienced in gender and generational relationships once the family arrives in the new country (Falicov, 2007).

b) The community context: A "loss of social capital "(Falicov, 2007, p.164) is likely to be experienced when the family moves from one country to another.The availability of technology allows transnationals the opportunity to rebuild this over time either through real or virtual spaces; whilst connections to the community left behind are more possible. Falicov (2007) further argues that to cope with this immigrants are likely to rebuild their ethnic community networks in their countries of destination. Connections to such community networks have been shown to correlate highly with mental health (Vega, Kolody, Valle & Weir, 1991).

c) The cultural-sociopolitical context: In the past two decades family therapy has increasingly focused on issues of cultural diversity as well as taking on a more socio-political frame. This is likely to be as a result of the more postmodern and critical approaches that have developed in the greater field of Psychology. Falicov's (2007) definition of what constitutes cultural diversity is very comprehensive, namely, "Cultural diversity is concerned with honoring (own highlighting) difference in values, beliefs, and meaning systems based on ethnicity, religion, occupation, political ideology, or other value-based and meaning-imparting contexts. They bring with them many complex and diverse values in relation to gender, parenting, and religious practices that provide crucial psychological and practical resources. Values may also pose constraints in their original cultures or in contact with the new culture" (p.166). This awareness of cultural diversity is meant to encourage therapists to look beyond their own accepted ways of practice questioning their own prejudices and stereotypes as they acquire more cultural competence (Falicov, 2007).

In addition a socio-political approach would be cognizant of the type of racism and discrimination that immigrants are likely to experience in a new country as well as the power differences and differential access to resources; these are likely to have a strong impact on the physical and mental health of immigrant families (Falicov, 2007).

MULTICULTURAL COUNSELING CONSIDERATIONS

Sue (in Pedersen & Carey, 2003) is concerned that although there seem to be a number of works on multicultural counseling and psychotherapy, there seem to be few relevant texts specifically on multicultural school counseling. Canada, Allen Heath, Money, Annandale, Fischer and Young (2007) argue that one of the challenges in, "providing effective counseling services sensitive to the context of diverse backgrounds requires an understanding of what diversity is and how diversity impacts student and family perceptions "(p.13).

I would like to return to Falicov's (2007) definition, namely, "Cultural diversity is concerned with honoring (own emphasis) differences in values, beliefs, and meaning systems based on ethnicity, religion, occupation, political ideology, or other value-base and meaning-imparting contexts"(Falicov, 2007, p.166) as I believe it provides one with an useful approach towards this dilemma as well as DiNicola's (1997) idea of "curiosity" when dealing with cultural diversity. Both these attitudes imply a respectful attitude towards difference and provide us with a conceptual framework when counseling within a multicultural context.

RELATIONSHIP TO THE SCHOOL BASED FAMILY COUNSELING MODEL

As an approach committed to understanding the complex relationship between school and family, it is important for School-based Family Counseling to take cognizance of the issues of diversity and multiculturalism which are so often linked to migration and transnationalism. It is in an ideal position to do so because its basic premise is that it is important to work with children in the context of family, school, peer and community systems using a family systems theoretical orientation (Gerrard, 1996).

With the background of the previous discussion in mind it is clear that issues of "home", belonging, culture and identity have a deep impact on individuals and their families. This becomes even more evident in increasingly multicultural societies deeply affected by the processes of migration. These processes will necessarily be at play in a school context, which is after all a microcosm of larger society.

FAMILY PREVENTION/INTERVENTION

As discussed earlier it is in the context of the family that norms and values closely linked to culture are acquired. The individual child in a school context is very much a product of that family, on the one hand with its own idiosyncratic culture as defined by DiNicola (1997); as well as a representative of a larger community from which the family comes and in which it resides. If the family comes from a culture which is more collectivistic, where group harmony, obedience and hierarchical relationships are valued over individual needs this may also be problematic in the more individualistic Western societies increasing the potential for intergenerational conflict as children absorb the new values especially in the school and peer context.

Families may be faced with the dilemma that they may want to encourage their children to acculturate quickly as this may lead to more success (for example academic performance, successful peer relationships, quick acquisition of the new language) while knowing that by acquiring the new culture this will mean loss of the original culture (for example loss of the mother tongue). The potential for conflict may be even higher during the period of adolescence where the potential for conflict between parents and children is already high (Hynie, 2006).

Children may become frustrated with the parents' lack of knowledge of the new culture, and may feel that they are in fact better able to navigate the new culture than their parents. This may lead to a situation where children feel that parents cannot provide them with adequate role modeling and may lead to further conflict and further alienation between the two (Hynie,2006). Stone et al (2005) however argue that in a family system where "transnationalism" is embraced the possibility of conflict between the two generations may be reduced. Children may regard their parents as "worthy carriers" of cultural knowledge from the country of origin. This might eliminate the conflict between those who are stuck in the past (the parents) and those who have adapted to the present (the children) (Marchetti-Mercer, 2009). It may also be useful to take note of the kind of the kind of stress that migrant families are likely to experience as described by writers such as Sluzki (1979) and Falicov (2007).

SCHOOL PREVENTION/INTERVENTION

Children who come from families outside the dominant cultural group have to become knowledgeable in the norms and accepted behaviors of the dominant culture. The school more often than not also represents the dominant culture and when looking at the functioning of the child within in this context it is important to consider whether it represents a place where the child feels at "home" and can belong or whether it is a place where the child feels alienated.

Adolescents are particularly at risk as peers and peer acceptance are highly valued. "Fitting in" and "belonging" are two very important needs experienced by adolescents. Consequently having to enter a new school system feeling different, while not perhaps being able to speak the local language and not understanding the accepted ways of behaving may be very traumatic for an adolescent (Marchetti-Mercer &Roos, 2006). Grinberg and Grinberg (1989) point out that during adolescence the effects of migration will be mostly seen in the school environment where the youth has to find and carve out a place for himself or herself.

This may result in children assimilate into the dominant culture much more quickly than adults as discussed earlier. This can be ascribed to a number of reasons amongst which the fact that being younger children are more flexible and adaptable but also that they do not want to stand out as different especially during the time of adolescence when children are particularly sensitive to the influence of the peer group.

The peer group probably provides the most important social context within which the child operates and which itself exhibits a very particular "culture." Research done in the U.S. following the Columbine school shooting highlighted the fact that there are very specific social groupings or a hierarchy of cliques in American high schools (Aronson, 2000). These are not necessarily inked to ethnic background, but it is easy for children to connect more to others from similar cultural backgrounds especially if the larger peer group is experienced as unwelcoming and hostile and if they once again feel they do not "belong". The impact of being an "outsider" during this developmental period may be enormous and receive serious attention.

COMMUNITY PREVENTION

It is especially at this level that we find specific cultural expressions of diversity as well an overall approach of how diversity is approached. If at a social level the child and the family are struggling with "belonging" and feeling at "home" these issues will have a great impact on their functioning and experiences within the school system. The family may also view with suspicion counselors who come from a different cultural background fearing prejudice and misunderstanding especially when language also becomes an issue. The experience of transnational families may be one of being torn between still being linked to the country of origin either virtually or by connecting to local ethnic communities as well as trying to integrate into the larger dominant receiving community.

Falicov (2007) is of the belief that communities can offer resources but they also can also provide problems such as gangs to other types of polarizations. A social-political sensitivity, which takes cognizance of the larger social discourses that may be at play in the communities in which the child and the family operate may be of great use in considering community aspects.

CHALLENGES AND SOLUTIONS

I believe that an awareness of the fact that people's experience of their world may differ greatly from ours, depending on the family, the community and the culture they come from and may have a large impact on the therapeutic process, is essential. In this respect some understanding and knowledge of the accepted norms and values associated with a specific ethnic group may be useful. It may also be useful to engage specifically with migrant families in a way that takes cognizance of the large body of work that exists on the impact on family life of migration and of the kinds of processes that people who migrate experience.

Furthermore I am also of the belief that one should enter any therapeutic relationship following a respectful position of curiosity as set out by DiNicola (1997) and "honoring" (Falicov, 2007) those differences that make us unique. This does not mean that we deny the professional training and "expertise" we carry with us, but rather that we never hope to fully know or understand the person in front of us before they have shared their story with us. Therefore multicultural competency is something that can only be hoped to be acquired as one engages in the therapeutic process and not merely from a textbook on diversity and counseling. Auerswald (1972) spoke of therapists having to be "non-blaming ecological detectives" (quoted in Falicov, 2007) and these words still hold true today as we attempt to make sense of the very complex world in which we find ourselves.

SUMMARY

In this chapter I have argued that it is important to acknowledge the importance of "home" in people's lives; as well as the fact that its meaning may vary greatly from person to person, from family to family and from culture to culture. It is important for SBF counselors to recognize this need to belong in people's lives in the context of the therapeutic encounter. Consequently a SBFC model should be sensitive to the fact that issues of belonging are becoming increasingly relevant in our globalized world where more people live transnational which impact significantly on their immediate experience of their world.

REFERENCES

Andolfi, M. (1997). Foreword: "Between two chairs". In V. DiNicola. *A stranger in the family*. (pp.vii-xi).New York: W.W.Norton& Co.

Angelou, M. (1986*). All God's children need traveling shoes*. New York: Vintage.

Aronson, E. (2000) *Nobody left to hate: Teaching compassion after Columbine*. New York: Henry Holt.

Barker, P. (1986). *Basic family therapy* (2nd ed.). London: Collins.

Bernstein, H. (1994). *The Rift: The exile experience of South Africans*. London: Jonathan Cape.

Bowen, M. (1978). *Family therapy in clinical practice*. New York: Aronson.

Bughra, D. (2004) Migration and mental health. *ActaPsychiatrica Scandinavia*, 109, 243-258.

Canada, M., Heath, M.A., Money, K., Fischer, L. & Young, E.L.(2006) Crisis intervention or students of diverse backgrounds: School Counselors' concerns. *Brief treatment and crisis intervention*, 7(1), 12-24

Castles, S., & Davidson, A. (2000). *Citizenship and migration: Globalization and the politics of belonging*. London: McMillan Press.

Christiansen, F. &Hedetoft, U. (2004). Introduction. In F. Christiansen, & U. Hedetoft (Eds.), *The politics of multiple belonging* (pp.1-19). Aldershot: Ashgate.

DiNicola, V. (1997). *A stranger in the family*. New York: W.W.Norton& Co.

Eco, U. (1997/2001). *Five moral pieces*. San Diego: Harcourt, Inc.

Falicov, C.J. (1995). Training to think culturally: A multidimensional comparative framework. *Family Process*, 34, 373-388.

Falicov, C.J (1998*). Latino Families in therapy: A guide to multicultural practice*. New York: Guilford Press.

Falicov, C. (2005). Emotional transnationalism and family identities. *Family Process*, 44(4), 399-406.

Falicov, C. (2007). Working with transnational immigrants: Expanding meanings of family, community, and culture. *Family Process*, 46(2), 157-171.

Foucault, M. (1988). Technologies of self. In L.Martin, H.Gutman&P.Hutton (Eds.), *Technologies of the self: A seminar with Michel Foucault* (pp.16-49).Amherst: The University of Massachusetts Press.

Foucault, M. (1988). The political technology of individuals. In L.Martin, H.Gutman&P.Hutton (Eds.), *Technologies of the self: A seminar with Michel Foucault* (pp.145-162). Amherst: The University of Massachusetts Press.

Framo, J.L. (1976). Family of origin as a therapeutic resource for adults in marital and family therapy: You can and should go home again. *Family Process*. 15, 193-210.

Framo, J.L. (1992*). Family-of origin therapy: An intergenerational approach*. New York: Brunner/Mazel.

Friedman, E. (1980).Systems and ceremonies. In E.A.Carter& M. McGoldrick (Eds.), *The family life cycle: A framework for family therapy* (pp429-460). New York: Gardner Press.

Friere, P. (1994). *The pedagogy of hope*. New York: Continuum

Giamatti, A.B. (1989). *Take time for paradise. Americans and their games*. New York: Summit.

Geertz, C. (1979). From a native's point of view: On the nature of anthropological understanding, In P. Rabinow& W.M. Sullivan (Eds.) *Interpretive Social Science* (pp.225-241). Berkeley: University of California Press.

Gerrard, B. (1996). School-Based Family Counseling: A new paradigm. University of San Francisco: Unpublished manuscript.

Glick Schiller, N., Basch, L., & Blanc-Szanton, C.(1992). Transnationalism: A new analytic framework for understanding migration. In N. Glick Shiller, L. Basch& C. Blanc-Szanton (Eds.), *Towards a transnational perspective on migration: Race, class, and nationalism reconsidered* (pp.1-24). New York: The New York Academy of Sciences.

Goldin, J. (2002, November). Belonging to two worlds: The experience of migration. *South African Psychiatry Review*.4-6.

Gordon, M.M.(1964.) *Assimilation in American Life*. New York , USA: O.U.P.

Grant White, L.(1958).*Dante: "The divine comedy" a new translation*. New York Pantheon.

Grinberg, L. &Grinberg, R. (1989). *Psychoanalytic perspectives on migration and exile*. New Haven: Yale University Press. Haley, J. (1980) *Leaving Home: The therapy of disturbed young people*. New York: McGraw and Hill.

Hedetoft, U. (2004). Discourses and images of belonging: Migrants between new racism, liberal nationalism and globalization. In F. Christiansen, & U. Hedetoft (Eds.), *The politics of multiple belonging* (pp.24-43). Aldershot: Ashgate.

Howard, G.S. (1991).Culture tales: A narrative approach to thinking cross-cultural psychology, and psychotherapy. *American Psychologist, 46*, 187-197.

Hynie, M (2006). From conflict to compromise: Immigrant families and the processes of acculturation In D.M. Taylor (Ed.). *Diversity with justice and harmony: A social psychological analysis*.(pp.97-123.).Ottawa: Canada: Department of citizenship and Immigration.

Ignatieff, M. (1994). *Blood and belonging: Journeys into the new nationalism*. London: Vintage

Kimmel, M.S., & Mahler, M. (2003) Adolescent masculinity, homophobia, and violence: Random school shootings, 1982-2001. The *American behavioral scientist, 46* (10)1439-1458

LaFramboise, T., Coleman, H.L., &Gerton, J.(1993). Psychological impact of biculturalism: evidence and theory. *Psychological Bulletin* 114(3): 395-412.

Laird, J. T. (1998).Theorizing culture: Narrative ideas and practice principles. In M. McGoldrick (Ed.*), Re-Visioning family therapy: Race, culture and gender in clinical practice* (pp.20-36). New York: The Guilford Press.

Magat, I.N. (1999). Israeli and Japanese immigrants to Canada: Home, belonging and the territorialization of identity. *Ethos*, 27(2), 119-144.

Mahler, M.S., Pine, F., & Bergman, A. (1975) *The psychological birth of the human infant: Symbiosis and individuation*. New York: Basic Books, Inc.

Marchetti-Mercer, M.C. (March, 2006) Looking for Home: A journey into nostalgia and (Be)longing (2006) ISDN 1-86864-634-9.

Marchetti-Mercer, M.C., &Roos, L. (September, 2006). Migration and mental health. *South African Journal of Psychiatry*, 12(3), 54-62.

Marchetti-Mercer, M.C., Hurlin, W. and Prinsloo, R. (2008). Looking for home in our families: Exploring the relational aspects of finding a place of belonging in a postmodern world. Paper presented at the XX International Family Therapy conference (Porto, Portugal, 26-20 March , 2008).

Marchetti-Mercer,M.C. (2009) South Africans in flux: Exploring the mental health impact of migration on family life. *African Journal of Psychiatry,* 12 (2), 129-134.

McGoldrick, M. (1993). Ethnicity, cultural diversity and normality. In F. Walsh, (Ed.), *Normal family processes* (pp.331-360). New York: The Guilford Press.

McGoldrick, M. (1998). Introduction: Re-visioning Family Therapy through a cultural lens. In M. McGoldrick, (Ed.), *Re-visioning family therapy: Race, culture and gender in clinical practice* (pp.3-19). New York: The Guilford Press.

McGoldrick, M. (1998). Belonging and liberation: Finding a place called "Home." In M., McGoldrick, (Ed.), *Re-visioning family therapy: Race, culture and gender in clinical practice* (pp215-228). New York: The Guilford Press.

McGoldrick, M. (27 October 2002). Culture: A challenge to concepts of normality. *Culture and normality*. www.MulticulturalFamily.org.

McGoldrick, M., & Carter, B. (1999). Self in context: The individual life cycle in systemic perspective. In B.Carter& M. McGoldrick (Eds.), *The expanded family life cycle. Individual, family and social perspectives* (pp.27-45). Boston: Allyn and Bacon.

McGoldrick, M. (1999). History, genograms, and the family life cycle. Freud in context. In B.Carter& M. McGoldrick (Eds.), *The expanded family life cycle. Individual, family and social perspectives* (pp.47-67). Boston: Allyn and Bacon.

McGoldrick, M., & Giordano, J. (1996). Overview: Ethnicity and family therapy. In M.McGoldrick, M., J.Giordano, & J. Pearce (Eds.), *Ethnicity and family therapy* (pp.1-30). New York: The Guilford Press.

Montalvo, B., & Gutierrez, M. (1983). A perspective for the use of the cultural dimension in family therapy. In C. Falicov (Ed.), *Cultural perspectives in family therapy* (pp.15-32). Rockville, MD. Aspen Systems.

Paré, D.A. (1995).Of families and other cultures: The shifting paradigm of family therapy. *Family Process,* 34(1), 1-19.

Pedersen, P.B.,& Carey, J.C.(Eds.).(2003). *Multicultural in schools: A practical handbook* (2nd ed.). Nedham Heights, MA: Allyn& Bacon.

Ramose, M. (1999*). African Philosophy through ubuntu*. Harare: Mond Books.

Rubenstein, R. (2001). *Home matters: Longing and belonging, nostalgia and mourning in women's fiction*. New York: Palgrave.

Sampson, E. (1993). Identity politics. Challenges to psychology's understanding. *American Psychologist.* 48(12), 1219-1230.

Schutzenberger, A.A. (2004) *La sindrome degli antenati.* Roma : Di Renzo Editore.

Skowron, E.A. (Fall, 2004). Differentiation of self, personal adjustment, problem solving, and ethnic group belonging among persons of color. *Journal of Counseling and Development*, 82, 447-456.

Sluzki,C. (1979).Migration and family conflict. *Family Process*, 18, 379-390.

Stone, E., Gomez, E., Hotzoglou, D., &Lipnitaky, J. (2005) Transnationalism as a motif in family stories. *Family Process*, 44(4): 381-398.

Sue, D.W., & Sue, D.(2003). *Counseling the culturally different: Theory and practice*(4th ed.).New York: John Wiley & Sons.

Tuan, Y. F. (1984). In place, out of place. In M Richardson (Ed.*) Experience and Symbol*. Baton Rouge, LA, Dept of Geography and Anthropology: Louisiana State University.

Vega, W.A. (1998). Lifetime prevalence of DSM IIIR psychiatric disorders among urban and Mexican Americans in California. *Archives of General Psychiatry*,15, 771-778.

Vega, W.A., Kolody, B., Valle, R., & Weir, J. (1991).Social networks, social support, and their relationship to depression among immigrant Mexican women. *Human Organization*, 50,154-162.

Westwood, S., &Phizacklea, A. (2000). *Trans-nationalism and the politics of belonging*. London: Routledge

Acknowledgement: The material is based on work supported by the National Research Foundation (NRF). Any opinion, findings and conclusions or recommendations expressed in this material are those of the author and therefore the NRF does not accept any liability in regard thereto.

Chapter 22
Teachers' Stories of Children Coping with Family Change: a Hong Kong Hybrid Case

Pattie Yuk Yee Luk-Fong

OVERVIEW: This chapter examines teachers' stories of children's coping with family change in Hong Kong where 'East meets West' in cultures and family relationships. This chapter argues for the use of the concept of hybridities in understanding the experiences of children in changing family situations in a hybrid context. Teachers' stories show that children in changing family situations are facing new kinds of difficulties from the mixing of modern family forms and traditional family values. Implications for School-based family counseling, teacher education, policy and practice are suggested.

BACKGROUND

An increasing number of children in Hong Kong are growing up in a variety of family forms such as single-parent families, divorced families, blended families, 'cross-border families' (a family with members living in China), 'astronaut families' (families with a parent living abroad) and grandparent/relative-headed families (Luk-Fong, 2000). Situated on the southern coast of China, Hong Kong has been a meeting place of people and ideas from East and West. Hong Kong has always been a transitory place, greatly affected by migrations of its population. During various periods of political unrest in China, Hong Kong had been a political refuge. Then it became a working place, and for some, a stepping stone to go abroad. The 1997 return to China saw many people leaving Hong Kong. Yet some of them returned after having acquired permanent residence in another country. The comings and goings help to put Hong Kong very much in the international arena. Indeed, Hong Kong has become a global city, with strong links to the outside. Post-1997 sees a closer relationship with China, with many jobs moved to China and more Mainland Chinese coming to live in Hong Kong. It is against this backdrop that this paper focuses discussion on four case stories from the typical changing family forms in Hong Kong which arise from its historical and geographical contexts. All four cases involve some form of family separation (a grandfather-headed globalised family; a joint-custody divorce family; a cross-border family and a father-headed repartnered family).

The number of children living in single-parent families rose from 52,826 in 1991 to about 103,500 in 2006. At the same time, the number of divorces rose from 6,295 cases in 1991 to 13,425 cases in 2001, and then up to 17,424 cases in 2006 (Hong Kong Census and Statistics Department, 2007). The actual proportion of single-parent families caused by divorce increased from 54.1% in 1991 to 76% in 2001. Since most single-parents are in the 30-49 age group, the chances of remarriage and cohabitation are great (Cheng, 1999) and the children are involved in difficult transitions. Moreover, the number of family violence cases and the number of cross-border marriages have also risen. The former rose from 1,253 cases in 1996 to 2,628 cases in 2005; while the latter rose from 19,203 cases in 1999 to 29,800 in 2005. It is not only the rise in absolute figures but also the rapidly increasing trend, that is of concern. Literature shows that whether in academic performance or school behavior, children growing up in two-parent families have better adjustment than children growing up in single-parent, mother-headed or stepfather-headed families (Zill, 1996). Literature on divorce and single parenting abounds, but there is not much literature devoted to the study of children in family separation situations. When there is family separation, the families are sometimes called 'pseudo-single families' signifying the lack of support from both parents in raising their children. This chapter attempts to fill the gap in the literature.

HYBRIDITIES AND THE HONG KONG CASE

The theoretical framework guiding this study is the concept of hybridity (Bhabha, 1996). Rowe and Schelling (1991, 231) define 'hybridisation' as 'the ways in which forms become separated from existing practices and recombine with new forms in practices.' Pieterse (1995, 62) further suggests that 'hybridisation as a perspective belongs to the fluid end of relations between cultures: it is the mixing of cultures and not their separateness that is emphasised.' In this sense, in the Hong Kong case there are mixes and interactions of 'Western' tendencies and 'Chinese traditions'. This evolving hybridity may also be described in terms of the Chinese idea of *yin-yang*, which can be used to explain dynamic change processes. In the present case, y*in* corresponds to the original Chinese family traditions whereas *yang* corresponds to incoming western traditions or modern family forms. The two traditions are constantly mixing, interacting and changing to reach equilibrium of harmony and balance. The equilibrium is represented by the Daoist symbol (Figure 22.1) of one wholeness divided into equal halves of black and white. Convergences of traditions would occur but divergences will remain. Thus, in each half of the whole, there is a dot of the opposite color signifying a seed of the opposite nature.

Figure 22.1 Daoist symbol of *yin-yang*

Hong Kong is a good case for studying hybridity as it has always been a place where East meets West. Under the 150 years of British colonialism up to 1997 westernisation has been grafted onto the indigenous Chinese culture. As a result, Hong Kong demonstrates hybridities in relation to families. Lee's (2000) notion of 'resilient familialism' which includes both an increasing dominance of nuclear families and the prevalence of traditional family values and norms with active mutual aid networks among kin and relatives is a classic example of hybridity in Hong Kong families. Thus, the boundary of the Hong Kong family is not restricted to the physical boundary of a household but extends outward to form a family network with the nuclear families of other kins (Chan and Lee, 1995). Moreover, nuclear family units, cross-border and astronaut families, decline in marriage and birth rates (for details, see Luk-Fong, 2000, 2005a; Sullivan, 2005) coexist with the patriarchal and child-centred Chinese families and the traditional cultural belief that 'family should be intact'. Given that family functioning in Hong Kong is influenced by both Chinese and Western traditions, in order to understand how Hong Kong children cope with family situations and changes, one has to start with the hybridities of the Hong Kong family context.

RELATIONSHIP TO THE SBFC MODEL

This chapter is about four cases of children facing family separation which is stressful to them and their families. The site of investigation is the primary school settings. This is done purposely as many scholars think that school is the best institution to help children cope during family changes and divorce and because it can provide a safe and secure environment, with regular routines and disciplines during periods of transitions and turmoil (Allers, 1982; Hetherington, 1987). This is in line with Dowling and Barnes (2000), who posit that a caring and supporting school environment, sensitive to the needs of students and family situations, is most helpful to children during family transitions. They consider it essential that schools should provide support to children in the changing familial contexts for two reasons. This is because in the child's mind, the two worlds of home and school are held together and what is happening in one context is constantly having an impact on the other. Moreover, schools often neglect the emotional factors which affect children's capacity for learning as they mainly focus on the cognitive development and academic performance of the children. The purpose of this research is to find out the actual school practices in helping children in stressful situations of family changes in the 'East meets West' context in Hong Kong. The school-based family counseling model was used as a framework to analyse the effectiveness of the current school practices both in prevention and intervention and in terms of whether the school support (school focus) and family support (family focus) can meet the needs of the students (child focus).

This study addresses the following research questions:

What is the experience of children in changing family situations in the Hong Kong context from the perceptions of primary school teachers?

How far do cases of family transitions exhibit features of hybridities? What issues are raised from the case stories about supporting children in changing familial situations?

What implications can be drawn for teacher education, policy and practice in a school-based family counseling framework?

THE FOUR CASES

This study used a qualitative case study methodology. A case study methodology is the best way to capture the uniqueness of Hong Kong. This is in agreement with Yang (1993, 33), who calls for the use of qualitative method 'in doing research for indigenous Chinese people because it can show the concrete details of the actual psychological and behavioural phenomena and their complex relationship in their social-cultural context.' Further, as this study is concerned with a new area of research, namely teachers' perceptions of school children coping with family situations, there are few categories and concepts from the literature to build on. Qualitative methodology is considered the most suitable approach in this situation. (Alasuutari, 1995).

Teachers' case stories of children's coping and adjustment in different familial situations is the main source of data used in this study. The stories represent snapshots of teachers' perceptions of children's struggles in difficult family situations. Stories are useful as they can embody children's lived experiences in their changing family situations and illustrate the kind of hybridities children are facing in the hybrid Hong Kong context. About narratives, Rosaldo (1986, 1998) puts it well, 'Narrative can provide a particular rich source of knowledge about the significance people find in their workaday lives.' Data in this study were obtained by asking school personnel to recall and retell stories of children in changing and difficult situations that impressed them most during their teaching careers. This way of recall has a great limitation in that data may have been lost or distorted by teachers' memories. The researcher is also aware that teachers have their own biases about divorce and alternative family forms (Drake, 1981; Luk-Fong, 2006). Indeed, it is the intention of this paper to capture the personal values of teachers about family types, because it is through the lenses of their biases that they provide care and support to children from these families. The case studies in this paper, from the teacher's perceptions, are to illuminate the actual mixing and blending of East and West contexts, to identify the actual experiencing of children in changing familial situations in the Hong Kong context and to propose implications for actions.

Four cases were selected from more than 10 typical cases narrated by the teachers. Illustrative stories of typical family types were chosen; they suffice to show the complex and multiple ways of families negotiating with the hybrid situations in Hong Kong. All cases were obtained from in-depth interviews with 30 primary school personnel in different age groups and working in different positions at school. Each story involved in-depth descriptions by one (a male or a female class teacher alone) or several (a mix of class teacher, guidance teacher, discipline teacher and school principal) school personnel. The triangulation of data from different personnel, if available, makes the data more rich and reliable. Both boys and girls at different levels, with father-, mother- or grand-father-headed families were included in the four cases.

For each case, the background information (about the story teller, the student and the school), the main difficulties that the child was facing, and the family structure and family relation as perceived by the teacher(s) will be given. It is important to include who tells the story and in what context, for as Narayan and George (2003, 126) put it well, 'People tell their stories according to their own feelings and the feelings of their audience.' All the four case stories are analysed using the framework of hybridities. All the names of the children are pseudonyms in order to protect the children and their families.

CASE 1: GRANDFATHER-HEADED GLOBALISED FAMILY

The following excerpt is a case story told by a female class teacher who has 15 years of teaching experience in a co-educational government primary school in the urban area of Hong Kong. The socio-economic status of the students' family is average.

Ah Ming was a primary six boy (primary 6 is the last year of elementary school. It is equivalent to Grade 6 in the US system). He wore untidy uniforms in summer, and did not wear jackets nor sweaters in winter. He often had no breakfast. He slept in class. Ah Ming's mother left for England to study and his father worked in China. He was taken care most of the time by his grandfather. Talking with the boy at length, the teacher found out that the grandfather was unable to find winter clothings for him. Ah Ming slept in class because his father took him to a karaoke in Shenzhen, across the border, the night before and they returned home during midnight. Ah Ming was very unhappy when he talked about his parents, and would be in tears when asked about his mother. Ah Ming was bright but chose to give up on himself in academic work.

When asked what she thought about the case, the teacher responded:

Maybe he felt being abandoned by his mother. Sometimes, I feel we have no ability to handle these problems. Although Ah Ming graduated from the school two years ago, I'm still worried about him. I feel very unhappy, I would give him clothes that my son had outgrown. If he had not eaten breakfast, I would give him some biscuits. I did not want him to feel my pity on him.

Hence, I only talked with him occasionally, avoiding others' notice. Like if he was lying on the table, I would ask if he was sick to show my care to him.

This case shows the separation of family members in an astronaut family impacted by the changing societal conditions in Hong Kong. As Hong Kong become more globalised and modernised, Ah Ming's mother could go abroad for study (reversal of traditional feminine role) which would be unthought of half a century ago. After Hong Kong was reunited with China in 1997, more people like Ah Ming's father have to cross the border to work in China. While the mother was abroad, the father and the grandfather (though he was willing to help) seemed incapable of looking after Ah Ming's healthy growth. Ah Ming lacked basic physical care, even proper meals and proper clothes. Moreover, family members were apparently not aware of, or were incapable of dealing with, Ah Ming's emotional needs and yearning for the 'loss' of his mother.

CASE 2: A JOINT-CUSTODY DIVORCE FAMILY

This story was told by a male class teacher in his early 30s. Students in Hong Kong are usually placed into classes of 35-40 students each in one academic year. Students belong to the same class although different subject teachers may be teaching them. A class teacher is the one that oversees the whole-person development of all students in his/her class. The school was a government co-educational school in an outlying district in Hong Kong. The socio-economic status of the student's family was low. This wasa divorce case of joint custody by both parents. Excerpts of the story are shown below.

Siu Keung was a primary six boy. He was unruly and talkative in class. He often ran around the classroom, at times kneeling down and lying on the floor and often failing to hand in homework. Siu Keung stayed with each of his parents half time. The teacher only saw either the father or the mother during parents' days. He saw both parents together only once during Siu Keung's graduation ceremony. The father drove Siu Keung to school and the mother sat with Siu Keung during the ceremony. The child seemed to lack love. He did participate in the guidance programme 'Space for growing up.' His case had been discussed in school for two years.

Case 2 is a example of co-parenting in a divorced family. Despite Siu Keung's restlessness, unruly behaviors in class and failures in handing in assignments, he managed to have good social relationships with friends. The teacher formulated his problem:

His problems with homework was related to the fact that he had missed too much work since primary one and so he lagged too far behind…Every year he just got by. His homework were copied from others. He would do homework that just required copying….Teachers tried to ask him to do homework during recess and after school, but he owed so many teachers' homework. Which teacher could he entertain? If he failed to hand in homework for me, I would not chase after him. Teachers' time was limited and they could not help him to make up for work missed in the previous years. Siu Keung never mentioned his parents' divorce to the teacher, but he wanted this class teacher to be his father. To this the male teacher reacted quite uncomfortably, I tell him to ask his father, I said, 'If your father heard you call everyone father, how would he think? How would he feel?' Siu Keung did not say a word. Siu Keung enjoyed talking to me and would keep order if I gave him sweets secretly in the staff room. When waiting for his father to pick him up after extra-curricular activities, he felt lonesome and being abandoned.

Siu Keung's showed some good adjustment which may be related to structures provided at home and in school. His parents negotiated a solution to attending his graduation. His participation in extra-curricular activities and guidance program in school apparently enhanced his relations with friends. The class teacher's care and support seemed important for alleviating some of Siu Keung's difficulties. However, the class teacher alone was not able to help Siu Keung keep up with his academic work nor ease his emotional stress from the family situation. This case demonstrated the ambivalence and emotional burden that both Siu Keung and the class teacher were experiencing. Although the parents seemed caring, they were not addressing Siu Keung's emotional needs. The class teacher cared about Siu Keung, but was very uncomfortable when Siu Keung called him father. Though the family was using a modern form of child custody, Sin Keung's silence about the divorce suggested there was a stigma attached to divorce by teachers and the child. Knowledge of the divorce by many people in the school might have created enormous stress for the child.

CASE 3: A CROSS-BORDER FAMILY

This story was told by an female discipline teacher, in her 40s, with over 20 years of experience. The discipline teacher is the person in charge of moral development and proper collective behaviors for students in the schools. Each school would have a discipline (Chinese traditions) and a counseling (Western traditions) team. The school is a Christian co-educational school in a new town.

Ping Heung was a gifted boy. However, he was unhappy and bad-tempered. As the only son in the family, he was pampered by his patriarchal father, who was a retired soldier. Deeply affected by the traditions of male dominance and preference for sons, the father looked down upon his wife and daughter. Following his father's example, Ping Heung was disrespectful to his mother, who could not control him. Thus, Ping Heung was treated as if he was a little emperor at home. When his father abandoned the family after meeting a woman across the border in China, Ping Heung became aggressive and hit his teachers and classmates. He was later referred to a school for children with behavior problems. I feel very sad that his giftedness was wasted. At first, all teachers accepted him but later on nobody wanted him. The discipline teacher talked to him and taught him how to handle his emotions, but to no avail. He was then referred to the school guidance officer and community resources. However, the support was still not enough for his adjustment.

This case shows how a chauvinistic father who upset the equilibrum at home led to the aggressive behaviors of his son in school. The mother did not have the power to discipline the son as he was pampered by his father. When the father finally abandoned the family, it was a loss too great for Ping Heung to bear. The case also shows that traditional patriarchal ideas still prevail in modern Hong Kong. After the return of Hong Kong to China in 1997, extra-marital affairs across the Hong Kong-China border became common. The unrespectable absence of a father figure in a patriarchal family had a great impact on the son. School support alone was inadequate to help the child.

CASE 4: FATHER-HEADED REPARTNERED

This case came from a Catholic girls' school in the urban area in Hong Kong. This school has a high reputation, with students from the middle/upper middle class. According to the principal children from divorced families in this school could generally manage well with adequate resources (such as domestic helpers). However, the school principal, the guidance teacher, and an experienced teacher all recalled one girl who had great difficulties in her adjustment. The story contributed by the three school personnel converged as follows:

Mei Ling was now a primary four girl living in a Children's Home. She had been a student of the school when she was in primary two, but she had repeated twice. She could not concentrate in class and often failed to hand in homework. Assessment showed that she has reasonable IQ. Her mother was invited to talk to the class teacher about her academic problems. Owing to marital discord, the mother later left the family. The father often beat the girl and demanded that she finished her homework even working till midnight. Mei Ling would be scolded for meeting with her mother. After his wife left, the father looked for a woman to take care of her two daughters because of his long working hours. He met one in the park. They later cohabitated. The woman wished to build a new family with Mei Ling's father and younger sister by placing Mei Ling in a Children's Home. The teacher thought that Mei Ling was bright and fluent in expression, but she could not concentrate on her studies because of her family situation.

All the school personnel in this case co-operated to help Mei Ling. The teacher and guidance teachers remarked that they would be like a mother to her; both gave her their telephone numbers. The guidance teacher would visit her in the Children's Home and let her own daughter talk with Mei Ling. The Principal tried to boost Mei Ling's self-esteem by publicly presenting the prize she won in the Children's Home to her during school assembly. All the school personnel said that they helped by loving Mei Ling more. They were angry that her father, though an educated doctor from China, could mistreat his own daughter in such a way.

This case as described by the personnel has evolved over a number of years, from the father fighting for custody of the daughters, then sending Mei Ling to a Children's Home. Meetings have been conducted by school personnel, a worker from the social welfare department, and a psychologist on issues relating to Mei Ling's adjustment and placement to different educational settings. Most probably the emotional tensions caused by parental conflicts, missing the non-custodian parent, readjustment to the 'step-mother', and separation from her younger sister were too great for Mei Ling to be able to concentrate on her studies. Again, this case demonstrated the father's lack of ability to take care of the children alone. A woman from the park was used to take care of his daughters.

DISCUSSION

New Family Forms Co-Existing with Traditional Family Values – Children's Problems Are Hidden
The case studies show that modern alternative family forms such as grand-parent headed family, pseudo-single parent families (in astronaut families), blended family, child abused family, and co-parenting were emerging. However, traditional family values such as 'family disgrace should not be disclosed' and 'families should be intact' were still strong as one can see that in Case 3, Siu Keung never talked about his own parents' divorce in school, and in Case 4, Mei Ling only talked about happy things in school.

With hybridities arising when new family forms co-exist with tradtional family values, these children suffered from their family situations. They preferred hiding their problems to receiving intervention or help from any third party. Only when their problems became acute did they become noticed by the teachers as 'problematic students'. Thus, most of the children's emotional difficulties were unknown. When problems surfaced, teachers only dealt with them as secrets.

Modern Family Forms But Traditional Family Values – New Forms of Care for Children Are Needed
The case studies managed to unveil some of the problems children are facing in the hybrid context of modern family forms with traditional family values, using the school as site of investigation. Children's family problems might not have been discovered if only the home was the site of investigation, as only families with serious problems might openly seek treatment in family services centres. All subjects in the four cases were suffering high emotional distress and having difficulties in their concentration and motivation for studies.

The ad-hoc ways in which teachers helped school children as 'fathers' or 'mothers' of a traditional family in the school context was highly inadequate. More sustained co-operative efforts from the families of the children must be elicited. The personal, sometimes intense ways that teachers took in these children, such as giving their own phone numbers, visiting students in the Children's Home and letting students to talk with their own children, perhaps relate to cultural traditions of Chinese teachers as proposed by Hayhoe (1999) and Luk-Fong (2005b). Chinese teachers' concerns go beyond students' academic knowledge to their whole person development (Cheng and Wong, 1996), including their moral development. The pleasing thing shown in this study is that teachers cared for their students very much. However, the close personal relationship with the students and a lack of boundaries between students and teachers created great stress for the teachers, particularly in view of the relatively large class size (32.2 students per class) in local schools (Education Bureau, 2006) and the heavy workload of the teachers. There is a great need to care for the teachers as 'carers'.

MULTICULTURAL COUNSELING ISSUES

Although all four cases involve ethnic Chinese, the multicultural issue in Hong Kong emerges in a very different way than in other parts of the world. As Hong Kong is becoming increasingly globalized, it is common to see in each family the influence of family members living abroad or living in Mainland China across the border. We can see in Case 1 how the astronaut family can induce changes on traditional family practices and cultures making it difficult for family members to adjust. Similarly, the actual difference in family values in the Mainland of China and Hong Kong created under the "One country, two system" since 1997 has created difficulties for cross-border families to adjust to the dominant cultures and values in Hong Kong.

SOCIAL JUSTICE SENSITIVITY

Despite role changes and the increasingly important status of women in the modern Hong Kong society, the family system did not seem to have changed accordingly. Traditional Chinese family values 'men take charge of the outside and women take charge of the inside of the family' and the caring role of woman as 'a good wife and mother' still prevail in the lived experiences of families. Fathers and grandfathers, though willing, could not competently take up the caring role for children. Of the four cases, two of them are father-headed families and they find taking care of children very difficult. Traditional Chinese ideas of male dominance were still significant in many families, particularly in cross-border families. Case 3 demonstrated that power relationships in the family could not be ignored when addressing a patriarchical and male-chavinistic family. In such a family, the mother was powerless to exert discipline on a son. The negotiations between traditional family values and changing family forms were often not easy.

IMPLICATIONS OF THIS STUDY

NEED FOR RECONFIGURATIONS OF 'FAMILY', 'WORKPLACE' AND 'GENDER AND POWER' IN THE HONG KONG HYBRID CONTEXT

The above case studies have shown in concrete detail how family separations induced by divorce, remarriages, globalisation of workforce, and cross-border marriages are giving challenges to children's academic and healthy development and how teachers are responding to the families when parents cannot cope with the provision of child care. Without reconfiguration of gender role, family, workplace and power relationships, 'resilient familialism' alone is inadequate in helping families to nurture their children. Tu's (2002) call for a reconfiguration of family and gender is very apt here. In his words:

> I think one important implication for the rise of feminism as a form of humanism, is not simply the quest of gender equality, but a fundamental transformation of what is a family, what is a public place, for work, basic nature of human relationships, even the pattern of authority and power (p. 160).

Perhaps a good starting point for action is the awareness of the multiple manifestations of 'families' in Hong Kong. In the re-configurations of 'families', one crucial question to ask is how the nurturing of children can best be supported in a culture where 'family disgrace should not be disclosed' is the norm.

TRAINING NEEDS OF TEACHERS

Teachers are stressed and overwhelmed and they need to be supported. In pre-service and in-service teaching training teachers must be made aware of how the changing family terrains are affecting the children they teach. They should also be taught skills in understanding and sensitively responding to these children in emotional stress. Moreover, children's academic and emotional problems must be tackled hand-in-hand. School principals and administrators must ensure that policies and practices enhance a culture of acceptance and non-discrimination for all children and families.

NEED FOR A SBFC PERSPECTIVE IN SCHOOLS

 School is the place where children's problems of adjusting to family changes emerges. School must respond to these problems using a school-based family counselling perspective. At present, schools and teachers seemed not be be able to respond to students' emotional needs in family situations in particular. They should also be taught the current research findings about the risks and resilience of children in changing family situations and know their roles and boundaries in helping children. School counselling personnel must be trained in family counseling and family education knowledge and skills so as to better support changing families. Children and their families should be taught new ways to adapt to family separations including being more flexible with changes, and learning new structures, and children and parents learning new ways of connecting to one another in a separated family. (Olson, 2000).

COMPREHENSIVE COORDINATED POLICIES AND COOPERATIVE EFFORTS FROM FAMILY, SCHOOL AND SOCIETY

In this era of changing family and gender relationships, Hong Kong policy makers have to recognize that children are embedded in the family and school systems which are in turn embedded in the hybridised Hong Kong society. In formulating policies in supporting the academic and personal development of children, the roles played by home, school and society, and how their efforts can be coordinated, should be the focus. Some starting points for action may include the school system using the close personal relationship of teachers, especially class teachers, with students in the school setting, but, at the same time, finding ways to relieve teachers' workload. In the home front it would benefit the children if mothers' changing roles in work can be acknowledged at home and the caring roles of fathers can be enhanced and encouraged. One practical issue is perhaps to provide the necessary child caring skills to non-traditional carers (like fathers and grandfathers). For the larger society, more community education about the increasing diversity in family forms, better child support policies, and a family-friendly support environment should be initiated in response to the changing family terrain. The situation may be more stressful in Hong Kong as compared with the West, because the changes in families as a result of industralisation and globalisation are compressed within a much shorter time span of the last fifty years in contrast to more than a hundred years in the West (Lau, 2005). Moreover, the changes are taking place in families embedded in deep-rooted traditional Chinese family values.

SUMMARY

The case stories have provided rich data embedded in their naturalistic settings. This paper has demonstrated in the lived experiences of children how the traditional family values cannot keep pace with rapidly changing modern family forms. It has argued that new kinds of problems were created in the changing hybridised familial contexts in Hong Kong. New ways of coping with the problems are required. In terms of methodology, this study has attempted to understand children's coping with changing familial situations through teachers' perceptions. As such, it has highlighted children's and teachers' voices and difficulties that would otherwise not be heard. It also calls for the need to use a school-based family counseling framework in helping children in changing family situations. This way of data collection is inadequate as a lot of data might have been missed by interviewing the school personnel only. Future directions can include studying the voices of the trio of parents, teachers and children to add to the thickness of data. Another limitation of this study is the way that the subjects were recruited. As subjects were recruited on a voluntary basis, the study might have self-selected teachers who perceive children's family problems as serious. Moreover, students who were coping well would not be identified by the teachers as children are generally not too ready to disclose their problems in the Chinese context. Last but not least, this study is very small in scale and hence only exploratory in nature. The purpose of this study is to raise issues rather than to generalize. More large-scaled quantitative and qualitative studies and indeed, longitudinal studies are needed before results can be generalized.

Although this chapter is about Hong Kong, it is hoped that it will spark discussions on similar issues in parallel settings in the world, particularly in areas where Confucian heritage has met modernization. The ultimate goal is to search for ways in which schools and families can start to help the coping of children with methods suitable to hybrid cultures and changing contexts.

REFERENCES

Alasuutari, P. 1995. *Researching culture*. Sage: London.
Allers, R.D. 1982. *Divorce, children, and the School*. Princeton, NJ: Princeton Book Co.
Bhabha, H.K. 1996. Cultures in-between. In *Questions of cultural identity*, ed. S. Hall and P. du Gay, 53-61. London: Sage.
Chan, H., and R.L. Lee. 1995. Hong Kong families: At the crossroads of modernism and transitionalism. *Journal of Comparative Family Studies* 26: 83-99.
Cheng, K.M., and K.C. Wong. 1996. School effectiveness in East Asia. *Journal of Educational Administration* 34: 32-49.
Cheng, K.M. 1999. Culture matters: A cultural perspective of aims of education for Hong Kong (synopsis, draft). Paper presented at the International Conference on Teacher Education, February 22-24, in Hong Kong.

Dowling, E., and G.G. Barnes. 2000. *Working with children and parents through separation and divorce: The changing lives of children*. Macmillan: London.

Drake, E.A. 1981. Helping children cope with divorce: The role of the school. In *Children of separation and divorce: Management and treatment*, ed. I.R. Stuart and L.E. Abt, 147-172. New York: Van Nostrand.

Education Bureau. 2004. Comprehensive Student Guidance.
http://www.edb.gov.hk/index.aspx?langno=1&nodeID=1974

Education Bureau. 2006. Primary Education Figures.
http://www.edb.gov.hk/index.aspx?langno=1&nodeid=1038

Hayhoe, R. 1999. The teacher in Chinese society. Keynote address at International Conference on Teacher Education, February 22-24, in Hong Kong.

Hetherington, E.M. 1987. Family relations six years after divorce. In *Remarriage and stepparenting: Current research and theory*, ed. K. Pasley and M. Ihinger-Tallman, 185-205. New York: Guilford Press.

Hong Kong Census and Statistics Department. 2007. *Hong Kong annual digest of statistics*. Hong Kong: Hong Kong Government Printer.

Lau, Y.K. 2005. *Adolescent Development: Crisis and Turning Point* [in Chinese]. Taipei: Yang-Chih.

Lee, M.K. 2000. Hong Kong's family trends and their policy implications. Paper presented at Family Trends and Policies in OECD Countries: Issues and Lessons, in Hong Kong.

Luk-Fong, Y.Y.P. 2000. Family change and children's adjustment [in Chinese]. In *Teaching manual on sex education for kindergarten children*, ed. E. Tung, 112-23. Hong Kong: The Hong Kong Institute of Education.

Luk-Fong, Y.Y.P. 2005a. Family and primary school counseling from a systemic perspective. *Journal of Basic Education* 14(1): 101-20.

Luk-Fong, Y.Y.P. 2005b. Managing change in an integrated school – a Hong Kong hybrid experience. *International Journal of Inclusive Education* 9(1): 89-103.

Luk-Fong, Y.Y.P. 2006. Primary school teachers' perceptions of school children coping with changing family situations – A hybrid Hong Kong experience. *Social Psychology of Education* 9: 425-41.

Narayan, K., and George, K.M. 2003. Personal and folk narrative as cultural representation. In *Postmodern interviewing*, ed. J.F. Gubrium and J.A. Holstein, 123-40. Thousand Oaks: Sage Publications.

Olson, D. H. (2000). Circumplex model of marital and family systems. *Journal of Family Therapy*, (22), 144-167.

Pieterse, J.N. 1995. Globalization as hybridization. In *Globalization modernities*, ed. M. Featherstone, S. Lash, and R. Robertson, 45-68. London: Sage.

Rosaldo, R. 1986. Ilongot hunting as story and experience. In *The anthropology of experience*, ed. V.W. Turner and E.M. Bruner, 97-138. Urbana: University of Illinois Press.

Rowe, W., and V. Schelling. 1991. *Memory and modernity: Popular culture in Latin America*. London: Verso.

Sullivan, P.L. 2005.Culture, divorce, and family mediation in Hong Kong. *Family Court Review* 43: 109-123.

Tu, W.M. 2002. Confucianism in the twenty-first century: Dialogue among civilization and the public intellectual. In *Culture and humanity in the new millennium*, ed. S.T. Kwok and S. Chan, 155-66. Hong Kong: The Chinese University Press.

Yang, K.S. 1993. Why should we develop a local psychology for the Chinese? In *Development of a localized psychology* [in Chinese], ed. K.S. Yang, 6-88. Taipei: National Taiwan University Department of Psychology Local Psychology Study Centre.

Zill, N. 1996. Family change and student achievement: What we have learned, what it means for schools. In *Family-school links: How do they affect educational outcomes?*, ed. A. Booth and J.F. Dunn, 139-74. Mahwah, NJ: Lawrence Erlbaum Associates.

RESOURCES

Charbonneau, C. (2000). Siblings in family transitions. *Family Relations*, (49), 77-85.

Kelly, J.B. & Emery, R.E (2003) Children's Adjustment following divorce: Risk and Resilience Perspectives. *Family Relations,* 52 (4) 352-62

Masten, A. S. (2001) Ordinary magic: Resilience process in development. *American Psychologists,* 56 (3) 227-238

Pedro-Carroll, J. (2001). *The promotion of wellness in children and families: Challenges and opportunities.* Paper presented at the Annual Conference of the American Psychological Association, 109th, Sam Francisco, CA, August 24-28, 2001.

Chapter 23

Excluded Student-Excluded Parent: the Experiences and Reflections of Parents Whose Teenagers are Excluded from School

Andrew Smith

OVERVIEW: *This chapter explores research findings concerning parents' experiences of having a child excluded from school. These findings are discussed in the light of SBFC principles, and recommendations made for counseling practice.*

BACKGROUND

Research projects start in diverse ways. In 2007 I was having a conversation with a friend who, with her husband, are primary care-givers for their grandson. She was telling me some of what was happening for them at the time. Their grandson (then aged 14) had very recently been excluded from school, and the situation had had a major impact on both him and his grandparent 'parents'. The closing comment in the conversation was, "You know, there's a research project in this!" An initial cursory literature search reinforced that idea, in that I found very little evidence that researchers had explored families' experience of having a child excluded from school. Moreover, several writers have commented on that lack (Brown, 2007; Gordon, 2001; Knipe, Reynolds & Milner, 2007; McDonald & Thomas, 2003). Consequently, I made application to the New Zealand Families Commission for a research grant. This was approved, and the project started to unfold. But before moving to the project itself, let me set the scene.

Generally, when a school deems it appropriate to remove a young person from the school because of behavioral issues, processes fall into two categories: temporary suspension, and long-term or permanent 'exclusion'. Policies and processes vary slightly between Western nations. Internationally, increasing numbers of suspensions and exclusions through the 1980s and 1990s were reported (Brown, 2007; Gordon, 2001; Lloyd, 2000; Partington, 2001). These figures appear to have plateaued since 2000. Within this trend, it seems that rates of exclusion vary significantly both between nations (Parsons, 2005) and also between schools (Cullingford, 1999).

New Zealand has its own definitions as outlined by its Ministry of Education (2008), which closely parallel those of other nations:

Stand-down means the formal removal of a student from school for a specified period. Stand-downs of a particular student can total no more than 5 school days in a term or 10 school days in a year.

Suspension means the formal removal of a student from the school until the Board of Trustees decides the outcome at a suspension meeting.

Exclusion means the formal removal of a student aged under 16 from the school and the requirement that the student enrol elsewhere.

Expulsion means the formal removal of a student aged 16 or over from the school. If the student wishes to continue schooling he or she may enrol elsewhere.

Exclusion and expulsion are for the most serious cases only. (p. 3)

The New Zealand Education Acts (1989, 1998) define a three-fold purpose of these actions: to provide a range of responses, to minimise the disruption to school attendance, and to ensure that situations are dealt with in accordance with principles of natural justice. The MOE (2008) Guidelines for Principals clearly set out procedures which are set within principles of a child's right to free education, assisting all students to realise their full potential, ensuring access to good guidance and Counseling, and of taking "all reasonable steps" (p. 4) to keep parents informed of students' progress. New Zealand government policy guidelines note that exclusion of a student from school "can have far reaching consequences for the student (and for other members of their family)" (Ministry of Education, 2008, p. 5).

New Zealand statistics, as reported on the MOE 'Education Counts' website (Exclusions and expulsions from school, 2009) report an incidence of 2.7 students per 1,000 in 2000, and 2.2 / 1,000 in 2008. The graphic representation shows small fluctuations from year to year, suggesting that there has actually been very little change over the seven years.

Both in New Zealand and internationally, boys are excluded more often than girls. Minority ethnic groups, young people from disadvantaged or low socio-economic backgrounds and those in care are consistently over-represented in the statistics (Brodie&Berridge, 1996; Brown, 2007; Exclusions and expulsions from school, 2009; Gordon, 2001; Lloyd, 2000; Munn & Lloyd, 2005; Partington, 2001; Suspensions from school, 2009). Harrison (2004) and Partington (2001) believe that policy change and greater regulation have had minimal effect on rates of exclusion. Several authors have discussed the significance of school ethos. Munn and Lloyd (2005) have commented that school ethos can be 'including' or 'excluding' – often reflected in their formal exclusion figures. Berkeley (1999) believes that school ethos is more significant than government policy in determining exclusion rates, and adds that schools are not always consistent in their application of process or response to similar situations.

EXPERIENCES OF EXCLUSION

While Brown (2007) comments, "Effectively addressing these issues requires an understanding of what actually happens to students in the wake of school exclusion, some of which can only be learned from the young people themselves" (p. 434), writers note that students' voices are infrequently heard in discussion of the issue (Brown, 2007; Gordon, 2001; Knipe, Reynolds & Millar, 2007). A brief summary does not do justice to the young people concerned, but there are consistent themes across the studies around a sense of being rejected, an awareness of being responsible, and of awareness of and regret for the longer-term consequences (Gordon, 2001; Munn & Lloyd, 2005; Partington, 2001).

Turning to the voices of the families involved, the literature contains both 'anecdotal' accounts (A parent's story, 2002) and larger research studies (Brodie&Berridge, 1996; Gordon, 2001; McDonald & Thomas, 2003; Partington, 2001). McDonald and Thomas (2003) describe the parents' stories as "passionate, painful and poignant" (p. 108) – which would seem an appropriate summation not just of their study, but also of the other reports mentioned. They also comment that the parents' views communicated a sense of anger and powerlessness. They say that the interviews "offer a picture of a group of parents clearly traumatised by the experience of their children's exclusion" (p. 111). Alongside, and contributing to the emotions expressed, were concerns that time-frames for decision-making were lacking, and that little attention was paid to the present or future educational needs of their children, several of whom spent long periods out of school.

Another thread that seems consistent across the reports is the sense that parents often feel labelled and treated in the same way as they feel their children are labelled and treated – bad student, bad parent. The consequences of this are that parents can "feel themselves to be psychologically excluded from the school system" (Cullingford, 1999, p. 58).

SCHOOL AND FAMILY – THE BIGGER PICTURE

The literature indicates that teenagers who are excluded from school are more likely to come from home environments where there are socio-emotional or financial problems, and homes where there is less parental supervision (Stanley, Canham&Cureton, 2006). These writers, along with Gerrard (2008) observe that increased family stress leads to increased vulnerability in a young person, and consequently to an increased likelihood of 'acting out' at school. As Cullingford (1999) observes, disaffection is a gradual process, and once authority is questioned and a sense of power experienced, be it at home or school, the consequences flow from one setting to the other.

However, two reports challenge schools to be careful in the way they think of both themselves and parents in these debates. Firstly, a UK study (Tett, 2001) states that "a child's successful schooling should depend upon a great deal more than the efficacy of any individual parent" (p. 193 - original author's italics). She comments that it is too easy for schools to put the blame on parents if education appears unsuccessful. Tett also comments on the tendency of schools to pathologise parents who challenge or disagree with a school's decision, and to define a 'good parent' as one who conforms to school expectations. Secondly, Harrison (2004), in a New Zealand-based discussion, states:
The importance of family background in influencing student performance has been twisted by some New Zealand education academics into a reason for excusing poor performance by some schools. (p. 9)

Harrison (2004) adds that parents don't always make perfect decisions, but that overall they tend to make better decisions than distant professionals when it comes to the welfare of their children. He also believes that there is little evidence that economically-disadvantaged parents make poor choices in issues of schooling. Dyson and Robson (Links between…, 1999) report similar findings.

The availability of counseling services within schools varies not only between schools but also shows national patterns. In New Zealand, while the Education Act (1989) requires schools to provide access to good guidance and Counseling, there is no definition of what this would look like, and reports suggest that the provision of such services varies considerably. Hughes (1996) describes what he views as an increasing sense of invisibility and isolation experienced by school counselors. Crowe (2006) has described issues of increasing workload, and challenges related to the increasing complexity of the issues brought by students to the school counselor.

School counseling in NZ has worked primarily with the student client in isolation from her or his wider network of relationships. In an article in the New Zealand Association of Counsellors' newsletter in 1996, Winslade discusses issues around the rights of children, and the rights of parents to have a say in the Counseling provided for their children. While both legal and ethical aspects are addressed, the article clearly stresses the issue of parents' views of the student receiving Counseling, rather than the possibility of parents' involvement in Counseling. Crowe's (2006) exploration of issues facing NZ school counseling and counselors makes no mention of either parental involvement or parental views.

Fox and Butler (2009) describe the ebbing and flowing of attitudes and provision of school-based Counseling within the UK. They cite a 2006 survey which reported that "71% of schools now claim to offer 'therapeutic individual Counseling'" and comment that "provision at present is rather patchy, ad hoc and demand-led" (p.1). Fox and Butler contrast the UK picture with that of the USA, in which school-based counseling is a more accepted and available service. Increasing interest, especially in the USA, in School-Based Family Counseling (SBFC) - an integration of "school Counseling and family counseling models within a broad based systems meta-model" (Gerrard, 2008, p.1). is clearly relevant to this discussion.

RELATIONSHIP TO THE SBFC MODEL

The background to, and findings from the study reported here have specific relevance to two particular aspects of the SBFC model – the 'school-preventive' and 'family-remedial' quadrants. The first covers the area of school policy and process for handling situations when a student is challenging the status quo in a significant way. Two questions arise here: how does school policy and process position parents when a student is presenting challenging behavior? And – in the reality of a situation does the school follow its stated policy?

The second area of relevance - in the 'family-remedial' aspect of the SBFC model - concerns the contribution of school counselors in working with students and their families in situations where there is major disruption. How are counselors positioned in relation to school staff and to students? Do counselors see families as intrinsic to the 'client', and part of their responsibility of care?

Both these aspects link to underlying issues of how power is seen and used within the school context, and how the different contributors to an exclusion scenario conceptualise each other.

EVIDENCE-BASED SUPPORT

THE STUDY

This chapter focuses on the findings of a project which explored the experiences of a small group of New Zealand parents of excluded students - giving voice to their thoughts, feelings, hopes and concerns (Smith, 2008). The study adopted a phenomenological approach, in seeking "a glimpse of the lives behind some of the statistics" (Munn & Lloyd, 2005, p. 211). In keeping with Gadamer's (as cited in Sharkey, 2001) caution around reliance on pre-set standardised methods of interpretation, no formal analytical tool was used. Rather, reading and re-reading interview transcripts served to highlight themes.

The author acknowledges that in this study neither the students, nor the school staff involved in the situations described, were interviewed. I am aware that those other parties will have their own, potentially very different, but equally valid perspectives. The report therefore knowingly presents the views of one set of participants in a complex set of circumstances.

The alternative education system in New Zealand is a network of specialised service providers who offer a diverse range of programs for young people who are unable to be maintained within mainstream education for a variety of reasons. Funding is provided by the MOE via local area consortia of secondary schools. For this project an approach was made to one alternative education provider (from here on referred to as AEP). The positive response from the director resulted in AEP becoming the source of the participants. AEP, at the time of the study, had between 15 and 20 young people on its roll, referred from several different high schools.

Contact was established with the parents of teenagers who had been excluded from school, and interviews arranged. Eight interviews were conducted, lasting between 40 and 90 minutes. Interviews were audio-recorded, transcribed, and the transcripts sent back to the interviewees for checking and correction if desired. The interviews used a semi-structured format, based around questions that had been included in the participant letter:

What were the events and time frames around your child's exclusion?
How did the exclusion affect your family? – How did you feel about what was happening? –
What were the practical consequences for your family?
Were there support agencies involved?

As you reflect on what happened, how would you describe your sense of being involved in the process?

Do you have any suggestions concerning the process which would have made it more helpful for you as a family?

These questions were used as discussion-starters and the conversations allowed to unfold, clarifying and developing responses as they emerged. The parents have been given pseudonyms; their children are referred to by their relationship to the parent. All other names have been omitted. The interviewees comprised: 4 natural mothers (Linda, Anne-Marie, Michelle and Pam), who have partners (one of whom was part of the interview – Anne-Marie's partner, Seth); 1 step-mother (Carol), whose partner is the natural father - who at the last minute was unable to be present; 3 natural solo parents (Jessica, Terri [female] and Will). The young people concerned were five girls and three boys, all 14 or 15 at the time their parent/s were interviewed, who had come from four different schools to AEP.

FINDINGS

The intention in this section is to describe themes from the interviews. Firstly, general aspects will be considered. Subsequently, participants' experiences and comments more specifically related to the role of counseling and counselors will be addressed in greater detail. It is important to note that the parents spoke about the events in ways that communicated thoughtfulness, realism and care. They were aware of the complexity of the situations, and not blind to the challenges presented by their teenagers.

> Terri: "I know my son - I know he's a mouthy little shit and he does your head in, but he's not a bad, bad kid..."

While strong feelings were articulated, none of the parents appeared vindictive towards either the school or an individual.

EXCLUSION AND POSITIONING

In summary, one teenager had been formally excluded - Michelle's daughter. One parent had removed her daughter because she could see exclusion was inevitable and did not want her daughter to have that experience. Four students were 'sidelined' into alternative education following periods of stand-down, but prior to formal exclusion. Two young people were effectively barred from acceptance into a high school when they moved to the area on the basis of reputation or record. While there had only been one formal exclusion, all parents felt as if their child had been excluded. These routes to exclusion are diverse and do not neatly follow the MOE (2008) guidelines. They are, as Berkeley (1999) says, "Stories about not fitting in, stories which stubbornly refuse to fit in" (p. 19). Assuming that the MOE statistics (Exclusions and expulsions from school, 2009) are based on formal exclusions, these accounts cast doubt on whether the true extent of exclusion is appreciated. Parents reported that the teenagers had had significant time out of school, and that often the school had not provided support or resources for schoolwork to be carried on at home.

The language used by the parents seems to reflect an adversarial view of the school-parent interaction - a perception of 'them and us'.

> Michelle: "I got a phone call to say ... that **she was going up against the board**."
> (author's emphasis in bold)

The parents experienced the school acting not only as prosecutor, but also as judge and jury. While the Board of Trustees may nominally act as an impartial 'judge', when it was involved, the parents were unable to see the board members as being anything other than an extension of the school hierarchy. There were common threads of not being able to stand up to or disagree with the school view or decision, or of not really having much choice other than to acquiesce.

> Terri: "I feel really intimidated at schools, I always have done, I feel like - they probably don't even realise, but you feel like you're getting spoken down to..."

Not only did the parents report a feeling of 'them and us', but many had experienced a sense of being labelled by the schools in a negative way. Several parents talked about their feelings of powerlessness, of being talked down to, criticized, and blamed, and expressed varying levels of anger, frustration and grief. Jessica was very clear about her sense of being punished, and Linda had felt "bullied".

In contrast, several of the parents commented that stand-downs and exclusion are often not seen as punishment by their teenagers.

> Jessica: "Well, what did your mates say about that?" and she said, "They reckon I'm lucky" - and I actually heard one of them - "Oh, you're at home again, you lucky pig!"..."

IMPACT ON THE FAMILY

The parents reported significant stressing repercussions for the family from the exclusion process. It is obviously impossible to isolate the specific contribution of the school to the stress. However, their reports suggested that the exclusion process had exacerbated rather than alleviated an already stressful situation. The effects on the family were both emotional and practical. The emotional impact of feeling powerless and bullied has already been referred to.

Many of the group had experienced difficulties associated with work and/or the financial repercussions of exclusion.

> Michelle: "I'm self-employed, I had to have all that time off work ..."

The disruption is not just about being at home for anticipated longer periods of time when a child is stood-down or excluded, but also about the intermittent and more immediate demands of responding when a student is sent home, or a meeting is called. Will and Jessica were appreciative of empathetic and flexible employers – and would obviously have been much more affected by a 'harder line' response. While some might feel parents should stay at home to look after their children, this is easier said than done. Many parents are working in order to survive financially and to cover the basics, not the luxuries – and the financial burden is increased in situations where the time out of school is for an extended period.

The effect on the working situation, however, is not just about the financial implications. It is also about the person's sense of integrity and their reputation and credibility.

> Michelle: "People couldn't rely on me to turn up because, just randomly I'd have to say, "Look sorry, I can't make it" and so that wasn't very good..."

Another less obvious financial impact – to the community rather than the individual - is the cost of health care. Both Linda, and Pam's partner had suffered significant health issues and hospitalisation during the exclusion process, which would dramatically affect the hidden costs of exclusion.

One final consequence noted by the parents interviewed was the impact of parental experience on both the excluded teenager and also on younger siblings. As Cullingford (1999) points out, teenagers are not blind to the way their parents are treated by their school, and what they see is likely to influence their own view of, and response to school staff. Both Pam and Terri had been through the experience of an excluded child twice – and felt that the younger sibling had been influenced by watching the experience of the older teenager. Carol mentioned the hero-worship by her eight-year old of his older sibling. Michelle commented on how her younger child was worried that he was going to say or do something wrong that would add to the stress.

COMMUNICATION BETWEEN SCHOOL AND FAMILY

> Linda: "I think they could meet with the parents ….explain that this is a difficult situation…they need someone at the school that is going to stand up and say, "We are here to help you parents with these difficult kids"… "

Several of the parents interviewed commented that they would have hoped for, if not expected, a greater level of communication from the school prior to the situation of a stand-down being implemented – they wanted to know what was happening. At the point where the school instituted a stand-down process, many of the parents, even in situations where they felt the school had communicated reasonably, did not seem particularly well-informed about how the process worked. Of concern is that several of them commented that either what they had discovered had been the result of their initiative, or that they really had no idea where to go to find information. Several had used family members or other families in similar situations, as a resource. It is perhaps not surprising, then, that one of the recurring suggestions made in the interviews related to communication.

> Michelle: "I think there should be an information pack that goes out to all parents… about how if anything happens, what they can do, who they can turn to."

Three parents spoke about the importance of a consistent point of contact.

> Jessica: "They said I could have a meeting with the guidance counsellor but every time I tried to ring him to get an appointment, the guidance counsellor wasn't available …it's like a business, you press button this and button …I wanted one person at the school… …the sort of support I wanted would have been more than meetings."

Michelle had had experience at previous schools of developing action plans to support her daughter, but her more recent experience had not been so positive.

> Michelle: "The school didn't get in contact with any of the services that they said they would, the school didn't do anything."

Michelle, however, still retained faith in the possibilities.

> "Having all the services that can be involved work together and come up with one action plan and I think that if there was someone in the schools doing that, talking with parents, the student and perhaps bringing in services that would assist with that student and how to keep that student in school…"

COUNSELING SUPPORT

The parents' experiences of the provision of counseling differed widely. The availability of counseling was not unfamiliar to some of the parents - sometimes the counseling was within the school, and sometimes from an external agency. Pam's daughter had been to Counseling in the past, but in Pam's view: "...that wasn't really working for her."

Parents commented on their own response to the possibility of counseling:

> Will: "Nine times out of ten I would try and deal with it myself...I wouldn't go to counsellors or something like that."

Other parents reported that no counseling support had been offered. Some had taken the initiative themselves to seek help.

> Terri: "There's just no offer of any help, like counseling or anything ...I actually took my kids to family counseling."

One parent told of the school counselor who had visited their home 'off the record' to see how the family was doing. Another parent talked about the member of staff at the school who ran outdoor education activities and with whom her daughter connected and communicated well, but whom left the school under unclear circumstances.

CHALLENGES AND SOLUTIONS

This section makes some general observations before more specific recommendations are proposed. Significantly one of the challenges in developing this project was in sourcing participants. My initial approach was to three secondary schools. The response from each was along the lines of, "Good idea for a project, but we will not give permission for you to talk to parents of students we have excluded." This response does not indicate a willingness on the part of these schools to receive feedback about their own processes and while it is obviously not fair to generalise from these particular schools, it does not give great confidence when considering schools' openness to evaluate their own processes and to review issues of power, and how they are perceived by significant stakeholders.

As previously noted, the parents whose voices have been heard in the research literature reviewed describe a sense of invisibility and powerlessness when their teenagers were excluded from school. The comparative lack of parents' voices within the literature reinforces that lack of 'voice'. The parents in this study echo that same sense. There is a significant challenge for schools and school counselors to ensure that this invisibility is not allowed to continue.

These reflections raise questions concerning the ways in which parents are seen – either as problems or partners. The contrasting discourses around exclusion merit further attention. Underpinning philosophies influence policy and also subconsciously orientate people into particular patterns of relating. The self-reported experiences of parents in this study indicate that in practice, if not necessarily by intent, the schools involved seem to have created an adversarial and excluding ethos around exclusion, which had negatively impacted the families. Such an ethos may make life simpler for the school in the short term, but is likely to be counter-productive for all concerned in the longer view. Taken together, these concerns need to be considered seriously by school governance and management – the bodies and individuals who either intentionally or by default create the ethos of any school. In addition, school counselors would be wise to reflect both on their own positioning within these situations, and also on their ability to influence school policy and practice, taking up the social justice and advocacy component of their role. The SBFC model is ideally placed to stimulate collaborative ways of working. Further research is warranted that explores both the benefits and challenges of the approach in specific situations such as those which may involve exclusion.

MULTICULTURAL COUNSELING CONSIDERATIONS

Considering the issue from a multi-cultural perspective, as previously mentioned young people from minority ethnic group are often excluded more frequently than those from the dominant culture. This is true of the New Zealand context in general, and specifically true in this study – five of the eight parent participants would identify as Maori. To embark on an exploration of the reasons for these differences would be to engage with an extremely complex and potentially emotive debate – one which is beyond the scope of this chapter. However, simplistically, cultural perspectives affect students' and their parents' views of education in general and their school in particular. Equally, cultural perspectives influence staff and counselors' views of students and their families.

While much has been written on the broad issue of multicultural Counseling it seems there is less research specifically addressing multicultural issues in school Counseling. Despite the considerable attention to bi-cultural issues in the education of Maori and Pasifika young people in New Zealand, there seems to be little research that explores appropriate models and practices of school Counseling for these students. Bishop and Berryman (2006) identified relationship with teachers as the "most influential factor" (p.254) affecting performance in school. This characteristic had been identified also by Hawk, Cowley, Hill and Sutherland (2002), who qualified the element by referring to "the right kind" of relationship – expressed specifically as empathy, caring and respect. Hawk et al talk about the importance of reciprocity – when teachers live confidence in, and loyalty to, students, mixed with high expectations, there is a higher likelihood that these characteristics will be reciprocated. While this work addressed the student-teacher relationship it would seem very appropriate to transpose the findings to the student-school counselor context.

RECOMMENDATIONS

The situations around exclusion in which families find themselves clearly have the potential to overwhelm the resources of the family itself. Most schools are generally not equipped as a social service agencies to deal with complex, often long-standing, situations. Traditionally, school counselors do not have the time, expertise or resources to respond adequately to the situations exemplified by the families in this study. However, for schools to simply wash their hands of the situation or seek to pass the responsibility for involvement elsewhere is not a response calculated to improve the long-term well-being of family, student, or, for that matter, the school itself. The SBFC model with its systemic approach is well positioned to recognise and address the challenges in a positive manner. The way of working needs to include cooperation, clear conceptualisation, good communication, and consistent coordination.

1. Cooperation: building on the potential of parents as partners, there would appear to be a significant body of international empirical research that demonstrates the positive outcomes for all concerned arising from cooperative, multi-agency approaches (e.g., Milbourne, 2005; Stanley, Canham&Cureton, 2006; Van Hoose&Legrand, 2000; Vulliamy& Webb, 2003). SBFC sits as a specific model within this broader framework. Admittedly, in the current study, some of the families accessed other agencies for assistance. However, this seems to have been at the initiative of the families themselves and to have happened in a somewhat random fashion, with little evidence of collaboration or inter-agency communication. The SBF Counseling team can act as a key point of contact and cooperation, drawing in available resources.

2. Clear conceptualisation: as previously mentioned, discourses that inherently problematise parents and apportion blame on the family are unhelpful. There is need for objective assessment. The challenge obviously is to be able to provide and communicate such assessment without creating defensive position-taking. Also required are strategies that overcome the resistance to Counseling illustrated by participants Will and Pam.

An important aspect of this is the issue of triangulation. Gerrard (2008) discusses the the potential development of triangulation between family, school and counselor. With respect to this issue, writers (as cited in Gerrard, 2008) have seen SBFC as having potential advantages over other patterns of multi-external-agency involvement. SBFC is suggested as being less liable to triangulation "because the school-based family counsellor is not seen as a "third party" but rather viewed as part of the school system" (p. 2). However, it is important to bear in mind that if parents see the school system as antagonistic and dominating, this "being part of the system" is inherently problematic. Further exploration of such dynamics is called for.

3. Communication: While information may be theoretically accessible, such as on a website or in written brochures and leaflets, it would appear that greater attention could be given to connecting families with those sources of information and support. The simple existence of such resources cannot be assumed to equate to engagement with them by families. Additionally, the parents in this study reflected a desire for communication that is relational, not simply informational. This leads to the final point.

4. As mentioned by Michelle and Anne-Marie, whatever form multi-disciplinary approaches take, *Coordination and Consistency* are important. If a school takes responsibility for working in this way, it goes a long way to reduce overlap, confusion and unclear communication. Inevitably staff leave and are replaced, and policies and processes evolve over time, but such changes somehow need to keep the well-being of the student at the centre of the picture.

SUMMARY

The parents who were interviewed are clearly under no illusions that these are easy situations to resolve or that it is only a case of finding the appropriate magic wand to 'make it all better'. However, the parents challenge the commonly-held discourse that it is the family situation that is to blame for student behavioral difficulties - and that problem children come from problem parents. There is much in the interviews to advocate not simply relating to parents as people, but rather moving towards accepting them as partners. These parents communicate care and commitment, linked with a long-term knowledge and understanding of their children.

Schools concerned not only for student academic achievement but also for social well-being need to be aware of parental perceptions and, as those perceived to be the power-holders in the situations discussed, need to be the initiators of redressing the power dynamic. Parental well-being, student well-being and what happens at school are inextricably linked. One parent, Anne-Marie, talked about feeling like "David going up against Goliath". While parental resilience and hope may win out - in the original story David was the victor in the situation - educational policy and, more importantly, school practice could be such that parents do not need to see themselves as David confronting Goliath in the first place.

In conclusion, it is worth noting that the parents interviewed communicated a sense of hope - a belief that both the systems they had encountered could be different and also that their teenagers, through alternative education if not in mainstream schooling, could make something of their lives. The challenge for schools, counselors and other involved agencies is to relate and work in ways that, rather than quashing constructive possibilities, create positive reality out of that hope. The SBFC model is ideally suited to contribute to new ways of handling these challenging situations.

I wish to thank the parents who shared their stories so openly, and wish them all well for their on-going parenting journey. My thanks, too, to the New Zealand Families Commission for their support of the project.

REFERENCES

A parent's story. (2002, Autumn). Education Links, 64, 39. Retrieved from http://web.ebscohost.com/ehost/pdfviewer/pdfviewer?vid=10&hid=8&sid=c2a6e13c-3f0a-416e-8005-51c68e4b3d62%40sessionmgr10

Berkeley, R. (1999). Not fitting in: Exclusions from school, a local study. Paper presented at the British Educational Association Conference, Brighton, England, September 2-5.

Bishop, R., & Berryman, M. (2006). *Culture speaks, cultural relationships and classroom learning.* Wellington, New Zealand: Huia Publishers.

Brodie, I., &Berridge, D. (1996).*School exclusion: Research themes and issues.* UK: University of Luton Press.

Bromell, D., & Hyland, M. (2007, March). *Social inclusion and participation: A guide for policy and planning.* Wellington, New Zealand: Ministry of Social Development.

Brown, T. (2007). Lost and turned out: Academic, social and emotional experiences of students excluded from school. *Urban Education*, 42(5), 432-455.

Cole, A. L., & Knowles, J. G. (Eds.). (2001*). Lives in context: The art of life history research.* Walnut Creek, CA: AltaMira Press.

Crowe, A. (2006). Guidance and Counseling in New Zealand schools: Exploring the issues. *New Zealand Journal of Counseling*, 26(3), 16-25.

Cullingford, C. (1999). *The causes of exclusion: Home, school and the development of young criminals.* London, England: Kogan Page.

Exclusions and expulsions from school. (2009). Retrieved from http://www.educationcounts.govt.nz/indicators/student_participation/schooling/1947

Gerrard, B. (2008). School-based family counseling: Overview, trends, and recommendations for future research. *International Journal for School-Based Family Counseling*, 1, 2-15.

Goebert, D., Bell, C., Hishinuma, E., Nahulu, L., Johnson, R., Foster, J.& Andrade, N.(2004). Influence of family adversity on school-related behavioural problems among multi-ethnic high school students. *School Psychology International*, 25(2), 193-206.

Gordon, A. (2001). School exclusions in England: Children's voices and adult solutions? *Educational Studies*, 27(1), 69-85.

Harrison, M. (2004). *Education matters: Government, markets and New Zealand schools.* Wellington, New Zealand: Education Forum.

Hawk, K., Cowley, E., Hill, J., & Sutherland, S. (2002). The importance of the teacher/student relationship for Maori and Pasifika students. *SET Research Information for teachers, 3,* 44-49.

Hughes, C. (1996). The colonisation of the school counselor's role. *Newsletter of the New Zealand Association of Counsellors*, 17(1), 40-41.

Information for parents: Suspension....(2010, January). Retrieved from http://www.minedu.govt.nz/~/media/MinEdu/Files/EducationSectors/PrimarySecondary/StandDo wnSuspensionExclusionExpulsions/SuspensionsParentInfoWEB.pdf

Inter-agency working to prevent school exclusion.(2001, September). Retrieved from http://www.jrf.org.uk/knowledge/findings/social policy/961.asp

Knipe, D., Reynolds, M., & Milner, S. (2007). Exclusion in schools in Northern Ireland: The pupils' voice. Research Papers in Education, 22(4), 407-424.

Kvale, S. (1996). *Interviews: An introduction to qualitative research interviewing*. Thousand Oaks, CA: Sage.

Links between school, family and the community: A review of the evidence. (1999, November). Retrieved from http://www.jrf.org.uk/knlwledge/findings/socialpolicy/N19.asp

Lloyd, G. (2000). Gender and exclusion from school. In J. Salisbury & S. Riddell (Eds.), *Gender, policy and educational change: Shifting agendas in the UK and Europe* (pp. 257-273). London: Routledge.

McDonald, T., & Thomas, G. (2003).Parents' reflections on their children being excluded. *Emotional and Behavioural Difficulties*, 8(2), 108-119.

Milbourne, L. (2005, December). Children, families and inter-agency work: Experiences of partnership work in primary education settings. *British Educational Research Journal*, 31(6), 675-695.

Ministry of Education.(2008). Guidelines for principals and Boards of Trustees of state and state integrated schools. Retrieved from http://www.minedu.govt.nz/NZEducation/EducationPolicies/Schools/StanddownsSuspensionsExcl usionsExpulsions.aspx

Munn, P., & Lloyd, G. (2005). Exclusion and excluded pupils. *British Educational Research Journal*, 31(2), 205-221.

Parents of suspended pupils should stay at home says Blair. (2005, July 22) *Education,* 188, 2. Retrieved from http://web.ebscohost.com/ehost/pdfviewer/pdfviewer?vid=8&hid=8&sid=f903aa24-f1d5-4b31-9014-8c5ddb0c10bc%40sessionmgr13

Parsons, C. (2005, June). School exclusion: The will to punish. *British Journal of Educational Studies*, 53(2), 187-211.

Partington, G. (2001, December). Student suspensions: The influence on students and their parents. *Australian Journal of Education*, 45(3), 323. Retrieved from http://find.galegroup.com/gps/infomark.do?&contentSet=IACDocuments&type=retrieve&tabID=T 002&prodId=IPS&docId=A85060412&source=gale&srcprod=ITOF&userGroupName=per_bil&versi on=1.0

Sharkey, P. (2001). Hermeneutic phenomenology. In R. Barnacle (Ed*.), Phenomenology*.(chap. 2). Melbourne, Australia:RMIT University Press.

Suspension from school.(2009, August). Retrieved from http://www,educationcounts.edcentre.govt.nz/indicators/student_participation/schooling/53413

Stanley, M., Canham, D., &Cureton, V. (2006, February).Assessing prevalence of emotional and behavioural problems in suspended middle school students. *The Journal of School Nursing*, 22(1), 40-47.

Tett, L. (2001, May/June). Parents as problems or parents as people? Parental involvement programmes, schools and adult educators. *International Journal of Lifelong Education*, 20(3), 188-198.

Van Hoose, J., &Legrand, P. (2000, January). It takes parents, the whole village, and school to raise the children. *Middle School Journal*, 31(3), 32-37.

Vulliamy, G., & Webb, R. (2003, Winter). Supporting disaffected pupils: Perspectives from the pupils, their parents and their teachers. *Educational Research*, 45(3), 275-286.

Winslade, J. (1996). The school counsellor and parents. *Newsletter of the New Zealand Association of Counsellors*, 17(1), 32-34.

Chapter 24

Assessing Individual or Family Dynamics through the Collage Life-Story Elicitation Technique (CLET)

Gertina J. van Schalkwyk

OVERVIEW: The Collage Life-Story Elicitation Technique (CLET) is an auto-ethnographic and representational technique that scaffolds the process of narrating significant relationships and attachments in everyday life of children, adolescent and adults. Based on the theoretical underpinnings of narrative psychology, social constructionism and symbolic interactionism, the CLET provides a way in which participants can express and perform narratives involving cognitive, motivational and affective aspects of autobiographical remembering as they engage in both collage-making and storytelling. The CLET brings to light rich and vivid stories about the self and relationships in a variety of settings such as the family and the school, and provides the counselor and researcher access to perceptions that lurk below the level of awareness or that are often suppressed because of fears of retribution. Thus, the CLET can serve as tool for intake interviewing and treatment planning, externalizing conflicting relationships and problems, and fits well within the School-based Family Counseling (SBFC) model for preventive and remedial purposes.

BACKGROUND

Telling stories—life stories, stories about key events, stories about one's family or school, or stories about significant attachments—has become a key feature of ethnographic inquiry and narrative therapy for different population groups (Clandinin & Connelly, 2000; McAdams, 2001, 2006). The basic premise is that story telling is a mechanism by which experiences are rendered meaningful within some form of structure, interweaving physical, cognitive and affective aspects of development across the lifespan (Anderson & Gehart, 2007; Taylor, 2006; White, 2007). Storytelling provides a framework for studying humans as relational beings and in the context and content of their self-defining memories (Bohn & Berntsen, 2008; Bruner, 2010; Gergen & Gergen, 2006; Habermas & Bluck, 2000; Kulkofsky & Klemfuss, 2008; McLean & Pasupathi, 2010). It is the integrative configuration of self-in-the-world and the psychosocial consequences of the co-constructed, relational self.

A challenge for many counselors, however, is finding ways to elicit reliable and detailed narratives that provide access to individual's experiences and perceptions of relationships to others, as well as externalizing the underlying problem (Brannen, Mooney, & Statham, 2009; Chan, 2004; White, 2007). Some client populations also experience difficulty telling their stories due to a number of obstacles such as age, suppressing a past filled with trauma, discontent and emotional cut-off, cultural prohibitions, or lack of discursive modes for expressing themselves in language of the dominant group (or counselor) (Monk, Winslade, Crocket, & Epston, 1997; Van Schalkwyk, 2010). For example, children and adolescents are only starting the storytelling process and are often constrained by a fear of retribution should they disclose their vulnerabilities (Bohn & Berntsen, 2008; Kulkofsky & Klemfuss, 2008). Although adults might have developed greater interpretive capabilities and can tell an integrative life story, they are often constrained by cultural and societal cues that prevent or inhibit self-disclosure (Bauer, McAdams, & Pals, 2008).

In view of these (and other) obstacles, the Collage Life-story Elicitation Technique (CLET) was developed as a way to explore life-story remembering in a way that could overcome the reluctance of some—specifically those in distress or in cross-cultural settings—to tell the full story and disclose or externalize the underlying problematic (Van Schalkwyk, 2010). Within this technique, I accept that collage making is a valid social action, a narrative performance that provides a channel for making sense of the past and integrating experiences with the present and an anticipated future (Eisner, 2002; Fivush, 1991; Monk et al., 1997; Weber, 2008). Collage making combines with conversation or storytelling to generate rich descriptions and vivid memories. It is a kind of 'performance', in which the perceptions emerge in relation to the multiple voices of the social and the private self. In a collaborative process of narrating both non-verbal and verbal recollections of the past, the CLET engages the individual or family in co-constructing stories for interpretation and co-action.

Thus, the purpose of the CLET is to explore what lies beneath the level of awareness and gain access to experiences and perceptions of real-life relationships, events and attachments that could shed light on the dynamic conflict and cause for concern. Based on life story remembering (McAdams, 1993), narrative psychology (McLean & Pasupathi, 2010; Monk et al., 1997; Lieblich, McAdams, & Josselson, 2004) and the theoretical underpinnings of social constructionism (Gergen, 2000), the objective with the CLET is to gain a greater understanding of how the individual co-constructs his or her reality for everyday living. Children, adolescents and adults alike can be quite creative and resourceful when disclosing their distresses in a playful and engaging manner (Bauer, McAdams, & Pals, 2008; Brannen et al., 2009; Powell & Snow, 2007; White, 2007). Through life-story remembering using the CLET, individuals and groups represent their perceptions and interpretations of local customs and practices, attitudes, relationships and interactions that emerge in interactive systems and in different settings such as the home, at school and in recreational environments (Van Schalkwyk, 2010).

PROGRAM DESCRIPTION

The CLET is a plausible and integrative method to study the experiences and perceptions of individuals and groups (e.g., the family). "It provides scope for collecting and analyzing self-defining memories and expressions or representations of self, involving autobiographical memories, as well as cognitive, motivational and affective aspects as the individual engages in collaborative process of (co)constructing life narratives" (Van Schalkwyk, 2010, p. 676). Through a process of scaffolding, the individual or group is provided with a mechanism supporting and aiding remembering and narrating significant events, relationships and attachments to people and objects using different modes of expression. Thus, following the sequential steps outlined below, the CLET can uncover memories from the past that have or could have significant meanings to the individual and a bearing on the underlying problematic causing distress in the present. Whether conducted as a face-to-face semi-structured interview with the individual or family or in a written format with small (focus) groups, the procedures unfold in the same manner following five steps outlined below. The counselor should familiarize him or herself with the steps as well as the subsequent analysis and interpretation before proceeding.

PROCEDURE

The CLET unfolds in five non-negotiable sequential steps. Step 1 entails the making of a collage, followed by 'storytelling' (step 2), positioning of the dialogical self (step 3), juxtaposition (step 4), and self-reflection (step 5). The individual completes each step before commencing with the next one all the time collaborating with the counselor in constructing and interpreting their stories. Below I explain each step for collecting the narratives (data) in more detail. The tasks for each of the steps are explained to the individual using simple and easy language to ensure understanding, and can easily be translated into the native language of the individual in counseling.

Following the explication of procedures for collecting stories, I explain the analytic strategy for making sense of the non-verbal and verbal narratives collected utilizing the CLET. This analytic strategy provides a broad overview of how the counselor can use the materials to gain insight in the client's everyday functioning in different settings. However, it should be noted that the CLET should not be interpreted rigidly as it is aimed at hypothesis generating rather than formal diagnosis. Additional strategies might be necessary should one suspect more severe forms of pathology. Nonetheless, the CLET is useful for generating provisional hypotheses that can be explored further during the counseling process.

STEPS FOR CONDUCTING THE CLET

Preparation. Prior to conducting the CLET semi-structured interview, it is essential to determine the focus area or topic. In this regard, the counselor can focus on any particular area for the narrations that are relevant to the referral issue and/or the topic under investigation. Focus areas usually involve relationships and attachments, developmental issue, settings, events, and so forth. It is best to have a focus area at the outset that can be clearly communicated to the individual or group participating in this process. Furthermore, prepare all materials necessary for proceeding smoothly through each step. Apart from sound knowledge of the CLET steps and their sequence, the following preparations are important:

a) Collect a number of magazines, journals and newspapers to be used for collage making. There is no restriction on the kind of magazines and it is not necessary to have the same magazines for all individuals. However, it is advisable to collect those magazines with similar content for each individual to allow sufficient scope for selecting pictures and images for the collage making (see also discussion below in Step 1 of CLET procedures). Alternatively collect a range of images publicly available (e.g., on the Internet) and representing a range of categories. It is advisable to collect 20+ images of (i) people (individuals, dyads, triads, groups), (ii) human-like figures (cartoons), (iii) settings and events with people (e.g., celebration, eating), (iv) objects and artefacts with no human involvement, (v) any other relevant images to the focus area for the narration.

b) Materials for collage making: blank A3 (or A4) paper, scissors, glue, pen/pencil and crayons (for drawing if needed).

c) Voice recorder for audio recording the conversation (in the case of an individual or group face-to-face interview). Voice recording is helpful for later transcription creating the field texts for analysis and is strongly advised since writing down all narratives can interfere in the smooth flow of the procedures. Video recording is optional although advised for children with serious disabilities such as Autism Spectrum Disorder (ASD) and to obtain further material for behavioral observation. However, recording can only be done with consent from the individual or, in the case of children, the parent or guardian.

Setting. Prepare the right setting that is private, has sufficient space and furniture, and is not noisy. The interview can be conducted at the individual 's home or in a public place where facilities are available. As far as possible, avoid interferences during the execution of the CLET, whether from parents or teachers when working with a child, children when working with adults, or any other outside noises and disturbances (e.g., phone calls).

Step 1: Collage making

The first step in the CLET entails the making of a collage. The adjacent column reflects the basic instructions for collage making and encourages the individual's agency in selecting images and/or cuttings from the magazines and print media provided for making a collage.

Instructions for collage making in the CLET project

> Create your own life story (or focus area) collage. Use at least 8-10 pictures, images, cuttings (also text) and drawings. Try to answer the question:
> *"How does this picture/image/drawing represent something important or memorable about _____ (focus area) in my life?"*
>
> You are free to paste the images in any way you want on the paper provided. You can also make some drawings on your collage if you want to. Take your time but try to do this as quickly as possible so that we can proceed with the next part.

The collage is a non-verbal narrative in the form of a poster or visual representation of the focus area—i.e., the phenomenon identified as the topic for inquiry. For example, exploring children's perceptions of family life, the focus of collage-making will be *the family* and the child will select pictures, images or cuttings (also text) and drawings from the available magazines that represent her or his perceptions of family life. Collage-making takes approximately 20-30 minutes, depending on the situation, the individual's age and level of functioning, and the topic. Making a collage aims to stimulate remembering and sets the individual—even adult individuals—at ease for the next steps in the CLET process. Although 8-10 images should be sufficient to elicit rich and saturated narratives, more images are also possible and some contexts (focus areas) require 10-15 images for the collage-making. It is also possible to ask the older participants to make the collage at home and bring it to the next session when the further CLET steps unfold in a semi-structured interview setting. When asking the participant to make the collage at home, it is advisable not to present Steps 2 to 5 at the outset but execute these steps when the participant attends the next session.

The CLET makes use of locally relevant magazines and print media and assumes basic motor skills for cutting and pasting images on the collage. As described above, the use of local print media is important as these provide valuable socio-cultural cues that would not be available if images are pre-determined through prior selection from culturally irrelevant sources. Counselors who want to use the CLET are advised to collect magazines and other print media over a period of time and from whichever sources available in the local context. For example, ask the local newsstand owner for copies of magazines after the expiration date, or get friends to provide their old magazines instead of discarding them in the dustbin. Magazines are social products indigenous to the culture in which they are published and thus contain cues that are reminiscent of social construction of everyday life for the individual (Threadgold, 2003). Therefore, it is advisable to use magazines that have relevance to the participant's daily life and with which he or she is familiar in the local context and, if possible, contains writing in the participant's native language. Locally familiar magazines provide the participant with the freedom to narrate her or his own non-verbal story using culturally relevant cues instead of predetermined categories—i.e., when the counselor selects and presents images from other sources such as the internet to the client.

As indicated above, there is no restriction on the kind of magazines used for the collage making although counselors should preferably not use magazines with sensitive information such as explicit sexually-related images. The nature of the self-selected images or pictures, the pasting of these images on the collage and their relationship to one another, as well as the construction of the collage as a whole represents the participant's autobiographical remembering of the phenomenon and will be interpreted through the sense-making process described below. The counselor can also ask the participant to bring her or his own photos, picture, images and cuttings (also text) from magazines to the interview session. This approach works well with older children, adolescents and adults, although some also prefer to rather use magazine clippings in order to maintain confidentiality and avoid self-disclosure. When working with young children, those who do not have the cognitive-motor skills for cutting images from a magazine or children previously diagnosed with cognitive impairment, the counselor can choose to pre-select and cut-out images of different type and nature (see Table 25.1) and provide these during the session to the child for pasting and/or further cutting. Some children might also need assistance with pasting the images. Nonetheless, the counselor should take care not to impose any prescriptions or advice about how to make the collage (i.e., pictures to choose, where to paste an image, and so on) and allow the participant sufficient freedom to do this in her or his own way.

Step 2: Storytelling

In Step 2 the individual engages actively in constructing micro-narratives stimulated by the images on the collage. In a semi-structured interview setting, the counselor asks the participant to describe each picture/image on the collage as best they can.	**Ask the following questions:** *Tell a short story about the picture/drawing on the collage.* *Why did you choose this picture or drawing to represent _____ (focus area)?* *What makes this picture or drawing important to you as a representation of ___ (focus area)?*

The individual narrates a story about each image on the collage, giving reasons for selecting them, describing thoughts, and feelings and the meanings each image brings out and explaining the significance of the image in her or his life and in relation to the focus area. Images on the collage are numbered consecutively as the narratives unfold, providing a point of reference for later steps in the CLET and for analytic purposes. The narrating takes place in the language with which the participant feels comfortable (e.g., native language or English), and should allow the participant to tell whatever comes to mind as the authentic author of her/his own story (McAdams, 1993). The co-constructor— that is, the counselor—supports the narrator demonstrating appropriate responses affirming the participant's knowledge about her or his own memories regarding the focus area or phenomenon.

Step 3: Positioning the self and eliciting silent voices

The third step continues the autobiographical remembering and reminiscing, asking the participant to comment on two issues: A place on the collage where she or he would like to position the self. An image he or she could not find but would have liked to add to the collage.	**Ask the following questions:** *Where would you put yourself (a picture of yourself if you had one) in this collage at this point in time?* *What image would you like to add if you could find the right one?*

Mark the selected position clearly and ask the participant to give reasons, meanings and emotions related to this positioning of the self. As explained below in the analytic strategy, the individual's self-positioning provides some insight into her or his ownership of and involvement in the reported memories and perceptions of self-in-the-world of everyday living along two dimensions of the player-spectator orientation and the close-distanced self-other relationships. Discuss also the image the participant would have liked to add asking about the meanings and emotions such an image would have evoked. The silent voice often refers to a suppressed memory or relationship and alerts the counselor to further explore if not during the execution of the CLET, then later in counseling. For example, when remembering family relationships one could explore further why a particular family member is not mentioned or depicted in the collage.

Step 4: Juxtaposition (comparing similarities and differences)

In this step, the participant reflects upon the dynamic conflict portrayed in the similarities and differences of images on the collage. After selecting three images, ask the participant to describe the similarities and differences and to give reasons.	**Ask the participant to:** *Select two pictures/images with similar meanings, and one picture/image with an opposing (different) meaning.* *What are the differences and similarities between these images?*

The counselor should again mark and/or number the similar and different images on the collage for later reference. If the individual has difficulty selecting similar and different pictures/images for this step (e.g., younger children) the counselor can assist with the task. Select two similar images that the participant focused on most during the storytelling stage (Step 2) and an opposing image as one he or she skipped over very quickly. Alternatively, select two images of positive meanings and one with a negative meaning. Reflecting upon the differences and similarities explore the dialogue between narrative voices and inter-subjectivities (Markova, 2003)—that is, the dialogue between voices from the past with those of the present, voices that may be part of the outside or the inside world of the self (Hermans, 2001), or voices that tell of a conflict yet to be discovered. It is an important step to uncover or externalize the potential problem. Although comparing differences and similarities once only should be sufficient to uncover such dynamic conflict, repeating the step two or three times could elicit further meanings regarding the problem saturated narratives underlying the representations on the collage.

Step 5: Reflection and Closure

For the final step in the CLET interview, the individual gets a chance to reflect upon the process of making the collage and telling her or his story, and to add further information she or he might think relevant to the topic. This step also provides some form of debriefing, and allows the individual to ask questions about things that created confusion during the collage making and storytelling.	**Ask the participant:** *How did you feel when making this collage and telling your stories?* *What do you feel now that we are almost done?* *Can you think of anything you would like to add that you did not include previously?*

During the execution of the CLET, emotions may emerge caused by disturbing or difficult events in the participant's life. The counselor should be sensitive and empathic in these emotional states, and preferably not prompt for further elaboration if it appears to be a difficult topic for the child. Debriefing is imperative and should be available at the participant's request, particularly if the CLET is conducted for research purposes rather than as an intake interview for potential clients. Throughout the process of conducting the CLET, the counselor can use appropriate prompts as a form of conversational scaffolding and encourage reflection and self-understanding. However, avoid expanding the parameters of the focus area as this can create confusion for the individual as well for later analysis. It is also advisable, in the case of a face-to-face interview, to record the conversations for later transcription—and translation if necessary. Furthermore, the individual can be invited to read the transcript of the interview as soon as it is completed. This will give the individual an opportunity to ensure that you have captured her or his stories correctly in writing, and provide her or him a chance to add or change something should they wish to do so.

Although narrative inquiry or storytelling is a plausible and integrative framework for exploring experiences and possible problems, the CLET adds a scaffolding process to life story remembering that helps to overcome perceived obstacles that some client populations have with autobiographical remembering. The collage (non-verbal) and the storytelling (verbal) thus provide multiple stories for each case, allowing for case study analytic procedures to follow (see *Interpretation of CLET* below). The CLET can also be combined with other diagnostic tools to gain a deeper understanding of the problem or as confirmation for interpretations. After completion of the CLET interview, the counselor is encouraged to compose field notes and analytic memos pertaining the experience and impressions gleaned from doing the CLET with the individual or family. This adds a further data source for interpretation, as each case solicits its own reflections and interpretations.

INTERPRETATION OF CLET NARRATIVE TEXTS

The purpose of this section is to present an explication of the analytic strategy for analyzing and interpreting the CLET case. The objective of analysis and interpretation is to make sense of the data and to build a valid and compelling argument for further action and co-action (e.g., treatment planning). Each CLET interview follows a central question or focus area. For example, in a study exploring children's perceptions of family life, the central question could be *"How do children in middle childhood perceive the family in which they grow up?"* (Van Schalkwyk, 2011). Children in middle childhood aged 9-12 years and living with their families in different cultures could tell their stories following the steps in the CLET, and reveal both similar and different perceptions about family life in their culture. Their perceptions not only reveal local customs of childcare and practices in the family, but also attitudes, relationships and interactions that emerged in the child-family interactive system in different settings such as the home, at school and in recreational environments (Mulvaney, 2011; Van Schalkwyk & Lijadi, 2013). Some of these stories also required further attention by a local counselor particularly when family relationships were distressful to the child.

TRANSCRIPTION AND TRANSLATION

Moving from speech to text entails transcription of interview material. It is advisable, even in a counseling setting, to transcribe the spoken word into text as an important part of analyzing and interpreting the content of the CLET and provide evidence for further action. The functions of a transcript are as follows:

Helping us to take note of a particular phenomena

Providing accessible data archive material (i.e., empirical data of an interview)

Providing quick access to a range of interactional episodes that can be inspected for comparative purposes

Providing the reader with limited but useful access to phenomena discussed in analysis

Alternatively the counselor can refer back to the audio recording during analysis and interpretation, although this can be difficult for a longer interview. Translation will also be necessary if the CLET was not conducted in English or in the language of the counselor. The translation entails a verbatim translation where the entire transcript is translated to capture the inherent meanings and intent of the narrator. Different procedures exist for translation of narratives, and the counselor should use the one most suitable for the textual data obtained through the CLET.

MAKING SENSE OF THE CLET NARRATIVE TEXTS

The CLET data, when appropriately completed in a sequential manner as described above, provides the counselor with a holistic single-case study containing three embedded units analysis for examination and interpretation (Figure 1) (Baxter & Jack, 2008; Yin, 2009). The first unit of analysis pertains to the collage as a non-verbal narrative and represents the nature and content of the participant's autobiographical memories. For example, as a non-verbal narrative, the collage contains information about significant people (individuals and groups), objects-in-the world, settings and events, the relationships of self with others, the cognitive functions relevant to organizing memories in coherent fashion, and the underlying meanings that the individual has difficulty verbalizing.

The second unit of analysis concerns to the stories the participant told for each image. These are micro-narratives stimulated by the images on the collage and representing the participant's authentic memories and interpretations of past events as they influence the present and anticipated future functioning of the participant. The story grid as a combination of all the steps of the CLET constitutes the third unit of analysis and represents the interweaving of a full but realistic range of memories with the cognitive, motivational and affective aspects of the self-in-the-world. Systematically analyzing and interpreting the case will give the counselor access to different layers of memories and stories—also problem-saturated stories—that affect functioning in different settings. Whereas the underlying dynamic conflict and problem saturated narratives might otherwise go unobserved, utilizing the CLET and making sense of the data bring to light that which the counselor needs to address through the therapeutic process. The case analysis and sense-making process of the CLET unfolds in different sequential phases as the counselor organizes the data for a holistic single-case analysis and explore the deeper meanings and connotations elicited through autobiographical remembering (Miles & Huberman,

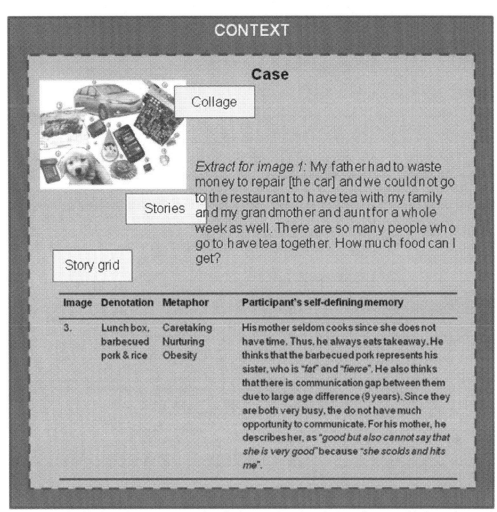

CONTEXT

Case

Collage

Extract for image 1: My father had to waste money to repair [the car] and we could not go to the restaurant to have tea with my family and my grandmother and aunt for a whole week as well. There are so many people who go to have tea together. How much food can I get?

Stories

Story grid

Image	Denotation	Metaphor	Participant's self-defining memory
3.	Lunch box, barbecued pork & rice	Caretaking Nurturing Obesity	His mother seldom cooks since she does not have time. Thus, he always eats takeaway. He thinks that the barbecued pork represents his sister, who is "fat" and "fierce". He also thinks that there is communication gap between them due to large age difference (9 years). Since they are both very busy, the do not have much opportunity to communicate. For his mother, he describes her, as "good but also cannot say that she is very good" because "she scolds and hits me".

Figure 1 Embedded single-case protocol with three units of analysis and permeable boundary with the context or setting

1994; Van Schalkwyk, 2010; Yin 2009). The analytic strategy developed for analyzing CLET data is described below. It is a coherent and systematic way to explore each unit of analysis (collage, stories and story grid) along 14 categories for coding the various units of analysis, and interpreting the participant's range of memories in a given context and about the specified phenomenon or focus area in response to context-specific question. It also allows the counselor to identify the underlying conflict or problem of which the participant is yet unaware but where the counselor wishes to target her or his intervention strategies.

Phase 1: Analyzing the Collage. The first phase involves analyzing and coding the collage as non-verbal narrative (unit of analysis 1) while temporarily ignoring or bracketing the verbal micro-narratives. Read the collage as a stand-alone non-verbal narrative while observing and coding Categories 1 to 7 as listed in Table 24.1. The analysis of the collage takes place independent from the stories

Table 24.1 Categories for analyzing the collage as non-verbal narrative of the CLET

Category	Description	Analytic action
Number of images	The number of images indicates the participant's adherence to prescriptions, where fewer images could indicate the level of cognitive functioning required for autobiographical remembering and/or distress resulting in repression of memories.	
Nature of images	Categorise the nature of images representing one of the following categories: - human characters (e.g., people, individuals, groups, cartoons), - settings and life events (e.g., travel, celebration involving humans) - non-human characters (e.g., animals, non-human cartoons) - objects/artifacts, - scenery (e.g., nature), and - other (e.g., not fiting any of the above)	List the denotations for each image and assign them to one of the six groups and count images in terms of the six groups. Depending on the context and/or topic, further groups could be added for a more in-depth understanding of the denotations and connotations (see also the analysis of the story grid in phase 3 of the analytic strategy).
Proximity	The overall snse of self-other closeness where a numerical value of 1 represents closeness in relation to people, and 2 represents self-object/artifact/ scenery closeness.	Coding: 1 = self-other closeness 2 = self-object closeness Note: >50% images with humans could be interpreted as closeness to people and would be interpreted somewhat differently than closeness to objects, artifacts or scenery depending on the topic or focus of the CLET. However, this will only be done in the final phase of analysis and interpretation.
Narrative tone	The overall emotional content of the non-verbal (collage) narrative where 0 reflects a neutral emotive tone, 1 reflects a positive tone, and 2 reflects a negative tone	Coding: 1 = positive narrative tone 2 = negative narrative tone
Construction	The overall sense of structure in the collage depicting the underlying cognitive organization of memories related to the topic, and where 1 represents a sequential and 2 a random organization of the collage.	Coding: 1 = sequential (i.e., ordered clockwise or row-by-row) 2 = random (i.e., triggered by memories and not sequential)
Coherence	The overall sense that the individual's descriptive efforts in performing a non-verbal (collage) narrative were related to the topic (1) or unrelated to the topic	Coding: 1 = related to the topic 2 = unrelated to the topic

	or focus area (2).	
Self-positioning	The position on the collage where the individual positioned the self (step 3) and in relation to the centre of the collage or on the periphery of the collage.	Coding: 1 = close to centre of collage 2 = on the periphery of the collage *Note: See also the interpretation of self-positioning below.*

(micro-narratives) to avoid being influenced by the story-telling and missing some of the deeper meanings communicated in the non-verbal narrating. Potential interpretations for each category are described below.

In the CLET, the collage is the first unit of analysis including symbolic meanings and representations that describe the dialogical self and involves cognitive, motivational and affective aspects of autobiographical memories. "Both social and personal voices, as well as dominant and conflicting positions emerge in the rich 'text' and metaphors represented in the pictures and images posted on the collage as a form of narrative performance" (Van Schalkwyk, 2010, p. 680). The collage emerges as a representation of self-in-the-world and is part of the doing of a certain kind of action, the performance of which would not normally be described by just 'saying' or 'describing' something. Thus, the collage represents not only the actual content of the images (denotations), but also the symbolic meanings (connotations) that emerge from the participant's interactions with the context. Whether the context pertains to the family, the school, the society or other cultural cues, using images from locally relevant magazines for making a collage captures the underlying feelings, meanings, thoughts and actions implied by the connotations for the 'speaker' (the individual) and the other (the counselor) and as a representation of the context. Therefore, the interpretation of each category in Table 25.1 would depend heavily on the counselor's knowledge of and expertise in the context.

Interpreting the collage aims at generating hypotheses for further exploration and cannot provide sufficient evidence for diagnostic purposes. In this regard, for example, a child's collage about *the family* containing mostly objects and artifacts with very few (if any) people could generate hypotheses about poor attachment formation and relationships with significant others. The great distances between images pertains to how the child perceives and experiences her or his relationship to, for example, family members. In this regard, big spaces between images could hypothetically indicate poor relationships and a lack of warmth in the family as supported by the narrative tone of the memories. Moving to the construction and the coherence in Table 25.1, the collage represents more information about the cognitive aspects of remembering and the motivations in relation to others that lurks below the surface. Here one could hypothesize lower levels or even poor cognitive functioning when images are disjointed, irrational and unrelated to the focus of the collage making, while also understanding the deeper meanings emerging from a narrow or full range of memories about the focus area. Thus, several hypotheses emerge that could be explored when conducting Phase 2 (see below) of this analytic strategy and/or implementing further a variety of assessment strategies.

The previous paragraph describes the collage of a child that is most likely disturbed and in need of intervention for closing the gap between self and other. On the other hand, the child's collage about the family containing images of people (also human-like images such as cartoons), positive emotions, connectivity (overlapping images) and coherent construction provides the counselor with areas of strength that can be supported through preventive interventions. For the most part, however, the collage represents the symbolic meanings of the autobiographical memories that are important to the individual. Interpretation should always be done with sensitivity to the focus of the inquiry (reason for using the CLET), the context within which the CLET was executed, and further analysis of the micro-narratives discussed below. The counselor who is familiar with the context and culture and has experience interpreting narrative performances will add as many notes and comments to the collage analysis as possible, all of which will help when interpreting the case in more depth.

Phase 2: Analyzing the verbal micro-narratives. The aim of analyzing the stories (micro-narratives) that the individual told about each image/picture on the collage is to find the voice of the client in a particular time, setting or context (Clandinin & Connelly, 2000). The next phase in the sense-making process therefore involves reading and re-reading the narratives as the second unit of analysis and to gain a deeper understanding of the participant's autobiographical memories (Van Schalkwyk, 2010). Here the counselor or researcher asks about the substance of the individual's stories, the meanings these stories have for the client, and the symbolic meanings and metaphors embedded in the micro-narratives. Meanings, in this regard, emerge from the positive or negative associations, high or low points, qualities adopted as self-defining attributes, and so on. The analysis of micro-narratives takes place independent from the collage to avoid being influenced by the non-verbal narrative and missing some of the deeper meanings communicated in the story-telling.

Table 25.2 lists Categories 8 to 11 for the purpose of analyzing the micro-narratives and serve as possible interpretive codes likely to emerge from reading the stories. However, as with other analytic procedures in narrative inquiry, the counselor should be sensitive to any other possible categories that could emerge from an in-depth analysis of the stories we live by. For example, in the CLET about family life, who are the characters (people) in each micro-narrative and how does the individual relate to these characters? What role does the individual ascribe to the self in relation to the world he/she lives in (e.g., central character, spectator, hero, villain, perpetrator, victim and so on)? How does the plot in each micro-narrative and the CLET narrative as a whole unfold? What solutions have been found for difficult situations in the past and how are these transferred into the present and prospective future? It is not possible for me to explicate all potential questions for analyzing the micro-narratives within the scope of this chapter. Nonetheless, I believe that the experienced counselor will have developed her or his own expertise analyzing verbal narratives as these stand at the center of all clinical interviews and intervention strategies.

Apart from coding the micro-narratives according to the categories listed in Table 24.2, the counselor also adds further comments and summarizes the narrative content for inclusion in the final phase of the CLET analytic strategy, the story grid.

Phase 3: The story grid as a summary of the case. The final phase of the sense-making process entails creating a story grid for the case (Du Preez & Roos, 2008; Van Schalkwyk & Lijadi, 2013). The story grid is a unique protocol for each case consisting of:

> The background information about the case (e.g., demographics);
> The collage;
> A table consisting of 4 columns containing the (i) image number, (ii) denotation inventory for each picture/image on the collage, (iii) the metaphor, symbolic meanings and/or cultural connotations associated with each picture/image, and (iv) the micro-narratives for each picture/image; and
> A transcription of Steps 3 to 5 of the CLET.

In order to create a story grid, the counselor (or researcher) reads the field texts (collage and micro-narratives) several times for the actual and symbolic meanings adding words, phrases, adjectives, or descriptive terms in the margins or in analytic memos. On the story grid and in the table format suggest in point 3 above, compile an inventory of denotations (actual meanings) for the images on the collage using descriptive terms. These will most likely correspond with the nature of the image (see Table 25.1, Category 2). The metaphor for each image is catalogued in the next column. Here one adds symbolic meanings or cultural connotations implied by the denotation of the image or picture. Compile a list of adjectives that reflect the metaphors the image holds in the local culture and any other significant meanings relevant to the context. The key question to ask oneself is *"What are the contextual meanings manifested in the symbolic aspects of each image on the collage?"* The metaphors are culturally specific and could reveal a depth of meanings otherwise ignored when merely looking at the literal (denotation) meanings of the images on the collage. For example, food can carry both

Table 24.2 Categories for analyzing the verbal micro-narratives of the CLET

Category	Description	Analytic action
Proximity	The overall sense of the relationship between self and others expressed in micro-narratives (stories) and depicting memories of distance and closeness.	Coding: 1 = self-other closeness 2 = self-object closeness
Narrative tone	The overall emotional content of the verbal narrative (stories, unit of analysis 2) in terms of positive or negative memories.	Coding: List micro-narratives with positive tone List micro-narratives with negative tone in parentheses
Construction	The overall sense of storylines as chronological or as a random sequence of events but not chronological.	Coding: 1 = storylines are mostly chronological 2 = storylines are mostly a sequence of events but not chronological
Coherence	The overall sense of the micro-narratives and the participant's descriptive efforts as representing a full but realistic range of memories about the topic or focus area.	Coding: 1 = related to the topic 2 = unrelated to the topic

positive and negative meanings depending on how it is presented—a single, lonely bowl of soup devoid of other contextual clues represents loneliness and isolation, whereas a plate filled with various delicacies and with other contextual clues could represent community and togetherness for the child telling stories about the family. The core content and meanings of each micro-narrative are added in column 4 of the table in the story grid together with extracts in the individual's own voice. Complete the story grid by adding the narratives that ensued from Steps 3 to 5 on the CLET story grid together with analytic memos or notes about underlying meanings.

Each protocol, consisting of the collage, the table summarizing the denotations, connotations, micro-narratives and analytic memos, as well as the Steps 3 to 5 provides the third unit of analysis for the final thematic analysis and interpretation. This final analysis of the story grid of a CLET protocol is done in terms of Categories 12 to 14 as listed in Table 24.3, and provides further access to the substance, content and meanings related to the focus area.

The third unit of analysis in the CLET analytic strategy aims at exploring the positioning of self (Category 12), the silent voice(s) (Category 13) and the dynamic conflict (Category 14). Interpretation of these categories gives the counselor insight into the how the individual's perceptions of self-in-the-

Table 24.3   Categories for analyzing the story grid of the CLET

Category	Description	Analytic action
Positioning of self	The representation of self on two dimensions: A – player-spectator B – distance-closeness to others (people)	DIMENSION A Spectator – self on periphery of narratives DIMENSION B Self in distant relation to others — Self in close relation to others Player – self as central character in narratives
Silent voice	The recognition and nature of the silent voice—the voice that is absent from the narratives.	List representations of significant memories that were silent and concerning: - people (individuals and groups), - settings or life events (e.g., travel) - objects/artifacts, and - scenery (e.g., nature)
Dynamic conflict	The conflict or problem relevant to the topic.	Note the possible underlying conflict as expressed by the participant and other hypotheses ensuing from the full exposition of the CLET and worthy of further exploration in the therapeutic context

world, ownership of her/his memories, and absence of significant others could affect the individual's memories and everyday functioning. It also explicates the dynamic conflict and potential problematic that would inform the treatment planning. For example, the individual's positioning of him or herself (Category 12) on the edge or periphery of the collage indicates a spectator orientation (dimension A), while the proximity of self to inanimate objects or non-human characters rather than human figures could reflect a distance in self-other relationships (dimension B) and tell a story about how he or she perceives and experiences the self-in-the world of everyday living. Alternatively, positioning the self in the center of the collage (player-orientation) and in close proximity to others could reflect a secure attachment formation and an available emotional support system.

Analyzing the silent voice, dynamic conflict and possible congruence or incongruence between non-verbal (unit of analysis 1) and verbal (unit of analysis 2) narratives serves to develop further hypotheses or arguments for the nature of an intervention that might follow. Whereas the non-verbal narrative (collage) often reveals what lies below the surface of awareness, it is possible that the participant tells her or his stories (micro-narratives) quite selectively based on what they think the audience wants to hear or how the culture informs self-disclosure. Here the CLET provides the most significant contribution to eliciting that which lurks below the surface or is often suppressed for fear of retribution. For example, the child posting mostly objects in the collage but telling stories of warmth and affection in parent-child relations represents an incongruent tale that should be further explored. Another child, pasting only one picture (despite much encouragement to do more) and then telling of his mother's love and affection and the siblings' care for him, is most likely unaware of his distrust, isolation and withdrawal from the world (see Figure 2). For this child and his family, the incongruence between non-verbal and verbal narratives reveals a deep-seated distress that urgently needs remedial attention if he is to function optimally within the school environment. On the other hand, comparing the units of analysis in the CLET also reveals, through the collage and micro-narratives, the strengths of family relations upon which a child experiencing distress in the school environment can draw to develop his or her agency and optimal functioning in different settings.

BUILDING A COMPELLING CASE

The interpretations of CLET case materials evolves from rigorously reading each unit of analysis (i.e., the collage, the micro-narratives and the story grid), taking cognizance of the existing literature and theoretical frameworks, and reflexivity to build a compelling case for further co-action (e.g., Watt, 2007). Thus, the counselor should adopt a critical reflective position when analyzing the case, and check and re-check interpretations with the original collage, micro-narratives, and literature. Collaborating with the others (e.g., other counselors or a multi-disciplinary team) improves the credibility of the case. Collaborators can independently analyze the case following the analytic strategy outlined above, provide further background information about the context, and assist in identifying the problems relevant to the intervention processes.

Furthermore and as indicated above, the CLET is not a diagnostic tool, but a screening tool for intake interviewing that provides a rich source of hypotheses for further exploration either through clinical interviewing or additional assessment strategies. Performances on the CLET are not true or false, that is, they are not truth-evaluable. Instead, they are subjective meaning-making actions or part of the doing of a certain kind of co-action, the performance of which would not normally be described by just 'saying' or 'describing' something. When something is wrong with them then they are 'happy' or 'unhappy', not right or wrong.

The CLET is a powerful expressive channel for conveying non-verbal messages about the self and for modulating emotional impact on everyday functioning (Page, 2001; Raggatt, 2007). It is not only an individual movement but also a process that is context-shaped and context renewing. Both counselor and client gain insights from collaborating in the sense-making process, which helps with developing a less problem-saturated life story and optimal functioning in different everyday life settings.

RELATIONSHIP TO THE SBFC MODEL

The CLET fits well within the SBFC model described in in this book. As indicated above, the CLET provides a viable means to conceptualize a case through a theoretical lens appropriate to SBFC and for hypothesizing the client's problems and strengths. Although not a diagnostic tool in itself, the CLET affords the SBFC professional with multiple hypotheses to follow up in further diagnosis of the case. The CLET also offers general guidance for goal-setting and developing a meaningful and attainable goal for counseling. It can also be used effectively the determine whether these goals have been met by executing the CLET again at the end of the intervention to see if problem-saturated narratives have been transformed to strength-based narratives guiding the improved functioning of the individual in her/his

Case of Mark

Collage

Stories

Extract for image 1: [Can you tell me the story of the collage, each picture? How about this one?]
Ate his things *[Pardon?]* He has eaten his thing ... Ice-cream
[Why did you choose this?]
... ... [Hhm?] ... ... [What does this represent in your home?]... ... [Hhm? You don't know?]* (Shakes his head)

Story grid

No	Denotation	Metaphor	Participant's self-defining memory
4.	Flower (small feint drawing)	Nature Separate from others	*[Okay, let's talk about other things first. How about this flower?]* ... ... [This flower?] ... ... [What does the flower represent? Can you tell me?]* ... ... (shakes his head) *[Why did you draw this flower?]* I like to draw *[You like to draw. Then do you like the flower?]* (Nods) *[What kind of flower do you like?]* ... ... [Hhm?] ... Lotus *[Lotus. Have you seen a lotus flower?]* I have seen it on TV *[So, have you seen it on the river?]* No *[Why do you like lotus?]* It is pretty *[I see. What color do you like?]* ... ... [Hhm?] ... ... [What color have you seen?]* I have only seen one color *[What is that?]* I don't remember *[You don't remember. Don't you know what color you have seen?]* Maybe pink

world. Thus, the CLET can be used in any quadrant of the SBFC model based on whether the counselor is exploring school-focused or family-focused, remedial or preventive case conceptualization. For example, the CLET can be utilized in each of the quadrants in the following ways:

School-Prevention: Utilise the CLET in teacher consultation to explore underlying areas of stress and teacher practices/customs, as well as plan interventions that can prevent problems for the individual and/or students.

School-Intervention: Utilise the CLET to identify problem situations and where intervention is clearly required given the consequences of such problems within the school setting. Most School Psychology programs do not include sufficient training for how to work with all stakeholders independently and collaboratively. The CLET provides an opportunity to explore the underlying dynamics as well as the strengths and weaknesses that are available to the various stakeholders (i.e., teacher, child, family and school).

Family-Prevention: The family members can individually or collectively participate in the CLET, and identify strengths for developing skills to prevent future problems.

Family-Intervention: The CLET can, for example, enable parents and children to explore their perceptions of family life, parenting style and customs of care giving, and to promote family change when problem-saturated perceptions are having a negative effect on a student.

Since the CLET is still a fairly newly developed technique in narrative inquiry, many possibilities are open to how the counselor can utilize it for establishing a plausible and compelling case for further action, whether as intervention, psycho-education or consultation. In the Child-remedial Focus area, the counselor utilizes the CLET to explore the underlying dynamic conflict or problem that brought the child to the intervention setting. Whatever the referral problem might be, the CLET can provide access to the problematic that has not yet surfaced or has not been observed by other observation strategies. However, as indicated above, the CLET is not a diagnostic tool and in the case of more severe or diverse problems should be used in conjunction with other assessment strategies to verify hypotheses generated through the analytic strategy. When used in conjunction with other assessments, the SBFC professional can obtain more rigorous and in-depth understanding of the case and focus her or his treatment planning for either remedial or preventive purposes. Thus, the counselor can act on a more sophisticated level of intervention in the SBFC Model quadrants.

EVIDENCE-BASED SUPPORT

Apart from its utility within the counseling context, the CLET has great potential as research method in different contexts and for various populations. As a collaborative inquiry tool, the CLET was developed to explore life story remembering in cross-cultural settings where various obstacles prevented verbal narrating. Combining non-verbal and verbal strategies to elicit life stories thus provided a way to access populations otherwise excluded from participating in ethnographic research projects. Van Schalkwyk (2010) explicated the utility of the CLET with a group of emerging adults in late adolescence. In this study, the CLET was executed in the written format with a group of students studying in English as a non-native language. Participating in the project enabled these young people to reflect on their past and integrate this with the present in view of an anticipated future (Habermas & Bluck, 2000). Through the collage-making, their remembering was stimulated so as to elicit rich narratives that would otherwise have been difficult to perform given the cultural inhibition towards self-disclosure.

Lijadi and Van Schalkwyk (2013) explored the relationship experiences of Third Culture Kids growing up in a high-mibiliy lifestyle and as so-called global nomads, and found the CLET a useful tool to elicit rich narratives from participants who were initially reluctant to tell their stories. Exploring the family life of three families living with autism, Lao and Van Schalkwyk (2012) utilized the CLET to gather multiple voices—that is, the voice of the mother and the voice of an older sibling. The three units of analysis provided a rich source of data to gain a deeper understanding of the challenges and distress these families experience in their local context. The CLET has also been implemented with adults to explore connectedness and alienation within the family life, social networking, and the work context (Bauer et al., 2008; Ow & Katz, 1999; Van Schalkwyk, 2013).

Until recently, the CLET has only been executed with non-clinical populations although the analytic strategy revealed underlying problematic that might otherwise not have been noticeable with these groups. Thus, although evidence with clinical samples is not yet available, the technique has shown potential to uncover conflicts that the client and/or the referral agency have not yet uncovered. Counselors using the technique with clinical population should therefore execute the analysis alongside further diagnostic measurements to confirm interpretations.

MULTICULTURAL COUNSELING CONSIDERATIONS

The original rationale for developing the CLET was to conduct narrative research in cross-cultural settings. It was therefore designed to fit well within different cultures and is sensitive to socio-cultural cues through the use of locally relevant magazines for the collage-making (Ho, Peng, Lai, & Chan, 2001). Conducting a study of children's perceptions across four different cultures, Van Schalkwyk and Lijadi (2013) explored the utility of the CLET to elicit rich narratives despite other potential differences there may exist between the children. The authors found that the CLET works equally well with children in China and Africa, and despite the variation in cognitive functioning of the different groups. Their study also revealed that implementation of the CLET can be done by multiple fieldworkers who were adequately trained to execute the procedures as outlined above in the native language of the participants. Although some of the finer nuances of narratives are lost in translation of the verbal text, the collage offers a rich source of non-verbal narration that can overcome the limitations of translation. Furthermore, as with any assessment in psychological counseling and intervention, ethical considerations should be taken into account prior to conducting the CLET. When working with children, parents should be appropriately informed of procedures and give consent for recording the semi-structured interview. Confidentiality should be evident on all fronts to protect the rights of the participant. This could imply changing names and personal details about the child or the family prior to soliciting collaboration from others to also analyze the CLET or when discussing a case in a multi-disciplinary setting.

CHALLENGES AND SOLUTIONS

One of the challenges is to appropriately execute the sequential steps of the CLET when asking for written narratives instead of conducting a semi-structured interview. Some client populations find it difficult to verbalize their stories in written format. For example, young children and those who have to write in their non-native language might not have sufficient command of the language or an adequate vocabulary to express themselves fully in writing (Van Schalkwyk & Lijadi, 2013). Other clinical populations such as substance abusers, those with minimal education, and those who are developmentally challenged (e.g., ASD) could also be hindered in expressing themselves in written form. Nonetheless, the written format works well with adolescents and adults in non-clinical populations and those with adequate language proficiency. In the written format, the CLET can also be assigned as a self-reflective (homework) activity forming part of an ongoing intervention strategy. When conducted in the written format, steps 2 to 5 of the CLET are carefully structured in a booklet where the participant can add her or his stories as they proceed through the different steps.

Another challenge to the execution of the CLET is the reluctance of adults to engage in playful behavior such as collage-making. Cultural prohibitions, task-orientation and reluctance to self-disclose or emotional expressiveness disenable the adult striving for control over her or his environment to engage in actions considered to be 'childish'. Nonetheless, with sufficient encouragement adults will collaborate. Even if collaborating with initial reluctance, the adult participant soon discovers the power of the CLET to scaffold memories and produce insight regarding issues otherwise suppressed (Van Schalkwyk, 2013).

SUMMARY

This chapter describes the procedures and analytical strategy for implementing the Collage Life story Elicitation Technique within the SBFC Model. I developed the CLET to prompt autobiographical remembering in different settings and with varying client populations. It combines collage-making with storytelling to support the narrating process and to elicit rich and vivid stories and metaphors about the past in the present and with a prospective future in mind (Van Schalkwyk, 2010). Participants become co-actors as they reflect upon their life stories and co-construct a sense of meaning about the phenomenon that focuses the inquiry. Collage making is a way of dialoguing that overcomes the inhibitions of verbal communication by utilizing an alternative mode of expression. In a cross-cultural setting, where language could pose problems, or when conducting narrative inquiry with clinical populations who have difficulty with self-disclosure it has great value for uncovering underlying local processes and social interactions and relationships.

Finally, the interpretations will be context-specific and no generalizations are possible to non-local populations. Rather, the purpose is not to find universal trends or patterns but to build a reasonable and compelling case for treatment planning and intervention that could follow the implementation of the CLET. By presenting a significant case for intervention purposes, the counselor makes pragmatic use of the available resources to plan and execute interventions. The CLET adds a range of very useful representations and communication regarding positive and negative experiences, attachments to significant people, settings and actions, successes or failures, future aspirations and many more that contribute to an understanding of the client's daily functioning. It is a collaborative process of inquiry, actively and fully involving the client in the process of co-constructing stories, and provides the counselor access to the individual's authentic autobiography—the significant events, beliefs, internal and external views of the self, and core constructs regarding the nature of the world and reality (Berg, 2009; McAdams, 1993, 2001; Pasupathi, 2006).

REFERENCES

Clandinin, D. J., & Connelly, F. M. (2000). *Narrative Inquiry*. San Francisco: Jossey-Bass.

Baxter P., & Jack, S. (2008). Qualitative Case Study Methodology: Study Design and Implementation for Novice Researchers. *The Qualitative Report,* 13(4), 544-559. http://www.nova.edu/ssss/QR/QR13-4/baxter.pdf

Bauer J. J., McAdams, P., & Pals, J. L. (2008). Narrative Identity and Eudaimonic Well-being. *Journal of Happiness Studies, 9,* 81-104. doi: 10.1007/s10902-006-9021-6

Bohn, A., & Berntsen, D. (2008). Life story development in childhood: The development of life story abilities and the acquisition of cultural life scripts from late middle childhood to adolescence. *Developmental Psychology, 44*(4), 1135-1147. doi: 10.1037/0012-1649.44.4.1135

Brannen, J., Mooney, A., & Statham, J. (2009). Childhood Experiences: a Commitment To Caring and Care Work with Vulnerable Children. *Childhood, 16*(3), 377-393. doi:10.1177/0907568209335317.

Bruner, J. (2010). Narrative, Culture and Mind. In D. F. Schiffrin & A. De Nylund (Eds.), *Telling Stories: Language, Narrative, and Social Life*. Washington, DC: Georgetown University Press.

Chan, E. (2004). Narratives of Experience: how culture matters to children's development. *Contemporary Issues in Early Childhood, 5*(2), 145-159. doi:10.2304/ciec.2004.5.2.3

Du Preez, E., & Roos,V. (2008). The development of counsellor identity – a visual expression. *South African Journal of Psychology, 38*(4), 699-709.

Eisner, E. W. (2002). *The Arts and the Creation of Mind*. New Haven: Yale University Press.

Fivush, R. (1991). The social construction of personal narratives. *Journal of Developmental Psychology, 37*(1), 59-81.

Gergen, K. J. (2000). *An invitation to social construction*. London: Sage Publications.

Gergen, M., & Gergen, K. J. (2006). Narratives as action. *Narrative Inquiry, 16*(1), 112-121. doi: http://dx.doi.org/10.1075/ni.16.1.15ger

Habermas, T., & Bluck, S. (2000). Getting a life: The emergence of the life story in adolescence. *Psychological Bulletin, 126*, 748-769. doi: 10.1037/0033-2909.126.5.748

Ho, D. Y. F., Peng, S. Q., Lai, A. C., & Chan, S. F. (2001). Indigenization and beyond: Methodological relationalism in the study of personality across cultures. *Journal of Personality, 69*, 925-953. doi: 10.1111/1467-6494.696170

Hermans, H. J. (2001). The dialogical self: Toward a theory of personal and cultural positioning. *Culture & Psychology, 7*, 243-81.

Kulkofsky, S., & Klemfuss, J. Z. (2008). What the stories children tell can tell about their memory: Narrative skill and young children's suggestibility. *Developmental Psychology, 44*(5), 1442-1456. doi: 10.1037/a0012849

Lao, N. G. A., & Van Schalkwyk, G. J. (2012). Living with autism in Macao—The experiences of families living with autism. Paper presented at the ICP2012, Cape Town, 22-27 July 2012.

Lieblich, A., McAdams, D. P., & Josselson, R. (2004). *Healing plots: The narrative basis of psychotherapy*. Washington, DC: American Psychological Association.

Lijadi, A. A., & Van Schalkwyk, G. J. (2013). Narratives of Third Culture Kids: Friendships and relation-ships. Unpublished paper available from the authors at gjvsumac@gmail.com

Markova, I. (2003). Constitution of the Self: Intersubjectivity and Dialogicality. *Culture & Psychology, 9*(3), 249-259.

McAdams, D. P. (1993). *The stories we live by: Personal myths and the making of the self*. New York: Morrow.

McAdams, D. P. (2001). The psychology of life stories. *Review of General Psychology, 5*, 100–122. doi: 10.1037//l089-2680.5.2.100.

McAdams, D. P. (2006). The role of narrative in personality psychology today. *Narrative Inquiry, 16*(1), 11-18. doi: http://dx.doi.org/10.1075/ni.16.1.04mca

McLean, K. C., & Pasupathi, M. (Eds.) (2010). *Narrative development in adolescence: Creating the storied self*. New York: Springer.

Miles, M. B., & Huberman, A. M. (1994). *Qualitative Data Analysis* (2nd ed.). Thousand Oaks, CA: Sage.

Monk, G., Winslade, J., Crocket, K., & Epston, D. (Eds.) (1997). *Narrative therapy in practice: The archaeology of hope*. San Francisco: Jossey-Bass.

Mulvaney, M. K. (2011). Narrative processes across childhood. *Early Child Development and Care, 181*(9), 1153-1161. doi:10.1080/03004430.2010.507312

Ow, R., & Katz, D. (1999). Family secrets and the disclosure of distressful information in Chinese families. *Families in Society, 80*(6), 620-628.

Page, T. F. (2001). The social meaning of children's narratives: a review of the attachment-based narrative story stem technique. *Child and Adolescent Social Work Journal, 18*(3), 171-187. doi: 10.1023/A:1011006402275

Powell, M. B., & Snow, P. C. (2007). Guide to questioning children during the free narrative phase of an investigative interview. *Australian Psychologist, 42*(1), 57-65. doi: 10.1080/00050060600976032

Raggatt, P. T. F. (2007). Forms of positioning in the dialogical self: A system of classification and the strange case of Dame Edna Everage. *Theory & Psychology, 17*(3), 355-382.

Taylor, S. (2006). Narrative as construction and discursive resource. *Narrative Inquiry, 16* (1), 94-102. doi: http://dx.doi.org/10.1075/ni.16.1.13tay

Threadgold, T. (2003). Cultural Studies, Critical Theory and Critical Discourse Analysis: Histories, Remembering and Futures. *Linguistik Online, 14*(2), available at:
http://www.linguistik-online.de/14_03/threadgold.html [Retrieved on March 16, 2004]

Van Schalkwyk, G. J. (2010). Collage Life Story Elicitation Technique: A representational technique for scaffolding autobiographical memories. *The Qualitative Report, 15*(3), 675-695. Retrieved from http://www.nova.edu/ssss/QR/QR15-3/vanschalkwyk.pdf

Van Schalkwyk, G. J. (2011). Children's Perceptions of Family Life in Macao, Zhuhai and Gaborone. Paper presented at NASP, February 2011 in San Francisco, USA

Van Schalkwyk, G. J. (2013). Connectedness and alienation in the Collage Life-story Eliciation Technique with adults. Paper presented at the ACP2013, Osaka (Japan), 23-31 March 2013.

Van Schalkwyk, G. J., & Lijadi, A. A. (2013). Utilization of the Collage Life Story Elicitation Technique in Different Cultures. Unpublished paper available from the authors at gjvsumac@gmail.com

Watt, D. (2007). On becoming a qualitative researcher: The value of reflexivity. *The Qualitative Report, 12*, 82-101. Retrieved on November 4, 2008, from http://www.nova.edu/ssss/QR/QR12-1/watt.pdf

Weber, S. (2008). Using images in research. In J. G. Knowles & A. L. Cole (Eds.), *Handbook of the Arts in Qualitative Research: Perspectives, Methodologies, Examples and Issues* (pp. 41-54). London: Sage Press.

White, M. (2007). *Maps of narrative practice*. New York: W. W. Norton & Company.

Yin, R. K. (2009). *Case Study Research: Design and Methods*. Sage Inc: California

PART VII

SCHOOL-BASED FAMILY COUNSELING: SPECIFIC APPLICATIONS

B. FAMILY-INTERVENTION APPLICATIONS

SCHOOL FOCUS

School-Prevention	School-Intervention
Family-Prevention	**Family-Intervention**

PREVENTION FOCUS

INTERVENTION FOCUS

FAMILY FOCUS

Chapter 25

Family Involvement in School-Based Treatment of Childhood Trauma

Theresa Kruczek

OVERVIEW: *Positive family support is considered a buffer for stressful life events and lack of family/caregiver support can result in an increased risk for serious mental illness following childhood trauma. Given the frequency with which young people today experience traumatic events, it is important that we develop school-based models of trauma intervention that include families. This chapter will review guidelines for family involvement in school-based treatment of childhood trauma. Recommended treatment strategies include providing psycho-education for family members about trauma responses, helping the family re-establish a climate of safety, involving the family in counter-conditioning of fear responses, and helping the family to contextualize the trauma. The ultimate goal of this treatment model is to re-establish normative development for the child and within the family life cycle.*

BACKGROUND

Today many students directly experience traumatic life events both personally and within their communities and an even greater number are indirectly exposed to traumatic events via powerful media images. This direct and indirect exposure to trauma has the potential to undermine both the educational and personal achievement of students (Cook-Cottone, 2004).While positive family support is considered a buffer for stressful life events, lack of family/caregiver support can result in an increased risk for serious mental illness following childhood trauma (Wasserstein & La Greca, 1998).

There are many types of traumatic events that students can encounter in their lives. These events include natural and technological disasters (e.g., earthquakes, hurricanes, ferry boat accidents), exposure to war, sexual and physical abuse or interpersonal violence, community violence, life-threatening illnesses and medical procedures (Pynoos, 1994). Terr (1991) has proposed a two category conceptual framework for classifying traumatic events. Type I events are typically short-term, unexpected, single incidents and a quick recovery is more likely from this type of trauma exposure. Type II events are more prolonged, chronic, or repetitive experiences such as prolonged natural disasters or repeated sexual victimization. Those students who experience Type II trauma are more likely to demonstrate severe stress reactions and difficulty with adjustment. However, more severe stress reactions are possible for students encountering Type I stressors that result in loss of a significant other (e.g., death of a parent) or loss of function (e.g., loss of a limb or paralysis).

CHILD-BASED RISK AND PROTECTIVE FACTORS

Age and developmental factors have been suggested as risk factors for trauma and development of trauma reactions. However, research is inconclusive with regard to the relationship between age at the time of trauma exposure and the development of stress disorders. Several authors have found no support for age at trauma exposure as a risk factor (Foa, Keane, & Friedman, 2000; Garrison, Bryant, Addy, Spurrier, Freedy, & Kilpatrick, 1995; Silverman & La Greca, 2002; Yule, Perrin & Smith, 1999). Others suggest that there is up to a 3 times greater likelihood of development of PTSD when trauma exposure occurs before age 11 (Davidson & Smith, 1990).

Some have even argued that age serves as a protective factor in younger children as they are unable to comprehend and appreciate the full extent of the danger (Davis & Siegel, 2000). The memory literature lends some support to this latter perspective as there is significant evidence that autobiographic memory for events in the past is based predominantly on reconstructive processes (Loftus & Ketcham, 1994). That is, we tend to combine fragments of actual memory with broader cognitive knowledge, beliefs and expectations to form a meaningful account of what really happened. Further, with highly charged emotional events three factors facilitate more accurate recall 1) the personal significance of the event, 2) the uniqueness or distinctiveness of the event and 3) selective rehearsal of the memory (Bower & Sivers, 1998). Traumatic events tend to be emotionally charged and Type I traumatic events in particular meet the criteria for uniqueness or distinctiveness. Given the developmental level of a child at the age of the trauma, their limited cognitive abilities and awareness may serve as a buffer to prevent more extensive and meaningful encoding and retrieval of traumatic memories. In this sense, family members and caregivers have the potential to either reinforce or diminish both the child's memory of the event and influence their interpretation and meaning of the significance of the event to the child's self concept and life perspective.

There is extensive empirical evidence suggesting that the child's cognitive appraisal of the traumatic event can either hinder or facilitate adaptive response to the trauma (Pandit & Shah, 2000; Silverman & La Greca, 2002; Stallard, 2000; Tolin & Foa, 2002; Udwin, Boyle, Yule, Bolton & O'Ryan, 2000). As suggested from the memory literature, family and caregivers have great potential to adaptively influence the child's cognitive appraisal of the traumatic event. Not surprisingly, there also is evidence that higher levels of cognitive ability serve as a protective factor in the development of PTSD (Yule, et al., 1999), as these children likely possess greater cognitive capacities for re-interpretation of meaning of the event. Related protective factors include positive self-esteem, problem solving and communication skills, an internal locus of control, and a history of adaptive coping (Clark & Miller, 1998; Silverman & La Greca, 2002). Conversely, pre-existing academic difficulties, behavior problems and attention difficulties seem to be associated with increased risk for development of PTSD following trauma exposure (Silverman & La Greca, 2002).

FAMILY-BASED RISK AND PROTECTIVE FACTORS

Most would agree that violence within the family is a traumatic event for children and that there is an intergenerational propensity to transmit aggressive patterns of problem resolution. It is beyond the scope and purpose of this chapter to review the literature on systemic interventions with abusive families. However, it is important to note that family violence is one of the major sources of Type II trauma and that children who witness domestic violence are at an increased risk for development of PTSD (Wasserstein & La Greca, 1998). Family violence is most certainly then a major a risk factor for childhood trauma reactions. Additionally, there are a host of other family factors that seem to moderate a child's reaction to trauma. The child's perception of possible danger or fear for a parent's safety has been shown to exacerbate trauma reactions with Type I trauma (Silverman & La Greca, 2002). Other factors such as parent's marital status, parent's psychological functioning, family stability and parental level of education can all serve as both risk and protective factors in child and adolescent response to trauma (Davis & Siegel, 2000; Elklit, 2002; Silverman & La Greca, 2002).

The most important factor mediating a child or teenager's response to trauma appears to be parent and caregiver reactions to the event (Davis & Siegel, 2000; Silverman & La Greca, 2002, van der Kolk, 2003). Research has long demonstrated that positive family support can be a protective factor, while a lack of family/caregiver support can result in an increased risk for serious mental illnesses (Wasserstein & La Greca, 1998). Support can come from the individual's immediate family or may come from a wider network of caregivers or supportive individuals within the community (de Silva, 1999).

Caregivers can include aunts, uncles, supportive foster parents or grandparents (Pandit & Shah, 2000). Parent and caregiver reactions consist of two components, the reaction to the child her/himself and the reaction to the traumatic event. Parent and caregiver reactions to the child that consist of validation, nurturance, and support serve to enhance adaptive coping. Further, parents and caregivers who are able to demonstrate positive coping strategies in response to the stressor themselves, provide not only healthy role models for coping, but also help the child to regain the feelings of safety and predictability that are necessary for healthy development (van der Kolk, 2003).

PROGRAM DESCRIPTION

Family involvement in school-based trauma interventions start with helping the family understand trauma reactions in order to understand their child's, and perhaps their own, response to the trauma. This increased understanding will help normalize their and their child's trauma reaction. Psycho-educational groups (for both the parents and children) should include information to help them understand the basis of stress disorders as well as the basic signs and symptoms of stress disorders. Educating students and their caregivers about the trauma accommodation syndromes will help provide a context for the healing process. Awareness of the aforementioned risk and protective factors for successful coping can help caregivers assess their family's circumstances and point the way to systemic interventions to reduce risk factors and enhance protective factors. A basic review of relevant information to include in the psycho-educational groups as well as a model for family assessment and intervention follows.

POST-TRAUMATIC STRESS DISORDER AND ACUTE STRESS DISORDER

Theoretical models for the development of the stress disorders stem from stress reaction theory or as it is more popularly known the "fight or flight" response. The *general adaptation syndrome* (GAS) was first proposed by Hans Selye (1952) to describe the human response to chronic stressors. Our physiological response to stress is mediated by the sympathetic nervous system and the general stress response represents the body's typical defensive posture in the face of stressors. Environmental stressors trigger characteristic limbic system responses that prepare the body for "fight or flight". Limbic system activity, particularly in the amygdala results in automatic physiological and psychological stress reactions that are minimally influenced by higher cortical functions. (See van der Kolk (2003) for an extensive review of the neurobiological bases of trauma response in children.) The PTSD symptoms of hyperarousal, intrusive memories, and nightmares are thought to occur as a result of hyper-responsive action in the amygdala (Cohen, 2001). Additionally, stressful experiences, particularly those that are uncontrollable and unpredictable, result in greater adrenergic activity and affect those brain regions involved in emotion, arousal, and attention (Donnelly, Amaya-Jackson, & March, 1999). These reactions are thought to underlie "fear conditioning" responses (LeDoux, 1996) or the classical conditioning of fear reactions to stimuli that approximate the original trauma or stressor (Foa, Zinbarg, &Rothbaum, 1992).

The neurobiological systems regulating this stress response are probably not as adaptive or well developed in children (Perry, 1994). Additionally, childhood exposure to trauma can adversely impact the neurobiological development of children (van der Kolk, 2003). A child's developing brain is responsible for adaptively organizing and learning information from the environment (Perry, Pollard, Blakley& Baker, 1995). When a child's development is interrupted by traumatic life events, he/she may (in the absence of mediating protective factors) develop maladaptive patterns of coping with stress, most typically displayed as hyperarousal or detachment (van der Kolk, 2003). These maladaptive response patterns interfere with the child's capacity for adaptive coping with subsequent life stressors and are reflected as developmental deficits. Specifically, these children display deficits in capacity for emotional self-regulation, learning and memory, social relationships as well as an increased vulnerability to physical illness (van der Kolk, 2003).

A subset of those children exposed to traumatic events will develop the clinical syndrome of PTSD and even more are likely to have acute stress reactions or develop an Acute Stress Disorder (ASD). In both PTSD and ASD an individual is exposed to a traumatic event and displays a similar symptom cluster. However, in ASD the symptoms occur within the first month after experiencing the trauma and do not persist beyond four weeks. In PTSD the symptoms persist longer than one month. PTSD symptoms generally fall within three categories: 1) re-experiencing the trauma, which includes flashbacks, intrusive thoughts, nightmares, and an exaggerated startle response, 2) avoiding stimuli related to the trauma and numbing, which includes feeling detached or estranged from others and deriving significantly less pleasure from previously enjoyed activities, and 3) hyper-arousal, which includes irritability, hyper-vigilance, sleep and concentration disturbance. The symptoms of PTSD in adolescents are fairly consistent with adult symptomatology (Amaya-Jackson & March, 1995).

The *Diagnostic and Statistical Manual of Mental Disorders* (*DSM IV-TR: American Psychiatric Association, 1994*) estimates suggest that 3 to 58% of those experiencing a traumatic life event will develop PTSD. The prevalence of PTSD in the general population of adolescents is estimated at 6.3% (Reinherz, Giaconia, Lefkowitz, Pakiz, & Frost, 1993). Unfortunately there are no epidemiological investigations of the prevalence of PTSD in the general population of children. One problem with estimating prevalence in the general child survivor population is that while some children experiencing Type I trauma demonstrate classic PTSD symptoms, children experiencing Type II trauma are more likely to display the aforementioned broad developmental delays rather than specific PTSD symptoms (van der Kolk, 2003), therefore it is more difficult to determine prevalence in the general population. There also is some suggestion that children and adolescents may alternate between periods of re-experiencing and avoidance/numbing symptoms, making them appear asymptomatic (Cohen, 1998) and further complicating the diagnostic picture.

TRAUMA ACCOMMODATION SYNDROME

Miller and Veltkamp (1988, 1993 as cited in Clark & Miller, 1998) have elaborated a specific Trauma Accommodation Syndrome for children and adolescents. This syndrome describes a stage theory of adaptation to traumatic stressors. Stage I involves the actual experience of the traumatic event. At Stage II the young person may be dealing with the aftermath of physical injuries sustained in the trauma and he/she often experiences psychological fear, horror, and helplessness. After the actual trauma and the acute reaction to the trauma, a third stage begins that is characterized by a period of intrusive thoughts and feelings related to the trauma. During this third stage the young person often re-enacts the trauma, has frightening dreams, avoids activities related to the trauma, re-experiences thoughts and feelings from the trauma, and displays disorganized and/or agitated behavior. Stage IV heralds the beginning of successful accommodation. In this stage the child or teenager is able to use cognitive reasoning to re-evaluate both the original trauma and their subsequent re-experiencing of the trauma. It is at this stage that the young person may begin to mourn losses associated with the trauma and work to find meaning from the experience. The final stage (V) involves successful accommodation or resolution of the traumatic issues. By this stage the child or teen is using coping strategies to deal with the aftermath of the trauma and has integrated the traumatic experience within his or her overall life experience and identity.

Summit (1983) described the Child Sexual Abuse Accommodation Syndrome (CSAAS) or a model of accommodation that is specific to child sexual abuse. This model also has five phases which include, secrecy, helplessness, accommodation, delayed disclosure, and retraction. During the accommodation phase the young person is most likely to suffer dissociative experiences and repress memories about the abuse, particularly if her/his disclosure to family and caretakers is met with disbelief, rejection, and continued abuse or threats of violence by the perpetrator. These children and teens are at significant risk for developing PTSD, and even long term personality changes, in reaction to the trauma of child sexual abuse (Briere, 1997).

FAMILY INVOLVEMENT IN TREATMENT

Family involvement in school-based treatment of childhood trauma should incorporate psycho-education about trauma reactions as described above and be grounded in family systems theory. In particular, core family systems principles and knowledge of the normative family life cycle tasks should inform family oriented trauma interventions, as the ultimate treatment goal is to maintain (or return to) a healthy developmental trajectory for both the family and individual child. Barnhill's (1979) dimensions of healthy family functioning will be briefly reviewed to highlight core systems principles. Those elements of Carter and McGoldrick's (2005) family life cycle model most relevant to trauma work will be briefly reviewed as this model can be useful in school-based family practice with many western cultural groups.

Barnhill (1979) articulated eight common factors of the varied family systems theories. He organized these factors into four core processes each comprised of two dimensions. First, identity processes include the healthy dimensions of individuation (vs. enmeshment or disengagement) and mutuality (vs. isolation). In healthy families, individuals have a clearly individuated sense of self in relation to others. It is important to note that what constitutes a "healthy" sense of self varies across cultural groups (i.e., collectivist vs. individualistic societies). When a child and his/her family experience traumatic events it is important to help each member articulate an individuated response to the trauma in addition to exploring shared aspects of response. Trauma survivors frequently experience a sense of isolation and disconnection from others and family involvement in treatment can help prevent such isolation.

Information processing consists of the dimensions of communication and perception. Barnhill (1979) described healthy families as those demonstrating clear (vs. unclear or distorted) perception of events or interactions and clear communication about their experiences. Perceptual distortions in particular often occur when children experience trauma. Issues relevant to promoting clear perception and communication will follow in the next section that reviews specific intervention strategies. The third family process is role functioning, in which healthy families demonstrate role reciprocity (vs. unclear or conflicted roles) and clear generational boundaries (vs. breached, vague, or unclear generational boundaries). Intergenerational family violence often results in breached generational boundaries. Finally, the change processes refer to how the family solves problems and copes with stressors. According to Barnhill, healthy families as have a stable, but flexible (as opposed to disorganized and/or rigid) approach to problem solution. Certainly traumatic life events create considerable stress for the child and his/her family and even otherwise "healthy" families may need assistance developing adaptive responses.

The concept of family response to stressors is also a critical component of Carter and McGoldrick's (2005) family life cycle model of family functioning. These authors distinguish between two types of stressors, vertical and horizontal. Vertical stressors are those which influence the family across levels of systems and time, while horizontal stressors are developmental and unfold as time progresses. Examples of individual level vertical stressors include biological predispositions and abilities. Family level vertical stressors include trans-generationally transmitted patterns of behavior and relationships. Horizontal stressors consist of both normative developmental processes (e.g., life cycle transitions) and unpredictable events such as traumatic experiences. Both Type I and Type II traumatic events would be considered horizontal stressors in this model.

At any given life stage there are centrifugal forces which propel an individual away from the family system and centripetal forces that pull the individual toward the family. At certain life stages the centrifugal forces are normative and an expected part of development (i.e., leaving home; single young adults, families with adolescents, and launching children and moving on). See Carter and McGoldrick (2005) for a more extensive review of the specific stages of the family life cycle as well as associated emotional processes and developmental tasks. While traumatic life events can exert centrifugal forces on an individual, they more typically exert a centripetal force on the individual, pulling them back into the family system. This centripetal force can be counter to normative centrifugal developmental changes when the traumatic event occurs at a life stage where the normative developmental shift requires moving away from the family.

RELATIONSHIP TO THE SBFC MODEL

This chapter provides recommendations for family involvement in school-based trauma treatment. These recommendations are grounded in both the trauma and family systems literature. Further, family involvement is beginning to be recognized as an important component of school-based trauma treatment (Morris & McKee, 2009; Saxe, Ellis, Fogler, &Navalta, 2012). Some authors are even proposing an ecological approach to the treatment of trauma (Hobfoll, Walter, & Horsey, 2008; Hoffman & Kruczek, 2011). This ecological approach includes family involvement as one component of a more comprehensive approach to intervention. However, while family involvement has increasingly been recommended as an ancillary component to school-based trauma programming, there is no current model for family involvement that is grounded in both trauma *and* family systems theory.

EVIDENCE-BASED SUPPORT

The reaction any given child or adolescent has to the traumatic event is moderated by many variables including the type of stressor and whether the stressor occurs as a single, acute event or as chronic, repeated events. Consequently, student and family interventions will differ based on trauma type. The school setting has been recommended as an ideal setting to provide group-trauma focused programming for students (Avinger & Jones, 2007; Cohen & Mannarino, 2011; Yule, 2001). Several models for student-focused trauma intervention have been proposed and evaluated (e.g., Akin-Little & Somerville, 2011; Berger & Gelkopf, 2009; Boyd-Webb, 2011; Charwastra, Goldfarb, Petroch, &Cloitre, 2010; Dean et. al., 2008; Jaycox et. al 2010; Layne, et.al., 2008). Trauma Focused-Cognitive Behavior Therapy (TF-CBT) is the only intervention approach identified as "well established" for the treatment of PTSD in children and teens (Silverman et.al, 2008). TF-CBT includes conjoint parent involvement, but this approach has not been widely adapted for use in schools.

MULTICULTURAL COUNSELING CONSIDERATIONS

In addition to establishing physical safety, it is important to restore a perceptual and emotional sense of safety. Again, this therapeutic goal will be more difficult with some populations. The establishment of a sense of safety and security in minority groups may be more difficult if they have experienced poverty, discrimination, and/or oppression (also vertical stressors). These groups appear to be more vulnerable to stress reactions. Rabalais, Ruggerio and Scotti (2002)'s review of the literature suggested that African American and Hispanic American youth were at increased risk for developing PTSD following traumatic life events and these minority groups seemed less likely to experience a decrease in PTSD symptoms over time when compared to Caucasians. However, it is important to note that an emphasis on extended kin networks, spirituality, positive family relationships, and culture can serve as powerful mechanisms to counteract these negative experiences and can foster an enhanced sense of safety and security. (Gonzales & Kim, 1997). There also is preliminary evidence suggesting that religion can enhance adaptive coping with trauma (de Silva, 1999).

Finally, there is some evidence that it may be more difficult to establish a sense of safety in women and girls following traumatic experiences. Females seem to assign more self-blame following a traumatic event and tend to evaluate the world as more dangerous or negative than their male counterparts (Tolin & Foa, 2002). These gender differences in cognitive appraisal of safety and responsibility may in part be due to differences in the frequency and type of trauma experienced by males (e.g., physical assault is most frequent) and females (e.g., sexual assault is most frequent). Girls also consistently display greater symptoms of anxiety, depression, and distress following traumatic events (Elklit, 2002; Davis & Siegel, 2000; Foa, et al., 2000; Pandit & Shah, 2000; Silverman & La Greca, 2002; Yule, et al., 1999) regardless of whether the experience is a natural disaster or repeated, personal trauma (Garrison, et al., 1995). While further research is needed to identify whether these gender differences are due to cultural factors, the type of traumatic experience or "true" gender differences (Clark & Miller, 1998; Foa et al., 2000; Silverman & La Greca, 2002), it is clear that different cognitive treatment strategies are necessary to re-establish a sense of safety and security in male and female students.

CHALLENGES AND SOLUTIONS

The biggest barrier to successful implementation of school-based family treatment of trauma is stakeholder buy in. More specifically, garnering the support of school personnel and families for this mode of intervention. Both school's and families struggle with integrating family trauma treatment into the normal school day. As such, these interventions are best provided in the evening, after school and work hours. Additionally, the various ages as well as levels of functioning of different family members can make for challenges in the psycho-educational programming. This challenge can be addressed by providing concurrent age specific psycho-educational groups in the case of mass trauma or meet with developmentally similar family subsystems with individual trauma. Similarly, there are times when different family subsystems need to be the focus of counseling sessions. In both these instances making provisions for childcare, when indicated, can facilitate family engagement.

PROCEDURE

FAMILY INVOLVEMENT IN CHILD AND ADOLESCENT TRAUMA INTERVENTIONS

As described in the Program section of this chapter. Family involvement should be grounded in an understanding of trauma reactions and family and developmental systems theories. Initial, interventions with families should focus on providing psycho-educational material to parents and children/teens about the typical characteristics of trauma response and the course of adjustment to trauma. Further, therapists providing family trauma interventions should be conducting an assessment of each family's unique response to the traumatic event. The core elements of trauma treatment which therapists need to actively integrate in their family trauma therapy are presented below.

SAFETY

The first intervention priority is re-establishing safety for the child and family. Ideally, physical safety is initially re-established as it is difficult to reduce and counteract stress responses in an unsafe and continually stressful environment. There are some settings where re-establishing physical safety is difficult, however, and students from these environments will likely struggle more with stress disorders. Horowitz, Weine & Jekel (1995) suggested that youth (e.g., those living in urban and war zones) who experience frequent and repetitive traumatic events {a vertical stressor in Carter & McGoldrick's (2005) model} in their community or *compounded community trauma* have an increased risk for developing PTSD following a specific trauma. These authors found rates of PTSD symptomatology as high as 67% in their sample of minority, urban females.

Regardless of specific vulnerabilities and difficulties with re-establishing a sense of safety, there are certain strategies that can be implemented within the family. When the child is demonstrating a stress reaction, parents and caregivers can begin by providing developmentally appropriate behavioral responses that are physically soothing (e.g., holding, rocking, patting in younger children). At this time is important to talk to the child or teen in a calm and re-assuring manner. This behavioral and interpersonal stance communicates a sense of safety and predictability even in the face of external stress and traumatic events. It is important to note that the physical soothing responses may need to be modified for children who have been physically or sexually abused. These children may not initially experience a sense of safety when being touched by a caregiver, even a well intentioned and nurturing caregiver. A long-term therapeutic goal will be working to develop comfort with healthy touch (Gil, 1996), but some children initially may need more verbal soothing (vs. physical). Additionally, children who have experienced trauma may develop an enhanced sense of physical safety by participating in activities where they can demonstrate their physical prowess (van der Kolk, 2003).

After initial soothing responses, it is important to establish boundaries, rules, and limits for the child's behavior and response to the trauma in order to help him/her develop a better capacity for emotional self regulation and impulse control (van der Kolk, 2003). It will be easier to re-establish the child's physical, emotional, and cognitive sense of safety when there was a healthy parent-child attachment relationship prior to the trauma. In the absence of pre-existing positive attachment relationships, it may be necessary to establish a trusting, nurturant caregiver-child relationship in order for the child to respond to these overtures to re-establish safety.

COUNTER-CONDITIONING

Most contemporary models of PTSD in adults incorporate elements of traditional learning theory with the current memory and cognition literature (Berliner, Hyman, Thomas, & Fitzgerald, 2003; Bower & Sivers, 1998; Hackman & Holmes, 2004). While these models can serve as a basis for understanding PTSD in children, it is necessary to incorporate elements of child development and family systems theory when working with child trauma survivors. Again, an extensive review of this literature is beyond the scope of this manuscript (see Brewin & Holmes, 2003 for a review of contemporary models of PTSD and Bower & Sivers, 1998 for a review of the impact of trauma on cognitive processes, especially memory). The key elements of this literature as pertain to family involvement in treatment of trauma involve enlisting the family's aid when the child is 1) re-experiencing the trauma via flashbacks and dissociative processes and 2) avoiding environmental stimuli associated with the trauma.

Flashbacks and dissociation are extremely disturbing experiences both for child trauma survivors and their families. During flashbacks, the child or teen experiences intrusive memories associated with their traumatic experiences. These memories include vivid recall of the traumatic event and are highly affectively charged. The experience induces significant fear and distress in the young person. Family members witnessing a flashback often feel helpless and overwhelmed by their child's response and their lack of ability to relieve the child's distress. Current memory literature suggests that because the traumatic memory is encoded in association with fear, these memories are then more likely to be retrieved in a state dependent fashion. That is, flashbacks are more likely to occur when the child trauma survivor feels fearful or encounters environmental stimuli or cognitions associated with fear (Bower & Sivers, 1998), guilt, shame, disgust, sadness, and anger (Grey, Holmes, & Brewin, 2001). Further, the memories associated with trauma often occur as implicit vs. explicit memories. That is, they can occur involuntarily or without the child's conscious attempt at recall (Bower & Sivers, 1998). The family can be instrumental in helping identify those stimuli and situations that produce the affective responses that stimulate these implicit memories in their children. Parents and caregivers can be utilized to monitor the child's reactions in an attempt to identify flashback triggers. They can then support the child to implement anxiety reduction and emotional regulation procedures either in anticipation of or at the onset of the negative affect producing experiences. In this sense the family can serve to facilitate prevention of flashbacks in the child.

Dissociation the other hand involves the child's emotional and cognitive disconnection from trauma. Briere (1992) described three types of dissociation: disengagement, detachment or numbing, and observation. Disengagement refers to "spacing-out" and losing awareness of one's surroundings. Detachment or numbing involves a separation between the affective and cognitive content of the event. These children lose touch with the negative affect associated with the event and subsequent memories of the event. Observation involves a process of disconnection between the mind and body. These trauma survivors describe themselves as "watching" the traumatic event occur rather than being an actor in the event. Bower & Sivers (1998) have suggested that the process of dissociation may be related to autobiographic and episodic memory processes whereby the memory of the traumatic event is encoded without the associations with a feeling of consciousness and self (autobiographic) that episodic memories typically contain. Children and teens experiencing traumatic events may be particularly vulnerable these dissociative processes as their cognitive capacity for a sense of self or "me", and consequently autobiographical memory, is less well developed than adults (Howe & Courage, 1997).

As with flashbacks, parents and caregivers can facilitate adaptive coping with dissociation. With disengagement, young people are typically not aware of those situations and experiences associated with "spacing-out". Gil (1991) normalizes dissociation as a coping mechanism and asserts that it becomes maladaptive when we are not able to exercise control over the experience. She suggests a cognitive behavioral approach whereby the young person identifies environmental triggers for the dissociative episodes and then practices controlling the dissociative process while experiencing those triggers. As with flashbacks, since the child is often not consciously aware of the triggers, the family can help identify environmental triggers as well as help the child develop increased awareness of the thoughts and feelings associated with dissociation. Parents and caregivers are in a much better position to facilitate increased awareness as they can work with the child in situ, when they are experiencing dissociative episodes.

Finally, flashbacks and dissociation are frequently triggered by negative associational cues. These negative associational cues can be environmental stimuli, emotional experiences, or cognitions (thoughts, beliefs, perceptions, etc.). Positive associational cues can be used to counteract these negative associational cues. These positive associational cues are those environmental stimuli, emotional experiences, and cognitions associated with positive memories and situations. Families can be engaged to help the child develop positive associational cues in an attempt to counteract the negative cues associated with the child's traumatic experience. These cues can take the form of enjoyable activities as well as tangible representations of the child's adaptive coping. Tangible cues can facilitate long term adaptive functioning and generalizability as they are concrete associations the child can carry in the daily environment.

CONTEXTUALIZING THE TRAUMA

Treatment models for recovery from trauma tend to emphasize cognitive behavioral approaches. The models identified as most effective often combine anxiety management techniques with exposure and/or counter-conditioning techniques (Kruczek, Vitanza, &Salsman, 2008). However, it is important to note there is a paucity of research evaluating most other treatment models. One of the primary cognitive behavioral elements of treatment involves evaluating thoughts and feelings related to the traumatic experience in order to contextualize the trauma. Often the first step in providing a context for the trauma is to help the child and family recognize the external nature of the trauma. In cases of accidents and disasters, the trauma is discussed as an event external to the child and family that happened to them. When the traumatic event involves abuse, it is important for the child and family to externalize responsibility for the trauma by identifying that the abuse perpetrator did something to the child or teen that was hurtful and precipitated their traumatic reaction.

Another interesting approach adapted from treatment with adult trauma survivors (e.g., Foa, Molnar & Cashman, 1995) involves use of narrative techniques. There is mixed evidence about the use of trauma-focused narratives with children. Salloum & Overstreet (2012) found that the addition of trauma-focused narratives did not result in a significant or incremental gain over a coping skills alone approach with children. Deblinger, Mannarino, Cohen, Runyon, and Steer (2011) used two "doses" (8 and 16 sessions) of TF-CBT with and without inclusion of a trauma narrative (TN). The eight session intervention with the TN was most effective at reducing parents' abuse specific distress. However the 16 sessions without the TN was the most effective overall in promoting parental efficacy and minimizing externalizing behavior problems in the child survivors. It may be that trauma-focused narratives are less useful in facilitating adaptive coping, but helping children and families develop a narrative that places the traumatic experience within the broader context of their life experiences may be more useful. Developing a context for the trauma is particularly important given the often fragmented and limited nature of children's memories surrounding their traumatic experiences.

Recall the research on autobiographical memory that suggests a "reconstructive" nature with these memory processes (Loftus & Ketcham, 1994). Related research on emotion and memory may help explain further why these memories are incomplete and call for subsequent reconstruction. While events that arouse significant emotion lead to improved memory about the event, there can be an element of selectivity to the memory. That is, during an event that arouses significant emotionality, not all aspects of the situation will be equally attended to. Those elements of the situation that are most salient to the individual experiencing the event are best attended to and elaborated (Bower &Sivers, 1998). This selective attention bias likely results in incomplete memories of the stressful event and in an attempt to develop a coherent memory for the event the individual turns to her/his previously developed cognitive schemas about the world. Cognitive schemas include knowledge, beliefs, and attitudes that are used to understand and make predictions about the world. They are thought to develop from our interactions with caregivers and our early environment. They also guide our behavioral choices. In children both memory capabilities and cognitive schema are less well developed than in adults and adolescents.

The majority of the cognitive behavioral treatment models for PTSD in children and teens are provided in a group format and include interventions designed to facilitate memory consolidation (Kruczek, Vitanza, & Salsman, 2008). Given the fragility of children's memory in general and for traumatic events in particular *and* the impact of trauma on the family as a whole, it seems remiss to exclude parents and caregivers from the memory consolidation process. Even when experienced individually, a child's trauma experience has an impact on the whole family, particularly parents and caregivers. Family involvement in the reconstructive memory process not only can foster cohesion within the family, but can also facilitate the family's capacity to find meaning in the experience. The Deblingeret. al (2011) finding that a brief (eight session) time of attention to the narrative facilitated parents' abuse specific distress is consistent with this notion. Long term healthy adaptation for the child and family depends on their capacity to maintain overall healthy family functioning in spite of the stressor of trauma as well as their ability to contextualize the trauma as only one of many self defining life experiences.

Social cognitive theory supports the child and family's need to incorporate the traumatic event within their overall belief system. Janoff-Bulman (1992) suggests that children who have had positive attachment relationships with their caregivers develop core beliefs that the world is a just and benevolent place. When these children and teens experience Type I traumatic events, they must adjust and adapt their core belief systems to incorporate this new, adverse experience. Given that these children start with positive core expectations, beliefs and knowledge bases, they are in a position to construe their traumatic memories in an adaptive fashion. Parents and caregivers can facilitate this process by communicating cognitive reframes of the event and openly discussing mutual perceptions of the event.

When children experience Type II traumatic events (or perhaps even compounded community trauma) in the absence of positive attachment relationships, they may not develop core belief systems that are healthy and adaptive. While subsequent trauma may not alter these children's core belief system, it may reinforce their maladaptive self and world perceptions. Counselors working with these children and their families may need to work on fostering more healthy perceptual sets and re-orient them to their strengths and to adaptive solutions. When these families experience vertical stressors associated with trans-generational patterns of violence, counselors may need to work with both the child and family to foster healthy identity development beyond that of a "victim" or even "survivor". When these families are able to expand their self concept to include elements unrelated to the abuse, they will be able to develop a more balanced, healthy self perception and identity.

SUMMARY

The family remains both an untapped resource in and potentially neglected element of school-based treatment of trauma. Family involvement has great potential to support and enhance a student's capacity to develop adaptive strategies for coping with their traumatic life experience. Further, students do not experience trauma in isolation of their families. Even when the trauma is experienced individually by the student, the long term effects of the trauma often impact family functioning. Schools have long been recognized as a logical place to address trauma in children and teens. Few models to date, however, have integrated family systems and trauma literature in an attempt to provide guidelines for family involvement of school-based trauma interventions. This chapter is a preliminary attempt to provide one such model of treatment in order to re-establish normative development for the child and within the family life cycle.

REFERENCES

Amaya-Jackson, L., & March, J. (1995). Posttraumatic stress disorder in adolescents: Risk factors, diagnosis, and intervention. *Adolescent Medicine, 6,* 251-269.

American Psychiatric Association. (2000). *Diagnostic and Statistical Manual of Mental Disorders* (4th ed., text revisions). Washington, DC: Author.

Avinger, K.A. & Jones, R.A. (2007). Group treatment of sexually abused adolescent girls: A review of outcome studies. *The American Journal of Family Therapy, 35,* 315-326.

Barnhill, L.R. (1979). Healthy family systems. *Family Coordinator, 28(1),* 94-100.

Bower, G.H., & Sivers, H. (1998).Cognitive impact of traumatic events. *Development and Psychopathology, 10,* 625-653.

Brewin, C.R., & Holmes, E.A. (2003).Psychological theories of posttraumatic stress disorder.*Clinical Psychology Review, 23(3),* 339-376.

Briere, J. (1992). *Child Abuse Trauma.* Newbury Park, CA: Sage Publications.

Briere, J. (1997). *Psychological Assessment of Adult Posttraumatic States.* Washington, DC: American Psychological Association.

Carter, B., & McGoldrick, M. (2005). Overview: the expanded family life cycle: Individual, family and social perspectives. In B. Carter & M. McGoldrick (Eds.) *The Expanded Family Life Cycle: Individual, family, and social perspectives* (3rd ed., pp.1-26). New York: Allyn and Bacon Classics.

Clark, D. B., & Miller, T. W. (1998). Stress response and adaptation in children: Theoretical Models. In T.W. Miller (Ed.) *Children of Trauma: Stressful life events and their effects on children and adolescents* (pp. 3-29). Madison, CT: International Universities Press, Inc.

Cohen, J. A. (1998). Practice parameters for the assessment and treatment of children and adolescents with posttraumatic stress disorder. *Journal of the American Academy of Child and Adolescent Psychiatry, 37,* 4S-26S.

Cohen, J. A. (2001). Pharmacologic treatment of traumatized children. *Trauma, Violence, and Abuse, 2(2),* 155-171.

Cook-Cottone, C. (2004). Childhood Posttraumatic Stress Disorder: Diagnosis, Treatment, and School Reintegration. *School Psychology Review, 33(1),* 127-139.

Davidson, S. & Smith, R. (1990). Traumatic experiences in psychiatric outpatients. *Journal of Traumatic Stress Studies, 3,* 459-475.

Davis, L. & Siegel, L.J. (2000). Posttraumatic stress disorder in children and adolescents: A review and analysis. *Clinical Child and Family Psychology Review, 3(3),* 135-154.

de Silva, P. (1999). Cultural aspects of posttraumatic stress disorder. In W. Yule (Ed.), *Post-traumatic stress disorders: Concepts and therapy* (pp. 116-137). New York: John Wiley & Sons.

Donnelly, C.I., Amaya-Jackson, L., & March, J.S. (1999). Psychopharmacology of pediatric posttraumatic stress disorder. *Journal of Child and Adolescent Psychopharmacology, 9(3),* 203-220.

Elklit, A. (2002). Victimization and PTSD in a Danish national youth probability sample. *Journal of the American Academy of Child and Adolescent Psychiatry, 41*(2), 174-181.

Foa, E. B., Keane, T. M., & Friedman, M. J. (2000). Introduction. In. E. B. Foa, T. M. Keane, & M. J. Friedman (Eds.), *Effective treatments for PTSD: Practice guidelines from the International Society for Traumatic Stress Studies* (pp. 106-138). New York: Guilford Press.

Foa, E.B., Molnar, C., &Cashman, L. (1995). Change in rape narratives during exposure therapy for post-traumatic stress disorder. *Journal of Traumatic Stress, 8,* 675-690.

Foa, E.B., Zinbarg, R., &Rothbaum, B.O. (1992). Uncontrollability and unpredictability in post-traumatic stress disorder: An animal model. *Psychological Bulletin, 112,* 218-238.

Garrison, C. Z., Bryant, E. S., Addy, C. L., Spurrier, P. G., Freedy, J. R., & Kilpatrick, D. G. (1995). Posttraumatic stress disorder in adolescents after Hurricane Andrew. *Journal of the American Academy of Child and Adolescent Psychiatry, 34*(9), 1193-1201.

Gil, E. (1991).*The healing power of play: Working with abused children.* New York, NY: Guilford Press.

Gil, E. (1996).*Systemic treatment of families who abuse.* San Francisco: Josey-Bass Publishers.

Gonzales, N. & Kim, L. (1997). Stress and coping in an ethnic minority context. In S.A. Wlochik& I.N. Sandler (Eds.), *Handbook of children's coping: Linking theory and intervention* (pp. 481-511). New York: Plenum Press.

Grey, N., Holmes, E., &Brewin, C. (2001). Peri-traumatic emotional "hot spots" in memory. *Behavioural and Cognitive Psychotherapy, 29(3),* 367-372.

Hackman, E.A., & Holmes, A. (2004). Reflecting on imagery: A clinical perspective and overview. *Memory, 12(4),*389-402.

Horowitz, K., Weine, S., & Jekel, J. (1995).PTSD symptoms in urban adolescent girls. *Journal of the American Academy of Child and Adolescent Psychiatry, 34*(10), 1353-1361.

Howe, M.L., & Courage, M.L. (1997). The emergence and early development of autobiographical memory. *Psychological Review, 104,*n 499-523.

Janoff-Bulman, R. (1992). *Shattered assumptions: Towards a new psychology of trauma.* New York: Free Press.

Kruczek, T.,Vitanza, S., &Salsman, J. (2008).Post-traumatic stress disorder in children.In Gullotta, T. & Blau, G. (Eds), *Handbook of childhood behavioral issues: Evidence-based approaches to prevention and treatment.* New York, NY, US: Routledge/Taylor & Francis Group.

Loftus, E., &Ketcham, K. (1994). *The myth of repressed memory: False memories and allegations of sexual abuse.* New York: St. Martin's Press.

LeDoux, J.E. (1996). *The emotional brain: The mysterious underpinnings of emotional life.* New York: Simon & Schuster.

Pandit, S., & Shah, L. (2000). Post-traumatic stress disorder: causes and aetiological factors. In K.N. Dwivedi (Ed.), *Post-traumatic stress disorder in children and adolescents* (pp. 25-38). London, England: Whurr Publishers, Ltd.

Perry, B.D. (1994). Neurobiological sequelae of childhood trauma: PTSD in children. In M.M. Murburg (Ed.), *Catecholamine function in posttraumatic stress disorder: Emerging concepts* (pp. 223-255). Washington, DC: American Psychiatric Press.

Perry, B., Pollard, R., Blakley, T., & Baker, W. (1995). Childhood trauma, the neurobiology of adaptation and use-dependent development of the brain: How states become traits. *Infant Mental Health Journal, 16(4),* 271-291.

Pynoos, R.S. (1994). Traumatic stress and developmental psychopathology in children and adolescents. In R.S. Pynoos (Ed.), *Posttraumatic stress disorder: A clinical review* (pp. 64-98). Lutherville, MD: The Sidran Press.

Rablais, A.E., Ruggerio, K.J., &Scotti, J.R. (2002). Multicultural issues in the response of children to disasters. In A.M. LaGreca, W.K. Silverman, E.M. Vernberg, and MC. Roberts (Eds.), *Helping children cope with disasters and terrorism* (pp. 73-100). Washington, DC: American Psychological Association.

Reinherz, H.Z., Giaconia, R.M., Lefkowitz, E.S., Pakiz, B., & Frost, A.K. (1993). Prevalence of psychiatric disorders in a community population of older adolescents. *Journal of the American Academy of Child and Adolescent Psychiatry, 32,* 369-377.

Selye, H. (1952). *The Story of the Adaptation Syndrome.*Montreal, Canada: Acta, Inc.

Silverman, W. K., & La Greca, A. K. (2002). Children experiencing disasters: Definitions, reactions, and predictors of outcomes. In A.M. LaGreca, W.K. Silverman, E.M. Vernberg, and MC. Roberts (Eds.), *Helping children cope with disasters and terrorism* (pp. 11-34). Washington, DC: American Psychological Association.

Stallard, P. (2000). Debriefing adolescents after critical life events. In B. Raphael & J. P. Wilson (Eds.), *Psychological debriefing: Theory, practice, and evidence* (pp. 213-224). New York: Cambridge University Press.

Summit, R.C. (1983). The child sexual abuse accommodation syndrome. *Child Abuse and Neglect, 7,* 177-193.

Terr, L.C. (1991). Childhood traumas: An outline and overview. *American Journal of Psychiatry, 148,* 10-19.

Tolin, D. E., &Foa, E. B. (2002). Gender and PTSD: A cognitive model.In R. Kimmerling, P. Ouimette, and J. Wolfe (Eds.), *Gender and PTSD* (pp. 76-97). NewYork: Guilford Press.

Udwin, O., Boyle, S., Yule, W., Bolton, D., &O'Ryan, D. (2000). Risk factors for long-term psychological effects of a disaster experienced in adolescence: Predictors of post-traumatic stress disorder. *Journal of Child Psychology and Psychiatry, 41*(8), 969-979.

van der Kolk, B.A. (2003). The neurobiology of childhood trauma and abuse. *Child and Adolescent Psychiatric Clinics of North America, 12,* 293-317.

Wasserstein, S. B., & La Greca, A. M. (1998). Hurricane Andrew: Parent conflict as a moderator of children's adjustment. *Hispanic Journal of Behavioral Sciences, 20*(2), 212-224.

Yule, W. (2001). Post-traumatic stress disorder in children and adolescents. *International Review of Psychiatry, 13*, 194-200.

Yule, W., Perrin, S., & Smith, P. (1999). Post-traumatic stress reactions in children and adolescents. In W. Yule (Ed.), *Post-traumatic stress disorders* (pp. 25-50).New York: John Wiley & Sons.

RESOURCES

The following organizations contain a host of resources and recommendations for the treatment of child and adolescent trauma and can be accessed at the links below.

American Academy of Child and Adolescent Psychiatry
http://www.aacap.org/cs/root/facts_for_families/posttraumatic_stress_disorder_ptsd

American Counseling Association
http://www.counseling.org/sub/dmh/resources.aspx

American Psychological Association
Professionals
http://www.apa.org/pi/families/resources/task-force/child-trauma.aspx
Parents
http://www.apa.org/about/gr/issues/cyf/child-trauma.pdf

American School Counseling Association
http://www.schoolcounselor.org/content.asp?pl=327&contentid=327

National Child Traumatic Stress Network
http://www.nctsn.org/

Chapter 26
Therapeutic Storytelling Intervention
Group Therapy

Ron Phillips

OVERVIEW: *Therapeutic Storytelling Intervention (TSI) is a strategy that guides adolescents on their quest for achieving identity. The book Gem of the First Water is the journey of an unnamed Boy on his journey of self discovery. The Boy enacts the issues and struggles of life and for the listeners/readers his responses to each dilemma serve as the platform for meaningful group discussion and even more importantly personal mindful consideration.*

BACKGROUND

Many past innovations result from great need. I stumbled into creating the TSI process because the traditional group therapeutic approach did not work for me.

> *Is it working? No? Then change what you are doing.*
> -William Glasser MD

My wife Mary and I founded Creative Alternatives Inc in 1976 as a residential treatment facility for emotionally disturbed children located in northern California. Creative Alternatives served as a wonderful laboratory for developing a new adaptation to a very old form of childhood education. Storytelling is age old and until the advent of television and the Hi Tech games revolution, was the model for transmitting the stories, values and traditions of one generation to the next. From Creative Alternatives inception in 1976 it grew rapidly, and by 1980 we had 65 children from all over California. We wanted our delivery of care to be integrated, so in the late 70's I went to the University of San Francisco (USF) to become a qualified therapist. My USF education was first class and I achieved my Masters of Family Therapy (MFT). However it did not equip me with the tools necessary for running group therapy sessions with multi-problem kids who are historically and universally resistant to therapeutic interventions. The USF training in the facilitation of groups was based on Dr. Irvin D Yalom's model of group therapy (adult model), which emphasizes peer developed rules, group boundaries and structure.

I hypothesized and considered that the best model of intervention for my population was a group format. This thinking was based on empirical fact that peers greatly influence each other by what they say or don't say, by the way they look, and by what they do. The idea was right; however my model to achieve an effective culture of therapy was wrong. Dr. Irvin Yalom's protocols for running effective groups work well with adults and motivated adolescents; however, I immediately learned they did not work with multi-problem adolescents. The success of the group using his model is dependant on each individual's level of self disclosure and agreement by the group members on the rules of engagement and group rules of confidentiality. Forget it! From the very moment I began every kid in all 6 of the initial groups started formulating an exit procedure out of the group and in all 6 groups' chaos was their response. Why didn't Yalom's proven method work? Adolescents are a totally different developmental group. Adolescents strive to be similar. Check out groups of kids walking together at any mall. In all groupings of meandering kids they are dressed similarly; the last thing an adolescent will do is strive to be different.

So the instant I started setting up rules for the group based on them sharing their deep 'stuff'- they started dropping out. This explains the poverty of literature on successful groups run with multi-problem teens; there isn't data (that I'm aware of) because there aren't any successful groups of any consistency or duration run. Teens vote with their feet. Before me was an enactment of my hypothesis - the mighty power of peer influence. Adolescents do indeed influence each other. They told me with their collective actions that they were not about to agree to the group rules and would fight tooth and nail to knock over the group therapy. The reason for this is also very clear - they were afraid of being revealed, they fear humiliation.

I learned from William Glasser that if what you are doing isn't working - then change. I applied this to the obvious failure of my initial start at running group therapy. What adolescent would risk putting themselves into a position of exposure? It didn't work nor will the adult model ever work with adolescents. The developmental issues of adolescence made the idea of self-revealing so developmentally wrong. I still believed that group therapy for teens was so right, but how to get it to work? I applied the great lesson I learned while practicing Reality Therapy and changed my therapeutic approach.

My early groups based on an adult proven approach didn't work and each of my six weekly groups were more like a "shark frenzy" than therapy and I was the bait; there was no effective life change occurring. In fact the most frequent words were, "Fuck you!" I reluctantly persevered and after two or three groups of sheer stress in order to fill time I shifted from a topic of pure boredom to telling a story. I stumbled into storytelling and from that week it's been my life's work.

I started telling a story and the very moment I started painting mind pictures, the kids' listened. Not only did they hear what I was saying, they were interested and asked questions and responded to questions without the ever present opposition and defiance. They immediately began participating in the new form of group therapy session with enjoyment and without attitude. Early into the onset of TSI it became apparent I was actually talking to these kids on the *other side of their attitude*. The front door approach didn't work, so, metaphorically speaking, I took TSI 'through the bathroom window' and I've been going 'in and out the bathroom window' running groups using exactly the same story and approach since 1985. What started out originally as a survival method, is now a refined sophisticated psychological intervention that invades the imagination of listeners and works freely in the listeners' unconscious mind.

From the beginning I wanted each story to have some therapeutic meaning or life lesson, so that we could have a bit of a discussion, thus meeting a group therapy definition. To my great surprise not only did they listen but were able to relate to the presented issues and the story led to meaningful post-story discussion. It was even of greater surprise to discover that the next week they would retain last week's content and demanded continuity by wanting to know how the unnamed 'Boy' got from where he was last week to the present place. The listeners wanted connection, they insisted on the stories becoming a journey. Suddenly the penny dropped. My interns, Dan Brewer MFT., and John Hopper MFT and I realized that our kids were some of California's most *therapized* kids and they were listening to learn. We quickly realized that this approach was effective because as we learned later, they were listening from an absolutely undefended and totally receptive altered state of consciousness. Once insight occurred I started saturating the story with universal lessons of life.

THE NEW ZEALAND ERA

As *way leads to way* Mary, 3 kids and I left California in 1991 and moved to New Zealand, for a year's working holiday. We did not know one single soul in New Zealand so naturally TSI started with a blank slate. I started working for the Ministry of Education as a school psychologist in Northland, three hours north of Auckland. I went to the ten schools up the east coast of northland and asked the principals how I could be of most service. Expecting to hear that they wanted me to do the typical psychometric testing I was surprised that they preferred me to work with kids they felt had potential but were problematic. I started using TSI in all ten schools. The ministry wanted me to test yet the principals wanted something different; "we know what the test will say, so why not try and help the kids with their issues of well being".

Also in that first year the New Zealand police and New Zealand Dare Foundation took TSI on as a national policing strategy they called *Dare To Make Change*. Since the project took several years of training to implement nationally we stayed in New Zealand. *Dare to Make Change* was used throughout New Zealand by Police education officers and Dare presenters for over ten years. In 1996 I started using TSI at Whirinaki the tertiary child and adolescent mental health clinic that services all of South Auckland with a population of 500,000 multi ethnic people. This is an area having both high crime rates and rampant drug use. For the last 16 years I have run hundreds of TSI groups with multi-problem youth and adolescents. The group compositions have been varied, same sex groups, mixed sex groups, homogeneous topic groups (for example: all with major suicide presentations, eating disorder, ADHD, ODD, school refusal, etc).

MULTICULTURAL COUNSELING CONSIDERATIONS

TSI has been used in a variety of settings with a variety of ethnic groups. I recognize the verbosity of saying that the content is gender, ethnic, religious and social-status blind. The issues and dilemmas the Boy enacts are the issues everyone faces boy or girl rich or poor black or white, Jew or Christian.

In my early years at Creative Alternatives the ethnic mix was divided into thirds. We worked with mostly boys of Anglo, Black and Latino heritage. For the last 21 years TSI has been delivered to an even greater mix of ethnic backgrounds. The gender mix and social status mix has been greater also. At Creative Alternatives the clients were primarily from lower socio-economic families. In New Zealand the mix is varied. For example, I presently work in 10 high schools all over the greater South Auckland region. The gender split is about 60% male and 40% female. Some of my groups are all Polynesian and Maori clients including Samoan, Tongan, Tokelauan, Niuean, Fijian, and Maori from various tribes. The present composition of the groups is mostly same sex. However 4 of the groups are mixed sex. One of the groups is from an upper middleclass school with mostly professional parents. In all my groups the material is accepted in the same manner. The students are color blind to the characters and I'm often told they mindfully visualize the Boy as being of their own color. Kids identify with the Boy, they internalize the lessons and in many cases they re-direct their behaviors not because they are being told too but because they endogenously decide too.

RELATIONSHIP TO THE SBFC MODEL

Therapeutic Storytelling Intervention meets criteria as both a preventive and remedial counseling approach. TSI uses the book *Gem of the First Water* as the vehicle for engagement and content introduction within the story's context. *Gem of the First Water* is a purpose built journey with embedded themes and relevant issues that the Boy enacts for the group participants. The material is preventive in nature because life experiences that are yet to be encountered by the young participants are thought about, discussed and decisions of how to best tackle the issues are played out for the group members in advance of the personal experience. Over the course of TSI's utilization, many participants have related how the group experience prepared them in advance for life's actual event.

The TSI orientation is also very remedial and is like looking in a mirror. Kids see themselves and endogenously determine to change. Each lesson offers remedies and solutions to serious personal problems. Kids change not because a powerful force is insisting on it, but they change because they have mindfully considered that what they are doing is not working and that there are better behavioral alternatives.

Over the last five years I have moved from TSI running primarily with groups at the clinic, to running a majority of groups in the community. Presently I run twelve groups per semester in high schools all over South Auckland. The constellation of each group is determined by school personnel. Most often the referring agent is the School Guidance Counselor (SGC), who identifies and organizes between 8 to 12 students to participate. The other professionals who organize their school for TSI are School Social Workers (3) and (1) RTLB (Resource Learning and Behavior Specialist). These professionals also attend each group. They triage any mental health or academic concerns to parents, teachers, and administration. The nature of the TSI/ *Gem Journey* stimulates thinking and emotions of the listener and primes the guided group discussion. If a student discloses information of a sensitive nature I will encourage the participant to discuss the issue in private after group with their School Guidance Counselor and should the nature of what is disclosed be beyond the professional scope of the SGC they make a referral to Whirinaki. Generally since I know the student I will inherit the case. The group actually reduces the number of mental health referrals because issues are often satisfactorily resolved in the group setting. The Gem journey is psycho-educational with the positive outcome of fewer clinic referrals.

PROCEDURE

Most new group members come to the group apprehensive, resistant and thinking "how will I get out of this mess I'm about to get into?" The new group members are exactly like the original kids I worked with back in the mid-eighties. They attend the first group with fear and their pervading thought is that they don't want to be there. Therefore my entire first group approach is unique and designed to establish effective engagement. As I've mentioned my approach is unique to most group therapies. Typically I can sit down with a diverse and unknown circle of adolescents/latency youth and within 10 minutes have the Gem Journey started with everyone knowing pretty much everything they need to know.

GETTING STARTED: GROUND RULES

Step 1

I learn everyone's name. It's actually very simple to learn 8 to 10 names.

Step 2

Promise: I tell them, "I am going to give each of you something worth more than Gold. Yep! I said it, more than gold." I then ask randomly of a group participant, "Hey Jim do you believe me?" The common answer with arms folded protectively across chest is "hell no". To which I respond: "I don't blame you, I wouldn't believe me either - however you won't forget I said this on the first day. Yep, more than Gold!"

<u>Step 3</u>

The rules: 1. My rules are: make yourself comfortable. "I'm going to take you on a journey and you are going to dig it! Close your eyes if you want- sit on the floor if you want.
However….I do ask that you stay in your own circle. By that I mean………When Jim's talking I wouldn't dream of talking and when I'm……………" I often then tail off without finishing sentence. The leaving off technique is interesting because you can empirically watch the kids putting words to finish off the unspoken sentence.

<u>Step 4</u>

The Paradox: The all important paradox message is, don't bullshit yourself or the process. If I ask you a question that you don't think is anyone's business, especially mine or you can't think of an answer - then I insist that you say 'pass'. I then add; ever been in class and a teacher asks you a question and your mind goes blank—*duh what's up Doc*? What should you do? "PASS." "The one thing I do ask if you do give an answer, it's gotta be what you really think and feel. If you bullshit me or yourself you'll miss the…." I often only half complete a sentence relying on unconscious process to complete and consolidate the theme.

Then without any more talk, I fire into the process and start telling the first chapter. Students visibly relax when I begin. I believe everyone enjoys a story, and I can without reservation make that statement after telling the exact same story since 1985. After the ever so brief introduction the students realize that they won't be embarrassed from the anxiety and fear of being revealed and that it's alleviated by simply being able to just say "pass". Interestingly many kids later relate that they initially decided to pass on every question for the duration of the whole group. Once these brief non-intimidating rules, promises and paradoxes are introduced most kids relax to the point that some even close their eyes and get in a comfortable position and listen, all this is observable by their clear body language. I then proceed to paint wonderful mind pictures in the telling of *Gem of the First Water*.

I also make the declaration, "I will never embarrass you, so come to group and relax; that's a promise." It is my belief that the simple combination of beginning instructions, paves the way for group success by being so non-threatening it gives the story telling process an opportunity to succeed. I also re-enforce this premise by doing a round at the end of the first session asking each kid if the group was as bad as they thought it was going to be. I then go on to add it will never get any heavier than today. I don't want to '*psychologize you*' '*alphabetize you*' or '*mesmerize you*'…I just want to tell you a story. Generally the kids respond by stating it wasn't nearly as bad as they thought it would be and bingo the group is off the ground.

THE JOURNEY BEGINS: GENERAL SESSION

After the brief introduction the initial group is run essentially the same as general sessions. All groups are predictable in format. It's the predictability and structure that create a safe, non-threatening environment that adolescents soon learn to enjoy and not fear. Keeping this safe environment is paramount to group success. For example, if you have a group room that is subject to disturbances, your group is likely to fail. Keeping interruptions to a minimum is essential. All cell phones turned off, the land line taken off the hook and even a do not disturb sign on the door are all key group issues. The facilitator must model the requests by turning off his/her phone and not attending to distractions, with the message that what we are now about to do or are doing is something more important than anything else.

Warm up: I generally run groups on a weekly basis, having found it is important to have time to allow the themes to breathe. This allows time for the issues to get thoroughly worked over in mindful unconscious process. Running groups with no time between them is less impacting than groups with a good 'time' gap.

To start off a group session I do rounds asking everyone *"what has been the best thing in your life over the last week?"*

I then start with a recap of the last story with questions. Kids like to answer non threatening questions that are simple. For example in chapter two, the Boy has a tattoo of a multi-piece puzzle on the palm of his left hand. In groups down the line, I will ask an individual or the group as a whole; "Say, what was on the Boy's hand?" That would be a generalized question the entire group is free to respond to. Or I might ask Jimmy "what's one word to describe the boy", or "what's one word to describe how you are a little bit like the boy?" If I notice Jimmy faltering, I rescue, "if you can't think of anything just pass, no big thing." After bringing the group up to speed to where we left off, I then launch into the next segment.

Step 2

Story: I tell the story in the next chapter or chapters. Note, some story sessions involve more than one chapter. For example in the eighth session, I tell three chapters: 8, 9, 10. In the ninth session I tell 11, 12 and 13. The talking book (set of 5 CD's of author telling the story) follows the session sequence.

Step 3

Facilitated Discussions: The discussion component of the TSI group is very important. Not only do students/clients listen from an unconscious undefended position, they are also listening to learn. The accompanying Guide has numerous already proven questions that if skillfully presented results in interesting discussions. The quality of these are often so healing in nature I shake my head in wonder. I do not coax or insist or push post group discussion. If, after I've put everything I wish the students to mindfully consider 'on the table' and for whatever reason no flow of conversation comes about, I end the session with a session close down procedure.

Since every one of the participants is new to the process I maintain a very non-threatening interactive position. For the first several groups I emphasize and reinforce the pass rule. Early in the group journey process, my first questions are easy to answer and mostly require only a single word reply. "Ok, Jimmy give me one word to describe when those old people in Foulicia's dungeon first got stuck?" If Jimmy doesn't pass and yet seems keen to respond, only hesitant, I might reduce the stress by next asking, "Did they first get stuck when they were young or old?" Most often participants will comply with a nod or a yeah. Each chapter is purpose built with key themes and guided questions created to simulate thinking and discussion. There is a story guide which highlights themes, important lesson points, and questions I use to stimulate discussion.

Step 4

Session close down: Most stories' finish leaving the listeners' wondering what's going to happen next, which is exactly the impression I want the kids to leave with. Once I assess that the pertinent material has been covered and have adequately asked all the key questions, I then close by doing a round asking each student/client *"what are you going to take home with* you?" If a student says "I don't know" or "Nothing?" I give them a post group suggestion, a question for them to think about; a theme I wish to embed that is relevant to the story of the day. For example, if the session's story centers on the listeners' becoming aware of what they think about, I construct a post group suggestive thought. I might ask Jill (if she stated she wasn't sure exactly what she was taking home) "Hey Jill why don't you consider tonight right before you go off to sleep - you know that very quiet time just before you nod off - *think about what you say to your self the instant you are asked by one of your parents to do something you don't want to do.* Think about what happens next? Is it a battle? Are you in the habit of thinking *I don't feel like it* to almost everything you are asked to do? Is it an easy thinking habit to get into? What if instead of, *I don't feel like it, you can't make me,* Jill, why don't you say to yourself, *Oh ok."*

I do try to ask at next start-up if Jill did explore the question. I am always amazed at how often a post group question is considered and reported about at the next session. The scope of post group suggestions is enormous and the beauty of the method is that these suggestions can be tailored to suit the kid. Although the post-group question was directed to Jill her question had a contemplative impact on all the other members. It is also interesting how often a post-group question for one child will be mindfully considered by others. Now after years of running groups, I tailor a question for a specific student and expect it to be considered by others if the question strikes a personal chord. The post-group question I liken to going into a shoe store, some of the questions fit perfectly while others aren't even considered because they already resolved their position on the issue or developmentally are not ready to even consider.

CHAPTER CONTENT EXAMPLES

There are twenty six purpose built chapters in *Gem of the First Water.* All the chapters have importance however some are important for Journey connective/segway reasons with minor therapeutic lessons, while others introduce profound life lessons with object lessons in the form of learning models. In this brief overview I've chosen two chapters to highlight. Chapter 16 entitled *Worms Wolves* and Chapter 20 *entitled, Outskirts of Splendora.* The chapters leading up to *Worms Wolves* are instructional chapters full of life principles. *The Pool of Right Decisions* (Chapter 14) theme is establishing the concept that good choices/decisions result in positive self image and good feelings. Chapter 15 *Desert of Simple Choice* exposes the internal struggle between what a person should do coming into conflict with what they feel like doing. The Boy is confronted with three dilemmas (moral, pride/ego, altruistic). In each case he makes good choices.

My University of San Francisco degree had a family therapy emphasis which influenced aspects of the Gem Journey. In the first year I was developing the TSI group journey process it became obvious about midway through the journey, that students were developing expectations of each chapter's dilemma. Scripts, and a state of habituation was forming and settling in amongst the participants resulting in listeners losing their intensity for the journey.

The Gem Journey development in the first year was dynamic and evolving with every new episode so when a kid made the unsolicited statement in the post *Desert of Simple Choice* (Chapter 15) discussion; "that the Boy is just a 'do good candy ass,' he just always does what everyone wants him to do, you can tell me the story and I'll tell you what he does." I agreed, and woke up to what was happening and created the next story with a major unexpected event in fact so unexpected the boy who highlighted the script was totally surprised. From a systemic stand point I was scripted and the next story *Worm's Wolves* totally caught the listeners 'off guard.' The script of expectation breaks, resulting in renewed listening/learning intensity.

"The Boy wakes up on the wrong side of the campfire. He's tired of listening, he's tired of all the effort he has been putting forth, he's sick of the uphill hassle. He is in a terrible mood; the way he feels, the content of his thoughts and certainly his actions are all negative - he is full of attitude, easily pissed off - everything is annoying."

This chapter paints a mental picture of the flow chart of a *bad choice*. His "Me Day" intensifies and he arrives at the first cactus where he makes a choice based on what *he feels like doing* rather than what he innately *knows he should do*. The Boy goes down hill full of the dangerous endogenous *I don't care* attitude. The Fox warns him numerous times that this isn't the right way, however his mind conversation is full of 'I don't care thoughts' which over-ride rational thinking and he simply doesn't listen and continues on his wrong path. The fox finally realizes the Boy is not going to turn around and accepts it. Several times he reminds the Boy that this was supposed to be the easiest part of the journey. Wolves surround and drive the Boy and the fox up a cactus. This chapter ends with the Boy experiencing the consequences of a seriously bad choice. *Worms Wolves* is a wonderful metaphor of the "how, when, why's, of a bad decision. The result of his 'Me Day' not only affects him it also greatly affects the fox. The flow of this chapter mirrors life and serves as a wonderful teaching model. The journey is full of equally powerful mind pictures that provide easy unopposed learning scenes that flow into natural post story discussion within the context of the group and probably more importantly carries on in individual mindfulness throughout the week.

Posted on my website are both *Worms Wolves* and the Chapter 16 guide. Please read the chapter and then mindfully answer the guide questions. If you have an audience, read the chapter to them and then facilitate a discussion from the guide questions (www.tsi.co.nz).

Below is a flow chart of the bad choice (Figure 26.1). The moment the Boy awoke he had an attitude. His negative thinking produced negative feelings that resulted in anger, lies, and blame dominating his actions and decisions. Chapter 16 was purpose built to model the steps leading to loss of direction and trouble. The Boy had a habit of making decisions based on doing what he felt like doing. His choice offers participants a clear unambiguous mind picture that is integrated into new thinking and behaviors.

The second example I've selected to demonstrate the depth and scope of journey content is chapter 20 *The Outskirts of Splendora*. Again I would ask the reader to refer to the website: www.tsi.co.nz where all four components of chapter 20 will be available for review. The order I would like you to follow is first to read the chapter. Then watch the commentary of the themes, lessons and key questions that I ask the students. Which ones achieve best practice use of the chapter? Next watch the Christchurch video that highlights one segment of the chapter. Finally, read the guide and mindfully workout your answer to the questions and teaching. Each chapter has a self contained lesson and some chapters like Chapter 20, have numerous talking points.

A wonderful aspect to the journey theme is that chapters or segment of chapters can be used to fit appropriate therapeutic situations. Therapists are from time to time thrust into situations that require some form of brilliance to help achieve meaning to the occasion. One example might be: yearly it seems I'm faced with a situation where the clients/students have experienced a recent trauma and I might use the "Canyon of Sadness" vignette from chapter 20.

In March of 2010 Christchurch New Zealand experienced the most devastating urban earthquake which literally flattened the Central business section of the city. People were killed and there were many serious injuries. Entire residential suburbs were evacuated and condemned, displacing thousands of families. Almost all the historic building was damaged beyond repair. The people of Christchurch and Canterbury region were traumatized. The Young New Zealanders foundation and TSI created a helpful kit sent to all the schools in the region. The video will give the readers an idea of how excerpts from the Gem Journey can be used.

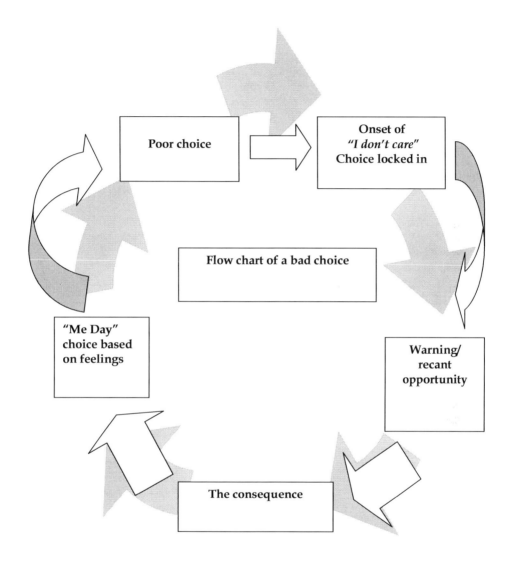

The boxes in the diagram contain the following text:
- Poor choice
- Onset of *"I don't care"* Choice locked in
- Flow chart of a bad choice
- Warning/ recant opportunity
- "Me Day" choice based on feelings
- The consequence

Figure 26.1 Flow Chart of a Bad Choice

RATIONALE

Once kids engage they really get into the journey and look forward to the process without resistance. Each chapter is purpose built to convey essential life lessons. Embedded in the easy to visualize stories are; teaching themes, life principles', and models of behavioral instruction all conveyed in the context of the journey. A big reason that students become engaged is because each chapter leaves the participant with a degree of suspense.

As a child I loved the cartoon *Crusader Rabbit and Rags the Tiger.* The cartoon always left me wondering what was going to happen next. Each segment finished with either one or both the heroes in dire straits. Rags hanging on a limb over a cliff he couldn't possibly survive should he fall. Silly, silly stuff, however the picture lodged in my mind all week, compelling me to see the next episode.

Now for a story for you; When I was about 10 we lived in a tiny little sleepy village south of San Francisco called Sharps Park now part of Pacifica. It was Saturday morning early and my mates and I were on the beach heading north. I had my dad's work watch on to let me know when I had to start heading home to see the cartoon. All week long I looked forward to finding out how the dilemma was resolved. Well here we were walking just beyond the water mark and we spotted several hundred yards up the beach a giant something that shouldn't be there, a gigantic whale. Naturally we were all over it, for the whale represented the ultimate in discovery for the captains of play. I was in a personal quandary knowing my distance home and the morning marching rapidly on. Finally my desire to see the cartoon overpowered me and I leaped off the whale and headed home. My mates thought I was brain dead leaving the treasure.

The Gem Journey acts on the unconscious in exactly the same way. It captures the imagination, causing the participants to mindfully consider the embedded issues of the moment and also considering them all week long. Most leave group wondering what will happen next?

Unconscious State of Listening: The magic of storytelling is that individuals actually go into an altered state of consciousness - a subdued state where they listen to the story with singular focus. It is thought that a listener can be thinking many times faster than another person talking. Experience and client feedback leads me to believe this to be factual. Over the years and from numerous participants I have received feedback that while the story is being told, a very interesting event happens to them deep in their minds. A transformation of thinking transpires unconsciously. The listener sees 'the boy' and his dilemma as common to their dilemmas. Without bringing attention to it or having to highlight the importance of what the Boy is experiencing, an individual's thinking changes from hearing a story of a Boy, a third person experience, into hearing the story vicariously transforming into the role of the Boy enacting the story dilemma, as though it was themselves wrestling with the alternative choices. This feedback is from both boys and girls. I have heard countless times, "hey Ron when you tell the story I become the boy". Another interesting comment that I've heard numerous time is the girls confuse the gender and respond to my questions referring to 'the boy' as 'the girl.' One police education officer from the South Island changed the peer hero from 'The Boy' to 'The Girl". He related the journey worked just as well having the hero a girl. What I'm attempting to relate is similar to getting lost in a book. When reading we get "totally into it", we take that adventure; we envisage those dangers and marvel at the grandeurs, all as though we were actually there in a first person role. What I consider even more terrific is this vicarious first person experience is even more intense with storytelling. Once the story starts, listeners easily fall into the altered state of consciousness, experiencing the story as though looking into a mirror. I believe it happens to almost all the participants who do the groups. My sense is that the intense identification begins from the very onset of starting to relate the day's yarn. Because listeners' insert themselves into the journey they personalize and tailor the lessons to their own experiences.

Once the story begins, an observer can easily identify a softening of mood. Behavioral changes occur, and the changes are sudden and obvious (they can be termed empirical). Body positions shift and adjust to make the listener more comfortable, noise levels lessen, muscles relax and idiosyncratic behaviors increase; for example, one listener might start rubbing a hand on his/her face or scratch an arm or be gently rocking, interlocking fingers in a repeated manner. Colleagues over the twenty-five years I've been running TSI groups collaborate this observation. "Its like once you start telling the story they zone out and become hypnotized," commented a recent co-facilitator. Students listen without interference from the usual culprits: anger, denial, projection; before my eyes I can see defense mechanisms relax allowing mindfulness in its purest form to transpire. Once I realized that this methodology worked, I started saturating/embedding the Journey with all kinds of important lessons, themes and models of instruction. I was talking to kids and being listened too.

State of Identification: The state of identification is achieved in almost every clinical session. Once the story starts all the listener's cares, frustrations, fears, unresolved conflicts etc. simply drift away for a brief period of time. The power of the story causes a profound change from defense mechanisms dominating thoughts, to the state of mindfulness. I can think of no better example of the story altering consciousness' of the participants than one group I ran at Berkeley Lodge (a Creative Alternative group home where I had my practice) in about 1987. Two separate groups of kids arrived a bit early for the group and had to wait outside the door because I was engaged. All of a sudden all hell broke loose right at the door. I rushed over to discover that two teenage boys had punched each other. Both boys got in a great hit. One boy received a serious split lip (later required stitches) and the other boy a massive black eye. After the drama of separating them, neither boy wanted to miss out on the next story. We allowed them to continue after everyone agreed that at the first hassle one or both were gone from the group. The boys immediately settled each with ice towels and they listened without incident. They even participated in the post group discussion. However at the very conclusion of the group they eyed each other and the conflict resumed.

It's the sweet state of identification that makes the gem journey so powerful because information is so easily transmitted from facilitator to recipient. In the altered state listeners are absorbing the information and because there is no interference a facilitator can be creative and all kinds of ancillary information that supports the themes can be inserted within the group context. For example in Chapter 2 *The Spiders Web* the Boy is trapped by an enormous Spider that looks down at him and says, "Welcome to now sucker!" The Boy then responds to stress/fear/frustration etc in the same manner he does in ordinary time. He "goes off" - massive tantrum behavior - swearing, rushing randomly around, throwing dirt and sticks as the Spider looks down and laughs causing its massive belly to giggle like a plate of jello. After some group discussion, participants' arrive at the conclusion that the Boy merely acted in the same manner he usually does, an enactment of his normal responses. Participants are easily introduced to an ancillary discussion on how anger actually works. The 'fight or flight' reaction can be described and discussed. It's a miracle what your body does the instant you perceive stress. Sympathetic and parasympathetic nervous systems kick in and you get ready to fight or run for your life.

"Do you know what your body does? You should find out, it's amazing."

Because the group is receptive I can do some wonderful teaching. In the session of the Spider's Web I actually go through the series of the instant body changes that prepares a person to fight for their lives or haul….. Listeners can easily see how their instant emotional response to say "turn off the computer" is a huge overreaction. The journey and its discussions provide opportunity for teaching and learning insight.

"Can a person get in the habit of getting angry?"
"Should a person get that angry over being asked to take out the garbage? Turn off the computer, come to dinner now?"
"What do you say to yourself when you are asked to do something you don't want to do?"
"Do you light up like a Christmas tree?"
"Why do they call anger management courses anger management courses?"

The story is wonderful in allowing extended education of the receptive listeners. For example I might do a round asking each member what car they would choose if money was no object. Later in this focused discussion I would come back to their car choice and ask them if every time they got into their new corvette they'd rev it up past the red line?
"What would you be doing to your new car?"
"Are you in the habit of getting angry over little stuff?"
"Ever get very angry and 45 minutes later ask yourself why you got so angry over that little thing?"

The Journey allows numerous opportunities both within the story being told and in post group discussion to relate important information. I may in the midst of telling the days story and slip/drop into the story a little axiom knowing the listeners are totally open to consideration. The journey allows for stories within the story. I share little axioms in an almost subliminal manner during states of pure rapport, the time where everyone is on the same page. Every group session offers moments of pure engagement and often during this unopposed moment (and sensing the opportunity) I will out of the "clear blue sky" insert little axioms or a short story within the story into the journey context without missing a beat. Or I might at groups' end as they are exiting, say to someone, little axioms like:
"Pretty is as pretty does."
'Quick to listen, slow to speak, and slow to get angry'
'Don't doubt in the dark what you know to be true in the light'
"Make good choices and you'll see the world - make lousy choices and you'll get to   know South Auckland really well."
"You know you guys make me a rich man"

Or personal individual stuff:
"Pretty amazing that Jim went home and cleaned his room."
"Can you believe that Samantha went to school every day last week?"

In the state of connection I do lots of prophecy setting for individuals.
 "Wow! Some of you because you took this journey will get on a different flight and will see the world. Some of you are going to do real important work" etc.

I have fun with kids on the journey - it's a very fun process that most kids dig.

CHALLENGES AND SOLUTIONS

Discipline problems are rare, but they certainly do occur. Kids oppose the process for several reasons and are simply not going to co operate regardless of the therapist's skills in circumventing resistance. It may be that the kid has something they'd much rather do at the time slot and the time conflict is insurmountable. This population of kids never settle into the group. I believe that all behavior has meaning and I question kids who present large initial resistance. Generally I will wait until after group however at times it necessary to find out why sooner.

Genuinely asking often gets a logical explanation that quite often I agree with; a kid might be part of a team and the team holds practice at 3:30 on Tuesday. I too would rather be playing baseball with their team or going to drama class at this time and agree with them that now *is* a very lousy time and *not* the right time for them to be doing the group. I do not sacrifice the group by struggling for control with the individual. I never think that my stuff is more important to them than their stuff.

Another common reason for resistance is oppositional defiant kids in the habit of being disruptive. I will let them know that they will tell me next group by what they do if they want to take the journey at another time; "no worries if you don't." Last year I had two boys who made the choice based on their actions not to continue and both did stop. However the other 6 kids continued and benefited. I might add both the boys want to do a group this year based on the information they heard from those that continued.

EVIDENCE-BASED SUPPORT

In early 1997 I was quietly running several groups a week at Campbell Lodge - now Whirinaki the child and adolescent mental health clinic services for South Auckland. Bruce Hart a therapist colleague was watching the numbers of youth consistently attending group and one day told me, "Ron I searched the mental health literature and nowhere can I find the levels of group compliance you are having." Up until that exact point in time and space I paid no attention to the phenomena of attendance. His comment produced instant insight. *Gem of the First Water* is having profound effect on listeners and was having the same impact on the members as the *Crusader Rabbit* cartoon had on me, and they came to group because their imagination was captured. I now started paying attention and realized numerous examples of compliance were commonplace during the course of every group. The young adolescent on the run from home or residential placement shows up at group. Another common example is students who come to group while still ill. Or the student who only comes to school on group day or the house bound client that ventures out for group. The TSI process gets past the number one hurdle: the story is heard and lodges in the mind in conscious and unconscious form. An individual's imagination has been accessed.

Following Bruce's observation, several research papers were written studying TSI. In 1997 Sarah Fortune, a clinical psychologist in the service undertook naturalistic outcome study of TSI in the clinical setting. Below are the results. This study was conducted within the group of colleagues at Campbell Lodge and now called Whirinaki Counties Manukau's child and adolescent mental health service. There was no financial backing for this study it was conducted by colleagues' intrigued by the amazing compliance numbers initially compiled by the secretary for administrative reasons.

SETTING AND PARTICIPANTS

Catchment area: This study was based on 347 children and adolescents who attended TSI group therapy at a public outpatient child and adolescent mental health service in South Auckland, New Zealand. The catchment area for this service was at that time populated by more than 400,000 of which more than one third were under 20 years. At that time European/Pakeha made up 52% of the community, Pacific peoples 27%, Maori 17% and Asians 15% of the community. The rates of unemployment (10.1% in this area vs. 7.5% nationally), single parent families (23% vs. 19%), number of people living in each house (3.3 vs. 2.7) and proportion of adults with no educational qualifications (29% vs. 27.6%) were higher in this community compared with other parts of New Zealand (Statistics New Zealand, 2002). It is acknowledged that the local context will influence the wider applicability of this information.

The Clinic: A multidisciplinary team including child psychiatrists, clinical psychologists, psychiatric nurses, social workers and family therapists worked with children, adolescents and their families who represented the 3-5% of the population in greatest need of psychiatric services. Children and adolescents up to the age of 20 years (if still in school) were treated using a combination of crisis interventions, family therapy, group therapy, medication and individual therapy. Attempts were made to involve the wider systems of care for the young person including the family, school, social work agency, police and health care providers with which they have contact. Inpatient admissions are possible at a regional child and adolescent psychiatric unit.

Selection of participants: Patients were assessed by two mental health clinicians as part of usual clinic practices and a treatment plan generated which may include any combination of family therapy, group therapy, medication, or individual therapy. All patients who attended the clinic between 1997 and 2001 and who were referred to group therapy were included in this study.

Procedure and Measures: Demographic data was collected from routine clinical records. Individual attendance data at each group session was collected by administrative staff. A clinical profile of patients attending TSI was generated in 1999 as part of quality improvement using a using a pre and post intervention design. Questionnaires were given to group members and their parents attending the initial group session and again at the completion of the group process. Parents of all patients were asked to complete the Childhood Behaviour Checklist (CBCL). Children were asked to complete the Childhood Depression Inventory (CDI) and adolescents completed these measures and the McMaster Family Assessment Device (FAD) and Beck Scale for Suicide Ideation (BSSI). These measures were found to have acceptable reliability with this population with Cronbach alpha ranging from .83 (FAD) to .95 (BSSI).

Psychiatric diagnoses were not routinely generated by clinicians during the period of this study and are therefore not reported. However another clinical audit in this service around the same time suggested that nearly 50% of patients presented with a mood disorder, 17% presented with disruptive behaviours, including conduct disorder and oppositional defiant disorder, 7% had PTSD and 27% experienced difficulties such as childhood sexual abuse, parent/child relationship issues or neglect (Fortune, 2002). This population was also known to experience high rates of known risk factors for psychosocial distress such as suicide behaviour, substance abuse, parental psychopathology, physical abuse and childhood sexual abuse (Fortune, 2002). The early TSI groups were particularly targeted at boys, but over the period of the study TSI was increasingly utilised with both girls and boys. One quarter (n = 78) of group participants were Maori and two thirds European/Pakeha (n = 238). Two thirds of patients attending the group were adolescents and one third was under the age of 12 years.

Table 26.1 Demographic profile of group participants

	1997		1998		1999		2000		2001		Total	
Variable	N	%	N	%	N	%	N	%	N	%	N	%
Male	51	70	37	67	71	56	18	60	36	57	213	61
Female	22	30	18	33	55	44	12	40	27	43	134	39
Maori	15	21	11	20	27	21	10	33	15	24	78	23
Pacific Island	4	6	2	4	6	5	2	7	4	6	18	5
Asian	2	3	-	-	7	6	1	3	3	5	13	4
European / Pakeha	52	71	42	76	86	68	17	57	41	65	238	69

Between three and six groups were completed each calendar year with variance reflecting fluctuating staffing numbers, particularly in 2000. The groups were conducted over an average of 16 sessions could be condensed to 9 sessions if required or extended for up to 20 sessions dependant on the requirements of the group members and clinicians.

Table 26.2 Duration and number of participants in each group 1997 – 2001

Variable	Year of completion				
	1997	1998	1999	2000	2001
Total number of groups conducted	12	6	13	3	6
Average number of sessions	17	15	16	15	16
Range	10 - 19	11 - 20	11 - 19	14 - 16	9 - 18
Average number of patients per group	6	9	10	10	11
Range	3 - 11	6 - 13	3 - 15	8 - 12	8 - 16

Three out of every five patients attended more than 60% of sessions and were described as 'graduates' with no significant difference in rates of graduation between males and females. Half of non-graduates had legitimate reasons for dropping out of the group such as moving out of the area or the family having significant problems with transport. Average attendance among patients who commenced TSI was 65% from 1997 - 2001. Among graduates average attendance rates were between 86% - 89% which allows for one session missed due to illness and another to attend a school camp or similar.

Maori were more likely than other ethnic groups to begin the TSI group but not graduate while Pacific Island children and adolescents were more likely to be referred to the group by their key worker and never commence the group ($x2$ (6, N = 347) = 34.32, p = .000).

Table 26.3 Attendance and retention rates for group participants 1997 – 2001

	Year of TSI completion				
Variable	1997	1998	1999	2000	2001
Total Number of Participants	73	55	126	30	63
N	52	27	70	20	37
Graduates	71%	48%	56%	67%	58%
N	15	19	35	10	21
Non Graduates	21%	34%	28%	33%	32%
N	6	10	19	0	5
Referred but Did Not Start	8%	18%	15%	0%	8%
Average attendance	78%	64%	56%	69%	59%

From Figure 26.2 it can be seen that average attendance at group sessions declined with an increasing number of sessions, but not among those who graduated from the programme. It appears that successful engagement with the therapeutic process can be defined by a return after session three.

Pre and post test data were available for a small sub-set of 46 children and adolescents. Due to the small sample size caution should be used in interpreting the following results; using the CBCL measure, parents rated significant reductions in withdrawn (t(25) = 3.05, p = .005), somatic (t(25) = 2.50, p = .02) and anxious/depressed behaviours (t(25) = 2.55, p = .02) among their offspring. Parents also rated their children has having fewer attentional difficulties (t(25) = 2.88, p = .008). Parents reported an overall improvement in their child's behaviour at the completion of the group compared with at the beginning of the group process (t(25) = 3.15, p = .001).

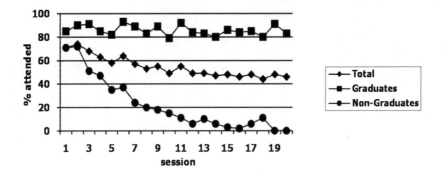

Figure 26.2   Average attendance rates per session for graduates, non-graduates and total sample

Table 26. 4   CBCL scores pre and post group intervention

Clinical subscale	Pre		Post		
	Mean	SD	Mean	SD	T
Withdrawn	63.27	10.26	58.54	7.97	3.05**
Somatic	61.19	8.04	56.61	8.77	2.51**
Anxious/depressed	64.23	9.77	60.00	9.91	2.55**
Social problems	62.31	11.16	58.65	9.52	1.77
Thought problems	61.00	8.99	57.84	7.41	2.04*
Attention problems	64.81	9.05	60.81	7.23	2.89**
Delinquent behaviours	66.00	8.83	65.03	8.67	0.64
Aggressive behaviours	65.65	10.45	63.26	9.30	1.47
Total T score	67.15	8.38	61.65	11.30	3.14**
Internal T score	64.85	8.41	57.27	12.70	3.61***
External T score	66.23	9.30	63.19	11.66	1.79
* p < .05 ** p < .01 *** p < .001					

The relatively small number of children and adolescents who completed the CDI before and after the TSI group rated themselves as significantly less depressed at follow-up (t(33) = 2.41, p = .02) with the strongest effect seen in the domain of perceived ineffectiveness where the mean score fell from 2.97 (SD = 2.29) to 1.76 (SD = 1.78) (t(36) = 3.10, p = .004).

Adolescents perceived an improvement in the way in which their family functioned at follow-up using the McMaster Family Assessment Device (t(21) = 2.21, p = .04). The strongest improvements, among the small number of respondents, were seen in the extent to which adolescents felt the roles of family members were clear and congruent (t(21) = 2.77, p = .01) and the degree to which family members were affectively connected and involved with each other (t(21) = 2.69, p = .01).

Table 26. 5   Childhood Depression Inventory scores pre and post group

Clinical subscale	Pre		Post		
	Mean	SD	Mean	SD	T
Negative mood	3.03	2.15	2.19	2.36	1.89
Interpersonal problems	1.62	1.28	1.08	1.36	1.85
Ineffectiveness	2.97	2.29	1.76	1.78	3.10**
Anhedonia	4.11	3.25	3.02	2.33	2.19**
Negative self esteem	1.76	1.96	1.10	1.52	1.81
Total CDI score	13.5	8.79	9.65	8.36	2.41*
* p < .05 ** p < .01 *** p < .001					

Table 26. 6   Family functioning as perceived by the adolescents

Clinical subscale	Pre		Post		
	Mean	SD	Mean	SD	T
Problem solving	2.36	0.57	2.10	0.47	2.07*
Communication	2.34	0.36	2.11	0.53	2.17*
Roles	2.53	0.33	2.22	0.57	2.77**
Affective responsiveness	2.28	0.48	2.08	0.74	1.19
Affective involvement	2.43	0.51	2.05	0.62	2.69**
Behaviour control	2.20	0.94	1.84	0.59	1.81
General functioning	2.26	0.54	1.98	0.63	2.21*
* p < .05 ** p < .01 *** p < .001					

Adolescents reported a significant reduction in their overall suicidality following the group compared with prior to attending the group (t (17) = 2.73, p = .01). Caution should be taken in interpreting these results, due to the small sample size.

SUMMARY

Gem of the First Water and the supporting guide is the first of three similarly constructed stories that highlight the issues of our lives and make up the Splendora Trilogy. Hopefully this glance into the working content of Gem and the TSI process that delivers the themes and lessons will stimulate your interest to find out more.

The research is what it is: a five year study developed by work mates interested in understanding the empirical results they were seeing week in and week out. No funds or special extras were given to them, only the pure motivation of investigating the phenomenon of teenagers attending a therapeutic group held after a long school day at a mental health clinic often a long way from their school and home. Why in the world would 60 % of the kids who start, come to 90% of the sessions over a four month period?

Whakatika: arise stand up start your journey.

REFERENCES

Abraham, P. P., Lepisto, B. L., & Schultz, L. (1995). Adolescents perceptions of process and speciality group therapy. *Psychotherapy*, 32(1), 70 – 76.

Beautrais, A. (2000). The Canterbury suicide project: aims, overview and progress. *Community Mental Health in New Zealand*, 8(2), 32 – 39.

Coatsworth, J. D., Santisteban, D. A., McBride, C. K., & Szapocznik, J. (2001). Brief strategic family therapy versus community control: engagement, retention and an exploration of the moderating role of adolescent symptom severity. *Family Process*, 40(3), 313 – 332.

Fortune, S. A. (2002). Suicidal behaviour among a clinical sample of children and adolescents in New Zealand. Unpublished report: TSI International.

Glasser, W. (1965). *Reality Therapy.* New York: Harper and Row.

Glasser, W. (1984). Take Effective Control of Your Life. New York: Harper Collins.

King, C. A., Hovey, J. D., Brand, E., & Wilson, R. (1997). Suicidal adolescents after hospitalization: Parent and family impacts on treatment follow-through. *Journal of the American Academy of Child & Adolescent Psychiatry*, 36(1), 85-93.

Mishna, F., Kaiman, J., Little, S., & Tarshis, E. (1994). Group therapy with adolescents who havd learning disabilities and social/emotional problems. *Journal of Child and Adolescent Group Therapy*, 4(2), 117 – 131.

Phillips, R. (1989). *Gem of the First Water a Fable for Our Times* (Third ed.). Auckland: Therapeutic Story Telling International.

Rotheram-Borus, M. J., Piacentini, J., Van Rossem, R., Graae, F., Cantwell, C., Castro-Blanco, D., et al. (1999). Treatment adherence among Latina female adolescent suicide attempters. *Suicide & Life-Threatening Behavior*, 29(4), 293 – 311.

Spirito, A., Plummer, B., Gispert, M., Levy, S., & et al. (1992). Adolescent suicide attempts: Outcomes at follow-up. *American Journal of Orthopsychiatry*, 62(3), 464-468.

Statistics New Zealand. (2002). Manukau City Census 2001 area data. Wellington: Government Print.

Trautman, P. D., Stewart, N., & Morishima, A. (1993). Are adolescent suicide attempters noncompliant with outpatient care? *Journal of the American Academy of Child & Adolescent Psychiatry*, 32(1), 89 – 94.

Yalom, I. (2005). *The Theory and Practice of Group Psychotherapy. New York: Basic Books*

RESOURCES

If you too are interested, check into the 'journey that everyone should take.'
All materials are available through the website: www.tsi.co.nz

Chapter 27
Creativity and Healing:
Expressive Arts and Families

Nancy Iverson and Andrea Bass

OVERVIEW: This chapter describes practical ways SBFC professionals can use expressive arts with children and families to help them deal with grief and loss.

INTRODUCTION

> "My Dad
>
> I love my dad higher than the sky, further than the stars,
> and deeper than the oceans.
> My dad was the kindest person I have ever known.
> He was also my best friend…
> Thank you, Dad, for giving me life and being the best father you can.
> You will always be in my heart. "

Devastated by his father's death, as 11 year old Sho Kulko shared his poem during his father's memorial service, he used words to help reconnect to lifelines of love and gratitude and to start his monumental journey of healing from loss. His writing embodies the restoration inherent in accessing beauty and resilience. When we work with children and families, we have the opportunity to affirm for them that they have the gifts of art within and around them at all times. How can we help them access the deep wisdom that is innate in artful exploration and expression? How can we nurture our own capacity to use our minds, hearts, and spirits synergistically so that we may be truly present for our families and nourish our connection to compassion and wisdom?

BACKGROUND

With words, music, pictures, and in a myriad of other ways, art accompanies both our seemingly mundane everyday activities and our profound life-changing experiences and invites us to explore the deep undercurrents of life, conflict, connection, and well-being. Prehistoric cave paintings, textiles and design, tribal chanting and dance, the tombs, temples, and pyramids of Egypt, Greek drama, film, photography, and iTunes are all reminders that the arts have been an integral part of life throughout the history of civilization. We must, of course, bring the best of our knowledge and expertise to our work with families, but we miss so much when we limit ourselves merely to theories, reviewing clinical notes, scheduling appointments, and writing evaluations. When we restrict our focus, we may feel only the defeat of discord and overlook the pockets of spirit that inspire courage and resilience—both our own and our children's and their families'.

The expressive arts, including visual art, music, dance/movement, poetry/creative writing, theater/film, and sandplay, access healing potential through the imaginative realm and the creative process. Applicable to psychotherapy, counseling, health care, and education, an integrated arts approach involves the use of artistic modalities to foster self-expression, healing, and growth. Information about programs for specialized training in expressive arts therapy is available through such organizations as the American Dance Therapy Association, the American Music Therapy Association, the National Drama Therapy Association, the National Association for Poetry Therapy, and the International Expressive Arts Therapy Association.

Rather than relegating the use of artful modalities to certified specialists only, counselors who have not had extensive training in these therapies may develop simple practices to enrich their interactions with students and families. Opportunities abound to integrate expressive arts activities into school based family counseling as counselors familiarize themselves with these practices and build them into their work. By recognizing personal areas of experience and expertise and trusting our skills, knowledge and intuition, we can adapt expressive arts exercises to the needs of our clients and students. For example, knowing how different art modalities tend to facilitate different processes among individuals may help inform the design of a session. An unstructured medium such as paint or clay often facilitates spontaneity, loosening of control and an activation of unconscious psychological material while a more structured medium such as collage or drawing with colored pencils will often promote a greater experience of mastery and control; certain musical tones and rhythms tend to be energizing, while others are more relaxing. By developing a variety of creative techniques with clients and encouraging them to focus on the process rather than the finished product or their training or talent (or perceived lack of), we can help provide a doorway into the intrinsic healing power of the creative process. Above all, our ability to be present with and attuned to our students and families with a sense of respect, encouragement and wonder helps create an environment that enables clients to feel safe to explore their inner world.

RELATIONSHIP TO THE SBFC MODEL

The expressive arts can be used in all four quadrants of the SBFC model. They can be used to help students in school-based support groups discuss loss (School-Remedial) as well as a primary intervention in counseling sessions with students or families (Family Remedial). In addition, expressive arts can be integrated into preventive workshops dealing with loss with students or families (as a way to facilitate discussion and teach coping skills (School-Preventive and Family-Preventive).

PROCEDURE

Following are descriptions of activities Iverson and Bass have used with individuals, groups, and families. Although these practices may be used in a somewhat 'cookbook' fashion, we encourage some specific guidelines:

1) Try these out with colleagues and adapt them to your personal 'style' related to your experience.
2) Tailor use of expressive art intervention to the client's background, setting, and treatment goals.
3) Resist the tendency to project conclusions about content. Facilitate clients' exploration, discovery, and sharing of their own interpretations.

4) Nurture your own creativity and skills and those of your students and families to develop modifications of these practices that are unique to you and the families with whom you work.

5) In addition to the usual standards of group work such as respectful listening, confidentiality, etc., setting parameters specific to responding to art expression in a nonjudgemental fashion is essential.

FAMILY WRITING: PROMPTS

Writing together in a family circle invites the possibility of discovering together vulnerabilities and strengths, trusting shared expressions, and restoring relationships easily shattered when disease and or death dominate. In her work with pediatric hospice, Iverson developed this practice, using it with a circle of family and friends around the bedside of an ill patient or in a writing circle following the death of a loved one.

Materials: Pens or pencils, writing paper

Activity: Explain the procedure to the group. Name the person for whom the group is focused--the person who is ill or has died. The counselor reads a prompt, and everyone will start with that phrase and write, uninterrupted, for 3 minutes, with the facilitator serving as time-keeper. The writing may be in whatever style is most comfortable for each participant. Remind the group that this is an opportunity to reflect and express rather than a demand to produce a perfectly crafted literary piece. Each group member may revisit their writing at another time and elaborate, polish, and edit as they choose. Depending on the size of the group and the amount of time, 4-5 prompts may be used. Following the writing practice, encourage participants to share their writing, with the understanding that anyone who prefers to pass may do so. The counselor is a group member in terms of doing the writing and contributing to the sharing. As participants read, all others listen, with no comments regarding content or writing criticism.

Example: These were written by family members around the bedside of a young adult hospice patient.

Prompt: I remember...

> I remember growing up on Bright street
> And experiencing laughter with him.
> When he first got sick
> And us being able to experience Disney World
> With my brother.
> (sister)

> I remember the ninja suits and spilled milk—
> The games on the dead end and
> The trips to Stonestown.
> Love.
> Funny.
> Beverly Hills Cop. LUL!
> The swimming lessons and the bee stings in the park.
> I always remember because I never forget love...
> My brother...
> I remember my brother—every part...

I remember, I remember, I remember...
I just remember so many things
And I feel good that I have these moments.
They truly last forever...
I remember...
Hilarious times,
Silly moments of laughter.
        (sister)

I remember when Gerald first went to the beach.
He screamed because the sand was touching his feet.
I remember one Fourth of July.
We lit sparklers.
He screamed at them.
(They scared him.
I remember when he first got into the pool
I had trouble getting him out.
I remember the Thanksgiving we spent together and some Christmases.
        (mother)

I remember the first time I met Gerald.
He was standing in front of his house.
His dad introduced us.
The first thing I saw was his dimples.
I knew I was hooked.
He has this infectious smile.
That was 10 years ago.
I remember Gerald always walking through the house
Doing the 'Carlton dance'—
That's the character from Fresh Prince sitcom comedy show.
I remember when Gerald gave his life to Christ.
He, his dad, and I all joined church together in October, 1996.
        (stepmother)

I remember
So strong
So private
So giving
So inviting
So direct to the point
So unassuming
So layed back
So prompt
So responsible
Being able to walk
Being able to talk
Being able to express your thoughts

Being able to play basketball
And play video games with a big smile on your face
Kicking your sister out of your room
        (father)

I remember coming into this room
just a few days ago
and knowing
Love lives here.
Kindness lives here.
Courage lives here.
I remember family times in our homes
and in others' homes
And the great gift of gratitude
When people can join together,
Care for one another
And receive that care.
I remember
Way back when I was young
And my grandfather was sick
And love circled his bed
And flowed through the house.
I remember missing him
But also cherishing many wonderful memories
And feeling sure that
He was OK.
I remember
That no matter what's happened
Hard times
Happy times
I've always known
That he was OK
And so were we.
        (Nancy Iverson)

Prompt: I wish…

I wish I could go back to all the fun
I've had with my big brother
Because even though most of those times
Were spent just sitting in a room,
It meant so much.
I wish I could hear his responses to what we're writing
Because I know it would make me laugh.

I wish we had forever to be together on earth.
We won't, but
In Heaven, we'll have eternity.

(sister)

I wish I had more opportunities to spend more time
With my funny and loving brother Gerald.
Although I live on the other side of the US
He knows that I love him with all my heart.
I wish I could remember more good times growing up with him.
            (sister)

I wish that I could be more like Gerald.
I wish that I could take away his pains.
I wish that one day I could have done more with him—
ball games, bowling, etc.
I wish that we could have spent more time together.
I   wish that I had more love to give him.
            (stepfather)

I wish I could have another 10 years X 10
Because the young boy who I helped raise
Was on his way to being a
Great and awesome adult.
Being able to experience the growth and
Seeing the wisdom and maturity in him
Has been such a thrill.
However,
I do not question God's choices.
Gerald will be that awesome adult right by God's side.
            (stepmother)

I wish
You may all sit in the love and joy
Filling this moment.
I wish
Even in hard times
And tears
The joy will stay
Deep in your soul.

I wish
You will always know
The great gift of love
You give
And receive
As you care
So devotedly
Day in and
Day out.

I wish
This may be
The hardest time
You ever face.
And that
Courage
And kindness
Compassion
And love
Warm memories
And the making of
New ones
Will carry you
Always.
                    (Nancy Iverson)

Other prompts include:
'I love...'
'I hope...'
'thank you ...'
'I didn't know...'
'I always thought....'

An alternative is to read a poem together, such as the following one by Sheenagh Pugh, and then use the first line of the poem as a prompt.

SOMETIMES

Sometimes things don't go, after all,
from bad to worse. Some years, muscadel
faces down frost; green thrives; the crops don't fail.
Sometimes a man aims high, and all goes well.

A people sometimes will step back from war,
elect an honest man, decide they care
enough, that they can't leave some stranger poor.
Some men become what they were born for.

Sometimes our best intentions do not go
amiss; sometimes we do as we meant to.
The sun will sometimes melt a field of sorrow
that seemed hard frozen; may it happen for you.

Example, using the opening line, written after the death of a 19 year old by her sister:

Sometimes things don't go, after all,
From bad to worse.
Sometimes they go so differently than

you could have planned
that you can only wonder what
to make of it all.

Some days a bird may
alight on your outstretched
hand
and for an instant
there is nothing else.
Then it is gone
and you can only wonder what
it meant.

FAMILY DRAWING AND WRITING: GINGERBREAD PERSON, QUALITIES

From a simple drawing exercise that Iverson learned to do with young children, she adapted this activity to include writing and engage participants from youth to elders.

Materials: Drawing paper, colored markers, pens or pencils, copy of J. Ruth Gendler's *The Book of Qualities*.

Activity: Invite one person to be the 'recorder' for the group. Compile two lists--one of 'Feelings We Don't Like to Have" and one of "Feelings We Like to Have." Give each participant a sheet of blank paper and instruct them to draw the outline of a 'gingerbread person' with two blank boxes on each side (see figure 27.1).

Figure 27.1 Outline of Gingerbread Person with Blank Boxes

Label each of the two boxes on the right with feelings from the list of "Feelings We Like to Have" and the two boxes on the left with two from the list of "Feelings We Don't Like to Have." Choose a color to represent each feeling and color the box to correspond with its label. Each participant chooses the four feelings they will use (see figure 27.2).

Figure 27.2 Gingerbread Person with Feelings and Colors

Starting with the first box, invite each person to color into the gingerbread outline the places he or she experiences that feeling in their body. ("When I'm happy, my heart feels happy, I have a big smile, my hair feels bright and shiny, I want to reach out to everyone, and I feel like skipping!"; see figure 27.3)

Figure 27.3 Happy Gingerbread Person

Color into the outline the next feeling: ("When I'm loving, I see love and I can show love through my eyes. I smile, and my heart feels full of love. I feel it in my arms--I just want to hug everyone. And I feel good all the way down my legs right to the tips of my toes."; see figure 27.4).

Figure 27.4 Loving Gingerbread Person

Use the color in the third box to draw in that feeling. ("When I'm sad I have tears running down my face, and I can't smile. My heart feels sad, and I feel like have a big weight in my stomach. I feel really heavy--like I have big bricks in my feet."; see figure 27.4).

Figure 27.4 Sad Gingerbread Person

Finish the drawing with the fourth box. ("My head feels like it's going to explode when I'm really mad. My ears close up and I can't hear anything good from anybody. I don't see anything nice and I don't say anything nice. My hands clench up into fists. My heart squeezes tight and mean. My stomach feels like it's burning on fire. My feet feel like they want to kick the whole world."; see figure 27.5).

Figure 27.5 Angry Gingerbread Person

After everyone has completed drawing in all four feelings, invite the group members to share their drawings and talk about them. Depending on the size of the group and the age and attention span of participants, decide whether to invite each person to choose just one feeling to share or to encourage sharing of all four feelings in each drawing. If time allows, after everyone has shared, reflect on color choices that people have used for feelings (one person may use black for 'mad' while another uses red) and where and how we each experience feelings in our bodies, acknowledging both similarities and differences as demonstrated in this activity.

Ruth Gendler's *The Book of Qualities*, in which Gendler personifies 74 qualities, such as resignation, joy, and pleasure, inspires the writing component to this activity. Invite up to three group members to select at random a quality from the book and read it aloud. Starting with the first feeling in this or her gingerbread outline, each participant writes for three minutes, timed by the counselor, modeling Gendler's style. Continue with the second, third and fourth feelings. Complete this activity with the invitation for participants to read what they've written. The counselor participates and shares in this activity as a group member.

Example: An 18 year old hospice patient wrote about despair:

"Despair is an old tigris. She once was strong, but now has seen all the horrors of reality. Her stripes make it easy for her to hide from those who want her gone. She stays with those who feed her, but out of caution she lashes out at them, sometimes taking an arm or a leg of them. This makes her bigger though she does not want power. She hates her self for existing, and yet she still tries so hard to stay alive because she's afraid of not existing."

Her father, introduced despair in this way:

> "Despair is a small stooped gray man. You might see him with the homeless vet in the park. He is often with those who have sold their souls for things. Don't be deceived, though. He has great power, and he watches you. When he speaks his words can drive into your center and lodge there. They freeze your soul. If you let despair speak to you he will transform you into a cheerless, grumpy, smelly person who has forgotten what it means to live. Despair is a recluse. He hides in the corner at parties and never shares a toast or a drink in celebration."

Her 16 year old brother described confusion and happiness:

> "Confusion is easily made and released. It bounces in your head ricocheting off your skull destroying your thoughts.
> Happiness lifts your head and pushes all bad things out your mouth. It spreads through your chest and arms to break you free."

Her 20 year old sister personified disappointment and joy:

> "Disappointment lives downstairs and I have to pass him on the way out. He doesn't say much, just reminds me that he's there. Sometimes he stands outside my door. I tell him I'm really busy and we'll talk later so he goes downstairs and sits in the lobby and waits for a better time.
> Joy may talk a lot, but I don't mind. She knows the best stories anyway. She showed me a bird's nest once and gave me a piece of blue sea glass at the   beach. Her eyes are ever so keen."

Her mother wrote this:

> "Joy isn't happiness. She isn't everything going swimmingly. Joy comes from truth and hope and knowing you are loved. Joy wakes up early in the morning, goes outside and listens to the birds in the morning quiet, and then has the strength to go on and look into the face of tragedy and suffering. Before Joy came into her own she was always disappointed and angry at the world, but now she has a foundation, a timeless underpinning that keeps her anchored in the truth of God's unfathomable love for her."

And, as part of their circle, Iverson also wrote about joy:

> "Joy doesn't always wear purple, but she does today. She's wanting to wear something rich and deep so she won't be confused—as she so often is—with her second cousins Happiness and Acquisition. They often wear royal blue, which Joy would wear too, except she knows it's important that she stand out more on her own. She's the one who can always be available. Even if you can't find her at home right away, you can check with Gratitude. Gratitude always knows how to find Joy. Joy can walk arm in arm with profound Sadness, with setbacks and frustrations, and she generously invites Hope to accompany her on many of her journeys."

GROUP VISUAL ART: COLLAGE-MAKING

The following activity is an example of an expressive arts intermodal approach that is useful for individuals and families dealing with conflict, learning goal-setting, acknowledging accomplishment, and attending to transition and loss. It moves from a guided meditation into an art therapy experiential and concludes with processing and sharing of the experience with other participants.

Materials: Colored construction paper (2 sheets per person), felt-tipped pens or pastels, glue sticks. For alternative collage-making, scissors and magazines, photographs, and cards that can be cut and pasted.

Activity: Set the tone for the activity with a reflection such as:

"Please get comfortable in your seats, place both feet on the floor, and take three slow deep breaths. Give yourself time to just arrive and be in this room. Feel the support of the cushions or seat beneath and behind you. Imagine that with each inhale, you are able to bring in relaxing energy and with each exhale, you are able to let go of any tension or tightness you might be carrying... so that you can become more and more relaxed. Notice each foot making contact with the ground. Imagine that roots have sprouted from the bottom of each foot extending themselves deep into the core of the earth. Also imagine that at the top or crown of your head you are able to open to the wisdom of a universal force or energy that is larger than your individual self."

Include an invitation to explore more deeply a specific theme to bring focus to the topic of the group. The example below is for bereavement.

1. Pass around colored construction paper and instruct group members to each choose two different colored sheets of paper. Invite each participant to draw the images that appeared or their "internal terrain" during the guided meditation. Remind them that there is no right or wrong way to do this, to simply accept and trust their experience and not worry about whether they have experience or skill in art. What is most important is the process itself rather than the finished product.

2. Upon completion of drawings, ask group members to now draw on second sheet of paper a symbol that represents their thoughts and internal images during the reflection. Give examples such as a boy who drew his grandmother as a tree because she was sturdy and grounded, a girl who drew her father as a chef's hat because he loved to bake and just opened his own bakery, or an adult who drew an empty barrel to represent the loss of her job at a winery.

3. When second drawings have been completed, ask members to tear them up into several pieces and notice how that feels as they do so. (They should not tear up first drawings of internal landscape). Expect a strong reaction.

4. Next instruct participants to glue the torn pieces of paper onto first drawing of "internal landscape" in any way they wish. They do not need to glue every single piece of torn drawing but should include pieces with significant images.

5. Instruct group or family members to split into dyads or triads to discuss their experiences during the guided meditation, drawing, tearing, and incorporation of torn pieces into original drawing. State the time allotted for this, and, at the end of that period, invite participants back into the group to share collectively. Spread drawings out on table or floor; invite members to walk around and silently view each other's drawings. Each participant may then describe their experience of witnessing the drawings. Offer guidelines to responses in terms of questions such as "What did you learn about...," "What inspired you?" "What was hard for you?" and other directed open-ended questions. If a group member prefers to reply nonverbally, movement, sound, and drawing may be alternative forms of expression. If time allows, the group may construct a collective poem or collage. As an alternative, participants may make a collage of images from magazines, cards, photos, etc., rather than from their own drawing.

Example: Following the centering meditation, this reflection may be used to bring focus to loss and transition:

"I'd like to invite you to think about a loss, ending or goodbye you've had in your life - recent or from the past. It can be a loss from the death of someone in your life or some other type of loss or transition... the ending of a relationship, a job, a move, changing schools, the loss of health or anything else. Just notice the emotions that come up for you when you think about this loss. Do your feelings have a color? Shape? Texture? Are they located in a particular part of your body or spread throughout? Do they have a weight? Are they still or do they move throughout the body? Would there be sounds that go with this movement? Are there words? Now imagine your body as a vessel that can hold and carry all these different emotions. What would that look like? Whenever you feel ready now, taking as much time as you need, allow yourself to slowly come back to being here in this room feeling awake and refreshed... and slowly open the eyes."

With a focus on loss, following the first drawing of their 'internal terrain,' invite group members to draw a symbol that represents their loved one who died or the loss with which they are working. A student whose brother died in a shooting made this collage (figure 27.6) in a San Francisco school-based bereavement group:

Figure 27.6 Collage of Student Whose Brother Died

Following the death of her grandmother, a granddaughter created this (figure 27.7):

Figure 27.7 Collage of Granddaughter Following Death of Grandmother

Processing the activity is invaluable. When asked how they felt about or what they learned as they tore up their second drawings and glued the pieces onto their original drawings, group members offered responses such as, "This is about learning to let go of our loved ones", "Now this person lives inside of us" or "We carry them with us forever".

GROUP WRITING AND DRAWING: FIVE WISHES

This expressive arts activity is readily adaptable to different ages and is especially suited for multigenerational work.

Materials: Colored construction paper, waterproof Sharpie pens of many colors. For group display, add poster board or fabric and appropriate materials such as glue, thread, stapler and staples, etc.

Activity: Instruct students and/or family members to trace the outline of their hand onto a sheet of colored construction paper. If done within family context, parents/guardians and children, grandparents and children or two siblings can trace each other's hands onto paper.

Ask them to cut out hand and write a wish inside each digit:

Thumb: a wish that you have for yourself.

Index: a wish that you have for a loved one.

Third finger: a wish that you have for family or friends of loved.

Ring finger: a wish that you have for people around the world.

Pinkie: a wish that you have for the earth.

Instruct participants to draw something connected with their wishes in the center of the hand cutout. Next, invite students and families to share their creations with each other and discuss their five wishes. Encourage family members to voice wishes they have for each other and/or guess what each family member might wish for themselves or others.

To conclude with a group display, each participant glues their 'hand' to display material (poster board, Tibetan prayer flag, quilt background.) Counselors may choose to include poetry and/or songs about hands to the group display process.

Variations: Write a wish within each finger pertaining to a specific global issue such as world hunger, violence, racism, poverty, etc. Write a hope, dream, or goal on each finger. Invite teams to outline each partners' hand on the same paper, with fingers interfacing.

Example: Middle school children in San Francisco composed these hands Figure 27.8):

Figure 27.8 Collage Made by Middle School Children

Parent and young child team drawing Figure 27.9):

Figure 27.9 Parent and Child Drawing

GROUP MUSIC PRACTICE

Music is an almost universal component of daily life and yet often is conspicuously absent from counseling and therapy practices. Incorporating practices of making music by composing and/or playing an instrument, singing, and moving to sound and rhythm expands the realm of music as a resource. The following activities involve listening.

Materials: CD player, recorded music, paper, pens, pencils, markers, paint and brushes.

Activity: Choose two contrasting pieces of music, one that is loud and/or dissonant and one that is tranquil and/or harmonious. Ask one person to be the recorder. Instruct group members to listen and notice how they are feeling as they hear the first piece, and then play 1-2 minutes of the loud/dissonant piece. Going clockwise around the group, invite each participant to use one word or a short phrase to describe how he or she felt as they heard the music; the recorder makes a list of each word offered in the circle. Play 1-2 minutes of the tranquil/harmonious piece, and, this time going counterclockwise, invite each participant to relate a feeling evoked by this piece and create a second list. Compare and discuss the two lists, noting the capacity of sound to influence mood, feelings, and body reactions. Depending on time and group composition, replay each piece of music with the instruction to draw, move, or write as inspired by the sound.

Activity: Instruct each member to bring a favorite recording to the next session--one that helps them deal with stress, conflict, disappointment, or loss or give voice to their triumphs, passions, gratitudes, and joys. In the group, one member at a time introduces his or her piece in terms of why he or she chose it and what it evokes for her/him. Everyone listens and, depending on the size of the group and time constraints, after the piece has finished, may talk about feelings and responses that came up for them as they listened. The next student or family member shares their selection in a similar fashion until everyone in the group has had a turn. Again, depending on time constraints, replay all pieces without interruption while group members write, draw, paint, or dance.

MULTICULTURAL COUNSELING CONSIDERATIONS

It is important to remember that while all ethnic groups value some form of expressive art, some groups may place a greater emphasis on a particular expressive art. For example, one ethnic group might have a strong emphasis on music, but not writing. Members of that group will more likely feel comfortable with the group music practice exercise rather than the "I remember" writing exercise.

SUMMARY

Engaging in expressive art, whether music, visual, prose, poetry, or dance, assists in making the unconscious conscious, allowing unexplored issues and needs to surface, facilitating a kinesthetic and cathartic release and unleashing creative energy necessary to cope with the challenges of daily living. When we work artfully with children and families we can provide opportunities to express deep feelings, fears, and dreams through art, poetry, music, movement and we can collectively witness the hopes, heartbreaks, and wonders we encounter in life. Creative expressions may become infused with symbols and images of profound meaning and set into motion a healing process that almost has a life of its own. In the "creative zone", each of us can be fully present in the moment, lose our concept of linear time and surrender to a "flow" where we become vehicles for not only the expression of our own personal mythology but also the archetypal (universal) themes and images of the collective unconscious that can inform, inspire and guide us along our journeys.

The activities in this chapter are presented as guidelines for school-based family counseling projects. Although they may be followed step by step without alteration, the richest experiences occur as each counselor and group work together to collaborate in creativity, never overlooking the opportunity to recognize and develop artful expression in every moment and interchange.

Note: Color versions of figures in this chapter may be viewed at:
http://www.usfca.edu/soe/ctrs_institutes/center_child_family_development/ (Using Expressive Arts with Families)

REFERENCES

Darley, S. and Heath, W. (2008). *The expressive arts activity book: A resource for professionals.* Philadelphia, PA: Jessica Kingsley Publishers.

Dower, L.(2001). *I will remember you: What to do when someone you love dies.* A guidebook through grief for teens. New York,NY: Scholastic Inc.

Fitzgerald, H.(2000). *The grieving teen: A guide for teenagers and their friends.* New York,NY: Simon and Schuster , Fireside Books.

Fitzgerald, H.(2000). *Grief at school: Resource manual.* Washington, DC: American Hospice Foundation.

Ganin, B. and Heath, W. (1999). *Art and healing: Using expressive art to heal your body, mind, and spirit.* New York,NY: Three Rivers Press.

Gendler, J. R. (1988). *The book of qualities.* Berkeley, CA: Turquoise Mountain Publications.

Gersie, A. (1991). *Storymaking in bereavement: Dragons fight in the meadow.* London,UK: Jessica Kingsley Publishers.

Leeds, J. (2010). *The power of sound: How to be healthy and productive using music and sound.* Updated second edition., Rochester, VT: Healing Arts Press.

Numeroff, L.and Harpham, W.(1999). *The hope tree: Kids talk about breast cancer.* New York,NY: Simon and Schuster.

O'Toole, D. (1995). *Facing change: Falling apart and coming together again in the teen years.* Burnsville, North Carolina: Compassion Press.

Pugh, S. (1990). *Selected Poems.* Bridgend, Wales: Seren Press.

Sourkes, B. (1995). *Armfuls of time: The psychological experience of the child with a life threatening illness.* Pittsburgh,PA: University of Pittsburgh Press.

Sourkes, B. (1982). *The deepening shade: Psychological aspects of life-threatening illness.* Pittsburgh,PA: University of Pittsburgh Press.

The Dougy Center. (2004). *Waving goodbye; An activities manual.* Portland, Oregon: The National Center for Grieving Children and Families.

Traisman, E. (1992). *Fire in my heart, ice in my veins.* Omaha, Nebraska: Centering Corporation.

RESOURCES

Professional Expressive Arts Organizations:
American Art Therapy Association
www.arttherapy.org
American Dance Therapy Association
www.adta.org
American Music Therapy Association
www.musictherapy.org
American Society of Group Psychotherapy and Psychodrama
www.asgpp.org
International Expressive Arts Therapy Association
www.ieata.org
National Association for Drama Therapy
www.nadt.org
National Association for Poetry Therapy
www.poetrytherapy.org
Sandplay Therapists of America
www.sandplay.org

Chapter 28
Resilience-Oriented Family Systems Approach:
A Model for School-Based Family Counseling with
Parents and Siblings of Children with
a Life-Threatening Illness

Martha J. Markward

OVERVIEW: This chapter provides the background and rationale for school-based family counseling with families in which there is a child who has a life-threatening illness. Despite the lack of definitive evidence for effective practice, the major proposition in the chapter is that a resilience-oriented family systems approach has utility in helping family members recognize resilience in coping with the life-threatening illness of a child. Likewise, another proposition is that this approach has particular utility in working with ethnic-minority families, as well as gay/lesbian families. In emphasizing narrative and the use of metaphor, this chapter illustrates how the clinician helped a family explore beliefs about a child's illness, the organization of the family's roles and needs, and communication about the illness relative to the child's diagnosis and family relationships that resulted in recognition of resilience in the family.

BACKGROUND

School-based counselors are challenged to address the needs of families in which there is a child who has a life-threatening illness. Estimates suggest that 50 in 100,000 children live with a life-threatening illness (Himelstein, 2006), and in this context, the parents/guardians of those children matter when one considers the decisions they make regarding the curative and palliative care of children with life-threatening illnesses. Even though information is needed to gain understanding about *how* parents participate in collaborative decision making regarding children who are ill, who may die, and who are dying (Freudtner (2010), we know that families in which there is major change experience considerable stress and must cope with the circumstances that accompany that change.

This may be especially true when one takes into account the unique role and responsibility that parents have had in the lives of their children prior to the onset of illness. For example, the sense of responsibility and contribution to the child's life may be taken away from parents in the attempt to cure the illness, and instead, is placed with medical service providers. In addition, a sibling may feel a sense of responsibility for the illness of his/her sibling or feel abandoned in being left with extended family members or neighbors during the illness trajectory (Himelstein, 2006). In this regard, school-based family counseling with a focus on providing support to the family is a means of helping members negotiate the illness experience.

PROGRAM AND CASE DESCRIPTION

Numerous experts have proposed using a *resilience-oriented family systems approach* to address health problems in families wherein the family is the *central unit of care* (Kazak, Simms, & Rourke, 2002;

McDaniel, Campbell, Hepworth, & Lorenz, 2005; Rolland &Walsh, 2005; Walsh, 2006). In using this approach, service providers can engage in work that strengthens resilience in families, and this is especially needed in families in which there is a child with a life-threatening illness. As such, the clinician's objectives are to help the family *meet the many challenges of the child's illness over time* and *put the illness in its place*. The clinician can begin the resilience-oriented family systems approach by answering the following questions:

What is the effect of the child's illness on the family relative to areas of functioning?
What is the illness experience for the parents? Ill child? Sibling(s)?
How can parents/guardians shelter their relationship in such a way that they can cope with stress over time?
How can parents approach siblings about the possibility that the ill child might die?
How can relatives, friends, and social resources be mobilized?

Meeting the challenges of the child's illness requires that the clinician be flexible in meeting the needs of the family at particular points in time, depending on the trajectory of the illness. In the process, it might be necessary for the clinician to meet with individual members, couples, or the family as a system/unit. As the illness takes its course, Rolland (1994) noted that it is necessary for the clinician to understand that the phases of the illness must be linked with both the individual and family life cycle. This takes on particular importance if clinicians want to engage with parents to help them cope with the illness experience as one crisis replaces another.

By comparison, putting the illness in its place may require that clinicians help members of the family gain a perspective on, or meaning of, the illness that does not define the family or its members. In order for the family to "bounce forward," Walsh (2006) noted that the family members must learn to negotiate the "terrain" of the illness world (p.226). For example, each family member may want to establish boundaries that determine with whom, when, and where s/he will discuss concerns associated with the child's illness. This can be a means of preserving some sense of normalcy for each family member.

It is also important for the clinician to encourage family members to frame the child's illness as an *"unwelcome intruder"* in an attempt to allow all members of the family to join forces against the child's illness. In turn, this allows family members to regain control of their lives over time and with the progression of the child's illness (Walsh, 2006, p. 228). In using a family resilience approach that externalizes the child's illness, the goals are to manage illness, reduce stress, and strengthen individual and family well-being (see White & Epston, 1990; Walsh, 2006).

In the process of achieving those goals, it is necessary for those who work with a family in which there is an ill child to focus on the *belief systems in the family, the organizational patterns in the family,* and *communication within and outside the family* (Walsh, 2006). Belief systems include beliefs about life/death, the role of helping professionals in the meeting the challenges of the family, and the hopes/fears of family members. Organizational patterns in the family will change (who does what), and change will require each family member to adapt the way the family functions. Last and perhaps most important, there must be open communication in the family in order for members to make decisions about the child's care over time.

> *What are the family's beliefs in general, as well as beliefs about life and death?*
> *What the organization patterns in the family, and how have they changed with illness?*
> *What is the communication like among family members, and especially relative to illness?*

The following vignette focuses on a white family of European background in which there is a child who is 2 years of age and who has received treatment for childhood cancer. In this regard, the results in one study show that European American parents are more likely than African American parents to accept the recommendations of physicians, though this difference was not significant (Moseley, Church, Hempel, Yuan, Goold, & Freed, 2004). To some extent, the dependence of parents on physicians regarding the treatment/care of an ill child may prevent the family from identifying its own resilience, especially in terms of decision-making regarding the care of the child in the context of family functioning.

CASE VIGNETTE

The Miller family resides in a small community of approximately 1500 people in the Midwestern United States. The family has a son John who is 2 years of age and who has been diagnosed with and treated for a childhood cancer at St. Jude's Children Hospital in Memphis, Tennessee, a 6-hour drive from the community. The family came to the attention of the school social worker when the 4th grade teacher referred Kristin, the sister of the ill child, to the social worker for support due to her "needy" behaviors. In meeting with Kristin, the fourth grader, it was apparent that John's illness had placed considerable strain on the family unit, and the author asked her to see if her parents, Angela and Christopher, might be interested in meeting with me to discuss what help, if any, they need to cope with John's illness. The next day Kristin shared that Angela, her mother, would appreciate the social worker visiting with her in the home due to her caring for John. The social worker visited with mother in the home three days later, and the following excerpt exemplifies a portion of the dialogue between the service provider and John's mother.

Clinician: How do you think John's illness has affected the family as a unit?

Mother: One thing is that I don't pay the same amount of attention to Kristin as I did before he got sick. I don't sleep because I constantly worry about John.

Clinician: As you probably know, the teachers and I are paying special attention to Kristin. Do you and your husband discuss the prognosis of John's illness with Kristin?

Mother: We are grateful for the attention you and others are giving Kristin. If you can discuss John's illness with her, that is okay. We have no more appointments at St. Jude's.

Clinician: How do you think your husband is doing with John's illness?

Mother: He works late much of the time, and he is more and more quiet when he is home. I saw him crying the other day. I can't believe what John's illness has done to our family!

Clinician: If you are willing to meet with me again, I wonder if we might discuss John's illness as the "unwelcome intruder" into the family. In this way, it might allow you, your husband, and Kristin to join forces against the illness, and in the process, allow everyone to gain more family strength in coping with the situation. What do you think?

Mother: Yes, that might work.

Clinician: Let me know about a good time to meet again.

Angela, John's mother, was not sleeping, which likely affected her ability to function as well as she would like. She was aware that she and her husband were not paying as much attention to Kristin as they did before John's illness, and as a result, Kristin's need for attention in the school setting increased. Father appeared to be withdrawing more and more, and thus, this likely put more pressure on his relationship with Angela, John, and Kristin.

How can parents/guardians shelter their relationship in such a way that they can cope with stress over time?

One way these parents could shelter their relationship is through communication, but it seemed that Christopher was withdrawing and that Angela was too fatigued to initiate communication. At this point in time, it was unclear what has been said to John or to Kristin about the illness.

How can parents approach siblings about the possibility that the ill child might die?

It was helpful for family members to begin referring to the cancer as the Unwelcome Intruder. This allowed family members to have a common enemy and begin to use their resilience to address the "enemy." It also depersonalized the problem. It was unclear what the child's prognosis is.

How can relatives, friends, and social resources be mobilized?

With the referral from Kristin's teachers, social resources have begun to be mobilized.

The initial meeting with Mrs. Brown allowed the clinician to answer several basic questions about the family's resilience. Based on this information, there are several areas that warrant attention: (a) the parental relationship, (b) communication in the family, (c) understanding of the prognosis, and (d) the resources available to the family. With these questions answered, a service provider might want to explore the belief system in the family regarding John's illness. In the meeting with the family, the service provider might engage with family members to discuss beliefs about the "unwelcome intruder" in the family. This could include dialogue about beliefs related to hope and spirituality; the way the family is now functioning in light of the child's illness, and how the family members are communicating with each other and those outside the family system. In this case, Kristin and her parents were able to meet the next week, and the following are excerpts from the discussion during the meeting.

Clinician: I am glad to see all of you, and I hope you are doing well.

Mother: We are managing.

Kristin: I am glad we are meeting at school!

Clinician: So am I!

Clinician: When we met last time, Angela, we agreed to refer to John's illness as the "unwelcome intruder," and I wonder if we might discuss today each family member's beliefs about the "intruder." What do each one of you think about the possibility that the intruder will go away and John will be okay?

Kristin: I think that the intruder will go away and that John will be okay because I say prayers for him. God will take care of him.

Clinician: It sounds as if you have much hope for John to be well again.

Kristin: I do!

Clinician: What do you think, Christopher?

Father: Well, he is no longer receiving treatments to fight the, uh, intruder, so I don't know.

Mother: But there is still hope, especially if we continue to pray.

Clinician: You all have some hope that the intruder will eventually leave the family and you believe that your prayers will help, but what have the doctors told you about the intruder? "No longer receiving treatments" could mean that the intruder is leaving for good or that the intruder is here to stay. The next time we meet, maybe we can discuss this further.

Father: I think Angela wants to believe the intruder is gone for good, and I don't know. I have not said this before, but this is what I think.

Clinician: Perhaps it will be helpful for you to reconnect with the doctor at St. Jude's in order to more clearly understand whether or not the intruder will leave the family. This will help each of you adjust to the intruder one way or another. This will also help you know how the family will work in the days ahead and the extent to which you will need resources, possibly from your church.

What is the status of the parental relationship and communication in the family?

In this excerpt, one can see that the parents disagreed to an extent about the prognosis for John. At that point in work with this family, it was unclear as to whether or not this disagreement was a function of spiritual beliefs that focused on hope, especially Angela's spiritual beliefs, a lack of communication between parents/medical providers, Angela's denial, or pessimism on the part of Christopher. In either case, there seemed to be a lack of communication between the parents, and in turn, this resulted to an extent in a lack of honest communication with Kristin.

What is the parents' understanding about the prognosis for John?

There seemed to be a lack of understanding about the prognosis for John. In order to build on the resilience of the family, clarification about the prognosis was necessary, and in this case, the clinician encouraged the parents to check with the doctors at St. Jude's before the next meeting. As Walsh (2006) noted, when beliefs about the prognosis are polarized, there is potential for conflict among family members in making decisions in the future, such as how the family functions and/or the resources that the family need to fight the "intruder." This is not atypical, but because this results in the reduction of resilience, clarification about the prognosis was essential.

What are the resources available to the family?

Based on the responses of Kristin and her mother regarding hope, religion/spirituality seemed important. Depending on clarification regarding prognosis, the clinician will question in the future the extent to which the family belongs to a church and the extent to which church members can/will be supportive of the family as they negotiate the illness experience. At this point, Kristin had support at school, and the clinician believed that the family had a support system in a church, and at the very least, in a relationship with God.

After the second meeting, the clinician wrote a letter to the family that summarized what they had addressed in meetings up to this point, specifically emphasizing the need for clarification regarding the prognosis for John. Knowing the prognosis is essential in order for the family to reorganize roles and functions, if necessary, and communicate more effectively. The following excerpts are from the dialogue in the next meeting.

Clinician: Christopher, if you were going to tell a story about John at this point, what would you tell?

Father: [Christopher begins to cry] I would say that John has been a special person in our lives, and we are so grateful to have him for two years. Miracles do happen. We will continue to deal with the intruder as best we can, but I will miss my son if the miracle does not happen.

Clinician: Angela, if you were going to tell a story about John, what would you tell?

Mother: [also begins to cry] John is such a sweet boy, and he has brought us such joy! I continue to believe that he will be okay, even though I know what the doctors have told us. I see John growing up and graduating from high school, going to college, getting married, and having children.

Clinician: What will your story tell, Kristin?

Kristin: I think John will be a beautiful angel in heaven, and he will watch over me always.

Clinician: Your stories suggest that the family may need more resources in coping with the unwelcome intruder in your lives. Christopher, in your story of John, what type of help do you think the family will need in order to deal with the unwelcome intruder?

Father: I know that Angela is not sleeping much due to caring for John and worrying about him, so I think she can use some help with John during the day. Maybe we can also get help from the church with meals down the road.

Mother: I know I can use help, but I want to spend as much time with John as possible, but maybe the church could help with meals.

Kristin: I can help more around the house.

Mother: No, you need to pay attention to your school activities.

Clinician: Christopher, what do you see as your own needs down the road?

Father: I need to make time for me and John.

What is the clarification about the prognosis?

Rather than asking the family members whether or not they contacted the doctor at St. Jude's, the clinician asked family members to tell a story about John. In their stories, it was apparent they were told that the prognosis for John was not positive. The storytelling strategy allowed family members to have more honest communication, though Angela, John's mother, still struggled at this point with the prognosis. Her hope and faith was an important aspect of her ability to cope with the unwelcome intruder.

With more clarification about the prognosis, what are the resources the family will need to be resilient against the unwelcome intruder?

Christopher, John's father, recognized that his wife was not sleeping, and as a result, he thought that they could turn to the church for help. In response to this, his wife indicated that she wanted to spend as much time with John as possible, which was quite understandable. Even so, she indicated that having help with meals would be welcome. She did not want Kristin put in the adult role of helping at home; rather, she wanted Kristin to concentrate on her school activities.

RELATIONSHIP TO THE SBFC MODEL

Within the context of the family-remedial focus of SBFC, there is a need for school-based family counseling with parents whose child has a life-threatening illness. With this focus, the major emphasis is on using interventions that promote family support to help a student, even though the family may not be the source of stress for the student. Many children with life-threatening illnesses receive treatment in large hospitals in metro areas, such as Memphis, Tennessee in this situation, but when the treatment regimen is finished, the family returns to the community and attempt to function as they had before the child's illness. Unfortunately, those families may have little support as they attempt to "bounce forward" rather than "bounce back" to life before the child's illness (Walsh, 2006, p. 222). Often, teachers learn of the illness via communication with a sibling or another parent in the community, and in turn, teachers refer the sibling to supportive personnel, such as school counselor, social worker, nurse, psychologist, or other person in a supportive role. When this occurs, it seems optimum for supportive personnel to use a resilience-oriented family systems approach in working with the family.

This work focuses on the need to understand the "psychosocial bridge" that can connect families and community resources. Campbell (2003) emphasized the impact of illness on the family, and in this context, the need to highlight the family's strengths and spirituality (Walsh, 2006). In this regard, Kleinman (1988) referred to the "illness experience" as the extent to which the ill member and other members of the family are able to live with and manage the challenges of the illness over time. Clinicians in school settings can use a resilience-oriented family systems approach in working with a family in which there is a child who has a life-threatening illness (Walsh, 2006, p. 222).

EVIDENCE-BASED SUPPORT

The underlying premise of this approach is that the family is a system, and therefore, the focus of the approach is on the family unit/system per se. As such, the major assumption here is that change in one family member will affect change in all, and as one would expect, the child's illness/child results in inevitable change in how the family functions. Second, this approach allows the "helper" to integrate a variety of intervention strategies that have been proven to work, such as cognitive behavioral therapy (CBT). However, given that the situation changes with the trajectory of the child's illness, a more process-oriented approach seems warranted in work with families in which there is a child with a life-threatening illness. Unfortunately, there is much less evidence to support intervention approaches, such as narrative and solution-focused approaches, that are process-oriented.

Rolland (1994) proposed a framework for evaluating resilience-oriented intervention with families who deal with an ill child or one who has a disability. As such, this framework highlights the interconnectedness of practical, emotional, and interpersonal demands over time, and there is considerable support for attending to the family system as the unit of care relative to resilience of the family and all of its members. Others have supported this notion as well (Kazak, Simms, & Rourke, 2002; McDaniel, Campbell, Hepworth, & Lorenz, 2005; Rolland & Walsh, 2005; Walsh, 2006). Although this suggests the need to account for the intertwining of many aspects of family life as it relates to the illness experience, it poses challenges for those trying to measure the effectiveness of the resilience-oriented family systems approach.

MULTICULTURAL COUNSELING CONSIDERATIONS

Many of the same considerations that were in play in using the resilience-oriented family systems approach with a Midwestern white family will be in play with an ethnic-minority family, primarily because the focus is on the family system/unit. However, in work with ethnic-minority families and gay/lesbian families who have a child with a life-threatening illness, three implications are especially salient. First, those families may be less likely than European Americans to seek help from supportive personnel in schools due to negative experiences that result from institutional biases and prejudices. This may prohibit any family member from seeking and/or accessing the support that might have utility for a family to recognize its resilience.

In fact, the second consideration is that culture will be the metaphor for work with an ethnic minority family whose child has a life-threatening illness; more specifically, culture will be central to the work rather than peripheral or additive (Laird, 2000). In this regard, the cultural beliefs, values, and practices in ethnic-minority families, such as rituals, stories, kinship patterns, and family relationships, take on special salience. For example, the perspectives of African American families on death and dying may be very different than those of Asian American families. Clearly, one can see that a resilience-oriented family systems approach to work with families allows for the clinician to take into account the cultural background of families, especially when s/he emphasizes the narratives of family members.

The third consideration in working with non-traditional and non-white families is that interpersonal injustice must be taken into account, primarily because work with an ethnic-minority family whose child has a life-threatening illness will likely reflect the oppression and lack of opportunities they have experienced in the community and society. This requires that those who work with ethnic-minority families, as well as gay and lesbian families, utilize a narrative stance to understand how and why decisions are made about the child's care relative to the trajectory of the illness. In using a narrative stance, the clinician avoids pathology or blame and relies on basic parameters common to most families, including ecological niche, acculturation, and life-cycle events (Falicov, 1995).

CHALLENGES AND SOLUTIONS

Markward and Benner (under review) conducted a systematic review of literature that focused specifically on the perspectives of parents about making decisions regarding the curative and palliative care of their children. They identified the following five inter-related decision-making themes: (a) ambiguity (hope v. uncertainty), (b) honest communication, (c) the need for knowledge and/or advocacy, (d) inclusion in the decision-making process, and (e) parent-child/family relationships. The authors concluded that while research is critically needed to understand how parents make decisions about the care of ill children, especially as it relates to ambiguity, attention (or lack thereof) given to parents and siblings seems to be a missing link in addressing the needs of the family in which there is a child with a life-threatening illness. Therefore, the greatest challenge in working with all families in which a child has a life-threatening illness is in understanding how the family as a unit makes decisions regarding the curative and/or palliative (end-of-life) care of the child.

Another challenge is in measuring the effectiveness of the resilience-oriented approach in working with families in which there is very ill child. Wherein the family is treated as the "subject" in a single-subject design, this can be accomplished to some extent if the clinician uses a measure of family coping or resilience at various points in working with a family, especially when s/he takes into account the factors external to the resilience-oriented family systems approach. In the meantime, clinicians who use this approach with its emphasis on narrative can be flexible and adaptive to the realities in families in which child has a life-threatening illness. Despite the emphasis on process of exploration in the resilience-oriented family systems approach, there are constructs that can be measured in using this approach in work with families. For example, those working with families in which there is a child with a life-threatening illness could ask family members to complete a measure of resilience. Anyone can complete the *14-Item Resilience Scale* (RS-14, Wagnild & Young, 1987) at http://www.resilience.com. Respondents will be asked to rate the extent to which they agree with statements, such as "I usually manage one way or another, I feel I can handle many things at a time," and "my life has meaning (7= Strongly Agree; 1 = Strongly Disagree).

Similarly, a measure of the family's ability to cope with crisis could be used to measure the ability of families to cope with the child's illness at various points in the illness trajectory/experience. The *Family Crisis Oriented Personal Scales (*F-COPES, McCubbin, Olson, & Larsen, 1991) can be used to identify problem solving and behavioral strategies used by families when faced with problems or crises.

This scale has 30 items that describe a variety of coping behaviors that individuals may use in times of stress or crisis and those behaviors are categorized as "acquiring social support, reframing, seeking spiritual support, mobilizing to acquire and accept help," and "passive appraisal."

Overall reliability of the F-COPES using Cronbach's Alpha ranges from .77-.86. Individual subscales had alpha's ranging from .63-.83. Overall test-retest reliability is .81 with individual scales ranging from .61-.95. Respondents will be asked to rate their agreement with statements, such as "sharing our difficulties with relatives, seeking encouragement and support from friends," and "knowing I/we have the power to solve major problems (5 = Strongly Agree; 1 = Strongly Disagree). The instrument can be used as a pre-post test to measure change over time (see Appendix A for permission to use this instrument).

Other constructs that can be measured include but not limited to communication, family functioning, and decision-making. With this said, the primary objective of the clinician is to focus on exploration using strategies that are family-centered. In this case, narrative strategies were used.

Conclusions

Within the context of the family-remedial focus of school-based family counseling with the focus on the family to support a student, several conclusions can be drawn about the use of the resilience-oriented family systems approach as a means of focusing on a family to support a student whose young brother has been treated for childhood cancer. First, the resilience-oriented family systems approach allowed the clinician to be flexible in meeting with family members individually and collectively. Second, the clinician was able to help the family put the illness in its place by externalizing the illness from the family, which allowed the family to "bounce forward" rather than "bounce backward." Last, in exploring family members' beliefs about the child's illness, the organization of the family roles and needs, and communication about the illness relative to the child's diagnosis and family relationships, the clinician helped the family clarify that the prognosis for John was poor.

Implications

One implication of the family work described in this chapter is that the family in which there is a child with a life-threatening illness warrants the attention of trained school-based clinicians, including psychologists, social workers, and counselors. Another implication is that in using the resilience-oriented family systems approach to intervention, the clinician can promote family support that helps a student in the school setting. In a family in which there is a child who has a life-threatening illness, the family per se is not the source of stress for the student. In fact, the work with family suggests the need to externalize the child's illness from the family and treat it as an intrusion into family life. Last, while the clinician in this case used techniques associated with narrative therapy, clinicians can use an eclectic, pragmatic approach to help the family "bounce forward."

RECOMMENDATIONS

Periodically, school-based clinicians can check with teachers to see if there are students who reside in families in which there is a child with a chronic or life-threatening illness; clinicians should consider using an approach to intervention that focuses on the family (versus the student in the family) as the unit of care; and last, any intervention approach can be used, but modalities that encourage families to explore and reframe the impact of the child's illness on the family unit, and in turn, on the sibling in the school setting are recommended.

REFERENCES

Campbell, T. (2003).The effectiveness of family interventions for physical disorders. *Journal of and Family Therapy,29*(2), 263-281.

Falicov, C. (1995). Training to think culturally: A multi-dimensional framework. *Family Process,34*.373-388.

Himelstein, B. (2006). Palliative care for infants, children, adolescents, and their families. *Journal of Palliative Medicine, 9*(1), 163-181. DOI:10.1089/jpm.2006.9.163.

Kazak, A., Simms, S.,& Rourke, M. (2002). Family systems practice in pediatric psychology. *Journal of Pediatric Psychology, 27*, 133-143.

Kleinman, A. (1988). *Illness narratives: Suffering, healing, and the human condition.* New York: Basic Books.

Laird,J.(2000). Culture and narrative as metaphors for clinical practice with families. In D. Demo, K. Allen, & M. Fine (Eds.), *Handbook of family diversity* (pp.338358). New York: Oxford University Press.

Markward, M., & Benner, K. (under review). *Perspectives of parents on decision-making about the care of children with life-threatening illnesses: A systematic review of literature.*

McCubbin, H., Olson, D., & Larson, A. (1982). *F-Cope: Family coping strategies.* St. Paul, MN: University of Minnesota.

McDaniel, S., Campbell, T., Hepworth, J., & Lorenz, A. (2005). *Family-oriented primary care.* (2nd ed.). New York: Springer.

Moseley, K., Church, A., Hempel, B., Yuan, H., Goold, S., & Freed, G. (2001). End-of-life choices for African American and white infants in a neonatal intensive-care unit: A pilot study. *Journal of National Medical Association, 96*, 933-937.

Rolland, J. (1994). *Families, illness, and disability: An integrative treatment model.* New York: Basic Books.

Rolland, J., & Walsh, F. (2005). Systemic training for healthcare professionals: The ChicagoCenter for Family Health approach. *Family Process, 44*(3), 283-301.

Wagnild, G., & Young, (1987). *The Resilience Scale user's guide.* Worden, MT: The Resilience Center.

Walsh, F. (2006). *Strengthening family resilience.*(2nd ed.). New York: The Guilford Press.

White, M., & Epston, D. (1990). *Narrative means to therapeutic ends.* New York: Norton.

Appendix A

http://www. resilience.com This link pasted as an address will allow an individual family member to use the instrument online. This individual will be asked to provide educational level, age, and gender.

Contact Information to obtain permission to use the *F-Copes* scales:

Family Stress Coping and Health Project
1300 Linden Drive
University of Wisconsin-Madison
Madison, WI 53706 (608)262-5070

PART VII

SCHOOL-BASED FAMILY COUNSELING: SPECIFIC APPLICATIONS

C. SCHOOL-INTERVENTION APPLICATIONS

SCHOOL FOCUS

School-Prevention	**School-Intervention**
Family-Prevention	Family-Intervention

PREVENTION FOCUS

INTERVENTION FOCUS

FAMILY FOCUS

Chapter 29
The Calgary Transitions Mental Health Classrooms:
A 17 Year Old Collaborative Program

Teresita A. José

OVERVIEW: This chapter provides an overview of the Calgary Transitions Program, a collaborative partnership between two Calgary school boards and several community agencies at its inception. The four transitions mental health classrooms are designed to provide a nurturing therapeutic classroom environment for elementary and junior high school students with significant internalizing mental health challenges. My experience working as a psychologist and member of the classroom core team in one of the four mental health classrooms from 1997 – 2000 is described.

BACKGROUND

I first learned about the Transitions Mental Health Program from my Program Manager, Gay Blauel, also a child psychologist, when the project was first imagined, and the proposal for funding was being worked on by the partnership. This included the Calgary Board of Education, the Calgary Catholic School Board, the Provincial Mental Health Board's Family Adolescent and Children's Program, the Interfaith Family Support Services, Alberta Children's Hospital, William Roper Hull Child and Family Services, Woods Homes, and the Young Adult Program, Foothills Hospital. I was working as a clinical child psychologist with the Northwest Family Adolescent and Children's Services (FACS), now known as the Child Adolescent Addictions Mental Health Program (CAAMHP). As one of the more senior clinicians with the FACS Team, with several years of work experience in school based mental health programs and residential school treatment programs, Ms. Blauel asked me as well as another colleague, Mel Lipsey, a clinical social worker from my team with years of experience running therapy groups, to participate in some of the partnerships' earlier meetings. She asked us to provide feedback on the Transitions proposal. For example we had long discussions on issues such as the use of group sessions in the classrooms, the possible role of mental health professionals from the FACS program, and more specifically the function or role of the mental health clinician in the service delivery of the program.

BASIS FOR THE TRANSITIONS MENTAL HEALTH CLASSROOMS PROPOSAL

An interagency group consisting of the members of this collaborative project was formed in response to their felt need to go beyond the confines of their programs and work with other agencies to better serve the children and families they worked with. The group was working together for awhile and was "comfortable with each other" when the Provincial Mental Health Board announced the availability of funding for collaborative projects. This group was therefore quite ready to take advantage of this opportunity to realize their hopes[1].

This interagency group was interested in the San Diego New Beginnings Program, an interagency partnership between schools and community agencies designed to serve the needs of at risk children and their families (1990). In the early nineteen nineties, their project was considered 'new thinking.'[2].

After inviting a member of the San Diego New Beginnings group (Payzant, 1992), to come to Calgary to share strategies for interagency collaboration with schools, the Calgary partnership prepared the Transitions Program proposal for four mental health classrooms. With input from the group, Ms. Blauel was given the task of writing up the proposal. Two other collaborative projects known as Opening Doors, a one stop service delivery model involving schools and social service agencies designed to assist children at risk and their families, and Bridging the Gap, a program for transitional youth who struggle with mental health difficulties were also proposed around the same time[3].

While there was no actual research or pilot study done before starting the mental health classrooms, the proposal cited references to support the proposal. This included Dan Offord's work from the Ontario Health Study suggesting that a child with poor school performance has 3.1 times the odds of having a psychiatric disorder compared to children without poor school performance (1990). It also cites Thompson's (1992) study of Alberta children suggesting a prevalence rate of childhood mental illness in the range of 10.8 % to 25.4%. Kinney, et al's (1992) article on the use of individualized academic and treatment planning for serving children with emotional disturbance was mentioned. As well, Kanfer and Grimm (1980) were cited when discussing treatment motivation, suggesting that it improves when clients believe they have responsibility for their outcome. Trivette et al (1990) article was noted in discussing the importance of a strength based approach when working with children and their families, especially when they can identify resources within themselves[4].

PROGRAM DESCRIPTION

The Calgary Transitions Program is a seventeen year old collaborative project consisting of four mental health classrooms located in a regular community based classroom: one elementary classroom and one junior high school classroom that operates under the aegis of the Calgary Board of Education (CBE), and one elementary and one junior high school classroom that functions under the Calgary Catholic School District (CCSD). At its inception, the CBE mental health classrooms were located at Maple Ridge Elementary School, and Sir John A. MacDonald Jr. High School. CCSD mental health classrooms were housed at St. Margaret Elementary School and St. James Jr. High School.

The purpose of the transitions program is to provide children with severe mental health difficulties a safe treatment focused classroom environment that assists them in identifying their own emotional issues, learning more acceptable coping strategies, and building on their ability to take charge of their lives. Some examples include children who are phobic, highly anxious with excessive worries or fears, depressed, cry easily, are selectively mute or withdrawn, and who may also be refusing to attend school. Components of the program include an individualized academic and treatment plan, a focus on strengths and self improvement, social skills training, individual, family and group therapy, in home support and case coordination with a residential/hospital program for children returning from residential or hospital settings.

The three other program components involve transitioning students to the regular classes in the host school, and finally transitioning the student to a community school, as well as follow up services. The core team of each mental health classroom is made up of a teacher specialist, the teaching assistant (also with a special education background), the in-home support staff, (who works closely with the family and serve as the link between home and school), and a mental health professional who provides counseling to the students and families on an as needed basis, as well as consultation to the team. The school principal and administrative staff of each host school plays a vital role in the day to day functioning of this classroom. A psychiatric consultant attached to the Family Adolescent and Children's team, (now Child Adolescent Addictions Mental Health Program) provides psychiatric consultation to three of the classrooms on an as needed basis[5].

STEPS IN ESTABLISHING THE TRANSITIONS PROGRAM: 1996-1997

Seventeen years ago, shortly after funding was received from the Provincial Mental Health Board [6], the management team, made up of the partnerships' representatives began to meet more frequently in order to begin doing the hard work of establishing a contract, the policy and procedures manual and launching the four mental health classrooms. The two school boards secured the location for the four mental health classrooms. In short, members of the management team ensured that the roles and responsibilities they had identified for themselves were in place. The following is a list of the partnership and the roles they agreed to take for the Transitions Classrooms[7].

ROLES AND RESPONSIBILITIES OF THE TWO SCHOOL BOARDS AND SIX COMMUNITY AGENCIES WITH THE TRANSITIONS CLASSROOMS 1996-2005

As a collaborative endeavor the Transitions Program team agreed to share the responsibilities of running the program. This involved assuming responsibility for funding staffing, consultation, supervision, and administration. Representatives of the partnership were made up of the Transitions Program Management Committee and in charge of the program's operation. The program is unique in that each service provider reports directly to their respective schools and community agencies. For example, the teaching staff consisting of the teacher specialist and the special education assistant reports to their respective school principals and school boards, the mental health professional reports to the manager of the Family Adolescent Team and the in-home support staff reports to the manager of the Inter Faith Youth and Family Services, see Figure 29.1.

The Calgary Board of Education provided education to approximately 95,000 students per year at the inception of the Transitions classrooms. Its mission is to ensure individual student development through effective education. In addition to the regular instructional programs in community schools, there are a number of specialized programs to address diverse student needs. Within the Calgary Board of Education, the Student Services Unit is committed to linking educational programs for youth at risk.

Calgary Roman Catholic School District at the programs ' inception provided a range of educational services to 36,650 children and youth, based on a mission statement which supports education that is focused on the holistic needs of children from a Catholic perspective. Student Services exists to provide expertise, assistance and support for students whose special needs are beyond the scope of school-based resources. There is a strong commitment to optimizing the opportunities for these students in their learning, growth and development.

In 1996, both the Calgary Board of Education and the Calgary Catholic School District agreed to collaborate with eight other city agencies and programs to establish four mental health classrooms. Both school boards provide instructional supports in the form of teacher specialists, teaching aides, plus administrative supports. Estimated in-kind dollars at the program's inception was $300,000.

Teachers and teaching assistants with special education background for the four classrooms were selected and hired by the two school boards. The Provincial Mental Health Board's Family Adolescent and Children Services, now known as Alberta Health Services, Child Adolescent Addictions Mental Health Program, agreed to provide mental health consultation and treatment services required for two classrooms, as well as the psychiatric consultation services required for all the classrooms. Estimated in-kind dollars at the start of the program was $ 24, 000.00. Alberta Children's Hospital agreed to provide the in-home support services for one classroom as well as the support necessary to ensure an effective transition of students admitted to the hospital's mental health program to the mental health classrooms. Estimated in- kind dollars at the start of the program was $19,000.00.

Figure 29.1 Organizational Chart for Transitions Program

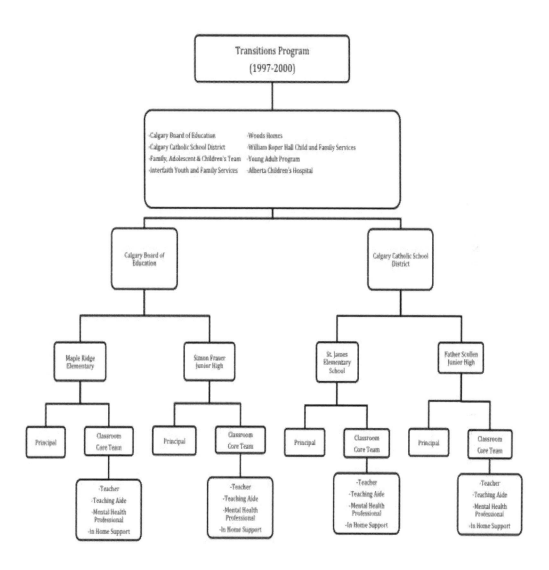

Interfaith Youth and Family Service agreed to provide supervision and support to in home support workers hired through funding. The link with Interfaith Youth and Family Services provided an opportunity for the in-home support staff to connect with in home workers from other programs, such as COMPASS, a community parent school support program and the Behavior classes, which in turn increased their opportunities for staff development and support. In kind contributions included donated client comforts such as bedding and bikes, participation in social events for the purpose of skill development around Christmas and Halloween, as well as summer months when activities sponsored by the agency would be available to Transitions students. At the program's inception, Interfaith also assumed the role of fiscal agent for funds earmarked for the Transitions Classrooms, such as extra school supplies, and for hiring some in-home support workers.

Woods Homes, a not-for-profit residential treatment and educational facility committed to participating as a member of the transitions treatment team when families who have been referred to the program have also been involved with their services, such as the Community Response Team and the Stabilization Program. Woods Homes has also offered to provide consultation in specialty areas such as substance abuse or sexualized behaviors. Estimated in-kind dollars at the program's inception was $ 7,000.00. William Roper Hull Child and Family Services, also a residential treatment and educational facility, committed to participating as a member of the treatment team when families have been involved with their agency. Young Adult Program at the Foothills Hospital agreed to provide their expertise when families have been involved with their program. The management committee met regularly to ensure the establishment of the four mental health classrooms in 1997, and a policy and procedures manual for the program was written[viii].

Referrals and Screening: Referrals to the program are drawn from the schools, community agencies, residential or hospital programs within the Calgary catchment area. It is expected that the referring school or agency has informed the family about the possibility of their child attending a transitions classroom and has obtained consent to share relevant information with the screening team. Referrals that fit the mandate are collected by Student Services and all pertinent information they gather, or the referring school or agency collected, are brought forward to the screening committee.

The screening team consists of the family support staff, mental Health professional, teacher, and teacher aide of the particular transitions classroom concerned, the student services consultant/specialist for the school board concerned, and a representative of the referring community school or agency, as well as the student, and his or her parents. Significant professionals involved with the child may also attend this screening session [ix].

Requested screening information includes a psychological or psychiatric assessment report, results of a current behavioral inventory, such as the Achenbach, Behavior Adaptation Scale for Children. An academic assessment or current individual program plan is also required. A severe disabilities assessment may also be required. Any other relevant assessments and other reports from the referring agency, e.g., medical, speech, occupational therapy, etc. are considered helpful[x].

STEPS TAKEN TO ESTABLISH THE TRANSITIONS PROGRAM AT SIR JOHN A. MACDONALD JR. HIGH SCHOOL

Charlotte Arbuckle was teaching with the CBE at that time and was hired to be the first teacher at CBE'S Junior High Transitions Mental Health Classroom. At that time she had twelve years of teaching experience and a Master's degree in Educational Counseling with a specialization in Adolescent Mental Health. Additionally she was credentialing to be an educational psychologist. Students attending this classroom were in Grades 7, 8, & 9, and Ms Arbuckle taught all the subjects. Catherine Brown, with a degree in Fine Arts, a strong art background and course work in educational counseling, was chosen to fill the position as teaching aide. Terry Calderon, a social worker, was appointed to be the in-home support worker at its inception, and Mel Lipsey, a clinical social worker was appointed to be the first mental health professional from the Family Adolescent Children's team to be part of this classroom team. Dr. Susan Carpenter a psychiatric consultant with the FACS Program was appointed the consulting psychiatrist for the program.

THE TRANSITIONS MENTAL HEALTH CLASSROOM AT SIMON FRASER JR. HIGH SCHOOL 1997-2000

After Mr. Lipsey left the FACS team, in 1997, I was appointed to take his place. This special classroom had also just moved to their new host school, Simon Fraser Junior High School, from Sir John A. Macdonald when I joined the team as psychologist, working with the core staff and the students. I spent two afternoons a week, Mondays and Fridays, with the children and staff, providing individual counseling to students and meeting with the team. The classroom's teachers and in home support staff remained the same; however, being in a new host school meant a new principal, administrative staff, and teaching staff. This move was considered good as the new classroom was spacious and situated across from the school's science room. The teaching staff of the mental health classroom reported to the new principal who was most helpful to the transitions program, especially as she had a solid background working with children experiencing emotional and behavioral difficulties and thus was able to provide good support for the mental health classroom. While we all reported to different organizations, we were also responsible to the management committee of the partnership, where the transitions program was concerned.

The Simon Fraser Jr. High School transitions classroom's working philosophy as practiced and articulated by the core team members involved a strong focus on collaboration and integration for the best interest of the child. In this set up, it meant that there were deliberate and planned attempts to ensure the safety of the children and program staff (Jose, Arbuckle, Brown & Wagner, 2000).

Classroom Climate at Simon Fraser Jr. High School: 1997 – 1999: Dr Mahoney, a group consultant with the SFJH program was trying to take a reading on the school and classroom climate when he first entered the "space" of the mental health classroom, from how much room the transitions students gave him in the hallway, how the secretary handled him in the main office, to the call to tell Ms. Arbuckle that he was on his way up to the classroom, and the introductions, getting under way and the description of the program. He described his classroom experience in the following way:

> It was a pleasure to see the many positive attributes that had been built into this classroom. The most effective characteristics were the complimentary tandem approach of the teacher and teacher-aide, plus the effective and superior educational match of curriculum with a sophisticated emotional sensitivity to creating a psychological climate that fostered the educational learning. It was visible in how the teachers planned, it was visible in Dr. Jose's work of supporting the growth of personal characteristics in the students which improved their likelihood of learning.

Dr. Mahoney went on to further describe his impressions of how this classroom was working:

> It was obvious that a spirit of openness, truthfulness, respect and affection existed in this classroom at several levels. Teacher to student, student to mental health therapist to teacher, mental health therapist to students, mental health therapist to other mental health therapists. A climate of learning was evident, not to be confused with a classroom with no structure, no expectations, no real work achievement levels, no correction of inappropriate behavior.

> This effective learning climate was developed as far as I could see, from the efforts of the teacher and teacher-aide developing a team style that was very respectful of the defenses of the students so was patient as frail egos took longer to come around but set a standard for behavior and book learning was not an insulting "watering down." The wish coming clearly

from the mental health worker, the teachers, etc. gave a strong message of support and caring that the student had to take self improvement seriously as their caretakers did too[xi].

RELATIONSHIP TO THE SBFC MODEL

The two most powerful systems that impact a child's life are his family and his school. The essence of school based family counseling approach as described by Gerrard (2000) involves:

> helping children succeed in school and integrates school counseling and family counseling models within a broad based systems meta-model that is used to conceptualize the child's problems in the context of all his or her interpersonal networks: family, peer group, classroom, school teacher principal, other students and community. (p.1).

The way the Calgary transitions classrooms are set up, speaks to its strong commitment to the school-based family counseling approach described above, where a wrap around service is provided to at risk children and their families involved in the program. This is made possible by the efforts of many individuals: the teacher and teaching aide in the specialized classrooms, as well as the mental health staff and in home-support staff that form the core team. Additionally, the transitions class enjoyed the support of the school principal, administrative staff, and the teachers in the host school especially when the transitions students began to integrate into the mainstream regular classes at this school. As well, the psychiatric consultant supplied by the FACS team provided psychiatric services to the children and their families on an as needed basis. These consultations were arranged by the mental health professional. Other health providers from the community, such as psychologists and psychiatrists already involved with the transitions students and families, as well as hospital, residential staff were invited to attend profile meetings on the student. During these meetings, the student's overall adjustment and progress in the program was discussed with his or her parents, the core classroom team health professionals, and educators involved with the student.

In examining SBFC model, described in Chapter 1 of this book the Transitions Program may be classified as school based, with a school remedial focus as well as a family remedial focus. It is school based in that the collaborative classrooms operate in a host community school. It is school remedial in that students admitted to the program struggle with their academic work and mental health issues that negatively affect their school performance. Thus, the mental health classroom's function is two-pronged in that it addresses both educational and therapeutic needs of the student. The overarching goal is to facilitate the student's integration into a regular classroom at the host school and eventually promote return to his or her regular community school.

The Transitions Program is also family-remedial in focus because when a child has a mental health issue, usually there is a family mental health issue, or the family struggles to deal with the child's mental health issue. The mental health professional may be called upon to facilitate a psychiatric consultation or provide family therapy. The in-home support staff provides help to the family by way of supporting family members, for example, providing mental health support, or other types of supports, such as accessing certain services, or problem solving for the family, e.g., finding camps, medical referrals, etc. One example of this is family A where there was a lot of anxiety demonstrated by family members, particularly one of the parents, who was even more anxious than the child attending the program. Child A had trouble adjusting to the mental health classroom and appeared stuck and unable to do school work or relate to peers. After the in-home support staff addressed the family subsystem's main issue, which was severe anxiety in one of the parents that made day to day life difficult for the entire family to manage, student A began to move forward in his school work and his relationship with peers. In this case the in home-support staff helped the family member connect with a psychiatrist and following diagnosis and treatment, the parental subsystem improved to the point that the couple started to go on coffee dates. Then every family member's functioning improved. The support staff noted that the house was no longer in shambles, one of the parents was no longer withdrawn, and student A did not need all of the toys he took to school every day for comfort[xii].

It is important to note that the Family Adolescent Treatment Team, (now the Child Adolescent Mental Health Program) that is involved in the partnership and provides the mental health staff to two of the mental health classrooms, as well as the psychiatric consultant to three of the current mental health classrooms, practice in the tradition of school- based family counseling. This is because historically, the CAAMHP's day to day clinical practice of involving the child's family, school and community is rooted in the Child Guidance Clinics model that has been in Alberta since the 1930's (Dechant, 2006) and has a similar philosophy to the Adlerian Child Guidance Clinics that started in Vienna.

EVIDENCE-BASED SUPPORT

STUDENT DATA

Available data in 1998 provides information about how twelve Maple Ridge Elementary students and Simon Fraser Jr. High students rated themselves at pre- transitions time and post transitions time. Using a 1-5 Likert scale, students registered an average rating of 43.4% before attending the transitions class. After attending transitions class, students reported an average rating of 83%   suggesting that they felt better in all domains, including confidence, up from 46.7 % to 86.2%; self knowledge from 50% to 85%; advocacy from 46.8% to 85%; self expression from 43.3% to 83.3%, and skills from 35% to 78.3% (see Figure 29.2).

The available data on Figure 29.3 showed that in most categories the same students felt better "A lot" and "A Little" on the following variables: do better in school (91.7%), like school more (75%) feel better about self (100%),understand self (83.3%). understand behavior (83.3%), learn new ways of coping (91.7%), feel more independent (100%), get along better with adults (100%) and get along better with kids (75%).

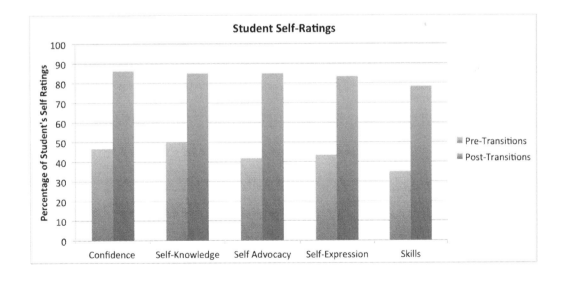

Figure 29.2 Transitions Program Student Data (1998).

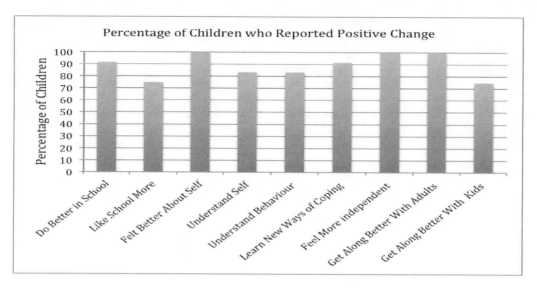

Figure 29.3 Percentage of Children Who reported Positive Change (1998)

PARENT DATA

The parent Satisfaction Survey (Figure 29.4) shows that in almost all categories, parents on average were 82 % satisfied with the transitions program on nine variables. This included parent/guardian involvement in the selection process (100 %), parent guardian inclusion in the plan to achieve child's goals (92%), open and honest sharing of information with parents/guardians about their child (92 %), availability and flexibility of staff towards child (92 %), amount of communication between parents/guardians and program staff (82 %), the identification and work towards their child goals (82%), helping their child to develop and implement new strategies to achieve those goals ((91%), effectiveness in helping the family as a whole (67 %), and helping child become more independent (100%).

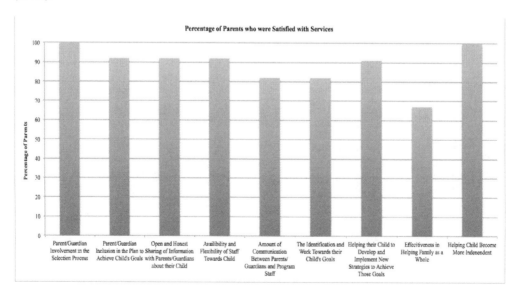

Figure 29.4. Percentage of Parents Who were Satisfied with service (1998)

While longitudinal data is not available at this time, it is worthwhile noting that although the proposal for initial funding was one year, the Transitions Mental Health Classrooms have received ongoing funding over seventeen years and that the classrooms appear to be well used by students. One of the changes noted by Lori Watson-Roe, the current manager for the CAAMHP Student Partnership Programs is the reduction in the number of agencies that form the collaborative from eight agencies to the current four agencies that are involved with the program[xiii].

MULTICULTURAL COUNSELING CONSIDERATIONS

Calgary is a multicultural society, with 22 percent of its population identifying themselves as visible minority in the 2006 Statistics Canada Census. This included Chinese, South Asian, Black, Filipino, Latin American, Southeast Asian, Arab, West Asian, Korean, and Japanese. The aboriginal population is not included under this designation (Statistics Canada, 2006). At the proposal stage of the Transitions program, aboriginal and immigrant referrals were carefully considered and noted and that the Transitions Program has access to the school boards' Aboriginal and Cultural Liaison Workers. Furthermore, it went on to say that these diversity workers could provide consultation, support and or information to access other culturally appropriate resources as necessary[xiv].

While these resources are available today, during my three year involvement with SFJH transitions class, the majority of the students who attended this classroom were Caucasians, with only one South American student and one aboriginal student. When this aboriginal student first joined this classroom, he was very shy and withdrawn. It took awhile for him to open up, even when everyone tried hard to help him feel comfortable. It was only through the discovery of his special talent, which was his drawing, that helped him open up. Both staff and students who were amazed at his exquisite eagle drawing praised him. This made him feel good and shortly after this discovery he began to participate in the classroom lessons and activities. Art work was used a lot in this classroom in the same way that Igoa (1995) used art in her classroom to help students to bring out the inner world of the child and help them have a voice, as well as the way that Iverson (2006) made use of drawings in her work with children dealing with bereavement.

During the first three years of my involvement with the SFJH classroom (1991-2000), 70% of the students in this classroom were male and only 30% female. Another snapshot taken in 2005 – 2006 showed a similar trend where 83% of the entire Transitions Program was male (Jose & Rosettis, 2006). There is limited research on why there seems to be an over representation of males in programs for students with emotional disorders (McIntyre & Tong, 1998). Subotsky (as cited in Abel, 1996) found that one of the three psychiatric clinics in the Camberwell Health District Area, England, that was funded by the Education Authority, had more referrals from schools in connection with poor behaviours, attainment, and attendance which are all common in boys. This clinic has the lowest proportion of female new cases (30%). Oswald et al (2003) suggested that the under identification of girls within the IDEA (Individuals with Disabilities Education Act) " may occur because the problems girls present are not recognized by school personnel as the type of problem typically identified under the current definition of educational disability (Oswald et al., 2003, pp.231-232).Note that while most of the students at Simon Fraser Jr. High School were male, most of the staff in the classrooms and in-home support staff was female, consisting of three Caucasians and one Southeast Asian. This was the case at its inception and in 2000. Having a male teacher in the classroom may be useful for dealing with large boys who may at times be acting out. For example, one of the big male students in this classroom barricaded one of the teachers and students inside the classroom. One wonders if this situation would have happened if there was a strong male presence in the classroom. It is difficult to draw conclusions as to why there are fewer visible minorities that attended this particular classroom. It is possible that the program has not been tested with other multicultural groups in Calgary. This could be an area for possible research to see if the program meets the needs of children and families from varying ethnic groups.

CHALLENGES AND SOLUTIONS

Collaborative programs are known to be complex with challenges to overcome as noted by Pounder (1997), Porter & Epp (2000), and Weist, et al (2012).

CHALLENGES RELATED TO TIME

Time was one challenge the partnership had to deal with twice in 1996.

Challenge: Time was a major issue at the proposal stage. When the Provincial Mental Health funding was announced in 1996, there was the usual problem of having too little time to write a proposal and do an in depth research or pilot project.
Solution: This problem was resolved by way of hard work and more frequent meetings with the members of the partnership. Ms. Blauel was appointed to write the proposal with input from the partners, as the group felt that because she was already working as a manager with the Provincial Mental Health Board, and that she would have a good understanding of management issues involved in the proposal writing. This process was shortened because the group knew each other and were comfortable working with each other, and highly motivated to apply for funding to achieve their common goal of finding ways to better serve at risk children and their families[xv].

Challenge: The second known challenge was also related to time. The group was trying to draw up a legal contract for the new program quickly. They found out that drawing a legal contract would take a really long time and interfere with the funding and program launch.
Solution: They resolved their dilemma by taking the proposal to each of their respective agencies for their lawyer's input. This resulted in a decision to draw up a letter of understanding which did not take as much time. Later on when they were no longer pressed for time, a formal contract was prepared[xvi]. The policy and procedures manual also helped to facilitate the establishment and operation of the program on the classroom level[xvii].

SOME CHALLENGES AT SIMON FRASER JR. HIGH MENTAL HEALTH CLASSROOM: 1997-2000

During the period from 1997-1998, the transitions classroom enjoyed much stability due to the good working relationship between the core team members, the school principal, and school staff in general. The challenges I remember centered around students. One challenge was on how to teach and integrate the mental health component with the required school curriculum, staff changes, and the rest of the challenges were student based.

Challenge: Integrating the mental health curriculum with the academic curriculum. This transitions classroom was designed to be a therapeutic classroom, one that addressed the educational needs of grade 7, 8, 9 students. The challenge of integrating the mental health curriculum with the academic curriculum fell on the teachers shoulders.
Solution: As Ms Arbuckle, was given the freedom to create the class according to parameters set by the school and management committee, she was able to provide the leadership to address this challenge. Using a creative approach Ms. Arbuckle and Ms. Brown were able to weave curriculum and components of therapy together. An example of this was the "mask project" in English. First the students were asked to read the book called Mask, a curriculum requirement. Then they watched a film called "The Mask" and later they did art work on the mask. The students were instructed to create a mask made of paper maché then paint or decorate it. Furthermore, the class was instructed to show what others would see on the outside part of the mask. Inside the mask the students were instructed to depict a picture or write what others could not see. This was a successful project in that it resulted in

much discussion about the student's characteristics and feelings that others do not see. This was cathartic for the students and resulted in one student writing a moving poem about moving on.

Challenge: Difficulty integrating transitions students to the regular classroom. Integrating transitions students into regular classes in the host school was another challenge. Students preferred to stay in the safe confines of the transitions classroom at SFJH.
Solution: This problem was inadvertently resolved. The transitions classroom was located across from Ms. Martin's Science classroom where a lot of animals were housed. The transitions students were interested in volunteering to look after the animals at time which involved feeding them. One day I walked into the transitions classroom and was horrified to see that each of the students had a snake wrapped around their necks and bodies. I refused to enter the room as I am afraid of snakes; however I was informed that since the students felt comfortable with the animals in Ms. Martins Science room, the transitions students were happy to integrate in her classroom[xviii].

Challenge: A student's obsessive behaviours interfering with school work. The problem was addressing CC's obsession and preoccupations which were interfering with his school work. CC was obsessed with fishing and would only talk about fishing, and then move on to golfing after a few weeks or months.
Solution: It became clear to the team that CC's major reinforcer was money and that he was quite interested in food at that time. A job was found for him working in the school's cafeteria, which helped him to move on in his schoolwork and socially. This change was depicted in a self portrait. The earlier self portrait was about an immature looking person with sharp teeth showing. A later drawing of self portrayed a well groomed and confident young man (Arbuckle, Jose, Brown, Wagner, 2000).

Challenge: a student's need for classroom control. A student needed to control the classroom. One day this resulted in him barricading one of the teachers, as well as the students, into the classroom. Principal's office help had to be requested. Since this student was huge, and had a strong need to control, it was obvious that the classroom staff and children would not be safe with him present in the class.
Solution: He was discharged from the transitions class, however, the principal was able to find a regular class within the host school for him to be contained, and still continue with his education. This saved face for him and his family, as he was still at SFJH even if he was asked to leave the mental health classroom.

Challenge: Student M's deteriorating functioning. Parents and school personnel were concerned that this student was having trouble doing his school work and his parents reported aggressive behaviors at home. Both school and home reported deterioration in his functioning.
Solution: This problem was addressed by referring this student for psychiatric consultation. Medication was prescribed and more individual and family work done, resulting in some improvement in class and at home.

Challenge: Numerous staff changes September 1998 – June 2000. This time period was characterized by ongoing staff changes: a total of eight changes within two school years. This presented many challenges for this mental health classroom at SFJH. Both students and staff found it difficult to cope with the numerous changes. It was understandable that the parents and children for this classroom openly expressed their feelings of being incredibly upset over the decision to once again change the teacher for this class, after they struggled with the back and forth changes in recent months. Several children from this class allegedly skipped classes, or refused to return to this class in 2000 on account of perceived problems with having a new teacher and the perception that only the teaching aide was doing the job. There was a need for one staff member to fill in the vacuum and assume a leadership role for the class and one staff member described herself as feeling like the wicked step-mother after the favorite teacher left.

Solution: To address the issues that came about during this time period, the program was fortunate to have Dr. Mahoney's expertise with group work and his experience with this particular mental health classroom before this difficult time. Staff meetings were held regularly at this time to talk about staff's feelings and work on some solutions as a group. In essence the new core group had to work on rebuilding the classroom. This meant a lot of hard work on everyone's part. After the core team staff was working again, the students began to settle down, and the classroom was back on track again.

PROCEDURE

Following are some recommended steps in establishing a similar transitions program:

1. A pilot study of the proposed school mental health partnership should be done to determine strengths and weaknesses of the program design. This preliminary study will provide basic information about the project, on which the partnership can base its decisions.

2. The next step in establishing a collaborative partnership like the Transitions Program is finding a strong, energetic, and resourceful leader with excellent management and social skills. This is especially important since it is well known that collaborative programs are by nature complex and require a lot of time, energy, commitment, and ongoing hard work for project sustainability. The more partners there are, the more challenges there are.

3. Finding committed partners for the collaborative is the next step. This means partners who have the necessary resources to offer the partnership. Management experience from among the partners that sit around the table would be an asset, as partnerships like this require a commitment of resources, staff, funding, etc. Strong interest and motivation in the project is also helpful.

4. Finding a funding source is essential especially if the partners are not going to be able to fully provide the resources required for this collaborative project.

5. Legal Advice from the partnership is essential in drawing up the partnership contract. This can come from the partners' individual agencies. Time to write up a contract takes time and should be kept in mind especially when timelines are tight.

6. Ongoing management of the program should be mapped out ahead of time, to ensure program continuity and sustainability. For example the partnership will have to address the issue of what happens when the initial management leaves, Who will ensure that management function is maintained and sustained? This could be addressed in the Policy and Procedures Manual. Special attention should be given on how the actual mental health classroom ought to operate, to ensure that program goals are adhered to. For example, these mental health classrooms have a dual function in addressing the students' curriculum and maintaining a therapeutic milieu to address their mental health issues. What special staff qualifications should be required, not only at its inception, but later on as the program is more established? More importantly, who ensures that the appropriate staff is hired? Is there a management audit mechanism established to monitor program adherence?

7. Since services are school sited, staff involved should be cognizant of "principalese." This means acknowledging and adapting to the school culture, and the principal's role as the primary administrator of the entire school.

8. Evaluation is an important component in any type of service delivery like this collaborative. It is imperative that program monitoring be done, and that the information on demographics and

evaluations is kept in one location for easy access. In a collaborative like this, where everyone is responsible for monitoring and evaluating the program, tracking information for the program can be most difficult, especially after some agencies decide to leave the program.

SUMMARY

The Calgary Transitions Mental Health Classrooms function as school-based family counseling that is school-sited, with a school and family remedial focus. This program that is designed to meet the academic and therapeutic needs of students from grades one to nine in Calgary continues to be delivered even though the partnership has been reduced to four, from the eight agencies at its inception. The fact that the program is seventeen years old is proof that it is filling a need and is well supported by the remaining partnership. This also speaks to the passion and dedication of staff and the current partnerships' commitment to the program. This chapter offers information on how the program was established, and the programs' challenges at its inception. It also takes a close look at one of the four mental health classrooms and outlines some of the challenges encountered and how they were resolved.

REFERENCES

Abel, K., Buszewicz, M., Davison, S., Johnson, S., & Staples, E. (Eds.). (1996). *Planning community mental*
> *health services for women: A multiprofessional handbook.* New York: NY: Routledge.

Dechant, G. (2006). *Winters children*: The emergence of children's mental health services in Alberta
> 1905 – 2005. Edmonton, AB: The Muttart Foundation.

Gerrard, B. (2008). School based family counseling: overview, trends, and recommendations for future
> research. *International Journal for School Based Family Counseling,* 1 (1), 1-30.

Igoa, C. (1995). *The inner world of the immigrant child.* Mawah, New Jersey: Lawrence Erlbaum
> Associates, Inc.

Iverson, N. (2008, August). *Creativity and Healing: Expressive arts & families*. Oxford symposium in
> school-based family counseling, Brasenose College Oxford University.

Jose, T. A., Arbuckle, C., Brown, C., & Wagner, L. (2000, November). *Building resiliency in a transitions mental health classroom.* Paper presented at the 2nd Annual Mental Health Conference, Sheraton Cavalier Hotel, Calgary, AB.

Jose, T., & Rosettis, A. (2006, August). *Calgary mental health transitions classroom*. Oxford symposium in
> school-based family counseling, Brasenose College, Oxford University.

Kanfer, F. H., & Grimm, L. G. (1978). Freedom of choice and behavioral change. *Journal of Consulting & Clinical Psychology,* 46 (5), 873 – 878. doi: 10.1037/0022-006X.46.5.873

Kinney, J. M., Haapala, D., & Boath, C. L. (1991). *Keeping families together: The home builders model.*
> New York, NY: Adline de Gruyter.

McIntyre, T & Tong, V. (1998). Where the boys are: Do cross-gender misunderstandings of language and
> behavior patterns contribute to the overrepresentation of males in programs for students with emotional and behavioral disorders? *Education & treatment of children, 21:3.*

Offord, D. R., Boyle, M. H., & Racine, Y. A. (1991). Children at risk: Schools reaching out. *Education Today,* 3, 17-18.

Oswald, D. P., Best, A. M., Coutinho, M. J. & Nagle, H. A. (2003). Trends in the special education rates of
> boys and girls: A call for research and change. Exceptionality: A Special Education Journal, 11:4,
> 223-237. doi:10.1207/S15327035EX1104_3

Payzant, T. (1992). New Beginnings in San Diego: developing a strategy for interagency collaboration. *Phi*

Delta Kappan, 74 (2), 139 – 146.

Porter, G., Epp, L. & Bryan, S. (2000). Collaboration among mental health professional: A necessity, not luxury. *Professional School Counseling,* 3 (5) 315 – 322. Retreived from http: // courses. Unt.edu/bullock/edsp5620/module7/art 3. Pdf.

Pounder, D. G. (1998). Restructuring schools for collaboration: promises and pitfalls. Albany NY: State University of New York Press.

Statistics Canada. (2006). 2006 census. Retreived March 6, 2012, from http://www12.statcan. gc.ca/census – reconsement/ 2006/dp-pd/prof/92-591/details/page.cfm?L...

Trivette, C. M., Dunst, C. J., Deal, A. G., Hamer, W., & Propet, S. (1990). Assessing famil strengths and family style. *Topics in Early Childhood Special Education,* 10 (1) 16 – 35. doi 10.1177/027112149001000103

Thompson, A. (1992). Emotional disturbance in a sample of children in the care of child welfare. A report submitted to the Edmonton Region, Family and Social Services. Retrieved from http://www.socialproblemindex.ualberta.ca/ChildCW160Kids.pdf

Weist, M. D., Mellin, E. A., Chambers, M. S., Lever, N. A., Haber, D., & Blabber, C. (2012). Challenges to collaboration in school mental health and strategies for overcoming them. *Journal of School Health,* 82 (2), 97 – 105, doi: 10.1111/j.1746 – 1561. 2011.00672. x

Endnotes
[1] G. C. Blauel (personal communication, March 17, 2012)
[1] G. Ghitan (personal communication, February 28, 2012)
[1] G. C. Blauel (personal communication, February 26, 2012) & G. Ghitan (personal communication, February 28, (2012)
[1] G.C. Blauel (personal communication, January 3, 2012)
[1] G. C. Blauel (personal communication. January 3. 2012)
[1] E. Grant (personal communication, June 24, 1996)
[1] G. C. Blauel (personal communications, January 3, 2012) & C. Arbuckle (personal communication, February 24, 2012)
[1] G. C. Blauel (personal communication, March 7, 2012)
[1] C. Arbuckle (personal communication, March 1, 2012)
[1] C. Arbuckle (personal communication, March 1, 2012)
[1] K. Mahoney (personal communication, February 5, 1999)
[1] L. Wagner (personal communication, February 27, 2012)
[1] L .Watson-Roe (personal communication January 12, 2012)
[1] G.C. Blauel (personal communication, January 2, 2012)
[1] G. C. Blauel (personal communication, March 4, 2012)
[1] G. Ghitan (personal communication, February 29, 2012) & G.C. Blauel (personal communication, March 7, 2012)
[1] C. Arbuckle (personal communication, March 2, 2012)
[1] C. Brown (personal communication, February 28, 2012)

RESOURCES

Programs Similar to Transitions Mental Health Classrooms

Chiumento, A., Nelki, J., Dutton, C., & Hughes, G. (2011). School based mental health service for refugee and asylum seeking children: multi-agency working, lessons for good practice. *Journal of Public Mental Health,* 10 (3), 104-174.doi:10.1108/17465721111175047

A guide to the development of school based mental health partnership. (2003). Retrieved March 9,2012, from the Northshore Child and Family Guidance Center Web site: http://www.northshorechildguidance.org/SpecEdTechManual%20(1).pdf

Background, advice, strategies for collaboration in schools, and other agencies

Porter, G., Epp, L., & Bryan, S. (2000). Collaboration among mental health Professionals: A necessity, not
    luxury. *Professional School Counseling,* 3 (5) 315-322.
    Retrievedfromhttp://courses.unt.edu/bullock/edsp5620/module7/art3.pdf
Pounder, D. G. (1998). *Restructuring schools for collaboration: promises and pitfalls.* Albany, NY: State
    University of New York Press.
Weist, M. D., Mellin, E. A. Chambers, M. S., Lever, N. A., Haber, D., & Blaber, C. (2012). Challenges to
    collaboration in school mental health and strategies for overcoming them. *Journal of School Health,*
    82 (2), 97 – 105. doi:10.1111/j.1746-1561.2011.00672.x
Yifeng, W., & Kutcher, S. (2011). Comprehensive school mental health in an integrated "school based
    pathway to care." Model for Canadian Secondary Schools. *Mc Gill Journal of Education,* 46 (2) 213 –
    229. Retrieved from http://www.erudit.org/revue/mje/2011/v46/n2/1006436ar.pdf

Studies on School and Agency Collaboration

Mellin, E., Weist, M. D. (2011). Exploring school mental health collaboration in urban community: A
    social capital perspective. *School Mental Health,* 3, 81 – 92. doi: 10.1007/s 12310 – 011, 9049 – 6.
Sloeper, P. (2004). Facilitators & barriers for coordinated multi-agency services.*Health & Development*,
    30 (6), 571 – 580. doi: 10.1111/j.1365-2214.2004.00468.x
Storch, E. A., & Crisp, H. L. (2004). Taking it to the schools. Transporting empirically supported
    treatments for childhood psychopathology in the school setting. *Clinical Child & Family Psychology
    Review,* 7 (4), 191 – 193. doi: 10.1007/s10567-004-6084-y

Contact for Current Calgary Transitions Mental Health Program

Lori Watson Roe: Lori.WatsonRoe@albertahealthservices.ca

Chapter 30

Therapeutic Interventions Following an Incident of Violence in a School: A South African Case Study

Maria Marchetti-Mercer

OVERVIEW: *In this chapter I will describe the process of a therapeutic intervention carried out in order to treat children from a primary school who had been exposed to the real life drama created by an armed attempt robbery. The therapeutic team comprised two trainers and nine postgraduate students all of whom spent two weeks in the school system following the traumatic events created by the shooting incident. During this period of time the therapeutic team worked to address the support needs of the different members of the school community, inter alia pupils, teachers and parents, via a range of specially designed therapeutic interventions. In this process a number of interesting observations were made regarding the challenges posed by trauma work in a multilayered system. The aim of this chapter is to extract some therapeutic guidelines for counselors/therapists who may be called upon to provide trauma counseling in an inherently complex environment, such as school, in the aftermath of violence.*

BACKGROUND

Entering a school community in the aftermath of a traumatic event may be a challenging task for mental health professionals such as School-Based Family Counselors. In this type of situation therapeutic intervention must be aimed at different levels and must be mindful of the specific needs of the client system. Therapists and counselors may tend to enter a system in a manner that is colored by their own perceptions of what the client system may need rather than be guided by the actual needs of the client. Furthermore their views regarding peoples' reactions to trauma are largely informed by their training and existing theories on trauma and how to work with people exposed to it.

In this chapter I would like to illustrate with the aid of a case study that, when intervening in a complex community such as a school, it is important for therapists to enter from a position of not-knowing as advocated by post-modern writers such as Anderson and Goolishian (1992). I will therefore use the theoretical framework of social constructionism to argue that the counselor(s) and the client system are collaborators in the process of therapy, thus equally contributing to it (White &Epston, 1990). Overlooking this, especially in the case of trauma work, may lead to a situation where, instead of facilitating a healing process in the system, more trauma is in fact created.

CASE DESCRIPTION

The case study I wish to discuss for the purpose of illustration took place outside Pretoria in South Africa. The therapeutic team that was involved consisted of two clinical psychologists/trainers and eight graduate students in Clinical Psychology.(In South Africa a Master's degree leads to registration as either a clinical, counseling, educational or an industrial psychologist).

BACKGROUND INFORMATION

On Monday, 10 May 1999, a primary school in the countryside outside Pretoria was the target of an attempted robbery, when a number of armed men tried to rob a cash-in-hand transit van that was being used to courier money from the school premises. In South Africa money is often transported in such security vehicles. More than ten armed men appeared at the school entrance in five cars and threatened the security guards who had come to collect the monies from the school financial department. A small war, as described by the onlookers, ensued and more than 60 shots were fired between the security guards and the robbers who were carrying AK 47 and R5 rifles as well as pistols. The robbers managed to take 30 money trunks from the van, which were fortunately later discovered by the police. One of the robbers was shot in the foot at the scene of the crime whilst his accomplices, although managing to flee at the time, were later apprehended by the police. In the meantime the school principal, learning of the commotion, grabbed a pistol from his office and also came running to the scene. The school secretary immediately phoned the police who reacted promptly and this resulted in the subsequent swift apprehension of the robbers. This was not the first example of attempted robbery at the school but the other incidents had taken place without violence. A large number of the children directly witnessed the shooting as the grade 1 and 2 classes (6-7 year olds) faced the grounds where the shooting took place. Initially, many of the youngsters said that they thought the noise came from fireworks, later realizing it was a serious shooting. Fortunately the teachers reacted and got the children lie down on the floor, thus preventing injury. The shooting was also heard by children in the other classes bit they did not register what was happening and were barely overwhelmed by the noise. Parents were immediately informed of the incident and many of them rushed to the school to take stock of what had happened and to take their children home. The incident made headline news in most local newspapers, inter alia held, 12th May 1999.

In the aftermath of the shooting, the school became the focus of a lot of media mention as well as falling under the eye of community leaders and politicians. This event seemed to highlight the vulnerability of rural schools, many of which are fairly isolated and lack proper security. The principal of the school commented that the schools had become soft targets for incidents of violence. Furthermore this event took place in the South African social context, which is already characterized by high levels of violence (Pelser& de Kock, 2000). This was also a period following the Columbine shooting incident in America and there was therefore heightened public awareness around school violence. The general public was consequently very shocked by this event and many role players wanted to come involved. A representative from the Department of Education, the Minister of Safety and Security and the commissioner of Police all visited the school two days after the shooting and promised support in terms of added security as well as psychological services.

As members of a Psychology department at a nearby University we became aware of the incident and decide that this would be an ideal opportunity to provide much needed community assistance as well as a chance for our graduate students to be exposed to a large scale therapeutic intervention. I contacted the principal of the school and offered him our assistance. He appeared keen to have the University involved as opposed to the police service, he felt that the latter was offering assistance owing to political pressure rather than because of genuine interest in the welfare of the children.

Together with a colleague we set up the logistics for the project. In the meantime the police service contacted me as they initially wanted a joint co-operation on the effort. However it was later decided to leave the matter entirely to our department. At this time we envisaged carrying out a crisis intervention as is usually indicated following a population's exposure to a stressful event. An example of this is short-term crisis therapy, where the therapist is very active, helping to clarify the problem for the client, giving suggestions for plans of actions, giving reassurance and also giving information and emotional support (Carson, Butcher &Mineka, 1996). By definition this is an intensive and short-term intervention. The two trainers held an in-depth discussion with the students explaining the nature of this type of intervention. We emphasized that we would be working together on this project as a team and that we had full confidence in their therapeutic abilities. We also explained to them that two weeks would be the time limit on our team's presence at the school. Later this decision became critical as there was a lot of pressure from them the students to remain involved with the school on a long-term basis.

Phase 1: Initial contact with the school. The day after contacting the school the University team visited the school. An individual meeting had been arranged with the school principal in order to assess his needs as well as to explain what kind of psychological assistance the team could offer. At this stage we envisaged working only with the children who had directly witnessed the shooting. As we arrived at the school we were ushered into the staff room where all the staff members were present (approximately 30 people) and I was asked by the principal to address them. Addressing a large group of people was not quite what I expected but I presented the staff with my assessment of the situation. I was also careful to emphasize the fact that the team had come in order to address their needs and it was therefore very important that they make those clear to us. I shared some ideas of what we thought would be important but also listened carefully to their suggestions. They had many concerns regarding how to deal with their pupils following the shooting. It became clear that even the children who had not directly witnessed the shooting had been deeply affected.

After the presentation the principal, who seemed very open to the ideas presented, held an in-depth discussion with me. Although, on the surface, the discussion seemed to focus on the events surrounding the shooting, it soon became apparent that the principal was very frustrated with the authorities, who had provided very little help before the incident and were eager to jump in now that the media was involved. It was also clear that he had been greatly shaken by the event but had to keep up a brave front for the sake of those around him. He told me emphatically that he was fine and did not need any psychological assistance. In fact this meeting turned out to be quite a long intense debriefing session where he shared many of his feelings around the event with me.

Phase 2: Group debriefing with the children. The day after the meeting with the school teachers the team went to the school in groups of three and addressed classes of the children who had actually witnessed the shooting incident. As group debriefing is an accepted manner of trauma work (Udwin, 1993) it was felt that this would be the most effective manner to reach all the children who had directly witnessed this event. The intervention was aimed at the following:

> Allowing the children to express their feelings regarding the shooting incident in a non-threatening context;
> Allowing them to regain some sense of control over their environment; and
> Normalizing the experience for them as a group by allowing them to see that their classmates had experienced similar feelings of fear and anxiety.

Pynoos and Eth (1986) argue that allowing the child to develop an increased sense of security, competence and mastery following a traumatic event is regarded as a desirable goal of trauma work with children. In keeping with the literature (for example Lipovsky, 1992; Pynoos& Eth, 1986; Terr, 1989) it was decided to use a developmentally appropriate technique, such as drawings, which would allow the children to express their feelings around the shootings in a non-threatening manner.

Each child was given the opportunity to draw a picture of what had happened and given a chance to talk about his/her picture to the rest of the class. Team members provided each child with a lot of positive reinforcement throughout the process. After this each child was asked to draw a picture describing what he or she would do if he/she were the chief of the police to make the school safer for the children. It was a felt that this exercise would provide the children with a sense of empowerment as they would feel involved in decision-making about safety in schools. These second sets of pictures revealed similar recurring trends, such as big policemen with large guns, fierce police dogs, high fences around the school building and so forth.

The teachers also assisted during this process and the team gave them a lot of positive reinforcement for the very quick way in which they had reacted in order to protect the children. They were in fact very shaken after the incident as they had feared for their own as well as the children's safety. In fact they had responded quite effectively to the situation by having the children lie down on the floor immediately and managed to keep a reasonable calm atmosphere.

Phase 3 Individual assessment of children. The next step was to ask teachers to identify children in the other classes whom they felt were experiencing particularly negative feelings around the shooting incident. This offer was also made to the children who had been the target of the group intervention as certain children through diagnostic interviews and projective techniques such as the draw-a-person test or the kinetic family test and then make recommendations for the day for an entire week. Following the incident a number of children also refused to come to school and their parents had contacted us for advice as to how address the problem.

Phase 4: Group intervention with teachers. The next part of the intervention was to address the needs of the teachers at the school. As mentioned earlier the teachers seemed to have experienced a serious crisis surrounding their roles as caregivers. Moreover they seemed to experience their place of work as no longer safe. It was therefore decided to hold group sessions with the different teachers led by two co-therapists. The value of group therapy is widely recorded in the literature, for example Yalom (1995), and it was considered important for teachers to share their own feelings with another and ultimately to normalize their own experiences of the event. The groups were open and discussions centered around the teachers' feelings regarding the shooting. The level of emotional intensity seemed to differ from group to group but it was interesting to note that the male teachers tried very hard to mask their feelings of powerlessness by indulging in the language of bravado. An example of this was the military theme commonly expressed by a majority of male teachers, who saw their military experience as having exposed them to far more dangerous situations. However it became clear to the therapists that they had in fact been deeply affected by the incident.

A group was also run with the black workers at the school (for example janitors and cleaning staff) whom we feared might easily have been ignored in the aftermath of the event. This group was led by a therapist fluent in African languages thus allowing people the comfort to speak in their mother tongue.

Phase 5: Parents' evening. It has been widely argued in the literature that involving the parents in the process following their children's experience of trauma is of paramount importance to the therapeutic endeavor (Leibowitz, Mendelsohn & Michelson, 1999; Udwin, 1993). A parents' evening was therefore organized inorder for parents to come up with their concerns and pose questions to the team. Individual time was also allocated to parents who wanted to speak privately to members of the team. It was felt that it would be important to make the parents aware of the possible symptoms of post-traumatic stress disorder that the children might experience later on and also to give them some tips on how to deal in a psychologically supportive manner with children exposed to such trauma.

An information sheet listing typical symptoms which parents should watch out for in the following weeks was also drawn up by the team. This included the typical DSM-IV diagnostic criteria (American Psychiatric Association, 1994) as well as some guidelines on how to deal with anxiety in their children. Disappointingly the turnout proved to be rather poor. This can be attributed to a number of factors. Firstly the security situation in the area may have discouraged people from coming out in the evening. Secondly parents with pressing concerns had already had the opportunity to discuss their concerns with the team members earlier on. The handout drawn was however sent to all the school's parents and included important information, such as the telephone numbers where team members could be contacted should there be a need for further inquiries.

Phase 6: Exiting the school system. The next step was the exit from the system. This process was quite difficult for many of the students. A number of them felt that they could not leave the children without further therapeutic interventions. Some suggested starting a clinic at the school where they could work as part of their practicum. (It must be noted that the school is more than an hour's drive from the University and would therefore have been very difficult to reach on a regular basis). This led to quite a heated group discussion regarding our responsibilities as therapists and what our future definition relationship with the school was going to be.

Phase 7: Students' feedback. At the end of the two weeks the students were asked to give the team leaders feedback on their experiences at the school. It was deemed essential to hear the stories of the students who, as therapists in training, had been faced with quite a complex therapeutic process, involving different client populations and different types of interventions. This feedback gave us some significant insights into the importance of this type of work as part of the training process. Two main themes seemed to be recurrent in all the students' feed-back, namely:

Anxiety at the unfamiliar situation

The students' comments showed that they had in fact experienced a lot of stress in regard to their introduction into a community where so much was expected of them.

> *"The thought of working with young children was quite daunting."*
>
> *"I was quite enthusiastic about going to the school...but the flipside of this coin was the fear that I did not possess the skills to be effective, and indeed that I might only worsen the situation."*

The value of the learning experience

The strongest theme identified in the students' feedback was the value of this community intervention in relation to their feelings of self-confidence and indeed confidence as budding therapists. It is important to note that, throughout the process, the team leaders treated them as full competent professional people and regarded them as equal members of the team.

> *"Facilitating the groups was a new experience...it was amazing to see the group through this process I did learn to trust my abilities, but most importantly I realized that I have the skills."*
>
> *"Having gone through this experience my confidence has been boosted and I am now of the opinion that I did possess adequate therapeutic skills and have gained a lot of this process."*
>
> *"I was glad to get involved in the community, not only for the theoretical and practical experience but also because it was very satisfying to provide help during a time of crisis."*
>
> *"The fact that the lecturers put trust in our abilities as therapists created a sense of self- worth in the group as well as positive feelings of self."*
>
> *"It seems in some way that the experience bonded us together as a group and also gave us a boost of confidence, because we were treated at all times by both our lecturers and the staff at the school as professionals who had something to offer. I think this is an important aspect of the training process as in some ways it dispels the myth that you will one day 'magically' become a therapist, as if this were something bestowed upon one pursuant to attaining some higher truth."*

CHALLENGES AND SOLUTIONS

The following challenges were encountered during the different phases of the intervention and this is how they were approached:

PHASE 1: INITIAL MEETING WITH THE SCHOOL

It became evident after the first contact with the school that the therapeutic intervention would have to address the school system on different levels and not only the children who had directly witnessed the shooting. The needs of the other children and of the teachers as well as the parents would have to be addressed. Given that the project was also aimed at giving our graduate psychology students a real "hands on" opportunity to develop their skills as systemically orientated therapists and also had to be taken into consideration when planning the intervention. It was therefore decided to hold discussions with the team members at the end of each day wherein we could discuss the events of the day. Students were also encouraged to seek supervision at any time during the course of the intervention.

After the initial introduction to the school I became very aware of the fact that there is a real danger that, when "experts" move in after people have suffered a traumatic experience as they may risk creating more trauma by emphasizing the helplessness and the neediness of the clients. By simply entering the system as the "expert" on trauma the counselor may inadvertently communicate the message that there is something wrong with the client and that the counselor is the only one who can fix it. One must always be sensitive to the fact that a person's experience of stress and trauma may be highly individual and that people also have access to resilience (Walsh, 2003) of which a counselor may not be aware.

This first contact with the school therefore highlighted the fact that when entering such a system one must let oneself be guided by the needs of the needs of the clients as they emerge and be flexible enough to respond to them as they rise. One can almost speak of an element of "therapeutic flexibility" which is necessary when working with a large system. If one's initial plans are too rigid and too perspective they may not be adequate to address the wide range of needs of the clients and may eventually be rejected.

PHASE 2: GROUP INTERVENTIONS WITH THE CHILDREN

As a group the team was fairly satisfied with this phase of the intervention. The students had felt quite intimidated about working with children in a group context prior to the sessions but had been reinforced by the seemingly positive impact of the intervention. However we did pick that the teachers had been deeply affected by the incident as it had impinged on their sense of feelings such as fear/anxiety as well as anger at having been a target of violence. Consequently the clinical team realized that the teachers would have to receive very specific therapeutic attention from the team.

PHASE 3: INDIVIDUAL ASSESSMENT OF CHILDREN

As the students began assessing the children more and more clients presented for assistance. It soon became clear that the school system had decided to make use of the psychological services now available to them. Therefore both parents and teachers alike had decided to refer children with problems unrelated to the shooting incident. We became aware of this process fairly quickly but decided that given the limited resources available to this community it would be wise to provide our services even to those whose needs were not closely related to the shooting. Because the team felt that some of the children no longer needed therapy the offer was made to the school that we would provide services free of charge to any child wishing to come to the University Counseling Unit. (Interestingly nobody took up this offer in the long term).

This trend once again highlighted the fact the needs of a community may be different than what has been envisaged by the therapist and during the therapeutic process the therapist must be able to respond to the evolving demands of the clients.

PHASE 4: GROUP SESSIONS WITH TEACHERS AND STAFF

In general the feedback from the group sessions was positive and the teachers felt that they had also had the chance to express their feelings surrounding the incident. This was an important focus of the intervention as it might have been otherwise all too easy to focus only on the children while ignoring the adults. The South African context is also of such a nature that it is really socially acceptable for men to express feelings of anxiety or fear.

PHASE 5: PARENTS' EVENING

The team had worked hard to prepare for the parents' evening and had also made personal sacrifices in making themselves available in the evening. Many of the students were disappointed that the turnout had not been better. Again the team was faced with a situation in which they had had very specific needs of the clients had been quite different. We held an in-depth discussion with the students following the evening. Interestingly we were once again approached by individual parents who had concerns, not directly connected to the shooting incident, but who had an obvious need to talk to a therapist. Once again it became very clear that this community had a serious need for psychological services independent of any needs that may have arisen as a consequence of the shooting incident.

PHASE 6: EXITING THE SYSTEM

It became apparent to us as trainers that, given the intensity of this type of intervention, we should have predicted that the students might became very emotionally involved with the school. This was their first opportunity to work fairly independently as therapists and as their trainers we should have spent more time discussing their roles and the boundaries and time limits of this type of intervention. The team leaders felt that allowing students to continue to work at the school at this time would merely have reinforced a sense of powerlessness in the system rather enhancing resilience. The trainers' assessment at the time was that the school was in fact quite a strong supportive community and that it possessed enough resilience to work through any further problems precipitated by the crisis. There was also a strong message communicated by the school's principal that now was the time to terminate therapy.

PHASE 7: STUDENTS' FEEDBACK

The students' comments highlighted the importance in the process of training of the practical application of theoretical concepts. It became evident that the students were simultaneously aware not only of their position and potential as therapists but also of the complexity of the community intervention. By allowing them to function independently as professionals the trainers provided a context for growth and self-development, while at the same time providing an indispensable service to a community in need.

PROCEDURE

The following questions may be posed when having to deal with incidents of violence in a school context:

> How does a counselor/therapist enter a school system after a traumatic event in a manner that is respectful and does not create further trauma?

> What is the role of the counselor/therapist in a school context following a traumatic event?

> How does a counselor/therapist include the families in this therapeutic process?

> What are the implications of a traumatic event for the relationship between school and parents?

1. GUIDELINES FOR ENTERING THE SCHOOL SYSTEM

There are a number of theories on trauma work especially with regard to children (for example Lipovsky, 1992; McFarlane, 1994; Pynoos & Eth, 1986; Terr, 1989) as well the specific diagnostic criteria set out in the DSM-IV defining post-traumatic stress (American Psychiatric Association, 1994):

> Persistent re-experiencing of the event through flashbacks, invasive and repetitive thoughts and nightmares;
> Avoidance of specific factors or reminders associated with the event or the development of related fears and phobias;
> A general numbing of overall responsiveness is often experienced, with children appearing lethargic and uninterested in previously enjoyable activities;
> Social withdrawal may also be observed;
> Symptoms of increased arousal, with children experiencing difficulties sleeping, becoming irritable and touchy, finding it difficult to concentrate and generally appearing over alert to any forms of danger are also often observed.

These are the guidelines that inform counselors/therapists when working with people who have been exposed to traumatic events. However useful or even necessary these theories may be as part of our training and work they only represent some of the "voices" with which to speak about trauma. As a counselor/therapist one must always be sensitive to the fact that the client may bring a very different story after been exposed to a violent event. Individuals will react dissimilarly after being exposed to a violent event. A number of factors may influence individuals' reactions such as previous exposure to trauma, personality factors, support systems and other mediating factors. Individual experiences must therefore be addressed specifically: when entering a large system such as a school it is also important to remember that different subsystems such as teachers, children and parents may have specific needs which may have to be addressed accordingly.

As discussed earlier I hypothesized that by our mere entrance into the school as "experts" we might have communicated the message to the members of the school that they were helpless and unable to deal with the aftermath of the experience. Immediately after the exposure to trauma the client may be disorientated and may feel powerless (DSM-IV: American Psychiatric Association, 1994). Theories of trauma debriefing are prescriptive and encourage therapists to follow specific guidelines when dealing with clients. However when applying such interventions the counselor/therapist must be careful not to exacerbate feelings of powerlessness; rather a process of co-operation and co-operation between therapists and the school system must be emphasized, so that a process of healing can more effectively be put into place.

2. THE ROLE OF THE COUNSELOR/THERAPIST IN A SCHOOL EXPOSED TO VIOLENCE

In recent years there have been a number of violent incidents in schools all over the world. These have ranged from students going on killing sprees of fellow students and teachers outsiders entering the school and injuring students and staff. These events cause great shock to communities, since children or young people are the victims. Furthermore, schools are traditionally perceived by parents and society as secure nurturing environments. When these safe havens are violated this impacts not only the school system but also the larger communities within which schools operate.
Researchers such as Ochberg (1991) have written about the impact that trauma may have on the survivors' social network.

The therapeutic plan should therefore be guided by the school community, which consists of staff and children as well as parents. A high priority should be the involvement of the families as this is the context into which children have to return, and this can certainly aid the therapeutic process.

McFarlane (1988) also argues that the treatment objectives of the therapist in this situation should be, amongst others, to facilitator rather than the expert. It is important to emphasize from the beginning one's confidence in the system's ability to heal itself. Figley (1988) also argues that the treatment objectives of the therapist in this situation should be, amongst others, to facilitate a process of recovery as well as self-reliance. It is also important to emphasize that the presence of the therapist/counselor in the system will be brief. One must also be able to assess when the system has reached a "therapeutic saturation point" and therefore needs no further input from the therapist/counselor.

A counselor/therapist may also have to deal with his/her own feelings during the therapy as well as feelings of sadness around having to terminate the therapy. The intensity of such an intervention may cause certain bonds to become forged between the counselor/therapist and members of the school community. It was obviously very difficult for our students to leave feeling that so much more was still needed by individual children. In this process the counselor/therapist must therefore find a balance between certain guidelines which are informed by the theoretical training and the need to be adaptable in one's therapy given the requirements of the specific context with which he/she is working.

3. THE ROLE OF FAMILIES WHEN WORKING WITH A SCHOOL SYSTEM EXPOSED TO VIOLENCE

When working with a school exposed to trauma it is equally important to work with children in the context of their family. It has been argued in relevant literature that an important mediating factor in children's responses to trauma is the family context of the child and especially the parent's reaction to the traumatic event (Stallard & law, 1994). Figley (1988) argues that the family can play an important therapeutic role in detecting the symptoms of trauma and helping the child through a process of resolution. Leibowitz et al (1999) point out (a) that the parents might also manifest a response to the trauma experienced by the child, and (b) that this response impacts upon the child's reaction to the event. Terr (1989) argues that families have their own grief responses after trauma and their own process of adjustment, which may make the child's response to trauma more complicated. Furthermore, as Udwin (1993) points out, the level of adjustment of parents is to be considered a significant determinant of the child's adjustment, while of course the converse may also be true as the child's emotional state can similarly impact upon the parents. Other researchers have also shown that the nature of mothers' coping responses has a particularly significant impact on the way in which children cope with a stressful environment(Punamaki & Suleiman, 1990). In the case where parents are themselves experiencing personal problems and may thus be emotionally distant from the child, this may help exacerbate the negative consequences of the trauma (Van der Kolk, Penny & Herman, 1991).

The family remains the primary context within which child functions: traditional views of family therapy have always emphasized that any therapy aimed at a child must always take place in the context of the family or at least be mindful of the family system (for example Minuchin, 1974). This does not that one always has the luxury to work with the entire family system. It does however imply that any therapeutic intervention with a child must consider the specific family dynamics of which he/she is part.

4. IMPLICATIONS FOR THE RELATIONSHIP BETWEEN SCHOOL AND FAMILY

Exposure of a school system to a traumatic event may deeply influence the relationship between the school and the families of the children. In our case many parents directly or indirectly blamed the school for poor security measures, which may have placed their children at risk. Although these accusations proved to be unfounded, they may rather have been a reflection of the deep emotional distress experienced by parents following their children's traumatic event. Newberger, Geremy, Waterman and Newberger, (1993) strongly emphasize the fact that it is of primary importance to address the psychological distress of the primary caregivers as a core competent of the treatment of the child. These feelings may however hinder the healing process as children may find themselves in the middle of conflict given they are dual members of both the school and family systems. Feeling torn between these two may place additional emotional demands upon the children. Leibowitz, et al. (1999) also emphasize the significance of the response of the parents upon the child's response to trauma.

In the aftermath of school violence the strongest emphasis may be on the children while the feelings and experiences of the teachers may take second place. This may lead to teachers resenting the families' aggressive feelings even more. Teachers' perceptions and role definitions as caregivers are also deeply affected by the trauma. They may question themselves as to whether or not they had acted responsibly or if they could have done more to protect the children from possible harm. In a situation where children have been hurt or died teachers may even experience a strong sense of survivor's guilt in addition to feeling that they had not done enough to protect the children. Feelings of guilt following a traumatic event, particularly where a perceived failure to protect others is involved, may prove extremely intense (Carson et al., 1996). It is important that teachers and families be allowed to communicate their respective feelings with one other so that a resolution may be reached that will allow the school to continue functioning effectively in future and give the children a feeling of safety. This process should be facilitated by the counselor/therapist.

RELATIONSHIP TO THE SBFC MODEL

It is particularly after a school has been exposed to trauma that the importance of viewing a school as a complex system made up of interlinking subsystems becomes apparent. This case study highlights the fact that any work with children must incorporate the family system as well as taking into consideration the relationship between school and family. Any trauma intervention done in isolation without an acknowledgment of the mutual influences of family, school and community will fail to be fully beneficial to the client(s). In this respect the findings associated with this case study support the theoretical premises of the School-Based Family Counseling model.

SUMMARY

In this chapter I have tried to illustrate certain guidelines, which hopefully will help other counselors/therapists who may have to work with a school system following a traumatic event. I have tried to base my argument mainly upon the personal experience gained via the case study as well as other theoretical perspectives.

Working with a community, which has been exposed to trauma is not easy for a counselor/therapist. We were fortunate that no one had been hurt in the particular case study analyzed as this would have made the intervention much more difficult. When working with trauma it remains essential to emphasize the strengths and resources of the client(s).

Finally the exposure to this specific community intervention allowed me to reflect on my role as a therapist and a trainer. As a therapist I began the intervention by thinking I knew more than the people I was working with (or for) and realized that the client has untapped resources and is the real expert in the therapeutic encounter. As a trainer I was humbled by my own students' creativity and strength as well as by the warmth and compassion they showed toward their clients.

Hopefully this experience will be of benefit to counselors working from a School-Based Family Counseling model.

REFERENCES

American Psychiatric Association (1994). *Diagnostic and statistical manual of mental disorders.* 4th edition, Washington, DC.

Anderson, H. & Goolishian H. A. (1992). The client is the expert: A not-knowing approach to therapy. In S. McNamee & K. Gergen (Eds.), *Social construction and the therapeutic process* (pp.25-39). Newbury Park, CA: sage Publications.

Beeld (11th May 1999). Wilde Skietgeval by Skool. Bevreesde kinders Wil Nou Nie Teruggaan Nie (Wild Shooting Incident at School. Terrified Children Do Not Want to Go Back)

Carson, R.C., Butcher, J.N., & Mineka, S. (1996). *Abnormal psychology and modern Life*. 10th edition, New York: HarperCollins College publishers.

Figley, C.R. (1998). Post-traumatic family therapy. In F.M. Ochberg (Ed.), *Post-traumatic therapy and victims of violence* (pp.83 – 109). New York: Brunner/Mazel.

Leibowitz, S., Mendelsohn, M., & Michelson, C. (1999). Child rape: Extending the therapeutic intervention to Include the mother-child dyad. *South African Journal of Psychology*, 29 (3): 103-108.

Lipovsky, J.A (1992). Assessment and treatment of post-traumatic stress disorder in child survivors of sexual assault. In D.W. Foy (Ed.). *Treating PSTD: Cognitive-behavioral strategies* (pp.127-164). New York: The Guilford Press.

McFarlane, A.C. (1994). Individual psychotherapy for post-traumatic stress disorder. *Psychiatric Clinics of Northern America*, 17:393-408.

Minuchin, S. (1974). *Families and family therapy*. Cambridge, MA: Harvard University Press.

Newberger, C.M., Geremy, I.M., Waterman, C.M., & Newberger, E.H. (1993). Mothers of sexually abused children: Trauma and repair in a longitudinal perspective. *American Journal of Orthopsychiatry*, 63: 92-102.

Ochberg, FM. (1991. Post-traumatic therapy. *Psychotherapy*, 28: 5-15.

Pelser, A., & de Kock, C. (2000). Violence in South Africa: A note on some trends in the 1990s. *Acta Criminologica*, 13(1): 80-93.

Punamaki, R. & Suleiman, R. (1990). Predictors and effectiveness of coping with political violence amongst Palestinian children. *British Journal of Social Psychology*, 29: 67-77.

Pynoos, R.S., & Eth, S. (1996). Witness to violence: The child interview. *Journal of the American Academy of Child Psychiatry*, 26:306-319.

Stallard, P. & Law, F. (1994). The psychological effects of trauma on children. *Children in Society*, 8: 89-97.

Terr, L.C. (1989). Treating psychic trauma in children: A preliminary discussion. *Journal of Traumatic Stress*, 2: 3-20.

Chapter 31
SI SE PUEDE: A SERVICE LEARNING
SCHOOL SUPPORT PROJECT

Nancy Iverson and Andrea Bass

OVERVIEW: *This chapter describes a School-Intervention approach to helping students deal with grief and loss issues.*

BACKGROUND

Loss creates uncertainty like no other. Children are especially vulnerable to the tremendous upheaval that the death of a loved one causes. From such basic questions as 'Where will I live?' and "Who will take me to school?' to grappling with conceptualizing the finality of death and exploring the meaning and purpose of life, children and families are called to reconfigure their daily lives and their relationships with one another in their homes and their communities in the face of bereavement. Unresolved childhood grief can set the stage for a lifetime of internal and external manifestations of emotional distress. Poor academic performance, difficulty concentrating and focusing, increased acting out behaviors, isolation and withdrawal, interpersonal difficulties, somatic complaints and post-traumatic stress disorder symptoms are some of the many grief responses bereaved students demonstrate. According to the National Alliance for Grieving Children, youth who are offered emotional support following a death are 20 times less likely to develop behavioral disorders that lead to aggressive and violent acts (Center For Disease Control, US). How can we best champion our schools in sustaining supportive communities to help youths, families, and staff navigate through the grieving process?

No one, not even a child, is immune to loss. The death of a family member or close friend will impact as many as 9 out of 10 youth by the time they finish school. An article in the 1/29/12 issue of the San Francisco Chronicle states that 1 in 6 students surveyed in seven San Francisco middle schools this year "experienced community violence, abuse, the death of a loved one, war or other traumatic event, putting them at risk for posttraumatic stress disorder or other trauma-related problems. On average five or six children in every classroom are challenged with mental, physical or emotional symptoms related to stressful events in their lives outside school, regardless of race, family income or neighborhood." ('Studying Trauma in Middle Schools," San Francisco Chronicle, January 29, 2012, p. C1-3.) Recognizing the inherent nature of loss in life, we are compelled to provide outreach, support, and intervention as early as possible to help children, within their families and communities, develop resources to assist them in meeting life's inevitable losses with grace and resilience.

Learning is the 'primary occupation' of every child. An article entitled 'School Health Services' in the March 2003 issue of Contemporary Pediatrics (Vol. 20, No. 3,p. 61) lists two of the eight components of a coordinated school health program as 'counseling, psychological, and social services' and 'family and community involvement." An optimal school setting would support the child and family living with illness and/or loss. For various reasons, many youth are not willing or able to make use of counseling centers or community clinics, and it is imperative that we reach out and provide support to them within their school environment.

In San Francisco, pediatrician Nancy Iverson developed, coordinated, and facilitated "Living with Illness/Living with Loss" program through the California Pacific Medical Center's Institute for Health and Healing from 1995-2008. This program for families living with life-threatening illness and loss centered around support groups held simultaneously, but independently, for parents and children.

The adult group focused on talking about illness in respect to feelings and family dynamics, with special attention on parenting and discussions about developmental aspects of children's experiences and perceptions about illness and death; the children's group included an activity or project relevant to feelings, illness, death, or relationship with family, friends, or medical staff.

For over a decade, we have seen the development and initial success of grief support groups within schools. In 2001, in response to the multiple--and often traumatic--losses faced by youth in the San Francisco Bay area, Hospice By the Bay began partnering with the San Francisco Unified School District to provide bereavement outreach and support in the public schools. Andrea Bass, their youth bereavement counselor, has coordinated and facilitated "Coping with Loss" groups for students in twelve middle and high schools as well as education and training for families, teachers, intern, and staff.

Incorporating expressive arts activities, each group helps promote the four tasks of grieving (William Worden: Grief Counseling and Grief Therapy). With the training of additional graduate school interns to facilitate groups, this program has continued to expand within the San Francisco school system.

The context of school-based family counseling provides a superb model for extending in-school programs to include parent and family support groups. During the Oxford Symposium in School-Based Family Counseling in August 2003, Iverson proposed the development of in-school programs, recommending school-based support services for families, counselors, and school staff (including non-faculty staff such as custodial and food services), incorporating concepts, experiences, and insights from of out-of-school family programs and in-school bereavement experiences.

Just as hospital-based program provided medical professionals with an introduction to and experience with family systems and support services for those living with illness and loss, a school-based program would provide learning opportunities and participation for school staff working with these children. As children who are living with illness or loss are identified in the school, their families would be contacted, and students and parents would be invited to join ongoing groups. A school-based family counselor would coordinate and facilitate the groups; counseling students and trainees and community- based therapists or interns would also serve as facilitators. For some children group work alone is not a sufficient resource, and, as has been the case at times in our hospital-based program, additional assistance such as individual therapy may be appropriate.

Teacher education and support would also be components of the program, not with the expectation that teachers would be expected to lead groups or do intensive counseling but to help classroom staff enhance competency in recognizing behaviors consistent with children's struggles with living with family illness and loss and to gain ease in communicating about these issues. Teachers and group staff would meet together for two to three sessions with a facilitator experienced in grief, loss, and group work to explore and deepen their own resources for healing. After these preliminary sessions, the counseling staff would work with children and parent groups in the school, using the pilot program as a model and making appropriate adaptations. Teachers would continue to meet with a facilitator on a monthly basis throughout the school year; cases would be presented and discussed in these meetings with an emphasis on cultivating understanding as to how illness and death within a family impacts a child's school life and performance and how to provide the most favorable school services to optimize the experience for all involved.

In the spring of 2004, Judy Scheffel, a doctoral student in the education program at the University of San Francisco (USF), responded to Iverson's proposal and offered to partner in a pilot program. Her contacts with schools involved in USF's school-based family counseling programs led to an invitation to meet in November 2004 with the teaching staff of EXCEL Academy, a San Francisco charter high school. Through a series of conversations a plan emerged for a pilot project. Although differing in some key points from Iverson's original proposal, a team agreed that the invitation to develop a support program at EXCEL Academy offered a place to start and accepted the invitation. SI SE PUEDE, a service learning class, evolved as a pilot program based on this proposal in 2005.

RELATIONSHIP TO THE SBFC MODEL

Disruption in the family system inevitably impacts a child's school performance. Bereavement creates havoc in the family unit. Schoolwork suffers; students, parents, and teachers doubt that academic performance will ever be restored. And yet, the topics of sickness, trauma, and death are often not 'safe' ones, and many parents, teachers, school counselors and other school staff feel poorly equipped to navigate conversations with youth through this terrain. "We also had to face teachers and classmates, who may have felt distinctly uncomfortable with death, not knowing how to talk about death in the classroom situation or on the school playground." (Gersie, Alida, 1991, Storymaking in Bereavement: Dragons Fight in the Meadow, p. 140). Children, parents, and teachers who have witnessed and accompanied others going through similar life events may have an easier time regaining and maintaining confidence about abilities and performance. Ways of incorporating components of the SFBC model include the following:

A) SCHOOL FOCUS

Teaching the topics of loss, death and the grieving process as part of the school curriculum each semester creates a foundation for a successful program. In classes and group counseling, students have opportunities to share their personal experiences with loss and grief and how they adapt to the many changes in their lives as a result of these losses. Classes with discussions regarding healthy coping skills, self-care and ways to support others who are mourning the loss of a loved one follow. Students are taught ways to identify and communicate their feelings and needs to peers and family members. Peer counseling training programs are another avenue for providing and receiving support and education within the school and larger community.

Teacher education and support must be fundamental components of a school-based support program, not with the expectation that teachers would be expected to lead groups or do intensive counseling but they would demonstrate enhanced competency in recognizing behaviors consistent with children's struggles with living with family illness and loss and to gain ease in communicating about these issues. When teachers and group leaders meet together with a facilitator experienced in grief, loss, and group work, they may explore and deepen their own resources for healing. By continuing to meet with a facilitator on a monthly basis throughout the school year; staff may present and discuss cases, with an emphasis on cultivating understanding as to how illness and death within a family impacts a child's school life and performance and how to provide the most favorable school services to optimize the experience for all involved. Artist residency programs in the schools allow community artists, writers, dancers, musicians and performers to inspire and empower youth through creative expressions of loss and grief.

B) PREVENTIVE FOCUS

As families and students learn stress management/ relaxation techniques, they increase their ability to deal with the anxiety that accompanies loss and change. As teachers, school staff and counselors benefit from education on the impact of loss, they become more skillful in being resources to interrupt the cycle of bereavement, dysfunction, and failure.

C) REMEDIAL FOCUS

As children who are living with illness or loss are identified in the school, their families are contacted, and students and parents are invited to join ongoing groups. A school-based family counselor coordinates and facilitates the groups; counseling students and trainees and community-based therapists or interns may also serve as facilitators. For some children group work alone is not a sufficient resource and additional assistance such as individual therapy may be appropriate.

D) FAMILY FOCUS

Integration of parents/guardians (and grandparents) through education and participation is essential. Parenting classes and PTA presentations provide information about developmental tasks and how child development is impacted by loss. Through pre and post "Coping with Loss" group questionnaires, caregivers have the opportunity to share information, concerns, and hopes regarding their child's functioning at home and in school. In parent support groups, adults may cultivate ease in talking with each other and with their children about challenges and feelings regarding illness and death. This program may also be helpful by providing information about community resources, including neighborhood clinics and organizations that offer couple and family therapy.

MULTICULTURAL COUNSELING CONSIDERATIONS

While feelings of sorrow are universally inherent within loss, cultural beliefs, traditions, and values inform people's expression of grief and their attempts to cope with it. It is important for us to be culturally sensitive and competent in interacting with grieving youth and their families. Editors Doka and Tucci state, "Every culture has norms that suggest what types of behaviors are acceptable as an expression of grief. In some cultures, intense emotional displays are considered appropriate; in others, stoicism is encouraged... Cultures also offer different methods for adapting to or coping with a loss, beginning with the rituals that surround dying and the immediate period after the death. Cultural norms may include the type of support traditionally given to the bereaved, the expectations placed on the bereaved, the understanding of grief prevalent in the culture, rituals to mark or recognize anniversaries or other milestones in the grieving process, and receptiveness to interventions such as counseling or support groups." (LIVING WITH GRIEF by the Hospice Foundation of America) School staff and families do best by exploring and meeting cultural expectations, beliefs and needs.

When discussing specific cultural beliefs and practices we must refrain from generalizations or stereotyping. Some examples of culturally specific perspectives on grief and bereavement, though, may be helpful as a starting point. A focus on individuality, glorification of youth, and aversion to death in US mainstream culture carries an implicit set of expectations related to grieving. People of other ethnicities and backgrounds, even though living in the US-- sometimes 2nd and 3rd generation-- hold different values and may not subscribe to similar assumptions. For example, African-American traditions concerning death draw from many cultures, ethnicities, and religious backgrounds. Friends and family of the deceased often gather at the home to offer support and share in the common grief. Music, songs and hymns may be played or sung at a wake followed by a shared meal among bereaved loved ones. In both Hispanic/Latin- American cultures and African- American cultures, grief is usually expressed with great emotion while stoic attitudes are more common among Asian-Americans and those with Northern European ancestry. In Muslim culture, it is permissible to cry and express grief over the death of a loved one; however extreme expressions of grief are discouraged. Funerals are seen as very important opportunities to grieve, pay respect to the deceased and express faith in God. Muslims often comfort the bereaved person by visiting them, strengthening their faith, offering them food and reciting the Qur'an. For many Latin- American families the concept of "taking care of our own" is very important; when a family member is ill or has died, the family's obligation is to take control of the situation. This sometimes means that the bereaved child may not be able to receive outside help such as counseling or a support group despite attempts to provide grief education and describe the benefits of a grief support group to parents or guardians.

As we offer our support to students and families, we are charged to consider the following: What emotions and behaviors are seen as normal grief responses? What are their families' beliefs about death? What type of ceremonies are performed before, during and after death? Who is expected and/or allowed to participate? Is grief expressed quietly and privately or loudly and publicly? Are people of different ages or genders expected to grieve differently? How long are family members expected to grieve and what new roles are family members expected to assume? What special days or dates will be significant for the bereaved family and what types of verbal or written condolences are considered appropriate?

Students who attend the San Francisco public schools are composed of many races, ethnicities and cultures including African-American, Latin- American, Native- American, Asian , Pacific Islander, Middle- Eastern, Caucasian, Christian, Jewish, Muslim, and Buddhist. Customs and traditions from each student's family and heritage are often shared and honored in the grief support groups they attend.

Spirituality predominates throughout much of the Mexican/Latin American culture where attachments endure following a death. A relationship between the living and the dead continues through prayer, visits to the grave, and holidays such as Dia de Los Muertos, in which it is believed that the spirits of deceased loved ones return to their family's homes to be greeted by their favorite foods and other special objects. Encountering the ghosts of departed loved ones is seen as a very natural part of this life, culture and belief system. The following vignette illustrates the ways in which a child's response to death is impacted by background and heritage:

> The Hospice By The Bay's "Coping With Loss Group" created altars for Day of the Dead (Dia de los Muertos), One of the group members, 14 year old Estella, spoke about her family's tradition of baking pan de muerto, "bread of the dead" on this occasion. As she shared the bread that her mother had baked the night before, she told a story: "About a year ago, my dead grandmother's ghost came back to visit our home. When I walked into our bathroom, I suddenly discovered her taking a shower there!" When asked if it was shocking to see her grandmother's spirit, Estella replied: " No! It was not a surprise at all for me to see her ghost. What was so shocking was seeing my grandmother NAKED!"

Working with grieving children and families carries a responsibility for us to be mindful of our own personal and cultural assumptions and biases, to understand and respect the beliefs and wishes of the family, and to involve family members in the process as much as possible. For example, while we might naturally encourage a grieving student to attend a loved one's funeral, this may, for them, be a time fraught with anxiety or confusion if they are reuniting with conflicting family members or anticipating that opposing gang members will be part of the gathering. We may learn that students will not do bereavement homework or take the writing or artwork they create in groups home to save if personal boundaries and privacy are not available within the culture of their family. We must also realize that certain races or cultures may have a mistrust of authority figures such as teachers and other school staff and are more likely to seek help from clergy or other religious institutions within their community. By having an awareness of various cultural and religious perspectives on death and mourning, our interventions will be appropriate and relevant to the cultural context of the children and families being served.

PROCEDURE

Any program developed within a school must fit within the framework of that system's regulations: find out what they are. In the San Francisco school district, a mandatory orientation, Memorandum of Understanding, Site Agreement, background security check and Live Scan fingerprinting must be completed and filed with the district before a group through an organization such as Hospice By The Bay can be offered at any public school. It may several months to receive district approval, so it is wise to plan ahead.

Whether through contacts with schools already involved in a school- based family counseling program or through a community organization such as hospice, initial communication must include the Principal and counseling staff. Explore with them the relevance of a grief support group in their school. Have many of their students have suffered losses? What about a need for an anticipatory grief support group for students with terminally ill family members? Describe the structure, goals and benefits of a program. If you have a curriculum for each session, offer to share this with school staff. Describe proposed in-service presentations on helping school staff to recognize behaviors of students impacted by loss and to support grieving students and families.

Promote avenues of student referrals. Provide guidelines contextualizing loss and students' emotional, physical, cognitive, behavioral, spiritual and relational responses so that appropriate referrals may be made by teachers, counselors, ancillary staff, parents, or guardians. You may invite students to learn about the program and self-refer through brief classroom sessions introducing loss-related topics and the support program and/or through flyers, preferably designed by students.

Before including a student in your program, request that a designated school staff member, usually a counselor, teacher, or student advisor, call the child's parent or guardian, describe what will be offered and possible benefits for the child and family and obtain verbal permission for their child to be interviewed. When a student is selected for participation, provide a packet of information to that student to bring home to their parent or guardian, contents of which include a letter describing the program, a parental consent form permitting the child to participate, and a pre and post questionnaire to evaluate the experience. No student will be allowed to participate without a signed parental consent form.

By conducting individual student interviews, counselors may help to determine appropriateness for program participation and begin establishing rapport. Assessing responses to the following questions helps guide group member selection:

> Has a friend or someone in your family died?
> Was the death expected or sudden?
> When and how did it happen?
> What other losses have happened for you?

Additional questions for the counselor to consider include:

> Is the student able to talk about the loss and share personal feelings?
> Is it too soon after the loss for a student to enter a group?
> How likely is it for this child that listening to others share their stories of loss
> and grief will trigger feelings of overwhelm?
> Does this child show sufficient coping skills?
> Would this student benefit from individual counseling prior to joining a group?
> Will this student be too disruptive?
> Does the child's attendance record suggest ability to attend group consistently?
> What would the student's comfort level be if a group is unbalanced in relation to age,
> > race, or gender?
> Will this child's family be supportive of their participation in group?

PROGRAM DESCRIPTION: SI SE PUEDE

In their 2005 pilot program, Iverson and Scheffel offered SI SE PUEDE, a 'service learning class' elective for high school sophomores. Meeting on Thursday afternoons for an hour and twenty-five minutes, every Thursday (except two falling in school break weeks) during the second semester of the 2004-2005 school year (January 27-June 9), Scheffel and Iverson conducted these sessions. As neither of them was credentialed as a high school teacher, AC, an EXCEL faculty member, agreed to be present in the classroom throughout the term, as would the student services coordinator, JL. Integral to the experience would be the service learning project; we discussed that this could be a community workshop about loss for families which the students would organize and conduct.

In December 2004, in ten-minute sessions in each classroom (six classrooms in all), Iverson and Scheffel introduced themselves, led a brief discussion about loss, and invited interested students to participate in designing this pilot program. Several students, a teacher, and the student services coordinator (JL) joined us. During this meeting the students chose the name for the class; Si Se Puede!

(Yes, you can!) We suggested that the teens develop questions for which this could be the response, such as:

> Can I ever have a good day again after my mom died?
> Can I help a friend who is upset because his parents got divorced?
> Can I know what to say to my friend who has to move to another city?
> Can I survive my dad having cancer?
> Can I get my parents to understand how I feel when they're fighting over what happens to me when they split up?
> Can I ever 'get over' being so mad about being robbed?

The students agreed to coordinate activities with JL to inform classmates about SI SE PUEDE and to invite them to participate.

An alternative to enlisting student participation in a bereavement program is to work from an established curriculum. In that case, a counselor would tell students:

"A support group for students who have lost a loved one will be starting at your school on this date during this class period. We will meet for 8 weeks once a week. Everyone in the group has experienced the loss of a loved one; many have lost more than one person. We have offered these groups in different schools in your city and many students have found it to be very helpful to be with other students who have lost a loved one, like yourself. Although there is not a wrong or right way to grieve and we all move through the grieving process in our own unique way, you will probably find that the other students in your group are able to really understand what you are going through because they have also experienced loss and have had similar feelings as you. Each meeting will have a different topic such as the ways we grieve, memories, changes in ourselves and our families as a result of the loss, how different cultures grieve including beliefs about death and afterlife, and healthy ways we can cope with loss and change. We will also be doing different creative activities in each group such as drawing, painting, collage, writing and movement as a way to express feelings that may be hard to put into words. Do you think you might be interested in joining this group?"

As with the hospital-based support groups Iverson coordinated, she designed SI SE PUEDE's weekly meetings to create a safe, supportive environment for students to explore and develop ease in communicating about their feelings and experiences with living with loss. Inherent to these groups would be the tenets of safety, confidentiality, no advice-giving, listening, and caring. Anticipating that loss issues related to family illness or death may be too confining for the students' experience, we broadened our conversations about loss to include issues such as divorce, moving, school transitions, and theft.

They defined their objectives:
Students will

Learn a vocabulary of grief and loss terms
Recognize the universal nature of loss and grief
Learn to recognize loss feelings
Learn to recognize loss behaviors
Learn to identify the style and patterns in which they respond to loss
Learn common ways people avoid grieving
Develop verbal skills for discussing loss and grief
Learn cultural differences and similarities in responding to loss
Identify loss communication and behavior styles within their families of origin
Learn to identify the tools of grieving
Recognize the role of the arts in healing loss

Develop greater confidence in their ability to respond to the losses of others
Learn to develop greater personal compassion
Learn to find and accept peer support in the process of grieving

They established the 'rules':
Confidentiality
No advice-giving
No judging
Respectful listening
No interrupting
They initiated each session with a review of these guidelines.

Iverson chose *Tuesdays with Morrie*, by Mitch Albon, as the 'core text', intending to follow Morrie's story together as a class and to explore key themes regarding loss as they evolved in the book. Iverson and Scheffel experimented with several formats in the first few meetings and developed a framework for each session. Following a check-in and discussion of the 'rules', the group read from *Tuesdays with Morrie*—initially entire chapters but then excerpts that Iverson selected for each week. Choosing a theme relevant to the reading (such as 'Community', 'Regrets', or 'Meaning'), they directed an activity, most commonly an art or writing project. One afternoon, starting with Morrie's question, "Why is everyone so afraid to talk about dying?" students and adults did a ten-minute free-write, followed by participants sharing their writing and joining in a group discussion. In another session, after reading the chapter "We Say Goodbye," some students chose to write goodbye letters---either to someone to whom they wished to express farewell wishes or what they would like their own 'goodbye' to say. During that project, one teen suggested writing goodbye letters to one another the last day of SI SE PUEDE, voicing her recognition and sadness that the group would not be together again after that day; the team incorporated this into the final class activity.

Within the first few weeks of SI SE PUEDE, Iverson and Sheffel realized they did not have the necessary school organization and support to develop a community workshop as the service learning project. Through facilitated discussion in SI SE PUEDE's classroom sessions, the students reached a consensus; they chose to focus on helping other teens in their grieving process by creating a booklet and film in which they told their stories and shared from their experience in this program. Working with a volunteer cameraman, the group devoted two class sessions to filming and compiling materials for their booklet. Each student, Iverson, Sheffel, and AC received a copy of the completed (unedited) DVD and the booklet at the end of the term, and the students agreed that their materials could be provided as a resource to schools, hospitals, and other settings in which teens are exploring loss issues.

The following outline was used for both the book and the film:

INTRODUCTIONS

    Our Class
    Our Loss Histories

WHAT WE'VE LEARNED

    From the class
        From each other
        From *Tuesdays with Morrie*
    Outside the class

    Class Themes

What, who helps
What, who doesn't help
Feelings
Regrets
Family
Friends
Community
Crying
Fear
Meaning
Dying
Customs
Love
Saying goodbye
Memories

IDEAS FOR OTHER TEENS EXPERIENCING LOSS

PROGRAM DESCRIPTION: EIGHT WEEK LOSS CURRICULUM

In her programs with the San Francisco schools, Bass offered an eight week curriculum with the following format:

Group I: Introductions: Group starts with warm-up activity. Participants recognize what they share in common, ranging from favorite hobbies or food to losing a parent, sibling , relative or friend. Give pre-group questionnaires to each student to fill out. Review group rules/guidelines. Each student shares their name, grade, what they hope to gain from being in group, and a brief history of who died and when and how they died. Give each child a journal and drawing materials for decorating its cover and encourage writing any thoughts, feelings, or memories that they have about their loved one(s). Request that students bring a photo of their deceased loved one to the next group.

Group II: Memories: After brief check-ins by group members, give students cardboard or cigar boxes to decorate with paint and various materials. Invite the students to glue photos of their loved one outside or inside the box and to write memories or qualities of their loved one on different strips of paper to be placed inside box along with special objects that belonged to or remind them of their loved ones. Group sharing of boxes and memories follows along with time for writing in journals. Alternatives: memory bowls or altars.

Group III: The Grieving Process: Begin group with a discussion about the different ways that grief manifests in terms of emotions, thoughts, physical responses, and behaviors. Encourage each student to share and write on hanging poster board, first about an emotion they felt following the death of their loved one and then about other responses to loss such as "tired, want to be alone, loss of appetite, fighting more, difficulty concentrating," etc. Additional activities may include drawing or writing about inner and outer self in relation to grieving process, drawing or tracing a body outline of body and where one experiences different emotions, and mapping a personal grief journey.

Group IV: Coping Skills: Part I: Follow a review of the previous week's discussion with an exploration of coping skills as described in a list given to students. Ask students to circle healthy and unhealthy coping skills they have utilized when faced with painful emotions or other challenges such as "talk to someone I trust, write, listen to music, take a walk, drugs or alcohol, fighting, isolating", as well as other coping skills not listed. Group sharing and discussion follows. Journal writing concludes group.

Group V: Coping Skills: Part II: Begin session with "Pass Around Drawing" activity in which students write and draw a particular challenge with which they are struggling related to their loss. As the drawings are passed around the group, each student may write suggestions in response. When each student has their own drawing, with feedback, returned to them, invite them to share their responses to suggestions. Depending upon content of sharing, teach and practice with the group one of the following coping skills: relaxation techniques, mindfulness training, anger management or non-violent communication skills.

Group VI: Adjusting to Change: Give each student a large sheet of paper divided into three sections: Where I Was, Where I Am Now, and Where I Want To Be. Ask them to draw and write about what they, their families, and their lives were like before their loss, how they see themselves and their lives since their loss, and what their hopes and goals are for their future in the corresponding sections. Facilitate the group in the sharing of drawings and discussion.

Group VII: Imaginary Journey With Loved One: Facilitate a guided visualization by inviting students to imagine themselves walking down a path leading to a safe and protected meadow where they are able to reunite with their loved one(s) who have died. Offer them an opportunity to communicate important things to their loved one(s) and to ask any questions they desire. Suggest that their loved one tells them something very important to remember during difficult times. Invite them to ask their loved ones whether they would be willing to return to this special place to meet with them again and then to acknowledge appreciations and goodbyes, and guide students back into the group. Encourage them to write and draw about their experiences, including the important guidance they received from their loved one. Group sharing of drawings follows. If time allows, discussion about cross-cultural beliefs about death and the afterlife concludes group. Ask group members whether they would like to have a goodbye party with refreshments for the final group.

Group VIII: Goodbyes: Give students a post-group questionnaire to complete. During a snack time, review group learning and experiences and ask each student to reflect what he/she gained from attending group. Students and facilitator write appreciations to each student in goodbye cards that each participant keeps. Conduct a closing ritual which includes a group reading of a poem honoring loved ones who have died.

EVIDENCE-BASED SUPPORT

Although no formal evaluation process was implemented for Si Se Puede, Iverson did document her own observations. Despite the many challenges that emerged during the term, she rated this project as a successful pilot program, commenting after the first session, "I was so impressed with their presence and their willingness to participate." After another session she wrote, "It really was amazing. I suggested they talk from either things that they noticed in the story or from their own family or personal experience. B started by saying he didn't want to share anything personal, and by the end of the hour he had shared so much. It seemed like they had all really listened to TUESDAYS—and there was lots of good material in that to 'prime the pump'."   As losses occurred during the semester, several teens brought photos, obituaries, and news clippings from home to share with our group. One student commented several times throughout the term, "I'm so glad we have this class. It really lets you open your mind. And you can say stuff knowin' everyone isn't gonna go messin' with your stuff."

Iverson recommends significant alterations in planning, staffing, and resources for future programs, but ultimately what matters most is the students' experience, and she had no doubt that their participation in SI SE PUEDE, with all its limitations, provided an invaluable opportunity for these teens to cultivate their abilities to heal loss. This is reflected in her notes prior to our last session: "Their active participation and sharing has consistently been so rich in each session, and they have developed such a cohesion as a group and have gone to some pretty profound places in their writings, drawings, and discussions---their active participation, especially considering the makeup of the class and the uncharted territory we're all navigating with this, has been extraordinary. I don't get the sense that any of them, even the students who first seemed very detached from the group, are just showing up because they have to; each student seems very engaged. It feels like very precious time and an experience they may not get soon again in their family or friendship circles, and, in a way, this experience may have to last them a lifetime----or at least part of it."

CHALLENGES AND SOLUTIONS

Both rich rewards and notable challenges are integral to the inclusion of grief support programs within the school. Some of the difficulties may be inherent to a specific institution and others more universal.

RELATIONSHIP WITH SCHOOL STAFF

School staff, especially teachers, often play a key factor in student participation. The more they understand the importance of bereavement support, the more they will be able to encourage their students generally and in consistent participation in a grief program. Although educating teachers, principals, counselors, and other school staff about the purpose, content, and structure of bereavement programs is essential, time and workload constraints may not allow for this. Both prior to the start of the SI SE PUEUE sessions and throughout the semester Iverson and Scheffel did not have sufficient communication with school staff to develop clarity regarding class plans and structure, expectations, and evaluations for student participation. This added confusion and frustration to many of the conversations, especially in the first two months of the term.

Consistent communication with school staff and counselors throughout the program duration is important but may be difficult to achieve. In the hospital support groups Iverson had coordinated for families living with illness and loss, she or another member of the facilitator staff communicated between sessions with group members; this provided the team with updates regarding significant events for families and of special concerns that may need addressing. SI SE PUEDE included no avenue for this. Not only was the counseling intern not present in the classroom but also she was not accessible by phone or email, and Iverson and Scheffel had no opportunities to discover or recognize shared concerns. For a few weeks AC was available for a pre-meeting thirty minutes before each class; his schedule changed and, aside from occasional emails, he was unavailable for updates. Bass' experience
has been that whether through unexpected absence, other duties such as crisis intervention, or required meeting attendance, counselors have not always been able to be available for assistance or the usual exchange of information. Communication and consistency falter when counselors are assigned to different schools each year.

Iverson and Scheffel also encountered challenges in that the format of Si Se Puede, designed for student participation only, did not allow inclusion of staff education and support as components of the program. AC, the assigned teacher, did not have a specialized background and/or training in grief and loss and group work. He did acknowledge that his experience with Si Se Puede contributed to his deeper understanding of the impact loss has on a child's school life, and he was able to explore and deepen his own resources for healing. Although extending this learning to the entire school community--including, in addition to teachers, staff such as custodians, cooks, and aids--would help optimize the cultivation of healthy and helpful school services and environments, this remained a deficit in the SI SE PUEDE project. Training and then relying on the school's counselors and interns to conduct these programs would ease burdens for individual teachers while broadening the base of support for students and staff. Students and educators face enormous pressures regarding academic performance, and In a format such as Bass uses, with groups being held during class time, teachers may be very resistant to students' missing one and/or successive classes and may withhold permission for a student to attend a particular group because of testing, low grades, field trip, an important project, etc. Meeting this challenge with flexibility is helpful, and, when possible, Bass has scheduled groups to meet in alternating periods---e.g.1st period in the 1st, 3rd, 5th, and 7th sessions and 2nd period in the others.

Ongoing and post-program evaluation by faculty may be nonexistent due to the extreme demands already inherent for educators. During the first two years in which grief groups were offered at a San Francisco middle school, teachers and counselors were provided a pre and post-group questionnaire regarding their students' group participation; no one turned in a written response.

SCHEDULING CONSIDERATIONS

Scheduling considerations offer additional challenges. The choice of time to hold sessions is of paramount importance. Bass found that scheduling a group during lunch period when students would prefer to socialize with peers resulted in poor attendance. Transition time between classes is essential, both to allow students to get from one class to another and to 'regroup' from what may be an intense emotional sojourn back into the more usual classroom situations. SI SE PUEDE met during the last period of the day, so students did not face an abrupt transition between grief work and regular classroom activities. Often a school schedule mandates a maximum session time 50-60 minutes. If students are late arriving, even less time is available for group. Integrating latecomers into group poses challenges as well.

ATTENDANCE

Group cohesiveness and stability is compromised when students are frequently absent, truant, suspended or discontinue mid-way through group. Iverson and Scheffel noted that all SI SE PUEDE students were never present in any single session throughout the term—usually two to three were absent, and one student was suspended from school during this term. Staff reported this is as representative of the general attendance habits of the students. The abrupt discontinuance of a student's participation, whether due to parental wishes, family relocation, school suspension, or other causes forfeits the opportunity for goodbyes and closure for that child and for the group.

PHYSICAL ENVIRONMENT

Finding any classroom for a group to meet regularly each week is problematic in many overcrowded schools, and securing one that fills the prerequisites of being consistently available, quiet, clean, well-lit, warm, ventilated, private, and furnished with a large table and chairs for art projects heightens the challenge. EXCEL Academy used space carved out of another high school, and not only were classrooms often noisy or uncomfortable but also Iverson and Scheffel encountered frequent inconsistencies in classroom location and availability. Some afternoons a nonparticipating teacher was in the room doing computer or paper work. (As the students gained familiarity and confidence with the group and the guidelines, they took the lead in maintaining privacy for the group and politely requesting that uninvolved people leave the room.)

One must also be prepared for the many inevitable disruptions that can occur in a school environment such as intercom announcements, fire drills, last-minute schedule changes such as an assembly or shortened class period, other students knocking on doors during a session, and raucous or disruptive hallway conversations. If the group meets in a multi-use classroom, the space may only be available for exactly the length of the class period, with no extra set-up or clean-up time allotted. Sessions may have to end prematurely to allow sufficient time to rearrange tables and chairs into the usual classroom setting.

RESOURCES

With school underfunding and cutbacks, personnel resources are often stretched to limit and do not match the needs for a grief program. Although conversations had started with EXCEL based on participation in USF's counseling program, the intern's available hours did not match with the classroom schedule; Iverson and Scheffel had no counselor presence throughout the SI SE PUEDE project. JS, the student services coordinator with whom they had had all initial conversations and whom they understood would be present and participating throughout all the classes and the service learning project, could not reconfigure her schedule and did not attend any of the sessions. And, AC, whose presence in the group developed into a 'perfect fit', was a part of SI SE PUEDE, not because of special interest or training but somewhat randomly based on scheduling logistics and the principal's assignment.

Iverson and Scheffel had planned to co-facilitate each session, but an unforeseen change in Scheffel's schedule in February left her unavailable for almost all Thursdays except those for which Iverson was scheduled to be out of town. Iverson's subsequent increased workload and the need for AC to accept added responsibilities added to the challenge of this experience. Although initial plans for SI SE PUEDE specified a student-run workshop for their families as the service learning component of the course, sufficient resources in terms of meeting space, advance planning and promotion, and staffing did not materialize, and the program was unable to fulfill the service learning goal. More often than not, resources such as art supplies, books, and journals are not available through the schools. The persons running the programs must both arrange for or personally donate such supplies and transport the materials to the classroom. In a densely populated area such as San Francisco, parking difficulties in some neighborhoods add to the challenges for team leaders, especially when they must transport all their own teaching and project materials to and from each session.

FAMILY/COMMUNITY INVOLVEMENT

The lack of family and school community involvement in SI SE PUEDE demonstrates a great gap between the original proposal and this pilot program. Conducting the sessions as a class rather than as support groups resulted in the exclusion of family members and a missed opportunity to explore and deepen grieving processes collectively within the home. As resources did not permit running a family workshop, parental involvement could not materialize in that format.

In the hospice program with which Bass participates, parent participation has been encouraged through pre and post-group questionnaires that they are asked to complete regarding their child's functioning at home and school. During the past four years, approximately 25%-50% of the designated parents have not responded. Of those who did respond, most shared their concerns about their child and hopes regarding group participation. The hospice-based projects do not include any accompanying parent/guardian group programs.

Documented parental consent is mandatory for student grief group participation. Although the group team sends home packets that include the pre and post questionnaires and consent form along with a stamped self- addressed envelope, many parents do not fill out and return the forms, resulting in exclusion of their child from the program. Parents' failure to return evaluation forms hampers ability to evaluate the impact of participating in bereavement support.

SUMMARY

The theme of grief is relevant to children and adolescents. Within SI SE PUEDE's first round of introductions, five of the six students identified a family death as a loss issue; two spoke of recent parental death. During the next month, two more students joined our group, one of whom related a recent sibling death. Although bereavement was clearly an agenda among the class members, we also encouraged identifying their broader experiences with loss.

Clearly an urgent need calls us to provide crisis intervention, emotional support, education, and collaboration with community resources for students and their families. Since most of today's youth in mainstream cultures spend the majority of their time in school and often are not willing or able to make use of counseling centers or community clinics for various reasons, we must reach out and provide support to them within their school environment. In-school bereavement programs offered to the many students facing ongoing loss and trauma in their daily lives have enabled them to learn about grief and loss, find a safe place among peers to share feelings and concerns about their losses, provide support to each other, and develop healthier coping skills. As children have developed to demonstrate greater compassion, empathy and appreciation for life and each other, they have discovered commonalities in their journeys through grief and have learned to accept and transcend racial, ethnic, cultural, religious and class differences.

Many children, parents, and facilitators have touched one another's lives through their involvement in support groups. Programs differ as to group members, facilitators, structure and intention and, like living organisms, transition at certain stages in their growth and development. As we learn and adapt through our experiences with illness, loss, and support services for those encountering these life situations, we can continue to explore ways to cultivate new visions and enhance existing services.

The poet J. B. Yeats says: "We should not make light of the troubles of children. They are worse than ours, because we can see the end of our trouble and they can never see any end." (Yeats, W.B., 1955, Reveries over Childhood and Youth, p. 5) Although we may wish that all children will only have 'small' troubles, many children will experience personally or through a family member the tremendous challenge of living with a life-limiting illness or loss. We cannot prevent the enormous demands for these children and their families but we can help guide them through their troubles and ease their pain and ours by exploring ways to connect, share our stories, cultivate our resources, build and sustain community, and promote healing. As we reflect on and learn from SI SE PUEDE and other pioneer programs, we can continue to seek ways to enhance existing services, cultivate new resources, and explore new horizons within our schools. We can build programs that leave us saying, as Iverson wrote after one class: "Class summary today: WOW!!! That was our exclamation to each other at the end today, and it was a shared, mutual, eye-sparkling heartfelt WOW!!"

RESOURCES

Albom, M. (1997). *Tuesdays with Morrie.* New York:Doubleday.

Barron, T.A. (2000). *Where is grandpa?* New York: Philomel Books.

Brown, L. K. & Marc, . (1996) *When dinosaurs die: A guide to understanding death.* New York: Little, Brown and Company.

Byrock, I. (1997). *Dying well: The prospect for growth at the end of life.* New York: Riverhead Books, New

York.

Children from the Center for Attitudinal Healing. (1991). *Advice to doctors and other big people.* Berkeley, California: Celestial Arts Publishing .

Children from the Center for Attitudinal Healing. (1978). *There is a rainbow behind every dark cloud.* Berkeley, California: Celestial Arts Publishing.

Children Who Have Brothers and Sisters with a Life-Threatening Illness. (1982). *Straight from the siblings: Another look at the rainbow.* Berkeley, California: Celestial Arts Publishing.

Christ, G. H. (2000).*Healing children's grief: Surviving a parent's death from cancer.* Oxford: Oxford University Press.

Curtis, J. L.(1998). *Today I feel silly and other moods that make my day.* Joanna Cotler Books.

Davies, B. (1999). *Shadows in the sun.* Philadelphia: Taylor and Francis.

Death and dying: San Francisco medicine. (2002). *Journal of the San Francisco Medical Society*, Vol. 75, No. 8, October.

DeVita-Raeburn, E. (2004). *The empty room: Surviving the loss of a brother or sister at any age*. New York: Scribner.

Didion, J. (2005). *The year of magical thinking*. New York: Alfred A. Knopf.

Dower, L. (2001). *I will remember you: What to do when someone you love dies: A guidebook through grief for teens*. New York: Scholastic Inc.

Fadiman, A. (1997). *The Spirit catches you and you fall down*. New York: Farrar Strauss and Giroux.

Fawzy, F. I., et al, (1993). Malignant melanoma: Effects of an early structured intervention, coping, and affective state on recurrence and survival six years later. *Archives of General Psychiatry, 50*, September: 681-689.

Fitzgerald, H. (2000). *The grieving teen: A guide for teenagers and their friends*. New York: Fireside Books, Simon and Schuster.

Fitzgerald, H.(2000). *Grief at school: Resource manual*. Washington, DC: American Hospice Foundation .

Gersie, A. (1991). *Storymaking in bereavement: Dragons fight in the meadow*. London: Jessica Kingsley Publishers.

Harper, B. C. (1977). *Death: The coping mechanism of the health professional*. Greenville, South Carolina: Southeastern University Press, Inc.,

Heegaard, M. (1991). *When someone has a very serious illness: Children can learn to cope with loss and change.* Minneapolis: Woodland Press.

Heegaard, M., *When someone very special dies: Children can learn to cope with grief*. Woodland Press, Minneapolis, 1988.

Hospice of Lancaster County (1995). *A Teacher's Guide to the Grieving Student: Guidelines and Suggestions for School Personnel Grades K-12*. Hospice of Lancaster County, Pennsylvania, 1995.

Kubler-Ross, Elisabeth (1978). *To Live Until We Say Good-Bye*. Prentice-Hall, Inc., Englewood Cliffs, New Jersey.

Krementz, Jill (1988). *How It Feels When A Parent Dies* New York: Alfred A. Knopf.

Lear, Martha Weinman (1980). *Heartsounds*. New York: Simon and Schuster.

Levine, Stephen (1982). *Who Dies?* New York: Anchor Press.

Miller, Suki and Ober, Doris (1999). *Finding hope when a child dies: What other cultures can teach us*. New York: Simon and Schuster.

Numeroff, Laura, and Harpham, Wendy S. (1999). The hope tree: Kids talk about breast cancer. New York: Simon and Schuster.

Picoult, Jodi (2005*). My sister's keeper*. New York: Washington Square Press.

Ornish, Dean (1997). Love and survival: The scientific basis for the healing power of intimacy. New York:
     HarperCollins Publishers.

O'Toole, Donna (1995*). Facing change: Falling apart and coming together again in the teen years*. Burnsville, North Carolina: Compassion Press.

Pinkson, Tom Soloway (1998*). "Do they celebrate Christmas in Heaven?": Spiritual rite of passage teachings from children with life-threatening illness*. Woodacre, California: Wakan Press.

Pipher, Mary (1996). *The shelter of each other: Rebuilding our families.* New York: Ballantine Books.

Remen, Rachel Naomi (1996). *Kitchen table wisdom: Stories that heal*. New York: Riverhead Books.

Silverman, Phyllis Rolfe (2000). *Never too young to know: Death in children's lives.* Oxford: Oxford University Press.

Sourkes, Barbara M. (1995). Armfuls of time: The psychological experience of the child with a life-threatening Illness. Pittsburg: University of Pittsburgh Press.

Sourkes, Barbara M. (1982). The deepening shade: Psychologicalaspects of life-threatening Illness. Pittsburg: University of Pittsburgh Press.

Spiegel, David, Draemer, Helena C., Bloom, Joan R., and Gottheli,Ellen (1989). Effect of psychological treatment on survival of patients with metastatic breast cancer, *The Lancet*, October 14: 888-89.

The Dougy Center (2004). *Waving goodbye: An activities manual*. Portland, Oregon: The National Center for Grieving Children and Families.

Traisman, Enid S. (1992). *Fire in my heart, ice in my veins*. Omaha, Nebraska: Centering Corporation

Varley, Susan (1984). *Badger's parting gifts*. New York: Lothrup, Lee and Shepard Books.

Viorst, Judith (1971). *The tenth good thing about Barney*. New York: Simon and Schuster.

Willner-Pardo, Gina (1996*). Hunting grandma's treasures*. New York: Clarion Books.

Worden, William (2001). *Grief counseling and grief therapy: A handbook for the mental health practitioner*. New York: Springer.

Chapter 32
Crisis Intervention on Campus:
A School-Based Family Counseling Approach

Christopher Trailer Jr.

OVERVIEW: This chapter discusses three crises that took place in a school-based setting. One involved the murder of a grade 4 student during the same week as the 9/11 World Trade Center terrorist attack. Another involved the sudden death of a beloved classroom teacher and the other a suspected kidnapping. In all three crises I was the clinical supervisor for the SBFC trainees and interns who made the crisis interventions in the schools.

CRISIS #1: THE MURDER OF A GRADE 4 STUDENT

BACKGROUND

A grade 4 student in a school participating in a SBFC outreach program was murdered by her father.

PRESENTING ISSUES

There were four presenting issues: 1) the clinical supervisor must mobilize a group of SBFC trainees he is about to meet for the first time to 2) provide crisis intervention at an elementary school (K-8); 3) the supervision group has two trainees from New York, one of whom has a brother who works in one of the World Trade Center towers; and 4) I will be activated by the American Red Cross Disaster Mental Health Team to provide critical incident debriefing at the San Francisco International Airport.

CLINICAL OBJECTIVES

The clinical objectives in the first crisis are: 1) to minimize and arrest the psychological fallout from the attack and deaths; 2) provide an opportunity for various segments of the school culture to express and defuse their feelings, against the backdrop of the country's national shock of the 9-11 terrorist attack; and 3) to provide school-based family counselors with a hands-on crisis intervention experience.

RELATIONSHIP TO THE SBFC MODEL

This event, while untimely and tragic, both on a local and national basis, provided a rich opportunity for SBFC counseling trainees to provide crucial therapeutic support to those in great need of their services. This first crisis will demonstrate a number of SBFC Model components: 1) School-Prevention with classroom meetings and support groups; 2) School Remedial with teacher consultation, group counseling and crisis intervention, as well as 3) Family Preventive with parent education; and 4) Family Remedial with parent consultation.

THE CRISIS INTERVENTION

On the morning of Tuesday, September 11, 2001 I met for the first time with my newly assigned school-based trainees for the academic year 2001-02. Over the weekend, I had been forewarned that the father of a 4th grade student at one of our Catholic schools killed the student, her mother and 3 siblings and then shot himself. That would have been enough, but there was "breaking news" reaching the west coast that terrorists had crashed two passenger airliners into each of the two World Trade Center towers in New York City. To complicate matters further, two of the new trainees were from New York and one of them had a brother who worked in one of the towers. Ordinarily, the first day of supervision would be for introductions, but this day was very different. I would have to process the thoughts and feelings of the new trainees and then mobilize a team of trainees to go to the school to assist faculty and staff to process the emotional fallout and grief from the murder/suicide as well as the 9/11 attack and deaths.

In addition, I was a member of the American Red Cross Disaster Mental Health Team and was about to be called out to provide crisis intervention work at the San Francisco International Airport to deal with yet unfolding developments stemming from United Air Lines Flight 93 (Newark to San Francisco) which crashed into a field nears Shanksville, Pennsylvania killing all aboard.

By the time the group met that Tuesday at 8:30am, most had gotten word of the attacks back east. I knew I would be called away to provide crisis intervention shortly, yet I had to welcome the new trainees, process their emotions (especially the two female students from New York), brief them on the murder/suicide which had occurred over the previous weekend and send them to the school to help school officials deal with the murdered child's classmates.

As I learned that two of the newly assigned trainees were from New York and that one was quite concerned about her brother, I knew I owed it to them to process their concerns and worries for family and friends back home. Having taken the time to process their concerns and advising them to call home, the trainee whose brother worked in the World Trade Center discovered her brother had called in sick that morning and was not there at the time of the attack. With that established the group as a whole took a collective sigh of relief and turned their attention to a briefing on "crisis intervention".

Having been trained in the Jeffrey Mitchell method of crisis intervention and debriefing, I described the process of both large and small group debriefings and how in each the debriefer begins with "what happened?", "what did you see...hear" on a sensory level, then begins to probe deeper as to "what did you think?" and finally, "what did you feel?" The trainees had to be given a rudimentary understanding of the differences between "therapy" and "crisis intervention"; that there would be no history taking, other than to inquire about the murdered student and memories associated with her; and that while there might be need for further psychological support and therapy, it would not be provided by these trainees, but would be the result of referrals to other therapists in the community.

As part of the debriefing, and in considering the tender age of these youngsters, processing of memories they had of their murdered classmate would have to be probed delicately. Issues such as: had they had an argument or falling out with the murdered classmate recently; had they had plans to do something with her (e.g., an athletic event, birthday party, etc.) that was now no longer possible; and how were they dealing with how she died—murdered by her own father! It was a difficult lesson for children averaging between 9 and 10 years of age to grasp.

The faculty, especially those who had previously taught the student as well as her current teacher, would have to be given their own opportunity to deal with their feelings on a one-to-one basis.

Then there was the matter of the empty desk; what should be done with it? Should it be allowed to be a "shrine"? Should it be removed or a new student assigned to it? And, what about the parents of these children; what should they be told to do in helping their children? These were all questions and issues that would have to be anticipated in attempting to attend to the emotional fallout for school administrators, students and their parents.

By 9:45am, armed with this "quick and dirty" orientation to crisis intervention, a team of trainees were on their way to the school of the murdered child where a colleague supervisor would meet and direct their efforts. I was, as expected, told to report to the San Francisco International Airport to meet up with the other members of the American Red Cross Disaster Mental Health Team.

When the trainees arrived at the school, they were met by my colleague from the Center for Child and Family Development (also an SBFC supervisor) and the principal who briefed them on the student and her class and how the faculty seemed to be doing. The trainees then went to the classroom (School- Remedial: crisis intervention) where they first introduced themselves to the class then began a large group debriefing allowing the children to express their thoughts and feelings regarding the tragic news. Following that, they spread out in pairs of twos to the other classes to deal with the feelings of the other students who either knew the girl or her siblings and had their own thoughts and feelings about the murders. Along the way, students identified as having a "more difficult time" were allowed to meet individually with the trainees who were now becoming "grief counselors".

A parents' meeting was called for that night (Family-Intervention: Parent Consultation) and representatives of the USF Center provided a presentation on how to best deal with the emotional fallout of this tragic event on their children and this faith community. After all, the family was known in the community, they had been not only fellow parishioners, but neighbors and the parents of their children's playmates. Parents were encouraged to allow their children to ask questions and were advised they did not have to answer as much as listen (Family-Prevention: Parent Education). It was suggested that they answer their child's questions with questions, thereby processing the child's thoughts and feelings without advising them how they "should" feel.

Parents were also given the opportunity to express their own thoughts and feelings and given information as to the likely post-event symptoms and behaviors that could result, such things as sleep disorders, changes in appetite, increased irritability, difficulty concentrating, etc. These were not offered as *predictions*, but as *possibilities*, so that if they did occur parents would not be unduly concerned, but would simply attend to their child's distressed reactions.

COUNSELING OUTCOME

Although the shock to this faith community and school could not be entirely eliminated, the quick response of the USF Center trainees did provide the much needed psychological support to school administrators, faculty, students and their families in order to minimize the emotional and psychological fallout from this tragic event.

CRISIS #2: THE SUDDEN DEATH OF A BELOVED TEACHER

BACKGROUND

A beloved teacher had gone with her family on a cruise during the Easter break from one of our Catholic schools. On the eve of school resuming after the break, the SBFC trainee assigned to that school was called by the principal and informed of the sudden, tragic death of the teacher while on the cruise. The principal asked what should be done. The trainee contacted me and together we developed a plan of action in support of the school culture.

PRESENTING ISSUES

The Administration, faculty and student body of a Catholic school was about to return from Easter Break and learn that their beloved 5th grade teacher has suddenly died while on a cruise with her family. The principal, who was feeling the full effect of the loss, wasn't sure how to approach the loss and asked the trainee and supervisor for a consultation meeting the next morning.

CLINICAL OBJECTIVES

Clinical objectives include: 1) reassuring the principal; 2) consulting with the faculty; 3) providing the deceased teacher's class with a forum within which to express their feelings; 4) providing other students who have had this teacher in the past with a chance to express their feelings of loss; and 5) providing a forum for the school culture to express their sense of loss in order to give "license" to their process of bereavement.

RELATIONSHIP TO THE SBFC MODEL

In addressing the needs of this school culture at the time of mourning, the following components of the SBFC model were used: 1) School-Intervention with consultation with principal and faculty; 2) School-Intervention with crisis intervention; and 3) School-Prevention with classroom meetings.

THE CRISIS INTERVENTION

The trainee and supervisor reported to the school as requested well before the beginning of the school day in order to discuss and decide upon a plan of action for addressing the loss. It was decided that I would meet with the faculty along with the principal and trainee, both of whom are part of the culture and, therefore, affected by the loss. While the meeting was designed to provide an expression of grief, all recognized the fact that immediately following the meeting, the teachers will go to their respective classrooms to deal with their students' grief.

Just before going into session with the faculty, the trainee said to me, "Here's a picture of the teacher." To my amazement, I recognized her as a fellow-parishioner from my home parish and suddenly I wasn't so removed as I had been moments before. I said a few words regarding what the faculty can expect as part of their need to mourn, even as they carry out their roles as educators. Then the discussion turns to what they expect from their students and how they might address those expressions of loss and grief.

Several of the teachers, especially those who had worked with the deceased teacher spoke of how much they loved her and respected her dedication to the school and its students. Several also spoke about what an important role she had played in welcoming them to the faculty when they were new to the school and how she mentored them. Although we provided them with a time and place (in the school library) to express and briefly process their feelings, the principal, supervisor and trainee were all very aware they would be going out to the schoolyard momentarily to pick up their classes and begin the school day, so we turned their attention to what they were anticipating from their students and how they might best handle it.

Because this was a Catholic school, it provided both faculty and students with a learning opportunity, though difficult and sad in nature. It provided an opportunity to apply a faith dimension to what had taken place and brought to mind several lessons such as not to take Life for granted; we're not promised or guaranteed a certain number of years on the planet. It was also an opportunity to discuss the notion (on an age-appropriate basis) of the belief in Life-after-Death (a basis tenant of Christian faith). Then, the trainee and supervisor went with the principal to meet the 5th graders who were about to learn the fate of their teacher.

The principal brought the students in and they immediately sensed something was amiss. The principal broke the news to the class very sensitively and with compassion, but there was no way to prevent—nor was it our goal—to prevent their anguish and tears. The shock was apparent, after all "teachers don't die". Still, in time, they were able to share their favorite stories of their teacher and even laugh a bit. Later in the day, a letter went out to the parents from the principal, sharing the tragic news with them. In it, the principal offered some suggestions as to what parents might expect to see and hear from their children and ways to tend to their concerns.

CLINICAL OUTCOMES

This sad and unexpected event required a quick and caring response to the fallen teacher's colleagues and students as well as the school culture in general. Several things contributed to enabling a favorable outcome: 1) the principal was not "shy" or too proud to admit she wasn't sure how best to handle the situation (after all, she lost a good friend and colleague too); 2) the trainee got in touch immediately with his clinical supervisor, giving both some time in which to formulate a plan of action to submit to the principal; 3) the principal was provided with a variety of choices with which to address the students and faculty which empowered her and recognized her leadership role, yet provided her with a measure of support as well; 4) similarly, the faculty was recognized for their loss, even as they prepared to attend to their students' thoughts and feelings; and 5) even with minimal preparation and process, the action plan encouraged everyone to support one another in taking in their shared tragic loss, and be there for each other both in mourning and recovery. Though tragic, this event gave everyone a chance to find consolation and comfort in their religious beliefs.

CRISIS #3: THE KIDNAPPING OF A STUDENT

BACKGROUND

As in the preceding crisis, the SBFC trainee assigned to a Catholic school was contacted on the evening prior to school reconvening after an extended break; in this case the Christmas break. Word came from the principal that one of the school's students, an 8th grade female student, had been kidnapped. The principal was not sure how best to handle the situation and asked for support from the USF Center.

PRESENTING ISSUES

Kidnapping is among the worst fears of parents and educators and makes everyone feel vulnerable to the unknown stranger who violates every sense of human civility. This makes for a very charged atmosphere within any community and hysteria very often accompanies this kind of crisis. Rumors, conjecture, and fear inevitably runs rampant if not handled quickly and effectively. Authorities will tell you that the first hours are critically important and valuable in contributing to the maximum possibility of a positive outcome: the return of the kidnapped person.

CLINICAL OBJECTIVES

Clinical objectives in this event called for: 1) forming a quick response team to report to the school; 2) working with the principal who in turn was working with the family of the missing girl and police to try to best assess the facts in order to deal with the psychological upset of the school culture and greater community; 3) the team would need to work with the faculty in assuaging the concerns of students (K-8) on a developmentally appropriate cognitive level; 4) parents would need to be reassured about what school administrators were doing and that their child's school was still safe; 5) finding a way to prevent and minimize fear, anxiety, rumors and wild speculation that could promote hysteria.

RELATIONSHIP TO THE SBFC MODEL

In this crisis, the following SBFC components were implemented: 1) School-Intervention with consultation with teachers and crisis intervention; 2) School-Prevention with classroom meetings and support groups; 3) Family-Intervention with parent consultation; and 4) Family-Prevention with parent education.

THE CRISIS INTERVENTION

Following the initial call from the trainee to the clinical supervisor, the USF Center's telephone tree was activated to recruit as many SBFC trainees and interns as possible due to having to cover so many grade levels as soon as possible upon the team's arrival at the school. Fortunately a number of trainees and interns made themselves available for duty the next morning and met at the school at the agreed upon hour (prior to the commencement of the school day) in order to meet with the principal and the faculty to be briefed and to establish an action plan for classroom interventions.

The principal and faculty were very open and welcoming of the Center's trainees and interns and were introduced to those assigned to their classes. Following the briefing in which it was disclosed that there was some suspicion that an "older male" that had been obsessed with the missing girl might be involved as he was also "missing", the team spread out across the school to begin to process the students' feelings. Wherever possible the trainees/interns were sent out in two-person teams in order to support each other and deal with approximately 30 students per classroom.

Fanning out across the school, trainees and interns went into their assigned classrooms with the teachers and began to process how each grade was doing. A pattern that developed early was that the younger children, due to their capacity for "magical thinking" suffered from "magical fears" including that the "kidnapper" would come back and get them. Some of the younger students who had older siblings who were playmates of the missing girl and her younger sister (who was also a student at the school in the 7th grade) were afraid that the "kidnapper" would know where they lived and come back for them.

As trainees and interns reported back their findings and impressions from their classes, it became apparent that students were dealing with the crisis pretty much according to what was anticipated based on developmental expectations; the older the student, the less irrational their fears. What was a bit surprising and more than a bit disturbing was new information the trainees and interns were reporting back from the upper division grades. Classmates of the missing girl seemed to have the view that the girl was not "kidnapped" at all, but had run off with her older boyfriend and that she had been upset with her parents and their insistence in working her at the family restaurant.

By late morning, it was suggested by myself and approved of by the principal and faculty that a parents' meeting would be held that night in the school's auditorium. I agreed to be there with as many colleagues as were able to attend. It began to be increasingly clear that the rumors of the girl having run off with her older boyfriend was shared by a majority of the parents and that there were indications that the family of the missing girl was being judged rather harshly by other school parents. With this in mind, precautions as to rumor control and the potential for unkind or insensitive statements or accusations had to be anticipated and a plan as to how to deal with such eventualities needed to be in place whether the family of the missing girl was in attendance that night or not.

Part of the strategy surrounding the parents' meeting included that as teachers greeted parents of their respective students that they keep an ear out for any such negative or gossipy comments and try to squelch such remarks and speculation, instead asking parents to be more sympathetic to the parents of the missing girl being alarmed about their daughter being missing whatever the reason. That strategy was extremely effective in knocking down unkind and unnecessary speculation, not only about why the girl was missing, but also in not unfairly judging the family of the missing girl. In the course of the meeting that evening, the principal shared what was known and what was being done to sort through wide-ranging reports surrounding events leading up to the time the girl went missing. Other parents, adhering to the request to be "Christian" in sharing the sense of loss and confusion with the girl's family refrained from wild speculation and unhelpful gossip and participants left with a greater sense of camaraderie and communal concern as well as a reassurance that everything that could be done was being done.

CLINICAL OUTCOMES

The intervention for this particular crisis was successful due to: 1) the early request and notice by the principal to the trainee and her supervisor; 2) the openness to assistance from not only the principal, but faculty as well (welcoming trainees and interns into their classrooms); 3) consultation with and planning that incorporated the principal and her faculty; 4) having a satisfactory number of counselors to cover the age range of students K-8 on a developmentally appropriate basis; 5) the development of facts and impressions coming out of the classroom meetings that gave school administrators a more accurate picture of what had actually happened and an early warning of some negative and counter-productive attitudes toward the missing girl and her family. Success in this case could be seen in the school-culture of support at a time of uncertainty, the reassurance of parents and their children at an age-appropriate level, and the reminder to the community to be kind and supportive of one another, especially as members of a Catholic/Christian faith community.

SUMMARY

These three crises demonstrate what can be accomplished by SBFC trainees and interns with minimal administrative support during times of crisis in the schools. Although educators and school administrators as trained professionals are skilled in dealing with a wide variety of issues and problems that occur on school campuses, there are those times when they are also swept up in crisis that challenge even the best trained and well-prepared professionals due to their being part of the school-culture and therefore experience the fallout from tragic events affecting the school on a deeper level than those invited to come in to assist at such difficult times. Having a quick response team prepared to assist in such crisis events is good for both those in training and those in need and should be part of every SBFC professional's training.

Chapter 33
Group Intervention to Address the Emotional Aspects of Children with Learning Disorders and their Parents

Zipora Shechtman

OVERVIEW: This chapter focuses on children diagnosed with learning disabilities who struggle with learning difficulties as well as with social and emotional challenges. It also discusses the challenges their parents face in the process of parenting them. Group intervention is offered to help children and their parents cope more effectively with the disability and research is presented to support the evidence-base of such groups.

BACKGROUND

Children and adolescents diagnosed with learning disabilities face a wide array of difficulties, in academic, social, emotional, and behavioral aspects of everyday life. Specifically, the characteristics of these children include high levels of social rejection and loneliness (Estell et al., 2008), mood disturbance and depression (Sideridi, 2007), adjustment difficulties of both an internalizing and externalizing nature (Auerbach et al., 2008), and lower academic achievements then other children of their age (Leichtentritt& Shechtman, 2010).

For parents of children with LD, coping and caring for them pose continuing daily challenges: they experience higher stress levels compared to parents of children without LD (Shechtman & Gilat, 2005), express a sense of helplessness (Bandura et al., 1996), and feel more anxious and depressed (Al-Yagon, 2007). As a result, their parental functioning is impaired and becomes less efficient.

Academic difficulties of children with LD are the most recognized and therefore serve as the target of treatment. Children with LD are often tutored by expert in teaching, individually or in small groups, under the assumption that improved academic achievement will have a positive impact on children's self-esteem, improve interpersonal relationships and social status, and lead to fewer emotional difficulties (Morgan et al., 2008). Although the association between academic success and socio-emotional well-being is well known and widely documented (Baker et al., 2007; Durlak et al., 2011; Elias & Arnold, 2006), association does not point to causation, thus, one may look at it the other way around: addressing the socio-emotional difficulties of children with LD may improve their academic achievements. Such perception of the situation is still less common in the school. Moreover, when socio-emotional difficulties are addressed, they are mostly of a psycho-educational nature in which children are trained in social skills. I would like to propose that children with LD need more then this; their emotional needs must be addressed before they can be "fixed".

To address the social and emotional needs of children with LD, it is offered, in this chapter, to use counseling groups. Group is a natural setting for children. The group process provides opportunities for cathartic experiences, a sense of belonging, a place to receive support, learn from each other, and develop hope. Being in a group in which children share similar difficulties, where they are liked and appreciated, is of great importance. Indeed, in a series of large scale studies we demonstrated that children improved in social adjustment, in social competence, in social status and in academic achievement (Shechtman, 2007). Improvement in academic achievement is particularly interesting because we do not work on academic skills. It seems that it is the improvement in socio-emotional areas that affect academic achievement.

Intervention with parents follows the same philosophy, theory and practice. The focus is on emotions in regard to their child with LD. Our understanding is that freeing parents from anger, anxiety, guilt and shame, would change their communication with their child and lead to the child's improvement. Studies confirmed these expectations; following participation in a group parents showed a reduction in stress, a decreased in the perception of the child's difficulties, and increased coping skills (Shechtman & Gilat, 2005; Danino & Shechtman, 2011). Overall, affective group interventions proved to be effective and efficient.

RELATIONSHIP TO THE SBFC MODEL

The SBFC model pertains to two major target groups for intervention: children and their parents. The intervention can be preventive or remedial. Preventive classroom and school group interventions are extremely important (Durlak et al., 2011) and actually the most frequently used in school (Kulic, Dagley, & Horne, 2001). However, children with serious challenges, such as learning disabilities, and their parents seem to need more rigorous interventions. In the current chapter we discuss counseling groups for children and their parents; these groups are growth-engendering and remedial and in terms of the SBFC Model fit into the School-Intervention and Family-Intervention quadrants. The type of group is supportive-expressive (Shechtman, 2007) aimed to enhance self-understanding which may in turn lead to behavior change. Group support, as well as other therapeutic factors (e. g. altruism, universality, catharsis, interpersonal learning; Yalom& Leszcz, 2005) are the forces that lead toward change of participants (children and parents alike) in the group. The SBFC model suggests that school is more than a place to achieve academic skills and knowledge. The current chapter suggests that Family-Intervention and School-Intervention group support can improve children's and parents' lives, including in the arena of academic achievements.

PROFILES OF CHILDREN WITH LD IN GROUP

Today I can tell you that I am a student with learning disabilities of every possible sort. I graduated from elementary school knowing that I am a problem child and that learning is not for me and will never be. I know that everyone thought I was just lazy; no one thought that it is simply difficult for me. The letters jump in front of my eyes and I can hardly combine them into a word and I don't understand what I read. With time, learning became more complicated and I just did not manage. I was ashamed. What could I say? That I cannot read and write? When I manage to write I cannot read my own handwriting. Once in class, the teacher came over, looked at it, and said: What a scribble! Then I understood very quickly that it is better to be considered lazy and even arrogant than stupid.

These are the words of Dan, spoken in one of the sessions of a group of seventh graders, designed for students with learning disabilities. His monologue has many of the elements characterizing students with LD: the learning difficulties and the fear of admitting them; the shame and embarrassment; the threat to his self-image; and the disappointment of self and others. Like many students with LD, Dan used misbehavior to mask his disabilities, because the most devastating feeling is to feel stupid. And no one really expected him to change—until now. In a group of children with similar difficulties, who talk openly about their difficulties and express similar feelings of frustration and embarrassment, Dan is able to admit, for the first time, that he has LD and to understand the ways he compensates for his lack of success in academic achievement.

Following identification and expression of his emotions, Dan is also able to state goals for possible change. Yet, the issue he brings up is not his academic performance, but rather his problems with friendship. Because he is not well accepted by his classmates and feels quite lonely and rejected, he has joined a group of youngsters on the verge of breaking the law. He does not like what they do, but nevertheless goes along with them. He now asks the group members to help him in his efforts to resist these youngsters. The group appears to provide him with a new sense of belonging and support which he needs in order to be able to disengage from his "friends". Armed with social support, he makes the decision to give up his mask and deal with his issues in an open and direct way. He indeed becomes the best learner in the group, demonstrating progress in behavior as well as in scholastic achievements. In classes where he has a supportive teacher, he does extremely well. While Dan could gain a sense of universality in another type of group as well, it is the unstructured form of treatment focused on emotions, rather than pre-planned content, that has broadened for him the scope of issues to deal with. He can select the issues that are unique to his life, which helps him reduce the emotional burden and free his energies to cope with his difficulties.

Ellen is a 13-year old boy in seventh grade, diagnosed with a LD. He often complains about stomach ache--the cause of his too many absentees from school. "It feels as if I had swallowed the sun, so much it burns in my stomach", he says. As a result of missing classes he fails on most subjects. He is often angry and impulsive. An interview with the boy revealed that he is highly rejected by his peers, feels lonely during recess, and most importantly, blames himself for his parents' divorce "I know my father left home because he was ashamed of me", he said.

Helping this boy with his academic failure would do very little for him; freeing him from disturbing thoughts would do a better service, which cannot be achieved through guidance and skills training. Interventions must focus on the exploration of emotions and reflecting on them (Greenberg, 2001; Elliot, 2001).

Finally, Sandy, a teenager in another group, shares his experience of being interviewed in the process of admission to a new school. He badly wants to be accepted to this vocational school, where he has a better chance of succeeding; in fact, it is his only chance of receiving a high school diploma. Upon arrival at the school, he found out that there were several tests to take and an interview with the school principal, which scared him. In the counseling group, he reports that he skipped some of the tests because "they did not seem relevant" and he did not cooperate in the interview because "the principal was mean". Like many other children with LD, Sandy has developed a sense of helplessness, and gave up his chances for admission even before trying. He played it "cool" and disguised his fears as lack of interest, when actually he wanted very much to be admitted. Why? Because it is easier to reject than be rejected. It feels better to say "I am not interested" than "I cannot make it". The group works very hard to help him explore his real emotions and admit that it is actually very important for him to be accepted there. They also help him develop some insight into his distorted behavior. Finally, they encourage him to take a second chance and ask for another interview with the school principal. In a role play, he practices the skills of a constructive and open interviewee and is encouraged to emphasize his real desire to be admitted. In the end, Sandy is successful and is accepted into the new school.

PROCEDURE

There is considerable empirical evidence that children with LD differ from normally achieving children in terms of behavior and personality variables. Due to difficulties in academic achievements and lack of appropriate social skills, they experience more negative affect, which in turn impairs their academic and social performance (Yasutake & Bryan, 1995). They often demonstrate high rates of anger, anxiety, and depression (Fisher, Allen, &Kose, 1996), low self-efficacy (Zimmerman, 1995), low self-esteem (Elbaum & Vaughn, 2001), high rates of loneliness and rejection (Margalit & Efrati, 1996), and low self-control (Bender & Wall, 1994). These are affective processes that have negative impact on school performance (Grolnik & Ryan, 1990). Indeed, research has widely documented the relation between cognitive and affective variables in learning and points particularly to the above variables (Durlak et al., 2011). Often, therefore, researchers have concluded their studies with the recommendation to treat students with LD in small groups.

Many schools, however, do not assume the role of mental health support and focus instead on excellence in education. These schools normally treat children with academic dysfunctions by offering increased teaching assistance and support, failing to recognize that the learning process contains both a cognitive and an affective component (Elias & Arnold, 2006; Zins & Elias, 2006). In view of the multiplicity of difficulties that LD children face, as well as the salience of the affective component, it is clear that these components also need to be treated.

When schools do assume the role of helping these children with their affective difficulties, it is usually provided within a cognitive-behavioral orientation with a strong focus on learning and social skills (Kazdin & Weisz, 2003). CBT group is defined as therapy that uses the dynamics of the group format, in addition to common cognitive-behavioral techniques, such as challenging thoughts, setting goals, problem solving, and risk assessment, to change distorted, maladaptive, and dysfunctional beliefs, attitudes, and behavior (Van Dam-Bagger & Kraaimaat, 2000). Even though practiced in groups, it is a task-oriented model, content focused, and largely structured, designed to seek problem resolution for the individual, while the group provides validation (Petrocelli, 2002). The model places an emphasis on the learning process, skill rehearsal, modeling, self-talk, and relaxation techniques (Kendall, Aschenbrand, & Hudson, 2003).

Educational/problem-solving groups

One such educational program was developed in Israel (Alyagon & Bracha, 1996). The program is aimed at developing coping skills with academic tasks and social adjustment. Based on the problem-solving model (Kazdin, 2003), the intervention includes three major topics: strength building (session 1-3), examination of coping patterns at times of difficulty, frustration, and failure (sessions 4-6), and practicing with the problem-solving model (sessions 7-15). In the initial stage children, for example, draw their own portraits, note some of their strengths in each part of their body (e.g., "I am a strong runner"), and then share a few of the strengths with the group. In the middle stage, the children engage, for example, in the Facing a Difficulty activity. Cards with sentences describing a difficulty in school are presented ("I did not understand my homework"; "I failed the math test), and each child is asked to select one and share with the group his/her way of coping. The group then discusses similarities and differences in coping strategies. Finally, in the third stage of the group, the children practice the problem-solving model. For example, they are presented with a picture of a boy facing a wall, and are then asked to identify the problem, to find alternatives for coping, to evaluate the pros and cons for each option, and to select the best solution. Finally, they are asked to apply the problem-solving process to one of their own social or learning problems. Such programs are effective and help children with LD cope better. However, in this chapter I offer counseling groups, which operate in a different way.

COUNSELING GROUPS

In congruence with the expressive-supportive model, our groups are aimed at releasing negative emotions, sharing disturbing experiences, and exploring personal difficulties not necessarily related to learning or social difficulties. Cathartic experiences are encouraged and used in the process of affective exploration. Insight is intensified by sharing the personal experiences of other group members and the leader, as well as through the exchange of constructive feedback. Action is intensified by exploring one's own coping strategies and by considering alternative strategies offered by others.

While the process is largely unstructured, activities are offered for each session. The initial stage (sessions 1-6) is aimed at building self-esteem, similar to the educational groups, but it also contains activities designed to build relationships and group cohesion, to develop a language of feelings and self-expressiveness, and to develop norms of interpersonal interaction, the exchange of feedback, and support. At the working stage (sessions 7-13), children share personal experiences of their choice, not limited to learning problems. One child might select test anxiety as an issue to explore, another might consults the group on a social difficulty, and yet another may choose to talk about his relationship with his father. That is, each child raises his/her unique concern or problem. Finally (sessions 14-15), children summarize gains in the group, declare goals for future improvement, and say goodbye to each other.

This counseling form of group intervention differs from educational groups in several major respects. First, the intervention does not focus on learning difficulties, and is not structured around specific issues of LD. The assumption is that students with LD are first and foremost children who may have various developmental or situational difficulties, including LD. Second, the focus is on emotions, because we believe that the roots of the difficulty and the key to change lie within the affective domain of human functioning. Finally, therapeutic interaction among group members and positive interpersonal support is strongly encouraged, as we believe that change in the individual is more a function of the group interaction and interpersonal positive experiences than of learning specific skills. Illustration of the process

One counseling group consists of seven eighth graders: five boys and two girls. Five participants have been diagnosed as learning disabled with emotional difficulties. Three of these are also diagnosed with ADHD and medication has been recommended for them. One boy and one girl are not learning disabled, but have been evaluated as troubled children. The group meets for 15 one-hour sessions after school in the counseling room.

The group, labeled "Children Help Children," is introduced as an opportunity to talk about thoughts, feelings, and difficulties in children's lives. Participants are told that they have been selected owing to their ability to help themselves and others. Such a positive presentation of the group encourages members at the onset of therapy and instills a sense of hope. It conveys a message that no one is going to teach them something that will make them fail yet again. For children with a history of failure and getting into trouble, such a positive welcome is extremely important.

The activities at the initial stage aim at developing the language of feelings, building trust, and developing group norms. The children play the Circle of Emotions game, in which a circle is divided into four parts. As they stand in each part, they state a feeling they have in the here-and-now about the group. Both anxiety and excitement are expressed. The children are a bit anxious about the unknown, but are also happy to be selected, and they are looking forward to the activities and games promised. They then play the My Ideal Group game to establish norms of constructive work. They mention issues such as arriving on time, not leaving the session, expressing honest feelings, and treating everyone with respect. Shari, the counselor, adds the issue of confidentiality, and they close the session with the We Promise activity, in which they all promise to keep secrets in the group.

In the next sessions, the children continue developing a climate of trust. They play the Legacy of My Name, which makes them feel more intimate with each other, and they interview each other in pairs to promote self-disclosure. Processing of the difficulties in this activity reveals interesting self-learning. Kathy admits, "I am afraid to be the first to disclose." Timmy says, "I was afraid that no one will invite me." And Jordan states, "I was afraid I would be rejected and so I preferred to wait to be invited." These reactions are typical of children with LD, reflecting their deep sense of social rejection, low trust of self and others, and low self-esteem.

The next session focuses on identifying emotions. Many children, in general, and children with LD in particular, lack a language of emotions. This limits their ability to express emotions and to understand them. The children play with picture cards and with a Bingo of Emotions to enhance their vocabulary and their identification of feelings. Susan says, "I am frustrated and feel hopeless because I fail the science exams." Johnny says, "I feel lonely and I don't feel good about it (but now I don't feel that lonely)." The group seems to already take a place in his life and ease his sense of loneliness. Larry expresses his pride for being able to perform on stage, singing and dancing, and the group members respond with encouragement and reinforcement, reflecting the beginnings of spontaneous feedback exchange. Shari, the counselor, feels that they can now move to the working stage and deal with some of the major issues they have presented—namely, loneliness, a sense of failure, and low self-esteem.

The next session therefore centers on self-esteem. The counselor asks the children to give themselves awards for things that they appreciate in themselves, and she encourages group members to enhance their sense of worth by expanding upon the given award. Here are some of the reactions following the activity:

- *I feel good because, although I do good things, I never expressed them in front of others.*
- *I found that I had the patience to listen to others and was interested in what they said.*
- *I usually talk only with my mother about personal issues, because I trust no one; here I had an opportunity to share with other people and it felt good.*

Then Susan says, "I know that people always see the dark side of me, they hear my screaming and talking back. Now I shared for the first time something good about myself." This leads to several spontaneous reactions among group members. "I am in your class. I can help you when people say something negative about you," Kathy says. "You are kind of a leader and a very important group member," adds Larry. Timmy states: "I did not know you are so vulnerable. On the surface you seem so cool. I like you more this way." "I am sensitive, too. I feel much like you," says Marc. This has been an extremely meaningful session for Susan. Supported with social acceptance, her self-esteem is enhanced, and she becomes less restless in the group.

One of the next sessions takes place in the music room. Following a session that seemed too superficial to her, Shari is looking for a way to make this one more creative. The children are at first confused in the large room and look to her for guidance. Children with LD easily get distracted and need clear limits, but Shari decides to let them figure out the rules. After a few minutes in which they inspect the drums, each picks one up and starts playing, trying to connect with the other group members. Timmy suggests they play a feeling game, in which they should take turns using the drum to express their feelings, and the others will have to guess what the feeling is. The group gladly accepts the idea. Jordan begins by banging extremely hard on the drum. The group identifies anger, and he says: "Too often people do not listen to what I say, so I like to get on people's nerves." In response, Larry also beats on his drum with much anger, saying "I'm with you. We are not treated fairly. The teachers don't like us." Others soon join and create a quite angry communication. This is followed by an open discussion of their difficulties with schooling and with authority figures in the school.

Shari feels that this is a turning point in the group process. Group cohesion was enhanced, and the children actually took over leadership of the group in a very constructive way. They were able to follow the rules of a constructive group with minimal intervention of the leader, which is not very typical of children with LD and particularly those with ADHD. Indeed, when, in the next session, a new girl asks to join the group, they refuse. Susan explains: "I know she may feel bad, but we need to be honest in this group, and honestly, I would not feel comfortable with a new group member." Marc, an extremely withdrawn boy, adds, "At this point, I can talk about everything in the group. I feel connected, and I've gained a new friend. I don't want to change it." Johnny confirms this: "I've been with him for years, but only here in the group, when he talked about his feelings, did I discover what a good person he is. We are very close friends now."

At termination, Shari asks the children about critical incidents in the group. The drum session is mentioned as one that helped them to connect. "Since then I feel close to the people in the group, and when I have a bad day, I turn to them," says Larry. Other children mentioned interpersonal learning, group cohesiveness, acceptance and support, and catharsis.

All these children have behavior problems. They were described by teachers as having severe attention and discipline problems, a high level of arousal and aggression, low self-esteem, extreme withdrawal, high anxiety and loneliness. These issues came up in the process, but the attention deficits and discipline problems were hardly there. Rather, their interactions are typical of a "regular" group with social and emotional difficulties. These gains may be attributed to the counselor, who was sensitive, supportive and creative, as well as to the group, which created cohesiveness and norms of support.

A second illustration involves a group of seven 16-year-old girls, all diagnosed with LD, who dropped out of a middle school and are currently in a special vocational program. All have a long history of failure in school. Nonetheless, the dominant issues that come up during the therapy process are relationships with parents and peers, and only towards the end of the intervention does the issue of learning difficulties emerge. The girls in this group speak of parent-daughter relations characterized by lack of communication, harsh discipline, mistrust, and even violence. They relate how they have reacted by lying, drinking alcohol, taking drugs, driving without a license, and running away.

The initial sessions of this group are dominated by anger directed at their parents; few feelings are expressed on a deeper level, and there is little evidence of insight. This low level of communication changes in the fourth session, when they work with the book, *The Soul Bird* (Snunit, 1999). Martha shares her basic strategy of constant lying to her parents and expresses feelings of sadness and fear for not being able to be honest with them. Other group members present a variety of coping strategies, mostly negative. Only after Mindy, the counselor, insists that the group is not really listening to Martha's feelings and not hearing her sadness and pain do they start listening and sharing similar feelings. After several role plays, it becomes clear that the girls have replaced their hostile reactions to their parents with a more open communication pattern.

At another session, Judy, the most silent group member, shares her experience of extortion:
I am very lonely most of the time, I do not have friends, and when these two guys asked me for my money, I gave it to them, even though it left me hungry all day and I had to walk home [it took an hour]. The next day they asked for more money, which I did not have. They said they will come back tomorrow. They were nice and friendly, and I wanted to give them the money, but since I did not have it, I did not come to school for several days. Eventually, I consulted with the school counselor and I did not see them anymore. Judy's motivation to give away her money is typical of children with learning disabilities, because of their sense of loneliness. She misjudged the situation, perhaps because of her low self-esteem or even her cognitive difficulties. The group offers powerful support for her courage to speak with the counselor and for being who she is:
- *This is the first time I hear you. You are so delicate. I liked listening to you.*
- *I would also be afraid to report them and I admire your courage.*
- *I was very moved when you talked and liked the way you expressed yourself. You were interesting.*

Such feedback is meaningful beyond the reported incident. Judy felt valued and liked, and considering her sense of loneliness and history of withdrawal, this is an important group event for her.
At another session, the girls are playing with SAGA cards. Keren selects a card of a clown and one of a prison. She says she feels happy when she gets away from her troubles and come to the group. But she is sad because she feels rejected by classmates ("not here" she adds); she feels used by other girls who take from her but never give back or invite her over: "I am slow in learning and have no confidence to respond even when I know the answer. This has been going on since third grade. It makes me feel frustrated, even violent sometimes." This self-disclosure leads to a wide sense of identification and other girls express similar feelings. Donna shares her sense of incompetence, even stupidity, and Gail tells of her poor self-image and low expectations for the future. There are also supportive, warm, and caring reactions. Donna acknowledges Karen's honest self-disclosure and expresses appreciation of Karen's great ability to articulate her feelings. Carla empathizes with her regarding her low sense of self-efficacy, but urges her to continue striving for academic achievement, because it will make a better life for her.

In the next session, Carla raises the topic of academic success, but Mindy, the counselor, notices that Carla is also expressing much anger. When she reflects on those feelings, Carla begins to cry. After a long silence, she shares with the group a recent incident in which her mother was violent, and tells them that she has left home and refuses to go back. The most disturbing message she has received from her mother is that she is disappointed in her and has lost all hope for her future. Carla feels that her mother's attitude has a devastating impact on her motivation to make an effort. To deal with the situation constructively, Mindy uses a book that offers various coping patterns. Carla selects the strategy of avoiding the problem rather than dealing with it. The group provides her with immediate feedback, pointing out that she is choosing to run away. She understands the feedback and agrees to involve the school authorities and confront her mother. Eight days later, following her mother's visit to school and constructive confrontation with her, Carla returns home.

In sum, children with LD have common problems including academic difficulties, social isolation, and low self-esteem. Yet, they also have unique difficulties, some of which are more disturbing to them than academic achievements. There are developmental and situational problems that seriously hinder their performance in school. It is true that, through progress in schooling, some of these problems may diminish, but how do you keep students on task when they feel so vulnerable, so helpless, and so hopeless? When asked at termination what they take from the group, LD children mention friendship, connectedness, warmth, and support. This is not to suggest that they do not need to develop more effective coping and problem-solving skills. Such skills are indeed a part of the group process, but what appears more effective is the exchange of empathy, the provision of social and emotional support, and the enhancement of self-esteem. These interpersonal processes are highly related to academic achievement, as our clinical experience and research show (see more below).

THE UNIQUE CHARACTERISTICS OF GROUPS WITH LD STUDENTS

Most children with LD have difficulty functioning in a group, as in life. Following continuous experiences of academic failure and stormy relationships with authority figures in the school and at home, they find it hard to trust the counselor. They are frustrated and angry and have little hope that things can change for them. With peers, too, they often have a history of failure, so it is not easy to trust other kids. Those children who also have an attention disorder and hyperactivity find it even more frustrating, because they are unable to control themselves, even when they want to behave well.

Take the case of Sam, who has ADHD. He insists on attending the group, but finds it difficult to calm down. He walks around the room restlessly, interrupting the discussion. At a certain point, Jodie, the counselor, suggests that he leave for a few moments to calm down, but he refuses and continues wandering around the room. At the end of the session, when Jodie gives out "awards," she rewards Sam for his persistent participation in the group, despite his difficulties. In return, he gives her an award "for being accepting and so different from other teachers". I know that many psychologists would consider this to be reinforcement of negative behavior, but this counselor chose to focus on the bright side, on the positive intentions of the child, and rightly so. I fully agree with Malekoff (2004) that working on the strengths of the child rather than the deficits is much more effective in producing change in a child or adolescent's behavior. Indeed, this was a turning point in Sam's behavior in the group. He was encouraged by Jodie's positive attitude and made great efforts to control himself.

Support and acceptance are not always sufficient, however. For example, in another group in which three of the six boys are diagnosed with ADHD, it is more difficult to progress with the group process, because several children have similar difficulties controlling themselves. Ed wants very much to be in the group. Being a very intelligent boy, he understands the group rules, but finds it difficult to control himself. His attitude to peers is critical and rude; he insults the other group members with abusive language, and he bullies some of them. At one point, he discloses a secret but immediately regrets this, and does not show up the next time. When he is convinced that the secret has not leaked out, he comes back, destroying the delicate discipline that has since been established in the group with much effort. Margo, the counselor, feels that he is a threat to the group process and asks him to leave. In a later private conversation, Ed convinces her to give him another chance. But the next time, Ed himself recognizes that he cannot control himself, and he leaves the group for good. Whether it was the difficult group composition (50% ADHD boys) or Ed's particularly difficult disabilities that created the problem, it was impossible to keep this boy in the group despite the very sensitive therapeutic approach.

In general, it is more difficult to conduct counseling and psychotherapy groups for children with LD because of problems of attendance, discipline, and attention. Therefore, the groups should be kept small, and much attention should be given to group composition. Pre-group screening and individual interviews may help eliminate prospective members who would not benefit from the group. If possible, co-leading can be very helpful, so that one leader can provide individual attention to the very needy group members. Just sitting down next to a highly aroused or restless child can help. Despite these difficulties, groups for LD children are successful. We know this from children's feedback and our research outcomes.

CHILDREN'S FEEDBACK

Attending a faculty meeting a year after her group terminated, a counselor noted that all the children from her group are doing extremely well in school. Excited about this positive feedback, she decided to investigate how they were actually helped in the group. She contacted them and interviewed each. Here are some of their responses:

Wendy: Following each session I felt more confident, less anxious on tests. I am also more open with my friends, and get to establish closer and deeper relationships with them.

Ruth: The meetings helped me change socially and in school. I am happier, less stressful during exams and I have more friends. My improvement in school also improved my relationships with teachers. I liked the group because it enabled me to express my feelings. I learned a lot about myself, and I realized that other people also have similar problems.

Delia: They asked me what this group is, and I really didn't know how to define it. We simply talked and we helped each other a lot. I used to be very moody; today I am different. I talk more freely with girls and I've improved in academic achievement. Now that I've overcome both social and academic difficulties, I know I can overcome any difficulty. I kind of trust myself more, and when needed, I know where to turn for help. I learned to admit to my difficulties and, when needed, to make a change. I also learned to think before I act, and this is the most important thing I learned in the group.

The above feedback incorporates all the goals we have for such groups. The children resolved social issues, increased academic achievements, enhanced trust in themselves and others, increased self-confidence and self-efficacy, and gained self-control. In some respects, such gains have unique meaning for children with LD, but in many other respects, they reflect developmental issues of any children their age.

In a group of younger children, feedback is obtained through a game. The counselor displays various objects and asks the children to select the one that best describes what the group has been for them. Gary selects a box of chocolate, because it was such a sweet experience. Cindy chooses a package of rice to express the connection between group members. Corey selects a seesaw, expressing the ups and downs in the group, and indicating that they ended at on top. This is only a sample of feedback provided by children to show the efficacy of such groups. More can be learn from our intensive research on groups with LD children.

EVIDENCE-BASED SUPPORT FOR GROUPS WITH CHILDREN WITH LD

The first study (Shechtman, Gilat, Fos, & Flasher, 1996) on children with LD was aimed to measure self-esteem, social status, and self-control of 142 low-achieving children of whom two-third were diagnosed as learning disabled. Academic achievements were measured only as a by product, because of the well known association between academic achievement and social and emotional variables. The sample population of 142 children was randomly divided into experimental and control groups. While both groups received 4-6 weekly hours of academic assistance by expert teachers, only the 73 children in the experimental group also participated in group counseling of an expressive-supportive nature. They were grouped by age level, creating 11 mixed-gender groups. Results indicated an overall significant difference between the experimental (counseling) and control groups, with higher gains for the former on all measures: scores in language and math, self-concept, locus of control, and social acceptance, and these gains were sustained at follow-up.

While gains on socio-emotional measures were expected in such groups, academic achievements were beyond our expectations. The average grades of the experimental group moved from failing to almost average (math: from 50 to 63 at termination and to 65 at follow-up, 6-9 months later; language: from 58 to 68 and 69). There was no change in the control group. These gains were confirmed in national tests, which are usually perceived as more objective measures than teachers' grades. In addition, we compared the percentages of experimental and control failing pupils who received passing marks (60 and above) at the end of the intervention and at follow-up. Results indicated that about 70% of the pupils in the experimental group who initially failed received a passing math grade at termination, and this percentage remained constant at follow-up. Parallel percentages for the control group were 15% and 12%, respectively. The improvement was equally clear for language: the proportions of pupils in the experimental group whose grades improved from failing to passing was about 80%and 60%, in comparison to 13% and 10% in the control group.

The results of this study clearly indicate the contribution of group counseling of an expressive-supportive nature to children's progress in academic achievement, as well as on social and emotional variables. Gains in academic performance after treatment of affective variables, without specific focus on academic issues, make the results particularly interesting. Whereas 4-6 weekly extra-help sessions focusing on scholastic performance did not significantly improve grades or test scores, the addition of the weekly group session did. Because there were no initial differences between the experimental and control groups, and because the only obvious difference between them was the group treatment, it is reasonable to attribute the outcomes to the intervention. The progress made on the affective and social variables, although not directly linked to the outcomes on academic achievements, may provide some explanation for these outcomes. The children involved in the study displayed affective difficulties along with learning difficulties. Improved self-esteem, self-control, and particularly social status can positively affect children's academic achievements. Indeed, children's feedback on the group experience clearly supports this assumption.

These results bear a significant message for educators who normally address learning dysfunctions with increased teaching assistance. It seems that these children's social and emotional needs must also be addressed. Another important message is that counseling groups of an affective focus are effective. This is important to state in light of the prevailing modes of cognitive-behavioral treatments.

The next study (Shechtman & Pastor, 2005) expanded upon the previous research by comparing counseling treatment of LD children to cognitive-behavioral group therapy. The study comprised 200 children from second to sixth grade. All were diagnosed with learning disabilities and were receiving treatment in a learning center. Some received one-hour assistance with academic achievements twice a week; others received academic assistance along with CBT group treatment or affective group counseling; and the rest were on a waiting list for academic assistance and meanwhile received one of the two group treatments. Thus, the 200 children were randomly assigned to five comparison conditions: academic assistance only; academic assistance + group treatment (both types); and treatment of both types without academic assistance. Two more comparisons were made between all children who received CBT and all children who received affective group counseling. The last two comparison groups entailed a reclassification of the second and third groups, to allow the comparison between treatments.

In this study, too, we measured academic progress, this time with the expectation that affective groups would have a positive effect on achievements, but questioning whether it is the particular type of intervention offered that makes a difference. Overall, all children moved from a failing (around 40) to a passing (around 60) grade in reading, following all types of treatments. However, progress was significantly different for the comparison groups. The group that received only group treatment gained more than the group that received only academic assistance, and of the two types, affective therapy was more effective than CBT group treatment. A similar result was obtained for progress in math. The most striking result was that academic assistance was least effective in generating gains on scholastic achievement, while affective therapy, which does not focus on learning, achieved the highest gains.

Results on affective measures were along the same lines, which, of course, could be expected. We would not expect progress in adjustment behavior, self-efficacy, or social status following academic assistance only. Indeed, all group treatments were more effective than no group treatment, but on most of these measures, too, affective group counseling was more effective than CBT groups.

In this same study, we also analyzed the process of client and therapist functioning, in order to help us understand results. We found less client resistance and more affective exploration and insight in the affective therapy groups, and more cognitive exploration in the CBT groups. These results provide evidence that the two types of treatment indeed do what they aim to do. Affective group therapy is meant to focus on affect and to achieve some insight; and the climate of sharing and trust usually reduces resistance. Conversely, cognitive therapies focus on cognition, thoughts, and perceptions. Moreover, as affective exploration and insight are considered more constructive behaviors (Hill & O'Brien, 1999), they may also explain some of the advantages seen in the outcomes for the affective therapy groups.

As expected, therapists used different skills in the two types of treatment. There was more encouragement, reflection of feelings, and interpretations in the affective therapy groups and more information and guidance in the CBT groups. Leaders operated within their theoretical orientations and used their helping skills with particular aims. Since reflection of feelings, encouragement and interpretation are also more appreciated by clients (Hill & O'Brien, 1999), this result, too, may explain the effectiveness of affective group therapy.

These results are congruent with the feedback we received from the LD children. They seem to tire of being reminded of their academic failure. The affective and social issues seem to be of more concern to them than their academic performance. Perhaps it is time to address the real issues of this population.

Support for the importance of the affective processes in the group experience was found in a recent study (Shechtman &Katz, 2006) involving a large number of students with ADHD. Results indicated gains on social competence following group treatment compared to a wait-list group. More important, however, was the finding that these gains were associated with children's bonding with both the counselor and with other group members. This result adds strength to the importance of relationships in the group, as reflected so clearly in children's feedback.

Finally, in a recent study (Leichtentritt & Shechtman, 2010) involving 40 small groups and over 250 students we found that children showed progress in academic achievement and in social competence, as well as a reduction in externalizing and internalizing symptoms. Interestingly 20 of these groups were composed of students with LD. No difference in outcomes was revealed between the children with LD and their counterparts. Moreover, there was no difference between the children with and without learning disabilities on the process variables as well. That is, the engagement of children with LD in the group process, their bonding with the therapist and the group members, and their therapeutic work was not different from the non-LD children.

WORKING WITH PARENTS OF CHILDREN WITH LD IN GROUP

Some of the children with LD constitute a daily challenge for their parents, due to academic, social, emotional and behavioral difficulties (Mcphail & Stone, 1995; Morrison & Cosden, 1997; Turnbull, Hart, & Lapkin, 2003). Parents, of these children are under great stress (Adelizzi & Goss, 2001; Al-Yagon, 2007; Brannan, Heflinger & Bickman, 1997), often feel helpless and depressed (Bandura, Barbaranelli, Caprara, & Pastorelli, 1996; Turnbull, & Turnbull, 1986), and as a result their parental functioning is less effective (Barkley et al., 1991; Stone, 1997). Parent child relationships directly affect the level of problems children demonstrate (Barkley, 1997). The more parents are attuned to their children's needs, are supportive and warm, the less the child demonstrates emotional and social difficulties (Morrison & Cosden, 1997). The more parents are authoritative and punitive, the more the child shows adjustment symptoms (Eisenberg, Fabes, and Murphy, 1996; Stone, 1997).The problem is that parents of children with LD show adjustment problems as well. Compared to parents of non-LD they are under higher stress, tend to blame themselves more often and express less satisfaction of their parental role, demonstrate a lower level of self-efficacy and a sense of helplessness (Bandura et al., 1996), and feel more anxious and depressed (Al-Yagon, 2007). As a result they are less supportive of their children and more punitive (Barkley et al., 1991).

Assistance to such parents of children with LD is not very common; most assistance is addressing children with LD, mainly with their academic difficulties. The interventions that are reported in the literature are mainly educational, aimed at training parents how to cope with their children. The reported outcomes are positive; educational interventions with parents of autistic children, for example, showed a decrease in parental stress (Baker et al., 2005; Feldman & Werner,2002). Another cognitive group intervention with parents of retarded children (Nixon & Singer, 1993) indicated a decrease in parental self-blame, negative thoughts, and depression symptoms. Barkely and colleagues (1992) compared three types of treatments for parents of children with ADHD--a behavioral management treatment, training in problem solving and communication, and family therapy. All interventions were effective in reducing negative communication, conflict, anger, and improved adjustment of children and decreased mothers' level of depression. Webster-Stratton (1984; 1985)used video presentations to train parents of children with conduct disorder. The results pointed to improved coping skills and child's problem solving skills.

In our work with parents we assume the same theoretical approach to treatment as we do with children. We use an integrative approach, treatment focuses on emotions, and in the group format we apply the two principles of self-expressiveness and interpersonal support. The focus of these groups is the parent, rather than the child. The goal is to help parents change their interaction with the child, which can be achieved through the development of insight and which will eventually lead to change in behavior.

Parents come in to the group with the illusion that by miracle they will get an immediate solution to their child's difficulties. They look for guidance and advice. It is easier for parents to see the child as the "identified patient' rather seeing themselves in a therapy process. Here they are, in a group of strangers, unexpectedly asked to look into themselves. Why do we think we can make them work?
We build on the therapeutic factors that are evident in a group process, including universality, altruism, hope, group cohesion, interpersonal learning, and catharsis, among others (Yalom & Leszcz, 2005).

Parents learn quite soon that they are not alone in the difficult situation, that there is no reason to be ashamed or feel guilty about it. Once members start to disclose their difficulties and show their vulnerabilities, other group members try to help, sometimes in an altruistic way. The disclosure of personal issues leads to group cohesion, a general sense of liking and trust about each other. The sense of belonging through sharing, sometimes through highly emotional cathartic experiences, increases even more the sense of trust and universality, and help other group members to become engaged in the group process through identification and imitation processes. The more cohesive the group more hope develops for each group member. Members become eager to see how people view them and want to learn more about themselves, either through self-understanding or through feedback provided by group members. Once people feel safe in the group and empowered by the support provided by group members, they are also willing to make changes in their behavior.
The following is an illustration of one such group.

Groups develop in stages. At the initial stage people are suspicious and therefore cautious. They are placed in a group of strangers, yet knowing that all parents have children with LD they start by asking very practical questions. At this point, they focus on the child's difficulties —social,low self - concept, behavior problems, complains from teachers. They are confused about their parental role- "should we be strict with the child, put more limits, punish, or demand more? They tend towards an authoritarian approach perhaps to limit their sense of helplessness. They express frustration and helplessness and turn much anger towards the therapists who do not provide solutions at this point.
Gradually, group members start talking about their feelings, guilt, anxiety, and helplessness. They share difficult situations with the child, learn to listen to each other, develop empathy, and try to help. The more they feel safe and comfortable in the group the more they become engaged emotionally. Many take the opportunity to go through emotional catharsis while sharing their concerns, sometimes for the first time in their life. One mother, Sylvia, shares her conflictual communication with her son-a young

man. The group provides feedback regarding her overprotective approach, on one hand, and her dependence on him, on the other hand (she is a widow). "He is already a man but you still talk to him as if he was a child", says one. She understands her mistakes and makes a plan to change her behavior. Another controlling person in the group, Marta, takes too much time of the sessions, and although members and the leaders point to her disturbing behavior she doesn't stop. At the sixth session she comes in late, interrupts the process, and immediately takes over the group. Another quite withdrawn group member, gets up and leaves the room angrily. At the next session the behavior of both members is explored. The man admits that this is a typical behavior for him: "I stay silent until I cannot bear it any more then I explode…when I do it to my child he gets really scared". He understands his avoiding behavior and its consequences. The woman was surprised, asking "why didn't you say something?" Group members told her that they all tried gently but she couldn't hear them. She then shared with the group her difficult childhood in a family of seven siblings. "If I wouldn't take the time I would never be heard", she said. With her 7 years old son a similar pattern of communications exists. She went on disclosing—"yesterday I talked to him and he suddenly shut me off with a scream "you only talk, can you stop and listen to me once?" She combined the two incidents understanding that she needs to work on her listening skills.

Gail, a very gentle woman, whose husband refused to join the group, decided that she is not going to let him continue with the abuse behavior towards their son. She shares with the group her assertive conversation with him. Group members expressed their appreciation of her newly gained behavior. Her progress brought hope into the room, and several mothers made decisions to follow her steps.

Dina, came with her husband to the group sessions. He was soon engaged in the group but she lagged much behind. She missed sessions and when she was present she was rude and cynical. She shared her home experiences totally detached from feelings, so she got from the group a laugh rather than empathy. A turning point in the group process occurred when the therapist directly approached her asking if she feels part of the group. "I am not part of the group and I experience more difficulties than anyone here" she responded (she has three diagnosed children with various disabilities). Her very honest sharing led to a positive reaction from the group; they acknowledged her difficulties and expressed their appreciation for being able to cope with the situation while holding a full-time job. For the first time she felt understood and accepted. Since then she came regularly to the sessions and became engaged actively in the group process. She came to the understanding that her anger and rudeness is a defense mechanism that only pushes people away from her. At termination she summarized "The group was a gift for me, a place I could be myself".

People tend to play out in the group the role they take in life outside the group. One of the group members, Mikel, played out the" wise man". He quickly understood any situation, providing interpretations in a critical manner, bringing his creative way as the ultimate example of child rearing. Although the group was impressed with his good ideas they expressed dislike and rejection. It was clear that he is not aware of his behavior, until the session in which he told his story about his childhood. It turned out that he was a difficult child with various disabilities, failed school and dropped out at an early stage. He talked about his failures with tears, stressing the gap between his abilities and actual achievements. The group loved him for stepping out of fake role he played so far and provide him with a lot of positive feedback. At the end of treatment he admitted that he changed his communication with his son and wife who was also present in the group.

At a certain point the group is guided to talk about their child's strengths, something very unusual for them. Interestingly, most of them could identify unique talents in their children and understood they need to encourage the children to focus more on success than on failure. They found talents in music, sports, arts, and cooking. This positive shift of their perceptions of the children was important for their own relaxation as well as for hopes towards the future.

As one can see, the focus of this stage is on the parents. They gradually learned to give up their expectations to get instant solutions to their difficulties and learned to rely on others in the group and particularly on themselves. At termination they expressed pride of being courageous, of taking the time to learn about self, of being able to take charge of their lives, and change their communication with the difficult child. Specifically, they mentioned an increase in listening skills and acceptance, self-understanding and understanding of others, and the acquisition of parental skills.

EVIDENCE-BASED SUPPORT FOR GROUPS WITH PARENTS

In our first group with parents of children with LD (Shechtman & Gilat, 2005) we conducted supportive-expressive groups with 56 mothers in 10 sessions. Furthermore, these groups were compared with psycho-educational groups with about the same number of mothers. Results indicated that on all measures of parental stress, mothers in the counseling expressive-supportive group gained more than mothers in the psycho-educational group. They reduced their level of stress, gained control of the child's behavior, and perceived the child as less problematic than the other mothers. Moreover, children's feedback confirmed the progress made in mother-child relationships. Another interesting outcome was the progress made by fathers on all these dimensions, although they themselves did not take part in the intervention. It seems that the influence of the group on mothers had a broad effect, including the father and the child (recall the example of the mother who initiated an assertive conversation with her husband). The process measures in this study indicated that catharsis and interpersonal learning were the therapeutic factors most valued by the mothers, supporting the type of intervention provided to them.

In a more recent study (Danino & Shechtman, 2011) 97 parents participating in seven small groups (12 sessions) were compared to 31 parents on a waiting list for treatment. Results indicated more favorable outcomes for parents treated in groups, compared to control. Parents treated in groups improved their coping strategies with children's emotions and reduced the level of stress compared to non-treated parents These results sustained at follow up-six months later. Moreover, when the therapeutic factors as perceived by parents were analyzed, insight appeared the most important factor in group. These results point to the importance of self-understanding in improving parents coping with the difficulties their children with LD present.

MULTICULTURAL COUNSELING CONSIDERATIONS

Multiculturalism has become an important discipline and a primary source for explaining human development and functioning. In the context of group counseling, cultural influences can clearly impact behavior and the group process. Self-disclosure is a fundamental behavior in groups, the force that underlies all therapeutic factors (Yalom & Leszcz, 2005), and is expected of all members. Moreover, group members are expected to provide honest and direct feedback to each other, challenge each other, and take risks. But all these are Western ideas about group processes that may not fit other cultures. The conclusion in the literature suggests culturally-sensitive group counseling tailored to the values and norms of specific cultures.

The Arab culture, for example, is considered a non-Western culture, known as a collectivistic society, in which family and society may be expected to obscure group functioning. Several studies were conducted with the Arab population in Israel, including children and adults, to investigate the impact of the Arab culture on group functioning. It was expected that the Arab participants would be less self-disclosing than their Jewish counterparts and therefore would gain less from the group process. In a study with adolescents (Shechtman, Hyradin, & Zina, 2003) groups of Arab adolescents were compared with Jewish groups. In contrast to our expectation, Arab adolescents disclosed more than the Jewish ones, in most areas studied, including on family issues, which is a very sensitive area. Their gains from therapy were similar to their Jewish counterparts. In another study with university students-trainees in counseling (Shechtman & Halevi, 2006), Arab trainees reported greater intention to self- disclose, their goals for the course were more personal than academic (similar to the Jewish students), and they were less resistant to therapy. The really important finding here is that behavior in group was not restricted by culture; on the contrary, a high need for group counseling appears in the

Arab participants. Although these studies are limited to only one cultural group, a clear suggestion emerges—to refrain from premature conclusions regarding the employment of psychodynamic process groups in such cultural groups, as suggested in the literature (e.g. Dwairy, 1998). More research is needed in the area of multiculturalism and group counseling.

SUMMARY AND CHALLENGES

This chapter described counseling groups for children with LD and for their parents that focused on their social and emotional concerns rather than their academic difficulties. The clinical illustrations point to the importance of processes that are free of pre-planned content and based on self-expressiveness and intensive interpersonal interaction and support.

The results of our research clearly support affective group counseling for children with LD and for their parents. Such groups appear to be more effective than training groups, which are more commonly used. The implications of these results are both theoretical and practical. Theoretically, it seems logical to conclude that students with LD are first of all children or adolescents; they also have LD. Thus, they display a wide range of emotional and social needs along with the disability. Addressing these needs seems to be more effective than providing academic assistance. Practically, it appears that such groups can be conducted in a school setting. They are not much longer than educational groups, and trained counselors can lead them effectively. They should also be recommended on the grounds of cost effectiveness.

The greatest challenge to the implementation of such groups in the school is the fear of school personnel to deal with emotions. Rogers already in 1980, in his book "A way of being" stipulated that schools invite the head to school but insist on leaving emotions out of it. To a great extent, this is the situation also nowadays. A shift in perception of the school roles and a shift from cognitive-behavioral theories of treatment to a more integrative model of treatment are needed to permit counseling groups to flourish in the school.

The second and related challenge is the lack of trained counselors to conduct process-oriented group. Groups with children are different from adult groups; considering developmental stages of children it is clear that the group process has to be tailored to their abilities and needs. Specific strategies of intervention (e.g. therapeutic cards; Shechtman, 2007) are needed with children to compensate over the lack of content and structure in such groups.

Similar challenges exist to conducting parental groups. Schools refrain from taking a leading role in helping parents in a proactive and meaningful way. They do provide individual consultation when needed, but the SBFC model is not applied most of the time. Considering the effectiveness of these groups for parents and their children, a shift in the perceptions of educators regarding school roles is needed, allowing parents to bring their emotions to school. The groups we offer are short-term therefore trained counselors, who are specially skilled to conduct process groups with parents, are needed.

More research with these unique populations is important. It is particularly interesting to compare client behavior, content of problems, therapist interventions, and therapeutic factors. Such information would help counselors work more effectively with children with learning disabilities and their parents.

REFERENCES

Adelizzi, J.U., & Goss, D.B. (2001). *Parenting children with learning disabilities*. Westport, CT. & London: Bergin & Garvey.

Al Yagon, M. (2007). Socio-emotional and behavioral adjustment among school-age children with learning disabilities: the moderating role of maternal personal resources. *Journal of Special Education*, 40, 205-218.

Alyagon, M., & Bracha, I. (1996). *The enhancement of social skills and adjustment*. Tel Aviv, Israel:

Ramot (Hebrew).

Auerbach, J. G., Gross-Tsur, V., Manor, O., & Shalev, R. S. (2008). Emotional and behavioral characteristics over a six year period in youths with persistent and non-persistent dyscalculia. *Journal of Learning Disabilities, 41*, 263-273.

Baker-Ericzen, M. J., Brookman-Frazee, L. & Stahmer, A.(2005). Stress levels and adaptability in parents of toddlers with and without Autism Spectrum Disorders. *Research & Practice for Persons with Severe Disabilities*, 30(4), 194-204

Bakker, J. T. A., Denessen, E., Bosman, A. M. T., Krijger, E., & Bouts, L. (2007). Sociometric status and self-image of children with specific and general learning difficulties in Dutch general and special education classes. *Learning Disability Quarterly, 30*, 47-62.

Bandura, A., Barbaranelli, C., Caprara, G. V., & Pastorelli, C.(1996). Multifaceted impact of self-efficacy beliefs on academic functioning. *Child Development*, 67, 1206-1222.

Barkley, R. A., Fischer, M., Edelbrock, C., & Smallish, L. (1991). The adolescent outcome of hyperactive children diagnosed by research criteria: 3. Mother-child interactions, family conflicts and maternal psychopathology. *Journal of Child Psychology and Psychiatry and Allied Disciplines*, 32, 233-255.

Barkley, R. A., Guevremont, D. C., Anastopoulos, A. D., Fletcher, K. E. (1992). A comparison of three family therapy programs for treating family conflicts in adolescents with Attention-Deficit Hyperactivity Disorder. *Journal of Counseling and Clinical Psychology, 60*, 3, 450-462.

Barkley, R. A.(1997). *ADHD and the nature of self-control.* New York, NY: Guilford.

Bender, W. N., & Wall, M. E. (1994). Social emotional development of students with learning disabilities. *Learning Disability Quarterly, 17*, 323-341.

Brannan, A . M., Heflinger, C. A; Bickman, L. (1997) The Caregiver Strain Questionnaire: Measuring the impact on the family of living with a child with serious emotional disturbance. *Journal of Emotional and Behavioral Disorders, 5*, 4, 212-22

Danino, M., & Shechtman, Z. (2011). Counseling parents of children with LD: A comparison of group and individual couching. Unpublished manuscript.

Durlak,J. A., Weissberg, R. P., Dymnicki, A. B., Taylor, R. D., & Schellinger, K. B. (2011). The impact of enhancing students' social and emotional learning: A meta-analysis of school-based universal interventions. *Child Development*, 82, 405-432.

Dwairy, m. (1998).*Cross-cultural counseling: The Arab-Palestinian case*. New-York: Haworth.

Eisenberg, N., Fabes, R. A., & Murphy, B. C. (1996). Parents' reactions to children's negative emotion: Relations to children's social competence and comforting behavior *Child Development,* 67, 2227-2247.

Elbaum, B., & Vaughn, S. (2001). School-based interventions to enhance the self-concept of students with learning disabilities: A meta-analysis. *The Elementary School Journal, 101*(3), 303-329.

Estell, D. B., Jones, M. H., Pearl, R. A., Van Acker, R., Farmer, T. W., & Rodkin, P. R. (2008). Peer groups, popularity, and social preference: Trajectories of social functioning among students with and without learning disabilities. *Journal of Learning Disabilities, 41*, 5-14.

Elias, M., & Arnold, H. (2006) (Eds.). *The educator's guide to emotional intelligence and academic achievement*. Thousand Oaks, CA: Corwin Press.

Elliott, R. (2001). The effectiveness of humanistic therapies: A Meta-analysis. In D. J. Cain (Ed.), *Humanistic psychotherapies: Handbook of research and practice* (pp. 57-81), Washington, DC: American Psychological Association.

Feldman, F. A., & Werner, S. E. (2002). Collateral effects of behavioral parent training on families of children with developmental disabilities and behavior disorders. *Behavioral Interventions*, 17, 75-83.

Fisher, B. L., Allen, R., &Kose, G. (1996). The relationship between anxiety and problem-solving skills in children with and without learning disabilities. *Journal of Learning Disabilities, 29*, 439-446.

Grolnik, W. S., & Ryan, R. M. (1990). Self-perceptions, motivation, and adjustment in children with learning disabilities: A multiple group comparison study. *Journal of Learning Disabilities, 23,* 177-

183.

Greenberg, L. S. (2002). *Emotion-focused therapy: Coaching clients to work through their feelings*. Washington, DC. American Psychology Association.

Hill, C. E., &O'Brien, K. (1999). *Helping skills*. Washington, D.C.: American

Kazdin, A. E., & Weisz, J. R. (2003). Context and background of evidence-based psychotherapies for children and adolescent. In A. E. Kazdin & J. R. Weisz (Eds.), *Evidence-based psychotherapies for children and adolescents* (pp. 3-20), New York: Guilford Press.

Kendall, P. C., Aschenbrand, S. G., & Hudson, J. L. (2003). Child-focused treatment of anxiety. In A. E. Kazdin& J. R. Weisz (Eds.), *Evidence-based psychotherapies for children and adolescents* (pp. 81-100). New York: Guilford Press.

Kulic, k. R., Dagley, J. C., & Horne, A. M. (2001). Prevention groups with children and adolescents. *Journal for Specialists in Group Work, 26,* 211-218.

Leichtentritt, J., & Shechtman, Z. (2009).Children With and Without Learning Disabilities: A Comparisonof Processes and Outcomes Following Group Counseling. *Journal of Learning Disabilities,* 43, 169- 179.

Margalit, M., &Efrati, M. (1996). Loneliness, coherence and companionship among children with learning disorders. *Educational Psychology, 16,* 69-79.

McPhail, J. C. & Stone, C. A. (1995). The self-concept of adolescents with learning disabilities: A review of the literature and a call for theoretical elaboration. In E. Scruggs & M. A. Mastropieri (Eds.) *Advances in learning and behavior disorders* (Vol. 9, pp. 193-226). Greenwich, CT: JAI Press.

Morgan, P. L., Farkas, G., Tufis, P. A., &Sperling, R. A. (2008). Are reading and behavior problems risk factors for each other? *Journal of Learning Disabilities, 41, 417-436.*

Morrison, G. M., Cosden, M. A.(1997). Risk, resilience, and adjustment of individuals with learning disabilities. *Learning Disability Quarterly, 20,* 43-60.

Nixon, C. D. & Singer, G. H. (1993). Group cognitive behavioral treatment for excessive parental self-blame and guilt. *American journal of Mental Retardation, 97*(6), 665-672.

Petrocelli, J. V. (2002). Effectiveness of group cognitive-behavioral therapy for general symptomatology: A meta-analysis. *Journal for Specialists in Group Work, 27*(1), 95-115.

Rogers, C. (1980). *A way of being.* Boston: Houghton Mifflin.

Shechtman, Z. (2007). Group counseling with children and adolescents. Mahva, New Jersey: Erlbaum

Shechtman, Z., & Katz, E. (2007). Therapeutic bonding in group as an explanatory variable of progress in the social competence of students with learning disabilities. *Group Dynamics: Theory. Research, and Practice, 11,* 117-128.

Shechtman, Z. & Gilat, I. (2005). The effectiveness of counseling groups in reducing stress of parents of children with learning disabilities. (2005). *Group Dynamics: Theory, Research, and Practice*, 9, 275-286.

Shechtman, Z., Gilat, I., Fos, L., & Flasher, A. (1996). Brief group therapy with low-achieving elementary school children. *Journal of Counseling Psychology, 43,* 376-382.

Shechtman, Z., &Halevi, H. (2006).Functioning in the group comparing Arab and Jewish trainees in a counseling program.*Group Dynamics, 10,* 181-193.

Shechtman, Z., Hiradin, I., & Zina, S. (2003). The impact of culture on group behavior: A comparison of three ethnic groups. *Journal of Counseling & Development, 81,* 208-216.

Shechtman, Z., & Pastor, R. (2005). Cognitive-behavioral and humanistic group treatment for children with learning disabilities: A comparison of outcome and process. *Journal of Counseling Psychology, 52,* 322-336.

Sideridis, G. D. (2007). Why are student with LD depressed? *Journal of Learning disabilities,* 40, 526-539

Stone, C. A. (1997). Correspondences among parent, teacher, and student perceptions of adolescents' learning disabilities. *Journal of Learning Disabilities, 30*(6), 660-669.

Turnbull, M., Hart, D. & Lapkin, S. (2003). Grade 6 French immersion students' performance on large-scale Reading, Writing and Mathematics tests: Building explanations. *Alberta Journal of Educational Research*, 49, 6-23.

Van Dam-Baggen, R., & Kraaimaat, F. (2000). Group social skills training or cognitive group therapy as the clinical treatment of choice for generalized social phobia. *Journal of Anxiety Disorders, 14*, 437-451. Developmental sequences in small groups.

Webster-Stratton, C. (1984). Randomized Trail of two parent training programs for families with conduct-disordered children. *Journal of Consulting and Clinical Psychology, 52*, 666-678.

Webster-Stratton, C. (1985). Predictors of treatment outcome in parent training for conduct disordered children. *Behavior Therapy, 16*, 223-243.

Yalom, I., Leszcz, M. (2005). *The Theory and Practice of Group Psychotherapy*. (5th ed.) New York, Basic Books.

Yasutake, D., & Bryan, T. (1995). The influence of affect on the achievement and behavior of students with learning disabilities. *Journal of Learning Disabilities, 28*, 329-334.

Zimmerman, B. J. (1995). Self-efficacy and educational development. In A. Bandura (Ed.), *Self-efficacy in changing societies* (pp. 202-231). Cambridge: Cambridge University Press.

Zins, J. E, & Elias, M. J. (2006). Social and emotional learning: Promoting the development of all students. Journal of Educational and Psychological Consultation, *17*, 233-255.

PART VII

SCHOOL-BASED FAMILY COUNSELING: SPECIFIC APPLICATIONS

D. FAMILY-PREVENTION APPLICATIONS

SCHOOL FOCUS

School-Prevention	School-Intervention
Family-Prevention	Family-Intervention

PREVENTION FOCUS

INTERVENTION FOCUS

FAMILY FOCUS

Chapter 34
Promoting School Success through Mentor Families

Dale R. Fryxell

OVERVIEW: *This chapter describes a unique school-based mentoring program, the Project Kako'o Family Mentoring Program. This program focused on building strong families by matching mentor families with other families who were considered at risk or were struggling with stressful events or situations.*

BACKGROUND

Project Kako'o (meaning "to support") was developed at an elementary school on the Island of Oahu, in Hawaii. At the time the project was initiated, the 27-year-old school was experiencing a rapid shift in the profile in its 598 students, with over 40% of the students participating in the Free and Reduced Lunch Program. Additionally, over 10% of the students lived below the poverty level. Student ethnicity at the school was mixed with Filipino, Caucasian and Hawaiian/part-Hawaiian students comprising 60% of the total enrollment. Beginning a year before the project started, ongoing community forums were held to build a vision for the school and surrounding community and to discuss both current and future needs of the school and community. Many students, parents, community representatives, and school staff members actively participated in these meetings. One of the major needs identified during this process was the need for the school to play a more active role in strengthening and supporting families in the community. This decision was based on the premise that strong families will in turn nurture healthy, confident, and successful children.

There are several important reasons why mentoring was selected as the model to provide support to the school's children and families. First, it was thought that due to the tremendous cultural diversity at this school, mentoring would provide an opportunity to tailor services and supports that would be more culturally sensitive and appropriate. Oftentimes, mentors, or in the case of this project – mentor families, can be matched with mentee families based on similar cultural backgrounds. This often leads to not only a quicker development of meaningful relationships but also to stronger bonds between mentors and mentees. Secondly, mentoring allows services to be flexible in both content and dosage. Since mentor families spend time working individually with their mentee families, it is possible to adjust the areas where attention will be focused based on the individual needs of the mentee families. Mentor families also have the flexibility to provide increased services to their mentee families during crisis periods or when additional services are needed. Thirdly, due to the stigma that many families attach to receiving services from "professionals," it was thought that many families would be more comfortable seeking support and working with mentor families who have had similar experiences and backgrounds.

Mentors can be differentiated from teachers, counselors, and psychologists based on the differing roles that they play. Mentors often take on some of the roles of these professionals but their roles can also include coaching, advising, and even advocating for their mentees. Mentors can also serve as trainers, friends, companions, guides, challengers, and positive role models. Since mentors are not professional helpers they are able to provide flexible services including serving as tutors one day, confidants the following day, and role models the next. Historically, the term "mentor" appears to have originated from Homer's the Odyssey in which Ulysses selected his trusted friend, Mentor, to serve as a guide, guard, and teacher for his son, Telemachus, while he was away on his adventures. Over time and across the globe mentors have been known by different names including "sensi," "master," "guru," "coach," "sponsor," "tutor," and "patron" (Torrance, Goff & Satterfield, 2005).

Lev Vygotsky, provided important insight into the way that individuals learn and develop. He hypothesized that individuals acquire knowledge about their worlds by participating in activities with others who are more skilled (Vygotsky, 1978). Vygotsky found that the discoveries or skills of others, which he called cultural tools, get passed on to less skilled others through social interaction. Through this process of social guidance children, youth and even adults are able to internalize the skills of others as well as the cultural wisdom of the society in which they live in. This social guidance serves as the basis for much of what happens during a mentoring relationship.

A landmark research project conducted in Hawaii, that has become known as the Kauai Longitudinal Study, provided some important insight into the significance of establishing a relationship with important others as a way to improve resiliency in youth (Werner & Smith, 1992). This study has followed 698 infants born on the Hawaiian island of Kauai in 1955. The researchers have followed these individuals for over 30 years in an attempt to discover how some individuals can overcome challenging families and environments to become psychologically and emotionally healthy adults. An important finding of this study has been that children who were found to have at least one caring person in their lives, who accepted them for who they were regardless of behavioral, temperamental, physical, or mental challenges were more likely to become resilient, successful adults. The authors of the study thought that all children can be helped to become more resilient if interested others provide encouragement, model appropriate behavior, and teach communication and self-help skills. Family mentoring can certainly provide this relationship to not only children but to parents who are also often in need of support and positive relationships.

Mentoring has been described as a relationship between a pair of unrelated individuals which takes place on a regular basis over an extended period of time. For this project, the relationship has been expanded from just individual relationships to relationships between entire families. Mentoring has been characterized as a "special bond of mutual commitment" that has "an emotional character of respect, loyalty, and identification" (Hamilton, 1990). The results from empirical studies examining the outcomes of mentoring projects have provided strong evidence of its efficacy in preventing or reducing many different types of social problems including: juvenile delinquency (e.g., Benard, 1996; Grossman & Tierney, 1998; Hawkins & Weiss, 1985; Kumpfer, 1996,; Tierney, Grossman, & Resch, 1995); serious childhood and adolescent behavior problems (Benard, 1993; Lefkowitz, 1986; McPartland & Nettlees, 1991; Office of Juvenile Justice and Delinquency Prevention, 1998; Walsh, 1989); drug prevention (Kumpfer, 1996), as well as addressing the isolation that people often experience (Ferguson, 1990). Other benefits from many of these and other mentoring studies have shown improvements in academic outcomes, peer relationships, and in strengthening families.

In summary, mentoring has proven to be an ideal model for providing prevention and intervention programs for children, youth and families. A well-planned and coordinated mentoring program with clear strategies that relate activities to desired outcomes and provides ongoing support for mentors was deemed to be the perfect solution for meeting the school's needs.

PROGRAM DESCRIPTION

The overall goal of Project Kako'o was to build a strong school-community partnership that would enhance the skills and knowledge base of parents, address the diverse needs of the local children, and build a community of lifelong learners who are committed to their children, schools, and communities. This goal was in line with several state and national initiatives including the Goals 2000 objective of establishing partnerships with families, businesses, agencies, and community organizations. The Goals 2000: Educate America Act (P.L. 103-227), was a law signed on March 31, 1994 by President Clinton which provided resources to states and communities to ensure that all students would reach their full potential. A partnership between the Parent Teacher Association (PTA), the School Community

Networking Center (PCNC) and the project was established to facilitate active participation in the project.

With the financial support of the Victoria S. and Bradley L. Geist Foundation, the project was in existence for 3 years actively supporting, training, and nurturing many families in the school's community. What made this project unique was that instead of using a traditional mentoring model where one individual is paired with another individual, entire families were trained to be mentor families who were then paired with mentee families. The project started with the selection and recruitment of a core group of mentor families who were not only interested in strengthening their own families but also committed to helping other families. These twelve families participated in a year-long training program in which they met monthly to develop skills and strategies to not only strengthen their own families but to eventually pass on to the families they would be mentoring. These topics that were the focus of the trainings included: (1) developing strong communication skills, (2) problem solving, (3) conflict resolution, (4) conducting family meetings, (5) building trust and respect, (6) promoting responsibility, (7) successful child rearing strategies, (8) supporting children to be active learners, (9) relieving stress. In addition to these core topics, other areas that were included as part of the mentor training related to special topics such as preventing drug and alcohol use, dealing with homework hassles, sibling rivalry, friendships skills and a variety of parenting techniques and strategies.

SAMPLE FAMILY NIGHT AGENDA- TOPIC: STRESS MANAGEMENT

5:30 – 6:15	Potluck Dinner (Filipino Theme)
6:15 – 7:00	Introductory Activity – Wire Stress Sculpture (Families working together to build a wire sculpture that represents stress in their family)
7:00 – 7:30	What stresses me out! (Parent and children groups separate) Handout: hassles sheet Brainstorm ideas for managing stress Parent and children groups report out
7:30 – 7:45	Chillers – Introduce and practice stress reduction techniques guided imagery deep breathing muscle relaxation exercise meditation counting music
7:45 – 8:00	Family Action Planning - Fill out "Family Action Plan" sheets
8:00 – 8:30	Make Stress Balls – Made with balloons and rice
8:30	Evaluation – Fill out evaluation sheet

During the second year of the project, the mentor families were matched with one or two mentee families (see Figure 1).

Figure 1. Kako'o Family Mentoring Project Model

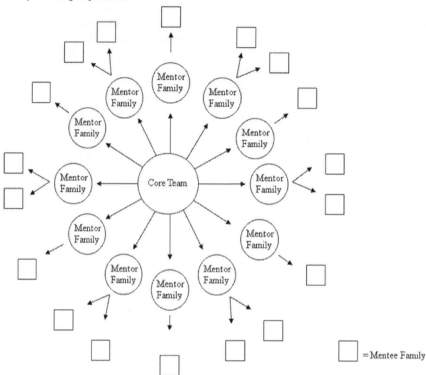

The mentee families were referred to the program by teachers, counselors and administrators based on the perceived needs of the family. The families were identified based on having a child who was "at risk" for social or academic failure and was also experiencing some type of crisis (i.e., divorce, unemployment) or lack of social support (i.e., new to the community) at home. In addition, families could self-nominate themselves as potential mentee families based on their perceived need for support. During the second year both the mentor and mentee families continued to meet at monthly gatherings to learn new skills, develop new relationships, and strengthen their families. In addition, special events were planned such as a weekend family retreat, a day at the waterpark, and community service projects to facilitate interaction and growth. Mentor and mentee families were also encouraged to meet regularly on their own and engage in activities like going to the beach or having a picnic.

During the last year (3rd year) the project was expanded into the larger community to include the entire school district complex which included four elementary schools and the middle and high schools into which they feed. The project relied on an ongoing planning strategy which enabled it to remain flexible and meet the changing needs of the project and community. The planning committee was made up of children and youth, parents, teachers, administrators, community members, and two psychologists. The Kako'o mentoring project also established important partnerships with several community organizations including the Senior Citizens Club, the City and County Parks and Recreation Division, the Estate of James Campbell, the Rotary Club, and the YMCA's Communities in Schools program.

RELATIONSHIP TO THE SBFC MODEL

Project Kako'o operated at both the Family-Intervention and Family-Prevention levels of the SBFC model. At the remedial-intervention level, families who were having various difficulties were identified by teachers, counselors, and administrators, to participate in the program. Some of the risk factors used to identify potential families to participate as Mentee Families were: a recent divorce or separation, new families moving into the community who did not have a social support network, families with children who had identified social and behavioral difficulties.

At the Family–Prevention level, families were selected to be mentor families because they were identified by teachers, counselors and/or administrators as being strong, supportive families who were willing to help other families. To build the skills of these families even further, they spent an entire year working with the program to explore some of their strengths and weakness and build new skills to further strengthen their own family. The mentor families learned new communication, problem solving, conflict resolution and other skills to not only share with their mentor families but to also strengthen their own.

EVIDENCE-BASED SUPPORT

It is very difficult to look at the impact that a program such as this has on the participants, the school, and the broader community. The evidence-base for this project was based primarily on evaluations completed by member families as they participated in monthly events and activities. The evaluations asked each member of each family how they felt what they had just learned about and experienced would impact them and their relationships with their families and others. These evaluations were followed by having families complete homework assignments which helped them incorporate new skills into their daily lives. Family journals were also used to keep running records of family growth and development. At monthly events, families were also asked to say something about how they have been able to incorporate new information and skills into their family.

Comments from evaluations included statements such as: "Not only has my family grown but we were also able to reach out and help another family." "It has been exciting seeing my children realize that they can help other people," and "I like the grassroots philosophy of this program where we can learn new skills and then use them to help families in our own community." From these comments and the other qualitative information gathering strategies that were utilized, we were able to see that families were learning new material, incorporating that material into their lives, sharing the information with others, and becoming stronger more skilled families.

MULTICULTURAL COUNSELING CONSIDERATIONS

Hawaii is a very culturally diverse State which was reflected in the makeup of the school where the project was implemented. The school and project participants included a diverse cultural mix including Chinese, Japanese, African-American, Filipino, Caucasian and Hawaiian/part-Hawaiian families. The major approach that was utilized to ensure a culturally sensitive program was to have a culturally diverse team of people developing, organizing and implementing the program. Another strategy that was often incorporated into project activities was to have families talk about how a new skill or strategy would work for their particular family and culture. By sharing this information everyone was able to learn more about other cultures and expand their cultural sensitivity.

CHALLENGES AND SOLUTIONS

The two major obstacles that this project faced were (1) changes in the school's leadership and (2) maintaining funding for the project. A major key to implementing and maintaining a school-based mentoring program is having a leader or a team of committed individuals who value the program and want to see it succeed. In the case of this project, the Principal of the school was very committed to the project and its goals and objectives. When the Principal transferred to a new job, much of the momentum for the project was lost.

Funding was another obstacle for this project which required a large investment of time and energy to organize and manage. The project was fortunate to receive funding for three years but when the outside financial support for the project ended, it was difficult to continue the project. As stated earlier, it is very difficult to demonstrate how a project like this actually impacts the learning of a particular student. For many school-based projects, making this connection is very important for securing funding.

Future efforts to replicate the program will need to work towards institutionalizing the program as one of the services that the school provides. By institutionalizing the program and building it into the budget of the school, the program would be more resistant to changes in school leadership and the availability of outside funding. Budgeting for and hiring a Project Coordinator at the school who would be responsible for building and maintaining the family mentoring program would also help to ensure its success.

PROCEDURE

Family mentoring is strongly recommended for any school that is trying to support families, build family participation, and improve school-family partnerships. The first step in starting a family mentoring program at your school is to assemble a leadership team that is representative of the school and community and is committed to building a successful program. Providing informational sessions for all of the schools staff and parents is also important in order for everyone to understand the project and it's goals.

The establishment of successful mentoring programs have been found to be based on the inclusion of several important programmatic factors. One of the components that the literature often cites as important for the success of a mentoring project is the development of well articulated, clear, and achievable goals that focus on developing the skills or competence of the mentees (Bernard, 1993; Brindis, Barth, & Loomis,1987; Hamilton, 1990). Based on a review of Project Kako'o and other types of mentoring programs, the following core elements have been identified as important in order to achieve positive mentoring outcomes:

1. Mentoring is particularly effective when intervening with children and their families as early as possible and before major problems arise.

2. Maintaining a consistent level of contact between mentor families and mentee families, typically involving meetings 3-4 times per month for one or more hours per meeting.

3. The mentoring program has a well thought out structure which includes a project management plan, policies, and procedures.

4. Standards and procedures are established for screening of mentor families, orientation and training of mentor families, matching of the mentor and mentee families, and the required frequency of meetings between mentor and mentee families.

5. Mentor families are trained in communication skills, behavioral management skills, interpersonal skills, and evaluation skills enabling them to identify needs of the mentee families.

6. Mentor families are matched with mentee families taking into account the preferences of both families. Considerations regarding appropriate matches are based on factors such as the racial, cultural, and religious backgrounds of the families.

7. In addition to providing social support and friendship, mentor families are encouraged to assist their mentee families in developing specific competencies (i.e., problem solving skills, conflict resolution skills) which will increase positive relationships and interactions in the families.

8. Efforts are made to ensure that caring relationships are developed between the mentor and mentee families that promote improvement in all areas of the family's life.

9. Ongoing supervision and support of each mentoring match is provided by project personnel who maintain frequent contact with all of the families.

10. When assistance is requested or when difficulties arise extra support and referral services are provided.

SUMMARY

The students, parents and staff who participated in The Kako'o Family Mentoring Program were committed to building a strong school community composed of happy and healthy families who would support and nurture capable, inquisitive, and productive children. From a core group of mentor families a web of support was developed where many families in the school community were supported and strengthened.

During the first phase (year 1) of the project twelve families were selected and trained to serve as mentor families. These mentor families worked together to learn new skills and techniques to not only help their own families function better but that they could also pass on and share with other families. The mentor families focused on learning many new skills including those related to improving communication, problem solving, and conflict resolution skills. In addition, the mentor families were encouraged to implement family meetings and to plan for more opportunities to spend quality time together.

Phase 2 (years 2 and 3) of the project involved linking mentor families with other families in the community that were in need of support or nurturing. The project staff continued to support the mentor and mentee families with ongoing training and consultation as well as organizing group activities where both mentor and mentee families could engage with each other. Through these planned activities and events, as well as through activities that the mentor and mentee families set up for themselves, both families were able to grow and develop.

REFERENCES

Benard, B. (1993). Fostering resiliency in kids. *Educational Leadership, 51* (3), pp. 43-48.

Benard, B. (1999). Mentoring: New study shows the power of relationship to make a difference. In N. Henderson, B. Benard, N. Sharp-Light (Eds.), *Resiliency in Action* (pp. 93-99). Gorham, ME: Resiliency in Action, Inc

Brindis, C., Barth, R., & Loomis, A. (1987). Continuous counseling: Case management with teenage parents. *The Journal of Contemporary Social Work, 68* (3), 164-172.

Ferguson, R. (1990). The case for community-based programs that inform and motivate Black male youth. Washington, DC: The Urban Institute.

Grossman, J. B., & Tierney, J. P. (1998). Does mentoring work? An impact study of the Big Brothers Big Sisters Program. *Evaluation Review, 22* (3), 403-426.

Hamilton, S. F. (1990). *Apprenticeship for adulthood*. New York: Free Press.

Hawkins, J. D., Catalano, R. F., & Miller, J. Y. (1992). Risk and protective factors for alcohol and other drug problems in adolescence and early adulthood: Implications for substance abuse prevention. *Psychological Bulletin, 112* (1), 64-105.

Kumpfer, K. L. (1996). Effectiveness of a culturally tailored, family-focused substance abuse program: The strengthening families program. Paper presented at the National Conference on Drug Abuse Prevention Research. Washington, D.C.

Lefkowitz, G. (1986). *Tough change: Growing up on your own in America*. New York: Free Press.

McPartland, J., & Nettles, S. (1991). Using community adults as advocates or mentors for at-risk middle school students: A two-year evaluation of Project Raise. *American Journal of Education, 99* (4), 568-586.

Office of Juvenile Justice and Delinquency Prevention (1998). *Juvenile mentoring Program: 1998 Report to Congress*. Washington, DC: US Department of Justice.

Tierney, J. P., Grossman, J. B., & Resch, N. L. (1995). *Making a difference: An impact study of Big Brothers/Big Sisters*. Philadelphia, PA: Public/Private Ventures.

Torrance, E. P., Goff, K., & Satterfield, N. B (2005). *Multicultural mentoring of the gifted and talented*. Waco, TX: Prufrock Press.

Vygotsky, L. (1978). Interaction *between learning and development: Mind and society*. Cambridge, MA: Harvard University Press

Walsh, J. (1989). *Connections: Linking youth with Caring Adults*. Oakland, CA: Urban Strategies Council.

Werner, E. E., & Smith, R. S. (1992). *Overcoming the odds: High risk children from birth to adulthood*. Ithaca, NY: Cornell University Press.

RESOURCES

NATIONAL CLEARINGHOUSE ON FAMILIES & YOUTH (http://ncfy.acf.hhs.gov/topics/mentoring) - The National Clearinghouse on Families & Youth (NCFY) provides free information for communities, organizations, and individuals interested in developing new and effective strategies for supporting young people and their families. NCFY was established by the Family and Youth Services Bureau (FYSB), U.S. Department of Health and Human Services to link those interested in youth issues with the resources they need to better serve young people, families, and communities.

MENTOR (www.mentoring.org) - MENTOR/National Mentoring Partnership has been working to expand the world of quality mentoring. MENTOR is acknowledged as the nation's premier advocate and resource for the expansion of mentoring initiatives. MENTOR works to provide the support and tools that mentoring organizations need to effectively serve young people in their communities.

Chapter 35
Developing Migrant Family Resilience

Hans Everts

OVERVIEW: *This chapter describes the New Zealand-based Migrant Family Resilience (MFR) project and its relationship with SBFC. It encompasses an integrated number of preventive, psycho-educational programs, designed to enhance the resilience of migrant families, facilitate the integration of children into the local educational system, and build the capacity of associated helping agencies. Some of this chapter cites directly from an article written by the author in International Journal for School-Based Family Counseling (Everts, 2008). We hope that our New Zealand experience contributes to the world-wide development of SBFC-related activities. The author welcomes discussion of any issues raised in this chapter, and is happy to share MFR resources with others who have a suitable professional background.*

BACKGROUND

This chapter represents the conceptual and applied journey of a project team that developed in 2000, comprising the author as project coordinator and senior academic/professional, and a group of post-graduate students in counseling at the University of Auckland, representing a range of migrant communities and all of them mature adults with prior professional experience in their countries of origin. Our project journey started with the team's concern about the school system's receptivity to the arrival in New Zealand of an increasing number of overseas-born students, both migrant and short term fee-paying ones – many from East Asia, and especially ethnic Chinese and Korean. An analysis of pertinent school-based peer support programs highlighted the need to attend also to what was happening in students' families as they adapted to life in the local community. For this we needed a comprehensive model of family functioning, as a conceptual basis for the development of a series of preventive psycho-educational programs that addressed different aspects of the family system. While we started with developing a core parenting program, this soon expanded to address different types of parent, youth, and the parenting couple. We also expanded our focus from migrant families to include refugees, addressed in more detail in chapter 10. These interventions then link back into fostering the adjustment of children in schools. Doing all this represents both the concept and application of SBFC, and much of this project's rationale, underpinning research, programs and practical applications fortuitously coincided with the development of the Oxford Symposia in SBFC over the last ten years. While the project is based in New Zealand, it is our experience that its circumstances are similar to many other communities and countries that have experienced immigration, especially from Asia. The reader is cautioned, however, to examine critically the relevance of the chapter's content to any other community with which they are involved.

MIGRATION, MIGRATING FAMILIES, AND THE RECIPIENT COMMUNITY

Migration is a world-wide and increasingly common phenomenon which profoundly affects the family as a fundamental unit of society. Some migration is regional, and economic opportunity has depleted many rural areas while filling up urban centers, sometimes creating mega-cities in the process. Urban drift has often forced extended family systems to split up into more nuclear units, living in smaller spaces, and in greater isolation from each other. In most cases, however, families remain within the same cultural environment, continue to speak the same language, and stay within familiar social, educational and political systems. Where families migrate from one country to another, additional stresses accrue. The motivation to move may be the same, but a family often faces extra challenges in the form of a foreign language, differences in educational and social systems, different cultural and historical traditions, and a greater sense of being alien and disadvantaged. Both these forms of migration are voluntary. Some migration is, however, involuntary and an increasing number of families are forced to migrate in order to escape war, persecution or disaster. Where that happens, families commonly face yet further challenges. Some of these may be physical (disease, death, poverty), and some may be psychological (personal trauma, family break-up, long-term limbo in transit camps). This is the background against which the MFR project evolved, and the literature at the time on which we drew.

MIGRANT CHILDREN IN THE EDUCATIONAL SYSTEM

Whatever the form of migration, the presence of migrant families in a recipient community has a significant effect on its institutions, including schools. Children with a different language and learning background challenge the educational system – its curriculum, classroom practices and the skills required of the educator. In many high schools in New Zealand, the so-called Peer Support program, run by senior students in the school, seeks to provide supportive care for new students from the first day of their arrival at school. The author's involvement in this area started with a survey of the effectiveness of this program (Everts, 2003a, 2008), which indicated that it met a variety of needs for domestic students. However, it was equally clear that migrant and fee-paying international students required a more tailor-made program, as well as an effective "buddy" system. The results of this survey were used after 2003 in the continued development and evaluation of school-based programs for overseas-born youth to enhance their wellbeing and integration into the local community. Some of this addressed the needs of international students from other countries who come to New Zealand to continue their schooling in an English-speaking system (Everts, 2004a). In a Ministry of Education-supported project conducted in five local high schools (Everts, 2004b), we tracked and evaluated different experimental versions of such programs. We found that their worth was demonstrated in all participating schools, especially when integrated with individual counseling, peer support programs, culture clubs, and senior staff support. Several other school-based programs were developed and trialed in Auckland around that time. Sylvia Chu addressed Hong Kong migrants with her Life Skills for Chinese Adolescent Migrants program (Chu, 2003). Aditi Satyapal, a South African school counselor, ran a 6-session "Knowing Me, Knowing You" program for a group of South African adolescents (Satyapal, 2006). Nyunt Naign was the only one who developed and ran the "Settling In" program for Burmese migrant youth in the community (Naign, 2004). The results of these various projects indicated that, while a significant and effective contribution can be made by school-based programs, the family and the wider community remained underserved, both conceptually and in practice. It is here that the MFR project has targeted its contribution.

MIGRANT CHILDREN IN THEIR FAMILIES

Migrant children in western countries like New Zealand face several major challenges (Chu, 2002; Vong, 2003) - a new language to learn (for some); ambivalent parental attitudes; a local peer group which is not very interested in foreigners; a very different learning style; and stereotyped expectations from some that they will behave like a "model minority" (Sue, 2002). For young people, also facing the normal challenges of being an adolescent, this combination of challenges is very demanding on their sense of identity and belonging. Nevertheless, many adjust relatively quickly and well. In Shih and Tai's (2002) sample, for instance, the children surveyed appreciated the less competitive schooling system; they were becoming more intrinsically motivated, and challenged family traditions from a more bicultural perspective. For many Chinese migrant children, developing a deeper sense of belonging to a family and an ethnic group allows them to achieve a satisfactory sense of personal and ethnic identity - even as covert and overt negative messages from the majority ethnic peer group threaten the immigrant child's self-esteem and ethnic identity (Chu, 2002) and lead to their isolation. Thus, for both

Chinese migrant children and their parents, the young person's sense of identity and self-worth is very dependent on the balance that is struck between the demands of the peer group and those of the parents.

THE INTEGRITY OF THE MIGRANT FAMILY SYSTEM

The child is an inextricable part of the family system as it struggles to adapt to life in a new community, while at the same time attending to its three core tasks - of meeting the needs of its members, meeting the requirements of the new community, and maintaining itself as a functioning unit (Everts, 2003). All core components of the family system are affected:

> 1.Individual members may be challenged in terms of their values, needs, thinking processes, physical wellbeing, spirituality, and self worth.

> 2.The actual range of family members available to make things happen is often depleted as extended family members are left behind, and parents work long hours.

> 3.Parent couples may struggle to meet each other's intimacy needs and maintain strong leadership when their status in the new environment is uncertain.

> 4.Child rearing norms and ways of using discipline are often questioned.

> 5.Gender roles may be very different.

> 6.Traditional communication skills and decision making strategies are commonly tested, and may clash with those found in the new society.

All in all, the family's entire paradigm or system may be challenged, seen as inadequate, or deemed inappropriate in the new community. A child's wellbeing and ability to cope with a new educational system is strongly dependent on the family system's integrity. It is therefore necessary for an educator or school-based counselor to understand family systems in order to assess a child's functioning, and select an appropriate family-orientated intervention strategy.

THE COUPLE'S RELATIONSHIP IN MIGRANT FAMILIES

Most commonly, the parenting couple (if present) is primarily responsible for the family's success in adapting to life in a new country. Individually, however, each of them may struggle to cope with culture shock, cognitive overload, and feelings of inadequacy in the face of a very dissimilar life style, living environment, climate, language, educational/legal/medical systems, and transportation. In a study of 25 Chinese couples who had been in New Zealand for up to 10 years (Wong & Everts, 2002), several talked about being "completely lost". Isolation, loss of support systems, and homesickness can create sadness or depression. Under-employment, unemployment, exploitation or discrimination at work, and racism in the community may provoke negative attitudes and undercut a migrant couple's self-image and self-esteem. Diminished earning power by the breadwinner can challenge the family's hierarchy and create tension in the marriage system, made worse by changes in gender role when women may acculturate faster than men. Couple relationships may become overloaded as a lack of social support forces partners to become more dependent on each other. In spite of emotional commitment to each other, a couple's communication and decision making skills can deteriorate.

Thus, in working with migrant families, educators and helping professionals like SBFCs must be aware of the pivotal role played by the parenting couple in enhancing a child's ability to adapt successfully to life in a new educational environment. Both the wellbeing of a couple's relationship and their ability to provide effective leadership must be addressed in any SBFC intervention strategy – an issue that is discussed further in chapter 10.

PATTERNS OF PARENTING IN MIGRANT FAMILIES

The above stresses faced by many couples help to make their task of parenting more complex and vexed. For one, the family hierarchical structure may be reversed and the boundary of the parenting subgroup becomes confused, due to the parents' slower acculturation and lower level of fluency in English. Children may become "cultural brokers", interpreting the new culture and language for their parents. In addition, many migrant parents typically wish to maintain an emotional closeness with their children. For example, the emphasis on collectivism and interdependence in Chinese culture may lead them to be more protective and supervisory toward their children in comparison with Western parents (Chiu, 1987). Their rapidly Westernizing children, however, may be rebellious toward parental authority and demand more freedom and independence. Some parents may perceive such behavior by their children as disobedient and disloyal. Thus, intergenerational conflicts and tensions are easily provoked if immigrant parents fail to acknowledge their children's needs and renegotiate their emotional relationship with the children. Chinese parents also constantly face the internal conflict of whether to protect their children or to promote independence as done by Western parents (Wu, 2001). Thus, traditional norms and rules are often challenged in a new context, and many migrant Chinese parents find it difficult when they sense their children growing away from Chinese values of conforming, filial piety, and educational priorities (Miller, Yang and Chen, 1997; Sue, 1997; and Wu, 2001). Even in Shih and Tai's New Zealand sample (Shih & Tai, 2002), the parents yearned for more information about New Zealand culture, values and skills to help them in their parenting. They wanted more confidence in using firm but warm parenting practices, as in discipline and control. At the same time, they wanted to support their children as they faced conflicting cultural values and the challenge of slowly establishing a positive ethnic identity, and being accepted by their New Zealand or "Kiwi" peers. Taken together, this highlights how families face challenges to their total family paradigm or model (Lin & Fu, 1990; Wu, 2001). The successful resolution of such family paradigm conflict is crucially important for parents and children alike.

WHAT IS NEEDED?

Against the background of this complex body of literature, it was necessary for our project team to ascertain what migrant families needed (or not) in terms of support from helping professionals. To this end, an initial survey of some 75 parents and 50 children from Korea, Taiwan and Sri Lanka provided information on family adaptation. Parents from all three groups (Kim, 2001) said that family relationships had improved since coming to New Zealand; that they had become more accepting towards their children, but had retained a strong commitment to education and the maintenance of cultural values. Among the children, by far the majority declared that relationships with both parents had improved since coming to New Zealand. Both parents and children wished they had received more early information on aspects of daily life in New Zealand.

These findings indicated to us that most families felt that they had coped reasonably well with the process of settling into New Zealand society and that, for many, there was no urgent need or wish for more drastic therapeutic intervention in family relationships. In fact, such intervention was unfamiliar to them and was regarded with suspicion. They valued education rather than therapy as the best means of making change. Thus we chose a strength-orientated model to guide us in working with these migrant families, and to develop preventive programs to help fill the gap in resources which they had indicated. The research results also indicated that the initial period of a year or two provides a golden opportunity for such preventive work, comprising a limited program of information giving, skill acquisition, emotional support, and community development to strengthen families. If a family learns during that time, it is likely to avoid the development of more serious problems at a later point. For anyone wishing to work with such migrant communities, a prior analysis of how it sees its needs is therefore vitally important.

MIGRANT FAMILY RESILIENCE AS A CONCEPTUAL FRAMEWORK

We have adopted the notion of Migrant Family Resilience (MFR), derived from Froma Walsh's work on family resilience (1996, 2006), as a core framework in our project at both a conceptual and a practical level. It is, of course, based on a family system perspective which guides our analysis of what happens to families as they migrate, as well as our rationale for intervention. Systemically, the family is seen as a functioning unit, whose integrity must be preserved if it is successfully to carry out its tasks of meeting the needs of members and the requirements of society, and of maintaining structural coherence in the face of change (Everts, 2003, 2004d). The concept of resilience lends focus to the way in which we work with family systems. It emphasizes strength and how this can be developed. The results of our migrant family surveys indicate that many families do develop resilience, or new strength, through the very fact of having to face challenges. As Froma Walsh notes "Family resilience is forged *through* adversity, not *despite* it." (Walsh, 1996, 2006). Thus the challenge of migration can be seen as a time of positive crisis, when judicious intervention facilitates the development of systemic strengths, and prevents the development of more serious problems (Everts & Wu, 2004). In addition, the positive connotation of resilience is very much in tune with Asian, especially Chinese, values which emphasize hardiness and the maintenance of an optimistic perspective. Such strength-orientated preventive action often takes the form of more structured training or education, rather than traditional counseling. Education and training are familiar and desirable forms of making change for Asian families. Thus Migrant Family Resilience (MFR) is a construct which focuses on identifying and developing systemic strength in migrant families, with particular emphasis on personal resourcefulness, relational intimacy, effective communication, stable but flexible structure, and community support. As such it is highly compatible with SBFC (Everts, 2007).

PROGRAM DESCRIPTION

DESCRIPTION OF PROGRAMS DEVELOPED TO DATE

Different programs have been developed by the MFR project team for different family subsystems, though all derive from the same rationale. While most have been used within different migrant communities, some have focused on the needs of refugee families (see also chapter 18). This section describes programs developed for various client groups, as well as the process of training group facilitators from different migrant groups, and empowering migrant community organizations.

THE PARENTING PROGRAM

As noted earlier, the most urgent need expressed by migrant community members was for training in parenting skills, using a psycho-educational rather than a therapeutic process. Thus the parenting program was first developed in 2003/2004 from several tentative outlines (eg, Everts & Tai, 2003; Tai, 2004) and, after evaluation of its effectiveness, revised in 2007 (MFR, 2007). Subsequently, it has been modified to meet the specific needs of different client populations – including Burmese (Everts, 2009a), Iranian (Everts, 2009b), and even a mixed group of refugees from Sudan, Ethiopia and Iraq. The program manual comprises an introductory rationale, detailed guidelines for all sessions (introduction, the standard eight sessions, and follow-up), handouts and worksheets for each session, session and program evaluation forms, ethical requirements, attendance certificates, and a bibliography.

Apart from having an appropriate rationale underpinning the program (described above), the following issues require consideration by a SBFC practitioner for this kind of program:

Clientele – differences in age, parenting experience, education (even literacy), occupational background and cultural tradition demand very different ways of handling the same core material. Some applications have involved fewer sessions, a weekend rather than a weekly session format, minimal handouts, less discussion, more action practice, and the use of translators when working with refugee groups. In some groups we have had parents, grandparents, teenage children, and single adults all together in the group – something which provides a great opportunity to work in a family systems manner. Our rationale-based intention to help participants take responsibility for their own decision making and actions may run counter to their traditional customs, and requires careful negotiation – with emphasis on helping families adapt to succeed in a western-style community. The use of a fairly structured program means that more urgent and compelling personal needs cannot be accommodated readily, and may need to be redirected, or addressed in a different way. Unsurprisingly, women attend programs more readily than men, so that the leader must address the men and children through the woman in order to maximize systemic change. With some groups, like Afghans, it has been important to provide separate groups for men and women. In this case, the men (as heads of the household) attended first, then recommended that their wives also had a group; our crowning success came when we were subsequently able to run a combined group! In other variations on the theme, one group was run specifically for single parents (Tai & Everts, 2010), another developed for Korean fathers (Lim, 2010). In all instances, however, the same core themes run through the program and the same basic psycho-educational format is followed.

Process – while structured, the program must be flexibly responsive to the needs of participants, which are shared at the start. The program aims to stimulate all facets of the participants' functioning - have them be fully alert, think critically, and make their own action decisions. Our experience is that it is a very powerful experience during the initial period of adjustment in a new country. But it is only an introductory one, and requires later consolidation through various activities (as discussed below).

Leadership – we have found that the most effective leader is somebody who comes from the same cultural background as the participants, but who has professional qualifications that are recognized in the host country. It needs to be somebody who embodies essential components of both cultures, and who can model the process of integrating them. Most importantly, having such a leader allows the program to be presented in the language of the recipient group, and in a culturally meaningful manner. Conceptually, we stress four aspects of good leadership that we expect to be evident – high levels of personal caring and teaching ability, and moderate levels of participant challenge and of process structuring. These qualities and skills are assessed in potential leaders, shaped during the process of leader training, and assessed in program evaluation. Leaders are inducted through a process of apprentice training, and required to undertake professional supervision. We typically use co-leaders, either somebody who is training to be a leader, or somebody who has a senior role in the recipient community and who will help affirm and consolidate the program's teachings (see below).

Evaluation - protocols are available for the evaluation of sessions by participants and leaders, and for the evaluation of the whole program – with attention to overall value, the usefulness of individual session and teaching techniques, leadership skills, and gains made through participation (see appendix 1).

Attendance certificate - all those who have attended at least two thirds of sessions receive an attendance certificate. Such certificates and their formal presentation are rituals that are highly valued by all our participant communities; a celebratory meal, to which participants contribute food, is similarly fitting.

The standard program contains eight sessions that cover the following topics:
1. *Introduction* – setting group goals; stages of migration; family tasks; understanding children.
2. *Responsible parenting and couple resilience* –things that work, and a conceptual model.
3. *The power of encouragement.*
4. *Effective discipline* – why children misbehave; setting limits and consequences; strategies.

5. *Communication training* – problem ownership; effective and ineffective communication.
6. *Communication training* – I-messages; win-win solutions.
7. *Home-school relationships* - issues for families and schools.
8. *Conclusion* – summary, evaluation, certificates, celebration.

Each individual session is carefully structured to provide continuity with previous ones and comprises teaching points (made orally and in handouts), sharing of participants' personal experiences that illustrate content themes covered, leaders' personal illustrative examples and demonstrations of pertinent techniques, discussion of principles and illustrations, preparation of at-home practice, and a final summary, and group sharing of what they have learned from the session (see Appendix 2). In the example illustrated, the group comprised 14 Iranians, mostly mothers, but also 3 grandparents (including the solitary male). Most of the group had migrated to New Zealand voluntarily, but some were refugees. Most spoke reasonable to good English, and were economically successful. The program was run in the house of one grandparent couple, who were also the co-leader's parents. Each session started with refreshments while participants arrived. The author was leader, while the co-leader was a senior figure in the local Iranian community. Rapport with and respect for the leader as a non-Iranian was based on his academic status, his own migrant background, his experience of parenting and grand-parenting, and his previous work with migrant groups. The author spoke in English, the co-leader translated as required, and discussion took place in both Farsi and English, mostly the former. That discussion was lively, especially since this was the program's third session, and participants were eager to take on board new perspectives as well as have their existing parenting experiences validated. For example, there was considerable debate over how praise fitted in with their current values and life style, alongside (or in conflict with) a tradition emphasis on punishment rather than praise as the best means of discipline. This example illustrates several principles of MFR parenting program rationale, and the flexibility with which this must be applied with a particular clientele – all or part of which may be relevant to the reader of this chapter.

THE GRANDPARENTING PROGRAM

A version of the above parenting program has been developed in conjunction with a local branch of the Age Concern organization (MFR, 2010). It has been delivered to two groups of Chinese grandparents to date. The nature of the resource material and process of operation are essentially similar to the parenting program, and the eight sessions cover much the same ground – except that they are geared to the nature and needs of Chinese migrant grandparents in New Zealand. After the induction phase, this program is now run by professional staff of Age Concern. Such a program is a natural extension of the parenting one and very relevant for many migrant and refugee families – where grandparents are actively involved in child rearing in New Zealand, often live with or near the rest of the family, but are less fluent in English, relatively isolated from the mainstream community, more inclined to keep to traditional values and customs, and therefore likely to be in conflict with or alienated by younger family members.

COUPLE RELATIONSHIP STRENGTHENING PROGRAMS

It is impossible to work with migrant or refugee parents as they seek to develop their parenting skills without considering the quality of their own relationship. It is a tenet of the MFR project rationale that this issue be addressed in its own right, alongside parenting and alongside youth empowerment (as below). Each of these themes has its own focal rationale, and in the MFR model couple relationship strengthening is based on the concept of couple resilience. This issue is addressed in detail in chapter 18, but it should be noted here that several pertinent programs have been developed. Our experience is that migrant couples are reluctant to discuss the details of their own relationship in the more public arena of a group. We have therefore incorporated the theme of couple functioning into the parenting program (see above), with emphasis on the fact that effective parenting depends in part of the ability of the parenting couple to work together as a team. This is the focus of one of the early sessions, and has worked well for us. We also emphasize and illustrate the importance of couple teamwork elsewhere in the program.

YOUTH EMPOWERMENT PROGRAMS

The third theme within the MFR project's conceptual framework focuses on youth empowerment. It recognizes that, in parallel with their parents, young people go through their own process of cultural adaptation, and that this occurs on top of their normal process of personal development. Migrant youth live simultaneously in the two worlds of school and family that SBFC addresses. Some of such youth's adaptation takes place at school, and is the focus of many school-based programs, as discussed in this chapter's background section. Some of this takes place within the family and wider community, and has been specifically targeted by the MFR project. Our work with youth occurs alongside our work with parents and is aimed at the same goals of effective family functioning - where each member gets their needs met, the wider community's requirements (eg. educational) are addressed, and the family as a system maintains a structure that works. In our work with migrant youth, the MFR project has identified a number of core issues that challenge those of school age, and we have developed these into program sessions within the Building Youth Resilience program (MFR 2007). In addition, the project has worked with a specific group of young adults to develop a program that addresses their needs. Both programs are described below.

Building Youth Resilience: As indicated in the "Migrant children in the education system" section, the MFR project built on a range of experimental programs to establish its own Building Youth Resilience program. The core rationale is, of course, the same as the Parenting program. Its clientele includes pre-adolescents (aged 9 to 12) and adolescents (aged 13 to 17), and the core program has been modified somewhat to meet the characteristics and needs of both groups. The program has also been structured into two formats, one comprising eight 2-hour sessions for groups run in the community, the other comprising nine to ten shortened 45-60 minute sessions for groups run in schools. The Leader Manual contains an introductory letter for leaders and co-leaders, a conceptual background, detailed guidelines for each session, handouts, PowerPoint summary statements, evaluation forms, a leader contract, ethical guidelines, attendance certificates, and a bibliography. Co-leaders for programs run to date have included mostly community leaders and school staff; these are not aiming to run programs themselves, but have an important role in their communities to support learning outcomes in the environment in which the young participants function. So far, the Building Youth Resilience program has been run with 7 groups of Chinese, South African, Burmese and Afghan participants; some of these have been in the country for less than a year, some have been in New Zealand for as long as ten years. Three have been run in schools, four in community youth organizations. Minor modifications have been made to the program in its different forms as a result of these experiences.

The core program consists of eight sessions; half address the young person's growing bi-cultural identity, half address family relationships and communication skills:

1. *Valuing my migrant side*
2. *Valuing my Kiwi (New Zealand) side*
3. *Being whole, strong and resilient*
4. *Real friendship*
5. *Dealing with prejudice and bullying*
6. *Good communication – active listening skills*
7. *Good communication – I statements*
8. *Win-win solutions, conclusion and celebration*

Each individual session is structured in a manner which is similar to sessions in the Parenting program. A copy of session 5 on Dealing with Prejudice and Bullying has been included in this chapter's appendices (see Appendix 3). This is a sensitive issue for many migrant youth, as noted in our earlier survey work, and can be particularly painful for refugees. It is also one that is often not talked about much, even though it causes strong and varied reactions. Parents, uncertain themselves in a new country, may be at a loss on how to advise their children, and problem incidents may be ignored if not repressed. Addressing prejudice and bullying is therefore important in our program, especially after consideration in prior sessions of participants' increasingly bi-cultural identities, the importance of positive self-esteem, and the identification of sound friendships. By this stage in the program's process, young people are usually pretty forthcoming in their sharing and supportive of each other – as reflected in the session's structure. Developing a positive response to prejudice and bullying, sanctioned by an authoritative leader and supported by a within-community adult with status, is greatly appreciated by participants and, indirectly, their parents. As noted in the section on evaluation below, this is particularly true of young people during the first year of their adjustment to life in a new country.

Empowering Kowi Youth: The MFR project team recognized that neither parenting nor youth empowerment programs attended to the cohort of young adult migrants who have needs of their own, but who are also in a strategically important position to help their younger peers. Fortuitously, we met up with the Kowiana Association of New Zealand ("Kowi" stands for Korean Kiwi, denoting the successful integration of both cultures). This Association seeks to celebrate and promote its multicultural identity. At its 2008 Conference the author presented a workshop on "Migration and the challenge to family wellness". This flowed through into a survey of Association members, titled "The Kowi Experience" which assessed the satisfactions and difficulties experienced by young adult Kowis, what they needed to be successful, what experiences helped them in the process, and how young adult Kowis might help their adolescent peers (Everts & Kim, 2009). After the presentation of survey results at the 2009 Kowiana Association Conference, a group of its members participated in the development of a single-session "Empowering Kowi Youth" workshop (MFR, 2009) for adolescent Kowis in local high schools (see Appendix 4). This workshop has been presented at three high schools to date, and refined in the process. It runs for some 90 minutes, is led by a professional Korean counselor, assisted by a group of Kowiana Association members, and with a relevant member of school staff (eg. counselor or Korean teacher) responsible for follow-up and the integration of workshop learnings with pertinent school activities. The participants are normally senior Kowi students. The session comprises a PowerPoint presentation of the survey findings, the personal sharing of practical examples by Kowiana Association members, small group discussion of student experiences and workshop presentation points, and planning of further activities. After running these three workshops, the MFR project team has handed the program over to the Kowiana Association to be used in its ongoing community work.

MIGRANT COMMUNITY EMPOWERMENT

Beyond providing preventive psycho-educational programs for members of migrant and refugee communities, the MFR project is committed to a process of empowerment for migrant community organizations. Part of its philosophy is to develop professional services where these are lacking, train members of existing community and educational organizations to run them (if they have appropriate professional qualifications), give them free use of programs once these are adequately validated, then step back and leave the organizations to carry on the good work. The Kowiana project is one example of such empowerment. Migrant community empowerment has been undertaken by the MFR project at three levels:

Training the trainers: Within each migrant or refugee community there are resource people who have a leadership role because they are in traditional leadership positions, or because they have pertinent qualifications and, hopefully, are in a position to help or train their community members in the process of adapting to life in the new community. These people do not have the professional qualifications that would enable them to run MFR programs. Nevertheless, the generalization of learnings from MFR programs requires that community resource people have some understanding of its core content, and can provide some support for its use in family, educational and religious life. So far, the MFR project team has involved two groups of resource personnel from migrant and refugee communities, and taken them through an intensive 6-hour overview of core MFR program components (listening skills, the power of encouragement, dealing with arguments, strong couples/good parents, effective discipline, and the dangers of anger). The first instance involved a group of refugee community resource people from a variety of backgrounds. The second group comprised a range of professionally trained counselors, working for an Asian Family Services agency. Some of the latter took the subsequent step of training as group facilitators (below). As noted in previous sections, a similar process of "training the trainer" has sometimes been undertaken by having the person involved as an informal co-leader in a group.

Training group facilitators: The MFR project specifies that group facilitators must be able to handle both aspects of its psycho-educational programs. They must be educators, able to teach cognitive information and behavioral skills. They must also have the psychological and counseling skills needed to deal with client values, emotional needs and personal vulnerabilities. To manage both tasks, we say that group facilitators must have had personal experience of migration or a migration-like process. They must have had prior tertiary training in one of the helping professions such as psychology, counseling, social work, medicine, religion, or education. They must have also undertaken a process of self-examination, counseling or personal development, so that issues in MFR programs have been successfully faced by them. That may involve them having been participants in such a program. Potential facilitators are then taken on as apprentice co-leaders. Their level of responsibility in actively leading a program is increased as they demonstrate capability. When leader evaluation and participant feedback indicate appropriate competence, new facilitators are certificated and permitted to run programs themselves. Such programs continue to be owned under copyright by the MFR project. Leaders may use them free of charge, on condition that they continue to receive professional supervision, and that the delivery of each program is evaluated, with the results returned to the MFR project.

Empowering community organizations or educational institutions: At a broad community level, the MFR project (like many other SBFC-related teams) has a responsibility to facilitate social change within organizational contexts. Where possible, we will come in and run our specialized programs, train resource personnel and facilitators, and run workshops on aspects of MFR as required – especially for people in leadership roles. We have run such workshops for senior school personnel, church leaders, and officials in migrant community organizations. While this at least ensures support for the running of MFR programs, it is our hope that it may contribute to the constructive evolution of organizational culture. We then step back and support the organization or institution involved in running MFR programs as appropriate – as with the Kowiana Association. For anybody working in this field, the same challenge beckons.

RELATIONSHIP TO THE SBFC MODEL

The focus in the MFR project is primarily on prevention with families in terms of Gerrard's paradigm of SBFC (Gerrard, 2008), though some of its work (especially with children) involves working directly with educational institutions. Conceptually and practically, this requires one to stretch across a wide spectrum that ranges from education systems and individual schools on one extreme end, through the individual child, into the family as a system (comprising several subsystems), and finally into the community institutions that support the family. Such a stretch poses a challenge to SBFC and MFR to provide an intervention process that is detailed, comprehensive and flexible; practitioners who, individually or collectively, can provide an appropriate service; agencies with sufficient vision and working brief; and training programs that are sufficiently focused, thorough and comprehensive enough to match that vision (Everts, 2006). For people working in this field, including the MFR project, the SBFC framework provides a significant anchor point.

More specifically, the SBFC framework requires inclusion of a comprehensive model of family functioning that allows its different parts to be addressed through different but interrelated intervention programs. Beyond the family, the SBFC framework must link in with the community agencies that represent and address families, including religious, social and cultural ones. These wider community systems have received little attention in the SBFC literature (Gerrard, 2008), but are natural extensions of the family system. As noted above, the MFR project has had to address these in its intervention activities. With respect to schools, our experience reinforces the notion that a broad orientation must be taken. For example, we have found ourselves working with educational institutions that include public schools as well as private ones associated with the Christian or Muslim faith, and with broadly educational organizations that devote themselves to teaching the language, history and culture of a child's country of origin. We have worked with the educational section of the refugee reception centre where all newly arrived refugees in New Zealand spend their first six weeks in intense induction – a place at the very forefront of preventive work with families. In each such organization, the challenge for us and those working from a SBFC perspective is to strengthen its ability to address the migrant child's personal, family and educational needs. With such a broad working brief, it is difficult to keep all the balls in the air, and we have found it easy to have a child's school life fade into the background while we focus on its family and associated community organizations. Any one of us can only achieve so much, but it behooves us to take collective responsibility for completing SBFC's loop that stretches across child, school and family.

EVIDENCE-BASED SUPPORT

Evaluation has been an inherent part of running MFR programs, where such evaluation is practicable and likely to be valid. However, any preventive, time-limited, psycho-educational program is likely to have an impact that is short term rather than lasting by itself. Such programs need follow-up, purposeful generalization, or linking in with other activities. When working with migrant or refugee clients, further complications arise in the process of evaluation. Social desirability in the form of being polite and "saying the right thing" is always present, and language or educational limitations may impede fullness of expression. While desirable, we have not collected longer-term follow up data on our programs. The evaluations reported below suffer from all these limitations. We typically use a mixture of quantitative and qualitative measures. Client feedback is collected most consistently, while informal leader feedback during or after a program is normally obtained but not reported here.

PARENTING PROGRAMS

A comprehensive evaluation was carried out on the fundamental Parenting program in 2007 (Kim & Everts, 2007). In it, both participants and leaders confirmed the validity and effectiveness of the essential structure, content, and leadership of the Parenting program as then constituted. Its provisions for cognitive input, personal sharing and support, and practical skill learning addressed the varied needs that participants brought. Strong leadership, incorporating a range of counseling and educational skills, was needed to manage the complexities of group process. The program needed some development of content, leader style and group processes, which were incorporated into the 2007 revision of the Parenting program (MFR, 2007). Typical of more recent program evaluations is that run for the Iranian parents noted above (Everts, 2009b). Participants consistently liked its sessions and presentation strategies, appreciated a positive leadership style, and sought to put into action listening skills, setting rules, being positive (friendly, calm, patient) with the children, and discussing matters with their husbands. These actions were still strongly present at a four-week follow up. In 2010, a group of Chinese parents attended a program at a local high school. Most reported (Tai, 2010) learning "a lot" and found the topics of encouragement, discipline, listening and home-school relationships (important for SBFC) especially useful. Teaching presentations and group discussion were appreciated, and leadership style (caring, challenge, teaching and organization) was affirmed. Participants reported being "reasonably successful" in being more attentive, thoughtful, calm, and making I-statements. In 2011 a community-based program was run for a group of Ethiopian men (Saeid, 2011). They liked the program a "lot" or "reasonably well", and found the sessions on understanding children and families, encouragement, listening skills and win-win solutions most helpful. They rated the variety of teaching techniques and leadership style highly. Most rated themselves as clearly successful in implementing a range of program learnings.

THE GRANDPARENTING PROGRAM

The second of the grandparenting programs was run in 2011 (Tai & Lai, 2011). Most participants rated it having learned a "reasonable" amount, and especially liked the sessions on responsible parenting for grandparents, encouragement, and communication. For them, teaching, group discussion and handouts were helpful, as well as sound leadership style. They reported themselves as "reasonably successful" or "OK" in being more affirmative, listening better and self-sharing more.

YOUTH PROGRAMS

The Building Youth Resilience program has been run with 7 different groups. In general terms, the evaluation data suggests that it is most effective when provided within the first year of young migrants arriving in the host country. In one instance, two programs were run in a middle school by its counselor (an immigrant from South Africa herself) for 11-13 year old South African and Korean migrants respectively (van Zyl, 2008). All liked the program "a lot", with all topics except Family Rules (surprise!) appreciated. Participants liked the use of a variety of facilitation techniques, especially group discussion and drawing. The program was seen to be successful in its overall objective of helping immigrant young people integrate their new Kiwi side with their existing culture and celebrating both, in fostering new friendships, and in building resilience by teaching strategies on how to deal with bullying and teasing. Parents expressed appreciation for the opportunity given their children to openly address such topics. Another program was run for Afghan children, from both sexes and representing two languages (Saeid, 2008). It was run in a community centre as part of its language school. Most topics were well liked, PowerPoint slides captured attention, and the use of cultural proverbs and religious quotes added meaning to content themes. Teachers and parents reported that children had improved in terms of integrating and celebrating their Afghan and Kiwi sides, avoiding bullying, and practiced active listening and effective communication. The program's general use also highlights the value of running parenting and youth programs in tandem, of integrating their content, and of having local peers participate in some sessions. This counters the danger of a program like this being seen as subversive by parents who do not participate in their own program. While logistics militate against it in many instances, one successful program has been run for Afghan mothers and daughters together. Combining parents and children in the one program remains a valid idea whose time is yet to come in the life of the MFR project.

Each "Empowering Kowi Youth" program has also been evaluated. In the most recent one (Kim, 2011), the participating Korean high school students said that on average they learned a "reasonable amount", and found all aspects of the process useful. The members of the Kowiana Association, who co-facilitated the session, reported gains in their own confidence and presentation skills. Evaluation of all three programs run to date suggests that sharing personal experiences by older Kowis, together with small and large group discussion, and a brief PowerPoint presentation, is most valuable. This form of youth empowerment is important because of its multiple impacts – it strengthens both migrant adolescents and young adults, and enhances the role of school counselors. The program can also be used with parents and community agencies, though this has not been done by the MFR project to date.

MIGRANT COMMUNITY EMPOWERMENT

In the training-the-trainers category, two groups of resource personnel have undergone the program. The group of refugee community resource people, varied in experiential background, evaluated the program and liked its content and the way it was taught. However, in spite of good intentions, a follow-up session four months later showed that most had not applied much of the material. In fact, they needed and received a solid refresher course. The second group, of professional counselors in an Asian Family Services agency, also liked the program and the way it was taught, but demonstrated a deeper insight into how to apply it in their personal and professional lives than the first group. Follow-up of these programs is yet to take place.

No systematic evaluation of the training of group facilitators has taken place, because of the intensely personal nature of the process involved. Group facilitators have, however, continued to run programs in community settings where they could be paid for their work. The effects of workshops on empowering community organizations or educational institutions is equally difficult to assess, since the organizations involved are often large and engaged in a variety of activities. It is fair to say that, where the MFR project team does not provide continuing input, provision of its programs tends to fade.

MULTICULTURAL COUNSELING CONSIDERATIONS

In line with the themes set out by Marcel Soriano on cultural congruence in SBFC (Soriano, 2004), the entire MFR project is multicultural in nature. Its team members represent different cultural communities. The project trustees include New Zealanders of Taiwanese, Korean, Afghan and Dutch extraction. We include migrants and refugees, and have been in New Zealand for varying periods of time. All, except for the Dutch-born author, have strong connections with our own ethnic communities and occupy leadership positions of varying kinds. We represent Christian, Muslim and Buddhist faiths. We all have post-graduate qualifications in at least two professions – including medicine, psychology, counseling, social work, the ministry, and even dentistry. The very nature of our team is diverse in origin, but united in its commitment to the development of New Zealand as a multi-cultural community, and competent in the practical application of the MFR project's aims. As such, the project team sees itself as an agent of empowerment for community organizations or educational institutions which need but do not have the resources that the project has developed. From that starting point, supported by the SBFC framework, we have found that core values, program content, group leadership, session process, language used, and other agencies worked with, are all colored by the multicultural context in which we work. This has been evident in every preceding section of this chapter. Our experience is, no doubt, typical of the one that many SBFCs find themselves in. Some of our rationale or practice may be culturally embedded in the New Zealand context, and needs translating into or be critiqued from the perspective of other contexts. What is challenging for us, though, is to find what in our work is culturally relative, and what is universal. We constantly strive to find the latter as a common base when working with diverse migrant and refugee groups - what must be accepted as non-negotiable, and what can be negotiated in a program. Much session process is spent identifying that and helping participants think their way through the issues involved in such a way that they can more easily accommodate to life in a multicultural community.

CHALLENGES AND SOLUTIONS

Our project, like other similar ones in the SBFC-related area, has experienced its fair share of challenges and obstacles during the past ten years of its life. Our solutions, insofar as we have them, may not be yours. These are some of the challenges, not necessarily listed in order of priority:

Conceptual integrity and clarity – without a comprehensive conceptual framework, our work would lack integrity. The MFR framework, based on a systemic model of individual and family functioning (Everts, 2003), took many years to develop but has provided a secure underpinning for our practical work.

A compatible team at the core of the project – it has taken a group of people who have experienced similar life challenges, who share similar values and world views, who are prepared to collaborate rather than compete, and who have the time to put into the project that is needed (always a challenge!). Such a team, not large, takes time to find one other and grow together.

A constant need for promotion – in this area of work there is constant stress, pressure and change. We needed a core of people who constantly promoted, supported clients, and advocated with community agencies who had their own agendas. In our own case, the MFR project team has suffered recently from attrition, and thus a diminution in its capacity to promote the cause.

Having and training the right leaders – it is hard to get the right combination of personal qualities, life experiences and professional skills required to make a good leader; somebody who can be a teacher, model, counselor and manager all at the same time. We developed a clear and experiential process of induction, but found that there is no single recipe for success.

Unrealistic expectations by participants – for a quick fix or instant expert advice, which take away from a participant the responsibility for their own actions. As in other forms of cross-cultural counseling, our programs emphasize constantly the need for participants to take such responsibility.

The fluid dividing line between psycho-educational prevention and therapeutic treatment – in spite of selection, program participants sometimes display signs of serious disturbance during a session that cannot be managed within the confines of the program. This necessitates the availability at all times of alternative therapeutic options, especially when working with refugees who may need multiple forms of help – all of which can hopefully be coordinated.

Sufficient funding or salaried team members – to keep the project afloat. We were fortunate in that we had enough salaried people on board, and an attractive project to sell. But we were never rich, and seldom had enough forward funding to write a long term business plan.

The short term nature of psycho-educational preventive work - on its own, the results of our programs can disappear within a disappointingly short time. Programs must be followed through systematically by other activities, or informally by those around the participants. This is why a comprehensive systemic approach has more chance of lasting success.

Limited empirical follow up – associated with the above is the project's lack of systematic follow-up research to ascertain the effects of programs some time afterwards.

SUMMARY

The MFR project is one that has gradually evolved in response to the needs of the migrant and refugee communities that have settled in increasing numbers in New Zealand. This evolution has involved a great deal of experiential learning. Throughout that process, the SBFC framework has provided us with an invaluable conceptual anchor, and the Institute's annual Symposia are a precious opportunity to share experiences and update our world views. It is fair to say, however, that the MFR project and its development in the New Zealand context have been relatively unique from the SBFC perspective. While unique in some ways, our experience suggests that the issues we have encountered are universal, and that our response to them has many parallels with what is taking place in other parts of the world.

The elements of the MFR project that we believe have been central to its nature, and important in its modest success include the following: leadership by a multicultural and multi-professional team; a comprehensive conceptual framework; working through skilled leaders from within the client communities; a diverse but interrelated range of interventions; an emphasis on psycho-educational preventive programs where appropriate; the empowerment of existing resource personnel and community agencies; recognizing that a range of agencies are required in order to effect change within the triad of child, family, and school; flexibility in adapting to circumstance; and a commitment to accountability and professionalism.

In our work we are limited by the modest size of the project team, and have lost impetus as a result of the disestablishment of the charitable trust that provided funding. However it is critically important at this stage of the project's evolution that our experiences are laid alongside those of our colleagues within the international SBFC community - to enable mutual learning, and to inspire further creative initiatives in our common quest to develop healthy multicultural societies.

PROCEDURE FOR FURTHER CONSULTATION

Should the reader of this chapter be interested in comparing their own experiences with those of the MFR project, or wish to replicate any aspect of our project, we recommend that they inform the author of their background, work context, and professional involvement. This should establish common ground, and raise issues of client characteristics, conceptual rationale and practical applications. We anticipate that there would much to share and learn from each other. Any action project that emerges from that process is likely to be of benefit to both parties.

REFERENCES

Chiu, L. H. (1987). Child-rearing attitudes of Chinese, Chinese American, and Anglo-American mothers. *International Journal of Psychology, 22,* 409-419.

Chu, S. (2002). Adaptation problems of Chinese immigrant students in New Zealand high schools. *New Zealand Journal of Counselling, 23,* 39-46.

Chu, S. (2003). *A Life Skills Training Programme for Chinese migrant students in New Zealand.* Auckland: University of Auckland, Unpublished EdD Manuscript.

Everts, H. (2003a). *Integrating pastoral care in schools with the enhancement of family resilience - a New Zealand project for migrant families.* Paper delivered at the First Oxford Symposium in School-Based Family Counselling, Keble College, Oxford.

Everts, J.F. (2003b). An integrated Model of Functioning for use in counselling and Reaction Pattern Research. Auckland: University of Auckland: Research Paper.

Everts, J. F. (2004a). The pastoral needs of international students in New Zealand secondary schools. *New Zealand Journal of Counselling 25, 2,* 54-73.

Everts, H. (2004b). *The development and evaluation of peer group-based resources to meet the pastoral needs of International Students in selected New Zealand secondary schools.* Wellington: Ministry of Education: Research Report.

Everts, H. (2004c). *Vision and challenge in School-Based Family Counselling.* Paper presented at the Second Annual Oxford Symposium in SBFC. Oxford: Brasenose College.

Everts, H. (2004d). *Migant Family Resilience.* Paper presented at the Inaugural International Asian Health Conference. New Zealand: Auckland, November.

Everts, H. (2006). *The Contribution of the Oxford Symposia to School-Based Family Counselling: Development of a Vision and its Implications for Research.* Paper presented at the Fourth Annual Oxford Symposium in SBFC. Oxford: Brasenose College.

Everts, J.F. (2007). *Applying Principles of School-Based Family Counselling to Preventive Intervention with Migrant and Refugee Families.* Paper presented at the Fifth Oxford Symposium in School-Based Family Counselling. Hong Kong: University of Hong Kong, June.

Everts, J.F. (2008). Integrating supportive care in schools with the enhancement of family resilience – A New Zealand project for immigrant families. *International Journal for School-Based Family Counseling, 1,* 57-64.

Everts, J.F. (2009a). *An evaluation of the Parenting Programme for Burmese parents.* Auckland: University of Auckland, Faculty of Education: Research Report.

Everts, J.F. (2009b). *An evaluation of the Parenting Programme for Iranian parents.* Auckland: University   of Auckland, Faculty of Education: Research Report.

Everts, H. & Kim, H. (2009). *The Kowi Experience.* Kowiana Association Annual Conference,
University of Auckland, New Zealand, July.

Everts, J.F. & Tai, J. (2003). A Parenting Programme for migrant families. Auckland: University of
Auckland, Faculty of Education: Draft Program.

Everts, H. & Wu, P. (2004). *Identity and resilience in families facing cultural transition through migration - with illustrative reference to Chinese families in New Zealand and Taiwan.* Paper presented at
the   Third Biennial International Conference on Intercultural Research, National Taiwan Normal
University, Taipei, May.

Gerrard, B. (2008). School-Based Family Counseling: Overview, trends, and recommendations for future
research. *International Journal for School-Based Family Counseling,1,* 6-24.

Kim, H. (2001). *Parenting skills and couple relationships of Korean parents who have migrated with adolescent children to New Zealand.* Auckland: University of Auckland: unpublished MEd
dissertation.

Kim, H. (2011). *An evaluation of the Empowering Kowi Youth Programme.* Auckland: University of
Auckland, Faculty of Education: Research Report.

Kim, H. & Everts, J.F. (2007). *An evaluation of the Parenting Programme.* Auckland: University of
Auckland, Faculty of Education: Research Report.

Lim, G. (2010). *Parenting Programme for Korean Fathers.* Auckland, New Zealand: University of
Auckland, Faculty of Education: Draft Program.

Lin, C.Y., & Fu, V. R. (1990). A comparison of child-rearing practices among Chinese, immigrant Chinese,
and Caucasian-American parents. *Child Development, 61,* 433-39.

Migrant Family Resilience Project (2007). *Parenting Programme.* Auckland: University of Auckland,
Faculty of Education: Program Manual.

Migrant Family Resilience Project (2008). *Building Youth Resilience Programme.* Auckland: University of
Auckland, Faculty of Education: Program Manual.

Migrant Family Resilience Project (2009). *Empowering Kowi Youth Programme.* Auckland: University of
Auckland, Faculty of Education: Program Manual.

Migrant Family Resilience Project (2010). *Parenting for Grandparents Programme.* Auckland: University
of Auckland, Faculty of Education: Program Manual.

Miller, G., Yang, J., & Chen, M. (1997). Counseling Taiwan Chinese in America. *Counselor Education and
Supervision, 37,* 22-34.

Nyunt Naing Thein (2006). *The "Settling In" Refugee Youth Programme - A study of the development and   evaluation of the programme for refugee youth in the Burmese refugee community, New Zealand.*
Auckland: University of Auckland: Unpublished Masters research paper.

Saeid, A. (2008). *An evaluation of the Building Youth Resilience Programme for Afghan children.*
Auckland: University of Auckland, Faculty of Education: Research Report.

Saeid, A. (2010). *An evaluation of the Parenting Programme for Afghan men.* Auckland: University of
Auckland, Faculty of Education: Research Report.

Satyapal, A. (2006). *"Knowing Me Knowing You" – South African Migrant Youth Programme* Auckland:
The University of Auckland: Unpublished Masters research paper.

Shih, S. & Tai, J. (2002). *Migrant Family Resilience: A study of the process af adaptation for 25 Taiwanese   migrant families in New Zealand.* Auckland: University of Auckland: Unpublished
Manuscript.

Soriano, M. (2004). *School-Based Family Counseling: A caring, culturally congruent bridge to diverse
communities.* Paper presented at the Second Annual Oxford Symposium in SBFC. Oxford:
Brasenose College.

Sue, D. (1997). Counseling strategies for Chinese Americans. In C. C. Lee (Ed.), *Multicultural issues in
counseling: New approaches to diversity (2nd ed.).* VA: American Counseling Association.

Tai, J. (2004). *Effective parenting for Chinese families.* Auckland: University of Auckland: unpublished MEd. Dissertation.

Tai, J. (2010). *An evaluation of the Parenting for Single Parents Programme.* Auckland: University of Auckland, Faculty of Education: Research Report.

Tai, J. & Lai, J. (2011). *An evaluation of the Parenting for Grandparents Programme.* Auckland: University of Auckland, Faculty of Education: Research Report.

Vong, C. (2002). The impact of migration on the Chinese family. *New Zealand Journal of Counselling, 23,* 21-24.

Walsh, F. (1996). The concept of family resilience: Crisis and challenge. *Family Process, 35,* 261-281.

Walsh, F. (2006). *Strengthening family resilience (2nd ed).* New York: Guilford.

Wong, J. & Everts, H. (2002). How Chinese families develop resilience. *New Zealand Journal of Counselling, 23,* 25-32.

Wu, S. J. (2001). Parenting in Chinese American families. In N. B. Webb, *Culturally diverse parent-child and family relationships.* NY: Columbia University Press.

Van Zyl, L. (2008). *An evaluation of the Building Youth Resilience Programme for South African and Korean youth.* Auckland: University of Auckland, Faculty of Education: Research Report.

APPENDIX (1)   Parenting Program Evaluation

University of Auckland - Faculty of Education
Migrant Family Resilience Project

PARENTING PROGRAMME - PROGRAMME EVALUATION FORM

1. How much have you learned in this programme that is useful for you?   (circle)

a lot   a reasonable   something   not   nothing
                 amount   much

2. How useful has each of the topics been for you? (for each topic, circle one   number,
from 7 (very useful) to 1 (no use).

Topics	very useful	7	6	5	4	3	2	1no use
Understanding our family in a changing culture		7	6	5	4	3	2	1
Understanding our children		7	6	5	4	3	2	1
Responsible parenting		7	6	5	4	3	2	1
The power of encouragement		7	6	5	4	3	2	1
Effective discipline		7	6	5	4	3	2	1
Communication training - listening skills		7	6	5	4	3	2	1
Communication training - self-expression skills		7	6	5	4	3	2	1
Communication training - win-win skills		7	6	5	4	3	2	1

3. How useful have the following techniques been? (For each, circle one number)

Techniques	very useful	7	6	5	4	3	2	1no use
Teaching presentations			7	6	5	4	3	2	1
Group discussions			7	6	5	4	3	2	1
Handout notes			7	6	5	4	3	2	1
Homework			7	6	5	4	3	2	1
Having these group members			7	6	5	4	3	2	1

Please turn over

4. How do you rate the leadership style?   (for each, circle one number)

Leader Caring - warmth, trustworthiness, attention to all group members
(very strong) 7   6   5   4   3   2   1 (weak)

Leader Challenge - for group members to try new ways of thinking or doing things
(very strong) 7   6   5   4   3   2   1 (weak)

Leader Teaching Skills - being clear, practical; personal wisdom
(very strong) 7   6   5   4   3   2   1 (weak)

Leader Organisation Skills - managing time, preparation for sessions
(very strong) 7   6   5   4   3   2   1 (weak)

5. What do you now do differently as a result of participating in this programme? (please describe)

6. How successful have these changes been so far? (circle one)

| very Successful | reasonably successful | OK | little change | no change | things have got worse |

7. If anything, what would be a useful follow-up from this programme for you?

8. Any other comments about this programme?

APPENDIX (2)   Parenting Program – Session III (Iranian group)
LEADER GUIDELINES

Session III: The Power of Praise

AIM OF SESSION
To understand, appreciate and apply the skills of praise and encouragement.

SESSION STRUCTURE (2-hour session)
Follow-up from previous week and introduction to this session (20 mins)
Personal experience of praise and encouragement (30 mins)
What to do and not do when you give praise (30 mins)
Personal application (20 mins)
Summary (20 mins)

Follow-up from previous week and introduction to this session (20 mins)
Welcome; discuss home activities from last session; introduce this week's theme in the context of the wider programme. Hans shares image of tree.

Personal experience of praise and encouragement (30 mins)
Ask participants in two small groups to share one example each of when they were given praise or encouragement in the last week. Who gave it? What for? How did it feel to be praised? Leader collates information.
Information is shared in the large group.
Discuss and connect with section 1 in the handout, and why everybody needs praise.

What to do and not do when you give praise (30 mins)
Hans and Neda demonstrate what to do; ask for comments.
Go through sections 2 and 3 in the handout.
Hans and Neda demonstrate what not to do; ask for comments.
Go through section 4 in the handout.

Personal application (20 mins)
In two small groups, have participants share what they can/should do to give more praise or encouragement to their children (and others in the family).

Summary (20 mins)
Do a round in which each participant shares one thing they learned in this session that is important for them. Affirm each. How will they share learnings with their husbands and family? Put this session into wider programme context and note next week's topic.

© Migrant Family Resilience Programme (2009)

Migrant Family Resilience - Parenting Programme 2009 – T3 Iranian Group

Session III Handout

THE POWER OF PRAISE

What all children (and parents) need

ATTENTION   -   (for example, being listened to)

ACCEPTANCE   -   (for who they are, as family members)

APPROVAL   -   (for being successful and for trying)

AFFECTION   -   (for who they are, not for what done)

Giving praise or encouragement – what to do
Praise children for what they do, for what they try to do, and for who they are.
Look for chances to praise and encourage your child (catch them being good).
Tell them what they did, and why it is good.
Be honest in what you say; speak the truth.

The results of praise or encouragement
Your child will understand more about what is good or bad to do, will be more motivated to do good things, will feel happier, will relax more physically, and will feel better as a person.
Your child and you will feel better about each other.

Giving praise or encouragement – what not to do
Don't give too much or too little praise.
Don't give praise or encouragement for things that are not true, or that are wrong.
Don't praise or encourage when you don't mean it.

© Migrant Family Resilience Programme (2009)

Parenting Programme 2009 – T3 Iranian Group, Session III Handout (Farsi)

مکالمه و خوب گوش دادن
والدین خوب بودن:

در خانواده عشق بهتر از عصبانیت است .
قدردانی و پاداش بهتر از تنبیه است .
رشد شخصیتی فرزندتان از درون متداوم تر از کنترل فرزندتان از بیرون است .
عشق و احترام اکتسابی است نه با اصرار و زور والدین .
اگر می خواهید همه جوره در خدمت فرزندان باشید، به آنها گوش بدهید .

برای خوب گوش دادن و در میان گذاشتن افکار چه باید کرد:

زمانی درست و مکانی درست را برای صحبت انتخاب کنید .
با رفتارتان، حرکت های بدنتان و صورتتان نشان دهید که با دقت گوش می دهید .
فرزندتان را تشویق به در میان گذاشتن افکار و احساستشان کنید .

599

. اطمینان حاصل کنید که به طور کامل متوجه منظور فرزندتان شدید
. از فرزتتان به خاطر به در میان گذاشتن افکار و احساستشان تشکر کنید.

زمانی که شما خوب گوش دهید:

. فرزند شما خوشحال میشود که به او گوش داده شده، مورد احترام واقع شده و
می فهمد که عاشقش هستید
. فرزند شما متقابلاً به شما احترام می گذارد و دوستتان خواهد داشت
. ارتباط و عشق بین شما و فرزندتان بهتر خواهد شد
. والدین خوبی خواهید بود

خوب گوش ندادن۔ چکار نباید کرد:

. موشکافی و نکته سنجی نکنید، به فرزندتان نگویید که بد یا بی ارزش هستند
. سریعاً به فرزندتان نگویید که چه کند، این زمان گوش دادن است.
. تظاهر به گوش دادن و اهمیت دادن به فرزندتان نکنید وقتی که حقیقتاً اینگونه نیستید.

نتیجه بد گوش دادن:

. فرزند شما احساس بدی می کند، عصبانی می شود و فکر می کند که گول خورده و به شما اعتماد نمی کند.
. مکالمات بین شما لطمه می خورد و درنتیجه ارتباطتان لطمه می خورد

APPENDIX (3) BUILDING YOUTH RESILIENCE PROGRAM – Session V

Migrant Family Resilience Project
Building Youth Resilience Programme (Brief Edition)

LEADER GUIDELINES

Session V: Dealing with Prejudice and Bullying

AIM OF SESSION
To identify patterns of prejudice and bullying, and their underlying motivation. To explore a range of options in dealing with prejudice and bullying. To evaluate these options, and connect the themes from that the preceding sessions with them.

SESSION STRUCTURE (for a 45 minute session)
Welcome and introduction (10 mins)
The experience of prejudice and bullying (10 mins)
Dealing with prejudice and bullying (20 mins)
Practical application (5 mins)

Welcome and introduction (10 mins)
Welcome
Any questions, issues or relevant events since last session?
Brief statement of session aim

The experience of prejudice and bullying (10 mins)
Do this with the whole group. Ask them what examples of prejudice (ie. negative attitudes) and bullying (ie. actual actions) they have run into this year. Write these down briefly on the board. When you have a good range of them, stop. Express your empathy, and affirm them for sharing painful experiences.

Analyse what is on the board. What are the patterns? What are the feelings that underlie prejudice and bullying? Eg. ignorance, misinformation, fear, jealousy.

Dealing with prejudice and bullying (20 mins)
Ask the group to share examples of how they have dealt with prejudice and bullying. At this stage, just note examples and write them on the board until you have a good range.
Now go to the Handout and PP, and relate to what the group has said.

Practical application (5 mins)
Do a round, each participant shares one thing that they have learned today.
Draw attention to the task for next time.
Affirm group achievements, give farewell and bestwishes.

© Migrant Family Resilience Project

Building Youth Resilience Programme – Brief Edition
Session V - Handout
DEALING WITH PREJUDICE AND BULLYING
The following are some ideas for dealing with prejudice and bullying. They are not listed in order of priority, and they are not foolproof. Other options may exist.

Be strong and resilient
Remember who you are and the strengths you have. You have a rich personality because you have two sides and two cultures to draw on. You have learned important skills and qualities in coping with the challenges of migration.
Take pride in what you have achieved as a migrant, and in your good qualities. Be positive and tough. If you are strong and resilient, nobody can hurt you.

Develop "I'OK, you're OK" relationships
Find other people, of all cultures, who are "winners" – who have a positive attitude and who want to get on with others. They are the best kind of friends.
Be a really good friend yourself. Be positive, affirm your friends, have a "Get on with" attitude. This is the best defence against an "Us versus Them" or a "loser" attitude.

Join in with the locals
Join in with the locals where you can, whether this is in class activities, projects, hobbies, sports, cultural activities.
Learn the skills needed to join in – English language, sports skills etc.
Accept that you have to make most of the moves. While this may not seem fair, that is how it is, and you have to make the effort to join in.
Contribute to the way that local groups and activities work. Offer to help in the classroom, school, clubs, events.

Stand up for your culture
Inform others about your culture, beliefs, customs and lifestyle.
Support cultural celebrations and social events; visit each other's homes.

Avoid trouble

Where possible, ignore insults and bullying. Hold yourself together proudly and let it bounce off you - like water off a duck's back.

Where possible, avoid confrontations or situations where you know that trouble is brewing.

Avoid retaliation – it only inflames the situation and plays right into the hands of the bullies.

Avoid developing group situations where it becomes an "Us versus them" conflict. That undermines any "Getting on with each other" approach.

Be smart

Recognise that standing tall yourself, joining in, and developing good friendships are the most positive and successful ways of defeating prejudice and bullying in the long run. Being prejudiced and being a bully yourself only makes the problem worse.

Where action is needed, go to the authorities – teachers, leaders, counsellors, the principal, your parents, community leaders. Have good evidence, and make sure that your own attitudes and behaviour are good in the face of prejudice and bullying by others. People in authority have much more power to act. But keep up the pressure if nothing happens.

FOR NEXT TIME

Of the different suggestions listed above, which are ones that you are already doing? Take pride in that.

What else are you already doing that protects you against prejudice and bullying? Affirm yourself for any of that.

What are suggestions that you yourself could do more of? Be realistic. It is better to succeed in one thing that is small but important, than to fail in something that is worthwhile but too big. If there is one such new activity that you might undertake, what might it be?

What are others already doing that you can support? Some things are best tackled by others, but you can be part of encouraging that bigger effort.

© Migrant Family Resilience Project

APPENDIX (4) EMPOWERING KOWI YOUTH MEETING OUTLINE

This meeting is part of a collaborative project between the Diversity Trust, the Kowiana Association, and (name of school or organisation). Its aim is to help young Kowis (Korean-Kiwis) in schools, community organisations and churches develop the skills and qualities they need to deal with life challenges. A typical meeting's outline is as follows:

Introduction
Introduction of presenters, statement of Korean Youth Empowerment Project aims, reference to research underpinnings, overview of meeting structure.

PowerPoint presentation
PowerPoint presentation of findings from the Kowi Experience survey, with reference to the suggested profile of a successful Kowi, the qualities and skills needed when facing life challenges, what hinders the development of strength and happiness, and how to support young Kowis – when you are a parent, teacher or friend.

Personal sharing

Personal sharing by facilitators (mostly members of the Kowiana Association) of specific life experiences which they have gone through in striving to develop strength and happiness as Kowis.

Small group discussion
Small group sharing, led by facilitators, of participant experiences and goals, what gets in the way of being empowered as a Kowi, consideration of how the experience of older Kowis is (or is not) of help, support for making one's vision a reality, and discussion of what further help participants may need.

How this meeting can be best conducted is discussed beforehand by providers and recipients. Normally it is run as a single session. At the start, meetings will be run through high schools, featuring a single 1½ hour session, along the above lines, to which young Kowis (and possibly their parents) are invited. Participants will be given a handout, containing the results from the Kowi Experience Survey, to take home for further discussion. Meetings can also be provided through community organisations or churches. It should be remembered that running a meeting is largely done on a voluntary basis.

PART VII

SCHOOL-BASED FAMILY COUNSELING: SPECIFIC APPLICATIONS

E. SCHOOL-PREVENTION APPLICATIONS

SCHOOL FOCUS

School-Prevention	School-Intervention
Family-Prevention	Family-Intervention

PREVENTION FOCUS

INTERVENTION FOCUS

FAMILY FOCUS

Chapter 36
Kiwi ACE: A School-Based Preventive Depression Program

Barbara Woods

OVERVIEW: *This chapter describes the Kiwi Ace Program which is based on the Australian ACE Program. Over a 13 year period, these programs have provided school-based resilience training to more than 4,000 students.*

BACKGROUND

In the wake of the murder of a student, the murders of several adults and the suicide of a young person from the area, all within the space of a month, that left large numbers of the school population where I work, shocked and devastated, I searched for ways that would assist the students to navigate their way through their distress. My hope was not in any sense about "fast-tracking" their natural grief processes but about helping them with the meanings they were making about their experiences over time.

The program that took my interest, and that used school counselors working with mental health professionals as co-facilitators, was the *ACE (Adolescents Coping with Emotions)* program (Kowalenko, et al, 2002). It had been trialled by a consortium of Australian Health Department, University, and Department of Education and Training leaders with promising results in Australia (Kowalenko, et al, 2005).

PROGRAM DESCRIPTION

Following discussions with the researchers and an examination of the program, I went to Australia and met with participating students and facilitators. They were able to answer questions that I had about possible stigma for participating students and ease of delivery for facilitators. The program involved the prior screening of a cohort of students for depressive symptoms and the offering of the program to those students identified as being at risk of depression. It appeared to be very well received by both facilitators and students.

On returning to New Zealand I made informal approaches to local school counselors and mental health professionals to see what support there would be for running the program locally. The feedback was positive and I then obtained a grant from the New Zealand government to trial the program, and was given six months in which to contract six schools, train facilitators, implement, evaluate and report back on the program!

PROGRAM IMPLEMENTATION AND CONTENT

The *Kiwi ACE* program is a school-based indicated preventive depression program used with adolescents identified as experiencing depressive symptoms. An "indicated" program is one that is offered to those identified as being in need of assistance; "universal" programs are offered to a whole cohort. Small groups of up to ten students meet with two facilitators (the school counselor is always one of the facilitators) for 1½ hours each week during school time for eight weeks. Each student is supplied with a Student Workbook and, using a variety of exercises, role-plays, rehearsals and structured personal discussions, learns cognitive-behavioral, social and problem-solving skills.

Students are taught to understand the relationship between thinking, feeling and behavior, to challenge beliefs and unrealistic thinking, to problem-solve and develop the social skills of assertiveness, negotiation and compromise. The generation of alternative solutions to problems and the learning of a more adaptive attributional style are important aspects of the program. Enhancing personal efficacy, self-monitoring, recognising personal strengths and achievements, learning how to change their negative coping strategies, and using self-reward also form part of the program. Students have the opportunity within the safety of the group to rehearse and share strategies, and to learn from and support each other.

Each session begins and ends with a recapitulation of content from the previous session to reinforce learning and the program is presented in an atmosphere of fun, with teaching and practice of concepts being interspersed with games and rewards of confectionery, and praise being given to participants when they get a "right" answer, do "homework" tasks or participate fully.

Participants showed improvement in depressive symptoms and coping skills across ethnicity and gender. There was a reduction in the use of "non-productive" coping skills for girls and for Maori and a smaller reduction in their use for boys overall. All gains appeared to be maintained at eight-weeks follow-up (Woods, 2001). However, non-Maori male students' use of non-productive coping strategies increased slightly over the test period. The reasons for this increase are not known but a North American study of adolescent coping strategies (Copeland & Hess, 1995) may offer some explanation. The study showed that coping strategies differed for males and females and that males were more likely to use avoidance of problems that included the use of drugs and diversions as stress relief or coping strategies. While this study may not be generalisable to New Zealand adolescents it offered an idea for consideration that could explain the disparity in coping styles because anecdotal evidence from school counselors at the time of the trial indicated that problematic drug and alcohol use was a frequently recurring topic in the groups, in particular for males. It could be that attendance at the groups heightened the boys' awareness of the depressive feelings that they were experiencing, that these feelings had previously been denied or ignored by them and that they then used substances to cope with their increased awareness of these depressive feelings.

Students identified learnings in assertiveness, connecting with others, getting on better with families, rewarding themselves, thinking through situations, feeling better about themselves, reducing isolation and managing feelings better. They felt more positive and saw this as continuing in the future, believing that they would cope better as a result.

School counselors reported that a benefit of the screening process was that many students identified at that point had previously not been receiving help and that this had enabled them to be offered much-needed support. They reported other benefits: students who had been "isolates" at earlier sessions, but who by the end of the program were well integrated into the group; participants who had brought in friends who previously had had no contact with the counselor, and one group member who had not participated actively in program sessions but who had returned post-group to report that he was very depressed. It was the counselor's belief that he would not have come in had he not been a participant in the program. The other benefit was the increased confidence in the use of CBT that the counselors experienced after being up-skilled, and the consequent "flow-on" to their clients.

The program was well received in New Zealand by both students and education and health professionals and this was evidenced by the high recruitment and retention rates and the comments received from all groups post-intervention. Mental health professionals who had worked as co-facilitators in the groups with the school counselors were very supportive of the program and keen to see it incorporated into the national education curriculum. They believed that going into the schools and working alongside the school counselors had been very helpful in that it had opened up channels of communication and eased the way for referral between the two services. As a result of the findings of this first study and the feedback received, I decided to further modify the program and to trial it again with a follow-up at one-year.

2005 TRIAL

Feedback about problematic drug and alcohol use amongst participants in the earlier trial prompted me to include a section called "Changing Bad Habits" based on Sobell & Sobell's Guided Self-Change Program (1993), Blyth's Smashed or Stoned (2001) and techniques from Motivational Interviewing (Miller & Rollnick, 2002) in the revised program. *Kiwi ACE* targets students at the age of regular, rather than habitual, usage of substances and it thereby has the potential to offer a protective function in terms of drug and alcohol abuse. My hope was that its inclusion would serve several functions: it would offer an opportunity for students to discuss issues that bothered them; it would "normalise" bad habits and frame them as "learned" behaviors (and therefore able to be "unlearned"); it would acknowledge the possibilities of lapse and relapse (which would help the students to accept themselves and their pace of change) and it would reinforce the knowledge for students that there was at least one adult in the school environment to whom they could go if they wished to persist with any changes they wished to make. These points were highlighted with the facilitators during their training.

The "Changing Bad Habits" section above can be used to assist with making changes in a variety of behaviors and I decided that rather than focus only on drugs and alcohol, it would be of more benefit and less "threatening" to students to have a broader focus on unspecified habits or behaviors, such as "wanting to do more exercise" or "not doing enough study". Students were asked to identify something they would like to change about the particular behavior and to explore positive and negative consequences to themselves and others of the behavior. They were asked to set small, achievable goals, to identify supports for change in their lives and to draw up an Action Plan that included "triggers" for risk, and risk management strategies that explored options for the behavior and the consequences of those options. The idea of lapse and relapse was introduced with the message that if they "slipped up, then tomorrow was another day" (in which they could begin again). This process helped to counter the faulty "all or nothing" thinking that students were learning to challenge as part of the program. This session was placed third in the eight sessions in order to allow for on-going support and review of goals to continue over a period of weeks. While the prospect of changing entrenched habits in a few sessions is unlikely, there is usefulness in reinforcing for students early in the program the notions that habits can be changed, that it is acceptable and normal to have undesired habits and that there are trusted adults available who can assist them in the process of change.

A further change made was to increase the emphasis on the use of pleasurable activities because of the success currently being achieved in the reduction of depressive symptomatology with the use of these activities (Jacobson, et al, 2001). Each week a "game" was made of the process with students competing to come up with five new ways that they could enjoy themselves with rewards for those who came up with five ideas first. Students rated their pleasure before and after taking part in these activities, and as with the "Changing Bad Habits" section, a brief check-in time was allocated at the start of subsequent sessions to emphasise the importance of the activities.

Program content: An outline of the program, session-by-session, that demonstrates the developmental nature of the learning, follows.

Session 1: The first session of the program has a group-building component, and focuses on the identification of thoughts and feelings and the generation of alternative responses to various scenarios. An example from one of the scenarios uses a girl called "Seli" who hears "Aroha and Kate whispering in the library" and the girls both look in her direction as she walks closer. Students are invited to write responses (alone, in pairs or threes - as they choose) that they might have, by completing the sentences:

"I could think …", "I could also think…", and "I could feel …", "I could also feel …"

Session 2: This session continues this theme with students being encouraged through the use of worksheets to challenge their own personal negative beliefs and to examine the evidence for and against these beliefs. The notion of "thinking errors" is introduced and students are invited to call on their internalised resources through such questions as "What would your friends and family say?" and "What would you tell a friend?" They then begin generating alternative responses to their negative beliefs and scaling is used to measure feelings before and after the exercise. A "Fun form" is introduced with students using a ranking scale to measure feelings before and after pleasurable activities and students are encouraged to compete in generating five ways in which they can have more pleasurable experiences in each day. The idea is promoted that "moments" of pleasure are worthwhile and that moments of pleasure need not incur a high cost financially.

Session 3: The third session has a "check-in" time about the use during the previous weeks of "Realistic Thinking" (the name given to the process of challenging thoughts and generating alternative solutions) and of pleasurable activities. Students are invited to generate new ways for the coming week that they can increase their pleasurable activities and more thinking errors are introduced, followed by the section focusing on changing "bad" habits. Students choose a habit they would like to change, and are offered a range of ideas to stimulate their thinking. They are asked to complete a "balance sheet" about the habit, of "good things about it" and "not so good things about it" and this activity in itself is often productive in terms of beginning to change motivations. Students then complete the sentence: "I want to change because …" and are asked to set a small, achievable goal for themselves for the coming week. They use scaling to explore the importance of the goal and their confidence in achieving it. Supports are identified, and "triggers" listed. Students are encouraged to recall the last time they engaged in the behaviors, the triggers at that time and the immediate and delayed consequences that followed. An Action Plan is drawn up with optional behaviors and consequences, triggers and management strategies. A Back-up Plan is called for, and the idea of relapse introduced.

Session 4: Activities around the development of social skills - and an awareness of cultural differences relating to these – are introduced, with exercises and role plays focusing on listening skills, meeting people and dealing with conflict. A sample scenario is:

"Matt lives with his mother and father. Lately, he has been more aware that his parents seem to be arguing more. Last night, there was a huge fight, they both seemed really angry and there was a lot of shouting. His father took off in the car and his mum shut herself in the bedroom for ages. They didn't speak at all this morning, and Matt hasn't been able to get his mind off what is happening – he feels really down and expects the worst."

Students are asked how Matt might be feeling and what some of his thoughts might be. They check out the evidence that Matt has using the "Realistic Thinking" formula they have learnt. Then they are asked about how Matt might cope if there was real violence or separation - how to communicate with parents, especially the parent in danger, and what support networks are available (police, family, friends, counselors). Phone numbers and contact details for sources of help are provided by the group facilitators.

Session 5: This session focuses on assertiveness exercises, and once more there is a focus on cultural difference. An example of this is around the use of eye contact: in many "Western" societies a child is required to look an adult in the eye when being rebuked, and this is seen as a sign that the child is paying attention to what is being communicated - the act of looking away, or downwards, might indicate that the child is avoiding the full import of the message. In Maori and Pacific societies, the behavior of a child who looked an adult in the eye while being rebuked would be seen as confrontational and the "correct" way of receiving this sort of communication would be to look down while being spoken to (Massey University, 2006). Issues of safety and appropriateness are explored, and the notions of passive, aggressive, and assertive behaviour are introduced using role-play and rehearsal to aid learning. A sample situation is "A friend borrowed one of your CDs and scratched it and you want them to replace it".

Some students are not comfortable using role-play and group facilitators are encouraged to allow students to work in ways that are enabling for them to learn. Those students who are not comfortable acting out a scenario could write out a dialogue or describe verbally to the rest of group the different responses that might occur in various scenarios. Facilitators report that in all groups there are some students who are enthusiastic participants in role-plays and students in most groups who are not and that the flexibility of approach as described above allowed all to participate in the learning.

Session 6: Negotiation and compromise, skills that build on the learning about assertiveness, are practised and activities are undertaken that focus on the building of self-esteem. Students are encouraged to look at core beliefs that affect their feelings about themselves and this links back to earlier learning and practice with the challenging of negative thinking.

Session 7: This session includes a review of negotiation and social skills and offers a schema for problem-solving using role play and rehearsal. Students work through the schema from examples that include:
"A Science assignment is due. It is a large project that is worth 30% of the year's mark. You have been putting it off and you now have one week before the assignment is due."
"While your parents are out, you invite friends over without your parents' permission and they accidentally break a window."

Session 8: The final session of the program reviews the problem-solving strategies learnt in Session 7 and has students demonstrate in groups through the use of role-plays, songs or posters the four key concepts of the program, i.e., that emotions result from how we think and interpret experience; that some thoughts are unrealistic and can be challenged; that our behavior can be assertive, aggressive or passive and that we can use problem-solving skills to help with practical solutions. This activity reinforces the previous learning. Students draw up a list of supports available to them, both personally and in the community, with contact details, and then share what they personally have learnt in the program. They give each other written feedback on something they like about each other, are presented with a certificate of completion in communication and problem-solving skills and then enjoy a shared lunch together. This concludes the program.

RELATIONSHIP TO THE SBFC MODEL

The Kiwi ACE program fits into the SBFC Model under the School-Prevention quadrant. This quadrant refers to interventions that focus on teaching students and/or teachers skills that could prevent future problems. The identification of students at risk of depression through the screening process that occurs prior to the implementation of the Kiwi ACE program means that students in need of assistance are able to be offered the opportunity to learn ways of managing troubling feelings and situations, thus potentially assisting with the prevention of some future problems. The program seeks to develop resilience skills in participating students, thereby serving a preventive function with students.

EVIDENCE-BASED SUPPORT

The *Kiwi ACE* program operates from a skills deficit and cognitive distortion model and uses personal and social skills competence training based around the use of CBT taught in a small group setting. The cognitive-behavioral focus is drawn from the psychological and sociological models of depression - the stress-diathesis model (Nemeroff, 1998) - and the purpose of this focus is to assist participants to address the cognitive attributional style they use to appraise events, causality and future. Increasing their ability to recognise and challenge faulty thinking patterns has the potential to have an impact on other constructs of depression – belief in the self, somatic symptoms, social problems and psychomotor retardation and to enable them to deal with stress and life events (Young et al., 2006). Cognitive restructuring has been found to be effective in reducing levels of depression in young people as has training in psychosocial skills, and the incorporation of both into the same program would seem to offer "double protection."

The question of whether to offer an indicated or universal program ultimately can come down to pragmatic considerations of personnel and resources. While there is some evidence that universal programs have a positive influence on the school climate overall (Cohen et al., 2007) and the social skills offered in effective universal programs benefit more students than are reached through indicated programs, the costs in terms of time and resources to implement such programs means that indicated programs are currently much more likely to be well received and implemented in New Zealand schools.

2005 TRIAL

All Year 10 students (average age 14 years) in eight secondary schools were offered screening for depressive symptoms with the Children's Depression Inventory (CDI) a standardised self-report questionnaire, using a passive consent process. A cut-off T score of 63 was used and students scoring over this point were deemed to be at risk of clinical depression. This cut-off point allowed for the selection ratio of true and false positives from a normative population to be maintained, minimising the number of false positives. The CDI measures mood, interpersonal problems, ineffectiveness, anhedonia and self esteem. The Adolescent Coping Scale (ACS) that measures problem-solving, coping by reference to others and non-productive coping was used with the CDI at four test points after screening to measure change.

At one-year follow-up, participating students had significantly improved scores on the CDI and this was effective across gender and ethnicity (Woods & Jose, 2011). The findings were supported by data from teachers reporting participating students as appearing less withdrawn, anxious and depressed; displaying fewer mood changes; having fewer attention problems; disrupting others in the classroom less; being less disobedient and aggressive in class; showing evidence of poor school work less and getting along better with other students.

Student focus group feedback included: "not cutting any more", "not having big tempys now", being "much more relaxed and don't really care what people care about me", "speaking differently to my mother", "I don't give up on it – try to solve problems in every way possible", "I talk to people instead of keeping it inside", "I actually like life now", "not doing a runner", "managing anger a lot better", and "cutting down (alcohol and drug use)".

Facilitators described changes in student help-seeking behaviors and social interactions, in student confidence and in the development of trust and listening skills. This was particularly noticeable with a boy diagnosed with Asperger's Syndrome who was reported to have made social gains. Students reported to counselors months after the cessation of the program that they continued to find the thinking processes that were taught very useful.

MULTICULTURAL COUNSELING CONSIDERATIONS

In New Zealand we have a particular ethnic mix: there is a predominantly Caucasian population (80%) with 14.7% identifying as Maori (the indigenous peoples of New Zealand), 6.5% as Pacific peoples, 6.6% as from Asian groups, and .7% as "Other" (Statistics New Zealand, 2002). As a matter of interest, the national census from which these figures are drawn notes that a proportion of individuals (7.9%) identify with more than one ethnic background. The categories of ethnicity described above, that mingle notions of "blood", culture, nationality, race, ancestry, identity and citizenship, are still being clarified across government departments. This ethnic mix means that results from use of the program with New Zealand young people may differ from results obtained in other parts of the world.

Prior to implementing the program, I embarked on a consultation process with representatives from the local community - kaumatua (elders) and others from the mana whenua (Maori from the area), representatives from Pacific peoples and other cultural groups - to evaluate the suitability of the program for use in New Zealand. The link between cultural consultation and competence and the success of an intervention has been clearly identified by The Institute of Medicine, an arm of the United States National Academy of Science (Mrazek & Haggerty, 1994). All those consulted had experience in working with youth in the mental health arena and they offered input on both the wording and layout of the Australian Facilitators' Handbooks and Student Workbooks as well as on the implementation of the program. Cross-cultural, mixed gender focus groups of students were also set up to review the Student Workbooks.

The suggestions from all groups consisted mainly of making small changes to words and pictures, in reducing the number of words to a page and in using Maori and Pacific Island names and cultural designs to replace those used in the Australian workbooks. I made other changes to make the books more relevant for New Zealand young people such as through the use of Maori proverbs and changing the wording on some of the worksheets. The Australian CBT worksheets, for example, asked students "To think of a more balanced way of looking at an issue", "What are the chances?" and to "Change places" and these were altered to read: "What would your friends and family say?" and "What would you tell a friend?" This was more appropriate for the New Zealand cultural mix for whom family connections have a strong influence. The essence and sequence of the program, however, remained unchanged. Acknowledgement was also made of the different rules operating in the Maori and Pacific and European cultures in terms of assertiveness behaviour.

Maori involvement at this preliminary stage of the trial led to the setting up of a parallel *Kiwi ACE* program being offered for Maori students and being facilitated by Maori counselors. As part of strengthening cultural identity and engaging in political analysis at an age-appropriate level, the effects of colonisation were woven into the course content where this didn't distract from the main functions of the group.

CHALLENGES AND SOLUTIONS

Consultation: It was a challenge finding the people to consult with culturally in the early stages. I was aware that with various tribal groups and offices in the area it could be difficult to make sure that all persons of influence were consulted.
Solution: I contacted relevant government Ministries and asked for names, then went to various NGOs and mental health groups and did the same. It came down to asking lots of people and groups who needed to be consulted and distilling from there. I set up a small focus group of adults and met separately with kaumatua (elders) and Maori mental health professionals. In schools, I consulted with focus groups of students selected across age, gender, sexual orientation and ethnicity.

Who to contact in the schools? You need someone who has the power to make decisions about directions in which the school will move, staffing and funding. If you write a letter "cold turkey", chances are it will be one of many that will arrive on the principal's or administrator's desk and be overlooked. While the program offers valuable support with one of the important conditions that a school must meet – that of providing a safe environment for its students – schools have so many demands on them that yet another program from an unknown source can be "shelved" for later…
Solution: The school counselors are the people who will carry most of the workload in the school. If they are "on board" with the process, it could be useful for them to approach their principal first and for you to speak to your proposal with them later. Having all the supporting infrastructure ready to go

(Student Workbooks, Facilitator Handbooks, timelines, letters home for parents, questionnaires, etc.,) is vital so that it is then just a "join the dots" exercise for the schools.

Screening Questionnaire: There is a need for a New Zealand adolescent depression inventory. The students found the wording on some of the questions in the CDI strange and wrote comments on the questionnaires. The cost to schools of purchasing and administering the CDI would be prohibitive and so would also mitigate against its use.
Solution: The Center for Epidemiologic Studies have put out the CES-Depression Scale which has good reliability and validity and is free to download on the internet. It requires scoring but a capable computer programmer could write a program to do this cheaply for a school.

Skilled facilitation: This is of prime importance and ideally the group will have a psychologist from a community mental health unit working with the school counselor leading a group of up to ten students. The current over-stretched state of the community mental health services in New Zealand means that their psychologists simply are not on offer.
Solution: Solutions that have worked include the school counselor working alone with a smaller group of five to six students, counselors in nearby schools co-facilitating groups in each other's schools, educational professionals such as Resource Teachers of Learning and Behavior coming in and co-facilitating with the school counselor, and getting funding to pay for psychologists (this was a "one-off" small-scale, and unlikely to recur).

PROCEDURE

If you are thinking about introducing the Kiwi ACE program into your school, I would recommend you consider the following steps.

1. It would be useful to see what is already being done for young people in the area, and to undertake a needs analysis. What is the history in the area? How does this impact on what is happening now? What is the socio-economic background? What is the cultural mix in the community? Consult, consult, consult - with cultural groups, at government Ministry level, and as widely as possible. Use broadly-based focus groups to get feedback on the program content. It is necessary to have input and "buy-in" from members of these various communities in order for the program to have meaning and the support it needs.

2. When you have an understanding of the community's needs and resources, then you can look at where the program fits and what needs to be tweaked and added or removed. When ready to choose schools, it could be useful to take the following steps:

3. Contact the school counselors. (In New Zealand schools, most counselors report directly to the principal). If the counselor is "on board" with it, they can discuss your written proposal, including a copy of the screening tool, with their principals (with whom you can later meet) and the idea can then be launched with the school community – Boards of Trustees, proprietors, staff, caregivers and students, through a variety of means: meetings, newsletters and assemblies. Staff support is desirable for release of students from class. Staff need to be assured the programme won't happen at the same time each week so students won't miss the same class. I think it is important to introduce the program to caregivers as a resilience program so that they don't become concerned that their young person has a diagnosis of depression if they are invited to participate. It may be that the key figures identified in your schools are not the counselors but they must have access to and influence with administrators or principals who are making decisions about policy and finance.

4. Offer proposed letters for parents, assembly and classroom talks, newsletter articles and evaluation tools so that the implementation process is eased.

5. Give schools a timeline setting out processes to be followed that includes:
    Staff briefing
    Article in school newsletter
    Student assembly briefing
    Facilitator Training (give out Facilitator Manuals and Student Handbooks)
    Consent letters to give to students to take home
    Student screening and Information Sheets for students
    Scoring of screening questionnaires
    Notification to school counselors of students scoring over the cut-off point
    Interviewing of all high-scoring students
    Program session timing and any testing required
    Follow-up for students not attending program
    Evaluation
    "Booster shot" three months post-group

SUMMARY

The *Kiwi ACE* program is a school-based indicated preventive depression program used with adolescents identified as experiencing depressive symptoms. Small groups of up to ten students meet with two facilitators (the school counselor is always one of the facilitators) for 1½ hours each week during school time for eight weeks. Each student is supplied with a Student Workbook and, using a variety of exercises, role-plays, rehearsals and structured personal discussions, learns cognitive-behavioral, social and problem-solving skills. The program is based on the Australian *ACE* program which has provided school-based resilience training to more than 4,000 students over a period of 13 years. Implementation requires an understanding of the community's needs and resources and a thorough consultation process in order for the program to have a good "fit".

REFERENCES

Blyth, S. (2001). *Smashed or Stoned*. Wellington: Alcohol & Drug Advisory Council.

Cohen, R., Kincaid, D., & Childs, K. E. (2007). Measuring School-wide Positive Behavior Support Implementation: Development and Validation of the Benchmarks of Quality. *Journal of Positive Behavior Interventions, 9,* (4) 203-213.

Copeland, E. P. & Hess, R. S. (1995). Differences in young adolescents' coping strategies based on gender and ethnicity. *Journal of Early Adolescence, 15,* (2) 203-219.

Jacobson, N. S., Martell, C. R., & Dimidjian, S. (2001). Behavioral Activation Treatment for Depression: Returning to Contextual Roots. *American Psychological Association, 8,* (3) 255-270.

Kowalenko, N., Wignall, A., Rapee, R., Simmons, J., Whitefield, K. & Steinehouse, R. (2002) *Working with Schools to Promote Emotional health & Prevent Depression: The ACE Program (Adolescents Coping with Emotions) Youth Studies Australia, 21,* 31-38.

Kowalenko, N., Rapee, R. M., Simmons, J., Wignall, A., Hoge, R., Whitefield, K., Starling, J., Stonehouse, R., & Baillie, A. J. (2005). Short-term Effectiveness of a School-based Early Intervention Program for Adolescent Depression. *Clin Child Psychol Psychiatry, 10, 1, 493-508.*

Massey University. (2006). *Health & Counselling*. Retrieved on 7 March 2007 from http://www.massey.ac.nz/massey/students/student-services/health/resources/listening.cfm.

Miller, W. R., & Rollnick, S. (2002). *Motivational Interviewing: Preparing People for Change*. New York: The Guilford Press.

Mrazek, P. J. & Haggerty, R. J. (1994). Reducing Risks for Mental Disorders: Frontiers for Preventive Intervention Research. 1st. Ed. Washington D.C.: National Academy Press.

Nemeroff, C. B. (1998). Psychopharmacology of affective disorders in the 21st century. *Biological Psychiatry, 44,* 517–525.

Sobell, M. B. & L. C. (1993). *Problem Drinkers: Guided Self-Change Treatment.* New York: The Guilford Press.

Stark, K. D., Rouse, L. W., & Livingston, R. (1991). Treatment of Depression During Childhood and Adolescence: Cognitive-Behavioral Procedures for the Individual and Family. In *Child and Adolescent Therapy: Cognitive-behavioral Procedures,* Kendall, P. C. (Ed.) New York: Guilford Press.

Woods, B. & Jose, P. E. (2011). Effectiveness of a School-Based Indicated Early Intervention Program for Maori and Pacific Adolescents. *Journal of Pacific Rim Psychology, 5,* (1) 40-50.

Young, J. F., Mufson, L., & Davies, M. (2006). Efficacy of Interpersonal Psychotherapy-Adolescent Skills Training: an indicated preventive intervention for depression. *Journal of Child Psychology and Psychiatry, 47,* (12) 1254-1262.

RESOURCES

Kiwi ACE Facilitator's Manual and Student Workbook. Please contact the writer at barbara.woods@stmaryswellington.school.nz

Woods, B. R. (2001). *Kiwi ACE – An Indicated Preventive Depression Programme in Schools.* Report to Ministry of Education, New Zealand.

Chapter 37
Coping with School Bullying:
Students and Experts' Views on Effective Strategies

Phillip Slee

OVERVIEW: *This chapter describes a strengths-based approach to coping with bullying using the SBFC Model as a meta-framework. The focus for the intervention is School-Prevention and School-Intervention. This chapter gives an overview of current research on school bullying and cyber-bullying and describes a study contrasting student and expert views on bullying. In addition the chapter outlines specific recommendations for best practices in developing anti-bullying programs.*

BACKGROUND

Overviews of research are clear that bullying occurs in every school, and that there are significant negative physical and mental health outcomes associated with it (Beaty & Alexeyev, 2008; Carter, 2011). As such it is imperative to develop successful school-based intervention strategies to help students cope with bullying, including the emergent form of cyber-bullying. Research suggests however, that students have a very limited repertoire of strategies for dealing with bullying generally (Owens, Shute, & Slee, 2004; Kanetsuna, Smith & Morita, 2006). This chapter outlines what is currently known about bullying, including cyber-bullying, its impact on students, and a classroom intervention to assist and support students to cope with bullying, and implications for schools.

Bullying has been conceived broadly as the systematic abuse of power (Smith , Cowie, Olafsson, & Liefooghe, 2002). It is a deliberate form of aggressive behavior, perpetrated by a more powerful individual or group that is unfair or unjustified and is typically repeated. The severity of bullying extends along a continuum from acts that are comparatively mild, as in insensitive teasing or taunting, to extremely severe, as in repeated violent physical assaults or deliberate and unjustifiable total exclusion by peers. Bullying may be classified as direct, as in face-to-face physical and verbal harassment, or indirect as in unfair exclusion and rumour spreading.

Most recently, the latest iteration of bullying: cyber-bullying, involves the deliberate (mis)use of technology to target another person, e.g. the sending of anonymous and abusive messages by email. Researchers (e.g. Campbell, 2005; Cross et al., 2009; Spears et al., 2008; 2009) have drawn attention to the emergent forms of cyber-bullying and the new understandings regarding definitional issues that have arisen as a result. For example the notion that the act must be 'repeated' is called into question when, as part of cyber-bullying, one incident can go viral. Power differentials now operate across and though technologies, and deliberate intent can now be demonstrated both privately (between individuals) and publically (via the world wide web and social networking sites), verbally and non-verbally (through images); covertly and overtly (through deliberate stalking overtly or anonymously). Indeed the latest technologies have shifted cyber-bullying from computers in rooms, to a totally integrated, mobile platform.

SCHOOL BULLYING: A PHYSICALLY HARMFUL, EMOTIONALLY HURTFUL AND SOCIALLY ISOLATING EXPERIENCE

In Australia and internationally the issue of school bullying is a significant concern of educators and students. Research (Cross et al, 2009; Slee, 2003) indicates that bullying is an all too frequent facet of young people's lives. More particularly the Australian Covert Bullying Prevalence Study (ACBPS) reports that just over one quarter (27%) of school students aged 8 to 14- years were bullied and 9% bullied others on a frequent basis (every few weeks or more often) (Cross et al., 2009).

Spears, Slee, Owens and Johnson (2008; 2009) through their qualitative study, highlighted the relationship cost of covert and cyber-bullying. Incidence of bullying rates are self-reported as highest in the primary years and in the early years of secondary school. In an early meta-analytic review of twenty years of research Hawker and Boulton (2000) concluded that it was clear that victimisation was positively associated with depression, loneliness, anxiety, low self esteem and poor social self concept. They concluded by noting that cross-sectional studies " … demonstrate that victims of peer aggression suffer a variety of feelings of psychosocial distress. They feel more anxious, socially anxious, depressed, lonely and worse about themselves than non-victims" (Hawker & Boulton, 2000, p. 453). They go on to note that "The evidence suggests that these feelings occur among victims of both sexes, of all age groups, and of all subtypes of aggression" (p.453). Reviews of research have largely confirmed the initial findings reported by Hawker & Boulton (e.g. Cross et al, 2011)

CYBER-BULLYING: A NEW MANIFESTATION OF AN OLD PROBLEM

Defined as repeated, harmful interactions which are deliberately offensive, humiliating, threatening and power-assertive, cyber-bullying interactions are enacted using electronic equipment, such as cell (mobile) phones or the Internet, by one or more individuals towards another. Cyber-bullying can take the form of instant or email messages, images, videos, calls, excluding or preventing someone to be part of a group or an online community (Spears et al., 2011; Cross et al., 2011). Scientific research into the prevalence and consequences associated with cyber-bullying is increasing each year and, as such, we are beginning to understand more about these behaviors. It appears that the risk of being exposed to these behaviors is greatest during the school years with particular risk associated with transition years.

In contrast to face-to-face bullying, the limits of cyber-bullying are difficult to define. For instance, a single image can be forwarded countless times to innumerable people, a message can be pervasive and difficult to stop, an aggressor can remain unidentified hiding through multiple profiles, maintaining anonymity and making it harder for the victim to defend, escape or identify (and as a result, act to stop the behavior). Furthermore, cyber-bullying behaviors can change and assume new forms according to different interactional settings, highlighting both the overt and covert nature of these behavior (Spears et al, 2008; 2009). For example, abrupt and violent threats are often made using instant messages or malicious calls.

It is important to note that while young people are often considered the masters of the cyber-world (especially the socializing aspects of it) they are the ones that are at greatest risk of being exposed to cyber-bullying behaviors. In addition, they are often the ones responsible for engaging in cyber-bullying and other inappropriate behaviors. Furthermore, there is evidence that a large proportion of those who engage in cyber-bullying behavior do so against those individuals who are considered friends. Spears et al (2008; 2009) found that bullying behavior cycled between school and online (cyber) and back again, suggesting a clear link with existing relationships. In addition, research evidence at the present time is a little conflicting with some evidence suggesting that although there is an overlap between those who engage in face-to-face and cyber-bullying, a large number of those who engage in cyber-bullying behavior or were victimized were not involved in face-to-face bullying (Campbell et al,

2010).Furthermore the impact of cyber-bullying on mental health and emotional response, is only just beginning to be understood, though it has been posited that it will be greater, possibly due to the 24/7 nature of it, the anonymity aspects and the broader audience available, not to mention the power that the written and visual electronic media can have (Spears et al 2008; 2009; Cross, 2009; Campbell,2010).

COPING WITH SCHOOL BULLYING

A criticism directed at research relating to school bullying is that it is essentially a-theoretical. In fact, various approaches addressing the matter of interventions are generally underpinned by some theoretical understanding that that can be identified in terms of social learning theory, humanistic theory or systems based models (Slee, & Shute, 2003). The position adopted in the present chapter is that schools are 'relationship saturated' environments and school bullying is a relationship issue (Murray-Harvey & Slee, 2010) The pivotal role of relationships in the student's learning points to the need for schools to not only have policies and procedures for dealing with aggressive behaviour, but to also include a positive relationship-building dimension to the interactions among teachers and students and between students at school (Slee, 2001).

Interventions may be categorized broadly according to whether their purpose is primarily to prevent bullying from happening or alternatively to deal with cases of bullying if and when they occur. However, a rigid distinction cannot be made; for instance, disciplinary actions taken when a case of bullying is identified may impact not only the person being treated but may also make it less likely that others will bully; that is, it may also have a preventative function. Some interventions are not primarily directed towards changing the behavior of individuals who become involved in bullying, but are concerned rather with establishing an environment or ethos in which bullying is less likely, for instance by developing in members of the school community (including both teachers and parents) a better understanding of the problem and promoting more pro-social attitudes and empathic feelings towards others; or alternatively by reducing the motivation to bully by involving students more deeply in school-related study. These may be described as preventative measures. Many programs include both preventative and remedial elements.

Adapting a model described by Mrazek and Haggerty (1994) interventions may be targeted:
a) universally at whole populations
b) selectively at a population at risk
c) indicatively at 'high-risk' individuals
a) and (b) are usually identified in terms of 'prevention' whereas (c) encompasses 'early intervention'

Universal Programs: are targeted to the general public or a whole population group that has not been identified on the basis of individual risk e.g. childhood immunization.
Populations at Risk: Here the interventions are directed towards individuals or sub-groups of a population known to be at risk of developing problems e.g. literacy programs directed toward children from economically depressed areas
'High Risk' Individuals: Programs are directed specifically toward high risk individuals who may already be presenting with signs or symptoms e.g. programs to prevent depression in children who have one or both clinically depressed parents.

Generally as one moves across the continuum from universal preventative programs to targeted programs for high risk individuals the size of the population receiving the interventions decreases, while the degree of the psychological problems increases in severity. To date then it has been argued that school bullying and it now appears cyber-bullying as its latest manifestation is an all too frequent aspect of young people's lives and that it has a negative impact on the wellbeing of all those involved.

Evidence has been presented that schools are a very obvious settings for wellbeing and health promotion activities and that evidence-based initiatives indicate that teachers can effectively deliver

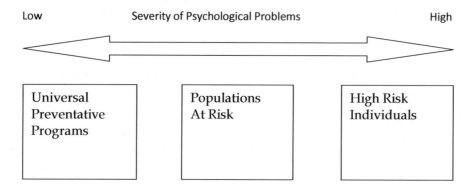

Low   Severity of Psychological Problems   High

| Universal Preventative Programs | Populations At Risk | High Risk Individuals |

Figure 1. The Intervention Continuum

programs that make a difference to the wellbeing of young people. It has been argued that it is important to nuance how we understand interventions in order to maximise their impact. An important facet of such nuancing, is understanding the dynamics underpinning how young people cope with school bullying. Thus programs which target the improvement in the ways in which young people cope with these behaviors is important.

RELATIONSHIP TO THE SBFC MODEL

This chapter focuses on interventions that are required in a school after the issue of school bullying has clearly developed. School communities become aware of the issue of bullying in various ways. For example, a bullying incident or local or national campaigns can draw attention to the issue. Typically a 'champion' emerges in the form of a student, teacher or parent who picks up the issue of bullying and drives the change process. Thus, in relation to the SBFC model the focus is upon the School Prevention and the School Intervention areas of the SBFC model.

EVIDENCE-BASED SUPPORT

According to Lazarus and Folkman (1984) coping relates to how one deals with stress, where stress refers to environmental elements that impact on physical or psychological functioning in a disruptive manner. Coping strategies may be categorised as "approach" or "avoidance" (Causey &Dubow, 1992; Lazarus, 1984) where "approach" includes positive strategies which may decrease the likelihood of continued victimisation, such as seeking help or support from others to stop the victimisation. Not quite so effective are "avoidance" approaches, such as denial and refusal to think about an incident after it has happened. However, as Kochenderfer-Ladd and Ladd (2001) suggest, how effective each strategy might be is dependent on the context, and any strategy which is used which reduces the bullying may be beneficial, while any that results in no change may be harmful. Coping strategies are dependent on internal (self-esteem, intelligence, personality) and external (social support, changes in circumstances) mechanisms and these influence the success of coping (Folkman, Lazarus, Gruen & DeLongis, 1986).

The coping resources of children may be severely taxed by repeated experiences of victimisation (Lazarus, 1984). Bullying incidents which are frequent and occur over long periods of time, overwhelm the coping capabilities of victims. The type of bullying directed at victims, such as name calling or physical bullying, may also influence how well one copes (Kochenderfer-Ladd & Ladd, 2001). An important element of many anti-bullying programs is encouraging victims to tell someone so that they can be helped to sort out a bullying situation (Glover, Gough, Johnson, & Cartwright, 2000). Indeed, this is the number one coping strategy reported by trainee teachers as the tactic they would most recommend to students (Nicolaides, Toda, & Smith, 2002; Spears, Campbell, Slee, & Tangen, 2010). In addition to this, victims are also encouraged to speak to their parents or guardians and in some schools peer support systems have been developed to counsel or advise other pupils (Naylor & Cowie, 1999; Sharp & Smith, 1994). However, many victims do not seek help. This could be due to a fear of retaliation from bullies and shame over peers' perceptions of them (Bijttebier & Vertommen, 1998; Naylor & Cowie, 1999, Naylor, Cowie, & del Key, 2001). Smith and Shu (2000) found that around 30% of bullied pupils in English schools told no-one, and this was more likely amongst boys (40%) than girls (20%). Cross et al. (2009) note that students in Australia report that only in rare cases does the bullying stop when an adult is told with almost 50% indicating it stays the same, while in some instances it gets worse.

In an Australian study (Murray-Harvey, Skrzypiec, & Slee, 2012) involving 1223 students across Years 8 to10 in three South Australian high schools students completed a 26 item Coping with Bullying questionnaire about how they dealt with bullying and 82 informed professionals (IPs e.g. school counselors, researchers) rated the effectiveness of each strategy along with its applicability to different bullying types (physical, verbal, social, covert). Informed professionals generally agreed on which were effective and ineffective strategies, with consensus as well, that the same strategies were appropriate for all types of bullying. Productive Other-focused strategies were regarded by informed professionals as most effective for coping with bullying. Among these were strategies such as talking to family members or professionals outside school, talking to teachers and counselors at school and using the school's anti-bullying and harassment policies and procedures; all indicative of students eliciting support from others who are well positioned to act for or on behalf of them. However, it was found that seriously bullied students reported under-using the Productive-Other Focused strategies rated by informed professionals as effective and instead reported using non-productive strategies such as avoidance and denial. More research is needed to provide evidence about whether telling someone actually helps victims escape from victimisation, particularly given the prominence accorded to it in much school anti-bullying work.

SOME SPECULATIONS CONCERNIBG COPING WITH CYBER-BULLYING

As noted earlier the matter of cyber-bullying may in fact raise particular questions with regard to coping, given its 24/7 nature, virtual anonymity and the broader audience available, not to mention the power that the written and visual electronic media can have. Education authorities and parent advocates will frequently propose simplistic measures to assist with coping in terms of 'banning' 'blocking or restricting access to technology. Some of the complexities of the issues are encapsulated in Campbell et al's (2010) attention to the legal aspects in their discussion of the criminal and civil law aspects as applied to cyber-bullying. As Spears et al (2011) have noted in developing an understanding of the issues associated with cyber-bullying (including coping) it is imperative to listen to the 'voices' of the stakeholders, that is the young people themselves.

A SCHOOL BULLYING INTERVENTION WITH YEAR 8 AND 9 CLASSES

Over two school terms in 2008-09 the University researchers collaborated with a school coordinator and school counselor to design and deliver, to Year 8 & 9 students, a 'Coping with School Bullying intervention'. In Term 2 professional development was provided to all year 8 & 9 home group teachers regarding the 'Coping with School Bullying' program to be run in Term 3. Lesson plans were provided including excerpts from the DVD 'Coping with School Bullying'. Five of the home groups ran a program called 'Coping with School Bullying' and 4 of the groups ran a program called 'Dealing with Bullying'. In the 'Coping with Bullying' groups the DVD was used to coach and practice specific skills relating to coping. In the 'Dealing with Bullying' groups the DVD was used as a general discussion starter but no specific activities were taught and practiced for dealing with bullying. Pre, post and a 3 month follow-up questionnaire assessed the level of bullying and coping strategies . In related research in the schools, data was collected regarding the multiple ways in which students reported they were bullied and the relationship to coping. Data was also collected regarding the coping strategies that 'seriously' bullied students use compared with what school counsellors would advise.

Results of the School Intervention: In the 10 week pastoral care program there was a decline in 'serious bullying' as a result of the intervention. In the 10 week program the decline was greatest in the 'Coping with School Bullying' intervention which explicitly taught coping strategies.

Students reported that:
> "We learned: ... to stay calm and not get angry - to not panic and to think
> ... to not let bullies get the satisfaction of seeing your emotions - to be a little bit more confident in dealing with bullying."

Teachers reported:
> "It was good to revisit some of the successful and failed 'coping techniques' exhibited in the video. Students had a pretty good retention. Overall: a very successful exercise."

Strategies rated as effective by counselors that are not frequently used by bullied students:
> Talk to a professional at school
> Use the school bullying policy

Strategies rated as ineffective by experts that are frequently used by bullied students:
> Wish for a miracle
> Hope the bullying will sort itself out

Students bullied in multiple ways are significantly more likely to report they are 'not coping.'Girls use a wider range of coping strategies than boys.

Discussion: Interventions that teach coping skills in an explicit manner were more effective than those which teach about bullying generally. Students who are bullied use a different array of coping strategies than those which experts advocate. Students bullied in multiple ways are coping less well than other bullied students.

*Some Implications for school practice:*As Murray-Harvey and Slee (2010, p.271) have noted "...it is important that schools provide an environment that makes it possible for their students to thrive and to achieve, not only academically but in all ways that relate to their overall well-being". It is well accepted that education is positively related to health, and that schools play a key role in promoting healthy behaviors and attitudes. The responsibility of educators as reported by The United Nations' Convention on the Rights of the Child (United Nations, 1991) is for protecting children's quality of life and their rights to be educated in a safe environment, free from all forms of violence, victimisation, harassment, and neglect is understood (Cross et al., 2011). The National Safe schools Framework (2010) affirms the need for all Australian schools to provide a learning environment free from bullying and harassment. Given the sheer quantity of research and the ready availability of anti-bullying programs the daunting task facing school administrators concerns how to choose the best quality programs that are underpinned by an evidence-base, and how these may translate into effective anti-cyber-bullying approaches. In considering a program the following factors should be considered:

a) whether the program has an identifiable theoretical base
b) whether there have been independent evaluations conducted of the program
c) the extent to which the program identifies the 'pill and dose', that is the number , nature, and quality of the lessons
d) whether the program is developmentally appropriate

SUMMARY

School bullying, including emergent forms of cyber-bullying, is an all too frequent aspect of young people's lives and it has a negative impact on the wellbeing of all those involved. Evidence with regard to transnational research indicates that schools are a very obvious setting for wellbeing and health promotion activities, and that teachers can effectively deliver evidence-based programs that make a difference to the wellbeing of young people. Australia is one of the few countries in the world to have in place a national framework (National Safe Schools Framework) within which to consider the matter of the wellbeing of young people in our schools. To continue to provide leadership in the field of matters that affect the wellbeing of our students, it is very important to maintain a focus on research to inform our practice. In particular, the contemporary issue of cyber-bullying is one that requires urgent attention to meet the needs of the young people affected, the families involved and the educational institutions which are at the forefront in addressing the matter at both a policy and practical level.

REFERENCES

Askell-Williams,H., Russell, A., Dix, K.L., Slee, P.T., Spears, B.A., Lawson, M.J., Owens, L.D., & Gregory, K. (2008) Early challenges in evaluating the KidsMatter national mental health promotion initiative in Australian primary schools. *International Journal of Mental Health Promotion.* 10,35-44.

Campbell, M. A. (2005). Cyber bullying: An old problem in a new guise? *Australian Journal of Guidance & Counselling, 15,* 84-114.

Campbell, M. A., Cross, D., Spears, B., & Slee, P (2010). *Cyber-bullying- legal implications for schools.* CSE Occasional Paper, 118. Melbourne, CSE.

Causey, D. L., & Dubow, E. F. (1992). Development of a self-report coping measure for elementary school children. *Journal of Clinical Child Psychology, 21:,*47-59.

Cross, D., Shaw, T., Hearn, L., Epstein, M., Monks, H., Lester, L., Thomas. (2009). Australian Covert Bullying Prevalence Study (ACBPS). Retrieved 4th June, 2009, from http://www.deewr.gov.au/Schooling/NationalSafeSchools/Pages/research.aspx

Cross, D., Monks, H., Campbell, M. A., Spears, B., & Slee, P.T (2010). *School-Based strategies to address cyber-bullying.* CSE Occasional Papers, 118.Melbourne, CSE.

Cross, D., Epstein, M., Hearn, L., Slee, P.T., Shaw, T., Monks, H., & Schwartz, T. (2011). National safe schools framework: Policy and practice to reduce bullying in Australian schools. *International Journal of Behavioural Development,* 1-7.

Durlak, J. A., & DuPre, E. P. (2008). Implementation matters: A review of research on the influence of implementation on program outcomes and factors affecting implementation. *American Journal of Community Psychology, 41,* 327-350.

Durlak, J. A., Weissberg, R. P., Dymnicki, A. B., Taylor, R. D., & Schellinger, K. B. (2011). The impact of enhancing students' social and emotional learning: A meta-analysis of school-based universal interventions. *Child Development, 82*, 405-432.

Folkman, S., Lazarus, R. S., Gruen, R. J., & DeLongis, A. (1986).Appraisal, coping, health status, and psychological symptoms. *Journal of Personality and Social Psychology, 50,* 571-579.

Glover, D., Gough, G., Johnson, M. ,& Cartwright, N. (2000). Bullying in 25 secondary schools: Incidence, impact and intervention. *Educational Research, 42*) 141-156.

Harris, J. R. (1995). Where is the child's environment? A group socialization theory of development. *Psychological Review, 102,* 458-489.

Hawker, S. J., & Boulton, M. (2000). Twenty years' research on peer victimisation and psychosocial maladjustment: A meta-analytic review of cross-sectional studies. *Journal Child Psychology & Psychiatry, 41*, 441-455.

Kochenderfer -Ladd, B., & Ladd, G. W. (2001). 'ariations in peer victimization: Relations to children's maladjustment. in J. Juvonen & S. Graham (Eds.), *Peer harassment in school*, (pp. 25-48). London: The Guilford Press.

Lazarus, R. S. (1984).The stress and coping paradigm. In J. M. Joffe, G. W. Albee & L. C. Kelly (Eds.), *Readings in primary prevention of psychopathology(* pp. 131-156). Hanover, NH: University Press of New England.

Lazarus, R. S.,& Folkman, S. (1984). *Stress appraisal and coping.* New York: Springer.

Mrazek, P. J., & Haggerty, R. J. (Eds.). (1994). *Reducing risks for mental disorders: Frontiers for preventive intervention research.* . Washington, DC: National Academy Press.

Murray-Harvey, R., & Slee, P.T. (2010). School and home relationships and their impact on school bullying. *School Psychology International, 31* , 271-295.

Murray-Harvey, R., Skrzypiec, G., & Slee, P.T. (2012). Effective and ineffective coping with bullying strategies assessed by informed professionals and their use by victimized students. *Australian Journal of Guidance & Counselling*. In press.

Naylor, P.,& Cowie, H. (1999). The effectiveness of peer support systems in challenging bullying in schools: the perspectives and experiences of teachers and pupils'. Journal of Adolescence, 22, 467-48

Naylor, P., Cowie, H. ,& del Rey, R. (2001).Coping strategies of secondary school children in response to being bullied. *Child Psychology and Psychiatry Review ,6* 114–120.

Nicolaides, S., Toda, Y., & Smith, P.K. (2002).Knowledge and attitudes about school bullying in trainee teachers. *British Journal of Educational Psychology, 72*:105-18.

Owens, L., Shute, R.,& Slee, P. T. (2000). 'I'm in and you're out': Explanations for teenage girls' indirect aggression. *Psychology, Evolution & Gender, 2,* 19-46.

Owens, L., Shute, R., & Slee, P. T. (2004). Girls' aggressive behavior. *The Prevention Researcher,11,,* 9-12.

Resnick, L. (2010). Nested learning systems for the thinking curriculum. *Educational researcher,. 39* 183-197.

Slee, P.T.,& Mohyla, J. (2007). *The PEACE Pack: an evaluation to reduce bullying in four Australian primary schools.* Educational Research, 49 *103-114.*

Slee, P.T., & Shute, R (2003). *Theories in child development.* London: Guilford.

Slee, P.T., Murray-Harvey, R., Dix, K., & Van Deur, P (2012). Quality assurance for KidsMatter primary. Unpublished report.

Smith, P. K., & Shu, S. (2000).What good schools can do about bullying: Findings from a survey in English schools after a decade of research and action. *Childhood ,7*:193-212.

Smith, P., Cowie, H., Olafsson, & Liefooghe, (2002). Definitions of bullying: A comparison of terms used, and age and gender differences, in a fourteen-country international comparison. *Child Development, 73,* 1119-1133.

Spears, B.A. & Dix, K.L. (2008, September). *Project Officers Facilitating Change in Schools*. Symposium: Evaluating Whole School Approaches to Mental Health Promotion: Transferring Learning to Practice at the From Margins to Mainstream: 5th World Conference on the Promotion of Mental Health and the Prevention of Mental and Behavioural Disorders, Melbourne.

Spears, B.A., Campbell, M., Slee, P.T. & Tangen, D. (2010,April). The net gen: Pre-service teachers' understanding of face-to-face and cyber-bullying. Presented at the National Centre Against Bullying Conference: Navigating the Maze: Cybersafety and Wellbeing solutions for schools: Melbourne.

Spears, B ., Slee, P., Campbell, M. A., & Cross D. (2011). *Educational change and youth voice: Informing school action on cyber-bullying* . CSE Occasional Papers Melbourne

Tremblay, R. E., Hartup, W. W., & Archer, J. (Eds.). (2005). *Developmental origins of aggression*. New York: Guilford Press.

Wandersman, A., Duffy, J., Flaspohler, P., Noonan, R., Lubell, K., Stillman, L., Blachman, M., Dunville, R., & Saul, J. (2008). Bridging the gap between prevention research and practice: The interactive systems framework for dissemination and implementation. *American Journal of Community Psychology, 41*,171–181.

RESOURCES

Shute, R., Slee, P.T., Murray-Harvey, R., & Dix, K (eds.) (2011). *Mental health and well being: Educational perspectives*. Adelaide: Shannon Press.

Slee, P.T. Campbell, M., & Spears, B (2012). Child, adolescent and family development. Melbourne: Cambridge University Press.

Slee, P.T., Flanagan, A., & Mitchell, B. (1995). Stressed out and growing up. A video/discussion resource package. Flinders University. Adelaide.

Slee, P.T. ,Murray-Harvey, R. Lawson, D., & Mitchell, B. (1997). Stressed out and coping in families. A video/discussion resource package. Flinders University. Adelaide.

Slee, P.T. (1997). The P.E.A.C.E. Pack. A programme for reducing bullying in our Schools. 1nd. edt. Flinders University. Adelaide.

Wotherspoon, A. Slee, P.T. ,Shute, R. & Owens, L. (2005). 'Best Practice in Anti-Bullying Prevention. Flinders University. Adelaide.

Slee, P.T. ,Shute, R. Wotherspoon, A.. (2002). 'Very Mixed Emotions' A discussion about bullying and young children. Commonwealth Attorney General's Department. Canberra.

Wotherspoon, A. Slee, P.T. ,& Murray-Harvey, R.. (2006). 'Coping with school Bullying. Flinders University. Adelaide.

Web sites
http://www.caper.com.au

Chapter 38
The Hong Kong "Uncle Long Legs"
Letter Box Project

Frederick Ka Ching Yeung, Queenie Lai Kwan Chan, and Daby Kwan Wah Tam

OVERVIEW: *This chapter introduces the "Uncle Long Legs' Letter Box" project launched by the Evangelical Lutheran Church Social Service (Hong Kong) since 1994. Inspired by a television cartoon program called "Uncle Long Legs[1]", a totally child-centered letter counseling service aiming at providing long-term friendship and guidance to children was established and it turns out to be a great blessing to the children and the volunteers of the project. Up to Dec. 2011, there were totally 46,000 letters mailed by over 14,000 children to the Letter Box. This chapter shares the operation and working experience of Uncle Long Legs' Letter Box and reviews the strengths and limitations of letter counseling service to children.*

"People who've had happy childhoods are wonderful, but they're bland... An unhappy childhood compels you to use your imagination to create a world in which you can be happy. Use your old grief. That's the gift you're given."

-Baron Patrick Maynard Stuart Blackett

BACKGROUND

Dear Uncle Long Legs,

How are you, this is the first time I write to you, I hope I can see you personally. I am the best friend of Mary who writes to you frequently and she introduce you to me, why they call you Uncle Long Legs, I have seen you at the TV cartoon, I think there is no Uncle Long Legs in the real world. I really love to make friend with you.

My mother disserted me and the family, the temperament of my father is very hot and I dare not to share or talk with him. Mary told me that Uncle Long Legs is very understanding and helpful, so I write to you immediately. I hope you can help me and can share my deepest feelings.   (From a boy of 10)

Dear Uncle Long Legs,

I am very stressful as my parents have serious conflicts currently. I was scared when my mother told me that she was seeking help from social worker and she was thinking to divorce with my father. I was very

---

[1] The cartoon was based on Jean Webster's classic book, "Daddy Long Legs". In the Chinese culture, the name "Uncle Long Legs" is a better translation than "Daddy Long Legs".

disturbed as I cannot stop thinking what should I do if my parents really separated. What will happen to my family? Father Day is coming, I really would like to choose a present for him to make him happier. Can you give me some advices? (From a boy of 10)

Dear Uncle Long Legs,

My Chinese, English and Mathematics were failed in most of my examinations. My parents and my elder sister were all angry with me and scolding me seriously. However, I have no motivation to do the assignments and revision, my mother doesn't like me. I don't like myself too. (From a girl of 7)

The letters above are some typical letter samples that mail to Uncle Long Legs' Letter Box. Soon after reading a few sample letters, you will be convinced that all the volunteer and staff of the Letter Box Project will not question the value and impact of the service. Currently, we have about 500 active volunteers to reply about 300 letters that emailed to Uncle Long Legs Letter Box every month, the demand as well as the support to the Project has never been stopped since its inception in 1994.

We all know that during the growing up process, children face many challenges. They need support and guidance from adults whom they can trust. Many children feel not secure enough to disclose their worries even to their parents or teachers, and in most case their peers also could not be mature enough to provide good guidance to solve the children's problem. In order to rich out to the children in need of support and guidance, Uncle Long Legs' Letter Box was set up to provide letter counseling service for children aged from around 8 to 15 years Using letters as the medium, children are encouraged to seek help from "Uncle Long Legs" when they are facing problems related to family, friendship and study. In letters, children are often more willing to disclose their personal feelings and problems than they are in face-to-face contacts. A lot of studies have shown that if timely assistance is not provided to children at risk, then normal social, emotional and cognitive developmental processes will be affected (e.g. Barrett, 1998; Barrett, 1999; Robinson et al., 2011; Sharp & Cowie, 1998).

Although "Writing as a form of therapeutic intervention does not have an especially long, rich, or varied history" (L'Abate, 1992, p. 6), Michael White and David Epston's work in early 1990s did well demonstrate the therapeutic power of letter (White & Epston, 1990). In the past two decades, there were many studies provided more evidence to show that letter can be an important therapeutic mean and have significant therapeutic results in different aspects (e.g. Allan & Bertoia, 1992; Bennion, 1998; Bobier, C., Dowell, J. & Craig, B., 2009; Cleveland, A.S., 2011; France, Cadieax & Allen, 1995; Goldberg, 2000; L'Abate, 1992; Hoffman, Hinkie & Kress, 2010; Lenhoff, 2011; Nau, 1997; Oliver et al., 2007; Petronio & Bradford, 1993; Sloman & Pipitone, 1991; Zimmerman & Shepherd, 1993).

A letter, no matter sent out or not, already has a therapeutic effect (Paul, Christensen & Falk, 2000). Letter writing helps the writer to organize fragmented experience into a cohesive story. The process can help the writer confront his or her problem and ultimately, change his or her life (Vance, 1998). Allan & Betoia (1992) suggest that writing letters provides children with a structure for commenting on their inner feelings, the demands of the outer world, and the struggle between the two realities; therefore the writing process is a powerful vehicle for healing and self-growth. Rasmussen also (1992) proposes that letter writing can also be used for self-guided personal therapy, because the letter writing process can become a process of desensitization to painful conflicts and traumatic experiences, and finally free the writer from the negative effects of his or her undesirable personal experience.

The letter writing process also has great cathartic value as the letter is a good medium through which to express deep personal feelings. In a study comparing writing and therapy transcripts in terms of narrative and narrative transformation, written narratives tend to be more emotionally involved, self-descriptive, and exploratory than spoken therapeutic interaction (Bennion, 1998). Therefore, writing letters to Uncle Long Legs Letter Box can serve as an effective strategy for children to articulate their feelings and inner concerns, especially when they believe that their letter will be read by an understanding and caring "Uncle" who will continue to be there to provide guidance and support.

From a narrative perspective, letter counseling is a process of writing and receiving letters in such a way that the client's experience of, and relationship to, their problems are transformed. Both the volunteer and the client join together to construct a new story in which the client has more power, freedom and alternatives to manage his or her difficulties (Bennion, 1998; Diamond, 1997; Friedman, 1992). In order to maximize the healing potential of each reply, the volunteer has to write it carefully (Lown & Britton, 1991; Rasmussen & Tomm, 1992; Sloman & Pipitone, 1991); the content and wording must be selected thoughtfully, in Karl Tom's words, "To bring experiences and events that promise to be resourceful, and to promote those kinds of 'stories' that have healing potential (White & Epston, 1990, p. ix)."

In essence we see writing letters to Uncle Long Legs as a story-construction process which includes three major components: writing the letter, waiting for the reply, and receiving the reply. In this process, the client is considered not as a passive child, but as an active agent who creates new meanings through writing letters to and receiving replies from a symbolic figure, Uncle Long Legs.

PROGRAM DESCRIPTION

Based on Jean Webster's classic book, "Daddy Long Legs", a cartoon version call "Uncle Long Legs" was broadcasted in Hong Kong in 1994. Uncle Long Legs is about an orphan named Judy, who wrote to her mysterious guardian, Uncle Long Legs, to share about her everyday life. Letter was the only way that Judy could communicate with this significant secret person. As the cartoon was very popular, nearly all the children know who is Uncle Long Legs and love him. Inspired by the Uncle Long Legs' story, a children and youth service center of the Evangelical Lutheran Church Social Service (Hong Kong) borrowed the identity of Uncle Long Legs and started a letter box service for children to write their concerns and make friend with Uncle Long Legs. The project Uncle Long Legs Letter Box turns out to be a great success and Uncle Long Legs continues to be the best friend of thousands of Hong Kong children for the last 18 years.

In reviewing the last 18 years of experience, five core areas are crucial to the success of the Letter Box which are: (1) The core characters of Uncle Long Legs; (2) the relationship between Uncle Long Legs and the child; (3) recruitment, training and monitoring of Uncle Long Legs volunteers;(4) letter procession procedures; and (5) promotion of the Letter Box and Uncle Long Legs' image.

THE CORE CHARACTER OF UNCLE LONG LEGS

Consistent with the image portrayed in Jean Webster's "Daddy Long Legs" and the objectives of the Letter Box, we carefully decided that the definitive character of Uncle Long Legs should be an approachable, caring and wise adult who is willing to listen to children whole-heartedly. That is why so many children liked him and, therefore, this should be the guiding principle in our letter counseling service. These characteristics are consistent with Carl Roger's person centered (Roger, 1951, 1961, 1980) approach and are emphasized throughout the recruitment, training and supervising process with our Uncle Long Legs volunteers.

THE RELATIONSHIP BETWEEN UNCLE LONG LEGS AND THE CHILD

Because we are aiming at establishing a long term guidance friendship with our children, we assign a designated volunteer to every new child who writes to Uncle Long Legs Letter Box. As a result, some children continue to connect with their Uncle Long Legs even when they become teenagers and the long term friendship somehow transform Uncle Long Legs to be as significant as a real uncle of their own.

Box 38.1: Uncle Long Legs in the eyes of children

"Uncle Long Legs is a very kind and helpful person who would try his best to solve our difficulties. Sometimes I found he like a "magic machine" which could absorb all my sadness. He helped me from impasses and I have grown a lot after knowing this "Uncle". (From a girl of 13)

"I trusted Uncle Long Legs very much as he was my good listener. When I was unhappy, I wrote to him...... afterwards, I could release all my pressure and felt better. (From a girl of 16)

"Uncle Long Legs become my best pen-friend since I was studying at primary two, no matter happy or unhappy, I will write to him and looking for his reply. We have already been the pen-friend for six years, he is the only one who accompanied me in all my happiness and sadness. This dear Uncle Long Legs lives in Hong Kong who has a special letter box for keeping contact with me. Uncle Long Legs, I would like to say thank you to you! "(From a girl of 15)

Moreover, as letter is the only mean that Judy can communicate with Uncle Long Legs, we also think that we should keep on maintaining this relationship between our Uncle Long Legs volunteers and their children. Hence, we closely monitor all the letters and replies and make sure that they only use letters to communicate throughout the service. The relationship is child directed as the role of Uncle Long Legs volunteer only reply child's letter and will not actively write to the child without receiving a letter from the child first. We believe that this kind of secret and child directed relationship is the essence of this Letter Box and also make this letter writing process interesting and therapeutic.

RECRUITMENT, TRAINING AND MONITORING OF UNCLE LONG LEGS VOLUNTEERS

Much effort has been made to recruit, select and train the volunteer team for the Letter Box service. At this stage, we have about 500 volunteers; most of them are social workers or teachers. In order to ensure the quality of our Uncle Long Legs service, regular training is provided for the volunteers. Each volunteer is expected to be committed to the mission and value of this letter box service. Each is equipped with basic knowledge about the concept of letter counseling. Narrative perspective (White & Epston, 1990; White, 1995) and client-centered approach (Roger, 1951, 1961) are used as our basic counseling strategies, in which we see letter counseling as a meaningful construction process. We believe that children have strength and potential to overcome their problems when they are given an adequate amount of guidance, especially from someone who is caring and supportive. The following are the core attitudes that we expect our Uncle Long Legs representatives to adopt, in writing replies to our children:

> To write each reply whole-heartedly and use every word with great care; write every word with regard to its healing impact on the receiver (Lown & Britton, 1991).

To be a good listener and supporter by showing empathy for, acceptance of and respect towards each child.

To validate and normalize the client's experiences and difficulties.

To be strength oriented; to use no criticism but to try to identify the strengths reflected in   the child's letter.

To reinforce actions, and affirm a positive attitude toward life (France et al., 1995).

Because our volunteers have a lot of opportunities to know the secrets of those children sending letter to the Letter Box, they need to be very risk sensitive which such as any form of child abuse, self-destructive behavior or suicidal tendencies. Once any potential risk is identified, they have to inform our social worker immediately; prompt action will be taken to contact the child or the child's family, to provide immediate assistance or crisis intervention.

LETTER PROCESSION PROCEDURES

Every month, on average, the Letter Box receives about 300 letters. Each incoming letter goes through a number of standard procedures. After receiving a letter, we first record the basic information of the writer and categorize the letter according to its theme or problem nature (e.g. study, family, interpersonal relationships etc.). If the letter comes from a new child, a new volunteer is assigned. In order to maintain a sense of continuity and to enable a trusting relationship, a specific volunteer is assigned to each child and the volunteer follows the child's letters in the future. If the letter is a reply to our letter, or a letter about a new problem from an existing client, the letter is sent to the responsible volunteer. In all cases, only a photocopy of the letter is given to the respective volunteer, and all the original letters are kept by the central management for filing. After receiving a child's letter, we make sure that the child gets a reply within three weeks' time. The responsible volunteer has to write the reply as soon as possible and send it to the central management. In order to guarantee the quality of each reply letter, a responsible worker form the Letter Box will be assigned to prove read every reply letter once before sending to the respective child. Moreover, a photocopy of the reply will be kept in the central office of the Letter Box. Except for the responsible volunteer, the responsible staff members and consultants of the program, all the information is kept confidential.

PROMOTION OF THE LETTER BOX AND UNCLE LONG LEGS' IMAGE

The major promotion strategies (see Table 38.1)for the Letter Box are:

1) Promoting the service through primary and secondary schools talks, also by designing Uncle Long Legs' pencils, book marks, writing pads and souvenirs to encourage the students to write to Uncle Long Legs. This is the most frequently used strategy and the result is also significant.

2) Organizing Uncle Long Legs' programs such as game stalls, carnivals, singing contests, drawing or writing competitions etc. In these activities, we tried to incorporate themes that matched Uncle Long Legs' image, for instance, a carnival promoting friendship, a singing competition focused on love, a writing competition for Mother's Day or Father's Day, to promote parent-child relationships. We hoped that such programs would help to build up Uncle Long Legs' image as a loving and caring adult.

3) Publicizing the service through mass media such as children's magazines, radio and television interviews, to consolidate Uncle Long Legs' caring image.

Table 38.1 Promotion and training activities conducted in 2011.

Uncle Long Legs' Event	Quantity	Total Persons Served
School Educational Talks	99 talks	14774
Public Promotion Activity	13 sessions	5314
Volunteer Reunion Gathering	18 sessions	250
Letter Counseling Training Course	27 sessions	491

RELATIONSHIP TO THE SBFC MODEL

Uncle-Long-Legs' Letter Box basically is a 100% child-centered service as we solely use letter as the main service medium between the children and our volunteers. It is hoped that a long-term one to one child initiated relationship can be established so that guidance and support can be provided timely and continuously to the child in all aspects of life (e.g. individual, peer, school-related and family) and the Letter Box can serve a wide range of functions from preventive, development to remedial. Hence, we believe that, using the SBFC model, Uncle-Long-Legs' Letter Box is mainly child-centered and can intervene at all four levels, however, judging from the content of letters and the service delivery model, the interventions are relatively more on family-preventive and school-preventive. In addition to the guidance support service to children, we also organize a lot of training and workshop for teachers and parents (please refer to Table 38.1) which can serve as a powerful platform between school and family to understand the needs of their children. We believe that the SBFC model is a good framework for us to examine how the Letter Box can further enhance its unique characteristics to work with school and parents in the future.

EVIDENCE-BASED SUPPORT

In order to give a clearer picture of the latest operation of the Letter Box, we have listed the statistics of the letters received and the nature of the letters in Table 38.2 and Table 38.3 below:

Table 38.2   Statistics of Uncle Long Legs' Letter Box in 2011

Letters received	3442 (750 letters from new service user)	
Served persons	1680 (1344 girls and 336 boys)	
Volunteers involved	482 volunteers	
Age of children	7-9 years old	30%
	10-12 years old	49%
	13-15 years old	17%
	16 years old or above	4%
Frequency of letters writing	1-3 letters per year	87.5%
	4-5 letters per year	6.9%
	6-9 letters per year	4%
	10 or above letters per year	1.5%

Table 38.3   The nature of the content of the letters received in 2011

Natures	Number of Letters	%
Relationship with Uncle Long Legs	931	16%
Peer relationship	549	9%
Love affairs	202	3%
Daily life sharing	1138	19%
Poor Self-Image	215	4%
Family life / Parent-child relationship	812	14%
School life sharing	832	14%
Study problems / Academic pressures	1058	18%
Social hot issue sharing	133	2%
Parents' marital relationship / financial status	51	1%
Others	26	0%

On the whole, most of the children indicated a very positive evaluation toward Uncle Long Legs' Letter Box; 74% of them totally or strongly agreed that Uncle Long Legs could support them, 56% of them agreed that their problem solving ability had been improved, 85% of them satisfied with the service and 63% of them would recommend Uncle Long Legs to their friend too. In addition to the survey result, below are some extracts of the children's sharing about their relationship and impression about Uncle Long Legs collected in the 15thanniversary celebration of the Letter Box in 2009:

"I have known Uncle Long Legs for two year. I could still remember that I had asked more than twenty questions in my first letter to this "unknown Uncle". I would write to him whenever I had difficulties and each time he would help me to solve them completely. However, Uncle Long Legs would not reply me about his personal particular as he had to keep his identity confidential to me. No matter what, our friendship was accumulated by letters to letters. I hope more children, youth and even adult can make friend Uncle Long Legs. The more you share, the less you worry!" (Siu Ting, a girl of 12)

"I did not know much about the appearance and background of Uncle Long Legs but I felt a lot of support and encouragement from him through letters. The energy of letters was so strong which enhanced our trustful relationship. Every time I felt sad and disappointed, I would think about him and wanted to write to him immediately. I hope, I could keep on writing to maintain the relationship with Uncle Long Legs forever. (Tse Ying, a girl of 19)

"Times goes by, Uncle Long Legs Letter Box has been over 15 years. Because of this letter box, I kept on writing and loved to use letters for sharing. Although the science of communications developed and changed day by day, letters writing might be out in one day. I still insisted that only letters of hand-writing was the most sincere communication channel with others. Letters could keep people heart to heart as you could keep the letters forever. In my experience, I found that Uncle Long Legs not only my pen friend, he was also my "old friend" who listened and understood me for over ten years. I hope all of Uncle's pen friends would not forget him forever. (Sze Kei, a girl of 20)

"I started writing to Uncle Long Legs when I was a primary student, we already have kept six years friendship. Every time I wanted to share with others, I would write to him and he would help me to ventilate and settle my difficulties. Sometimes I felt embarrassed to share with my family members, I

would talk to him too. Uncle Long Legs is my best friend and I hope our friendship will be forever". (Simon Yeung, a male of 15)

The Letter Box will conduct a survey to collect feedback and evaluation about the service annually, Table 38.4 shows the results of 2011's survey.

Table 38.4   Result of 2011 Service Evaluation Survey

Question (N = 139, conducted on 27th April, 2011)	Response					
	Totally Agree	Strongly Agree	Agree	Disagree	Strongly Disagree	Totally Disagree
Do you think that Uncle Long Legs can give you support or encouragement?	69 (49%)	35 (25%)	27 (19%)	7 (5%)	0	0
Do you think that Uncle Long Legs' Letter Box can help you to improve your problem solving ability?	39 (28%)	40 (28%)	41 (29%)	15 (11%)	0	1 (1%)
	Having Problem	Sharing unhappy feelings	Make Friend	Sharing Life experience	Curiosity	Others
Why you write to Uncle Long Legs' Letter Box? (Can choose more than one response)	64 (46%)	92 (66%)	73 (53%)	96 (69%)	47 (34%)	5 (4%)
	Yes		Consider		No	
Will you recommend the Letter Box service to your friends?	87 (63%)		46 (33%)		3 (2%)	
	Yes		Fair		No Response	
As a whole, satisfied with the service?	118 (85%)		18 (13%)		3 (2%)	

The above qualitative feedbacks from children are the best evidence of the success of the Letter Box. We think that the relationship between our children and their Uncle Long Legs is invaluable as they have grown together and shared a secret part of their special memory. Many children would like to keep

---

Box 38.2: Uncle Long Legs Volunteers' Sharing

"I have been the volunteers of Uncle Long Legs' Letter Box for few years. I found that this service very meaningful as I can witness the growth of many children. By comparing with our generation, children faced lots of pressure and challenge than before, including their study pressures and the over expectation of their parents. However, children were willing to share with Uncle Long Legs. Although we did not see each other, a very special relationship has been built up. I would like to use letters to give them support and encouragement in order to enhance their positive thinking. I believe that my devotion surely could enlighten children life and gave them some remarkable memories in their life". (Volunteer, Miss So Mei Ying)

"In the past 7 years of volunteer role of Uncle Long Legs, I have received over 100 letters from different children. Review this volunteer experience, there were full of ups and downs. When I read the letters from the poor children who were suffered from the family problems, I could share their helpless and sadness. Luckily, most of the letters sharing were full of happiness. Although they were facing many challenges, after the receiving my letters, they became strong and optimistic. In fact, I took more than gave in the past seven years. I have learnt how to use the perspective of children to understand them. I know that no one is perfect even adult could be wrong and mistreated their children. If we could start where the children are, we could understand what they want. I was so lucky to be one of the volunteer, hoping that you can share the happiness of being a volunteer in the coming future. (Volunteer, Mrs. and Mr. KO Sze Fung)

---

their friendship with Uncle Long Legs and some of them have become our Uncle Long Legs volunteers too. Box 38.3 also shows some feedback from the parents of our service users which is very positive. Indeed, we actively conduct promotional workshops to parents as parents' support is very important in Hong Kong.

MULTICULTURAL COUNSELING CONSIDERATIONS

As most of the children are Hong Kong born Chinese, there is little multicultural issue encountered in the Letter Box. However, some of the children are new immigrants from the mainland China, our volunteers have to be sensitive to their adjustment in Hong Kong and they are reminded to respect their different growing up experiences. We also tried to recruit some exchange university students from China to be the Uncle Long Legs for those children coming from the mainland China. Although most of the letters are written in Chinese, a small proportion of the letters are written in English and our volunteers will also use English to reply accordingly.

CHALLENGES AND SOLUTIONS

Letter writing is different from telephone counseling and face-to-face interviewing in that clients are not bound by time or space. In fact, we have received quite a number of letters from children not living in

Hong Kong. Children can choose whatever place and time are convenient for them to share feelings and difficulties. As the children do not need to face a volunteer directly, the labeling effect is reduced and mysterious nature of Uncle Long Legs increases their motivation to make friend and seek help from

---

Box 38.3: Sharing by the Service User's Parents

"I have two gifted children and they also have the general problems of gifted children; they are more self-centered, lack of patience, and have difficulties in articulate inner feels. Although I have spent a lot of time to communicate with them, but the effect is not good. After knowing the service of Uncle Long Legs Letter Box, I encouraged them to write to Uncle Long Legs. Out of my expectation, Uncle Long Legs become their best friend and Uncle Long Legs even know some their secrets that they wouldn't share with me. The best thing is that Uncle Long Legs successfully provide encouragement, emotional support and guidance that they desperately needed but unable to obtain by me. They are now much happier than before and I here sincerely thank Uncle Long Legs for his unfailing friendship and care. THANKS!" (Mrs. Lee)

"After making friend with Uncle Long Legs, my child has grown up suddenly, he is more able to follow my instruction and understand me more too. For example, he was under great academic pressure which I was not able to recognize, after Uncle Long Legs' encouragement and guidance, he is more willing to do his academic assignments and more motivated to study. I also become more understanding and patient in supervising his study. Sometimes, parents will be too emotionally involved and, as a result, may lead to many communication problems with their children. In such a situation, children are more willing to share their deep down feelings and problems with Uncle Long Legs. Uncle Long Legs, being a neutral adult figure, can help to comfort the children's pent-up emotions and to guide them to understand their parents more. My children are eager to wait for Uncle Long Legs' letters and they will read them many times. He surely is an uncle loved by many children." (Mrs. Ng)

Uncle Long Legs. Writing and receiving letters is a good means to build up intimate relationships with children (Lown & Britton, 1991; Shulman, Seiffge-Krenke, & Dimitrovski, 1994).

However, letter counseling has its limitations. Letter writing demands that a child has certain comprehension and writing abilities and this may discourage children whose writing ability is weak from using the service. As writing takes more time in which to express oneself than speaking, the letters from our clients are usually very short. Our volunteers have to provide counseling service based on very limited written information. Without any verbal and nonverbal information, accurate assessment of children's problem-intensity and emotional states is hindered. Moreover, it is also difficult for us to assess the authenticity of the messages, as our clients may exaggerate the risks involved, or the seriousness of their situations. Although a letter provides a good means by which to reach out to meet children's needs, letter counseling cannot replace the traditional counseling service. Due to the above limitations, our service tends to be supportive and preventive in nature.

Time is needed to answer a letter and send it back to the child. In order to keep high quality control, all reply letters have to be sent back to the central management to be inspected by a social worker before they are mailed out to our clients. It takes at least two to three weeks for the child to receive a reply from Uncle Long Legs. The Letter Box cannot give children a prompt response as in telephone counseling or a face-to-face interview. Moreover, the counseling input from a letter is not comparable to as the intensive as in a traditional face to face counseling service. However, we encourage children to write down their telephone number in their letter. Thus, we can contact a child by phone and offer immediate help in a crisis.

When we discover children who require prompt counseling service, we will refer them to our social workers to follow up. For urgent or serious problems, it is more appropriate for professional workers to contact the children and their family members directly, in order to provide a more intensive and immediate counseling service than letter counseling. For example, we received a letter from a 14 year-old girl, disclosing that she had been raped during a tour visit in Taiwan. No one knew about this secret and she dared not tell her parents about it. We decided to phone this girl directly and encouraged her to see a volunteer. With her consent, we arranged for a volunteer to provide a more intensive counseling service for her. Sometimes, confidentially might be violated in order to safeguard the best interest of the children.

As stated above, we need to closely monitor the quality of the replying letters, in addition to the heavy logistic and manual input to maintain the filing and related administrative system, certain degree of professional input from social workers are also required. Recruiting and training of volunteers are the core success factors for the Letter Box. You can see from Table 1, just in 2011, we had conducted 99 school educational talk and 13 public promotion activity to promote the Letter Box and to recruit volunteers and organized 18 sessions of volunteer reunion gathering and 27 sessions letter counseling training to our volunteers. That means a lot of hard works behind to support the smooth operation of the Letter Box.

In spite of these limitations, our Letter Box plays a unique role in providing a help-seeking alternative for children, as reflected in the number of letters received over the past few years. We are now living in a modern world that nearly everyone uses email and internet to communicate, there are also great development in email or on-line counseling service (e.g. Jones, 2009), the question of whether traditional hand-writing letter counseling service like Uncle Long Legs Letter Box should be continued or be on-lined has been coming up again and again from different people. Up to now, after careful review and reflection, we still believe that Uncle Long Legs Letter Box has its unique features and we would continue to use hand-written letter to deliver our love and support to our beloved children.

SUMMARY

Some people can express themselves better in writing than in speaking. In our experience, this is especially true for children. Our Uncle Long Legs' Letter Box provides a help-seeking alternative for children. Children can share their stress and feelings without talking to a volunteer directly. This helps to lessen their embarrassment and unpleasant feelings about seeking help. Being a caring and helpful adult, Uncle Long Legs not only helps children to ventilate their emotions, but also gives them timely and valuable guidance. Childhood is a stage of intellectual and moral development. Children need guidance and support to face challenges from the environment, and to establish their own value system. From our experience, many children do not have an adult whom they can trust and who will listen to them, comfort them and give them a sense of security. Uncle Long Legs is just the right person for this.

Besides helping children to release their feelings, letter writing also gives them time to calm down. According to France, Cadieax and Allen (1995), the letter counseling process is essentially one of focusing and refocusing the client's feelings, thoughts, and actions. The purpose is to allow the client an opportunity to reassess strengths, to focus on the positive, and to take responsibility for his or her actions. The process allows the client to reflect, experiment, and take action to solve his or her problem. The writing process enables him or her to have a better understanding of the problems and improve his or her self-understanding.

For most children, receiving a letter from a close friend or significant person is a highly satisfying event (Thomas, 1998). This is particularly true for children receiving Uncle Long Legs' reply. Reading Uncle Long Legs' reply is a special moment for most of our clients because they feel supported, understood and attended to. They are ready to take Uncle's advice, as they have waited for it for a few weeks. Many children wrote to our volunteers saying that they would keep the replies and re-read them many times. As the messages in the letter can be re-read many times, the therapeutic effects can be consolidated and expanded with each reading.

We can confidently say that letter counseling has its unique attraction and healing power to children in need and Uncle Long Legs Letter Box has provide invaluable friendship and guidance to thousands of Hong Kong children and will be continued to be a caring and loving Uncle to many more children in the future. We hope that the Letter Box experience can serve to illustrate how the SBFC model in real application to provide meaningful services to children, school and parents.

RESOURCES

We have set up an Uncle Long Legs' Letter Box website to promote the Letter Box and to updating the latest events and news of our service: http://service.elchk.org.hk/unclelongleg/html/main.html
We have also published books and journals to introduce the service since 1996 (e.g. Yeung, Cheng & Chau, 2003; Yeung, & Chau, 2004; Yeung, Cheng & Chau, 2004). Readers are welcome to contact the authors for any questions about the operation of the Letter Box.

REFERENCES

Allan, J. A., & Bertoia, J. (1992). *Written paths to healing: Education and Jungian child counseling.* Dallas, TX, USA: Spring Publications.

Barrett, J. H. W. (1998). New knowledge and research in child development. *Child and Family Social Work, 3(4)*, 267-276.

Barrett, J. H. W. (1999). New knowledge and research in child development, Part 2. *Child and Family Social Work, 4(2)*, 97-107.

Bennion, K. (1998). The use of letter writing technique in individual psychotherapy. *Dissertation Abstracts International: Section B: The Sciences and Engineering, 59(1-B)*, 410.

Bobier, C., Dowell, J., & Craig, B. (2009) Youth-, Family-, and Professional-Rated Utility of a Narrative Discharge Letter Written to Older Adolescent Psychiatric Inpatients. *Journal of Child and Adolescent Psychiatric Nursing 22(4)*, 182-189.

Cleveland, A.S. (2011). *Bibliotherapy for all: Using children's literature about loss and grieving to increase awareness, develop coping skills, and build community among elementary school students.* Webster University.

Diamond, J. P. (1997). Narrative means to sober ends: Language, interpretation, and letter writing in psychotherapy and recovery. *Dissertation Abstracts International Section A: Humanities and Social Sciences, 57(10-A)*, 4542.

France, M. H., Cadieax, J., & Allen, G. E. (1995). Letter therapy: A model for enhancing counseling intervention. *Journal of Counseling & Development, 73*, 317-318.

Friedman, S. (1992). Constructing solutions (stories) in brief family therapy. In S. H. Budman & M. F. Hoyt (Eds.), *The first session in brief therapy* . New York: Guilford Press.

Goldberg, D. (2000). "Emplotment": Letter writing with troubled adolescents and their families. *Clinical Child Psychology and Psychiatry, 5*(1), 63-76.

Hoffman, R., Hinkie, M.C., & Kress, V.W. (2010). Letter writing as an intervention in family therapy with adolescents who engage in nonsuicidal self-injury. Family Journal, 18 (1), 24.

Jones, G. (2009). *Online counselling : a handbook for practitioners*. Basingstoke.

L'Abate, L. (1992). *Programmed writing: A self-administered approach for interventions with individual, couples, and families*. Pacific Grove, CA: Brooks/Cole.

Lenhoff, J. (2011). *Dear perpetratror, A letter writing technique for female survivors of perpetrator inflicted violence*. Doctoral dissertation, Massachusetts School of Professional   Psychology.

Lown, N., & Britton, B. (1991). Engaging families through the letter writing technique. *Journal of Strategic and Systemic Therapies, 10(2)*, 43-48.

Nau, D. S. (1997). Andy writes to his amputated leg: Utilizing letter writing as an interventive technique in brief family therapy. *Journal of Family Psychotherapy, 8(1)*, 1-12.

Oliver, M., Nelson, K.W., Cade, R. & Cueva, C. (2007). Therapeutic letter writing from school counselors to students, parents, and teachers. *Professional School Counseling*, 19(5), 510- 516.

Paul, J. L., Christensen, L., & Falk, G. (2000). Accessing the intimate spaces of life in the   classroom through letters to former teachers: A protocol for uncovering hidden stories. In J. L. Paul & T. J. Smith (Eds.), *Stories out of school: Memories and reflections on care and   cruelty in the classroom* (pp. 15-26). Stamford, CT, US: Ablex Publishing Corp.

Petronio, S., & Bradford, L. (1993). Issues interfering with the use of written communication as a means of relational bonding between absentee divorced fathers and their children.   *Journal of Applied Communication Research, 21(2)*, 163-175.

Rasmussen, P. T., & Tomm, K. (1992). Guided letter writing: A long brief therapy method whereby clients carry out their own treatment. *Journal of Strategic and Systemic   Therapies, 11(4)*, 1-8.

Robinson, M., Mattes, E., Oddy, W.H., Pennell, C.E. et al. (2011). Prenatal stress and risk of behavioral morbidity from age 2 to 14 years: The influence of the number, type, and   timing of stressful life events. *Development and Psychopathology, 23 (2)*, 507-521.

Rogers, Carl. (1980). *A Way of Being*. Boston: Houghton Mifflin

Rogers, Carl. (1961). *On Becoming a Person: A Therapist's View of Psychotherapy*. London: Constable.

Rogers, Carl. (1951). *Client-centered Therapy: Its Current Practice, Implications and Theory*. London: Constable.

Sharp, S., & Cowie, H. (1998). *Counselling and supporting children in distress*. London: Sage.

Shulman, S., Seiffge-Krenke, I., & Dimitrovski, L. (1994). The functions of pen pals for   adolescents. *Journal of Psychology, 128(1)*, 89-100.

Sloman, L., & Pipitone, J. (1991). Letter writing in family therapy. *American Journal of Family Therapy, 19(1)*, 77-82.

Thomas, P. (1998). Writing letters to patients. *Psychiatric Bulletin, 22(9)*, 542-545.

Vance, T. (1998). *Letters home: How writing can change your life*. New York: Pantheon Books.

White, M., & Epston, D. (1990). *Narrative means to therapeutic ends*. New York: Norton.

White, M. (1995). 1995. *Re-Authoring Lives: Interviews and Essays*. Adelaide, South Australia: Dulwich Centre Publications.

Yeung, K.C., Cheng, S.F., & Chau, G.Y.Y (2003). Uncle Long Legs' letter box: A letter counseling   service for children in Hong Kong. *Child & Adolescent Social Work Journal. Vol. 20 (1)*, 37-   51.

Yeung, K.C., Wu Cheng, S. F. & Chau, Y.Y. (Eds.). (2004). *To Uncle-Long-Legs with Love: Letter Counselling Service from the Eyes of Children*. Hong Kong: Service Coordination Office of Evangelic Lutheran Church of Hong Kong.

Yeung, K.C., & Chau, G.Y.Y. (2004). Letters to my Uncle-Long-Legs': A case illustration of letter counseling to children. *Illinois Child Welfare. Vol. 1 (1)*, 79-89.

Zimmerman, T. S., & Shepherd, S. D. (1993). Externalizing the problem of bulimia: Conversation, drawing and letter writing in group therapy. *Journal of System Therapies, 12(1)*, 22-31.

PART VII

SCHOOL-BASED FAMILY COUNSELING: SPECIFIC APPLICATIONS

F. CASE STUDIES IN SCHOOL-BASED FAMILY COUNSELING

Chapter 39
The Girl Who Believed
She Would Never Be Good Enough

Heidi Petrow

OVERVIEW: *This chapter describes the use of a Family Counseling with Individuals approach to SBFC. The Circumplex Model and Psychological Type were used in case conceptualization. A step by step CBT Family Systems approach was used to help a student develop a more constructive relationship with her mother.*

PRESENTING PROBLEM

Maria, a fifteen-year-old Latina sophomore, was referred to me by one of the academic counselors during the first week of school for "wanting to talk with someone about personal issues."Maria experienced verbal abuse from her mother as a result over her being gay. Her mood had been depressed as a result of the tension with her mother and the stress of past romantic partners. Maria also exhibited self-harm behavior and had a pattern of co-dependency in relying on others for happiness despite abusive patterns of partner choice.

RELATIONSHIP TO THE SBFC MODEL

This case study highlights several modalities of the SBFC model. The first is the School-Prevention component in which I taught various stress management techniques and skills to my client throughout the course of treatment. The second element of the SBFC model that was utilized with my client was the School-Intervention facet in which I used different crisis interventions to reduce and eventually eliminate her self-harm behavior. The third component was the Family-Intervention element. This included primarily family counseling with the individual student, parent phone consultation for the no-self harm contract, and role-playing with the student assertion by me modeling her mother. Integrating all of these SBFC components into my treatment plan proved highly effective for my student to achieve individual and interpersonal success with those in her life at the end of termination.

BACKGROUND INFORMATION

Maria explained that she began cutting in the 7th grade due to the negative peer pressure she was around that made the cutting seem like it was a "good stress reliever" when her parents were arguing. Maria started dating in the 6th grade and became vulnerable to co-dependency issues due to extreme prior loneliness. She went on to say that her state of depression had been on and off for the past three years since the cutting began. In addition to coming out in her sexual orientation as being openly gay in the 8th grade, for which she was extremely bullied in junior high, she had a pattern of being in intense, short-term relationships with other openly gay females. These relationships have lasted from a week, to a month, and with her last relationship lasting two months.

Maria currently lived with her Father, George, her mother, Carol, and her three-year-old brother, Andrew, in a small home near the high school. Maria struggled academically and denied any presenting problems with her teachers. In addition, Maria had not reported any negative interaction with the Vice Principal or Assistant Principal for any behavioral issues.

THE FIRST SESSION

When Maria came to my office her affect was depressed with a level of sadness that indicated she was experiencing grief over a loss of some kind. She expressed that she was openly gay and was currently experiencing a difficult break-up with her last girlfriend that was particularly intense and destructive. Maria also divulged her history of cutting, which led to the past girlfriend not being able to cope with the underlying depression and self-harm behavior that Maria exhibited.

In addition to her poor peer relationships, Maria was experiencing stress at home also. Maria described her sexual orientation as a lesbian as being significantly stressful between her mother and herself. She felt pressure from her mother to be straight and did not feel supported in anyway by her mother to be gay. Her father, however, supported her decision and was understanding.

Maria also recalled the fights erupting between the two of them with Carol calling Maria derogatory names such as "Faggot," "Dyke," "Stupid Gay person," and other hurtful slurs, and constantly making fun of Maria being gay. Maria also said that her mother doesn't want the rest of the family to find out she is gay because they are religious. Maria felt that her mother was ashamed of her being her daughter and felt intense pressure from her to keep her lifestyle a secret. At the beginning of treatment Maria and her mother were fighting almost daily over the issue of Maria being gay and their communication had broken down almost completely.

As I was listening to Maria speak of the deep pain and hurt she experienced on almost a daily basis with the intense judgment she felt from her mother, I felt a deep compassion for this young girl. As a deeply committed woman of faith myself, I was seeing my client through a lens of overwhelming love and acceptance. I was keenly aware of my compassion towards this young girl in looking into her eyes and feeling the depth of her rejection by her mother and peers. Already, in this first session I was admiring my client's bravery, courage, and tenacity to persevere under adverse circumstances in holding fast to discovering her identity.

I was also very aware of this young girl's tendency towards self-harm and her current depressed mood, so I probed for further depth of any suicidal tendencies. After drawing her out she shared that she has had the thought of hanging herself in the past, but currently did not have a plan of intended harm. I asked if she had the means at home to hurt herself with and she said yes. I had her sign a "No Harm Contract" and call her father with her consent while she was in the room. My purpose was to make him aware of her fragile state so as to remove any ropes, while also alerting him and his wife to be sensitive to her at this time.

THE SBFC ASSESSMENT

My assessment of the tension between Carol and Maria lead me to conclude that Maria's unmet validation from her mother developed deep insecurities about herself that had resulted in to dependency issues in her personal relationships. As a result of Carol communicating to Maria that she is not acceptable to her as her daughter, Maria had a vulnerability in a poor self image which in turn lead me to recognize that she was also vulnerable in not asserting herself in peer relationships that are dysfunctional. The stress in these relationships could further impede her progress and success in school and in turn cause the self-harm behavior to remain cyclical. My initial DSM-IV TR diagnoses for Maria were an Identity Problem and Adjustment Disorder with Depressed Mood, in addition to the Parent-Child Relational Problem.

CIRCUMPLEX MODEL ASSESSMENT

I diagnosed this family within the Circumplex Model as "Structurally Connected" for several reasons. Maria described both of her parents as strict in their parenting style, but they allowed her to voice her opinion if things seem unfair. This told me that her parents were firm and consistent with being predictable with their reasonable consequences for raising their daughter, which indicated a Structured level on family adaptability. There are several reasons why I diagnosed this family as Connected. I asked Maria what she and her family did together for fun. She responded, "We eat dinner together during the week, go out to eat together, and they like to drive me and my friends around where we want to go." She also indicated that her parents do have an emotional closeness between them, that her parents like to be involved in her life, but they also respected her privacy. All these elements combined indicated a Connected level on family cohesion.

I diagnosed the relationship between George and Carol as being "Flexibly Connected" for several reasons. When I asked Maria about what she could tell me about her parent's relationship with each other, she said that even though her mom can be overpowering sometimes towards her, her parents do have an equal view of each other and the roles that they hold. I rated this relationship as Flexible on family adaptability. I also asked Maria how close her parents were emotionally. She said that they are committed to one another, and share and talk about things that are bothering them. I rated this relationship as Connected on cohesion.

I diagnosed the Father-Daughter dyad as "Structurally Connected." When I asked Maria what her relationship with her father was like she mentioned that he is strict, but he does listen to her when she complains about house rules .I rated this level of adaptability as Structured. I also asked Maria how connected she felt to her father and she said she feels more connected to him than to her mom. She said that he understands and is more accepting of her gay lifestyle. In addition, she felt supported by him more than her mom. She does feel like she can talk with him better than with her mother. He is much easier to approach because there is no judgment there. I rated this level of cohesion as Connected.

I diagnosed the relationship between Carol and Maria as "Rigid/Structurally Disengaged." Maria stated that she does know that her mom is strict, but she is not so strict that she's not flexible in making decisions about her. This suggests a more Structured diagnosis. However, there was an element of rigidity in Carol with being overly controlling and not being accepting of Maria's gay lifestyle. This was evident from the previous background examples of Carol's harsh and uncaring comments towards her daughter being a lesbian. I rated this relationship between Rigid and Structured on adaptability. The Disengaged element was clearly evident in this dyad especially with the amount of verbal attacks coming from Carol towards Maria, the lack of nurturance, the lack of emotional closeness between the two, and the heightened amount of tension involved over Maria being gay.

PSYCHOLOGICAL TYPE ASSESSMENT

I diagnosed Maria's Psychological Type as ENFJ for several reasons. As I have been drawing Maria out over the last 6 weeks through our sessions together, several things had stood out to me that gave me the impression that she was an Extrovert. She was highly social land loved to talk. Even when she had been upset about her intense female relationships, she shared a wide range of information about the 6 days that we had last seen each other. She seldom appeared overly serious when much turmoil was going on with her peers, which is a challenge for an introverted type. Overall, I definitely saw the strengths and challenges of Extroversion in Maria.

Maria had also given me the impression that she was an Intuitive type for several reasons. She was very original in her appearance with her style of hair, clothes, make-up, and accessories and was highly creative with her looks from week to week. In her relationship with her ex she showed impractical thinking and also being un-careful with herself and not getting her needs met. This can be a challenge with Intuitive types who can be flighty and dreamy. She had great insight into the pain and rejection of her mom's verbal attacks taking an effect on her. When asked if she thought that the stress of her mom's judgmental attitude could be playing into the depression and self-harm behaviors, she agreed that she could see that connection was contributing to her low self-esteem.

It is very clear that Maria was a Feeling type for many reasons. She had a huge heart of compassion for her peer group and reported numerous times how she would "drop everything to be there for them." She had mentioned that a lot of her peers turn to her for support when they are going through difficulties because they know she cares so much. With mom it was different, because she was easily hurt by the cold, uncaring, and blunt remarks that Carol made against her being gay. However, she very much felt connected to dad because there was harmony there between them. I also thought one of the challenges of her being a Feeling type was in being overly sentimental with her ex girlfriend who came back to trigger her each week with unnecessary drama. But overall, Maria's sweet, kind, sensitive and caring heart was what stands out the most when I assessed Maria as a Feeling type.

Finally, I diagnosed Maria as a Judging Type. She was very responsible and organized in her schoolwork. In the six weeks since I had been at the High School she had been there everyday except for one absence. I happened to observe Maria in class twice. She was respectful, focused, and engaged in the class discussion with the other students and was decisive in her answers when called upon. In addition, when I listened to Maria describe her interactions with her mother it seems like both of them can be overly opinionated about their different views, which can be a challenge for a Judging type when engaging in heated arguments.

COUNSELING GOALS

In forming the treatment goals for my client, I initially suggested to Maria that I bring her mother into my office either with myself or with the three of us. My client absolutely refused to involve her mother or even her father. To respect my client's wishes my goals were tailored to fit her needs with the hopes of joining mother and daughter together at a later time. The main goal was to move Maria and Carol from Structurally Disengaged to Structurally Separated. The second goal was to eliminate Maria's self-harm behavior. The third goal was to decrease her depression by increasing her self-esteem. The fourth goal was to reduce Maria's stress, by: a) reducing her fights with her mother; b) improving communication between daughter and mother; c) having Carol be more understanding of her daughter's gay lifestyle and decreasing the verbal abuse, and d) helping Maria generally to reconnect with her mother.

The following CBT counseling strategies were used with the purpose of helping Maria develop healthier coping skills to better manage her stress, increase her self-esteem and increase the overall health of her interpersonal relationships:

ABC's of Self-Esteem
Self-Esteem Bingo for Teens
Totika Self-Esteem game for Teens
Healthy Relationships Bingo for Teens
Healthy relationships list for client to formulate in her mind qualities she wants in a relationship
that would build her up and qualities that would tear her down

Reference to the Ten Traditional Stress-Reduction Methods list
Assessment of Troublesome Social Stimuli in Relationships
Systematic Muscle Relaxation
Talking in Type Cheat Sheet
DESC Confrontation (Assertion Skills Training)
Role Playing
Journaling thoughts and emotional triggers for depression and anger

In addition, I used Emotion Focused Therapy Strategies to bring awareness of maladaptive emotional regulation and help her release her repressed anger. In particular, we did collage work in processing the bullying experiences, co-dependency issues, and underlying sadness towards mom's verbal abuse.

COUNSELING PROCESS

I took Maria's specific type (ENFJ) into consideration with choosing particular interventions that would best fit her style of learning and communicating. I implemented my treatment plan for Maria over the course of six weeks seeing her twice a week. Each week had a different theme in order to slowly build up her ego strength so that she could eventually find the courage to assert herself with her mother's verbal abuse. Each week I referred to the "No Self Harm" contract and discussed with her at the beginning of each session if she had an impulse to cut during the week.

WEEK 1: SELF ESTEEM AND STRENGTH BUILDING WEEK

The theme of the first week and a half was "Self-Esteem and Strength Building Week." The purpose of this week was to increase my client's self worth and confidence in being a gay female by focusing on her positive attributes that made her uniquely her. This helped her move towards eliminating co-dependency issues related to romantic partners and encouraged her to see her own potential in spite of her mother's rejection and judgmental attitude. At the beginning of this week my client had an impulse to cut, however she used a prior intervention I gave her of holding an ice cube in the palm of her hand and feeling the pain of the cold numbing her hand instead of cutting.

I initially tried doing the "ABC's of Self-Esteem" with Maria, which is an intervention to get the client to creatively see positive attributes of her self that is linked with each letter of the alphabet. At this point, my client could not come up with one thing she liked about herself. I then modified my treatment plan by going on to play *Self-Esteem Bingo for Teens*. Maria responded well as an Intuitive and Feeling type with this game's creativity and originality by expressing herself with honest comments in regards to the benefits of self-esteem. She commented by saying, "It makes more sense to see the mistakes that I've made in past relationships as "opportunities for growth" (as the game describes), and not get so sad about my ex breaking up with me. Now I know to not say I love you so quickly and just say I like you."

In the Self-Esteem Bingo game Maria also identified her strengths as having a good sense of humor, being able to express herself fully, realizing that she does have potential, in addition to being able to talk things through in tough times. She also identified that her self-esteem is lowered when she relied too heavily on others for approval. Overall this exercise was very beneficial for Maria to learn that she does have a lot to offer others.

The next technique I had planned for Maria this week involved the game *Totika,* which is a self-esteem game that I thought would appeal to her Intuitive and Feeling personality. One of the questions that came up in this game that was very interesting was, "Who notices when you do something well?" Maria replied: "my Mom."I then said, "It makes a lot of sense why you would be so hurt when she attacks you verbally and how the tension gets to be too much between the two of you. However, it does also sound like she does really care about the details of the things you do well. Enough to tell you in her own way that she is proud of you." This dialogue opened Maria's heart a little more to see that her mom does have some nurturing aspects about her that communicate she does really care.

I also added an additional technique of playing *Healthy Relationships Bingo For Teens* with my client in order to draw out more of what a good relationship looks like in comparison to her previous relationships with ex-girlfriends. This was a great success as Maria began to see her pattern of picking unsafe people to be in relationship with .I also had Maria list out on a piece of paper the positive things she wants in a relationship and the negative things she doesn't want. This helped Maria see the previous ex girlfriend's controlling nature. I also used this list as a tool to guide Maria in choosing future romantic partners and to help Maria not to go back to her old habits of co-dependency. At the end of this week and a half I asked Maria how things were between her and her mom and she replied: "The fighting has improved some and mom is being less harassing."

WEEK 2: STRESS REDUCTION WEEK

The second week was "Stress Reduction Week." The purpose of this week was to give Maria better coping skills to manage stress with her peers and Carol's verbal abuse, to further eliminate her self-harm behavior, and to reduce her anxiety and depression. Maria reported no impulse to cut since we last met.

The first technique that I implemented was the Ten Traditional Stress-Reduction Methods list. This was a list of ways to reduce stress, four CBT techniques to reduce anxiety, and a compilation of positive self-statements for Maria to refer to when stress is high. Tapping into Maria's Extroverted Type we came up with positive ways that she could manage her stress by jogging, journaling her thoughts, and talking with her best friend.

The second technique I implemented was the Behavioral Assessment to identify her Troublesome Social Stimuli (TSS) with her Mom and the triggers in her body. This technique utilized Maria's Judging type in that I prepared ahead of time for this exercise and provided a clear and organized way to help her see her responses with her mom when stressed. Maria's TSS's were when her mom commands her, criticizes her and when her mother is unresponsive. Maria gave an example of her mom "getting in her face and ordering her to do all her chores at the same time." Her behavioral response was to yell back at her mom, to feel tension in her fists, and to notice that her breathing was heavy. Her stress response to her mom commanding her was to leave, fight back and to feel tension in her body. Her tolerant response was to just ignore her mom.

The second TSS that triggered Maria with her mom was criticism. Maria told me that when she cuts her hair short her mom tells her she looks ugly, looking like a boy, and grounds her from seeing her friends and doing any activities. Maria's behavioral response was to tell her mom that she is not ugly and that she just cuts her hair when she is bored. She then cries and gets sad and feels tension in her heart and that "it's breaking." Additionally, her breathing becomes slow. Her stress response was to leave, then to deny that it affects her, and to try and placate. Her tolerate response was to assert herself and tell her mom to please calm down.

The third TSS was unresponsiveness from Carol. The example was Maria asking for some food from Carol and Carol ignoring her and telling her to go sit down in front of her aunt. Maria's behavioral response was to ask her mom three times if she could "go get subway" and how she was hungry. Maria's tone was angry, she felt tension in her stomach and she had the urge to yell, but couldn't in front of the whole family because they would also start to criticize her. Her stress response was to fight, then leave, then feel the tension. Her tolerate response was to assert herself and ask her mom: "Mom please take me to get something to eat and I'll stop bothering you."

From this behavioral assessment it became clear that with these specific TSS's Maria responded by fighting back, wanting to leave, and then feeling tension in her fists, her chest, and her stomach. She also had a tolerate response pattern of asserting herself in a calm way to get what she wants with her mother. Maria said this exercise helped her to recognize her triggers for stress with her mom and notice in her body where the tension is so she can then respond assertively and calmly with her mother.

The next technique I implemented this week from the knowledge of the Behavioral Assessment was to help Maria develop a greater awareness of her Sensing (MBTI) function by helping her experience where she stores her tension in doing Systematic Muscle Relaxation (SMR) with her. After doing SMR, Maria was able to experience the relaxation exercise fully and notice afterwards that she also stores tension in her legs, feet, and her neck, in addition to her hands, stomach and chest. This told me that my client was extremely stressed and had much tension she stores throughout her body. She felt very relaxed after this exercise and said that she could do this when her mom stresses her by going into the bathroom or her room and practicing tensing up those parts of her body and then slowly letting them relax.

Overall, the techniques that were used this week had a deep impact on Maria and enabled her to have more tools at her disposal to cope with stress better and further eliminate her self-harm behavior, in addition to improving her relationship with her mom. After the success of this week's interventions, Maria now knew that when Carol stressed her she needed to take space, do deep breathing and do SMR.

WEEK 3: COMMUNICATION WEEK

The third week was "Communication Week." At the beginning of this week Maria reported feeling less stressed and able to manage with the techniques I taught her previously. Maria said that the tension had slowly been decreasing between Carol and herself. While the name-calling was still happening at this point in treatment, the fighting had gone down. The purpose of this week was to utilize talking in type with Carol's Psychological Type to improve communication and further decrease the fighting. This week my client reported no impulse to cut because of the no self-harm contract.

My first task this week was to assess Carol's Psychological Type from examples that Maria had described about her mother. I assessed Carol's Type as being ISTJ for several reasons. Maria described her mother as being overly serious which is a challenge for an Introverted Type. I also assessed Carol as being a Sensing Type from Maria's description of her mother as being practical and realistic. Maria described her mother being pessimistic, inflexible, and slow and dull, typical challenges experienced by Sensing types. I also assessed Carol as a Thinking type from Maria's perspective of her being very analytical, factual and consistent. Carol also exhibited the challenges of the Thinking type: being blunt, cold and uncaring and overly competitive, all behaviors she has shown towards Maria. Finally, I assessed Carol as being a Judging type. Maria described her mother as being decisive and taking charge with her family. Carol also exhibited the challenges of being overly opinionated, intrusive and very controlling. It makes a lot of sense after assessing Carol's Psychological Type of ISTJ as being very opposite to Maria's Type of ENFJ why they have a lot of issues and why they butt heads a lot of the time.

I modified my original intervention of a talking in type journal with my client to coming up with a communication cheat sheet to refer to when trying to talk with her mom. I realized that the journal would be too much for Maria and condensed what I knew about their different types into what would be more manageable for Maria with her homework load at school. With this knowledge of the different types I came up with specific ways Maria could communicate with her mother's type by compiling the cheat sheet for her to refer to on how to speak her mother's language and decrease the fighting.

From the book, *Just your Type* (Tieger & Barron-Tieger, 2000), which is a guide for couples to find balance in their different Psychological types, I identified suggestions that could be appropriately applied to understanding Maria and Carol as a mother-daughter dyad. I outlined the positive characteristic of having the ability to work well as a team with cleaning, cooking etc. using their organized Judging function that they have in common. I encouraged Maria to see the best in her mom and focus on what she does respect about her mom's personality.

I also encouraged Maria that she has the ability in her type to help her mom become more open to opposing viewpoints, and that Carol can help Maria develop a thicker skin and learn to take things less personally. In addition to pointing out the positive elements in regards to their two types, the book also aided in pointing out the vulnerabilities in their specific relationship. I pointed out to Maria that because their types are so opposite communication was going to be their biggest obstacle with Carol being a Thinking type and Maria being a Feeling type. In addition, Maria and Carol had different approaches to problem solving as Maria is an Intuitive type and Carol is a Sensing type, and I encouraged my client to be aware of those differences.

I also communicated to Maria that even in the midst of these differences she could help her mom by not being so quick to become emotionally upset. In addition, Carol could help Maria by not dismissing her feelings. I also pointed out to Maria how she can win over her ISTJ mom by encouraging her doing the chores her mom really wants done, by taking care of her personal things, and by tapping into her mom's Sensing type. The book also suggested that Intuitive types like Maria not exaggerate, but be clear and precise and use real examples when communicating (for example, with Carol). In addition, I encouraged Maria to recognize that because her mom is a Thinking type she can come across as blunt and that to help the situation she should try and not take things Carol says so personally.

Finally, I wrote out for Maria on her type cheat sheet to initiate with her mother a regular routine that they would both enjoy, such as jogging together or cooking together to bring closeness and to move from Disengaged to Separated in the Circumplex model. Maria thought that these suggestions would be very helpful for her to use with Carol and thanked me for spelling it out for her how to talk with her mom and get through to her in a more positive way. It was at this point that I started to notice a desire in Maria to reconnect with her mother, which was a huge improvement.

WEEK 4: ASSERTION TRAINING WEEK

The fourth week was "Assertion Training Week." At this point in treatment, Maria reported that she was practicing what we talked about with regards to communicating better with her mother. She was starting to notice a difference with her mother in that the fighting was continuing to decease and the wedge that was between them was getting smaller.

The purpose of this week was to teach Maria how to engage with her mother assertively, not aggressively, when tension is high in order to feel empowered in her own self that her opinion does matter and that she can stand up for herself when her mom is verbally abusing her. This week I utilized the DESC Confrontation (Bower, S.A, & Bower, G.H, 1991)with Maria as we processed how she wanted to confront her mother about the verbal abuse. Maria wrote out:

Describe:*(Describe what he/she did)* "When you call me a gay faggot."
Express:*(Describe how you felt about what was done and the tangible negative effect on you)* "I feel horrible. "Because it is offensive to me and showed me that you don't care."

Specify: *(Make a specific request for her/him to change behaviors)* "I would like you to stop calling me these names and be more respectful."

Consequences (Positive):*(State one positive consequence for her/him if she/he complies with your request)* "If you do that then I would share my feelings more openly with you."

Consequences (Negative): *(State a negative consequence for her/him that will occur is she/he doesn't comply with your request)* "If you are not willing to do that then I won't be comfortable telling you or sharing my feelings with you and I really want to tell you my feelings because I want to be closer to you again."

I thought this was very powerful coming from a sophomore who is realizing she really needs her mom to be more supportive of her. We then role-played the conversation several times with me being Carol. I asked Maria when would be a good time to talk with her mom one on one. She said she could do it that day after school when her mom was going to pick her up. Maria was feeling empowered enough with all the interventions utilized thus far to have the confidence to finally stand up for herself with her mother. At this point I also instructed Maria to ask her Mom if she could spend one on one time with her on a weekly basis just the two of them. We problem-solved what would be an enjoyable activity to do together. Maria came up with jogging with her mom, something that both of them used to do together a long time ago. We problem-solved when would be a good time for them to do that and Maria said that Sunday afternoons are usually the quietest at home.

So far at this point in the intervention my client demonstrated the desire to move from Disengaged to Separated in the Circumplex Model by asking Carol to have one on one time with her. In addition, Maria demonstrated the desire to move from Rigid to Structured by confronting Carol assertively about the verbal abuse and requesting a more democratic and stable relationship. I thought these were huge improvements on Maria's part without having the involvement of Carol at this point in any of the sessions.

WEEK 5: INCREASING COHESION

The theme of the fifth week was to move Maria and Carol from Disengaged towards Separated specifically in the area of emotional bonding and internal boundaries .Maria reported that she did not have a desire to cut anymore due to the no self-harm contract. She also reported that her mood had improved and she was not feeling depressed anymore. In addition, the student reported seeing her ex-girlfriend as an unsafe person and realized that she was not good for her. Up until this point Maria was going back and forth with her feelings for her ex. Her ex has been extremely manipulative towards Maria in playing her along every week and then deciding she wants to be with someone else. Maria finally realized that she was settling for someone that really did not care about her. This was a huge realization for my client. We continued to refer to the healthy relationships list that Maria came up with to further change her ideals of what she needs from a good relationship.

Maria also came back this week telling me of the huge success over the weekend with confronting her mother. Maria reported having some alone time with her mom shopping in a store for some hair products. Maria did the DESC confrontation with her mom like we practiced, and Carol acknowledged feeling bad that her name-calling affected Maria in such a destructive way. From what Maria told me about the interaction, her mom apologized for being so hurtful. Carol told Maria it has been hard for her to accept her decision to be gay because of her upbringing, but that she just needs time to get used to her decision. She said she would be more sensitive and not call her names anymore. Maria also reported asking her mom if she wanted to go jogging together again like they used to. Carol thought that was a great idea because she wanted to lose weight and she also wanted that closeness in their relationship that they used to have. This week was pivotal in moving Maria and Carol from Disengaged towards Separated and from Rigid to Structured.

WEEK 6: CELEBRATING SUCCESS

During the sixth week of intervention, Maria and I celebrated her success with the interventions she used in repairing her relationship with Carol. Maria reported experiencing significant improvement in her relationship with her mother. Not only were the interventions that were utilized in the project successful, the treatment goals were also all reached. Maria and Carol are now connecting more by jogging together once a week. Maria also reported a new romantic relationship where the new love interest called Carol and asked for her permission to date her daughter. Maria listened to the conversation and her mom was calm, respectful and responded to the new girlfriend's request by giving her "blessing." This proved that now not only did Maria and Carol's relationship improve, but now Carol had become more understanding and compassionate of her daughter's lifestyle. Additionally, the goal of moving the relationship from Rigid/Separated to a new Circumplex diagnosis of Structurally Connected became clearly evident.

In addition to Maria's relationship with her mom vastly improving, the cutting tendency is no longer an issue due to the enforcement of the no self-harm contract. Furthermore, Maria has also improved in her view of romantic relationships and has asserted herself in not playing along with her ex-girlfriend's games. At the time of this writing, Maria had chosen to abstain from romantic relationships for a time in order for her "heart to heal" from the pain of her past relationships. She truly discovered that she does not need a relationship to define her self-worth, that she is loveable just the way she is, and finally, that she has enough support in her family relationships and peer relationships.

RESOURCES

Bower, S.A, & Bower, G.H (1991), *Asserting yourself: A practical guide for positive change*, Reading, MA: Addison-Wesley Publishing Company.

Healthy Relationships Bingo for Teens. The Guidance Group. www.guidance-group.com.

Leutenberg, E.A., & Korb-Khalsa, K.L. *Self Esteem Bingo for Teens. An engaging and educational game about self esteem and ways to improve it*. The Guidance Group.www.guidance-group.com.

Totika: A Game of Fun, Skills, and Communication. The Guidance Group.
www.guidance-group.com.

Chapter 40

School-Based Family Counseling: An Integration of Psychodynamic, Cognitive-Behavioral and Family Systems Approaches

Salome Dineros

OVERVIEW:*Working in a school-based setting presents several challenges that are distinct from working in an outpatient setting. This case study provides a clinical analysis of how to effectively work with a severely dysfunctional and multi-problem adolescent and his family in a school-based setting using an integrative approach of psychodynamic, cognitive-behavioral and family systems approaches.*

PRESENTING PROBLEM

The adolescent presented here was referred by his teacher and required treatment services in a school-based setting due to the severity of his disturbances. His long history of major depression, suicidal ideation, and psychiatric hospitalizations warranted extensive long-term treatment (3-years in a school-based clinic and 1-year outpatient clinic). I was told he was exceedingly withdrawn at home and at school, and his persistent negativism, low self-worth and social isolation were apparent in all of his relationships.

BACKGROUND INFORMATION

Mathew is a fifteen-year-old Caucasian male, medium built, well groomed and articulate, who presented to the school-based mental health clinic. Accompanied by his Special Education teacher and mother, the client sought individual therapy due to the severity of his disturbances. This client had a long history of major depression, suicidal ideation, and psychiatric hospitalizations that interfered with his academic, emotional and social functioning.

Over the years, his low self-image and restricted range of emotional expression had worsened, and he often exhibited patterns of instability in interpersonal relationships. In addition, he frequently reported the following symptoms: irritability in mood, insomnia, anhedonia, low-energy, and fatigue. He demonstrated poor concentration in the classroom and in psychotherapy sessions. He often arrived to session talking about his depressive symptoms, lack of energy, and difficulty getting up each morning for school. He attributes his depression to not having a relationship, more specifically, not having a relationship with the "perfect" and "ideal" female.

Mathew lived with his biological mother and older brother, age 26. His parents divorced when he was 5 years old. Mathew reported having a strained relationship with his father, though he had been supportive both educationally, financially, and had been periodically involved with Mathew's hospitalizations. His father has a second family and they also live near Mathew. His mother is a clothing designer and works full-time. According to his mother, there were no problems with her pregnancy or delivery. She denied any significant previous medical or psychiatric problems; however, she reported signs of "separation-anxiety" in preschool that she attributed to the divorce. She also described her son as a "very needy" and "fragile" child, who was often sickly and required "all my attention, and constantly!" Mathew described being verbally mistreated by his older brother who he said got angry with him for weeks at a time. He also described a sense of frustration that the family had about his problem in recent years, feeling as though he was burdening them, saying at times they would be better off without him.

Mathew's psychiatric history include: three to 8 year history of recurrent major depressive disorder, and six psychiatric hospitalizations (1993, 1996, 1997, 1998, 1999, and 2000) for worsening depression, suicidal ideation, and thoughts of jumping off a building in 1999, which were precipitated by rejection from a female peer. He acknowledged hearing voices prior to his hospitalization in 1993, and had not heard voices since. In 1996, Mathew ingested twenty extra-strength ibuprofen and reported these ten days later. Additionally, he displayed numerous suicidal gestures, which were unknown to his family during that time. Mathew attended a day treatment facility for both hospitalizations in 1993 and 1996. In 1997, he was placed at a local High School's SED (Severe Emotionally Disturbed) classroom and was seen by this therapist thereafter. In addition, has a history of asthma and allergies to aspirin, ibuprofen, Advil, Neoprene, and nuts. Risperdal and Paxil minimally controlled his symptoms of depression due to poor compliance. He developed rashes when prescribed Prozac and reported increased depression with 350 mg of Effexor. His moods and symptoms appeared brighter and more stable once he was placed on a regimen of Wellbutrin 300 mg and Olanzapine 10 mg.

His school history included preschool experiences, special education services in a Special Day Class for learning disabilities (short attention span, difficulty listening, and ability to understand only when reading aloud), SED/Mental Health Services both at middle school and high school, and individual and family therapy. In 1998, Mathew worked at a local housewares store stocking merchandise for six months until his hospitalization subsequent to rejection by a female peer. In 1999, Mathew worked at a grocery store also stocking merchandise for three months until his hospitalization in 1999 for complaints of worsening depression and suicidal thoughts of jumping off a building.

THE FIRST SESSION

Mathew arrived on time his affect was mostly flat, bland and blunted, and his mood depressed. He presented with a glazed stare and rhythmic leg movements, and was easily distracted and annoyed by sudden surprising noises. He never smiled and was clearly depressed. His dark brown eyes looked straight into mine as he spoke. Mathew dressed appropriately; however, his black hair looked uncombed. His thought processes were disorganized and scattered with loose associations. He had limited insight, poor judgment, and poor problem-solving skills. Mathew often felt alone both in school and at home and he spent most of his time in isolation weight lifting, writing play-scripts, reading the bible, editing his video show, and playing with his dog. While he engaged in these activities daily, he often complained about being lonely and depressed. Mathew maintained few friendships from elementary, middle, and high schools.

In his first interview he told me his four previous therapists had not helped him at all. He also implied that our therapy may not help either. I replied, "I guess you feel I might fail you too just like your previous therapist?" He nodded in agreement, in a soft voice while staring straight at me, then said, "I don't think teachers or therapists can help me" as he shrugged his shoulders. I told him frankly, "I want to keep you in therapy to find out whether I'd be helpful or not." "What shall I do?" He shrugged and not a word for ten minutes. During the silence I realized William expected me to try to force him to talk, similarly as his teachers were trying to force him to be social. I respected his wish to withdraw, noticing my own withdrawn mood during this exchange. I also saw some positive aspects to the silence.

He responded, "I guess I'll come back here next week and see you once a week right?" I replied, "I'll be here."

THE SBFC ASSESSMENT

The Circumplex Model of marital and family systems was used to describe, through case illustrations, this writer's experience in this therapeutic endeavor. The three dimensions of the Circumplex Model, *cohesion, adaptability,* and *communication,* are used to assess family behavior in this case study. Family cohesion is defined as the "emotional bonding that family members have toward one another" (Olson, Russell & Sprenkle, 1989). In the Circumplex Model, emotional bonding, boundaries, coalitions, time, space, friends, decision-making, interests, and recreation are the variables used in diagnosing and assessing family cohesion dimensions. The level of cohesion ranges from low to high, with four levels: *disengaged* (very low) to *separated* (low to moderate) to *connected* (moderate to high) to *enmeshed* (very high) are shown in Figure 1. According to Olson, Russell and Sprenkle (1989), the central levels of cohesion (separated and connected) is the "optimal" family functioning, thus individuals are able to experience and balance being both independent from, and connected to, their families. The extremes (disengaged or enmeshed) are more problematic and unhealthy because the individual has no sense of self, is emotionally isolated from others, and lacks interdependence.

Family adaptability (change) as defined by Olson, Russell & Sprenkle (1989) is the ability of a family system to change its power structure, role relationships, and relationship rules in response to situational and developmental stress. The level of adaptability also ranges from low to high with four levels: *rigid* (very low) to *structured* (low to moderate) to *flexible* (moderate to high) to *chaotic* (very high) (see Figure 1). The central levels of adaptability (structured and flexible) are healthier family functioning, while the extremes (rigid and chaotic) are more problematic for families as they move through the family life cycle. Most "well-functioning" families maintain a balance between structure and flexibility (Olson, Russell & Sprenkle, 1989).

Family communication in the Circumplex Model is "considered critical for facilitating couples and families to move on the other two dimensions" (Olson, Russell & Sprenkle, 1989). In order for the family to achieve cohesion and adaptability, according to Olson, and colleagues, positive communication skills such as empathy, reflective listening, and supportive statements are necessary to enable families to share their changing needs within the family system. On the other hand, negative communication skills such as double messages, double binds, and negative criticism hinders family members from sharing their feelings and achieving healthier family functioning on these dimensions.

COUNSELING GOALS

In school, individual therapy focused on peer relationships and appropriate interactions, as well as interactions with his teacher (who often ignored Mathew due to her own difficulties with his depressive symptoms). Predominant use of psychodynamic intervention was the basis of treatment, but due to the complexity and nature of the case, family systems and cognitive behavioral approaches were integrated. The therapist provided a supportive environment for the client to develop healthy therapeutic attachments by exploring transference issues that evolved during treatment.

Significant improvement in the relationship between Mathew and his mother was observed over the course of treatment, as well as with his relationship to his teacher. For the first two years of treatment, family therapy focused on assisting his mother in understanding Mathew's illness, improving communication, and strengthening their ability to negotiate evolving needs within the family. Mathew was able to voice feelings of hopelessness and worthlessness related to his lack of meaningful relationships with his mother and female peers. His desire to have these relationships was explored and eventually supported by his mother, who recognized and acknowledged his need for maintaining meaningful relationships in his life. In the later months of the therapy, Mathew was able to recognize and express his abandonment issues and his feelings of anger towards his mother and father.

COUNSELING PROCESS

It is the view of this author that psychotherapy is an interpersonal relationship process that occurs between the client and therapist in a therapeutic setting. The adolescent in this case invariably involved the therapist in his conflicts with his teacher, peers and family members throughout the therapeutic process. Because of the severity of his disturbances, Mathew qualified for, and was referred by his teacher to the SED/Mental Health Partnership program in the school-based setting. His long history of major depression, suicidal ideation, and psychiatric hospitalizations warranted extensive long-term treatment.

In determining effective treatment intervention with this client it was important to involve both his teacher and mother to address school and family issues, respectively. The amount of time Mathew spent in the SED inclusive classroom, and the interaction between Mathew and his teacher, affected his dysfunctional behavior. It was evident from the beginning that the mother was overwhelmed with her son's disturbances, and she responded appropriately to the school's suggestions and recommendations for school-based treatment services.

EVALUATION OF THE TEACHER-CLIENT RELATIONSHIP

Treatment within the school system focused on the relationship between the teacher and Mathew. Mathew's severity of disturbances, history of major depression, suicidal ideation and attempts, and psychiatric hospitalizations qualified him for special education services in the SED inclusive classroom. The classroom consisted of seven adolescents (five males and two females), and most of his peers were diagnosed with oppositional defiant behavior, attention deficit hyperactivity disorder, and anxiety disorder. At first, Mathew seemed to be the only depressed client in the classroom. His teacher was observed to be more engaged with the students who overtly acted-out in the classroom than those students who were subdued and depressed. Therefore, the level of interaction between the teacher and Mathew was minimal.

In the early assessment phase of treatment, the therapist observed the teacher and client interaction. It was determined that the teacher often ignored Mathew in the classroom and had difficulty engaging with him positively; likewise, the client avoided the teacher by quietly writing in his journal or falling asleep in class. The therapist viewed this relationship as chaotically disengaged. To address this relationship between the teacher and client, systems and consultation approaches were used to work with Mathew and his teacher in the classroom. As treatment progressed, the teacher acknowledged her limitations with Mathew by admitting her anxiety and resistance to working with his depressive symptoms. She suggested that Mathew be treated in individual therapy twice a week during her class period.

An evaluation was obtained through several classroom observations and consultation interviews with his teacher and paraprofessional staff member in the classroom. Based on the Circumplex Model, it was determined that the relationship between the teacher and client was chaotically disengaged. Rather than assisting Mathew, the teacher would often instruct the paraprofessional to assist Mathew, thus avoiding interaction with him. On the cohesion dimension, the teacher and Mathew were very disconnected and disengaged, in that they frequently ignored and avoided each other in the classroom.

In terms of the adaptability dimension, the teacher-client relationship was seen as chaotic. The teacher viewed and treated William as a "severely disturbed" person not only in terms of his diagnosis, but her impression of him intensified by the mere fact that he did not "act-out". In addition, the teacher had limited hope for change. Communication was poor between Mathew and his teacher. During the course of treatment, most of the teachers' communication about Mathew's school difficulties was directed towards his therapist. Through frequent consultation with the teacher and continued individual therapy with Mathew twice a week, considerable changes in the teacher's attitude toward Mathew occurred. The teacher's anxiety and avoidance behavior ceased. There was a shift away from the extreme range of chaotically disengaged, and towards the mid-range and balanced range of structurally separated. Communication had improved in that there was mutual acknowledgment, respect and regard in the teacher-client relationship.

As the client improved in treatment, his teacher no longer ignored Mathew and his symptoms, and was able to engage him in a direct, sensitive and gentle way that allowed him to respond appropriately. For example, rather than delegating assistance of Mathew to the paraprofessional staff as in the past, the teacher made a point to address his needs personally, this communicated acceptance and helped to create a sense of belonging for Mathew. Her anxiety and resistance in working with Mathew had reduced. Likewise, Mathew's anxiety and depression had diminished. He had learned to be more assertive and express his feelings, increase eye contact and communication, and improve peer interaction and classroom participation over the years. Mathew successfully graduated from high school on time.

EVALUATION OF THE PARENT-CLIENT RELATIONSHIP

Because the parents are divorced and the relationship between Mathew and his father is strained and disengaged, and his father was unavailable for family therapy, the primary focus of treatment was Mathew's relationship with his mother. It was very important to Mathew that his mother understood his experiences. The mother complained that Mathew was often silent and "spaced-out" whenever she asked about his day in school. When he did not respond, she frequently felt compelled to "fill in the blanks" in order to understand him. The mother's inability to accept and tolerate Mathew's silence frustrated him whenever his mother interpreted his experience incorrectly. His mother was also frustrated by his inability to communicate effectively.

For the first two years of treatment, family therapy focused on helping Mathew's mother to understand his illness, improving communication, and strengthening their ability to negotiate evolving needs within the family. Mathew was able to voice his feelings of hopelessness and worthlessness related to his lack of meaningful relationships with his mother and female peers. His desire to have these relationships was explored and eventually supported by his mother, who recognized and acknowledged his need for maintaining meaningful relationships in his life.

Affective dependency and high symbiotic involvement in their relationship did not allow Mathew to have his unique experiences separate from his mother. The fear of destroying the perceived positive relationship with his mother actually resulted in poor communication. This pattern of communication led to Mathew's devalued experience of rejection and not being understood by his mother, and further silence and "spacing-out" behavior continued. Based on the Circumplex Model, the mother-son relationship was chaotically enmeshed. On the cohesion dimension scale, emotional bonding was very high and family involvement was also very high. The relationship between the mother and client demonstrated high dependence, loyalty, and enmeshment.

Mathew's mother also suffered from the lack of clear communication. Her frustration was reflected by her attempts to complete her son's thoughts in such a way that reflected her own preconceived ideas. Their relationship impinged on Mathew's sense of self, not allowing his own identity to develop and resulting in Mathew's isolation from others. Therefore, family therapy focused on assisting his mother in understanding Mathew's illness, improving communication, and strengthening their ability to negotiate evolving needs within the family. In terms of the adaptability dimension, the parent-client relationship was also seen as chaotic. The essential characteristics of the chaotic level of adaptability are lack of leadership, dramatic role shifts, erratic discipline, and too much change. Lack of leadership was reflected by the mother's inability to communicate her expectations, or provide an effective role model that Mathew could emulate. This was exacerbated by the dramatic role shifts that the mother exhibited such as trying to be a friend at times to Mathew, and other times acting as an authoritarian figure based on her own cycles of depression, anxiety and mood.

These dramatic role shifts resulted in corresponding forms of erratic discipline that took the form of psychological blackmail, to "punish" Mathew for "getting on my nerves". For example, the mother intentionally stayed late at work without informing her son, thereby creating a high level of anxiety and insecurity in Mathew. The lack of leadership, constant shifting of roles, the erratic discipline, and changes in the relationship resulted in a consistently changing unstable environment for William. This increased Mathew's insecurity, lack of confidence, inability to form appropriate relationships, and depression.

In the later months of the therapy, Mathew was able to recognize and express his abandonment issues and feelings of anger towards his mother and father. To address the chaotically enmeshed relationship between the parent and client, an integration of cognitive-behavioral and systems approaches was used. Once Mathew had sufficient ego strength and better insight to his experience, treatment techniques shifted to cognitive-behavioral interventions. He was able to use specific techniques, such as monitoring and logging negative self-talk and self-statements, when depressive symptoms returned. This shift did not occur until the client was in his fourth year of therapy.

EVALUATION OF THE CLIENT-THERAPIST

According to Luborsky (1984), "the main curative factors in psychodynamic psychotherapy come about through working toward three changes: achieving a helping relationship, achieving understanding, and incorporating the gains of treatment." Luborsky also believed that the more severe the client's illness, the more supportive therapy is required and less expressive therapy is needed. Psychotherapy with this client emphasized exploration of intra-psychic conflicts and how they were typically expressed in maladaptive personal relationships. The therapist provided a safe and supportive environment for Mathew to develop a healthy attachment through the exploration of transference, while maintaining therapeutic neutrality. The term transference is "an enactment of the client's intimate relationships of the past, the goal of the interpretation of transference is to help the client understand how these early relationships distort relationships in the present and most particularly with the therapist" (Miller, Luborsky, Barber & Docherty, 1993). Rather than understanding in order to interpret the client's experience, the therapist becomes a "curious student of the client's experience as well as his or her emergent capacity to notice, speak and understand" (Carrere, 1984). Themes presented by Mathew were also explored and analyzed.

Mathew was encouraged to talk about his story, and the goal for him was to put his experience into words. The therapeutic environment, as well as the evolving therapeutic relationship, provided a context that allowed Mathew to express his experience. From this approach, psychotherapy included verbal and nonverbal acknowledging, and joining and mirroring o his experience, in order for him to talk further about his experiences. According to Spotnitz and Meadow (1976), the therapeutic relationship is "conceived as a partnership, for the therapist to position himself or herself as a student of experience to be educated and informed". Silent interpretation was used by the therapist to analyze patterns and content presented by the client once his experience was verbalized. These interpretations were not shared with the client but rather it served as a way to understand his formulation of his experience and interpersonal relationships.

Sherman (1983) suggested, "Talking is facilitated when an analyst can communicate acceptance and understanding of the individual's experience by means of emotional communication". Carrere (1984) states that successful communication by the therapist is measured by the client's ability to continue talking productively. The ultimate goal is to give the client the freedom to explore his experience in a safe therapeutic environment in order to explore, elaborate, and understand his own experience. Change occurs when the client understands his experience. Throughout psychotherapy, the focus was on the client's experience. Timing was important, in that the therapist first accepted and tolerated Mathew's experience on his own terms. It was also quite helpful for the therapist to pay attention to her own counter-transference feelings and thoughts whenever the client was resistant to getting better. It was also important to note if suggestions of treatment interventions such as the use of cognitive-behavioral techniques (thoughts & behavioral logs of negative self-statements made by the client) were premature. Once Mathew experienced being understood in therapy, the therapist was able to integrate other treatment approaches, such as cognitive-behavioral techniques to monitor his negative self-statements and level of depression.

COUNSELING OUTCOME

The client chose to seek services at a school-based mental health clinic because of his needs and severity of his symptoms, as well as the proximity of the therapy site. Three years of individual therapy in a school-based setting and one year of therapy in an outpatient setting were provided, including consultation and family therapy. Mathew rarely missed therapy sessions, but he frequently missed school due to depressive symptoms when no therapy was scheduled. The first year of treatment the client was seen twice a week for individual therapy in school and twice a month with his mother for family therapy, and twice a month consultation with his special education teacher. The second and third year of treatment Mathew was seen once a week for individual therapy with once a month family therapy and teacher consultation. The fourth year of treatment Mathew was seen once a week for individual therapy. Several attempts of family therapy with his biological father and older sibling failed due to a lack of commitment.

Mathew was highly motivated to talk about his depression and symptoms and was overly self-critical. He often presented with a flat affect reporting on themes involving rejection by female peers and his difficulty being recognized and acknowledged. Initially, the focus of treatment was crisis intervention and reduction of symptoms, and emotional support for the family. The therapist emphasized open communication and facilitated family discussions about key relationship issues, including working with his teacher. The use of focused discussion as a means of resolving conflicts and differences of perception and opinion was explored and challenged during therapy sessions. Family therapy with the client and his mother focused on communication patterns, underlying meta-communication, and their understanding of Mathew's depression. In addition, treatment focused on helping his mother to reduce her anxiety, fear, and helping her to increase her ability to identify her own anger and rage whenever the client was re-hospitalized.

Mathew's relationship with his teacher also improved. Rather than ignoring Mathew and his symptoms, his teacher was able to engage him in a direct, sensitive and gentle way that allowed him to respond appropriately. For example, the teacher made eye contact and spoke in a sensitive and gentle manner when she delivered instructions to Mathew on class activity. Her anxiety and resistance in working with Mathew had reduced. Likewise Mathew's anxiety and depression had diminished. Over the treatment period, he had learned to be more assertive and express his feelings, increase eye contact and communication, and improve peer interaction and classroom participation. Mathew successfully graduated from high school on time. After four years, Mathew terminated counseling because the family experienced financial difficulties that made it difficult to continue treatment, and because their relationship problems had improved.

SUMMARY

Given Mathew's complex family situation, psychotherapy in a school-based setting provided the context and opportunity to gain additional and deeper information about his school and family experiences. It is my belief that the advantage of using an integrated approach to school-based family counseling is that the therapist is able to adapt to the changing needs of the client as they arise, particularly with more severe dysfunctional families.

Psychotherapy provided a safe and supportive environment for the client to freely explore his experience on his own terms. Mathew developed a sense of trust in the therapeutic relationship that allowed him to adapt positively to his environment, and improve relationships with his parent and teacher. An integrative approach to treatment in a school-based setting was utilized. Direct and frequent contact and consultation with the teacher and parent were necessary in the early phase of treatment. This strategy was implemented in order to assist Mathew with behavioral problems and conflicts that occurred in the school and at home.

One of the most problematic challenges Mathew endured was the rejection by his mother, teacher and peers. Most of his life he tried to make sense of his experience with others. He often assumed something was wrong with him emotionally, physically and socially. Mathew felt alone and isolated, and retreated *inward,* and internalized his negative experiences with others. This resulted in multiple psychological problems. Psychotherapy provided the environment to explore these experiences, and helped the client feel understood by the therapist. Once Mathew experienced being understood, change occurred internally, and his experience of others also changed.

Chapter 41
Organizational Development in Schools:
Impact on School-Based Family Counseling

Steven D. Pomerantz

OVERVIEW: *This chapter describes four case studies that illustrate the value of an organizational development perspective for School-Based Family Counseling.*

BACKGROUND

As effective as School Based Family Counseling (SBFC) is, there are times that all the work by the SBFC therapist/counselor (I use therapist or counselor to mean the same thing) can be negated by problems that exist with the school. These problems may come from a teacher's abusive treatment of students, unfair grading practices, or outright discrimination toward the student. Problems can also stem from the school's administration. The principal may have policies and procedures that enable or encourage disruptive behavior by students; and the culture of the school personnel, faculty, and administrators may discriminate toward a certain segment of the student population. The SBFC may make progress with a student but the organizational problems may limit the progress or actually reverse some of the progress made by the SBFC.

These organizational problems may require a strategy that is commonly referred to as organizational development (OD). Ironically, the OD strategy could borrow from the family systems model known as the Circumplex Model, which evaluates family relationships and interactions on three scales: cohesion, flexibility, and communication. Cohesion in a school setting reflects a team effort on the part of administration and faculty, and also relates to the students, parents, and community feeling connected to the school. Too connected, enmeshment, the organization will have difficulty being creative or innovative, especially if everyone thinks alike. Not enough cohesion, disengagement, the organization will have difficulty working as a team, being effective or efficient. Flexibility in a school setting refers to the rules and boundaries. Too many rules or too rigid of an implementation of the rules can lead to problems, too few rules or little implementation and follow-through on existing rules can lead to problems. Boundaries refer to respect and responsibility. In a school setting the students, parents, faculty, and administration need to feel respected by each other. The school setting could easily be evaluated in terms of family dynamics (see Figure 41.1 below).

The SBFC therapist has an opportunity to facilitate, intervene, or influence change and improvement in the school's ability to help the student learn and thrive at the school. In a very real sense the SBFC therapist could treat or influence the treatment of the school as if it was a dysfunctional family. The SBFC therapist could follow usual family therapy procedures when working to fix school dysfunction:

Listen and join with each family member,

Clarify the problem,

Use circular questioning by asking members of the family to consider the thoughts and feelings that other members might have about the situation or another member,

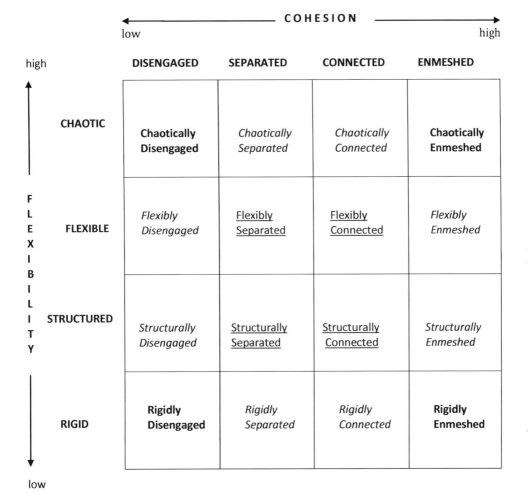

COHESION

low — high

	DISENGAGED	SEPARATED	CONNECTED	ENMESHED
CHAOTIC	**Chaotically Disengaged**	*Chaotically Separated*	*Chaotically Connected*	**Chaotically Enmeshed**
FLEXIBLE	*Flexibly Disengaged*	<u>Flexibly Separated</u>	<u>Flexibly Connected</u>	*Flexibly Enmeshed*
STRUCTURED	*Structurally Disengaged*	<u>Structurally Separated</u>	<u>Structurally Connected</u>	*Structurally Enmeshed*
RIGID	**Rigidly Disengaged**	*Rigidly Separated*	*Rigidly Connected*	**Rigidly Enmeshed**

Note: Bold: Extreme family/relationship types
Italics: Families/relationships with issues
Underlined: More functional families/relationships

Figure: 41.1 The Circumplex Model

Get agreement on what the problem is,

Brainstorm possible solutions; and

Help the family select a strategy to remedy the problem.

In family therapy there is usually agreement by family members to participate in the therapy. In the organization all members might not willingly participate in the problem solving. Therefore, the SBFC therapist may have to use interesting but ethical strategies to make unwilling members participate. The cases that will be discussed below are examples of how the SBFC therapist can influence a therapeutic intervention that increases the likelihood of a positive change, which will directly or indirectly benefit the student.

OD can take on a life of its own depending on the resistance from within the organization. Sometimes a fairly simple OD intervention is sufficient to improve the situation, and sometimes a more complex effort is needed. The SBFC therapist, a parent, or even the student could initiate simpler OD interventions. More complex interventions may require a professional consultant facilitator. In this chapter several OD interventions will be examined as case studies. The SBFC therapist may be in a key position to influence change by working with the student, parent, teacher, and/or the administrator. Though the cases below examine both simple and complex strategies, these examples should not be considered the only types of problems or strategies that could arise or be used. These cases only illustrate the additional impact that the SBFC therapist could have on the school family.

CASE # 1: UNREALISTICALLY HIGH GRADING STANDARDS AND REACHING FOR THE BRASS RING

A seventh grade student was experiencing frustration with her English teacher, who had very high expectations for written work. Five points was the maximum for an assignment, but the student never got a grade higher than three points. The student was frustrated and began losing confidence in her ability to do short essays, reports, and other written assignments. She stopped in to talk with the SBFC therapist who suggested the student talk directly with the teacher. When the student met with the teacher she was told that no student had ever received a grade higher than a three out of five points, and that the student needed to work harder if she wanted to earn five points.

The student struggled with her assignments for the English class, feeling that she would never be able to be successful. Assignment after assignment resulted in grades of three points. Her parents periodically asked how she was doing in school and she put them off by saying she was doing well.

The student had a follow-up session with the SBFC therapist. At the session the therapist asked if the student had talked with her English teacher. The student reported what was said. The therapist asked what the student had thought about doing next. The student said, "Give up, I guess." The therapist encouraged the student to consider some other options, and together they brainstormed. The options included a parent-teacher conference, having her parents review her work, and going with her parents to talk with the principal.

After several weeks of asking, the parents demanded to see some of the student's homework. The parents independently reviewed her written work and thought that she was doing very well, but noticed the three points out of five on each assignment. When asked what grade she was getting in English, the student replied, "I'm getting an F." Finally, the student opened up and expressed her frustration and disappointment with her English teacher. The parents thought this unreasonable based on the quality of work that the parents saw the student doing. The student suggested that one of the parents attend a counseling session so they could discuss this with the counselor.

The father met with the student and the SBFC therapist. The therapist suggested a parent-teacher conference and the father agreed. The therapist asked, "What will you say to the teacher?" The father said, "I'll ask how my daughter is doing and why she gets only 3 points out of 5." The therapist thought this would be a good beginning. The parents felt that a parent-teacher conference was in order and might be helpful in getting clarification of the teacher's expectations. The student agreed to this.

At the parent-teacher conference the father and daughter were present with the principal and the teacher. The father explained their concerns. The teacher stated that the student was doing work consistent with her grade level and would probably receive a B or A for the course. The father asked why she never got a grade higher than three points out of five? The teacher explained that no student had ever gotten a grade higher than three points. The teacher went on to explain that once a student even wrote a paper that brought her to tears, and that paper received a grade of three points out of five. The teacher explained that by not giving four or five points, the students would strive to do better and would eventually get a higher grade.

The father listened intently and when the teacher was finished with her explanation, the father said, "Shame on you, shame on you. Here you admit that a seventh grade student wrote such a moving paper that you were brought to tears, but you still gave this paper a grade of three points." The teacher seemed very surprised as the father continued to explain that at this age of 12 to 13 years old a student needs to believe that they could reach the brass ring. The father asked, "Have you ever heard the expression: reach for the brass ring?" "No." said the teacher. The father explained that it came from riding the merry-go-round, where there was a brass ring that would be available for riders on the periphery of the merry-go-round and when a rider's horse was high enough at just the right moment when the rider approached the brass ring, the rider could reach up and grab the ring. Collecting ten rings in one ride earned the rider a free ride. If the rider could not reach the brass ring, then he or she would give up and not try. "Shame on you for having your grading standard so high that a good student is giving up trying for the higher grade." The teacher had tears well up in her eyes, and as the father looked at her and then looked over at the principal, and the principal winked at the father as if to say you hit the target.

The teacher said that she would consider what the father had said, and the meeting ended cordially. A week later the student brought home a paper with a grade of five points out of five. The student was thrilled. About two months later the father ran into the principal in the grocery story and she asked him if things were better for his daughter, and he said, "yes she has gotten several fives and fours." The principal thanked the father for what he had said at the parent-teacher conference, and that the principal had talked with the teacher after the meeting and encouraged her to re-evaluate her grading practices.

ANALYSIS

The teacher had a problem with her grading practices and it caused good students to lose confidence in their own ability to reach for the higher grades. The teacher was well liked by students, so this made it harder for students to confront the teacher or to discuss the matter with their parents. The SBFC therapist helped encouraged the student to consider several options and still the student showed resistance by hesitating to talk with their parents until pressed by the parents. This encouragement by the SBFC therapist made it a bit easier for the student to open-up and to get the needed support from their parents. The teacher with five years experience teaching seventh grade English, had never had a parent confront her before about her grading philosophy even though the principal had discussed this with the teacher on several occasions. The teacher was motivated by this parent's confrontation and story about "reaching for the brass ring" to change her grading system.

In many cases parents can communicate concerns on behalf of their student, but in some cases parents may need coaching on how to approach the teacher and what to say. The SBFC therapist can help the parent practice what they will say through role-play exercises. Besides the influence of the parent, the principal has a key role in influencing teachers at their school. In this case, however, the teacher was well liked and well respected, and that made it more difficult for the principal to influence the teacher to modify their grading system.

CASE #2: CONFRONTING THE NON-SUPPORTIVE TEACHER

In this case a high school male student, 15 years old, was having difficulty in a history class, which was one of his favorite topics. The student felt that the teacher was picking on him. The student came to the SBFC to get some advice on what to do. The SBFC listened intently to the student describe specific behaviors and times of what the teacher did, which included saying to the student in front of the whole class, "You'll never amount to anything." "You're an embarrassment to the school." "Didn't your parents every teach you how to behave properly?" These comments, of course, made the student very embarrassed and angry, and the student became more defiant, which resulted in the teacher to make more negative comments and eventually send the student to the office. Once at the office the student met with the vice principal who counseled the student to not talk back to the instructor and to focus on doing what he was suppose to do, learn about history.

After the third referral to the office, the vice principal referred the student to SBFC. The SBFC therapist listened intently to the student's account of what happened and asked the student if he had thought about some options to dealing with this situation. The student said that he wanted out of this instructor's class. The SBFC therapist said, "That would be one option. Let's explore some others and then you can decide which you'd like to do." Together they brainstormed some possible options and came up with three that the student thought were feasible: 1) the student could talk to the teacher about feeling picked on by the teacher, 2) the student could inquire about transferring to another course; and 3) the student could show the teacher to be wrong by how well the student could behave in class.

The student chose the third choice and for several days didn't say a word in class and stayed on task the whole time, but the teacher continued making negative comments about him in front of the whole class. By the third day several students commented that the teacher was "unfairly picking on you and you should go to the principal." The student decided to talk with his academic counselor to see if he could be transferred out of this class and into another history class. He was told that would not be possible. So, when he met with his SBFC therapist the next day he reported what he had experienced and that he didn't believe that the teacher would be fair to him and stop picking on him.

The SBFC therapist asked the student if it would be okay for the therapist to come and observe what goes on in the classroom? The therapist explained that she would talk with the teacher about needing to observe a couple of students (the therapist was working with another student who was also in that class). The student agreed. Later that day the therapist had the opportunity to talk briefly with the teacher about needing to observe a couple of students in his class, and the teacher said, "Great. It's about time that someone came in to see what I have to deal with everyday."

So, the next day the therapist went in to observe and sat at the back of the classroom. The two students behaved very well and were on task the whole class period. The teacher, on the other hand, made the same types of degrading public comments about this student, right in the presence of the therapist. At the end of the class the therapist went up to the teacher and asked when the two could meet to talk about what she observed, and they agreed to meet later in the day.When the therapist met with the teacher she asked how the teacher thought things went. The teacher said, "He (used student's name) is never on task and always making jokes." The therapist asked if the teacher noticed that the student was sitting quietly and paying attention? "No, I didn't notice that," said the teacher.The therapist then pointed out what she observed of the student and what the teacher said about the student in front of the whole class, and asked if he recalled saying this? "Well, I didn't say that exactly, did I?" The teacher seemed puzzled. The therapist said, "Yes this was what you said." The teacher seemed perplexed. The therapist said, "I'm working with this student to correct their behavior and I need you to recognize the improvement that he is making. I, also, need you to stop making comments that can be perceived as degrading to this student, especially in front of the other students. Can I count on you?"The teacher said, "Thank you for this feedback. I wasn't aware of this."

Over next two weeks things improved dramatically for both the student and the teacher. The therapist had weekly follow-up sessions with the student to reinforce his good behavior and effort; and the therapist checked-in with the teacher two or three times each week to see how things were going. The teacher reported on student improvement and the student reported that the teacher was no longer picking on him and he was beginning to enjoy being in the class. The therapist continued to check-in with each of them on a weekly basis for the next two months. During this time the student opened up about other matters, which concerned friends and dating.

ANALYSIS

In this case the teacher was not aware of how the student's behavior was affecting him and how his behavior was affecting the student. By establishing rapport with each of them and asking permission to observe the class, the SBFC therapist was able to gain a perspective that both the teacher and student could respect, and therefore, be in a position for the therapist's feedback to be taken seriously. The therapist was both supportive to each, but also direct in her feedback to them. The therapist took a more Socratic approach by asking questions rather than instructing them on what to do. The therapist worked patiently with each of them and used a gentle confrontation with the teacher, and continued follow-up to support and monitor the steady improvement. This is clearly a role that the SBFC therapist can take.

CASE #3: CONFRONTING THE SCHOOL CULTURE OF DISCRIMINATION

In this case the school principal had received numerous complaints from parents and church leaders that students perceived that most teachers were prejudice and showed discrimination toward the students of color (mostly Black, African-American, and some Latino, Mexican-American). All of the teachers were Caucasian (white, Anglo-Saxon) at this 7th and 8th grade middle school in a suburban city, which was the home of an Air Force Base. The principal decided to hire a community member, a person of color, who could hopefully be a liaison between students and teachers. The person that was hired was well respected in the Black community, but her credentials only included some college. Her official title was Campus Monitor, but her role was that of a counselor, an untrained one at that. I'll refer to her as the Liaison, because what she actually did was to be a liaison between the students and teachers.

Within the first month of school the Liaison quickly established rapport with the students and daily was seen with students gathered around her. She did an excellent job of listening to student concerns, which included discriminatory comments by teachers toward students of color such as; "those little monkeys," "what can you expect from those kids, look at their parents," and "they're not very smart and won't amount to much. Students concerns focused on about ten of the teachers. Some students had even spoken to few trusted teachers who were supportive, but nothing was being done to stop the discriminatory behavior. So, the Liaison decided to talk with the principal, who seemed supportive but had no idea of what to do. The Liaison said she would talk with the concerned students and get their thoughts and report back to the principal.

The Liaison met with a large group of about 40 students and an idea emerged from their discussion to make a movie. Several students were taking an elective course on news reporting which included making a video. Over the next two months the students focused their anger and frustration on making the video, which was a series of interviews where students got to express their frustration and tell their stories of discriminatory behavior and comments from various teachers. The students even named the teachers who make the comments.

After much editing and review by the students and the Liaison, the video was shown to the principal. The principal and Liaison discussed what should be done and an idea surface that included bringing in an outside consultant who could work with the teachers in an "in-service training" just prior to the beginning of the spring semester. The Liaison knew of such a consultant who was also a Licensed Marriage Family Therapist. The fact that this consultant was also a Caucasian male would help the teachers establish rapport with him. The agenda for this training included the teachers watching the video that the students made and discussing their reactions with the consultant.

This training for 35 teachers began with an introduction by the principal in which he stated that numerous complaints had been received by students, parents, and community church leaders regarding teacher-student relations; and this training was designed as an opportunity to look at ways to improve those relations. The Liaison was presented and she introduced the consultant and his credentials. The consultant gave a brief overview of the agenda and his expectations for improved relations as an outcome of the training. He then gave a five-minute overview of perception and how it impacts communication. He used several images, including "the old woman, young woman" (see Figure 41.2 below) to illustrate how people can perceive the same thing differently. Some other figure ground images were shown to further emphasize the impact of perception (see Figure 41.3 below).

Figure 41.2

Figure 41.3

The consultant then discussed "diversity" and asked how many different ways that people are different. Participants offered many ways that people are different such as race, gender, age, education, language, physical appearance, etc. Then the consultant asked, "Can these differences impact a person's perception? If so, how?" There was considerable discussion that linked perception with prejudice and discrimination. This portion of the training lasted about 45 minutes. Then the student-made video was presented with a brief introduction by the Liaison, who emphasized that this video was an idea by the students and made by the students to express their views and feelings of how they perceive that teachers treat them. The 15-minute video, a compilation of short interviews by about 15 students, was shown. During the video a few teachers yelled, "This is crap." "I never said that."

At the conclusion of the video the consultant said, "Wow! This is quite unsettling. Let me hear your reactions." Many teachers thought it was a waste of time to allow the students to make such a video, and thought the criticisms were prejudicial and discriminatory. But a few courageous teachers spoke-up in support of student concerns, and the consultant added, "These are your students. They need your help, support, and guidance; and they don't feel you are giving that to them. What could you do differently that would help turn this around?" The consultant waited and slowly suggestions and discussion began to focus on what teachers could do and what help they needed so they could do their job more effectively. The three-hour training ended with a commitment from the principal and teachers to work together and with parents and community church leaders to help turn these perceptions around.

Coincidently, while this was happening at this school, the local police department was preparing a grant proposal to fund a SBFC program that would be run by the police department as an effort to lower the crime rate in the area. If funded the police department would hire a licensed psychotherapist to run the program, and several licensed psychotherapists to work in the schools and to supervise interns and trainees who would be SBFC therapists. The program was funded less than a year later.

The school, on its own, began making steps toward turning around student perceptions by having regular parent-teacher meetings, conflict mediation facilitated by the principal and the Liaison for some student-teacher problems, some teachers retired or transferred to another school, and some new teachers of color were hired. When the police department approached the school about the SBFC program, the principal welcomed it enthusiastically. An orientation was given to the teachers and separately to the students and parents about the purpose, scope, and limitations of the SBFC program. The SBFC program needed less than two months to become fully operational and has been successfully operating for over 20 years.

ANALYSIS

In this case the school had many problems and the students had few resources available to remedy those problems. A good intentioned principal thought that by giving the students an opportunity to vent their concerns would result in improvement, hired a Campus Monitor, a person of color from the local community. Though she lacked the professional training, she was the school's first SBFC therapist. The discrimination at the school was a highly sensitive issue and needed a highly sensitive approach to heighten teacher awareness and to offer the students an avenue to vent their feelings. The making of the video was that avenue and the in-service training provided by an outside consultant who could sensitively help the teacher see the need for change and provide them with an opportunity to do so.

CASE #4: SETTING UP A SCHOOL-WIDE DISCIPLINARY PROCESS

In this case a middle school did not have a SBFC program, but one of the teachers wanted to organize a conflict mediation program, so that students could learn to resolve their conflicts without having to use physical violence. The school's only method for handling student conflicts was to have the students talk with the principal or vice principal and then they were given some sort of punishment such as after school detention, suspension, of expulsion for very serious offenses. This was not effective, because the same students continued to be involved in problems, and when a first-time offender was sent to the office, the administrator had few options. So, the instructor proposed a course called "Peer Mediation" and she wrote a grant to have a license psychotherapist assist her with lesson planning and working with the students. The first class had 35 eighth grade students and met daily for 50 minutes. The therapist co-taught the class with the teacher on Fridays.

The majority of the 35 students were identified by the principal, vice principal, and academic counselor as having behavioral problems in classes and on campus. Most of the students did not want to be in the Peer Mediation course. The teacher and therapist perceived that these problem students had leadership skills that were being used for outcomes that got them into trouble. Redirecting these leadership skills was a primary goal of this class. The teacher and therapist used a "good cop, bad cop" approach. The teacher was the "bad cop" and was the enforcer of classroom behavior. The therapist lived in the community and frequently saw students at the grocery store, which gave them a chance for more rapport building. The teacher wasn't always the bad cop, and used her counseling skills with the students and worked well with the therapist to provide support and education to the students.

To foster and develop team building among the students, the teacher brought in an organizational development consultant to facilitate team-building exercises with the 35 students. These exercises included physical activities that required teamwork and the need to communicate. The students learned that communication was a key ingredient in forming an effective team. The consultant facilitated discussions after each exercise to emphasize what was learned. The students began to come together and develop interest in the Peer Mediation course.

Peer Mediation topics included lecturettes, discussions, hands-on activities, role plays, vignettes, guest presenters, and videos on active listening, conflict mediation, fighting fair, refusal skills, relationship issues, violence prevention, bullying awareness, substance abuse, suicide prevention, and problem solving. Most students started to appreciate that they were in the class by the end of the first month, and for some students it took two or three months. There were a few students who never got over the idea that they were put into this class saying, "There's nothing wrong with me. Why am I in the class?"

The Peer Mediation course was successful in teaching students how to have a discussion to resolve problems where the mediator listens to each participant and then brainstorms with them on how to resolve the problem. The administration did not allow any of the students to actually act as peer mediators, though all 35 were trained and volunteered to do mediation. The teacher and occasionally the therapist did mediation during the teacher's prep period. This was a limitation imposed by the administration. The Peer Mediation course continued for two years under a special grant. This program introduced the school district to the therapist and the benefits of providing mediation training and services.

Simultaneously with the Peer Mediation course the teacher also taught a course called AVID (Advancement Via Individual Determination). The AVID course focused on note taking and study techniques, and behavior in the classroom. The teacher saw the need for the middle school to have a coordinated effort on behavior management and study habit, so she invited her colleague teachers to attend an AVID training at the end of the summer vacation and just prior to the beginning of the new school year. The training focus of two behavior management techniques: 1) school rules with expected

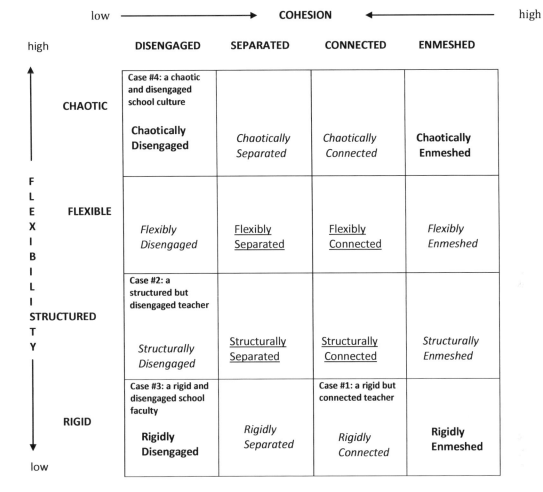

Figure: 41.4 Circumplex Model Assessment of the Four Cases

Note: Bold: Extreme family/relationship types
Italics: Families/relationships with issues
Underlined: More functional families/relationships

behavior posted in every classroom, 2) note taking techniques, which focused each teacher to organize their presentations in a similar fashion, and 3) binder checks, which required each student to have a binder of their work and regular inspections by each teacher. This school-wide effort resulted in improved test scores and student performance.

After the grant funding for the Peer Mediation ran out the school principal gave a lower priority to the Peer Mediation course, but a new school counselor was hired who had social work experience. This academic counselor provided some SBFC to students who expressed having a personal problem. This effort continued the focus on the need for psychotherapeutic counseling for students. At the same time the Peer Mediation therapist began talks with the school district administration about starting a SBFC program in the schools. It took several years before the school district gave permission for the therapist to begin a SBFC program at two high schools and two middle schools. Trust was a key factor in this decision as well as funding. The school district used money from truancy prevention funds to pay for the therapist to coordinate and supervise the graduate student therapists who provided the counseling. In the first year of the program the school principals and teachers saw clear benefits of the therapy in student focus, improved behavior and academic performance. The principals have used money from their own school budgets to continue to fund the SBFC program for the past seven years.

ANALYSIS

In this case the development of a SBFC program took many years and initial efforts did not necessarily have the end goal of a SBFC program in mind. Gradually, the administrative leaders saw the need and benefits of having a formal SBFC program that gave students an outlet to talk about their personal problems. The Peer Mediation course provided an introduction to the administration to the benefits of allowing students have a way to talk about their personal problems. This outlet helped the students get some perspective on how to deal with and handle their personal problems, which in turn gave them a chance to focus on improved behavior and academics. Additionally, the school needed a school-wide effort to coordinate behavior expectations and study habits in every classroom. The AVID program provided this opportunity.

SUMMARY

These cases clearly show a variety of OD efforts. These efforts are similar to those that would be used by a family therapist: 1) listening, paraphrasing, and summarizing; 2) identifying the problem causing the dysfunction (e.g. using the Circumplex Model: see figure 41.4); 3) problem solving with the family; and 4) providing some psycho-educational information. The external or internal OD consultant can use the same efforts when facilitating organizational improvement. These efforts are designed to help the organization and it's members to find the health functional balance between being rigidity and chaos, and the balance between being enmeshed and disengaged. Organizations, like families, must have some rules and procedures in order to accomplish the tasks that need to be done for their healthy survival. Each member must feel that they are receiving the support to accomplish their own personal goals as he or she is helping the organization (or family) succeed.

REFERENCES

Amatea, Ellen S. (1989). *Brief strategic intervention for school behavior problems*. San Francisco: Jossey-Bass.

Atkinson, Philip E. (1990*). Creating culture change: The key to successful total quality management*. Aspen, CO.: IFS Publications.

Barker, Joel (2000). *Wealth, innovation, and diversity.* DVD by Star Thrower.

Cummings, Thomas G. & Worley, Christopher G. (1993*). Organizational development and change.* Rochester, NY: West Publishing Company.

Olson, D. H. ,Russell, C.S. & Sprenkle, D.H. (Eds.). (1989). Circumplex model: Systemic assessment and treatment of families. Binghampton, N.Y.: Haworth Press.

Reddy, W. Brendan & Jamison, Kaleel (1988). *Team building: Blueprints for productivity and satisfaction. Tucson, AZ.: University Associates.*

Robbins, Stephen P. (1989*). Organizational behavior: Concepts, controversies, and applications.* New York: Prentice Hall.

Schwarz, Roger M. (1994*). The skilled facilitator: Practical wisdom for developing effective groups.* San Francisco: Jossey-Bass.

Chapter 42
A Day in the Life of a
School-Based Family Counselor

Sean Faulkner

OVERVIEW: *No day in the life of a School-Based Family Counselor is ever the same. Given the amount of different people in a school each day—from students, faculty, staff, and parents—and the occasional visitors like guest speakers and former students, the climate of a school can change in a heartbeat. A school-based family counselor must be flexible, as his or her agenda for the day can be thrown off by something as simple as a fire drill. To illustrate this point, I will share the events from a recent day on the job and then place them in the context of the Circumplex Model, the family systems model I was using for case conceptualization.*

No day in the life of a school-based family counselor is ever the same. Given the amount of different people in a school each day--from students, faculty, staff, and parents--and the occasional visitors like guest speakers and former students, the climate of a school can change in a heartbeat. A school-based family counselor must be flexible, as his or her agenda for the day can be thrown off by something as simple as a fire drill. To illustrate this point, I will share the events from a recent day on the job.

9:15 AM

I called down to the second grade class room for my first client of the day. His teacher informed me that he was absent, so I stopped by the third grade classroom to pick up a client I had planned to see later in the day named Alex. Alex is an 8-year-old boy referred by his teacher due to his explosive outbursts in class. He has a history of physical abuse at the hands of his biological father and refuses to talk about certain things from his past. Each week, he comes in my office, sits down, and asks if we can play a game. This was good for the first few sessions, as it allowed Alex to feel comfortable talking to me in a more casual setting. Now, however, it is a hindrance, as if I suggest we do anything that does not involve playing a game, he says he is bored and puts his head down in the table. On this particular day, I suggested we make a family tree (genogram) together. He seemed uncertain as to what a family tree was, but thinking it was Christmas related--it was mid-December--he was interested. This wound up being more beneficial than I had expected, as Alex told me about his entire family, including his mother's boyfriend, who he calls "Dad;" his biological father, who he only described as "being mean;" his aunts and uncles living in different parts of the country and world; and his many cousins. Learning this information helps me understand more about not only the people in his life, but also the different parts of the world he has roots in. At the end of the session, he asked if he could keep the family tree we had made.

9:50 AM

I brought Alex back to class and noticed the mother of one of my clients, Ms. Sanchez, dropping her son off from a doctor's appointment. Ms. Sanchez speaks very little English, but earlier in the school year, she visited the school secretary and asked her to interpret a conversation between us, as she had concerns regarding her son, Peter. In that meeting, Ms. Sanchez told me that Peter, a 7-year-old second grader, often mentioned that he was worried about his mother dying. Ms. Sanchez was in good health and there had been no deaths in the family, so she wanted me to talk to Peter about this to help alleviate some of his worries. During our third session, Peter brought up the concern he had that his mother would die. We explored this idea for the next two sessions before moving on to some other minor issues with which he was dealing.

When I saw Ms. Sanchez outside the office, I decided that this would be an ideal time to talk with her for a few minutes to get an update on how Peter has been doing at home, as the secretary who could act as our translator was right there. I greeted Ms. Sanchez and asked her if we could meet for a few minutes. We went into the secretary's office and I asked her if she could meet with us. Ms. Sanchez and I sat down and discussed how Peter was doing. I asked if he had brought up any concerns about his mother dying. She smiled and said that he had not mentioned anything about that in several weeks. I told her that I was happy to hear that and shared with her some of the observations I had made while working with Peter. She went on to explain a new concern she had. Peter had just started attending a new after-school program three days a week and when she drops him off there, he cries when she starts to leave. Since he started attending the program, he has started complaining about stomach aches. Ms. Sanchez took her son to the doctor's office that morning for testing, but they were unable to find any problems with his stomach. She theorized that Peter might be feeling intimidated by some of the older kids at the after-school program. As she was speaking, I heard a faint voice in the hallway say, "Mr. Sean!"

10:00 AM

Standing outside the secretary's office was Eric, a third grader I started seeing while he was in second grade. He was originally referred to me by the principal due to his misbehavior in the classroom, trouble relating to peers, and lack of focus in school. I excused myself from the secretary's office for a moment to speak with Eric. He told me that his teacher, Mrs. Piper, sent him to talk to me about "what had just happened in class." Unsure of what had transpired, I asked Eric to wait outside the secretary's office, thanked Ms. Sanchez for the conversation, and went to the third grade classroom to speak with Mrs. Piper. Eric followed me into the classroom and argued with Mrs. Piper as she explained the situation to me. The following conversation took place:

Therapist: Hello, Mrs. Piper. Eric told me that you wanted me to talk to him about something that had just happened in class.

Mrs. Piper: Yes, thank you. Eric has just been having a bad day—I don't know what it is. He's been getting up from his desk all day and running around the classroom. He's left the classroom a few times now without permission. And now he went to the back of the room and made a mess! He was back here throwing books against the wall and knocking toys over!

As she spoke, Mrs. Piper led me to the back of the classroom to show me what Eric had done. There were a few books lying open on the ground, covered by Legos and other small toys.

Eric: I didn't make the mess!

Mrs. Piper: Eric, enough! Jessica, Sally, and Billy separately told me that they saw you back here throwing things and knocking things over. See, Sean, he's just having a bad day and I'm not sure what's going on with him.

Eric: It's because my auntie in Mexico died!

Mrs. Piper: This is school property, Eric, and we don't do this at our school!

Realizing that this back and forth could continue all day and hearing what Eric had just shared, I politely intervened,

Therapist: Okay, Mrs. Piper, Eric and I are going to go up to my office and talk for a few minutes. I will bring him back down after, okay?

With that, Eric and I left the classroom and walked upstairs. Eric remained silent as we walked, which is very uncharacteristic of him. Usually upon sitting down with a client, I will be the one to initiate the conversation. In this instance, I remained silent and gave Eric the opportunity to begin talking when he was ready. I did this to reiterate to Eric that I was there to listen to him. After his teacher had been yelling at him and accusing him, I wanted to show him that I would not react like any other adult in his life would in a moment like this.

Not long after sitting down, Eric exclaimed, "I didn't make that mess in the back of the class!" I reminded Eric that he was not in trouble in my office and that we were there to talk about how he was feeling. Eric paused for a moment, looked at the ground, and said the most vulnerable thing he had said in our year and a half of work together: "Sometimes when I get so mad or sad, I feel like breaking thing, but I don't do it." I asked him if this had been one of those times he felt this way and he nodded his head. He told me that before school that morning, he had overheard his mother talking to someone about his aunt in Mexico, who he had never met but had heard a lot about, had recently died. He was dropped off at school with no other information on what had happened and sat in class for the next two hours thinking about what may have happened. I told Eric that if I were him, I would feel the same way. While that sounds like a cliché, Counseling 101, empathic response, it was the truth. If I had gone to work that day after finding out a family member had died, but no other information, I would have had a difficult time functioning properly, too, and I was decades older than Eric!

This simple but honest empathic response seemed to resonate in Eric, as he opened up about something he had avoided in our previous sessions: his classroom behaviors which his teachers had labeled as disruptive. He said, "You know why I get up and walk around in class and leave the classroom and yell sometimes?" I told him that I did not know, but if he wanted to tell me, I would love to hear. He explained that when his classmates are talking, it is hard for him to concentrate. To help himself calm him down so he can pay attention, he gets up and walks around the classroom or yells out something that he is thinking about. Eric said that the reason he had been in the back of the classroom when all the books and toys were thrown around was that he needed a few minutes to himself to calm down about his aunt. I commended him on finding something that helps him calm himself and asked him to tell me more about how this has helped him in the past.

After Eric indicated that he had not told Mrs. Piper about why he does some of the things he does in class, I asked him what he thought it would be like if he did tell her. He said that she would yell, "I don't care!" We discussed whether or not it could be helpful for Eric to tell his teacher that sometimes when he is feeling overwhelmed, he needs to be alone for a minute and if so, how he could share this message with Mrs. Piper. As we walked downstairs after the session, he decided that he did want to tell Mrs. Piper what we had talked about, but asked if I would stay in the room with him while he talked to her. He decided that he wanted to talk to Mrs. Piper right then because it was recess time and his classmates would be out of the classroom.

10:30 AM

I saw Mrs. Piper sitting at her desk in the classroom, so I lead Eric in and asked Mrs. Piper if she had a minute to talk. I told her that Eric and I had talked and he had something he wanted to share with her. In a quiet, insecure tone, Eric said, "Mrs. Piper, sometimes I get really mad and sad about things and I need to get up to make myself feel better." Mrs. Piper continued to reprimand Eric for his previous behavior—she told him that the classroom was a place for learning and he needed to respect that. Eric started to say something in a more confrontational tone than he started the conversation in and before the conversation could escalate, I calmly said, "Mrs. Piper, I think what Eric is trying to say is that when he is feeling a certain way during class, it becomes difficult for him to concentrate on his learning. Getting out of his desk and walking around helps him get some of his energy out so that he can sit back down and concentrate. Is that right, Eric?" Eric shook his head, indicating yes, and Mrs. Piper replied, "I know it can be hard for you to concentrate sometimes, Eric, and we only want the best for you here, but we can't have you running around the classroom and throwing things because it isn't safe for you and your classmates. Thank you for telling me this, though, and I will try to keep it in mind from now on. Do you want to go out for recess now?" Eric thanked his teacher and quickly left the classroom to enjoy the rest of the time he had left for recess.

After Eric exited the classroom, Mrs. Piper let out a loud sigh and thanked me for talking to Eric right away. We talked until her class came back from recess about different techniques to help Eric behave in class. After sharing some of her concerns with me, she opened up about the stress she was feeling in regards to her class. I listened to Mrs. Piper vent about how some of her students have been testing her patience and validated the way she was feeling. Sometimes, our work in the school is as much with the teachers as it is with the students and parents. In this moment, Mrs. Piper just needed someone to listen to how she was feeling without telling her what she should be doing differently. As her students filed back into the classroom, Mrs. Piper thanked me for my help. I ran to my office to make sure it was ready for my next client.

10:45 AM

My next client was Lisa, a fourth grader referred to counseling by her mother due to concerns over her daughter often seeming scared or nervous, often following loud noises. Lisa's parents are divorced, but remain on good terms. Lisa lives with her mother during the week and stays with her father and older sister on the weekends. Lisa's mother, Ms. Gomez, is a teacher's assistant at the school and I have built a good rapport with her since she began working in the school. Ms. Gomez felt comfortable talking to me and thought that her daughter would, too.

My session with Lisa started not unlike our five sessions had by talking about how her weekend was. She told me about visiting her father and playing with her dogs—her normal weekend activities. Lisa tells long stories about her dogs, often giving them human-like characteristics when talking about how they interact with the family. In passing, she mentioned that her father had hit her on the side of the neck a few nights earlier when she would not come to the kitchen table for dinner. This led in to a story about her dog being a picky-eater. While I continued to listen to Lisa's story, my mind started racing with questions regarding what Lisa had said about her father. Given the context of the following story, it was possible Lisa had been talking about her dog when she mentioned what her father had done, but I was not going to assume anything when a potential instance of child abuse was mentioned. I asked Lisa a few questions to clarify what she had said. According to Lisa, she had been watching videos on YouTube when her father called her to the dinner table. Lisa wanted to keep watching the videos and refused to come to the dinner table. Her father walked over to the computer and hit Lisa with his belt across the right side of her neck. She mentioned that she had been bruised by the belt, but as she was wearing a turtleneck, I did not see a bruise. Immediately, Lisa's sister and Ms. Gomez came to Lisa's aid, telling him to put the belt down and to never do that again. Lisa mentioned several times that nothing like this had ever happened before. It took several minutes to get this story from Lisa, however, as she would continued going off on tangents after answering my initial question. One of the stories Lisa told involved her sister doing something she described as "stupid" because she was "drunk or on drugs or something."

After I had assessed the situation and determined that what Lisa had told me did in fact warrant a call to my supervisor and a child protective services (CPS) report, I asked Lisa if she remembered one of the first things I had told her when we started counseling. She looked at me blankly, unsure of what I meant. I revisited the concept of confidentiality, briefly explaining it to her until she started to finish the explanation for me. I told her that what she had just told me was one of the circumstances for which I had to tell someone what we had talked about. Immediately, Lisa said, "Well, some of the stuff I said wasn't true—I was just joking around. My sister wasn't really drunk or anything." I asked her if she was joking around about anything else she had told me, and she said, "No." I then asked her if what she had told me about her father hitting her with a belt was true, and she said, "Yes, that really happened." While I still would have spoken to my supervisor and filed a CPS report had she answered negatively, I wanted to see if she would alter what she had reported after she mentioned that she was "joking around" about some of the things she said. She did not.

11:20 AM

After dropping Lisa back off at her classroom, I noticed Ms. Gomez using the copy machine alone in the main office. I greeted her and asked her if she could talk for a few minutes. We sat down at a table and, since the room we were in was not private, I started by telling her that if anyone walked in, I would stop talking about what we were about to talk about until the room was clear again. The following is my abbreviated recollection of our conversation:

Therapist: I just met with Lisa and she mentioned something that happened around dinner time on Sunday night.

Ms. Gomez: Laughs nervously. Oh, yes, that wasn't good, but everything is okay now and it wasn't a big deal.

Therapist: What exactly happened?

Ms. Gomez: Well, it was time for dinner and Lisa's father called her to come to the table. Lisa was on the computer watching some videos and did not want to come to the table and she kept yelling, "No! No! No!" Her dad walked over to the computer to get her and she got up and ran away. There was this little belt thing—I don't know what it is called, but we use it to hit against things to make noise to get our dog's attention. Anyways, it was sitting on the table and he grabbed it. He went to hit Lisa in the butt with it, but since she was running, he missed and it hit her in the neck. He had never done anything like that before and I yelled at him, "Arthur! Put that down!" He felt so bad—he started to cry! It had been a long day and with Lisa—she can be so hard sometimes. She always says, "No!" when we ask her to do anything. Arthur was so tired and I guess he just wasn't thinking.

Therapist: It sounds like it was a very stressful day. Raising kids isn't easy and sometimes as parents, we make mistakes. It sounds like the situation escalated in a way Arthur didn't intend it to.

Ms. Gomez: Yeah, he has never done something like this before. He felt so bad after. He was crying and saying, "What have I done? I didn't mean to do that," and he has high blood pressure, so I had to calm him down because I don't want him having a heart attack or anything.

Therapist: I hope he understands that it was just a mistake and is able to learn from this experience. Lisa has told me so many wonderful things about him and she loves spending time with him. I know this was an isolated incident and it doesn't sound like it will happen again, but unfortunately, this is something I have to report.

Ms. Gomez: Oh, no, it really wasn't a big deal. I don't think it needs to be reported.

Therapist: I know, and from what you've said, I don't think anything like this will happen again, but there are certain cases in which I am required by law to report things, and this is one of those cases. I wish I didn't have to report it because I know it could turn it in to something bigger than it really was, but I don't have a choice. I wanted to tell you about it before I made the report, though, so you would be aware of what was happening.

Ms. Gomez: Oh my. Are you sure you have to report it?

Therapist: I am going to call my supervisor to double-check with him that it is reportable, but I think it is unavoidable and I will have to report it. I know this is a difficult situation, though, so I will do my best to make sure that no one else in the school knows that this happened.

Ms. Gomez: Ah, I can't imagine what people will say if they find out about this!

Therapist: I know, and I will do my best to make this as easy as it possibly can be. When I file the report, I will tell them everything that you told me to make sure that they have an accurate and genuine picture of what happened. I am going to call my supervisor and I will come down to talk to you after, okay?

Ms. Gomez: Okay. Thank you, Sean.

12:00 PM

After speaking with Ms. Gomez, I called my supervisor, Steve Abrams, to share with him what had happened in the previous session, my meeting with Ms. Gomez, and what I planned to do next—call CPS to file a report. I told him that while I knew this was reportable and I was going to report it as mandated, I felt uneasy about doing so because Lisa's mother works in the school and I have built a strong rapport with her over the last several months. My concern was not only for the safety of my client, but also for the way the other school employees could react if and when they heard a CPS report had been filed for the daughter of a school employee. To prevent any possible backlash, I planned to not tell anyone at the school, other than Ms. Gomez, that I was filing the report. Steve assured me that my plan was the correct course of action to take and commended me for my concern over the possible ramifications this could have for Ms. Gomez at the school. He strongly suggested that I also tell the principal about the report, as if CPS were to send a police officer or social worker to the school to investigate it, the principal should know what was going on. I told Steve that I agreed with him and he thanked me for calling and told me to call back if I had any further questions.

12:10 PM

I left my office and found Ms. Gomez waiting for me in the main office. I told her that I did have to report what had happened, but that we could work together to make it go as smoothly as possible. I also told her that at the suggestion of my supervisor, I had to inform the principal that the report was being made. Ms. Gomez has some questions about this, but once I explained the rationale behind it, she understood the need for it. I offered to speak with the principal by myself, but suggested that it might be best if Ms. Gomez was part of the conversation as well. Ms. Gomez agreed and we went into the principal's office together.

The conversation with the principal, Sister Maria, was very similar to the initial conversation between Ms. Gomez and me. I started the conversation by saying, "I met with Lisa earlier today and I had some concerns which Ms. Gomez is going to share with you." Ms. Gomez explained exactly what had transpired on Sunday, starting with what the family did together during the afternoon, going through the incident with Arthur at dinner time, and ending with how she handled things with Arthur following the incident. Sister Maria, who herself has worked as a spiritual counselor, reacted to Ms. Gomez in a compassionate manner. She showed she understood how Arthur might have felt by sharing things that she has noticed in regards to Lisa's sometimes combative interactions with other students. She also gave Ms. Gomez some suggestions on different parenting techniques.

As the conversation between Sister Maria and Ms. Gomez came to an end, I told Sister Maria that we were telling her about this because I had to file a report on the incident. She gave me a puzzled look and said, "Are you sure? It sounds like everything has been taken care of and that this will never happen again, right Ms. Gomez?" As Ms. Gomez nodded, I reminded Sister Maria that as mandated reporters, we are obligated to report any suspicion of child abuse. Sister Maria immediately understood, saying, "Ah, okay, you're right. Okay then, Ms. Gomez, Sean has to file the report, but after that, it becomes confidential and we will not tell anyone about it. A social worker or police officer will probably come to the school to talk with Lisa and make sure she is all right and that should be the end of it." For the first time during this ordeal, Ms. Gomez began to tear up. I reiterated what Sister Maria said regarding the confidential nature of this, but made sure to let Ms. Gomez know that while CPS *may* send someone to the school, it is also possible that the family may just receive a phone call. I reassured her that Sister Maria and I would do whatever we could to help them through this. Ms. Gomez wiped her eyes and shared her concerns over how this could affect her ex-husband and his health. Sister Maria and I listened to Ms. Gomez and validated her feelings. I expressed my confliction with having to make the report, but reiterated that I was legally bound to do so.

1:00 PM

After my conversation with Sister Maria and Ms. Gomez, I gathered all of the information that I needed to make the CPS report from the student information cards in the main office. I went over the information with Ms. Gomez to ensure its accuracy and went into my office to prepare the report.

1:20 PM

Once I had completed the written report, I called the CPS hotline to make the report. Before making the report, I made sure to write down the name of the person I was speaking to so that I could note it in my progress notes. While the reporting process went fairly smoothly, I took a few precautions to ensure that nothing I reported could be taken out of context. When it came time to give the narrative description of the suspected abuse, I read the following statement, which I had prepared in advance:

> *Minor reported being on the computer watching videos on YouTube when it was time to eat dinner. Her parents asked her multiple times to come to the table, but she reports saying no. The suspect (minor's father) walked over to minor as minor got up and started to run away. Suspect picked up a miniature belt (used for making noise to get dog's attention) and hit the minor on the right side of her neck. Mother reported that the suspect had intended to hit the minor on the butt, but accidentally hit her neck when she ran. Mother reported suspect feeling extremely remorseful after the incident, crying, and apologizing to his daughter. Both the minor and her mother separately reported that this was the first and only instance of any physical abuse.*

I answered the follow-up questions the CPS worker asked, but did my best to not add much more than what was in my narrative description. When she asked questions related to what I thought--questions like "Do you think the minor is in imminent danger?"--I answered as factually-based as possible, but stressed the fact that I was giving them the report so that they could investigate the likelihood of danger.

Before ending the phone call, I asked the CPS worker where I should send my written report, which in the state of California, must be sent within 36 hours of making the telephonic report. The call lasted approximately 30 minutes, leaving me with just enough time to see one more client.

1:50 PM

I went down to the second grade classroom to pick up Peter, the son of Ms. Sanchez, who I had spoken to earlier that morning. Peter typically presents as a fun-loving, carefree, happy kid. Ever since our first session, he would skip down the hallway to my office. On this day, however, he was not skipping. He sat down and slouched in his chair with a solemn look on his face. I asked him how he was doing and he immediately started crying. I passed him the box of tissues that I keep on my desk and sat with him for a few minutes while he stopped crying. I asked him if he could tell me how he was feeling at that moment and he said, "My tummy hurts really bad," before sniffling and wiping tears from his eyes. We talked for a few minutes about what his stomach felt like, how long it had felt that way, and what he had tried to do to make it feel better. At his request, we played Connect 4. This seemed to take his mind off the pain for a few minutes, as he started smiling more. A few minutes later, however, he began to cry again and asked if I could take him to the office so he could call his mother to pick him up. I took him down to the office and waited with him while the secretary called Ms. Sanchez to pick Peter up. Once Peter was settled in the office, I told him that I hope he feels better and headed back to my office.

2:25 PM

Once I got to my office, I closed the door, sat down, and rested for a few minutes. As I wrote my progress notes for my clients, I reflected back on the day. This had been one of the busier days I had in recent memory, as I hadn't taken a break since I started my session with Alex that morning and the day kept moving from there. While I felt tired and ready to go home, I also felt a sense of accomplishment for everything I had done that day. It's not often that my day at the school takes so many drastic turns, and at one point earlier in my development as a school-based family therapist, I would have felt completely overwhelmed at the end of this day. At this point, however, I felt capable in everything that had come up that day. There was no way I could have prepared for a day like this, and I think that is some of the appeal that comes with this line of work. Every day is *completely* different. While some days may be mind-numbingly slow, other days, such as this, pass without having--or even feeling a need for--time to take a break. This day was the latter.

RELATIONSHIP TO THE SBFC MODEL

I approach each of my cases from a family systems perspective and develop goals and interventions based on the relationships my client has with key figures in his or her life. I have mapped out potential goals for each of the four clients I discussed and how I can best work towards these goals using the Circumplex Model of Marital & Family Systems within the SBFC framework (see Figure 41.1).

ALEX

I would classify the relationship between Alex and his classmates as Rigidly Separated. While I have not witnessed such behavior, his behavior has been described as explosive by his teacher. He is new to the school this year and aside from a few friends, has shown little loyalty to his classmates. He often works alone, but when he does work with his classmates, he typically tells them what they should do and how they should do it. He becomes upset if things are not done how he wants. According to his teacher, Alex views himself as the leader of the classroom. At snack time, his teacher reports that Alex insists on passing out the snacks to each student, when normally students get up to grab their own snacks. There have been incidents on the schoolyard where Alex has yelled at or hit classmates because of disagreements during soccer or basketball games.

My current goal is to move Alex's relationship with his class from Rigidly Separated to Structurally Separated. I will work to help Alex increase his comfort and flexibility in classroom roles, as his "leader of the class" mentality seems to be alienating him from some of his peers. In doing this, it will be important to show Alex that while he is sharing some of his perceived power, it does not mean that he is giving up any of the control he has in his own life.

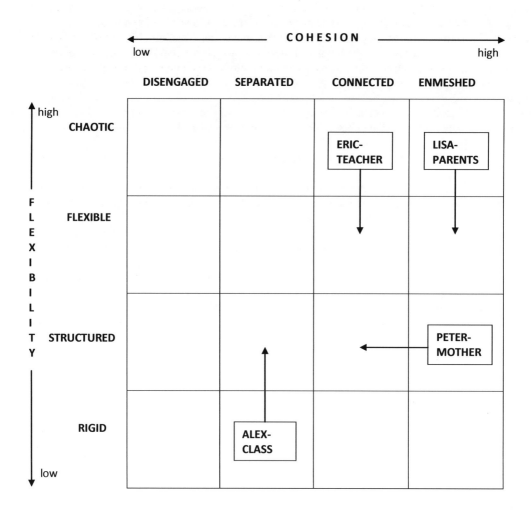

Figure 41.1 Circumplex Model Diagnoses and Goals

Note: ─────▶
indicates SBFC change direction

This work will be done primarily in the Family-Intervention quadrant in individual counseling with Alex, as I theorize that Alex's behavioral problems could be a result of the physical abuse he received. It is my thinking that if Alex is able to work through the trauma related to that, he may be more able to work through some of his behavioral issues. As the school year continues, the work could move into the School-Intervention quadrant with a counseling group with Alex and his classmates.

ERIC

The primary relationship interfering with Eric's schoolwork is his relationship with his teacher, Mrs. Piper. I would classify their relationship as Chaotically Connected. As the teacher, Mrs. Piper is clearly the leader, but Eric argues and fights for control in their interactions. There is no consistent form of discipline for Eric in the classroom. Eric is more dependent on Mrs. Piper than he likely knows, as she is responsible for teaching Eric and preparing him to move on in his education. Though their relationship is sometimes rough, they both show signs of loyalty to each other. Mrs. Piper has expressed the care she has for Eric, telling me that she wants to figure out the best way to help him achieve in school. I have also seen Eric run up to Mrs. Piper and give her a hug multiple times over the school year.

My current goal is to move Eric's relationship with his teacher from Chaotically Connected to Flexibly Connected. The work to achieve this goal will be in both the School-Intervention and Family-Intervention quadrants. The School-Intervention work will come in the form of consultations with Mrs. Piper. My goal in these consultations will be to help her set clear limits and appropriate consequences for Eric. I will stress the importance of following through with these changes consistently. Once the limits and consequences are determined, I will urge Mrs. Piper to sit down with Eric to explain these new rules and allow him the opportunity to make suggestions for possible changes to the rules before they become finalized. This will model compromising for Eric.

The work with Eric will be both School-Intervention and Family-Intervention in the form of individual counseling with Eric. Eric is likely to be unhappy with some of the changes that will be made and it is important that he has an opportunity to express unhappiness. The main focus with Eric right now, though, is to help him determine the things that get in the way of his learning. Eric was able to name some things that distract him in class, but I am sure there are other things that he is either unaware of or unable to express. Expressing these things will help me figure out skills I can teach him to work through the distractions. The Family-Intervention work would focus around helping Eric express and work through some of the stress he has at home, such as the death of his aunt, which he recently shared. I theorize that some of the things that distract him at school are related to things he has going on at home.

LISA

I would classify Lisa's current relationship with her parents as Chaotically Enmeshed. As parents, Ms. Gomez and her husband are the leaders of the family, but Lisa continuously challenges their authority. This causes the roles to shift dramatically, as both Lisa and her parents attempt to reassert their power. As evidenced by the recent first use of physical punishment, discipline is erratic at home. There is no established form of discipline. Rules in the house are made, but are not adhered to and change often. Even with all that, however, Lisa is very loyal to her family. She has mentioned numerous times that she likes spending time at both her mother's and her father's house. She talks about the different things she does with her parents and the fun that they have. It seems that problems arise when Lisa is told to do something that she doesn't want to do.

My current goal is to move Lisa's relationship with her parents from Chaotically Enmeshed to Flexibly Enmeshed. The work to achieve this goal will be in the Family-Intervention quadrant in the form of family and individual counseling. While it may be difficult to get Lisa's father into my office, I will be able to meet with Ms. Gomez on a regular basis. I plan to work together with both Lisa and her mother to define clear limits at home, with appropriate and realistic consequences for breaking those limits. Allowing Lisa to take part in this discussion helps model a shared leadership in the family. This is a trait that will become increasingly helpful for the Gomez family as Lisa gets older. I will also stress the importance of enforcing these defined limits with Ms. Gomez. If I am unable to see Lisa's father, I will coach Ms. Gomez in how she can explain the importance of these changes to her ex-husband. I will continue working with Lisa in individual counseling to give her a place to express her thoughts and feelings about these new rules at home. The way in which I implement this goal could change, however, based on the findings from the CPS report I filed. Depending on what, if any, actions CPS takes, I will alter my treatment plan accordingly.

PETER

I would classify the relationship between Peter and his mother as Structurally-Enmeshed. Peter and his mother genuinely seem to have a very close and loving relationship. Each week, Peter mentions the different games he plays with his mother at home. I have witnessed Ms. Sanchez walking her son home, holding his hand and carrying his backpack over her shoulder. The roles in the family seem to be clearly defined and stable.

My goal is to move Peter's relationship with his mother from Structurally-Enmeshed to Structurally-Connected. Given the strength of the relationship between Peter and his mother, the changes to meet this goal will be very minor. The work to achieve this goal will be in the Family-Intervention quadrant in the form of individual counseling. While his mother reported that Peter has not mentioned his fear of her dying recently, the constant worry he had about this, while age appropriate, could be a sign of dependency issues later in his life. As Peter grows up, it will be important that he feels comfortable having some separateness from his mother. Their emotional closeness is a major positive in his life, but he also needs to develop a sense of independence. To facilitate this change, I will explore with Peter what kinds of activities he does by himself and encourage him to pursue activities which promote independence. I will also stress the importance of his close bond with his mother, as that is something that does not need to change.

I also plan to do some School-Prevention work with Peter in the form of teaching him different ways to handle his stress. His reaction to his stomach pain was age appropriate, but it might be beneficial to start planting seeds for different ways of handling stress. I will start this process by talking to him about what kind of things make him feel mad, sad, or stressed out and what he does to calm himself. From there, I will teach him other strategies for calming himself, such as focusing on his breathing.

PART VII

SCHOOL-BASED FAMILY COUNSELING: SPECIFIC APPLICATIONS

G. EXAMPLES OF SCHOOL-BASED FAMILY COUNSELING PROGRAMS

CHAPTER 43

The Copper River Project: Laying the Foundation for School-Based Family Counseling with Alaska's Indigenous Populations

Allan A. Morotti

OVERVIEW:_This chapter describes an innovative collaboration between a school district and a university school counseling program to provide SBFC services to students in Alaska._

PROGRAM DESCRIPTION

The Copper River Project (CRP) was a collaborative effort between the Copper River School District (CRSD) and the Professional School Counseling Program at the University of Alaska Fairbanks to create a culturally responsive K-8 comprehensive developmental guidance and counseling program in the CRSD. Three hundred and eighty one K-8 students, 25 percent of whom identified as Alaska Native, attended eight schools in the district, which covers 24, 663 square miles. One project goal was to increase parent and community involvement in the education of these children. Various school-based family counseling strategies were utilized to help achieve this goal, including family counseling, psycho-educational presentations, and school/community agency partnerships. The project was funded by a grant from the U.S. Department of Education.

The Copper River Valley is located in interior rural Alaska. Its largest town, Glennallen, has a population of 450 inhabitants and is situated 200 miles northeast of Anchorage and 250 miles southeast of Fairbanks. The Copper River Valley and School District covers a land area of 24,663 square miles with a population of approximately 3,100 residents. This area is larger than the combined landmass of Massachusetts, Connecticut, Rhode Island, New Jersey, and Delaware.

The primary means for accessing the major communities of this region is by the Alaska Highway system. There is no public transportation or taxi service and the only airport in the area is unmanned and has no regularly scheduled flights. The typical ambulance run is approximately two hours. The roads are snow and ice-covered much of the year and daylight is limited to a few hours per day from November to March. Also, sustained sub-zero temperatures are the norm and cold spells of 50 degrees below zero (Fahrenheit scale) are not an uncommon experience.

Most communities in this area receive telephone service; however, there is no local television and only one local radio station. Municipal or borough governments are non-existent. On a voluntary basis citizens provide traditional public services (e.g., The Crossroads Medical Center). Weather permitting, itinerant medical professionals visit the region on a regular basis. Alaska Natives, predominately Athabaskan, comprise a considerable portion of the area's citizenry and cultural aspects of their heritage play an important role in the region's development. Alaska Native students constitute approximately 25% of the total pupil enrollment in the CRSD.

While CRP was conceptualized as a comprehensive guidance and counseling program, being preventive in nature, and built on academic career, as well as personal /social development domains

(American School Counselor Association, 2003; Gysbers & Henderson, 2000) in reality it also served as a mental health delivery system for students, parents, and school personnel in the region, by utilizing many school-based family counseling (SBFC) principles.

> SBFC is an approach to helping children succeed at school and overcome personal and interpersonal problems. SBFC integrates school counseling and family counseling models within a broad based systems meta-model that is used to conceptualize the child's problems in the context of all his or her interpersonal networks: family, peer group, classroom, school (teacher, principal, other students), and community. (Gerrard, 2008, p. 6)

Professional school counselors are trained in developmental psychology and while they traditionally engage in many therapeutic-like services during the school day, they are not charged with the responsibility of being mental health providers. However, the mental health needs of rural Alaskans often go unmet because of a shortage of trained professionals. In the Copper River region there are some agencies that do provide counseling services; however, individuals in need of services do not always believe that what they share at these agencies will be kept confidential, and therefore under utilize the available resources. School counseling services are no exception.

Developing trust between the school and the community is critical for the successful delivery of all social and educational services to Alaska's indigenous populations (Barnhardt & Kawagley, 2004; Erickson, 1987; Lipka, 2002; Villegas & Prieto, 2006). To lay the foundation for building trust and encouraging active parent and community involvement in the creation of the Copper River school counseling program, the two professional school counselors hired under the grant were asked to live in one of the smaller communities outside of Glennallen and to participate actively in as many of the region's community events as possible.

Through participation in community events such as the Copper Basin 300 Dogsled Race, the Chistochina Fun Days, and attendance at many sporting events, the school counselors were able to make contact with families not regularly involved in the school experiences of their children. They also made home visits and contacted parents by telephone on a regular basis. They coordinated the Copper Center Potlatch and met with Native elders and other community members to organize a variety of cultural events through the After School Club (e.g., Native dancing and singing, beading, and ice fishing) and the Bridging the Gap organization. The counselors were able to bridge many of the cultural gaps that existed between the school system and the community by displaying a willingness to become active members of their communities. These contacts helped to foster stronger parent and community relations with the school district, paralleling many of the recommendations found in the literature identified as ways to help build a SBFC program (Bryan & Holcomb-McCoy, 2004; Edwards & Foster, 1995; Evans & Carter, 1997). Furthermore, Carter and Perluss (2008) note that professional school counselors are "in a unique position to provide support and direction to families and schools in their mutual goal of maximizing the development of children….because of their daily presence at the school and their institutional role within the school system" (p. 49-50).

RELATIONSHIP TO THE SBFC MODEL

The CRP utilized all four domains of the SBFC Model. The school-prevention focus employed a combination of small group and entire classroom guidance activities. On the intervention side the two school counselors provided teacher consultation as needed, small group counseling activities, crisis intervention, and one-on-one counseling services. Topics addressed in both of these venues included: Strategies fo r academic success; social skills training; character education; understanding feelings, understanding self; anger management strategies; alcohol and drug awareness; conflict resolution activities; death and dying issues; parental divorce; peer pressure; and career education activities. The overarching goal of the grant's school focus was to help the students develop skills that would assist them in making socially constructive decisions throughout their lifetimes.

Family-prevention and intervention activities were also a central component of the CRP. Parent education groups were developed on a variety of topics, including: parenting strategies, well-baby care, child development, and how to improve family relations. Counselors provided both family counseling and consultation services to the students' parents and guardians. Demonstrations on the use of filial therapy were given at school and in the home if requested. Crisis and grief counseling were provided to individuals, families, and the larger community-at-large as the need arose. In addition, a Parent Resource Center was developed that housed a variety of self-help psycho-educational handouts. A Parent Resource Hour was held twice monthly for anyone in the community who might want assistance with any number of topics (e.g., higher education opportunities; family member experiencing suicidal ideation).

One of the primary footholds of the CRSD grant was the development of positive working relationships with students, families, staff, and community members. This goal was realized through a variety of means. The school counselors worked closely with numerous community organizations (e.g., Mt. Sanford Tribal Consortium, Wrangell Mountain Ministries, Copper River Native Association) to build partnerships on how to best help families in the Copper River Basin area. To increase community involvement in school programs the counselors met regularly with the CRP Advisory Board. They helped to integrate Native Elders and other community members into instructional roles through participation in the After School Club. Children attending the After School Club engaged in many traditional Alaskan Native activities, such as: dancing, singing, beading, weaving, metal working, and ice fishing.

EVIDENCE-BASED SUPPORT

A large amount of the literature supporting the CRP is interspersed throughout the chapter. Very little, if any, evidence-based support exists that is specific to Alaska Natives. "When examining research related to mental health practices, few published results and dissertation abstracts showing treatment modality with AI/AN [American Indians/Alaska Natives] populations exist" (Safran et al., 2009, cited in Gray & Rose, 2012, p. 85). Even those articles and books supposedly focusing on American Indian and Alaska Native populations seldom dedicate more than a few pages to addressing subjects specific to Alaska Natives (Trimble, 2012). In short, this group is usually lumped in with American Indians, implying a one-size fits all model to America's Indigenous peoples. "Therapists who work with AI/AN populations often use local culture and traditions in an attempt to adapt their therapeutic techniques to fit the unique needs of their clients" (Gray & Rose, 2012, p. 85). Therefore, because there is a lack of evidence-based research with America's Indigenous populations practitioners are forced to rely on various theoretical models that integrate Western models of therapy with traditional Native ways of healing specific to the individual's tribal affiliation. Nevertheless, few studies have been conducted assessing the validity and reliability of these treatment modalities with these populations (Gray & Rose, 2012).

However, there are more generic studies that support the integration of school, family, and community resources to better meet the educational needs of children. Steen and Noquera (2010) recommend a three prong approach to helping young children succeed academically, especially those children who may be experiencing socioeconomic hardships. They encourage the integration of the parents/guardians into the child's educational experience. Steen and Noquera also advocate for building community partnerships in order to develop after school and summer programs. Lastly, these authors note the importance of collaboration between school, family, and community in connecting children to needed health/medical services.

Dotson-Blake (2010) used an ethnographic approach to underscore the importance of school, family, and community collaborations in the academic success of Mexican-American children. The study explored the types of partnerships Mexican nationalists living in Veracruz developed as compared to Mexican immigrant families living in North Carolina. The importance of the study lies in the premise that school counselors are the educational professionals ideally suited for the development of positive relationships between these three entities in the United States. Ziomek-Daigle (2010) conducted a qualitative study that highlighted the benefits of intervention strategies that promoted higher levels of parental and family engagement in the educational experiences of their sons and daughters. These interventions were employed as a means to decrease the dropout rate of high school students. Ziomek-Daigle also recommended the development of graduation teams comprised of school personnel, family and community members as a way to encourage students to complete high school.

In sum, using cognitive-behavioral counseling strategies with ethnic minority clients, including AI/AN, that "emphasize self-appraisal and the meaning of events through an emphasis on self-efficacy can be useful..." (McDonald & Gonzalez, 2006, cited in Trimble, 2012, p. 194). The key element in the development of a positive sense of self and healthy functioning is a solid understanding of the context from which the individual emerges. SBFC professionals working with Indigenous populations must develop a working knowledge of the socio-historical, political, and economic factors that have interacted with and helped shape the worldview of the developing person, if they are to be effective practitioners with AI/AN populations.

MULTICULTURAL COUNSELING CONSIDERATIONS

Alaska Natives were once the dominant culture of the arctic and sub-arctic regions of North America, but are now a small sub-population of the American culture. Like every other indigenous group in what is now the United States, Alaska Natives have been exposed to numerous assimilation strategies (e.g., boarding schools) since coming under the rule of the federal government (Clarke, 2002: Klug & Whitfield, 2003; D.W. Sue & D. Sue, 2003). The debilitating effects of these assimilation efforts have resulted in multiple acculturation stressors leading to high suicide rates, substance abuse, and loss of traditional cultural practices (Manson, 2000; D.W. Sue & D. Sue, 2003; U.S. Department of Health and Human Services, 2001).

Although many Alaska Native communities continue to contend with such issues, their cultural traditions are embedded into the very fabric of the Alaskan way of life. Education continues to serve as one avenue open to Alaska Native youth for integrating two distinct ways of being, cultural traditions, values, and differing world views (e.g., traditional subsistence lifestyle versus American consumerism). Culturally congruent educational practices provide Alaska Native youth with one such way to realize this goal of merging cultures and avoiding a bifurcated sense of self (Morotti, 2006).

Alaska Native children are often described as being unmotivated in school due to their reluctance to compete against one another. In Native cultures, being competitive means putting oneself above the tribe and implies that the person is better than the tribe (D.W. Sue & D. Sue, 2003). This is one of the many value conflicts that indigenous youth face in school today. The underlying message for these youth is that to achieve academic success they must assimilate into the mainstream society (Kawagley, 1999). However, a person's identity and culture are intertwined, and a student with a strong sense of culture and self-worth does better socially and academically. Research studies indicate that Alaska Native children are more successful academically when their families maintain strong traditional values. (Barnhardt, 1981; Barnhardt & Kawagley, 2005; Barnhardt, Kawagley & Hill, 2000; Chance, 1966; Harkins, 1975: Kawagley, Norris-Tull, & Norris-Tull, 1998; Kleinfeld, 1979; Reyhner & Jacobs, 2002; Theobald & Howley, 1998).

To lessen the cultural conflict between the goals of public education and indigenous students' value systems, a goal like academic achievement can be presented as an extension of the traditional Native value of self-sufficiency through being able to help others. This process of value restructuring allows a student the opportunity to develop a framework of "stable core values that produces what education is all about—flexible personalities able to adapt to change, cope with special demands and stresses, and yet maintain coherent identity" (Kleinfeld, 1979, p. 133).

The validation of self and culture by representatives of the dominant society helps indigenous students to develop a secure sense of identity, confidence in abilities, and dignity of personhood (Kawagley, 1999). This is critical for healthy psychological development of the individual, because often times the messages indigenous and other ethnic minority youth receive from the dominant society are ones that disregard their value as members of the mainstream society.

> The messages from the school and the media, and other manifestations of Eurocentric society, present Yupiaq students with an unreal picture of the outside world as well as a distorted view of their own, which leads to a great deal of confusion for students about who they are and where they fit in the world. This loss of Yupiaq identity leads to guilt and shame at being Yupiaq. The resultant feelings of hurt, grief, and pain are locked in the mind to emerge as depression and apathy, which is further reinforced by the fear of failure in school, by ridicule from non-Natives, and by loss of spirituality. (Kawagley, 1999, p. 37)

Identity and culture are intrinsically linked. Therefore, educational experiences need to acknowledge the value of the student's culture of origin to help promote development of a more holistic self. It is not uncommon for the culturally diverse individual to feel competent among his or her own people, but experience feelings of inadequacy when interacting with representatives from the dominant culture. The dissonance created by this interface of cultures can result in the culturally diverse individual forming negative appraisals of self. Cultural differences affect an individual's perceptions and interactions with the environment impacting all aspects of a person's life, including how one learns (Barnhardt, 1997).

One way to offset the negative effects of cultural dissonance for Alaska Native youth is the development of a collaborative working relationship between all parties(i.e., teachers, students, parents, community members) affected by the school system (Agbo, 2001; Bemak & Cornely, 2002; Keys & Bemak, 1997; Lipka, 1998; Yazzie, 1999). This collaboration is necessary for creating a sense of ownership and responsibility towards students academic success (Villegas & Prieto, 2006). "Support of the schools by the community and parents is tied to the success of both schools and students" (Alaska Native Policy Center at the First Alaskans Institute, 2004, p. 95). This underscores the belief that "individual success and community success are interdependent and the recognition of community and school interdependence is vital for student success" (Russell, 2008, p.26). A result of this collaboration is the development of trust between all the stakeholders, because it signals a willingness to work together as equals demonstrating mutual respect towards all parties which is necessary for successful relationship building (Ansbacher & Ansbacher, 1956).

CHALLENGES AND SOLUTIONS

In rural Alaska professional educators come and go frequently. It is not an uncommon phenomenon for these individuals not only to change school districts, but also leave the state all together after a year or two of teaching. The three public universities that constitute the University of Alaska statewide system of higher education graduate approximately 20% of all the teachers needed every year in Alaska. Out-of-state educators who are often unfamiliar with Alaska and its indigenous populations usually fill the remaining educational vacancies. This unfamiliarity plays a significant role in teacher turnover. It is also a major factor that impedes the development of trust between Alaska's indigenous peoples and what is commonly known as the American K-12 educational system. Other factors that add to this distrust are a long list of socio-historical events that have resulted in Alaska Natives being subjugated to second-class citizenship on their own lands.

To lay the groundwork for building trusting relationships with the Alaska Natives living within the boundaries of the CRSD, the two professional school counselors were asked to live in one of the smaller communities and to become active participants in local activities. What the counselors had to do to be accepted by these individuals was to demonstrate that they were different than many of those educators who had preceded them. In essence, by demonstrating their willingness to become a part of the local community the counselors were saying we value your way of life.

A second challenge was developing culturally-appropriate counseling materials for classroom use. The Alaska Native Knowledge Network with its lists of cultural values specific to each of Alaska's indigenous populations was one resource that was utilized. Nevertheless, knowing a group's values and how those values are demonstrated are two completely different knowledge systems. Once again, this provided the two school counselors with opportunities to demonstrate their respect for these cultures by interacting with Native Elders and seeking their input on how to best teach these values.

The Copper River Basin has one of the highest rates of Fetal Alcohol Spectrum Disorder (FASD) in Alaska. It is common knowledge that this is a completely preventable disorder. However, one of the consequences of assimilation for America's indigenous populations has been the high rate of substance abuse due to the loss of their traditional ways of life. The loss of these traditions has often created a cultural vacuum for Indigenous populations, leading to a negative view of self and engagement in personally harmful behaviors. To meet this challenge the counselors provided parent education workshops, disseminated psycho-educational literature on the harmful effects of alcohol and others drugs during pregnancy, and worked closely with the Copper River Native Association (CRNA) in developing wrap-around services for families with FASD affected children.

At school the counselors integrated traditional Native values into their classroom activities. Grant funds were used to purchase and implement challenge activities (i.e., a ropes course) into the counseling curriculum to address the unique learning needs of FASD children. The counselors working in conjunction with the CRNA provided a summer camp for FASD children and their care providers, emphasizing traditional Athabascan ways of life as demonstrated by Native Elders. The counselors also taught transition skills to Head Start children identified as FASD. And lastly, one counselor worked with the CRNA during the summer months providing mental health services to FASD affected adults.

The biggest challenge facing the counselors, however, was the absence of any culturally-appropriate counseling curriculum materials for use with Alaska Native children. In addition, the counseling curriculum adopted by the Alaska School Counselor Association and endorsed by the state department of education lacked culture-specific activities pertinent to Alaska Natives. Furthermore, the above-mentioned document was solely school-focused and did not recommend any type of family counseling activities.

Using a model developed by one of the grant writers while teaching at a Catholic school in Eugene, Oregon (1982-87) the CRP undertook the challenge to integrate school and family counseling models. While the Oregon model did not include culture-specific activities, it did utilize family counseling and parent education modalities, besides traditional school counseling services (i.e., classroom guidance units, individual and small group counseling).

PROCEDURE

A theoretical underpinning of all professional school counseling programs is the premise that every student can benefit from school-wide guidance activities. In other words, guidance is prevention. Prevention activities often focus on addressing emerging critical issues that impact the entire school and surrounding community, as well as individual students and their families. Among K-12 students, these issues are frequently ecological in nature in that they concern factors that affect the general atmosphere of the schools and homes in which children and youth learn (Carter & Evans, 2008, p.26).

A primary goal of all prevention activities is to help students develop skills that will assist them in making socially responsible and well-reasoned decisions throughout their lifetimes. Nevertheless, for comprehensive school counseling programs to be effective, they must be tailored to meet the individual educational and developmental needs of each school population. The grant writers realized from the outset of conceptualizing this program that all stakeholders in the CRSD educational mission would have to have a voice and be asked to participate if the program was to meet with success. Building trust with the Alaska Native students and their families was central to program implementation. Teacher turnover in rural Alaskan school districts can run as high as 40% in any given year (Alaska Teacher Placement, 2008). Teachers coming from outside Alaska often lack the knowledge of how to teach in a culturally responsive manner. What the CRSD school counselors had to demonstrate to all stakeholders in the school system was a willingness to learn from them and then incorporate that learning into the counseling program.

The average K-8 student population in the district during the Copper River Project (CRP) was 380 students, spread across eight schools with the largest student population at the Glennallen schools (N=198) and the smallest at Chistochina and Gakona (N=11 students each). In addition to addressing the academic, career, and personal/social developmental concerns of the students, the CRP also addressed issues unique to rural schools in Alaska with a large Alaska Native population. Two of the most critical issues the CRP focused on were: (1) the cultural relevance of the program activities, and (2) the myriad of challenges facing school personnel, students and their families resulting from the effects of Fetal Alcohol Spectrum Disorder (FASD).

Public education in Alaska, like the rest of the United States, is built on a western scientific understanding of the world and is embedded with mainstream American values and cultural traditions. Many of these values and traditions are different from those held by indigenous youth. For example, two major differences apparent in the educational system are indigenous children's preference for working cooperatively with others as opposed to being in competition with them, and an emphasis on nonverbal communication (Garrett & Myers, 1996; Herring 1997; D.W. Sue & D. Sue, 2003).

Additionally, Alaska has been known for its high rate of children and adults afflicted with FASD for many years. In an assessment conducted by the Copper River Native Association during 1998, residents of all the Alaska Native villages in the region indicated that alcohol is a major social problem. Of 21 health and social problems respondents were asked to rate, lack of treatment for alcohol and alcohol abuse ranked as the number one threat to communities (James Lorence, personal communication, 5/28/2000). Furthermore, a 2002 study conducted by the State of Alaska found that 1.4 infants per 1000 live births were alcohol affected, and among Alaska Natives the rate was 4.8 infants per 1000 live births (State of Alaska Office of Fetal Alcohol Syndrome, 2005). In the Copper River Valley, the prevalence of FASD was estimated to be as high as 35% in children born to Alaska Native mothers (Alaska Native Commission, 2002). In one classroom of nine students, four of the children were identified as being FASD affected.

Students in rural communities face numerous challenges to realizing their academic goals (e.g., high absenteeism due to family responsibilities). To identify factors that might pose potential obstacles to student academic success, a needs assessment was conducted as the first step in developing the counseling program. School district personnel, students, parents and community members in the CRSD were surveyed, using a modified version of the Rye and Sparks (1999) needs assessment instruments. Eighty-five completed student responses were received for a 56.7% return rate. Sixty-four adults completed the survey for a 58.2% return rate. The assessment was conducted at the end of the 1999-2000 academic year and included in the grant proposal.

A sampling of student responses indicated that: 95% wanted help dealing with their feelings—especially anger; 94% wanted help understanding themselves; 94% wanted help understanding the dangers of drugs; 91% wanted help learning how to solve conflicts; 75% wanted help knowing how to deal with death and dying; and 66% wanted help in learning how to deal with parental divorce. Over 75% of the adult respondents thought students needed assistance understanding self; handling feelings positively; understanding the dangers of drugs; death and dying issues; parental divorce; conflict resolution; peer pressure; learning how to respond to people using drugs; and career opportunities in the community. Forty-seven percent of the adult respondents identified needing personal help with developing effective parenting skills.

While *The Comprehensive Counseling Program for Alaska Public Schools*(Alaska Department of Education & Early Development, 2001) provided the cornerstone for building the school counseling program, the success of the program was dependent on community acceptance. Therefore, a local advisory board was created to offer input on what the board members understood the needs of the children to be and what methods of education would most likely be successful. Counselors attended the annual advisory board meetings, besides meeting individually with community members when needed. In addition, the grant called for working closely with the local Native organizations, including the Copper River Native Association, the Mount Sanford Tribal Consortium, and the Chistochina Village Council. By working with these local agencies and organizations, counselors were able to develop a resource list of social services available in the area. This list was made available to all school personnel and community members for their use. Many of the key components of the CRP, if not all, are firmly based in the practice of SBFC. These included: classroom guidance activities addressing topics identified in the needs assessment; individual and small group counseling; integration of cultural awareness/appreciation activities into school activities; mentorships—adult-to-student and student-to-student; school counselor involvement in a variety of community activities; family education activities/presentations; crisis/trauma counseling services; collaboration with community service agencies and other professionals especially the Copper River region's Fetal Alcohol Syndrome/Effects Team.

Time and task analyses for the grant overall showed that program service fell into four basic categories: Classroom guidance activities (27%) focusing primarily on anger management, conflict resolution, and character education/social skills development; individual and small group counseling (28%) focusing primarily on in-school behavioral disruptions or crisis/traumatic events happening outside the school setting ; system support services (27%) which included dissemination of psycho-educational information to school personnel, parent education meetings/groups, family counseling, and participation in community events; and other activities (18%) such as travel between sites, professional development/supervision, and program paperwork. As can be seen from these figures, 82% of all program activities dealt with the delivery of counseling services to students, parents, community members-at-large and school personnel.

The Mental Health Profile (MHP) (Roberts & Morotti, 2001), a tracking instrument for identifying students' presenting concerns, was utilized as a starting point for developing many of the classroom activities and community presentations. On a yearly basis approximately 45% of all CRSD elementary school children participated in either individual or small group counseling. Of those students receiving counseling services, approximately half were seen for in-school behavioral disruptions. In addition, according to the MHP over 45% of those students receiving individual counseling presented with two or more major life stressors (e.g., parental divorce + physical abuse). "There is considerable research demonstrating that dysfunctional families (characterized by conflict, anxiety, low cohesion, and emotional problems of parents) are associated with a variety of problems affecting children" (Gerrard, 2008, p. 6). Other prominent presenting concerns included: All forms of child abuse; death or illness in family; potential harm to self or others through high risk behaviors; parental divorce, remarriage or separation issues; custody or other judicial proceedings; suicidal ideation; victimization; eating disorders; and depression.

Furthermore, the school counselors regularly provided counseling services to all community members during times of crisis. Grief recovery groups were open to all community members. These groups met weekly and were held December through February and March through May. One of the school counselors pursued specialized training in grief and loss therapy during the first summer the grant was in operation and was responsible for developing the community workshops on this topic. In 2001, information on basic grief responses of children, adolescents, and adults was made available to all community members at the funeral of a Glennallen high school student who died after a short illness.

Counseling services outside the school setting took many forms. The school counselors developed workshops on various topics and presented them in a variety of community settings. Some of the these activities included: The Parent Resource Center; the Parent Resource Hour offered bimonthly; workshops for Head Start parents on child development; community workshops on parenting skills and family relations, the effects of alcohol and drug use on children; and grief recovery work.

Communication with parents on many psycho-educational topics was also achieved through articles (e.g., the importance of children's play) in the local newspapers and school papers. In addition, a photography wall was created at each school so parents could see many of the activities the students took part in during the academic year.

Filial therapy was used to incorporate parents into the counseling process. Parents were taught how to communicate with their children through play. Counselors also visited homes and places of work to discuss counseling issues when requested by parents. Family counseling services were provided by one of the counselors, who received specialized training in play therapy, on a regular basis to eight families throughout the life of the grant.

Addressing ways to work more effectively with children impacted by FASD was a primary goal of the grant. Counselors participated in numerous professional trainings on FASD. They worked closely with local agencies especially the Copper River Native Association (CRNA). The counselors assisted in the delivery of services to identified individuals, besides taking an active role in developing various program activities to assist these individuals in improving their social skills.

Working with the CRNA, the counselors set up a FASD summer camp for children (ages 8-to-13) and their care providers emphasizing traditional Athabascan ways of life as demonstrated by community Elders. Counselors also taught transition skills to Head Start children identified as FASD throughout the school year. Likewise, to address the educational needs of this population counselors assisted in the facilitation of wrap-around services for these children.

On a school-wide basis challenge course activities (i.e., portable ropes course) were instituted as part of the regular academic program to address the unique learning needs of the FASD children. These experiential learning tasks helped to promote social skills development among all the students. In a sampling of 21 students who participated in these activities, 76% reported that the felt it helped them to learn how to work together better.

SUMMARY

During the four year time span (2000-04) of the Copper River School District's (CRSD) Elementary School Counseling Demonstration Grant (ESCDG), all the goals identified in the initial grant application were met to varying degrees of success. Overall, 10 of the 14 program objectives were accomplished as initially conceptualized in the grant application. These included: Development and delivery of guidance activities addressing topics identified in the needs assessment; delivery of individual and small group counseling services; reduction of student behaviors impeding academic performance; educational needs of Fetal Alcohol Spectrum Disordered (FASD) youth were addressed; development of a mentoring and transition program for the junior high school students; participation in numerous activities to bridge cultural gaps with local Alaska Native community; supervision and professional development opportunities for the elementary school counselors; dissemination of psycho-educational information to families; dissemination of information related to grant; and development of program accountability measures.

Objectives partially met included: Increasing students' awareness of career/occupational choices; increasing parent involvement in their student's educational experiences; ongoing meetings with local advisory board; and the development of a model for working with local agencies on an ongoing basis.

In reviewing the time and task analysis documentation throughout the life of the grant it was determined that the counselors spent 27% of their time delivering large group guidance activities, 28% in responsive services (i.e., individual and small group counseling), 27% in providing support services to teachers, administrators, and parents; this totals to 82% of their time being spent in direct student contact activities. The reminder of their time was spent in traveling (10%) from site to site, other assigned duties (7.25), and student assessments (.75%).

Community building was a primary objective of the grant. This was approached from a variety of avenues. A local advisory board was formed, parent education activities were initiated, adult-child mentorships were formed, and the counselors worked closely with numerous community agencies (e.g., Copper River Native Association, the Cross Road Medical Clinic, and Head Start) to more fully integrate the educational objectives of the school system into the wider community setting. The CRSD has a large Alaska Native population and their support of the counseling program's objectives was critical to its success. To facilitate this process the counselors engaged in many activities that utilized Native Elders to teach traditional cultural practices (e.g., dance, weaving, ice fishing). Counselors also incorporated Athabaskan values into their classroom guidance units to help bridge the cultural gap between school and the Native community.

Another primary goal of the CRSD school counseling program was to find more effective ways to meet the educational needs of FASD affected youth. The Copper River region has an exceptionally high rate of FASD children. Through the grant Deb Ivenson, a recognized expert in the State of Alaska on FASD, provided training and supervision on this subject to counselors, teachers, and parents. During 2002-03 academic year Ms. Ivenson met with the counselors on a regular basis to provide technical assistance, in addition to conducting a weeklong training on FASD.

Exposure to aggressive acts (e.g., bullying) was another obstacle to the development of a positive learning climate for CRSD students. To address this issue, the school counselors participated in specialized training on how to do functional behavioral assessments. Counselors learned how to develop individual student behavioral plans from this assessment process. Using the Mental Health Profile (Roberts & Morotti, 2001) as an indicator for counseling referrals, approximately 50% of all individual and small group counseling sessions dealt with in-school behavioral disruptions due to poor social skills development or peer relations. Other counseling needs identified through the use of this instrument included: Divorce/family issues, high-risk behaviors, high stress life experiences, all forms of abuse, and suicidal ideation. On average each year 45% of all elementary school-aged children in CRSD participated in one-on-one or small group counseling activities.

Upon review of the grant and its impact on the lives of the children attending the CRSD schools, it was the opinion of teachers, administrators, and students alike that this program produced positive change in the educational experiences of all parties involved. Due to a statewide budgetary shortfall in

2004, the CRSD was not able to continue funding the position of an elementary school counselor for the 2004-05 academic year, having to eliminate five certified teaching positions. However, support still remains high among administrators, teachers, and other educational personnel for seeking funding for at least a half-time counseling position in the elementary schools. Currently, one professional school counselor still continues to serve the educational needs of all 550 of the district's students.

In conclusion, the school is at the center of most community activities in rural Alaska. Even though the local school district was not able to continue funding the elementary school counseling position, the CRP did demonstrate that the theory and practice of SBFC could be successfully implemented in a rural Alaska school district with a sizeable indigenous population. This was accomplished largely through the efforts of the two grant funded school counselors, as demonstrated through their active participation in a variety of community activities. This engagement helped to facilitate the trust building process between school personnel and community members. It also made it possible for school and university personnel to more easily engage in ongoing evaluation of the program's effectiveness and to suggest new strategies for integrating school and community resources to all parties participating in the project. It is this very process of integrating school and community systems for the benefit of the child and his or her family that sets SBFC apart from traditional school counseling programs.

REFERENCES

Agbo, S.A. (2001). Enhancing success in American Indian students: Participatory Research at Awwesasne as part of the development of a culturally relevant Curriculum. *Journal of American Indian Education, 40,* 31-56. Retrieved June 21, 2008, from Ebsco Host database.

Alaska Department of Education and Early Development. (2001). *The comprehensive Counseling program for Alaska public schools (Rev. ed.).* Juneau, AK: Author.

Alaska Native Commission. (2002). *Commission on Child Protection.* Retrieved from http://www.hss.state.ak.us/press/2002/pr100302childprotection.htm,State of Alaska Dept. of Health & Social Services.

Alaska Native Policy Center at the First Alaskans Institute. (2004). *The status of Alaska Natives 2004: Our choices our future.* University of Alaska Anchorage: Institute of Social and Economic Research.

Alaska Teacher Placement. (2008). *Alaska teacher supply & demand.* Retrieved from http://alaskateacher.org/doku.php?id=supply_demand_&s=teacher%20turnover, University of Alaska Statewide: K-12 Outreach.

American School Counselor Association. (2003). *The ASCA national model: A framework for school counseling programs.* Alexandria, VA: Author.

Ansbacher, H.L. & Ansbacher, R.R. (1956). *The Individual psychology of Alfred Adler.* New York: Harper & Row.

Barnhardt, R. (1981). *Culture, community and the curriculum.* Retrieved from http:///www.ankn.uaf.edu/ccc2__, Alaska Native Knowledge Network, University of Alaska Fairbanks.

Barnhardt, R. (1997).*Teaching/Learning across cultures: Strategies for success.* Fairbanks, AK: Center for Cross-Cultural Studies, University of Alaska Fairbanks.

Barnhardt, R. Kawagley, A.O. (2004). Culture, chaos and complexity: Catalysts for change in indigenous education. *Cultural Survival Quarterly, 27* (4), 59-64.

Barnhardt, R. & Kawagley, A.O. (2005). Indigenous knowledge systems and Alaska Native ways of knowing. *Anthropology and Education Quarterly, 36* (1), 8-23.

Barnhardt, R., Kawagley, A.O., & Hill, F. (2000). Cultural standards and test scores. *Sharing Our Pathways, 5*(4), 1-4.

Bemak, F. & Cornely, L. (2002). The SAFI model as a critical link between marginalized families and schools: A literature review and strategies for school counselors. *Journal of Counseling and Development, 80* (3), 322-331.

Bryan, J. & Holcomb-McCoy, C. (2004). School counselors' perceptions of their involvement in school-family-community partnerships. *Professional School Counseling, 7* (3), 162-175.

Carter, M.J. & Evans, W.P. (2008). Implementing school-based family counseling: Strategies, activities and process considerations. *International Journal for School-Based Family Counseling, 1* (1), 25-39.

Carter, M.J. & Perluss, E. (2008). Developments in training school-based family counselors: The school-based family counseling (SBFC) graduate program at California State University, Los Angeles. *International Journal for School-Based Family Counseling, 1* (1), 49-56.

Chance, N. (1966). *The Eskimo of North America.* New York: Holt, Rinehart, & Winston.

Clarke, A.S. (2002). *Emotional distress among American Indian and Alaska Native students: Research findings. ERIC Digest.* Charleston, WV: ERIC Clearinghouse on Rural Education and Small Schools. (ERIC Document No. ED459988).

Dotson-Blake, K. (2010). Learning from each other: A portrait of family-school-community Partnerships in the United States and Mexico. *Professional School Counseling, 14*(1),101-114.

Erickson, F. (1987). Transformation and school success: The politics and culture of educational achievement. *Anthropology and Education Quarterly, 18* (4) Retrieved June 20, 2007 from Ebsco Host database.

Edwards, D. & Foster, M. (1995). Uniting the family and school systems: A process of empowering the school counselor. *School Counselor, 42* (4), 277-282.

Evans, W. & Carter, M. (1997). Urban SBFC: Role definition, practice applications, and training implications. *Journal of Counseling and Development, 75* (5), 366-374.

Garrett, M. & Myers, J. (1996). The rule of opposites: A paradigm for counseling Native Americans. *Journal of Multicultural Counseling and Development, 96,* 89-105.

Gerrard, B. (2008). School-based family counseling: Overview, trends, and recommendations for future research. *International Journal for School-Based Family Counseling, 1* (1)*,* 1, 6-24.

Gray, J., & Rose, W. (2012). Cultural adaptation for therapy with American Indians and Alaska Natives. *Journal of Multicultural Counseling and Development, 40*(2), 82-92.

Gysbers, N. & Henderson, P. (2000). *Developing and managing your school guidance program (3rd ed.).* Alexandria, VA: American Counseling Association.

Harkins, J.D. (1975). An analysis of the effect of the Yuk program of instruction upon student self-concept, student achievement, and parent-school rapport. *Dissertation Abstracts International, 36* (6-A), 3508-A. (University Mircofilms No. 71-5422).

Herring, R. (1997). *Counseling diverse ethnic youth: Synergetic strategies and interventions for school counselors.* New York: Harcourt Brace.

Kawagley, A.O. (1999). Alaska Native education: History and adaptation in the new millennium. *Journal of American Indian Education, 39*(1) 31-51.

Kawagley, A.O., Norris-Tull, D., & Norris-Tull, R. (1998). The indigenous worldview of Yupiaq culture: Its scientific nature and relevance to the practice and teaching of science. *Journal of Research in Science Teaching, 35*(2), 133-144.

Keys, S. & Bemak, F. (1997). School-family-community linked services: A school counseling role for changing times. *School Counselor, 44* (4), 255-263.

Kleinfeld, J. (1979). *Eskimo school on the Andreafsky: A study of effective bicultural education.* New York: Praeger.

Klug, B. & Whitfield, P. (2003). Widening the circle: Cultural relevant pedagogy for American Indian/Alaska Natives. *Journal of Multicultural Counseling and Development, 28,* 66-82.

Lipka, J. (2002). Schooling for self-determination: Research effects of including Native language and culture in the schools. *ERIC Digest.* Charleston, WV: ERIC Clearinghouse on Rural Education and Small Schools.

Lipka, J. (1998). *Transforming the culture of schools: Yup'ik Eskimo examples.* Mahwah, NJ: Lawrence Erlbaum Associates.

Manson, S. (2000). Mental health services for American Indians and Alaska Natives: Need, use, and barriers to effective care. *The Canadian Journal of Psychiatry, 45,* 617-626.

Morotti, A.A. (Fall 2006). Integrating culture into education: Self-concept formation in Alaska Native youth. *Forum on Public Policy Online.*
http://www.forumonpublicpolicy.com/papers.f06.html/child

Reyhner, J. & Jacobs, D. (2002). Preparing teachers of American Indian and Alaska Native students. *Action in Teacher Education, 24*(2), 85-93.

Roberts, Jr., W.B. & Morotti, A.A. (2001). What's your school's mental health profile? *The National Association of Secondary School Principals Bulletin, 85*(622), 59-68.

Russell, G. (2008). *Decolonizing UAF: Designing culturally responsive curriculum in a post secondary setting.* Unpublished master's project. Univ. of Alaska Fairbanks.

Rye, D. & Sparks, R. (1999). *Strengthening K-12 school counseling programs: A support systems approach.* Philadelphia, PA: Accelerated Development.

State of Alaska Office of Fetal Alcohol Syndrome. (2005). *Alaska's comprehensive FAS Project.* Retrieved from http://www.hss.state.ak.us/fas/AKfiveyrgoal/default.htm State of Alaska Health & Social Services, Office of Fetal Alcohol Syndrome.

Steen, S. & Noquera, P. (2010). A broader and broader approach to school reform: Expanded partnership roles for school counselors. *Professional School Counseling, 14*(1), 42-52.

Sue, D.W. & Sue, D. (2003).*Counseling the culturally diverse: Theory and practice* (4th ed.). New York: Wiley & Sons.

Theobald, P. & Howley, C. (1998). Public purpose and the preparation of teachers for rural schools. *The Teacher Educator, 33,* 150-164.

Trimble, J. (2012). Working with North American Indian and Alaska Native clients. (In M. Gallardo, C. Yeh, J. Trimble, & T. Parham (Eds.). *Culturally adaptive counseling Skills: Demonstrations of evidence-based practices,* 181-200. Thousand Oaks, CA:Sage.

U.S. Department of Health and Human Services (2001). Mental Health: Culture, race, and ethnicity. *Supplement to Mental Health: A Report of the Surgeon General.* Rockville, MD: Author.

Villegas, M. & Prieto, R. (2006). *Alaska Native student vitality: Community perspectives on supporting student success.* Alaska Native Policy Center at First Alaskans Institute. University of Alaska Anchorage.

Yazzie, T. (1999). Culturally appropriate curriculum: A research-based rationale. In K.G. Swisher & J.W. Tippeconnic III (Eds.), *Next steps: Research and practice to advance Indian education* (pp. 83-107). *ERIC Digest.* Charleston, WV: ERIC Clearinghouse on Rural Education and Small Schools. (ERIC Document No. ED427902)

Ziomek-Daigle, J. (2010). Schools, families, and communities affecting the dropout rate: Implications and strategies for family counselors. *Family Journal: Counseling and Therapy for Couples and Families, 18*(4), 377-385.

Chapter 44
The California State University, Los Angeles
Masters of Science Degree in
School-Based Family Counseling

Michael J. Carter and Emily J. Hernandez

OVERVIEW: This is a description of the Graduate Program in School-Based Family Counseling in the Charter College of Education at California State University, Los Angeles (CSULA). This was the first masters level graduate program to be developed in the USA.

BACKGROUND

During the latter part of the 20th century, many graduate programs were developed for School Counseling and Marriage and Family Therapy (MFT) throughout the U.S. There were also Clinical Social Work graduate programs, including some that focused on School Social Work. These programs had some similarities in knowledge base and coursework, but were distinctly different in most areas, especially in the area of clinical training.

Graduate programs in School Counseling tended to focus solely on school-aged children and on the traditional individual and group guidance/counseling model. Most School Social Work graduate programs were focused on the traditional individual diagnosis model and worked mostly with children who were "psychiatrically involved", although some worked with parents in some capacity. Most MFT graduate programs also provided clinical training in working with children and adults in individual and group therapy, with some focus on family therapy. These programs, however, typically did not specifically address school-related problems or the process of working with school personnel.

For those MFT graduate programs that did teach family therapy, training typically focused primarily upon understanding family dynamics and providing traditional family therapy to improve family functioning. Many families would come initially to address a crisis situation, but once the initial crisis had abated, they seemed to no longer understand the value of continued counseling. While school issues often constituted the presenting problem, assessments did not consistently obtain input from the teacher or other school system personnel and interventions were typically limited to the family system. Children often improved in school, perhaps as a result of the improved family functioning, but it was often difficult to retain the family's involvement in counseling because the direct benefits for the child's educational progress was not readily apparent to the family. Consequently, these families did not

---

Note: This chapter is based on an article published in the International Journal for School-Based Family Counseling, Volume I, Number 1, 2008.

experience much second order change and soon experienced another crisis, which resulted in the child experiencing further difficulties in school. Work with some families revealed obstacles such as ineffective teachers, institutional racism, or other problems related to the school system. Because of the limited role of the MFT related to the school, these obstacles were rarely dealt with and continued to plague the lives of the children and their families and they discontinued family counseling.

These experiences revealed some of the limitations of traditional family counseling approaches in resolving school-related problems. Some professionals in the schools point to these limitations and conclude that family system issues should not be dealt with by school personnel. We feel that this is a simplistic and untenable position, however, because it is clear that children are most affected by the two major systems in their lives: their family and their school. As children become adolescents, their peer group has a greater impact on their lives, but the school is still the predominant setting for their social interactions and their family situation still has a significant impact on their development.

In light of these factors, it seems clear that school support personnel (i.e., school counselors and school psychologists) can be in a unique position to provide support and direction to families and schools in their mutual goal of maximizing the development of children. At many schools, particularly at the elementary level, school counselors might be in the best position to help families because of their daily presence at the school and their institutional role within the school system. A number of obstacles appeared to prevent them from being effective in this regard, including time constraints, non-counseling job requirements, and lack of administrative support. A critical problem, however, was that most school counselors lacked the training and experience in the family counseling skills necessary to identify and address these issues effectively. Conversely, while some MFT's may have had the necessary training and experience to help families, most were unaware of how to integrate this work into the mission of the school (i.e. to maximize student's academic achievement). Because of this, most of these mental health professionals lacked the credibility necessary to effectively intervene with the school in addressing school-related problems. What was needed was a mental health professional who had the combination of MFT training and experience and the skills and competence in school counseling necessary to help families and schools to work collaboratively in specific procedures to help children overcome obstacles to learning.

THE SBFC MODEL

In the mid-1990's, several models were developed that attempted to integrate family counseling in the schools. A specific school-based family counseling (SBFC) model was described in detail over the next few years (Carter & Evans, 1995; Evans & Carter, 1997; Carter & Evans, 2008). Consistent with earlier concepts of school-based family counseling, this model essentially focuses efforts on integrating the work of family and school systems in order to address barriers to learning and maximize the social and academic development of children. Specific issues are addressed through prevention and postvention (intervention) activities with school staff, parents and students. Prevention activities focus on addressing critical issues through large group meetings with teachers, staff, parents and students. Postvention activities usually focus on addressing individual students' problems in development and behavior by first attempting to maximize collaboration between the members of the school and family systems that are most likely to influence the child's development. Developing this sense of collaboration requires the SBFC professional to help both teachers and parents to understand their shared goals and common strategies in helping children to learn.

This model focused on the process of school-based family counseling and the requisite skills and experience that school support professionals would need to effectively implement the model. Specific aspects of training were described and it was felt that school counselors and school psychologists might be able to implement the model with additional training. However, as the authors gained more experience in implementing the model in public schools, it became more apparent that the model required a professional with a high degree of specific training in school-based family counseling. While previous papers indicated that this professional might currently be a "school counselor", "school psychologist", or "marriage and family therapist", the most recent paper refers to the professional as a School-Based Family Counselor, a role that is hoped will someday be formally recognized as vital to our schools. This person might already serve as one of the professionals mentioned above, but would have to have substantial additional training and the allocation of the time necessary to fulfill the SBFC role. Most programs that train these professionals, however, do not provide the breadth of training necessary to effectively implement the multi-faceted role of the SBFC professional.

In 1997, Evans and Carter discussed the historical lack of family counseling and practicum curricula in school counseling or school psychology programs which directly inhibited most school counselors and school psychologists from engaging in counseling interactions with families. Several authors advocated additional training for school professionals to address this discrepancy, and there were attempts to include family counseling training in school counseling programs (Hinkle & Wells, 1995; Nicoll, 1992; Palmo, Lowry, Weldon & Scioscia, 1988). Helping school-based professionals adjust to the more active role of a change agent, enhancing competencies in systems theory and family intervention techniques, and providing family counseling internships also were recommended (Cleghorn& Levin, 1973; Goldenburg & Goldenburg, 1991; Hinkle, 1993. See Hinkle & Wells (1995) for a review of training competencies in family counseling for school counselors.

Another critical component in operationalizing school-based family counseling, as outlined in the articles by Carter & Evans, is the high level of personal development and complex array of skills that are required of a person who wishes to be a SBFC professional. For many of the urban school sites in which we and our interns have worked, the implicit focus of school-based family counseling has been on facilitating interactions with families where a high level of conflict and confrontation are often the norm. This requires that SBFC professionals be keenly aware of their own issues, and have resolved these sufficiently in order to remain objective when working with troubled families. Awareness of one's own personal dynamics is critical to the process of helping families and typically involves a great deal of personal exploration and development.

In light of the above factors, some advocated for greater use of family counselors in the schools. SBFC professionals, however, also must learn to deal with a wider range of concerns and constituencies in promoting student development than do most family counselors. In addition to the student's personal development, the domains of career development, academic progress, and socialization are often expected to be addressed by the school. Although focusing on student development is primary to the role of the SBFC professional, attention also must be paid to the needs and concerns of teachers, administrators, and other school personnel. These complex factors of school systems are not typically addressed in traditional MFCC training programs.

It was apparent, then, that most academic and clinical programs geared for the preparation of traditional school or family counselors did not necessarily provide the wide range of knowledge and skills required for school-based family counseling to be effective (O'Callaghan, 1994; Palmo et al., 1988; Stevens-Smith, Hinkle & Stahmann, 1993). Integration of these specialties is critical to preparing professionals who can operate effectively in school and family environments. These circumstances led to the understanding that a new type of professional training program was needed in order to improve the delivery of counseling services to families and schools. The School-Based Family Counseling Program at CSULA is an attempt to prepare professional counselors with the expertise in family therapy and school counseling necessary to implement the school-based family counseling model. In 1993, the School-Based Family Counseling Graduate Program was first developed at CSULA and included courses for the study of School Counseling and Marriage, Family, and Child Counseling. Since then, the program has been refined and modified to meet current accreditation requirements and to incorporate new findings in SBFC.

THE SBFC TRAINING PROGRAM AT CALIFORNIA STATE UNIVERSITY, LOS ANGELES

The SBFC Program at CSULA was designed to provide a diverse curriculum that would prepare counselors to act as a connective force involving families, schools, and communities in education. The CSULA SBFC program also developed close alliances with the school districts and school sites involved with SBFC intern placements. This provided the opportunity for the SBFC program to improve and adjust the curriculum, training, and supervision of interns to better meet school and community needs. The program focused on helping students to develop the specific counseling skills that facilitate the individual and systemic changes that are crucial to the school-based family counseling model. This coursework and training was primarily applied to school environments with as many school-related examples as possible. All of the coursework in the CSULA SBFC Graduate Program is contained in Appendix A and is organized according to the SBFC framework.

SEQUENCING OF STUDENT EXPERIENCES THROUGHOUT THE SBFC GRADUATE PROGRAM

At its inception, the SBFC program essentially comprised two separate programs with some overlapping course content and competencies. As we learned more about the practice of school-based family counseling, we began to integrate school counseling and family counseling into specific courses, particularly the more clinically-oriented courses such as COUN 505 (Practicum in Counseling), COUN 520 (Introduction to Family Evaluation), COUN 521 (Advanced Marriage and Family Counseling), and COUN 523 (Family Counseling Laboratory). These courses are taken in sequence and provide a continuous learning experience in School-Based Family Counseling. Following is a description of the sequence of training that a student goes through in the CSULA SBFC program.

ADVISEMENT AND APPLICATION PROCESS BEFORE ADMISSION

Before a student comes to CSULA, they can obtain advisement information from a variety of sources. A basic description of the program and requirements and timelines for admission is available from the Division office or on the Internet. In addition, prospective applicants are encouraged to speak directly with the Coordinator of the Program by making an appointment with him.

After the deadline for applications has passed, the Admissions Committee screens all applications to assess the suitability of the candidate to be included in the interview process. Areas assessed include Grade Point Average, previous experience, an autobiographical statement and their answers to specific questions regarding the applicants' view of their own strengths and weaknesses. This screening process results in a list of applicants who are best qualified for an interview. Over the past twenty years, there have been an average of between 60 and 100 applicants each year for the 24 positions. In the Spring of 2003, there were 125 applicants to the program, of which 83 were interviewed. In the Spring of 2013, while most programs experienced extreme reductions in the number of applicants, the SBFC graduate program at CSULA received over 75 applicants of which 61 were qualified enough to be interviewed. Historically, applicants with a grade point average of 3.0 or better are selected for interviews, although this depends on the quality of the applicants for each year's cohorts. Those applicants selected receive a 20-30 minute individual interview with at least two faculty members. The purpose of the interview is to assess the applicants' knowledge and experience of the Marriage and Family Therapy and the School Counseling professions, their awareness of their own cultural and historical background and their understanding of other cultural factors, and their ability to demonstrate the interpersonal skills and level of openness and self-reflection necessary to be an effective SBFC. While no specific undergraduate major is required for acceptance, there are four prerequisite courses for the program, which may be satisfied by undergraduate coursework. These include: abnormal psychology, counseling or psychological theories, statistics, and foundations of Special Education. While completion of these courses is not required before acceptance into the SBFC program, applicants are encouraged to complete the courses as soon as possible.

THE COHORT MODEL AND ORIENTATION PROCESS

One of the most important aspects of the CSULA-SBFC program is the use of "cohort" groups. Following the completion of interviews, 24 students are selected for "conditional" acceptance and separated into two cohorts of 12 students each. These cohorts go through a specific sequence of classes with at least one cohort class per quarter, usually with the same professor who also serves as their academic advisor. The cohorts are intended to provide a supportive and safe environment where students have the opportunity to learn more about themselves through close interactions with others. The cohort approach also can provide long-term opportunities to network with others as students and as professionals. This professional networking may be more critical to SBFC's because of the need to create clear and firm boundaries with school staff in order to maintain the objectivity necessary to implement the SBFC model.

Soon after acceptance, all students attend an orientation meeting that provides information about their development as SBFC's and the sequence of graduate coursework. This meeting is begun with introductions that include the student's name, where they received their undergraduate degree and what major, and one thing they like to do for fun. This last element is important because it reminds the students of the need to retain some balance in their lives even as they begin an arduous program of graduate study and training. Promoting this balanced perspective will also be important in their work with families who are often primarily focused on deficits and problems when they come in for counseling. Students are also provided information on how to become members of professional organizations such as the American Counseling Association, the California Association of Marriage and Family Therapists, and the American School Counselors Association (ASCA).

At the beginning of the Fall academic quarter, students take two courses that they must demonstrate competence in before they are "officially" admitted to the program along with Counseling 520, Introduction to Family Evaluation and Counseling. These probationary courses are Counseling 400A (Human Development across the Life Span), a lecture course in human development and Counseling 505 (Practicum in Counseling), an introductory course with role-play experience in providing and receiving counseling. If a student fails to demonstrate competence in these courses during the Fall quarter, they may be advised as to what they need to do to establish competence or they may be dismissed from the program, depending on the level of difficulty that they are experiencing with the courses.

THE SBFC COHORT SEQUENCE

The SBFC students begin their Cohort Sequence in the Fall academic quarter. As mentioned above, the first Cohort class is Counseling 505, Practicum in Counseling. This course teaches the generic clinical skills of counseling through an experiential process that encourages students to use some of their own personal issues in role-plays with their cohort-mates. This course also provides an introduction to the school counseling and family therapy professions and addresses legal and ethical aspects as well as other competencies.

Following Counseling 505, the students take Counseling 506, Individual Counseling Strategies. This course provides an orientation to individual counseling theory, crisis counseling, conflict resolution and other aspects of counseling. Following Counseling 506, students take Counseling 516, Group Counseling. Counseling 516 provides orientation and practice in understanding group dynamics and implementation of therapeutic and curriculum group processes for both small and large groups.

THE SBFC CLINICAL TRAINING EXPERIENCE

Also beginning in the Fall quarter of their first year, students take a sequence of clinically-oriented courses that comprise the majority of their clinical training in SBFC. These courses are Counseling 520, Counseling 521 and two quarters of Counseling 523. These courses are taught by one instructor. The consistency of having the same instructor throughout this sequence appears to be critical to providing an integrated and meaningful clinical training experience. It enables the instructor and student to work together for a prolonged period of time that provides close clinical supervision and mentoring of the student's development as a clinician.

Counseling 520 is an introduction to family evaluation and systems theory and school-based family counseling procedures and practice. The two cohorts are combined into one group for this lecture class. Students are given an introduction into the leadership role of counselors, and an overview of the SBFC role, definition and practice. In Counseling 520, students are taught a generic family evaluation system developed by Karpel and Strauss (1983), based on the contextual family therapy of Ivan Boszormenyi-Nagy (1981), that assesses the family in four dimensions: Factual, Individual, Systemic, and Ethical. This also involves clinical training in how to access these dimensions through interviews with the family as a whole and individually. Students are then required to write a family evaluation paper on their own family of origin. The family evaluation paper is a comprehensive, objective study of their own family of origin (i.e., the family consisting of the student, siblings, parents, and grandparents).

Students are asked to focus on a time in their family's history when a problem clearly existed and that they clearly remember. They are asked to imagine that their family sought counseling to address this problem and then to act as if they are the family counselor that the family sees. Their task is to write a comprehensive and objective evaluation of the family from the perspective of the family counselor. They must include the following: 1) a genogram of the family including the grandparents, parents' generation and the student's generation; 2) a description of the presenting problem and identification of the stage(s) in the developmental life cycle that the family was in when the problem occurred. If the family is in more than one stage, determine which is most important and why; 3) a multidimensional analysis and description of the family's current structure and dynamics (i.e. Factual, Individual, Systemic and Ethical dimensions) with respect to the presenting problem, cultural and historical factors, and any other issues that may have identified; and 4) a description of the most important issues for the family as the therapist sees them, including how the presenting problem fits in (e.g., separation anxiety resulting from Father-Child symbiosis). According to students, this assignment has proven to be one of the most difficult but informative tasks that they experience in the program. More importantly, it is critical to their analysis of counter-transference when they work directly with families later in the program (i.e.; Counseling 523).

During the Counseling 520 course, students are assigned to co-therapy teams that will operate in tandem for the next three academic quarters, which encompasses the majority of their clinical training in SBFC. There is specific discussion of co-therapy relationships and the opportunities and challenges associated with these. In their co-therapy teams, students participate in role-plays of the opening sessions, which provide the structure of the SBFC experience. They are also taught the theories of Minuchin and Bowen, Solution-focused and Narrative family therapies, and the Experiential family therapies of Whitaker and Satir.

During the quarter following Counseling 520, students take two related courses: Counseling 521 and Counseling 523. The cohorts are again combined into Counseling 521 "Advanced Marriage and

Family Counseling, which is a lecture course in marriage and family counseling that coincides with Counseling 523, which is the family counseling laboratory course. Students are separated into different sections of Counseling 523, but all have the same instructor as they have in Counseling 521. Counseling 521 provides students with additional knowledge of marriage and family theories, but also emphasizes the application of these to role of the SBFC and the specific procedures that encompass this role. These theories are more easily understood through writing case-studies that apply different family therapy theories to vignettes and by applying concepts to the specific family that the students are working with in Counseling 523. Students are also required to develop and present the results of an SBFC Evaluation with a family that they are working with in Counseling 523. This evaluation also assesses aspects of the school system and leads to the development of a home and school –oriented treatment plan with specific strategies to address these issues.

Counseling 523 is "Family Counseling Laboratory", and students take the course for two consecutive quarters, which enables them to work with families on a weekly basis for almost 6 months. These courses provide the opportunity for students to work in the CSULA Counseling and Assessment Clinic with families from the community who are referred for school-related problems in children such as behavioral or social problems or other difficulties involving the family. Students work in co-therapy teams under the direct supervision of licensed faculty members who are able to directly observe their work through live cameras and videotape. The students receive clinical supervision before and after seeing two families, and the supervisor at times may model appropriate techniques through direct interaction with the families. During the first quarter of Counseling 523 in the Winter quarter, students complete a family evaluation, contact the school to complete the SBFC Interview, and complete an assessment of school related issues. They then develop a specific SBFC Treatment plan that leads to initial implementation of SBFC strategies.

During the second quarter of Counseling 523 in the Spring quarter, students continue to work with the same families to evaluate and monitor the progress of the family and school in addressing the presenting problem. This provides the opportunity to more fully explore and address deeper issues related to the family and schools' functioning that may affect the child's development. These may include marital conflict, communication problems within the family or school system or other issues such as domestic violence, substance abuse or gang involvement. Students learn about the process of termination and referral for additional interventions and how to help the family to follow through with recommendations through the use of a report that is presented and given to the family at the final session. Some families are able to continue counseling at the Clinic and the student-clinicians of these families learn how to transfer these cases to other counselors. The COUN 523 courses are the cornerstone of our clinical training in school-based family counseling.

During the Winter and Spring quarters of the first year, students also undergo preparation to begin their fieldwork experiences. This includes discussion of the requirements of fieldwork, appropriate placements, how to be proactive in the supervision process, and the need for malpractice insurance. These and additional components of fieldwork are contained in the Fieldwork Manuals for School Counseling and Marriage and Family Therapy. These manuals contain all of the competencies that students must learn to demonstrate and forms for evaluation and documentation.

Upon completion of all coursework, students typically take the Comprehensive Examinations for the Masters of Science degree. Students are allowed to complete a thesis in place of these exams, but they are strongly encouraged to begin this process in their first year and only if they feel confident in their writing skills and level of self-motivation. The Comprehensive Examinations consist of a Core Exam and the SBFC Option Exam and is modeled after the California State Board of Behavioral Sciences' Exam for the MFT license. The Core Exam is multiple-choice in format and covers all of the Required Core classes. The SBFC Option Exam is a case study format that assesses their ability to demonstrate their understanding and application of school counseling and family counseling theories and diagnosis of individual pathology through the use of the DSM-IV.

CONTENT AREAS IN THE CSULA SBFC PROGRAM

In addition to the courses described above, the CSULA SBFC graduate program focuses on developing the following content areas:

1) Experiences that enable the counselors to learn more about their own cultural and historical backgrounds to identify biases that they may have in their own worldview and how these might affect their interactions with others. In order to be effective in today's urban schools, counselors must be open to utilizing information from a number of sources without prejudice in order to forge relevant and workable solutions. While this aspect of counselor development is infused within most courses in the program, courses that specifically address this area are Counseling 503, Counseling 505, and Counseling 520. Counseling 503 is a course in Sociological and Cultural Factors in Counseling that has a primary emphasis on helping students to become more aware of their own cultural identity and bias as well as learning more about other cultures.

2) Training in the skills of facilitation and mediation that would allow the SBFC to conduct large group meetings to address issues critical to the school and community. Students are required to make a number of presentations within their courses, but specific training in these areas occurs in Counseling 516, Counseling 520, and Counseling 521. Counseling 516 is the Group Counseling course that includes facilitation and mediation in groups and also requires the students to present to the large group.

3) The study of systems, with specific training of those skills necessary for interacting effectively with families, educational institutions, and community and government agencies. This would include understanding the structure and processes of families and other systems, how to facilitate organizational change within systems, and how to improve collaboration among systems. These areas are primarily addressed with the Counseling 520, Counseling 521 and Counseling 581. Counseling 581 is the Seminar in Pupil Personnel Services course that addresses issues related to the school system.

4) Training in the process of improving the school-family-community connection. This involves providing counseling and educational services to the family at the school site, fostering a team approach within the school to maximize student success, and networking with community-based organizations. While these areas are initially addressed in Counseling 520 and Counseling 521, the majority of this training occurs during students' fieldwork experiences in school counseling and marriage and family therapy (Counseling 586S and Counseling 589).

5) Specific instruction in the range of family dynamics that affect a child's cognitive, emotional and social development. This would include identification of high-risk behaviors, prevention strategies, and effective interventions. Theoretical concepts are applied to school-related situations in order to maximize their relevance to counseling in the schools. For example, discussion of family counseling techniques could revolve around presenting problems that impact child success in the classroom. This specific focus on school-related content also would provide a more extensive knowledge base of specific family factors and their relation to school problems. These areas are primarily addressed in Counseling 520, Counseling 521, and Counseling 523, with additional training as part of the students' fieldwork experiences in school counseling and marriage and family therapy (Counseling 586S and Counseling 589).

Additional training components are also included to help fulfill the multifaceted role of the SBFC. These include the development and implementation of classroom-focused prevention and intervention strategies; crisis counseling; support for student and staff transitions; the identification of community resources and the appropriate use of referrals in school settings; and ethical, legal, and "turf" issues related to school-based family counseling.

AN INTERVIEW WITH A GRADUATE OF THE CSULA SBFC GRADUATE PROGRAM

Recently, an interview was conducted with a graduate of the CSULA SBFC Graduate Program, Emily Hernandez, MS, MFT. Following are some sample responses to questions about the graduate's experience in the program.

Interviewer (Carter): "Could you describe your experience as a graduate student in the Cal State LA school-based family counseling program from the beginning?"

Emily: "I had a really great experience in the program... One of the things about the program that I think I attribute my career successes to had to do with the cohort approach that they used. It was a small group of students attached to one advisor that we received support from throughout the entire program. Having access to your professors and your instructors on a regular basis, they were there for you whenever you needed anything. With the cohort, you not only become very good friends and colleagues but it's also a professional network. When there's a job opening and they're looking for someone, the first people that they contact are your cohort members, people that you've experienced learning with and have grown close to. To this day, I still keep in contact with most of the members from my cohort."

Interviewer:"What was the clinical training in family therapy like in both lecture and in your lab experience?"

Emily: "I'll never forget that class (COUN 520-Introduction to Family Evaluation) because it incorporated a lot of theory but there was also a lot of application as well and a lot of writing. The class really challenged you to use the theory and apply it to your writing. I remember that we learned to use the genogram and I was thinking, what am I going to use this for? I've never seen anybody use this? Then, when I was actually doing therapy as an intern in my clinical supervision groups, a lot of the other people in the group that didn't come from our program, they didn't even know what a genogram was or even how to use it. So that was something where I felt like I had an edge on the others."

"We worked in the clinic that was on campus and everybody was really nervous about the whole thing and we had a partner, a co-therapist. It was interesting because it was taking what you learned in the books and then actually going into a supervised setting that had a video camera in each of the rooms. We were nervous just about the process of being in front of a live person, and being videotaped, but we were very well prepared for that first session. I remember that we talked and processed over and over what to do in the first session. It wasn't like we were just thrown in;we were well equipped in terms of what to do. Once we got in there, things fell into place and all the nervousness and anxiety about knowing that you're being watched and on camera, it just kind of went away. It also ended up being very relieving because if you did need assistance, you knew that you just had to look up and glance towards the camera and within seconds there would be your advisor assisting you. One of the things that we did experience in that clinical setting was doing therapy in Spanish. We had a young woman where we had to do a suicidal assessment with her. It was a very intense setting, but I felt fortunate that I got to experience that with my advisor and professor kind of with me but not really with me. It was kind of like somebody holding your hand, but on the other side of the door."

Interviewer:"How prepared did you feel for field work with marriage and family therapy and school counseling when you finished your first year when it was time for fieldwork?"

Emily: "In the beginning of the program when we would talk about fieldwork, I was nervous about it. I was thinking, "What am I going to do, I don't know anything?" But by the time fieldwork came around, those feelings were completely gone. I think part of it was because we were prepared so much. There was a lot of discussion in our advisory group; you knew what to expect and you were prepared to go into the situation: what to say, what to bring, and what you would be doing. I felt that it was a continued learning experience. It was an extension of what I was doing in the clinic and in my classes. I felt really well prepared for the fieldwork setting."

"My fieldwork placement was a really unique experience because I feel that I got to work with so many different staff at the school. I worked with their school psychologist and I did a lot of job shadowing and really just understanding how a school works. Every school has its own culture and its own way of working and I really had never been in that setting. I also got to do home visitations, which was a really good experience because when you talk about school-based family counseling, you can't get more real than going on home visits, sitting in a family's living room with a child, the family, and just getting into some family counseling right in their home. It's really bringing the school into the home. That is, in essence, school-based family counseling. I did classroom observations in different classrooms and I was able to see students and how they may act or behave differently when they're around their peers. I got the opportunity to go into classrooms and work with different teachers on classroom management and some behavior support for students. One of the classes that we took, the behavior analysis class (COUN 501), was really helpful for me to develop a solid foundation in understanding behavior. It was just one fieldwork experience, but in so many different capacities I was really able to apply so many things from the courses that we took. "

Interviewer: "How prepared did you feel after graduating for your first job in the schools?"

Emily:"I felt very prepared. I learned about the job when I was asked to come into an orientation meeting a quarter before the program actually started. We had guest speakers that were in the field talk about what they had done with their degree. What are the potentials and the options that you have with this credential, with this degree? One person was a PSA counselor: Pupil, Services and Attendance counselor. When the guest speaker described her job in schools, that she works with families and that they do home visitation, I said that's what I want to do. So when we graduated, I started a position as a PSA counselor with the Los Angeles Unified School District. Upon starting that position, there was really no training at all. You were given an assignment, I actually had 3 schools, and you sink or swim. Had I not had the extensive training and experience I got through the program, I think I would not have been prepared for this experience."

Interviewer: "How much do you think your experience in the clinic with families while you were at Cal State LA prepared you in your job in comparison to peers who had not received that training?"

Emily: "I definitely felt better prepared and it was very apparent in supervision groups. Things that other interns were struggling with or needed more experience with, I felt confident in those areas. I felt like I had a strong foundation in terms of building more knowledge of what we were learning in our intern supervision groups. I feel that without my training I would not have been successful at that job. I had peers that were still trying to learn the criteria for some of the different diagnoses and how to ask questions to get there and I just felt that that was something that was a strength for me because of our classes. It has been crucial for me in terms of getting jobs, passing my licensure exam, and working as a therapist. The program really emphasized a systems approach. You can't just work with the child, you need to work with the whole child, the family and the school. I felt that I was prepared once I went into the school system to work with teachers because I had already done that in my fieldwork. I felt confident in what to do with the teachers and the experience of working in classrooms so I was able to negotiate those things once I was in a school setting. I felt comfortable working with parents and I feel that they felt comfortable in working with me also. With administrators, it really had to do with professionalism, our level of knowledge and what we learned at our fieldwork. Because the fieldwork experience was a quality experience, you knew what to do when you were in a real setting. I worked with the principal and assistant principals and really integrated the fieldwork experience into the school setting. I think that because of that, I had a very positive experience at the school. After my first year working with LA Unified as a PSA counselor, I felt comfortable in managing and working with administrators because I had already done it and understood expectations. Working with administrators is crucial to our role, because they need to understand and value the role of support services for students."

Interviewer: "How prepared did you feel for getting a job in family counseling or as an MFT?"

Emily: "After my first year with the school system, I really wanted to pursue my marriage and family therapy license, and wanted to get some core clinical experience. I had always wanted to work in foster care and with probation youth. So I transitioned from the school system and got a job in foster care and probation and found that I was really able to apply what I learned in my classes in that setting. When I returned to the school system, I came back much more prepared, really capable of handling any situation. There were some students, foster youth, that were referred for therapeutic services and I was able to provide therapy not only to the foster youth, but also to their biological parents to help on the path to family reunification. So that was a really interesting experience in working with the biological parents, minors and foster parents. This was not easy. There were some pretty volatile situations that we worked through. And that's where I was able to use my genogram and a lot of what we learned in our family therapy classes."

Interviewer: "Is there anything else you would like to add about your graduate experience at Cal State Los Angeles?

Emily: "One of the things I just wanted to emphasize was the cohort experience, how invaluable that was to the program. One of the other things is the relationships with your advisor and with your peers. Even though it is a big university and a big program in an urban area, it didn't feel that way. It felt intimate and informal even though it's a very formalized and structured program and could seem very overwhelming. The three years went by so quickly because I felt that you were supported through the whole process. I also want to focus on the quality of the education and knowledge level of the professors. I really think that this program does an excellent job, is affordable, and delivers quality education in comparison to other programs, especially in terms of preparing to pursue the licensure in marriage and family therapy. When I studied for my licensing exam, I started reviewing all of my notes, our papers that we had to write and our books from the program. That's how I studied for my licensure exam, and I passed on the first time. I used our course materials from five years prior, coupled with the experience I had obtained, and my clinical supervision, and I passed. That's how I feel about the caliber and quality of the program, it was a rigorous program that prepared you for the professional world. If you fully engage in the program, and it's difficult not to because of the structure and close relationships with professors and peers, you will receive an excellent preparation in this profession. You will have a deep understanding of the theoretical concepts and be able to apply what you have learned. The program also gave me options. I completed the Pupil Personnel Credential in School Counseling, the Child Welfare and Attendance Authorization and the MFT coursework because I wanted to have options in life, have the most opportunities and doors open to me. I feel that I was very well prepared for my future because of this program and that I had many paths available to pursue because of it."

ACCREDITATION OF THE SBFC GRADUATE PROGRAM

The SBFC program is clearly a work in progress and has undergone many modifications in order to be consistent with the changing requirements of state agencies, which regulate school counseling and marriage and family therapy. The Masters of Science degree in SBFC satisfies the academic requirement for the California State Marriage and Family Therapist (MFT) License, which also requires 3000 hours of supervised experience, at least 1500 of which must be completed after earning the Masters degree.

Imbedded in this Masters degree is all the coursework necessary to earn the California State Pupil Personnel Services (PPS) Credential in School Counseling with the Advanced Authorization in Child Welfare and Attendance (CWA). The PPS credential provides the qualifications necessary to work as a school counselor in grades K-12 in the public schools. The CWA authorization is necessary in many school districts in order to work in the Pupil Services and Attendance (PSA) divisions.

In California, the Marriage and Family Therapy License is administrated by the California State Board of Behavioral Sciences (BBS), which requires that the Masters degree address specific content areas, some of which were recently added in August 2012. In addition to these requirements, the SBFC program must also meet all of the requirements for the California State Pupil Personnel Services (PPS) Credential in School Counseling with Advanced Authorization in Child Welfare and Attendance. The California Commission on Teacher Credentialing (CTC) administrates this credential.

Over the years, the CTC has made major and extensive revisions in these requirements, which have been integrated into the CSULA SBFC Graduate program. The Masters of Science in Counseling: MFT Option has been approved by the BBS since its inception and was recently recognized as having met all of the new BBS requirements for MFT graduate programs. Since 1993, the School-Based Family Counseling Graduate Program has also been accredited by the Council on Accreditation of Counseling and Related Educational Programs (CACREP) for School Counseling.

EMPLOYMENT OF SBFC GRADUATES

Upon completion of the SBFC program, most graduates obtain jobs as School Counselors or Marriage and Family Therapy Interns without any formal assistance from the CSULA program. We are in the process of compiling data regarding our graduates and the evaluations of their competence by employers, but anecdotal information is uniformly positive. Despite severe funding shortages in most of Los Angeles' school districts and in many non-profit counseling agencies, almost all of our recent graduates who have applied for counseling positions have been hired. In addition, some of our students, usually those who are bilingual, are offered jobs while they are still in the process of completing their degree, usually as a result of their fieldwork experiences.

Discussions with administrators at these schools indicate their appreciation of our students' clinical skill and creativity in meeting the needs of the students and the school staff. While most school counselors deal primarily with administrative functions and paperwork, our students seem to be chosen to deal with the major crises and conflicts that occur at their school. We believe that this is because of their clinical experience in working with families during the COUN 523 courses. The cases that our students deal with often include intense issues of crisis and conflict including domestic violence, chronic substance abuse, severe marital and familial conflict and gang involvement and violence. Students report that the experience of working with these families in a relatively safe learning environment with the support of a co-therapist and direct supervision provides them with a great deal of confidence when they work in the schools or other settings.

DEVELOPMENT OF SBFC POSITIONS

One of the most frequent questions we are asked is about the existence of School-Based Family Counselor positions in the schools. As discussed previously, there is no formal classification such as this, although we look forward to the day when this is a reality. There are, however, many school counselors who are doing this work on either a part-time or full-time basis. For the past 20 years, we have tried to develop SBFC positions through two major pathways: through direct interactions with school district boards and administrators and through continued clinical training and support in SBFC practice for graduates after they are hired as school counselors. We have actively promoted the SBFC concept as a part of several school reform initiatives in the hopes of creating more SBFC positions in the schools. We have not been very successful in this regard for several reasons, but most often because of the low priority that most California districts place on school counseling. Some of this may be related to the common perception that school counselors do not make a significant impact on the lives of most students and teachers. We believe that this perception is often inaccurate, particularly when the counselor has received extensive clinical training in working with systems. The success of our recent graduates in the schools seems to support our view and we have seen more and more administrators and school boards who seem to be interested in the SBFC concept.

The most effective means of implementing the SBFC concept has been through the work of our graduates when they are hired as school counselors. For the past 20 years, we have provided some graduates with ongoing training and consultation in the SBFC model through weekly group meetings with SBFC faculty. In order to receive this training, the graduates must obtain written administrator approval to be included in this supervision group. When these graduates begin their employment, we usually advise them to assess the school climate and the willingness of the administrators to change the way they provide school counseling services.

Some graduates have directly presented the SBFC concept to their administrators as an alternative to the traditional approach and have obtained permission to implement the SBFC model, although typically at a somewhat reduced level. This reduction is usually caused by other duties of school counselors such as scheduling of classes, or monitoring of playground interactions. Most of our graduates, however, enter jobs whose duties are already rigidly proscribed by the school staff or administrators. We encourage these graduates to work within this existing paradigm until they have earned the familiarity and respect of the school staff. This is frequently the most critical aspect of the process of altering the status quo of the school system. Once the graduate has been accepted, they can then offer alternative strategies to replace those that may be ineffective. This requires an evaluation of the success of current procedures and explanation of the alternative SBFC model to school staff and parents.

For example, one graduate entered a job where the principal gave her a list of the 30-40 groups with students that she was expected to run each week. She initially accepted this challenge, but also began to take data on the effectiveness of these group interventions, particularly in terms of the rate of recidivism for behavior problems and subsequent re-referral for services for these students. After six months, she presented this data to the principal with an explanation of possible causes and strategies to address these. Because she had already established her credibility as a team player and as a counselor who was clinically capable and willing to address the most difficult crises and conflicts with the school, she was allowed to pilot a new approach. This graduate now spends about 70 % of her time involved in SBFC activities.

Another graduate began working as a School Psychologist (she had earned this credential prior to her enrollment in the SBFC program). She was allowed one day a week to provide counseling to the Special Education students and soon began to integrate SBFC procedures into her work. She did not receive much support from administrators, however, until she was able to show data indicating that there was a significant reduction in student problems and fewer fair hearing cases against the district for those families that she worked with. The district ended up hiring her as their District Counselor with a primary emphasis on working with members of high-risk families.

CHALLENGES AND SOLUTIONS

There have been a number of challenges to training graduate students and others in SBFC. One of the biggest challenges has been the dual-faceted nature of school-based family counseling and the tendency for organizations to work within a "silo" mentality where counseling is considered either family therapy or school guidance counseling. It is often difficult for administrators and practitioners in the schools and mental health agencies to conceptualize how a single practitioner can operate effectively in both of these clinical environments. This has also been a challenge for those institutions responsible for accrediting MFT and school counseling graduate programs.

For example, the Council on Accreditation of Counseling and Related Educational Programs (CACREP) has accredited the CSULA SBFC graduate program in School Counseling for over 20 years. In 2003, the CSULA SBFC program intended to apply for accreditation by CACREP's International Association of Marriage and Family Therapists (IAMFT) in MFT as well as CACREP's accreditation in School Counseling. After receiving the program documents, however, there seemed to be much confusion on the part of the CACREP evaluators as to how one program could satisfy the content areas in both fields. For example, how could a Group Therapy course cover group counseling with children in a school setting and with adults in a mental health agency or how could a course in Family Counseling with Children satisfy the content of a course in Guidance Counseling with Elementary School Students? Despite our explanations, this confusion appeared to have the potential to sabotage both accreditation processes, so the application for CACREP accreditation in MFT was withdrawn. We were again reaccredited in School Counseling by CACREP and continue to have separate accreditation by the California State Board of Behavioral Sciences.

SUMMARY

The CSULA SBFC training program has made a great deal of progress over the past 10 years in learning how to train counselors to become effective agents of change in families and school. There also have been many obstacles along the way. These include bureaucratic challenges in schools and universities, fear of schools in dealing directly with families who are experiencing difficulty, and some reticence on the part of many school counselors and administrators to change the way they operate. We believe, however, that confronting these obstacles in an open and cooperative manner often provides an opportunity to gain consensus on the need to reach out to children and their families to improve the quality of their lives and the sense of accomplishment of our hard-working school staffs. We feel that most of our graduates can be highly effective agents of change who can directly address many of the barriers to student achievement while also improving the quality of the home-school partnership. We are still in our infancy, but look forward to continued improvement in our ability to train clinically adept SBFC professionals who can improve our schools if given the opportunity.

REFERENCES

Boszormenyi-Nagy, I. (1981). Contextual therapy: Therapeutic leverages in mobilizing trust. *The American Family*.

Carter, M.J., & Evans, W.P. (1995). School-based family counseling: Helping teachers improve student success in the urban classroom. *National Forum of Teacher Education Journal, 5*, 3-11.

Carter, M.J., & Evans, W.P. (2008). *Implementing School-Based Family Counseling: Strategies, activities, and process considerations.* International Journal for School-Based Family Counseling, Volume 1, Number 1.

Cleghorn, J., & Levin, S. (1973). Training therapists by setting learning objectives. *American Journal of Orthopsychiatry, 43*, 439-446.

Evans, W.P. & Carter, M.J. (1997). Urban school-based family counseling: Role definition, practice applications, and training implications. *Journal of Counseling and Development, May/June (75)*, 366-374.

Goldenburg, I., & Goldenburg, H. (1991). *Family Therapy: Overview* (3rd ed.). Pacific Grove, CA: Books/Cole.

Hinkle, J. S. (1993). Training school counselors to do family counseling. *Elementary School Guidance & Counseling, 27*, 252-257.

Hinkle, J. S., & Wells, M. E. (1995). *Family counseling in the schools: Effective strategies and interventions for counselors, psychologists and therapists.* University of North Carolina at Greensboro, NC: ERIC/CASS.

Karpel, M. & Strauss, E. (1983). *Family Evaluation.* New York: Psychology Press.

Nicoll, W. G. (1992).A family counseling and consultation model for school counselors.*The School Counselor, 39*, 351-361.

O'Callaghan, J. B. (1994). School-based collaboration with families: An effective model for a society in crisis. *The Family Journal: Counseling and Therapy for Couples and Families, 2*, 286-300.

Palmo, A. J., Lowry, L. A., Weldon, D. P., & Scioscia, T. M. (1984). Schools and family: Future perspectives for school counselors. *The School Counselor, 34*, 272-284.

Stevens-Smith, P., Hinkle, J. S., & Stahmann, R. F. (1993). A comparison of professional accreditation standards in marriage and family counseling and therapy.*Counselor Education and Supervision, 33*, 116-126.

APPENDIX A   CSULA courses across the SBFC Model

School Intervention
COUN 501 Behavior Analysis in School, Home and Agency Settings (4)
COUN 503 Sociological and Cultural Factors in Counseling (4)
COUN 505 Practicum: Counseling (3)
COUN 589 Site Practicum in Marriage, Family and Child Counseling (6)
COUN 403 The Psychosocial Dynamics of Child Maltreatment and Family Violence (4)
COUN 506 Individual Counseling Strategies (4)
COUN 516 Group Counseling (4)
COUN 522 Family Counseling with Children (4)
COUN 581 Seminar: Leadership in Pupil Personnel Services (4)
COUN 586S Supervised Field Experience in School Counseling (9)
COUN 586W Supervised Field Experience in Child Welfare and Attendance (3)
COUN 465 Addiction Counseling (4)

School Prevention
COUN 400A Lifespan Human Development (4)
COUN 400B Lifespan Human Development (4)
COUN 428 Measurement Issues in Counseling (4)
COUN 503 Sociological and Cultural Factors in Counseling (4)
COUN 529 Principles of Research and Program Evaluation in Counseling (4)
COUN 460 Laws Relating to the Child and Family (4)
COUN 557 Career Education and Guidance in School Counseling (4)
COUN 581 Seminar: Leadership in Pupil Personnel Services (4)
COUN 586S Supervised Field Experience in School Counseling (9)
COUN 465 Addiction Counseling (4)

Family Intervention

COUN 505 Practicum: Counseling (3)

COUN 589 Site Practicum in Marriage, Family and Child Counseling (6)

COUN 403 The Psychosocial Dynamics of Child Maltreatment and Family Violence (4)

COUN 520 Introduction to Family Evaluation and Counseling (4)

COUN 521 Advanced Family and Marriage Counseling (4)

COUN 522 Family Counseling with Children (4)

COUN 523 Family Counseling Laboratory (6)

COUN 538 Seminar: Methods of Diagnostic Assessment in Counseling (4)

COUN 539 Psychopharmacology for Counselors (3)

COUN 552 Counseling and Human Sexuality (4)

COUN 589 Site Practicum in Marriage, Family and Child Counseling (3)

COUN 465 Addiction Counseling (4)

Family Prevention

COUN 503 Sociological and Cultural Factors in Counseling (4)

COUN 400A Lifespan Human Development (4)

COUN 400B Lifespan Human Development (4)

COUN 460 Laws Relating to the Child and Family (4)

COUN 529 Principles of Research and Program Evaluation in Counseling (4)

COUN 521 Advanced Family and Marriage Counseling (4)

COUN 552 Counseling and Human Sexuality (4)

COUN 589 Site Practicum in Marriage, Family and Child Counseling (3)

COUN 465 Addiction Counseling (4)

Chapter 45
Mission Possible:
a 30 Year University-Schools Partnership in School-Based Family Counseling

Brian A. Gerrard

OVERVIEW: *This chapter describes the University of San Francisco Mission Possible Program which, over a 28 year period, provided school-based family counseling to more than 100 Bay area schools and 10,000 children and families.*

BACKGROUND

I first learned about school-based family counseling (SBFC) while I was a graduate student in the Counseling Psychology Department at the University of British Columbia in 1974. The chair of the department, Dr. John Friesen, had hired me as a research assistant and assigned me the task of helping him develop a grant proposal to develop a community counseling center that would be physically located on a school campus in Richmond School District. I remember preparing a drawing of what the counseling center floor plan would look like. The Center would be staffed by UBC masters and doctoral counseling students who would provide counseling to the school students and their families. The idea of placing family counseling students on a school campus seemed to me quite brilliant.

In 1983, while working as an assistant professor in the Counseling Psychology Department in the School of Education at the University of San Francisco, I received a small grant for the Balboa High School Family Counseling Project. The grant paid for a licensed psychologist to supervise 10 USF masters level marital and family therapy students who were placed at Balboa High School (a public school in San Francisco) in order to work with the students and families. The project was a disaster because none of the 2 school counselors in the school would refer to my SBFC professionals. I realized later that the principal was in conflict with the school counselors and had an agenda (that I had missed) which was to have the USF SBFC professionals provide the kind of counseling that the principal felt was lacking.

In 1984, together with my colleague Dr. Emily Girault, we initiated the *Catholic Schools Family Counseling Project*. The impetus for the project came when a Catholic principal phoned me (I was the MFT Coordinator at the time) and asked me if I could send her school a counselor. When she told me that she met monthly with a group of 14 Catholic school principals in a group called the Mission Cluster schools (so called because these schools were based in the Mission district of San Francisco- a mostly Latino, low-income area), I asked her if they could use 14 counselors (as that was how many I had in my family therapy class). I attended the very next principals' meeting in order to explain the type of services a SBFC professional could provide. I felt a little intimidated when I met with the principals and found they were all nuns wearing white habits. I was moved by the way we all held hands around a large conference table during an opening prayer. I made a 15 minute presentation and, noting what seemed to be a stony-faced response from the principals, returned to the university. The contact principal called the next day and asked to have the 14 SBFC professionals assigned to the schools. This was the beginning of the program we called *Mission Possible*.

PROGRAM DESCRIPTION

1984-1986: THE CATHOLIC SCHOOLS FAMILY COUNSELING PROJECT

Basic Program Structure: In 1984 the basic structure of the Mission Possible Program consisted of:
1) MFT trainees in the second year of a 2 year MFT degree program. During the second year each MFT trainee was expected to find a community placement where they could see clients under licensed supervision and accumulate about 200 hours of client contact. About half of the Mission Possible trainees come from USF and the rest come from other bay area universities.
2) A licensed mental health professional who provided group supervision (2 hours per week) to the trainees (with a maximum of 8 in a supervision group).
3) Schools willing to accept MFT trainees as the school counselor
4) An administrative director who provided program oversight
  Each SBFC trainee counselor was placed in a school for 2 days a week (approximately 6 hours a day). The SBFC trainee provided individual counseling for students who were self referred or referred by teachers, parents, or the principal. Each school was expected to provide a room for private counseling sessions for the students and their parents/guardians.

Program Funding: During this early phase pilot of the program we had no funding. The main expense of the licensed supervisor was initially covered by the Dean of the School of Education who loaned us Dr. George Boisson, an organizational consultant he had retained. Dr. Boisson had a doctorate in Organizational Development, was a licensed MFT, and had been an Assistant Superintendent of the San Francisco Unified School District. At the end of academic year 1984-85 the Catholic principals were enthusiastic about the program and asked for trainees to return the following year. In our discussions with principals, we noticed that they frequently expressed appreciation of the fact that the SBFC professionals were able to help students with family problems that seemed to be impeding the students' learning.
  In 1986 Dr. Boisson implemented a fee-based strategy by asking the principal to pay something for the counseling service. No school was denied service because of an inability to pay. If a school could not pay initially, Dr. Boisson would place the SBFC professional in the school during the fall semester for free. In the spring, Dr. Boisson would meet with the principal again and ask if the school could pay any amount. Some schools initially paid only $100 or $200 for 200 hours of counseling service. Invariably, the principals found the SBFC counseling service to be of value and they would be able to secure funding to help pay for the service.
  Because we were working with mostly poor schools, it was necessary to obtain foundation grant funding to underwrite program expenses. Our Dean was supportive of the program and facilitated our obtaining grant-writing assistance from the university's Development division. From about 1990 to 2011 the average amount of grants received by Mission Possible has been $20,000 per year. During that same period the funding received from schools has averaged about $2500 per school. That is, the funding for the program has always been a joint schools and university effort. The university makes an additional contribution in the form of: a) a quarter time release for the Executive Director (who is a faculty member); b) two graduate assistants; and c) payment of insurance coverage for the staff and trainees/interns.

1986-1990: THE SAN FRANCISCO SCHOOLS FAMILY COUNSELING PROGRAM

During this period the program expanded into public schools. The 30 schools participating in Mission Possible at this point were equally divided between Catholic and public schools. Consistent funding from foundations and an increase in funding support from the participating schools had now put the program on a solid financial footing. Because the number of participating schools had doubled, the number of supervision groups increased to four. The additional funding also provided for individual supervision (1 hour per week) for each trainee. An in-service training program was added to balance their academic family counseling training with training on how to work within the culture of Catholic and public schools.

1991-2013: THE CENTER FOR CHILD & FAMILY DEVELOPMENT

During this phase the Center was given a $15,000 donation from our Dean, Dr. Paul Warren, to enable us to build a counseling center in the basement of St. Paul's Church in the mission district. At this location the Center for Child & Family Development (CCFD) maintained its administrative headquarters, in addition to two Mission Possible service programs: the School Outreach Program and the Community Counseling Center. The School Outreach Program was a continuation of the basic original Mission Possible program that places SBFC trainees in schools. The Community Counseling Center (CCC) program was added in order to provide a place for SBFC counseling for a) parents/guardians who could not come to a school for counseling during the day, and b) more serious cases that could be referred to the CCC for SBFC by more experienced interns.

Currently, the organizational structure of the Center for Child and Family Development is shown as Chart 45.1. The Center is affiliated with the Counseling Psychology Department but is formally administered under the office of the Dean for the School of Education. The mission statement of the Center is:

> The USF Center for Child and Family Development is committed to the academic, psychological, social, and spiritual development of children and families through teaching, research, and direct service programs in School-Based Family Counseling. Our purpose is to provide children and families (particularly under-served children and families) with a variety of culturally sensitive family counseling services).

As can be seen in the organizational chart Mission Possible is the name for the two main SBFC direct service programs: the School Outreach Program and the Community Counseling Center. There are, however, three additional programs. The Oxford Symposium in SBFC which is an international SBFC association sponsored by the Institute for School-Based Family Counseling (and co-sponsored by the CCFD). The Oxford Symposium, which meets at Brasenose College, Oxford University in even years, and other international sites in odd-numbered years, is an association of more that 100 SBFC practitioners and scholars from 15 countries. The Program for the Prevention of School and Family Violence is coordinated by Cloe Madanes. The TEAM (Therapists Educating and Motivating) Program, coordinated by Dr. Nancy Rosenbledt, provides psycho-educational workshops to schools.

During this 20 year period the CCFD has been based at 5 different locations and is currently located on the 4th floor of Mercy High School, a Catholic girls' school, in San Francisco. Since 1984 Mission Possible has served more than 10,000 children and their families in over 100 bay area schools. Approximately 30 schools have hired their Mission Possible trainee as the school counselor.

RELATIONSHIP TO THE SBFC MODEL

This approach to SBFC is described in Chapter 1 as School-Sited: University-School Collaboration. The SBFC professionals in *Mission Possible* work mainly in the Family-Intervention focus area. This is because these MFT trainees receive extensive coursework in their academic program on working remedially with children and families. In most California MFT programs there is no coursework related to working in

Chart 45.1 Organizational Chart for USF Center for Child and Family Development

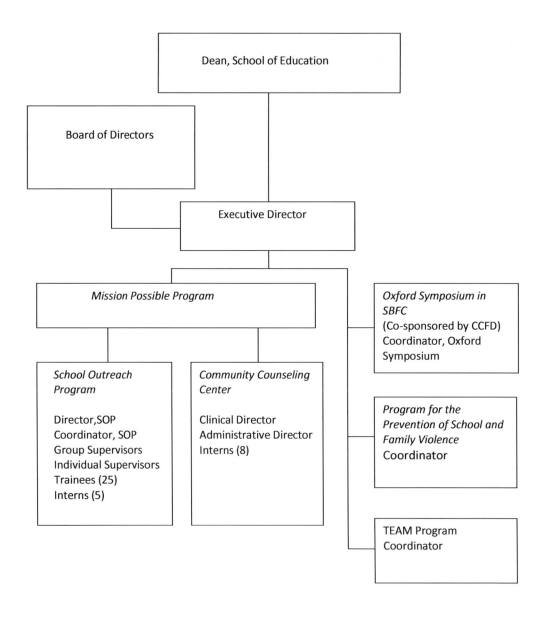

schools, as that is seen as a separate field of counseling, i.e. school counseling. The average caseload of a Mission Possible SBFC professional is 14 students (in a school of an average size of 500 students). The clients referred are generally experiencing severe family-related problems: e.g. marital discord, divorce, child abuse, death of a family member, etc.

The in-service training program includes workshops that deal with other quadrants of the SBFC Model. For example, there are: a) presentations on how to deal with cyber-bullying through parent education training (*Family-Prevention focus*); b) presentations on teacher consultation (*School-Intervention focus*); and c) presentations on how to conduct a stress reduction presentation with students (*School-Prevention focus*). These are all areas that lie outside traditional MFT training. Unfortunately, because the amount of time devoted to in-service training is limited to about 5 hours per month, the training in these 3 quadrants is at best an introduction. To address this problem in 2009 we hired Dr. Nancy Rosenbledt, a licensed psychologist and family therapist with a school counseling credential. Dr. Rosenbledt subsequently developed a program called TEAM (Therapists Educating and Motivating) for experienced Mission Possible interns (who have graduated and have prior SBFC experience). TEAM provides schools with parent, teacher, and student workshops with a preventive focus on topics such as parent effectiveness, family communication (*Family-Prevention focus*) and bullying, classroom management, handling parent-teacher conflict (*School-Prevention focus*). The addition of the TEAM program provides schools with a more sophisticated level of intervention in the SBFC Model quadrants that are not adequately covered in a traditional MFT academic program.

BASIC SOCIO-DEMOGRAPHIC DATA

At the end of each school year we collect basic socio-demographic data on the clients served. Data from 2011-12 is shown as Figures 45.1-45.8. Figure 45.1 shows client ages. Figure 45.2 displays client ethnicity. Figures 45.3 and 45.4 show presenting problems and risk factors. As can be seen in Figures 45.3 and 45.4 family problems figure significantly in the lives of the children seen for counseling. The dominant presenting problems (in rank order) are:

1. Family problems
2. Difficulty with peers
3. Anxiety
4. Low self esteem,shyness
5. Classroom behavior problems
6. Underachieving, poor grades

The dominant risk factors for these clients (in rank order) are:

1. Absent parent
2. Divorce
3. Financial difficulties
4. Single-parent family
5. Marital conflict
6. Step-parent in family
7. Death of family member/friend

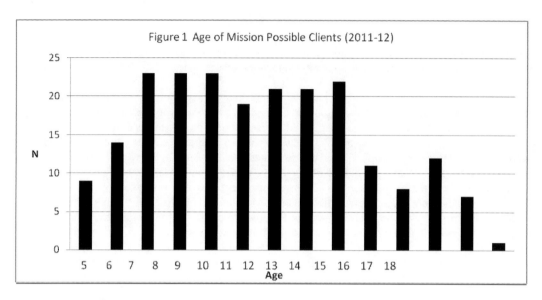

Figure 45.1 Age of Mission Possible Clients (2011-12)

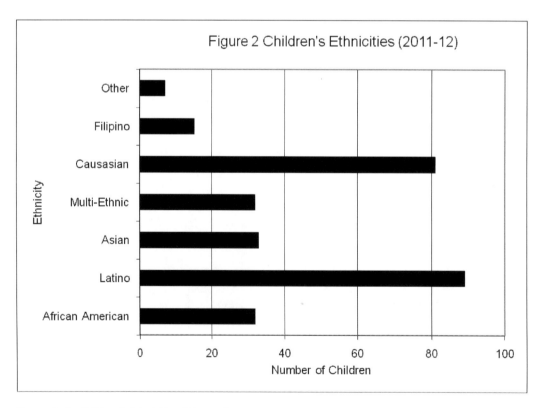

Figure 45.2 Children's Ethnicities (2011-12)

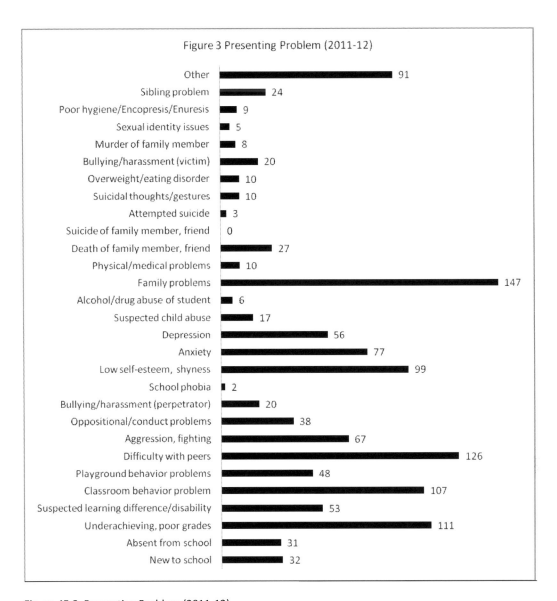

Figure 45.3 Presenting Problem (2011-12)

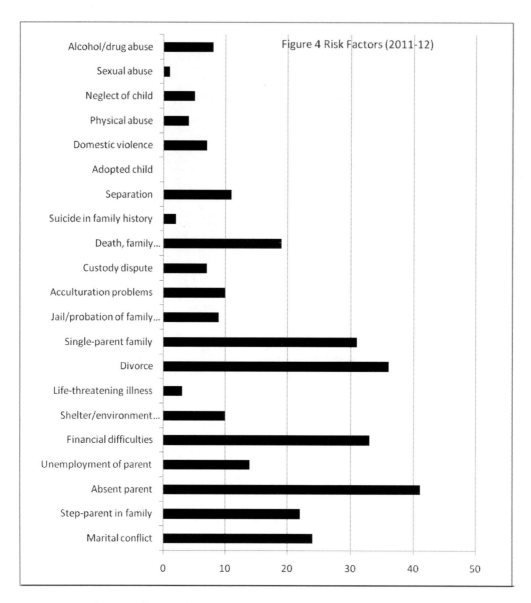

Figure 45.4   Risk Factors (2011-12)

Our experience is that in a majority of the clients we see in the schools the problems with peers, classroom behavior, and poor grades are intimately involved with family problems, in particular problems between the parents.

EVIDENCE-BASED SUPPORT

In addition, each SBFC professional completes a 1-4 rating scale assessing the client's before counseling and after counseling status on Grades, Self-Esteem, At-Home Behavior, and Classroom Behavior (see Figures 45.5-45.8). This is admittedly soft data since it is based solely on counselor report.

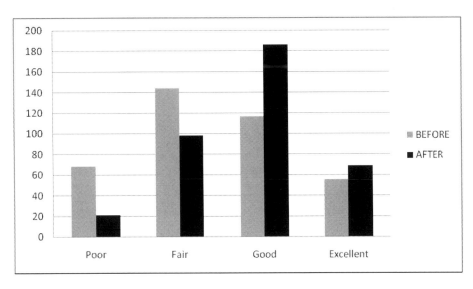

Figure 45.5: Counselor Evaluation of Student Grades

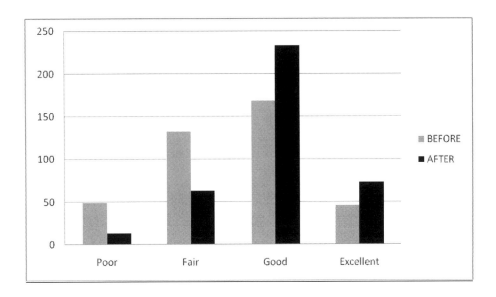

Figure45.6: Counselor Evaluation of Student Classroom Behavior

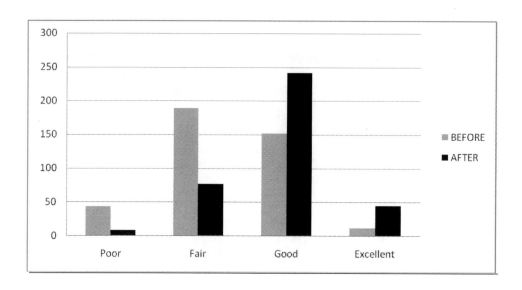

Figure 45.7 Counselor Evaluation of Student Self-Esteem

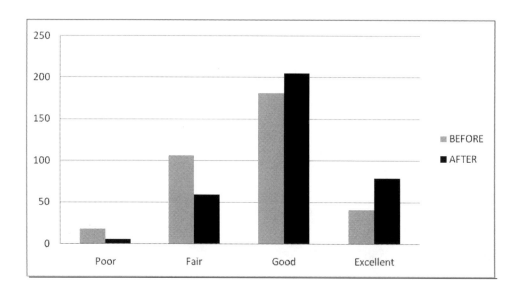

Figure 45.8 Counselor Evaluation of At-Home Behavior

Using a causal-comparative research design Almonte (2005) examined the effect of number of family sessions on Mission Possible SBFC professional ratings of grades, at-home behavior, classroom behavior, and GAF scores. SBFC professionals who saw the family at least twice had significantly better outcomes than counselors who saw the family once or not at all (see Table 45.1).

Table 45.1   Almonte (2005) Study Comparing Number of Family Sessions with Gain Scores (Post - Pre Scores) for SBFC professional Ratings of Grades, Classroom Behavior, At-home Behavior, and GAF Scores

Outcome Measure	No. of Family Sessions		
	2 or more	1 or less	p
GRADES	1.00	.21	.0003
CLASSROOM BEHAVIOR	1.20	.40	.02
AT-HOME BEHAVIOR	.90	.25	.001
GAF SCORES	7.80	4.80	.0003

MULTICULTURAL COUNSELING CONSIDERATIONS

The Center's mission statement includes the sentence:" Our purpose is to provide children and families (particularly under-served children and families) with a variety of culturally sensitive family counseling services)." This reflects a commitment of the Mission Possible program and staff from its beginnings in 1984 to provide SBFC counseling to populations that normally are underserved.

Most of the Center's clients live in the Mission District – one of the most pluralistic, yet difficult neighborhoods in which to live in San Francisco. The violent crime rate in the Mission is among the highest in San Francisco and gang activity is a constant concern for the residents. It has the highest concentration of children and is one of the poorest San Francisco neighborhoods. According to the 2000 Census, approximately 50 percent of Mission District families fell in the low income bracket, averaging an annual income of $32,000. Approximately 80 % of the children seen in the Mission Possible program are minority. Without proper mental health intervention and counseling – like that which the Center provides – children begin to fail academically and lose their self-esteem and confidence. The Center exists to remedy this social injustice.

There are few influences in a child's life that are as oppressive as a destructive family environment. The Center exists to transform children's destructive family environments so that children can grow academically, emotionally, socially, and spiritually. This focus on helping at-risk children, and their families, so that children can succeed at school, is congruent with the Jesuit Foundation's mission of promoting justice and undoing the negative effects of "oppressive social systems and unjust structural realities". The USF trainees and interns who work in the Mission Possible program have a unique opportunity to work with children and families that do not normally receive counseling services because they are poor and minority. This opportunity to help underserved children and families is a major reason the USF students choose the Center as their counseling placement.

In the early phase of Mission Possible (1984-1998) the majority of SBFC professionals (90%) were Caucasian. Currently about 70% of SBFC professionals are Caucasian. This reflects the ethnicity of the student body at the University of San Francisco. However, 80% of the Mission Possible clients are minority students (see Table 1). All MFT trainees in California are required to take a course in cross-cultural counseling as part of their academic training. We found this to be insufficient preparation for SBFC trainees working primarily with minority clients. Consequently we instituted in-service workshops that deal specifically with effective ways to work with minority clients. For example, Almonte's (2005) Personalismo Training program was developed specifically to help SBFC professionals relate more effectively and personally when interacting with Latino and other minority clients. The Personalismo in-service training included skill-based exercises involving role playing with minority actors who performed the roles of parents/guardians.

Because Mission Possible trainees graduate after their 9 month traineeship, the following year a new group of university trainees come into the program and need to complete the in-service training program. Before going out to a school, trainees are given a detailed orientation to the culture of Catholic, private, and public schools. This is important because the MFT trainees are not exposed to any coursework on schools in a traditional MFT academic program.

CHALLENGES AND SOLUTIONS

During the 28 years of the Mission Possible Program, it faced many serious challenges. The fact that the program continues to exist is because we were able to identify solutions to these challenges. There were four key challenges that had to be overcome:

1. Challenges with colleagues

2. Challenges with administration

3. Funding challenges

4. Training Challenges

CHALLENGES WITH COLLEAGUES

Because SBFC is a synthesis of family counseling and school counseling approaches, it is potentially threatening to traditional educators and mental health professionals who believe that there is only one correct way to approach schools or families. This opposition appeared in the early years of Mission Possible in several forms: as a motion at a department meeting to not support an early version of the SBFC program (the motion was not approved); as a program coordinator's decision to not send their students to Mission Possible for internships; and as demands that the meetings of Mission Possible staff be reported in detail at department meetings. Although these challenges only came from a few colleagues, they opened the door to the possibility that a Mission Possible program that was departmentally based could quickly cease to exist.

Solution: I am not exactly sure how I did this, but I convinced the dean, who was aware of the many difficulties between different personalities in the department, to administratively base the program under the dean's office. This meant that in my role as Executive Director I was directly accountable to the dean, not my department. This effectively restricted any potential departmental interference in the operation of Mission Possible. In the years that followed the colleagues who had originally undermined the Mission Possible program became much more supportive, in part I believe, because of the program's demonstrated success and the fact that it provided traineeship placements for about 40% of the departments MFT students.

CHALLENGES WITH ADMINISTRATION

After the Mission Possible program had been successfully operating for about 5 years, we encountered a serious challenge in the form of a falling out with a highly placed university administrator. I believe part of the problem was that a colleague who had been less than supportive of the Mission Possible program had won the administrator's favor and ear with their own creative project. As can be seen from the organizational chart, losing the support of a "higher-up" is dangerous and often fatal to a program's continuance. This administrator supported one attempt by a colleague to block counseling students from doing internships in the Center. On another occasion, this administrator removed the Center from the Development office's funding priority list (and during that year the Center received a grant of only $5000 ($15,000 below the amount we usually received).

Solution: We formed two boards for the Center: an Executive or working board chaired by Sr. Mary Peter Traviss, who was Chair of the Institute for Catholic Educational Leadership, a prestigious program at USF, a Jesuit university. For additional protection, we established a second Honorary Advisory Board, chaired by Fr. John LoSchiavo, Chancellor of USF and former USF president. The presence of both of these boards helped to make the Mission Possible program more effective because of the expertise of the various board members, some of whom were principals and influential members of the community. However, the nature of these two boards would make it very difficult for an administrator to make any unreasonable attempt to eliminate Mission Possible. I was aided in this solution by Dr. George Boisson who was Associate Director of the Center. Dr. Boisson was a 30 year veteran of the San Francisco Unified School District where he had served as an Assistant Superintendent while obtaining his doctorate in Organizational Development. He understood political dynamics in organizations and I learned a great deal about organizational survival from his wisdom.

During this period we also had on our board, Dr. Jackie Shinefield. She had been a trainee in the program, then a Group Supervisor, finally a board member. Dr. Shinefield, who had been Chair of the San Francisco Opera Board, has special skills at planning successful fundraising dinners. Over a period of 15 years she hosted 7 glamorous Awards Dinners for the Center generally held at the St. Francis Hotel in Union Square. Not only did these dinners generate funds for the Center, they also helped to melt the ice with the administrator who spoke at each dinner which was often attended by the Mayor of San Francisco and the President of USF.

FUNDING CHALLENGES

The first two challenges were of a more political nature. Funding challenges, which plague profit and non-profit organizations alike are critical to deal with. Effectively dealing with them one year does not mean that they will not return, like the rock Sisyphus would repeatedly roll uphill only to see it roll back down again and again. The yearly cost of administering the Center's programs averages about $110,000, most of this covering salary costs for program staff and supervisors. Yearly income from participating schools and from clients seen in the Community Counseling Center programs averages about $90,000; income from grants averages about $20,000. A dip in income from any of the three sources immediately puts the program into a deficit. During the Center's 30 year history there have been two large deficit periods, both occurring after we had to move the Community Counseling Center to a new location and consequently lost significant CCC income (due to a drop in clients).

Solution: During both deficit periods, I placed - with board support - all staff on a 30%-50% salary reduction in order to turn in a balanced budget. The staff, whose salaries are all part-time (ranging from 3 hours/week to 10 hours/week) understood the need for this type of crisis budgeting and have been supportive. The deans also were supportive. One dean managed to get our deficit removed by the university. Another dean permitted the Center to carry the deficit until we were able to pay it off and matched the Center dollar for dollar in paying it down. One of our deficit phases occurred during the 2010 recession when the university itself was experiencing financial difficulties. At a time like this a program, no matter how creative or effective, can easily end up on the chopping block when university accountants take a cold hard look at budgets.

I believe that the Center has survived the chopping block during these deficit moments for the following reasons: a) the university and the San Francisco schools view the Mission Possible program as providing a valuable community service which meets a critical need of the schools as well as fulfilling the university mission of service to the community. In San Francisco Catholic and public schools the ratio of school counselors to students is approximately 1:400. The ratio recommended by the American Counseling Association is 1:200. This means that many students who need counseling do not receive it. In the schools served by the USF Center for Child and Family Development, the Mission Possible counselor is often the only counselor in the school. By the time the Center experienced its deficits (in 1996 and in 2010) the Center had established a positive reputation. A previous USF president once referred to the Center as a "jewel in the crown of the university." When the deficits occurred the higher-ups probably viewed the Center more as a thorn in the university's side, but the positive reputation helped to buffer this image; b) the Board and I have demonstrated that we are willing to cut salaries in order to balance budgets; c) the Center has over its 28 years consistently generated a solid stream of income from school fees and from grants (totaling more than $1.4 million); and d) the Mission Possible program has provided a valuable traineeship site for more than 300 USF MFT students. That is, the Mission Possible traineeship program directly supports the university academic MFT program.

TRAINING CHALLENGES

The Mission Possible program has two main aims: providing SBFC service to schools and providing SBFC training to university students. The use of MFT trainees who are not given SBFC training in their academic program (a traditional MFT program that has little or no focus on schools) poses a challenge because a) these SBFC professionals are relatively inexperienced (when they enter a school as the SBFC professional they are seeing their first clients), and b) some of the MFT coursework that would be of use to them hasn't been taken yet. For example, for many years the trainees from USF did not complete the introductory course in conjoint family counseling until they had been in a school placement for 4 months. The USF courses that focused on Parent Consultation and Group Counseling were not completed until the final month of the SBFC traineeship. This means that the majority of SBFC trainees enter Mission Possible with only rudimentary family counseling skills. Because the USF MFT program (like many in California) is a two year 48 unit program and the traineeship is completed in the second year, there are of necessity core MFT courses that are taken after a student has begun a traineeship and is seeing clients.

The in-service training consists of only about 50 hours spread over the traineeship period. Each trainee in currently in the second year of their MFT degree program and attending courses two days a week, while completing a 20 hour per week traineeship with Mission Possible, and - for some trainees - holding a part-time job to pay for their degree. Consequently, increasing the in-service training programs hours is not realistic. Because trainees graduate from the university at the end of their traineeship, and only a few return to Mission Possible for another year as interns, the schools that participate in mission Possible are staffed mainly by trainees rather than experienced interns.

Solution: In the early years of Mission Possible our in-service training program was mostly didactic. Currently it is strongly skill-based with emphasis on role-playing specific SBFC skills such as making the first phone call to a parent or conducting an initial parent/guardian interview. In addition, the group and individual supervisors are highly experienced in SBFC and most have been with the program for more than 10 years. The trainees who apply for Mission Possible are interviewed by the Director of the School Outreach Program, Judy Giampaoli, MFT who is a licensed family therapist and a former principal. This combination of skills enables her to make judgments about the suitability of a trainee for a particular school. Not every trainee who applies to the program is accepted. Those who are accepted are screened for maturity and aptitude for working with minority clients in a school context. In addition, each Mission Possible trainee is carefully matched with a school and its principal.

PROCEDURE

These are the some of the basic steps I would recommend to anyone wanting to develop a Mission Possible SBFC program from the university end:

1. Do a pilot project in one school to test out the feasibility of the program. If you are successful, other principals will hear about it and you will have no trouble expanding. Consider building your SBFC program in a series of steps to reduce opposition: e.g. project, program, Center.

2. Assemble a staff team that understands SBFC and is loyal to you and each other.

3. Select an outstanding group supervisor for the first group of SBFC counseling trainees. It is critical that the supervisor understand how to work with both schools and families.

4. Obtain support for the program from your department chair and dean. Keep them in the loop as you develop the program.

5. Learn to talk "principalese." That is, appreciate that principals work in an organizational culture different from universities. If you lack this skill consider developing a partnership with someone with principal or school administration experience who can act as your liaison with principals.

6. Develop a funding base for the program through grants or direct fees to schools. This step is critical to the long term survival of your program. Grants come and go and rarely provide a stable income source.

7. Recognize that you may encounter resistance and opposition from colleagues and other mental health professionals who feel threatened by a counseling approach that is different from their training. Develop an understanding of political and organizational dynamics. My experience is that most counselors and professors are very naïve about dealing with organizational conflict and political in-fighting. In dealing with political battle in universities I have found an understanding of military history to be invaluable and I often recommend Sun Tzu's *The Art of War* to students and colleagues dealing with organizational aggression. As a program administrator you should understand basic Sun Tzu concepts like: "Don't attack when the enemy is strong." Failure to grasp this could mean annihilation of your program.

SUMMARY

Mission Possible is one of the six types of SBFC delivery program. As a school-sited program staffed by university SBFC trainees it has two distinct advantages. First, it provides schools with an affordable SBFC professional. In San Francisco about half of the Mission Possible schools would have no school counselor if it were not for this program. Many schools in California had severe budgets cutbacks due to the 2010 recession and given a choice between eliminating a teacher or eliminating a counselor in order to balance a school budget, most principals will eliminate the counselor. Second, it provides MFT trainees with basic training in SBFC that they would not otherwise receive in their traditional MFT programs.

Mission Possible has served over 15,000 children and families in the San Francisco bay area and most of these children and families are underserved and minority. The success of the program - which has lasted 30 years - is because the trainees, interns, and staff are passionate about helping children succeed in school and because they understand that they are pioneering a new approach to counseling that empowers children through interventions linking home and school. In 1984 when Mission Possible began, no mental health agencies in San Francisco were actively involved working with family counselors in schools. Today there are few large mental health agencies in San Francisco that are not involved in some form of SBFC and school outreach. Mission Possible's involvement in over 100 bay area schools has played a major role in modeling the value of a SBFC approach for other agencies. Over 30 of these schools have hired their Mission Possible trainee/intern and each year an average of 25 principals dedicate a line in their budget in order to have a SBFC professional work in their schools.

The longevity of Mission Possible is also due to the cohesion among staff and board members. The program has had many ups and downs, fiscal and political. In order for a program to survive this kind of turbulence the stakeholders must have a shared vision and a loyalty to each other and the program. This is the key to the resilience of the Mission Possible program.

RESOURCES

http://www.usfca.edu/soe/ctrs_institutes/center_child_family_development/
>   This is the USF Center for Child & Family Development website. Browsing this site will give a feel for the Center's programs.

http://usftherapist.wordpress.com/
>   This is the blog website for the Center's Community Counseling Center

CCFD Staff (2011) *Mission Possible Traineeship/Internship Orientation Manual* (2011) DVD and hard copy, San Francisco: Center for Child & Family Development, University of San Francisco.
>   This is the orientation manual given to all SBFC trainees/interns. It contains basic information concerning their SBFC role in the schools including a variety of forms for assessment, case management, evaluation and child abuse reporting.

Contents
1. Directory
2. To Do List
3. Becoming Part of School Culture
4. Tips from 2nd Year Interns
5. Counselor Checklist
6. Client Referral Form (Teacher/Parent)
7. Classroom Behavior Checklist
8. Parental Consent Form (English)

9. Parental Consent Form (Spanish)
10. Release of Information Form
11. Basic Client data Form (BCDF)
12. BCDF Tally Sheet
13. Global Assessment of Functioning Scale
14. Counseling Summary Notes
15. MFT Supervisor Responsibilities
16. MFT Weekly Summary of Hours
17. MFT Experience Verification
18. California Child Abuse and Neglect Reporting
19. When to Report Sexual Activity
20. Child Abuse Assessment and Reporting
21. Child Abuse Reporting Guidelines
22. Suspected Child Abuse Reporting Form
23. Counseling Hotlines
24. CAMFT Ethical Standards
25. Trainee/Intern Program Evaluation

To obtain a copy of this manual contact the author at gerrardb@usfca.edu.

You tube interviews with members of the Center for Child and Family Development (CCFD) Community:

Fr. John LoSchiavo, Chancellor: University of San Francisco and former Chair: Board of Directors, CCFD
http://www.youtube.com/watch?v=7qYS-4ChE7k

Dr. Betty Taylor, Professor, School of Education and CCFD Board Member
http://www.youtube.com/watch?v=1eYl4l1q6B0

Dr. Eugene Muscat, Professor School of Business and CCFD Board Member
http://www.youtube.com/watch?v=PGaggQg40_l

Judy Giampaoli, LMFT, Director: Mission Possible School Outreach Program
http://www.youtube.com/watch?v=yQMyKMKQ-qQ

Chris Trailer, LMFT, Clinical Director and Group supervisor
http://www.youtube.com/watch?v=M1TKBZO0OQs

Steve Abrams, LMFT Group Supervisor
http://www.youtube.com/watch?v=L8rm09twJJg

Dr. Nancy Rosenbledt, Parent Education Consultant
http://www.youtube.com/watch?v=9cTbKCZ1aAY

Dr. Cori Bussolari, MFT Coordinator, Counseling Psychology Department, University of San Francisco
http://www.youtube.com/watch?v=8xAay2KkwOw

Sheena Sattarpour, MFT trainee
http://www.youtube.com/watch?v=iZzOzTCP1js

Judy Giampaoli, LMFT, former principal of Francisco Middle School, San Francisco
http://www.youtube.com/watch?v=XEycFrZ79sc

Sr. Sister Leonarda Montealto, OP   principal of Holy Angels School, Colma
http://www.youtube.com/watch?v=sfpHp2fzE1M

Dr. Brian Gerrard, Executive Director, CCFD
http://www.youtube.com/watch?v=xEwBPBvGcyk

Chapter 46
Joining School-Based Counseling Teams: School Certification for Connecticut Marriage and Family Therapists

Kathleen C. Laundy, Ralph S. Cohen and Katharine Bishop

OVERVIEW: Marriage and Family Therapy (MFT) is a relative "newcomer" to the cadre of mental health professionals who provide school-based family counseling and therapy services to improve educational outcomes for students. Although for many years MFTs have provided contracted services to school systems, they joined allied mental health colleagues as certified employees of school systems in the United States in 2007. This chapter chronicles the fifteen year journey to certification in Connecticut, the first state to pass school certification for MFTs in the US. Challenges and merits of multidisciplinary school collaboration to boost student achievement are highlighted, and a school-based systems theory to guide school-based family practice is illustrated. The chapter offers preliminary research to suggest the presence of multidisciplinary support for MFTs and the need for collaborative practice in schools.

BACKGROUND

In his thorough review of literature regarding family systems-based school counseling, Gerrard (2008) summarizes six main types of School Based Family Counseling (SBFC) which are used in schools to boost student achievement. These include in-service trainings, staff with family therapy training, university-school collaboratives, agency-school collaboratives, and agency and private practice types of contracted services. Historically, many such services have been provided through contracted services developed by the six US licensed mental health professionals at universities, agencies, clinics and private practices, rather than by full time employed mental health professional teams within the schools. Although many valuable programs have been developed, contracted programs are more subject to the threat of termination or alteration when funding ceases and/or school priorities change. Programs and services initiated by full time employed special services staffs can potentially provide safeguards to preserve sustainability and improve such programs and services.

In Connecticut, the Department of Public Health (DPH) licenses the six mental health professions of counseling, marriage and family therapy, nursing, psychiatry, psychology and social work for entry-level practice. Licenses are required across most clinical settings to provide mental health diagnostic, treatment and consultation services to children, adolescents, adults and families.

In addition, the Connecticut State Department of Education requires education certification for all special services staff pursuing full-time school employment. Until recently in New England, however, school counselors, school psychologists, and school social workers were the only mental health professions eligible for certified full time employment in schools, although ironically none of these three professions are required yet to be licensed by the Connecticut DPH in order to be hired for full time employment in public schools. The full complement of multidisciplinary teams of mental health professionals has therefore yet to be developed in schools across New England, the US, and beyond, making it difficult to fully utilize systems-based interventions in education.

Marriage and Family Therapy (MFT) is a relative "newcomer" to the cadre of mental health professionals who provide school-based family counseling and therapy services. Although for many years MFTs have provided contracted services to school systems, Connecticut became the first state in the USA to certify licensed marriage and family therapists (MFTs) for full time employment in American public schools in 2007.

This chapter chronicles the fifteen year journey of Connecticut MFTs to join school-based family counseling teams as certified mental health clinicians. It summarizes the value and challenges of multidisciplinary collaboration to boost student achievement. It introduces a model called the Longitudinal Overview of Growth in Systems (LOGS), designed as a systems-based template for mental health practice in schools and described more in depth in Chapter 48. This chapter also provides preliminary data to support educators' support for MFTs in schools as well as recommendations for multidisciplinary programs and services designed to remove constraints to learning, build healthy relationships between schools and families, and improve academic functioning in students.

Connecticut's path to certification led us to Gerrard, Everts, Carter and others' work in School-Based Family Counseling. Through the Oxford Symposium we met many mental health professionals dedicated to promoting family friendly and systems-based services to children and families in schools around the world. Although we borrowed from US models of medical family therapy (Rolland, 1994, & McDaniel, Hepworth & Doherty, 1992) and the common factors of Metaframeworks (Breunlin, Schwartz, & Mac Kune-Karrer, 1992), to develop our school-based systems theory prior to meeting SBFC colleagues, we find our work to be compatible with other authors' family systems-based work in this handbook. We have utilized divergent yet complimentary paths to arrive at a common place in order to best serve the mental health needs of children and families in schools.

Carter and Evans note that "children are most affected by two major systems in their lives: their family and their school" (2008, p. 1). We believe that it behooves clinicians in school systems to develop multidisciplinary models of service for *all* children in their natural settings, regardless of their special needs. Our collective mission is to promote healthy school functioning and achievement in children, and to strengthen school team and family collaboration on behalf of that achievement.

Over the past century, six mental health professions (counseling, marriage and family therapy, nursing, psychiatry, psychology and social work) have all become licensed in the USA to provide clinical services to children, adolescents and adults. Mental health professionals have developed creative ways to collaborate with educators to boost student achievement through the provision of school-based family counseling (SBFC), family therapy, and other family-systems based services. (Laundy, Nelson & Abucewicz, 2011, Gerrard, 2008, Carter & Evans, 2008, Carter & Perluss, 2008).

Since 1975 in the US, Public Law 94-142 has mandated that all children have a right to education, regardless of what special needs they have. Since that time, multidisciplinary teams have been created in US school districts to assess and service children with special needs so that they have access to education along with their typical peers. Schools have hired certified school counselors, school psychologists, and school social workers along with special educators, occupational therapists, and other learning specialists that school districts deem important for their multidisciplinary teams. The success of these teams has been evidenced by the growth in special education budgets, programs and services in the past forty years. The presence of these teams has become increasingly necessary as rising health care costs in America have left so many children and families underinsured or with no insurance for mental health care. Schools are increasingly becoming the place where children receive health care services.

In his article reviewing the school-based family counseling and therapy literature, Gerrard (2008) notes that some services are offered *directly* in schools by licensed and certified mental health professionals, and some others represent *contracted* university, agency and private practice partnerships with licensed mental health clinicians *outside* of school buildings (p. 14, and 28-29). Gerrard notes that a broad range of traditional family therapy approaches can be applied to school settings. However, he cautions that family-based counseling is difficult to do, and that SBFC needs specialized training to deliver effectively in school systems (p.3).

Gerrard adds that there is a growing interest in School-Based Family Counseling (SBFC) that cuts across disciplines of school counseling, school psychology, family therapy, school social work, and special education. He notes that school practitioners in each of these fields are writing about the importance of a family systems theoretical viewpoint in working with children with school difficulties (p.14).

Carter and Perluss (2008) summarize several authors' views of the need for specialized family systems training in their seminal article on (SBFC). They summarize several authors' view (O'Callahaghn, 1994, Palmo et al., 1998, Stevens-Smith, Hinkle and Stahmann, 1993) that "academic or clinical programs geared for the preparation of traditional school or family counselors do not necessarily provide the wide range of knowledge and skills required for school-based family counseling to be effective" (p. 3). These authors call for integration of specialties in order to best prepare mental health professionals to function effectively with both school and family systems (p. 3).

Connecticut clinicians from all six mental health professions are eligible to provide *contracted* family counseling and therapy services to school systems in one of these delivery models, if they are licensed by the Department of Public Health and have the specialized training and interest. But until recently, only school counselors, school psychologists and school social workers have been *school-certified* as *full time employees* in Connecticut school systems. In 2007, Connecticut became the first state in the US to certify licensed marriage and family therapists (MFTs) for full time employment in American public schools, and several other states are now enacting similar legislation. Here we summarize Connecticut's fifteen year journey of advocating for the inclusion of MFTs on school-based family counseling teams as certified mental health clinicians.

We introduce the models of service delivery we utilized to pilot school-based family counseling/therapy programs in Connecticut schools in Chapter 48, and describe the course of study we have established at CCSU for graduate and postgraduate MFTs who are interested in school-based practice. We chronicle how we achieved MFT school certification, and address the challenges we faced while passing legislation.

Different school systems in Connecticut required different programs and services as we placed students in schools across the state. We developed a metamodel for systems-based family practice in schools that we applied in these pilot programs. Based on the common-factors principles from *Metaframeworks: Transcending the models of family* therapy (Breunlin, Schwartz, & Mac Kune-Karrer, 1992), we developed the Longitudinal Overview of Growth in Systems (LOGS). LOGS is a model that helps clinicians to rank order systemic constraints in students' lives which interfere with their school achievement, and helps guide the sequence and development of school and family-based interventions to remove those constraints.

We integrated LOGS with principles from medical family therapy to address individual and family life cycle needs in families with chronic illnesses and disabilities. These principles have utility for all mental health and education professionals in a variety of school settings. They fit well with the SBFC Model, and can be utilized in preventive as well as remedial ways with students, families and school systems. Medical family therapy techniques and the LOGS Model will be further described in Chapter 48.

Finally, we provide preliminary data from a recent Connecticut schools study regarding educators' initial attitudes about MFTs and multidisciplinary collaboration. This research was collected shortly after certification, in order to understand educators' attitudes as well as raise awareness about how multidisciplinary family-centered practice in schools removes constraints to learning, builds healthy relationships between schools and families, and improves academic functioning.

When reviewing the literature on school-based family counseling and therapy, Gerrard notes that school-based family counseling services "occur in a variety of ways, but what all have in common is the emphasis on linking family intervention with school intervention" (2008, p. 14). Medicine in the US is beginning to recognize the importance of collaborative care for families through a systems-based network called "medical home" (Deloitte Center for Health Solutions, 2010), and similar collaborative educational models have been mandated through PL 94-142 in schools for almost forty years. By tracing one profession's path to school certification and multidisciplinary team participation, the goal of this chapter is to document the value-added service provided by the *full* complement of credentialed mental health teams who offer family-friendly and systems-based service in schools to boost academic achievement.

CHRONOLOGY OF THE PROCESS

Ralph Cohen and Kathleen Laundy served together on the Connecticut Association for Marriage and Family Therapy (CTAMFT) Board of Directors during the 1990s, the period when state licensure for MFTs, counselors and social workers across the US was a major national initiative. Laundy was president of CTAMFT shortly after licensure, and the Board at that time was tracking and supporting new practice arenas for licensed MFTs. When Cohen joined the CTAMFT Board as the Director of the Family Therapy Program at Central Connecticut State University (CCSU), he became the Chair of a newly created Advocacy Committee. This committee was developed to facilitate employment opportunities for MFTs in schools, state government, and other nontraditional settings. Laundy later joined the CCSU family therapy faculty following her presidency.

Following an initial period of holding "town meetings" and conducting a membership survey across Connecticut to collect data about MFT programs and services to schools, Cohen asked Laundy to co-chair Advocacy Committee with him, in order to pursue school certification with more collaborative energy. Laundy's first degree was in special education, and as a licensed psychologist and family therapist in private practice, she provided consultation services to several school districts in southeastern Connecticut. In her practice, she participated in a variety of districts' Planning and Placement Team (PPTs) and other special meetings, and she provided other specialized programs and services for students and their families. Her special area of interest is medical family therapy with families with chronic illnesses. Multidisciplinary collaboration with school systems convinced Laundy of the worth of family-centered and family-friendly health care and education for children with complex needs, and she readily agreed to help Cohen co-chair the Advocacy Committee.

Together, Cohen and Laundy enlisted other MFT students and CTAMFT members, developed a "Fact Sheet", and set up a grass-roots effort to market MFTs to school districts. CTAMFT devoted lobbying hours and leadership, and legislators were enlisted as sponsors for the bill. The state Commissioner of Education and several superintendents were also enlisted as supporters of the legislation.

Because his clinical background involved working in schools, Cohen often placed graduate MFT students in school systems for internship training. School districts in Connecticut have utilized MFT services through direct contracting or collaborative "sharing" with youth service bureaus (YSBs) and other social service agencies for over several decades. Many MFTs complete internships in school systems along with their allied mental health colleagues, and they continue to service schools after graduation through subsequent employment at the YSBs, that are regulated by the State Department of Education in Connecticut. Together, Cohen and Laundy helped establish and supervise MFT school placements that incorporated several of Gerrard's types of school-based family counseling services (namely in-service trainings, university-school collaboratives, agency-school collaboratives, and agency and private practice services and programs for students and families).

But schools were not able to hire MFTs after graduation directly, because until 2007 there was no school certification credential for MFTs, as there is for other mental health disciplines (counseling, school psychology, and social work). As the newest mental health profession, MFTs have come to the school accreditation process later than our allied mental health colleagues. As older professions more traditionally affiliated with education, the disciplines of school counseling, psychology and social work have been accredited by the Connecticut State Department of Education for several years. When Connecticut MFTs and schools realized the need to develop a similar credential, they decided to pursue School MFT accreditation, with the goal of developing a more full complement of mental health team members to school systems for their special education (SPED) teams.

Concurrent with this division advocacy work, Laundy was participating in the creation of a Youth Service Bureau in her home town, where local school and community leaders recognized the need for its creation. Westbrook was the only local shoreline town that did not have its own social service agency at that time and clinical services often had to be obtained outside of the local town. Kit Bishop, principal at Daisy Ingraham Elementary School and colleague, asked if Laundy could help provide her with some part-time clinical help at her school. When asked if she could utilize an MFT intern, to which we had access at CCSU, she asked, "What's an MFT"? That was the beginning of a generative and rich collaboration that has grown exponentially over the past decade.

Bishop was agreeable to providing supervision and space for an intern, and an MFT from CCSU soon volunteered to complete her supervised training in the school. Ellen Flanagan-Cecchini joined the school team as a second year practicum student. In three summer months, Flanagan-Cecchini accumulated 20 families for treatment at Bishop's school, which helped document the need for the creation of the Westbrook YSB. Soon, school colleagues at the middle and high school began requesting services, and Bishop joined Laundy and other community leaders in Westbrook as its first YSB Board of Directors. Over the next three years, Westbrook's Educational Reference Group Scores comparing the amount out-of-district placements went down, in comparison with towns of similar size. The Coordinator of Special Services at Westbrook High School, Chet Bialicki, attributed this cost-saving trend to the collaborative and preventive team planning which now included MFTs. Those cost savings factored positively into the development of a close relationship between the youth service bureau and the school system, and they were also viewed favorably by legislators when school certification legislation for MFTs was passed.

The Westbrook YSB became a reality in 2001 and staff and programs grew quickly. It now employs three professional staff and CCSU provides up to10 MFT intern/practicum students per year to the school and agency for training and service, under the clinical direction of Michelle Ciak. About 35 individual sessions are held weekly with students at the agency and
about 100 additional students are serviced by group programs at the schools and at the agency.
The YSB agency provides over 5,050 hours of service yearly to children and families (based on annualized clinical record keeping statistics reported by Jacqueline Ward, their Executive Director). Because the town of Westbrook also houses a program for students with neurocognitive disorders, and Bishop and Laundy were former special educators with special interest in chronic disabilities, the agency developed a niche market of service to youngsters with autism spectrum disorders and their families.

MFT students split their time between the schools and the agency. They have shared caseloads across the elementary, middle and high schools, and they have become active and valued members of the multidisciplinary teams in the Westbrook School System. They continue to administer and develop five of the six types of school-based family counseling services that Gerrard describes in his literature review.

While the Westbrook YSB was established, Laundy, Bishop and Cohen developed serendipitous relationships with local and state legislators in their respective districts. One such legislator, who grew up in Westbrook, volunteered to hand-deliver the original application for the Westbrook YSB to the State Department of Education, as a service to his constituency. This legislator then submitted a bill to the state legislature for MFT school certification, unbeknownst to our Advocacy Committee. He later helped co-sponsor subsequent MFT school certification bills during his tenure in the legislature.

Prior to that same legislative session, Cohen's State Representative approached Cohen at his West Hartford home when the legislator was canvassing for election. Cohen gave him an MFT fact sheet that the Advocacy Committee had just developed. Also unbeknownst to the CTAMFT Advocacy Committee, this representative introduced another MFT school certification bill that year. He has been a strong supporter of the three MFT bills that he has helped introduce each year. He later became Co-Chair of the Education Committee where the bill was first heard and he helped shepherd the bill into law. Another legislative ally was a local school psychologist colleague by profession who also utilized and appreciated multidisciplinary collaboration.

When the bills were introduced, Bishop joined the CTAMFT Advocacy Committee to testify at the Capital and collaborate with our lobbyists on behalf of the legislation. Strong opposition was first encountered by both the legislature as well as other allied mental health clinicians who feared competition for jobs they considered their exclusive domain. The CTAMFT Advocacy Committee then employed the collaborative testimony of allied mental health and other education colleagues with whom we worked. We wanted to stress the value of systems-based multidisciplinary collaboration and teamwork in schools, and how we found that it is *well* supported in school systems where MFTs are actually working (Laundy, Nelson, & Abucewicz, 2011, p. 390).

For instance, when managed care first came to Connecticut in 1993, the Connecticut mental health professions established the Connecticut Council of Mental Health Providers (CCMHP). They built a collaborative multidisciplinary committee with representatives from the six mental health professions to collectively advocate for services affecting children and families, as well as for the accountability standards we wanted to establish through licensure and certification. Our Advocacy Committee enlisted their support for the certification process.

In their lobbying efforts, the Advocacy Committee made liberal use of the CCMHP, as well as their CTAMFT members who were dually credentialed as counselors, nurses, psychologists, psychiatrists, and social workers, in addition to holding MFT licenses. The group discovered that the MFT profession had a higher density of mental health clinicians with dual licenses than any of our other fellow mental health colleagues. This served as a key ingredient for establishing their credibility in school systems and building collaborative rather than competitive relationships with their colleagues. These colleagues have been invaluable in helping CTAMFT to pass the school certification legislation and many of them are currently practicing collaboratively in schools in some capacity.

Over the five years of introducing legislation, they developed gradually more strategic interventions in our lobbying efforts. For the first few years, they testified about who MFTs are and how school MFT certification will empower school administrators to hire from the full talent pool of mental health professionals. Later, with the help of the CTAMFT lobbying firm, they attached the bill to a larger education bill that the governor, a strong proponent of children and education, supported. The third certification bill passed after many years of intense legislative advocacy, and intense multidisciplinary collaboration. Over fifty MFT students, clinicians and CTAMFT Board members and lobbyists worked together for well over a decade to make the dream a reality. In 2007, as Public Act No. 07-241, An Act Concerning Minor Changes to the Education Statutes was enacted.

Regulations have now been written by the State Department of Education (SDE) to fully implement the law. Cohen worked with Central Connecticut State University (CCSU) officials in the School of Education and Professional Studies and the State Department of Education to develop a course of study to meet the regulations standards. As of 2011, CCSU has developed a specialized training track for MFTs who want to pursue school-based certification. Box 46.1 below illustrates the sequence of coursework that has been pre-approved at CCSU (by the State Department of Education Certification Bureau) for the Educator Certificate for Marriage and Family Therapists. It meets the requirements specified in the regulations.

This course sequence was negotiated with the Department of Higher Education for pre-approval at CCSU. Other Connecticut universities negotiate their own course sequence that meets the State Department of Education's interpretation of the regulations.

In addition to meeting these course and practicum requirements, persons interested in the MFT School Certification must also obtain their professional practice license (LMFT) through the Department of Public Health after graduation, currently the only mental health profession required to do so. For students enrolled in the MFT program, one course would count toward the required elective; there are two extra courses required beyond the regular MFT curriculum (6 credit hours). Standards for school MFT certification are higher than for other mental health groups in Connecticut. The State Department of Education is considering raising the standards in like fashion in the next few years for the allied mental health professions already accredited.

EVIDENCE-BASED SUPPORT

PRELIMINARY FINDINGS FROM CONNECTICUT

A study was conducted shortly after school MFT certification in Connecticut, in order to investigate educators' initial perceptions about MFT services to students, families and

---

Box 46.1: Sequence of CCSU Courses required for Connecticut School Certification

---

1) **MFT 592** : School-Based Family Counseling - MFT practice and intervention in public schools, school-based systems theory, learning theory, state and federal education laws pertaining to the health and education of children, and statutory requirements for mandated reporting, suspensions/ expulsions, and school/district accountability; strategies for communicating and collaborating with families about students' progress; school-based ethics, and policies and procedures governing special and general ed. services for collaboration, referral and placement.

2) **MFT 593** : School-Based Marriage and Family Therapy Practicum and Seminar I -
Supervision of Marriage and Family practice in public schools with direct client contact.
Covers school-based learning and systems theories, federal and state education laws
(e.g., Individuals with Disabilities Education Act (IDEA) and Americans with Disabilities Act (ADA); professional ethics and code of professional responsibility for
educators; Family Education Rights and Privacy Act (FERPA); statutory requirements for mandated reporting, suspensions and expulsions; and school and district accountability. This fulfills 1/2 of the required 300 hours of practicum for state certification.

3) **MFT 594** : School-Based Marriage and Family Therapy Practicum and Seminar II:
School-Based Marriage and Family Therapy Practicum and Seminar II Spring.

This is a continuation of the two-semester School-Based Marriage and Family Therapy Practicum and Seminar. Further development of content areas covered in MFT 593. It fulfills the second 1/2 of the required 300 hours of practicum for state certification.

4) **Practicum Placements:** Students must be placed in a public school for a minimum of

300 clock hours (obtained through the MFT program's requirement of 12 hours per

week). MFT 593 and MFT 594 seminar meets the state's requirement for "joint

supervision" between the school and the MFT program.

5) **ED 515 :** School Law - School Law addresses the legal bases of education and provides an understanding of federal, state, and local laws applicable to

teachers and pupils of public school. Primary emphasis is placed on Connecticut statutes

and judicial interpretations.

6) **SPED 501:** Education of the Special Learner – Education of the Exceptional Learner

Examines growth and development of students with disabilities, including those

identified as gifted and talented, and methods for assessing, planning for and working

effectively with these students. Meets State of Connecticut requirement for teacher

certification (10 hours of off-campus field experience required). CT law requires

fingerprinting and a criminal background check for the field experiences in this class.

Fingerprinting must be completed prior to the beginning of class.

7) **PSY 512 :** Seminar in Developmental Psychology - Study of human development from conception through old age, including analysis of theory and research findings. This

course is already a requirement of the MFT program's regular curriculum.

8) **Post-Grads :** MFT-post-master's students undertaking school certification may enroll in the special school certificate program in the MFT program at CCSU. Post grads take the required courses and the program refers the student to various school-based sites for 300 hours of practicum training.

multidisciplinary school teams in public schools in Connecticut. The goal was to obtain baseline data to utilize for training MFTs for school-based practice.

Methodology: The study was conducted in five Connecticut school systems where the bulk of MFT graduate students from Central Connecticut State University train to become certified school service providers. Two suburban and three urban schools were represented in the study sample. A total 154 surveys were completed; 113 surveys were completed by elementary and middle school personnel and 41 were completed by high school professionals. Participants were asked to complete demographic information which included participants' professional school roles, years of professional experience, and highest level of education achieved. The survey consisted of 10 statements describing various opinions about MFT services in their schools. Participants were asked to respond to statements by utilizing a Likert Scale to report their perceptions. The categories were then collapsed into three categories (Agree, Undecided and Disagree) for statistical analysis. Survey questions are included in the RESOURCES section at the end of this chapter.

Findings & Recommendations: The majority of school staff members surveyed reported that MFTs will deliver valuable support to teachers (74%) and students with behavioral challenges (72%). Survey participants reported from 70 – 85% agreement that MFT services to families will improve student outcomes. Support was stronger among both administrators and allied mental health, special education and support staffs than among general educators. It was also stronger in seasoned school professionals than among educators with less experience with teams in school systems.

Survey respondents, including allied mental health professionals, were somewhat undecided about the potential duplication of services that mental health clinicians in schools may create. Findings from this study suggest that the *"necessary redundancies"* inherent in the skill sets of MFTs, school counselors, psychologists, and social workers, as well as the unique roles that each mental health discipline plays, all need to be better understood. Mental health professionals have overlapping skill sets in individual, group and family counseling which we have described as "necessary redundancies", as well as unique skills relative to their discipline. More sophisticated understanding about how disciplines can *collectively* and *uniquely* boost student achievement needs to occur before multidisciplinary collaboration can be utilized in comprehensive and efficient ways.

Nonetheless, multidisciplinary support for MFTs from school counselors, psychologists and social workers was surprisingly high in this study (83%), particularly given the opposition that was experienced in *legislative* attempts to enact MFT school certification legislation. These findings suggest that multidisciplinary teams are valued by schools where such teams function actively. Despite the small sample size of the survey, it provided support for the presence of MFTs on multidisciplinary school teams.

Clarity about MFT roles in schools was less well understood among general education survey respondents (43% undecided) and administrators (50% undecided) than it was among allied mental health staff members and support staff. In all likelihood, this finding reflects the historic artifact of special education growth resulting in more specialization and some drift away from regular education since the first special education mandate (Public Law 94-142) was enacted in 1975. Since that time, general education teachers have tended to interact less with special education staff than allied health care and support staff and administrators do, and they have therefore become less clear about specific roles and contributions of MFTs as well as special education staff.

Since the current Response to Intervention (RtI) federal initiative in America represents a systems-based mandate to re-integrate special and regular education by providing more collaborative, preventive services to all students who need them within general education, the timing for MFT school certification and multidisciplinary team building seems particularly appropriate. With MFT training and research emphasis on evidence-based treatment with a wide range of systems, it is fitting that MFT clinicians who have family-strengthening expertise are beginning to join school staffs, where their skills match current educational "best practice" patterns.

Findings from the survey suggest several opportunities for school practice and research. First, there needs to be more full understanding about professional mental health roles and how the professions work together. There is a need for professional development regarding the specific and collective skill sets of multidisciplinary team professionals in school systems. Particular emphasis should be placed on training general education teachers, who currently have less direct exposure to multidisciplinary school team members than special services staff. In-service training should target those with least amount of experience with multidisciplinary collaboration

Future research should explore the impact of MFTs' unique family strengthening skills and clinical expertise with multiple systems. As these variables are better measured, the value-added contributions of MFTs to school multidisciplinary teams and academic achievement will be better understood, appreciated and utilized. Teachers, students and families should all be included in research. Outcome data should be collected from a broad base of sources to measure how MFT services make a difference in promoting school achievement, as well as to calibrate the optimal roles MFTs can play on school multidisciplinary teams. Research should include other school systems in Connecticut, as well as other states and countries where MFTs provide school-based practice. Connecticut was the first state in United States to enact legislation to certify school MFTs for full time employment, and other states are rapidly enacting similar legislation. More comprehensive scientific inquiry is recommended, in order to fully support better educational outcomes for students as well as to track the impact MFTs and other mental health professions are having on American schools.

School-based family programs and services need to be tailored to the unique systemic needs of each local school system. Although many system-based family mental health services are relevant for all schools, each school system presents its own unique needs and constraints. For instance, Westbrook began adopting MFTs and family-based services a decade ago because of the convergence of clinical needs in the town at that time, the wisdom and foresight of a school principal, and the availability of MFT students for internships in the school system.

Across the state in urban Hartford, another resourceful principal learned about MFT school certification in 2007. Robert Travaglini headed a K – 9 public school in downtown Hartford. Naylor School is a professional development school with strong ties to CCSU. Many undergraduate and graduate educators-in-training cycled through Naylor School every year, and several are hired by that school upon graduation. The school houses a rich cultural mixture of students and 27 different languages are spoken at Naylor. It is also a neighborhood school where a large number of children walk to school. Travaglini wanted to attract more family support for Naylor's students and their school activities and he requested that MFTs join his school team when the certification law was passed in 2007. Through negotiations with CCSU, we agreed to hold the MFT practicum seminar at Naylor to "immerse" students in the Naylor culture, and to more actively introduce MFTs and systems-based family programs to the Naylor culture.

During the first year, MFTs seeking school certification sought clinical placements at Naylor School and programs soon were developed. One student who lived within walking distance of the school and knew the Naylor neighborhood endeared herself to students and teachers because of her bilingual background in Portugal. Another student developed programs for parents of students on the autistic spectrum. She organized a program on Asperger's Syndrome one evening, encouraging families to bring food to share from their home countries. Over 120 people attended that program, a first for Naylor School.

During another evening program that year that same MFT student (who had a background in art) designed a three dimensional display of the LOGS Model. She secured flags from the countries represented at Naylor and had students place them on the LOGS Model in the "cultural" ring of the concentric circles. From these activities she organized several follow-up groups for parents and students on the autistic spectrum.

Another student designed leadership programs for girls that Naylor referred to as "frequent flyers". These were girls who would leave class and wander throughout the building, often getting into trouble with teachers and other students. Several of these girls came from families who had members who were part of gangs and some of the middle girls were involved with bullying younger students. Our CCSU MFT student started groups for these young women and that first year truancy went down and grades went up. The next year that MFT graduate student created a mentoring program from that group of girls, where the older adolescents were entrusted with orienting the younger girls to middle school and adolescence. Better school attendance and higher grades were sustained.

Another MFT graduate student was concerned about some of the cultural constraints between the primarily Caucasian teaching staff and the rich cultural backgrounds of the Naylor student body. Utilizing a component of Metaframeworks called Internal Family Systems, she began to do continuing education workshops with teachers designed to address some of the cultural constraints that contributed to a stressful teacher-student atmosphere. Significant gains were reported here too, by both teachers and students. Teachers reported higher comfort levels and less distress when teaching children from different cultural backgrounds.

In the years since Naylor has housed MFTs-in-training there has developed an MFT Department that now trains a group of student practicum/intern MFTs. Naylor now funds leadership of that department, and has reported that building neighborhood sustainability has increased since school-based family counseling clinicians have joined the school staff. School-based MFTs have been placed at several other urban, suburban and rural schools in Connecticut, in addition to our primary placements at Westbrook and Naylor Schools. It is critically important that there be a goodness of fit between school needs and the talent pool of school-based family counselors, just as is true for all special service staff in schools. The culture of school systems is quite different from other clinical settings. Mental health professionals need to be prepared that academic achievement is the goal of education and that mental health clinicians are "guests" in school systems. Scheduling constraints, role overlap among disciplines, and other issues that characterize school culture make school-based family counseling and other mental health work in schools unique. But despite these challenges, school-based family counseling can be instrumental in boosting school achievement.

SUMMARY AND IMPLICATIONS

There are logistical issues and scheduling problems to manage, both with pursuing a path to school certification, as well as to the process of building multidisciplinary teams to assess and services children within schools. But the value of many professional eyes on children with special needs and the collective support and skill that provides to families cannot be underestimated. Comprehensive team planning early in a child's life can prevent untold complications later, and failure to do so can become an unbearable drain on the energy, hope and creativity of the families and school systems of these students. Proactive collaborative planning can actually prevent mental health issues from developing or intensifying. Due process, hospitalizations, and out-of-district placements cannot always be avoided, but a collaborative "ounce of prevention" by a multidisciplinary team can provide "a pound of proactive cure" for children with complex health and educational needs.

When Laundy became the first school social worker in a southeastern Connecticut town forty years ago, Public Law 94-142 had not yet been enacted. Only doctoral level mental health clinicians (psychiatrists and psychologists) were Department of Public Health licensed, and the mental health clinicians practicing in schools held no state certification from the State Department of Education in Connecticut. Family therapy was just beginning to emerge as a field and profession, and was more often than not adapted as a specialization by its founding psychiatrists, psychologists, social workers and later counselors. Since the 1970s, the professions of counseling, marriage and family therapy, and social work have all pursued certification and licensure with the Connecticut Department of Public Health, as well as accreditation with the State Department of Education in Connecticut.

The field and profession of marriage and family therapy have evolved from a start as seminars and free-standing postgraduate programs in the 1970s to departments within Graduate Schools of Education, Counseling, School Psychology and Social Work. Connecticut has also witnessed the emergence of five graduate schools of family therapy since the 1970s. The Connecticut Department of Public Health licensed MFTs, counselors and social workers within a two year period from 1996-98, with much collective lobbying from our allied mental health professions. Licensure and vendorship laws in the last decade have enabled our allied health care professions to participate with equity in health care service delivery to children and families in private practice, agency and inpatient and other settings.

Because each state government has different regulatory bodies for mental health professions, pursuing school MFT certification is taking different routes for MFT professionals and the American Association for Marriage and Family Therapy (AAMFT) divisions across the US and outside the country. Within the US, each state has its own licensure and certification requirements, as do other countries. In order to pursue school certification it is important to know the systems in which you practice, whether it is your school system, your state or province, and/or your country. What has worked in Connecticut has been developing a vision for certification, utilizing the active support of AAMFT and state division leadership and committees. A competent lobbying firm is essential as well.

Primarily, however, it takes a dedicated group of collaborative colleagues, who make liberal use of the systems-based training to develop a structure, build healthy relationships, and communicate clearly and tenaciously about what is needed. It is what makes for the development of healthy families, as well as the creation of a healthy school certification law for MFTs. Family therapists call that an elegant isomorph.

RESOURCES

School Survey: School mental health administrators and clinicians vary across states and countries. Below is the survey that was utilized for schools in Connecticut. Contact Kathleen C. Laundy, PsyD at klaundy@snet.net for permission to use the survey. More about this survey is published in:

Laundy, K.C., Nelson, W., & Abucewicz, D. (2011). Building Collaborative Mental Health Teams
    in Schools through MFT School Certification: Initial Findings. *Contemporary Family
    Therapy: An International Journal, 33(4)*:384-399. DOI 10.1007/s10591-011-9158-2.

Marriage and Family Therapist Interns Public School Survey

Marriage and Family Therapy students and graduates from Central Connecticut State University have recently begun training and/or are providing services at your school. As part of the effort to evaluate their contributions to the services and supports being provided to your school community, we are requesting that you take a few minutes to complete this survey. The information garnered from the survey will be used to help to better understand the impact of the interns' work upon your school community. We thank you for taking the time to complete the survey. Please place the completed survey in the envelope provided and return it to _____ by _____.

Demographic Data

Professional Role, Please check all that apply.

General Education Teacher___, Special Education Teacher ___,
Related Services Provider ___, Student Support Staff ___.

Years of Professional Experience, please check one:

0 to 5___, 6 to 15 ___, 16 to 25+ ___,

Highest level of Education, please check the highest level achieved:

High School Diploma___, Bachelors ___, Masters ___,
Advanced Degree (6th Year or Doctorate) ___,

Please respond to the following statements by indicating if you strongly agree, agree, are undecided, disagree, or strongly disagree.

I am aware of the availability of support for students, teachers, and parents from Marriage and Family Therapist interns in the school.

Strongly agree___ , Agree___ , Undecided___, Disagree___ , Strongly disagree ___

I understand the role of the Marriage and Family Therapist interns in the school.

Strongly agree___ , Agree___ , Undecided___, Disagree___ , Strongly disagree ___

I believe Marriage and Family Therapist Interns will deliver valuable support to teachers working with children with academic and emotional challenges.
Strongly agree___ , Agree___ , Undecided___ , Disagree___ , Strongly disagree ___

I believe Marriage and Family Therapist Interns will deliver valuable support to students with disabilities who are experiencing difficulties with academic and emotional challenges.
Strongly agree___ , Agree___ , Undecided___ , Disagree___ , Strongly disagree ___

I believe Marriage and Family Therapist Interns will deliver valuable support to general education students who are experiencing difficulties with academic and emotional challenges.
Strongly agree___ , Agree___ , Undecided___ , Disagree___ , Strongly disagree ___

I believe Marriage and Family Therapist Interns will enhance the work of the School Social Worker.
Strongly agree___ , Agree___ , Undecided___ , Disagree___ , Strongly disagree ___
I believe Marriage and Family Therapist Interns will enhance the work of the School Psychologist.
Strongly agree___ , Agree___ , Undecided___ , Disagree___ , Strongly disagree ___

I believe Marriage and Family Therapist Interns have the same skill set as School Counselors and School Social Workers.
Strongly agree___ , Agree___ , Undecided___ , Disagree___ , Strongly disagree ___

I believe Marriage and Family Therapist Interns' work with families will improve educational out-comes for students.
Strongly agree___ , Agree___ , Undecided___ , Disagree___ , Strongly disagree ___

I believe the contributions of Marriage and Family Therapist Interns represent a duplication of services that are already being provided by the School Counselor and School Social Worker.
Strongly agree___ , Agree___ , Undecided___ , Disagree___ , Strongly disagree ___

Connecticut State Department of Education web information:To learn more about school certification for various school professionals, this web site offers information for Connecticut's certification laws and regulations. www.sde.ct.gov Laws and regulations vary widely across states in the US and in other countries.

REFERENCES

Alexander, K. & Alexander, M.D. (2005). *American public school law, eighth edition.* Belmont, CA: Wadsworth Cengage Learning

Anderson, W., Chitwood, S. & Hayden, D. (1997). *Negotiating the special education maze: A guide for parents and teachers.* Bethesda: Woodbine House.

Boyd-Franklin, N. & Hafer Bry, B. (2000). *Reaching out in family therapy: Home-Based, school, and community interventions/* New York: The Guilford Press.

Breunlin, D.C., Schwartz, R.C., Mac Kune-Karrer, B. (1992). *Metaframeworks: Transcending the models of family therapy.* San Francisco, Jossey-Bass Publishers.

Carlson, C. (1992) *The handbook of family-school intervention: A systems perspective.* Boston: Allyn and Bacon, pg.18.

Carter, M.J., & Evans, W.P. (2008, August). Implementing school-based family   counseling: Strategies, activities, and process considerations. *International   Journal for School-   Based Family Counseling, 1,* 1-22.

Carter, M.J., & Perluss, E.   (2008, August).   Developments   in   training   school-based   family counselors: The school-based family counseling (SBFC) graduate program at California   State University, Los Angeles. *International Journal for School-Based Family   Counseling, 1,* 1-12.

Connecticut   State   Department   of   Education   (Bureau   of   School   and   District   Improvements). (February,   2008,   Executive   summary). *Using   scientific   research-based   interventions: Improving education for **all** students, Connecticut's framework for RtI.* Retrieved from   http— www.sde.ct.gov-sde-pdf-pressroom-SRBI_full.pdf.url .

Fine, M.J. & Carlson, C., (Eds.).   (1992). *Handbook   of   family-school   interventions: A   systems perspective.* Boston: Allyn & Bacon.

Fletcher-Janzen, E. & Reynolds, C.R. (Eds.). (2008).   Neuropsychological perspectives on learning disabilities in the era of RtI: Recommendations for diagnosis and intervention. Hoboken, New Jersey: John Wiley & Sons.

Gerrard, B. A. (2008, August).   School-based   family   counseling: Overview,   trends,   and recommendations   for   future   research. *International   Journal   for   School-Based   Family Counseling. 1,* 1-30.

House, A.E. (1999). *DSM-IV Diagnosis in the schools.* New York: The Guilford Press.

Kennedy, A. (2008) Opening School Doors to MFTS. *Counseling Today.*

Laundy, K.C., Nelson, W., & Abucewicz, D. (2011). Building Collaborative Mental Health Teams   in Schools through MFT School Certification: Initial Findings. *Contemporary Family   Therapy:An International Journal, 33(4):384-399. DOI 10.1007/s10591-011-9158-2.*

Laundy, K.C. (May/June, 2009). Supervision Bulletin: Family therapy in schools. AAMFT Family   therapy magazine, 8 (3)41-43.

McDaniel, S., Hepworth, J., & Doherty, W. (1992). *Medical family therapy: A biopsychosocial approach to families and health problems.* New York: Basic Books.

Mukherjee, S., Lightfoot, J., & Sloper, P. (2000). The inclusion of pupils with a chronic health condition in mainstream school: What does it mean for teachers? *Educational   Research, 42*(1), 59-72. doi:10.1080/001318800363917.

National Association of State Directors of Special Education, Inc. (2005). *Response to intervention: Policy considerations and implementation.* Alexandria, VA.www.nasde.org

Quealy-Berge, D., & Caldwell, K. (2004). Mock interdisciplinary staffing: educating for interprofessional   collaboration. *Counselor   Education   &   Supervision,   43*(4),   310-320. Retrieved from Academic Search Premier database.

Rolland, J.S.   (1994). *Families, Illness and Disability: An integrative treatment model.* New York: Basic Books.

Salmon, G., & Kirby, A. (2008). Schools: Central to providing comprehensive CAMH services in   the future? *Child & Adolescent Mental Health, 13*(3), 107-114. doi:10.1111/j.1475-3588.2007.00468.x.

Seligman, M. & Darling, R.B. (1997). *Ordinary families, special children: A systems approach to childhood disability, Second Edition.* New York: Guilford Press.

Turnbull, R.H. (1993). *Free and appropriate public education: The law and children with disabilities*   (4th ed.). Denver: Love Publishing Company.

Wright, P. & Wright, P. (2007). *Wrightslaw: Special education law (2nd ed.).* Hartfield, VA: Harbor House Law Press, Inc.

Wright, P. and Wright, P. (2007) *From emotions to advocacy: The special education survival   guide.* Hartfield: Harbor House Law Press, Inc

Chapter 47

Connecticut MFT Models for School-Based Family Counseling: Medical Family Therapy and the Longitudinal Overview of Growth in Systems (LOGs)

Kathleen C. Laundy

OVERVIEW: *Prior to our collaboration with the Oxford group of School-Based Family Counseling clinicians, school-based MFTs in Connecticut utilized two bodies of family systems literature to develop theory for school-based MFT state certification. We utilized techniques from medical family therapy (McDaniel, Hepworth, & Doherty, 1992, Rolland, 1994) and elements of Metaframeworks theory, a common-factors "meta" model developed Breunlin, Schwartz, & Mac Kune-Karrer (1992). We learned that they compliment the parent/teacher/family/student consultation and treatment concepts from the SBFC Model. More theory is now needed to adequately prepare all mental health disciplines for multidisciplinary team collaboration in schools in order to boost student achievement. This chapter outlines elements of medical family therapy techniques as well as our LOGs Model adaptation of Metaframeworks theory, which we developed for multidisciplinary mental health work in schools. Whether offering preventive or remedial services to children and families or to school systems, medical family therapy techniques and the LOGs Model can serve to inform mental health professionals about the systemic variables they need to consider and the techniques they can use when providing collaborative school-based family counseling services.*

BACKGROUND

At first glance, it may seem unusual to include a chapter about health care and medical family therapy in a book about school-based family counseling. Many students with special educational needs have accompanying long-term health care issues, however, and many children with special health needs also develop special education needs. The last half century has witnessed an explosion of advanced technology and research in medicine and health care. With the help of advanced reproductive and neonatal technology, premature infants now survive at a growing rate. According to Genel et al., Preterm birth remains the leading cause of later-life developmental disabilities, yet its causes remain largely unknown and unpreventable and its incidence is increasing. As a result, the burden of lifelong problems and their financial costs that stem frompreterm birth are growing exponentially. (2008, p.845).

Coinciding with these trends is an increase in poverty and incidence of under and non-insured children and families. A recent estimate in Health Affairs (Kenney, Lynch, Cook, & Phong, 2010) suggested that five million children in the United States are eligible for Medicaid or the Children's Health Insurance Program (SCHIP), but are uninsured because they are not enrolled in either plan. Despite evidence from Head Start, Birth to 3, and other preschool programs that early prevention is both effective and cost efficient (Anderson, Chirwood & Hayden, 1997, pp. 88-93, Seligman & Darling, 1997, pp. 160-161), many children do not receive adequate health care and education in America's current health care milieu.

Schools have therefore increasingly become the setting where health care needs are first recognized and addressed. Rones and Hoagwood (2000) noted that schools are commonly regarded as the primary providers of mental health services for children and youth. They report research that only 16% of children receive any mental health services at all, and 70 – 80% of those psychosocial services are provided at school. Burns et al. suggest that "schools may function as the de facto mental health system for children and adolescents" (1996, p.147).

The rise of chronic illnesses has created the need for more complex and specialized diagnostic, treatment and educational services to better manage those illnesses over time. In order to be sustainable and cost effective, however, such services must also be well-monitored and delivered within a comprehensive, evidence-based framework of interventions. In other words, the success of diagnosis and treatment of chronic disorders is predicated on the development of *specialized collaborative care, based on good science, which is well coordinated* over time.

The medical specialties of pediatrics and family medicine were the leaders in the creation of the "medical home" concept, which was first developed in 1967 by the American Academy of Pediatrics. The goal of the medical home model is to reduce the cost of unmanaged chronic health disorders by streamlining and coordinating services over time. Noting that 45% of the population of our country has a chronic medical condition of some sort (Deloitte, 2008), physicians endorsing the medical home concept recommend that *primary care professionals* provide the *bulk* of diagnostic and treatment services, as well as coordinate the care of their patients over time. Schools can be important team players in the development of that system of care.

Children need to be healthy in order to learn with consistency. It seems logical to provide some of the health care services in the primary system where children function, and where comprehensive educational services are already being delivered. Some Connecticut schools have begun to incorporate health clinics into their schools in order to provide the basic medical, mental health and dental care necessary for children to attend school regularly. A growing number of hospital, community and school-based practices across the US are emerging that incorporate parallel policies and programs across the fields of health care and education. They utilize multidisciplinary collaboration to more comprehensively educate, diagnose and treat children and families who struggle with acute and chronic illnesses. The medical family therapy literature provides rich material from which to view and address the impact that chronic disabilities and illnesses can have on children and families across the life span.

Preliminary research findings about health and educational outcomes utilizing the "pediatric medical home" concept are encouraging. In a report of a three year pilot study of 300 families in 10 pediatric practices utilizing medical home practices in New Hampshire (McAllister, Scherrieb & Cooley, 2009), parents of children with special health needs reported that their children experienced better school attendance and fewer hospitalizations. The parents also reported less worry about their children's health. A review article of 30 studies by Homer et al. (2008) also provided support that medical home practices improve health outcomes for children with special needs and their families. Improvements were noted in improved health status, efficiency of service provision, and family functioning and satisfaction.

MEDICAL FAMILY THERAPY MODEL

We adapted two components of medical family therapy for use in school-based systems theory. They include John Rolland's chronic illness typology, and techniques from McDaniel, Hepworth and Doherty's *Medical Family Therapy* text (1992). These techniques can be used in any of Gerrard's six types of SBFC. Case examples will be cited for the Connecticut school systems where we place MFT graduate students.

Rolland provided a valuable way to conceptualize the impact of chronic illness on families over time. He categorized long-term medical illnesses into a schema that is useful for clinicians who treat families coping with chronic health disorders (Rolland, 1984), which is illustrated on the next page. This typology of disorders includes a consideration of one of the three ways a chronic illness can manifest itself. The first category is *Progressive*, where the illness follows a downward path of deterioration. A disorder such as Alzheimer's, which follows a path of deteriorating cognitive functioning, classifies as *progressive*. The second category is called *Relapsing*, where episodes of acute distress may be followed by a return to baseline functioning. Asthma falls into the Relapsing category. Another disorder, such as multiple sclerosis, may be ultimately *progressive*, but may initially follow a *relapsing* path. Here, episodes of the disorder may be followed by return to baseline functioning for quite some time before loss of functioning occurs. A third type of manifestation is a *Constant* type of disorder such as familial hyperlipidemia. Here, the abnormally high lipid levels which occur congenitally in some families are constant, although adverse symptoms may be entirely silent until a coronary event occurs (Laundy, 1989).

Rolland next classifies chronic illnesses according to the symptom *severity*. He classifies them according to whether they are *Incapacitating*, such as a myocardial infarction, or *Non- incapacitating*, such as atopic dermatitis, commonly known as eczema. He then breaks illnesses down further into more specific categories which include *Fatal, Shortened life, Possibly fatal, and Nonfatal.* The *Fatal* category includes illnesses such as Stage Four metastatic cancer. An example of *Shortened life, possibly fatal* includes Type I childhood diabetes mellitus, and the *Nonfatal* category includes disorders such as mild asthma. Rolland's model is illustrated below as figure 47.1.

We utilize Rolland's typology to sensitize and inform students about the role of chronic illness in children's and families' lives, and how these illnesses can affect children's functioning in school. We utilize the personal experience students have had in their own lives, and then expand their appreciation of how the wider array of chronic illnesses and disabilities can impact children and families over time.

We have students brainstorm as many chronic illnesses as they can imagine. We then have them plug their list into Rolland's typology. We utilize family genograms to examine the impact that chronic illnesses can have on students' own families, as a prelude to appreciating how that information and experience translates more generally to planning for children and schools. Other techniques from medical family therapy are useful for school-based practice. These techniques are listed below (see Figure 47.2).

Chronic Illness Typology

		Incapacitating		Non-Incapacitating	
		Acute	Gradual	Acute	Gradual
Progressive	Fatal				
Relapsing					
Progressive	Shortened Life Possibly Fatal				
Relapsing					
Constant					
Progressive	Non-fatal				
Relapsing					
Constant					

Source: Rolland, J.S. (1987, June). *Chronic illness and the life cycle: A conceptual framework.* Family Process, 26, 203-221. [CD-ROM]. Family Process, 1 - 36, Copyright 1998.

Figure 47.1   Rolland's Chronic Illness Typology

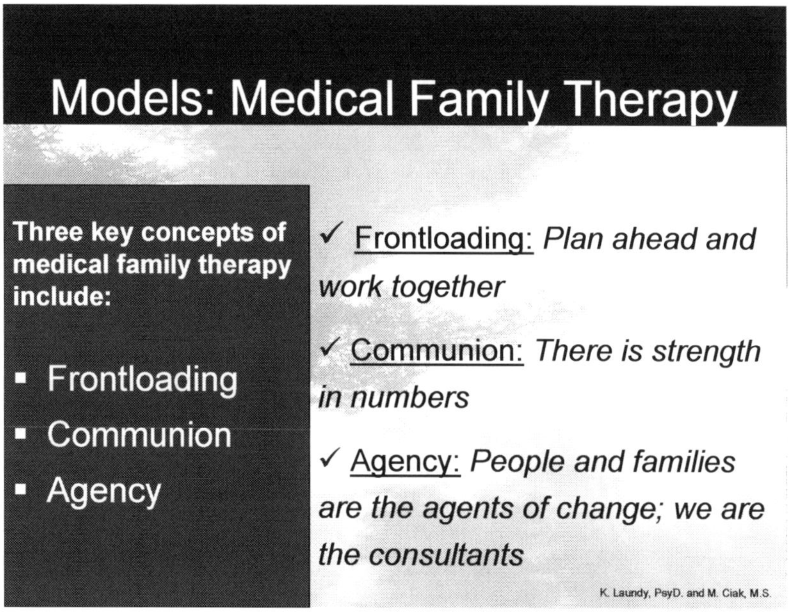

Figure 47.2   Models of Medical Family Therapy

Schools typically create multidisciplinary child study teams to begin the assessment for children with special needs, a process which involves obtaining informed consent forms from families. When schools contract with health care providers of specialized diagnostic or treatment services, they routinely obtain signed release of information forms from the families of the child they refer. At the first appointment, those of us who contract privately with schools also obtain reciprocal signed release forms, and we inquire who else provides service to them on the child's behalf. We typically begin building the multidisciplinary health care/educational team at that point. We stress that health care and education is too complicated for any one of our disciplines alone, and that we want to provide as much support to the child and family as we can. We use the term *frontloading* to support the family from the point in time when the child is referred, whether we are working within schools or are in practice outside of school systems. We utilize the data we collect in order to more comprehensively assess, track and evaluate the interventions we provide. *Frontloading* is the first step in building evidence-based treatment strategies, which is being increasingly incorporated in evidence-based interventions in education and health care. It is routinely used in schools in Planning and Placement Teams to assess children with special needs. It is also used in medical settings where complex treatment planning is required.

McDaniel, Hepworth and Doherty (1992) promote two other key medical family therapy goals that we have adopted for use in school-based professional service. The first involves promoting the concept of *agency,* first coined by Richard Totman, to describe active involvement in one's own health care. McDaniel et al. expanded this notion to include supporting and strengthening the *family's ability* to actively manage chronic health problems in a family member (pp. 9-10, 206-209). Building a sense of *agency* strengthens a family's confidence and competence to manage its family member's chronic illness or disability.

A related concept is that of enhancing *communion* in families experiencing health care crises. This notion refers both to the psychological family bonds of communication that are nurtured over the course of a chronic illness, as well as the resilience that can foster better health outcomes through team collaboration. As McDaniel, Hepworth and Doherty note, "the quality of social relationships appears to be the most powerful psychosocial factor in health and illness" (p. 10). Serious medical crises can isolate families, deplete their resources, and challenge their ability to communicate within and outside of their family. But, according to the authors, "serious illnesses and disabilities provide opportunities for resolving old conflicts and for forging new levels of healthy family bonding" (p.10). Promoting *agency* and *communion* through medical family therapy can help mitigate stressors and can actually strengthen families over the course of the illness.

Whether MFT students are placed directly in schools from Central Connecticut State University (CCSU), or whether they are placed through agencies, clinics and private practices where they complete their practicum and internship experience, they learn these medical family therapy concepts in their pre-internship classes. They then integrate these family systems-based ideas as they attend school meetings, become sensitized to cultural variations in families, and develop experience at multidisciplinary team building. These concepts are easily taught to multidisciplinary teams, which can strengthen the productivity of their planning and service provision.

The other major meta-model we have developed for school-based family work is the Longitudinal Overview of Growth in Systems (LOGS). In the past generation of family therapy literature, theorists have evolved beyond creating *specific* therapy models to developing *integrated* paradigms for clinicians to employ *across* various settings. Systems thinkers frequently illustrate their family therapy concepts as concentric circles, which represent spheres of influence that impact individuals and families.

Medical family therapists McDaniel, Hepworth and Doherty (1992), adapted Engel's biopsychosocial model of layers of influence on health into a circular pattern describing both the stages of family adjustment to illness and health, as well as players who need to be considered in health care. Those players include the patients, the health care system, *and family members.* Seaburn et al. (1996) developed a circular web of collaborative treatment that they call a "culture of collaboration" (p.8). They emphasize the importance of creating a non-hierarchical web of teams of medical and mental health care providers, patients and families as participating treatment team collaborators. Their circular model was developed as an alternative to the more traditional and linear model in medicine, where the hierarchy is more triangular and is headed by physicians.

Family therapists Boyd-Franklin and Hafer Bry (2000) developed what they called a Multisystems Model, which is illustrated as another concentric pattern of circles incorporating the layers of systems which have impact on an individual's functioning. Their Multisystems Model includes subsystem layers of immediate and extended family households, nonblood kin and friends, church and community resources, and social service agencies and other outside systems (p. 5). This model illustrates the authors' conceptualization of how to provide comprehensive family therapy in a variety of home-based, school and community settings.

LONGITUDINAL OVERVIEW OF GROWTH IN SYSTEMS (LOGS) MODEL

Borrowing from this body of medical and general family therapy literature, we created a circular prototype for work in schools called the Longitudinal Overview of Growth in Systems (LOGS) Model. To fully consider the needs of children with special needs across their school careers, we needed a growth-oriented paradigm that incorporates temporal as well as dimensional elements. LOGS is a school-based meta-model which incorporates several systemic levels of influence across the life cycle of a child and his/her family.

It is loosely based on another systemic metamodel of family therapy described in _Metaframeworks_: _Transcending the Models of Family Therapy_ (Breunlin, Schwartz, & Mac Kune-Karrer, 1997). This text forms a core curriculum component of the training that graduate MFT students receive at Central Connecticut State University (CCSU). Metaframeworks incorporates several spheres of influence which affect human systems, including individual, developmental, gender, and cultural dimensions of a person's life. Metaframeworks also includes a dimension involving the sequential patterns of behavior that families exhibit, as well as a description of the structural organization of a student's family and social milieu (p. 23).

We illustrate these elements in our LOGS Model as an elongated log, which contains a trunk with concentric circles across one end depicting the age-rings of the tree's trunk. In the LOGS Model, the trunk itself represents the life cycle development of both the individual child and her/his family. It helps frame the concurrent developmental needs and processes which occur in children and families. The concentric rings represent the individual, family, school, community and cultural dimensions of a child's functioning included in the Metaframeworks paradigm (See Figure 47.3).

The LOGS model is useful for identifying, targeting and tracking clinical interventions in schools. It can be utilized with case conceptualizations of any quadrant of the SBFC Model. Students are asked to examine the referrals they receive through the LOGS lens, and to design interventions that they clinically address over time.

We utilize the LOGS Model to help ground students in their understanding about the impact of many layers of systems on child and family functioning. We examine cases through the LOGS lens, then begin to prioritize and rank order best practices over time. Because students graduate and leave school systems every year, the LOGS Model helps to establish continuity over time in cases that have multiple needs and dimensions.

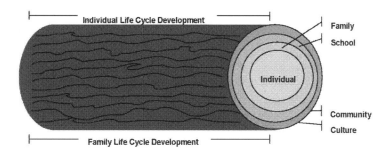

Figure 47.3 The Longitudinal Overview of Growth in Systems (LOGS) Model

LOGS Model Instructions:

1. Using a case of your choosing with a school, family, remedial or preventive focus, apply the LOGS model to determine how you would intervene in a case. Which elements provide the most to least constraints?

2. What systemic intervention should take priority, or is there more than one area that should be addressed concurrently?

3. Rank interventions in order below, from most to least important, with brief descriptor of intervention.

Systems	Rank	Intervention(s)
Individual Development		
Family Life Cycle Development		
Individual		
Family		
School		
Community		
Culture		

CASE EXAMPLE

Our case example involves a high school sophomore named Gabriel, who was referred to me for a triennial evaluation by his school system. Gabe was diagnosed with Asperger's Disorder, which can be classified on Rolland's typology as a *Constant* Disorder with a potentially *Incapacitating* but *Non-fatal* course. Gabe is the only adopted son of professional parents. He was diagnosed with Asperger's as a fifth grader in his former school system in another state, although his parents suspected early after his adoption as an infant that his development seemed uneven and delayed. Although Gabe spoke early, his fine and gross motor development skills were delayed, as well as his behavior in social situations. He was easily over-stimulated by sights, sounds and people. His frustration tolerance was low, and he experienced frequent "meltdowns". His parents described these as dramatic temper tantrums which included such self-injurious behavior as hitting his head against walls and pounding his fists on his head.

Gabe showed the discomfort with transitions and tendency to focus on details instead of the bigger picture that many students with Asperger's show. Although school reports indicated that he was bright, particularly in language arts and social studies, Gabe made inconsistent progress in public elementary school. As he approached middle school, his parents placed him in a small private school to provide more structure and less overwhelming stimulation for Gabe.

From his infancy on, Gabe's parents became informed advocates and active seekers of support for his emotional and educational needs. They joined an Asperger's network for parents and educators in their state, which had progressive legislation as well as grass roots organizations for families and professionals involved with children on the autistic spectrum. When Gabe and his family relocated to our state, his parents sought help from the local school system where they moved. Fortunately, the Director of Special Services was skilled at building multidisciplinary school teams. She convened a team meeting and asked me to complete an updated psychological evaluation of Gabe, in order to support his transition to his new school and develop needed academic and other support services.

Gabe's scores on his psychological evaluation placed him in the Superior Range of cognitive functioning on the Verbal Comprehension Scale. His score on the Perceptual Organization Scale, the nonverbal domain, was compromised by his difficulty completing test items with speed and accuracy. Gabe also received significantly lowered scores on scales measuring his working memory and his ability to process and synthesize information accurately and with precision, as is common in Asperger's Disorder. But he showed no major signs of having specific learning disabilities. In fact, his scores on achievement testing measures were generally higher than his measured abilities, with the exception of mathematical calculations.

These findings affirmed what we observed in Gabe's behavior and performance at school. That is, Gabe did well with oral discussions in class and he had expectations that he would achieve in his new school. He chose to attend his school team meetings, and Gabe enjoyed talking with the adults around the table in that setting.

But Gabe had consistent difficulty operating under timed conditions on tests in class, and he was not able to complete assignments by their due dates. Gabe's ability to process competing stimuli, particularly in unstructured social situations such as the cafeteria, was significantly impaired. When he had to "think on his feet", especially in novel situations, Gabe's mood and behavior quickly decompensated. He became anxious, had difficulty remaining seated and paced around the room, becoming more agitated as he paced. His anxiety would build until he began to cry or shout, bang his head against a wall or curse or hit himself.

At such times, Gabe needed to leave the school setting. His mother would pick him up at school, often early in the day, and he would remain home for the rest of the school day. During the eruptions at school, Gabe was oblivious to the effects of his behavior on other students or teachers. But he became embarrassed and guilt- stricken later, when his behavior calmed and he reconstructed the events of the meltdown.

Gabe's Special Services Director first established a special plan for him, called a 504 Plan. This is a plan established under an amended component of the US federal special education law, Public Law 94-142 which requires the development of special services for students with handicaps. It fit into Gerrard's SBFC Model under the School-Remedial category of interventions. Gabe's plan included specific tutoring with special teachers in school. This resource was created to help Gabe process, comprehend, and complete assignments with more efficiency.

In addition, Gabe and his family were referred to me for supportive individual and family therapy, and his parents were referred to the Parent Support Group for students with spectrum disorders at a local social service agency and led by our MFT graduate students. Here we incorporated both Family-Remedial and Family-Preventive interventions of the SBFC Model, to help Gabe's family solve social problems he encountered and to help Gabe and his parents avoid some of the difficulties they encountered as new community members with a family member with autism.

Next, The Special Education Director realized that Gabe's behavior, although frightening to other students, did not fit into the same category as other potentially violent behaviors which warranted suspension under the school's Zero Tolerance Policy. She worked with the team to construct a safety plan for Gabe in school, so that he didn't lose valuable learning opportunities by having to leave the school milieu where he could practice more adaptive behaviors. The school counselor, nurse, psychologist, and social worker all collaborated to help Gabe recognize when he felt "triggered" and his behavior started to escalate at school. He was invited to proceed to one of their offices to cool off, rather than being sent to the office for dismissal from school. Because Gabe was a good writer, we composed a one-page "de-briefing" outline to have him complete after meltdown incidents. His assignment was to use the outline to reconstruct what happened, and devise a written plan for what to do the next time a meltdown occurred as a preparation for re-entry to classes. His school psychologist volunteered to liaison with me about his school behavior, so that we could mutually reinforce this safety plan. We incorporated both School-Intervention and School-Prevention interventions from SBFC in our multidisciplinary collaborations.

Gabe needed to leave school only twice after that. In a few weeks, he began to achieve success in managing his self-injurious episodes. At a 504 meeting held one month later, Gabe suggested that he might make amends with classmates who observed his meltdowns by giving testimonials in class about Asperger's Disorder to his peers. We all agreed that orienting his classmates to the nature of Asperger's could be good for Gabe as well as his classmates. Gabe's lectures to his classmates were well received, with the interesting result that other students *also* began opening up in class about general issues that affected *them*. It was a wonderful preventive opportunity that Gabe himself initiated to offer bullying prevention meetings in his classroom.

Gabe continued utilizing opportunities such as this to build his social confidence and skills. At the agency he was invited to mentor other newly diagnosed young people with Asperger's Disorder and his parents did the same with other parents in the support group at the youth service agency. By his senior year Gabe's friendship base expanded somewhat and he began to take a few more social risks. After a period of much trepidation and anxiety he decided to attend his senior prom with a group of his friends. Although he continued to have difficulty completing assignments on time, Gabe's grades improved sufficiently that he graduated with his class and he was accepted at a state university to begin college.

For Gabe and his family several areas of the LOGS Model were employed to help him adapt to his new school and function with more success. Gabe's individual behavior needed immediate attention, which was addressed skillfully through the wisdom and direction of his Special Services Director and his multidisciplinary team. Establishing clarity about Gabe's academic strengths and needs through an updated psycho- educational evaluation helped us create a 504 plan. Schools regularly employ such team planning meetings, and they have well documented methods for tracking students' progress. Family therapists also employ these collaborative techniques to address all relational aspects of a young person's functioning, utilizing the goal of strengthening the family as a central tenet of clinical work. Such collaboration illustrates the medical family therapy techniques of *Frontloading, Agency* and *Communion.*

A major strength of this case was Gabe's parents, who graciously brought a wealth of knowledge about Asperger's Disorder to the team, as well as strong family support for their son. They modeled well the notion of *Agency*, whereby the confidence they brought from their former advocacy efforts encouraged the school team and *further* developed their own sense of *Advocacy.*

We were able to create and employ a plan with *all* team members' active input and support as soon as he entered the school system. Such *Frontloading* or comprehensive planning served to apply system-wide interventions to Gabe. Such systemic planning at the beginning of his school year served to facilitate Gabe's willingness to manage his meltdowns earlier and with more success. Active inclusion of Gabe's family served to increase their sense of *Communion* with Gabe's team at school.

We utilized the family and school rings of the LOGS Model to specifically target Gabe's individual needs. Gabe's parents brought valuable skills and information about Asperger's Disorder from the *culture* of the state where they used to live which served to make the frontloading process more valued, efficient and productive. Our family therapy and consultation with Gabe's parents illustrates some Family-Remedial and Family-Preventive we utilized together to help Gabe function better in school.

Regarding life cycle aspects of LOGS, Gabe's family was ready to begin the "launching" process of their son as he graduated from high school and transitioned to college. Gabe, however, as often happens with bright students with Asperger's, was understandably anxious about the big changes in his life. His parents relied on the collective support of the agency MFTs and school team to help them prepare Gabe for graduation and the college transition. They scheduled several family sessions the summer after graduation to rehearse as a family what Gabe needed to do to make a successful transition to college.

For this case we were able to provide remedial tutoring and counseling services (School and Family Preventive and Remedial SBFC) as well as preventive mental health services by his team to keep Gabe in school and boost his achievement. We worked with his teachers to address classroom management and stress management for Gabe. Team consultation with his teachers at school meetings and informal "curbside consults" helped Gabe's teachers understand his behavior. For Gabe's parents, we provided remedial counseling with me and with our contracted MFTs in a parent support group, which helped them navigate Gabe's last two years of high school and transition into college. We utilized an array of multidisciplinary team interventions (with both school employees and contracted clinicians) to boost Gabe's achievement, keep him in school, and help him graduate with his peers.

Medical family therapy and the LOGS Model fit well in public education as well as the SBFC Model. They illustrate the possibilities of integrating *all* services provided to children in schools, and serve as a template for *how* each discipline can fit together on a child's behalf over time to help that child achieve. Concurrent school services for a child may include, for example, a paraprofessional in the classroom to help a child sustain attention, occupational therapy to improve fine motor skills, a social skills group led by an MFT, school psychologist, counselor or school social worker, a parent support group led by an MFT or other school mental health clinician, and psychological testing provided by a school psychologist, as occurred with Gabe's case. The LOGS Model accommodates all of those services and helps locate where and when they can be offered during a child's school career, and blends well with the array of SBFC interventions listed throughout this book.

Services may change yearly through a child's Individual Educational Plan (IEP), 504 Plan, or other tracking mechanism. Individual, family, school and other variables will inevitably change over time. Interventions at one stage of development (such as protection from bullying by limiting a child's activities) may, in fact, impede that child's progress as the child becomes healthier and more mature.

The LOGS Model is a useful mnemonic to help integrate and calibrate the services extending *throughout* a student's academic career, particularly for those students with chronic educational and health needs (as illustrated in Rolland's typology). Any teacher or clinician may apply their particular skills to a specific service or need in a linear, sequential way, such as a social skills group or a behavioral management feedback system.

But with the LOGS framework, a professional or parent can more easily fit their expertise holistically into the *full* context of the child's education over time. It provides a school-based systems perspective to academic performance and achievement. Medical family therapy offers some valuable techniques for joining with families to provide more comprehensive school-based services. And the SBFC Model adds valuable information about where to direct interventions to children and families in schools. The three models serve complimentary functions and provide valuable resources to mental health clinicians who practice in school systems.

REFERENCES

Anderson, W., Chitwood, S. & Hayden, D. (1997). *Negotiating the special education maze: A guide for parents and teachers.* Bethesda: Woodbine House.

Boyd-Franklin, N. & Hafer Bry, B. (2000). *Reaching out in family therapy: Home- based, school, and community interventions.* New York: The Guilford Press.

Breunlin, D.D, Schwartz, R.C., & Mac Kune-Karrer, B. (1997). *Metaframeworks: Transcending the models of family therapy.* San Francisco: Jossey-Bass.

Burns, B.J., Costello, E.J., Angold, A., Tweed., D., et al. (1995). Children's mental health service use across sectors. (Chevy Chase). *Health Affairs, 14(30),* 147 – 159.

Deloitte Center for Health Solutions. (2010). The Medical Home: Disruptive Innovation for a new primary care model. Retrieved from http://www.deloitte.com.assets.Dcom-UnitedStates/LocalAssets/Document/us_chs_MedicalHome_w.pdf

Doherty, W.J. & Baird, M.A. (1987). *Family-centered medical care: A clinical casebook.* New York: Guilford.

Genel, M., McCaffree, M.A., Hendricks, K., Dennery, P.A., Hay, Jr.,W.W., Stanton, B., Szilagyi, P.G., & Jenkins, R.R. (2008). A national agenda for America's children and adolescents in 2008: Recommendations from the 15th annual public policy plenary symposium, Annual meeting of the Pediatric Academic Societies, May 3, 2008. *Pediatrics: Official Journal of the American Academy of Pediatrics, 122, 4, 843-849.*

Homer, C.J., Klatka, K., Romm, D., Kuhlthau, K., Bloom, S., Newacheck, P., Van Cleave,J.,& Perrin, J.M. (October, 2008). A review of the evidence for the medical home for children with special health care needs. *Pediatrics.* 122 (4), 3922-e937 (doi:10.1542/peds.2007-3762)

Kenney, G.M., Lynch, V., Cook, A & Phong, S. (2010). Who and where are the children yet to enroll in Medicaid and the Children's Health Insurance Program? *Health Affairs, published online September 3, 2010, Project Hope .* doi: 10.1377/hlthaff.2010.0747.

Laundy, K.C. (1990). *The relationship between family psychosocial functioning and compliance with treatment for familial hyperlipidemia. (Doctoral dissertation).* Dissertation Abstracts International. 50 – 10B, 4774. University Microfilms No. 8923642).

McAllister, J., Sherrieb, K. & Cooley, C. (2009). Improvement in the family-centered medical home enhances outcomes for children and youth with special healthcare needs. *Journal of Ambulatory Care Management.* 32(3), 188-196.

McDaniel, S., Hepworth, J., & Doherty, W. (1992). *Medical family therapy: A biopsychosocial approach to families with health problems.* New York: Basic Books.

Rolland, J.S. (1994). *Families, illness, and disability: An integrative treatment model.* New York: Basic Books.

Rolland, J.S. (1984). Toward a psychosocial typology of chronic and life-threatening illness. *Family Systems Medicine, (2)245-62. Reprinted with permission of Family Process, Inc.*

Rones, M., & Hoagwood, K. (2000). School-based mental health services: A research review. *Clinical Child & Family Psychology Review,* 34, 223, 241.

Seaburn, D.B., Lorenz, A.D., Gunn, W.B., JR., Gawinski, B.A., & Mauksch. (1996). *Models of Collaboration: A guide for mental health professionals working with health care practitioners.* New York: Basic Books.

Seligman, M. & Darling, (1997). *Ordinary families, special children: A systems approach to childhood disability, Second Edition.* New York: Guilford Press.

Volkmar, F. & Wiesner, L. (2009). *A Practical Guide to Autism: What Every Parent, Family Member and Teacher Needs to Know.* New Jersey, John Wiley & Sons, Inc.

Yapko, Diane. (2003). *Understanding autism spectrum disorders: Frequently asked questions.* London and Philadelphia: Jessica Kingsley Publishers.

RESOURCES

Medical Family Therapy: Medical family therapy is being increasingly incorporated across hospital and outpatient settings in the U.S., and an updated text from McDaniels, Hepworth and Doherty is currently in press.

Longitudinal Overview of Growth in Systems (LOGS): Was developed by MFT faculty and students over the first five years of school-based MFT practice in Connecticut. For more information about LOGS, contact Kathleen Laundy, PsyD at klaundy@snet.net.

Autism Spectrum Disorders: There are growing resources to acquaint clinicians with the autism spectrum disorders. Jessica Kingsley Publishers offers many books and games to introduce clinicians to autistic spectrum disorders and offer treatment resources. World renowned expert on autism, Fred Volkmar and his wife Lisa Wiesner recently published A *Practical Guide to Autism: What Every Parent, Family Member and Teacher Needs to Know* (2009). New Jersey, John Wiley & Sons, Inc. This is another valuable resource to help clinicians become familiar with autistic spectrum disorders.

Chapter 48
Mission Possible:
A Private Practice SBFC Model

Christine L. Tippett

OVERVIEW: This chapter describes the history and progress of Mission Possible in the Sacramento Valley, where since 1994, it has been functioning in a private practice model, providing SBFC mental health services to youth and families in elementary and secondary schools throughout Sacramento and San Joaquin Counties.

BACKGROUND

I first became aware of the likelihood that youth and families would be well served by having mental health services available within the school system when I was a graduate student in Social Work in the mid 1970's. When I became licensed as both a Licensed Clinical Social Worker and a Marriage and Family Therapist (in 1979 and 1980), I blended the skills to address family systems in work with clients in whatever constructs they formed. Shortly thereafter, AB 3632 passed in California, beginning an era of team building among educators, mental health providers, social service case managers and families to become "whole family helpers" for at-risk youth. At that time I was the Coordinator for Mental Health Services for Children and Adolescents for Sacramento County, so I felt honored to be in the position to implement this legislation and the challenges it presented.

I left that administrative position to become a parent myself, and soon entered the world of school-based interaction from three different viewpoints:

Therapist: Some of my clients were (and continue to be) students from preschool through college ages; as a result, collaboration and consultation have been part of my practice for decades.

Parent: From the time my son entered kindergarten until he graduated from eighth grade, I volunteered in his classroom as the "Tuesday mom," and thus became the example of the helper during the situations throughout the years.

Professor: When I began teaching at the University of San Francisco in 1992, at the Sacramento Campus, in the Marriage and Family Therapy Program, I began hearing about the wonderful work being done at the Mission Possible Program within the Center for Child and Family on the main campus under the direction of Dr. Brian Gerrard. Our students in Sacramento could certainly benefit from such a wonderful placement opportunity, and our local schools could certainly benefit from such a great resource for USF trainees to provide on-site help. However, I knew that the overhead expenses of having a Center to run were costly, and that the administrative cost of having a faculty member in place to oversee a center was prohibitive so...

I decided to create a local program with a very modest budget, to fit the harsh reality of the declining economy, and offer it to a district dear to my heart, to see if it could help meet some of the unmet needs of the community.

It remains true that approximately 10% of children and adolescents in the United States will meet criteria for a mental health disorder during their school years [National Institute of Mental Health, 2004], and, regardless of a formal diagnosis, 12% to 22% of youth under age 18 have a need for mental health intervention to address emotional or behavioral difficulties (Christner, 2009), I met with Dr. Brian Gerrard and Dr. Steven Pomerantz, and obtained support to create *Mission Possible* as it has evolved in the Sacramento Valley. This model is a school based youth and family counseling program operating on elementary, middle and high school campuses with high risk students, to facilitate their success academically, socially, behaviorally and emotionally as they progress through the developmental stages of competency and identity discovery. The program brings trainees and interns from the University of San Francisco graduate program in Marriage and Family Therapy, at the Sacramento Campus, under the supervision of a private practitioner, and contracts with local school districts to provide mental health services on designated school sites.

More than 25% of school children experience moderate to severe school adjustment problems due to emotional difficulties, and children who do not experience early school success are at risk of school failure, dropping out, becoming drug addicted and delinquent, and developing serious emotional disorders, which result in costly burdens to society (Drewes, 2001a, in Christner, 2009); thus, after meeting with Brian Gerrard to learn about the Center for Child and Family in San Francisco, and interviewing with staff there to learn how the Center and school based services operated, I approached the Natomas Unified School District to begin this venture in 2004. I presented the well documented position that mental health providers might serve as mediators and facilitators between families and the schools (Boyd-Franklin, 2000). At that time, the school counselor/student ratio in California was 1:951, and the "recommended school counselor/student ratio was 1:250 (Counseling Today, 2005). In 2012-13 the school counselor student ratio was 1: 945 (see Figure 48.1).

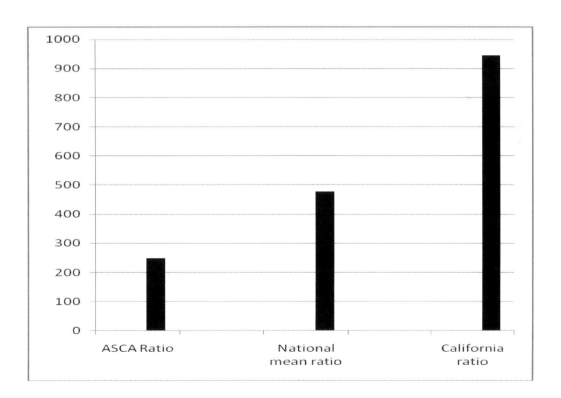

Figure 48.1 School Counselor/Student Ratios

In the Sacramento community, there are four Special Education Local Planning Areas, encompassing seventeen school districts, within which some overlapping charter schools operate. Each of these stakeholders understands that school is the equivalent of a workplace for children and adolescents. If the youth learn how to handle the challenges experienced while in school, they will be able to handle employment and further challenges later on (Boyd-Franklin, 2000). Further, mental health is directly related to children's learning and development. It intersects with interpersonal relationships, socio-emotional skills, behavior, academic motivation, learning, mental illness, crisis prevention and response, school safety and substance abuse. Each of these issues affects not only the success and well-being of the individual student but also the school climate and outcomes for all students (www.counseling.org, 2010). As Coordinator for Mental Health Services for Children and Adolescents, I had worked closely with the SELPA (Special Education Local Planning Area) Directors in implementing AB 3632 (later PL 26.5). This helped me understand the importance of teambuilding on school sites, and increased my desire to bring mental health services as an adjunct to the already overstressed academic counseling load that existed at those school sites.

PROGRAM DESCRIPTION

This model was proposed to the Natomas Unified School District, to be piloted in one elementary school, one middle school and one high school, in order to reach the K-12 range of student population. However, when presented to the District for initial consideration, with benefit for "at risk youth", the population that was identified fit with what has been researched by Christner & Rosemary (2009)

> …adolescents with mental health disorders are at increased risk for poor
> academic achievement as well as continued mental disability. Many youth
> who suffer from mental disorders also end up in the juvenile justice system,
> an outcome that could be prevented if they were treated while still in school.
> These young people are also at increased risk for substance abuse and failing
> to complete school.

While schools remain focused, as they should, on TEACHING students, they are becoming increasingly aware that, the 10-25% of the population of those being taught with emotional distress/disturbance will be better taught IF/WHEN their socio-emotional issues are addressed as part of their ongoing growth-promoting experience. Thus, when *Mission Possible* was presented to the Natomas Unified School District, as an opportunity to have a graduate level trainee at a school site two days each week, providing mental health services to youth and their families, freeing academic counselors to do the college prep work that was mandated by the State, and charging the district ONLY for the cost of supervising the trainees, the contract was approved, and the placements were selected to start at both middle schools and both high schools, to reach the most at risk youth first.

Learning supports have been shown to be directly effective in reducing barriers to learning and overall success. Resources, strategies, and practices that provide physical social and intellectual support to learning, teaching and emotional interaction can reengage disconnected students (www.louisianaschools.net). *Mission Possible* is helping the whole child succeed, by accepting referrals from the designated site link from each school, from teachers through that designee, from a referral box with a confidential slot so that youth may self refer, from administrators who may contact the trainee directly, from parents who may contact the school, or from other students who may request help with conflict resolution.

The SBFC approach requires volunteer time from the trainee counselors, who receive graduate school credit for their experience with *Mission Possible.* Over the years, some of them have devoted such extraordinary effort to this project that they have stayed an additional year to share their skills with this community. In addition, this model requires a contract between each district or charter school and the supervising clinician, so that the contracted supervision will be compensated. The annual cost for supervising approximates $4500 (@$75.00 per hour). This cost is far less than would be charged for any agency overhead or for any third party billing or eligibility determination, so *Mission Possible* makes it possible for more youth to be served, more effectively, with more efficiency, more easily.

Since 2004, the program has served over 1200 youth and families, and saved several lives. The services that have been performed have varied, and the interventions have been flexible. The client issues have included:

self-injury
peer conflict (sometimes escalating to physical aggression/suspension
parental separation/divorce
foreclosure/homelessness
abuse (physical, sexual, emotional)
relational harassment
gang activity
bullying
serious emotional disturbance
cultural shock (transition to/from differing continents
grief (loss of significant caregiver)
chronic truancy
school failure (not turning in completed work)
substance use/abuse)
mood disturbance (depression, anxiety)

Empirical evidence shows that intervention with early adolescents with early warning signs, like those identified above, e.g., truancy, poor grades, behavioral problems, and difficulty getting along at home and/or school, will have an increased probability of developing *severe* problems later on (Boyd-Franklin, 2000). Further, middle school youth are seen as good targets for identification for help; if they begin to disengage, and then repeat a grade due to academic failure (e.g., not turning in completed work), poor attendance, discipline referrals or any of the other issues referenced above, then the more generalized problems can be anticipated (Boyd-Franklin, 2000).

RELATIONSHIP TO THE SBFC MODEL

Mission Possible in the Sacramento Valley relates to the SBFC model in a holistic manner, in that the program works to help the whole child succeed within his or her real world, which incorporates the ecosystem within which the child survives and grows. While doing this, the child is growing through either the developmental stage of industry or identity, so how much or how little the guardians are actually in attendance during the therapy sessions differs on a case by case basis. Nonetheless, the family is a crucial component of assessment and treatment. How this looks in terms of the SBFC model follows:

Promoting self esteem: *Family Prevention; School Prevention*
Improving attendance: *School Prevention*

Improving behavior: *School Prevention; School Intervention*
Increasing grades: *School Intervention; School Prevention*

Community employed or contracted mental health providers focus their work on a student's "global mental health" and how it impacts family, community, and school functioning (www.counseling.org, 2010). The school setting, into which the *Mission Possible* volunteer trainees have entered for the past eight years, provides ample teachable moments to introduce and reinforce rational thinking concepts, which can be generalized to wide problem solving situations (Christner, 2009). Also called therapy moments, these examples from daily interactions are brought into sessions to process and facilitate growth.

Boyd-Franklin and Hafer-Bry, among others, have identified numerous socio-emotional learning competencies that can translate well from school based interventions to school, family, and community success: Self awareness: identification and recognition of one's own emotions, recognition of strengths in self and others, sense of self-efficacy and self confidence; Social awareness: empathy, respect for others, and perspective taking; Responsible decision making: evaluation and reflection and personal and ethical responsibility; Self management: impulse control, stress management, persistence, goal setting, and motivation; Relationship skills, cooperation, help seeking and providing, and communicating (Christner, 2009).

PROGRAM DESCRIPTION

The trainees I select for *Mission Possible* may come from a variety of backgrounds. They will be working in districts that serve clients from very diverse cultures; the original schools I approached for the pilot project had been known to serve students with 32 first languages on entry to first grade. All of the trainees and interns who have since worked with *Mission Possible* in its expansion through the Valley have been allowed the opportunity to learn and grow while providing a great benefit to the community. Because of their placement in schools away from the place where supervision occurs, they must possess the following skill set in addition to the knowledge, skills and abilities they are learning as part of their graduate training in marriage and family therapy, in order to succeed in this valuable work:

initiative
self confidence
willingness to work as a team member
ability to ask for help when needed
flexibility
self awareness

Trainees and/or interns commit to work at their designated schools for the duration of the school year; they may choose to extend on a yearly basis if the fit is mutually agreeable. However, for continuity of therapeutic benefit for students/clients being served onsite, the commitment goes from year to year, rather than changing throughout the year as much as possible. Teambuilding among staff and administration is enhanced by this practice; *Mission Possible* has come to be known as the favorite program of those who come in and out of the schools but who, unlike us, do not seem to maintain a consistent link with either students or staff.

This consistency, and the delivery of those socio-emotional supports which were referenced earlier, are thus shown to be linked to the development of a positive school climate (Christner, 2009) as the bond between *Mission Possible* and the school sites reveals. This was clearly evident during a very low economic point in 2009, when 48 of the 52 school counselors in the Natomas Unified School District were given pink slips. The School Board sadly had to withdraw funding from Mission Possible in order to retain the remaining 4 counselors and try to comply with the mandates for scheduling and college readiness with just 4 employees. Since the cost for *Mission Possible* had continued to be kept so skeletal, and the services were considered so crucial, each of the sites approached their site councils and secured school funding to keep the program onsite. Thus *Mission Possible* has remained intact through the Valley economic crisis, and has welcomed back the 48 academic counselors when they returned this Spring! Those counselors kept the student/academic counselor ratio in the 1/850 range for academic readiness, and left *Mission Possible* available to help with socio-emotional issues.

CASE EXAMPLES

Confidentiality is the cornerstone of the psychotherapeutic relationship. This is basic knowledge for all allied health and mental health professionals. However, when counselors work with other professionals, the meaning of this standard, and the implications of violating it, can either strengthen alliances or create barriers to effective work with student/client/families. Thus, the standard that fits for school based mental health practitioners is that therapists should be careful to share *with informed consent only, unless in excepted circumstances* only information that benefits the client (Boyd-Franklin, 2000). The case examples included here have been disguised to preserve client anonymity, while retaining sufficient detail to alert the reader to the systemic collaboration exhibited in implementing the humanistic systems perspective in school based mental health intervention.

AMBROSE

One morning I was visiting one of the high schools, getting ready for the mid-term evaluation meeting. In order to make efficient use of the time away from my office, my trainee and I had scheduled her weekly supervision meeting to be held there, on campus, prior to the start of her time with students that day. One of her clients that year was Ambrose, an African American youth who had moved to California from Texas to live with his maternal aunt following the sad loss of his mother due to a brain aneurysm. He was feeling lost and without energy, and was not responding to the "tough love" approach his aunt was providing in an attempt to help him move forward in life. As a senior in high school, he had been doing well in Texas, was athletic and academically successful, and friendly; however, since moving to California, he noticed a change, with little energy for previous activities or interests. He was not interested in involving his aunt in counseling; for fear that she would consider him "weak" and be even more disappointed in him than she already appeared. The trainee and I devised a plan to work with the client and his aunt symbolically, in order to help him address his distress, reground, and decide his next steps. He wrote a practice dialogue with his aunt, and then role-played it with the trainee, playing both roles in succession. After expressing the feelings in session, he did this task at home, and returned with a greater sense of calm.

On the day I was at the high school, there was a quiet knock at the door; with my permission, the trainee opened the door. Standing outside was a very polite Ambrose, asking if she would be willing to write a letter on his behalf for admission to a university in Northern California! She arranged a meeting with him for later that day, and then we strategized. I encouraged her to talk with her site link and his academic counselor, sharing only the information that would be to his benefit, and with his informed consent, so that no one would think that collusion rather than collaboration occurred.

Then I encouraged her to think what she would like to ask him before she wrote the letter, and she said: "Why would you like to go to college most?" I supported her in posing this question, emphasizing the <u>most</u>, and she did just that. When they met, and he answered, "I want to learn to do something so that I can give back to the community. My mom would have liked that." She incorporated that into the letter, read it to him, and sent it to the university. A few months later, he received an early acceptance letter! He felt a return of his energy, and no longer felt like running back to Texas.

ANGER MANAGEMENT GROUP

One of the trainees was working with several youth at a middle school who had been referred for difficulty with anger management and/or defiant behavior. He noticed that they did well in individual counseling, but had difficulty managing interpersonal interaction. In supervision, we talked about the developmental challenge of identity growth through group diffusion, which eventually emerges into identity emergence later; I suggested that he create a peer group to simulate a slice of life, and use the situations that are brought into group to problem solve and then generalize therefrom. Very soon, an incident occurred that could not have been done by anyone other than peers → One student was describing his difficulty in getting to school on time; all of his "buddies" were commiserating, and saying things like, "Oh, man, that's hard, can you get a clock?...Or, can someone help you get up?...Or, how come no one helps you not get in trouble?" Then, when the 'victim' began berating his Mom, calling her a "****ing *****, who should just get the **** out of my room", the <u>kids</u> said, in the quietest voices heard ever thus far, "Oh, man, you can't talk to your Mom, that way. If I did that, I'd get smacked into the wall." Just hearing other kids say that garbage talk was not OK was enough to unstick a group member from his position; the trainee was able to facilitate by being present rather than lecturing or overcontrolling. During the course of the group, tools such as a hacky sack [a golf-sized, soft, pliable ball which feels soft yet is comforting to hold and comes in a variety of earth friendly colors],(to show who had the floor for talking), a thumb-ball [a round ball with words plastered all over it; whoever catches it selects the word covered by his "thumb" which elicits feedback on a topic], anger bingo [one of a series of bingo games used with youth to teach wider examples of triggers and options for affect management] and worksheets were used as needed, but the greatest gifts came from the mouths of the participants themselves.

JOSIE

This youth had been seen by a *Mission Possible* trainee in a prior year. When the next year began, he requested services again, because he was beginning to feel increasingly despondent, depressed and, eventually suicidal. The trainees are taught to assess for self harm and suicidality, and also to call for consultation as needed. A copy of the *Self Injury Contract* is shown as Box 48.1

When it became clear that this client could not remain safe from self harm, the trainee contacted me. We agreed that it was time to initiate a Welfare and Institutions Code§5150. WIC§5150 authorizes mental health persons in California to help clients who, as a result of serious emotional disturbance, pose evidence of grave, imminent, lethal danger to self or others, and thus require evaluation of need for care and custody in a facility designated to provide 24 hour services for no more than 72 hours before review, be taken to such facility for evaluation and possible detention and care. The following steps were taken:

1. The Sacramento County 911 5150 assistance operator was contacted;
2. The client's mother was contacted;
3. The trainee had the client come to the phone so that I could talk with him and let him know that the police would be coming to help him get to a place where people will be with him 24 hours a day until his feelings become manageable; the police will be coming to him to help him (not to arrest him; the phone is on speaker phone so that the trainee's messages matched my statements to this vulnerable client;

4. The trainee let the site link know just the emergent details so that when the police arrive on campus, there is no escalated drama;

5. I follow up with the trainee once the client has been transported from the school site, to debrief the process.

Box 48.1 Self Injury Contract

Self Injury Contract

This is my self-injury contract. I have agreed to carry it around with me and refer to it when I am upset and feel like hurting myself. I won't guarantee that I will never hurt myself, but I guarantee that I will read and do what I've agreed to do in this contract before I hurt myself.

I feel the impulse to hurt myself because:

I think it will help me to get through this moment, but it will cost me:

Before I hurt myself, I can:

Four people I can call before I hurt myself are:

Name: Phone #

Name: Phone #

Name: Phone #

Name: Phone #

One thing that I can try, that has worked before and is almost always comforting to me, is:

The most important reminder for me is:

_____   _____
Client Signature   *Date*   *Witness Signature*   *Date*

In this case, the client was hospitalized, stabilized, and returned to school. The client and his mother have consistently worked toward success for the remainder of the school year, with collaboration from clinical, teaching and administrative support. This particular mom has requested input from me regarding a complicated third party entanglement (insurance billing for the hospital stay that started, lapsed, and then asked about "preexisting conditions" for a teen a with serious emotional disturbance warranted a consultation that no trainee should be expected to provide. The whole child is being considered in the nest of his high school environment, with such respect that he regularly refers his friends to "his *Mission Possible* counselor, and when a sticky ethical dilemma occurs for him, he asks her to check with "Miss Christine".

EVIDENCE-BASED SUPPORT

The USF trainees have worked at the schools as mental health providers, and become integral members of the helping community, for the past eight years. During one of our presentations to the Natomas Unified School District School Board, the program was called "a Godsend", to a resounding ovation of applause from appreciative community members. The services provided at each school include individual counseling, family counseling, group counseling, crisis intervention, community collaboration and referral, consultation with staff and administration, and program development. In addition, twice during each year, I visit each school to do program evaluation with the identified site link personnel and program administrator, to assure program effectiveness and plan for future success. The qualitative instruments utilized for feedback are shown below in Figure 48.2.

In addition, during 2011-12, a pilot research project has begun, to learn if there is a way to quantitatively measure those standards that were identified earlier in this chapter of whole child success. The tool for gathering this data has been given to each of the *Mission Possible* interns and trainees, with instructions to complete it (maintaining confidentiality and gathering it solely based on client interviews) on those clients they saw for three or more times during the past school year. The tool is shown below in Figure 48.3. Measuring success is difficult, because whole child success includes the student's perspective on what constitutes success, and that may be very different from what might be desired by the referral source. However, we were very interested in gathering this information, to see what the results revealed. As can be seen from Figure 48.4, counselor ratings showed significant increases for self-esteem, attendance, pro-social behavior, and grades.

Figure 48.2   Mission Possible Qualitative Evaluations

Mission Possible Mid-Term Evaluation Tool

*Site Visited:*_____   *Date:*_____

*Contact Person:*_____

What is working well?	What could we improve?
{this goes on an 8 ½ x 11" sheet, and is used for note taking during a scheduled meeting at mid-year in the school calendar, to allow any possible change).	

Mission Possible End of Term Evaluation Tool

What worked well this year?	What would you like to see next year?
{as before, this goes on an 8 ½ " sheet, and forms the basis for discussion, with awareness of the limitations posed by the state of the economy and the priority given to socio-emotional needs of students and families within the school setting).	

Figure 48.3   Data Recording Sheet Mission Possible Pilot Project,2011-2012

Data Recording Sheet Mission Possible Pilot Project
Instructions: This year I would like to begin seeing how helpful we are at working to engage whole children in succeeding with various aspects of their functional lives. Without reducing their sense of selves to "what they can do for us" I just want to naturally capture aspects (on entry and discharge from service, as these issues become available to us in the course of clinical inquiry) of difficulty that would impinge on their ability to have *happy healthy lives.*

Therefore, please record using a 0-5 rating scale (o=low, 5=high), for clients with whom you connect for the 3-session intake and make a treatment agreement (thus becoming an "entry"client), their functioning in the categories below. Similarly, note their functioning on end of treatment. We will then compare the ratings during this pilot, seeing within the entire *Mission Possible Program*, the impact of our services with the clients we serve.

Client:_____

Characteristic Rated	Self Esteem	Attendance	Behavior (Antisocial-Prosocial)	Grades (e.g., one course or overall)
Entry rating				
Discharge rating				

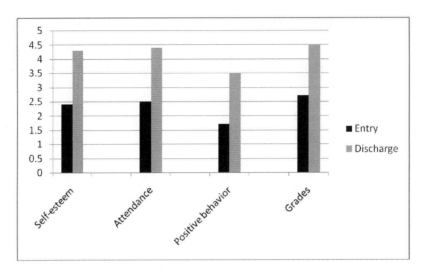

Figure 48.4   Pilot Project Results 2011-2012

difficulties, or pressure from others to leave the area. This break in services has created a mid-year shift each time it has occurred, and has taken some time to repair.

Mental health providers speak a language that is unique to our profession, and it sometimes comes across as though we consider ourselves better than other professions. I actually respect and appreciate the work that my colleagues do; otherwise I would neither have spent nine years helping in my son's classroom each week, all day, nor would I continue to work with children and go to their schools to work with their teachers (as I have done since 1980). However, the challenge remains to adhere to our standards while working at the setting where everyone else speaks educator-talk, and learn to understand that, just as we learn to adjust our communication to that of our clients from whatever background they honor us with their sharing. Similarly, we need to value the educational culture within which we are welcomed to provide our services.

The supervision is external to the actual practice, so I must select the trainees with care for the process for clients to go well, and for trainees to be effective. If I choose unwisely, *Mission Possible* may not be invited back for another year. If I supervise inattentively, the trainees will not learn and grow. If I do not help them learn new skills, the clients will not benefit.

As discussed earlier in this chapter, measuring success is difficult, because whole child success includes the student's perspective on what constitutes success, and that may be very different from what might be desired by the referral source. We will continue the data gathering methods referenced herein to monitor progress for three years, and assess our findings from 2004-2014.

Billing changes each year as staff at each school changes. Because I am in private practice, I do the billing for supervision on a monthly basis. At various times throughout the year, staffing changes occur; however, the way I learn this is that an invoice remains unpaid. The amount of time necessary to figure this out and correct this constitutes pro bono service to the community, because I do not want to create a financial burden for this very efficient program; yet it is challenging to offer a service and figure out how to be compensated for it.

Sometimes having a solo operation can be isolating. When asked why the concept isn't more widespread, a part of me responds, "I wish it was, because it certainly could be replicated, if only people would carry this dream into their community and start one district at a time." Yet another part understands that it requires perseverance, organization, and stamina to continue to pursue the dream when the details become cumbersome. Nonetheless, the benefits FAR outweigh the challenges, as can be seen by the case examples given. These were three of over 1,200. I hope that the program lasts for years to come.

REFERENCES

American Counseling Association (2010). *An overview of school-based mental health services.* www.counseling.org.

Boyd-Franklin, N. & Hafer-Bry, B. (2000). *Reaching out in family therapy: Home-based, school, and community Interventions.* The Guilford Press, New York.

Christner, R. & Christner, R. (Eds.) (2009). *School-based mental health: A practitioner's guide to comparative practices.* New York: Routledge.

Pastorek, P.(2009). *Louisiana's comprehensive learning supports system: The design document.* www.louisianaschools.net.

RESOURCES

http://smhp.psych.ucla.edu/pdfdocs
This is the link to H.S. Adelman & L. Taylor's wonderful website; once you are part of this network, you will receive well documented research about school based information from educators, clinicians and community members who work together for whole child success.

Rigby, K. (2011). *Bullying in Schools: Six Methods of Intervention.* Northampton,UK:Loggerhead Productions, Ltd.
This is a 45 minute DVD by Ken Rigby, with a comprehensive booklet which I have used with my interns and trainees in group supervision both in the field and at the University in traineeship courses.

Berman, A. , Jobes, D. & Silverman,M. (2006). *Adolescent Suicide: Assessment and Intervention.* New York: American Psychological Association*.*
This is a very informative text written by Berman, Jobes and Silverman which I rotate among the trainees when then enter *Mission Possible.* It helps prepare them for the *No Self Injury Contracts* that soon become part of our work.

Scaife, J. (2001).*Supervision in the mental health professions: A practitioner's guide*. New York: Routledge.
As a private practitioner, I find it useful to be a lifelong learner about how to be the best nurturer I can be to the next generation of therapists. Joyce Scaifes' book helps with this.

Potter-Effron, R. (2007). *Rage: A Step by Step Guide to Overcoming Explosive Anger.*Oakland, CA: New Harbinger
This is a very readable guide to help introduce trainees to the work of affect management. Potter-Effron writes well and the book gets used regularly.

Huang, C. & Lynch, J. (1999). *TAO Mentoring: Cultivate Collaborative Relationships in All Areas of Your Life*. Cambridge, MA: Da Capo Press.

This is another example of a supervision book, which generalizes to wider use. Huang   and Lynch are wonderful authors and examples.

Igoa, C. (1995).*The Inner World of the Immigrant Child*. New York: Routledge.
Cristina Igoa presented at Oxford in 2006. She shared this example of helping whole   children   learn and grow in her classroom in Hayward, CA. I share this with the trainees to help them join with their clients equally respectfully.

Pipher, M. & Ross, R. (2005). *Reviving Ophelia: Saving the Selves of Adolescent Girls.* New York:
    Riverhead.
Mary Pipher wrote with clarity and compassion about this painful, very prevalent treatment issue.

Anaya, R. (1999). *Bless Me, Ultima.* New York: Warner Books.
Rudolfo Anaya is one of the premier Hispanic authors. I regularly share his two novels so that the trainees can learn how a major population in the Natomas Unified School District are raised to dream. In that way, some of the messages that are shared have another layer of respect.

D'Ambrosio, R. (1970*). No Language But a Cry*. New York: Dell.
        Trainees regularly want to know "what should I <u>do</u> when the door closes for the first   time?" Dr. D'Ambrosio answers this perfectly, as he waits patiently for two years for his very abused client to find her way through abuse to him. This book has been well read and loved.

Many workbooks, handouts and articles are used for training and group enhancement throughout the year. Hopefully these resources will enhance your SBFC work as well.

Chapter 49
The M.Ed. Specialization
in School-Based Family Counseling
at the Hong Kong Institute of Education

Pattie Luk-Fong Yuk Yee

OVERVIEW: This chapter describes a Master in Education Specialization entitled 'School-Based Family Counseling' that the author designed in 2011 at the Hong Kong Institute of Education as an example of School-Based Family Counseling in the context of an educational institution. The target participants of this specialization included school principals, NGO workers, social workers, teachers and school personnel working in home-school collaboration areas, as well as fresh graduates particularly from the Hong Kong Institute of Education. The program also anticipated participants from Mainland China or overseas. The program as originally designed, however, was not implemented due to several challenges. The chapter describes these challenges and proposes solutions that may be helpful to anyone developing a School-Based Family Counseling program.

BACKGROUND

The specialization 'School-Based Family Counseling' was launched in 2011 by the Department of Special Needs and Counseling in the Hong Kong Institute of Education as one of the specializations (together with the specialization in Special Education and Gifted Education) in the Master of Education Program in the institute. This Specialization is in response to the public policy in Hong Kong which calls for cherishing the family and enhancing family harmony. "Cherishing the family is a core value of our community, and family harmony is the foundation of social harmony" (Policy Address by Chief Executive: 2006-2007, Paragraph 35). In the Chief Executive's Policy Address, a preventive and pro-active approach is advocated. "To tackle social problems, it is necessary to start with supporting and strengthening the family: fostering a sense of responsibility and obligation in every family member, nurturing care and love, and developing a relationship of mutual support." (Paragraph 36) In the Policy Address of 2007-2008, as reported by Hong Kong Economic Times on Oct. 4, 2007, the Government will set up a high-powered Family Affairs Committee to coordinate and promote family-friendly policies in Hong Kong and this Committee will be headed by the Chief Secretary of Administration. If Hong Kong society is to cherish the family, a best starting point is to provide comprehensive and co-coordinated learning in the area.

As in other parts in the world, families in Hong Kong are facing the stresses of rapid social and economic changes. An increasing number of children in Hong Kong are growing up in a variety of family forms such as single-parent families, divorced families, blended families, cross border families[2], newly

---

[2] A cross border family is one with family members living in Mainland China

arrived families, astronaut families[3] and grand parent/relative headed families (Luk-Fong, 2000; Leung, Leung & Chan, 2007). Moreover, the number of family violence cases and the number of cross-border marriages have also risen. Parents from dual income families have difficulties juggling between home and work. The re-negotiation of gender roles in the family is often not easy. Work-home balance becomes increasingly an issue for all. Schools and teachers are facing new challenges when teaching children in changing family situations. In order to support these children, teachers and schools have to be well prepared in working with parents, and the families need to be supported by home-school partnership, parent education, counseling and other social services.

As Hong Kong has become more affluent and parents are having fewer children, parents' expectations on their children's education are extremely high, particularly in the Chinese cultural context that emphasizes learning outcomes. Parents want to involve themselves in their children's learning and well equip themselves for their educational roles at home and in school. There is an increasing demand for family education, parenting education and home-school cooperation from parents (Pang, 2004). In a survey conducted by the Hong Kong Council of Social Services (1999), 55.2% of parents indicated that they had great difficulties in parenting their children, while indeed 10% to13% of 4 year-old children displayed behavior that should be further evaluated for diagnosis of potentially significant psychopathology. Parents are extremely concerned about children's behavior problems (Leung, Leung, Chan, Tso & Ip, 2005). Other studies also indicate that parenting stresses are associated with children's academic performance (Hong Kong Boys' and Girls' Association Family Life Education Committee, 2000) and the amount of social support available to parents.

The Hong Kong Institute of Education is well placed to develop 'School-Based Family Counseling' because it can provide a link between a child's school education and home education, which are both as important for the whole person development of the child. Family is a primary context in which individual socialization and development take place. It is, perhaps, the principal medium through which culture, society and social changes affect the individual. It would be most beneficial to all if school, family and the wider community can join hands in facilitating the education of the child. *There is no comprehensive counseling course in Hong Kong to train school personnel to help parents and families in supporting children's learning and development.* This 'School-Based Family Counseling' Specialization is to fill this gap in education provision.

THE HONG KONG INSTITUTE OF EDUCATION'S MASTER IN EDUCATION (MEd) PROGRAM

The Hong Kong Institute of Education is a self-accrediting publicly-funded institution primarily offering degree and postgraduate level programs in Education. She is the main provider of school teachers in Hong Kong – 80% of trained kindergarten teachers, 84% of primary school teachers, and 30% of secondary school teachers (HKIEd's web page). The Master in Education (MEd) is designed to strengthen the executive capabilities of experienced educators through the examinations of new insights in theory, practice and leadership. Participants are expected to take 8 modules (24 credit points) to complete the program. There are two compulsory core modules namely:

International Perspectives on Educational Reform

Introduction to Research Methods

---

[3] An astronaut family is one with a parent abroad.

There is a wide spectrum of Specialization including:

      Assessment and Evaluation
      Curriculum and Innovative Teaching
      Early Childhood Education
      Educational Management and Leadership
      Educational and Developmental Psychology
      Gifted Education
      International Education
      Life and Spirituality Education
      Philosophy and Education
      Professional and Vocational Education
      Special Education
      School-Based Family Counseling

Participants can opt to take any 4 modules from the program plus a dissertation /major project in place of two elective modules or they can also choose to take double specializations (each specialization with 3 modules) to make up the 6 modules.

SPECIALIZATION DESCRIPTION

Aims of the Specialization: The 'School-Based Family Counseling' Specialization *provides participants with opportunities and experiences* to display an understanding of the ways in which pupil development, well being, and learning are enhanced by *pro-active family-school collaboration.* The specialization requires participants to work with parents to foster respectful and productive family-school collaboration to enhance pupils' development.

General Statement: Participants learn that one of the most effective ways to promote student learning is to involve parents and families in their children's education. By keeping parents and families informed and asking for their input and feedback, participants realize they can empower parents and make their voices heard. The 'School-Based Family Counseling' Specialization emphasizes the importance of building these collaborative relationships, using counseling theories and skills related to both the school and family systems, as it facilitates more positive student outcomes. Participants also learn that collaboration must be made not only on an individual level, but also at a school-based level, where parents and families feel like the whole school is working towards the best education for their children.

EXPECTED OUTCOMES

Expected Outcomes: Knowledge and skills that participants will have developed as a result of completing the specialization

      Acquire basic knowledge concerning individuals and families in their own and other cultures; learn how the family, the workplace, the community and the larger culture affect and are affected by the individual
      Develop basic counseling knowledge and skills
      Be aware of resources and strategies to support and strengthen the family
      Understand problems related to families such as child and spouse abuse, drug addiction, and divorce
      Examine effective strategies in helping students and parents through prevention and intervention

Explore moral, ethical, and legal issues participants will face as teachers/professionals and evaluate alternative approaches to promoting optimal development

PROGRAM STRUCTURE AND CURRICULUM

The 'School-based Family Counseling' Specialization comprises three compulsory taught modules. The three modules are:
    A) Negotiation-based parent education and family support
    B) Parent education: Theory, practice and research
    C) Supporting parents and families with diverse needs.

Negotiation- based parent education and family support: participants will examine the theories and research related to parenting, well being, as well as the concepts of healthy, resilient and dysfunctional families in this module. A special focus will be on counseling for supporting the changing family contexts as well as the hybrid "East meets West" family and education contexts in Hong Kong.

Parent Education: Theory, practice and research: adopts a scientist-practitioner model and takes participants through a critical review of the major counseling perspectives in parent education. Participants will also be introduced to evidence-based parent education programs both internationally and locally in Hong Kong. The module also examines skills, strategies, formats and techniques in the delivery of parent education.

Supporting parents and families with diverse needs: examines the needs of parents and families that might require additional support to help their children succeed, such as new immigrant families, lone-parent families, low income families, ethnic minority families, cross-border families, families with domestic violence, and families with children with special education needs. Local and overseas models and strategies of support and counseling for families with different needs will be reviewed and evaluated.

ASSESSMENT

The three modules have the following assessment requirements:

Negotiation-based parent education and family support
a) Conduct a literature review of children's/adolescents' voices on any chosen theme in families, parenting or family support. Using theories learnt in this module, propose counseling strategies to promote children's/adolescents' emotional well being in the Hong Kong context. (3000 words) 80%
b) Draw a three generation genogram of your family. Reflect on the changes in expectations of parents, parenting styles and contextual factors for the well being and health of parents and children in the three generations. Expound on the insights you gain from doing this exercise in understanding parenting issues in contemporary Hong Kong. (1000words;20%).

Parent Education: Theory, practice and research
Based on a given parent education program, participants are required to modify it to suit the needs of the parents they are working with. The program has to be implemented. Based on evidence collected during the study, participants are expected to write a report on the effectiveness of the program (4000 words; 100%).

Supporting parents and families with diverse needs
Using counseling theories learnt in this module, propose an action plan for helping any one type of parents and families with diverse needs. The action plan should include prevention as well as intervention, skills and evaluation strategies. Try it out in the actual setting and provide suggestions for improvement. (4000words; 100%).

RELATIONSHIP TO THE SBFC MODEL

From the aims of the specialization and the content of the modules, it can be seen that the School-based Family Counseling specialization incorporates School-Intervention, School-Prevention, Family-Intervention and Family Prevention approaches. In essence, the specialization emphasizes an ecological or systems approach and focuses on the linkage between the family and the school systems.

Negotiation Based Parent Education and Family Support brings out the impact of the changing contexts of the families, including how work overspills into home and how work-life balance issues affect both parents and school personnel. At the same time the module also highlights how both schools and families must address the 'East meets West' contexts in schooling in Hong Kong. It highlights the importance of both prevention and remediation in schools as well as in home as illustrated by the use of the word education to signify prevention and the use of the word support to denote remediation.

Parent Education-Theory, practice and research emphasizes prevention. This module is for all students. The module is very important as parents are often the first teachers of children and their relationships with their children and the way they organize learning and activities for their children are of vital importance for their children's healthy growth and development. Many children's and adolescents' problems might have been avoided if parents have a wider repertoire of knowledge and skills in educating their children in the first place.

Supporting parents and families with diverse needs takes a more remedial approach as the title of the module suggests. Children from diverse types of families will be highlighted for support so that all children will be provided with equal chances of participation and success in schools.

EVIDENCE-BASED SUPPORT

The specialization stresses evidence-based practices. There are few training programs with School-Based Family Counseling as THE program title hence it is difficult to borrow evidence-based materials directly from other programs. School-Based Family Counseling as a specialization in the HKIEd is an attempt to provide educators with basic counseling training to work with families when they are facilitating children's/adolescents' growth and development. The specialization refers to Western theories on the one hand; it also collects local Hong Kong data in schools and/or with particular family groups on the other hand. Furthermore, it emphasizes trying out theories in the actual contexts and action learning. As a new development in the education setting, it is hoped that this specialization will help not only in building up data that are useful in the Hong Kong contexts but also provide data that will be helpful to other cultural settings.

MULTICULTURAL COUNSELING CONSIDERATIONS

This specialization emphasizes cultural contexts as well as the interplay of the 'global' with the 'local' in education and in families support. It particularly highlights the meeting of the Chinese Confucian traditions with Western values when an essentially Western education system was grafted onto Hong Kong in her 150 years of colonial history under the British rule (up till 1997), together with the global educational reforms since the 1990s, creating new hybrids which present both challenges and possibilities. The specialization emphasizes diverse family types: in particular marginal family types such as new immigrant families, lone-parent families, low income families, ethnic minority families, cross-border families, family with domestic violence, and families having children with special education needs. In essence, it advocates equal opportunities in education for all students.

PROCEDURE: THE MAKING OF THE SBFC SPECIALIZATION

The 'school-based family counseling specialization' was initially proposed in 2011 as 'Parent Education and Family Support'. The idea was first put forward by Dr I-Wah Pang who is an educator in the area of Home School Collaboration in the Department of Educational Policy and Leadership in the Institute. The specialization adopted a cross-departmental and a multi-disciplinary approach including faculty members from the Department of Special Needs and Counseling, the Department of Educational Policy and Leadership and the Department of Early Childhood. Initially, the specialization offered five modules from which participants elected any four. The five modules were:

    A) Parent education and family support (now called Negotiated-Based Parent Education and
       Family Support)
    B) Family relationships
    C) School-family-community collaboration
    D) Parent Education: Theory, practice and research
    E) Supporting parents and families with diverse needs

The specialization however was to be in the custody of the Department of Special Needs and Counseling, which had developed four modules of the specialization (apart from 'School-family-Community Collaboration' which was in the custody of the Educational Policy and Leadership Department.

       Unfortunately, when the specialization was to start in the year 2011 - 2012 there were not enough applicants to offer the specialization. Efforts were then made to improve as well as to publicize the specialization. Consultancy was sought and there were suggestions to add more practical skills to the modules. Around that time, I came to know about the work of scholars of Oxford Symposium on School-Based Family Counseling and thought our specialization was closely aligned with the ethos of their thinking and hence proposed the changing of the title of the Specialization to highlight the focus of the Specialization in 2011. This coincided with the Oxford Symposium which took place at the University of Hong Kong in 2011 and provided an opportune time to promote School-Based Family Counseling to the Hong Kong counseling professionals. A School-Based Family Counseling Symposium was launched by the Special Needs and Counselling Department of the Hong Kong Institute of Education on 25 June, 2011. In the morning, a symposium titled "Negotiations and Integrations between 'old' and 'new'" was held with three keynote speakers: 'Overview of School-Based Family Counseling' by Dr Brian Gerrard (USA), 'Building Resilience in Migrant Families – An illustration of School-Based Family Counseling in action' by Dr. Hans Everts (New Zealand) and 'Intergenerational Negotiations and Integrations in School-Based Family Counseling' by Dr Yuk King Lau (Hong Kong). In the afternoon, a school-based family skill workshop entitled 'Couple Resilience Psycho-Social Education Workshop' was conducted by Dr Hans Everts. Subsequently, I was invited to give a talk on School-Based Family Counseling to guidance professionals in Hong Kong on Dec 6, 2012.

In the year 2012-13, there were 8 applicants to the specialization. Many applicants were social workers and they liked the specialization because it would fill the missing gap that concerns the development of children in relationship to both school and family systems. The department wished to start the first cohort with this small number but as I was not available for teaching in the fall semester because of my retirement arrangement, the specialization was not offered. In 2012, due to the pressure from the Graduate School for each department to offer only one specialization, the three specializations planned by our department, namely Special Needs, Gifted Education and School-Based Family Counseling, were combined to make one Area of Focus, namely Special Needs, Giftedness and Counseling. Not many elements of School-Based Family Counseling were left in the combined specialization.

CHALLENGES AND SOLUTIONS

The brief history about the development of the School-Based Family Counseling Specialization in our Institute shows that there were four main challenges that I and the counseling team faced. They were: lack of support from inside, competition from outside, the politics in education and the difficulties to recruit faculty members who can teach the specialization. The positive side was that some staff development in the area of School-Based Family Counseling has been started in our department and in Hong Kong, and the underlying principles of School-Based Family Counseling can continue to flourish under different names and umbrellas. The real possibilities clearly lie in the need of school-based family counseling which teachers and parents should soon come to recognize.

CHALLENGES

Lack of support from inside: There are six faculty members in our department's counseling team. Four were faculty members: two associate professors and two assistance professors. The other two members were teaching fellows who had not yet obtained their doctoral degrees. There was only one faculty member other than myself who specialized in parent education but she did not take a systems perspective. An expert in Parenting Education who earlier wrote the module "*Supporting parents and families with diverse needs*" had left the Institute three years ago. Hence, there were not enough faculty members who could teach the specialization.

Competition from outside: As discussed above, there were 12 specializations in the Master in Education Program of the Institute. There were also 4 master programs offered by the Faculty of Arts and Science and 4 other offered by the Faculty of Humanities. Hence, many specializations in the Institute were competing for students. Moreover, it was up to the Graduate School to make final decisions on what was to be taught, who were qualified to teach the programs (such as whether they were associate professors and active researchers) and how many specialization(s) each department could offer. In the year 2011-2012, the program structure was changed to offering a double specialization option to fit the demands from Hong Kong schools for various specializations in a teacher. To adjust for the double specialization option, each specialization was changed to comprise three rather than four modules. In year 2012, the Graduate School decided that each department could offer only one specialization. Hence, there were competitions from one's own department as well as competitions from other departments. Our department's response was to take an easy way out by combining the three specializations into one Focus area: Special Needs, Giftedness and Counseling, which in fact took away the main essence of School-Based Family Counseling from its existing modules.

Politics in education: From the experience of developing of the School-Based Family Specialization in our Institute, it can be seen that the decision to offer a specialization is very often political, responding to assumed market needs rather than educational goals and principles. It is not easy to convince the administration at the top the need and the robustness of a specialization. Very often, it is the Graduate School that imposes constraints for setting up   the specialization. The combination of three specializations into one in our department seemed a bit absurd as a specialization in one combined specialization becomes no specialization. The purpose for this combination was perhaps to make sure that the three expertise areas in our department each had an equal share. . As I had retired from the Institute when this change was made, I was not able to suggest alternative proposals such as offering the three specializations in three different years and/or according to the demand from the students. The very fact that the faculty members who could teach the School-Based Family Counseling Specialization had left made it difficult to continue to offer the Specialization however much school-based family counseling was needed in Hong Kong.

Recruitment of faculty in SBFC: Though anticipating my retirement, it was really difficult to find replacement that has expertise in general counseling as well as family counseling. Moreover, another difficulty with this program is that it is not an accredited counseling program and candidates interested to be a counselor would not enroll in this program. School personnel doing work in the area of home-school collaboration are not prepared to invest in this program even if it is useful for their work as the program is a costly investment both in terms of time and money.

SOLUTIONS

Staff Development on School-Based Family Counseling: Although the School-Based Family Counseling Specialization has not been realized so far, all colleagues of the counseling team benefited by attending the full day symposium on School-Based Family Counseling. More that 50 social workers and other counseling professionals outside the Institute also benefited from the seminar and workshop of the day. Moreover, two members of the counseling team were able to attend the Oxford Symposium that was based in Hong Kong University on 2012. Guidance personnel from over 100 primary schools in primary schools in Hong Kong were also introduced to the concept of School-Based Family Counseling in a talk organized by the Guidance and Discipline section of the Education Bureau given by myself in Dec 2012. The Education Bureau also mentioned the possibilities of using School-Based Family Counseling as framework to support schools if extra funding was allocated to guidance services in schools.

School-Based Family Counseling in different packages and formats: Our journey of the development of a School-Based Family Counseling MEd Specialization was wrought with ever-changing circumstantial difficulties in the department and in the institute; however, the needs for a School-Based Family Counseling perspective for Hong Kong teachers remained solely unchanged. I resorted to packaging the essence and core elements of school-based family counseling in different formats and packages. For example, I tried to incorporate the needs and strategies of working with parents and families when I was asked to run staff development workshops on 'managing diversity'. Likewise I would bring out the needs to highlight the significant roles played by parents and families when invited to talk about Invitation Education in the International Alliance of Invitational Education to be held in Hong Kong in Nov 2012. I am also planning to advocate school-based family counseling to family therapists in the Consortium of Institutes of Family in Asia bi-annual conference to be held in Dec 2012. In all these endeavors, I highlight the importance of taking as starting point the hybrid 'East meets West' contexts in Hong Kong as culture is embedded in all counseling including school-based family counseling.

LESSONS LEARNED FROM THE DEVELOPMENT OF THE SPECIALIZATION

Find a space to foster School-Based Family Counseling Perspectives for teachers and school personnel: From the above discussion, it can be seen that developing a School-Based Family Counseling Specialization is difficult because a MEd program is mainly about education and is not about training of counselor. However, it is without doubt that there is a need to foster school-based family counseling perspectives to facilitate whole person development and education of pupils in schools. Elements that are included in the three modules of the specialization are indeed contents and strategies that principals, senior teachers and regular teachers need to know and acquire though the depth of knowledge and skills needed may differ.

Funding source: As the Master in Education programs in the Hong Kong Institute of Education are all self-funded programs, it is difficult to expect teachers/principals to invest in a program that is not directly related to their teaching qualifications or promotion requirements. Hence, it might be more feasible to try to obtain funding for school-based family counseling enhancement from other sources, such as from government's tender programs for teacher development organized by the Education Bureau, or from the Guidance and Discipline Section in the Education Bureau. The recent demands for staff development for Managing Diversity and Invitational Education, particularly in primary schools in Hong Kong, may be good starting points.

Linking counselors, teachers (school personnel) and parents: In order to have School-Based Family Counseling implemented in schools, it is essential to distinguish the different training needs for school principals, counselors, counseling teachers, regular teachers and parents. Unless the different stakeholders can be provided with the necessary training and perspectives, it is difficult to truly give each child the support that he/she needs in order to succeed in his/her schooling, in the sense of a whole person education for his/her future. The road to this ideal is long but it is encouraging to see the journey has already started.

SUMMARY

This chapter describes a MEd Specialization on School-Based Family Counseling in the Master in Education Program in the Hong Kong Institution of Education. It lays out the program objectives, contents and assessments of the program. It also traces the development of the specialization, highlighting both the challenges and opportunities. It ends by indicating future directions of development of School-Based Family Counseling perspectives for principals, counselors, regular teachers and parents.

REFERENCES

Hong Kong Council of Social Service (1999). Report on parenting survey. Retrieved June 13, 2003, from www.hkcss.org.hk/views/survey/html.

Hong Kong Chief Executive (2006). The 2006-07 policy address. Hong Kong : Hong Kong Administrative Region.

Hong Kong Boys' and Girls Association Family Life Education Committee, 2000). Mental health of parents of preschool children: survey report on parenting stress and its management].   Hong Kong Boys and Girls Association.

Leung, C., Leung, S.S.L. & Chan R. (2007). The adaptation of mainland Chinese immigrant parents of preschool children in Hong Kong. *E-Journal of Applied Psychology, 3*(1), 43-57.

Leung, C., Leung, S., Chan, R., Tso, K. & Ip, F. (2005). Child behaviour and parenting stress in Hong Kong families with young children. *Hong Kong Medical Journal, 11*(5), 373-380.

Luk-Fong, Y. Y. (2000). Family Change and Children's Adjustment. In E. Tung (Ed.), *Teaching   Manual on Sex Education for Kindergarten Children* (pp. 112-123). Hong Kong: HKIEd. (in Chinese)

Pang, I, W. (2004). School-family-community partnership in Hong Kong: Perspectives and challenges. *Education Research for Policy and Practice 3*, 109-125.

Appendix I: Negotiated Based Parent Education and Family Support

THE HONG KONG INSTITUTE OF EDUCATION

Course Outline

Programme Title   : Master of Education
Course Title   : Negotiated Based Parent Education and Family Support
[Maximum length including space: English – 60 characters; Chinese – 30 characters.]
Department   : EPCL
Credit Points   : 3
Contact Hours   : 39
Pre-requisite(s)   : Nil
[If applicable.]
Level   :
[If applicable. For example, for Discipline Studies under the BEd Core Curriculum, there are three levels of courses to reflect the progression of study or the extent of in-depth knowledge.]

Synopsis
Participants will examine the theories and research related to parenting, wellbeing, as well as healthy, resilient and dysfunctional families in this course. A special focus will be on counselling for supporting the changing contexts of families and the hybrid "East meets West" contexts in Hong Kong.

Objectives
Learn theories and research related to parenting, wellbeing, health and disease as well as healthy, resilient and dysfunctional families;
Acquire knowledge of the changing contexts of families and their impact on parents and children's wellbeing;
Learn how the family, the workplace, the community and the larger culture affect and are affected by the individuals;
Be aware of the particular issues affecting families and parenting in Hong Kong arising from its particular "East meets West" contexts;
Be aware of the need for negotiations in parent education and family support.

Content
Theories and research related to parenting, wellbeing, as well as healthy, resilient and dysfunctional families;
The changing families and parenting contexts and the negotiations of differences;
Children's/adolescent's voices on families, parenting or family support: implications for policy and intervention strategies;
Ecological approach in understanding the family: the individual, the family, the workplace, the community and the larger culture;
Generation changes of families, children and parent well-being: policy implications and actions;
Contemporary issues related to parent education and family support in the Hong Kong contexts: parents' high expectations on their children's education and work-life balance/work-life integration.

Recommended Reading

Bichanan, A and Hudson, B (Ed.). (2000). *Promoting Children's emotional wellbeing: Messages from research*. Oxford: Oxford University Press.

Brannen, J., Moss, P., Money, A. (2004). *Working and caring over the twentieth century: Change and continuity in four-generation families. The Future of Work Series*. London: Palgrave Macmillan.

Chan, C. M. S. (2004). Issues of preschool parents' education in Hong Kong in the 21st century. *Contemporary Issues in Early Childhood-Special Edition of Asia Pacific Issues* (online Journal), 5 (2), pp 257-263.

Chan, C. M. S. (2004). Establishing health promoting preschool to promote children's health (in Chinese). *Hong Kong Journal of Early Childhood*, Vol.3 No.2, pp 36-40.

Smolensky, E. and Gootman, J. A., National Research Council (US), Committee on Family and Work Policies (US), (2003). *Working families and growing kids: Caring for children and adolescents* (1st ed.). National Academies Press.

Gerson, K. (2002). Moral Dilemmas, Moral Strategies, and the Transformation of Gender: Lessons from Two Generations of Work and Family Change. *Gender & Society*, 16 (8).

Edwards. A. J. (1989). *The second handbook on parent education*. SanDiego: Academic Press.

Leira, A. (2002). *Working parents and the welfare state: Family change and policy reform in Scandinavia*. Cambridge University Press.

Hansen, K. V. (2006). Not-So-Nuclear Families: Class, Gender, and Networks of Care. *Contemporary Sociology*, 35 (3), 257-258.

Luk-Fong, Y. Y.P. (2008). Initial development of a model of care and support for primary school children in changing familial situations: A Hong Kong hybrid case. *Pastoral Care in Education*, 26(4), 281-295.

Luk-Fong, Y. Y. P. (2005). A search for new ways in describing parent-child relationships: voices from principals, teachers, guidance professionals, parents and pupils. *Childhood*, 12(1), 111-137.

Phillipson, S. (2009). *Role of parents in children's academic achievement: A specific sociocultural context*. Köln, Germany: LAP LAMBERT Academic Publishing.

Roffey, S. (Ed.). (2002). *School Behaviour and Families: Frameworks for working together*. London: David Fulton.

Roggman, L. A., Boyce, L. K., & Innocenti, M. S. (2008*). Developmental parenting: A guide for early childhood practitioners*. Baltimore, Md: Paul H. Brookes Pub. Co.

Winston, L., Tietze, R., Perlstein, S., & Kaplan, M. (2001). *Grandpartners: Intergenerational learning and civic renewal, K-6*. Portsmouth, NH: Heinemann.

Web resources

Ackerman Family Institute
http://www.ackerman.org/professionals/books.html
Consortium of Institutes on Family in the Asian Region Ltd. Newsletter Issue No.26.
http://www.cifa-net.org.
http://www.cifa-net.org/cifa/pdf/Issue%2026.pdf

Appendix II: Parent Education: Theory, Practice and Research

THE HONG KONG INSTITUTE OF EDUCATION

Course Outline

Programme Title : Master of Education
Course Title : Parent Education: Theory, Practice and Research
[Maximum length including space: English – 60 characters; Chinese – 30 characters.]
Department : EPCL
Credit Points : 3
Contact Hours : 39
Pre-requisite(s) :
[If applicable.]
Level :
[If applicable. For example, for Discipline Studies under the BEd Core Curriculum, there are three levels of courses to reflect the progression of study or the extent of in-depth knowledge.]

Synopsis

This course adopts a scientist-practitioner model and takes participants through a critical review of the major counselling theories in parent education. Participants will also be introduced to evidence-based parent education programmes internationally and in Hong Kong. It also examines skills, strategies, formats and techniques in the delivery of parent education.

Objectives

Acquire knowledge and critique major counselling theories in parent education;
Review and appraise research on the efficacy of parent education programmes in promoting children's optimal development; be familiarized with evidence based parent education programmes in Hong Kong;
Acquire skills, strategies, format and techniques in the delivery of parent education;
Observe moral, ethical and legal standards in service delivery.

Assessment

Based on a given parent education programme, participants are required to modify it to suit the needs of the parents they are working with. The programme has to be implemented. Based on evidence collected during the study, participants are expected to write a report on the effectiveness of the programme. (4000 words) 100%

Recommended Reading

Campbell, D., Palm, G. F. (2004). *Group parent education: Promoting parent learning and support.* Thousand Oaks, California, London, New Delhi: Sage Publications, Inc.
Cheung, S. K. (2001). Parent education programmes in Hong Kong: Are they effective? *Hong Kong Journal of Social Work,* 35 (nos. 1 & 2), 85–96.
Fine, M. J., Lee, S. W. (2001). *Handbook of diversity in parent education: The changing faces of parenting and parent education.* Orlando, Florida: Academic Press.
Giridhar, C. H., Sharma, R. S. (2005). *Encyclopaedia of education in the new millennium.* New Delhi: Commonwealth Publishers.
Kuczynski, L. (2003). *Handbook of dynamics in parent-child relations.* Thousand Oaks, Calif: Sage.

Rockwell, R. E., & Kniepkamp, J. R. (2003). *Partnering with parents: Easy programs to involve parents in the early learning process*. Beltsville, Md: Gryphon House.

Roggman, L. A., Boyce, L. K., & Innocenti, M. S. (2008). *Developmental parenting: A guide for early childhood practitioners*. Baltimore, Md: Paul H. Brookes Pub. Co.

Smith, L. M., Wells, W. M. (1997). *Urban parent education: dilemmas and resolutions.* USA: Hampton Press, Inc.

Web resources

An Outcome Evaluation of the Implementation of the Triple P-Positive Parenting Program in Hong Kong
http://dx.doi.org/10.1111/j.1545-5300.2003.00531.x
Parent Education Database
http://parented.sw.hku.hk/
Quality Parenting leaflet
http://www.women.gov.hk/download/QualityParenting_Leaflet.pdf
Study on Core Life Values for Parenting Education
http://www.women.gov.hk/download/press_release_060904_final_e.pdf
University of Minnesota : Online Parent Education Courses
http://www.cehd.umn.edu/CI/Programs/FYC/parent.html
Work of the Education Department on Parent Education
http://www.women.gov.hk/download/woc03-02e.pdf

Appendix III: Supporting Parents and Families with Diverse Needs

Programme Title   : Master of Education
Course Title   : Supporting Parents and Families with Diverse Needs
[Maximum length including space: English – 60 characters; Chinese – 30 characters.]
Department   : EPCL
Credit Points   : 3
Contact Hours   : 39
Pre-requisite(s)   :
[If applicable.]
Level   :
[If applicable. For example, for Discipline Studies under the BEd Core Curriculum, there are three levels of courses to reflect the progression of study or the extent of in-depth knowledge.]

Synopsis
This course examines the needs of parents and families which might need additional support, such as new immigrant families, lone-parent families, low income families, ethnic minority families, cross-border families, domestic violence, and families with children with special education needs. Local and overseas models and strategies of support and counseling for families with different needs will be reviewed and evaluated.

Objectives
To be aware of and embrace diverse types of families
Be able to assess the needs of parents and families which might need additional support;
Communicate and consult with parents and family members;
To be aware of and able to make use of resources and strategies to support parents and families with diverse needs;

To be aware of moral, ethical and legal issues when supporting parents and family members.

Content

Other kinds of families: representation of family in school culture and curriculum;

Parents and families wellbeing and children/adolescent optimal development;

Needs of parents and families which might need additional support: new immigrant families, lone-parent families, low income families, ethnic minority families, cross-border families, domestic violence, and families with children with special education needs;

Communication and consultation with parents: evidence based models and practices;

Resources and strategies to support diverse families: international and local models; prevention and intervention;

Moral, ethical and legal issues in supporting diverse families.

Assessment

Using counselling theories learnt in this course, propose an action plan for helping any one type of parents and families with diverse needs. The action plan should include prevention as well as intervention, skills and evaluation strategies. Try it out in the actual setting and provide suggestions for improvement. (4000words) 100%

Required Text

Turner-Vorbeck, T., & Miller Marsh, M. (2008). *Other kinds of families: Embracing diversity in schools.* New York: Teachers College Press.

Recommended Readings

Boult, B. (2006). *176 ways to involve parents: Practical strategies for partnering with families* (2nd ed.). Thousand Oaks, Calif: Corwin Press.

Callard-Szulgit, R. (2003). *Parenting and teaching the gifted.* Lanham, Md: Scarecrow Press.

Digman, C., & Soan, S. (2008). *Working with parents: A guide for education professionals.* London: Sage.

Dukes, C., Smith, M., & Smith, S. (2007). *Working with parents of children with special educational needs.* London: Paul Chapman.

Fiedler, C. R., Simpson, R. L., & Clark, D. M. (2007). *Parents and families of children with disabilities: Effective school-based support services.* Upper Saddle River, N.J: Pearson Merrill/Prentice Hall.

Grant, K. B., & Ray, J. (2010). *Home, school, and community collaboration: Culturally responsive family involvement.* Thousand Oaks, Calif: Sage Publications.

Hamner, T. J., & Turner, P. H. (2001*). Parenting in contemporary society* (4th ed.). Boston, MA: Allyn and Bacon.

Hong Kong (China). Education Dept. (2001*). Information guide to support services for students with special educational needs in ordinary schools.* Hong Kong: Education Dept.

Hong Kong (China). Social Welfare Dept. & University of Hong Kong. Dept. of Social Work and Social Administration. *Study on child abuse and spouse battering.* Hong Kong: Social Welfare Dept.

Hong Kong Committee on Children's Rights. (2005). *NGO report of the Hong Kong special administrative region under the convention on the rights of the child.* Hong Kong: the Hong Kong Committee on Children's Rights.

Jacobs, E. H. (2000). *ADHD: Helping parents help their children.* Northvale, N.J: Jason Aronson.

Hong Kong Committee on Children's Rights. (2005). *NGO report of the Hong Kong special administrative region under the convention on the rights of the child.* Hong Kong: the Hong Kong Committee on Children's Rights.

Jeynes, W. (2002). *Divorce, family structure, and the academic success of children.* New York: Haworth Press.

Li, J. (2009). *Parental expectations of Chinese immigrants for children's school achievement: Sociocultural context, psychological adjustment, and educational consequences.* Lewiston, NY: Edwin Mellen Press.

Luk-Fong, Y. Y. P. (2006b). Primary school teachers' perceptions of school children coping with changing family situations – a hybrid Hong Kong experience. *Social Psychology of Education*, 9, 425-441.

Manzon, M., & Comparative Education Research Centre. (2004). *Building alliances: Schools, parents and communities in Hong Kong and Singapore.* Hong Kong: Comparative Education Research Centre, The University of Hong Kong.

Olsen, G. W., & Fuller, M. L. (2008). *Home-school relations: Working successfully with parents and families* (3rd ed.). Boston, Mass: Pearson/Allyn and Bacon.

Porter, L. (2008). *Teacher-parent collaboration: Early childhood to adolescence.* Camberwell, Vic: ACER Press.

Pryor, J., & Rodgers, B. (2001). *Children in changing families: Life after parental separation.* Oxford, England: Blackwell Publishers.

Rockwell, R. E., & Kniepkamp, J. R. (2003). *Partnering with parents: Easy programs to involve parents in the early learning process.* Beltsville, Md: Gryphon House.

Sandieson, R., Sharpe, V., Hourcade, J. J., & Council for Exceptional Children. Division on Developmental Disabilities. (2004). *Foundations, teachers, and families in developmental disabilities.* Austin, Tex: PRO-ED.

Smith, T. E. C. (2006). *Families and children with special needs: Professional and family partnerships.* Upper Saddle River, N.J: Pearson/Merrill Prentice Hall.

University of Hong Kong. Dept. of Social Work and Social Administration. (2005). *Study on child abuse and spouse battering: Report on findings of household survey.* Hong Kong: Dept. of Social Work and Social Administration, The University of Hong Kong.

Winter, J. (2006). *Breakthrough parenting for children with special needs: Raising the bar of expectations.* San Francisco, Calif: Jossey-Bass.

Web resources

Children, Youth and Family Consortium
http://www.cyfc.umn.edu/schoolage/resources/supporting.html
Early Childhood Special Education/Diversity Materials With an Emphasis on Partnerships with Families
http://www.education.uiowa.edu/crl/bibliographies/pdf/specialed_print1.pdf
Future of School Psychology Task force on Family-School Partnerships
http://fsp.unl.edu/future_index.html

Chapter 50
The Origins of SBFC in Southern California:
A Practical Partnership, Leadership
and School Reform

Marcel Soriano

OVERVIEW: *This chapter describes the typical challenges found in schools where counseling in general, and family counseling specifically, is often met with hostile, unsupportive attitudes that limit the domain of schools to "the three R's" and nothing else. The chapter outlines ways that counselors and counselor educators can take advantage of the myriad initiatives possible under the category of school reform, including those efforts on prevention stemming from empirical research on mental health and schools (e.g., Adelman & Taylor, 1998; 2012), as well as those that focus on student health and wellness with an urgent appeal to the importance of mental health in relation to achievement (e.g., Hurwitz & Weston, 2011). The key aspect of these school reform initiatives is the recognition of the need for a paradigm shift in counseling and an understanding that school-based services provide an effective way to move about eliminating substantial barriers to student achievement while at the same time ensuring healthy growth and development of <u>all</u> children and their families. The author provides an illustration on ways to initiate structural change in a school district as well as a counselor-education institution. The chapter focuses on the author's experience in two districts where he worked as a counselor and school administrator, as well as an educator at California State University, Los Angeles.*

BACKGROUND

I first learned about the need for school reform as a practicing school counselor when I realized that many of the problems my counselees encountered were not of their own doing or due to personal or family's deficiencies. Rather, their problems were due to the fundamental structure of schools and their seeming lack of awareness of the challenges children and their families faced. These observations were later confirmed by reviews of the literature as I worked on my administrative credential and later as a practicing administrator. Ironically, my work as an educator was preceded earlier by my entry into another "service" profession as a California Youth Authority Parole Agent (CYA). It was here that I learned how many of the problems faced by families in our society are partly due to the social institutions that purport to help them. The so-called "rehabilitation schools" where I worked (e.g., the Nelles School and Reception Center in Norwalk, California, or the "Youth Training School" in Chino, California) were not designed to assess need and to rehabilitate, but more to punish incarcerated youth. Many of these children, as the youngest I supervised was 13 years old, were victims of abuse or neglect within their families and communities, as much as victims of inadequate schools and poorly prepared teachers.

Subsequently, I again confirmed my suspicions about the failing public schools when I began to conduct research and teach leadership courses at California State University, Los Angeles. As one such research effort would tell us, "the problems in the schools are but a reflection of the problems in society; therefore, the solution to these problems must be systemic, collaborative and inclusive of the entire community and its institutions (Soriano, Soriano & Jimenez, 1994). From those early days to the present time, I remain convinced that learning is immanent and that all children can indeed learn and be successful, often in spite their schools. In other words, the problems in learning lie not in the children themselves, but in the barriers placed in front of them. These barriers include poverty, poorly trained teachers, culturally incompetent professionals and the lack of or insufficient linkage between the school and the community. The result is that the child is victimized by an inadequately organized system that lacks vision. In the words of Buckminster Fuller (in Cohen & Filpczak, 1971), schools should be organized so that children and their families who come to them solve their problems by environmental reform, instead of individual reform. Referring to a visionary school-community reform, Fuller states: "...the school design was organized on the basis that he [the leader] would help the individuals who came there as students to see what their problems were and to see how these problems could be solved by environmental reform instead of individual reform (p. xiv).

THE JOURNEY INTO SCHOOL COUNSELING

In the late '70's and early '80's when I began my professional service as a school counselor, I realized that the traditional training model of counseling which I and many others had received at the university was not only insufficient but also inadequate. The model suggested a simplistic guidance-based approach for framing and solving "student problems," that simply ignored other fundamental factors associated with culture, extended family systems, socio-economic and social justice issues affecting the child. I saw multifaceted problems requiring a consideration of the whole family as my charge, but was handed a single tool with which to respond. I call this the "silo" training model which fails to envision viable solutions that embrace the whole family, or which fail to recognize the intimate relationship families played in student behavior and wellbeing. It is for this reason that I fell in love with the notion of re-framing student problems at school as "family" problems which required family focused interventions. Appropriate family interventions, I also learned, require community-based interventions that involve diverse agencies, businesses, civic leaders and profit and not for profit public agencies that reflect a motivation and desire to make a positive difference in the lives of children and their families.

In 1982, as a practicing counselor at Chino High School, I began exploring ways to more effectively reach out to students and their families by developing a counselor-led drop-in "Advocate Center" at school. This center was designed for those students who were disengaged from school and were on their way to dropping-out of school (some actually had done so). This was forged with the collaboration of "Dick" Vaniman, a very effective, sensitive teacher who taught psychology and social psychology. Our relationship grew, both personally and professionally, as we thought of ways to reach out to those students who were on the edge or who felt marginalized by the system. The result was a wonderful Peer Counseling Program that successfully trained "Peer Counselors" and reached out to students who were outside our reach as professionals, but were reachable by students themselves. In this manner we were able to address student needs in ways that neither he nor I alone could do so.

Soon after this experience I was asked by my district superintendent to go back to school and obtain an administrative credential and help address some of the district's problems, including drop-outs, intergroup ethnic conflict and lack of parental participation in schools. The result was a community-wide drop-out recovery and family support collaborative program that was essentially paid for by the community and the funds accrued from recovered Average Daily Apportionment (ADA), or state school support that would be lost when students are not in school. The collaborative included agreements with the City of Chino, the San Bernardino County Department of Mental Health and the Department of Social Services; it also included Chino Youth Services, a non-profit counseling agency, and the local Ecumenical Council which provided faith-based counseling services to appropriate families in the community.

This period of my professional service was also the first time that I realized that many of the problems in learning or disengagement from school were due to mental health issues impacting the student and his/her family. Thus the program we designed began with what I called the "Needs Assessment Profile" (NAP) for each student and his/her family. I vividly recalled "Squeekie," my wonderful administrative assistant who worked with me at Buena Vista Continuation High School telling teachers we "needed to "NAP" a student, referring to the family assessment we did in determining why he/she was not being successful. When the needs were social services related, the collaborative responded with services provided in a creative and motivating manner. For example, I had cross referenced the goals and objectives in high school courses and found that many of these could be appropriately "taught" through personal or family counseling. This effort not only de-stigmatized counseling, but also offered academic rewards for participation in counseling. Students were offered high school credit for engaging in personal or family counseling!

After I left the Chino Unified School District I again had the fortunate experience of beginning a school-based program designed to meet the needs of my new community in the Garvey School District. Using what I had learned in Chino and realizing the complexity of contemporary families' needs, I formed another collaborative in the San Gabriel Valley, home of the Garvey School District. The district straddled three cities and portions of unincorporated Los Angeles County, including Rosemead, Monterrey Park and San Gabriel. With an extremely poor funding base, Garvey was struggling to meet the emotional and learning needs of highly diverse children and their families. Garvey was said to be the "first stop" for many Vietnamese, Chinese and Latino immigrant children coming from many Asian and Latin American countries. The district provided one half-time counselor to handle all school and family related problems. This was not only inadequate, but highly misleading to the community in thinking their children's needs would be appropriately addressed. My work was again cut out for me!

PROGRAM DESCRIPTION

For many years, research on school reform has focused on many areas of public education. These range from school configuration and teacher training to curriculum and instructional strategies; from categorical program implementation ranging from early childhood education and bilingual education to Title 1 for the economically disadvantaged and special education. However, despite all efforts to improve student outcomes and achievement, most efforts have amounted to mere "tinkering" at the edges of the same model, often defining "the problem" in an analogous definition of the three blind men defining the elephant based on the area of the animal they touched. Research accumulated from the Annenberg Foundation Challenge on school reform, as well as the Center for Mental Health in Schools suggests that while much is known about the elements necessary for effective schools, many of these school reform efforts fail to address the actual psychosocial barriers to achievement (Phillips, Reyes & Clarke, 2009; Adelman & Taylor, 1998; 2011). One of the most formidable barriers to student achievement is child and adolescent health, including mental health (Hurwitz & Weston, 2011). In my long public service career I have served as parole agent, school counselor, school principal, school district coordinator of student services, assistant superintendent of student services and finally as professor of educational leadership and counseling at California State University, Los Angeles. In all these diverse roles, and now as a counselor educator, I have seen the results of community failure to meet the needs of young people. I saw among them gifted young people on probation or parole whose schools and community agencies failed them; I have also seen the success of effective systems of care with families that have thrived when their needs were met. What follows then is a description of how school reform can help integrate the community, families and schools in order to meet the needs of children and their families and help narrow the achievement gap in public education.

THE NOAH MODEL OF SERVICE

Using the NOAH model which I learned from the VISTA program (Volunteers in Service to America), I established what I called the "Interagency Communication Council" (ICC), a community-wide collaborative. NOAH stands for "need overlap analysis in the helping process" (Pearce & Amato, 1980). The model teaches us that any organization, agency or individual or group has identifiable needs, even if those needs are in the form of the profit motive. As an illustration, imagine three circles, each representing an organization and each overlapping the other (see Figure 50.1). Each organization represented by each circle represents a set of needs. One might need to be seen as an upstanding, responsible agency doing a profitable business but also serving the community. Another might be a non-profit agency seeking access to the clients it must serve based on streams of funding with specific objectives. The other might be a school with a "captive audience" of children and their families, all representing a myriad set of diverse needs. The NOAH model suggests that where the three circles overlap there is a central core of overlapping needs potentially met by the needs of the other. The needs of families might appropriately be met through access for the agencies seeking to serve the community. The needs of the profit motivated agency might be met by "allowing" it to be seen as a responsible corporate citizen, generously giving back to the community. This is often seen in marketing campaigns. When I presented this model to my superintendents in both districts I served (Chino and Garvey school systems), I received full support to engage in this collaborative effort.

This is indeed what happened in the Chino and Garvey School Districts after presenting the concept to the newly formed Interagency Communication Council. In the case of Garvey Schools, armed with the help of Ingleside Hospital located in Rosemead, I was able to obtain free space to provide family counseling in the community. Thanks to Brian Gerrard and Cal State, LA, I was able to obtain interns and trainees in order to provide counseling to the children and families in my district. I in turn provided clinical supervision and training in order to meet their practice needs in the "real world". Significantly, it was this fortuitous event that brought me to meet and get to know Brian over a Chinese lunch. The result was the importation from San Francisco of the "Mission Possible" model to the California State University, Los Angeles and a long, intimate friendship with Brian.

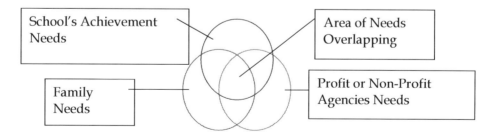

Figure 50.1
The NOAH Model

RELATIONSHIP TO THE SBFC MODEL

In the fall of 1989 I was recruited to join the faculty in the School of Education at California State University, Los Angeles. This was after meeting Brian Gerrard and adopting the Mission Possible model of School Based Family Counseling into our Southern California Garvey School District. Prior to leaving Garvey, Brian and I had developed "guidelines" for implementing a Mission Possible program, and presented these guidelines to the Governing Board. Approval by board action was necessary as it involved a "memorandum of understanding" (MOU) which spelled out the expectations of each organization, including the district and California State University's College of Education. The guidelines were necessary in order to avoid conflict between counselors and school personnel, as well as to help identify appropriate expectations, from counselors and supervisors, as well as from principals and parents with respect to the services to be provided. The MOU also addressed issues related to liability and insurance coverage. This MOU was later supplemented with a "Resource and Evaluation Handbook: Culture-Sensitive School-Based Metal Health Services (Soriano, 1993). This handbook included the specific guidelines for a successful school-based program targeting preventive supports for students, parents and school personnel. It also included an essential "must read" collection of articles in order to provide counselors and school personnel with a common base of knowledge about school-based services.

MISSION POSSIBLE GUIDELINES: THE "HOW TO" FOR A COLLABORATIVE SBFC PROGRAM

The "Mission Possible" MOU and its guidelines were presented to the Garvey School District Board of Education and were approved, thanks to the excellent presentation by Brian Gerrard and our collaborative illustration of the NOAH model reflecting benefits to each entity. What follows is a step by step illustration of what needs to be done to meet the challenges posed when different organizational cultures work together, and to avoid irreparable ruptures in these organizational relationships.

Keep administrative and community leadership informed. As a practicing educator, I know the importance of close communication with my superintendent and the Garvey Board of Education. Fortunately, I had cultivated a good working relationship with Virginia Gutierrez, a Garvey Board Member who was very committed to the parents in the community. These two individuals were very critically helpful when the time came to discuss and approve the recommendation in support of Mission Possible. However, a cautionary comment should be made about "surprises" to administrators. Do not communicate with board members before your superintendent! This could be very embarrassing and damaging to your credibility if the board member "surprises" your superintendent with program proposals from subordinates rather than from him/her.

Work closely with your principals and their administrative assistants. It is important to develop "collaborative goals" when designing a school-based family counseling program (SBFC). Starting with a discussion about the rationale for SBFC, its benefits and desired outcomes (e.g., better student readiness to learn), it is important to also learn from the principal and administrative assistant, teachers and parents about the specific needs, special circumstances in the community and an exploration of how SBFC could address these needs. In other words, it is important to avoid a "one size fits all" mentality. What works well in the Mission District of San Francisco may not work in the urban context of Los Angeles and Rosemead.

Think of logistical needs of the counselor, as well as the needs of the school. This implies an understanding and sensitivity to the different "cultures" coming together, that of the educator and that of the clinician. Schools see their mission and promote a culture for learning, for socializing children and, given today's political realities, for measured and demonstrated achievement gains. Counselors, on the other hand, see the child's emotional struggles, lack of confidence and/or family turmoil as the main impediments to wellness and student success. Don't assume, however, that this vision is understood by the principal, the teacher or even parents themselves. As a clinician I am often reminded of how blind I can be to my own family's issues and yet see them clearly in the families I serve.

Take time to talk about what the counselor needs, such as appropriate space, privacy conducive to good counseling, appropriate informed consent and releases and treatment agreements. And finally discuss ways to evaluate expected outcomes. Moreover, take time to listen to the school's concerns for limited student time out from instruction, space limitations and develop a protocol for providing services. The Garvey Schools Mission Possible program developed a specific guide to services by providing a statement to the administrator in the form of a "Dear Principal" and one to the counselor in the form of a "Dear Counselor" format.

Whenever possible, try to involve the community. Research conducted by a panel of educators, including this author, clearly suggests that the problems in the schools are but a reflection of the problems in society; it also suggests that the solution to those problems lies in the collaboration among all community stakeholders (CCTC, 1998). Thus if other community agencies are to be involved, make sure you provide them with an orientation to the program, needs to be addressed and work with their staff to explore mutually beneficial collaboration. Also define and communicate expectations, as discussed above.

Establish guidelines for formative and summative or outcome evaluation. When Mission possible was established in the Garvey School District, immediate plans were formulated for evaluation, thanks to a federally funded program that required a strong evaluation component. This requirement gave stature to the Mission Possible program and led to the changes in training of school counselors at California State University, Los Angeles. This was the case since the training of school counselors was wedded to an old model that pretty much excluded working with parents in a counseling capacity. The traditional school counselor model focused on student focused interventions and only minor involvement of parents by way of informing and obtaining permission to work with their children. The new SBFC model reframed the "client" as the whole family, not only the student. This essentially meant re-structuring the traditional school counselor training program into a "family counseling program" that is inclusive of both, individual and family work, as well as strong involvement of the school's professionals serving the student.

Concluding this section on reform efforts in relation to SBFC, children learn because it is in their nature to learn; it is the barriers they encounter, be it familial, community or organizational, that impedes their achievement. According to the National Assembly on School-Based Health Care (2011), "Children spend a major part of their day in school, so schools must be prepared to address their mental health, as well as health needs" as an urgent matter (p.3). The SBFC model works well because it elevates the importance of psychological and family well-being as essential ingredients to student achievement.

EVIDENCE-BASED SUPPORT

Philosophically speaking, I am convinced of the veracity of the Jungian concept of "synchronicity" or meaningful coincidences (DeLaszlo, 1959). How Brian and I would meet, develop a close friendship and help usher changes in the way school counselors are taught at Cal State, Los Angeles is truly synchronous. As outlined by Dr. Gerrard, the university-school partnership model for SBFC was the result of creative and purposeful initiatives by committed professionals who worked with Brian in San Francisco. However, the model was the brainchild of Brian Gerrard as he worked with his students in the Mission District of San Francisco (see Chapter 45 for a detailed description of the University of San Francisco Mission Possible program). However, when Brian took a leave of absence from the University of San Francisco and took a position as professor of Counselor Education at California State University in the early 1980's, he began efforts to "export" and implement the model within the metropolitan Los Angeles area. He approached Dr. Ray Hillis, the department chair at the time, to see if he knew of a district that would be receptive to the model. Previously I had approached the university with a complaint that the university was not preparing counselors adequately in the area of cultural competence. This was based on my experience working with interns placed under my supervision in the Garvey School District where I worked as the Assistant Superintendent of Student Services. Dr. Hillis referred him to me and met over a Chinese lunch. The rest, as it is often said, is history! Brian and I immediately developed plans to implement Mission Possible in the Garvey School District. Ironically, once we had implemented the program, and having received a major multi-year grant from the Office of Substance Abuse Prevention, Brian returned to the University of San Francisco, vacating his position at California State University, Los Angeles. Soon after, Dr. Roy Mayer and Randall Lindsey, the new Chair and Associate Chair, recruited me to join the faculty at Cal State, Los Angeles.

The evidence of effectiveness of the SBFC model was soon to be made clear when as a new faculty member and as Principal Investigator of the Mission Possible Project I, along with other faculty members, helped Dr. Hillis to develop a completely new Masters Degree in school-based family counseling, a program that embraced the SBFC model. The external funding secured from the Office of Substance Abuse Prevention (OSEP) was intended to target "high risk" gang affiliated students or students at risk for drug abuse. The project was part of an initiative entitled Gang Risk Intervention Project Program (GRIPP), a project which required rigorous evaluation. The results of this project clearly demonstrated the importance of interventions targeting the entire family, not merely the student "at risk". Measures included academic engagement and performance (i.e., GPA and attendance), improved family communication and relationships, greater family involvement in the community and improved self-esteem (OSEP/GRIPP Final Report, 1996).

Interestingly, through Brian's initial influence and my joining the CSULA faculty, California State University developed the first of now several Masters Degree programs (i.e., Phillips Institute, CSUSF). Moreover, since the mid 1990's, the focus of Cal State L.A.'s School Based Family Counseling program has become one of preparing school counselors who earn the Pupil Personnel Services Credential, the Child Welfare and Attendance Authorization, and eligibility to be licensed as a Marriage and Family Therapists.

MULTICULTURAL COUNSELING CONSIDERATIONS

There are many empirical and theoretical reasons for asserting that SBFC is more culturally sensitive and appropriate when serving ethnic minorities than the traditional medical model of counseling and psychotherapy (Soriano, Soriano & Jimenez, 1994; Soriano & Hong, 2010). The literature has consistently catalogued the tendency for Western Psychology trained clinicians to pathologize ethnic minorities (Sue, 2011). Additionally, many ethnic minorities, including Asian, Latino and Middle Eastern immigrant communities hold strong stigmas against psychology and counseling, adding to the resistance to seek help from counselors in the traditional community clinics. However, the same cultural groups place a high value on education and hold educators in high esteem. I recall the high respect afforded me when visiting schools while traveling in Mexico and later in Spain. Students would automatically stand up when I was entering their classrooms. When conversing with parents, they often attended carefully to my opinions and suggestions for student improvement, even in the realm of emotional or behavioral problems. It's been my experience that when families are offered "help" at school with the intent to help their children achieve academic excellence, they immediately line up to receive this help from the local SBFC professional. Thus compliance and receptiveness increases when providing counseling services in the form of psycho-educational interventions designed to empower parents and increase collaboration between school and home.

School-Based Family Counselors are able to serve ethnic minorities as a result of cultural adaptations to the basic counseling relationship and a change in the context from clinic to home school. Additionally, being at the school, SBFC professionals are ahead of the curve in reaching students early, rather than waiting until a "problem" occurs and the student is referred out to a clinician. The value of school-based family counseling as a culturally appropriate model for serving diverse communities is evident in the following essential elements not present in traditional models for providing mental health services:

SBFC IS "SYSTEMS BASED"

This reflects the important recognition of SBFC as a more inclusive model that frames a child's problem as a family system's problem and therefore the solution lies in a whole family response. Collectivistic cultures, as Triandis (1995) reminds us, don't see the individual as the important unit of discourse, but the entire family or kinship system.

SBFC IS A MORE CONGRUENT MODEL OF HELPING

When culturally diverse immigrant families from collectivistic cultures have a problem they don't rush to the local mental health agency for help. In fact, seeking "therapy" or a counseling professional is not the first thing they think of, as there is a strong stigma against counseling, psychology and psychiatry. On the one hand, seeing a counseling psychologist amounts to admitting one is crazy. On the other hand, collectivistic cultures healing ways are more practical and traditional. When seeking help for an emotional problem, one seeks a priest, an elder family member or simply handles the problem within the family. However, when provided with access to "education" as a way to solve problems, families are eager to accept this help since they place a high value on education and they tend to have high respect for the educator.

SBFC PROVIDES EARLY INTERVENTION

SBFC provides early intervention, thus preventing problems from becoming more difficult and causing more damage. Children constitute an early warning system that alerts professionals about the child's problems. Children somatize, act out, act in and generally reflect through their behavior and academic performance when they are affected by problems in the community or the home. Therefore, a school-based family counselor is able to quickly respond to the problems before they fester and cause more harm. These and many other factors make SBFC a culturally sensitive and appropriate model for serving Latino, African American, Asian and Middle Eastern families, among other collectivistic families. However, aside from its culturally appropriate stance, SBFC is an appropriate and effective model for helping to promote healthy children and families.

CHALLENGES AND SOLUTIONS

There are numerous challenges confronting School Based Family Counseling models. These lie essentially in what Joel Barker (1994) calls the "paradigm effect." The paradigm of school counseling or marriage family counseling calls for a silo model response, not a family system response. The "counseling paradigm" blinds us to the possibility of a system response. The same paradigm blinds us into seeing only that intervention handed to us by our training. As the saying goes, if all we have is a hammer, everything begins to look like nails! The challenge is to envision the whole person and the whole family as our charge. The solution lies in seeing this vision and acting accordingly. The challenge is for us to step out of our silos and learn to collaborate with our allied professionals, paraprofessionals and parents. We must learn to collaborate with teachers, doctors, business leaders, parents and children themselves.

The other challenge facing the SBFC professional is that of leadership. Visionary leadership is essential in order to teach and model by example. A visionary leader is a person with strong vision, as well as effective communication strong relational skills. He/she must be able to share his or her perspective not as "the truth" but as his/her truth. I am told that despite all advances in engineering, when erecting a high-rise building, engineers must still share with their scopes where to place the joining bolt for a span. The engineer reportedly says to a second engineer in the distance, "from my present viewpoint, I see the need for the support to be "X" distance higher (or lower, as the case may be), how do you see it from your perspective?" In other words, despite the knowledge and computational data about stress, distance, sagging nature of steel, etc., one still must communicate for the edifice to stand sound and straight. Thus it is with the implementation of any new way of solving problems, including those using SBFC. Communication is essential in order to effectively face challenges in schools and communities.

TYPES OF CHALLENGES AND WAYS TO RESPOND

Schools are organizations just like any other organization. They possess an organizational culture; they have a history and a behavioral repertoire that helps members feel connected with a sense of value and purpose. There are many types of organizations, but all of them have a common feature. Organizations are "organismic" in nature and so, as with any organism, they are oriented to survive, even if they are seen as "dysfunctional" from the societal point of view. However, this organismic desire to survive requires leaders who have vision, courage and strong interpersonal influencing skills. They lead by example, not by shaming or hostile confrontation. Let us look at some types of organizations and ways to respond.

The Rigid Organization. Some organizations are rigid and tend to remain stuck with "the way we do business" mentality, regardless of conditions changing in the social environment. For example, South Central Los Angeles was for years an African American community and so, the culture of the schools reflected a cultural world view of this community. However, the radical changes in demographics led to South Central Los Angeles to become a Latino and essentially newcomer region. Despite these changes in cultural climate, the schools remained wedded to an African American world view, serving a community that does not exist. For example, in South Central Los Angeles, a community that was once predominantly African American, is now 99% Latino(a). However, the school administrators, City Council members and County Board of Supervisors and other governing leaders in this area are either African American or Euro-American! Moreover, when families express concern for the lack of cultural sensitivity and absence of a Latino voice at the top, the response tends to invoke the prevailing antagonistic view used by the Supreme Court against Affirmative Action by labeling the community's request as "race-based representation". This rigidity not only silences active Latino participation, but also hurts children and families by de-valuing their participation. It also frustrates educators' efforts to increase parent involvement in those schools. The solution lies in counselors forging partnerships with community leaders by engaging them in asking the question I discussed for engineers when building a high rise building: "from my perspective I see a Hispanic/Latino community seeking understanding, validation and support, what do you see from your perspective?" It is these questions posed in a non-threatening manner that result in change.

The Chaotic Organization. As with the rigid organization, the chaotic organization is typically one that is responding to change in a disorganized manner, thereby lacking in a focused vision. This leads to inconsistent direction and a sense of purpose. They are what some sociologists have labeled "neurotic organizations" since they fail to satisfy their members or to meet significant target goals. When a chaotic organization is a school, it fails to meet its mission to educate <u>all</u> children, often allowing groups of children to fall through the proverbial cracks of the system. SBFC leaders can help these organizations by immersing themselves as team members of the teaching and leadership community and by sharing their visions. An SBFC professional might say at a faculty meeting, "I am concerned about significant numbers of students not meeting standards of success as others. I am wondering if others of you see this? Perhaps we can join forces and address this together? My vision is to see all children succeed. Maybe we can get parents and community leaders to help us." In other words, the vision has to be shared, the conditions must be identified and the voiceless given voice.

There are many other examples of schools as organizations facing enormous challenges. Many of these schools have leaders-in-waiting that should rise and join hands with others who share the vision. Many of these visionaries may not be educators, but rather members of the community. The old paradigm of schools containing professionals with blinders, trained in silos based on rigid professional dogma must change to a new paradigm based on collaboration and interdisciplinary team work. The role of the SBFC professional is to define his/her charge as that of a facilitator of change, an ombudsperson with the school, the family and the community. The SBFC professional understands his/her role as a systems-oriented person who envisions the next paradigm of schooling, one whose inherent nature is that of an inclusive community of professionals and families. This professional sees the links between multiple professionals with their own organizational systems and understands the importance of linking them with the schools.

SUMMARY

This chapter provides two examples of ways to promote the SBFC model of services using the NOAH or needs overlap analysis in the helping process model. The chapter illustrates the importance of changing the paradigm of "counseling" into a more systems-oriented model that allows for multiple visions of helping families, especially those from non western cultures.

REFERENCES

Adelman, H.S. & Taylor, L. (1998). Reframing mental health in schools and expanding school reform. *Educational Psychologist*, 33(4), 135-152.

Barker, J. (1994). *The Business of Paradigms*. New York: Chart House.

Calfee, C., Wittwer, F & Meredith, M. (1998). *Building a Full-Service School: A Step-By-Step Guide*. San Francisco, CA: Jossey-Bass, Inc.

Cohen, H. I. & Filipczak, J. (1971*). A New Learning Environment*. San Francisco, CA: Jossey-Bass, Inc.

Cowen, E.L., Hightower, A.D., Pedro-Carroll, J.A., Work, W.C., Wyman, P.A. & Haffey, W.G. (1996). *School-Based Prevention for Children at Risk: The Primary Mental Health Project.* Washington, DC: American Psychological Association.

Dryfoos, J.G. (1994). *Full-Service Schools: A revolution in health and social services for children, youth, and families.* San Francisco, CA: Jossey-Bass, Inc.

Fine, M. J. & Carlson, C. (Eds.). (1992). *The handbook of family-school intervention: A systems perspective.* Boston, MA: Allyn & Bacon.

Hong, G.K., Garcia, M., Soriano, M. (in press). Responding to the challenge: Preparing mental health professionals for the changing U.S. demongraphics. Chapter in Cuellar & F.A. Paniagua (Eds.), *Handbook of multicultural mental health: Assessment and treatment of diverse populations* (2nd Edition). San Diego, CA: Academic Press.

Hurwitz, L. & Weston, K. (2001*). Issue Brief: Using coordinated school health to promote mental health for all students.* National Assembly on School-Based Health Care. US Department of Health and Human Services.

Pearce, P. I. & Amato, P. R. (1980). A Taxonomy of Helping: A Multidimensional Scaling Analysis. *Social Psychology Quarterly*, 43 (4), 363-371.

Rubenstein, G. (2008). *Full-Service Schools: Where success is more than academic.* Retreived from http://www.edutopia.org/whats-next-2008-communityservices.

Soriano, M., Pir, T., Hong, G. & Carter, M. (1993*). Mission Possible: Resource and evaluation handbook for culture-sensitive school-based mental health services*. Los Angeles, CA: California State University, Los Angeles.

Soriano, M. & Soriano, F.I. & Jimenez, R. (1994). School violence among culturally diverse populations, *National School Psychology Review*, 23 (2), 216-235.

Triandis, H.C. (1995*). Individualism & collectivism.* Boulder, CO: Westview Press, Inc.

PART IX

FUTURE DEVELOPMENTS IN SCHOOL-BASED FAMILY COUNSELING

Chapter 51
School Counseling and Family Services in
Southeast Asia: Towards the Development of
School-Based Family Counseling

Gertina J. van Schalkwyk

OVERVIEW: *School counseling and family services in Southeast Asia are still greatly underrepresented in the literature, most likely because the field is not yet fully developed as elsewhere in the world. In most Pacific Rim countries such as Thailand, Malaysia, Philippines, Macao and others some psychological services are provided by educational psychologists, school counselors and teacher-counselors but their training and expertise leave much to be desired. At present, school psychology is not a recognized profession within these territories, and Van Schalkwyk and D'Amato (2013) note that "school psychology services and the functions of school psychologists providing assessment, consultation and intervention for children and their families are still greatly underdeveloped" (p. x). School counseling and family services are often non-existent or managed by non-government organizations with limited resources. In this chapter I present an overview of the current status of school psychological and family services in some of these Southeast Asian countries and examine some recommendations for the development of School-Based Family Counseling (SBFC) in the region.*

BACKGROUND

In this chapter, I aim to explore the provision of school counseling and family services in Southeast Asia. Mental health services, school counseling and family therapy are relatively new to most Pacific Rim countries despite the growth and development of these services over the past 20 to 30 years in regions such as Hong Kong and Taiwan (Chan, 2005; Ding, Kuo & Van Dyke, 2008; Luk-Fong & Lung, 2003), and in Singapore (Chong, Lee, Tan, Wong, & Yeo, 2013). For example, Macao—a Special Administrative Region of the People's Republic of China situated in the Pearl River delta—is still lagging behind in the scope of school-based counseling, training, licensure, and opportunities for continuing professional development and supervision (Chang, Van Schalkwyk & Tran, 2006). Specialized mental health services, specifically school-based child and family interventions have limited exposure (Van Schalkwyk, 2011). There is also a dearth of research specific to this and other regions in Southeast Asia such as Malaysia, the Philippines and Thailand, and in Mainland China. One could certainly ask: *Where is school psychology and school-based family counseling in Asia?* (Van Schalkwyk & D'Amato, 2013).

School psychology and school counseling have a long history in the west (see Fagan & Wise, 2007; Merrell, Ervin & Gimpel, 2006). The National Association of School Psychologists in the United States (NASP) explains that the central focus of the school psychologist is on helping "children and youth succeed academically, socially, behaviorally, and emotionally" (www.nasponline.org). School psychologists collaborate with educators, parents and other professionals to support learning and strengthen connections between home, school, and the community for all students. The International School Psychology Association (ISPA) also aims to "promote the use of sound psychological principles in education, encourage communication between professionals committed to improving children's mental health and well-being, [and develop] recourses of school psychology [to] initiate and promote cooperation with organizations committed to similar purposes" (http://www.ispaweb.org/). School counseling, on the other hand, refers to work done primarily with secondary school students in providing academic and vocational guidance (Chan, 2005; Luk-Fong & Lung, 2003). School counselors in the US and elsewhere are often required to have a teaching certificate and teaching experience (Fagan & Wise, 2007). A more recent endeavor is school-based family counseling that expands school psychology and counseling practices to address the child's problems in the "context of all his or her interpersonal networks: family, peer group, classroom, school and community" (Gerrard, 2008, p. 1). Nonetheless, the development of school-based child and family psychological services in the international arena has been and still is very much associated with a country's domestic conditions, both economically and socially.

In Asian countries, school psychology and school counseling have a short history and there is a dearth of scholarly articles on the growth and development of these fields in the region (Van Schalkwyk & D'Amato, 2013). There also appears to be some confusion regarding the role and function of school psychologists and school counselors, and a blurring of boundaries between school psychology, school counseling, and school social work (Chong et al., 2013; Ding et al., 2008; Leeuwerke & Shi, 2010; Low, Kok, & Lee, 2013). In the People's Republic of China (PRC), Hong Kong and Taiwan school psychological services are, for example, performed by school counselors and vary greatly depending on the culture and attributed value of mental health services in these regions (Chan, 2005; D'Amato, Van Schalkwyk, Zhao & Hu, 2013; Lam & Yuen, 2004; Wang & D'Amato, 2013). Career guidance and school counseling overlap with school psychology particularly regarding assessment, intervention and prevention (Luk-Fong & Lung, 2003; Ni, Jones, & Bruning, 2012).

In their recent review of the state of the art of school psychology and school counseling in Pacific Rim countries, Van Schalkwyk and D'Amato (2013) conclude that there is an "obvious need for systematic mental health services, particularly for children and youth and their families" (p. 123). A review of the literature indicates a critical need to develop programs and training opportunities that enable and empower professional psychologists to provide the necessary services with recognition of the diversity of these Asian cultures in the Pacific Rim. Ding and colleagues (2008) note that "causal pathways linking culture, social economy, professional perspectives and political ideas to the practice of school psychology" (p. 592) should be considered when developing both services and training. Furthermore, people who are still firmly embedded in Confucian Heritage Cultures also demonstrate particular adversity to help-seeking behavior while education in Asia in general progressed along different lines further hampering the development of psychology and school psychology in Asian countries. School-based family counseling (SBFC) is also non-existent except for recent endeavors at the Hong Kong Institute for Education (personal communication with Pattie Luk-Fong, 2011).

Early developments in **Mainland China** reveal the establishment of a Division of School Psychology within the Chinese Psychological Society (Lin, 1995). However, in their historical overview of the status quo of school psychological practices in Mainland China, D'Amato and colleagues (2013) assert that there is still a great gap in the provision of coherent and consistent professional services amongst those practicing as so-called school psychologists. For the most part, school counseling and family services in China form part of mental health education in schools and deal primarily with children in the mainstream school system while little assistance exist for children with learning disabilities or families struggling with demand of the opening up of China to global initiatives. Whereas education is highly valued amongst the Chinese people and firmly embedded in the incremental theory model (Dweck, Chiu, and Hong, 1995; Hong, Chiu, Dweck, Lin, & Wan, 1999; Norenzayan, Choi, & Nisbett, 2002), there is little room for considering the needs of Chinese children, youths and families with special needs. It seems that the Chinese education system and therefore also the endeavors to provide mental health services are still firmly rooted in the belief that traits, intelligence and ability are malleable and academic success is determined more by effort and practice, rather than intelligence and ability. China's mental health education is hampered by ideological and political constraints, and provides little or no opportunities to assist those with learning disabilities or other problems, and even less in terms of school counseling and family services (Chan, 2005; Ding et al., 2008).

School psychology has somewhat more visibility in **Taiwan** where landmark events such as the compulsory education system and a free-market economy contributed to the status quo of school-based family counseling services (Wang & D'Amato, 2013). In their quest for developing a more indigenous psychology, Taiwanese psychologists have been hard at work to integrate school guidance and counseling programs that can offer comprehensive mental health services in schools and to families in need. However, there still appears to be some confusion and a blurring of boundaries regarding the role and function of school psychologists and school counselors where school-based child and family services are greatly dependent on the culture and attributed value of mental health services (Ding et al., 2008; Leeuwerke & Shi, 2010).

It seems that to date school psychology is maybe best developed in two regions with previous colonial ties to the United Kingdom. **Hong Kong** has a well-developed educational psychology component in their higher education system with graduate-level training and an established system for regulation and licensing of professionals working in school-related settings (Chan, 2005; Ding et al., 2008; Luk-Fong & Lung, 2003). Recent developments in school-based family counseling also explicate greater collaboration between professional practice and parents for the development of appropriate and relevant school-based child and family interventions (Luk-Fong, 2013; Wong, Lam, Leung, Ho & Au-Yeung, in press).

In **Singapore**, advanced-level educational psychology aims to train professionals who can provide psychological services to school-aged children at all levels and in particular support diverse student learning needs and special education needs within the mainstream school system (Chong et al., 2013; Ooi, Ang, Ibrahim, et al., in press). Although incorporating families in the services are still somewhat lagging, Singapore "seemingly has a well-developed framework for school psychology professionals to execute their expected roles and functions" (Van Schalkwyk & D'Amato, 2013, p. 127).

However, despite the positive developments in some regions, other areas in Southeast Asia are still lagging far behind in their provision of school-based child and family counseling. Low, Kok and Lee (2013) mention the absence of school psychology in the Malaysian educational system and consider the express need for a multi-faceted framework that would enable professionals to provide more comprehensive psychological services to the culturally diversion children and youths, and families in **Malaysia**. They conclude that a holistic approach integrating school, family, the local community and training institutions would greatly benefit the mental health services, and advocate for more collaboration between Southeast Asian countries in the development and establishment of school-based family counseling in the region. A similar situation prevails in the **Philippines** where school psychology training also need to consider the unique psychosocial issues faced by children of migrant parents—that is, the children of Overseas Filipino Workers (OFW) (Tarroja & Fernando, 2013). The Philippines have a particular need for appropriately and adequately dealing with the absence of parental support for school-aged children and the subsequent special needs of children and youths in this country.

Two countries where school psychology and school-based child and family services are slowly on the rise, is **Thailand** (Tangdhanakanond, Archwamety, McFarland, & Beckman, 2013) and **South Korea** (Tangdhanakanond & Dong, in press). In Thailand most psychological services are still provided by guidance teachers, while special education teachers with limited specific training are assigned duties to carry out intervention practices for children with learning disabilities at different grade levels (Van Schalkwyk & D'Amato, 2013). Korean and Thai college students and school psychology practitioners are also still confused about the roles and functions expected of those providing mental health services to special needs children, particularly through counseling, intervention and consultation with parents and teachers within school-related settings.

The above overview of the status quo in some Southeast Asian countries set the stage for exploring the needs and building a case for the development of school-based family counseling in Asia. Only a few countries are mentioned above, which for the most part is due to the absence of research literature pertaining other regions such Vietnam, Cambodia, Indonesia, Myanmar/Burma, Laos, Nepal and even India. The International School Psychology Association (ISPA) has made some inroads in these regions in recent years but there is still much work to be done for school-based family services to systematically provide mental health services and assist children and youth to develop to their fullest potential. As Van Schalkwyk and D'Amato (2013) conclude in a recent publication it seems that maybe the most important need is "to develop programs that would lead to graduate level training in school psychology while simultaneously acknowledging the diversity of these Asian cultures" (p. 128). Therefore the next section will address some of the most pressing needs and recommendations regarding such development and in order to establish the groundwork for school-based family counselors to develop these Asian countries to their fullest potential.

A CASE STUDY: SCHOOL COUNSELING IN MACAO

Macao is an enclave of about 28 square kilometers on the South China coast consisting predominantly of Chinese citizens. In 1999, Macao became a Special Administration Region of the PRC after more than 450 years of Portuguese administrative rule. Under the Portuguese, the education system and mental health services has been different from that in the PRC in that it focused mainly on European and religious-oriented practices (Van Schalkwyk, Tran & Chang, 2006). With the dawn of the 21st century, access to the education system has become more equal to all classes and both genders, and the government has paid much attention to developing an integrated and holistic education system that will benefit all people in society (Direcção dos Serviços de Educação e Juventude [DSEJ] (i.e., Education and Youth Affairs Bureau), 2011). In the 2011 scholastic year, Macao had a total of 79 schools with 11 government schools and 68 private, predominantly religious-oriented schools serving children from age 3 (kindergarten) to age 18 (senior secondary). The school-going population totaled 76,214, which was about 5.6% less than the previous year (2008/2009) (DSEJ, 2011; Direcção dos Serviços de Estatística e Censos [DSEC] (i.e., Statistics and Census Service of Macao SAR Government), 2010). Approximately 85% of students attended public or private schools funded by the Government's free education for 15 years scheme. Although the total number of students has decreased, the number of teachers increased by approximately 4.78% resulting in a teacher-student ratio of about 1:16.3.

There are, as far as I could determine, no school psychologists officially working in any of the schools, although teachers with advanced training in educational psychology and school counseling are evident in some schools. Psychological counseling and assessment for the school-going population are provided through the Centre for Psycho-Pedagogical Support and Special Education of the Education and Youth Affairs Bureau (DSEJ, 2011). The DSEJ has sponsored eight non-government organizations and schools to hire school counselors. These counselors, holding a bachelor degree in either psychology or social work (Chang et al, 2006), provide school counseling services for 79 schools, and according to the 2011 statistics there were about 126.5 school counselors in total (DSEJ, 2011). Some doctoral level clinical psychologists trained in the US have been employed by the DSEJ as consultants and supervisors. The school counselors provide psychological services and preventive and developmental guidance programs through all school grades with no distinction between private and public schools (DSEJ, 2011). A prescribed *Handbook for School Counseling* explicates the daily tasks. According to these prescriptions, the school counselor is required to offer individual, group and crisis counseling, developmentally appropriate classroom and small-group presentations (e.g., psycho-education), assessment for school placement, and teacher and parent consultation. This certainly is a different role than for most western countries. There is also very little research specific to this region regarding any school psychology, psychological services or school-based child and family services (Van Schalkwyk, 2011).

EXPLORING SCHOOL-BASED CHILD AND FAMILY INTERVENTIONS IN MACAO

Adopting a qualitative approach, I explored the perceptions and shared meanings in the verbal (interviews) and non-verbal (written) accounts of three teachers and seven school counselors in Macao (Clandinin & Connelly, 2000). The aim was not to conduct an in-depth study or to generalize but to gain a deeper understanding of the current situation and the gaps in providing school-based mental health services to children and their families within the school setting in Macao (Van Schalkwyk, 2013). As such, I identified relevant participants through using a non-probability purposive sampling strategy (e.g., see Onwuegbuzie & Leech, 2007). The age range for the three female teachers was between 52 and 56 years, while the school counselors' ages ranged between 23 and 27 years and included three males and four females. Except for one teacher who has a Diploma in Teaching, all other participants had a Bachelor degree with a major in either education (i.e., teachers) or psychology (i.e., school counselors).

A research assistant conducted semi-structured face-to-face interviews with the three teachers and four school counselors in Cantonese, the native language of participants. The three remaining school counselors provided written responses in English. The interviews and written stories focused on the viewpoints of participants based on the central question: *How do school counselors serve the Macao school children and their families?* Additional questions related to specific experiences regarding the tasks and responsibilities, case management, frustrations and rewards, and training needs of school counselors. Acknowledging the ethical principles required for qualitative research (Clandinnin & Connelly, 2000), I provided all participants with an information leaflet explaining their privacy protection, anonymity and confidentiality of the information they provided. Participation was voluntary and participants did not receive any compensation. Written consent was obtained from all participants allowing the research assistant to audio record the interviews and the researcher to use the information (both verbal and written) for study purposes.

The research assistant transcribed all the Chinese materials and translated them into English to generate the field texts for analysis. Working with the translated texts does have a limitation because some of the language features—the intrinsic nuances and meanings of language—cannot be captured (Haiman, 2005). Many words in the Chinese language are difficult to translate in their full meaning into English. Nonetheless, since the research assistant is a native speaker and collaborated in the thematic analysis and interpretation, we could refer back to the original recordings and transcripts in Chinese to verify credibility of interpretations (Van Schalkwyk & Sit, 2013). This enhanced trustworthiness of the analysis within the local context (Clandinin & Connelly, 2000).

The psychology community in Macao is quite small and the majority of school counselors currently employed in schools is recent graduates from a local university. Thus, as a university educator I am quite familiar with the local scenario having trained several cohorts in recent years. In order to limit potential bias and maintain anonymity, I assigned pseudonyms to each participant. Furthermore and in collaboration with the research assistant, I undertook an in-depth thematic analysis in which we independently analyzed and compared the field texts using an iterative and inductive approach (Larkin, Eatough & Osborn, 2011). Continuous critical reflection further allowed for analytic generalization using the eco-systemic model proposed by Low (2009). Cognizance of the existing literature in the fields of school counseling and school-based family counseling also allowed for verification and trustworthiness of interpretations (Carter & Perluss, 2008; Ding et al., 2008; Fagan & Wise, 2007; Gerrard, 2008; Ni et al., 2012). Referring to examples from the participants' accounts (in *italics* below), I identified several themes that show the ways in which school counselors in Macao provide psychological services to schoolchildren and their families, as well as the perceived needs for establishing school-based child and family services.

SCHOOL-BASED CHILD AND FAMILY SERVICES IN MACAO

Integrating extracts from the participants' reports, I describe here the situation of school-based child and family counseling in Macao in 2011-2012 when the study was conducted. The themes that emerged relate to the ways in which school counselors served children and their families, and the perceptions of both teachers and school counselors regarding the value added through providing mental health services within the school context. Given the limited training they received prior to an appointment as school counselor, I also discuss the needs of the school counselors as reflected in the seven participants' reports. Although the needs of the Macao school counselors I interviewed for this case should not be generalized to all school counselors (in Macao or elsewhere), reviewing the meager literature available on school-based child and family services in Southeast Asia allowed me to make some recommendations for how training institutions could proceed to adequately equip current and future school-based child and family counselors (see below).

School counseling services in Macao. A school counselor participant summarized the job description as follows: "*According to the DSEJ requirement, each school counselor has to handle 50 cases at school and organize a minimum of 25 activities per year for students at the school.* Another school counselor added that they *needed to assist the school dealing with teachers' and students' emotional, behavioral and family problems, holding activities for preventive and developmental outcomes … and building positive values.*" In their capacity as school counselors albeit with limited training, their main task was to provide psychological counseling to children with needs varying from academic and behavioral problems to interpersonal relationship and family problems. The counselors commented on providing developmentally appropriate interventions based on the assessment of the student's mental health condition at the time. For the most part these services amounted to a kind of band aid aimed at covering up serious wounds elsewhere (e.g., a dysfunctional family system). High-risk cases were referred to the DSEJ and/or school for follow up, and in severe cases a student might be expelled before any kind of intervention could run its course.

Cases could "*be referred by class advisors, discovered by the counselor* (the counselor identifies cases by her or himself) *or self-committed* (a needy student actively seeking out help)." The class advisor or teacher usually had some basic understanding of the child's needs and the school counselor would meet with the relevant teacher to explore the nature of specific problems. As one teacher commented, students "*would even work with the school doctor, head-teacher of the class, and the religious teacher.*" Because many student problems in school originated within the family, the school counselor also interacted with parents. The counselor needed to regularly report on the progress of individual sessions with the student to assure the parents (and the teachers) that they were providing the necessary interventions. Furthermore, they needed to enlist the help of parents in resolving the student's problems and even conducted family therapy when necessary. This happened despite the school counselor not having had the appropriate training to provide any form of family therapy and often grappling in the dark when interceding on behalf of the child with either the school or the family.

For interventions, the school counselor relied on meager therapeutic strategies and often found it disenabling because of insufficient training and supervision with most of them trained at the Bachelor level in psychology (Gora, Sawatzky & Hague, 1992; Leeuwerke & Shi, 2010; Low, 2009). Nonetheless, the teacher's in this study all agreed that the school counselor's intervention with parents was most helpful to the smooth running of the school. The school also relied heavily on the school counselor to talk with the parents when problems arose between students and teachers or when the student violated any of the school's regulations. In Macao, the relationship between teachers and parents was often strained and parents might not listen to teachers calmly when there was something wrong with their children. However, when communicating with the counselor, parents accepted information with greater ease. They seemingly perceived the counselors as more caring and compassionate as opposed to teachers who were perceived as punitive and too busy. The school counselors, on the other hand, perceived this mediation role as though they were acting "*as a bridge,*" and reportedly found this role stressful and troublesome particularly since they have not yet developed efficient skills to deal with all parties involved (Van Schalkwyk, 2011).

In the current education system in Macao, the school counselors provided a valuable and necessary service to children and their families (DSEJ, 2011). The teachers believed, for example, that "*counselors are necessary in schools*" and were there to "*help teachers to handle some extra problems.*" School counselors in Macao contributed greatly to the development of mental health in schools through the workshops they presented and the counseling they provided to individual students. Both the teachers and school counselors who participated in this study perceived the need of providing additional psychological services to the school population. However, participants in this study all agreed that school counselors were inadequately equipped to deal with the various tasks expected of them.

Psycho-education and mental health services. Apart from the casework they had to do, the school counselor also had to conduct individual and group activities. The nature of activities varied according to the developmental needs of the students in a particular school. The focus was on psycho-education including, as one counselor commented, "*talks in the hall, small group sessions, or go somewhere else to pay a visit.*" Psycho-education and/or workshops reached a larger group and were preventive in nature, (Montoya, Colom & Ferrin, 2011; Ni et al., 2012). These activities are organized through the school and scheduled according to available time slots on the calendar. The objectives of class discussions, talks, small group sessions and even off-campus visits were to enhance positive values and contributed towards the growth and development of the students. Broadly described as activities, the school counselor had flexibility regarding what to offer during the seminars, workshops and talks.

According to DSEJ (2011), the most frequently held activity was about sex education, followed by peer support groups, social relationships, developmental adaptation, drug avoidance, internet addiction and volunteer work, career planning. For these events, school counselors had to do the necessary research, provided appropriate planning documents (including budget allocation), liaised with different people within the school context, and presented the activities often to large groups of students. As one counselor commented, "*I have to organize some group workshops about different topics frequently. In each semester, I have to do a 40 minute presentations in every class. I think that was the most effective way for students to learn.*" However, conducting psycho-education development groups required special (personal) skills to "*control the situation*" and some counselors had trouble communicating in large groups. As a teacher commented, "*the counselor in our school is having a problem with his communication skills—it is not good enough.*" Thus, even with the preventive interventions there seemed to be a need for more focused training that would enable the school counselor to provide adequate services to children, their families, and the school.

Building a Compelling Case. Although providing psychological counseling to needy students was for the most part quite rewarding, the school counselors in Macao reported some frustration on their jobs. Despite being valued within the school setting, the school counselors perceived some role confusion that restricted them from fully serving the client population they had to deal with—that is, the school (teachers), the children, and the families. Based on the four domains in the ecosystems framework proposed by Low (2009) and reviewing the meager literature related to school-based child and family counseling in Southeast Asia, the next section focuses on the identification of the areas where urgent attention was required to address the multitude of needs both in the client population and the school counselors (Figure 51.1).

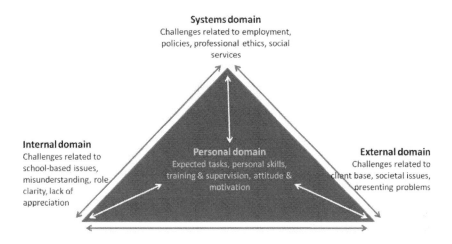

Systems domain
Challenges related to employment, policies, professional ethics, social services

Internal domain
Challenges related to school-based issues, misunderstanding, role clarity, lack of appreciation

Personal domain
Expected tasks, personal skills, training & supervision, attitude & motivation

External domain
Challenges related to client base, societal issues, presenting problems

Figure 51.1   Four domains of challenges that school counselors face in Macao (adapted from Low, 2009)

In the **personal domain**, school counselors faced the challenge of inadequate training and insufficient supervision. All the Southeast Asian communities thus far reviewed report limited training and inadequate expertise for their roles and the functions they had to act upon (e.g., Low et al., 2013; Tarroja & Fernando, 2013; Van Schalkwyk & Sit, 2013; Wang & D'Amato, 2013). As one counselor in Macao commented, "*most frustrating is that there is not enough training for me. I help students all day long, but sometimes I feel tired or frustrated about having too much negative thinking*." For the most part they lacked most of the competencies or skills expected of a SBFC professional (see Chapter 1)— that is, someone who had a systems focus, was strength based and multi-culturally sensitive, could enter into partnership with parents, advocated for the child, and promoted positive transformation in the school. Existing training models did not address, for example, school psychological assessment, parent consultation or family counseling. With insufficient training, and perceiving themselves as inadequate and inferior, school counselors in Macao also experienced high turnover amongst their colleagues, something that seriously affected their personal wellbeing and motivation for the job.

The **internal domain** of challenges related to the lack of role clarity and misunderstanding that school counselors had to face in the communities they served. For example, in Macao school counseling and school psychology were not seen as a professional vocations and this diminished the self-worth of counselors whether working in the school setting or in the community. Some even indicated a sense of inferiority, believing there was little recognition and support for their profession, even though the schools and administration formally promoted the importance of mental health services in school-related settings (D'Amato et al., 2013). Mental health professionals in Macao such as school social workers and clinical psychologists (and even teachers) perceived the school counselors as lacking proper training to provide the interventions needed to help disturbed children or those with special needs (Van Schalkwyk & Sit, 2013). Although gradually emerging as important providers of mental health services, school counselors had to face issues related to the definition of their professional roles and clearly defined boundaries ((Tangdhanakanond et al., 2013; Tangdhanakanond & Dong, in press). In some cases the counselors also had limited if any training in education. This positioned them as outsiders in the school setting where they were employed to provide counseling services to the children. They were not considered as a member of the professional team (i.e., the teachers) and with their background in psychology (rather than education) were seen as different and even unwelcome guests (Tarroja, & Fernando, 2013). As Fagan and Wise (2007) have argued, they were merely visitors tolerated by staff members in the school. Although this was not unique to Southeast Asian countries, these challenges might serve as roadblocks to the development of SBFC in the region (Gerrard, 2008; Gysbers, & Henderson, 2001; Low, 2009; Low et al., 2013).

Bunce and Willower (2001) also posed that misunderstanding and lack of role clarity were key issues pertaining how school counselors experienced their role and function in the school setting. Even though the teachers in Macao commented that the counselors provided a necessary service in schools, they still had a rather vague perception of the actual nature and qualifications required to practice as a school counselor causing much role ambiguity amongst school counselors. Teachers' acceptance of school counselors was important and in the absence of recognition from the largest group of professionals in the school, the school counselors experienced constantly having to defend their position (Chan, 2005; Low, 2009). Rather, the school counselor was perceived as a teacher's aide, "*a kind of supplement to education in the school*" or as the "*janitor, a person who lacks knowledge ... only having some skills for talking and making money through chit-chat*". Similar experiences had been reported for educational psychologists in Hong Kong (Luk-Fong & Lung, 2003).

In the **external domain**, school counselors were challenged by ineffective working styles and difficulties to adapt to the many professionals and parents with whom they regularly interacted within the school setting (e.g., children, teachers, agency representatives). Moreover, they felt inadequately equipped to deal with the various tasks expected of them. Ethical challenges also surfaced when different parties, specifically the school staff were "*dissatisfied about how counselors have to maintain privacy for the cases they see.*" There was also the uncertainty of so-called unrelated tasks that kept them from providing the psychological services they were employed to do. For example, although report writing was common for school counselors, having to satisfy the expectations of both the agency assigning them to the school as well as school staff posed another challenge within the school-related work environment. A school counselor in Macao commented "*counselors could spend about 40% of their time on writing reports and proposals.*" In this city, they had a so-called dual-employment status, and had to please "*two bosses. This situation bothers the school counselors a lot. It is because the agency has a set of rules and requirements for case management and counseling services. On the other hand, the schools also have another set of rules. Therefore, the counselor is always in a dilemma.*"

Finally and in the **systems domain**, dramatic and rapid changes were taking place in Southeast Asian countries in recent years (e.g., economic boom, globalization, etc.). These systemic changes and societal and global trends posed further challenges to school counselors who wanted to serve children, youths and families in school-related settings (Low et al., 2013; Tarroja & Fernando, 2013; Van Schalkwyk, 2011; Van Schalkwyk & Sit, 2013). As elsewhere (Low, 2009), schools in Macao included a diverse student population with a continuous flow of migrants from Mainland China and other Southeast Asian countries (DSEC, 2009), and a booming gaming industry that lured students towards earning "fast money" (Van Schalkwyk et al., 2006). Multiple societal changes in recent years also influenced the nature of presenting problems (Chong et al., 2013; Low et al., 2013; Luk-Fong, 2013; Tarroja & Fernando, 2013). Furthermore, striving for international recognition tertiary education institutions often provided training in English and in western models of psychology. However, the counselors had to practice in Chinese Heritage Cultures firmly embedded in Eastern philosophies and had to operate in the local dialect (Luk-Fong, 2005; Sun, 2008). This posed a further challenge regarding case management, writing progress reports and client confidentiality, and, as the counselors in Macao noted, there was a constant need to adapt to the conflicting cultures, rules and policies in their everyday practice of school-based child and family counseling within the school setting.

CHALLENGES AND SOLUTIONS

I conclude the explication of identified needs with an excerpt from one of Macao's young school counselors who aptly described the challenges and needs within the local context.

> "I think it is necessary to officially introduce the work of school counselor to the public—citizens, teachers, headmasters and others. The role of school counselor is not clear and there is always some misunderstanding about the school counselor's profession. This kind of value does actually affect the enthusiasm of school counselors, since we are treated as an extra work force at school, even though we have to focus on counseling. Moreover, the minimum requirement to become a school counselor is a bachelor degree, which is not sufficient. People also do not know psychology and counseling and therefore even staff at school may assume anyone can become the school counselor. I think role clarification and further training are crucially important, and the DSEJ may actually help to develop specialist school psychologists, as they are the authority in Macao."

The above extract resonated with the situation in other Southeast Asian countries and provided the basis for the recommendations below in the hope that the future development of SBFC in these countries will emerge with confidence.

First, given the scope of services required from psychologists and school counselors in Asia, it is highly recommended that these countries consider implementing the School-Based Family Counseling (SBFC) model. The SBFC model resonates well with suggestions to integrate school, family, community and training institutions (Low, Kok, & Lee, 2013) and with a culture-sensitive approach to prevention and remediation (Van Schalkwyk & D'Amato, 2013). In a culture where the value of children tops the agenda and family life is revered as essential to community building (Van Schalkwyk, 2010), adopting the SBFC model would allow mental health professionals to adequately and appropriately advocate for the child, the family, and the school, and work with parents and families to help children succeed in school (Low, Kok, & Lee, 2013; Tarroja, & Fernando, 2013; Van Schalkwyk, 2011). Thus, pursuing SBFC training and developing diagnostic tools and interventions focusing on strengths, multi-cultural sensitivity, partnerships, and openness to transformation both within the community and in the school, the SBFC school counselors and family therapists could encourage success for the child not only in the school setting but in life in general (Gerrard, 2008; Morotti, 2010).

Second, local universities should take the lead and train professionals to meet the needs of the school-going population and their families. Establishing graduate programs and professional development in all aspects of providing psychological services both within school settings and in the community is an urgent need for both the professionals and the public. Focusing the training on the strengths of SBFC would greatly aid in the preparation of those who have to work with the school and the family in order to maximize outcomes for the child (Carter & Perluss, 2008; Minke, 2010). Such training should adopt a scientist-practitioner model in which SBFC is embedded and foster the advancement of practices that meets international standards and are locally relevant (Carter & Evans, 2008; D'Amato et al., 2013; Everts, 2008; Gerrard, 2008; Lam & Yuen, 2004; Leeuwerke & Shi, 2010; Luk-Fong & Lung, 2003; Merrell et al., 2006).

Third, there should be recognition by the authorities, mental health professionals and the community concerning the role and function of school counselors and in particular of the SBFC professional. This could best be achieved through establishing the necessary frameworks for licensing and registration of clinical psychologists, school psychologists and SBFC professionals in the regions. Cross-border collaboration between professionals should also be encouraged to strengthen the support and gain recognition from local authorities (Everts, 2008; Smith, 2011). External review by professional associations and internal and external regulations (e.g., licensure) could ensure that SBFC professionals will have the expertise required for the services they provide to the school-going population, their families and the school itself.

Fourthly, it is important that structures are established for continuing professional development in all areas of SBFC counseling. Apart from establishing guidelines for training and licensure, continuous training should be locally and regionally available for up-to-date interventions appropriate within the contexts. Continuous training should also be available to enable SBFC professionals for consultation with the various stakeholders. Following the primary focus of SBFC model, continuous professional development should integrate a family and school focus, as well as a prevention and remediation approach. Thus, not only school counselors but also family counselors could gain a greater understanding of the four quadrants delineating the areas in which SBFC professionals typically work (Gerrard, 2008; Carter, Evans, Zapata, & Taifa, 2011).

Finally, research in Southeast Asia should be encouraged to ensure the development of indigenous models and appropriate diagnostic tools and intervention strategies within the Asian schools and settings. Apart from expanding the available assessments and normative adaptations, research in SBFC should explore the prospects of interventions that will benefit all participants (i.e., the school, the child, and the family) coming from a Confucian Heritage Culture.

SUMMARY

The chapter explored the situation with regard to school-related services to children, youths and their families in Southeast Asian countries and the case of Macao. With school psychology a non-existent practice in most countries except in some universities, school counselors share similar challenges in all domains of the ecosystems framework (Low, 2009; Van Schalkwyk & D'Amato, 2013). Considering the interaction between the personal, the internal, the external and the systems domains revealed some of the enabling and disabling forces at play. There is a major gap in mental health services in Asia, particularly in School-Based Family Counseling. Advancement of such mental health services in Asia and in locally relevant interventions should be pursued avidly with the help of international expertise available at most universities in the regions. The authorities and communities in these countries should also recognize the needs and participate in rectifying the role confusion and disenabling forces currently existing among school counselors and psychologists. Regular discussions between stakeholders in the different domains should work towards enhancing policies and guidelines, and influence the development of SBFC in a positive manner. Further research is important and should investigate the areas of concern among mental health service providers in Southeast Asia, as well as the challenges and constraints experienced by school counselors in offering mental health services to children and their families both within the school and in the community. There is also a need for base line research regarding the value the SBFC model can bring to local communities and collaboration across borders to strengthen the practice of those already in the field.

REFERENCES

Bunce, C. A., & Willower, D. J. (2001). Counselor subcultures in schools. *Journal of Educational Administration, 39*, 472-487.

Carter, M. J., & Evans, W. P. (2008). Implementing School-Based Family Counseling: Strategies, activities, and process considerations. *International Journal for School-Based Family Counseling, 1,*

1-22. Available at: http://www.schoolbasedfamilycounseling.com/journal.html

Carter, M. J., & Perluss, E. (2008). Developments in training School-Based Family Counselors: The School-Based Family Counseling (SBFC) graduate program at California State University, Los Angeles. *International Journal for School-Based Family Counseling, 1,* 1-13. Available at: http://www.schoolbasedfamilycounseling.com/journal.html

Carter, M. J., Evans, W. P., Zapata, J., & Taifa, A. (2011). School-Based Family Counseling Evaluation: Warm feelings, perilous paradigms and empirical hopes. *International Journal for School-Based Family Counseling, 3,* 1-12. Available at:
http://www.schoolbasedfamilycounseling.com/journal.html

Chan, D. W. (2005). Conceptions of counseling among Chinese secondary school teachers in Hong Kong. *International Journal for the Advancement of Counseling, 27,* 311-322. doi:10.1007/s10447-005-3189-z

Chang, K., Van Schalkwyk, G. J., & Tran, E. (2006). Developing Psychological Mindfulness in Macao: Needs and Challenges. *Chinese Cross Currents,* November 2006, 28-47.

Chong, W. H., Lee, B. O., Tan, S. Y., Wong, S. S., & Yeo, L. S. (2013). School psychology and school-based child and family interventions in Singapore. *School Psychology International, 34*(2), 177-189. doi: 10.1177/0143034312453397

Clandinin, D. J., & Connelly, F. M. (2000). *Narrative Inquiry.* San Francisco: Jossey-Bass.

D'Amato, R. C., Van Schalkwyk, G. J., Zhao, B. Y., & Hu, J. (2013). Understanding the development of school psychology in mainland China. *School Psychology International, 34*(2), 131-144. doi: 10.1177/0143034312453392

Ding, Y., Kuo, Y-L., & Van Dyke, D. C. (2008). School psychology in China (PRC), Hong Kong and Taiwan. *School Psychology International, 29,* 529-548. doi:10.1177/0143034308099200

DSEC (2010). Direcção dos Serviços de Estatística e Censos (Statistics and Census Service of Macao SAR Government). Retrieved October 2010 from: www.dsec.gov.mo/Statistic.aspx

DSEJ (2011). Direcção dos Serviços de Educação e Juventude (Education and Youth Bureau). Retrieved September 2011 from: http://www.dsej.gov.mo/

Dweck, C. S., Chiu, C., & Hong, Y. (1995). Implicit theories and their role in judgments and reactions: A world from two perspectives. *Psychological Inquiry, 6,* 267–285.

Everts, H. (2008). Integrating supportive care in schools with the enhancement of family resilience – a New Zealand project for immigrant families. *International Journal for School-Based Family Counseling, 1,* 1-13. Available at: http://www.schoolbasedfamilycounseling.com/journal.html

Fagan, T. K., & Wise, P. S. (Eds.) (2007). *School Psychology: Past, Present and Future* (3rd ed.). Washington, DC: National Association of School Psychologists.

Gerrard, B. (2008). School-Based Family Counseling: overview, trends and recommendations for future research. *International Journal for School-Based Family Counseling, 1,* 1-30. Available at: http://www.schoolbasedfamilycounseling.com/journal.html

Gora, R., Sawatzky, D., & Hague, W. (1992). School counselors' perceptions of their effectiveness. *Canadian Journal of Counseling, 26,* 5-14.

Gysbers, N. C., & Henderson, P. (2001). Comprehensive guidance and counseling programs: A rich history and a bright future. *Professional School Counseling, l4,* 246-256.

Haiman, J. (2005). Losses in translation. *Culture & Psychology, 11,* 111-116. doi:10.1177/1354067X05050755

Hong, Y. Y., Chiu, C. Y., Dweck, C. S., Lin, D., & Wan, W. (1999). Implicit theories, attributions, and coping: A meaning system approach. *Journal of Personality and Social Psychology, 77,* 588 – 599.

Lam, S. F., & Yuen, M. (2004). Continuing professional development in school psychology: Perspective from Hong Kong. *School Psychology International, 25,* 480-494. doi:10.1177/0143034304048781

Larkin, M., Eatough, V., & Osborn, M. (2011). Interpretative phenomenological analysis and embodied, active, situated cognition. *Theory & Psychology, 21*, 318-337. doi:10.1177/0959354310377544

Leeuwerke, W., & Shi, Q. (2010). The practice and perceptions of school counselors: A view from urban China. *International Journal for the Advancement of Counseling, 32*, 75-89. doi:10.1007/s10447-009-9091-3

Low, P. K. (2009). Considering the challenges of counseling practice in schools. *International Journal for the Advancement of Counseling, 31*, 71-79. doi:10.1007/s10447-009-9069-1

Low, S. K., Kok, J. K., & Lee, M. N. (2013). A holistic approach to school-based counseling and guidance services in Malaysia. *School Psychology International, 34*(2), 190-201. doi: 10.1177/0143034312453398

Luk-Fong, P. Y. Y. (2005). Globalization and localization enmeshed - Towards a framework for the development of guidance curriculum in Hong Kong. GLOBALIZATION, SOCIETIES AND EDUCATION, 3, 83-100. doi:10.1080/14767720500046344

Luk-Fong, P. Y. Y. (2013). "External conditions affecting a harmonious family." Lessons learnt from a school-based parent education program in Hong Kong. *School Psychology International, 34*(2), 166-176. doi: 10.1177/0143034312453396

Luk-Fong, P. Y. Y., & Lung, C. L. (2003). The initial development of an instrument for the evaluation of guidance and counseling services in schools. *School Psychology International, 24*, 292-312. doi:10.1177/01430343030243003

Merrell, K. W., Ervin, R. A., & Gimpel, G. A. (2006). *School Psychology for the 21st Century: Foundations and Practices*. New York: The Guilford Press.

Montoya, A., Colom, F., & Ferrin, M. (2011). Is psycho education for parents and teachers of children and adolescents with ADHD efficacious? A systematic literature review. *European Psychiatry, 26*, 135-200. doi:10.1016/j.eurpsy.2010.10.005

Morotti, A. (2010). The Copper River Project: Laying the foundation for School-Based Family Counseling with Alaska's indigenous populations. *International Journal for School-Based Family Counseling, 2*, 1-13. Available at: http://www.schoolbasedfamilycounseling.com/journal.html

Ni, H., Jones, C., & Bruning, R. (2012). Chinese teachers' evaluation criteria as reflected in narrative student evaluations: Implications for psychological services in schools. *School Psychology International, online first February 2012*, 1-16. doi:10.1177/0143034312437079

Norenzayan, A., Choi, I., & Nisbett, R. E. (2002). Cultural similarities and differences in social inference: Evidence from behavioral predictions and lay theories of behavior. *Personality and Social Psychology Bulletin, 28*, 109–120.

Oakland, T. (2007). International School Psychology. In T. K. Fagan & P. S. Wise (Eds.), *School Psychology: Past, Present and Future,* (3rd ed.), (pp.339-365). Washington, DC: National Association of School Psychologists.

Onwuegbuzie, A. J., & Leech, N. L. (2007). Sampling designs in qualitative research: making the sampling process more public. *The Qualitative Report, 12*, 238-254. Retrieved from: http://www.nova.edu/ssss/QR/QR12-2/onwuegbuzie1.pdf

Ooi, Y. P., Ang, R. P., Ibrahim, N. H., Koh, D., Lee, P. Y., Ong, L. P., Wong, G., & Fung, D. S. S. (in press). The continued development and practice of school psychology in Singapore: Using REACH as an illustration. *School Psychology International* (accepted for publication).

Smith, A. (2011). The experience and reflections of parents whose teenagers are excluded from school, with particular attention to the place of counseling. *International Journal for School-Based Family Counseling, 3*, 1-14. Available at: http://www.schoolbasedfamilycounseling.com/journal.html

Sun, C.T. (2008). *Themes in Chinese Psychology*. Singapore: Cengage Learning.

Tarroja, M. C. H., & Fernando, K. C. (2013). Providing psychological services for children of Overseas Filipino Workers (OFWs): a challenge for school psychologists in the Philippines. *School Psychology International, 34*(2), 202-212. doi: 10.1177/0143034312453399

Van Schalkwyk, G. J. (2010). Mapping Chinese family systems and parental involvement in educational settings in Macao. *International Journal of School-based Family Counseling, 2*, 1-20. Available at: http://www.schoolbasedfamilycounseling.com/journal.html

Van Schalkwyk, G. J. (2011). Saving face: hierarchical positioning in family-school relationships in Macao. *International Journal of School-based Family Counseling, 3*, 1-12. Available at: http://www.schoolbasedfamilycounseling.com/journal.html

Van Schalkwyk, G. J., & D'Amato, R. C. (2013). Providing psychological services and counseling in Pacific Rim countries: Where is school psychology in Asia? *School Psychology International, 34*(2), 123-130. doi: 10.1177/0143034312453389

Van Schalkwyk, G. J., & Sit, H. H. Y. (2013). School counseling in Macao. *School Psychology International, 34*(2), 154-165. doi: 10.1177/0143034312453395

Van Schalkwyk, G. J., Tran, E., & Chang, K. (2006). The impact of Macao gaming industry on family life: An exploratory study. *China Perspectives, 64* (March-April), 2-12.

Wang, Y., & D'Amato, R. C. (2013). Providing comprehensive school psychology services in the Republic of Taiwan. *School Psychology International, 34*(2), 145-153. doi: 10.1177/014303412453394

Wong, B. P. H., Lam, S-F., Leung, D., Ho, D., & Au-Yeung, P. (in press). School psychology and the enhancement of community integration in Hong Kong: Coping strategies of Chinese parents of children with Autism Spectrum Disorders. *School Psychology International* (accepted for publication).

Made in the USA
Las Vegas, NV
15 February 2024

85837296R00453